PhET SIMULATIONS

Available in the Pearson eText and in the Study Area of MasteringPhysics

Extended Edition includes Chapters 1–44. Standard Edition includes Chapters 1–37.
Three-volume edition: Volume 1 includes Chapters 1–20, Volume 2 includes Chapters 21–37,
and Volume 3 includes Chapters 37–44.

*Indicates an associated tutorial is available in the MasteringPhysics Item Library.

APPLICATIONS

Hugh D. Young • Roger A. Freedman

Sears and Zemansky's University Physics with Modern Physics
Phys 157

Fourth Custom Edition for the University of British Columbia

Taken from:
*Sears and Zemansky's University Physics with
Modern Physics*, Fourteenth Edition
by Hugh D. Young and Roger A. Freedman,
with contributions by A. Lewis Ford

Cover Art: Courtesy of Joseph Giacomin/Getty Images.

Taken from:

Sears and Zemansky's University Physics with Modern Physics, Fourteenth Edition
by Hugh D. Young and Roger A. Freedman, with contributions by A. Lewis Ford
Copyright © 2016, 2014, 2012 by Pearson Education, Inc.
New York, New York 10013

Pearson Learning Solutions, 330 Hudson Street, New York, New York 10013
A Pearson Education Company
www.pearsoned.com

Printed in Canada

1 2 3 4 5 6 7 8 9 10 V092 16 15

000200010271967688

SK/CC

ISBN 10: 1-323-19253-0
ISBN 13: 978-1-323-19253-5

BRIEF CONTENTS

VOLUME 1: Chapters 6, 11, 14–16 • VOLUME 2: Chapters 17-20, 33, 35

ABOUT THE AUTHORS

Roger A. Freedman is a Lecturer in Physics at the University of California, Santa Barbara. He was an undergraduate at the University of California campuses in San Diego and Los Angeles and did his doctoral research in nuclear theory at Stanford University under the direction of Professor J. Dirk Walecka. Dr. Freedman came to UCSB in 1981 after three years of teaching and doing research at the University of Washington.

At UCSB, Dr. Freedman has taught in both the Department of Physics and the College of Creative Studies, a branch of the university intended for highly gifted and motivated undergraduates. He has published research in nuclear physics, elementary particle physics, and laser physics. In recent years, he has worked to make physics lectures a more interactive experience through the use of classroom response systems and pre-lecture videos.

In the 1970s Dr. Freedman worked as a comic book letterer and helped organize the San Diego Comic-Con (now the world's largest popular culture convention) during its first few years. Today, when not in the classroom or slaving over a computer, Dr. Freedman can be found either flying (he holds a commercial pilot's license) or with his wife, Caroline, cheering on the rowers of UCSB Men's and Women's Crew.

IN MEMORIAM: HUGH YOUNG (1930–2013)

Hugh D. Young was Emeritus Professor of Physics at Carnegie Mellon University. He earned both his undergraduate and graduate degrees from that university. He earned his Ph.D. in fundamental particle theory under the direction of the late Richard Cutkosky. Dr. Young joined the faculty of Carnegie Mellon in 1956 and retired in 2004. He also had two visiting professorships at the University of California, Berkeley.

Dr. Young's career was centered entirely on undergraduate education. He wrote several undergraduate-level textbooks, and in 1973 he became a coauthor with Francis Sears and Mark Zemansky for their well-known introductory textbooks. In addition to his role on Sears and Zemansky's *University Physics,* he was the author of Sears and Zemansky's *College Physics.*

Dr. Young earned a bachelor's degree in organ performance from Carnegie Mellon in 1972 and spent several years as Associate Organist at St. Paul's Cathedral in Pittsburgh. He often ventured into the wilderness to hike, climb, or go caving with students in Carnegie Mellon's Explorers Club, which he founded as a graduate student and later advised. Dr. Young and his wife, Alice, hosted up to 50 students each year for Thanksgiving dinners in their home.

Always gracious, Dr. Young expressed his appreciation earnestly: "I want to extend my heartfelt thanks to my colleagues at Carnegie Mellon, especially Professors Robert Kraemer, Bruce Sherwood, Ruth Chabay, Helmut Vogel, and Brian Quinn, for many stimulating discussions about physics pedagogy and for their support and encouragement during the writing of several successive editions of this book. I am equally indebted to the many generations of Carnegie Mellon students who have helped me learn what good teaching and good writing are, by showing me what works and what doesn't. It is always a joy and a privilege to express my gratitude to my wife, Alice, and our children, Gretchen and Rebecca, for their love, support, and emotional sustenance during the writing of several successive editions of this book. May all men and women be blessed with love such as theirs." We at Pearson appreciated his professionalism, good nature, and collaboration. He will be missed.

A. Lewis Ford is Professor of Physics at Texas A&M University. He received a B.A. from Rice University in 1968 and a Ph.D. in chemical physics from the University of Texas at Austin in 1972. After a one-year postdoc at Harvard University, he joined the Texas A&M physics faculty in 1973 and has been there ever since. Professor Ford has specialized in theoretical atomic physics—in particular, atomic collisions. At Texas A&M he has taught a variety of undergraduate and graduate courses, but primarily introductory physics.

DETAILED CONTENTS

20   THE SECOND LAW OF THERMODYNAMICS   647

23   ENTROPY   684

OPTICS

33   THE NATURE AND PROPAGATION OF LIGHT   1078

35   INTERFERENCE   1160

APPENDICES

? A baseball pitcher does work with his throwing arm to give the ball a property called kinetic energy, which depends on the ball's mass and speed. Which has the greatest kinetic energy? (i) A ball of mass 0.145 kg moving at 20.0 m/s; (ii) a smaller ball of mass 0.0145 kg moving at 200 m/s; (iii) a larger ball of mass 1.45 kg moving at 2.00 m/s; (iv) all three balls have the same kinetic energy; (v) it depends on the directions in which the balls move.

6 WORK AND KINETIC ENERGY

LEARNING GOALS

Looking forward at …

6.1 What it means for a force to do work on a body, and how to calculate the amount of work done.

6.2 The definition of the kinetic energy (energy of motion) of a body, and how the total work done on a body changes the body's kinetic energy.

6.3 How to use the relationship between total work and change in kinetic energy when the forces are not constant, the body follows a curved path, or both.

6.4 How to solve problems involving power (the rate of doing work).

Suppose you try to find the speed of an arrow that has been shot from a bow. You apply Newton's laws and all the problem-solving techniques that we've learned, but you run across a major stumbling block: After the archer releases the arrow, the bow string exerts a *varying* force that depends on the arrow's position. As a result, the simple methods that we've learned aren't enough to calculate the speed. Never fear; we aren't by any means finished with mechanics, and there are other methods for dealing with such problems.

The new method that we're about to introduce uses the ideas of *work* and *energy*. The importance of the energy idea stems from the *principle of conservation of energy*: Energy is a quantity that can be converted from one form to another but cannot be created or destroyed. In an automobile engine, chemical energy stored in the fuel is converted partially to the energy of the automobile's motion and partially to thermal energy. In a microwave oven, electromagnetic energy obtained from your power company is converted to thermal energy of the food being cooked. In these and all other processes, the *total* energy—the sum of all energy present in all different forms—remains the same. No exception has ever been found.

We'll use the energy idea throughout the rest of this book to study a tremendous range of physical phenomena. This idea will help you understand how automotive engines work, how a camera's flash unit can produce a short burst of light, and the meaning of Einstein's famous equation $E = mc^2$.

In this chapter, though, our concentration will be on mechanics. We'll learn about one important form of energy called *kinetic energy,* or energy of motion, and how it relates to the concept of *work*. We'll also consider *power*, which is the time rate of doing work. In Chapter 7 we'll expand these ideas into a deeper understanding of the concepts of energy and the conservation of energy.

6.1 WORK

You'd probably agree that it's hard work to pull a heavy sofa across the room, to lift a stack of encyclopedias from the floor to a high shelf, or to push a stalled car off the road. Indeed, all of these examples agree with the everyday meaning of *work*—any activity that requires muscular or mental effort.

In physics, work has a much more precise definition. By making use of this definition we'll find that in any motion, no matter how complicated, the total work done on a particle by all forces that act on it equals the change in its *kinetic energy*—a quantity that's related to the particle's mass and speed. This relationship holds even when the forces acting on the particle aren't constant, a situation that can be difficult or impossible to handle with the techniques you learned in Chapters 4 and 5. The ideas of work and kinetic energy enable us to solve problems in mechanics that we could not have attempted before.

In this section we'll see how work is defined and how to calculate work in a variety of situations involving *constant* forces. Later in this chapter we'll relate work and kinetic energy, and then apply these ideas to problems in which the forces are *not* constant.

The three examples of work described above—pulling a sofa, lifting encyclopedias, and pushing a car—have something in common. In each case you do work by exerting a *force* on a body while that body *moves* from one place to another—that is, undergoes a *displacement* (**Fig. 6.1**). You do more work if the force is greater (you push harder on the car) or if the displacement is greater (you push the car farther down the road).

The physicist's definition of work is based on these observations. Consider a body that undergoes a displacement of magnitude s along a straight line. (For now, we'll assume that any body we discuss can be treated as a particle so that we can ignore any rotation or changes in shape of the body.) While the body moves, a constant force $\vec{F}$ acts on it in the same direction as the displacement $\vec{s}$ (**Fig. 6.2**). We define the **work** W done by this constant force under these circumstances as the product of the force magnitude F and the displacement magnitude s:

$$W = Fs \qquad \text{(constant force in direction of straight-line displacement)} \qquad (6.1)$$

The work done on the body is greater if either the force F or the displacement s is greater, in agreement with our observations above.

CAUTION **Work = W, weight = w** Don't confuse uppercase W (work) with lowercase w (weight). Though the symbols are similar, work and weight are different quantities. ▮

The SI unit of work is the **joule** (abbreviated J, pronounced "jool," and named in honor of the 19th-century English physicist James Prescott Joule). From Eq. (6.1) we see that in any system of units, the unit of work is the unit of force multiplied by the unit of distance. In SI units the unit of force is the newton and the unit of distance is the meter, so 1 joule is equivalent to 1 *newton-meter* (N·m):

$$1 \text{ joule} = (1 \text{ newton})(1 \text{ meter}) \quad \text{or} \quad 1 \text{ J} = 1 \text{ N} \cdot \text{m}$$

If you lift an object with a weight of 1 N (about the weight of a medium-sized apple) a distance of 1 m at a constant speed, you exert a 1-N force on the object in the same direction as its 1-m displacement and so do 1 J of work on it.

As an illustration of Eq. (6.1), think of a person pushing a stalled car. If he pushes the car through a displacement $\vec{s}$ with a constant force $\vec{F}$ in the direction of motion, the amount of work he does on the car is given by Eq. (6.1): $W = Fs$.

6.1 These people are doing work as they push on the car because they exert a force on the car as it moves.

6.2 The work done by a constant force acting in the same direction as the displacement

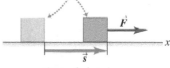

If a body moves through a displacement $\vec{s}$ while a constant force $\vec{F}$ acts on it in the same direction ...

... the work done by the force on the body is $W = Fs$.

BIO **Application Work and Muscle Fibers** Our ability to do work with our bodies comes from our skeletal muscles. The fiberlike cells of skeletal muscle, shown in this micrograph, can shorten, causing the muscle as a whole to contract and to exert force on the tendons to which it attaches. Muscle can exert a force of about 0.3 N per square millimeter of cross-sectional area: The greater the cross-sectional area, the more fibers the muscle has and the more force it can exert when it contracts.

6.3 The work done by a constant force acting at an angle to the displacement.

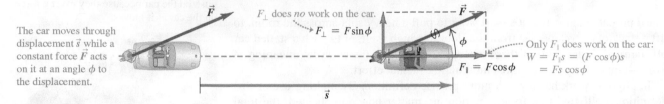

The car moves through displacement $\vec{s}$ while a constant force $\vec{F}$ acts on it at an angle ϕ to the displacement.

$F_\perp$ does *no* work on the car.

$F_\perp = F\sin\phi$

$F_\parallel = F\cos\phi$

Only $F_\parallel$ does work on the car:
$W = F_\parallel s = (F\cos\phi)s$
$= Fs\cos\phi$

But what if the person pushes at an angle ϕ to the car's displacement (**Fig. 6.3**)? Then $\vec{F}$ has a component $F_\parallel = F\cos\phi$ in the direction of the displacement $\vec{s}$ and a component $F_\perp = F\sin\phi$ that acts perpendicular to $\vec{s}$. (Other forces must act on the car so that it moves along $\vec{s}$, not in the direction of $\vec{F}$. We're interested in only the work that the person does, however, so we'll consider only the force he exerts.) Only the parallel component $F_\parallel$ is effective in moving the car, so we define the work as the product of this force component and the magnitude of the displacement. Hence $W = F_\parallel s = (F\cos\phi)s$, or

Work done on a particle by **constant force** $\vec{F}$ during **straight-line displacement** $\vec{s}$ $\qquad W = Fs\cos\phi \qquad$ ⟵ Magnitude of $\vec{F}$ / Angle between $\vec{F}$ and $\vec{s}$ / Magnitude of $\vec{s}$ $\qquad$ (6.2)

If $\phi = 0$, so that $\vec{F}$ and $\vec{s}$ are in the same direction, then $\cos\phi = 1$ and we are back to Eq. (6.1).

Equation (6.2) has the form of the *scalar product* of two vectors, which we introduced in Section 1.10: $\vec{A} \cdot \vec{B} = AB\cos\phi$. You may want to review that definition. Hence we can write Eq. (6.2) more compactly as

Work done on a particle by **constant force** $\vec{F}$ during **straight-line displacement** $\vec{s}$ $\qquad W = \vec{F} \cdot \vec{s} \qquad$ (6.3)

Scalar product (dot product) of vectors $\vec{F}$ and $\vec{s}$

CAUTION **Work is a scalar** An essential point: Work is a *scalar* quantity, even though it's calculated from two vector quantities (force and displacement). A 5-N force toward the east acting on a body that moves 6 m to the east does the same amount of work as a 5-N force toward the north acting on a body that moves 6 m to the north. ∎

EXAMPLE 6.1 **WORK DONE BY A CONSTANT FORCE**

(a) Steve exerts a steady force of magnitude 210 N (about 47 lb) on the stalled car in Fig. 6.3 as he pushes it a distance of 18 m. The car also has a flat tire, so to make the car track straight Steve must push at an angle of 30° to the direction of motion. How much work does Steve do? (b) In a helpful mood, Steve pushes a second stalled car with a steady force $\vec{F} = (160\text{ N})\hat{\imath} - (40\text{ N})\hat{\jmath}$. The displacement of the car is $\vec{s} = (14\text{ m})\hat{\imath} + (11\text{ m})\hat{\jmath}$. How much work does Steve do in this case?

SOLUTION

IDENTIFY and SET UP: In both parts (a) and (b), the target variable is the work W done by Steve. In each case the force is constant and the displacement is along a straight line, so we can use Eq. (6.2) or (6.3). The angle between $\vec{F}$ and $\vec{s}$ is given in part (a), so we can apply Eq. (6.2) directly. In part (b) both $\vec{F}$ and $\vec{s}$ are given in terms

of components, so it's best to calculate the scalar product by using Eq. (1.19): $\vec{A} \cdot \vec{B} = A_xB_x + A_yB_y + A_zB_z$.

EXECUTE: (a) From Eq. (6.2),

$$W = Fs\cos\phi = (210\text{ N})(18\text{ m})\cos 30° = 3.3 \times 10^3\text{ J}$$

(b) The components of $\vec{F}$ are $F_x = 160$ N and $F_y = -40$ N, and the components of $\vec{s}$ are $x = 14$ m and $y = 11$ m. (There are no z-components for either vector.) Hence, using Eqs. (1.19) and (6.3), we have

$$W = \vec{F} \cdot \vec{s} = F_x x + F_y y$$
$$= (160\text{ N})(14\text{ m}) + (-40\text{ N})(11\text{ m})$$
$$= 1.8 \times 10^3\text{ J}$$

EVALUATE: In each case the work that Steve does is more than 1000 J. This shows that 1 joule is a rather small amount of work.

6.4 A constant force $\vec{F}$ can do positive, negative, or zero work depending on the angle between $\vec{F}$ and the displacement $\vec{s}$.

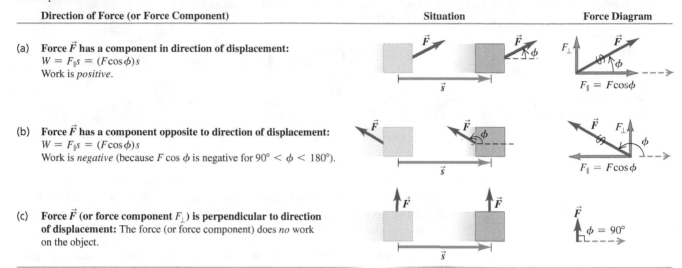

Direction of Force (or Force Component)	Situation	Force Diagram
(a) **Force $\vec{F}$ has a component in direction of displacement:** $W = F_{\parallel}s = (F\cos\phi)s$ Work is *positive*.		
(b) **Force $\vec{F}$ has a component opposite to direction of displacement:** $W = F_{\parallel}s = (F\cos\phi)s$ Work is *negative* (because $F\cos\phi$ is negative for $90° < \phi < 180°$).		
(c) **Force $\vec{F}$ (or force component $F_{\perp}$) is perpendicular to direction of displacement:** The force (or force component) does *no* work on the object.		

Work: Positive, Negative, or Zero

In Example 6.1 the work done in pushing the cars was positive. But it's important to understand that work can also be negative or zero. This is the essential way in which work as defined in physics differs from the "everyday" definition of work. When the force has a component in the *same direction* as the displacement (ϕ between 0° and 90°), $\cos\phi$ in Eq. (6.2) is positive and the work W is *positive* (**Fig. 6.4a**). When the force has a component *opposite* to the displacement (ϕ between 90° and 180°), $\cos\phi$ is negative and the work is *negative* (Fig. 6.4b). When the force is *perpendicular* to the displacement, $\phi = 90°$ and the work done by the force is *zero* (Fig. 6.4c). The cases of zero work and negative work bear closer examination, so let's look at some examples.

There are many situations in which forces act but do zero work. You might think it's "hard work" to hold a barbell motionless in the air for 5 minutes (**Fig. 6.5**). But in fact, you aren't doing any work on the barbell because there is no displacement. (Holding the barbell requires you to keep the muscles of your arms contracted, and this consumes energy stored in carbohydrates and fat within your body. As these energy stores are used up, your muscles feel fatigued even though you do no work on the barbell.) Even when you carry a book while you walk with constant velocity on a level floor, you do no work on the book. It has a displacement, but the (vertical) supporting force that you exert on the book has no component in the direction of the (horizontal) motion. Then $\phi = 90°$ in Eq. (6.2), and $\cos\phi = 0$. When a body slides along a surface, the work done on the body by the normal force is zero; and when a ball on a string moves in uniform circular motion, the work done on the ball by the tension in the string is also zero. In both cases the work is zero because the force has no component in the direction of motion.

What does it mean to do *negative* work? The answer comes from Newton's third law of motion. When a weightlifter lowers a barbell as in **Fig. 6.6a** (next page), his hands and the barbell move together with the same displacement $\vec{s}$. The barbell exerts a force $\vec{F}_{\text{barbell on hands}}$ on his hands in the same direction as the hands' displacement, so the work done by the *barbell* on his *hands* is positive (Fig. 6.6b). But by Newton's third law the weightlifter's hands exert an equal and opposite force $\vec{F}_{\text{hands on barbell}} = -\vec{F}_{\text{barbell on hands}}$ on the barbell (Fig. 6.6c). This force, which keeps the barbell from crashing to the floor, acts opposite to the barbell's displacement. Thus the work done by his *hands* on the *barbell* is negative. Because the weightlifter's hands and the barbell have the same displacement, the

6.5 A weightlifter does no work on a barbell as long as he holds it stationary.

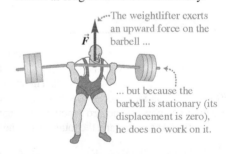

The weightlifter exerts an upward force on the barbell ...

... but because the barbell is stationary (its displacement is zero), he does no work on it.

6.6 This weightlifter's hands do negative work on a barbell as the barbell does positive work on his hands.

(a) A weightlifter lowers a barbell to the floor.

(b) The barbell does *positive* work on the weightlifter's hands.

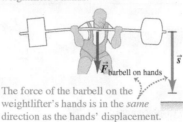

The force of the barbell on the weightlifter's hands is in the *same* direction as the hands' displacement.

(c) The weightlifter's hands do *negative* work on the barbell.

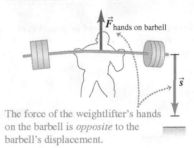

$\vec{F}_{\text{hands on barbell}}$

The force of the weightlifter's hands on the barbell is *opposite* to the barbell's displacement.

work that his hands do on the barbell is just the negative of the work that the barbell does on his hands. In general, when one body does negative work on a second body, the second body does an equal amount of *positive* work on the first body.

CAUTION **Keep track of who's doing the work** We always speak of work done *on* a particular body *by* a specific force. Always specify exactly what force is doing the work. When you lift a book, you exert an upward force on it and the book's displacement is upward, so the work done by the lifting force on the book is positive. But the work done by the *gravitational* force (weight) on a book being lifted is *negative* because the downward gravitational force is opposite to the upward displacement. ∎

Total Work

How do we calculate work when *several* forces act on a body? One way is to use Eq. (6.2) or (6.3) to compute the work done by each separate force. Then, because work is a scalar quantity, the *total* work W_{tot} done on the body by all the forces is the algebraic sum of the quantities of work done by the individual forces. An alternative way to find the total work W_{tot} is to compute the vector sum of the forces (that is, the net force) and then use this vector sum as $\vec{F}$ in Eq. (6.2) or (6.3). The following example illustrates both of these techniques.

DATA *SPEAKS*

Positive, Negative, and Zero Work

When students were given a problem that required them to find the work done by a constant force during a straight-line displacement, more than 59% gave an incorrect answer. Common errors:

• Forgetting that a force does negative work if it acts opposite to the direction of the object's displacement.

• Forgetting that, even if a force is present, it does zero work if it acts perpendicular to the direction of the displacement.

EXAMPLE 6.2 WORK DONE BY SEVERAL FORCES

A farmer hitches her tractor to a sled loaded with firewood and pulls it a distance of 20 m along level ground (**Fig. 6.7a**). The total weight of sled and load is 14,700 N. The tractor exerts a constant 5000-N force at an angle of 36.9° above the horizontal. A 3500-N friction force opposes the sled's motion. Find the work done by each force acting on the sled and the total work done by all the forces.

6.7 Calculating the work done on a sled of firewood being pulled by a tractor.

(a)

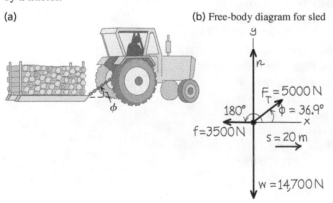

(b) Free-body diagram for sled

$F_T = 5000$ N
$\phi = 36.9°$
$180°$
$f = 3500$ N
$s = 20$ m
$w = 14{,}700$ N

SOLUTION

IDENTIFY and SET UP: Each force is constant and the sled's displacement is along a straight line, so we can use the ideas of this section to calculate the work. We'll find the total work in two ways: (1) by adding the work done on the sled by each force and (2) by finding the work done by the net force on the sled. We first draw a free-body diagram showing all of the forces acting on the sled, and we choose a coordinate system (Fig. 6.7b). For each force—weight, normal force, force of the tractor, and friction force—we know the angle between the displacement (in the positive *x*-direction) and the force. Hence we can use Eq. (6.2) to calculate the work each force does.

As in Chapter 5, we'll find the net force by adding the components of the four forces. Newton's second law tells us that because the sled's motion is purely horizontal, the net force can have only a horizontal component.

EXECUTE: (1) The work W_w done by the weight is zero because its direction is perpendicular to the displacement (compare Fig. 6.4c). For the same reason, the work W_n done by the normal force is also zero. (Note that we don't need to calculate the magnitude n to conclude this.) So $W_w = W_n = 0$.

That leaves the work W_T done by the force F_T exerted by the tractor and the work W_f done by the friction force f. From Eq. (6.2),

$$W_T = F_T s \cos 36.9° = (5000\text{ N})(20\text{ m})(0.800) = 80{,}000\text{ N} \cdot \text{m}$$
$$= 80\text{ kJ}$$

The friction force $\vec{f}$ is opposite to the displacement, so for this force $\phi = 180°$ and $\cos\phi = -1$. Again from Eq. (6.2),

$$W_f = fs \cos 180° = (3500\text{ N})(20\text{ m})(-1) = -70{,}000\text{ N} \cdot \text{m}$$
$$= -70\text{ kJ}$$

The total work W_{tot} done on the sled by all forces is the *algebraic* sum of the work done by the individual forces:

$$W_{\text{tot}} = W_w + W_n + W_T + W_f = 0 + 0 + 80\text{ kJ} + (-70\text{ kJ})$$
$$= 10\text{ kJ}$$

(2) In the second approach, we first find the *vector* sum of all the forces (the net force) and then use it to compute the total work. It's easiest to find the net force by using components. From Fig. 6.7b,

$$\Sigma F_x = F_T \cos\phi + (-f) = (5000\text{ N})\cos 36.9° - 3500\text{ N}$$
$$= 500\text{ N}$$

$$\Sigma F_y = F_T \sin\phi + n + (-w)$$
$$= (5000\text{ N})\sin 36.9° + n - 14{,}700\text{ N}$$

We don't need the second equation; we know that the y-component of force is perpendicular to the displacement, so it does no work. Besides, there is no y-component of acceleration, so ΣF_y must be zero anyway. The total work is therefore the work done by the total x-component:

$$W_{\text{tot}} = (\Sigma\vec{F}) \cdot \vec{s} = (\Sigma F_x)s = (500\text{ N})(20\text{ m}) = 10{,}000\text{ J}$$
$$= 10\text{ kJ}$$

EVALUATE: We get the same result for W_{tot} with either method, as we should. Note that the net force in the x-direction is *not* zero, and so the sled must accelerate as it moves. In Section 6.2 we'll return to this example and see how to use the concept of work to explore the sled's changes of speed.

TEST YOUR UNDERSTANDING OF SECTION 6.1   An electron moves in a straight line toward the east with a constant speed of 8×10^7 m/s. It has electric, magnetic, and gravitational forces acting on it. During a 1-m displacement, the total work done on the electron is (i) positive; (ii) negative; (iii) zero; (iv) not enough information is given. ▌

6.2 KINETIC ENERGY AND THE WORK–ENERGY THEOREM

The total work done on a body by external forces is related to the body's displacement—that is, to changes in its position. But the total work is also related to changes in the *speed* of the body. To see this, consider **Fig. 6.8**, which shows a block sliding on a frictionless table. The forces acting on the block are its weight $\vec{w}$, the normal force $\vec{n}$, and the force $\vec{F}$ exerted on it by the hand.

PhET: The Ramp

In Fig. 6.8a the net force on the block is in the direction of its motion. From Newton's second law, this means that the block speeds up; from Eq. (6.1), this also means that the total work W_{tot} done on the block is positive. The total work

6.8 The relationship between the total work done on a body and how the body's speed changes.

(a)

A block slides to the right on a frictionless surface.

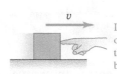

If you push to the right on the block as it moves, the net force on the block is to the right.

• The total work done on the block during a displacement $\vec{s}$ is positive: $W_{\text{tot}} > 0$.
• The block speeds up.

(b)

If you push to the left on the block as it moves, the net force on the block is to the left.

• The total work done on the block during a displacement $\vec{s}$ is negative: $W_{\text{tot}} < 0$.
• The block slows down.

(c)

If you push straight down on the block as it moves, the net force on the block is zero.

• The total work done on the block during a displacement $\vec{s}$ is zero: $W_{\text{tot}} = 0$.
• The block's speed stays the same.

is *negative* in Fig. 6.8b because the net force opposes the displacement; in this case the block slows down. The net force is zero in Fig. 6.8c, so the speed of the block stays the same and the total work done on the block is zero. We can conclude that *when a particle undergoes a displacement, it speeds up if* $W_{tot} > 0$, *slows down if* $W_{tot} < 0$, *and maintains the same speed if* $W_{tot} = 0$.

Let's make this more quantitative. In **Fig. 6.9** a particle with mass m moves along the x-axis under the action of a constant net force with magnitude F that points in the positive x-direction. The particle's acceleration is constant and given by Newton's second law (Section 4.3): $F = ma_x$. As the particle moves from point x_1 to x_2, it undergoes a displacement $s = x_2 - x_1$ and its speed changes from v_1 to v_2. Using a constant-acceleration equation from Section 2.4, Eq. (2.13), and replacing v_{0x} by v_1, v_x by v_2, and $(x - x_0)$ by s, we have

$$v_2^2 = v_1^2 + 2a_x s$$

$$a_x = \frac{v_2^2 - v_1^2}{2s}$$

When we multiply this equation by m and equate ma_x to the net force F, we find

$$F = ma_x = m\frac{v_2^2 - v_1^2}{2s} \quad \text{and}$$

$$Fs = \tfrac{1}{2}mv_2^2 - \tfrac{1}{2}mv_1^2 \tag{6.4}$$

In Eq. (6.4) the product Fs is the work done by the net force F and thus is equal to the total work W_{tot} done by all the forces acting on the particle. The quantity $\tfrac{1}{2}mv^2$ is called the **kinetic energy** K of the particle:

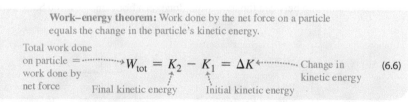

Kinetic energy ⋯⋯▸ $K = \tfrac{1}{2}mv^2$ ⋯⋯ Mass of particle
of a particle ⋯⋯ Speed of particle $\tag{6.5}$

Like work, the kinetic energy of a particle is a scalar quantity; it depends on only the particle's mass and speed, not its direction of motion (**Fig. 6.10**). Kinetic energy can never be negative, and it is zero only when the particle is at rest.

We can now interpret Eq. (6.4) in terms of work and kinetic energy. The first term on the right side of Eq. (6.4) is $K_2 = \tfrac{1}{2}mv_2^2$, the final kinetic energy of the particle (that is, after the displacement). The second term is the initial kinetic energy, $K_1 = \tfrac{1}{2}mv_1^2$, and the difference between these terms is the *change* in kinetic energy. So Eq. (6.4) says:

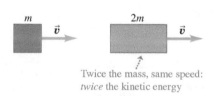

Work–energy theorem: Work done by the net force on a particle equals the change in the particle's kinetic energy.

Total work done
on particle = ⋯⋯▸ $W_{tot} = K_2 - K_1 = \Delta K$ ◂⋯⋯ Change in $\tag{6.6}$
work done by   kinetic energy
net force   Final kinetic energy   Initial kinetic energy

This **work–energy theorem** agrees with our observations about the block in Fig. 6.8. When W_{tot} is *positive*, the kinetic energy *increases* (the final kinetic energy K_2 is greater than the initial kinetic energy K_1) and the particle is going faster at the end of the displacement than at the beginning. When W_{tot} is *negative*, the kinetic energy *decreases* (K_2 is less than K_1) and the speed is less after the displacement. When $W_{tot} = 0$, the kinetic energy stays the same ($K_1 = K_2$) and the speed is unchanged. Note that the work–energy theorem by itself tells us only about changes in *speed*, not velocity, since the kinetic energy doesn't depend on the direction of motion.

From Eq. (6.4) or Eq. (6.6), kinetic energy and work must have the same units. Hence the joule is the SI unit of both work and kinetic energy (and, as we will see

6.9 A constant net force $\vec{F}$ does work on a moving body.

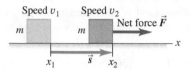

6.10 Comparing the kinetic energy $K = \tfrac{1}{2}mv^2$ of different bodies.

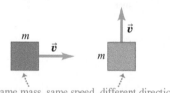

Same mass, same speed, different directions of motion: *same* kinetic energy

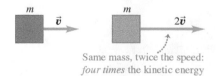

Twice the mass, same speed: *twice* the kinetic energy

Same mass, twice the speed: *four times* the kinetic energy

later, of all kinds of energy). To verify this, note that in SI the quantity $K = \frac{1}{2}mv^2$ has units $\text{kg} \cdot (\text{m/s})^2$ or $\text{kg} \cdot \text{m}^2/\text{s}^2$; we recall that $1\,\text{N} = 1\,\text{kg} \cdot \text{m/s}^2$, so

$$1\,\text{J} = 1\,\text{N} \cdot \text{m} = 1\,(\text{kg} \cdot \text{m/s}^2) \cdot \text{m} = 1\,\text{kg} \cdot \text{m}^2/\text{s}^2$$

Because we used Newton's laws in deriving the work–energy theorem, we can use this theorem only in an inertial frame of reference. Note that the work–energy theorem is valid in *any* inertial frame, but the values of W_{tot} and $K_2 - K_1$ may differ from one inertial frame to another (because the displacement and speed of a body may be different in different frames).

We've derived the work–energy theorem for the special case of straight-line motion with constant forces, and in the following examples we'll apply it to this special case only. We'll find in the next section that the theorem is valid even when the forces are not constant and the particle's trajectory is curved.

PROBLEM-SOLVING STRATEGY 6.1 | WORK AND KINETIC ENERGY

IDENTIFY *the relevant concepts:* The work–energy theorem, $W_{\text{tot}} = K_2 - K_1$, is extremely useful when you want to relate a body's speed v_1 at one point in its motion to its speed v_2 at a different point. (It's less useful for problems that involve the *time* it takes a body to go from point 1 to point 2 because the work–energy theorem doesn't involve time at all. For such problems it's usually best to use the relationships among time, position, velocity, and acceleration described in Chapters 2 and 3.)

SET UP *the problem* using the following steps:
1. Identify the initial and final positions of the body, and draw a free-body diagram showing all the forces that act on the body.
2. Choose a coordinate system. (If the motion is along a straight line, it's usually easiest to have both the initial and final positions lie along one of the axes.)
3. List the unknown and known quantities, and decide which unknowns are your target variables. The target variable may be the body's initial or final speed, the magnitude of one of the forces acting on the body, or the body's displacement.

EXECUTE *the solution:* Calculate the work W done by each force. If the force is constant and the displacement is a straight line, you can use Eq. (6.2) or Eq. (6.3). (Later in this chapter we'll see how to handle varying forces and curved trajectories.) Be sure to check signs; W must be positive if the force has a component in the direction of the displacement, negative if the force has a component opposite to the displacement, and zero if the force and displacement are perpendicular.

Add the amounts of work done by each force to find the total work W_{tot}. Sometimes it's easier to calculate the vector sum of the forces (the net force) and then find the work done by the net force; this value is also equal to W_{tot}.

Write expressions for the initial and final kinetic energies, K_1 and K_2. Note that kinetic energy involves *mass,* not *weight;* if you are given the body's weight, use $w = mg$ to find the mass.

Finally, use Eq. (6.6), $W_{\text{tot}} = K_2 - K_1$, and Eq. (6.5), $K = \frac{1}{2}mv^2$, to solve for the target variable. Remember that the right-hand side of Eq. (6.6) represents the change of the body's kinetic energy between points 1 and 2; that is, it is the *final* kinetic energy minus the *initial* kinetic energy, never the other way around. (If you can predict the sign of W_{tot}, you can predict whether the body speeds up or slows down.)

EVALUATE *your answer:* Check whether your answer makes sense. Remember that kinetic energy $K = \frac{1}{2}mv^2$ can never be negative. If you come up with a negative value of K, perhaps you interchanged the initial and final kinetic energies in $W_{\text{tot}} = K_2 - K_1$ or made a sign error in one of the work calculations.

EXAMPLE 6.3   USING WORK AND ENERGY TO CALCULATE SPEED

Let's look again at the sled in Fig. 6.7 and our results from Example 6.2. Suppose the sled's initial speed v_1 is 2.0 m/s. What is the speed of the sled after it moves 20 m?

SOLUTION

IDENTIFY and SET UP: We'll use the work–energy theorem, Eq. (6.6), $W_{\text{tot}} = K_2 - K_1$, since we are given the initial speed $v_1 = 2.0$ m/s and want to find the final speed v_2. **Figure 6.11** shows our sketch of the situation. The motion is in the positive x-direction. In Example 6.2 we calculated the total work done by all the forces: $W_{\text{tot}} = 10$ kJ. Hence the kinetic energy of the sled and its load must increase by 10 kJ, and the speed of the sled must also increase.

6.11 Our sketch for this problem.

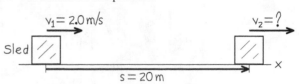

EXECUTE: To write expressions for the initial and final kinetic energies, we need the mass of the sled and load. The combined *weight* is 14,700 N, so the mass is

$$m = \frac{w}{g} = \frac{14{,}700\,\text{N}}{9.8\,\text{m/s}^2} = 1500\,\text{kg}$$

Continued

Then the initial kinetic energy K_1 is

$$K_1 = \tfrac{1}{2}mv_1^2 = \tfrac{1}{2}(1500 \text{ kg})(2.0 \text{ m/s})^2 = 3000 \text{ kg} \cdot \text{m}^2/\text{s}^2$$

$$= 3000 \text{ J}$$

The final kinetic energy K_2 is

$$K_2 = \tfrac{1}{2}mv_2^2 = \tfrac{1}{2}(1500 \text{ kg})v_2^2$$

The work–energy theorem, Eq. (6.6), gives

$$K_2 = K_1 + W_{\text{tot}} = 3000 \text{ J} + 10{,}000 \text{ J} = 13{,}000 \text{ J}$$

Setting these two expressions for K_2 equal, substituting $1 \text{ J} = 1 \text{ kg} \cdot \text{m}^2/\text{s}^2$, and solving for the final speed v_2, we find

$$v_2 = 4.2 \text{ m/s}$$

EVALUATE: The total work is positive, so the kinetic energy increases ($K_2 > K_1$) and the speed increases ($v_2 > v_1$).

This problem can also be solved without the work–energy theorem. We can find the acceleration from $\Sigma\vec{F} = m\vec{a}$ and then use the equations of motion for constant acceleration to find v_2. Since the acceleration is along the x-axis,

$$a = a_x = \frac{\Sigma F_x}{m} = \frac{500 \text{ N}}{1500 \text{ kg}} = 0.333 \text{ m/s}^2$$

Then, using Eq. (2.13),

$$v_2^2 = v_1^2 + 2as = (2.0 \text{ m/s})^2 + 2(0.333 \text{ m/s}^2)(20 \text{ m})$$

$$= 17.3 \text{ m}^2/\text{s}^2$$

$$v_2 = 4.2 \text{ m/s}$$

This is the same result we obtained with the work–energy approach, but there we avoided the intermediate step of finding the acceleration. You will find several other examples in this chapter and the next that *can* be done without using energy considerations but that are easier when energy methods are used. When a problem can be done by two methods, doing it by both methods (as we did here) is a good way to check your work.

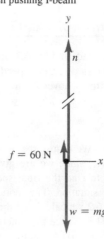

EXAMPLE 6.4   FORCES ON A HAMMERHEAD

The 200-kg steel hammerhead of a pile driver is lifted 3.00 m above the top of a vertical I-beam being driven into the ground (**Fig. 6.12a**). The hammerhead is then dropped, driving the I-beam 7.4 cm deeper into the ground. The vertical guide rails exert a constant 60-N friction force on the hammerhead. Use the work–energy theorem to find (a) the speed of the hammerhead just as it hits the I-beam and (b) the average force the hammerhead exerts on the I-beam. Ignore the effects of the air.

SOLUTION

IDENTIFY: We'll use the work–energy theorem to relate the hammerhead's speed at different locations and the forces acting on it.

There are *three* locations of interest: point 1, where the hammerhead starts from rest; point 2, where it first contacts the I-beam; and point 3, where the hammerhead and I-beam come to a halt (Fig. 6.12a). The two target variables are the hammerhead's speed at point 2 and the average force the hammerhead exerts between points 2 and 3. Hence we'll apply the work–energy theorem twice: once for the motion from 1 to 2, and once for the motion from 2 to 3.

SET UP: Figure 6.12b shows the vertical forces on the hammerhead as it falls from point 1 to point 2. (We can ignore any horizontal forces that may be present because they do no work as the hammerhead moves vertically.) For this part of the motion, our target variable is the hammerhead's final speed v_2.

6.12 (a) A pile driver pounds an I-beam into the ground. (b), (c) Free-body diagrams. Vector lengths are not to scale.

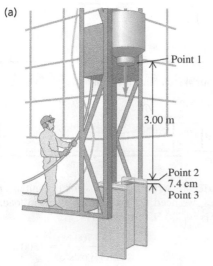

(a)

Point 1

3.00 m

Point 2
7.4 cm
Point 3

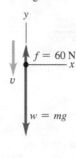

(b) Free-body diagram for falling hammerhead

y

$f = 60 \text{ N}$

x

v

$w = mg$

(c) Free-body diagram for hammerhead when pushing I-beam

y

n

$f = 60 \text{ N}$

x

$w = mg$

Figure 6.12c shows the vertical forces on the hammerhead during the motion from point 2 to point 3. In addition to the forces shown in Fig. 6.12b, the I-beam exerts an upward normal force of magnitude n on the hammerhead. This force actually varies as the hammerhead comes to a halt, but for simplicity we'll treat n as a constant. Hence n represents the *average* value of this upward force during the motion. Our target variable for this part of the motion is the force that the *hammerhead* exerts on the I-beam; it is the reaction force to the normal force exerted by the I-beam, so by Newton's third law its magnitude is also n.

EXECUTE: (a) From point 1 to point 2, the vertical forces are the downward weight $w = mg = (200 \text{ kg})(9.8 \text{ m/s}^2) = 1960 \text{ N}$ and the upward friction force $f = 60 \text{ N}$. Thus the net downward force is $w - f = 1900 \text{ N}$. The displacement of the hammerhead from point 1 to point 2 is downward and equal to $s_{12} = 3.00 \text{ m}$. The total work done on the hammerhead between point 1 and point 2 is then

$$W_{\text{tot}} = (w - f)s_{12} = (1900 \text{ N})(3.00 \text{ m}) = 5700 \text{ J}$$

At point 1 the hammerhead is at rest, so its initial kinetic energy K_1 is zero. Hence the kinetic energy K_2 at point 2 equals the total work done on the hammerhead between points 1 and 2:

$$W_{\text{tot}} = K_2 - K_1 = K_2 - 0 = \tfrac{1}{2}mv_2^2 - 0$$

$$v_2 = \sqrt{\frac{2W_{\text{tot}}}{m}} = \sqrt{\frac{2(5700 \text{ J})}{200 \text{ kg}}} = 7.55 \text{ m/s}$$

This is the hammerhead's speed at point 2, just as it hits the I-beam.

(b) As the hammerhead moves downward from point 2 to point 3, its displacement is $s_{23} = 7.4 \text{ cm} = 0.074 \text{ m}$ and the net downward force acting on it is $w - f - n$ (Fig. 6.12c). The total work done on the hammerhead during this displacement is

$$W_{\text{tot}} = (w - f - n)s_{23}$$

The initial kinetic energy for this part of the motion is K_2, which from part (a) equals 5700 J. The final kinetic energy is $K_3 = 0$ (the hammerhead ends at rest). From the work–energy theorem,

$$W_{\text{tot}} = (w - f - n)s_{23} = K_3 - K_2$$

$$n = w - f - \frac{K_3 - K_2}{s_{23}}$$

$$= 1960 \text{ N} - 60 \text{ N} - \frac{0 \text{ J} - 5700 \text{ J}}{0.074 \text{ m}} = 79,000 \text{ N}$$

The downward force that the hammerhead exerts on the I-beam has this same magnitude, 79,000 N (about 9 tons)—more than 40 times the weight of the hammerhead.

EVALUATE: The net change in the hammerhead's kinetic energy from point 1 to point 3 is zero; a relatively small net force does positive work over a large distance, and then a much larger net force does negative work over a much smaller distance. The same thing happens if you speed up your car gradually and then drive it into a brick wall. The very large force needed to reduce the kinetic energy to zero over a short distance is what does the damage to your car—and possibly to you.

The Meaning of Kinetic Energy

Example 6.4 gives insight into the physical meaning of kinetic energy. The hammerhead is dropped from rest, and its kinetic energy when it hits the I-beam equals the total work done on it up to that point by the net force. This result is true in general: To accelerate a particle of mass m from rest (zero kinetic energy) up to a speed v, the total work done on it must equal the change in kinetic energy from zero to $K = \tfrac{1}{2}mv^2$:

$$W_{\text{tot}} = K - 0 = K$$

So *the kinetic energy of a particle is equal to the total work that was done to accelerate it from rest to its present speed* (**Fig. 6.13**). The definition $K = \tfrac{1}{2}mv^2$, Eq. (6.5), wasn't chosen at random; it's the *only* definition that agrees with this interpretation of kinetic energy.

In the second part of Example 6.4 the kinetic energy of the hammerhead did work on the I-beam and drove it into the ground. This gives us another interpretation of kinetic energy: *The kinetic energy of a particle is equal to the total work that particle can do in the process of being brought to rest.* This is why you pull your hand and arm backward when you catch a ball. As the ball comes to rest, it does an amount of work (force times distance) on your hand equal to the ball's initial kinetic energy. By pulling your hand back, you maximize the distance over which the force acts and so minimize the force on your hand.

6.13 Imparting kinetic energy to a cue ball.

When a billiards player hits a cue ball at rest, the ball's kinetic energy after being hit is equal to the work that was done on it by the cue.

The greater the force exerted by the cue and the greater the distance the ball moves while in contact with it, the greater the ball's kinetic energy.

CONCEPTUAL EXAMPLE 6.5 **COMPARING KINETIC ENERGIES**

Two iceboats like the one in Example 5.6 (Section 5.2) hold a race on a frictionless horizontal lake (**Fig. 6.14**). The two iceboats have masses m and $2m$. The iceboats have identical sails, so the wind exerts the same constant force $\vec{F}$ on each iceboat. They start from rest and cross the finish line a distance s away. Which iceboat crosses the finish line with greater kinetic energy?

SOLUTION

If you use the definition of kinetic energy, $K = \frac{1}{2}mv^2$, Eq. (6.5), the answer to this problem isn't obvious. The iceboat of mass $2m$

6.14 A race between iceboats.

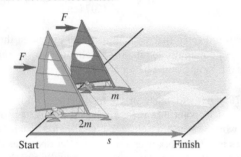

has greater mass, so you might guess that it has greater kinetic energy at the finish line. But the lighter iceboat, of mass m, has greater acceleration and crosses the finish line with a greater speed, so you might guess that *this* iceboat has the greater kinetic energy. How can we decide?

The key is to remember that *the kinetic energy of a particle is equal to the total work done to accelerate it from rest*. Both iceboats travel the same distance s from rest, and only the horizontal force F in the direction of motion does work on either iceboat. Hence the total work done between the starting line and the finish line is the *same* for each iceboat, $W_{\text{tot}} = Fs$. At the finish line, each iceboat has a kinetic energy equal to the work W_{tot} done on it, because each iceboat started from rest. So both iceboats have the *same* kinetic energy at the finish line!

You might think this is a "trick" question, but it isn't. If you really understand the meanings of quantities such as kinetic energy, you can solve problems more easily and with better insight.

Notice that we didn't need to know anything about how much time each iceboat took to reach the finish line. This is because the work–energy theorem makes no direct reference to time, only to displacement. In fact the iceboat of mass m has greater acceleration and so takes less time to reach the finish line than does the iceboat of mass $2m$.

Work and Kinetic Energy in Composite Systems

In this section we've been careful to apply the work–energy theorem only to bodies that we can represent as *particles*—that is, as moving point masses. New subtleties appear for more complex systems that have to be represented as many particles with different motions. We can't go into these subtleties in detail in this chapter, but here's an example.

Suppose a boy stands on frictionless roller skates on a level surface, facing a rigid wall (**Fig. 6.15**). He pushes against the wall, which makes him move to the right. The forces acting on him are his weight $\vec{w}$, the upward normal forces $\vec{n}_1$ and $\vec{n}_2$ exerted by the ground on his skates, and the horizontal force $\vec{F}$ exerted on him by the wall. There is no vertical displacement, so $\vec{w}$, $\vec{n}_1$, and $\vec{n}_2$ do no work. Force $\vec{F}$ accelerates him to the right, but the parts of his body where that force is applied (the boy's hands) do not move while the force acts. Thus the force $\vec{F}$ also does no work. Where, then, does the boy's kinetic energy come from?

The explanation is that it's not adequate to represent the boy as a single point mass. Different parts of the boy's body have different motions; his hands remain stationary against the wall while his torso is moving away from the wall. The various parts of his body interact with each other, and one part can exert forces and do work on another part. Therefore the *total* kinetic energy of this *composite* system of body parts can change, even though no work is done by forces applied by bodies (such as the wall) that are outside the system. In Chapter 8 we'll consider further the motion of a collection of particles that interact with each other. We'll discover that just as for the boy in this example, the total kinetic energy of such a system can change even when no work is done on any part of the system by anything outside it.

6.15 The external forces acting on a skater pushing off a wall. The work done by these forces is zero, but the skater's kinetic energy changes nonetheless.

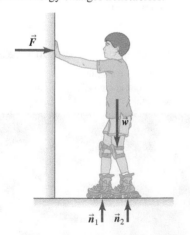

TEST YOUR UNDERSTANDING OF SECTION 6.2 Rank the following bodies in order of their kinetic energy, from least to greatest. (i) A 2.0-kg body moving at 5.0 m/s; (ii) a 1.0-kg body that initially was at rest and then had 30 J of work done on it; (iii) a 1.0-kg body that initially was moving at 4.0 m/s and then had 20 J of work done on it; (iv) a 2.0-kg body that initially was moving at 10 m/s and then did 80 J of work on another body. ▮

6.3 WORK AND ENERGY WITH VARYING FORCES

So far we've considered work done by *constant forces* only. But what happens when you stretch a spring? The more you stretch it, the harder you have to pull, so the force you exert is *not* constant as the spring is stretched. We've also restricted our discussion to *straight-line* motion. There are many situations in which a body moves along a curved path and is acted on by a force that varies in magnitude, direction, or both. We need to be able to compute the work done by the force in these more general cases. Fortunately, the work–energy theorem holds true even when forces are varying and when the body's path is not straight.

Work Done by a Varying Force, Straight-Line Motion

To add only one complication at a time, let's consider straight-line motion along the x-axis with a force whose x-component F_x may change as the body moves. (A real-life example is driving a car along a straight road with stop signs, so the driver has to alternately step on the gas and apply the brakes.) Suppose a particle moves along the x-axis from point x_1 to x_2 (**Fig. 6.16a**). Figure 6.16b is a graph of the x-component of force as a function of the particle's coordinate x. To find the work done by this force, we divide the total displacement into narrow segments Δx_a, Δx_b, and so on (Fig. 6.16c). We approximate the work done by the force during segment Δx_a as the average x-component of force F_{ax} in that segment multiplied by the x-displacement Δx_a. We do this for each segment and then add the results for all the segments. The work done by the force in the total displacement from x_1 to x_2 is approximately

$$W = F_{ax}\Delta x_a + F_{bx}\Delta x_b + \cdots$$

In the limit that the number of segments becomes very large and the width of each becomes very small, this sum becomes the *integral* of F_x from x_1 to x_2:

Work done on a particle by a **varying x-component of force** F_x **during straight-line displacement** along x-axis ....➤
Upper limit = final position
$$W = \int_{x_1}^{x_2} F_x\,dx$$
Integral of x-component of force
Lower limit = initial position
(6.7)

Note that $F_{ax}\Delta x_a$ represents the *area* of the first vertical strip in Fig. 6.16c and that the integral in Eq. (6.7) represents the area under the curve of Fig. 6.16b between x_1 and x_2. *On such a graph of force as a function of position, the total work done by the force is represented by the area under the curve between the initial and final positions.* Alternatively, the work W equals the average force that acts over the entire displacement, multiplied by the displacement.

In the special case that F_x, the x-component of the force, is constant, we can take it outside the integral in Eq. (6.7):

$$W = \int_{x_1}^{x_2} F_x\,dx = F_x\int_{x_1}^{x_2} dx = F_x(x_2 - x_1) \quad \text{(constant force)}$$

But $x_2 - x_1 = s$, the total displacement of the particle. So in the case of a constant force F, Eq. (6.7) says that $W = Fs$, in agreement with Eq. (6.1). The interpretation of work as the area under the curve of F_x as a function of x also holds for a constant force: $W = Fs$ is the area of a rectangle of height F and width s (**Fig. 6.17**).

Now let's apply these ideas to the stretched spring. To keep a spring stretched beyond its unstretched length by an amount x, we have to apply a force of equal

6.16 Calculating the work done by a varying force F_x in the x-direction as a particle moves from x_1 to x_2.

(a) A particle moves from x_1 to x_2 in response to a changing force in the x-direction.

(b) The force F_x varies with position x ...

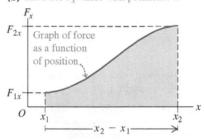

(c) ... but over a short displacement Δx, the force is essentially constant.

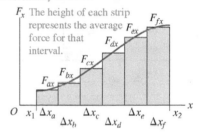

PhET: Molecular Motors

PhET: Stretching DNA

6.17 The work done by a constant force F in the x-direction as a particle moves from x_1 to x_2.

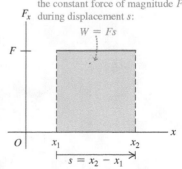

6.18 The force needed to stretch an ideal spring is proportional to the spring's elongation: $F_x = kx$.

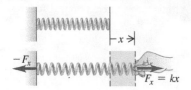

magnitude at each end (**Fig. 6.18**). If the elongation x is not too great, the force we apply to the right-hand end has an x-component directly proportional to x:

$$F_x = kx \quad \text{(force required to stretch a spring)} \quad (6.8)$$

where k is a constant called the **force constant** (or spring constant) of the spring. The units of k are force divided by distance: N/m in SI units. A floppy toy spring such as a Slinky™ has a force constant of about 1 N/m; for the much stiffer springs in an automobile's suspension, k is about 10^5 N/m. The observation that force is directly proportional to elongation for elongations that are not too great was made by Robert Hooke in 1678 and is known as **Hooke's law.** It really shouldn't be called a "law," since it's a statement about a specific device and not a fundamental law of nature. Real springs don't always obey Eq. (6.8) precisely, but it's still a useful idealized model. We'll discuss Hooke's law more fully in Chapter 11.

To stretch a spring, we must do work. We apply equal and opposite forces to the ends of the spring and gradually increase the forces. We hold the left end stationary, so the force we apply at this end does no work. The force at the moving end *does* do work. **Figure 6.19** is a graph of F_x as a function of x, the elongation of the spring. The work done by this force when the elongation goes from zero to a maximum value X is

6.19 Calculating the work done to stretch a spring by a length X.

The area under the graph represents the work done on the spring as the spring is stretched from $x = 0$ to a maximum value X:

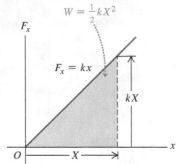

$$W = \int_0^X F_x \, dx = \int_0^X kx \, dx = \tfrac{1}{2}kX^2 \quad (6.9)$$

We can also obtain this result graphically. The area of the shaded triangle in Fig. 6.19, representing the total work done by the force, is equal to half the product of the base and altitude, or

$$W = \tfrac{1}{2}(X)(kX) = \tfrac{1}{2}kX^2$$

This equation also says that the work is the *average* force $kX/2$ multiplied by the total displacement X. We see that the total work is proportional to the *square* of the final elongation X. To stretch an ideal spring by 2 cm, you must do four times as much work as is needed to stretch it by 1 cm.

Equation (6.9) assumes that the spring was originally unstretched. If initially the spring is already stretched a distance x_1, the work we must do to stretch it to a greater elongation x_2 (**Fig. 6.20a**) is

$$W = \int_{x_1}^{x_2} F_x \, dx = \int_{x_1}^{x_2} kx \, dx = \tfrac{1}{2}kx_2^2 - \tfrac{1}{2}kx_1^2 \quad (6.10)$$

Use your knowledge of geometry to convince yourself that the trapezoidal area under the graph in Fig. 6.20b is given by the expression in Eq. (6.10).

6.20 Calculating the work done to stretch a spring from one elongation to a greater one.

(a) Stretching a spring from elongation x_1 to elongation x_2

(b) Force-versus-distance graph

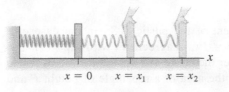

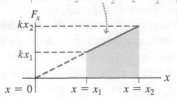

The trapezoidal area under the graph represents the work done on the spring to stretch it from $x = x_1$ to $x = x_2$: $W = \tfrac{1}{2}kx_2^2 - \tfrac{1}{2}kx_1^2$.

If the spring has spaces between the coils when it is unstretched, then it can also be compressed, and Hooke's law holds for compression as well as stretching. In this case the force and displacement are in the opposite directions from those shown in Fig. 6.18, so both F_x and x in Eq. (6.8) are negative. Since both F_x and x are reversed, the force again is in the same direction as the displacement, and the work done by F_x is again positive. So the total work is still given by Eq. (6.9) or (6.10), even when X is negative or either or both of x_1 and x_2 are negative.

CAUTION **Work done *on* a spring vs. work done *by* a spring** Equation (6.10) gives the work that *you* must do *on* a spring to change its length. If you stretch a spring that's originally relaxed, then $x_1 = 0$, $x_2 > 0$, and $W > 0$: The force you apply to one end of the spring is in the same direction as the displacement, and the work you do is positive. By contrast, the work that the *spring* does on whatever it's attached to is given by the *negative* of Eq. (6.10). Thus, as you pull on the spring, the spring does negative work on you. ∎

EXAMPLE 6.6   WORK DONE ON A SPRING SCALE

A woman weighing 600 N steps on a bathroom scale that contains a stiff spring (**Fig. 6.21**). In equilibrium, the spring is compressed 1.0 cm under her weight. Find the force constant of the spring and the total work done on it during the compression.

SOLUTION

IDENTIFY and **SET UP:** In equilibrium the upward force exerted by the spring balances the downward force of the woman's weight. We'll use this principle and Eq. (6.8) to determine the force constant k, and we'll use Eq. (6.10) to calculate the work W that the woman does on the spring to compress it. We take positive values of x to correspond to elongation (upward in Fig. 6.21), so that both the displacement of the end of the spring (x) and the x-component of the force that the woman exerts on it (F_x) are negative. The applied force and the displacement are in the same direction, so the work done on the spring will be positive.

EXECUTE: The top of the spring is displaced by $x = -1.0$ cm $= -0.010$ m, and the woman exerts a force $F_x = -600$ N on the spring. From Eq. (6.8) the force constant is then

$$k = \frac{F_x}{x} = \frac{-600 \text{ N}}{-0.010 \text{ m}} = 6.0 \times 10^4 \text{ N/m}$$

Then, using $x_1 = 0$ and $x_2 = -0.010$ m in Eq. (6.10), we have

$$W = \tfrac{1}{2}kx_2^2 - \tfrac{1}{2}kx_1^2$$
$$= \tfrac{1}{2}(6.0 \times 10^4 \text{ N/m})(-0.010 \text{ m})^2 - 0 = 3.0 \text{ J}$$

EVALUATE: The work done is positive, as expected. Our arbitrary choice of the positive direction has no effect on the answer for W. You can test this by taking the positive x-direction to be downward, corresponding to compression. Do you get the same values for k and W as we found here?

6.21 Compressing a spring in a bathroom scale.

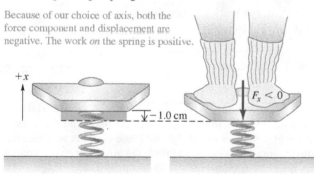

Because of our choice of axis, both the force component and displacement are negative. The work *on* the spring is positive.

$+x$

-1.0 cm

$F_x < 0$

Work–Energy Theorem for Straight-Line Motion, Varying Forces

In Section 6.2 we derived the work–energy theorem, $W_{\text{tot}} = K_2 - K_1$, for the special case of straight-line motion with a constant net force. We can now prove that this theorem is true even when the force varies with position. As in Section 6.2, let's consider a particle that undergoes a displacement x while being acted on by a net force with x-component F_x, which we now allow to vary. Just as in Fig. 6.16, we divide the total displacement x into a large number of small segments Δx. We can apply the work–energy theorem, Eq. (6.6), to each segment because the value

Muscles exert forces via the tendons that attach them to bones. A tendon consists of long, stiff, elastic collagen fibers. The graph shows how the tendon from the hind leg of a wallaby (a small kangaroo-like marsupial) stretches in response to an applied force. The tendon does not exhibit the simple, straight-line behavior of an ideal spring, so the work it does has to be found by integration [Eq. (6.7)]. The tendon exerts less force while relaxing than while stretching. As a result, the relaxing tendon does only about 93% of the work that was done to stretch it.

Force exerted by tendon (N)

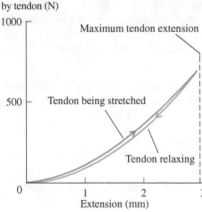

of F_x in each small segment is approximately constant. The change in kinetic energy in segment Δx_a is equal to the work $F_{ax}\Delta x_a$, and so on. The total change of kinetic energy is the sum of the changes in the individual segments, and thus is equal to the total work done on the particle during the entire displacement. So $W_{tot} = \Delta K$ holds for varying forces as well as for constant ones.

Here's an alternative derivation of the work–energy theorem for a force that may vary with position. It involves making a change of variable from x to v_x in the work integral. Note first that the acceleration a of the particle can be expressed in various ways, using $a_x = dv_x/dt$, $v_x = dx/dt$, and the chain rule for derivatives:

$$a_x = \frac{dv_x}{dt} = \frac{dv_x}{dx}\frac{dx}{dt} = v_x\frac{dv_x}{dx} \tag{6.11}$$

From this result, Eq. (6.7) tells us that the total work done by the *net* force F_x is

$$W_{tot} = \int_{x_1}^{x_2} F_x\,dx = \int_{x_1}^{x_2} ma_x\,dx = \int_{x_1}^{x_2} mv_x\frac{dv_x}{dx}\,dx \tag{6.12}$$

Now $(dv_x/dx)dx$ is the change in velocity dv_x during the displacement dx, so we can make that substitution in Eq. (6.12). This changes the integration variable from x to v_x, so we change the limits from x_1 and x_2 to the corresponding x-velocities v_1 and v_2:

$$W_{tot} = \int_{v_1}^{v_2} mv_x\,dv_x$$

The integral of $v_x\,dv_x$ is just $v_x^2/2$. Substituting the upper and lower limits, we finally find

$$W_{tot} = \tfrac{1}{2}mv_2^2 - \tfrac{1}{2}mv_1^2 \tag{6.13}$$

This is the same as Eq. (6.6), so the work–energy theorem is valid even without the assumption that the net force is constant.

EXAMPLE 6.7 MOTION WITH A VARYING FORCE

An air-track glider of mass 0.100 kg is attached to the end of a horizontal air track by a spring with force constant 20.0 N/m (**Fig. 6.22a**). Initially the spring is unstretched and the glider is moving at 1.50 m/s to the right. Find the maximum distance d that the glider moves to the right (a) if the air track is turned on, so that there is no friction, and (b) if the air is turned off, so that there is kinetic friction with coefficient $\mu_k = 0.47$.

6.22 (a) A glider attached to an air track by a spring. (b), (c) Our free-body diagrams.

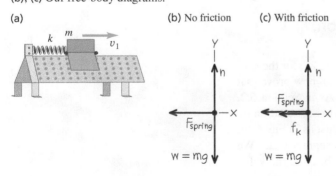

SOLUTION

IDENTIFY and SET UP: The force exerted by the spring is not constant, so we *cannot* use the constant-acceleration formulas of Chapter 2 to solve this problem. Instead, we'll use the work–energy theorem, since the total work done involves the distance moved (our target variable). In Figs. 6.22b and 6.22c we choose the positive x-direction to be to the right (in the direction of the glider's motion). We take $x = 0$ at the glider's initial position (where the spring is unstretched) and $x = d$ (the target variable) at the position where the glider stops. The motion is purely horizontal, so only the horizontal forces do work. Note that Eq. (6.10) gives the work done by the *glider* on the *spring* as it stretches; to use the work–energy theorem we need the work done by the *spring* on the *glider*, which is the negative of Eq. (6.10). We expect the glider to move farther without friction than with friction.

EXECUTE: (a) Equation (6.10) says that as the glider moves from $x_1 = 0$ to $x_2 = d$, it does an amount of work $W = \frac{1}{2}kd^2 - \frac{1}{2}k(0)^2 = \frac{1}{2}kd^2$ on the spring. The amount of work that the *spring* does on the *glider* is the negative of this, $-\frac{1}{2}kd^2$. The spring stretches until the glider comes instantaneously to rest, so the final kinetic energy K_2 is zero. The initial kinetic energy is $\frac{1}{2}mv_1^2$, where $v_1 - 1.50$ m/s is the glider's initial speed. From the work–energy theorem,

$$-\tfrac{1}{2}kd^2 = 0 - \tfrac{1}{2}mv_1^2$$

We solve for the distance d the glider moves:

$$d = v_1\sqrt{\frac{m}{k}} = (1.50 \text{ m/s})\sqrt{\frac{0.100 \text{ kg}}{20.0 \text{ N/m}}}$$

$$= 0.106 \text{ m} = 10.6 \text{ cm}$$

The stretched spring subsequently pulls the glider back to the left, so the glider is at rest only instantaneously.

(b) If the air is turned off, we must include the work done by the kinetic friction force. The normal force n is equal in magnitude to the weight of the glider, since the track is horizontal and there are no other vertical forces. Hence the kinetic friction force has constant magnitude $f_k = \mu_k n = \mu_k mg$. The friction force is directed opposite to the displacement, so the work done by friction is

$$W_{\text{fric}} = f_k d \cos 180° = -f_k d = -\mu_k mgd$$

The total work is the sum of W_{fric} and the work done by the spring, $-\frac{1}{2}kd^2$. The work–energy theorem then says that

$$-\mu_k mgd - \tfrac{1}{2}kd^2 = 0 - \tfrac{1}{2}mv_1^2 \qquad \text{or}$$

$$\tfrac{1}{2}kd^2 + \mu_k mgd - \tfrac{1}{2}mv_1^2 = 0$$

This is a quadratic equation for d. The solutions are

$$d = -\frac{\mu_k mg}{k} \pm \sqrt{\left(\frac{\mu_k mg}{k}\right)^2 + \frac{mv_1^2}{k}}$$

We have

$$\frac{\mu_k mg}{k} = \frac{(0.47)(0.100 \text{ kg})(9.80 \text{ m/s}^2)}{20.0 \text{ N/m}} = 0.02303 \text{ m}$$

$$\frac{mv_1^2}{k} = \frac{(0.100 \text{ kg})(1.50 \text{ m/s})^2}{20.0 \text{ N/m}} = 0.01125 \text{ m}^2$$

so

$$d = -(0.02303 \text{ m}) \pm \sqrt{(0.02303 \text{ m})^2 + 0.01125 \text{ m}^2}$$

$$= 0.086 \text{ m} \quad \text{or} \quad -0.132 \text{ m}$$

The quantity d is a positive displacement, so only the positive value of d makes sense. Thus with friction the glider moves a distance $d = 0.086$ m $= 8.6$ cm.

EVALUATE: If we set $\mu_k = 0$, our algebraic solution for d in part (b) reduces to $d = v_1\sqrt{m/k}$, the zero-friction result from part (a). With friction, the glider goes a shorter distance. Again the glider stops instantaneously, and again the spring force pulls it toward the left; whether it moves or not depends on how great the *static* friction force is. How large would the coefficient of static friction μ_s have to be to keep the glider from springing back to the left?

Work-Energy Theorem for Motion Along a Curve

We can generalize our definition of work further to include a force that varies in direction as well as magnitude, and a displacement that lies along a curved path. **Figure 6.23a** shows a particle moving from P_1 to P_2 along a curve. We divide the curve between these points into many infinitesimal vector displacements, and we call a typical one of these $d\vec{l}$. Each $d\vec{l}$ is tangent to the path at its position. Let $\vec{F}$ be the force at a typical point along the path, and let ϕ be the angle between $\vec{F}$ and $d\vec{l}$ at this point. Then the small element of work dW done on the particle during the displacement $d\vec{l}$ may be written as

$$dW = \vec{F} \cdot d\vec{l} = F\cos\phi\, dl = F_{\parallel}\, dl$$

where $F_{\parallel} = F\cos\phi$ is the component of $\vec{F}$ in the direction parallel to $d\vec{l}$ (Fig. 6.23b). The work done by $\vec{F}$ on the particle as it moves from P_1 to P_2 is

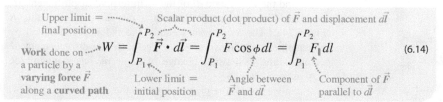

Upper limit = final position · Scalar product (dot product) of $\vec{F}$ and displacement $d\vec{l}$

Work done on a particle by a **varying force** $\vec{F}$ along a **curved path**

$$W = \int_{P_1}^{P_2} \vec{F} \cdot d\vec{l} = \int_{P_1}^{P_2} F\cos\phi\, dl = \int_{P_1}^{P_2} F_{\parallel}\, dl \qquad (6.14)$$

Lower limit = initial position · Angle between $\vec{F}$ and $d\vec{l}$ · Component of $\vec{F}$ parallel to $d\vec{l}$

The integral in Eq. (6.14) (shown in three versions) is called a *line integral*. We'll see shortly how to evaluate an integral of this kind.

6.23 A particle moves along a curved path from point P_1 to P_2, acted on by a force $\vec{F}$ that varies in magnitude and direction.

(a)

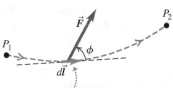

During an infinitesimal displacement $d\vec{l}$, the force $\vec{F}$ does work dW on the particle:

$$dW = \vec{F} \cdot d\vec{l} = F\cos\phi\, dl$$

(b)

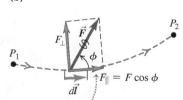

Only the component of $\vec{F}$ parallel to the displacement, $F_{\parallel} = F\cos\phi$, contributes to the work done by $\vec{F}$.

We can now show that the work–energy theorem, Eq. (6.6), holds true even with varying forces and a displacement along a curved path. The force $\vec{F}$ is essentially constant over any given infinitesimal segment $d\vec{l}$ of the path, so we can apply the work–energy theorem for straight-line motion to that segment. Thus the change in the particle's kinetic energy K over that segment equals the work $dW = F_{\parallel} dl = \vec{F} \cdot d\vec{l}$ done on the particle. Adding up these infinitesimal quantities of work from all the segments along the whole path gives the total work done, Eq. (6.14), which equals the total change in kinetic energy over the whole path. So $W_{\text{tot}} = \Delta K = K_2 - K_1$ is true *in general,* no matter what the path and no matter what the character of the forces. This can be proved more rigorously by using steps like those in Eqs. (6.11) through (6.13).

Note that only the component of the net force parallel to the path, $F_{\parallel}$, does work on the particle, so only this component can change the speed and kinetic energy of the particle. The component perpendicular to the path, $F_{\perp} = F\sin\phi$, has no effect on the particle's speed; it acts only to change the particle's direction.

To evaluate the line integral in Eq. (6.14) in a specific problem, we need some sort of detailed description of the path and of the way in which $\vec{F}$ varies along the path. We usually express the line integral in terms of some scalar variable, as in the following example.

EXAMPLE 6.8 MOTION ON A CURVED PATH

At a family picnic you are appointed to push your obnoxious cousin Throckmorton in a swing (**Fig. 6.24a**). His weight is w, the length of the chains is R, and you push Throcky until the chains make an angle θ_0 with the vertical. To do this, you exert a varying horizontal force $\vec{F}$ that starts at zero and gradually increases just enough that Throcky and the swing move very slowly and remain very nearly in equilibrium throughout the process. (a) What is the total work done on Throcky by all forces? (b) What is the work done by the tension T in the chains? (c) What is the work you do by exerting force $\vec{F}$? (Ignore the weight of the chains and seat.)

SOLUTION

IDENTIFY and SET UP: The motion is along a curve, so we'll use Eq. (6.14) to calculate the work done by the net force, by the tension force, and by the force $\vec{F}$. Figure 6.24b shows our free-body diagram and coordinate system for some arbitrary point in Throcky's motion. We have replaced the sum of the tensions in the two chains with a single tension T.

6.24 (a) Pushing cousin Throckmorton in a swing. (b) Our free-body diagram.

(a)

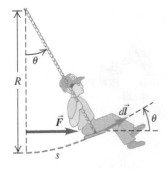

(b) Free-body diagram for Throckmorton (neglecting the weight of the chains and seat)

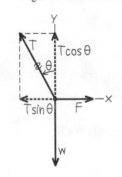

EXECUTE: (a) There are two ways to find the total work done during the motion: (1) by calculating the work done by each force and then adding those quantities, and (2) by calculating the work done by the net force. The second approach is far easier here because Throcky is nearly in equilibrium at every point. Hence the net force on him is zero, the integral of the net force in Eq. (6.14) is zero, and the total work done on him is zero.

(b) It's also easy to find the work done by the chain tension T because this force is perpendicular to the direction of motion at all points along the path. Hence at all points the angle between the chain tension and the displacement vector $d\vec{l}$ is 90° and the scalar product in Eq. (6.14) is zero. Thus the chain tension does zero work.

(c) To compute the work done by $\vec{F}$, we need to calculate the line integral in Eq. (6.14). Inside the integral is the quantity $F\cos\phi\,dl$; let's see how to express each term in this quantity.

Figure 6.24a shows that the angle between $\vec{F}$ and $d\vec{l}$ is θ, so we replace ϕ in Eq. (6.14) with θ. The value of θ changes as Throcky moves.

To find the magnitude F of force $\vec{F}$, note that the net force on Throcky is zero (he is nearly in equilibrium at all points), so $\Sigma F_x = 0$ and $\Sigma F_y = 0$. From Fig. 6.24b,

$$\Sigma F_x = F + (-T\sin\theta) = 0 \qquad \Sigma F_y = T\cos\theta + (-w) = 0$$

If you eliminate T from these two equations, you can show that $F = w\tan\theta$. As the angle θ increases, the tangent increases and F increases (you have to push harder).

To find the magnitude dl of the infinitesimal displacement $d\vec{l}$, note that Throcky moves through a circular arc of radius R (Fig. 6.24a). The arc length s equals the radius R multiplied by the length θ (in radians): $s = R\theta$. Therefore the displacement $d\vec{l}$ corresponding to a small change of angle $d\theta$ has a magnitude $dl = ds = R\,d\theta$.

When we put all the pieces together, the integral in Eq. (6.14) becomes

$$W = \int_{P_1}^{P_2} F\cos\phi\,dl = \int_0^{\theta_0} (w\tan\theta)\cos\theta(R\,d\theta) = \int_0^{\theta_0} wR\sin\theta\,d\theta$$

(Recall that $\tan\theta = \sin\theta/\cos\theta$, so $\tan\theta\cos\theta = \sin\theta$.) We've converted the *line* integral into an *ordinary* integral in terms of the angle θ. The limits of integration are from the starting position at $\theta = 0$ to the final position at $\theta = \theta_0$. The final result is

$$W = wR\int_0^{\theta_0}\sin\theta\,d\theta = -wR\cos\theta\Big|_0^{\theta_0} = -wR(\cos\theta_0 - 1)$$

$$= wR(1 - \cos\theta_0)$$

EVALUATE: If $\theta_0 = 0$, there is no displacement; then $\cos\theta_0 = 1$ and $W = 0$, as we should expect. As θ_0 increases, $\cos\theta_0$ decreases and $W = wR(1 - \cos\theta_0)$ increases. So the farther along the arc you push Throcky, the more work you do. You can confirm that the quantity $R(1 - \cos\theta_0)$ is equal to h, the increase in Throcky's height during the displacement. So the work that you do to raise Throcky is just equal to his weight multiplied by the height that you raise him.

We can check our results by calculating the work done by the force of gravity $\vec{w}$. From part (a) the total work done on Throcky is zero, and from part (b) the work done by tension is zero. So gravity must do a negative amount of work that just balances the positive work done by the force $\vec{F}$ that we calculated in part (c).

For variety, let's calculate the work done by gravity by using the form of Eq. (6.14) that involves the quantity $\vec{F} \cdot d\vec{l}$, and express the force $\vec{w}$ and displacement $d\vec{l}$ in terms of their x- and y-components. The force of gravity has zero x-component and a y-component of $-w$. Figure 6.24a shows that $d\vec{l}$ has a magnitude of ds, an x-component of $ds\cos\theta$, and a y-component of $ds\sin\theta$.

So

$$\vec{w} = \hat{\jmath}(-w)$$

$$d\vec{l} = \hat{\imath}(ds\cos\theta) + \hat{\jmath}(ds\sin\theta)$$

Use Eq. (1.19) to calculate the scalar product $\vec{w} \cdot d\vec{l}$:

$$\vec{w} \cdot d\vec{l} = (-w)(ds\sin\theta) = -w\sin\theta\,ds$$

Using $ds = R\,d\theta$, we find the work done by the force of gravity:

$$\int_{P_1}^{P_2}\vec{w}\cdot d\vec{l} = \int_0^{\theta_0}(-w\sin\theta)R\,d\theta = -wR\int_0^{\theta_0}\sin\theta\,d\theta$$

$$= -wR(1 - \cos\theta_0)$$

The work done by gravity is indeed the negative of the work done by force $\vec{F}$ that we calculated in part (c). Gravity does negative work because the force pulls downward while Throcky moves upward.

As we saw earlier, $R(1 - \cos\theta_0)$ is equal to h, the increase in Throcky's height during the displacement. So the work done by gravity along the curved path is $-mgh$, the *same* work that gravity would have done if Throcky had moved *straight upward* a distance h. This is an example of a more general result that we'll prove in Section 7.1.

TEST YOUR UNDERSTANDING OF SECTION 6.3 In Example 5.20 (Section 5.4) we examined a conical pendulum. The speed of the pendulum bob remains constant as it travels around the circle shown in Fig. 5.32a. (a) Over one complete circle, how much work does the tension force F do on the bob? (i) A positive amount; (ii) a negative amount; (iii) zero. (b) Over one complete circle, how much work does the weight do on the bob? (i) A positive amount; (ii) a negative amount; (iii) zero. ∎

6.4 POWER

The definition of work makes no reference to the passage of time. If you lift a barbell weighing 100 N through a vertical distance of 1.0 m at constant velocity, you do $(100\text{ N})(1.0\text{ m}) = 100\text{ J}$ of work whether it takes you 1 second, 1 hour, or 1 year to do it. But often we need to know how quickly work is done. We describe this in terms of *power*. In ordinary conversation the word "power" is often synonymous with "energy" or "force." In physics we use a much more precise definition: **Power** is the time *rate* at which work is done. Like work and energy, power is a scalar quantity.

The average work done per unit time, or **average power** P_{av}, is defined to be

$$P_{av} = \frac{\Delta W}{\Delta t} \qquad (6.15)$$

Average power during time interval Δt ⟶ P_{av}; ΔW ⟵ Work done during time interval; Δt ⟵ Duration of time interval

The rate at which work is done might not be constant. We define **instantaneous power** P as the quotient in Eq. (6.15) as Δt approaches zero:

$$P = \lim_{\Delta t \to 0}\frac{\Delta W}{\Delta t} = \frac{dW}{dt} \qquad (6.16)$$

Instantaneous power ⟶ P; Time rate of doing work

Average power over infinitesimally short time interval

The SI unit of power is the **watt** (W), named for the English inventor James Watt. One watt equals 1 joule per second: $1\text{ W} = 1\text{ J/s}$ (**Fig. 6.25**). The kilowatt $(1\text{ kW} = 10^3\text{ W})$ and the megawatt $(1\text{ MW} = 10^6\text{ W})$ are also commonly used.

6.25 The same amount of work is done in both of these situations, but the power (the rate at which work is done) is different.

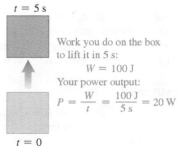

$t = 5\text{ s}$

Work you do on the box to lift it in 5 s:
$$W = 100\text{ J}$$
Your power output:
$$P = \frac{W}{t} = \frac{100\text{ J}}{5\text{ s}} = 20\text{ W}$$

$t = 0$

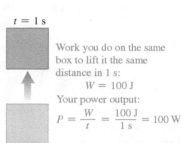

$t = 1\text{ s}$

Work you do on the same box to lift it the same distance in 1 s:
$$W = 100\text{ J}$$
Your power output:
$$P = \frac{W}{t} = \frac{100\text{ J}}{1\text{ s}} = 100\text{ W}$$

$t = 0$

6.26 A one-horsepower (746-W) propulsion system.

Application Muscle Power Skeletal muscles provide the power that makes animals move. Muscle fibers that rely on anaerobic metabolism do not require oxygen; they produce large amounts of power but are useful for short sprints only. Muscle fibers that metabolize aerobically use oxygen and produce smaller amounts of power for long intervals. Both fiber types are visible in a fish fillet: The pale (anaerobic) muscle is used for brief bursts of speed, while the darker (aerobic) muscle is used for sustained swimming.

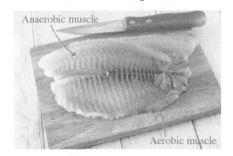

Anaerobic muscle

Aerobic muscle

Another common unit of power is the *horsepower* (hp) (**Fig. 6.26**). The value of this unit derives from experiments by James Watt, who measured that in one minute a horse could do an amount of work equivalent to lifting 33,000 pounds (lb) a distance of 1 foot (ft), or 33,000 ft · lb. Thus 1 hp = 33,000 ft · lb/min. Using 1 ft = 0.3048 m, 1 lb = 4.448 N, and 1 min = 60 s, we can show that

$$1 \text{ hp} = 746 \text{ W} = 0.746 \text{ kW}$$

The watt is a familiar unit of *electrical* power; a 100-W light bulb converts 100 J of electrical energy into light and heat each second. But there's nothing inherently electrical about a watt. A light bulb could be rated in horsepower, and an engine can be rated in kilowatts.

The *kilowatt-hour* (kW · h) is the usual commercial unit of electrical energy. One kilowatt-hour is the total work done in 1 hour (3600 s) when the power is 1 kilowatt (10^3 J/s), so

$$1 \text{ kW} \cdot \text{h} = (10^3 \text{ J/s})(3600 \text{ s}) = 3.6 \times 10^6 \text{ J} = 3.6 \text{ MJ}$$

The kilowatt-hour is a unit of *work* or *energy,* not power.

In mechanics we can also express power in terms of force and velocity. Suppose that a force $\vec{F}$ acts on a body while it undergoes a vector displacement $\Delta \vec{s}$. If $F_{\parallel}$ is the component of $\vec{F}$ tangent to the path (parallel to $\Delta \vec{s}$), then the work done by the force is $\Delta W = F_{\parallel} \Delta s$. The average power is

$$P_{\text{av}} = \frac{F_{\parallel} \Delta s}{\Delta t} = F_{\parallel} \frac{\Delta s}{\Delta t} = F_{\parallel} v_{\text{av}} \tag{6.17}$$

Instantaneous power P is the limit of this expression as $\Delta t \to 0$:

$$P = F_{\parallel} v \tag{6.18}$$

where v is the magnitude of the instantaneous velocity. We can also express Eq. (6.18) in terms of the scalar product:

Instantaneous power for a force doing work on a particle
$$P = \vec{F} \cdot \vec{v} \tag{6.19}$$
Force that acts on particle
Velocity of particle

EXAMPLE 6.9 **FORCE AND POWER**

Each of the four jet engines on an Airbus A380 airliner develops a thrust (a forward force on the airliner) of 322,000 N (72,000 lb). When the airplane is flying at 250 m/s (900 km/h, or roughly 560 mi/h), what horsepower does each engine develop?

SOLUTION

IDENTIFY, SET UP, and EXECUTE: Our target variable is the instantaneous power P, which is the rate at which the thrust does work. We use Eq. (6.18). The thrust is in the direction of motion, so $F_{\parallel}$ is just equal to the thrust. At $v = 250$ m/s, the power developed by each engine is

$$P = F_{\parallel} v = (3.22 \times 10^5 \text{ N})(250 \text{ m/s}) = 8.05 \times 10^7 \text{ W}$$

$$= (8.05 \times 10^7 \text{ W}) \frac{1 \text{ hp}}{746 \text{ W}} = 108,000 \text{ hp}$$

EVALUATE: The speed of modern airliners is directly related to the power of their engines (**Fig. 6.27**). The largest propeller-driven

6.27 (a) Propeller-driven and (b) jet airliners.

(a)

(b)

airliners of the 1950s had engines that each developed about 3400 hp (2.5×10^6 W), giving them maximum speeds of about 600 km/h (370 mi/h). Each engine on an Airbus A380 develops more than 30 times more power, enabling it to fly at about 900 km/h (560 mi/h) and to carry a much heavier load.

If the engines are at maximum thrust while the airliner is at rest on the ground so that $v = 0$, the engines develop *zero* power. Force and power are not the same thing!

EXAMPLE 6.10 A "POWER CLIMB"

A 50.0-kg marathon runner runs up the stairs to the top of Chicago's 443-m-tall Willis Tower, the second tallest building in the United States (**Fig. 6.28**). To lift herself to the top in 15.0 minutes, what must be her average power output? Express your answer in watts, in kilowatts, and in horsepower.

SOLUTION

IDENTIFY and SET UP: We'll treat the runner as a particle of mass m. Her average power output P_{av} must be enough to lift her at constant speed against gravity.

We can find P_{av} in two ways: (1) by determining how much work she must do and dividing that quantity by the elapsed time,

6.28 How much power is required to run up the stairs of Chicago's Willis Tower in 15 minutes?

as in Eq. (6.15), or (2) by calculating the average upward force she must exert (in the direction of the climb) and multiplying that quantity by her upward velocity, as in Eq. (6.17).

EXECUTE: (1) As in Example 6.8, lifting a mass m against gravity requires an amount of work equal to the weight mg multiplied by the height h it is lifted. Hence the work the runner must do is

$$W = mgh = (50.0 \text{ kg})(9.80 \text{ m/s}^2)(443 \text{ m})$$
$$= 2.17 \times 10^5 \text{ J}$$

She does this work in a time 15.0 min = 900 s, so from Eq. (6.15) the average power is

$$P_{av} = \frac{2.17 \times 10^5 \text{ J}}{900 \text{ s}} = 241 \text{ W} = 0.241 \text{ kW} = 0.323 \text{ hp}$$

(2) The force exerted is vertical and the average vertical component of velocity is $(443 \text{ m})/(900 \text{ s}) = 0.492 \text{ m/s}$, so from Eq. (6.17) the average power is

$$P_{av} = F_{\parallel}v_{av} = (mg)v_{av}$$
$$= (50.0 \text{ kg})(9.80 \text{ m/s}^2)(0.492 \text{ m/s}) = 241 \text{ W}$$

which is the same result as before.

EVALUATE: The runner's *total* power output will be several times greater than 241 W. The reason is that the runner isn't really a particle but a collection of parts that exert forces on each other and do work, such as the work done to inhale and exhale and to make her arms and legs swing. What we've calculated is only the part of her power output that lifts her to the top of the building.

TEST YOUR UNDERSTANDING OF SECTION 6.4 The air surrounding an airplane in flight exerts a drag force that acts opposite to the airplane's motion. When the Airbus A380 in Example 6.9 is flying in a straight line at a constant altitude at a constant 250 m/s, what is the rate at which the drag force does work on it? (i) 432,000 hp; (ii) 108,000 hp; (iii) 0; (iv) −108,000 hp; (v) −432,000 hp.

Work done by a force: When a constant force $\vec{F}$ acts on a particle that undergoes a straight-line displacement $\vec{s}$, the work done by the force on the particle is defined to be the scalar product of $\vec{F}$ and $\vec{s}$. The unit of work in SI units is 1 joule = 1 newton-meter (1 J = 1 N · m). Work is a scalar quantity; it can be positive or negative, but it has no direction in space. (See Examples 6.1 and 6.2.)

$$W = \vec{F} \cdot \vec{s} = Fs \cos\phi$$
$$\phi = \text{angle between } \vec{F} \text{ and } \vec{s}$$

(6.2), (6.3)

Kinetic energy: The kinetic energy K of a particle equals the amount of work required to accelerate the particle from rest to speed v. It is also equal to the amount of work the particle can do in the process of being brought to rest. Kinetic energy is a scalar that has no direction in space; it is always positive or zero. Its units are the same as the units of work: $1 \text{ J} = 1 \text{ N} \cdot \text{m} = 1 \text{ kg} \cdot \text{m}^2/\text{s}^2$.

$$K = \tfrac{1}{2}mv^2$$

(6.5)

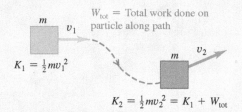

Doubling m doubles K.

Doubling v quadruples K.

The work–energy theorem: When forces act on a particle while it undergoes a displacement, the particle's kinetic energy changes by an amount equal to the total work done on the particle by all the forces. This relationship, called the work–energy theorem, is valid whether the forces are constant or varying and whether the particle moves along a straight or curved path. It is applicable only to bodies that can be treated as particles. (See Examples 6.3–6.5.)

$$W_{\text{tot}} = K_2 - K_1 = \Delta K$$

(6.6)

$W_{\text{tot}} = $ Total work done on particle along path

$$K_1 = \tfrac{1}{2}mv_1^2$$

$$K_2 = \tfrac{1}{2}mv_2^2 = K_1 + W_{\text{tot}}$$

Work done by a varying force or on a curved path: When a force varies during a straight-line displacement, the work done by the force is given by an integral, Eq. (6.7). (See Examples 6.6 and 6.7.) When a particle follows a curved path, the work done on it by a force $\vec{F}$ is given by an integral that involves the angle ϕ between the force and the displacement. This expression is valid even if the force magnitude and the angle ϕ vary during the displacement. (See Example 6.8.)

$$W = \int_{x_1}^{x_2} F_x \, dx$$

(6.7)

$$W = \int_{P_1}^{P_2} \vec{F} \cdot d\vec{l}$$

$$= \int_{P_1}^{P_2} F \cos\phi \, dl = \int_{P_1}^{P_2} F_\parallel \, dl$$

(6.14)

Area = Work done by force during displacement

Power: Power is the time rate of doing work. The average power P_{av} is the amount of work ΔW done in time Δt divided by that time. The instantaneous power is the limit of the average power as Δt goes to zero. When a force $\vec{F}$ acts on a particle moving with velocity $\vec{v}$, the instantaneous power (the rate at which the force does work) is the scalar product of $\vec{F}$ and $\vec{v}$. Like work and kinetic energy, power is a scalar quantity. The SI unit of power is 1 watt = 1 joule/second (1 W = 1 J/s). (See Examples 6.9 and 6.10.)

$$P_{\text{av}} = \frac{\Delta W}{\Delta t}$$

(6.15)

$$P = \lim_{\Delta t \to 0} \frac{\Delta W}{\Delta t} = \frac{dW}{dt}$$

(6.16)

$$P = \vec{F} \cdot \vec{v}$$

(6.19)

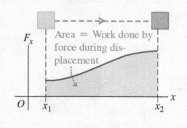

$t = 5 \text{ s}$

$t = 0$

Work you do on the box to lift it in 5 s:
$W = 100 \text{ J}$
Your power output:
$P = \dfrac{W}{t} = \dfrac{100 \text{ J}}{5 \text{ s}}$
$= 20 \text{ W}$

BRIDGING PROBLEM A SPRING THAT DISOBEYS HOOKE'S LAW

Consider a hanging spring of negligible mass that does *not* obey Hooke's law. When the spring is pulled downward by a distance x, the spring exerts an upward force of magnitude αx^2, where α is a positive constant. Initially the hanging spring is relaxed (not extended). We then attach a block of mass m to the spring and release the block. The block stretches the spring as it falls (**Fig. 6.29**). (a) How fast is the block moving when it has fallen a distance x_1? (b) At what rate does the spring do work on the block at this point? (c) Find the maximum distance x_2 that the spring stretches. (d) Will the block *remain* at the point found in part (c)?

SOLUTION GUIDE

IDENTIFY and SET UP

1. The spring force in this problem isn't constant, so you have to use the work–energy theorem. You'll also need Eq. (6.7) to find the work done by the spring over a given displacement.

6.29 The block is attached to a spring that does not obey Hooke's law.

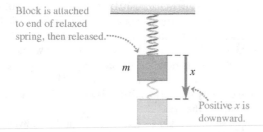

2. Draw a free-body diagram for the block, including your choice of coordinate axes. Note that x represents how far the spring is *stretched,* so choose the positive x-direction to be downward, as in Fig. 6.29. On your coordinate axis, label the points $x = x_1$ and $x = x_2$.
3. Make a list of the unknown quantities, and decide which of these are the target variables.

EXECUTE

4. Calculate the work done on the block by the spring as the block falls an arbitrary distance x. (The integral isn't a difficult one. Use Appendix B if you need a reminder.) Is the work done by the spring positive, negative, or zero?
5. Calculate the work done on the block by any other forces as the block falls an arbitrary distance x. Is this work positive, negative, or zero?
6. Use the work–energy theorem to find the target variables. (You'll also need an equation for power.) *Hint:* When the spring is at its maximum stretch, what is the speed of the block?
7. To answer part (d), consider the *net* force that acts on the block when it is at the point found in part (c).

EVALUATE

8. We learned in Section 2.5 that after an object dropped from rest has fallen freely a distance x_1, its speed is $\sqrt{2gx_1}$. Use this to decide whether your answer in part (a) makes sense. In addition, ask yourself whether the algebraic sign of your answer in part (b) makes sense.
9. Find the value of x where the net force on the block would be zero. How does this compare to your result for x_2? Is this consistent with your answer in part (d)?

Problems

For assigned homework and other learning materials, go to MasteringPhysics®.

•, ••, •••: Difficulty levels. **CP**: Cumulative problems incorporating material from earlier chapters. **CALC**: Problems requiring calculus. **DATA**: Problems involving real data, scientific evidence, experimental design, and/or statistical reasoning. **BIO**: Biosciences problems.

DISCUSSION QUESTIONS

Q6.1 The sign of many physical quantities depends on the choice of coordinates. For example, a_y for free-fall motion can be negative or positive, depending on whether we choose upward or downward as positive. Is the same true of work? In other words, can we make positive work negative by a different choice of coordinates? Explain.

Q6.2 An elevator is hoisted by its cables at constant speed. Is the total work done on the elevator positive, negative, or zero? Explain.

Q6.3 A rope tied to a body is pulled, causing the body to accelerate. But according to Newton's third law, the body pulls back on the rope with a force of equal magnitude and opposite direction. Is the total work done then zero? If so, how can the body's kinetic energy change? Explain.

Q6.4 If it takes total work W to give an object a speed v and kinetic energy K, starting from rest, what will be the object's speed (in terms of v) and kinetic energy (in terms of K) if we do twice as much work on it, again starting from rest?

Q6.5 If there is a net nonzero force on a moving object, can the total work done on the object be zero? Explain, using an example.

Q6.6 In Example 5.5 (Section 5.1), how does the work done on the bucket by the tension in the cable compare with the work done on the cart by the tension in the cable?

Q6.7 In the conical pendulum of Example 5.20 (Section 5.4), which of the forces do work on the bob while it is swinging?

Q6.8 For the cases shown in **Fig. Q6.8**, the object is released from rest at the top and feels no friction or air resistance. In which (if any) cases will the mass have (i) the greatest speed at the bottom and (ii) the most work done on it by the time it reaches the bottom?

Figure **Q6.8**

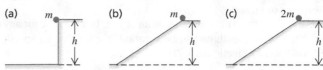

Q6.9 A force $\vec{F}$ is in the x-direction and has a magnitude that depends on x. Sketch a possible graph of F versus x such that the force does zero work on an object that moves from x_1 to x_2, even though the force magnitude is not zero at all x in this range.

Q6.10 Does a car's kinetic energy change more when the car speeds up from 10 to 15 m/s or from 15 to 20 m/s? Explain.

Q6.11 A falling brick has a mass of 1.5 kg and is moving straight downward with a speed of 5.0 m/s. A 1.5-kg physics book is sliding across the floor with a speed of 5.0 m/s. A 1.5-kg melon is traveling with a horizontal velocity component 3.0 m/s to the right and a vertical component 4.0 m/s upward. Do all of these objects have the same velocity? Do all of them have the same kinetic energy? For both questions, give your reasoning.

Q6.12 Can the *total* work done on an object during a displacement be negative? Explain. If the total work is negative, can its magnitude be larger than the initial kinetic energy of the object? Explain.

Q6.13 A net force acts on an object and accelerates it from rest to a speed v_1. In doing so, the force does an amount of work W_1. By what factor must the work done on the object be increased to produce three times the final speed, with the object again starting from rest?

Q6.14 A truck speeding down the highway has a lot of kinetic energy relative to a stopped state trooper but no kinetic energy relative to the truck driver. In these two frames of reference, is the same amount of work required to stop the truck? Explain.

Q6.15 You are holding a briefcase by the handle, with your arm straight down by your side. Does the force your hand exerts do work on the briefcase when (a) you walk at a constant speed down a horizontal hallway and (b) you ride an escalator from the first to second floor of a building? In both cases justify your answer.

Q6.16 When a book slides along a tabletop, the force of friction does negative work on it. Can friction ever do *positive* work? Explain. (*Hint:* Think of a box in the back of an accelerating truck.)

Q6.17 Time yourself while running up a flight of steps, and compute the average rate at which you do work against the force of gravity. Express your answer in watts and in horsepower.

Q6.18 Fractured Physics. Many terms from physics are badly misused in everyday language. In both cases, explain the errors involved. (a) A *strong* person is called *powerful*. What is wrong with this use of *power*? (b) When a worker carries a bag of concrete along a level construction site, people say he did a lot of *work*. Did he?

Q6.19 An advertisement for a portable electrical generating unit claims that the unit's diesel engine produces 28,000 hp to drive an electrical generator that produces 30 MW of electrical power. Is this possible? Explain.

Q6.20 A car speeds up while the engine delivers constant power. Is the acceleration greater at the beginning of this process or at the end? Explain.

Q6.21 Consider a graph of instantaneous power versus time, with the vertical P-axis starting at $P = 0$. What is the physical significance of the area under the P-versus-t curve between vertical lines at t_1 and t_2? How could you find the average power from the graph? Draw a P-versus-t curve that consists of two straight-line sections and for which the peak power is equal to twice the average power.

Q6.22 A nonzero net force acts on an object. Is it possible for any of the following quantities to be constant: the object's (a) speed; (b) velocity; (c) kinetic energy?

Q6.23 When a certain force is applied to an ideal spring, the spring stretches a distance x from its unstretched length and does work W. If instead twice the force is applied, what distance (in terms of x) does the spring stretch from its unstretched length, and how much work (in terms of W) is required to stretch it this distance?

Q6.24 If work W is required to stretch a spring a distance x from its unstretched length, what work (in terms of W) is required to stretch the spring an *additional* distance x?

EXERCISES

Section 6.1 Work

6.1 • You push your physics book 1.50 m along a horizontal tabletop with a horizontal push of 2.40 N while the opposing force of friction is 0.600 N. How much work does each of the following forces do on the book: (a) your 2.40-N push, (b) the friction force, (c) the normal force from the tabletop, and (d) gravity? (e) What is the net work done on the book?

6.2 • Using a cable with a tension of 1350 N, a tow truck pulls a car 5.00 km along a horizontal roadway. (a) How much work does the cable do on the car if it pulls horizontally? If it pulls at 35.0° above the horizontal? (b) How much work does the cable do on the tow truck in both cases of part (a)? (c) How much work does gravity do on the car in part (a)?

6.3 • A factory worker pushes a 30.0-kg crate a distance of 4.5 m along a level floor at constant velocity by pushing horizontally on it. The coefficient of kinetic friction between the crate and the floor is 0.25. (a) What magnitude of force must the worker apply? (b) How much work is done on the crate by this force? (c) How much work is done on the crate by friction? (d) How much work is done on the crate by the normal force? By gravity? (e) What is the total work done on the crate?

6.4 •• Suppose the worker in Exercise 6.3 pushes downward at an angle of 30° below the horizontal. (a) What magnitude of force must the worker apply to move the crate at constant velocity? (b) How much work is done on the crate by this force when the crate is pushed a distance of 4.5 m? (c) How much work is done on the crate by friction during this displacement? (d) How much work is done on the crate by the normal force? By gravity? (e) What is the total work done on the crate?

6.5 •• A 75.0-kg painter climbs a ladder that is 2.75 m long and leans against a vertical wall. The ladder makes a 30.0° angle with the wall. (a) How much work does gravity do on the painter? (b) Does the answer to part (a) depend on whether the painter climbs at constant speed or accelerates up the ladder?

6.6 •• Two tugboats pull a disabled supertanker. Each tug exerts a constant force of 1.80×10^6 N, one 14° west of north and the other 14° east of north, as they pull the tanker 0.75 km toward the north. What is the total work they do on the supertanker?

6.7 • Two blocks are connected by a very light string passing over a massless and frictionless pulley (**Fig. E6.7**). Traveling at constant speed, the 20.0-N block moves 75.0 cm to the right and the 12.0-N block moves 75.0 cm downward. How much work is done (a) on the 12.0-N block by (i) gravity and (ii) the tension in the string? (b) How much work is done on the 20.0-N block by

Figure **E6.7**

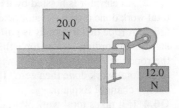

(i) gravity, (ii) the tension in the string, (iii) friction, and (iv) the normal force? (c) Find the total work done on each block.

6.8 •• A loaded grocery cart is rolling across a parking lot in a strong wind. You apply a constant force $\vec{F} = (30\,\text{N})\hat{\imath} - (40\,\text{N})\hat{\jmath}$ to the cart as it undergoes a displacement $\vec{s} = (-9.0\,\text{m})\hat{\imath} - (3.0\,\text{m})\hat{\jmath}$. How much work does the force you apply do on the grocery cart?

6.9 • A 0.800-kg ball is tied to the end of a string 1.60 m long and swung in a vertical circle. (a) During one complete circle, starting anywhere, calculate the total work done on the ball by (i) the tension in the string and (ii) gravity. (b) Repeat part (a) for motion along the semicircle from the lowest to the highest point on the path.

6.10 •• A 12.0-kg package in a mail-sorting room slides 2.00 m down a chute that is inclined at 53.0° below the horizontal. The coefficient of kinetic friction between the package and the chute's surface is 0.40. Calculate the work done on the package by (a) friction, (b) gravity, and (c) the normal force. (d) What is the net work done on the package?

6.11 • A 128.0-N carton is pulled up a frictionless baggage ramp inclined at 30.0° above the horizontal by a rope exerting a 72.0-N pull parallel to the ramp's surface. If the carton travels 5.20 m along the surface of the ramp, calculate the work done on it by (a) the rope, (b) gravity, and (c) the normal force of the ramp. (d) What is the net work done on the carton? (e) Suppose that the rope is angled at 50.0° above the horizontal, instead of being parallel to the ramp's surface. How much work does the rope do on the carton in this case?

6.12 •• A boxed 10.0-kg computer monitor is dragged by friction 5.50 m upward along a conveyor belt inclined at an angle of 36.9° above the horizontal. If the monitor's speed is a constant 2.10 cm/s, how much work is done on the monitor by (a) friction, (b) gravity, and (c) the normal force of the conveyor belt?

6.13 •• A large crate sits on the floor of a warehouse. Paul and Bob apply constant horizontal forces to the crate. The force applied by Paul has magnitude 48.0 N and direction 61.0° south of west. How much work does Paul's force do during a displacement of the crate that is 12.0 m in the direction 22.0° east of north?

6.14 •• You apply a constant force $\vec{F} = (-68.0\,\text{N})\hat{\imath} + (36.0\,\text{N})\hat{\jmath}$ to a 380-kg car as the car travels 48.0 m in a direction that is 240.0° counterclockwise from the +x-axis. How much work does the force you apply do on the car?

6.15 •• On a farm, you are pushing on a stubborn pig with a constant horizontal force with magnitude 30.0 N and direction 37.0° counterclockwise from the +x-axis. How much work does this force do during a displacement of the pig that is (a) $\vec{s} = (5.00\,\text{m})\hat{\imath}$; (b) $\vec{s} = -(6.00\,\text{m})\hat{\jmath}$; (c) $\vec{s} = -(2.00\,\text{m})\hat{\imath} + (4.00\,\text{m})\hat{\jmath}$?

Section 6.2 Kinetic Energy and the Work-Energy Theorem

6.16 •• A 1.50-kg book is sliding along a rough horizontal surface. At point A it is moving at 3.21 m/s, and at point B it has slowed to 1.25 m/s. (a) How much work was done on the book between A and B? (b) If -0.750 J of work is done on the book from B to C, how fast is it moving at point C? (c) How fast would it be moving at C if $+0.750$ J of work was done on it from B to C?

6.17 •• BIO **Animal Energy.** Adult cheetahs, the fastest of the great cats, have a mass of about 70 kg and have been clocked to run at up to 72 mi/h (32 m/s). (a) How many joules of kinetic energy does such a swift cheetah have? (b) By what factor would its kinetic energy change if its speed were doubled?

6.18 • **Some Typical Kinetic Energies.** (a) In the Bohr model of the atom, the ground-state electron in hydrogen has an orbital speed of 2190 km/s. What is its kinetic energy? (Consult Appendix F.) (b) If you drop a 1.0-kg weight (about 2 lb) from a height of 1.0 m, how many joules of kinetic energy will it have when it reaches the ground? (c) Is it reasonable that a 30-kg child could run fast enough to have 100 J of kinetic energy?

6.19 • **Meteor Crater.** About 50,000 years ago, a meteor crashed into the earth near present-day Flagstaff, Arizona. Measurements from 2005 estimate that this meteor had a mass of about 1.4×10^8 kg (around 150,000 tons) and hit the ground at a speed of 12 km/s. (a) How much kinetic energy did this meteor deliver to the ground? (b) How does this energy compare to the energy released by a 1.0-megaton nuclear bomb? (A megaton bomb releases the same amount of energy as a million tons of TNT, and 1.0 ton of TNT releases 4.184×10^9 J of energy.)

6.20 • A 4.80-kg watermelon is dropped from rest from the roof of an 18.0-m-tall building and feels no appreciable air resistance. (a) Calculate the work done by gravity on the watermelon during its displacement from the roof to the ground. (b) Just before it strikes the ground, what is the watermelon's (i) kinetic energy and (ii) speed? (c) Which of the answers in parts (a) and (b) would be *different* if there were appreciable air resistance?

6.21 •• Use the work–energy theorem to solve each of these problems. You can use Newton's laws to check your answers. Neglect air resistance in all cases. (a) A branch falls from the top of a 95.0-m-tall redwood tree, starting from rest. How fast is it moving when it reaches the ground? (b) A volcano ejects a boulder directly upward 525 m into the air. How fast was the boulder moving just as it left the volcano?

6.22 •• Use the work–energy theorem to solve each of these problems. You can use Newton's laws to check your answers. (a) A skier moving at 5.00 m/s encounters a long, rough horizontal patch of snow having a coefficient of kinetic friction of 0.220 with her skis. How far does she travel on this patch before stopping? (b) Suppose the rough patch in part (a) was only 2.90 m long. How fast would the skier be moving when she reached the end of the patch? (c) At the base of a frictionless icy hill that rises at 25.0° above the horizontal, a toboggan has a speed of 12.0 m/s toward the hill. How high vertically above the base will it go before stopping?

6.23 •• You are a member of an Alpine Rescue Team. You must project a box of supplies up an incline of constant slope angle α so that it reaches a stranded skier who is a vertical distance h above the bottom of the incline. The incline is slippery, but there is some friction present, with kinetic friction coefficient μ_k. Use the work–energy theorem to calculate the minimum speed you must give the box at the bottom of the incline so that it will reach the skier. Express your answer in terms of g, h, μ_k, and α.

6.24 •• You throw a 3.00-N rock vertically into the air from ground level. You observe that when it is 15.0 m above the ground, it is traveling at 25.0 m/s upward. Use the work–energy theorem to find (a) the rock's speed just as it left the ground and (b) its maximum height.

6.25 • A sled with mass 12.00 kg moves in a straight line on a frictionless, horizontal surface. At one point in its path, its speed is 4.00 m/s; after it has traveled 2.50 m beyond this point, its speed is 6.00 m/s. Use the work–energy theorem to find the force acting on the sled, assuming that this force is constant and that it acts in the direction of the sled's motion.

6.26 •• A mass m slides down a smooth inclined plane from an initial vertical height h, making an angle α with the horizontal. (a) The work done by a force is the sum of the work done by the components of the force. Consider the components of gravity parallel and perpendicular to the surface of the plane. Calculate the work done on the mass by each of the components, and use these results to show that the work done by gravity is exactly the same as if the mass had fallen straight down through the air from a height h. (b) Use the work–energy theorem to prove that the speed of the mass at the bottom of the incline is the same as if the mass had been dropped from height h, independent of the angle α of the incline. Explain how this speed can be independent of the slope angle. (c) Use the results of part (b) to find the speed of a rock that slides down an icy frictionless hill, starting from rest 15.0 m above the bottom.

6.27 • A 12-pack of Omni-Cola (mass 4.30 kg) is initially at rest on a horizontal floor. It is then pushed in a straight line for 1.20 m by a trained dog that exerts a horizontal force with magnitude 36.0 N. Use the work–energy theorem to find the final speed of the 12-pack if (a) there is no friction between the 12-pack and the floor, and (b) the coefficient of kinetic friction between the 12-pack and the floor is 0.30.

6.28 •• A soccer ball with mass 0.420 kg is initially moving with speed 2.00 m/s. A soccer player kicks the ball, exerting a constant force of magnitude 40.0 N in the same direction as the ball's motion. Over what distance must the player's foot be in contact with the ball to increase the ball's speed to 6.00 m/s?

6.29 • A little red wagon with mass 7.00 kg moves in a straight line on a frictionless horizontal surface. It has an initial speed of 4.00 m/s and then is pushed 3.0 m in the direction of the initial velocity by a force with a magnitude of 10.0 N. (a) Use the work–energy theorem to calculate the wagon's final speed. (b) Calculate the acceleration produced by the force. Use this acceleration in the kinematic relationships of Chapter 2 to calculate the wagon's final speed. Compare this result to that calculated in part (a).

6.30 •• A block of ice with mass 2.00 kg slides 1.35 m down an inclined plane that slopes downward at an angle of 36.9° below the horizontal. If the block of ice starts from rest, what is its final speed? Ignore friction.

6.31 • **Stopping Distance.** A car is traveling on a level road with speed v_0 at the instant when the brakes lock, so that the tires slide rather than roll. (a) Use the work–energy theorem to calculate the minimum stopping distance of the car in terms of v_0, g, and the coefficient of kinetic friction μ_k between the tires and the road. (b) By what factor would the minimum stopping distance change if (i) the coefficient of kinetic friction were doubled, or (ii) the initial speed were doubled, or (iii) both the coefficient of kinetic friction and the initial speed were doubled?

6.32 •• A 30.0-kg crate is initially moving with a velocity that has magnitude 3.90 m/s in a direction 37.0° west of north. How much work must be done on the crate to change its velocity to 5.62 m/s in a direction 63.0° south of east?

Section 6.3 Work and Energy with Varying Forces

6.33 • BIO **Heart Repair.** A surgeon is using material from a donated heart to repair a patient's damaged aorta and needs to know the elastic characteristics of this aortal material. Tests performed on a 16.0-cm strip of the donated aorta reveal that it stretches 3.75 cm when a 1.50-N pull is exerted on it. (a) What is the force constant of this strip of aortal material? (b) If the maximum distance it will be able to stretch when it replaces the aorta in the damaged heart is 1.14 cm, what is the greatest force it will be able to exert there?

6.34 •• To stretch a spring 3.00 cm from its unstretched length, 12.0 J of work must be done. (a) What is the force constant of this spring? (b) What magnitude force is needed to stretch the spring 3.00 cm from its unstretched length? (c) How much work must be done to compress this spring 4.00 cm from its unstretched length, and what force is needed to compress it this distance?

6.35 • Three identical 8.50-kg masses are hung by three identical springs (**Fig. E6.35**). Each spring has a force constant of 7.80 kN/m and was 12.0 cm long before any masses were attached to it. (a) Draw a free-body diagram of each mass. (b) How long is each spring when hanging as shown? (*Hint:* First isolate only the bottom mass. Then treat the bottom two masses as a system. Finally, treat all three masses as a system.)

Figure E6.35

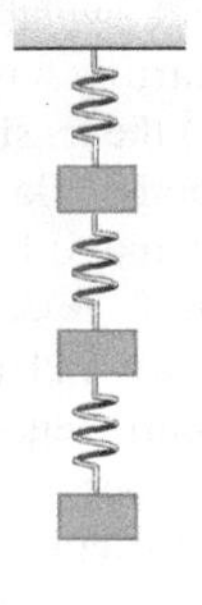

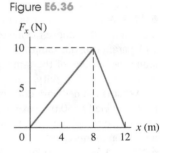

6.36 • A child applies a force $\vec{F}$ parallel to the x-axis to a 10.0-kg sled moving on the frozen surface of a small pond. As the child controls the speed of the sled, the x-component of the force she applies varies with the x-coordinate of the sled as shown in **Fig. E6.36**. Calculate the work done by $\vec{F}$ when the sled moves (a) from $x = 0$ to $x = 8.0$ m; (b) from $x = 8.0$ m to $x = 12.0$ m; (c) from $x = 0$ to 12.0 m.

Figure E6.36

6.37 •• Suppose the sled in Exercise 6.36 is initially at rest at $x = 0$. Use the work–energy theorem to find the speed of the sled at (a) $x = 8.0$ m and (b) $x = 12.0$ m. Ignore friction between the sled and the surface of the pond.

6.38 •• A spring of force constant 300.0 N/m and unstretched length 0.240 m is stretched by two forces, pulling in opposite directions at opposite ends of the spring, that increase to 15.0 N. How long will the spring now be, and how much work was required to stretch it that distance?

6.39 •• A 6.0-kg box moving at 3.0 m/s on a horizontal, frictionless surface runs into a light spring of force constant 75 N/cm. Use the work–energy theorem to find the maximum compression of the spring.

6.40 •• **Leg Presses.** As part of your daily workout, you lie on your back and push with your feet against a platform attached to two stiff springs arranged side by side so that they are parallel to each other. When you push the platform, you compress the springs. You do 80.0 J of work when you compress the springs 0.200 m from their uncompressed length. (a) What magnitude of force must you apply to hold the platform in this position? (b) How much *additional* work must you do to move the platform 0.200 m *farther,* and what maximum force must you apply?

6.41 •• (a) In Example 6.7 (Section 6.3) it was calculated that with the air track turned off, the glider travels 8.6 cm before it stops instantaneously. How large would the coefficient of static friction μ_s have to be to keep the glider from springing back to the left? (b) If the coefficient of static friction between the glider and the track is $\mu_s = 0.60$, what is the maximum initial speed v_1 that the glider can be given and still remain at rest after it stops instantaneously? With the air track turned off, the coefficient of kinetic friction is $\mu_k = 0.47$.

6.42 • A 4.00-kg block of ice is placed against a horizontal spring that has force constant $k = 200$ N/m and is compressed 0.025 m. The spring is released and accelerates the block along a horizontal surface. Ignore friction and the mass of the spring. (a) Calculate the work done on the block by the spring during the motion of the block from its initial position to where the spring has returned to its uncompressed length. (b) What is the speed of the block after it leaves the spring?

6.43 • A force $\vec{F}$ is applied to a 2.0-kg, radio-controlled model car parallel to the x-axis as it moves along a straight track. The x-component of the force varies with the x-coordinate of the car (**Fig. E6.43**). Calculate the work done by the force $\vec{F}$ when the car moves from (a) $x = 0$ to $x = 3.0$ m; (b) $x = 3.0$ m to $x = 4.0$ m; (c) $x = 4.0$ m to $x = 7.0$ m; (d) $x = 0$ to $x = 7.0$ m; (e) $x = 7.0$ m to $x = 2.0$ m.

Figure **E6.43**

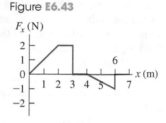

6.44 • Suppose the 2.0-kg model car in Exercise 6.43 is initially at rest at $x = 0$ and $\vec{F}$ is the net force acting on it. Use the work–energy theorem to find the speed of the car at (a) $x = 3.0$ m; (b) $x = 4.0$ m; (c) $x = 7.0$ m.

6.45 •• At a waterpark, sleds with riders are sent along a slippery, horizontal surface by the release of a large compressed spring. The spring, with force constant $k = 40.0$ N/cm and negligible mass, rests on the frictionless horizontal surface. One end is in contact with a stationary wall. A sled and rider with total mass 70.0 kg are pushed against the other end, compressing the spring 0.375 m. The sled is then released with zero initial velocity. What is the sled's speed when the spring (a) returns to its uncompressed length and (b) is still compressed 0.200 m?

6.46 • **Half of a Spring.** (a) Suppose you cut a massless ideal spring in half. If the full spring had a force constant k, what is the force constant of each half, in terms of k? (*Hint:* Think of the original spring as two equal halves, each producing the same force as the entire spring. Do you see why the forces must be equal?) (b) If you cut the spring into three equal segments instead, what is the force constant of each one, in terms of k?

6.47 •• A small glider is placed against a compressed spring at the bottom of an air track that slopes upward at an angle of 40.0° above the horizontal. The glider has mass 0.0900 kg. The spring has $k = 640$ N/m and negligible mass. When the spring is released, the glider travels a maximum distance of 1.80 m along the air track before sliding back down. Before reaching this maximum distance, the glider loses contact with the spring. (a) What distance was the spring originally compressed? (b) When the glider has traveled along the air track 0.80 m from its initial position against the compressed spring, is it still in contact with the spring? What is the kinetic energy of the glider at this point?

6.48 •• An ingenious bricklayer builds a device for shooting bricks up to the top of the wall where he is working. He places a brick on a vertical compressed spring with force constant $k = 450$ N/m and negligible mass. When the spring is released, the brick is propelled upward. If the brick has mass 1.80 kg and is to reach a maximum height of 3.6 m above its initial position on the compressed spring, what distance must the bricklayer compress the spring initially? (The brick loses contact with the spring when the spring returns to its uncompressed length. Why?)

6.49 •• CALC A force in the $+x$-direction with magnitude $F(x) = 18.0$ N $- (0.530$ N/m$)x$ is applied to a 6.00-kg box that is sitting on the horizontal, frictionless surface of a frozen lake. $F(x)$ is the only horizontal force on the box. If the box is initially at rest at $x = 0$, what is its speed after it has traveled 14.0 m?

Section 6.4 Power

6.50 •• A crate on a motorized cart starts from rest and moves with a constant eastward acceleration of $a = 2.80$ m/s². A worker assists the cart by pushing on the crate with a force that is eastward and has magnitude that depends on time according to $F(t) = (5.40$ N/s$)t$. What is the instantaneous power supplied by this force at $t = 5.00$ s?

6.51 • How many joules of energy does a 100-watt light bulb use per hour? How fast would a 70-kg person have to run to have that amount of kinetic energy?

6.52 •• BIO **Should You Walk or Run?** It is 5.0 km from your home to the physics lab. As part of your physical fitness program, you could run that distance at 10 km/h (which uses up energy at the rate of 700 W), or you could walk it leisurely at 3.0 km/h (which uses energy at 290 W). Which choice would burn up more energy, and how much energy (in joules) would it burn? Why does the more intense exercise burn up less energy than the less intense exercise?

6.53 •• **Magnetar.** On December 27, 2004, astronomers observed the greatest flash of light ever recorded from outside the solar system. It came from the highly magnetic neutron star SGR 1806-20 (a *magnetar*). During 0.20 s, this star released as much energy as our sun does in 250,000 years. If P is the average power output of our sun, what was the average power output (in terms of P) of this magnetar?

6.54 •• A 20.0-kg rock is sliding on a rough, horizontal surface at 8.00 m/s and eventually stops due to friction. The coefficient of kinetic friction between the rock and the surface is 0.200. What average power is produced by friction as the rock stops?

6.55 • A tandem (two-person) bicycle team must overcome a force of 165 N to maintain a speed of 9.00 m/s. Find the power required per rider, assuming that each contributes equally. Express your answer in watts and in horsepower.

6.56 •• When its 75-kW (100-hp) engine is generating full power, a small single-engine airplane with mass 700 kg gains altitude at a rate of 2.5 m/s (150 m/min, or 500 ft/min). What fraction of the engine power is being used to make the airplane climb? (The remainder is used to overcome the effects of air resistance and of inefficiencies in the propeller and engine.)

6.57 •• **Working Like a Horse.** Your job is to lift 30-kg crates a vertical distance of 0.90 m from the ground onto the bed of a truck. How many crates would you have to load onto the truck in 1 minute (a) for the average power output you use to lift the crates to equal 0.50 hp; (b) for an average power output of 100 W?

6.58 •• An elevator has mass 600 kg, not including passengers. The elevator is designed to ascend, at constant speed, a vertical distance of 20.0 m (five floors) in 16.0 s, and it is driven by a motor that can provide up to 40 hp to the elevator. What is the maximum number of passengers that can ride in the elevator? Assume that an average passenger has mass 65.0 kg.

6.59 •• A ski tow operates on a 15.0° slope of length 300 m. The rope moves at 12.0 km/h and provides power for 50 riders at one time, with an average mass per rider of 70.0 kg. Estimate the power required to operate the tow.

6.60 • You are applying a constant horizontal force $\vec{F} = (-8.00\ \text{N})\hat{\imath} + (3.00\ \text{N})\hat{\jmath}$ to a crate that is sliding on a factory floor. At the instant that the velocity of the crate is $\vec{v} = (3.20\ \text{m/s})\hat{\imath} + (2.20\ \text{m/s})\hat{\jmath}$, what is the instantaneous power supplied by this force?

6.61 • BIO While hovering, a typical flying insect applies an average force equal to twice its weight during each downward stroke. Take the mass of the insect to be 10 g, and assume the wings move an average downward distance of 1.0 cm during each stroke. Assuming 100 downward strokes per second, estimate the average power output of the insect.

PROBLEMS

6.62 ••• CALC A balky cow is leaving the barn as you try harder and harder to push her back in. In coordinates with the origin at the barn door, the cow walks from $x = 0$ to $x = 6.9$ m as you apply a force with x-component $F_x = -[20.0\ \text{N} + (3.0\ \text{N/m})x]$. How much work does the force you apply do on the cow during this displacement?

6.63 • A luggage handler pulls a 20.0-kg suitcase up a ramp inclined at $32.0°$ above the horizontal by a force $\vec{F}$ of magnitude 160 N that acts parallel to the ramp. The coefficient of kinetic friction between the ramp and the incline is $\mu_k = 0.300$. If the suitcase travels 3.80 m along the ramp, calculate (a) the work done on the suitcase by $\vec{F}$; (b) the work done on the suitcase by the gravitational force; (c) the work done on the suitcase by the normal force; (d) the work done on the suitcase by the friction force; (e) the total work done on the suitcase. (f) If the speed of the suitcase is zero at the bottom of the ramp, what is its speed after it has traveled 3.80 m along the ramp?

6.64 • BIO **Chin-ups.** While doing a chin-up, a man lifts his body 0.40 m. (a) How much work must the man do per kilogram of body mass? (b) The muscles involved in doing a chin-up can generate about 70 J of work per kilogram of muscle mass. If the man can just barely do a 0.40-m chin-up, what percentage of his body's mass do these muscles constitute? (For comparison, the *total* percentage of muscle in a typical 70-kg man with 14% body fat is about 43%.) (c) Repeat part (b) for the man's young son, who has arms half as long as his father's but whose muscles can also generate 70 J of work per kilogram of muscle mass. (d) Adults and children have about the same percentage of muscle in their bodies. Explain why children can commonly do chin-ups more easily than their fathers.

6.65 ••• Consider the blocks in Exercise 6.7 as they move 75.0 cm. Find the total work done on each one (a) if there is no friction between the table and the 20.0-N block, and (b) if $\mu_s = 0.500$ and $\mu_k = 0.325$ between the table and the 20.0-N block.

6.66 •• A 5.00-kg package slides 2.80 m down a long ramp that is inclined at $24.0°$ below the horizontal. The coefficient of kinetic friction between the package and the ramp is $\mu_k = 0.310$. Calculate (a) the work done on the package by friction; (b) the work done on the package by gravity; (c) the work done on the package by the normal force; (d) the total work done on the package. (e) If the package has a speed of 2.20 m/s at the top of the ramp, what is its speed after it has slid 2.80 m down the ramp?

6.67 •• CP BIO **Whiplash Injuries.** When a car is hit from behind, its passengers undergo sudden forward acceleration, which can cause a severe neck injury known as *whiplash*. During normal acceleration, the neck muscles play a large role in accelerating the head so that the bones are not injured. But during a very sudden acceleration, the muscles do not react immediately because they are flexible; most of the accelerating force is provided by the neck bones. Experiments have shown that these bones will fracture if they absorb more than 8.0 J of energy. (a) If a car waiting at a stoplight is rear-ended in a collision that lasts for 10.0 ms, what is the greatest speed this car and its driver can reach without breaking neck bones if the driver's head has a mass of 5.0 kg (which is about right for a 70-kg person)? Express your answer in m/s and in mi/h. (b) What is the acceleration of the passengers during the collision in part (a), and how large a force is acting to accelerate their heads? Express the acceleration in m/s^2 and in g's.

6.68 •• CALC A net force along the x-axis that has x-component $F_x = -12.0\ \text{N} + (0.300\ \text{N/m}^2)x^2$ is applied to a 5.00-kg object that is initially at the origin and moving in the $-x$-direction with a speed of 6.00 m/s. What is the speed of the object when it reaches the point $x = 5.00$ m?

6.69 • CALC **Varying Coefficient of Friction.** A box is sliding with a speed of 4.50 m/s on a horizontal surface when, at point P, it encounters a rough section. The coefficient of friction there is not constant; it starts at 0.100 at P and increases linearly with distance past P, reaching a value of 0.600 at 12.5 m past point P. (a) Use the work–energy theorem to find how far this box slides before stopping. (b) What is the coefficient of friction at the stopping point? (c) How far would the box have slid if the friction coefficient didn't increase but instead had the constant value of 0.100?

6.70 •• CALC Consider a spring that does not obey Hooke's law very faithfully. One end of the spring is fixed. To keep the spring stretched or compressed an amount x, a force along the x-axis with x-component $F_x = kx - bx^2 + cx^3$ must be applied to the free end. Here $k = 100\ \text{N/m}$, $b = 700\ \text{N/m}^2$, and $c = 12{,}000\ \text{N/m}^3$. Note that $x > 0$ when the spring is stretched and $x < 0$ when it is compressed. How much work must be done (a) to stretch this spring by 0.050 m from its unstretched length? (b) To *compress* this spring by 0.050 m from its unstretched length? (c) Is it easier to stretch or compress this spring? Explain why in terms of the dependence of F_x on x. (Many real springs behave qualitatively in the same way.)

6.71 •• CP A small block with a mass of 0.0600 kg is attached to a cord passing through a hole in a frictionless, horizontal surface (**Fig. P6.71**). The block is originally revolving at a distance of 0.40 m from the hole with a speed of 0.70 m/s. The cord is then pulled from below, shortening the radius of the circle in which the block revolves to 0.10 m. At this new distance, the speed of the block is 2.80 m/s. (a) What is the tension in the cord in the original situation, when the block has speed $v = 0.70$ m/s? (b) What is the tension in the cord in the final situation, when the block has speed $v = 2.80$ m/s? (c) How much work was done by the person who pulled on the cord?

Figure **P6.71**

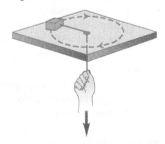

6.72 •• CALC **Proton Bombardment.** A proton with mass 1.67×10^{-27} kg is propelled at an initial speed of 3.00×10^5 m/s directly toward a uranium nucleus 5.00 m away. The proton is repelled by the uranium nucleus with a force of magnitude $F = \alpha/x^2$, where x is the separation between the two objects and $\alpha = 2.12 \times 10^{-26}\ \text{N} \cdot \text{m}^2$. Assume that the uranium nucleus remains at rest. (a) What is the speed of the proton when it is 8.00×10^{-10} m from the uranium nucleus? (b) As the proton approaches the uranium nucleus, the repulsive force slows down the proton until it comes momentarily to rest, after which the proton moves away from the uranium nucleus. How close to the uranium nucleus does the proton get? (c) What is the speed of the proton when it is again 5.00 m away from the uranium nucleus?

6.73 •• You are asked to design spring bumpers for the walls of a parking garage. A freely rolling 1200-kg car moving at 0.65 m/s is to compress the spring no more than 0.090 m before stopping. What should be the force constant of the spring? Assume that the spring has negligible mass.

6.74 •• You and your bicycle have combined mass 80.0 kg. When you reach the base of a bridge, you are traveling along the road at 5.00 m/s (**Fig. P6.74**). At the top of the bridge, you have climbed a vertical distance of 5.20 m and slowed to 1.50 m/s. Ignore work done by friction and any inefficiency in the bike or your legs. (a) What is the total work done on you and your bicycle when you go from the base to the top of the bridge? (b) How much work have you done with the force you apply to the pedals?

Figure **P6.74**

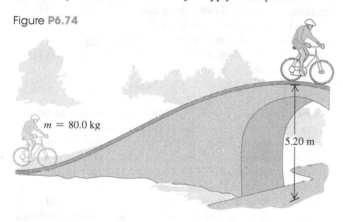

$m = 80.0$ kg

5.20 m

6.75 ••• A 2.50-kg textbook is forced against a horizontal spring of negligible mass and force constant 250 N/m, compressing the spring a distance of 0.250 m. When released, the textbook slides on a horizontal tabletop with coefficient of kinetic friction $\mu_k = 0.30$. Use the work–energy theorem to find how far the textbook moves from its initial position before it comes to rest.

6.76 •• The spring of a spring gun has force constant $k = 400$ N/m and negligible mass. The spring is compressed 6.00 cm, and a ball with mass 0.0300 kg is placed in the horizontal barrel against the compressed spring. The spring is then released, and the ball is propelled out the barrel of the gun. The barrel is 6.00 cm long, so the ball leaves the barrel at the same point that it loses contact with the spring. The gun is held so that the barrel is horizontal. (a) Calculate the speed with which the ball leaves the barrel if you can ignore friction. (b) Calculate the speed of the ball as it leaves the barrel if a constant resisting force of 6.00 N acts on the ball as it moves along the barrel. (c) For the situation in part (b), at what position along the barrel does the ball have the greatest speed, and what is that speed? (In this case, the maximum speed does not occur at the end of the barrel.)

6.77 •• One end of a horizontal spring with force constant 130.0 N/m is attached to a vertical wall. A 4.00-kg block sitting on the floor is placed against the spring. The coefficient of kinetic friction between the block and the floor is $\mu_k = 0.400$. You apply a constant force $\vec{F}$ to the block. $\vec{F}$ has magnitude $F = 82.0$ N and is directed toward the wall. At the instant that the spring is compressed 80.0 cm, what are (a) the speed of the block, and (b) the magnitude and direction of the block's acceleration?

6.78 •• One end of a horizontal spring with force constant 76.0 N/m is attached to a vertical post. A 2.00-kg block of frictionless ice is attached to the other end and rests on the floor. The spring is initially neither stretched nor compressed. A constant horizontal force of 54.0 N is then applied to the block, in the direction away from the post. (a) What is the speed of the block when the spring is stretched 0.400 m? (b) At that instant, what are the magnitude and direction of the acceleration of the block?

6.79 • A 5.00-kg block is moving at $v_0 = 6.00$ m/s along a frictionless, horizontal surface toward a spring with force constant $k = 500$ N/m that is attached to a wall (**Fig. P6.79**). The spring has negligible mass. (a) Find the maximum distance

Figure **P6.79**

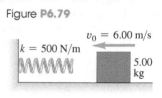

$v_0 = 6.00$ m/s
$k = 500$ N/m
5.00 kg

the spring will be compressed. (b) If the spring is to compress by no more than 0.150 m, what should be the maximum value of v_0?

6.80 ••• A physics professor is pushed up a ramp inclined upward at 30.0° above the horizontal as she sits in her desk chair, which slides on frictionless rollers. The combined mass of the professor and chair is 85.0 kg. She is pushed 2.50 m along the incline by a group of students who together exert a constant horizontal force of 600 N. The professor's speed at the bottom of the ramp is 2.00 m/s. Use the work–energy theorem to find her speed at the top of the ramp.

6.81 •• Consider the system shown in **Fig. P6.81**. The rope and pulley have negligible mass, and the pulley is frictionless. Initially the 6.00-kg block is moving downward and the 8.00-kg block is moving to the right, both with a speed of 0.900 m/s. The blocks come to rest after moving 2.00 m. Use the work–energy theorem to calculate the coefficient of kinetic friction between the 8.00-kg block and the tabletop.

Figure **P6.81**

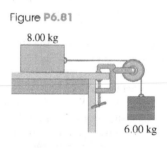

8.00 kg
6.00 kg

6.82 •• Consider the system shown in Fig. P6.81. The rope and pulley have negligible mass, and the pulley is frictionless. The coefficient of kinetic friction between the 8.00-kg block and the tabletop is $\mu_k = 0.250$. The blocks are released from rest. Use energy methods to calculate the speed of the 6.00-kg block after it has descended 1.50 m.

6.83 •• On an essentially frictionless, horizontal ice rink, a skater moving at 3.0 m/s encounters a rough patch that reduces her speed to 1.65 m/s due to a friction force that is 25% of her weight. Use the work–energy theorem to find the length of this rough patch.

6.84 •• BIO All birds, independent of their size, must maintain a power output of 10–25 watts per kilogram of body mass in order to fly by flapping their wings. (a) The Andean giant hummingbird (*Patagona gigas*) has mass 70 g and flaps its wings 10 times per second while hovering. Estimate the amount of work done by such a hummingbird in each wingbeat. (b) A 70-kg athlete can maintain a power output of 1.4 kW for no more than a few seconds; the *steady* power output of a typical athlete is only 500 W or so. Is it possible for a human-powered aircraft to fly for extended periods by flapping its wings? Explain.

6.85 •• A pump is required to lift 800 kg of water (about 210 gallons) per minute from a well 14.0 m deep and eject it with a speed of 18.0 m/s. (a) How much work is done per minute in lifting the water? (b) How much work is done in giving the water the kinetic energy it has when ejected? (c) What must be the power output of the pump?

6.86 ••• The Grand Coulee Dam is 1270 m long and 170 m high. The electrical power output from generators at its base is approximately 2000 MW. How many cubic meters of water must flow from the top of the dam per second to produce this amount of power if 92% of the work done on the water by gravity is converted to electrical energy? (Each cubic meter of water has a mass of 1000 kg.)

6.87 ••• A physics student spends part of her day walking between classes or for recreation, during which time she expends energy at an average rate of 280 W. The remainder of the day she is sitting in class, studying, or resting; during these activities, she expends energy at an average rate of 100 W. If she expends a total of 1.1×10^7 J of energy in a 24-hour day, how much of the day did she spend walking?

6.88 • CALC An object has several forces acting on it. One of these forces is $\vec{F} = \alpha xy\hat{\imath}$, a force in the x-direction whose magnitude depends on the position of the object, with $\alpha = 2.50 \text{ N/m}^2$. Calculate the work done on the object by this force for the following displacements of the object: (a) The object starts at the point ($x = 0$, $y = 3.00$ m) and moves parallel to the x-axis to the point ($x = 2.00$ m, $y = 3.00$ m). (b) The object starts at the point ($x = 2.00$ m, $y = 0$) and moves in the y-direction to the point ($x = 2.00$ m, $y = 3.00$ m). (c) The object starts at the origin and moves on the line $y = 1.5x$ to the point ($x = 2.00$ m, $y = 3.00$ m).

6.89 • BIO **Power of the Human Heart.** The human heart is a powerful and extremely reliable pump. Each day it takes in and discharges about 7500 L of blood. Assume that the work done by the heart is equal to the work required to lift this amount of blood a height equal to that of the average American woman (1.63 m). The density (mass per unit volume) of blood is $1.05 \times 10^3 \text{ kg/m}^3$. (a) How much work does the heart do in a day? (b) What is the heart's power output in watts?

6.90 •• DATA **Figure P6.90** shows the results of measuring the force F exerted on both ends of a rubber band to stretch it a distance x from its unstretched position. (Source: www.sciencebuddies.org) The data points are well fit by the equation $F = 33.55x^{0.4871}$, where F is in newtons and x is in meters. (a) Does this rubber band obey Hooke's law over the range of x shown in the graph? Explain. (b) The stiffness of a spring that obeys Hooke's law is measured by the value of its force constant k, where $k = F/x$. This can be written as $k = dF/dx$ to emphasize the quantities that are changing. Define $k_{\text{eff}} = dF/dx$ and calculate k_{eff} as a function of x for this rubber band. For a spring that obeys Hooke's law, k_{eff} is constant, independent of x. Does the stiffness of this band, as measured by k_{eff}, increase or decrease as x is increased, within the range of the data? (c) How much work must be done to stretch the rubber band from $x = 0$ to $x = 0.0400$ m? From $x = 0.0400$ m to $x = 0.0800$ m? (d) One end of the rubber band is attached to a stationary vertical rod, and the band is stretched horizontally 0.0800 m from its unstretched length. A 0.300-kg object on a horizontal, frictionless surface is attached to the free end of the rubber band and released from rest. What is the speed of the object after it has traveled 0.0400 m?

6.91 ••• DATA In a physics lab experiment, one end of a horizontal spring that obeys Hooke's law is attached to a wall. The spring is compressed 0.400 m, and a block with mass 0.300 kg is attached to it. The spring is then released, and the block moves along a horizontal surface. Electronic sensors measure the speed v of the block after it has traveled a distance d from its initial position against the compressed spring. The measured values are listed in the table. (a) The data show that the speed v of the block increases

d (m)	v (m/s)
0	0
0.05	0.85
0.10	1.11
0.15	1.24
0.25	1.26
0.30	1.14
0.35	0.90
0.40	0.36

and then decreases as the spring returns to its unstretched length. Explain why this happens, in terms of the work done on the block by the forces that act on it. (b) Use the work–energy theorem to derive an expression for v^2 in terms of d. (c) Use a computer graphing program (for example, Excel or Matlab) to graph the data as v^2 (vertical axis) versus d (horizontal axis). The equation that you derived in part (b) should show that v^2 is a quadratic function of d, so, in your graph, fit the data by a second-order polynomial (quadratic) and have the graphing program display the equation for this trendline. Use that equation to find the block's maximum speed v and the value of d at which this speed occurs. (d) By comparing the equation from the graphing program to the formula you derived in part (b), calculate the force constant k for the spring and the coefficient of kinetic friction for the friction force that the surface exerts on the block.

6.92 •• DATA For a physics lab experiment, four classmates run up the stairs from the basement to the top floor of their physics building—a vertical distance of 16.0 m. The classmates and their masses are: Tatiana, 50.2 kg; Bill, 68.2 kg; Ricardo, 81.8 kg; and Melanie, 59.1 kg. The time it takes each of them is shown in **Fig. P6.92**. (a) Considering only the work done against gravity, which person had the largest average power output? The smallest? (b) Chang is very fit and has mass 62.3 kg. If his average power output is 1.00 hp, how many seconds does it take him to run up the stairs?

Figure **P6.90**

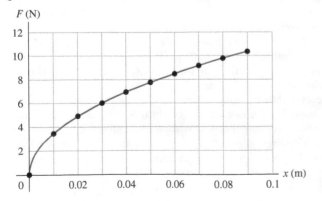

Figure **P6.92**

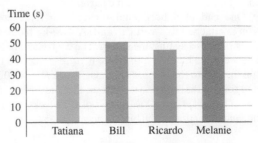

CHALLENGE PROBLEMS

6.93 ••• **CALC A Spring with Mass.** We usually ignore the kinetic energy of the moving coils of a spring, but let's try to get a reasonable approximation to this. Consider a spring of mass M, equilibrium length L_0, and force constant k. The work done to stretch or compress the spring by a distance L is $\frac{1}{2}kX^2$, where $X = L - L_0$. Consider a spring, as described above, that has one end fixed and the other end moving with speed v. Assume that the speed of points along the length of the spring varies linearly with distance l from the fixed end. Assume also that the mass M of the spring is distributed uniformly along the length of the spring. (a) Calculate the kinetic energy of the spring in terms of M and v. (*Hint:* Divide the spring into pieces of length dl; find the speed of each piece in terms of l, v, and L; find the mass of each piece in terms of dl, M, and L; and integrate from 0 to L. The result is *not* $\frac{1}{2}Mv^2$, since not all of the spring moves with the same speed.) In a spring gun, a spring of mass 0.243 kg and force constant 3200 N/m is compressed 2.50 cm from its unstretched length. When the trigger is pulled, the spring pushes horizontally on a 0.053-kg ball. The work done by friction is negligible. Calculate the ball's speed when the spring reaches its uncompressed length (b) ignoring the mass of the spring and (c) including, using the results of part (a), the mass of the spring. (d) In part (c), what is the final kinetic energy of the ball and of the spring?

6.94 ••• **CALC** An airplane in flight is subject to an air resistance force proportional to the square of its speed v. But there is an additional resistive force because the airplane has wings. Air flowing over the wings is pushed down and slightly forward, so from Newton's third law the air exerts a force on the wings and airplane that is up and slightly backward (**Fig. P6.94**). The upward force is the lift force that keeps the airplane aloft, and the backward force is called *induced drag*. At flying speeds, induced drag is inversely proportional to v^2, so the total air resistance force can be expressed by $F_{air} = \alpha v^2 + \beta/v^2$, where α and β are positive constants that depend on the shape and size of the airplane and the density of the air. For a Cessna 150, a small single-engine airplane, $\alpha = 0.30\ \text{N} \cdot \text{s}^2/\text{m}^2$ and $\beta = 3.5 \times 10^5\ \text{N} \cdot \text{m}^2/\text{s}^2$. In steady flight, the engine must provide a forward force that exactly balances the air resistance force. (a) Calculate the speed (in km/h) at which this airplane will have the maximum *range* (that is, travel the greatest distance) for a given quantity of fuel. (b) Calculate the speed (in km/h) for which the airplane will have the maximum *endurance* (that is, remain in the air the longest time).

Figure **P6.94**

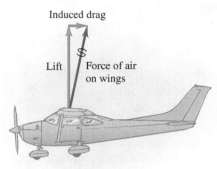

Induced drag

Lift

Force of air on wings

PASSAGE PROBLEMS

BIO **ENERGY OF LOCOMOTION.** On flat ground, a 70-kg person requires about 300 W of metabolic power to walk at a steady pace of 5.0 km/h (1.4 m/s). Using the same metabolic power output, that person can bicycle over the same ground at 15 km/h.

6.95 Based on the given data, how does the energy used in biking 1 km compare with that used in walking 1 km? Biking takes (a) $\frac{1}{3}$ of the energy of walking the same distance; (b) the same energy as walking the same distance; (c) 3 times the energy of walking the same distance; (d) 9 times the energy of walking the same distance.

6.96 A 70-kg person walks at a steady pace of 5.0 km/h on a treadmill at a 5.0% grade. (That is, the vertical distance covered is 5.0% of the horizontal distance covered.) If we assume the metabolic power required is equal to that required for walking on a flat surface plus the rate of doing work for the vertical climb, how much power is required? (a) 300 W; (b) 315 W; (c) 350 W; (d) 370 W.

6.97 How many times greater is the kinetic energy of the person when biking than when walking? Ignore the mass of the bike. (a) 1.7; (b) 3; (c) 6; (d) 9.

Answers

Chapter Opening Question ?

(ii) The expression for kinetic energy is $K = \frac{1}{2}mv^2$. If we calculate K for the three balls, we find (i) $K = \frac{1}{2}(0.145 \text{ kg}) \times (20.0 \text{ m/s})^2 = 29.0 \text{ kg} \cdot \text{m}^2/\text{s}^2 = 29.0 \text{ J}$, (ii) $K = \frac{1}{2}(0.0145 \text{ kg}) \times (200 \text{ m/s})^2 = 290 \text{ J}$, and (iii) $K = \frac{1}{2}(1.45 \text{ kg})(2.00 \text{ m/s})^2 = 2.90 \text{ J}$. The smaller ball has the least mass of all three, but it also has the greatest speed and so the most kinetic energy. Since kinetic energy is a scalar, it does not depend on the direction of motion.

Test Your Understanding Questions

6.1 (iii) The electron has constant velocity, so its acceleration is zero and (by Newton's second law) the net force on the electron is also zero. Therefore the total work done by all the forces (equal to the work done by the net force) must be zero as well. The individual forces may do nonzero work, but that's not what the question asks.

6.2 (iv), (i), (iii), (ii) Body (i) has kinetic energy $K = \frac{1}{2}mv^2 = \frac{1}{2}(2.0 \text{ kg})(5.0 \text{ m/s})^2 = 25 \text{ J}$. Body (ii) had zero kinetic energy initially and then had 30 J of work done on it, so its final kinetic energy is $K_2 = K_1 + W = 0 + 30 \text{ J} = 30 \text{ J}$. Body (iii) had initial kinetic energy $K_1 = \frac{1}{2}mv_1^2 = \frac{1}{2}(1.0 \text{ kg})(4.0 \text{ m/s})^2 = 8.0 \text{ J}$ and then had 20 J of work done on it, so its final kinetic energy is $K_2 = K_1 + W = 8.0 \text{ J} + 20 \text{ J} = 28 \text{ J}$. Body (iv) had initial kinetic energy $K_1 = \frac{1}{2}mv_1^2 = \frac{1}{2}(2.0 \text{ kg})(10 \text{ m/s})^2 = 100 \text{ J}$; when it did 80 J of work on another body, the other body did -80 J of work on body (iv), so the final kinetic energy of body (iv) is $K_2 = K_1 + W = 100 \text{ J} + (-80 \text{ J}) = 20 \text{ J}$.

6.3 (a) (iii), (b) (iii) At any point during the pendulum bob's motion, both the tension force and the weight act perpendicular to the motion—that is, perpendicular to an infinitesimal displacement $d\vec{l}$ of the bob. (In Fig. 5.32b, the displacement $d\vec{l}$ would be directed outward from the plane of the free-body diagram.) Hence for either force the scalar product inside the integral in Eq. (6.14) is $\vec{F} \cdot d\vec{l} = 0$, and the work done along any part of the circular path (including a complete circle) is $W = \int \vec{F} \cdot d\vec{l} = 0$.

6.4 (v) The airliner has a constant horizontal velocity, so the net horizontal force on it must be zero. Hence the backward drag force must have the same magnitude as the forward force due to the combined thrust of the four engines. This means that the drag force must do *negative* work on the airplane at the same rate that the combined thrust force does *positive* work. The combined thrust does work at a rate of $4(108,000 \text{ hp}) = 432,000 \text{ hp}$, so the drag force must do work at a rate of $-432,000 \text{ hp}$.

Bridging Problem

(a) $v_1 = \sqrt{\dfrac{2}{m}\left(mgx_1 - \frac{1}{3}\alpha x_1^3\right)} = \sqrt{2gx_1 - \dfrac{2\alpha x_1^3}{3m}}$

(b) $P = -F_{\text{spring}-1}v_1 = -\alpha x_1^2 \sqrt{2gx_1 - \dfrac{2\alpha x_1^3}{3m}}$

(c) $x_2 = \sqrt{\dfrac{3mg}{\alpha}}$ **(d)** No

? This Roman aqueduct uses the principle of the arch to sustain the weight of the structure and the water it carries. Are the blocks that make up the arch being (i) compressed, (ii) stretched, (iii) a combination of these, or (iv) neither compressed nor stretched?

11 EQUILIBRIUM AND ELASTICITY

LEARNING GOALS

Looking forward at ...

11.1 The conditions that must be satisfied for a body or structure to be in equilibrium.

11.2 What the center of gravity of a body is and how it relates to the body's stability.

11.3 How to solve problems that involve rigid bodies in equilibrium.

11.4 How to analyze situations in which a body is deformed by tension, compression, pressure, or shear.

11.5 What happens when a body is stretched so much that it deforms or breaks.

Looking back at ...

6.3 Hooke's law for an ideal spring.

We've devoted a good deal of effort to understanding why and how bodies accelerate in response to the forces that act on them. But very often we're interested in making sure that bodies *don't* accelerate. Any building, from a multistory skyscraper to the humblest shed, must be designed so that it won't topple over. Similar concerns arise with a suspension bridge, a ladder leaning against a wall, or a crane hoisting a bucket full of concrete.

A body that can be modeled as a *particle* is in equilibrium whenever the vector sum of the forces acting on it is zero. But for the situations we've just described, that condition isn't enough. If forces act at different points on an extended body, an additional requirement must be satisfied to ensure that the body has no tendency to *rotate:* The sum of the *torques* about any point must be zero. This requirement is based on the principles of rotational dynamics developed in Chapter 10. We can compute the torque due to the weight of a body by using the concept of center of gravity, which we introduce in this chapter.

Idealized rigid bodies don't bend, stretch, or squash when forces act on them. But all real materials are *elastic* and do deform to some extent. Elastic properties of materials are tremendously important. You want the wings of an airplane to be able to bend a little, but you'd rather not have them break off. Tendons in your limbs need to stretch when you exercise, but they must return to their relaxed lengths when you stop. Many of the necessities of everyday life, from rubber bands to suspension bridges, depend on the elastic properties of materials. In this chapter we'll introduce the concepts of *stress, strain,* and *elastic modulus* and a simple principle called *Hooke's law,* which helps us predict what deformations will occur when forces are applied to a real (not perfectly rigid) body.

11.1 CONDITIONS FOR EQUILIBRIUM

11.1 To be in static equilibrium, a body at rest must satisfy *both* conditions for equilibrium: It can have no tendency to accelerate as a whole or to start rotating.

(a) This body is in static equilibrium.

Equilibrium conditions:

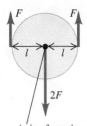

First condition satisfied: Net force = 0, so body at rest has no tendency to start moving as a whole.

Second condition satisfied: Net torque about the axis = 0, so body at rest has no tendency to start rotating.

Axis of rotation (perpendicular to figure)

(b) This body has no tendency to accelerate as a whole, but it has a tendency to start rotating.

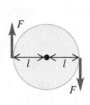

First condition satisfied: Net force = 0, so body at rest has no tendency to start moving as a whole.

Second condition NOT satisfied: There is a net clockwise torque about the axis, so body at rest will start rotating clockwise.

(c) This body has a tendency to accelerate as a whole but no tendency to start rotating.

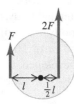

First condition NOT satisfied: There is a net upward force, so body at rest will start moving upward.

Second condition satisfied: Net torque about the axis = 0, so body at rest has no tendency to start rotating.

We learned in Sections 4.2 and 5.1 that a particle is in *equilibrium*—that is, the particle does not accelerate—in an inertial frame of reference if the vector sum of all the forces acting on the particle is zero, $\sum \vec{F} = 0$. For an *extended* body, the equivalent statement is that the center of mass of the body has zero acceleration if the vector sum of all external forces acting on the body is zero, as discussed in Section 8.5. This is often called the **first condition for equilibrium:**

> **First condition for equilibrium:** For the center of mass of a body at rest to remain at rest ...
>
> $$\sum \vec{F} = 0 \quad \longleftarrow \begin{array}{l} \textit{... net external force} \\ \textit{on the body must} \\ \textit{be zero.} \end{array}$$
>
> (11.1)

A second condition for an extended body to be in equilibrium is that the body must have no tendency to *rotate*. A rigid body that, in an inertial frame, is not rotating about a certain point has zero angular momentum about that point. If it is not to start rotating about that point, the rate of change of angular momentum must *also* be zero. From the discussion in Section 10.5, particularly Eq. (10.29), this means that the sum of torques due to all the external forces acting on the body must be zero. A rigid body in equilibrium can't have any tendency to start rotating about *any* point, so the sum of external torques must be zero about any point. This is the **second condition for equilibrium:**

> **Second condition for equilibrium:** For a nonrotating body to remain nonrotating ...
>
> $$\sum \vec{\tau} = 0 \quad \longleftarrow \begin{array}{l} \textit{... net external torque} \\ \textit{around any point on} \\ \textit{the body must be zero.} \end{array}$$
>
> (11.2)

In this chapter we'll apply the first and second conditions for equilibrium to situations in which a rigid body is at rest (no translation or rotation). Such a body is said to be in **static equilibrium** (**Fig. 11.1**). But the same conditions apply to a rigid body in uniform *translational* motion (without rotation), such as an airplane in flight with constant speed, direction, and altitude. Such a body is in equilibrium but is not static.

TEST YOUR UNDERSTANDING OF SECTION 11.1 Which situation satisfies both the first and second conditions for equilibrium? (i) A seagull gliding at a constant angle below the horizontal and at a constant speed; (ii) an automobile crankshaft turning at an increasing angular speed in the engine of a parked car; (iii) a thrown baseball that does not rotate as it sails through the air. ▮

11.2 CENTER OF GRAVITY

In most equilibrium problems, one of the forces acting on the body is its weight. We need to be able to calculate the *torque* of this force. The weight doesn't act at a single point; it is distributed over the entire body. But we can always calculate the torque due to the body's weight by assuming that the entire force of gravity (weight) is concentrated at a point called the **center of gravity** (abbreviated "cg"). The acceleration due to gravity decreases with altitude; but if we can ignore this variation over the vertical dimension of the body, then the body's center of gravity is identical to its *center of mass* (abbreviated "cm"), which we defined in Section 8.5. We stated this result without proof in Section 10.2, and now we'll prove it.

First let's review the definition of the center of mass. For a collection of particles with masses m_1, m_2, ... and coordinates (x_1, y_1, z_1), (x_2, y_2, z_2), ..., the coordinates x_{cm}, y_{cm}, and z_{cm} of the center of mass of the collection are

$$x_{cm} = \frac{m_1 x_1 + m_2 x_2 + m_3 x_3 + \cdots}{m_1 + m_2 + m_3 + \cdots} = \frac{\sum_i m_i x_i}{\sum_i m_i}$$

$$y_{cm} = \frac{m_1 y_1 + m_2 y_2 + m_3 y_3 + \cdots}{m_1 + m_2 + m_3 + \cdots} = \frac{\sum_i m_i y_i}{\sum_i m_i} \qquad \text{(center of mass)} \qquad (11.3)$$

$$z_{cm} = \frac{m_1 z_1 + m_2 z_2 + m_3 z_3 + \cdots}{m_1 + m_2 + m_3 + \cdots} = \frac{\sum_i m_i z_i}{\sum_i m_i}$$

Also, x_{cm}, y_{cm}, and z_{cm} are the components of the position vector $\vec{r}_{cm}$ of the center of mass, so Eqs. (11.3) are equivalent to the vector equation

Position vector of center of mass of a system of particles

Position vectors of individual particles

$$\vec{r}_{cm} = \frac{m_1 \vec{r}_1 + m_2 \vec{r}_2 + m_3 \vec{r}_3 + \cdots}{m_1 + m_2 + m_3 + \cdots} = \frac{\sum_i m_i \vec{r}_i}{\sum_i m_i} \qquad (11.4)$$

Masses of individual particles

Now consider the gravitational torque on a body of arbitrary shape (**Fig. 11.2**). We assume that the acceleration due to gravity $\vec{g}$ is the same at every point in the body. Every particle in the body experiences a gravitational force, and the total weight of the body is the vector sum of a large number of parallel forces. A typical particle has mass m_i and weight $\vec{w}_i = m_i \vec{g}$. If $\vec{r}_i$ is the position vector of this particle with respect to an arbitrary origin O, then the torque vector $\vec{\tau}_i$ of the weight $\vec{w}_i$ with respect to O is, from Eq. (10.3),

$$\vec{\tau}_i = \vec{r}_i \times \vec{w}_i = \vec{r}_i \times m_i \vec{g}$$

The *total* torque due to the gravitational forces on all the particles is

$$\vec{\tau} = \sum_i \vec{\tau}_i = \vec{r}_1 \times m_1 \vec{g} + \vec{r}_2 \times m_2 \vec{g} + \cdots$$

$$= (m_1 \vec{r}_1 + m_2 \vec{r}_2 + \cdots) \times \vec{g}$$

$$= \left(\sum_i m_i \vec{r}_i \right) \times \vec{g}$$

When we multiply and divide this by the total mass of the body,

$$M = m_1 + m_2 + \cdots = \sum_i m_i$$

we get

$$\vec{\tau} = \frac{m_1 \vec{r}_1 + m_2 \vec{r}_2 + \cdots}{m_1 + m_2 + \cdots} \times M\vec{g} = \frac{\sum_i m_i \vec{r}_i}{\sum_i m_i} \times M\vec{g}$$

11.2 The center of gravity (cg) and center of mass (cm) of an extended body.

The gravitational torque about O on a particle of mass m_i within the body is $\vec{\tau}_i = \vec{r}_i \times \vec{w}_i$.

If $\vec{g}$ has the same value at all points on the body, the cg is identical to the cm.

The net gravitational torque about O on the entire body is the same as if all the weight acted at the cg: $\vec{\tau} = \vec{r}_{cm} \times \vec{w}$.

11.3 The acceleration due to gravity at the bottom of the 452-m-tall Petronas Towers in Malaysia is only 0.014% greater than at the top. The center of gravity of the towers is only about 2 cm below the center of mass.

11.4 Finding the center of gravity of an irregularly shaped body—in this case, a coffee mug.

Where is the center of gravity of this mug?

① Suspend the mug from any point. A vertical line extending down from the point of suspension passes through the center of gravity.

② Now suspend the mug from a different point. A vertical line extending down from this point intersects the first line at the center of gravity (which is inside the mug).

Center of gravity

The fraction in this equation is just the position vector $\vec{r}_{cm}$ of the center of mass, with components x_{cm}, y_{cm}, and z_{cm}, as given by Eq. (11.4), and $M\vec{g}$ is equal to the total weight $\vec{w}$ of the body. Thus

$$\vec{\tau} = \vec{r}_{cm} \times M\vec{g} = \vec{r}_{cm} \times \vec{w} \qquad (11.5)$$

The total gravitational torque, given by Eq. (11.5), is the same as though the total weight $\vec{w}$ were acting at the position $\vec{r}_{cm}$ of the center of mass, which we also call the *center of gravity*. **If $\vec{g}$ has the same value at all points on a body, its center of gravity is identical to its center of mass.** Note, however, that the center of mass is defined independently of any gravitational effect.

While the value of $\vec{g}$ varies somewhat with elevation, the variation is extremely slight (**Fig. 11.3**). We'll assume throughout this chapter that the center of gravity and center of mass are identical unless explicitly stated otherwise.

Finding and Using the Center of Gravity

We can often use symmetry considerations to locate the center of gravity of a body, just as we did for the center of mass. The center of gravity of a homogeneous sphere, cube, or rectangular plate is at its geometric center. The center of gravity of a right circular cylinder or cone is on its axis of symmetry.

For a body with a more complex shape, we can sometimes locate the center of gravity by thinking of the body as being made of symmetrical pieces. For example, we could approximate the human body as a collection of solid cylinders, with a sphere for the head. Then we can locate the center of gravity of the combination with Eqs. (11.3), letting m_1, m_2, ... be the masses of the individual pieces and (x_1, y_1, z_1), (x_2, y_2, z_2), ... be the coordinates of their centers of gravity.

When a body in rotational equilibrium and acted on by gravity is supported or suspended at a single point, the center of gravity is always at or directly above or below the point of suspension. If it were anywhere else, the weight would have a torque with respect to the point of suspension, and the body could not be in rotational equilibrium. **Figure 11.4** shows an application of this idea.

Using the same reasoning, we can see that a body supported at several points must have its center of gravity somewhere within the area bounded by the supports. This explains why a car can drive on a straight but slanted road if the slant angle is relatively small (**Fig. 11.5a**) but will tip over if the angle is too steep (Fig. 11.5b). The truck in Fig. 11.5c has a higher center of gravity than the car and will tip over on a shallower incline.

The lower the center of gravity and the larger the area of support, the harder it is to overturn a body. Four-legged animals such as deer and horses have a large area of support bounded by their legs; hence they are naturally stable and need only small feet or hooves. Animals that walk on two legs, such as humans and birds, need relatively large feet to give them a reasonable area of support. If a

11.5 In (a) the center of gravity is within the area bounded by the supports, and the car is in equilibrium. The car in (b) and the truck in (c) will tip over because their centers of gravity lie outside the area of support.

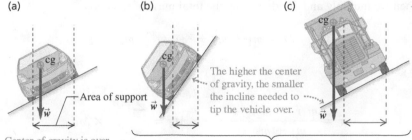

(a) Center of gravity is over the area of support: car is in equilibrium.

(b) (c) The higher the center of gravity, the smaller the incline needed to tip the vehicle over. Center of gravity is outside the area of support: vehicle tips over.

two-legged animal holds its body approximately horizontal, like a chicken or the dinosaur *Tyrannosaurus rex,* it must perform a balancing act as it walks to keep its center of gravity over the foot that is on the ground. A chicken does this by moving its head; *T. rex* probably did it by moving its massive tail.

DEMO

EXAMPLE 11.1 | WALKING THE PLANK

A uniform plank of length $L = 6.0$ m and mass $M = 90$ kg rests on sawhorses separated by $D = 1.5$ m and equidistant from the center of the plank. Cousin Throckmorton wants to stand on the right-hand end of the plank. If the plank is to remain at rest, how massive can Throckmorton be?

SOLUTION

IDENTIFY and SET UP: To just balance, Throckmorton's mass m must be such that the center of gravity of the plank–Throcky system is directly over the right-hand sawhorse (**Fig. 11.6**). We take the origin at C, the geometric center and center of gravity of the plank, and take the positive x-axis horizontally to the right. Then the centers of gravity of the plank and Throcky are at $x_P = 0$ and $x_T = L/2 = 3.0$ m, respectively, and the right-hand sawhorse is at

$x_S = D/2$. We'll use Eqs. (11.3) to locate the center of gravity x_{cg} of the plank–Throcky system.

EXECUTE: From the first of Eqs. (11.3),

$$x_{cg} = \frac{M(0) + m(L/2)}{M + m} = \frac{m}{M + m}\frac{L}{2}$$

We set $x_{cg} = x_S$ and solve for m:

$$\frac{m}{M + m}\frac{L}{2} = \frac{D}{2}$$

$$mL = (M + m)D$$

$$m = M\frac{D}{L - D} = (90 \text{ kg})\frac{1.5 \text{ m}}{6.0 \text{ m} - 1.5 \text{ m}} = 30 \text{ kg}$$

EVALUATE: As a check, let's repeat the calculation with the origin at the right-hand sawhorse. Now $x_S = 0$, $x_P = -D/2$, and $x_T = (L/2) - (D/2)$, and we require $x_{cg} = x_S = 0$:

$$x_{cg} = \frac{M(-D/2) + m[(L/2) - (D/2)]}{M + m} = 0$$

$$m = \frac{MD/2}{(L/2) - (D/2)} = M\frac{D}{L - D} = 30 \text{ kg}$$

The result doesn't depend on our choice of origin.

A 60-kg adult could stand only halfway between the right-hand sawhorse and the end of the plank. Can you see why?

11.6 Our sketch for this problem.

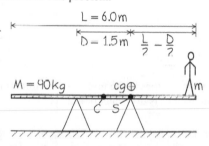

TEST YOUR UNDERSTANDING OF SECTION 11.2 A rock is attached to the left end of a uniform meter stick that has the same mass as the rock. In order for the combination of rock and meter stick to balance atop the triangular object in **Fig. 11.7**, how far from the left end of the stick should the triangular object be placed? (i) Less than 0.25 m; (ii) 0.25 m; (iii) between 0.25 m and 0.50 m; (iv) 0.50 m; (v) more than 0.50 m. ∎

11.7 At what point will the meter stick with rock attached be in balance?

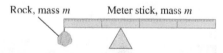

Rock, mass m \ Meter stick, mass m

11.3 SOLVING RIGID-BODY EQUILIBRIUM PROBLEMS

There are just two key conditions for rigid-body equilibrium: The vector sum of the forces on the body must be zero, and the sum of the torques about any point must be zero. To keep things simple, we'll restrict our attention to situations in which we can treat all forces as acting in a single plane, which we'll call the xy-plane. Then we need consider only the x- and y-components of force in Eq. (11.1), and in Eq. (11.2) we need consider only the z-components of torque (perpendicular to the plane). The first and second conditions for equilibrium are then

$$\Sigma F_x = 0 \quad \text{and} \quad \Sigma F_y = 0 \qquad \text{(first condition for equilibrium, forces in } xy\text{-plane)}$$

$$\Sigma \tau_z = 0 \qquad \text{(second condition for equilibrium, forces in } xy\text{-plane)}$$

(11.6)

CAUTION Choosing the reference point for calculating torques In equilibrium problems, the choice of reference point for calculating torques in $\Sigma \tau_z$ is completely arbitrary. But once you make your choice, you must use the *same* point to calculate *all* the torques on a body. Choose the point so as to simplify the calculations as much as possible. ∎

The challenge is to apply these simple conditions to specific problems. Problem-Solving Strategy 11.1 is very similar to the suggestions given in Section 5.1 for the equilibrium of a particle. You should compare it with Problem-Solving Strategy 10.1 (Section 10.2) for rotational dynamics problems.

PROBLEM-SOLVING STRATEGY 11.1 EQUILIBRIUM OF A RIGID BODY

IDENTIFY *the relevant concepts:* The first and second conditions for equilibrium ($\sum F_x = 0$, $\sum F_y = 0$, and $\sum \tau_z = 0$) are applicable to any rigid body that is not accelerating in space and not rotating.

SET UP *the problem* using the following steps:
1. Sketch the physical situation and identify the body in equilibrium to be analyzed. Sketch the body accurately; do *not* represent it as a point. Include dimensions.
2. Draw a free-body diagram showing all forces acting *on* the body. Show the point on the body at which each force acts.
3. Choose coordinate axes and specify their direction. Specify a positive direction of rotation for torques. Represent forces in terms of their components with respect to the chosen axes.
4. Choose a reference point about which to compute torques. Choose wisely; you can eliminate from your torque equation

any force whose line of action goes through the point you choose. The body doesn't actually have to be pivoted about an axis through the reference point.

EXECUTE *the solution* as follows:
1. Write equations expressing the equilibrium conditions. Remember that $\sum F_x = 0$, $\sum F_y = 0$, and $\sum \tau_z = 0$ are *separate* equations. You can compute the torque of a force by finding the torque of each of its components separately, each with its appropriate lever arm and sign, and adding the results.
2. To obtain as many equations as you have unknowns, you may need to compute torques with respect to two or more reference points; choose them wisely, too.

EVALUATE *your answer:* Check your results by writing $\sum \tau_z = 0$ with respect to a different reference point. You should get the same answers.

EXAMPLE 11.2   LOCATING YOUR CENTER OF GRAVITY WHILE YOU WORK OUT

The *plank* (**Fig. 11.8a**) is a great way to strengthen abdominal, back, and shoulder muscles. You can also use this exercise position to locate your center of gravity. Holding plank position with a scale under his toes and another under his forearms, one athlete measured that 66.0% of his weight was supported by his forearms and 34.0% by his toes. (That is, the total normal forces on his forearms and toes were $0.660w$ and $0.340w$, respectively, where w is the athlete's weight.) He is 1.80 m tall, and in plank position

11.8 An athlete in plank position.

(a)

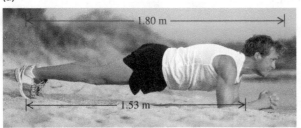

(b)

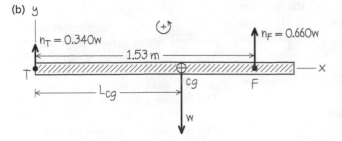

the distance from his toes to the middle of his forearms is 1.53 m. How far from his toes is his center of gravity?

SOLUTION

IDENTIFY and SET UP: We can use the two conditions for equilibrium, Eqs. (11.6), for an athlete at rest. So both the net force and net torque on the athlete are zero. Figure 11.8b shows a free-body diagram, including x- and y-axes and our convention that counterclockwise torques are positive. The weight w acts at the center of gravity, which is between the two supports (as it must be; see Section 11.2). Our target variable is the distance L_{cg}, the lever arm of the weight with respect to the toes T, so it is wise to take torques with respect to T. The torque due to the weight is negative (it tends to cause a clockwise rotation around T), and the torque due to the upward normal force at the forearms F is positive (it tends to cause a counterclockwise rotation around T).

EXECUTE: The first condition for equilibrium is satisfied (Fig. 11.8b): $\sum F_x = 0$ because there are no x-components and $\sum F_y = 0$ because $0.340w + 0.660w + (-w) = 0$. We write the torque equation and solve for L_{cg}:

$$\sum \tau_R = 0.340w(0) - wL_{cg} + 0.660w(1.53 \text{ m}) = 0$$
$$L_{cg} = 1.01 \text{ m}$$

EVALUATE: The center of gravity is slightly below our athlete's navel (as it is for most people) and closer to his forearms than to his toes, which is why his forearms support most of his weight. You can check our result by writing the torque equation about the forearms F. You'll find that his center of gravity is 0.52 m from his forearms, or $(1.53 \text{ m}) - (0.52 \text{ m}) = 1.01 \text{ m}$ from his toes.

EXAMPLE 11.3   WILL THE LADDER SLIP?

Sir Lancelot, who weighs 800 N, is assaulting a castle by climbing a uniform ladder that is 5.0 m long and weighs 180 N (**Fig. 11.9a**). The bottom of the ladder rests on a ledge and leans across the moat in equilibrium against a frictionless, vertical castle wall. The ladder makes an angle of 53.1° with the horizontal. Lancelot pauses one-third of the way up the ladder. (a) Find the normal and friction forces on the base of the ladder. (b) Find the minimum coefficient of static friction needed to prevent slipping at the base. (c) Find the magnitude and direction of the contact force on the base of the ladder.

SOLUTION

IDENTIFY and SET UP: The ladder–Lancelot system is stationary, so we can use the two conditions for equilibrium to solve part (a). In part (b), we need the relationship among the static friction force, coefficient of static friction, and normal force (see Section 5.3). In part (c), the contact force is the vector sum of the normal and friction forces acting at the base of the ladder, found in part (a). Figure 11.9b shows the free-body diagram, with x- and y-directions as shown and with counterclockwise torques taken to be positive. The ladder's center of gravity is at its geometric center. Lancelot's 800-N weight acts at a point one-third of the way up the ladder.

The wall exerts only a normal force n_1 on the top of the ladder. The forces on the base are an upward normal force n_2 and a static friction force f_s, which must point to the right to prevent slipping. The magnitudes n_2 and f_s are the target variables in part (a). From Eq. (5.4), these magnitudes are related by $f_s \leq \mu_s n_2$; the coefficient of static friction μ_s is the target variable in part (b).

EXECUTE: (a) From Eqs. (11.6), the first condition for equilibrium gives

$$\Sigma F_x = f_s + (-n_1) = 0$$
$$\Sigma F_y = n_2 + (-800 \text{ N}) + (-180 \text{ N}) = 0$$

These are two equations for the three unknowns n_1, n_2, and f_s. The second equation gives $n_2 = 980$ N. To obtain a third equation, we use the second condition for equilibrium. We take torques about point B, about which n_2 and f_s have no torque. The 53.1° angle creates a 3-4-5 right triangle, so from Fig. 11.9b the lever arm for the ladder's weight is 1.5 m, the lever arm for Lancelot's

weight is 1.0 m, and the lever arm for n_1 is 4.0 m. The torque equation for point B is then

$$\Sigma \tau_B = n_1(4.0 \text{ m}) - (180 \text{ N})(1.5 \text{ m})$$
$$- (800 \text{ N})(1.0 \text{ m}) + n_2(0) + f_s(0) = 0$$

Solving for n_1, we get $n_1 = 268$ N. We substitute this into the $\Sigma F_x = 0$ equation and get $f_s = 268$ N.

(b) The static friction force f_s cannot exceed $\mu_s n_2$, so the *minimum* coefficient of static friction to prevent slipping is

$$(\mu_s)_{min} = \frac{f_s}{n_2} = \frac{268 \text{ N}}{980 \text{ N}} = 0.27$$

(c) The components of the contact force $\vec{F}_B$ at the base are the static friction force f_s and the normal force n_2, so

$$\vec{F}_B = f_s \hat{\imath} + n_2 \hat{\jmath} = (268 \text{ N})\hat{\imath} + (980 \text{ N})\hat{\jmath}$$

The magnitude and direction of $\vec{F}_B$ (Fig. 11.9c) are

$$F_B = \sqrt{(268 \text{ N})^2 + (980 \text{ N})^2} = 1020 \text{ N}$$
$$\theta = \arctan\frac{980 \text{ N}}{268 \text{ N}} = 75°$$

EVALUATE: As Fig. 11.9c shows, the contact force $\vec{F}_B$ is *not* directed along the length of the ladder. Can you show that if $\vec{F}_B$ were directed along the ladder, there would be a net counterclockwise torque with respect to the top of the ladder, and equilibrium would be impossible?

As Lancelot climbs higher on the ladder, the lever arm and torque of his weight about B increase. This increases the values of n_1, f_s, and the required friction coefficient $(\mu_s)_{min}$, so the ladder is more and more likely to slip as he climbs (see Exercise 11.10). A simple way to make slipping less likely is to use a larger ladder angle (say, 75° rather than 53.1°). This decreases the lever arms with respect to B of the weights of the ladder and Lancelot and increases the lever arm of n_1, all of which decrease the required friction force.

If we had assumed friction on the wall as well as on the floor, the problem would be impossible to solve by using the equilibrium conditions alone. (Try it!) The difficulty is that it's no longer adequate to treat the body as being perfectly rigid. Another problem of this kind is a four-legged table; there's no way to use the equilibrium conditions alone to find the force on each separate leg.

11.9 (a) Sir Lancelot pauses a third of the way up the ladder, fearing it will slip. (b) Free-body diagram for the system of Sir Lancelot and the ladder. (c) The contact force at B is the superposition of the normal force and the static friction force.

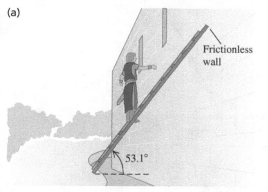

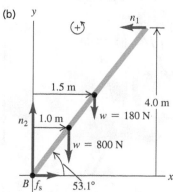

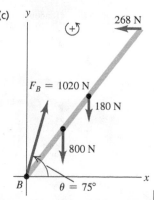

EXAMPLE 11.4 EQUILIBRIUM AND PUMPING IRON

Figure 11.10a shows a horizontal human arm lifting a dumbbell. The forearm is in equilibrium under the action of the weight $\vec{w}$ of the dumbbell, the tension $\vec{T}$ in the tendon connected to the biceps muscle, and the force $\vec{E}$ exerted on the forearm by the upper arm at the elbow joint. We ignore the weight of the forearm itself. (For clarity, in the drawing we've exaggerated the distance from the elbow to the point A where the tendon is attached.) Given the weight w and the angle θ between the tension force and the horizontal, find T and the two components of $\vec{E}$ (three unknown scalar quantities in all).

SOLUTION

IDENTIFY and SET UP: The system is at rest, so we use the conditions for equilibrium. We represent $\vec{T}$ and $\vec{E}$ in terms of their components (Fig. 11.10b). We guess that the directions of E_x and E_y are as shown; the signs of E_x and E_y as given by our solution will tell us the actual directions. Our target variables are T, E_x, and E_y.

EXECUTE: To find T, we take torques about the elbow joint so that the torque equation does not contain E_x, E_y, or T_x, then solve for T_y and hence T:

$$\sum \tau_{\text{elbow}} = Lw - DT_y = 0$$

$$T_y = \frac{Lw}{D} = T\sin\theta \quad \text{and} \quad T = \frac{Lw}{D\sin\theta}$$

To find E_x and E_y, we use the first conditions for equilibrium:

$$\sum F_x = T_x + (-E_x) = 0$$

$$E_x = T_x = T\cos\theta = \frac{Lw}{D\sin\theta}\cos\theta$$

$$= \frac{Lw}{D}\cot\theta = \frac{Lw}{D}\frac{D}{h} = \frac{Lw}{h}$$

$$\sum F_y = T_y + E_y + (-w) = 0$$

$$E_y = w - \frac{Lw}{D} = -\frac{(L-D)w}{D}$$

The negative sign for E_y tells us that it should actually point *down* in Fig. 11.10b.

EVALUATE: We can check our results for E_x and E_y by taking torques about points A and B, about both of which T has zero torque:

$$\sum \tau_A = (L-D)w + DE_y = 0 \quad \text{so} \quad E_y = -\frac{(L-D)w}{D}$$

$$\sum \tau_B = Lw - hE_x = 0 \quad \text{so} \quad E_x = \frac{Lw}{h}$$

As a realistic example, take $w = 200$ N, $D = 0.050$ m, $L = 0.30$ m, and $\theta = 80°$, so that $h = D\tan\theta = (0.050\text{ m})(5.67) = 0.28$ m. Using our results for T, E_x, and E_y, we find

$$T = \frac{Lw}{D\sin\theta} = \frac{(0.30\text{ m})(200\text{ N})}{(0.050\text{ m})(0.98)} = 1220\text{ N}$$

$$E_y = -\frac{(L-D)w}{D} = -\frac{(0.30\text{ m} - 0.050\text{ m})(200\text{ N})}{0.050\text{ m}}$$

$$= -1000\text{ N}$$

$$E_x = \frac{Lw}{h} = \frac{(0.30\text{ m})(200\text{ N})}{0.28\text{ m}} = 210\text{ N}$$

The magnitude of the force at the elbow is

$$E = \sqrt{E_x^2 + E_y^2} = 1020\text{ N}$$

Note that T and E are *much* larger than the 200-N weight of the dumbbell. A forearm weighs only about 20 N, so it was reasonable to ignore its weight.

11.10 (a) The situation. (b) Our free-body diagram for the forearm. The weight of the forearm is ignored, and the distance D is greatly exaggerated for clarity.

(a)

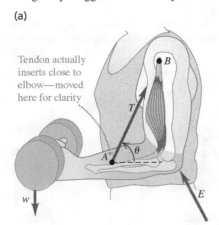

(b)

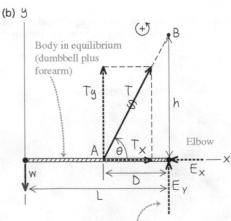

TEST YOUR UNDERSTANDING OF SECTION 11.3 A metal advertising sign (weight w) for a specialty shop is suspended from the end of a horizontal rod of length L and negligible mass (**Fig. 11.11**). The rod is supported by a cable at an angle θ from the horizontal and by a hinge at point P. Rank the following force magnitudes in order from greatest to smallest: (i) the weight w of the sign; (ii) the tension in the cable; (iii) the vertical component of force exerted on the rod by the hinge at P. ❚

11.11 What are the tension in the diagonal cable and the vertical component of force exerted by the hinge at P?

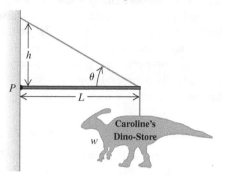

Caroline's Dino-Store

11.4 STRESS, STRAIN, AND ELASTIC MODULI

The rigid body is a useful idealized model, but the stretching, squeezing, and twisting of real bodies when forces are applied are often too important to ignore. **Figure 11.12** shows three examples. We want to study the relationship between the forces and deformations for each case.

You don't have to look far to find a deformable body; it's as plain as the nose on your face (**Fig. 11.13**). If you grasp the tip of your nose between your index finger and thumb, you'll find that the harder you pull your nose outward or push it inward, the more it stretches or compresses. Likewise, the harder you squeeze your index finger and thumb together, the more the tip of your nose compresses. If you try to twist the tip of your nose, you'll get a greater amount of twist if you apply stronger forces.

These observations illustrate a general rule. In each case you apply a **stress** to your nose; the amount of stress is a measure of the forces causing the deformation, on a "force per unit area" basis. And in each case the stress causes a deformation, or **strain.** More careful versions of the experiments with your nose suggest that for relatively small stresses, the resulting strain is proportional to the stress: The greater the deforming forces, the greater the resulting deformation. This proportionality is called **Hooke's law,** and the ratio of stress to strain is called the **elastic modulus:**

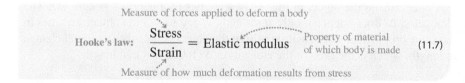

Measure of forces applied to deform a body

Hooke's law: $\dfrac{\text{Stress}}{\text{Strain}} = \text{Elastic modulus}$ Property of material of which body is made (11.7)

Measure of how much deformation results from stress

11.13 When you pinch your nose, the force per area that you apply to your nose is called *stress*. The fractional change in the size of your nose (the change in size divided by the initial size) is called *strain*. The deformation is *elastic* because your nose springs back to its initial size when you stop pinching.

11.12 Three types of stress. (a) Guitar strings under *tensile stress,* being stretched by forces acting at their ends. (b) A diver under *bulk stress,* being squeezed from all sides by forces due to water pressure. (c) A ribbon under *shear stress,* being deformed and eventually cut by forces exerted by the scissors.

The value of the elastic modulus depends on what the body is made of but not its shape or size. If a material returns to its original state after the stress is removed, it is called **elastic;** Hooke's law is a special case of elastic behavior. If a material instead remains deformed after the stress is removed, it is called **plastic.** Here we'll consider elastic behavior only; we'll return to plastic behavior in Section 11.5.

We used one form of Hooke's law in Section 6.3: The elongation of an ideal spring is proportional to the stretching force. Remember that Hooke's "law" is not really a general law; it is valid over only a limited range of stresses. In Section 11.5 we'll see what happens beyond that limited range.

Tensile and Compressive Stress and Strain

The simplest elastic behavior to understand is the stretching of a bar, rod, or wire when its ends are pulled (Fig. 11.12a). **Figure 11.14** shows an object that initially has uniform cross-sectional area A and length l_0. We then apply forces of equal magnitude $F_\perp$ but opposite directions at the ends (this ensures that the object has no tendency to move left or right). We say that the object is in **tension.** We've already talked a lot about tension in ropes and strings; it's the same concept here. The subscript $\perp$ is a reminder that the forces act perpendicular to the cross section.

We define the **tensile stress** at the cross section as the ratio of the force $F_\perp$ to the cross-sectional area A:

$$\text{Tensile stress} = \frac{F_\perp}{A} \quad (11.8)$$

This is a *scalar* quantity because $F_\perp$ is the *magnitude* of the force. The SI unit of stress is the **pascal** (abbreviated Pa and named for the 17th-century French scientist and philosopher Blaise Pascal). Equation (11.8) shows that 1 pascal equals 1 newton per square meter (N/m^2):

$$1 \text{ pascal} = 1 \text{ Pa} = 1 \text{ N/m}^2$$

In the British system the most common unit of stress is the pound per square inch (lb/in.^2 or psi). The conversion factors are

$$1 \text{ psi} = 6895 \text{ Pa} \quad \text{and} \quad 1 \text{ Pa} = 1.450 \times 10^{-4} \text{ psi}$$

The units of stress are the same as those of *pressure,* which we will encounter often in later chapters.

Under tension the object in Fig. 11.14 stretches to a length $l = l_0 + \Delta l$. The elongation Δl does not occur only at the ends; every part of the object stretches in the same proportion. The **tensile strain** of the object equals the fractional change in length, which is the ratio of the elongation Δl to the original length l_0:

$$\text{Tensile strain} = \frac{l - l_0}{l_0} = \frac{\Delta l}{l_0} \quad (11.9)$$

Tensile strain is stretch per unit length. It is a ratio of two lengths, always measured in the same units, and so is a pure (dimensionless) number with no units.

Experiment shows that for a sufficiently small tensile stress, stress and strain are proportional, as in Eq. (11.7). The corresponding elastic modulus is called **Young's modulus,** denoted by Y:

11.14 An object in tension. The net force on the object is zero, but the object deforms. The tensile stress (the ratio of the force to the cross-sectional area) produces a tensile strain (the elongation divided by the initial length). The elongation Δl is exaggerated for clarity.

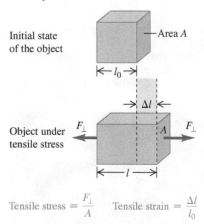

Initial state of the object — Area A

l_0

Δl

Object under tensile stress $F_\perp$ A $F_\perp$

l

Tensile stress $= \dfrac{F_\perp}{A}$ Tensile strain $= \dfrac{\Delta l}{l_0}$

BIO Application Young's Modulus of a Tendon The anterior tibial tendon connects your foot to the large muscle that runs along the side of your shinbone. (You can feel this tendon at the front of your ankle.) Measurements show that this tendon has a Young's modulus of 1.2×10^9 Pa, much less than for the metals listed in Table 11.1. Hence this tendon stretches substantially (up to 2.5% of its length) in response to the stresses experienced in walking and running.

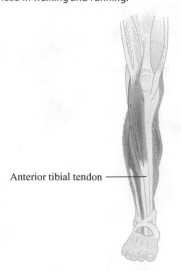

Anterior tibial tendon

$$\begin{array}{c} \text{Young's modulus} \\ \text{for tension} \end{array} \qquad \begin{array}{c} \text{Force applied perpendicular} \\ \text{to cross section} \end{array} \qquad \begin{array}{c} \text{Original length} \\ \text{(see Fig. 11.14)} \end{array}$$

$$Y = \frac{\text{Tensile stress}}{\text{Tensile strain}} = \frac{F_\perp/A}{\Delta l/l_0} = \frac{F_\perp}{A}\frac{l_0}{\Delta l} \quad (11.10)$$

Cross-sectional area of object   Elongation (see Fig. 11.14)

TABLE 11.1 Approximate Elastic Moduli

Material	Young's Modulus, Y (Pa)	Bulk Modulus, B (Pa)	Shear Modulus, S (Pa)
Aluminum	7.0×10^{10}	7.5×10^{10}	2.5×10^{10}
Brass	9.0×10^{10}	6.0×10^{10}	3.5×10^{10}
Copper	11×10^{10}	14×10^{10}	4.4×10^{10}
Iron	21×10^{10}	16×10^{10}	7.7×10^{10}
Lead	1.6×10^{10}	4.1×10^{10}	0.6×10^{10}
Nickel	21×10^{10}	17×10^{10}	7.8×10^{10}
Silicone rubber	0.001×10^{10}	0.2×10^{10}	0.0002×10^{10}
Steel	20×10^{10}	16×10^{10}	7.5×10^{10}
Tendon (typical)	0.12×10^{10}	—	—

Since strain is a pure number, the units of Young's modulus are the same as those of stress: force per unit area. **Table 11.1** lists some typical values. (This table also gives values of two other elastic moduli that we will discuss later in this chapter.) A material with a large value of Y is relatively unstretchable; a large stress is required for a given strain. For example, the value of Y for cast steel (2×10^{11} Pa) is much larger than that for a tendon (1.2×10^9 Pa).

When the forces on the ends of a bar are pushes rather than pulls (**Fig. 11.15**), the bar is in **compression** and the stress is a **compressive stress**. The **compressive strain** of an object in compression is defined in the same way as the tensile strain, but Δl has the opposite direction. Hooke's law and Eq. (11.10) are valid for compression as well as tension if the compressive stress is not too great. For many materials, Young's modulus has the same value for both tensile and compressive stresses. Composite materials such as concrete and stone are an exception; they can withstand compressive stresses but fail under comparable tensile stresses. Stone was the primary building material used by ancient civilizations such as the Babylonians, Assyrians, and Romans, so their structures had to be designed to avoid tensile stresses. Hence they used arches in doorways and bridges, where the weight of the overlying material compresses the stones of the arch together and does not place them under tension.

In many situations, bodies can experience both tensile and compressive stresses at the same time. For example, a horizontal beam supported at each end sags under its own weight. As a result, the top of the beam is under compression while the bottom of the beam is under tension (**Fig. 11.16a**). To minimize the stress and hence the bending strain, the top and bottom of the beam are given a large cross-sectional area. There is neither compression nor tension along the centerline of the beam, so this part can have a small cross section; this helps keep the weight of the beam to a minimum and further helps reduce the stress. The result is an I-beam of the familiar shape used in building construction (Fig. 11.16b).

11.15 An object in compression. The compressive stress and compressive strain are defined in the same way as tensile stress and strain (see Fig. 11.14), except that Δl now denotes the distance that the object contracts.

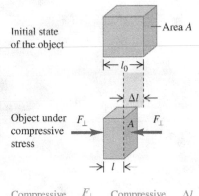

Initial state of the object — Area A

$\leftarrow l_0 \rightarrow$

$\rightarrow \Delta l \leftarrow$

Object under compressive stress $\quad F_\perp \quad A \quad F_\perp$

$\rightarrow l \leftarrow$

$$\text{Compressive} \atop \text{stress} = \frac{F_\perp}{A} \qquad \text{Compressive} \atop \text{strain} = \frac{\Delta l}{l_0}$$

(a)

Top of beam is under compression.

Beam's centerline is under neither tension nor compression.

Bottom of beam is under tension.

(b)

The top and bottom of an I-beam are broad to minimize the compressive and tensile stresses.

The beam can be narrow near its centerline, which is under neither compression nor tension.

11.16 (a) A beam supported at both ends is under both compression and tension. (b) The cross-sectional shape of an I-beam minimizes both stress and weight.

EXAMPLE 11.5 **TENSILE STRESS AND STRAIN**

A steel rod 2.0 m long has a cross-sectional area of 0.30 cm². It is hung by one end from a support, and a 550-kg milling machine is hung from its other end. Determine the stress on the rod and the resulting strain and elongation.

SOLUTION

IDENTIFY, SET UP, and EXECUTE: The rod is under tension, so we can use Eq. (11.8) to find the tensile stress; Eq. (11.9), with the value of Young's modulus Y for steel from Table 11.1, to find the corresponding strain; and Eq. (11.10) to find the elongation Δl:

$$\text{Tensile stress} = \frac{F_\perp}{A} = \frac{(550 \text{ kg})(9.8 \text{ m/s}^2)}{3.0 \times 10^{-5} \text{ m}^2} = 1.8 \times 10^8 \text{ Pa}$$

$$\text{Strain} = \frac{\Delta l}{l_0} = \frac{\text{Stress}}{Y} = \frac{1.8 \times 10^8 \text{ Pa}}{20 \times 10^{10} \text{ Pa}} = 9.0 \times 10^{-4}$$

$$\text{Elongation} = \Delta l = (\text{Strain}) \times l_0$$
$$= (9.0 \times 10^{-4})(2.0 \text{ m}) = 0.0018 \text{ m} = 1.8 \text{ mm}$$

EVALUATE: This small elongation, resulting from a load of over half a ton, is a testament to the stiffness of steel. (We've ignored the relatively small stress due to the weight of the rod itself.)

BIO Application Bulk Stress on an Anglerfish The anglerfish (*Melanocetus johnsoni*) is found in oceans throughout the world at depths as great as 1000 m, where the pressure (that is, the bulk stress) is about 100 atmospheres. Anglerfish are able to withstand such stress because they have no internal air spaces, unlike fish found in the upper ocean, where pressures are lower. The largest anglerfish are about 12 cm (5 in.) long.

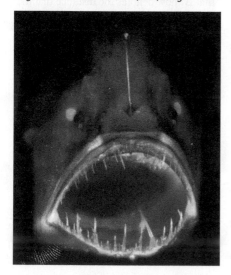

Bulk Stress and Strain

When a scuba diver plunges deep into the ocean, the water exerts nearly uniform pressure everywhere on his surface and squeezes him to a slightly smaller volume (see Fig. 11.12b). This is a different situation from the tensile and compressive stresses and strains we have discussed. The uniform pressure on all sides of the diver is a **bulk stress** (or **volume stress**), and the resulting deformation—a **bulk strain** (or **volume strain**)—is a change in his volume.

If an object is immersed in a fluid (liquid or gas) at rest, the fluid exerts a force on any part of the object's surface; this force is *perpendicular* to the surface. (If we tried to make the fluid exert a force parallel to the surface, the fluid would slip sideways to counteract the effort.) The force $F_\perp$ per unit area that the fluid exerts on an immersed object is called the **pressure** p in the fluid:

Pressure in a fluid $\cdots\blacktriangleright p = \dfrac{F_\perp}{A}$ ⟵ Force that fluid applies to surface of an immersed object
⟵ Area over which force is exerted (11.11)

Pressure has the same units as stress; commonly used units include 1 Pa ($= 1 \text{ N/m}^2$), 1 lb/in.² (1 psi), and 1 **atmosphere** (1 atm). One atmosphere is the approximate average pressure of the earth's atmosphere at sea level:

$$1 \text{ atmosphere} = 1 \text{ atm} = 1.013 \times 10^5 \text{ Pa} = 14.7 \text{ lb/in.}^2$$

CAUTION **Pressure vs. force** Unlike force, pressure has no intrinsic direction: The pressure on the surface of an immersed object is the same no matter how the surface is oriented. Hence pressure is a *scalar* quantity, not a vector quantity. ▮

The pressure in a fluid increases with depth. For example, the pressure in the ocean increases by about 1 atm every 10 m. If an immersed object is relatively small, however, we can ignore these pressure differences for purposes of calculating bulk stress. We'll then treat the pressure as having the same value at all points on an immersed object's surface.

Pressure plays the role of stress in a volume deformation. The corresponding strain is the fractional change in volume (**Fig. 11.17**)—that is, the ratio of the volume change ΔV to the original volume V_0:

$$\text{Bulk (volume) strain} = \frac{\Delta V}{V_0} \qquad (11.12)$$

Volume strain is the change in volume per unit volume. Like tensile or compressive strain, it is a pure number, without units.

When Hooke's law is obeyed, an increase in pressure (bulk stress) produces a *proportional* bulk strain (fractional change in volume). The corresponding elastic modulus (ratio of stress to strain) is called the **bulk modulus,** denoted by B. When the pressure on a body changes by a small amount Δp, from p_0 to $p_0 + \Delta p$, and the resulting bulk strain is $\Delta V/V_0$, Hooke's law takes the form

11.17 An object under bulk stress. Without the stress, the cube has volume V_0; when the stress is applied, the cube has a smaller volume V. The volume change ΔV is exaggerated for clarity.

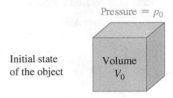

$$\underset{\substack{\text{Bulk modulus} \\ \text{for compression}}}{\longrightarrow} B = \frac{\text{Bulk stress}}{\text{Bulk strain}} = -\frac{\Delta p}{\Delta V/V_0} \quad \begin{array}{l}\text{Additional pressure} \\ \text{on object}\end{array} \qquad (11.13)$$

Change in volume (see Fig. 11.17) ⋯ Original volume (see Fig. 11.17)

We include a minus sign in this equation because an *increase* of pressure always causes a *decrease* in volume. In other words, if Δp is positive, ΔV is negative. The bulk modulus B itself is a positive quantity.

For small pressure changes in a solid or a liquid, we consider B to be constant. The bulk modulus of a *gas,* however, depends on the initial pressure p_0. Table 11.1 includes values of B for several solid materials. Its units, force per unit area, are the same as those of pressure (and of tensile or compressive stress).

The reciprocal of the bulk modulus is called the **compressibility** and is denoted by k. From Eq. (11.13),

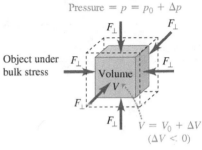

Bulk stress $= \Delta p$ Bulk strain $= \dfrac{\Delta V}{V_0}$

$$k = \frac{1}{B} = -\frac{\Delta V/V_0}{\Delta p} = -\frac{1}{V_0}\frac{\Delta V}{\Delta p} \quad \text{(compressibility)} \qquad (11.14)$$

Compressibility is the fractional decrease in volume, $-\Delta V/V_0$, per unit increase Δp in pressure. The units of compressibility are those of *reciprocal pressure,* Pa^{-1} or atm^{-1}.

Table 11.2 lists the values of compressibility k for several liquids. For example, the compressibility of water is $46.4 \times 10^{-6}\ \text{atm}^{-1}$, which means that the volume of water decreases by 46.4 parts per million for each 1-atmosphere increase in pressure. Materials with small bulk modulus B and large compressibility k are easiest to compress.

Compressibilities

TABLE 11.2	**of Liquids**	
	Compressibility, k	
Liquid	Pa^{-1}	atm^{-1}
Carbon disulfide	93×10^{-11}	94×10^{-6}
Ethyl alcohol	110×10^{-11}	111×10^{-6}
Glycerine	21×10^{-11}	21×10^{-6}
Mercury	3.7×10^{-11}	3.8×10^{-6}
Water	45.8×10^{-11}	46.4×10^{-6}

EXAMPLE 11.6   BULK STRESS AND STRAIN

A hydraulic press contains $0.25\ \text{m}^3$ (250 L) of oil. Find the decrease in the volume of the oil when it is subjected to a pressure increase $\Delta p = 1.6 \times 10^7\ \text{Pa}$ (about 160 atm or 2300 psi). The bulk modulus of the oil is $B = 5.0 \times 10^9\ \text{Pa}$ (about $5.0 \times 10^4\ \text{atm}$), and its compressibility is $k = 1/B = 20 \times 10^{-6}\ \text{atm}^{-1}$.

SOLUTION

IDENTIFY, SET UP, and EXECUTE: This example uses the ideas of bulk stress and strain. We are given both the bulk modulus and the compressibility, and our target variable is ΔV. Solving Eq. (11.13) for ΔV, we find

$$\Delta V = -\frac{V_0 \Delta p}{B} = -\frac{(0.25\ \text{m}^3)(1.6 \times 10^7\ \text{Pa})}{5.0 \times 10^9\ \text{Pa}}$$

$$= -8.0 \times 10^{-4}\ \text{m}^3 = -0.80\ \text{L}$$

Alternatively, we can use Eq. (11.14) with the approximate unit conversions given above:

$$\Delta V = -kV_0\Delta p = -(20 \times 10^{-6}\ \text{atm}^{-1})(0.25\ \text{m}^3)(160\ \text{atm})$$

$$= -8.0 \times 10^{-4}\ \text{m}^3$$

EVALUATE: The negative value of ΔV means that the volume decreases when the pressure increases. The 160-atm pressure increase is large, but the *fractional* volume change is very small:

$$\frac{\Delta V}{V_0} = \frac{-8.0 \times 10^{-4}\ \text{m}^3}{0.25\ \text{m}^3} = -0.0032 \quad \text{or} \quad -0.32\%$$

11.18 An object under shear stress. Forces are applied tangent to opposite surfaces of the object (in contrast to the situation in Fig. 11.14, in which the forces act perpendicular to the surfaces). The deformation x is exaggerated for clarity.

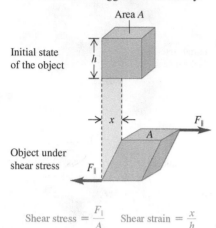

Shear Stress and Strain

The third kind of stress-strain situation is called *shear*. The ribbon in Fig. 11.12c is under **shear stress:** One part of the ribbon is being pushed up while an adjacent part is being pushed down, producing a deformation of the ribbon. **Figure 11.18** shows a body being deformed by a shear stress. In the figure, forces of equal magnitude but opposite direction act *tangent* to the surfaces of opposite ends of the object. We define the shear stress as the force $F_{\parallel}$ acting tangent to the surface divided by the area A on which it acts:

$$\text{Shear stress} = \frac{F_{\parallel}}{A} \qquad (11.15)$$

Shear stress, like the other two types of stress, is a force per unit area.

Figure 11.18 shows that one face of the object under shear stress is displaced by a distance x relative to the opposite face. We define **shear strain** as the ratio of the displacement x to the transverse dimension h:

$$\text{Shear strain} = \frac{x}{h} \qquad (11.16)$$

In real-life situations, x is typically much smaller than h. Like all strains, shear strain is a dimensionless number; it is a ratio of two lengths.

If the forces are small enough that Hooke's law is obeyed, the shear strain is *proportional* to the shear stress. The corresponding elastic modulus (ratio of shear stress to shear strain) is called the **shear modulus,** denoted by S:

Force applied tangent to surface of object ⋯⋯ Transverse dimension (see Fig. 11.18)

$$\text{Shear modulus for shear} \quad S = \frac{\text{Shear stress}}{\text{Shear strain}} = \frac{F_{\parallel}/A}{x/h} = \frac{F_{\parallel}}{A}\frac{h}{x} \qquad (11.17)$$

Area over which force is exerted ⋯⋯ Deformation (see Fig. 11.18)

Table 11.1 gives several values of shear modulus. For a given material, S is usually one-third to one-half as large as Young's modulus Y for tensile stress. Keep in mind that the concepts of shear stress, shear strain, and shear modulus apply to *solid* materials only. The reason is that *shear* refers to deforming an object that has a definite shape (see Fig. 11.18). This concept doesn't apply to gases and liquids, which do not have definite shapes.

EXAMPLE 11.7 **SHEAR STRESS AND STRAIN**

Suppose the object in Fig. 11.18 is the brass base plate of an outdoor sculpture that experiences shear forces in an earthquake. The plate is 0.80 m square and 0.50 cm thick. What is the force exerted on each of its edges if the resulting displacement x is 0.16 mm?

SOLUTION

IDENTIFY and SET UP: This example uses the relationship among shear stress, shear strain, and shear modulus. Our target variable is the force $F_{\parallel}$ exerted parallel to each edge, as shown in Fig. 11.18. We'll find the shear strain from Eq. (11.16), the shear stress from Eq. (11.17), and $F_{\parallel}$ from Eq. (11.15). Table 11.1 gives the shear modulus of brass. In Fig. 11.18, h represents the 0.80-m length of each side of the plate. The area A in Eq. (11.15) is the product of the 0.80-m length and the 0.50-cm thickness.

EXECUTE: From Eq. (11.16),

$$\text{Shear strain} = \frac{x}{h} = \frac{1.6 \times 10^{-4}\ \text{m}}{0.80\ \text{m}} = 2.0 \times 10^{-4}$$

From Eq. (11.17),

$$\text{Shear stress} = (\text{Shear strain}) \times S$$
$$= (2.0 \times 10^{-4})(3.5 \times 10^{10}\ \text{Pa}) = 7.0 \times 10^{6}\ \text{Pa}$$

Finally, from Eq. (11.15),

$$F_{\parallel} = (\text{Shear stress}) \times A$$
$$= (7.0 \times 10^{6}\ \text{Pa})(0.80\ \text{m})(0.0050\ \text{m}) = 2.8 \times 10^{4}\ \text{N}$$

EVALUATE: The shear force supplied by the earthquake is more than 3 tons! The large shear modulus of brass makes it hard to deform. Further, the plate is relatively thick (0.50 cm), so the area A is relatively large and a substantial force $F_{\parallel}$ is needed to provide the necessary stress $F_{\parallel}/A$.

11.5 ELASTICITY AND PLASTICITY

Hooke's law—the proportionality of stress and strain in elastic deformations—has a limited range of validity. In the preceding section we used phrases such as "if the forces are small enough that Hooke's law is obeyed." Just what *are* the limitations of Hooke's law? What's more, if you pull, squeeze, or twist *anything* hard enough, it will bend or break. Can we be more precise than that?

To address these questions, let's look at a graph of tensile stress as a function of tensile strain. **Figure 11.19** shows a typical graph of this kind for a metal such as copper or soft iron. The strain is shown as the *percent* elongation; the horizontal scale is not uniform beyond the first portion of the curve, up to a strain of less than 1%. The first portion is a straight line, indicating Hooke's law behavior with stress directly proportional to strain. This straight-line portion ends at point *a*; the stress at this point is called the *proportional limit*.

From *a* to *b*, stress and strain are no longer proportional, and Hooke's law is *not* obeyed. However, from *a* to *b* (and *O* to *a*), the behavior of the material is *elastic:* If the load is gradually removed starting at any point between *O* and *b*, the curve is retraced until the material returns to its original length. This elastic deformation is *reversible*.

Point *b*, the end of the elastic region, is called the *yield point;* the stress at the yield point is called the *elastic limit*. When we increase the stress beyond point *b*, the strain continues to increase. But if we remove the load at a point like *c* beyond the elastic limit, the material does *not* return to its original length. Instead, it follows the red line in Fig. 11.19. The material has deformed *irreversibly* and acquired a *permanent set*. This is the *plastic* behavior mentioned in Section 11.4.

Once the material has become plastic, a small additional stress produces a relatively large increase in strain, until a point *d* is reached at which *fracture* takes place. That's what happens if a steel guitar string in Fig. 11.12a is tightened too much: The string breaks at the fracture point. Steel is *brittle* because it breaks soon after reaching its elastic limit; other materials, such as soft iron, are *ductile*—they can be given a large permanent stretch without breaking. (The material depicted in Fig. 11.19 is ductile, since it can stretch by more than 30% before breaking.)

Unlike uniform materials such as metals, stretchable biological materials such as tendons and ligaments have no true plastic region. That's because these materials are made of a collection of microscopic fibers; when stressed beyond the elastic limit, the fibers tear apart from each other. (A torn ligament or tendon is one that has fractured in this way.)

If a material is still within its elastic region, something very curious can happen when it is stretched and then allowed to relax. **Figure 11.20** is a stress-strain curve for vulcanized rubber that has been stretched by more than seven times its original length. The stress is not proportional to the strain, but the behavior is elastic because when the load is removed, the material returns to its original length. However, the material follows *different* curves for increasing and decreasing stress. This is called *elastic hysteresis*. The work done by the material when it returns to its original shape is less than the work required to deform it; that's due to internal friction. Rubber with large elastic hysteresis is very useful for absorbing vibrations, such as in engine mounts and shock-absorber bushings for cars. Tendons display similar behavior.

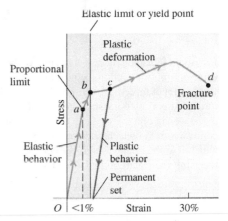

11.19 Typical stress-strain diagram for a ductile metal under tension.

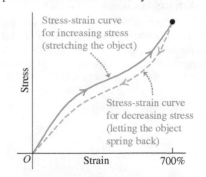

11.20 Typical stress-strain diagram for vulcanized rubber. The curves are different for increasing and decreasing stress, a phenomenon called elastic hysteresis.

TABLE 11.3	Approximate Breaking Stresses

Material	Breaking Stress (Pa or N/m²)
Aluminum	2.2×10^8
Brass	4.7×10^8
Glass	10×10^8
Iron	3.0×10^8
Steel	$5{-}20 \times 10^8$
Tendon (typical)	1×10^8

The stress required to cause actual fracture of a material is called the *breaking stress*, the *ultimate strength*, or (for tensile stress) the *tensile strength*. Two materials, such as two types of steel, may have very similar elastic constants but vastly different breaking stresses. **Table 11.3** gives typical values of breaking stress for several materials in tension. Comparing Tables 11.1 and 11.3 shows that iron and steel are comparably *stiff* (they have almost the same value of Young's modulus), but steel is *stronger* (it has a larger breaking stress than does iron).

TEST YOUR UNDERSTANDING OF SECTION 11.5   While parking your car, you accidentally back into a steel post. You pull forward until the car no longer touches the post and then get out to inspect the damage. What does your rear bumper look like if the strain in the impact was (a) less than at the proportional limit; (b) greater than at the proportional limit but less than at the yield point; (c) greater than at the yield point but less than at the fracture point; and (d) greater than at the fracture point? ❚

CHAPTER **11** SUMMARY

SOLUTIONS TO ALL EXAMPLES

Conditions for equilibrium: For a rigid body to be in equilibrium, two conditions must be satisfied. First, the vector sum of forces must be zero. Second, the sum of torques about any point must be zero. The torque due to the weight of a body can be found by assuming the entire weight is concentrated at the center of gravity, which is at the same point as the center of mass if $\vec{g}$ has the same value at all points. (See Examples 11.1–11.4.)

$$\sum \vec{F} = 0 \tag{11.1}$$

$$\sum \vec{\tau} = 0 \quad \text{about } any \text{ point} \tag{11.2}$$

$$\vec{r}_{\text{cm}} = \frac{m_1 \vec{r}_1 + m_2 \vec{r}_2 + m_3 \vec{r}_3 + \cdots}{m_1 + m_2 + m_3 + \cdots} \tag{11.4}$$

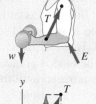

Stress, strain, and Hooke's law: Hooke's law states that in elastic deformations, stress (force per unit area) is proportional to strain (fractional deformation). The proportionality constant is called the elastic modulus.

$$\frac{\text{Stress}}{\text{Strain}} = \text{Elastic modulus} \tag{11.7}$$

Tensile and compressive stress: Tensile stress is tensile force per unit area, $F_\perp/A$. Tensile strain is fractional change in length, $\Delta l/l_0$. The elastic modulus for tension is called Young's modulus Y. Compressive stress and strain are defined in the same way. (See Example 11.5.)

$$Y = \frac{\text{Tensile stress}}{\text{Tensile strain}} = \frac{F_\perp/A}{\Delta l/l_0} = \frac{F_\perp}{A}\frac{l_0}{\Delta l} \tag{11.10}$$

Bulk stress: Pressure in a fluid is force per unit area. Bulk stress is pressure change, Δp, and bulk strain is fractional volume change, $\Delta V/V_0$. The elastic modulus for compression is called the bulk modulus, B. Compressibility, k, is the reciprocal of bulk modulus: $k = 1/B$. (See Example 11.6.)

$$p = \frac{F_\perp}{A} \tag{11.11}$$

$$B = \frac{\text{Bulk stress}}{\text{Bulk strain}} = -\frac{\Delta p}{\Delta V/V_0} \tag{11.13}$$

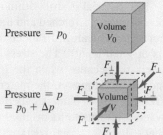
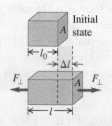

Shear stress: Shear stress is force per unit area, $F_\parallel/A$, for a force applied tangent to a surface. Shear strain is the displacement x of one side divided by the transverse dimension h. The elastic modulus for shear is called the shear modulus, S. (See Example 11.7.)

$$S = \frac{\text{Shear stress}}{\text{Shear strain}} = \frac{F_\parallel/A}{x/h} = \frac{F_\parallel}{A}\frac{h}{x} \quad (11.17)$$

The limits of Hooke's law: The proportional limit is the maximum stress for which stress and strain are proportional. Beyond the proportional limit, Hooke's law is not valid. The elastic limit is the stress beyond which irreversible deformation occurs. The breaking stress, or ultimate strength, is the stress at which the material breaks.

BRIDGING PROBLEM   IN EQUILIBRIUM AND UNDER STRESS

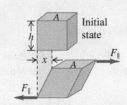

A horizontal, uniform, solid copper rod has an original length l_0, cross-sectional area A, Young's modulus Y, bulk modulus B, shear modulus S, and mass m. It is supported by a frictionless pivot at its right end and by a cable a distance $l_0/4$ from its left end (**Fig. 11.21**). Both pivot and cable are attached so that they exert their forces uniformly over the rod's cross section. The cable makes an angle θ with the rod and compresses it. (a) Find the tension in the cable. (b) Find the magnitude and direction of the force exerted by the pivot on the right end of the rod. How does this magnitude compare to the cable tension? How does this angle compare to θ? (c) Find the change in length of the rod due to the stresses exerted by the cable and pivot on the rod. (The length change is small compared to the original length l_0.) (d) By what factor would your answer in part (c) increase if the solid copper rod were twice as long but had the same cross-sectional area?

11.21 What are the forces on the rod? What are the stress and strain?

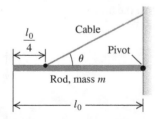

SOLUTION GUIDE

IDENTIFY and SET UP

1. Draw a free-body diagram for the rod. Be careful to place each force in the correct location.
2. List the unknown quantities, and decide which are the target variables.
3. What conditions must be met so that the rod remains at rest? What kind of stress (and resulting strain) is involved? Use your answers to select the appropriate equations.

EXECUTE

4. Use your equations to solve for the target variables. (*Hint:* You can make the solution easier by carefully choosing the point around which you calculate torques.)
5. Use trigonometry to decide whether the pivot force or the cable tension has the greater magnitude and whether the angle of the pivot force is greater than, less than, or equal to θ.

EVALUATE

6. Check whether your answers are reasonable. Which force, the cable tension or the pivot force, holds up more of the weight of the rod? Does this make sense?

Problems

For assigned homework and other learning materials, go to MasteringPhysics®.   **MP**

•, ••, •••: Difficulty levels. **CP**: Cumulative problems incorporating material from earlier chapters. **CALC**: Problems requiring calculus. **DATA**: Problems involving real data, scientific evidence, experimental design, and/or statistical reasoning. **BIO**: Biosciences problems.

DISCUSSION QUESTIONS

Q11.1 Does a rigid object in uniform rotation about a fixed axis satisfy the first and second conditions for equilibrium? Why? Does it then follow that every particle in this object is in equilibrium? Explain.

Q11.2 (a) Is it possible for an object to be in translational equilibrium (the first condition) but *not* in rotational equilibrium (the second condition)? Illustrate your answer with a simple example. (b) Can an object be in rotational equilibrium yet *not* in translational equilibrium? Justify your answer with a simple example.

Q11.3 Car tires are sometimes "balanced" on a machine that pivots the tire and wheel about the center. Weights are placed around the wheel rim until it does not tip from the horizontal plane. Discuss this procedure in terms of the center of gravity.

Q11.4 Does the center of gravity of a solid body always lie within the material of the body? If not, give a counterexample.

Q11.5 In Section 11.2 we always assumed that the value of g was the same at all points on the body. This is *not* a good approximation if the dimensions of the body are great enough, because the value of g decreases with altitude. If this is taken into account, will the center of gravity of a long, vertical rod be above, below, or at its center of mass? Explain how this can be used to keep the long axis of an orbiting spacecraft pointed toward the earth. (This would be useful for a weather satellite that must always keep its camera lens trained on the earth.) The moon is not exactly spherical but is somewhat elongated. Explain why this same effect is responsible for keeping the same face of the moon pointed toward the earth at all times.

Q11.6 You are balancing a wrench by suspending it at a single point. Is the equilibrium stable, unstable, or neutral if the point is above, at, or below the wrench's center of gravity? In each case give the reasoning behind your answer. (For rotation, a rigid body is in *stable* equilibrium if a small rotation of the body produces a torque that tends to return the body to equilibrium; it is in *unstable* equilibrium if a small rotation produces a torque that tends to take the body farther from equilibrium; and it is in *neutral* equilibrium if a small rotation produces no torque.)

Q11.7 You can probably stand flatfooted on the floor and then rise up and balance on your tiptoes. Why are you unable do it if your toes are touching the wall of your room? (Try it!)

Q11.8 You freely pivot a horseshoe from a horizontal nail through one of its nail holes. You then hang a long string with a weight at its bottom from the same nail, so that the string hangs vertically in front of the horseshoe without touching it. How do you know that the horseshoe's center of gravity is along the line behind the string? How can you locate the center of gravity by repeating the process at another nail hole? Will the center of gravity be within the solid material of the horseshoe?

Q11.9 An object consists of a ball of weight W glued to the end of a uniform bar also of weight W. If you release it from rest, with the bar horizontal, what will its behavior be as it falls if air resistance is negligible? Will it (a) remain horizontal; (b) rotate about its center of gravity; (c) rotate about the ball; or (d) rotate so that the ball swings downward? Explain your reasoning.

Q11.10 Suppose that the object in Question 11.9 is released from rest with the bar tilted at 60° above the horizontal with the ball at the upper end. As it is falling, will it (a) rotate about its center of gravity until it is horizontal; (b) rotate about its center of gravity until it is vertical with the ball at the bottom; (c) rotate about the ball until it is vertical with the ball at the bottom; or (d) remain at 60° above the horizontal?

Q11.11 Why must a water skier moving with constant velocity lean backward? What determines how far back she must lean? Draw a free-body diagram for the water skier to justify your answers.

Q11.12 In pioneer days, when a Conestoga wagon was stuck in the mud, people would grasp the wheel spokes and try to turn the wheels, rather than simply pushing the wagon. Why?

Q11.13 The mighty Zimbo claims to have leg muscles so strong that he can stand flat on his feet and lean forward to pick up an apple on the floor with his teeth. Should you pay to see him perform, or do you have any suspicions about his claim? Why?

Q11.14 Why is it easier to hold a 10-kg dumbbell in your hand at your side than it is to hold it with your arm extended horizontally?

Q11.15 Certain features of a person, such as height and mass, are fixed (at least over relatively long periods of time). Are the following features also fixed? (a) location of the center of gravity of the body; (b) moment of inertia of the body about an axis through the person's center of mass. Explain your reasoning.

Q11.16 During pregnancy, women often develop back pains from leaning backward while walking. Why do they have to walk this way?

Q11.17 Why is a tapered water glass with a narrow base easier to tip over than a glass with straight sides? Does it matter whether the glass is full or empty?

Q11.18 When a tall, heavy refrigerator is pushed across a rough floor, what factors determine whether it slides or tips?

Q11.19 A uniform beam is suspended horizontally and attached to a wall by a small hinge (**Fig. Q11.19**). What are the directions (upward or downward, and to the left or the right) of the components of the force that the hinge exerts *on the beam*? Explain.

Figure **Q11.19**

Center of mass

Hinge

Q11.20 If a metal wire has its length doubled and its diameter tripled, by what factor does its Young's modulus change?

Q11.21 A metal wire of diameter D stretches by 0.100 mm when supporting a weight W. If the same-length wire is used to support a weight three times as heavy, what would its diameter have to be (in terms of D) so it still stretches only 0.100 mm?

Q11.22 Compare the mechanical properties of a steel cable, made by twisting many thin wires together, with the properties of a solid steel rod of the same diameter. What advantages does each have?

Q11.23 The material in human bones and elephant bones is essentially the same, but an elephant has much thicker legs. Explain why, in terms of breaking stress.

Q11.24 There is a small but appreciable amount of elastic hysteresis in the large tendon at the back of a horse's leg. Explain how this can cause damage to the tendon if a horse runs too hard for too long a time.

Q11.25 When rubber mounting blocks are used to absorb machine vibrations through elastic hysteresis, as mentioned in Section 11.5, what becomes of the energy associated with the vibrations?

EXERCISES

Section 11.2 Center of Gravity

11.1 •• A 0.120-kg, 50.0-cm-long uniform bar has a small 0.055-kg mass glued to its left end and a small 0.110-kg mass glued to the other end. The two small masses can each be treated as point masses. You want to balance this system horizontally on a fulcrum placed just under its center of gravity. How far from the left end should the fulcrum be placed?

11.2 •• The center of gravity of a 5.00-kg irregular object is shown in **Fig. E11.2**. You need to move the center of gravity 2.20 cm to the left by gluing on a 1.50-kg mass, which will then be considered as part of the object. Where should the center of gravity of this additional mass be located?

Figure **E11.2**

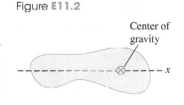

Center of gravity

11.3 • A uniform rod is 2.00 m long and has mass 1.80 kg. A 2.40-kg clamp is attached to the rod. How far should the center of gravity of the clamp be from the left-hand end of the rod in order for the center of gravity of the composite object to be 1.20 m from the left-hand end of the rod?

Section 11.3 Solving Rigid-Body Equilibrium Problems

11.4 • A uniform 300-N trapdoor in a floor is hinged at one side. Find the net upward force needed to begin to open it and the total force exerted on the door by the hinges (a) if the upward force is applied at the center and (b) if the upward force is applied at the center of the edge opposite the hinges.

11.5 •• **Raising a Ladder.** A ladder carried by a fire truck is 20.0 m long. The ladder weighs 3400 N and its center of gravity is at its center. The ladder is pivoted at one end (*A*) about a pin (**Fig. E11.5**); ignore the friction torque at the pin. The ladder is raised into position by a force applied by a hydraulic piston at *C*. Point *C* is 8.0 m from *A*, and the force $\vec{F}$ exerted by the piston makes an angle of 40° with the ladder. What magnitude must $\vec{F}$ have to just lift the ladder off the support bracket at *B*? Start with a free-body diagram of the ladder.

Figure **E11.5**

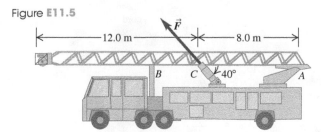

11.6 •• Two people are carrying a uniform wooden board that is 3.00 m long and weighs 160 N. If one person applies an upward force equal to 60 N at one end, at what point does the other person lift? Begin with a free-body diagram of the board.

11.7 •• Two people carry a heavy electric motor by placing it on a light board 2.00 m long. One person lifts at one end with a force of 400 N, and the other lifts the opposite end with a force of 600 N. (a) What is the weight of the motor, and where along the board is its center of gravity located? (b) Suppose the board is not light but weighs 200 N, with its center of gravity at its center, and the two people each exert the same forces as before. What is the weight of the motor in this case, and where is its center of gravity located?

11.8 •• A 60.0-cm, uniform, 50.0-N shelf is supported horizontally by two vertical wires attached to the sloping ceiling (**Fig. E11.8**). A very small 25.0-N tool is placed on the shelf midway between the points where the wires are attached to it. Find the tension in each wire. Begin by making a free-body diagram of the shelf.

Figure **E11.8**

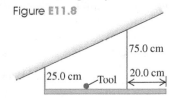

75.0 cm

25.0 cm   Tool   20.0 cm

11.9 •• A 350-N, uniform, 1.50-m bar is suspended horizontally by two vertical cables at each end. Cable *A* can support a maximum tension of 500.0 N without breaking, and cable *B* can support up to 400.0 N. You want to place a small weight on this bar. (a) What is the heaviest weight you can put on without breaking either cable, and (b) where should you put this weight?

11.10 •• A uniform ladder 5.0 m long rests against a frictionless, vertical wall with its lower end 3.0 m from the wall. The ladder weighs 160 N. The coefficient of static friction between the foot of the ladder and the ground is 0.40. A man weighing 740 N climbs slowly up the ladder. Start by drawing a free-body diagram of the ladder. (a) What is the maximum friction force that the ground can exert on the ladder at its lower end? (b) What is the actual friction force when the man has climbed 1.0 m along the ladder? (c) How far along the ladder can the man climb before the ladder starts to slip?

11.11 • A diving board 3.00 m long is supported at a point 1.00 m from the end, and a diver weighing 500 N stands at the free end (**Fig. E11.11**). The diving board is of uniform cross section and weighs 280 N. Find (a) the force at the support point and (b) the force at the left-hand end.

Figure **E11.11**

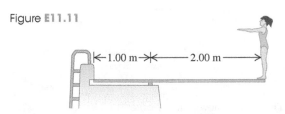

|← 1.00 m →|←   2.00 m   →|

11.12 • A uniform aluminum beam 9.00 m long, weighing 300 N, rests symmetrically on two supports 5.00 m apart (**Fig. E11.12**). A boy weighing 600 N starts at point *A* and walks toward the right.

Figure **E11.12**

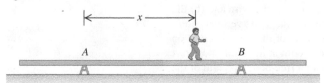

|←   *x*   →|

A   *B*

(a) In the same diagram construct two graphs showing the upward forces F_A and F_B exerted on the beam at points A and B, as functions of the coordinate x of the boy. Let 1 cm = 100 N vertically, and 1 cm = 1.00 m horizontally. (b) From your diagram, how far beyond point B can the boy walk before the beam tips? (c) How far from the right end of the beam should support B be placed so that the boy can walk just to the end of the beam without causing it to tip?

11.13 • Find the tension T in each cable and the magnitude and direction of the force exerted on the strut by the pivot in each of the arrangements in **Fig. E11.13**. In each case let w be the weight of the suspended crate full of priceless art objects. The strut is uniform and also has weight w. Start each case with a free-body diagram of the strut.

Figure **E11.13**

(a)   (b)

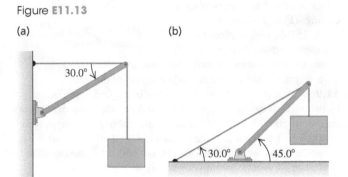

11.14 • The horizontal beam in **Fig. E11.14** weighs 190 N, and its center of gravity is at its center. Find (a) the tension in the cable and (b) the horizontal and vertical components of the force exerted on the beam at the wall.

Figure **E11.14**

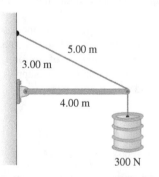

300 N

11.15 •• The boom shown in **Fig. E11.15** weighs 2600 N and is attached to a frictionless pivot at its lower end. It is not uniform; the distance of its center of gravity from the pivot is 35% of its length. Find (a) the tension in the guy wire and (b) the horizontal and vertical components of the force exerted on the boom at its lower end. Start with a free-body diagram of the boom.

Figure **E11.15**

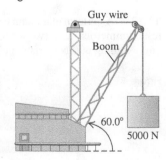

Guy wire

Boom

60.0°

5000 N

11.16 •• Suppose that you can lift no more than 650 N (around 150 lb) unaided. (a) How much can you lift using a 1.4-m-long wheelbarrow that weighs 80.0 N and whose center of gravity is 0.50 m from the center of the wheel (**Fig. E11.16**)? The center of gravity of the load carried in the wheelbarrow is also 0.50 m from the center of the wheel. (b) Where does the force come from to enable you to lift more than 650 N using the wheelbarrow?

Figure **E11.16**

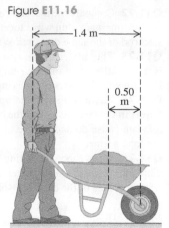

11.17 •• A 9.00-m-long uniform beam is hinged to a vertical wall and held horizontally by a 5.00-m-long cable attached to the wall 4.00 m above the hinge (**Fig. E11.17**). The metal of this cable has a test strength of 1.00 kN, which means that it will break if the tension in it exceeds that amount. (a) Draw a free-body diagram of the beam. (b) What is the heaviest beam that the cable can support in this configuration? (c) Find the horizontal and vertical components of the force the hinge exerts on the beam. Is the vertical component upward or downward?

Figure **E11.17**

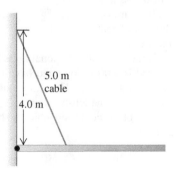

5.0 m cable

4.0 m

11.18 •• A 15,000-N crane pivots around a friction-free axle at its base and is supported by a cable making a 25° angle with the crane (**Fig. E11.18**). The crane is 16 m long and is not uniform, its center of gravity being 7.0 m from the axle as measured along the crane. The cable is attached 3.0 m from the upper end of the crane. When the crane is raised to 55° above the horizontal holding an 11,000-N pallet of bricks by a 2.2-m, very light cord, find (a) the tension in the cable and (b) the horizontal and vertical components of the force that the axle exerts on the crane. Start with a free-body diagram of the crane.

Figure **E11.18**

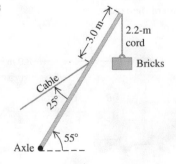

3.0 m

2.2-m cord

Bricks

Cable

25°

55°

Axle

11.19 •• A 3.00-m-long, 190-N, uniform rod at the zoo is held in a horizontal position by two ropes at its ends (**Fig. E11.19**). The left rope makes an angle of 150° with the rod, and the right rope makes an angle θ with the horizontal. A 90-N howler monkey (*Alouatta seniculus*) hangs motionless 0.50 m from the right end of the rod as he carefully studies you. Calculate the tensions in the two ropes and the angle θ. First make a free-body diagram of the rod.

Figure E11.19

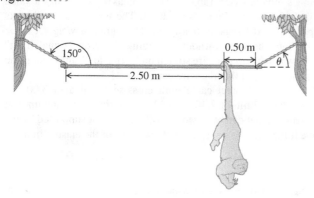

11.20 •• A nonuniform beam 4.50 m long and weighing 1.40 kN makes an angle of 25.0° below the horizontal. It is held in position by a frictionless pivot at its upper right end and by a cable 3.00 m farther down the beam and perpendicular to it (**Fig. E11.20**). The center of gravity of the beam is 2.00 m down the beam from the pivot. Lighting equipment exerts a 5.00-kN downward force on the lower left end of the beam. Find the tension T in the cable and the horizontal and vertical components of the force exerted on the beam by the pivot. Start by sketching a free-body diagram of the beam.

Figure E11.20

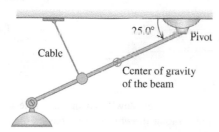

11.21 • **A Couple.** Two forces equal in magnitude and opposite in direction, acting on an object at two different points, form what is called a *couple*. Two antiparallel forces with equal magnitudes $F_1 = F_2 = 8.00$ N are applied to a rod as shown in **Fig. E11.21**. (a) What should the distance l between the forces be if they are to provide a net torque of 6.40 N·m about the left end of the rod? (b) Is the sense of this torque clockwise or counterclockwise? (c) Repeat parts (a) and (b) for a pivot at the point on the rod where $\vec{F}_2$ is applied.

Figure E11.21

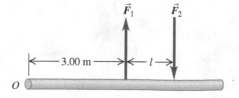

11.22 •• **BIO A Good Workout.** You are doing exercises on a Nautilus machine in a gym to strengthen your deltoid (shoulder) muscles. Your arms are raised vertically and can pivot around the shoulder joint, and you grasp the cable of the machine in your hand 64.0 cm from your shoulder joint. The deltoid muscle is attached to the humerus 15.0 cm from the shoulder joint and makes a 12.0° angle with that bone (**Fig. E11.22**). If you have set the tension in the cable of the machine to 36.0 N on each arm, what is the tension in each deltoid muscle if you simply hold your outstretched arms in place? (*Hint:* Start by making a clear free-body diagram of your arm.)

Figure E11.22

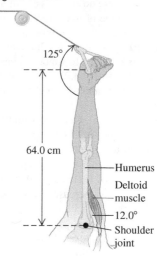

11.23 •• BIO **Neck Muscles.** A student bends her head at 40.0° from the vertical while intently reading her physics book, pivoting the head around the upper vertebra (point P in **Fig. E11.23**). Her head has a mass of 4.50 kg (which is typical), and its center of mass is 11.0 cm from the pivot point P. Her neck muscles are 1.50 cm from point P, as measured *perpendicular* to these muscles. The neck itself and the vertebrae are held vertical. (a) Draw a free-body diagram of the student's head. (b) Find the tension in her neck muscles.

Figure E11.23

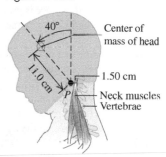

Section 11.4 Stress, Strain, and Elastic Moduli

11.24 • BIO **Biceps Muscle.** A relaxed biceps muscle requires a force of 25.0 N for an elongation of 3.0 cm; the same muscle under maximum tension requires a force of 500 N for the same elongation. Find Young's modulus for the muscle tissue under each of these conditions if the muscle is assumed to be a uniform cylinder with length 0.200 m and cross-sectional area 50.0 cm².

11.25 •• A circular steel wire 2.00 m long must stretch no more than 0.25 cm when a tensile force of 700 N is applied to each end of the wire. What minimum diameter is required for the wire?

11.26 •• Two circular rods, one steel and the other copper, are joined end to end. Each rod is 0.750 m long and 1.50 cm in diameter. The combination is subjected to a tensile force with magnitude 4000 N. For each rod, what are (a) the strain and (b) the elongation?

11.27 •• A metal rod that is 4.00 m long and 0.50 cm² in cross-sectional area is found to stretch 0.20 cm under a tension of 5000 N. What is Young's modulus for this metal?

11.28 •• **Stress on a Mountaineer's Rope.** A nylon rope used by mountaineers elongates 1.10 m under the weight of a 65.0-kg climber. If the rope is 45.0 m in length and 7.0 mm in diameter, what is Young's modulus for nylon?

11.29 ·· In constructing a large mobile, an artist hangs an aluminum sphere of mass 6.0 kg from a vertical steel wire 0.50 m long and 2.5×10^{-3} cm² in cross-sectional area. On the bottom of the sphere he attaches a similar steel wire, from which he hangs a brass cube of mass 10.0 kg. For each wire, compute (a) the tensile strain and (b) the elongation.

11.30 ·· A vertical, solid steel post 25 cm in diameter and 2.50 m long is required to support a load of 8000 kg. You can ignore the weight of the post. What are (a) the stress in the post; (b) the strain in the post; and (c) the change in the post's length when the load is applied?

11.31 ·· BIO **Compression of Human Bone.** The bulk modulus for bone is 15 GPa. (a) If a diver-in-training is put into a pressurized suit, by how much would the pressure have to be raised (in atmospheres) above atmospheric pressure to compress her bones by 0.10% of their original volume? (b) Given that the pressure in the ocean increases by 1.0×10^4 Pa for every meter of depth below the surface, how deep would this diver have to go for her bones to compress by 0.10%? Does it seem that bone compression is a problem she needs to be concerned with when diving?

11.32 · A solid gold bar is pulled up from the hold of the sunken RMS *Titanic.* (a) What happens to its volume as it goes from the pressure at the ship to the lower pressure at the ocean's surface? (b) The pressure difference is proportional to the depth. How many times greater would the volume change have been had the ship been twice as deep? (c) The bulk modulus of lead is one-fourth that of gold. Find the ratio of the volume change of a solid lead bar to that of a gold bar of equal volume for the same pressure change.

11.33 · A specimen of oil having an initial volume of 600 cm³ is subjected to a pressure increase of 3.6×10^6 Pa, and the volume is found to decrease by 0.45 cm³. What is the bulk modulus of the material? The compressibility?

11.34 ·· In the Challenger Deep of the Marianas Trench, the depth of seawater is 10.9 km and the pressure is 1.16×10^8 Pa (about 1.15×10^3 atm). (a) If a cubic meter of water is taken from the surface to this depth, what is the change in its volume? (Normal atmospheric pressure is about 1.0×10^5 Pa. Assume that k for seawater is the same as the freshwater value given in Table 11.2.) (b) What is the density of seawater at this depth? (At the surface, seawater has a density of 1.03×10^3 kg/m³.)

11.35 ·· A copper cube measures 6.00 cm on each side. The bottom face is held in place by very strong glue to a flat horizontal surface, while a horizontal force F is applied to the upper face parallel to one of the edges. (Consult Table 11.1.) (a) Show that the glue exerts a force F on the bottom face that is equal in magnitude but opposite to the force on the top face. (b) How large must F be to cause the cube to deform by 0.250 mm? (c) If the same experiment were performed on a lead cube of the same size as the copper one, by what distance would it deform for the same force as in part (b)?

11.36 ·· A square steel plate is 10.0 cm on a side and 0.500 cm thick. (a) Find the shear strain that results if a force of magnitude 9.0×10^5 N is applied to each of the four sides, parallel to the side. (b) Find the displacement x in centimeters.

11.37 · In lab tests on a 9.25-cm cube of a certain material, a force of 1375 N directed at 8.50° to the cube (**Fig. E11.37**) causes the cube to deform through an angle of 1.24°. What is the shear modulus of the material?

Figure **E11.37**

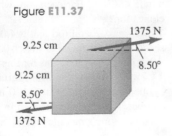

9.25 cm

9.25 cm

8.50°

1375 N

1375 N

8.50°

Section 11.5 Elasticity and Plasticity

11.38 ·· A brass wire is to withstand a tensile force of 350 N without breaking. What minimum diameter must the wire have?

11.39 ·· In a materials testing laboratory, a metal wire made from a new alloy is found to break when a tensile force of 90.8 N is applied perpendicular to each end. If the diameter of the wire is 1.84 mm, what is the breaking stress of the alloy?

11.40 · A 4.0-m-long steel wire has a cross-sectional area of 0.050 cm². Its proportional limit has a value of 0.0016 times its Young's modulus (see Table 11.1). Its breaking stress has a value of 0.0065 times its Young's modulus. The wire is fastened at its upper end and hangs vertically. (a) How great a weight can be hung from the wire without exceeding the proportional limit? (b) How much will the wire stretch under this load? (c) What is the maximum weight that the wire can support?

11.41 ·· CP A steel cable with cross-sectional area 3.00 cm² has an elastic limit of 2.40×10^8 Pa. Find the maximum upward acceleration that can be given a 1200-kg elevator supported by the cable if the stress is not to exceed one-third of the elastic limit.

PROBLEMS

11.42 ··· A door 1.00 m wide and 2.00 m high weighs 330 N and is supported by two hinges, one 0.50 m from the top and the other 0.50 m from the bottom. Each hinge supports half the total weight of the door. Assuming that the door's center of gravity is at its center, find the horizontal components of force exerted on the door by each hinge.

11.43 ··· A box of negligible mass rests at the left end of a 2.00-m, 25.0-kg plank (**Fig. P11.43**). The width of the box is 75.0 cm, and sand is to be distributed uniformly throughout it. The center of gravity of the nonuniform plank is 50.0 cm from the right end. What mass of sand should be put into the box so that the plank balances horizontally on a fulcrum placed just below its midpoint?

Figure **P11.43**

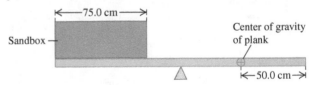

11.44 · Sir Lancelot rides slowly out of the castle at Camelot and onto the 12.0-m-long drawbridge that passes over the moat (**Fig. P11.44**). Unbeknownst to him, his enemies have partially severed the vertical cable holding up the front end of the bridge so that it will break under a tension of 5.80×10^3 N. The bridge has mass 200 kg and its center of gravity is at its center. Lancelot, his lance, his armor, and his horse together have a combined mass of 600 kg. Will the cable break before Lancelot reaches the end of the drawbridge? If so, how far from the castle end of the bridge will the center of gravity of the horse plus rider be when the cable breaks?

Figure **P11.44**

11.45 ••• **Mountain Climbing.** Mountaineers often use a rope to lower themselves down the face of a cliff (this is called *rappelling*). They do this with their body nearly horizontal and their feet pushing against the cliff (**Fig. P11.45**). Suppose that an 82.0-kg climber, who is 1.90 m tall and has a center of gravity 1.1 m from his feet, rappels down a vertical cliff with his body raised 35.0° above the horizontal. He holds the rope 1.40 m from his feet, and it makes a 25.0° angle with the cliff face. (a) What tension does his rope need to support? (b) Find the horizontal and vertical components of the force that the cliff face exerts on the climber's feet. (c) What minimum coefficient of static friction is needed to prevent the climber's feet from slipping on the cliff face if he has one foot at a time against the cliff?

Figure P11.45

11.46 •• A uniform, 8.0-m, 1150-kg beam is hinged to a wall and supported by a thin cable attached 2.0 m from the free end of the beam (**Fig. P11.46**). The beam is supported at an angle of 30.0° above the horizontal. (a) Draw a free-body diagram of the beam. (b) Find the tension in the cable. (c) How hard does the beam push inward on the wall?

Figure P11.46

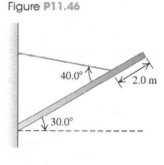

40.0° ⤡ 2.0 m
30.0°

11.47 •• A uniform, 255-N rod that is 2.00 m long carries a 225-N weight at its right end and an unknown weight W toward the left end (**Fig. P11.47**). When W is placed 50.0 cm from the left end of the rod, the system just balances horizontally when the fulcrum is located 75.0 cm from the right end. (a) Find W. (b) If W is now moved 25.0 cm to the right, how far and in what direction must the fulcrum be moved to restore balance?

Figure P11.47

W 225 N

11.48 ••• A claw hammer is used to pull a nail out of a board (**Fig. P11.48**). The nail is at an angle of 60° to the board, and a force $\vec{F}_1$ of magnitude 400 N applied to the nail is required to pull it from the board. The hammer head contacts the board at point A, which is 0.080 m from where the nail enters the board. A horizontal force $\vec{F}_2$ is applied to the hammer handle at a distance of 0.300 m above the board. What magnitude of force $\vec{F}_2$ is required to apply the required 400-N force (F_1) to the nail? (Ignore the weight of the hammer.)

Figure P11.48

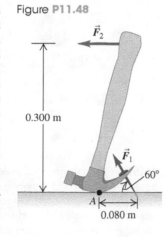

$\vec{F}_2$
0.300 m
$\vec{F}_1$
60°
A
0.080 m

11.49 •• You open a restaurant and hope to entice customers by hanging out a sign (**Fig. P11.49**). The uniform horizontal beam supporting the sign is 1.50 m long, has a mass of 16.0 kg, and is hinged to the wall. The sign itself is uniform with a mass of 28.0 kg and overall length of 1.20 m. The two wires supporting the sign are each 32.0 cm long, are 90.0 cm apart, and are equally spaced from the middle of the sign. The cable supporting the beam is 2.00 m long. (a) What minimum tension must your cable be able to support without having your sign come crashing down? (b) What minimum vertical force must the hinge be able to support without pulling out of the wall?

Figure P11.49

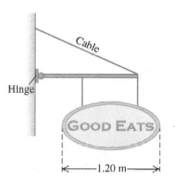

Cable
Hinge
GOOD EATS
⟵—1.20 m—⟶

11.50 • End A of the bar AB in **Fig. P11.50** rests on a frictionless horizontal surface, and end B is hinged. A horizontal force $\vec{F}$ of magnitude 220 N is exerted on end A. Ignore the weight of the bar. What are the horizontal and vertical components of the force exerted by the bar on the hinge at B?

Figure P11.50

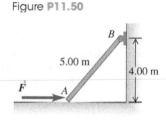

B
5.00 m
4.00 m
$\vec{F}$ A

11.51 •• BIO **Supporting a Broken Leg.** A therapist tells a 74-kg patient with a broken leg that he must have his leg in a cast suspended horizontally. For minimum discomfort, the leg should be supported by a vertical strap attached at the center of mass of the leg–cast system (**Fig. P11.51**). To comply with these instructions, the patient consults a table of typical mass distributions and finds that both upper legs (thighs) together typically account for 21.5% of body weight and the center of mass of each thigh is 18.0 cm from the hip joint. The patient also reads that the two lower legs (including the feet) are 14.0% of body weight, with a center of mass 69.0 cm from the hip joint. The cast has a mass of 5.50 kg, and its center of mass is 78.0 cm from the hip joint. How far from the hip joint should the supporting strap be attached to the cast?

Figure P11.51

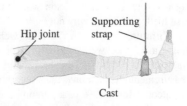

Hip joint   Supporting strap
Cast

11.52 · A Truck on a Drawbridge. A loaded cement mixer drives onto an old drawbridge, where it stalls with its center of gravity three-quarters of the way across the span. The truck driver radios for help, sets the handbrake, and waits. Meanwhile, a boat approaches, so the drawbridge is raised by means of a cable attached to the end opposite the hinge (**Fig. P11.52**). The drawbridge is 40.0 m long and has a mass of 18,000 kg; its center of gravity is at its midpoint. The cement mixer, with driver, has mass 30,000 kg. When the drawbridge has been raised to an angle of 30° above the horizontal, the cable makes an angle of 70° with the surface of the bridge. (a) What is the tension T in the cable when the drawbridge is held in this position? (b) What are the horizontal and vertical components of the force the hinge exerts on the span?

Figure **P11.52**

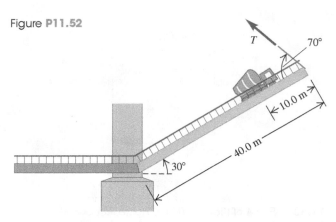

11.53 ·· BIO Leg Raises. In a simplified version of the musculature action in leg raises, the abdominal muscles pull on the femur (thigh bone) to raise the leg by pivoting it about one end (**Fig. P11.53**). When you are lying horizontally, these muscles make an angle of approximately 5° with the femur, and if you raise your legs, the muscles remain approximately horizontal, so the angle θ increases. Assume for simplicity that these muscles attach to the femur in only one place, 10 cm from the hip joint (although, in reality, the situation is more complicated). For a certain 80-kg person having a leg 90 cm long, the mass of the leg is 15 kg and its center of mass is 44 cm from his hip joint as measured along the leg. If the person raises his leg to 60° above the horizontal, the angle between the abdominal muscles and his femur would also be about 60°. (a) With his leg raised to 60°, find the tension in the abdominal muscle on each leg. Draw a free-body diagram. (b) When is the tension in this muscle greater: when the leg is raised to 60° or when the person just starts to raise it off the ground? Why? (Try this yourself.) (c) If the abdominal muscles attached to the femur were perfectly horizontal when a person was lying down, could the person raise his leg? Why or why not?

Figure **P11.53**

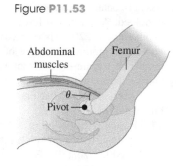

11.54 ·· BIO Pumping Iron. A 72.0-kg weightlifter doing arm raises holds a 7.50-kg weight. Her arm pivots around the elbow joint, starting 40.0° below the horizontal (**Fig. P11.54**). Biometric measurements have shown that, together, the forearms and the hands account for 6.00% of a person's weight. Since the

Figure **P11.54**

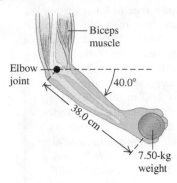

upper arm is held vertically, the biceps muscle always acts vertically and is attached to the bones of the forearm 5.50 cm from the elbow joint. The center of mass of this person's forearm–hand combination is 16.0 cm from the elbow joint, along the bones of the forearm, and she holds the weight 38.0 cm from her elbow joint. (a) Draw a free-body diagram of the forearm. (b) What force does the biceps muscle exert on the forearm? (c) Find the magnitude and direction of the force that the elbow joint exerts on the forearm. (d) As the weightlifter raises her arm toward a horizontal position, will the force in the biceps muscle increase, decrease, or stay the same? Why?

11.55 ·· BIO Back Pains During Pregnancy. Women often suffer from back pains during pregnancy. Model a woman (not including her fetus) as a uniform cylinder of diameter 30 cm and mass 60 kg. Model the fetus as a 10-kg sphere that is 25 cm in diameter and centered about 5 cm *outside* the front of the woman's body. (a) By how much does her pregnancy change the horizontal location of the woman's center of mass? (b) How does the change in part (a) affect the way the pregnant woman must stand and walk? In other words, what must she do to her posture to make up for her shifted center of mass? (c) Can you explain why she might have backaches?

11.56 · You are asked to design the decorative mobile shown in **Fig. P11.56**. The strings and rods have negligible weight, and the rods are to hang horizontally. (a) Draw a free-body diagram for each rod. (b) Find the weights of the balls A, B, and C. Find the tensions in the strings S_1, S_2, and S_3. (c) What can you say about the horizontal location of the mobile's center of gravity? Explain.

Figure **P11.56**

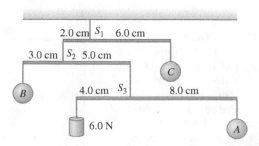

11.57 ·· A uniform, 7.5-m-long beam weighing 6490 N is hinged to a wall and supported by a thin cable attached 1.5 m from the free end of the beam. The cable runs between the beam and the wall and makes a 40° angle with the beam. What is the tension in the cable when the beam is at an angle of 30° above the horizontal?

11.58 •• **CP** A uniform drawbridge must be held at a 37° angle above the horizontal to allow ships to pass underneath. The drawbridge weighs 45,000 N and is 14.0 m long. A cable is connected 3.5 m from the hinge where the bridge pivots (measured along the bridge) and pulls horizontally on the bridge to hold it in place. (a) What is the tension in the cable? (b) Find the magnitude and direction of the force the hinge exerts on the bridge. (c) If the cable suddenly breaks, what is the magnitude of the angular acceleration of the drawbridge just after the cable breaks? (d) What is the angular speed of the drawbridge as it becomes horizontal?

11.59 •• **BIO Tendon-Stretching Exercises.** As part of an exercise program, a 75-kg person does toe raises in which he raises his entire body weight on the ball of one foot (**Fig. P11.59**). The Achilles tendon pulls straight upward on the heel bone of his foot. This tendon is 25 cm long and has a cross-sectional area of 78 mm² and a Young's modulus of 1470 MPa. (a) Draw a free-body diagram of the person's foot (everything below the ankle joint). Ignore the weight of the foot. (b) What force does the Achilles tendon exert on the heel during this exercise? Express your answer in newtons and in multiples of his weight. (c) By how many millimeters does the exercise stretch his Achilles tendon?

Figure **P11.59**

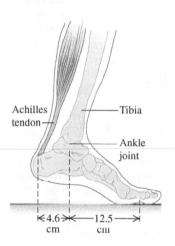

Achilles tendon—
—Tibia
—Ankle joint

|←4.6→|←—12.5—→|
  cm   cm

11.60 •• (a) In **Fig. P11.60** a 6.00-m-long, uniform beam is hanging from a point 1.00 m to the right of its center. The beam weighs 140 N and makes an angle of 30.0° with the vertical. At the right-hand end of the beam a 100.0-N weight is hung; an unknown weight w hangs at the left end. If the system is in equilibrium, what is w? You can ignore the thickness of the beam. (b) If the beam makes, instead, an angle of 45.0° with the vertical, what is w?

Figure **P11.60**

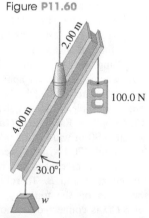

2.00 m

4.00 m

100.0 N

30.0°

w

11.61 ••• A uniform, horizontal flagpole 5.00 m long with a weight of 200 N is hinged to a vertical wall at one end. A 600-N stuntwoman hangs from its other end. The flagpole is supported by a guy wire running from its outer end to a point on the wall directly above the pole. (a) If the tension in this wire is not to exceed 1000 N, what is the minimum height above the pole at

which it may be fastened to the wall? (b) If the flagpole remains horizontal, by how many newtons would the tension be increased if the wire were fastened 0.50 m below this point?

11.62 • A holiday decoration consists of two shiny glass spheres with masses 0.0240 kg and 0.0360 kg suspended from a uniform rod with mass 0.120 kg and length 1.00 m (**Fig. P11.62**). The rod is suspended from the ceiling by a vertical cord at each end, so that it is horizontal. Calculate the tension in each of the cords A through F.

Figure **P11.62**

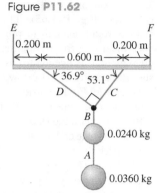

E F
0.200 m   0.200 m
|←—→|←—0.600 m—→|←—→|
36.9° 53.1°
D C
B
        0.0240 kg
A
        0.0360 kg

11.63 •• **BIO Downward-Facing Dog.** The yoga exercise "Downward-Facing Dog" requires stretching your hands straight out above your head and bending down to lean against the floor. This exercise is performed by a 750-N person as shown in **Fig. P11.63**. When he bends his body at the hip to a 90° angle between his legs and trunk, his legs, trunk, head, and arms have the dimensions indicated. Furthermore, his legs and feet weigh a total of 277 N, and their center of mass is 41 cm from his hip, measured along his legs. The person's trunk, head, and arms weigh 473 N, and their center of gravity is 65 cm from his hip, measured along the upper body. (a) Find the normal force that the floor exerts on each foot and on each hand, assuming that the person does not favor either hand or either foot. (b) Find the friction force on each foot and on each hand, assuming that it is the same on both feet and on both hands (but not necessarily the same on the feet as on the hands). [*Hint:* First treat his entire body as a system; then isolate his legs (or his upper body).]

Figure **P11.63**

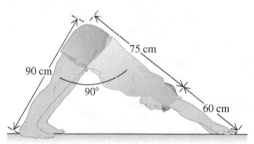

75 cm
90 cm
90°
60 cm

11.64 •• A uniform metal bar that is 8.00 m long and has mass 30.0 kg is attached at one end to the side of a building by a frictionless hinge. The bar is held at an angle of 64.0° above the horizontal by a thin, light cable that runs from the end of the bar opposite the hinge to a point on the wall that is above the hinge. The cable makes an angle of 37.0° with the bar. Your mass is 65.0 kg. You grab the bar near the hinge and hang beneath it, with your hands close together and your feet off the ground. To impress your friends, you intend to shift your hands slowly toward the top end of the bar. (a) If the cable breaks when its tension exceeds 455 N, how far from the upper end of the bar are you when the cable breaks? (b) Just before the cable breaks, what are the magnitude and direction of the resultant force that the hinge exerts on the bar?

11.65 • A worker wants to turn over a uniform, 1250-N, rectangular crate by pulling at 53.0° on one of its vertical sides (**Fig. P11.65**). The floor is rough enough to prevent the crate from slipping. (a) What pull is needed to just start the crate to tip? (b) How hard does the floor push upward on the crate? (c) Find the friction force on the crate. (d) What is the minimum coefficient of static friction needed to prevent the crate from slipping on the floor?

Figure **P11.65**

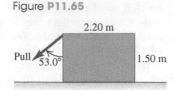

11.66 ••• One end of a uniform meter stick is placed against a vertical wall (**Fig. P11.66**). The other end is held by a lightweight cord that makes an angle θ with the stick. The coefficient of static friction between the end of the meter stick and the wall is 0.40. (a) What is the maximum value the angle θ can have if the stick is to remain in equilibrium? (b) Let the angle θ be 15°. A block of the same weight as the meter stick is suspended from the stick, as shown, at a distance x from the wall. What is the minimum value of x for which the stick will remain in equilibrium? (c) When $\theta = 15°$, how large must the coefficient of static friction be so that the block can be attached 10 cm from the left end of the stick without causing it to slip?

Figure **P11.66**

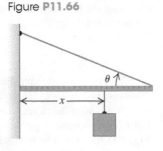

11.67 •• Two friends are carrying a 200-kg crate up a flight of stairs. The crate is 1.25 m long and 0.500 m high, and its center of gravity is at its center. The stairs make a 45.0° angle with respect to the floor. The crate also is carried at a 45.0° angle, so that its bottom side is parallel to the slope of the stairs (**Fig. P11.67**). If the force each person applies is vertical, what is the magnitude of each of these forces? Is it better to be the person above or below on the stairs?

Figure **P11.67**

11.68 •• BIO **Forearm.** In the human arm, the forearm and hand pivot about the elbow joint. Consider a simplified model in which the biceps muscle is attached to the forearm 3.80 cm from the elbow joint. Assume that the person's hand and forearm together weigh 15.0 N and that their center of gravity is 15.0 cm from the elbow (not quite halfway to the hand). The forearm is held horizontally at a right angle to the upper arm, with the biceps muscle exerting its force perpendicular to the forearm. (a) Draw a free-body diagram for the forearm, and find the force exerted by the biceps when the hand is empty. (b) Now the person holds an 80.0-N weight in his hand, with the forearm still horizontal. Assume that the center of gravity of this weight is 33.0 cm from the elbow. Draw a free-body diagram for the forearm, and find the force now exerted by the biceps. Explain why the biceps muscle needs to be very strong. (c) Under the conditions of part (b), find the magnitude and direction of the force that the elbow joint exerts on the forearm. (d) While holding the 80.0-N weight, the person

raises his forearm until it is at an angle of 53.0° above the horizontal. If the biceps muscle continues to exert its force perpendicular to the forearm, what is this force now? Has the force increased or decreased from its value in part (b)? Explain why this is so, and test your answer by doing this with your own arm.

11.69 •• BIO CALC Refer to the discussion of holding a dumbbell in Example 11.4 (Section 11.3). The maximum weight that can be held in this way is limited by the maximum allowable tendon tension T (determined by the strength of the tendons) and by the distance D from the elbow to where the tendon attaches to the forearm. (a) Let T_{max} represent the maximum value of the tendon tension. Use the results of Example 11.4 to express w_{max} (the maximum weight that can be held) in terms of T_{max}, L, D, and h. Your expression should *not* include the angle θ. (b) The tendons of different primates are attached to the forearm at different values of D. Calculate the derivative of w_{max} with respect to D, and determine whether the derivative is positive or negative. (c) A chimpanzee tendon is attached to the forearm at a point farther from the elbow than for humans. Use this to explain why chimpanzees have stronger arms than humans. (The disadvantage is that chimpanzees have less flexible arms than do humans.)

11.70 ••• In a city park a nonuniform wooden beam 4.00 m long is suspended horizontally by a light steel cable at each end. The cable at the left-hand end makes an angle of 30.0° with the vertical and has tension 620 N. The cable at the right-hand end of the beam makes an angle of 50.0° with the vertical. As an employee of the Parks and Recreation Department, you are asked to find the weight of the beam and the location of its center of gravity.

11.71 •• You are a summer intern for an architectural firm. An 8.00-m-long uniform steel rod is to be attached to a wall by a frictionless hinge at one end. The rod is to be held at 22.0° below the horizontal by a light cable that is attached to the end of the rod opposite the hinge. The cable makes an angle of 30.0° with the rod and is attached to the wall at a point above the hinge. The cable will break if its tension exceeds 650 N. (a) For what mass of the rod will the cable break? (b) If the rod has a mass that is 10.0 kg less than the value calculated in part (a), what are the magnitude and direction of the force that the hinge exerts on the rod?

11.72 •• You are trying to raise a bicycle wheel of mass m and radius R up over a curb of height h. To do this, you apply a horizontal force $\vec{F}$ (**Fig. P11.72**). What is the smallest magnitude of the force $\vec{F}$ that will succeed in raising the wheel onto the curb when the force is applied (a) at the center of the wheel and (b) at the top of the wheel? (c) In which case is less force required?

Figure **P11.72**

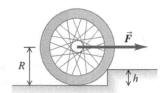

11.73 • **The Farmyard Gate.** A gate 4.00 m wide and 2.00 m high weighs 700 N. Its center of gravity is at its center, and it is hinged at A and B. To relieve the strain on the top hinge, a wire CD is connected as shown in **Fig. P11.73**. The tension in CD is increased until the horizontal force at hinge A is zero. What is (a) the tension in the wire CD;

Figure **P11.73**

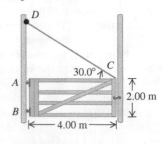

(b) the magnitude of the horizontal component of the force at hinge B; (c) the combined vertical force exerted by hinges A and B?

11.74 • If you put a uniform block at the edge of a table, the center of the block must be over the table for the block not to fall off. (a) If you stack two identical blocks at the table edge, the center of the top block must be over the bottom block, and the center of gravity of the two blocks together must be over the table. In terms of the length L of each block, what is the maximum overhang possible (**Fig. P11.74**)? (b) Repeat part (a) for three identical blocks and for four identical blocks. (c) Is it possible to make a stack of blocks such that the uppermost block is not directly over the table at all? How many blocks would it take to do this? (Try.)

Figure **P11.74**

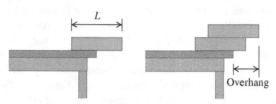

11.75 ••• Two uniform, 75.0-g marbles 2.00 cm in diameter are stacked as shown in **Fig. P11.75** in a container that is 3.00 cm wide. (a) Find the force that the container exerts on the marbles at the points of contact A, B, and C. (b) What force does each marble exert on the other?

Figure **P11.75**

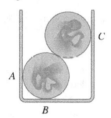

11.76 •• Two identical, uniform beams weighing 260 N each are connected at one end by a frictionless hinge. A light horizontal crossbar attached at the midpoints of the beams maintains an angle of 53.0° between the beams. The beams are suspended from the ceiling by vertical wires such that they form a "V" (**Fig. P11.76**). (a) What force does the crossbar exert on each beam? (b) Is the crossbar under tension or compression? (c) What force (magnitude and direction) does the hinge at point A exert on each beam?

Figure **P11.76**

11.77 • An engineer is designing a conveyor system for loading hay bales into a wagon (**Fig. P11.77**). Each bale is 0.25 m wide, 0.50 m high, and 0.80 m long (the dimension perpendicular to the plane of the figure), with mass 30.0 kg. The center of gravity of each bale is at its geometrical center. The coefficient of static friction between a bale and the conveyor belt is 0.60, and the belt moves with constant speed. (a) The angle β of the conveyor is slowly increased. At some critical angle a bale will tip (if it doesn't slip first), and at some different critical angle it will slip (if it doesn't tip first). Find the two critical angles and determine which happens at the smaller angle. (b) Would the outcome of part (a) be different if the coefficient of friction were 0.40?

Figure **P11.77**

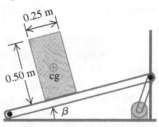

11.78 • A weight W is supported by attaching it to a vertical uniform metal pole by a thin cord passing over a pulley having negligible mass and friction. The cord is attached to the pole 40.0 cm below the top and pulls horizontally on it (**Fig. P11.78**). The pole is pivoted about a hinge at its base, is 1.75 m tall, and weighs 55.0 N. A thin wire connects the top of the pole to a vertical wall. The nail that holds this wire to the wall will pull out if an *outward* force greater than 22.0 N acts on it. (a) What is the greatest weight W that can be supported this way without pulling out the nail? (b) What is the *magnitude* of the force that the hinge exerts on the pole?

Figure **P11.78**

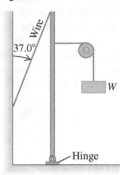

11.79 •• A garage door is mounted on an overhead rail (**Fig. P11.79**). The wheels at A and B have rusted so that they do not roll, but rather slide along the track. The coefficient of kinetic friction is 0.52. The distance between the wheels is 2.00 m, and each is 0.50 m from the vertical sides of the door. The door is uniform and weighs 950 N. It is pushed to the left at constant speed by a horizontal force $\vec{F}$. (a) If the distance h is 1.60 m, what is the vertical component of the force exerted on each wheel by the track? (b) Find the maximum value h can have without causing one wheel to leave the track.

Figure **P11.79**

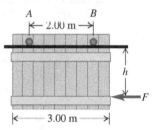

11.80 ••• **Pyramid Builders.** Ancient pyramid builders are balancing a uniform rectangular slab of stone tipped at an angle θ above the horizontal using a rope (**Fig. P11.80**). The rope is held by five workers who share the force equally. (a) If $\theta = 20.0°$, what force does each worker exert on the rope? (b) As θ increases, does each worker have to exert more or less force than in part (a), assuming they do not change the angle of the rope? Why? (c) At what angle do the workers need to exert *no force* to balance the slab? What happens if θ exceeds this value?

Figure **P11.80**

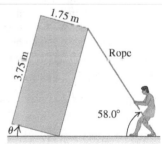

11.81 ••• CP A 12.0-kg mass, fastened to the end of an aluminum wire with an unstretched length of 0.70 m, is whirled in a vertical circle with a constant angular speed of 120 rev/min. The cross-sectional area of the wire is 0.014 cm². Calculate the elongation of the wire when the mass is (a) at the lowest point of the path and (b) at the highest point of its path.

11.82 •• **Hooke's Law for a Wire.** A wire of length l_0 and cross-sectional area A supports a hanging weight W. (a) Show that if the wire obeys Eq. (11.7), it behaves like a spring of force constant AY/l_0, where Y is Young's modulus for the wire material. (b) What would the force constant be for a 75.0-cm length of 16-gauge (diameter = 1.291 mm) copper wire? See Table 11.1. (c) What would W have to be to stretch the wire in part (b) by 1.25 mm?

11.83 ••• A 1.05-m-long rod of negligible weight is supported at its ends by wires A and B of equal length (**Fig. P11.83**). The cross-sectional area of A is 2.00 mm^2 and that of B is 4.00 mm^2. Young's modulus for wire A is 1.80×10^{11} Pa; that for B is 1.20×10^{11} Pa. At what point along the rod should a weight w be suspended to produce (a) equal stresses in A and B and (b) equal strains in A and B?

Figure **P11.83**

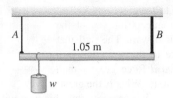

11.84 ••• CP An amusement park ride consists of airplane-shaped cars attached to steel rods (**Fig. P11.84**). Each rod has a length of 15.0 m and a cross-sectional area of 8.00 cm^2. (a) How much is each rod stretched when it is vertical and the ride is at rest? (Assume that each car plus two people seated in it has a total weight of 1900 N.) (b) When operating, the ride has a maximum angular speed of 12.0 rev/min. How much is the rod stretched then?

Figure **P11.84**

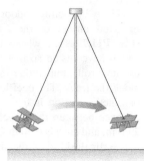

11.85 ••• CP BIO **Stress on the Shin Bone.** The compressive strength of our bones is important in everyday life. Young's modulus for bone is about 1.4×10^{10} Pa. Bone can take only about a 1.0% change in its length before fracturing. (a) What is the maximum force that can be applied to a bone whose minimum cross-sectional area is 3.0 cm^2? (This is approximately the cross-sectional area of a tibia, or shin bone, at its narrowest point.) (b) Estimate the maximum height from which a 70-kg man could jump and not fracture his tibia. Take the time between when he first touches the floor and when he has stopped to be 0.030 s, and assume that the stress on his two legs is distributed equally.

11.86 •• DATA You are to use a long, thin wire to build a pendulum in a science museum. The wire has an unstretched length of 22.0 m and a circular cross section of diameter 0.860 mm; it is made of an alloy that has a large breaking stress. One end of the wire will be attached to the ceiling, and a 9.50-kg metal sphere will be attached to the other end. As the pendulum swings back and forth, the wire's maximum angular displacement from the vertical will be 36.0°. You must determine the maximum amount the wire will stretch during this motion. So, before you attach the metal sphere, you suspend a test mass (mass m) from the wire's lower end. You then measure the increase in length Δl of the wire for several different test masses. **Figure P11.86**, a graph of Δl

Figure **P11.86**

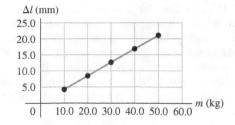

versus m, shows the results and the straight line that gives the best fit to the data. The equation for this line is $\Delta l = (0.422 \text{ mm/kg})m$. (a) Assume that $g = 9.80$ m/s^2, and use Fig. P11.86 to calculate Young's modulus Y for this wire. (b) You remove the test masses, attach the 9.50-kg sphere, and release the sphere from rest, with the wire displaced by 36.0°. Calculate the amount the wire will stretch as it swings through the vertical. Ignore air resistance.

11.87 •• DATA You need to measure the mass M of a 4.00-m-long bar. The bar has a square cross section but has some holes drilled along its length, so you suspect that its center of gravity isn't in the middle of the bar. The bar is too long for you to weigh on your scale. So, first you balance the bar on a knife-edge pivot and determine that the bar's center of gravity is 1.88 m from its left-hand end. You then place the bar on the pivot so that the point of support is 1.50 m from the left-hand end of the bar. Next you suspend a 2.00-kg mass (m_1) from the bar at a point 0.200 m from the left-hand end. Finally, you suspend a mass $m_2 = 1.00$ kg from the bar at a distance x from the left-hand end and adjust x so that the bar is balanced. You repeat this step for other values of m_2 and record each corresponding value of x. The table gives your results.

m_2 (kg)	1.00	1.50	2.00	2.50	3.00	4.00
x (m)	3.50	2.83	2.50	2.32	2.16	2.00

(a) Draw a free-body diagram for the bar when m_1 and m_2 are suspended from it. (b) Apply the static equilibrium equation $\sum \tau_z = 0$ with the axis at the location of the knife-edge pivot. Solve the equation for x as a function of m_2. (c) Plot x versus $1/m_2$. Use the slope of the best-fit straight line and the equation you derived in part (b) to calculate that bar's mass M. Use $g = 9.80$ m/s^2. (d) What is the y-intercept of the straight line that fits the data? Explain why it has this value.

11.88 ••• DATA You are a construction engineer working on the interior design of a retail store in a mall. A 2.00-m-long uniform bar of mass 8.50 kg is to be attached at one end to a wall, by means of a hinge that allows the bar to rotate freely with very little friction. The bar will be held in a horizontal position by a light cable from a point on the bar (a distance x from the hinge) to a point on the wall above the hinge. The cable makes an angle θ with the bar. The architect has proposed four possible ways to connect the cable and asked you to assess them:

Alternative	A	B	C	D
x (m)	2.00	1.50	0.75	0.50
θ (degrees)	30	60	37	75

(a) There is concern about the strength of the cable that will be required. Which set of x and θ values in the table produces the smallest tension in the cable? The greatest? (b) There is concern about the breaking strength of the sheetrock wall where the hinge will be attached. Which set of x and θ values produces the smallest horizontal component of the force the bar exerts on the hinge? The largest? (c) There is also concern about the required strength of the hinge and the strength of its attachment to the wall. Which set of x and θ values produces the smallest magnitude of the vertical component of the force the bar exerts on the hinge? The largest? (*Hint:* Does the direction of the vertical component of the force the hinge exerts on the bar depend on where along the bar the cable is attached?) (d) Is one of the alternatives given in the table preferable? Should any of the alternatives be avoided? Discuss.

CHALLENGE PROBLEMS

11.89 ••• Two ladders, 4.00 m and 3.00 m long, are hinged at point A and tied together by a horizontal rope 0.90 m above the floor (**Fig. P11.89**). The ladders weigh 480 N and 360 N, respectively, and the center of gravity of each is at its center. Assume that the floor is freshly waxed and frictionless. (a) Find the upward force at the bottom of each ladder. (b) Find the tension in the rope. (c) Find the magnitude of the force one ladder exerts on the other at point A. (d) If an 800-N painter stands at point A, find the tension in the horizontal rope.

Figure **P11.89**

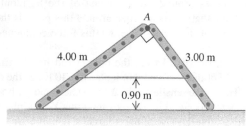

11.90 ••• **Knocking Over a Post.** One end of a post weighing 400 N and with height h rests on a rough horizontal surface with $\mu_s = 0.30$. The upper end is held by a rope fastened to the surface and making an angle of 36.9° with the post (**Fig. P11.90**). A horizontal force $\vec{F}$ is exerted on the post as

Figure **P11.90**

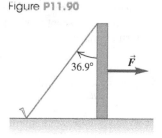

shown. (a) If the force $\vec{F}$ is applied at the midpoint of the post, what is the largest value it can have without causing the post to slip? (b) How large can the force be without causing the post to slip if its point of application is $\frac{6}{10}$ of the way from the ground to the top of the post? (c) Show that if the point of application of the force is too high, the post cannot be made to slip, no matter how great the force. Find the critical height for the point of application.

11.91 ••• CP An angler hangs a 4.50-kg fish from a vertical steel wire 1.50 m long and 5.00×10^{-3} cm^2 in cross-sectional area. The upper end of the wire is securely fastened to a support. (a) Calculate the amount the wire is stretched by the hanging fish. The angler now applies a varying force $\vec{F}$ at the lower end of the wire, pulling it very slowly downward by 0.500 mm from its equilibrium position. For this downward motion, calculate (b) the work done by gravity; (c) the work done by the force $\vec{F}$; (d) the work done by the force the wire exerts on the fish; and (e) the change in the elastic potential energy (the potential energy associated with the tensile stress in the wire). Compare the answers in parts (d) and (e).

BIO **TORQUES AND TUG-OF-WAR.** In a study of the biomechanics of the tug-of-war, a 2.0-m-tall, 80.0-kg competitor in the middle of the line is considered to be a rigid body leaning back at an angle of 30.0° to the vertical. The competitor is pulling on a rope that is held horizontal a distance of 1.5 m from his feet (as measured along the line of the body). At the moment shown in the figure, the man is stationary and the tension in the rope in front of him is $T_1 = 1160$ N. Since there is friction between the rope and his hands, the tension in the rope behind him, T_2, is not equal to T_1. His center of mass is halfway between his feet and the top of his head. The coefficient of static friction between his feet and the ground is 0.65.

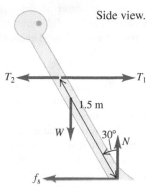

Side view.

11.92 What is tension T_2 in the rope behind him? (a) 590 N; (b) 650 N; (c) 860 N; (d) 1100 N.

11.93 If he leans slightly farther back (increasing the angle between his body and the vertical) but remains stationary in this new position, which of the following statements is true? Assume that the rope remains horizontal. (a) The difference between T_1 and T_2 will increase, balancing the increased torque about his feet that his weight produces when he leans farther back; (b) the difference between T_1 and T_2 will decrease, balancing the increased torque about his feet that his weight produces when he leans farther back; (c) neither T_1 nor T_2 will change, because no other forces are changing; (d) both T_1 and T_2 will change, but the difference between them will remain the same.

11.94 His body is again leaning back at 30.0° to the vertical, but now the height at which the rope is held above—but still parallel to—the ground is varied. The tension in the rope in front of the competitor (T_1) is measured as a function of the shortest distance between the rope and the ground (the holding height). Tension T_1 is found to decrease as the holding height increases. What could explain this observation? As the holding height increases, (a) the moment arm of the rope about his feet decreases due to the angle that his body makes with the vertical; (b) the moment arm of the weight about his feet decreases due to the angle that his body makes with the vertical; (c) a smaller tension in the rope is needed to produce a torque sufficient to balance the torque of the weight about his feet; (d) his center of mass moves down to compensate, so less tension in the rope is required to maintain equilibrium.

11.95 His body is leaning back at 30.0° to the vertical, but the coefficient of static friction between his feet and the ground is suddenly reduced to 0.50. What will happen? (a) His entire body will accelerate forward; (b) his feet will slip forward; (c) his feet will slip backward; (d) his feet will not slip.

Answers

Chapter Opening Question **?**

(i) Each stone in the arch is under compression, not tension. This is because the forces on the stones tend to push them inward toward the center of the arch and thus squeeze them together. Compared to a solid supporting wall, a wall with arches is just as strong yet much more economical to build.

Test Your Understanding Questions

11.1 (i) Situation (i) satisfies both equilibrium conditions because the seagull has zero acceleration (so $\Sigma \vec{F} = 0$) and no tendency to start rotating (so $\Sigma \vec{\tau} = 0$). Situation (ii) satisfies the first condition because the crankshaft as a whole does not accelerate through space, but it does not satisfy the second condition; the crankshaft has an angular acceleration, so $\Sigma \vec{\tau}$ is not zero. Situation (iii) satisfies the second condition (there is no tendency to rotate) but not the first one; the baseball accelerates in its flight (due to gravity and air resistance), so $\Sigma \vec{F}$ is not zero.

11.2 (ii) In equilibrium, the center of gravity must be at the point of support. Since the rock and meter stick have the same mass and hence the same weight, the center of gravity of the system is midway between their respective centers. The center of gravity of the meter stick alone is 0.50 m from the left end (that is, at the middle of the meter stick), so the center of gravity of the combination of rock and meter stick is 0.25 m from the left end.

11.3 (ii), (i), (iii) This is the same situation described in Example 11.4, with the rod replacing the forearm, the hinge replacing the elbow, and the cable replacing the tendon. The only difference is that the cable attachment point is at the end of the rod, so the distances D and L are identical. From Example 11.4, the tension is

$$T = \frac{Lw}{L\sin\theta} = \frac{w}{\sin\theta}$$

Since $\sin\theta$ is less than 1, the tension T is greater than the weight w. The vertical component of the force exerted by the hinge is

$$E_y = -\frac{(L - L)w}{L} = 0$$

In this situation, the hinge exerts *no* vertical force. To see this, calculate torques around the right end of the horizontal rod: The only force that exerts a torque around this point is the vertical component of the hinge force, so this force component must be zero.

11.4 (a) (iii), (b) (ii) In (a), the copper rod has 10 times the elongation Δl of the steel rod, but it also has 10 times the original length l_0. Hence the tensile strain $\Delta l/l_0$ is the same for both rods. In (b), the stress is equal to Young's modulus Y multiplied by the strain. From Table 11.1, steel has a larger value of Y, so a greater stress is required to produce the same strain.

11.5 In (a) and (b), the bumper will have sprung back to its original shape (although the paint may be scratched). In (c), the bumper will have a permanent dent or deformation. In (d), the bumper will be torn or broken.

Bridging Problem

(a) $T = \dfrac{2mg}{3\sin\theta}$

(b) $F = \dfrac{2mg}{3\sin\theta}\sqrt{\cos^2\theta + \tfrac{1}{4}\sin^2\theta}, \quad \phi = \arctan\left(\tfrac{1}{2}\tan\theta\right)$

(c) $\Delta l = \dfrac{2mgl_0}{3AY\tan\theta}$ (d) 4

? Dogs walk with much quicker strides than do humans. Is this primarily because, compared to human legs, dogs' legs (i) are shorter; (ii) are less massive; (iii) have a higher ratio of muscle to fat; (iv) have paws rather than toes; or (v) more than one of these?

14 PERIODIC MOTION

Many kinds of motion repeat themselves over and over: the vibration of a quartz crystal in a watch, the swinging pendulum of a grandfather clock, the sound vibrations produced by a clarinet or an organ pipe, and the back-and-forth motion of the pistons in a car engine. This kind of motion, called **periodic motion** or **oscillation,** is the subject of this chapter. Understanding periodic motion will be essential for our later study of waves, sound, alternating electric currents, and light.

A body that undergoes periodic motion always has a stable equilibrium position. When it is moved away from this position and released, a force or torque comes into play to pull it back toward equilibrium. But by the time it gets there, it has picked up some kinetic energy, so it overshoots, stopping somewhere on the other side, and is again pulled back toward equilibrium. Picture a ball rolling back and forth in a round bowl or a pendulum that swings back and forth past its straight-down position.

In this chapter we will concentrate on two simple examples of systems that can undergo periodic motions: spring-mass systems and pendulums. We will also study why oscillations often tend to die out with time and why some oscillations can build up to greater and greater displacements from equilibrium when periodically varying forces act.

14.1 DESCRIBING OSCILLATION

Figure 14.1 (next page) shows one of the simplest systems that can have periodic motion. A body with mass m rests on a frictionless horizontal guide system, such as a linear air track, so it can move along the x-axis only. The body is attached to a spring of negligible mass that can be either stretched or compressed. The left end of the spring is held fixed, and the right end is attached to the body. The spring force is the only horizontal force acting on the body; the vertical normal and gravitational forces always add to zero.

It's simplest to define our coordinate system so that the origin O is at the equilibrium position, where the spring is neither stretched nor compressed. Then x is

433

14.1 A system that can have periodic motion.

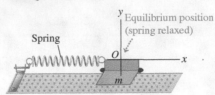

14.2 Model for periodic motion. When the body is displaced from its equilibrium position at $x = 0$, the spring exerts a restoring force back toward the equilibrium position.

(a)

$x > 0$: glider displaced to the right from the equilibrium position.

$F_x < 0$, so $a_x < 0$: stretched spring pulls glider toward equilibrium position.

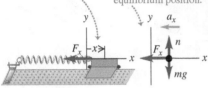

(b)

$x = 0$: The relaxed spring exerts no force on the glider, so the glider has zero acceleration.

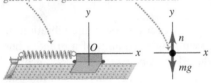

(c)

$x < 0$: glider displaced to the left from the equilibrium position.

$F_x > 0$, so $a_x > 0$: compressed spring pushes glider toward equilibrium position.

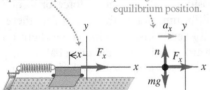

BIO Application Wing Frequencies
The ruby-throated hummingbird (*Archilochus colubris*) normally flaps its wings at about 50 Hz, producing the sound that gives hummingbirds their name. Insects can flap their wings at even faster rates, from 330 Hz for a house fly and 600 Hz for a mosquito to an amazing 1040 Hz for the tiny biting midge.

the *x*-component of the **displacement** of the body from equilibrium and is also the change in the length of the spring. The spring exerts a force on the body with *x*-component F_x, and the *x*-component of acceleration is $a_x = F_x/m$.

Figure 14.2 shows the body for three different displacements of the spring. Whenever the body is displaced from its equilibrium position, the spring force tends to restore it to the equilibrium position. We call a force with this character a **restoring force.** Oscillation can occur only when there is a restoring force tending to return the system to equilibrium.

Let's analyze how oscillation occurs in this system. If we displace the body to the right to $x = A$ and then let go, the net force and the acceleration are to the left (Fig. 14.2a). The speed increases as the body approaches the equilibrium position O. When the body is at O, the net force acting on it is zero (Fig. 14.2b), but because of its motion it *overshoots* the equilibrium position. On the other side of the equilibrium position the body is still moving to the left, but the net force and the acceleration are to the right (Fig. 14.2c); hence the speed decreases until the body comes to a stop. We will show later that with an ideal spring, the stopping point is at $x = -A$. The body then accelerates to the right, overshoots equilibrium again, and stops at the starting point $x = A$, ready to repeat the whole process. The body is oscillating! If there is no friction or other force to remove mechanical energy from the system, this motion repeats forever; the restoring force perpetually draws the body back toward the equilibrium position, only to have the body overshoot time after time.

In different situations the force may depend on the displacement x from equilibrium in different ways. But oscillation *always* occurs if the force is a *restoring* force that tends to return the system to equilibrium.

Amplitude, Period, Frequency, and Angular Frequency

Here are some terms that we'll use in discussing periodic motions of all kinds:

The **amplitude** of the motion, denoted by A, is the maximum magnitude of displacement from equilibrium—that is, the maximum value of $|x|$. It is always positive. If the spring in Fig. 14.2 is an ideal one, the total overall range of the motion is $2A$. The SI unit of A is the meter. A complete vibration, or **cycle,** is one complete round trip—say, from A to $-A$ and back to A, or from O to A, back through O to $-A$, and back to O. Note that motion from one side to the other (say, $-A$ to A) is a half-cycle, not a whole cycle.

The **period,** T, is the time to complete one cycle. It is always positive. The SI unit is the second, but it is sometimes expressed as "seconds per cycle."

The **frequency,** f, is the number of cycles in a unit of time. It is always positive. The SI unit of frequency is the *hertz,* named for the 19th-century German physicist Heinrich Hertz:

$$1 \text{ hertz} = 1 \text{ Hz} = 1 \text{ cycle/s} = 1 \text{ s}^{-1}$$

The **angular frequency,** ω, is 2π times the frequency:

$$\omega = 2\pi f$$

We'll learn shortly why ω is a useful quantity. It represents the rate of change of an angular quantity (not necessarily related to a rotational motion) that is always measured in radians, so its units are rad/s. Since f is in cycle/s, we may regard the number 2π as having units rad/cycle.

By definition, period and frequency are reciprocals of each other:

In periodic motion
frequency and period
are reciprocals of each other.
$$f = \frac{1}{T} \quad \overset{\text{Period}}{\nearrow} \quad T = \frac{1}{f}$$
Frequency
(14.1)

Also, from the definition of ω,

Angular frequency
related to frequency
and period
$$\omega = 2\pi f = \frac{2\pi}{T}$$
Frequency
Period
(14.2)

EXAMPLE 14.1   PERIOD, FREQUENCY, AND ANGULAR FREQUENCY

An ultrasonic transducer used for medical diagnosis oscillates at 6.7 MHz = 6.7×10^6 Hz. How long does each oscillation take, and what is the angular frequency?

SOLUTION

IDENTIFY and SET UP: The target variables are the period T and the angular frequency ω. We can find these from the given frequency f in Eqs. (14.1) and (14.2).

EXECUTE: From Eqs. (14.1) and (14.2),

$$T = \frac{1}{f} = \frac{1}{6.7 \times 10^6 \text{ Hz}} = 1.5 \times 10^{-7} \text{ s} = 0.15 \ \mu\text{s}$$

$$\omega = 2\pi f = 2\pi(6.7 \times 10^6 \text{ Hz})$$

$$= (2\pi \text{ rad/cycle})(6.7 \times 10^6 \text{ cycle/s}) = 4.2 \times 10^7 \text{ rad/s}$$

EVALUATE: This is a very rapid vibration, with large f and ω and small T. A slow vibration has small f and ω and large T.

TEST YOUR UNDERSTANDING OF SECTION 14.1   A body like that shown in Fig. 14.2 oscillates back and forth. For each of the following values of the body's x-velocity v_x and x-acceleration a_x, state whether its displacement x is positive, negative, or zero. (a) $v_x > 0$ and $a_x > 0$; (b) $v_x > 0$ and $a_x < 0$; (c) $v_x < 0$ and $a_x > 0$; (d) $v_x < 0$ and $a_x < 0$; (e) $v_x = 0$ and $a_x < 0$; (f) $v_x > 0$ and $a_x = 0$. ∎

14.2 SIMPLE HARMONIC MOTION

The simplest kind of oscillation occurs when the restoring force F_x is *directly proportional* to the displacement from equilibrium x. This happens if the spring in Figs. 14.1 and 14.2 is an ideal one that obeys *Hooke's law* (see Section 6.3). The constant of proportionality between F_x and x is the force constant k. On either side of the equilibrium position, F_x and x always have opposite signs. In Section 6.3 we represented the force acting *on* a stretched ideal spring as $F_x = kx$. The x-component of force the spring exerts *on the body* is the negative of this, so

Restoring force
exerted by an
ideal spring
$$F_x = -kx$$
x-component of force
Displacement
Force constant of spring
(14.3)

This equation gives the correct magnitude and sign of the force, whether x is positive, negative, or zero (**Fig. 14.3**). The force constant k is always positive and has units of N/m (a useful alternative set of units is kg/s²). We are assuming that there is no friction, so Eq. (14.3) gives the *net* force on the body.

14.3 An idealized spring exerts a restoring force that obeys Hooke's law, $F_x = -kx$. Oscillation with such a restoring force is called simple harmonic motion.

Restoring force F_x

$x < 0$
$F_x > 0$

Displacement x

O

$x > 0$
$F_x < 0$

The restoring force exerted by an idealized spring is directly proportional to the displacement (Hooke's law, $F_x = -kx$): the graph of F_x versus x is a straight line.

*When the restoring force is directly proportional to the displacement from equilibrium, as given by Eq. (14.3), the oscillation is called **simple harmonic motion (SHM)**.* The acceleration $a_x = d^2x/dt^2 = F_x/m$ of a body in SHM is

Equation for simple harmonic motion

x-component of acceleration

Force constant of restoring force

$$a_x = \frac{d^2x}{dt^2} = -\frac{k}{m}x \qquad (14.4)$$

Second derivative of displacement

Displacement

Mass of object

The minus sign means that, in SHM, the acceleration and displacement always have opposite signs. This acceleration is *not* constant, so don't even think of using the constant-acceleration equations from Chapter 2. We'll see shortly how to solve this equation to find the displacement x as a function of time. A body that undergoes simple harmonic motion is called a **harmonic oscillator.**

Why is simple harmonic motion important? Not all periodic motions are simple harmonic; in periodic motion in general, the restoring force depends on displacement in a more complicated way than in Eq. (14.3). But in many systems the restoring force is *approximately* proportional to displacement if the displacement is sufficiently small (**Fig. 14.4**). That is, if the amplitude is small enough, the oscillations of such systems are approximately simple harmonic and therefore approximately described by Eq. (14.4). Thus we can use SHM as an approximate model for many different periodic motions, such as the vibration of a tuning fork, the electric current in an alternating-current circuit, and the oscillations of atoms in molecules and solids.

Circular Motion and the Equations of SHM

To explore the properties of simple harmonic motion, we must express the displacement x of the oscillating body as a function of time, $x(t)$. The second derivative of this function, d^2x/dt^2, must be equal to $(-k/m)$ times the function itself, as required by Eq. (14.4). As we mentioned, the formulas for constant acceleration from Section 2.4 are no help because the acceleration changes constantly as the displacement x changes. Instead, we'll find $x(t)$ by noting that SHM is related to *uniform circular motion*, which we studied in Section 3.4.

Figure 14.5a shows a top view of a horizontal disk of radius A with a ball attached to its rim at point Q. The disk rotates with constant angular speed ω (measured in rad/s), so the ball moves in uniform circular motion. A horizontal

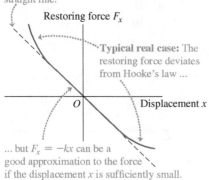

14.4 In most real oscillations Hooke's law applies provided the body doesn't move too far from equilibrium. In such a case small-amplitude oscillations are approximately simple harmonic.

Ideal case: The restoring force obeys Hooke's law ($F_x = -kx$), so the graph of F_x versus x is a straight line.

Restoring force F_x

Typical real case: The restoring force deviates from Hooke's law ...

O

Displacement x

... but $F_x = -kx$ can be a good approximation to the force if the displacement x is sufficiently small.

14.5 (a) Relating uniform circular motion and simple harmonic motion. (b) The ball's shadow moves exactly like a body oscillating on an ideal spring.

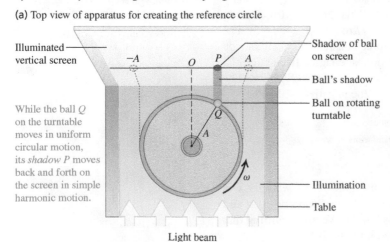

(a) Top view of apparatus for creating the reference circle

Illuminated vertical screen

$-A$ O P A

Shadow of ball on screen

Ball's shadow

Ball on rotating turntable

While the ball Q on the turntable moves in uniform circular motion, its *shadow P* moves back and forth on the screen in simple harmonic motion.

Q

A

ω

Illumination

Table

Light beam

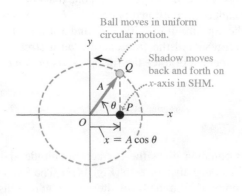

(b) An abstract representation of the motion in (a)

Ball moves in uniform circular motion.

y

Q

Shadow moves back and forth on x-axis in SHM.

A

θ P

O

x

$x = A \cos \theta$

light beam casts a shadow of the ball on a screen. The shadow at point P oscillates back and forth as the ball moves in a circle. We then arrange a body attached to an ideal spring, like the combination shown in Figs. 14.1 and 14.2, so that the body oscillates parallel to the shadow. We will prove that the motions of the body and of the ball's shadow are *identical* if the amplitude of the body's oscillation is equal to the disk radius A, and if the angular frequency $2\pi f$ of the oscillating body is equal to the angular speed ω of the rotating disk. That is, *simple harmonic motion is the projection of uniform circular motion onto a diameter.*

We can verify this remarkable statement by finding the acceleration of the shadow at P and comparing it to the acceleration of a body undergoing SHM, given by Eq. (14.4). The circle in which the ball moves so that its projection matches the motion of the oscillating body is called the **reference circle;** we will call the point Q the *reference point.* We take the reference circle to lie in the xy-plane, with the origin O at the center of the circle (Fig. 14.5b). At time t the vector OQ from the origin to reference point Q makes an angle θ with the positive x-axis. As point Q moves around the reference circle with constant angular speed ω, vector OQ rotates with the same angular speed. Such a rotating vector is called a **phasor.** (This term was in use long before the invention of the *Star Trek* stun gun with a similar name.) We'll use phasors again when we study alternating-current circuits in Chapter 31 and the interference of light in Chapters 35 and 36.

The x-component of the phasor at time t is just the x-coordinate of the point Q:

$$x = A\cos\theta \qquad (14.5)$$

This is also the x-coordinate of the shadow P, which is the *projection* of Q onto the x-axis. Hence the x-velocity of the shadow P along the x-axis is equal to the x-component of the velocity vector of point Q (**Fig. 14.6a**), and the x-acceleration of P is equal to the x-component of the acceleration vector of Q (Fig. 14.6b). Since point Q is in uniform circular motion, its acceleration vector $\vec{a}_Q$ is always directed toward O. Furthermore, the magnitude of $\vec{a}_Q$ is constant and given by the angular speed squared times the radius of the circle (see Section 9.3):

$$a_Q = \omega^2 A \qquad (14.6)$$

Figure 14.6b shows that the x-component of $\vec{a}_Q$ is $a_x = -a_Q\cos\theta$. Combining this with Eqs. (14.5) and (14.6), we get that the acceleration of point P is

$$a_x = -a_Q\cos\theta = -\omega^2 A\cos\theta \qquad \text{or} \qquad (14.7)$$

$$a_x = -\omega^2 x \qquad (14.8)$$

The acceleration of point P is directly proportional to the displacement x and always has the opposite sign. These are precisely the hallmarks of simple harmonic motion.

Equation (14.8) is *exactly* the same as Eq. (14.4) for the acceleration of a harmonic oscillator, provided that the angular speed ω of the reference point Q is related to the force constant k and mass m of the oscillating body by

$$\omega^2 = \frac{k}{m} \qquad \text{or} \qquad \omega = \sqrt{\frac{k}{m}} \qquad (14.9)$$

We have been using the same symbol ω for the angular *speed* of the reference point Q and the angular *frequency* of the oscillating point P. The reason is that these quantities are equal! If point Q makes one complete revolution in time T, then point P goes through one complete cycle of oscillation in the same time; hence T is the period of the oscillation. During time T the point Q moves through

14.6 The (a) x-velocity and (b) x-acceleration of the ball's shadow P (see Fig. 14.5) are the x-components of the velocity and acceleration vectors, respectively, of the ball Q.

(a) Using the reference circle to determine the x-velocity of point P

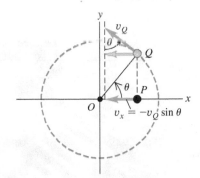

(b) Using the reference circle to determine the x-acceleration of point P

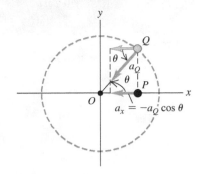

2π radians, so its angular speed is $\omega = 2\pi/T$. But this is the same as Eq. (14.2) for the angular frequency of the point P, which verifies our statement about the two interpretations of ω. This is why we introduced angular frequency in Section 14.1; this quantity makes the connection between oscillation and circular motion. So we reinterpret Eq. (14.9) as an expression for the angular frequency of simple harmonic motion:

$$\text{Angular frequency for simple harmonic motion} \qquad \omega = \sqrt{\frac{k}{m}} \qquad \overset{\text{Force constant of restoring force}}{\underset{\text{Mass of object}}{}} \qquad (14.10)$$

When you start a body oscillating in SHM, the value of ω is not yours to choose; it is predetermined by the values of k and m. The units of k are N/m or kg/s^2, so k/m is in (kg/s^2)/kg = s^{-2}. When we take the square root in Eq. (14.10), we get s^{-1}, or more properly rad/s because this is an *angular* frequency (recall that a radian is not a true unit).

According to Eqs. (14.1) and (14.2), the frequency f and period T are

$$\text{Frequency for simple harmonic motion} \qquad f = \frac{\overset{\text{Angular frequency}}{\omega}}{2\pi} = \frac{1}{2\pi}\sqrt{\frac{k}{m}} \qquad \overset{\text{Force constant of restoring force}}{\underset{\text{Mass of object}}{}} \qquad (14.11)$$

$$\text{Period for simple harmonic motion} \qquad T = \frac{1}{\underset{\text{Frequency}}{f}} = \frac{2\pi}{\underset{\text{Angular frequency}}{\omega}} = 2\pi\sqrt{\frac{m}{k}} \qquad \overset{\text{Mass of object}}{\underset{\text{Force constant of restoring force}}{}} \qquad (14.12)$$

We see from Eq. (14.12) that a larger mass m will have less acceleration and take a longer time for a complete cycle (**Fig. 14.7**). A stiffer spring (one with a larger force constant k) exerts a greater force at a given deformation x, causing greater acceleration and a shorter time T per cycle.

CAUTION **Don't confuse frequency and angular frequency** You can run into trouble if you don't make the distinction between frequency f and angular frequency $\omega = 2\pi f$. Frequency tells you how many cycles of oscillation occur per second, while angular frequency tells you how many radians per second this corresponds to on the reference circle. In solving problems, pay careful attention to whether the goal is to find f or ω. ▮

Period and Amplitude in SHM

Equations (14.11) and (14.12) show that the period and frequency of simple harmonic motion are completely determined by the mass m and the force constant k. *In simple harmonic motion the period and frequency do not depend on the amplitude A.* For given values of m and k, the time of one complete oscillation is the same whether the amplitude is large or small. Equation (14.3) shows why we should expect this. Larger A means that the body reaches larger values of $|x|$ and is subjected to larger restoring forces. This increases the average speed of the body over a complete cycle; this exactly compensates for having to travel a larger distance, so the same total time is involved.

The oscillations of a tuning fork are essentially simple harmonic motion, so it always vibrates with the same frequency, independent of amplitude. This is why a tuning fork can be used as a standard for musical pitch. If it were not for this characteristic of simple harmonic motion, it would be impossible to play most musical instruments in tune. If you encounter an oscillating body with a period that *does* depend on the amplitude, the oscillation is *not* simple harmonic motion.

14.7 The greater the mass m in a tuning fork's tines, the lower the frequency of oscillation $f = (1/2\pi)\sqrt{k/m}$ and the lower the pitch of the sound that the tuning fork produces.

Tines with large mass m: low frequency $f = 128$ Hz

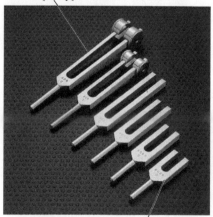

Tines with small mass m: high frequency $f = 4096$ Hz

EXAMPLE 14.2 ANGULAR FREQUENCY, FREQUENCY, AND PERIOD IN SHM

A spring is mounted horizontally, with its left end fixed. A spring balance attached to the free end and pulled toward the right (**Fig. 14.8a**) indicates that the stretching force is proportional to the displacement, and a force of 6.0 N causes a displacement of 0.030 m. We replace the spring balance with a 0.50-kg glider, pull it 0.020 m to the right along a frictionless air track, and release it from rest (Fig. 14.8b). (a) Find the force constant k of the spring. (b) Find the angular frequency ω, frequency f, and period T of the resulting oscillation.

SOLUTION

IDENTIFY and SET UP: Because the spring force (equal in magnitude to the stretching force) is proportional to the displacement, the motion is simple harmonic. We find k from Hooke's law,

14.8 (a) The force exerted *on* the spring (shown by the vector F) has x-component $F_x = +6.0$ N. The force exerted *by* the spring has x-component $F_x = -6.0$ N. (b) A glider is attached to the same spring and allowed to oscillate.

(a)

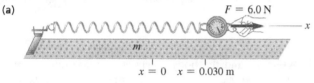

$$x = 0 \quad x = 0.030 \text{ m}$$

(b)

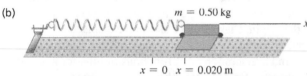

$$x = 0 \quad x = 0.020 \text{ m}$$

Eq. (14.3), and ω, f, and T from Eqs. (14.10), (14.11), and (14.12), respectively.

EXECUTE: (a) When $x = 0.030$ m, the force the spring exerts on the spring balance is $F_x = -6.0$ N. From Eq. (14.3),

$$k = -\frac{F_x}{x} = -\frac{-6.0 \text{ N}}{0.030 \text{ m}} = 200 \text{ N/m} = 200 \text{ kg/s}^2$$

(b) From Eq. (14.10), with $m = 0.50$ kg,

$$\omega = \sqrt{\frac{k}{m}} = \sqrt{\frac{200 \text{ kg/s}^2}{0.50 \text{ kg}}} = 20 \text{ rad/s}$$

$$f = \frac{\omega}{2\pi} = \frac{20 \text{ rad/s}}{2\pi \text{ rad/cycle}} = 3.2 \text{ cycle/s} = 3.2 \text{ Hz}$$

$$T = \frac{1}{f} = \frac{1}{3.2 \text{ cycle/s}} = 0.31 \text{ s}$$

EVALUATE: The amplitude of the oscillation is 0.020 m, the distance that we pulled the glider before releasing it. In SHM the angular frequency, frequency, and period are all independent of the amplitude. Note that a period is usually stated in "seconds" rather than "seconds per cycle."

Displacement, Velocity, and Acceleration in SHM

We still need to find the displacement x as a function of time for a harmonic oscillator. Equation (14.4) for a body in SHM along the x-axis is identical to Eq. (14.8) for the x-coordinate of the reference point in uniform circular motion with constant angular speed $\omega = \sqrt{k/m}$. Hence Eq. (14.5), $x = A\cos\theta$, describes the x-coordinate for both situations. If at $t = 0$ the phasor OQ makes an angle ϕ (the Greek letter phi) with the positive x-axis, then at any later time t this angle is $\theta = \omega t + \phi$. We substitute this into Eq. (14.5) to obtain

MP

PhET: Motion in 2D

Displacement in simple harmonic motion as a function of time ⟶ $x = A \cos (\omega t + \phi)$ ⟵ Amplitude, Time, Phase angle

Angular frequency $= \sqrt{k/m}$

$$(14.13)$$

14.9 Graph of x versus t [see Eq. (14.13)] for simple harmonic motion. The case shown has $\phi = 0$.

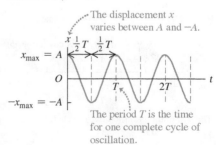

The displacement x varies between A and $-A$.

The period T is the time for one complete cycle of oscillation.

Figure 14.9 shows a graph of Eq. (14.13) for the particular case $\phi = 0$. We could also have written Eq. (14.13) in terms of a sine function rather than a cosine by using the identity $\cos\alpha = \sin(\alpha + \pi/2)$. *In simple harmonic motion the displacement is a periodic, sinusoidal function of time.* There are many other periodic functions, but none so simple as a sine or cosine function.

The value of the cosine function is always between -1 and 1, so in Eq. (14.13), x is always between $-A$ and A. This confirms that A is the amplitude of the motion.

14.10 Variations of simple harmonic motion. All cases shown have $\phi = 0$ [see Eq. (14.13)].

(a) Increasing m; same A and k

Mass m increases from curve 1 to 2 to 3. Increasing m alone increases the period.

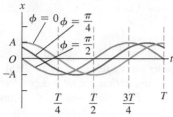

(b) Increasing k; same A and m

Force constant k increases from curve 1 to 2 to 3. Increasing k alone decreases the period.

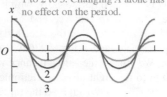

(c) Increasing A; same k and m

Amplitude A increases from curve 1 to 2 to 3. Changing A alone has no effect on the period.

The cosine function in Eq. (14.13) repeats itself whenever time t increases by one period T, or when $\omega t + \phi$ increases by 2π radians. Thus, if we start at time $t = 0$, the time T to complete one cycle is

$$\omega T = \sqrt{\frac{k}{m}} T = 2\pi \qquad \text{or} \qquad T = 2\pi \sqrt{\frac{m}{k}}$$

which is just Eq. (14.12). Changing either m or k changes the period T (**Figs. 14.10a** and 14.10b), but T does not depend on the amplitude A (Fig. 14.10c).

The constant ϕ in Eq. (14.13) is called the **phase angle.** It tells us at what point in the cycle the motion was at $t = 0$ (equivalent to where around the circle the point Q was at $t = 0$). We denote the displacement at $t = 0$ by x_0. Putting $t = 0$ and $x = x_0$ in Eq. (14.13), we get

$$x_0 = A \cos\phi \qquad (14.14)$$

If $\phi = 0$, then $x_0 = A\cos 0 = A$, and the body starts at its maximum positive displacement. If $\phi = \pi$, then $x_0 = A\cos\pi = -A$, and the particle starts at its maximum *negative* displacement. If $\phi = \pi/2$, then $x_0 = A\cos(\pi/2) = 0$, and the particle is initially at the origin. **Figure 14.11** shows the displacement x versus time for three different phase angles.

We find the velocity v_x and acceleration a_x as functions of time for a harmonic oscillator by taking derivatives of Eq. (14.13) with respect to time:

$$v_x = \frac{dx}{dt} = -\omega A \sin(\omega t + \phi) \qquad \text{(velocity in SHM)} \qquad (14.15)$$

$$a_x = \frac{dv_x}{dt} = \frac{d^2x}{dt^2} = -\omega^2 A \cos(\omega t + \phi) \qquad \text{(acceleration in SHM)} \qquad (14.16)$$

The velocity v_x oscillates between $v_{max} = +\omega A$ and $-v_{max} = -\omega A$, and the acceleration a_x oscillates between $a_{max} = +\omega^2 A$ and $-a_{max} = -\omega^2 A$ (**Fig. 14.12**). Comparing Eq. (14.16) with Eq. (14.13) and recalling that $\omega^2 = k/m$ from Eq. (14.9), we see that

$$a_x = -\omega^2 x = -\frac{k}{m}x$$

which is just Eq. (14.4) for simple harmonic motion. This confirms that Eq. (14.13) for x as a function of time is correct.

We actually derived Eq. (14.16) earlier in a geometrical way by taking the x-component of the acceleration vector of the reference point Q. This was done in Fig. 14.6b and Eq. (14.7) (recall that $\theta = \omega t + \phi$). In the same way, we could have derived Eq. (14.15) by taking the x-component of the velocity vector of Q, as shown in Fig. 14.6b. We'll leave the details for you to work out.

Note that the sinusoidal graph of displacement versus time (Fig. 14.12a) is shifted by one-quarter period from the graph of velocity versus time (Fig. 14.12b) and by one-half period from the graph of acceleration versus time (Fig. 14.12c).

14.11 Variations of simple harmonic motion: same m, k, and A but different phase angles ϕ.

These three curves show SHM with the same period T and amplitude A but with different phase angles ϕ.

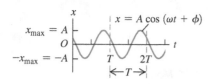

14.12 Graphs of (a) x versus t, (b) v_x versus t, and (c) a_x versus t for a body in SHM. For the motion depicted in these graphs, $\phi = \pi/3$.

(a) Displacement x as a function of time t

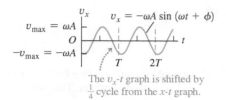

(b) Velocity v_x as a function of time t

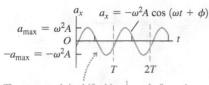

The v_x-t graph is shifted by $\frac{1}{4}$ cycle from the x-t graph.

(c) Acceleration a_x as a function of time t

The a_x-t graph is shifted by $\frac{1}{4}$ cycle from the v_x-t graph and by $\frac{1}{2}$ cycle from the x-t graph.

Figure 14.13 shows why this is so. When the body is passing through the equilibrium position so that $x = 0$, the velocity equals either v_{max} or $-v_{max}$ (depending on which way the body is moving) and the acceleration is zero. When the body is at either its most positive displacement, $x = +A$, or its most negative displacement, $x = -A$, the velocity is zero and the body is instantaneously at rest. At these points, the restoring force $F_x = -kx$ and the acceleration of the body have their maximum magnitudes. At $x = +A$ the acceleration is negative and equal to $-a_{max}$. At $x = -A$ the acceleration is positive: $a_x = +a_{max}$.

Here's how we can determine the amplitude A and phase angle ϕ for an oscillating body if we are given its initial displacement x_0 and initial velocity v_{0x}. The initial velocity v_{0x} is the velocity at time $t = 0$; putting $v_x = v_{0x}$ and $t = 0$ in Eq. (14.15), we find

$$v_{0x} = -\omega A \sin\phi \qquad (14.17)$$

To find ϕ, we divide Eq. (14.17) by Eq. (14.14). This eliminates A and gives an equation that we can solve for ϕ:

$$\frac{v_{0x}}{x_0} = \frac{\omega A \sin\phi}{A \cos\phi} = -\omega \tan\phi$$

$$\phi = \arctan\left(-\frac{v_{0x}}{\omega x_0}\right) \qquad \text{(phase angle in SHM)} \qquad (14.18)$$

It is also easy to find the amplitude A if we are given x_0 and v_{0x}. We'll sketch the derivation, and you can fill in the details. Square Eq. (14.14); then divide Eq. (14.17) by ω, square it, and add to the square of Eq. (14.14). The right side will be $A^2(\sin^2\phi + \cos^2\phi)$, which is equal to A^2. The final result is

$$A = \sqrt{x_0^2 + \frac{v_{0x}^2}{\omega^2}} \qquad \text{(amplitude in SHM)} \qquad (14.19)$$

Note that when the body has both an initial displacement x_0 and a nonzero initial velocity v_{0x}, the amplitude A is *not* equal to the initial displacement. That's reasonable; if you start the body at a positive x_0 but give it a positive velocity v_{0x}, it will go *farther* than x_0 before it turns and comes back, and so $A > x_0$.

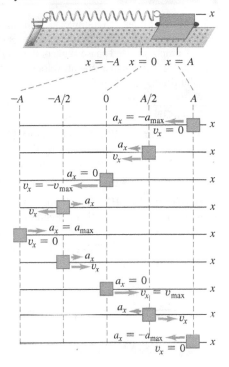

14.13 How x-velocity v_x and x-acceleration a_x vary during one cycle of SHM.

| PROBLEM-SOLVING STRATEGY 14.1 | SIMPLE HARMONIC MOTION I: DESCRIBING MOTION |

IDENTIFY *the relevant concepts:* An oscillating system undergoes simple harmonic motion (SHM) *only* if the restoring force is directly proportional to the displacement.

SET UP *the problem* using the following steps:
1. Identify the known and unknown quantities, and determine which are the target variables.
2. Distinguish between two kinds of quantities. *Properties of the system* include the mass m, the force constant k, and quantities derived from m and k, such as the period T, frequency f, and angular frequency ω. These are independent of *properties of the motion*, which describe how the system behaves when it is set into motion in a particular way; they include the amplitude A, maximum velocity v_{max}, and phase angle ϕ, and values of x, v_x, and a_x at particular times.
3. If necessary, define an x-axis as in Fig. 14.13, with the equilibrium position at $x = 0$.

EXECUTE *the solution* as follows:
1. Use the equations given in Sections 14.1 and 14.2 to solve for the target variables.
2. To find the values of x, v_x, and a_x at particular times, use Eqs. (14.13), (14.15), and (14.16), respectively. If both the initial displacement x_0 and initial velocity v_{0x} are given, determine ϕ and A from Eqs. (14.18) and (14.19). If the body has an initial positive displacement x_0 but zero initial velocity ($v_{0x} = 0$), then the amplitude is $A = x_0$ and the phase angle is $\phi = 0$. If it has an initial positive velocity v_{0x} but no initial displacement ($x_0 = 0$), the amplitude is $A = v_{0x}/\omega$ and the phase angle is $\phi = -\pi/2$. Express all phase angles in *radians*.

EVALUATE *your answer:* Make sure that your results are consistent. For example, suppose you used x_0 and v_{0x} to find general expressions for x and v_x at time t. If you substitute $t = 0$ into these expressions, you should get back the given values of x_0 and v_{0x}.

EXAMPLE 14.3 DESCRIBING SHM

We give the glider of Example 14.2 an initial displacement $x_0 = +0.015$ m and an initial velocity $v_{0x} = +0.40$ m/s. (a) Find the period, amplitude, and phase angle of the resulting motion. (b) Write equations for the displacement, velocity, and acceleration as functions of time.

SOLUTION

IDENTIFY and SET UP: As in Example 14.2, the oscillations are SHM. We use equations from this section and the given values $k = 200$ N/m, $m = 0.50$ kg, x_0, and v_{0x} to calculate the target variables A and ϕ and to obtain expressions for x, v_x, and a_x.

EXECUTE: (a) In SHM the period and angular frequency are *properties of the system* that depend on only k and m, not on the amplitude, and so are the same as in Example 14.2 ($T = 0.31$ s and $\omega = 20$ rad/s). From Eq. (14.19), the amplitude is

$$A = \sqrt{x_0^2 + \frac{v_{0x}^2}{\omega^2}} = \sqrt{(0.015 \text{ m})^2 + \frac{(0.40 \text{ m/s})^2}{(20 \text{ rad/s})^2}} = 0.025 \text{ m}$$

We use Eq. (14.18) to find the phase angle:

$$\phi = \arctan\left(-\frac{v_{0x}}{\omega x_0}\right)$$

$$= \arctan\left(-\frac{0.40 \text{ m/s}}{(20 \text{ rad/s})(0.015 \text{ m})}\right) = -53° = -0.93 \text{ rad}$$

(b) The displacement, velocity, and acceleration at any time are given by Eqs. (14.13), (14.15), and (14.16), respectively. We substitute the values of A, ω, and ϕ into these equations:

$$x = (0.025 \text{ m}) \cos[(20 \text{ rad/s})t - 0.93 \text{ rad}]$$
$$v_x = -(0.50 \text{ m/s}) \sin[(20 \text{ rad/s})t - 0.93 \text{ rad}]$$
$$a_x = -(10 \text{ m/s}^2) \cos[(20 \text{ rad/s})t - 0.93 \text{ rad}]$$

EVALUATE: You can check the expressions for x and v_x by confirming that if you substitute $t = 0$, they yield $x = x_0 = 0.015$ m and $v_x = v_{0x} = 0.40$ m/s.

DATA *SPEAKS*

Oscillations and SHM

When students were given a problem about oscillations and SHM, more than 26% gave an incorrect response. Common errors:

- Forgetting that the period T is the time for one complete cycle of motion, *not* the time to travel between $x = -A$ and $x = +A$.

- Not using Eq. (14.18) to determine the phase angle ϕ.

PhET: Masses & Springs

TEST YOUR UNDERSTANDING OF SECTION 14.2 A glider is attached to a spring as shown in Fig. 14.13. If the glider is moved to $x = 0.10$ m and released from rest at time $t = 0$, it will oscillate with amplitude $A = 0.10$ m and phase angle $\phi = 0$. (a) Suppose instead that at $t = 0$ the glider is at $x = 0.10$ m and is moving to the right in Fig. 14.13. In this situation is the amplitude greater than, less than, or equal to 0.10 m? Is the phase angle greater than, less than, or equal to zero? (b) Suppose instead that at $t = 0$ the glider is at $x = 0.10$ m and is moving to the left in Fig. 14.13. In this situation is the amplitude greater than, less than, or equal to 0.10 m? Is the phase angle greater than, less than, or equal to zero? ▮

14.3 ENERGY IN SIMPLE HARMONIC MOTION

We can learn even more about simple harmonic motion by using energy considerations. The only horizontal force on the body in SHM in Figs. 14.2 and 14.13 is the conservative force exerted by an ideal spring. The vertical forces do no work, so the total mechanical energy of the system is *conserved*. We also assume that the mass of the spring itself is negligible.

The kinetic energy of the body is $K = \frac{1}{2}mv^2$ and the potential energy of the spring is $U = \frac{1}{2}kx^2$, just as in Section 7.2. There are no nonconservative forces that do work, so the total mechanical energy $E = K + U$ is conserved:

$$E = \frac{1}{2}mv_x^2 + \frac{1}{2}kx^2 = \text{constant} \qquad (14.20)$$

(Since the motion is one-dimensional, $v^2 = v_x^2$.)

The total mechanical energy E is also directly related to the amplitude A of the motion. When the body reaches the point $x = A$, its maximum displacement from equilibrium, it momentarily stops as it turns back toward the equilibrium position. That is, when $x = A$ (or $-A$), $v_x = 0$. At this point the energy is entirely potential, and $E = \frac{1}{2}kA^2$. Because E is constant, it is equal to $\frac{1}{2}kA^2$ at any other point. Combining this expression with Eq. (14.20), we get

Total mechanical energy in simple harmonic motion

Mass · · · Force constant of restoring force

$$E = \frac{1}{2}mv_x^2 + \frac{1}{2}kx^2 = \frac{1}{2}kA^2 = \text{constant} \qquad (14.21)$$

Velocity   Displacement   Amplitude

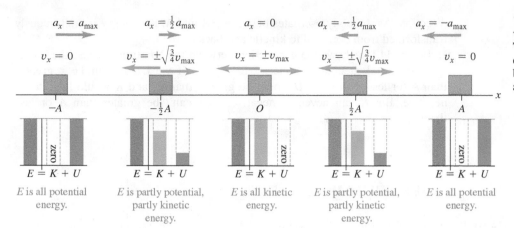

14.14 Graphs of E, K, and U versus displacement in SHM. The velocity of the body is *not* constant, so these images of the body at equally spaced positions are *not* equally spaced in time.

We can verify this equation by substituting x and v_x from Eqs. (14.13) and (14.15) and using $\omega^2 = k/m$ from Eq. (14.9):

$$E = \tfrac{1}{2}mv_x^2 + \tfrac{1}{2}kx^2 = \tfrac{1}{2}m[-\omega A \sin(\omega t + \phi)]^2 + \tfrac{1}{2}k[A\cos(\omega t + \phi)]^2$$

$$-\tfrac{1}{2}kA^2 \sin^2(\omega t + \phi) + \tfrac{1}{2}kA^2 \cos^2(\omega t + \phi) = \tfrac{1}{2}kA^2$$

(Recall that $\sin^2\alpha + \cos^2\alpha = 1$.) Hence our expressions for displacement and velocity in SHM are consistent with energy conservation, as they must be.

We can use Eq. (14.21) to solve for the velocity v_x of the body at a given displacement x:

$$v_x = \pm\sqrt{\frac{k}{m}}\sqrt{A^2 - x^2} \qquad (14.22)$$

The $\pm$ sign means that at a given value of x the body can be moving in either direction. For example, when $x = \pm A/2$,

$$v_x = \pm\sqrt{\frac{k}{m}}\sqrt{A^2 - \left(\mp\frac{A}{2}\right)^2} = \mp\sqrt{\frac{3}{4}}\sqrt{\frac{k}{m}}A$$

Equation (14.22) also shows that the *maximum* speed v_{max} occurs at $x = 0$. Using Eq. (14.10), $\omega = \sqrt{k/m}$, we find that

$$v_{max} = \sqrt{\frac{k}{m}}A = \omega A \qquad (14.23)$$

This agrees with Eq. (14.15): v_x oscillates between $-\omega A$ and $+\omega A$.

Interpreting *E*, *K*, and *U* in SHM

Figure 14.14 shows the energy quantities E, K, and U at $x = 0$, $x = \pm A/2$, and $x = \pm A$. **Figure 14.15** is a graphical display of Eq. (14.21); energy (kinetic, potential, and total) is plotted vertically and the coordinate x is plotted horizontally. The parabolic curve in Fig. 14.15a represents the potential energy $U = \tfrac{1}{2}kx^2$. The horizontal line represents the total mechanical energy E, which is constant and does not vary with x. At any value of x between $-A$ and A, the vertical distance from the x-axis to the parabola is U; since $E = K + U$, the remaining vertical distance up to the horizontal line is K. Figure 14.15b shows both K and U as functions of x. The horizontal line for E intersects the potential-energy curve at $x = -A$ and $x = A$, so at these points the energy is entirely potential, the kinetic energy is zero, and the body comes momentarily to rest before reversing

14.15 Kinetic energy K, potential energy U, and total mechanical energy E as functions of displacement for SHM. At each value of x the sum of the values of K and U equals the constant value of E. Can you show that the energy is half kinetic and half potential at $x = \pm\sqrt{\tfrac{1}{2}}A$?

(a) The potential energy U and total mechanical energy E for a body in SHM as a function of displacement x

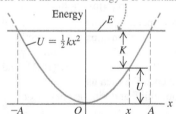

The total mechanical energy E is constant.

(b) The same graph as in **(a)**, showing kinetic energy K as well

At $x = \pm A$ the energy is all potential; $K = 0$.

At $x = 0$ the energy is all kinetic; $U = 0$.

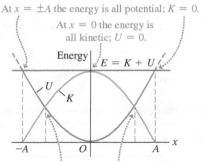

At these points the energy is half kinetic and half potential.

direction. As the body oscillates between $-A$ and A, the energy is continuously transformed from potential to kinetic and back again.

Figure 14.15a shows the connection between the amplitude A and the corresponding total mechanical energy $E = \frac{1}{2}kA^2$. If we tried to make x greater than A (or less than $-A$), U would be greater than E, and K would have to be negative. But K can never be negative, so x can't be greater than A or less than $-A$.

PROBLEM-SOLVING STRATEGY 14.2 | **SIMPLE HARMONIC MOTION II: ENERGY**

The SHM energy equation, Eq. (14.21), is a useful relationship among velocity, displacement, and total mechanical energy. If a problem requires you to relate displacement, velocity, and acceleration without reference to time, consider using Eq. (14.4) (from Newton's second law) or Eq. (14.21) (from energy conservation).

Because Eq. (14.21) involves x^2 and v_x^2, you must infer the *signs* of x and v_x from the situation. For instance, if the body is moving from the equilibrium position toward the point of greatest positive displacement, then x is positive and v_x is positive.

EXAMPLE 14.4 | VELOCITY, ACCELERATION, AND ENERGY IN SHM

(a) Find the maximum and minimum velocities attained by the oscillating glider of Example 14.2. (b) Find the maximum and minimum accelerations. (c) Find the velocity v_x and acceleration a_x when the glider is halfway from its initial position to the equilibrium position $x = 0$. (d) Find the total energy, potential energy, and kinetic energy at this position.

SOLUTION

IDENTIFY and SET UP: The problem concerns properties of the motion at specified *positions*, not at specified *times*, so we can use the energy relationships of this section. Figure 14.13 shows our choice of x-axis. The maximum displacement from equilibrium is $A = 0.020$ m. We use Eqs. (14.22) and (14.4) to find v_x and a_x for a given x. We then use Eq. (14.21) for given x and v_x to find the total, potential, and kinetic energies E, U, and K.

EXECUTE: (a) From Eq. (14.22), the velocity v_x at any displacement x is

$$v_x = \pm \sqrt{\frac{k}{m}} \sqrt{A^2 - x^2}$$

The glider's maximum *speed* occurs when it is moving through $x = 0$:

$$v_{max} = \sqrt{\frac{k}{m}}\, A = \sqrt{\frac{200 \text{ N/m}}{0.50 \text{ kg}}}(0.020 \text{ m}) = 0.40 \text{ m/s}$$

Its maximum and minimum (most negative) *velocities* are $+0.40$ m/s and -0.40 m/s, which occur when it is moving through $x = 0$ to the right and left, respectively.

(b) From Eq. (14.4), $a_x = -(k/m)x$. The glider's maximum (most positive) acceleration occurs at the most negative value of x, $x = -A$:

$$a_{max} = -\frac{k}{m}(-A) = -\frac{200 \text{ N/m}}{0.50 \text{ kg}}(-0.020 \text{ m}) = 8.0 \text{ m/s}^2$$

The minimum (most negative) acceleration is $a_{min} = -8.0$ m/s^2, which occurs at $x = +A = +0.020$ m.

(c) The point halfway from $x = x_0 = A$ to $x = 0$ is $x = A/2 = 0.010$ m. From Eq. (14.22), at this point

$$v_x = -\sqrt{\frac{200 \text{ N/m}}{0.50 \text{ kg}}}\sqrt{(0.020 \text{ m})^2 - (0.010 \text{ m})^2}$$

$$= -0.35 \text{ m/s}$$

We choose the negative square root because the glider is moving from $x = A$ toward $x = 0$. From Eq. (14.4),

$$a_x = -\frac{200 \text{ N/m}}{0.50 \text{ kg}}(0.010 \text{ m}) = -4.0 \text{ m/s}^2$$

Figure 14.14 shows the conditions at $x = 0$, $\pm A/2$, and $\pm A$.

(d) The energies are

$$E = \tfrac{1}{2}kA^2 = \tfrac{1}{2}(200 \text{ N/m})(0.020 \text{ m})^2 = 0.040 \text{ J}$$

$$U = \tfrac{1}{2}kx^2 = \tfrac{1}{2}(200 \text{ N/m})(0.010 \text{ m})^2 = 0.010 \text{ J}$$

$$K = \tfrac{1}{2}mv_x^2 = \tfrac{1}{2}(0.50 \text{ kg})(-0.35 \text{ m/s})^2 = 0.030 \text{ J}$$

EVALUATE: At $x = A/2$, the total energy is one-fourth potential energy and three-fourths kinetic energy. You can confirm this by inspecting Fig. 14.15b.

EXAMPLE 14.5 **ENERGY AND MOMENTUM IN SHM**

A block of mass M attached to a horizontal spring with force constant k is moving in SHM with amplitude A_1. As the block passes through its equilibrium position, a lump of putty of mass m is dropped from a small height and sticks to it. (a) Find the new amplitude and period of the motion. (b) Repeat part (a) if the putty is dropped onto the block when it is at one end of its path.

SOLUTION

IDENTIFY and SET UP: The problem involves the motion at a given position, not a given time, so we can use energy methods. **Figure 14.16** shows our sketches. Before the putty falls, the mechanical energy of the block–spring system is constant. In part (a), the putty–block collision is completely inelastic: The horizontal component of momentum is conserved, kinetic energy decreases, and the amount of mass that's oscillating increases. After the collision, the mechanical energy remains constant at its new value. In part (b) the oscillating mass also increases, but the block isn't moving when the putty is added; there is effectively no collision at all, and no mechanical energy is lost. We find the amplitude A_2 after each collision from the final energy of the system by using Eq. (14.21) and conservation of momentum. The period T_2 after the collision is the same in both parts (a) and (b) because the final mass is the same; we find it by using Eq. (14.12).

EXECUTE: (a) Before the collision the total mechanical energy of the block and spring is $E_1 = \frac{1}{2}kA_1^2$. The block is at $x = 0$, so $U = 0$ and the energy is purely kinetic (Fig. 14.16a). If we let v_1 be the speed of the block at this point, then $E_1 = \frac{1}{2}kA_1^2 = \frac{1}{2}Mv_1^2$ and

$$v_1 = \sqrt{\frac{k}{M}}A_1$$

During the collision the x-component of momentum of the block–putty system is conserved. (Why?) Just before the collision this component is the sum of Mv_1 (for the block) and zero (for the putty). Just after the collision the block and putty move together with speed v_2, so their combined x-component of momentum is $(M + m)v_2$. From conservation of momentum,

$$Mv_1 + 0 = (M + m)v_2 \quad \text{so} \quad v_2 = \frac{M}{M + m}v_1$$

The collision lasts a very short time, so the block and putty are still at the equilibrium position just after the collision. The energy is still purely kinetic but is *less* than before the collision:

$$E_2 = \frac{1}{2}(M + m)v_2^2 = \frac{1}{2}\frac{M^2}{M + m}v_1^2$$

$$= \frac{M}{M + m}\left(\frac{1}{2}Mv_1^2\right) = \left(\frac{M}{M + m}\right)E_1$$

14.16 Our sketches for this problem.

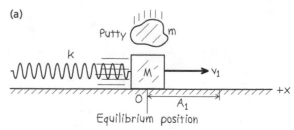

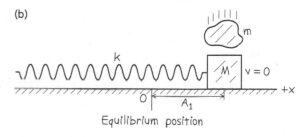

Since $E_2 = \frac{1}{2}kA_2^2$, where A_2 is the amplitude after the collision,

$$\frac{1}{2}kA_2^2 = \left(\frac{M}{M + m}\right)\frac{1}{2}kA_1^2$$

$$A_2 = A_1\sqrt{\frac{M}{M + m}}$$

From Eq. (14.12), the period of oscillation after the collision is

$$T_2 = 2\pi\sqrt{\frac{M + m}{k}}$$

(b) When the putty falls, the block is instantaneously at rest (Fig. 14.16b). The x-component of momentum is zero both before and after the collision. The block and putty have zero kinetic energy just before and just after the collision. The energy is all potential energy stored in the spring, so adding the putty has *no effect* on the mechanical energy. That is, $E_2 = E_1 = \frac{1}{2}kA_1^2$, and the amplitude is unchanged: $A_2 = A_1$. The period is again $T_2 = 2\pi\sqrt{(M + m)/k}$.

EVALUATE: Energy is lost in part (a) because the putty slides against the moving block during the collision, and energy is dissipated by kinetic friction. No energy is lost in part (b) because there is no sliding during the collision.

TEST YOUR UNDERSTANDING OF SECTION 14.3 (a) To double the total energy for a mass-spring system oscillating in SHM, by what factor must the amplitude increase? (i) 4; (ii) 2; (iii) $\sqrt{2} = 1.414$; (iv) $\sqrt[4]{2} = 1.189$. (b) By what factor will the frequency change due to this amplitude increase? (i) 4; (ii) 2; (iii) $\sqrt{2} = 1.414$; (iv) $\sqrt[4]{2} = 1.189$; (v) it does not change. ∎

14.17 A body attached to a hanging spring.

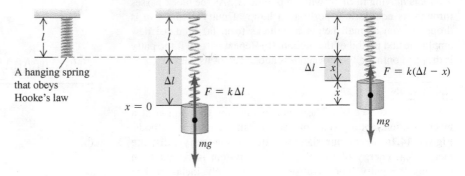

(a)

(b) A body is suspended from the spring. It is in equilibrium when the upward force exerted by the stretched spring equals the body's weight.

(c) If the body is displaced from equilibrium, the net force on the body is proportional to its displacement. The oscillations are SHM.

A hanging spring that obeys Hooke's law

$F = k \Delta l$

$x = 0$

$\Delta l - x$ $F = k(\Delta l - x)$

mg

mg

14.4 APPLICATIONS OF SIMPLE HARMONIC MOTION

So far, we've looked at a grand total of *one* situation in which simple harmonic motion (SHM) occurs: a body attached to an ideal horizontal spring. But SHM can occur in any system in which there is a restoring force that is directly proportional to the displacement from equilibrium, as given by Eq. (14.3), $F_x = -kx$. The restoring force originates in different ways in different situations, so we must find the force constant k for each case by examining the net force on the system. Once this is done, it's straightforward to find the angular frequency ω, frequency f, and period T; we just substitute the value of k into Eqs. (14.10), (14.11), and (14.12), respectively. Let's use these ideas to examine several examples of simple harmonic motion.

Vertical SHM

Suppose we hang a spring with force constant k (**Fig. 14.17a**) and suspend from it a body with mass m. Oscillations will now be vertical; will they still be SHM? In Fig. 14.17b the body hangs at rest, in equilibrium. In this position the spring is stretched an amount Δl just great enough that the spring's upward vertical force $k \Delta l$ on the body balances its weight mg:

$$k \Delta l = mg$$

Take $x = 0$ to be this equilibrium position and take the positive x-direction to be upward. When the body is a distance x *above* its equilibrium position (Fig. 14.17c), the extension of the spring is $\Delta l - x$. The upward force it exerts on the body is then $k(\Delta l - x)$, and the net x-component of force on the body is

$$F_{net} = k(\Delta l - x) + (-mg) = -kx$$

14.18 If the weight mg compresses the spring a distance Δl, the force constant is $k = mg/\Delta l$ and the angular frequency for vertical SHM is $\omega = \sqrt{k/m}$—the same as if the body were suspended from the spring (see Fig. 14.17).

A body is placed atop the spring. It is in equilibrium when the upward force exerted by the compressed spring equals the body's weight.

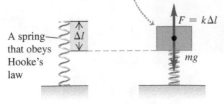

A spring that obeys Hooke's law

$F = k \Delta l$

mg

that is, a net downward force of magnitude kx. Similarly, when the body is *below* the equilibrium position, there is a net upward force with magnitude kx. In either case there is a restoring force with magnitude kx. If the body is set in vertical motion, it oscillates in SHM with the same angular frequency as though it were horizontal, $\omega = \sqrt{k/m}$. So vertical SHM doesn't differ in any essential way from horizontal SHM. The only real change is that the equilibrium position $x = 0$ no longer corresponds to the point at which the spring is unstretched. The same ideas hold if a body with weight mg is placed atop a compressible spring (**Fig. 14.18**) and compresses it a distance Δl.

EXAMPLE 14.6   VERTICAL SHM IN AN OLD CAR

The shock absorbers in an old car with mass 1000 kg are completely worn out. When a 980-N person climbs slowly into the car at its center of gravity, the car sinks 2.8 cm. The car (with the person aboard) hits a bump, and the car starts oscillating up and down in SHM. Model the car and person as a single body on a single spring, and find the period and frequency of the oscillation.

SOLUTION

IDENTIFY and SET UP: The situation is like that shown in Fig. 14.18. The compression of the spring when the person's weight is added tells us the force constant, which we can use to find the period and frequency (the target variables).

EXECUTE: When the force increases by 980 N, the spring compresses an additional 0.028 m, and the x coordinate of the car changes by −0.028 m. Hence the effective force constant (including the effect of the entire suspension) is

$$k = -\frac{F_x}{x} = -\frac{980\ \text{N}}{-0.028\ \text{m}} = 3.5 \times 10^4\ \text{kg/s}^2$$

The person's mass is $w/g = (980\ \text{N})/(9.8\ \text{m/s}^2) = 100$ kg. The *total* oscillating mass is $m = 1000\ \text{kg} + 100\ \text{kg} = 1100$ kg. The period T is

$$T = 2\pi\sqrt{\frac{m}{k}} = 2\pi\sqrt{\frac{1100\ \text{kg}}{3.5 \times 10^4\ \text{kg/s}^2}} = 1.11\ \text{s}$$

The frequency is $f = 1/T = 1/(1.11\ \text{s}) = 0.90$ Hz.

EVALUATE: A persistent oscillation with a period of about 1 second makes for a very unpleasant ride. The purpose of shock absorbers is to make such oscillations die out (see Section 14.7).

Angular SHM

A mechanical watch keeps time based on the oscillations of a balance wheel (**Fig. 14.19**). The wheel has a moment of inertia I about its axis. A coil spring exerts a restoring torque τ_z that is proportional to the angular displacement θ from the equilibrium position. We write $\tau_z = -\kappa\theta$, where κ (the Greek letter kappa) is a constant called the *torsion constant*. Using the rotational analog of Newton's second law for a rigid body, $\sum \tau_z = I\alpha_z = I\, d^2\theta/dt^2$, Eq. (10.7), we find

$$-\kappa\theta = I\alpha \quad \text{or} \quad \frac{d^2\theta}{dt^2} = -\frac{\kappa}{I}\theta$$

This equation is exactly the same as Eq. (14.4) for simple harmonic motion, with x replaced by θ and k/m replaced by κ/I. So we are dealing with a form of *angular* simple harmonic motion. The angular frequency ω and frequency f are given by Eqs. (14.10) and (14.11), respectively, with the same replacement:

14.19 The balance wheel of a mechanical watch. The spring exerts a restoring torque that is proportional to the angular displacement θ, so the motion is angular SHM.

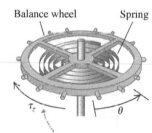

Balance wheel   Spring

τ_z θ

The spring torque τ_z opposes the angular displacement θ.

$$\underset{\substack{\text{Angular simple}\\\text{harmonic motion}}}{} \quad \overset{\text{Angular frequency}}{\omega = \sqrt{\frac{\kappa}{I}}} \quad \text{and} \quad \overset{\text{Frequency}}{f = \frac{1}{2\pi}\sqrt{\frac{\kappa}{I}}} \qquad (14.24)$$

Torsion constant divided by moment of inertia

The angular displacement θ as a function of time is given by

$$\theta = \Theta\cos(\omega t + \phi)$$

where Θ (the capital Greek letter theta) plays the role of an angular amplitude.

It's a good thing that the motion of a balance wheel *is* simple harmonic. If it weren't, the frequency might depend on the amplitude, and the watch would run too fast or too slow as the spring ran down.

Vibrations of Molecules

The following discussion of the vibrations of molecules uses the binomial theorem. If you aren't familiar with this theorem, you should read about it in the appropriate section of a math textbook.

14.20 (a) Two atoms with centers separated by r. (b) Potential energy U and (c) force F_r in the van der Waals interaction.

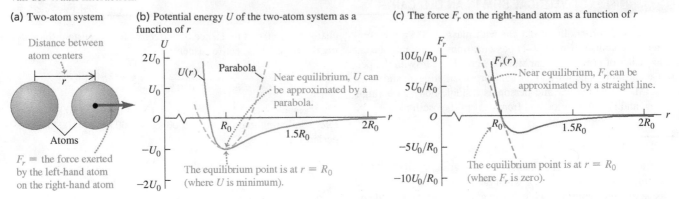

(a) Two-atom system

Distance between atom centers

r

Atoms

F_r = the force exerted by the left-hand atom on the right-hand atom

(b) Potential energy U of the two-atom system as a function of r

Parabola

$U(r)$

Near equilibrium, U can be approximated by a parabola.

The equilibrium point is at $r = R_0$ (where U is minimum).

(c) The force F_r on the right-hand atom as a function of r

$F_r(r)$

Near equilibrium, F_r can be approximated by a straight line.

The equilibrium point is at $r = R_0$ (where F_r is zero).

When two atoms are separated by a few atomic diameters, they can exert attractive forces on each other. But if the atoms are so close that their electron shells overlap, the atoms repel each other. Between these limits, there can be an equilibrium separation distance at which two atoms form a *molecule*. If these atoms are displaced slightly from equilibrium, they will oscillate.

Let's consider one type of interaction between atoms called the *van der Waals interaction*. Our immediate task here is to study oscillations, so we won't go into the details of how this interaction arises. Let the center of one atom be at the origin and let the center of the other atom be a distance r away (**Fig. 14.20a**); the equilibrium distance between centers is $r = R_0$. Experiment shows that the van der Waals interaction can be described by the potential-energy function

$$U = U_0\left[\left(\frac{R_0}{r}\right)^{12} - 2\left(\frac{R_0}{r}\right)^{6}\right] \tag{14.25}$$

where U_0 is a positive constant with units of joules. When the two atoms are very far apart, $U = 0$; when they are separated by the equilibrium distance $r = R_0$, $U = -U_0$. From Section 7.4, the force on the second atom is the negative derivative of Eq. (14.25):

$$F_r = -\frac{dU}{dr} = U_0\left[\frac{12R_0^{12}}{r^{13}} - 2\frac{6R_0^6}{r^7}\right] = 12\frac{U_0}{R_0}\left[\left(\frac{R_0}{r}\right)^{13} - \left(\frac{R_0}{r}\right)^{7}\right] \tag{14.26}$$

Figures 14.20b and 14.20c plot the potential energy and force, respectively. The force is positive for $r < R_0$ and negative for $r > R_0$, so it is a *restoring* force.

Let's examine the restoring force F_r in Eq. (14.26). We let x represent the displacement from equilibrium:

$$x = r - R_0 \quad \text{so} \quad r = R_0 + x$$

In terms of x, the force F_r in Eq. (14.26) becomes

$$F_r = 12\frac{U_0}{R_0}\left[\left(\frac{R_0}{R_0 + x}\right)^{13} - \left(\frac{R_0}{R_0 + x}\right)^{7}\right]$$

$$= 12\frac{U_0}{R_0}\left[\frac{1}{(1 + x/R_0)^{13}} - \frac{1}{(1 + x/R_0)^{7}}\right] \tag{14.27}$$

This looks nothing like Hooke's law, $F_x = -kx$, so we might be tempted to conclude that molecular oscillations cannot be SHM. But let us restrict ourselves to *small-amplitude* oscillations so that the absolute value of the displacement x is small in comparison to R_0 and the absolute value of the ratio x/R_0 is much less than 1. We can then simplify Eq. (14.27) by using the *binomial theorem:*

$$(1 + u)^n = 1 + nu + \frac{n(n-1)}{2!}u^2 + \frac{n(n-1)(n-2)}{3!}u^3 + \cdots \quad (14.28)$$

If $|u|$ is much less than 1, each successive term in Eq. (14.28) is much smaller than the one it follows, and we can safely approximate $(1 + u)^n$ by just the first two terms. In Eq. (14.27), u is replaced by x/R_0 and n equals -13 or -7, so

$$\frac{1}{(1 + x/R_0)^{13}} = (1 + x/R_0)^{-13} \approx 1 + (-13)\frac{x}{R_0}$$

$$\frac{1}{(1 + x/R_0)^{7}} = (1 + x/R_0)^{-7} \approx 1 + (-7)\frac{x}{R_0}$$

$$F_r \approx 12\frac{U_0}{R_0}\left[\left(1 + (-13)\frac{x}{R_0}\right) - \left(1 + (-7)\frac{x}{R_0}\right)\right] = -\left(\frac{72U_0}{R_0^2}\right)x \quad (14.29)$$

This is just Hooke's law, with force constant $k = 72U_0/R_0^2$. (Note that k has the correct units, J/m^2 or N/m.) So oscillations of molecules bound by the van der Waals interaction can be simple harmonic motion, provided that the amplitude is small in comparison to R_0 so that the approximation $|x/R_0| \ll 1$ used in the derivation of Eq. (14.29) is valid.

You can also use the binomial theorem to show that the potential energy U in Eq. (14.25) can be written as $U \approx \frac{1}{2}kx^2 + C$, where $C = -U_0$ and k is again equal to $72U_0/R_0^2$. Adding a constant to the potential-energy function has no effect on the physics, so the system of two atoms is fundamentally no different from a mass attached to a horizontal spring for which $U = \frac{1}{2}kx^2$.

EXAMPLE 14.7   MOLECULAR VIBRATION

Two argon atoms form the molecule Ar$_2$ as a result of a van der Waals interaction with $U_0 = 1.68 \times 10^{-21}$ J and $R_0 = 3.82 \times 10^{-10}$ m. Find the frequency of small oscillations of one Ar atom about its equilibrium position.

SOLUTION

IDENTIFY and SET UP: This is the situation shown in Fig. 14.20. Because the oscillations are small, we can use Eq. (14.29) to find the force constant k and Eq. (14.11) to find the frequency f of SHM.

EXECUTE: From Eq. (14.29),

$$k = \frac{72U_0}{R_0^2} = \frac{72(1.68 \times 10^{-21}\ \text{J})}{(3.82 \times 10^{-10}\ \text{m})^2} = 0.829\ \text{J/m}^2 = 0.829\ \text{N/m}$$

(This force constant is comparable to that of a loose toy spring like a Slinky™.) From Appendix D, the average atomic mass of argon is $(39.948\ \text{u})(1.66 \times 10^{-27}\ \text{kg/1 u}) = 6.63 \times 10^{-26}$ kg.

From Eq. (14.11), if one atom is fixed and the other oscillates,

$$f = \frac{1}{2\pi}\sqrt{\frac{k}{m}} = \frac{1}{2\pi}\sqrt{\frac{0.829\ \text{N/m}}{6.63 \times 10^{-26}\ \text{kg}}} = 5.63 \times 10^{11}\ \text{Hz}$$

EVALUATE: Our answer for f isn't quite right. If no net external force acts on the molecule, its center of mass (halfway between the atoms) doesn't accelerate, so *both* atoms must oscillate with the same amplitude in opposite directions. It turns out that we can account for this by replacing m with $m/2$ in our expression for f. This makes f larger by a factor of $\sqrt{2}$, so the correct frequency is $f = \sqrt{2}(5.63 \times 10^{11}\ \text{Hz}) = 7.96 \times 10^{11}$ Hz. What's more, on the atomic scale we must use *quantum mechanics* rather than Newtonian mechanics to describe motion; happily, quantum mechanics also yields $f = 7.96 \times 10^{11}$ Hz.

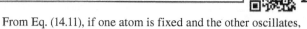

TEST YOUR UNDERSTANDING OF SECTION 14.4   A block attached to a hanging ideal spring oscillates up and down with a period of 10 s on earth. If you take the block and spring to Mars, where the acceleration due to gravity is only about 40% as large as on earth, what will be the new period of oscillation? (i) 10 s; (ii) more than 10 s; (iii) less than 10 s. ▮

14.21 The dynamics of a simple pendulum.

(a) A real pendulum

(b) An idealized simple pendulum

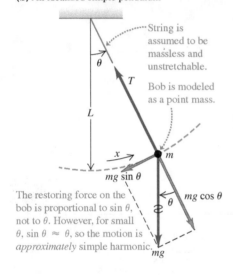

String is assumed to be massless and unstretchable.

Bob is modeled as a point mass.

The restoring force on the bob is proportional to $\sin\theta$, not to θ. However, for small θ, $\sin\theta \approx \theta$, so the motion is *approximately* simple harmonic.

14.22 For small angular displacements θ, the restoring force $F_\theta = -mg\sin\theta$ on a simple pendulum is approximately equal to $-mg\theta$; that is, it is approximately proportional to the displacement θ. Hence for small angles the oscillations are simple harmonic.

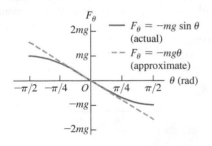

14.5 THE SIMPLE PENDULUM

A **simple pendulum** is an idealized model consisting of a point mass suspended by a massless, unstretchable string. When the point mass is pulled to one side of its straight-down equilibrium position and released, it oscillates about the equilibrium position. Familiar situations such as a wrecking ball on a crane's cable or a person on a swing (**Fig. 14.21a**) can be modeled as simple pendulums.

The path of the point mass (sometimes called a *pendulum bob*) is not a straight line but the arc of a circle with radius L equal to the length of the string (Fig. 14.21b). We use as our coordinate the distance x measured along the arc. If the motion is simple harmonic, the restoring force must be directly proportional to x or (because $x = L\theta$) to θ. Is it?

Figure 14.21b shows the radial and tangential components of the forces on the mass. The restoring force F_θ is the tangential component of the net force:

$$F_\theta = -mg\sin\theta \tag{14.30}$$

Gravity provides the restoring force F_θ; the tension T merely acts to make the point mass move in an arc. Since F_θ is proportional to $\sin\theta$, not to θ, the motion is *not* simple harmonic. However, if angle θ is *small*, $\sin\theta$ is very nearly equal to θ in radians (**Fig. 14.22**). (When $\theta = 0.1$ rad, about 6°, $\sin\theta = 0.998$. That's only 0.2% different.) With this approximation, Eq. (14.30) becomes

$$F_\theta = -mg\theta = -mg\frac{x}{L} = -\frac{mg}{L}x \tag{14.31}$$

The restoring force is then proportional to the coordinate for small displacements, and the force constant is $k = mg/L$. From Eq. (14.10) the angular frequency ω of a simple pendulum with small amplitude is

Angular frequency of simple pendulum, small amplitude
$$\omega = \sqrt{\frac{k}{m}} = \sqrt{\frac{mg/L}{m}} = \sqrt{\frac{g}{L}} \tag{14.32}$$
Acceleration due to gravity — Pendulum length — Pendulum mass (cancels)

The corresponding frequency and period relationships are

Frequency of simple pendulum, small amplitude
Angular frequency — Acceleration due to gravity
$$f = \frac{\omega}{2\pi} = \frac{1}{2\pi}\sqrt{\frac{g}{L}} \tag{14.33}$$
Pendulum length

Period of simple pendulum, small amplitude
Pendulum length
$$T = \frac{2\pi}{\omega} = \frac{1}{f} = 2\pi\sqrt{\frac{L}{g}} \tag{14.34}$$
Angular frequency — Frequency — Acceleration due to gravity

These expressions don't involve the *mass* of the particle. That's because the gravitational restoring force is proportional to m, so the mass appears on *both* sides of $\sum\vec{F} = m\vec{a}$ and cancels out. (The same physics explains why bodies of different masses fall with the same acceleration in a vacuum.) For small oscillations, the period of a pendulum for a given value of g is determined entirely by its length.

Equations (14.32) through (14.34) tell us that a long pendulum (large L) has a longer period than a shorter one. Increasing g increases the restoring force, causing the frequency to increase and the period to decrease.

The motion of a pendulum is only *approximately* simple harmonic. When the maximum angular displacement Θ (amplitude) is not small, the departures from simple harmonic motion can be substantial. In general, the period T is given by

$$T = 2\pi\sqrt{\frac{L}{g}}\left(1 + \frac{1^2}{2^2}\sin^2\frac{\Theta}{2} + \frac{1^2\cdot 3^2}{2^2\cdot 4^2}\sin^4\frac{\Theta}{2} + \cdots\right) \tag{14.35}$$

We can compute T to any desired degree of precision by taking enough terms in the series. You can confirm that when $\Theta = 15°$, the true period is longer than that given by the approximate Eq. (14.34) by less than 0.5%.

A pendulum is a useful timekeeper because the period is *very nearly* independent of amplitude, provided that the amplitude is small. Thus, as a pendulum clock runs down and the amplitude of the swings decreases a little, the clock still keeps very nearly correct time.

EXAMPLE 14.8 A SIMPLE PENDULUM

Find the period and frequency of a simple pendulum 1.000 m long at a location where $g = 9.800$ m/s^2.

SOLUTION

IDENTIFY and SET UP: This is a simple pendulum, so we can use Eq. (14.34) to determine the pendulum's period T from its length and Eq. (14.1) to find the frequency f from T.

EXECUTE: From Eqs. (14.34) and (14.1),

$$T = 2\pi \sqrt{\frac{L}{g}} = 2\pi \sqrt{\frac{1.000 \text{ m}}{9.800 \text{ m/s}^2}} = 2.007 \text{ s}$$

and

$$f = \frac{1}{T} = \frac{1}{2.007 \text{ s}} = 0.4983 \text{ Hz}$$

EVALUATE: The period is almost exactly 2 s. When the metric system was established, the second was *defined* as half the period of a 1-m simple pendulum. This was a poor standard, however, because the value of g varies from place to place. We discussed more modern time standards in Section 1.3.

TEST YOUR UNDERSTANDING OF SECTION 14.5   When a body oscillating on a horizontal spring passes through its equilibrium position, its acceleration is zero (see Fig. 14.2b). When the bob of an oscillating simple pendulum passes from left to right through its equilibrium position, is its acceleration (i) zero; (ii) to the left; (iii) to the right; (iv) upward; or (v) downward?

14.6 THE PHYSICAL PENDULUM

A **physical pendulum** is any *real* pendulum that uses an extended body, as contrasted to the idealized *simple* pendulum with all of its mass concentrated at a point. **Figure 14.23** shows a body of irregular shape pivoted so that it can turn without friction about an axis through point O. In equilibrium the center of gravity (cg) is directly below the pivot; in the position shown, the body is displaced from equilibrium by an angle θ, which we use as a coordinate for the system. The distance from O to the center of gravity is d, the moment of inertia of the body about the axis of rotation through O is I, and the total mass is m. When the body is displaced as shown, the weight mg causes a restoring torque

$$\tau_z = -(mg)(d\sin\theta) \tag{14.36}$$

The negative sign shows that the restoring torque is clockwise when the displacement is counterclockwise, and vice versa.

When the body is released, it oscillates about its equilibrium position. The motion is not simple harmonic because the torque τ_z is proportional to $\sin\theta$ rather than to θ itself. However, if θ is small, we can approximate $\sin\theta$ by θ in radians, just as we did in analyzing the simple pendulum. Then the motion is *approximately* simple harmonic. With this approximation,

$$\tau_z = -(mgd)\theta$$

From Section 10.2, the equation of motion is $\sum\tau_z = I\alpha_z$, so

$$-(mgd)\theta = I\alpha_z = I\frac{d^2\theta}{dt^2}$$

$$\frac{d^2\theta}{dt^2} = -\frac{mgd}{I}\theta \tag{14.37}$$

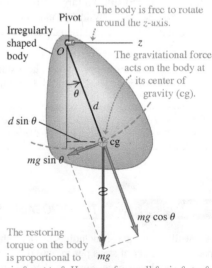

14.23 Dynamics of a physical pendulum.

The body is free to rotate around the z-axis.

Irregularly shaped body

The gravitational force acts on the body at its center of gravity (cg).

$d\sin\theta$

$mg\sin\theta$

$mg\cos\theta$

mg

The restoring torque on the body is proportional to $\sin\theta$, not to θ. However, for small θ, $\sin\theta \approx \theta$, so the motion is *approximately* simple harmonic.

Comparing this with Eq. (14.4), we see that the role of (k/m) for the spring-mass system is played here by the quantity (mgd/I). Thus the angular frequency is

Angular frequency of physical pendulum, small amplitude
Mass ⋯
Acceleration due to gravity

$$\omega = \sqrt{\frac{mgd}{I}}$$

Distance from rotation axis to center of gravity

Moment of inertia

(14.38)

The frequency f is $1/2\pi$ times this, and the period T is $1/f$:

Period of physical pendulum, small amplitude

Moment of inertia

$$T = 2\pi\sqrt{\frac{I}{mgd}}$$

Distance from rotation axis to center of gravity

Mass ⋯
Acceleration due to gravity

(14.39)

Equation (14.39) is the basis of a common method for experimentally determining the moment of inertia of a body with a complicated shape. First locate the center of gravity by balancing the body. Then suspend the body so that it is free to oscillate about an axis, and measure the period T of small-amplitude oscillations. Finally, use Eq. (14.39) to calculate the moment of inertia I of the body about this axis from T, the body's mass m, and the distance d from the axis to the center of gravity (see Exercise 14.55). Biomechanics researchers use this method to find the moments of inertia of an animal's limbs. This information is important for analyzing how an animal walks, as we'll see in the second of the two following examples.

EXAMPLE 14.9   PHYSICAL PENDULUM VERSUS SIMPLE PENDULUM

If the body in Fig. 14.23 is a uniform rod with length L, pivoted at one end, what is the period of its motion as a pendulum?

SOLUTION

IDENTIFY and SET UP: Our target variable is the oscillation period T of a rod that acts as a physical pendulum. We find the rod's moment of inertia in Table 9.2, and then determine T from Eq. (14.39).

EXECUTE: The moment of inertia of a uniform rod about an axis through one end is $I = \frac{1}{3}ML^2$. The distance from the pivot to the rod's center of gravity is $d = L/2$. Then from Eq. (14.39),

$$T = 2\pi\sqrt{\frac{I}{mgd}} = 2\pi\sqrt{\frac{\frac{1}{3}ML^2}{MgL/2}} = 2\pi\sqrt{\frac{2L}{3g}}$$

EVALUATE: If the rod is a meter stick ($L = 1.00$ m) and $g = 9.80$ m/s^2, then

$$T = 2\pi\sqrt{\frac{2(1.00 \text{ m})}{3(9.80 \text{ m/s}^2)}} = 1.64 \text{ s}$$

The period is smaller by a factor of $\sqrt{\frac{2}{3}} = 0.816$ than that of a simple pendulum of the same length (see Example 14.8). The rod's moment of inertia around one end, $I = \frac{1}{3}ML^2$, is one-third that of the simple pendulum, and the rod's cg is half as far from the pivot as that of the simple pendulum. You can show that, taken together in Eq. (14.39), these two differences account for the factor $\sqrt{\frac{2}{3}}$ by which the periods differ.

EXAMPLE 14.10   *TYRANNOSAURUS REX* AND THE PHYSICAL PENDULUM

All walking animals, including humans, have a natural walking pace—a number of steps per minute that is more comfortable than a faster or slower pace. Suppose that this pace corresponds to the oscillation of the leg as a physical pendulum. (a) How does this pace depend on the length L of the leg from hip to foot? Treat the leg as a uniform rod pivoted at the hip joint. (b) Fossil evidence shows that *T. rex,* a two-legged dinosaur that lived about 65 million years ago, had a leg length $L = 3.1$ m and a stride length $S = 4.0$ m (the distance from one footprint to the next print of the same foot; see **Fig. 14.24**). Estimate the walking speed of *T. rex.*

SOLUTION

IDENTIFY and SET UP: Our target variables are (a) the relationship between walking pace and leg length L and (b) the walking speed of *T. rex.* We treat the leg as a physical pendulum, with a period of oscillation as found in Example 14.9. We can find the walking speed from the period and the stride length.

EXECUTE: (a) From Example 14.9 the period of oscillation of the leg is $T = 2\pi\sqrt{2L/3g}$, which is proportional to $\sqrt{L}$. Each step

14.24 The walking speed of *Tyrannosaurus rex* can be estimated from leg length L and stride length S.

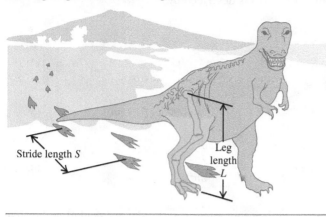

Stride length S

Leg length L

takes half of one period, so the walking pace (in steps per second) equals twice the oscillation frequency $f = 1/T$ and is proportional to $1/\sqrt{L}$. The longer the leg, the slower the pace.

(b) In our model, *T. rex* traveled one stride length S in a time

$$T = 2\pi\sqrt{\frac{2L}{3g}} = 2\pi\sqrt{\frac{2(3.1\text{ m})}{3(9.8\text{ m/s}^2)}} = 2.9\text{ s}$$

so its walking speed was

$$v = \frac{S}{T} = \frac{4.0\text{ m}}{2.9\text{ s}} = 1.4\text{ m/s} = 5.0\text{ km/h} = 3.1\text{ mi/h}$$

This is roughly the walking speed of an adult human.

EVALUATE: A uniform rod isn't a very good model for a leg. The legs of many animals, including both *T. rex* and humans, are tapered; there is more mass between hip and knee than between knee and foot. The center of mass is therefore less than $L/2$ from the hip; a reasonable guess would be about $L/4$. The moment of inertia is therefore *considerably* less than $ML^2/3$—say, $ML^2/15$. Use the analysis of Example 14.9 with these corrections; you'll get a shorter oscillation period and an even greater walking speed for *T. rex*.

TEST YOUR UNDERSTANDING OF SECTION 14.6 The center of gravity of a simple pendulum of mass m and length L is located at the pendulum bob, a distance L from the pivot point. The center of gravity of a uniform rod of the same mass m and length $2L$ pivoted at one end is also a distance L from the pivot point. Compared to the period of the simple pendulum, is the period of this uniform rod (i) longer; (ii) shorter; or (iii) the same? ❙

14.7 DAMPED OSCILLATIONS

The idealized oscillating systems we have discussed so far are frictionless. There are no nonconservative forces, the total mechanical energy is constant, and a system set into motion continues oscillating forever with no decrease in amplitude.

Real-world systems always have some dissipative forces, however, and oscillations die out with time unless we replace the dissipated mechanical energy (**Fig. 14.25**). A mechanical pendulum clock continues to run because potential energy stored in the spring or a hanging weight system replaces the mechanical energy lost due to friction in the pivot and the gears. But eventually the spring runs down or the weights reach the bottom of their travel. Then no more energy is available, and the pendulum swings decrease in amplitude and stop.

The decrease in amplitude caused by dissipative forces is called **damping** (*not* "dampening"), and the corresponding motion is called **damped oscillation.** The simplest case is a simple harmonic oscillator with a frictional damping force that is directly proportional to the *velocity* of the oscillating body. This behavior occurs in friction involving viscous fluid flow, such as in shock absorbers or sliding between oil-lubricated surfaces. We then have an additional force on the body due to friction, $F_x = -bv_x$, where $v_x = dx/dt$ is the velocity and b is a constant that describes the strength of the damping force. The negative sign shows that the force is always opposite in direction to the velocity. The *net* force on the body is then

$$\sum F_x = -kx - bv_x \tag{14.40}$$

and Newton's second law for the system is

$$-kx - bv_x = ma_x \quad \text{or} \quad -kx - b\frac{dx}{dt} = m\frac{d^2x}{dt^2} \tag{14.41}$$

Equation (14.41) is a differential equation for x; it's the same as Eq. (14.4), the equation for the acceleration in SHM, but with the added term $-bdx/dt$. We won't

14.25 A swinging bell left to itself will eventually stop oscillating due to damping forces (air resistance and friction at the point of suspension).

go into how to solve this equation; we'll just present the solution. If the damping force is relatively small, the motion is described by

$$\underset{\substack{\text{Displacement}\\\text{of oscillator,}\\\text{little damping}}}{} \quad \overset{\overset{\text{Initial}}{\text{amplitude}}}{} \quad \overset{\overset{\text{Damping}}{\text{constant}}}{} \quad \overset{\text{Mass}}{} \quad \overset{\text{Time}}{}$$
$$x = Ae^{-(b/2m)t}\cos(\omega' t + \phi) \tag{14.42}$$
$$\underset{\text{Angular frequency of damped oscillations}}{} \quad \underset{\text{Phase angle}}{}$$

The angular frequency of these damped oscillations is given by

$$\underset{\substack{\text{Angular frequency}\\\text{of oscillator,}\\\text{little damping}}}{} \quad \overset{\text{Force constant of restoring force}}{} \quad \overset{\text{Damping constant}}{}$$
$$\omega' = \sqrt{\frac{k}{m} - \frac{b^2}{4m^2}} \tag{14.43}$$
$$\underset{\text{Mass}}{}$$

You can verify that Eq. (14.42) is a solution of Eq. (14.41) by calculating the first and second derivatives of x, substituting them into Eq. (14.41), and checking whether the left and right sides are equal.

The motion described by Eq. (14.42) differs from the undamped case in two ways. First, the amplitude $Ae^{-(b/2m)t}$ is not constant but decreases with time because of the exponential factor $e^{-(b/2m)t}$. **Figure 14.26** is a graph of Eq. (14.42) for $\phi = 0$; the larger the value of b, the more quickly the amplitude decreases.

Second, the angular frequency ω', given by Eq. (14.43), is no longer equal to $\omega = \sqrt{k/m}$ but is somewhat smaller. It becomes zero when b becomes so large that

$$\frac{k}{m} - \frac{b^2}{4m^2} = 0 \quad \text{or} \quad b = 2\sqrt{km} \tag{14.44}$$

When Eq. (14.44) is satisfied, the condition is called **critical damping.** The system no longer oscillates but returns to its equilibrium position without oscillation when it is displaced and released.

If b is greater than $2\sqrt{km}$, the condition is called **overdamping.** Again there is no oscillation, but the system returns to equilibrium more slowly than with critical damping. For the overdamped case the solutions of Eq. (14.41) have the form

$$x = C_1 e^{-a_1 t} + C_2 e^{-a_2 t}$$

where C_1 and C_2 are constants that depend on the initial conditions and a_1 and a_2 are constants determined by m, k, and b.

When b is less than the critical value, as in Eq. (14.42), the condition is called **underdamping.** The system oscillates with steadily decreasing amplitude.

In a vibrating tuning fork or guitar string, it is usually desirable to have as little damping as possible. By contrast, damping plays a beneficial role in the oscillations of an automobile's suspension system. The shock absorbers provide a velocity-dependent damping force so that when the car goes over a bump, it doesn't continue bouncing forever (**Fig. 14.27**). For optimal passenger comfort, the system should be critically damped or slightly underdamped. Too much damping would be counterproductive; if the suspension is overdamped and the car hits a second bump just after the first one, the springs in the suspension will still be compressed somewhat from the first bump and will not be able to fully absorb the impact.

Energy in Damped Oscillations

In damped oscillations the damping force is nonconservative; the mechanical energy of the system is not constant but decreases continuously, approaching zero after a long time. To derive an expression for the rate of change of energy, we first write an expression for the total mechanical energy E at any instant:

$$E = \tfrac{1}{2}mv_x^2 + \tfrac{1}{2}kx^2$$

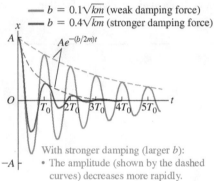

14.26 Graph of displacement versus time for an oscillator with little damping [see Eq. (14.42)] and with phase angle $\phi = 0$. The curves are for two values of the damping constant b.

— $b = 0.1\sqrt{km}$ (weak damping force)
— $b = 0.4\sqrt{km}$ (stronger damping force)

With stronger damping (larger b):
• The amplitude (shown by the dashed curves) decreases more rapidly.
• The period T increases (T_0 = period with zero damping).

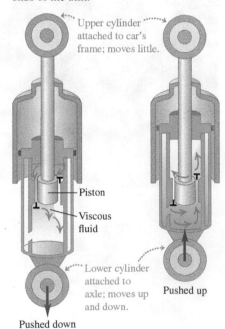

14.27 An automobile shock absorber. The viscous fluid causes a damping force that depends on the relative velocity of the two ends of the unit.

Upper cylinder attached to car's frame; moves little.

Piston

Viscous fluid

Lower cylinder attached to axle; moves up and down.

Pushed up

Pushed down

To find the rate of change of this quantity, we take its time derivative:

$$\frac{dE}{dt} = mv_x\frac{dv_x}{dt} + kx\frac{dx}{dt}$$

But $dv_x/dt = a_x$ and $dx/dt = v_x$, so

$$\frac{dE}{dt} = v_x(ma_x + kx)$$

From Eq. (14.41), $ma_x + kx = -bdx/dt = -bv_x$, so

$$\frac{dE}{dt} = v_x(-bv_x) = -bv_x^2 \qquad \text{(damped oscillations)} \qquad (14.45)$$

The right side of Eq. (14.45) is negative whenever the oscillating body is in motion, whether the x-velocity v_x is positive or negative. This shows that as the body moves, the energy decreases, though not at a uniform rate. The term $-bv_x^2 = (-bv_x)v_x$ (force times velocity) is the rate at which the damping force does (negative) work on the system (that is, the damping *power*). This equals the rate of change of the total mechanical energy of the system.

   Similar behavior occurs in electric circuits containing inductance, capacitance, and resistance. There is a natural frequency of oscillation, and the resistance plays the role of the damping constant b. We will study these circuits in detail in Chapters 30 and 31.

TEST YOUR UNDERSTANDING OF SECTION 14.7   An airplane is flying in a straight line at a constant altitude. If a wind gust strikes and raises the nose of the airplane, the nose will bob up and down until the airplane eventually returns to its original attitude. Are these oscillations (i) undamped; (ii) underdamped; (iii) critically damped; or (iv) overdamped? ∎

14.8 FORCED OSCILLATIONS AND RESONANCE

A damped oscillator left to itself will eventually stop moving. But we can maintain a constant-amplitude oscillation by applying a force that varies with time in a periodic way. As an example, consider your cousin Throckmorton on a playground swing. You can keep him swinging with constant amplitude by giving him a push once each cycle. We call this additional force a **driving force.**

Damped Oscillation with a Periodic Driving Force

If we apply a periodic driving force with angular frequency ω_d to a damped harmonic oscillator, the motion that results is called a **forced oscillation** or a *driven oscillation*. It is different from the motion that occurs when the system is simply displaced from equilibrium and then left alone, in which case the system oscillates with a **natural angular frequency** ω' determined by m, k, and b, as in Eq. (14.43). In a forced oscillation, however, the angular frequency with which the mass oscillates is equal to the driving angular frequency ω_d. This does *not* have to be equal to the natural angular frequency ω'. If you grab the ropes of Throckmorton's swing, you can force the swing to oscillate with any frequency you like.

   Suppose we force the oscillator to vibrate with an angular frequency ω_d that is nearly *equal* to the angular frequency ω' it would have with no driving force. What happens? The oscillator is naturally disposed to oscillate at $\omega = \omega'$, so we expect the amplitude of the resulting oscillation to be larger than when the two frequencies are very different. Detailed analysis and experiment show that this is just what happens. The easiest case to analyze is a *sinusoidally* varying force—say, $F(t) = F_{max}\cos\omega_d t$. If we vary the frequency ω_d of the driving force, the amplitude

BIO Application Forced Oscillations
This lady beetle (or "ladybug," family Coccinellidae) flies by means of a forced oscillation. Unlike the wings of birds, this insect's wings are extensions of its exoskeleton. Muscles attached to the inside of the exoskeleton apply a periodic driving force that deforms the exoskeleton rhythmically, causing the attached wings to beat up and down. The oscillation frequency of the wings and exoskeleton is the same as the frequency of the driving force.

14.28 Graph of the amplitude A of forced oscillation as a function of the angular frequency ω_d of the driving force. The horizontal axis shows the ratio of ω_d to the angular frequency $\omega = \sqrt{k/m}$ of an undamped oscillator. Each curve has a different value of the damping constant b.

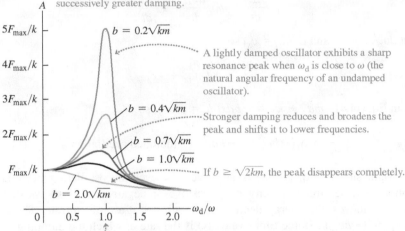

Each curve shows the amplitude A for an oscillator subjected to a driving force at various angular frequencies ω_d. Successive curves from blue to gold represent successively greater damping.

A lightly damped oscillator exhibits a sharp resonance peak when ω_d is close to ω (the natural angular frequency of an undamped oscillator).

Stronger damping reduces and broadens the peak and shifts it to lower frequencies.

If $b \geq \sqrt{2km}$, the peak disappears completely.

Driving frequency ω_d equals natural angular frequency ω of an undamped oscillator.

of the resulting forced oscillation varies in an interesting way (**Fig. 14.28**). When there is very little damping (small b), the amplitude goes through a sharp peak as the driving angular frequency ω_d nears the natural oscillation angular frequency ω'. When the damping is increased (larger b), the peak becomes broader and smaller in height and shifts toward lower frequencies.

Using more differential equations than we're ready for, we could find an expression for the amplitude A of the forced oscillation as a function of the driving angular frequency. Here is the result:

DEMO

Maximum value of driving force

Amplitude of a forced oscillator $\quad A = \dfrac{F_{max}}{\sqrt{(k - m\omega_d^2)^2 + b^2\omega_d^2}}$ Damping constant $\qquad$ (14.46)

Force constant of restoring force $\quad$ Mass $\quad$ Driving angular frequency

When $k - m\omega_d^2 = 0$, the first term under the radical is zero, so A has a maximum near $\omega_d = \sqrt{k/m}$. The height of the curve at this point is proportional to $1/b$; the less damping, the higher the peak. At the low-frequency extreme, when $\omega_d = 0$, we get $A = F_{max}/k$. This corresponds to a *constant* force F_{max} and a constant displacement $A = F_{max}/k$ from equilibrium, as we might expect.

Resonance and Its Consequences

The peaking of the amplitude at driving frequencies close to the natural frequency of the system is called **resonance.** Physics is full of examples of resonance; building up the oscillations of a child on a swing by pushing with a frequency equal to the swing's natural frequency is one. A vibrating rattle in a car that occurs only at a certain engine speed is another example. Inexpensive loudspeakers often have an annoying boom or buzz when a musical note coincides with the natural frequency of the speaker cone or housing. In Chapter 16 we will study examples of resonance that involve sound. Resonance also occurs in electric circuits, as we will see in Chapter 31; a tuned circuit in a radio receiver responds strongly to waves with frequencies near its natural frequency. This phenomenon lets us select one radio station and reject other stations.

Resonance in mechanical systems can be destructive. A company of soldiers once destroyed a bridge by marching across it in step; the frequency of their steps was close to a natural frequency of the bridge, and the resulting oscillation had large enough amplitude to tear the bridge apart. Ever since, marching soldiers have been ordered to break step before crossing a bridge. Some years ago,

BIO Application Canine Resonance Unlike humans, dogs have no sweat glands and so must pant in order to cool down. The frequency at which a dog pants is very close to the resonant frequency of its respiratory system. This causes the maximum amount of air inflow and outflow and so minimizes the effort that the dog must exert to cool itself.

vibrations of the engines of a particular type of airplane had just the right frequency to resonate with the natural frequencies of its wings. Large oscillations built up, and occasionally the wings fell off.

TEST YOUR UNDERSTANDING OF SECTION 14.8 When driven at a frequency near its natural frequency, an oscillator with very little damping has a much greater response than the same oscillator with more damping. When driven at a frequency that is much higher or lower than the natural frequency, which oscillator will have the greater response: (i) the one with very little damping or (ii) the one with more damping? ∎

CHAPTER 14 SUMMARY

SOLUTIONS TO ALL EXAMPLES

Periodic motion: Periodic motion is motion that repeats itself in a definite cycle. It occurs whenever a body has a stable equilibrium position and a restoring force that acts when the body is displaced from equilibrium. Period T is the time for one cycle. Frequency f is the number of cycles per unit time. Angular frequency ω is 2π times the frequency. (See Example 14.1.)

$$f = \frac{1}{T} \qquad T = \frac{1}{f} \tag{14.1}$$

$$\omega = 2\pi f = \frac{2\pi}{T} \tag{14.2}$$

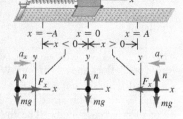

Simple harmonic motion: If the restoring force F_x in periodic motion is directly proportional to the displacement x, the motion is called simple harmonic motion (SHM). In many cases this condition is satisfied if the displacement from equilibrium is small. The angular frequency, frequency, and period in SHM do not depend on the amplitude but on only the mass m and force constant k. The displacement, velocity, and acceleration in SHM are sinusoidal functions of time; the amplitude A and phase angle ϕ of the oscillation are determined by the initial displacement and velocity of the body. (See Examples 14.2, 14.3, 14.6, and 14.7.)

$$F_x = -kx \tag{14.3}$$

$$a_x = \frac{F_x}{m} = -\frac{k}{m}x \tag{14.4}$$

$$\omega = \sqrt{\frac{k}{m}} \tag{14.10}$$

$$f = \frac{\omega}{2\pi} = \frac{1}{2\pi}\sqrt{\frac{k}{m}} \tag{14.11}$$

$$T = \frac{1}{f} = 2\pi\sqrt{\frac{m}{k}} \tag{14.12}$$

$$x = A\cos(\omega t + \phi) \tag{14.13}$$

Energy in simple harmonic motion: Energy is conserved in SHM. The total energy can be expressed in terms of the force constant k and amplitude A. (See Examples 14.4 and 14.5.)

$$E = \tfrac{1}{2}mv_x^2 + \tfrac{1}{2}kx^2 = \tfrac{1}{2}kA^2 = \text{constant} \tag{14.21}$$

Angular simple harmonic motion: In angular SHM, the frequency and angular frequency are related to the moment of inertia I and the torsion constant κ.

$$\omega = \sqrt{\frac{\kappa}{I}} \quad \text{and}$$

$$f = \frac{1}{2\pi}\sqrt{\frac{\kappa}{I}} \tag{14.24}$$

Balance wheel   Spring

Spring torque τ_z opposes angular displacement θ.

Simple pendulum: A simple pendulum consists of a point mass m at the end of a massless string of length L. Its motion is approximately simple harmonic for sufficiently small amplitude; the angular frequency, frequency, and period then depend on only g and L, not on the mass or amplitude. (See Example 14.8.)

$$\omega = \sqrt{\frac{g}{L}} \tag{14.32}$$

$$f = \frac{\omega}{2\pi} = \frac{1}{2\pi}\sqrt{\frac{g}{L}} \tag{14.33}$$

$$T = \frac{2\pi}{\omega} = \frac{1}{f} = 2\pi\sqrt{\frac{L}{g}} \tag{14.34}$$

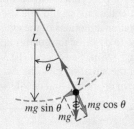

Physical pendulum: A physical pendulum is any body suspended from an axis of rotation. The angular frequency and period for small-amplitude oscillations are independent of amplitude but depend on the mass m, distance d from the axis of rotation to the center of gravity, and moment of inertia I about the axis. (See Examples 14.9 and 14.10.)

$$\omega = \sqrt{\frac{mgd}{I}} \qquad (14.38)$$

$$T = 2\pi \sqrt{\frac{I}{mgd}} \qquad (14.39)$$

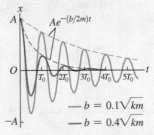

Damped oscillations: When a force $F_x = -bv_x$ is added to a simple harmonic oscillator, the motion is called a damped oscillation. If $b < 2\sqrt{km}$ (called underdamping), the system oscillates with a decaying amplitude and an angular frequency ω' that is lower than it would be without damping. If $b = 2\sqrt{km}$ (called critical damping) or $b > 2\sqrt{km}$ (called overdamping), when the system is displaced it returns to equilibrium without oscillating.

$$x = Ae^{-(b/2m)t}\cos(\omega' t + \phi) \qquad (14.42)$$

$$\omega' = \sqrt{\frac{k}{m} - \frac{b^2}{4m^2}} \qquad (14.43)$$

Forced oscillations and resonance: When a sinusoidally varying driving force is added to a damped harmonic oscillator, the resulting motion is called a forced oscillation or driven oscillation. The amplitude is a function of the driving frequency ω_d and reaches a peak at a driving frequency close to the natural frequency of the system. This behavior is called resonance.

$$A = \frac{F_{max}}{\sqrt{(k - m\omega_d^2)^2 + b^2\omega_d^2}} \qquad (14.46)$$

BRIDGING PROBLEM | **OSCILLATING AND ROLLING**

Two uniform, solid cylinders of radius R and total mass M are connected along their common axis by a short, light rod and rest on a horizontal tabletop (**Fig. 14.29**). A frictionless ring at the center of the rod is attached to a spring with force constant k; the other end of the spring is fixed. The cylinders are pulled to the left a distance x, stretching the spring, and then released from rest. Due to friction between the tabletop and the cylinders, the cylinders roll without slipping as they oscillate. Show that the motion of the center of mass of the cylinders is simple harmonic, and find its period.

14.29 Rolling cylinders attached to a spring.

SOLUTION GUIDE

IDENTIFY and SET UP

1. What condition must be satisfied for the motion of the center of mass of the cylinders to be simple harmonic?

2. Which equations should you use to describe the translational and rotational motions of the cylinders? Which equation should you use to describe the condition that the cylinders roll without slipping? (*Hint:* See Section 10.3.)

3. Sketch the situation and choose a coordinate system. List the unknown quantities and decide which is the target variable.

EXECUTE

4. Draw a free-body diagram for the cylinders when they are displaced a distance x from equilibrium.

5. Solve the equations to find an expression for the acceleration of the center of mass of the cylinders. What does this expression tell you?

6. Use your result from step 5 to find the period of oscillation of the center of mass of the cylinders.

EVALUATE

7. What would be the period of oscillation if there were no friction and the cylinders didn't roll? Is this period larger or smaller than your result from step 6? Is this reasonable?

Problems

•, ••, •••: Difficulty levels. **CP**: Cumulative problems incorporating material from earlier chapters. **CALC**: Problems requiring calculus. **DATA**: Problems involving real data, scientific evidence, experimental design, and/or statistical reasoning. **BIO**: Biosciences problems.

DISCUSSION QUESTIONS

Q14.1 An object is moving with SHM of amplitude A on the end of a spring. If the amplitude is doubled, what happens to the total distance the object travels in one period? What happens to the period? What happens to the maximum speed of the object? Discuss how these answers are related.

Q14.2 Think of several examples in everyday life of motions that are, at least approximately, simple harmonic. In what respects does each differ from SHM?

Q14.3 Does a tuning fork or similar tuning instrument undergo SHM? Why is this a crucial question for musicians?

Q14.4 A box containing a pebble is attached to an ideal horizontal spring and is oscillating on a friction-free air table. When the box has reached its maximum distance from the equilibrium point, the pebble is suddenly lifted out vertically without disturbing the box. Will the following characteristics of the motion increase, decrease, or remain the same in the subsequent motion of the box? Justify each answer. (a) Frequency; (b) period; (c) amplitude; (d) the maximum kinetic energy of the box; (e) the maximum speed of the box.

Q14.5 If a uniform spring is cut in half, what is the force constant of each half? Justify your answer. How would the frequency of SHM using a half-spring differ from the frequency using the same mass and the entire spring?

Q14.6 A glider is attached to a fixed ideal spring and oscillates on a horizontal, friction-free air track. A coin rests atop the glider and oscillates with it. At what points in the motion is the friction force on the coin greatest? The least? Justify your answers.

Q14.7 Two identical gliders on an air track are connected by an ideal spring. Could such a system undergo SHM? Explain. How would the period compare with that of a single glider attached to a spring whose other end is rigidly attached to a stationary object? Explain.

Q14.8 You are captured by Martians, taken into their ship, and put to sleep. You awake some time later and find yourself locked in a small room with no windows. All the Martians have left you with is your digital watch, your school ring, and your long silver-chain necklace. Explain how you can determine whether you are still on earth or have been transported to Mars.

Q14.9 The system shown in Fig. 14.17 is mounted in an elevator. What happens to the period of the motion (does it increase, decrease, or remain the same) if the elevator (a) accelerates upward at 5.0 m/s^2; (b) moves upward at a steady 5.0 m/s; (c) accelerates downward at 5.0 m/s^2? Justify your answers.

Q14.10 If a pendulum has a period of 2.5 s on earth, what would be its period in a space station orbiting the earth? If a mass hung from a vertical spring has a period of 5.0 s on earth, what would its period be in the space station? Justify your answers.

Q14.11 A simple pendulum is mounted in an elevator. What happens to the period of the pendulum (does it increase, decrease, or remain the same) if the elevator (a) accelerates upward at 5.0 m/s^2; (b) moves upward at a steady 5.0 m/s; (c) accelerates downward at 5.0 m/s^2; (d) accelerates downward at 9.8 m/s^2? Justify your answers.

Q14.12 What should you do to the length of the string of a simple pendulum to (a) double its frequency; (b) double its period; (c) double its angular frequency?

Q14.13 If a pendulum clock is taken to a mountaintop, does it gain or lose time, assuming it is correct at a lower elevation? Explain.

Q14.14 When the amplitude of a simple pendulum increases, should its period increase or decrease? Give a qualitative argument; do not rely on Eq. (14.35). Is your argument also valid for a physical pendulum?

Q14.15 Why do short dogs (like Chihuahuas) walk with quicker strides than do tall dogs (like Great Danes)?

Q14.16 At what point in the motion of a simple pendulum is the string tension greatest? Least? In each case give the reasoning behind your answer.

Q14.17 Could a standard of time be based on the period of a certain standard pendulum? What advantages and disadvantages would such a standard have compared to the actual present-day standard discussed in Section 1.3?

Q14.18 For a simple pendulum, clearly distinguish between ω (the angular speed) and ω (the angular frequency). Which is constant and which is variable?

Q14.19 In designing structures in an earthquake-prone region, how should the natural frequencies of oscillation of a structure relate to typical earthquake frequencies? Why? Should the structure have a large or small amount of damping?

EXERCISES

Section 14.1 Describing Oscillation

14.1 • **BIO** (a) **Music.** When a person sings, his or her vocal cords vibrate in a repetitive pattern that has the same frequency as the note that is sung. If someone sings the note B flat, which has a frequency of 466 Hz, how much time does it take the person's vocal cords to vibrate through one complete cycle, and what is the angular frequency of the cords? (b) **Hearing.** When sound waves strike the eardrum, this membrane vibrates with the same frequency as the sound. The highest pitch that young humans can hear has a period of 50.0 μs. What are the frequency and angular frequency of the vibrating eardrum for this sound? (c) **Vision.** When light having vibrations with angular frequency ranging from 2.7×10^{15} rad/s to 4.7×10^{15} rad/s strikes the retina of the eye, it stimulates the receptor cells there and is perceived as visible light. What are the limits of the period and frequency of this light? (d) **Ultrasound.** High-frequency sound waves (ultrasound) are used to probe the interior of the body, much as x rays do. To detect small objects such as tumors, a frequency of around 5.0 MHz is used. What are the period and angular frequency of the molecular vibrations caused by this pulse of sound?

14.2 • If an object on a horizontal, frictionless surface is attached to a spring, displaced, and then released, it will oscillate. If it is displaced 0.120 m from its equilibrium position and released with zero initial speed, then after 0.800 s its displacement is found to be 0.120 m on the opposite side, and it has passed the equilibrium position once during this interval. Find (a) the amplitude; (b) the period; (c) the frequency.

14.3 • The tip of a tuning fork goes through 440 complete vibrations in 0.500 s. Find the angular frequency and the period of the motion.

14.4 • The displacement of an oscillating object as a function of time is shown in **Fig. E14.4**. What are (a) the frequency; (b) the amplitude; (c) the period; (d) the angular frequency of this motion?

Figure **E14.4**

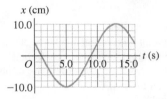

14.5 •• A machine part is undergoing SHM with a frequency of 4.00 Hz and amplitude 1.80 cm. How long does it take the part to go from $x = 0$ to $x = -1.80$ cm?

14.6 • BIO The wings of the blue-throated hummingbird (*Lampornis clemenciae*), which inhabits Mexico and the southwestern United States, beat at a rate of up to 900 times per minute. Calculate (a) the period of vibration of this bird's wings, (b) the frequency of the wings' vibration, and (c) the angular frequency of the bird's wing beats.

Section 14.2 Simple Harmonic Motion

14.7 • A 2.40-kg ball is attached to an unknown spring and allowed to oscillate. **Figure E14.7** shows a graph of the ball's position x as a function of time t. What are the oscillation's (a) period, (b) frequency, (c) angular frequency, and (d) amplitude? (e) What is the force constant of the spring?

Figure **E14.7**

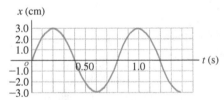

14.8 •• In a physics lab, you attach a 0.200-kg air-track glider to the end of an ideal spring of negligible mass and start it oscillating. The elapsed time from when the glider first moves through the equilibrium point to the second time it moves through that point is 2.60 s. Find the spring's force constant.

14.9 • When a body of unknown mass is attached to an ideal spring with force constant 120 N/m, it is found to vibrate with a frequency of 6.00 Hz. Find (a) the period of the motion; (b) the angular frequency; (c) the mass of the body.

14.10 • When a 0.750-kg mass oscillates on an ideal spring, the frequency is 1.75 Hz. What will the frequency be if 0.220 kg are (a) added to the original mass and (b) subtracted from the original mass? Try to solve this problem *without* finding the force constant of the spring.

14.11 •• An object is undergoing SHM with period 0.900 s and amplitude 0.320 m. At $t = 0$ the object is at $x = 0.320$ m and is instantaneously at rest. Calculate the time it takes the object to go (a) from $x = 0.320$ m to $x = 0.160$ m and (b) from $x = 0.160$ m to $x = 0$.

14.12 • A small block is attached to an ideal spring and is moving in SHM on a horizontal, frictionless surface. When the block is at $x = 0.280$ m, the acceleration of the block is -5.30 m/s^2. What is the frequency of the motion?

14.13 • A 2.00-kg, frictionless block is attached to an ideal spring with force constant 300 N/m. At $t = 0$ the spring is neither stretched nor compressed and the block is moving in the negative direction at 12.0 m/s. Find (a) the amplitude and (b) the phase angle. (c) Write an equation for the position as a function of time.

14.14 •• Repeat Exercise 14.13, but assume that at $t = 0$ the block has velocity -4.00 m/s and displacement $+0.200$ m.

14.15 • The point of the needle of a sewing machine moves in SHM along the x-axis with a frequency of 2.5 Hz. At $t = 0$ its position and velocity components are $+1.1$ cm and -15 cm/s, respectively. (a) Find the acceleration component of the needle at $t = 0$. (b) Write equations giving the position, velocity, and acceleration components of the point as a function of time.

14.16 •• A small block is attached to an ideal spring and is moving in SHM on a horizontal, frictionless surface. When the amplitude of the motion is 0.090 m, it takes the block 2.70 s to travel from $x = 0.090$ m to $x = -0.090$ m. If the amplitude is doubled, to 0.180 m, how long does it take the block to travel (a) from $x = 0.180$ m to $x = -0.180$ m and (b) from $x = 0.090$ m to $x = -0.090$ m?

14.17 • BIO **Weighing Astronauts.** This procedure has been used to "weigh" astronauts in space: A 42.5-kg chair is attached to a spring and allowed to oscillate. When it is empty, the chair takes 1.30 s to make one complete vibration. But with an astronaut sitting in it, with her feet off the floor, the chair takes 2.54 s for one cycle. What is the mass of the astronaut?

14.18 • A 0.400-kg object undergoing SHM has $a_x = -1.80$ m/s^2 when $x = 0.300$ m. What is the time for one oscillation?

14.19 • On a frictionless, horizontal air track, a glider oscillates at the end of an ideal spring of force constant 2.50 N/cm. The graph in **Fig. E14.19** shows the acceleration of the glider as a function of time. Find (a) the mass of the glider; (b) the maximum displacement of the glider from the equilibrium point; (c) the maximum force the spring exerts on the glider.

Figure **E14.19**

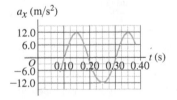

14.20 • A 0.500-kg mass on a spring has velocity as a function of time given by $v_x(t) = -(3.60$ cm/s$) \sin[(4.71$ rad/s$)t - (\pi/2)]$. What are (a) the period; (b) the amplitude; (c) the maximum acceleration of the mass; (d) the force constant of the spring?

14.21 • A 1.50-kg mass on a spring has displacement as a function of time given by

$$x(t) = (7.40 \text{ cm}) \cos[(4.16 \text{ rad/s})t - 2.42]$$

Find (a) the time for one complete vibration; (b) the force constant of the spring; (c) the maximum speed of the mass; (d) the maximum force on the mass; (e) the position, speed, and acceleration of the mass at $t = 1.00$ s; (f) the force on the mass at that time.

14.22 • BIO **Weighing a Virus.** In February 2004, scientists at Purdue University used a highly sensitive technique to measure the mass of a vaccinia virus (the kind used in smallpox vaccine). The procedure involved measuring the frequency of oscillation of a tiny sliver of silicon (just 30 nm long) with a laser, first without the virus and then after the virus had attached itself to the silicon.

The difference in mass caused a change in the frequency. We can model such a process as a mass on a spring. (a) Show that the ratio of the frequency with the virus attached (f_{S+V}) to the frequency without the virus (f_S) is given by $f_{S+V}/f_S = 1/\sqrt{1 + (m_V/m_S)}$, where m_V is the mass of the virus and m_S is the mass of the silicon sliver. Notice that it is *not* necessary to know or measure the force constant of the spring. (b) In some data, the silicon sliver has a mass of 2.10×10^{-16} g and a frequency of 2.00×10^{15} Hz without the virus and 2.87×10^{14} Hz with the virus. What is the mass of the virus, in grams and in femtograms?

14.23 •• **CALC Jerk.** A guitar string vibrates at a frequency of 440 Hz. A point at its center moves in SHM with an amplitude of 3.0 mm and a phase angle of zero. (a) Write an equation for the position of the center of the string as a function of time. (b) What are the maximum values of the magnitudes of the velocity and acceleration of the center of the string? (c) The derivative of the acceleration with respect to time is a quantity called the *jerk*. Write an equation for the jerk of the center of the string as a function of time, and find the maximum value of the magnitude of the jerk.

Section 14.3 Energy in Simple Harmonic Motion

14.24 •• For the oscillating object in Fig. E14.4, what are (a) its maximum speed and (b) its maximum acceleration?

14.25 • A small block is attached to an ideal spring and is moving in SHM on a horizontal frictionless surface. The amplitude of the motion is 0.165 m. The maximum speed of the block is 3.90 m/s. What is the maximum magnitude of the acceleration of the block?

14.26 • A small block is attached to an ideal spring and is moving in SHM on a horizontal, frictionless surface. The amplitude of the motion is 0.250 m and the period is 3.20 s. What are the speed and acceleration of the block when $x = 0.160$ m?

14.27 • A 0.150-kg toy is undergoing SHM on the end of a horizontal spring with force constant $k = 300$ N/m. When the toy is 0.0120 m from its equilibrium position, it is observed to have a speed of 0.400 m/s. What are the toy's (a) total energy at any point of its motion; (b) amplitude of motion; (c) maximum speed during its motion?

14.28 •• A harmonic oscillator has angular frequency ω and amplitude A. (a) What are the magnitudes of the displacement and velocity when the elastic potential energy is equal to the kinetic energy? (Assume that $U = 0$ at equilibrium.) (b) How often does this occur in each cycle? What is the time between occurrences? (c) At an instant when the displacement is equal to $A/2$, what fraction of the total energy of the system is kinetic and what fraction is potential?

14.29 • A 0.500-kg glider, attached to the end of an ideal spring with force constant $k = 450$ N/m, undergoes SHM with an amplitude of 0.040 m. Compute (a) the maximum speed of the glider; (b) the speed of the glider when it is at $x = -0.015$ m; (c) the magnitude of the maximum acceleration of the glider; (d) the acceleration of the glider at $x = -0.015$ m; (e) the total mechanical energy of the glider at any point in its motion.

14.30 •• A cheerleader waves her pom-pom in SHM with an amplitude of 18.0 cm and a frequency of 0.850 Hz. Find (a) the maximum magnitude of the acceleration and of the velocity; (b) the acceleration and speed when the pom-pom's coordinate is $x = +9.0$ cm; (c) the time required to move from the equilibrium position directly to a point 12.0 cm away. (d) Which of the quantities asked for in parts (a), (b), and (c) can be found by using the energy approach used in Section 14.3, and which cannot? Explain.

14.31 • CP For the situation described in part (a) of Example 14.5, what should be the value of the putty mass m so that the amplitude after the collision is one-half the original amplitude? For this value of m, what fraction of the original mechanical energy is converted into thermal energy?

14.32 •• A block with mass $m = 0.300$ kg is attached to one end of an ideal spring and moves on a horizontal frictionless surface. The other end of the spring is attached to a wall. When the block is at $x = +0.240$ m, its acceleration is $a_x = -12.0$ m/s^2 and its velocity is $v_x = +4.00$ m/s. What are (a) the spring's force constant k; (b) the amplitude of the motion; (c) the maximum speed of the block during its motion; and (d) the maximum magnitude of the block's acceleration during its motion?

14.33 •• You are watching an object that is moving in SHM. When the object is displaced 0.600 m to the right of its equilibrium position, it has a velocity of 2.20 m/s to the right and an acceleration of 8.40 m/s^2 to the left. How much farther from this point will the object move before it stops momentarily and then starts to move back to the left?

14.34 • A 2.00-kg frictionless block is attached to an ideal spring with force constant 315 N/m. Initially the spring is neither stretched nor compressed, but the block is moving in the negative direction at 12.0 m/s. Find (a) the amplitude of the motion, (b) the block's maximum acceleration, and (c) the maximum force the spring exerts on the block.

14.35 • A 2.00-kg frictionless block attached to an ideal spring with force constant 315 N/m is undergoing simple harmonic motion. When the block has displacement $+0.200$ m, it is moving in the negative x-direction with a speed of 4.00 m/s. Find (a) the amplitude of the motion; (b) the block's maximum acceleration; and (c) the maximum force the spring exerts on the block.

14.36 •• A mass is oscillating with amplitude A at the end of a spring. How far (in terms of A) is this mass from the equilibrium position of the spring when the elastic potential energy equals the kinetic energy?

Section 14.4 Applications of Simple Harmonic Motion

14.37 • A 175-g glider on a horizontal, frictionless air track is attached to a fixed ideal spring with force constant 155 N/m. At the instant you make measurements on the glider, it is moving at 0.815 m/s and is 3.00 cm from its equilibrium point. Use *energy conservation* to find (a) the amplitude of the motion and (b) the maximum speed of the glider. (c) What is the angular frequency of the oscillations?

14.38 • A proud deep-sea fisherman hangs a 65.0-kg fish from an ideal spring having negligible mass. The fish stretches the spring 0.180 m. (a) Find the force constant of the spring. The fish is now pulled down 5.00 cm and released. (b) What is the period of oscillation of the fish? (c) What is the maximum speed it will reach?

14.39 • A thrill-seeking cat with mass 4.00 kg is attached by a harness to an ideal spring of negligible mass and oscillates vertically in SHM. The amplitude is 0.050 m, and at the highest point of the motion the spring has its natural unstretched length. Calculate the elastic potential energy of the spring (take it to be zero for the unstretched spring), the kinetic energy of the cat, the gravitational potential energy of the system relative to the lowest point of the motion, and the sum of these three energies when the cat is (a) at its highest point; (b) at its lowest point; (c) at its equilibrium position.

14.40 •• A uniform, solid metal disk of mass 6.50 kg and diameter 24.0 cm hangs in a horizontal plane, supported at its center by a vertical metal wire. You find that it requires a horizontal force of 4.23 N tangent to the rim of the disk to turn it by 3.34°, thus twisting the wire. You now remove this force and release the disk from rest. (a) What is the torsion constant for the metal wire? (b) What are the frequency and period of the torsional oscillations of the disk? (c) Write the equation of motion for $\theta(t)$ for the disk.

14.41 •• A certain alarm clock ticks four times each second, with each tick representing half a period. The balance wheel consists of a thin rim with radius 0.55 cm, connected to the balance shaft by thin spokes of negligible mass. The total mass of the balance wheel is 0.90 g. (a) What is the moment of inertia of the balance wheel about its shaft? (b) What is the torsion constant of the coil spring (Fig. 14.19)?

14.42 • A thin metal disk with mass 2.00×10^{-3} kg and radius 2.20 cm is attached at its center to a long fiber (**Fig. E14.42**). The disk, when twisted and released, oscillates with a period of 1.00 s. Find the torsion constant of the fiber.

Figure **E14.42**

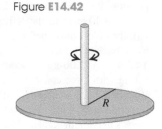

R

14.43 •• You want to find the moment of inertia of a complicated machine part about an axis through its center of mass. You suspend it from a wire along this axis. The wire has a torsion constant of 0.450 N·m/rad. You twist the part a small amount about this axis and let it go, timing 165 oscillations in 265 s. What is its moment of inertia?

14.44 •• CALC The balance wheel of a watch vibrates with an angular amplitude Θ, angular frequency ω, and phase angle $\phi = 0$. (a) Find expressions for the angular velocity $d\theta/dt$ and angular acceleration $d^2\theta/dt^2$ as functions of time. (b) Find the balance wheel's angular velocity and angular acceleration when its angular displacement is Θ, and when its angular displacement is $\Theta/2$ and θ is decreasing. (*Hint:* Sketch a graph of θ versus t.)

Section 14.5 The Simple Pendulum

14.45 •• You pull a simple pendulum 0.240 m long to the side through an angle of 3.50° and release it. (a) How much time does it take the pendulum bob to reach its highest speed? (b) How much time does it take if the pendulum is released at an angle of 1.75° instead of 3.50°?

14.46 • An 85.0-kg mountain climber plans to swing down, starting from rest, from a ledge using a light rope 6.50 m long. He holds one end of the rope, and the other end is tied higher up on a rock face. Since the ledge is not very far from the rock face, the rope makes a small angle with the vertical. At the lowest point of his swing, he plans to let go and drop a short distance to the ground. (a) How long after he begins his swing will the climber first reach his lowest point? (b) If he missed the first chance to drop off, how long after first beginning his swing will the climber reach his lowest point for the second time?

14.47 • A building in San Francisco has light fixtures consisting of small 2.35-kg bulbs with shades hanging from the ceiling at the end of light, thin cords 1.50 m long. If a minor earthquake occurs, how many swings per second will these fixtures make?

14.48 • **A Pendulum on Mars.** A certain simple pendulum has a period on the earth of 1.60 s. What is its period on the surface of Mars, where $g = 3.71$ m/s²?

14.49 • After landing on an unfamiliar planet, a space explorer constructs a simple pendulum of length 50.0 cm. She finds that the pendulum makes 100 complete swings in 136 s. What is the value of g on this planet?

14.50 •• In the laboratory, a student studies a pendulum by graphing the angle θ that the string makes with the vertical as a function of time t, obtaining the graph shown in **Fig. E14.50**. (a) What are the period, frequency, angular frequency, and amplitude of the pendulum's motion? (b) How long is the pendulum? (c) Is it possible to determine the mass of the bob?

Figure **E14.50**

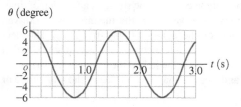

14.51 • A simple pendulum 2.00 m long swings through a maximum angle of 30.0° with the vertical. Calculate its period (a) assuming a small amplitude, and (b) using the first three terms of Eq. (14.35). (c) Which of the answers in parts (a) and (b) is more accurate? What is the percentage error of the less accurate answer compared with the more accurate one?

14.52 •• A small sphere with mass m is attached to a massless rod of length L that is pivoted at the top, forming a simple pendulum. The pendulum is pulled to one side so that the rod is at an angle θ from the vertical, and released from rest. (a) In a diagram, show the pendulum just after it is released. Draw vectors representing the *forces* acting on the small sphere and the *acceleration* of the sphere. Accuracy counts! At this point, what is the linear acceleration of the sphere? (b) Repeat part (a) for the instant when the pendulum rod is at an angle $\theta/2$ from the vertical. (c) Repeat part (a) for the instant when the pendulum rod is vertical. At this point, what is the linear speed of the sphere?

Section 14.6 The Physical Pendulum

14.53 • Two pendulums have the same dimensions (length L) and total mass (m). Pendulum A is a very small ball swinging at the end of a uniform massless bar. In pendulum B, half the mass is in the ball and half is in the uniform bar. Find the period of each pendulum for small oscillations. Which one takes longer for a swing?

14.54 •• We want to hang a thin hoop on a horizontal nail and have the hoop make one complete small-angle oscillation each 2.0 s. What must the hoop's radius be?

14.55 • A 1.80-kg connecting rod from a car engine is pivoted about a horizontal knife edge as shown in **Fig. E14.55**. The center of gravity of the rod was located by balancing and is 0.200 m from the pivot. When the rod is set into small-amplitude oscillation, it makes 100 complete swings in 120 s. Calculate the moment of inertia of the rod about the rotation axis through the pivot.

Figure **E14.55**

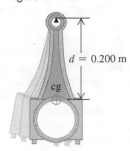

$d = 0.200$ m

cg

14.56 ·· A 1.80-kg monkey wrench is pivoted 0.250 m from its center of mass and allowed to swing as a physical pendulum. The period for small-angle oscillations is 0.940 s. (a) What is the moment of inertia of the wrench about an axis through the pivot? (b) If the wrench is initially displaced 0.400 rad from its equilibrium position, what is the angular speed of the wrench as it passes through the equilibrium position?

14.57 ·· The two pendulums shown in **Fig. E14.57** each consist of a uniform solid ball of mass M supported by a rigid massless rod, but the ball for pendulum A is very tiny while the ball for pendulum B is much larger. Find the period of each pendulum for small displacements. Which ball takes longer to complete a swing?

Figure E14.57

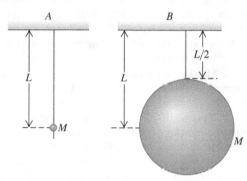

14.58 ·· CP A holiday ornament in the shape of a hollow sphere with mass $M = 0.015$ kg and radius $R = 0.050$ m is hung from a tree limb by a small loop of wire attached to the surface of the sphere. If the ornament is displaced a small distance and released, it swings back and forth as a physical pendulum with negligible friction. Calculate its period. (*Hint:* Use the parallel-axis theorem to find the moment of inertia of the sphere about the pivot at the tree limb.)

Section 14.7 Damped Oscillations

14.59 · A 1.35-kg object is attached to a horizontal spring of force constant 2.5 N/cm. The object is started oscillating by pulling it 6.0 cm from its equilibrium position and releasing it so that it is free to oscillate on a frictionless horizontal air track. You observe that after eight cycles its maximum displacement from equilibrium is only 3.5 cm. (a) How much energy has this system lost to damping during these eight cycles? (b) Where did the "lost" energy go? Explain physically how the system could have lost energy.

14.60 ·· A 50.0-g hard-boiled egg moves on the end of a spring with force constant $k = 25.0$ N/m. Its initial displacement is 0.300 m. A damping force $F_x = -bv_x$ acts on the egg, and the amplitude of the motion decreases to 0.100 m in 5.00 s. Calculate the magnitude of the damping constant b.

14.61 · An unhappy 0.300-kg rodent, moving on the end of a spring with force constant $k = 2.50$ N/m, is acted on by a damping force $F_x = -bv_x$. (a) If the constant b has the value 0.900 kg/s, what is the frequency of oscillation of the rodent? (b) For what value of the constant b will the motion be critically damped?

14.62 ·· A mass is vibrating at the end of a spring of force constant 225 N/m. **Figure E14.62** shows a graph of its position x as a function of time t. (a) At what times is the mass not moving? (b) How much energy did this system originally contain? (c) How much energy did the system lose between $t = 1.0$ s and $t = 4.0$ s? Where did this energy go?

Figure E14.62

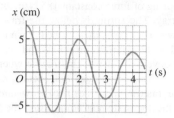

Section 14.8 Forced Oscillations and Resonance

14.63 · A sinusoidally varying driving force is applied to a damped harmonic oscillator of force constant k and mass m. If the damping constant has a value b_1, the amplitude is A_1 when the driving angular frequency equals $\sqrt{k/m}$. In terms of A_1, what is the amplitude for the same driving frequency and the same driving force amplitude F_{max}, if the damping constant is (a) $3b_1$ and (b) $b_1/2$?

PROBLEMS

14.64 ··· An object is undergoing SHM with period 0.300 s and amplitude 6.00 cm. At $t = 0$ the object is instantaneously at rest at $x = 6.00$ cm. Calculate the time it takes the object to go from $x = 6.00$ cm to $x = -1.50$ cm.

14.65 ·· An object is undergoing SHM with period 1.200 s and amplitude 0.600 m. At $t = 0$ the object is at $x = 0$ and is moving in the negative x-direction. How far is the object from the equilibrium position when $t = 0.480$ s?

14.66 · Four passengers with combined mass 250 kg compress the springs of a car with worn-out shock absorbers by 4.00 cm when they get in. Model the car and passengers as a single body on a single ideal spring. If the loaded car has a period of vibration of 1.92 s, what is the period of vibration of the empty car?

14.67 ·· At the end of a ride at a winter-theme amusement park, a sleigh with mass 250 kg (including two passengers) slides without friction along a horizontal, snow-covered surface. The sleigh hits one end of a light horizontal spring that obeys Hooke's law and has its other end attached to a wall. The sleigh latches onto the end of the spring and subsequently moves back and forth in SHM on the end of the spring until a braking mechanism is engaged, which brings the sleigh to rest. The frequency of the SHM is 0.225 Hz, and the amplitude is 0.950 m. (a) What was the speed of the sleigh just before it hit the end of the spring? (b) What is the maximum magnitude of the sleigh's acceleration during its SHM?

14.68 ·· CP A block with mass M rests on a frictionless surface and is connected to a horizontal spring of force constant k. The other end of the spring is attached to a wall (**Fig. P14.68**). A second block with mass m rests on top of the first block. The coefficient of static friction between the blocks is μ_s. Find the *maximum* amplitude of oscillation such that the top block will not slip on the bottom block.

Figure P14.68

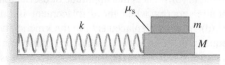

14.69 ••• A 1.50-kg, horizontal, uniform tray is attached to a vertical ideal spring of force constant 185 N/m and a 275-g metal ball is in the tray. The spring is below the tray, so it can oscillate up and down. The tray is then pushed down to point A, which is 15.0 cm below the equilibrium point, and released from rest. (a) How high above point A will the tray be when the metal ball leaves the tray? (*Hint:* This does *not* occur when the ball and tray reach their maximum speeds.) (b) How much time elapses between releasing the system at point A and the ball leaving the tray? (c) How fast is the ball moving just as it leaves the tray?

14.70 • CP A 10.0-kg mass is traveling to the right with a speed of 2.00 m/s on a smooth horizontal surface when it collides with and sticks to a second 10.0-kg mass that is initially at rest but is attached to a light spring with force constant 170.0 N/m. (a) Find the frequency, amplitude, and period of the subsequent oscillations. (b) How long does it take the system to return the first time to the position it had immediately after the collision?

14.71 ••• An apple weighs 1.00 N. When you hang it from the end of a long spring of force constant 1.50 N/m and negligible mass, it bounces up and down in SHM. If you stop the bouncing and let the apple swing from side to side through a small angle, the frequency of this simple pendulum is half the bounce frequency. (Because the angle is small, the back-and-forth swings do not cause any appreciable change in the length of the spring.) What is the unstretched length of the spring (with the apple removed)?

14.72 ••• CP **SHM of a Floating Object.** An object with height h, mass M, and a uniform cross-sectional area A floats upright in a liquid with density ρ. (a) Calculate the vertical distance from the surface of the liquid to the bottom of the floating object at equilibrium. (b) A downward force with magnitude F is applied to the top of the object. At the new equilibrium position, how much farther below the surface of the liquid is the bottom of the object than it was in part (a)? (Assume that some of the object remains above the surface of the liquid.) (c) Your result in part (b) shows that if the force is suddenly removed, the object will oscillate up and down in SHM. Calculate the period of this motion in terms of the density ρ of the liquid, the mass M, and the cross-sectional area A of the object. You can ignore the damping due to fluid friction (see Section 14.7).

14.73 •• CP A square object of mass m is constructed of four identical uniform thin sticks, each of length L, attached together. This object is hung on a hook at its upper corner (**Fig. P14.73**). If it is rotated slightly to the left and then released, at what frequency will it swing back and forth?

Figure **P14.73**

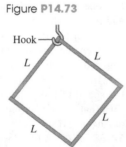

14.74 ••• An object with mass 0.200 kg is acted on by an elastic restoring force with force constant 10.0 N/m. (a) Graph elastic potential energy U as a function of displacement x over a range of x from -0.300 m to $+0.300$ m. On your graph, let 1 cm = 0.05 J vertically and 1 cm = 0.05 m horizontally. The object is set into oscillation with an initial potential energy of 0.140 J and an initial kinetic energy of 0.060 J. Answer the following questions by referring to the graph. (b) What is the amplitude of oscillation? (c) What is the potential energy when the displacement is one-half the amplitude? (d) At what displacement are the kinetic and potential energies equal? (e) What is the value of the phase angle ϕ if the initial velocity is positive and the initial displacement is negative?

14.75 • CALC A 2.00-kg bucket containing 10.0 kg of water is hanging from a vertical ideal spring of force constant 450 N/m and oscillating up and down with an amplitude of 3.00 cm. Suddenly the bucket springs a leak in the bottom such that water drops out at a steady rate of 2.00 g/s. When the bucket is half full, find (a) the period of oscillation and (b) the rate at which the period is changing with respect to time. Is the period getting longer or shorter? (c) What is the shortest period this system can have?

14.76 •• A uniform beam is suspended horizontally by two identical vertical springs that are attached between the ceiling and each end of the beam. The beam has mass 225 kg, and a 175-kg sack of gravel sits on the middle of it. The beam is oscillating in SHM with an amplitude of 40.0 cm and a frequency of 0.600 cycle/s. (a) The sack falls off the beam when the beam has its maximum upward displacement. What are the frequency and amplitude of the subsequent SHM of the beam? (b) If the sack instead falls off when the beam has its maximum speed, repeat part (a).

14.77 •• A 5.00-kg partridge is suspended from a pear tree by an ideal spring of negligible mass. When the partridge is pulled down 0.100 m below its equilibrium position and released, it vibrates with a period of 4.20 s. (a) What is its speed as it passes through the equilibrium position? (b) What is its acceleration when it is 0.050 m above the equilibrium position? (c) When it is moving upward, how much time is required for it to move from a point 0.050 m below its equilibrium position to a point 0.050 m above it? (d) The motion of the partridge is stopped, and then it is removed from the spring. How much does the spring shorten?

14.78 •• A 0.0200-kg bolt moves with SHM that has an amplitude of 0.240 m and a period of 1.500 s. The displacement of the bolt is $+0.240$ m when $t = 0$. Compute (a) the displacement of the bolt when $t = 0.500$ s; (b) the magnitude and direction of the force acting on the bolt when $t = 0.500$ s; (c) the minimum time required for the bolt to move from its initial position to the point where $x = -0.180$ m; (d) the speed of the bolt when $x = -0.180$ m.

14.79 •• CP **SHM of a Butcher's Scale.** A spring of negligible mass and force constant $k = 400$ N/m is hung vertically, and a 0.200-kg pan is suspended from its lower end. A butcher drops a 2.2-kg steak onto the pan from a height of 0.40 m. The steak makes a totally inelastic collision with the pan and sets the system into vertical SHM. What are (a) the speed of the pan and steak immediately after the collision; (b) the amplitude of the subsequent motion; (c) the period of that motion?

14.80 •• A 40.0-N force stretches a vertical spring 0.250 m. (a) What mass must be suspended from the spring so that the system will oscillate with a period of 1.00 s? (b) If the amplitude of the motion is 0.050 m and the period is that specified in part (a), where is the object and in what direction is it moving 0.35 s after it has passed the equilibrium position, moving downward? (c) What force (magnitude and direction) does the spring exert on the object when it is 0.030 m below the equilibrium position, moving upward?

14.81 •• **Don't Miss the Boat.** While on a visit to Minnesota ("Land of 10,000 Lakes"), you sign up to take an excursion around one of the larger lakes. When you go to the dock where the 1500-kg boat is tied, you find that the boat is bobbing up and down in the waves, executing simple harmonic motion with amplitude 20 cm. The boat takes 3.5 s to make one complete up-and-down cycle. When the boat is at its highest point, its deck is at the same height as the stationary dock. As you watch the boat bob up and down, you (mass 60 kg) begin to feel a bit woozy, due in part to the previous night's dinner of lutefisk. As a result, you refuse to board the boat unless the level of the boat's deck is within 10 cm of the dock level. How much time do you have to board the boat comfortably during each cycle of up-and-down motion?

14.82 • **CP** An interesting, though highly impractical example of oscillation is the motion of an object dropped down a hole that extends from one side of the earth, through its center, to the other side. With the assumption (not realistic) that the earth is a sphere of uniform density, prove that the motion is simple harmonic and find the period. [*Note:* The gravitational force on the object as a function of the object's distance r from the center of the earth was derived in Example 13.10 (Section 13.6). The motion is simple harmonic if the acceleration a_x and the displacement from equilibrium x are related by Eq. (14.8), and the period is then $T = 2\pi/\omega$.]

14.83 ••• **CP** A rifle bullet with mass 8.00 g and initial horizontal velocity 280 m/s strikes and embeds itself in a block with mass 0.992 kg that rests on a frictionless surface and is attached to one end of an ideal spring. The other end of the spring is attached to the wall. The impact compresses the spring a maximum distance of 15.0 cm. After the impact, the block moves in SHM. Calculate the period of this motion.

14.84 ••• **CP** Two uniform solid spheres, each with mass $M = 0.800$ kg and radius $R = 0.0800$ m, are connected by a short, light rod that is along a diameter of each sphere and are at rest on a horizontal tabletop. A spring with force constant $k = 160$ N/m has one end attached to the wall and the other end attached to a frictionless ring that passes over the rod at the center of mass of the spheres, which is midway between the centers of the two spheres. The spheres are each pulled the same distance from the wall, stretching the spring, and released. There is sufficient friction between the tabletop and the spheres for the spheres to roll without slipping as they move back and forth on the end of the spring. Show that the motion of the center of mass of the spheres is simple harmonic and calculate the period.

14.85 • **CP** In **Fig. P14.85** the upper ball is released from rest, collides with the stationary lower ball, and sticks to it. The strings are both 50.0 cm long. The upper ball has mass 2.00 kg, and it is initially 10.0 cm higher than the lower ball, which has mass 3.00 kg. Find the frequency and maximum angular displacement of the motion after the collision.

Figure **P14.85**

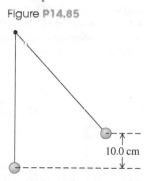

10.0 cm

14.86 •• **The Silently Ringing Bell.** A large, 34.0-kg bell is hung from a wooden beam so it can swing back and forth with negligible friction. The bell's center of mass is 0.60 m below the pivot. The bell's moment of inertia about an axis at the pivot is 18.0 kg · m^2. The clapper is a small, 1.8-kg mass attached to one end of a slender rod of length L and negligible mass. The other end of the rod is attached to the inside of the bell; the rod can swing freely about the same axis as the bell. What should be the length L of the clapper rod for the bell to ring silently—that is, for the period of oscillation for the bell to equal that of the clapper?

14.87 •• **CALC** A slender, uniform, metal rod with mass M is pivoted without friction about an axis through its midpoint and perpendicular to the rod. A horizontal spring with force constant k is attached to the lower end of the rod, with the other end

of the spring attached to a rigid support. If the rod is displaced by a small angle Θ from the vertical (**Fig. P14.87**) and released, show that it moves in angular SHM and calculate the period. (*Hint:* Assume that the angle Θ is small enough for the approximations $\sin\Theta \approx \Theta$ and $\cos\Theta \approx 1$ to be valid. The motion is simple harmonic if $d^2\theta/dt^2 = -\omega^2\theta$, and the period is then $T = 2\pi/\omega$.)

Figure **P14.87**

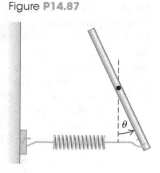

14.88 ••• Two identical thin rods, each with mass m and length L, are joined at right angles to form an L-shaped object. This object is balanced on top of a sharp edge (**Fig. P14.88**). If the L-shaped object is deflected slightly, it oscillates. Find the frequency of oscillation.

Figure **P14.88**

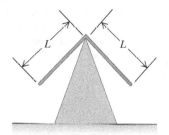

L L

14.89 •• **DATA** A mass m is attached to a spring of force constant 75 N/m and allowed to oscillate. **Figure P14.89** shows a graph of its velocity component v_x as a function of time t. Find (a) the period, (b) the frequency, and (c) the angular frequency of this motion. (d) What is the amplitude (in cm), and at what times does the mass reach this position? (e) Find the maximum acceleration magnitude of the mass and the times at which it occurs. (f) What is the value of m?

Figure **P14.89** v_x (cm/s)

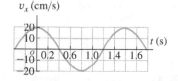

14.90 •• **DATA** You hang various masses m from the end of a vertical, 0.250-kg spring that obeys Hooke's law and is tapered, which means the diameter changes along the length of the spring. Since the mass of the spring is not negligible, you must replace m in the equation $T = 2\pi\sqrt{m/k}$ with $m + m_{\text{eff}}$, where m_{eff} is the effective mass of the oscillating spring. (See Challenge Problem 14.93.) You vary the mass m and measure the time for 10 complete oscillations, obtaining these data:

m (kg)	0.100	0.200	0.300	0.400	0.500
Time (s)	8.7	10.5	12.2	13.9	15.1

(a) Graph the square of the period T versus the mass suspended from the spring, and find the straight line of best fit. (b) From the slope of that line, determine the force constant of the spring. (c) From the vertical intercept of the line, determine the spring's effective mass. (d) What fraction is m_{eff} of the spring's mass? (e) If a 0.450-kg mass oscillates on the end of the spring, find its period, frequency, and angular frequency.

14.91 ••• **DATA** Experimenting with pendulums, you attach a light string to the ceiling and attach a small metal sphere to the lower end of the string. When you displace the sphere 2.00 m to the left, it nearly touches a vertical wall; with the string taut, you release the sphere from rest. The sphere swings back and forth as a simple pendulum, and you measure its period T. You repeat this act for strings of various lengths L, each time starting the motion with the sphere displaced 2.00 m to the left of the vertical position of the string. In each case the sphere's radius is very small compared with L. Your results are given in the table:

L (m)	12.00	10.00	8.00	6.00	5.00	4.00	3.00	2.50	2.30
T (s)	6.96	6.36	5.70	4.95	4.54	4.08	3.60	3.35	3.27

(a) For the five largest values of L, graph T^2 versus L. Explain why the data points fall close to a straight line. Does the slope of this line have the value you expected? (b) Add the remaining data to your graph. Explain why the data start to deviate from the straight-line fit as L decreases. To see this effect more clearly, plot T/T_0 versus L, where $T_0 = 2\pi\sqrt{L/g}$ and $g = 9.80 \text{ m/s}^2$. (c) Use your graph of T/T_0 versus L to estimate the angular amplitude of the pendulum (in degrees) for which the equation $T = 2\pi\sqrt{L/g}$ is in error by 5%.

CHALLENGE PROBLEMS

14.92 ••• **The Effective Force Constant of Two Springs.** Two springs with the same unstretched length but different force constants k_1 and k_2 are attached to a block with mass m on a level, frictionless surface. Calculate the effective force constant k_{eff} in each of the three cases (a), (b), and (c) depicted in **Fig. P14.92**. (The effective force constant is defined by $\Sigma F_x = -k_{eff}x$.) (d) An object with mass m, suspended from a uniform spring with a force constant k, vibrates with a frequency f_1. When the spring is cut in half and the same object is suspended from one of the halves, the frequency is f_2. What is the ratio f_1/f_2?

Figure **P14.92**

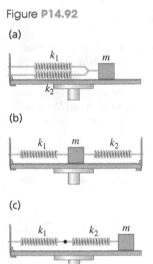

(a)

(b)

(c)

14.93 ••• **CALC A Spring with Mass.** The preceding problems in this chapter have assumed that the springs had negligible mass. But of course no spring is completely massless. To find the effect of the spring's mass, consider a spring with mass M, equilibrium length L_0, and spring constant k. When stretched or compressed to a length L, the potential energy is $\frac{1}{2}kx^2$, where $x = L - L_0$. (a) Consider a spring, as described above, that has one end fixed and the other end moving with speed v. Assume that the speed of points along the length of the spring varies linearly with distance l from the fixed end. Assume also that the mass M of the spring is distributed uniformly along the length of the spring. Calculate the kinetic energy of the spring in terms of M and v. (*Hint:* Divide the spring into pieces of length dl; find the speed of each piece in terms of l, v, and L; find the mass of each piece in terms of dl, M, and L; and integrate from 0 to L. The result is *not* $\frac{1}{2}Mv^2$, since not all of the spring moves with the same speed.) (b) Take the time derivative of the conservation of energy equation, Eq. (14.21), for a mass m moving on the end of a *massless* spring. By comparing your results to Eq. (14.8), which defines ω, show that the angular frequency of oscillation is $\omega = \sqrt{k/m}$. (c) Apply the procedure of part (b) to obtain the angular frequency of oscillation ω of the spring considered in part (a). If the *effective mass M'* of the spring is defined by $\omega = \sqrt{k/M'}$, what is M' in terms of M?

PASSAGE PROBLEMS

BIO "SEEING" SURFACES AT THE NANOSCALE. One technique for making images of surfaces at the nanometer scale, including membranes and biomolecules, is dynamic atomic force microscopy. In this technique, a small tip is attached to a cantilever, which is a flexible, rectangular slab supported at one end, like a diving board. The cantilever vibrates, so the tip moves up and down in simple harmonic motion. In one operating mode, the resonant frequency for a cantilever with force constant $k = 1000$ N/m is 100 kHz. As the oscillating tip is brought within a few nanometers of the surface of a sample (as shown in the figure), it experiences an attractive force from the surface. For an oscillation with a small amplitude (typically, 0.050 nm), the force F that the sample surface exerts on the tip varies linearly with the displacement x of the tip, $|F| = k_{surf}x$, where k_{surf} is the effective force constant for this force. The net force on the tip is therefore $(k + k_{surf})x$, and the frequency of the oscillation changes slightly due to the interaction with the surface. Measurements of the frequency as the tip moves over different parts of the sample's surface can provide information about the sample.

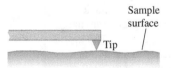

Sample surface
Tip

14.94 If we model the vibrating system as a mass on a spring, what is the mass necessary to achieve the desired resonant frequency when the tip is not interacting with the surface? (a) 25 ng; (b) 100 ng; (c) 2.5 μg; (d) 100 μg.

14.95 In the model of Problem 14.94, what is the mechanical energy of the vibration when the tip is not interacting with the surface? (a) 1.2×10^{-18} J; (b) 1.2×10^{-16} J; (c) 1.2×10^{-9} J; (d) 5.0×10^{-8} J.

14.96 By what percentage does the frequency of oscillation change if $k_{surf} = 5$ N/m? (a) 0.1%; (b) 0.2%; (c) 0.5%; (d) 1.0%.

Answers

Chapter Opening Question ?

(i) The back-and-forth motion of a leg during walking is like a physical pendulum, for which the oscillation period is $T = 2\pi\sqrt{I/mgd}$ [see Eq. (14.39)]. In this expression I is the moment of inertia of the pendulum, m is its mass, and d is the distance from the rotation axis to the pendulum center of mass. I is proportional to m, so the mass cancels out of this expression for T. Hence only the dimensions of the leg matter. (See Examples 14.9 and 14.10.)

Test Your Understanding Questions

14.1 **(a)** $x < 0$, **(b)** $x > 0$, **(c)** $x < 0$, **(d)** $x > 0$, **(e)** $x > 0$, **(f)** $x = 0$ Figure 14.2 shows that both the net x-component of force F_x and the x-acceleration a_x are positive when $x < 0$ (so the body is displaced to the left and the spring is compressed), while both F_x and a_x are negative when $x > 0$ (so the body is displaced to the right and the spring is stretched). Hence x and a_x always have *opposite* signs. This is true whether the object is moving to the right ($v_x > 0$), to the left ($v_x < 0$), or not at all ($v_x = 0$), since the force exerted by the spring depends on only whether it is compressed or stretched and by what distance. This explains the answers to (a) through (e). If the acceleration is zero as in (f), the net force must also be zero and so the spring must be relaxed; hence $x = 0$.

14.2 **(a)** $A > 0.10$ m, $\phi < 0$; **(b)** $A > 0.10$ m, $\phi > 0$ In both situations the initial ($t = 0$) x-velocity v_{0x} is nonzero, so from Eq. (14.19) the amplitude $A = \sqrt{x_0^2 + (v_{0x}^2/\omega^2)}$ is greater than the initial x-coordinate $x_0 = 0.10$ m. From Eq. (14.18) the phase angle is $\phi = \arctan(-v_{0x}/\omega x_0)$, which is positive if the quantity $-v_{0x}/\omega x_0$ (the argument of the arctangent function) is positive and negative if $-v_{0x}/\omega x_0$ is negative. In part (a) both x_0 and v_{0x} are positive, so $-v_{0x}/\omega x_0 < 0$ and $\phi < 0$. In part (b) x_0 is positive and v_{0x} is negative, so $-v_{0x}/\omega x_0 > 0$ and $\phi > 0$.

14.3 **(a) (iii)**, **(b) (v)**   To increase the total energy $E = \frac{1}{2}kA^2$ by a factor of 2, the amplitude A must increase by a factor of $\sqrt{2}$. Because the motion is SHM, changing the amplitude has no effect on the frequency.

14.4 **(i)**   The oscillation period of a body of mass m attached to a hanging spring of force constant k is given by $T = 2\pi\sqrt{m/k}$, the same expression as for a body attached to a horizontal spring. Neither m nor k changes when the apparatus is taken to Mars, so the period is unchanged. The only difference is that in equilibrium, the spring will stretch a shorter distance on Mars than on earth due to the weaker gravity.

14.5 **(iv)**   Just as for an object oscillating on a spring, at the equilibrium position the *speed* of a pendulum bob is instantaneously not changing (this is where the speed is maximum, so its derivative at this time is zero). But the *direction* of motion is changing because the pendulum bob follows a circular path. Hence the bob must have a component of acceleration perpendicular to the path and toward the center of the circle (see Section 3.4). To cause this acceleration at the equilibrium position when the string is vertical, the upward tension force at this position must be greater than the weight of the bob. This causes a net upward force on the bob and an upward acceleration toward the center of the circular path.

14.6 **(i)**   The period of a physical pendulum is given by Eq. (14.39), $T = 2\pi\sqrt{I/mgd}$. The distance $d = L$ from the pivot to the center of gravity is the same for both the rod and the simple pendulum, as is the mass m. Thus for any displacement angle θ the same restoring torque acts on both the rod and the simple pendulum. However, the rod has a greater moment of inertia: $I_{rod} = \frac{1}{3}m(2L)^2 = \frac{4}{3}mL^2$ and $I_{simple} = mL^2$ (all the mass of the pendulum is a distance L from the pivot). Hence the rod has a longer period.

14.7 **(ii)**   The oscillations are underdamped with a decreasing amplitude on each cycle of oscillation, like those graphed in Fig. 14.26. If the oscillations were undamped, they would continue indefinitely with the same amplitude. If they were critically damped or overdamped, the nose would not bob up and down but would return smoothly to the original equilibrium attitude without overshooting.

14.8 **(i)**   Figure 14.28 shows that the curve of amplitude versus driving frequency moves upward at *all* frequencies as the value of the damping constant b is decreased. Hence for fixed values of k and m, the oscillator with the least damping (smallest value of b) will have the greatest response at any driving frequency.

Bridging Problem

$T = 2\pi\sqrt{3M/2k}$

? When an earthquake strikes, the news of the event travels through the body of the earth in the form of seismic waves. Which aspects of a seismic wave determine how much power is carried by the wave: (i) the amplitude; (ii) the frequency; (iii) both the amplitude and the frequency; or (iv) neither the amplitude nor the frequency?

15 MECHANICAL WAVES

Ripples on a pond, musical sounds, seismic tremors triggered by an earthquake—all these are *wave* phenomena. Waves can occur whenever a system is disturbed from equilibrium and when the disturbance can travel, or *propagate*, from one region of the system to another. As a wave propagates, it carries energy. The energy in light waves from the sun warms the surface of our planet; the energy in seismic waves can crack our planet's crust.

This chapter and the next are about mechanical waves—waves that travel within some material called a *medium*. (Chapter 16 is concerned with sound, an important type of mechanical wave.) We'll begin this chapter by deriving the basic equations for describing waves, including the important special case of *sinusoidal* waves in which the wave pattern is a repeating sine or cosine function. To help us understand waves in general, we'll look at the simple case of waves that travel on a stretched string or rope.

Waves on a string are important in music. When a musician strums a guitar or bows a violin, she makes waves that travel in opposite directions along the instrument's strings. What happens when these oppositely directed waves overlap is called *interference*. We'll discover that sinusoidal waves can occur on a guitar or violin string only for certain special frequencies, called *normal-mode frequencies*, determined by the properties of the string. These normal-mode frequencies determine the pitch of the musical sounds that a stringed instrument produces. (In the next chapter we'll find that interference also helps explain the pitches of *wind* instruments such as pipe organs.)

Not all waves are mechanical in nature. *Electromagnetic* waves—including light, radio waves, infrared and ultraviolet radiation, and x rays—can propagate even in empty space, where there is *no* medium. We'll explore these and other nonmechanical waves in later chapters.

15.1 TYPES OF MECHANICAL WAVES

A **mechanical wave** is a disturbance that travels through some material or substance called the **medium** for the wave. As the wave travels through the medium, the particles that make up the medium undergo displacements of various kinds, depending on the nature of the wave.

15.1 Three ways to make a wave that moves to the right. **(a)** The hand moves the string up and then returns, producing a transverse wave. **(b)** The piston moves to the right, compressing the gas or liquid, and then returns, producing a longitudinal wave. **(c)** The board moves to the right and then returns, producing a combination of longitudinal and transverse waves.

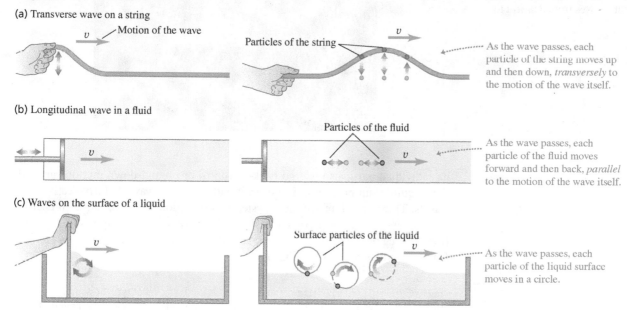

(a) Transverse wave on a string

As the wave passes, each particle of the string moves up and then down, *transversely* to the motion of the wave itself.

(b) Longitudinal wave in a fluid

As the wave passes, each particle of the fluid moves forward and then back, *parallel* to the motion of the wave itself.

(c) Waves on the surface of a liquid

As the wave passes, each particle of the liquid surface moves in a circle.

Figure 15.1 shows three varieties of mechanical waves. In Fig. 15.1a the medium is a string or rope under tension. If we give the left end a small upward shake or wiggle, the wiggle travels along the length of the string. Successive sections of string go through the same motion that we gave to the end, but at successively later times. Because the displacements of the medium are perpendicular or *transverse* to the direction of travel of the wave along the medium, this is called a **transverse wave.**

In Fig. 15.1b the medium is a liquid or gas in a tube with a rigid wall at the right end and a movable piston at the left end. If we give the piston a single back-and-forth motion, displacement and pressure fluctuations travel down the length of the medium. This time the motions of the particles of the medium are back and forth along the *same* direction that the wave travels. We call this a **longitudinal wave.**

In Fig. 15.1c the medium is a liquid in a channel, such as water in an irrigation ditch or canal. When we move the flat board at the left end forward and back once, a wave disturbance travels down the length of the channel. In this case the displacements of the water have *both* longitudinal and transverse components.

Each of these systems has an equilibrium state. For the stretched string it is the state in which the system is at rest, stretched out along a straight line. For the fluid in a tube it is a state in which the fluid is at rest with uniform pressure. And for the liquid in a trough it is a smooth, level water surface. In each case the wave motion is a disturbance from equilibrium that travels from one region of the medium to another. And in each case forces tend to restore the system to its equilibrium position when it is displaced, just as the force of gravity tends to pull a pendulum toward its straight-down equilibrium position when it is displaced.

These examples have three things in common. First, in each case the disturbance travels or *propagates* with a definite speed through the medium. This speed is called the speed of propagation, or simply the **wave speed.** Its value is determined in each case by the mechanical properties of the medium. We will use the symbol v for wave speed. (The wave speed is *not* the same as the speed with which particles move when they are disturbed by the wave. We'll return to this point in Section 15.3.) Second, the medium itself does not travel through space;

BIO **Application Waves on a Snake's Body** A snake moves itself along the ground by producing waves that travel backward along its body from its head to its tail. The waves remain stationary with respect to the ground as they push against the ground, so the snake moves forward.

15.2 "Doing the wave" at a sports stadium is an example of a mechanical wave: The disturbance propagates through the crowd, but there is no transport of matter (none of the spectators moves from one seat to another).

its individual particles undergo back-and-forth or up-and-down motions around their equilibrium positions. The overall pattern of the wave disturbance is what travels. Third, to set any of these systems into motion, we have to put in energy by doing mechanical work on the system. The wave motion transports this energy from one region of the medium to another. *Waves transport energy, but not matter, from one region to another* (**Fig. 15.2**).

TEST YOUR UNDERSTANDING OF SECTION 15.1 What type of wave is "the wave" shown in Fig. 15.2? (i) Transverse; (ii) longitudinal; (iii) a combination of transverse and longitudinal. ▮

15.2 PERIODIC WAVES

The transverse wave on a stretched string in Fig. 15.1a is an example of a *wave pulse.* The hand exerts a transverse force that shakes the string up and down just once, producing a single "wiggle," or pulse, that travels along the length of the string. The tension in the string restores its straight-line shape once the pulse has passed.

A more interesting situation develops when we give the free end of the string a repetitive, or *periodic,* motion. (You should review the discussion of periodic motion in Chapter 14 before going ahead.) Each particle in the string undergoes periodic motion as the wave propagates, and we have a **periodic wave.**

Periodic Transverse Waves

Suppose we move one end of the string up and down with *simple harmonic motion* (SHM) as in **Fig. 15.3**, with amplitude A, frequency f, angular frequency $\omega = 2\pi f$, and period $T = 1/f = 2\pi/\omega$. The wave that results is a symmetric sequence of *crests* and *troughs.* As we will see, periodic waves with SHM are

15.3 A block of mass m attached to a spring undergoes simple harmonic motion, producing a sinusoidal wave that travels to the right on the string. (In a real-life system a driving force would have to be applied to the block to replace the energy carried away by the wave.)

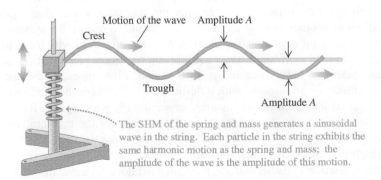

particularly easy to analyze; we call them **sinusoidal waves.** It turns out that *any* periodic wave can be represented as a combination of sinusoidal waves. So this kind of wave motion is worth special attention.

In Fig. 15.3 the wave is a *continuous succession* of transverse sinusoidal disturbances. **Figure 15.4** shows the shape of a part of the string near the left end at time intervals of $\frac{1}{8}$ of a period, for a total time of one period. The wave shape advances steadily toward the right, as indicated by the highlighted area. As the wave moves, any point on the string (any of the red dots, for example) oscillates up and down about its equilibrium position with simple harmonic motion. *When a sinusoidal wave passes through a medium, every particle in the medium undergoes simple harmonic motion with the same frequency.*

CAUTION **Wave motion vs. particle motion** Don't confuse the motion of the *transverse wave* along the string and the motion of a *particle* of the string. The wave moves with constant speed v *along* the length of the string, while the motion of the particle is simple harmonic and *transverse* (perpendicular) to the length of the string. ▌

For a periodic wave, the shape of the string at any instant is a repeating pattern. The **wavelength** λ (the Greek letter lambda) of the wave is the distance from one crest to the next, or from one trough to the next, or from any point to the corresponding point on the next repetition of the wave shape. The wave pattern travels with constant speed v and advances a distance of one wavelength λ in a time interval of one period T. So the wave speed is $v = \lambda/T$ or, because $f = 1/T$ from Eq. (14.1),

For a **periodic wave:**   Wave speed ⋯   ⋯Wavelength
$$v = \lambda f$$ ⋯Frequency   (15.1)

The speed of propagation equals the product of wavelength and frequency. The frequency is a property of the *entire* periodic wave because all points on the string oscillate with the same frequency f.

Waves on a string propagate in just one dimension (in Fig. 15.4, along the *x*-axis). But the ideas of frequency, wavelength, and amplitude apply equally well to waves that propagate in two or three dimensions. **Figure 15.5** shows a wave propagating in two dimensions on the surface of a tank of water. As with waves on a string, the wavelength is the distance from one crest to the next, and the amplitude is the height of a crest above the equilibrium level.

In many important situations including waves on a string, the wave speed v is determined entirely by the mechanical properties of the medium. In this case, increasing f causes λ to decrease so the product $v = \lambda f$ remains the same, and waves of *all* frequencies propagate with the same wave speed. In this chapter we will consider *only* waves of this kind. (In later chapters we'll study the propagation of light waves in transparent materials where the wave speed depends on frequency; this turns out to be the reason raindrops create a rainbow.)

15.4 A sinusoidal transverse wave traveling to the right along a string. The vertical scale is exaggerated.

The string is shown at time intervals of $\frac{1}{8}$ period for a total of one period T. The highlighting shows the motion of one wavelength of the wave.

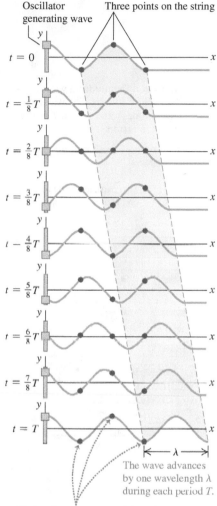

The wave advances by one wavelength λ during each period T.

Each point moves up and down in place. Particles one wavelength apart move in phase with each other.

15.5 A series of drops falling into water produces a periodic wave that spreads radially outward. The wave crests and troughs are concentric circles. The wavelength λ is the radial distance between adjacent crests or adjacent troughs.

15.6 Using an oscillating piston to make a sinusoidal longitudinal wave in a fluid.

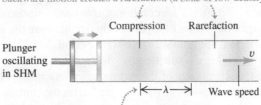

Forward motion of the plunger creates a compression (a zone of high density); backward motion creates a rarefaction (a zone of low density).

Wavelength λ is the distance between corresponding points on successive cycles.

15.7 A sinusoidal longitudinal wave traveling to the right in a fluid. The wave has the same amplitude A and period T as the oscillation of the piston.

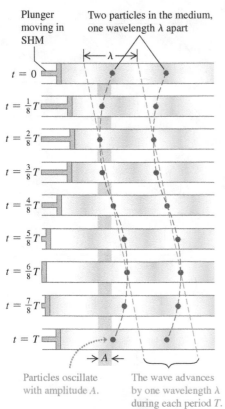

Longitudinal waves are shown at intervals of $\frac{1}{8}T$ for one period T.

Particles oscillate with amplitude A.

The wave advances by one wavelength λ during each period T.

Periodic Longitudinal Waves

To understand the mechanics of a periodic *longitudinal* wave, consider a long tube filled with a fluid, with a piston at the left end as in Fig. 15.1b. If we push the piston in, we compress the fluid near the piston, increasing the pressure in this region. This region then pushes against the neighboring region of fluid, and so on, and a wave pulse moves along the tube.

Now suppose we move the piston back and forth in SHM along a line parallel to the axis of the tube (**Fig. 15.6**). This motion forms regions in the fluid where the pressure and density are greater or less than the equilibrium values. We call a region of increased density a *compression;* a region of reduced density is a *rarefaction.* Figure 15.6 shows compressions as darkly shaded areas and rarefactions as lightly shaded areas. The wavelength is the distance from one compression to the next or from one rarefaction to the next.

Figure 15.7 shows the wave propagating in the fluid-filled tube at time intervals of $\frac{1}{8}$ of a period, for a total time of one period. The pattern of compressions and rarefactions moves steadily to the right, just like the pattern of crests and troughs in a sinusoidal transverse wave (compare Fig. 15.4). Each particle in the fluid oscillates in SHM parallel to the direction of wave propagation (that is, left and right) with the same amplitude A and period T as the piston. The particles shown by the two red dots in Fig. 15.7 are one wavelength apart, and so oscillate in phase with each other.

Just like the sinusoidal transverse wave shown in Fig. 15.4, in one period T the longitudinal wave in Fig. 15.7 travels one wavelength λ to the right. Hence the fundamental equation $v = \lambda f$ holds for longitudinal waves as well as for transverse waves, and indeed for *all* types of periodic waves. Just as for transverse waves, in this chapter and the next we will consider only situations in which the speed of longitudinal waves does not depend on the frequency.

EXAMPLE 15.1   WAVELENGTH OF A MUSICAL SOUND

Sound waves are longitudinal waves in air. The speed of sound depends on temperature; at 20°C it is 344 m/s (1130 ft/s). What is the wavelength of a sound wave in air at 20°C if the frequency is 262 Hz (the approximate frequency of middle C on a piano)?

SOLUTION

IDENTIFY and SET UP: This problem involves Eq. (15.1), $v = \lambda f$, which relates wave speed v, wavelength λ, and frequency f for a periodic wave. The target variable is the wavelength λ. We are given $v = 344$ m/s and $f = 262$ Hz $= 262$ s^{-1}.

EXECUTE: We solve Eq. (15.1) for λ:

$$\lambda = \frac{v}{f} = \frac{344 \text{ m/s}}{262 \text{ Hz}} = \frac{344 \text{ m/s}}{262 \text{ s}^{-1}} = 1.31 \text{ m}$$

EVALUATE: The speed v of sound waves does *not* depend on the frequency. Hence $\lambda = v/f$ says that wavelength changes in inverse proportion to frequency. As an example, high (soprano) C is two octaves above middle C. Each octave corresponds to a factor of 2 in frequency, so the frequency of high C is four times that of middle C: $f = 4(262 \text{ Hz}) = 1048$ Hz. Hence the *wavelength* of high C is *one-fourth* as large: $\lambda = (1.31 \text{ m})/4 = 0.328$ m.

If you double the wavelength of a wave on a particular string, what happens to the wave speed v and the frequency f? (i) v doubles and f is unchanged; (ii) v is unchanged and f doubles; (iii) v becomes one-half as great and f is unchanged; (iv) v is unchanged and f becomes one-half as great; (v) none of these. ▮

15.3 MATHEMATICAL DESCRIPTION OF A WAVE

Many characteristics of periodic waves can be described by using the concepts of wave speed, amplitude, period, frequency, and wavelength. Often, though, we need a more detailed description of the positions and motions of individual particles of the medium at particular times during wave propagation.

As a specific example, let's look at waves on a stretched string. If we ignore the sag of the string due to gravity, the equilibrium position of the string is along a straight line. We take this to be the x-axis of a coordinate system. Waves on a string are *transverse;* during wave motion a particle with equilibrium position x is displaced some distance y in the direction perpendicular to the x-axis. The value of y depends on which particle we are talking about (that is, y depends on x) and also on the time t when we look at it. Thus y is a *function* of both x and t; $y = y(x, t)$. We call $y(x, t)$ the **wave function** that describes the wave. If we know this function for a particular wave motion, we can use it to find the displacement (from equilibrium) of any particle at any time. From this we can find the velocity and acceleration of any particle, the shape of the string, and anything else we want to know about the behavior of the string at any time.

Wave Function for a Sinusoidal Wave

Let's see how to determine the form of the wave function for a sinusoidal wave. Suppose a sinusoidal wave travels from left to right (the direction of increasing x) along the string, as in **Fig. 15.8**. Every particle of the string oscillates in simple harmonic motion with the same amplitude and frequency. But the oscillations of particles at different points on the string are *not* all in step with each other. The particle at point B in Fig. 15.8 is at its maximum positive value of y at $t = 0$ and returns to $y = 0$ at $t = \frac{2}{8}T$; these same events occur for a particle at point A or point C at $t = \frac{4}{8}T$ and $t = \frac{6}{8}T$, exactly one half-period later. For any two particles of the string, the motion of the particle on the right (in terms of the wave, the "downstream" particle) lags behind the motion of the particle on the left by an amount proportional to the distance between the particles.

Hence the cyclic motions of various points on the string are out of step with each other by various fractions of a cycle. We call these differences *phase differences,* and we say that the *phase* of the motion is different for different points. For example, if one point has its maximum positive displacement at the same time that another has its maximum negative displacement, the two are a half-cycle out of phase. (This is the case for points A and B, or points B and C.)

Suppose that the displacement of a particle at the left end of the string ($x = 0$), where the wave originates, is given by

$$y(x = 0, t) = A\cos\omega t = A\cos 2\pi ft \qquad (15.2)$$

That is, the particle oscillates in SHM with amplitude A, frequency f, and angular frequency $\omega = 2\pi f$. The notation $y(x = 0, t)$ reminds us that the motion of this particle is a special case of the wave function $y(x, t)$ that describes the entire wave. At $t = 0$ the particle at $x = 0$ is at its maximum positive displacement ($y = A$) and is instantaneously at rest (because y is a maximum).

The wave disturbance travels from $x = 0$ to some point x to the right of the origin in an amount of time given by x/v, where v is the wave speed. So the motion of point x at time t is the same as the motion of point $x = 0$ at the earlier time $t - x/v$. Hence we can find the displacement of point x at time t

15.8 Tracking the oscillations of three points on a string as a sinusoidal wave propagates along it.

The string is shown at time intervals of $\frac{1}{8}$ period for a total of one period T.

by simply replacing t in Eq. (15.2) by $(t - x/v)$:

$$y(x, t) = A \cos \left[\omega \left(t - \frac{x}{v} \right) \right]$$

Because $\cos(-\theta) = \cos \theta$, we can rewrite the wave function as

Wave function for a sinusoidal wave propagating in +x-direction

Amplitude · · · Position · · · Time

$$y(x, t) = A \cos \left[\omega \left(\frac{x}{v} - t \right) \right] \qquad (15.3)$$

Angular frequency $= 2\pi f$ · · · Wave speed

The displacement $y(x, t)$ is a function of both the location x of the point and the time t. We could make Eq. (15.3) more general by allowing for different values of the phase angle, as we did for SHM in Section 14.2, but for now we omit this.

We can rewrite the wave function given by Eq. (15.3) in several different but useful forms. We can express it in terms of the period $T = 1/f$ and the wavelength $\lambda = v/f = 2\pi v/\omega$:

Wave function for a sinusoidal wave propagating in +x-direction

Amplitude · · Position · · Time

$$y(x, t) = A \cos \left[2\pi \left(\frac{x}{\lambda} - \frac{t}{T} \right) \right] \qquad (15.4)$$

Wavelength · · · · · Period

It's convenient to define a quantity k, called the **wave number**:

$$k = \frac{2\pi}{\lambda} \qquad \text{(wave number)} \qquad (15.5)$$

Substituting $\lambda = 2\pi/k$ and $f = \omega/2\pi$ into Eq. (15.1), $v = \lambda f$, gives

$$\omega = vk \qquad \text{(periodic wave)} \qquad (15.6)$$

We can then rewrite Eq. (15.4) as

Wave function for a sinusoidal wave propagating in +x-direction

Amplitude · · Position · · Time

$$y(x, t) = A \cos (kx - \omega t) \qquad (15.7)$$

Wave number $= 2\pi/\lambda$ · · · · Angular frequency $= 2\pi f$

Which of these various forms for the wave function $y(x, t)$ we use in any specific problem is a matter of convenience. Note that ω has units rad/s, so for unit consistency in Eqs. (15.6) and (15.7) the wave number k must have the units rad/m. (Warning: Some textbooks define the wave number as $1/\lambda$ rather than $2\pi/\lambda$.)

Graphing the Wave Function

Figure 15.9a graphs the wave function $y(x, t)$ as a function of x for a specific time t. This graph gives the displacement y of a particle from its equilibrium position as a function of the coordinate x of the particle. If the wave is a transverse wave on a string, the graph in Fig. 15.9a represents the shape of the string at that instant, like a flash photograph of the string. In particular, at time $t = 0$,

$$y(x, t = 0) = A \cos kx = A \cos 2\pi \frac{x}{\lambda}$$

Figure 15.9b is a graph of the wave function versus time t for a specific coordinate x. This graph gives the displacement y of the particle at x as a function of time; that is, it describes the motion of that particle. At position $x = 0$,

$$y(x = 0, t) = A \cos(-\omega t) = A \cos \omega t = A \cos 2\pi \frac{t}{T}$$

15.9 Two graphs of the wave function $y(x, t)$ in Eq. (15.7). **(a)** Graph of displacement y versus coordinate x at time $t = 0$. **(b)** Graph of displacement y versus time t at coordinate $x = 0$. The vertical scale is exaggerated in both (a) and (b).

(a) If we use Eq. (15.7) to plot y as a function of x for time $t = 0$, the curve shows the *shape* of the string at $t = 0$.

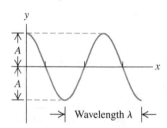

(b) If we use Eq. (15.7) to plot y as a function of t for position $x = 0$, the curve shows the *displacement y* of the particle at $x = 0$ as a function of time.

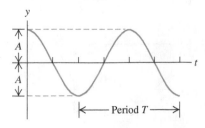

This is consistent with our original statement about the motion at $x = 0$, Eq. (15.2).

CAUTION **Wave graphs** Although they may look the same, Figs. 15.9a and 15.9b are *not* identical. Figure 15.9a is a picture of the shape of the string at $t = 0$, while Fig. 15.9b is a graph of the displacement y of a particle at $x = 0$ as a function of time. ▮

More on the Wave Function

We can modify Eqs. (15.3) through (15.7) to represent a wave traveling in the *negative x*-direction. In this case the displacement of point x at time t is the same as the motion of point $x = 0$ at the *later* time $(t + x/v)$, so in Eq. (15.2) we replace t by $(t + x/v)$. For a wave traveling in the negative x-direction,

$$y(x, t) = A \cos\left[\omega\left(\frac{x}{v} + t\right)\right] = A \cos\left[2\pi\left(\frac{x}{\lambda} + \frac{t}{T}\right)\right] = A \cos(kx + \omega t) \quad (15.8)$$

(sinusoidal wave moving in $-x$-direction)

In the expression $y(x, t) = A \cos(kx \pm \omega t)$ for a wave traveling in the $-x$- or $+x$-direction, the quantity $(kx \pm \omega t)$ is called the **phase.** It plays the role of an angular quantity (always measured in radians) in Eq. (15.7) or (15.8), and its value for any values of x and t determines what part of the sinusoidal cycle is occurring at a particular point and time. For a crest (where $y = A$ and the cosine function has the value 1), the phase could be 0, $\pm 2\pi$, $\pm 4\pi$, and so on; for a trough (where $y = -A$ and the cosine has the value -1), it could be $\pm\pi$, $\pm 3\pi$, $\pm 5\pi$, and so on.

The wave speed is the speed with which we have to move along with the wave to keep alongside a point of a given phase, such as a particular crest of a wave on a string. For a wave traveling in the $+x$-direction, that means $kx - \omega t =$ constant. Taking the derivative with respect to t, we find $k \, dx/dt = \omega$, or

$$\frac{dx}{dt} = \frac{\omega}{k}$$

Comparing this with Eq. (15.6), we see that dx/dt is equal to the speed v of the wave. Because of this relationship, v is sometimes called the *phase velocity* of the wave. (*Phase speed* would be a better term.)

PROBLEM-SOLVING STRATEGY 15.1 | **MECHANICAL WAVES**

IDENTIFY *the relevant concepts:* As always, identify the target variables; these may include mathematical *expressions* (for example, the wave function for a given situation). Note that wave problems fall into two categories. *Kinematics* problems, concerned with describing wave motion, involve wave speed v, wavelength λ (or wave number k), frequency f (or angular frequency ω), and amplitude A. They may also involve the position, velocity, and acceleration of individual particles in the medium. *Dynamics* problems also use concepts from Newton's laws. Later in this chapter we'll encounter problems that involve the relationship of wave speed to the mechanical properties of the medium.

SET UP *the problem* using the following steps:
1. List the given quantities. Sketch graphs of y versus x (like Fig. 15.9a) and of y versus t (like Fig. 15.9b), and label them with known values.
2. Identify useful equations. These may include Eq. (15.1) ($v = \lambda f$), Eq. (15.6) ($\omega = vk$), and Eqs. (15.3), (15.4), and

(15.7), which express the wave function in various forms. From the wave function, you can find the value of y at any point (value of x) and at any time t.
3. If you need to determine the wave speed v and don't know both λ and f, you may be able to use a relationship between v and the mechanical properties of the system. (In the next section we'll develop this relationship for waves on a string.)

EXECUTE *the solution:* Solve for the unknown quantities using the equations you've identified. To determine the wave function from Eq. (15.3), (15.4), or (15.7), you must know A and any two of v, λ, and f (or v, k, and ω).

EVALUATE *your answer:* Confirm that the values of v, f, and λ (or v, ω, and k) agree with the relationships given in Eq. (15.1) or (15.6). If you've calculated the wave function, check one or more special cases for which you can predict the results.

EXAMPLE 15.2   WAVE ON A CLOTHESLINE

Cousin Throckmorton holds one end of the clothesline taut and wiggles it up and down sinusoidally with frequency 2.00 Hz and amplitude 0.075 m. The wave speed on the clothesline is $v = 12.0$ m/s. At $t = 0$ Throcky's end has maximum positive displacement and is instantaneously at rest. Assume that no wave bounces back from the far end. (a) Find the wave amplitude A, angular frequency ω, period T, wavelength λ, and wave number k. (b) Write a wave function describing the wave. (c) Write equations for the displacement, as a function of time, of Throcky's end of the clothesline and of a point 3.00 m from that end.

SOLUTION

IDENTIFY and SET UP: This is a kinematics problem about the clothesline's wave motion. Throcky produces a sinusoidal wave that propagates along the clothesline, so we can use all of the expressions of this section. In part (a) our target variables are A, ω, T, λ, and k. We use the relationships $\omega = 2\pi f$, $f = 1/T$, $v = \lambda f$, and $k = 2\pi/\lambda$. In parts (b) and (c) our target "variables" are expressions for displacement, which we'll obtain from an appropriate equation for the wave function. We take the positive x-direction to be the direction in which the wave propagates, so either Eq. (15.4) or (15.7) will yield the desired expression. A photograph of the clothesline at time $t = 0$ would look like Fig. 15.9a, with the maximum displacement at $x = 0$ (the end that Throcky holds).

EXECUTE: (a) The wave amplitude and frequency are the same as for the oscillations of Throcky's end of the clothesline, $A = 0.075$ m and $f = 2.00$ Hz. Hence

$$\omega = 2\pi f = \left(2\pi \frac{\text{rad}}{\text{cycle}}\right)\left(2.00 \frac{\text{cycles}}{\text{s}}\right)$$

$$= 4.00\pi \text{ rad/s} = 12.6 \text{ rad/s}$$

The period is $T = 1/f = 0.500$ s, and from Eq. (15.1),

$$\lambda = \frac{v}{f} = \frac{12.0 \text{ m/s}}{2.00 \text{ s}^{-1}} = 6.00 \text{ m}$$

We find the wave number from Eq. (15.5) or (15.6):

$$k = \frac{2\pi}{\lambda} = \frac{2\pi \text{ rad}}{6.00 \text{ m}} = 1.05 \text{ rad/m}$$

or

$$k = \frac{\omega}{v} = \frac{4.00\pi \text{ rad/s}}{12.0 \text{ m/s}} = 1.05 \text{ rad/m}$$

(b) We write the wave function using Eq. (15.4) and the values of A, T, and λ from part (a):

$$y(x, t) = A\cos 2\pi\left(\frac{x}{\lambda} - \frac{t}{T}\right)$$

$$= (0.075 \text{ m})\cos 2\pi\left(\frac{x}{6.00 \text{ m}} - \frac{t}{0.500 \text{ s}}\right)$$

$$= (0.075 \text{ m})\cos[(1.05 \text{ rad/m})x - (12.6 \text{ rad/s})t]$$

We can also get this same expression from Eq. (15.7) by using the values of ω and k from part (a).

(c) We can find the displacement as a function of time at $x = 0$ and $x = +3.00$ m by substituting these values into the wave function from part (b):

$$y(x = 0, t) = (0.075 \text{ m})\cos 2\pi\left(\frac{0}{6.00 \text{ m}} - \frac{t}{0.500 \text{ s}}\right)$$

$$= (0.075 \text{ m})\cos(12.6 \text{ rad/s})t$$

$$y(x = +3.00 \text{ m}, t) = (0.075 \text{ m})\cos 2\pi\left(\frac{3.00 \text{ m}}{6.00 \text{ m}} - \frac{t}{0.500 \text{ s}}\right)$$

$$= (0.075 \text{ m})\cos[\pi - (12.6 \text{ rad/s})t]$$

$$= -(0.075 \text{ m})\cos(12.6 \text{ rad/s})t$$

EVALUATE: In part (b), the quantity $(1.05 \text{ rad/m})x - (12.6 \text{ rad/s})t$ is the *phase* of a point x on the string at time t. The two points in part (c) oscillate in SHM with the same frequency and amplitude, but their oscillations differ in phase by $(1.05 \text{ rad/m})(3.00 \text{ m}) = 3.15 \text{ rad} = \pi$ radians—that is, one half-cycle—because the points are separated by one half-wavelength: $\lambda/2 = (6.00 \text{ m})/2 = 3.00$ m. Thus, while a graph of y versus t for the point at $x = 0$ is a cosine curve (like Fig. 15.9b), a graph of y versus t for the point $x = 3.00$ m is a *negative* cosine curve (the same as a cosine curve shifted by one half-cycle).

Using the expression for $y(x = 0, t)$ in part (c), can you show that the end of the string at $x = 0$ is instantaneously at rest at $t = 0$, as stated at the beginning of this example? (*Hint:* Calculate the y-velocity at this point by taking the derivative of y with respect to t.)

Particle Velocity and Acceleration in a Sinusoidal Wave

From the wave function we can get an expression for the transverse velocity of any *particle* in a transverse wave. We call this v_y to distinguish it from the wave propagation speed v. To find the transverse velocity v_y at a particular point x, we take the derivative of the wave function $y(x, t)$ with respect to t, keeping x constant. If the wave function is

$$y(x, t) = A\cos(kx - \omega t)$$

then

$$v_y(x, t) = \frac{\partial y(x, t)}{\partial t} = \omega A\sin(kx - \omega t) \tag{15.9}$$

The ∂ in this expression is a modified d, used to remind us that $y(x, t)$ is a function of *two* variables and that we are allowing only one (t) to vary. The other (x) is constant because we are looking at a particular point on the string. This derivative is called a *partial derivative*. If you haven't yet encountered partial derivatives in your study of calculus, don't fret; it's a simple idea.

Equation (15.9) shows that the transverse velocity of a particle varies with time, as we expect for simple harmonic motion. The maximum particle speed is ωA; this can be greater than, less than, or equal to the wave speed v, depending on the amplitude and frequency of the wave.

The *acceleration* of any particle is the *second* partial derivative of $y(x, t)$ with respect to t:

$$a_y(x, t) = \frac{\partial^2 y(x, t)}{\partial t^2} = -\omega^2 A \cos(kx - \omega t)$$

$$= -\omega^2 y(x, t)$$

(15.10)

The acceleration of a particle equals $-\omega^2$ times its displacement, which is the result we obtained in Section 14.2 for simple harmonic motion.

We can also compute partial derivatives of $y(x, t)$ with respect to x, holding t constant. The first partial derivative $\partial y(x, t)/\partial x$ is the *slope* of the string at point x and at time t. The second partial derivative with respect to x tells us the *curvature* of the string:

$$\frac{\partial^2 y(x, t)}{\partial x^2} = -k^2 A \cos(kx - \omega t) = -k^2 y(x, t)$$

(15.11)

From Eqs. (15.10) and (15.11) and the relationship $\omega = vk$ we see that

$$\frac{\partial^2 y(x, t)/\partial t^2}{\partial^2 y(x, t)/\partial x^2} = \frac{\omega^2}{k^2} = v^2 \qquad \text{and}$$

Wave equation involves second partial derivatives of wave function:

Second derivative with respect to x

$$\frac{\partial^2 y(x, t)}{\partial x^2} = \frac{1}{v^2} \frac{\partial^2 y(x, t)}{\partial t^2}$$

Second derivative with respect to t

Wave speed

(15.12)

We've derived Eq. (15.12) for a wave traveling in the positive x-direction. You can show that the wave function for a sinusoidal wave propagating in the *negative* x-direction, $y(x, t) = A \cos(kx + \omega t)$, also satisfies this equation.

Equation (15.12), called the **wave equation,** is one of the most important equations in all of physics. Whenever it occurs, we know that a disturbance can propagate as a wave along the x-axis with wave speed v. The disturbance need not be a sinusoidal wave; we'll see in the next section that *any* wave on a string obeys Eq. (15.12), whether the wave is periodic or not. In Chapter 32 we will find that electric and magnetic fields satisfy the wave equation; the wave speed will turn out to be the speed of light, which will lead us to the conclusion that light is an electromagnetic wave.

Figure 15.10a (next page) shows the transverse velocity v_y and transverse acceleration a_y, given by Eqs. (15.9) and (15.10), for several points on a string as a sinusoidal wave passes along it. At points where the string has an upward curvature ($\partial^2 y/\partial x^2 > 0$), the acceleration is positive ($a_y = \partial^2 y/\partial t^2 > 0$); this follows from the wave equation, Eq. (15.12). For the same reason the acceleration is negative ($a_y = \partial^2 y/\partial t^2 < 0$) at points where the string has a downward curvature ($\partial^2 y/\partial x^2 < 0$), and the acceleration is zero ($a_y = \partial^2 y/\partial t^2 = 0$) at points of inflection where the curvature is zero ($\partial^2 y/\partial x^2 = 0$). Remember that v_y and a_y

15.10 (a) Another view of the wave at $t = 0$ in Fig. 15.9a. The vectors show the transverse velocity v_y and transverse acceleration a_y at several points on the string. (b) From $t = 0$ to $t = 0.05T$, a particle at point 1 is displaced to point 1′, a particle at point 2 is displaced to point 2′, and so on.

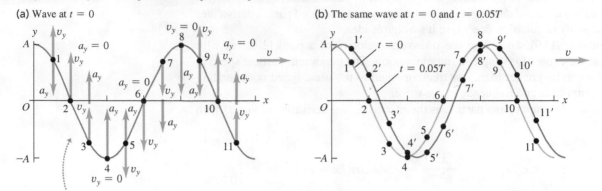

(a) Wave at $t = 0$

(b) The same wave at $t = 0$ and $t = 0.05T$

• Acceleration a_y at each point on the string is proportional to displacement y at that point.
• Acceleration is upward where string curves upward, downward where string curves downward.

are the *transverse* velocity and acceleration of points on the string; these points move along the y-direction, not along the propagation direction of the wave. Figure 15.10b shows these motions for several points on the string.

For *longitudinal* waves, the wave function $y(x, t)$ still measures the displacement of a particle of the medium from its equilibrium position. The difference is that for a longitudinal wave, this displacement is *parallel* to the x-axis instead of perpendicular to it. We'll discuss longitudinal waves in detail in Chapter 16.

TEST YOUR UNDERSTANDING OF SECTION 15.3 Figure 15.8 shows a sinusoidal wave of period T on a string at times $0, \frac{1}{8}T, \frac{2}{8}T, \frac{3}{8}T, \frac{4}{8}T, \frac{5}{8}T, \frac{6}{8}T, \frac{7}{8}T$, and T. (a) At which time is point A on the string moving upward with maximum speed? (b) At which time does point B on the string have the greatest upward acceleration? (c) At which time does point C on the string have a downward acceleration and a downward velocity? ∎

15.4 SPEED OF A TRANSVERSE WAVE

One of the key properties of any wave is the wave *speed*. Light waves in air have a much greater speed of propagation than do sound waves in air $(3.00 \times 10^8 \text{ m/s}$ versus $344 \text{ m/s})$; that's why you see the flash from a bolt of lightning before you hear the clap of thunder. In this section we'll see what determines the speed of propagation of one particular kind of wave: transverse waves on a string. The speed of these waves is important to understand because it is an essential part of analyzing stringed musical instruments, as we'll discuss later in this chapter. Furthermore, the speeds of many kinds of mechanical waves turn out to have the same basic mathematical expression as does the speed of waves on a string.

What determines the speed of transverse waves on a string are the *tension* in the string and its *mass per unit length* (also called *linear mass density*). Increasing the tension also increases the restoring forces that tend to straighten the string when it is disturbed, thus increasing the wave speed. Increasing the mass per unit length makes the motion more sluggish, and so decreases the wave speed. We'll develop the exact relationship among wave speed, tension, and mass per unit length by two different methods. The first is simple in concept and considers a specific wave shape; the second is more general but also more formal.

Wave Speed on a String: First Method

We consider a perfectly flexible string (**Fig. 15.11**). In the equilibrium position the tension is F and the linear mass density (mass per unit length) is μ. (When portions of the string are displaced from equilibrium, the mass per unit length

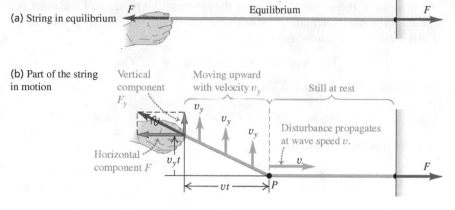

decreases a little, and the tension increases a little.) We ignore the weight of the string so that when the string is at rest in the equilibrium position, the string forms a perfectly straight line as in Fig. 15.11a.

Starting at time $t = 0$, we apply a constant upward force F_y at the left end of the string. We might expect that the end would move with constant acceleration; that would happen if the force were applied to a *point* mass. But here the effect of the force F_y is to set successively more and more mass in motion. The wave travels with constant speed v, so the division point P between moving and non-moving portions moves with the same constant speed v (Fig. 15.11b).

Figure 15.11b shows that all particles in the moving portion of the string move upward with constant *velocity* v_y, not constant acceleration. To see why this is so, we note that the *impulse* of the force F_y up to time t is $F_y t$. According to the impulse–momentum theorem (see Section 8.1), the impulse is equal to the change in the total transverse component of momentum of the moving part of the string. Because the system started with *zero* transverse momentum, this is equal to the total transverse momentum mv_y at time t:

$$\text{Transverse impulse} = \text{Transverse momentum}$$
$$F_y t = mv_y \tag{15.13}$$

The total momentum thus must increase proportionately with time. But since the division point P moves with constant speed, the length of string that is in motion and hence the total mass m in motion are also proportional to the time t that the force has been acting. So the *change* of momentum must be associated entirely with the increasing amount of mass in motion, not with an increasing velocity of an individual mass element. That is, mv_y changes because m, not v_y, changes.

At time t, the left end of the string has moved up a distance $v_y t$, and the boundary point P has advanced a distance vt. The total force at the left end of the string has components F and F_y. Why F? There is no motion in the direction along the length of the string, so there is no unbalanced horizontal force. Therefore F, the magnitude of the horizontal component, does not change when the string is displaced. In the displaced position the tension is $(F^2 + F_y^2)^{1/2}$; this is greater than F, so the string stretches somewhat.

To derive an expression for the wave speed v, we note that in Fig. 15.11b the right triangle whose vertex is at P, with sides $v_y t$ and vt, is similar to the right triangle whose vertex is at the position of the hand, with sides F_y and F. Hence

$$\frac{F_y}{F} = \frac{v_y t}{vt} \qquad F_y = F\frac{v_y}{v}$$

and

$$\text{Transverse impulse} = F_y t = F\frac{v_y}{v}t$$

15.12 These transmission cables have a relatively large amount of mass per unit length (μ) and a low tension (F). If the cables are disturbed—say, by a bird landing on them—transverse waves will travel along them at a slow speed $v = \sqrt{F/\mu}$.

The mass m of the moving portion of the string is the product of the mass per unit length μ and the length vt, or μvt. The transverse momentum is the product of this mass and the transverse velocity v_y:

$$\text{Transverse momentum} = mv_y = (\mu vt)v_y$$

Substituting these into Eq. (15.13), we obtain

$$F\frac{v_y}{v}t = \mu vtv_y$$

We solve this for the wave speed v:

Speed of a transverse wave on a string $\quad v = \sqrt{\dfrac{F}{\mu}} \quad$ Tension in string / Mass per unit length $\qquad$ (15.14)

Equation (15.14) confirms that the wave speed v increases when the tension F increases but decreases when the mass per unit length μ increases (**Fig. 15.12**).

Note that v_y does not appear in Eq. (15.14); thus the wave speed doesn't depend on v_y. Our calculation considered only a very special kind of pulse, but we can consider *any* shape of wave disturbance as a series of pulses with different values of v_y. So even though we derived Eq. (15.14) for a special case, it is valid for *any* transverse wave motion on a string, including the sinusoidal and other periodic waves we discussed in Section 15.3. Note also that the wave speed doesn't depend on the amplitude or frequency of the wave, in accordance with our assumptions in Section 15.3.

Wave Speed on a String: Second Method

Here is an alternative derivation of Eq. (15.14). If you aren't comfortable with partial derivatives, it can be omitted. We apply Newton's second law, $\sum \vec{F} = m\vec{a}$, to a small segment of string whose length in the equilibrium position is Δx (**Fig. 15.13**). The mass of the segment is $m = \mu \, \Delta x$. The x-components of the forces have equal magnitude F and add to zero because the motion is transverse and there is no component of acceleration in the x-direction. To obtain F_{1y} and F_{2y}, we note that the ratio F_{1y}/F is equal in magnitude to the *slope* of the string at point x and that F_{2y}/F is equal to the slope at point $x + \Delta x$. Taking proper account of signs, we find

15.13 Free-body diagram for a segment of string. The force at each end of the string is tangent to the string at the point of application.

The string to the right of the segment (not shown) exerts a force $\vec{F}_2$ on the segment.

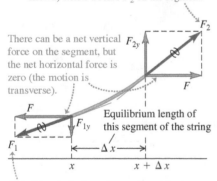

There can be a net vertical force on the segment, but the net horizontal force is zero (the motion is transverse).

Equilibrium length of this segment of the string

The string to the left of the segment (not shown) exerts a force $\vec{F}_1$ on the segment.

$$\frac{F_{1y}}{F} = -\left(\frac{\partial y}{\partial x}\right)_x \qquad \frac{F_{2y}}{F} = \left(\frac{\partial y}{\partial x}\right)_{x+\Delta x} \qquad (15.15)$$

The notation reminds us that the derivatives are evaluated at points x and $x + \Delta x$, respectively. From Eq. (15.15) we find that the net y-component of force is

$$F_y = F_{1y} + F_{2y} = F\left[\left(\frac{\partial y}{\partial x}\right)_{x+\Delta x} - \left(\frac{\partial y}{\partial x}\right)_x\right] \qquad (15.16)$$

We now equate F_y from Eq. (15.16) to the mass $\mu \, \Delta x$ times the y-component of acceleration $\partial^2 y / \partial t^2$:

$$F\left[\left(\frac{\partial y}{\partial x}\right)_{x+\Delta x} - \left(\frac{\partial y}{\partial x}\right)_x\right] = \mu \, \Delta x \frac{\partial^2 y}{\partial t^2} \qquad (15.17)$$

or, dividing Eq. (15.17) by $F\Delta x$,

$$\frac{\left(\frac{\partial y}{\partial x}\right)_{x+\Delta x} - \left(\frac{\partial y}{\partial x}\right)_x}{\Delta x} = \frac{\mu}{F}\frac{\partial^2 y}{\partial t^2} \qquad (15.18)$$

We now take the limit as $\Delta x \to 0$. In this limit, the left side of Eq. (15.18) becomes the derivative of $\partial y / \partial x$ with respect to x (at constant t)—that is, the *second* (partial) derivative of y with respect to x:

$$\frac{\partial^2 y}{\partial x^2} = \frac{\mu}{F}\frac{\partial^2 y}{\partial t^2} \qquad (15.19)$$

Now, Eq. (15.19) has exactly the same form as the *wave equation,* Eq. (15.12), that we derived at the end of Section 15.3. That equation and Eq. (15.19) describe the very same wave motion, so they must be identical. Comparing the two equations, we see that for this to be so, we must have

$$v = \sqrt{\frac{F}{\mu}}$$

which is the same expression as Eq. (15.14).

In going through this derivation, we didn't make any special assumptions about the shape of the wave. Since our derivation led us to rediscover Eq. (15.12), the wave equation, we conclude that the wave equation is valid for waves on a string that have *any* shape.

The Speed of Mechanical Waves

Equation (15.14) gives the wave speed for only the special case of mechanical waves on a stretched string or rope. Remarkably, it turns out that for many types of mechanical waves, including waves on a string, the expression for wave speed has the same general form:

$$v = \sqrt{\frac{\text{Restoring force returning the system to equilibrium}}{\text{Inertia resisting the return to equilibrium}}}$$

To interpret this expression, let's look at the now-familiar case of waves on a string. The tension F in the string plays the role of the restoring force; it tends to bring the string back to its undisturbed, equilibrium configuration. The mass of the string—or, more properly, the linear mass density μ—provides the inertia that prevents the string from returning instantaneously to equilibrium. Hence we have $v = \sqrt{F/\mu}$ for the speed of waves on a string.

In Chapter 16 we'll see a similar expression for the speed of sound waves in a gas. Roughly speaking, the gas pressure provides the force that tends to return the gas to its undisturbed state when a sound wave passes through. The inertia is provided by the density, or mass per unit volume, of the gas.

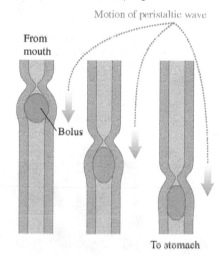

BIO Application Eating and Transverse Waves Swallowing food causes peristalsis, in which a transverse wave propagates down your esophagus. The wave is a radial contraction of the esophagus that pushes the bolus (the mass of swallowed food) toward the stomach. Unlike the speed of waves on a uniform string, the speed of this peristaltic wave is not constant: It averages about 3 cm/s in the upper esophagus, about 5 cm/s in the mid-esophagus, and about 2.5 cm/s in the lower esophagus.

EXAMPLE 15.3   **CALCULATING WAVE SPEED**

One end of a 2.00-kg rope is tied to a support at the top of a mine shaft 80.0 m deep (**Fig. 15.14**). The rope is stretched taut by a 20.0-kg box of rocks attached at the bottom. (a) A geologist at the bottom of the shaft signals to a colleague at the top by jerking the rope sideways. What is the speed of a transverse wave on the rope? (b) If a point on the rope is in transverse SHM with $f = 2.00$ Hz, how many cycles of the wave are there in the rope's length?

15.14 Using transverse waves to send signals along a vertical rope.

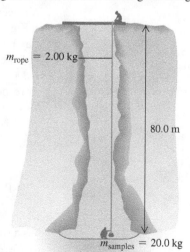

SOLUTION

IDENTIFY and SET UP: In part (a) we can find the wave speed (our target variable) by using the *dynamic* relationship $v = \sqrt{F/\mu}$ [Eq. (15.14)]. In part (b) we find the wavelength from the *kinematic* relationship $v = f\lambda$; from that we can find the target variable, the number of wavelengths that fit into the rope's 80.0-m length. We'll assume that the rope is massless (even though its weight is 10% that of the box), so that the box alone provides the tension in the rope.

Continued

EXECUTE: (a) The tension in the rope due to the box is

$$F = m_{box}g = (20.0 \text{ kg})(9.80 \text{ m/s}^2) = 196 \text{ N}$$

and the rope's linear mass density is

$$\mu = \frac{m_{rope}}{L} = \frac{2.00 \text{ kg}}{80.0 \text{ m}} = 0.0250 \text{ kg/m}$$

Hence, from Eq. (15.14), the wave speed is

$$v = \sqrt{\frac{F}{\mu}} = \sqrt{\frac{196 \text{ N}}{0.0250 \text{ kg/m}}} = 88.5 \text{ m/s}$$

(b) From Eq. (15.1), the wavelength is

$$\lambda = \frac{v}{f} = \frac{88.5 \text{ m/s}}{2.00 \text{ s}^{-1}} = 44.3 \text{ m}$$

There are $(80.0 \text{ m})/(44.3 \text{ m}) = 1.81$ wavelengths (that is, cycles of the wave) in the rope.

EVALUATE: Because of the rope's weight, its tension is greater at the top than at the bottom. Hence both the wave speed and the wavelength increase as a wave travels up the rope. If you take account of this, can you verify that the wave speed at the top of the rope is 92.9 m/s?

TEST YOUR UNDERSTANDING OF SECTION 15.4   The six strings of a guitar are the same length and under nearly the same tension, but they have different thicknesses. On which string do waves travel the fastest? (i) The thickest string; (ii) the thinnest string; (iii) the wave speed is the same on all strings. ∎

15.5 ENERGY IN WAVE MOTION

Every wave motion has *energy* associated with it. The energy we receive from sunlight and the destructive effects of ocean surf and earthquakes bear this out. To produce any of the wave motions we have discussed in this chapter, we have to apply a force to a portion of the wave medium; the point where the force is applied moves, so we do *work* on the system. As the wave propagates, each portion of the medium exerts a force and does work on the adjoining portion. In this way a wave can transport energy from one region of space to another.

As an example, let's look again at transverse waves on a string. How is energy transferred from one portion of the string to another? Picture a wave traveling from left to right (the positive x-direction) past a point a on the string (**Fig. 15.15a**). The string to the left of point a exerts a force on the string to the right of it, and vice versa. In Fig. 15.15b we show the components F_x and F_y of the force that the string to the left of a exerts on the string to the right of a. As in Figs. 15.11 and 15.13, the magnitude of the horizontal component F_x equals the tension F in the undisturbed string. Note that F_y/F is equal to the negative of the *slope* of the string at a, and this slope is also given by $\partial y/\partial x$. Putting these together, we have

$$F_y(x, t) = -F\frac{\partial y(x, t)}{\partial x} \tag{15.20}$$

We need the negative sign because F_y is negative when the slope is positive (as in Fig. 15.15b). We write the vertical force as $F_y(x, t)$ as a reminder that its value may be different at different points along the string and at different times.

When point a moves in the y-direction, the force F_y does *work* on this point and therefore transfers energy into the part of the string to the right of a. The corresponding power P (rate of doing work) at the point a is the transverse force $F_y(x, t)$ at a times the transverse velocity $v_y(x, t) = \partial y(x, t)/\partial t$ of that point:

$$P(x, t) = F_y(x, t)v_y(x, t) = -F\frac{\partial y(x, t)}{\partial x}\frac{\partial y(x, t)}{\partial t} \tag{15.21}$$

This power is the *instantaneous* rate at which energy is transferred along the string at position x and time t. Note that energy is transferred only at points where the string has a nonzero slope ($\partial y/\partial x$ is nonzero), so that the tension force has a transverse component, and where the string has a nonzero transverse velocity ($\partial y/\partial t$ is nonzero) so that the transverse force can do work.

BIO Application Surface Waves and the Swimming Speed of Ducks
When a duck swims, it necessarily produces waves on the surface of the water. The faster the duck swims, the larger the wave amplitude and the more power the duck must supply to produce these waves. The maximum power available from their leg muscles limits the maximum swimming speed of ducks to only about 0.7 m/s (2.5 km/h = 1.6 mi/h).

15.15 (a) Point a on a string carrying a wave from left to right. (b) The components of the force exerted on the part of the string to the right of point a by the part of the string to the left of point a.

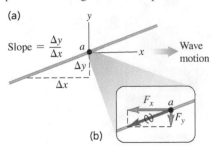

Equation (15.21) is valid for *any* wave on a string, sinusoidal or not. For a sinusoidal wave with wave function given by Eq. (15.7), we have

$$y(x, t) = A\cos(kx - \omega t)$$

$$\frac{\partial y(x, t)}{\partial x} = -kA\sin(kx - \omega t)$$

$$\frac{\partial y(x, t)}{\partial t} = \omega A\sin(kx - \omega t)$$

$$P(x, t) = Fk\omega A^2 \sin^2(kx - \omega t) \tag{15.22}$$

By using the relationships $\omega = vk$ and $v^2 = F/\mu$, we can also express Eq. (15.22) in the alternative form

$$P(x, t) = \sqrt{\mu F}\,\omega^2 A^2 \sin^2(kx - \omega t) \tag{15.23}$$

The $\sin^2$ function is never negative, so the instantaneous power in a sinusoidal wave is either positive (so that energy flows in the positive x-direction) or zero (at points where there is no energy transfer). Energy is never transferred in the direction opposite to the direction of wave propagation (**Fig. 15.16**).

The maximum value of the instantaneous power $P(x, t)$ occurs when the $\sin^2$ function has the value unity:

$$P_{max} = \sqrt{\mu F}\,\omega^2 A^2 \tag{15.24}$$

The *average* value of the $\sin^2$ function, averaged over any whole number of cycles, is $\frac{1}{2}$. Hence we see from Eq. (15.23) that the *average* power P_{av} is just one-half the maximum instantaneous power P_{max} (Fig. 15.16):

Average power, sinusoidal wave on a string
$$P_{av} = \frac{1}{2}\sqrt{\mu F}\,\omega^2 A^2 \tag{15.25}$$
Wave angular frequency · Wave amplitude · Mass per unit length · Tension in string

15.16 The instantaneous power $P(x, t)$ in a sinusoidal wave as given by Eq. (15.23), shown as a function of time at coordinate $x = 0$. The power is never negative, which means that energy never flows opposite to the direction of wave propagation.

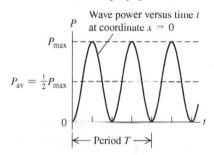

The average rate of energy transfer is proportional to the square of the amplitude and to the square of the frequency. This proportionality is a general result for mechanical waves of all types, including seismic waves (see the photo that opens this chapter). For a mechanical wave, the rate of energy transfer quadruples if the frequency is doubled (for the same amplitude) or if the amplitude is doubled (for the same frequency).

Electromagnetic waves turn out to be a bit different. While the average rate of energy transfer in an electromagnetic wave is proportional to the square of the amplitude, just as for mechanical waves, it is independent of the value of ω.

EXAMPLE 15.4 POWER IN A WAVE

(a) In Example 15.2 (Section 15.3), at what maximum rate does Throcky put energy into the clothesline? That is, what is his maximum instantaneous power? The linear mass density of the clothesline is $\mu = 0.250$ kg/m, and Throcky applies tension $F = 36.0$ N. (b) What is his average power? (c) As Throcky tires, the amplitude decreases. What is the average power when the amplitude is 7.50 mm?

SOLUTION

IDENTIFY and SET UP: In part (a) our target variable is the *maximum instantaneous* power P_{max}, while in parts (b) and (c) it

is the *average* power. For part (a) we'll use Eq. (15.24), and for parts (b) and (c) we'll use Eq. (15.25); Example 15.2 gives us all the needed quantities.

EXECUTE: (a) From Eq. (15.24),

$$P_{max} = \sqrt{\mu F}\,\omega^2 A^2$$
$$= \sqrt{(0.250\text{ kg/m})(36.0\text{ N})}\,(4.00\pi\text{ rad/s})^2(0.075\text{ m})^2$$
$$= 2.66\text{ W}$$

Continued

(b) From Eqs. (15.24) and (15.25), the average power is one-half of the maximum instantaneous power, so

$$P_{av} = \tfrac{1}{2}P_{max} = \tfrac{1}{2}(2.66 \text{ W}) = 1.33 \text{ W}$$

(c) The new amplitude is $\tfrac{1}{10}$ of the value we used in parts (a) and (b). From Eq. (15.25), the average power is proportional to A^2, so the new average power is

$$P_{av} = \left(\tfrac{1}{10}\right)^2(1.33 \text{ W}) = 0.0133 \text{ W} = 13.3 \text{ mW}$$

EVALUATE: Equation (15.23) shows that P_{max} occurs when $\sin^2(kx - \omega t) = 1$. At any given position x, this happens twice per period of the wave—once when the sine function is equal to $+1$, and once when it's equal to -1. The *minimum* instantaneous power is zero; this occurs when $\sin^2(kx - \omega t) = 0$, which also happens twice per period.

Can you confirm that the given values of μ and F give the wave speed mentioned in Example 15.2?

Wave Intensity

Waves on a string carry energy in one dimension (along the direction of the string). But other types of waves, including sound waves in air and seismic waves within the earth, carry energy across all three dimensions of space. For waves of this kind, we define the **intensity** (denoted by I) to be *the time average rate at which energy is transported by the wave, per unit area*, across a surface perpendicular to the direction of propagation. Intensity I is average power per unit area and is usually measured in watts per square meter (W/m^2).

15.17 The greater the distance from a wave source, the greater the area over which the wave power is distributed and the smaller the wave intensity.

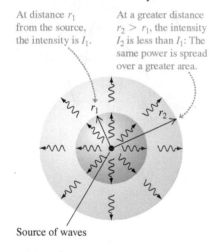

At distance r_1 from the source, the intensity is I_1.

At a greater distance $r_2 > r_1$, the intensity I_2 is less than I_1: The same power is spread over a greater area.

Source of waves

If waves spread out equally in all directions from a source, the intensity at a distance r from the source is inversely proportional to r^2 (**Fig. 15.17**). This result, called the *inverse-square law for intensity*, follows directly from energy conservation. If the power output of the source is P, then the average intensity I_1 through a sphere with radius r_1 and surface area $4\pi r_1^2$ is

$$I_1 = \frac{P}{4\pi r_1^2}$$

A similar expression gives the average intensity I_2 through a sphere with a different radius r_2. If no energy is absorbed between the two spheres, the power P must be the same for both, and

$$4\pi r_1^2 I_1 = 4\pi r_2^2 I_2$$

Inverse-square law for intensity:
Intensity is inversely proportional to the square of the distance from source.

Intensity at point 1 ⋯⋯► $\dfrac{I_1}{I_2} = \dfrac{r_2^2}{r_1^2}$ ◄⋯⋯ Distance from source to point 2

Intensity at point 2 ⋯⋯► ◄⋯⋯ Distance from source to point 1

(15.26)

EXAMPLE 15.5 THE INVERSE-SQUARE LAW

A siren on a tall pole radiates sound waves uniformly in all directions. At a distance of 15.0 m from the siren, the sound intensity is 0.250 W/m^2. At what distance is the intensity 0.010 W/m^2?

SOLUTION

IDENTIFY and SET UP: Because sound is radiated uniformly in all directions, we can use the inverse-square law, Eq. (15.26). At $r_1 = 15.0$ m the intensity is $I_1 = 0.250 \text{ W/m}^2$, and the target variable is the distance r_2 at which the intensity is $I_2 = 0.010 \text{ W/m}^2$.

EXECUTE: We solve Eq. (15.26) for r_2:

$$r_2 = r_1\sqrt{\frac{I_1}{I_2}} = (15.0 \text{ m})\sqrt{\frac{0.250 \text{ W/m}^2}{0.010 \text{ W/m}^2}} = 75.0 \text{ m}$$

EVALUATE: As a check on our answer, note that r_2 is five times greater than r_1. By the inverse-square law, the intensity I_2 should be $1/5^2 = 1/25$ as great as I_1, and indeed it is.

By using the inverse-square law, we've assumed that the sound waves travel in straight lines away from the siren. A more realistic solution, which is beyond our scope, would account for the reflection of sound waves from the ground.

15.18 Reflection of a wave pulse at a fixed end of a string. Time increases from top to bottom.

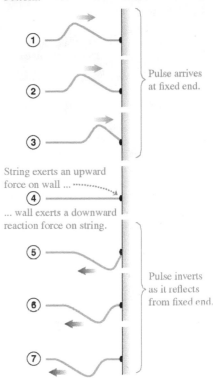

15.6 WAVE INTERFERENCE, BOUNDARY CONDITIONS, AND SUPERPOSITION

Up to this point we've been discussing waves that propagate continuously in the same direction. But when a wave strikes the boundaries of its medium, all or part of the wave is *reflected*. When you yell at a building wall or a cliff face some distance away, the sound wave is reflected from the rigid surface and you hear an echo. When you flip the end of a rope whose far end is tied to a rigid support, a pulse travels the length of the rope and is reflected back to you. In both cases, the initial and reflected waves overlap in the same region of the medium. We use the term **interference** to refer to what happens when two or more waves pass through the same region at the same time.

As a simple example of wave reflections and the role of the boundary of a wave medium, let's look again at transverse waves on a stretched string. What happens when a wave pulse or a sinusoidal wave arrives at the *end* of the string?

If the end is fastened to a rigid support as in **Fig. 15.18**, it is a *fixed* end that cannot move. The arriving wave exerts a force on the support (drawing 4 in Fig. 15.18); the reaction to this force, exerted by the support on the string, "kicks back" on the string and sets up a reflected pulse or wave traveling in the reverse direction (drawing 7). The reflected pulse moves in the opposite direction from the initial, or *incident*, pulse, and its displacement is also opposite.

The opposite situation from an end that is held stationary is a *free* end, one that is perfectly free to move in the direction perpendicular to the length of the string. For example, the string might be tied to a light ring that slides on a frictionless rod perpendicular to the string, as in **Fig. 15.19**. The ring and rod maintain the tension but exert no transverse force. When a wave arrives at this free end, the ring slides along the rod. The ring reaches a maximum displacement, and both it and the string come momentarily to rest, as in drawing 4 in Fig. 15.19. But the string is now stretched, giving increased tension, so the free end of the string is pulled back down, and again a reflected pulse is produced (drawing 7). As for a fixed end, the reflected pulse moves in the opposite direction from the initial pulse, but now the direction of the displacement is the same as for the initial pulse. The conditions at the end of the string, such as a rigid support or the complete absence of transverse force, are called **boundary conditions.**

The formation of the reflected pulse is similar to the overlap of two pulses traveling in opposite directions. **Figure 15.20** (next page) shows two pulses with the same shape, one inverted with respect to the other, traveling in opposite directions. As the pulses overlap and pass each other, the total displacement of the string is the *algebraic sum* of the displacements at that point in the individual pulses. Because these two pulses have the same shape, the total displacement at point *O* in the middle of the figure is zero at all times. Thus the motion of the left half

15.19 Reflection of a wave pulse at a free end of a string. Time increases from top to bottom. (Compare to Fig. 15.18.)

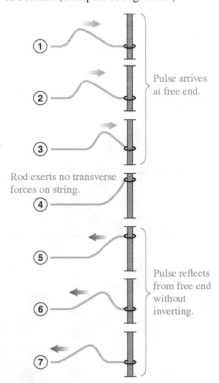

15.20 Overlap of two wave pulses—one right side up, one inverted—traveling in opposite directions. Time increases from top to bottom.

As the pulses overlap, the displacement of the string at any point is the algebraic sum of the displacements due to the individual pulses.

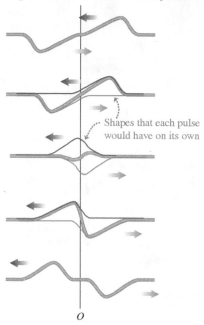

Shapes that each pulse would have on its own

O

15.21 Overlap of two wave pulses—both right side up—traveling in opposite directions. Time increases from top to bottom. Compare to Fig. 15.20.

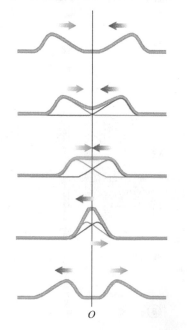

O

DEMO

of the string would be the same if we cut the string at point O, threw away the right side, and held the end at O fixed. The two pulses on the left side then correspond to the incident and reflected pulses, combining so that the total displacement at O is *always* zero. For this to occur, the reflected pulse must be inverted relative to the incident pulse, just as for reflection from the fixed end in Fig. 15.18.

Figure 15.21 shows two pulses with the same shape, traveling in opposite directions but *not* inverted relative to each other. The displacement at point O in the middle of the figure is not zero, but the slope of the string at this point is always zero. According to Eq. (15.20), this corresponds to the absence of any transverse force at this point. In this case the motion of the left half of the string would be the same as if we cut the string at point O and attached the end to a frictionless sliding ring (Fig. 15.19) that maintains tension without exerting any transverse force. In other words, this situation corresponds to reflection of a pulse at a free end of a string at point O. In this case the reflected pulse is *not* inverted.

The Principle of Superposition

Combining the displacements of the separate pulses at each point to obtain the actual displacement is an example of the **principle of superposition:** When two waves overlap, the actual displacement of any point on the string at any time is obtained by adding the displacement the point would have if only the first wave were present and the displacement it would have if only the second wave were present. In other words, the wave function $y(x, t)$ for the resulting motion is obtained by *adding* the two wave functions for the two separate waves:

Wave functions of two overlapping waves

Principle of superposition:
$$y(x, t) = y_1(x, t) + y_2(x, t) \tag{15.27}$$

Wave function of combined wave = sum of individual wave functions

Mathematically, this additive property of wave functions follows from the form of the wave equation, Eq. (15.12) or (15.19), which every physically possible wave function must satisfy. Specifically, the wave equation is *linear*; that is, it contains the function $y(x, t)$ only to the first power (there are no terms involving $y(x, t)^2$, $y(x, t)^{1/2}$, etc.). As a result, if any two functions $y_1(x, t)$ and $y_2(x, t)$ satisfy the wave equation separately, their sum $y_1(x, t) + y_2(x, t)$ also satisfies it and is therefore a physically possible motion. Because this principle depends on the linearity of the wave equation and the corresponding linear-combination property of its solutions, it is also called the *principle of linear superposition*. For some physical systems, such as a medium that does not obey Hooke's law, the wave equation is *not* linear; this principle does not hold for such systems.

The principle of superposition is of central importance in all types of waves. When a friend talks to you while you are listening to music, you can distinguish the speech and the music from each other. This is precisely because the total sound wave reaching your ears is the algebraic sum of the wave produced by your friend's voice and the wave produced by the speakers of your stereo. If two sound waves did *not* combine in this simple linear way, the sound you would hear in this situation would be a hopeless jumble. Superposition also applies to electromagnetic waves (such as light).

TEST YOUR UNDERSTANDING OF SECTION 15.6   **Figure 15.22** shows two wave pulses with different shapes traveling in different directions along a string. Make a series of sketches like Fig. 15.21 showing the shape of the string as the two pulses approach, overlap, and then pass each other. ▮

15.22 Two wave pulses with different shapes.

15.7 STANDING WAVES ON A STRING

We've looked at the reflection of a wave *pulse* on a string when it arrives at a boundary point (either a fixed end or a free end). Now let's consider what happens when a *sinusoidal* wave on a string is reflected by a fixed end. We'll again approach the problem by considering the superposition of two waves propagating through the string, one representing the incident wave and the other representing the wave reflected at the fixed end.

Figure 15.23 shows a string that is fixed at its left end. Its right end is moved up and down in simple harmonic motion to produce a wave that travels to the left; the wave reflected from the fixed end travels to the right. The resulting motion when the two waves combine no longer looks like two waves traveling in opposite directions. The string appears to be subdivided into segments, as in the time-exposure photographs of Figs. 15.23a, 15.23b, 15.23c, and 15.23d. Figure 15.23e shows two instantaneous shapes of the string in Fig. 15.23b. Let's compare this behavior with the waves we studied in Sections 15.1 through 15.5. In a wave that travels along the string, the amplitude is constant and the wave pattern moves with a speed equal to the wave speed. Here, instead, the wave pattern remains in the same position along the string and its amplitude fluctuates. There are particular points called **nodes** (labeled *N* in Fig. 15.23c) that never move at all. Midway between the nodes are points called **antinodes** (labeled *A* in Fig. 15.23e) where the amplitude of motion is greatest. Because the wave pattern doesn't appear to be moving in either direction along the string, it is called a **standing wave.** (To emphasize the difference, a wave that *does* move along the string is called a **traveling wave.**)

15.23 (a)–(d) Time exposures of standing waves in a stretched string. From (a) to (d), the frequency of oscillation of the right-hand end increases and the wavelength of the standing wave decreases. (e) The extremes of the motion of the standing wave in part (b), with nodes at the center and at the ends. The right-hand end of the string moves very little compared to the antinodes and so is essentially a node.

(a) String is one-half wavelength long.

(b) String is one wavelength long.

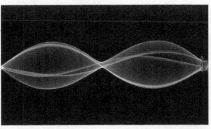

(c) String is one and a half wavelengths long.

(d) String is two wavelengths long.

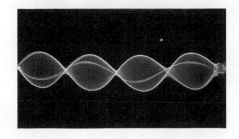

(e) The shape of the string in (b) at two different instants

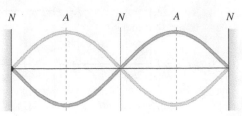

N = **nodes:** points at which the string never moves

A = **antinodes:** points at which the amplitude of string motion is greatest

The principle of superposition explains how the incident and reflected waves combine to form a standing wave. In **Fig. 15.24** the red curves show a wave traveling to the left. The blue curves show a wave traveling to the right with the same propagation speed, wavelength, and amplitude. The waves are shown at nine instants, $\frac{1}{16}$ of a period apart. At each point along the string, we add the displacements (the values of y) for the two separate waves; the result is the total wave on the string, shown in gold.

At certain instants, such as $t = \frac{1}{4}T$, the two wave patterns are exactly in phase with each other, and the shape of the string is a sine curve with twice the amplitude of either individual wave. At other instants, such as $t = \frac{1}{2}T$, the two waves are exactly out of phase with each other, and the total wave at that instant is zero. The resultant displacement is *always* zero at those places marked N at the bottom of Fig. 15.24. These are the *nodes*. At a node the displacements of the two waves in red and blue are always equal and opposite and cancel each other out. This cancellation is called **destructive interference.** Midway between the nodes are the points of *greatest* amplitude, or the *antinodes,* marked A. At the antinodes the displacements of the two waves in red and blue are always identical, giving a large resultant displacement; this phenomenon is called **constructive interference.** We can see from the figure that the distance between successive nodes or between successive antinodes is one half-wavelength, or $\lambda/2$.

15.24 Formation of a standing wave. A wave traveling to the left (red curves) combines with a wave traveling to the right (blue curves) to form a standing wave (gold curves).

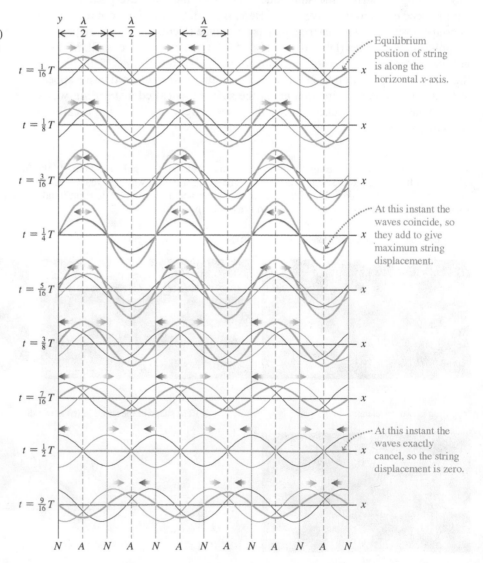

We can derive a wave function for the standing wave of Fig. 15.24 by adding the wave functions $y_1(x, t)$ and $y_2(x, t)$ for two waves with equal amplitude, period, and wavelength traveling in opposite directions. Here $y_1(x, t)$ (the red curves in Fig. 15.24) represents an incoming, or *incident,* wave traveling to the left along the $+x$-axis, arriving at the point $x = 0$ and being reflected; $y_2(x, t)$ (the blue curves in Fig. 15.24) represents the *reflected* wave traveling to the right from $x = 0$. We noted in Section 15.6 that the wave reflected from a fixed end of a string is inverted, so we give a negative sign to one of the waves:

$$y_1(x, t) = -A\cos(kx + \omega t) \qquad \text{(incident wave traveling to the left)}$$

$$y_2(x, t) = A\cos(kx - \omega t) \qquad \text{(reflected wave traveling to the right)}$$

The change in sign corresponds to a shift in *phase* of 180° or π radians. At $x = 0$ the motion from the reflected wave is $A\cos\omega t$ and the motion from the incident wave is $-A\cos\omega t$, which we can also write as $A\cos(\omega t + \pi)$. From Eq. (15.27), the wave function for the standing wave is the sum of the individual wave functions:

$$y(x, t) = y_1(x, t) + y_2(x, t) = A\left[-\cos(kx + \omega t) + \cos(kx - \omega t)\right]$$

We can rewrite each of the cosine terms by using the identities for the cosine of the sum and difference of two angles: $\cos(a \pm b) = \cos a \cos b \mp \sin a \sin b$. Applying these and combining terms, we obtain the wave function for the standing wave:

$$y(x, t) = y_1(x, t) + y_2(x, t) = (2A\sin kx)\sin\omega t \qquad \text{or}$$

Standing wave on a string, fixed end at $x = 0$:	Wave function Standing-wave amplitude $$y(x, t) = (A_{SW}\sin kx)\sin\omega t \dashleftarrow \text{Time}$$ Wave number ····· Position Angular frequency	(15.28)

The standing-wave amplitude A_{SW} is twice the amplitude A of either of the original traveling waves: $A_{SW} = 2A$.

Equation (15.28) has two factors: a function of x and a function of t. The factor $A_{SW}\sin kx$ shows that at each instant the shape of the string is a sine curve. But unlike a wave traveling along a string, the wave shape stays in the same position, oscillating up and down as described by the $\sin\omega t$ factor. This behavior is shown by the gold curves in Fig. 15.24. Each point in the string still undergoes simple harmonic motion, but all the points between any successive pair of nodes oscillate *in phase*. This is in contrast to the phase differences between oscillations of adjacent points that we see with a traveling wave.

We can use Eq. (15.28) to find the positions of the nodes; these are the points for which $\sin kx = 0$, so the displacement is *always* zero. This occurs when $kx = 0, \pi, 2\pi, 3\pi, \ldots$, or, using $k = 2\pi/\lambda$,

$$x = 0, \frac{\pi}{k}, \frac{2\pi}{k}, \frac{3\pi}{k}, \ldots$$

$$= 0, \frac{\lambda}{2}, \frac{2\lambda}{2}, \frac{3\lambda}{2}, \ldots$$

(nodes of a standing wave on a string, fixed end at $x = 0$)   (15.29)

In particular, there is a node at $x = 0$, as there should be, since this point is a fixed end of the string.

A standing wave, unlike a traveling wave, *does not* transfer energy from one end to the other. The two waves that form it would individually carry equal amounts of power in opposite directions. There is a local flow of energy from each node to the adjacent antinodes and back, but the *average* rate of energy transfer is zero at every point. If you use the wave function of Eq. (15.28) to evaluate the wave power given by Eq. (15.21), you will find that the average power is zero.

PROBLEM-SOLVING STRATEGY 15.2 **STANDING WAVES**

IDENTIFY *the relevant concepts:* Identify the target variables. Then determine whether the problem is purely *kinematic* (involving only such quantities as wave speed v, wavelength λ, and frequency f) or whether *dynamic* properties of the medium (such as F and μ for transverse waves on a string) are also involved.

SET UP *the problem* using the following steps:
1. Sketch the shape of the standing wave at a particular instant. This will help you visualize the nodes (label them N) and antinodes (A). The distance between adjacent nodes (or antinodes) is $\lambda/2$; the distance between a node and the adjacent antinode is $\lambda/4$.
2. Choose the equations you'll use. The wave function for the standing wave, like Eq. (15.28), is often useful.

3. You can determine the wave speed if you know λ and f (or, equivalently, $k = 2\pi/\lambda$ and $\omega = 2\pi f$) or if you know the relevant properties of the medium (for a string, F and μ).

EXECUTE *the solution:* Solve for the target variables. Once you've found the wave function, you can find the displacement y at any point x and at any time t. You can find the velocity and acceleration of a particle in the medium by taking the first and second partial derivatives of y with respect to time.

EVALUATE *your answer:* Compare your numerical answers with your sketch. Check that the wave function satisfies the boundary conditions (for example, the displacement should be zero at a fixed end).

EXAMPLE 15.6   STANDING WAVES ON A GUITAR STRING

A guitar string lies along the x-axis when in equilibrium. The end of the string at $x = 0$ (the bridge of the guitar) is fixed. A sinusoidal wave with amplitude $A = 0.750$ mm $= 7.50 \times 10^{-4}$ m and frequency $f = 440$ Hz, corresponding to the red curves in Fig. 15.24, travels along the string in the $-x$-direction at 143 m/s. It is reflected from the fixed end, and the superposition of the incident and reflected waves forms a standing wave. (a) Find the equation giving the displacement of a point on the string as a function of position and time. (b) Locate the nodes. (c) Find the amplitude of the standing wave and the maximum transverse velocity and acceleration.

SOLUTION

IDENTIFY and SET UP: This is a *kinematics* problem (see Problem-Solving Strategy 15.1 in Section 15.3). The target variables are: in part (a), the wave function of the standing wave; in part (b), the locations of the nodes; and in part (c), the maximum displacement y, transverse velocity v_y, and transverse acceleration a_y. Since there is a fixed end at $x = 0$, we can use Eqs. (15.28) and (15.29) to describe this standing wave. We will need the relationships $\omega = 2\pi f$, $v = \omega/k$, and $v = \lambda f$.

EXECUTE: (a) The standing-wave amplitude is $A_{SW} = 2A = 1.50 \times 10^{-3}$ m (twice the amplitude of either the incident or reflected wave). The angular frequency and wave number are

$$\omega = 2\pi f = (2\pi \text{ rad})(440 \text{ s}^{-1}) = 2760 \text{ rad/s}$$

$$k = \frac{\omega}{v} = \frac{2760 \text{ rad/s}}{143 \text{ m/s}} = 19.3 \text{ rad/m}$$

Equation (15.28) then gives

$$y(x, t) = (A_{SW} \sin kx) \sin \omega t$$

$$= [(1.50 \times 10^{-3} \text{ m}) \sin(19.3 \text{ rad/m})x] \sin(2760 \text{ rad/s})t$$

(b) From Eq. (15.29), the positions of the nodes are $x = 0$, $\lambda/2$, λ, $3\lambda/2$, ... The wavelength is $\lambda = v/f = (143 \text{ m/s})/(440 \text{ Hz}) = $

0.325 m, so the nodes are at $x = 0$, 0.163 m, 0.325 m, 0.488 m, ...

(c) From the expression for $y(x, t)$ in part (a), the maximum displacement from equilibrium is $A_{SW} = 1.50 \times 10^{-3}$ m $= 1.50$ mm. This occurs at the *antinodes,* which are midway between adjacent nodes (that is, at $x = 0.081$ m, 0.244 m, 0.406 m, ...).

For a particle on the string at any point x, the transverse (y-) velocity is

$$v_y(x, t) = \frac{\partial y(x, t)}{\partial t}$$

$$= [(1.50 \times 10^{-3} \text{ m}) \sin(19.3 \text{ rad/m})x]$$

$$\times [(2760 \text{ rad/s}) \cos(2760 \text{ rad/s})t]$$

$$= [(4.15 \text{ m/s}) \sin(19.3 \text{ rad/m})x] \cos(2760 \text{ rad/s})t$$

At an antinode, $\sin(19.3 \text{ rad/m})x = \pm 1$ and the transverse velocity varies between $+4.15$ m/s and -4.15 m/s. As is always the case in SHM, the maximum velocity occurs when the particle is passing through the equilibrium position ($y = 0$).

The transverse acceleration $a_y(x, t)$ is the *second* partial derivative of $y(x, t)$ with respect to time. You can show that

$$a_y(x, t) = \frac{\partial v_y(x, t)}{\partial t} = \frac{\partial^2 y(x, t)}{\partial t^2}$$

$$= [(-1.15 \times 10^4 \text{ m/s}^2) \sin(19.3 \text{ rad/m})x]$$

$$\times \sin(2760 \text{ rad/s})t$$

At the antinodes, the transverse acceleration varies between $+1.15 \times 10^4$ m/s^2 and -1.15×10^4 m/s^2.

EVALUATE: The maximum transverse velocity at an antinode is quite respectable (about 15 km/h, or 9.3 mi/h). But the maximum transverse acceleration is tremendous, 1170 times the acceleration due to gravity! Guitar strings are actually fixed at *both* ends; we'll see the consequences of this in the next section.

TEST YOUR UNDERSTANDING OF SECTION 15.7 Suppose the frequency of the standing wave in Example 15.6 were doubled from 440 Hz to 880 Hz. Would all of the nodes for $f = 440$ Hz also be nodes for $f = 880$ Hz? If so, would there be additional nodes for $f = 880$ Hz? If not, which nodes are absent for $f = 880$ Hz? ▮

15.8 NORMAL MODES OF A STRING

When we described standing waves on a string rigidly held at one end, as in Fig. 15.23, we made no assumptions about the length of the string or about what was happening at the other end. Let's now consider a string of a definite length L, rigidly held at *both* ends. Such strings are found in many musical instruments, including pianos, violins, and guitars. When a guitar string is plucked, a wave is produced in the string; this wave is reflected and re-reflected from the ends of the string, making a standing wave. This standing wave on the string in turn produces a sound wave in the air, with a frequency determined by the properties of the string. This is what makes stringed instruments so useful in making music.

To understand a standing wave on a string fixed at both ends, we first note that the standing wave must have a node at *both* ends of the string. We saw in the preceding section that adjacent nodes are one half-wavelength ($\lambda/2$) apart, so the length of the string must be $\lambda/2$, or $2(\lambda/2)$, or $3(\lambda/2)$, or in general some integer number of half-wavelengths:

$$L = n\frac{\lambda}{2} \quad (n = 1, 2, 3, \dots) \quad \text{(string fixed at both ends)} \quad (15.30)$$

That is, if a string with length L is fixed at both ends, a standing wave can exist only if its wavelength satisfies Eq. (15.30).

Solving this equation for λ and labeling the possible values of λ as λ_n, we find

$$\lambda_n = \frac{2L}{n} \quad (n = 1, 2, 3, \dots) \quad \text{(string fixed at both ends)} \quad (15.31)$$

Waves can exist on the string if the wavelength is *not* equal to one of these values, but there cannot be a steady wave pattern with nodes and antinodes, and the total wave cannot be a standing wave. Equation (15.31) is illustrated by the standing waves shown in Figs. 15.23a, 15.23b, 15.23c, and 15.23d; these represent $n = 1, 2, 3$, and 4, respectively.

Corresponding to the series of possible standing-wave wavelengths λ_n is a series of possible standing-wave frequencies f_n, each related to its corresponding wavelength by $f_n = v/\lambda_n$. The smallest frequency f_1 corresponds to the largest wavelength (the $n = 1$ case), $\lambda_1 = 2L$:

$$f_1 = \frac{v}{2L} \quad \text{(string fixed at both ends)} \quad (15.32)$$

This is called the **fundamental frequency.** The other standing-wave frequencies are $f_2 = 2v/2L$, $f_3 = 3v/2L$, and so on. These are all integer multiples of f_1, such as $2f_1$, $3f_1$, $4f_1$, and so on. We can express *all* the frequencies as

Standing-wave frequencies, string fixed at both ends:

$$\underset{\text{Length of string}}{f_n} = n\underset{\text{Wave speed}}{\frac{v}{2L}} = n\underset{\text{Fundamental frequency} = v/2L}{f_1} \quad (n = 1, 2, 3, \dots) \quad (15.33)$$

PhET: Fourier: Making Waves
PhET: Waves on a String

15.25 Each string of a violin naturally oscillates at its harmonic frequencies, producing sound waves in the air with the same frequencies.

These frequencies are called **harmonics,** and the series is called a **harmonic series.** Musicians sometimes call f_2, f_3, and so on **overtones;** f_2 is the second harmonic or the first overtone, f_3 is the third harmonic or the second overtone, and so on. The first harmonic is the same as the fundamental frequency (**Fig. 15.25**).

15.26 The first four normal modes of a string fixed at both ends. (Compare these to the photographs in Fig. 15.23.)

(a) $n = 1$: fundamental frequency, f_1

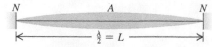

(b) $n = 2$: second harmonic, f_2 (first overtone)

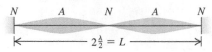

(c) $n = 3$: third harmonic, f_3 (second overtone)

(d) $n = 4$: fourth harmonic, f_4 (third overtone)

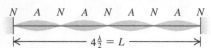

For a string with fixed ends at $x = 0$ and $x = L$, the wave function $y(x, t)$ of the nth standing wave is given by Eq. (15.28) (which satisfies the condition that there is a node at $x = 0$), with $\omega = \omega_n = 2\pi f_n$ and $k = k_n = 2\pi/\lambda_n$:

$$y_n(x, t) = A_{SW} \sin k_n x \sin \omega_n t \qquad (15.34)$$

You can confirm that this wave function has nodes at both $x = 0$ and $x = L$.

A **normal mode** of an oscillating system is a motion in which all particles of the system move sinusoidally with the same frequency. For a system made up of a string of length L fixed at both ends, each of the frequencies given by Eq. (15.33) corresponds to a possible normal-mode pattern. **Figure 15.26** shows the first four normal-mode patterns and their associated frequencies and wavelengths; these correspond to Eq. (15.34) with $n = 1, 2, 3$, and 4. By contrast, a harmonic oscillator, which has only one oscillating particle, has only one normal mode and one characteristic frequency. The string fixed at both ends has infinitely many normal modes ($n = 1, 2, 3, \ldots$) because it is made up of a very large (effectively infinite) number of particles. More complicated oscillating systems also have infinite numbers of normal modes, though with more complex normal-mode patterns (**Fig. 15.27**).

Complex Standing Waves

If we could displace a string so that its shape is the same as one of the normal-mode patterns and then release it, it would vibrate with the frequency of that mode. Such a vibrating string would displace the surrounding air with the same frequency, producing a traveling sinusoidal sound wave that your ears would perceive as a pure tone. But when a string is struck (as in a piano) or plucked (as is done to guitar strings), the shape of the displaced string is *not* one of the patterns in Fig. 15.26. The motion is therefore a combination or *superposition* of many normal modes. Several simple harmonic motions of different frequencies are present simultaneously, and the displacement of any point on the string is the superposition of the displacements associated with the individual modes. The sound produced by the vibrating string is likewise a superposition of traveling sinusoidal sound waves, which you perceive as a rich, complex tone with the fundamental frequency f_1. The standing wave on the string and the traveling sound wave in the air have similar **harmonic content** (the extent to which frequencies higher than the fundamental are present). The harmonic content depends on how the string is initially set into motion. If you pluck the strings of an acoustic guitar

15.27 Astronomers have discovered that the sun oscillates in several different normal modes. This computer simulation shows one such mode.

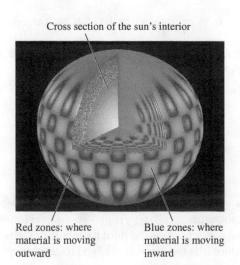

Cross section of the sun's interior

Red zones: where material is moving outward

Blue zones: where material is moving inward

in the normal location over the sound hole, the sound that you hear has a different harmonic content than if you pluck the strings next to the fixed end on the guitar body.

It is possible to represent every possible motion of the string as some superposition of normal-mode motions. Finding this representation for a given vibration pattern is called *harmonic analysis*. The sum of sinusoidal functions that represents a complex wave is called a *Fourier series*. **Figure 15.28** shows how a standing wave that is produced by plucking a guitar string of length L at a point $L/4$ from one end can be represented as a combination of sinusoidal functions.

Standing Waves and String Instruments

From Eq. (15.32), the fundamental frequency of a vibrating string is $f_1 = v/2L$. The speed v of waves on the string is determined by Eq. (15.14), $v = \sqrt{F/\mu}$. Combining these equations, we find

Fundamental frequency, string fixed at both ends

$$f_1 = \frac{1}{2L}\sqrt{\frac{F}{\mu}} \quad \begin{array}{l} \text{Tension in string} \\ \text{Mass per unit length} \end{array} \qquad (15.35)$$

Length of string

This is also the fundamental frequency of the sound wave created in the surrounding air by the vibrating string. The inverse dependence of frequency on length L is illustrated by the long strings of the bass (low-frequency) section of the piano or the bass viol compared with the shorter strings of the treble section of the piano or the violin (**Fig. 15.29**). The pitch of a violin or guitar is usually varied by pressing a string against the fingerboard with the fingers to change the length L of the vibrating portion of the string. Increasing the tension F increases the wave speed v and thus increases the frequency (and the pitch). All string instruments are "tuned" to the correct frequencies by varying the tension; you tighten the string to raise the pitch. Finally, increasing the mass per unit length μ decreases the wave speed and thus the frequency. The lower notes on a steel guitar are produced by thicker strings, and one reason for winding the bass strings of a piano with wire is to obtain the desired low frequency from a relatively short string.

Wind instruments such as saxophones and trombones also have normal modes. As for stringed instruments, the frequencies of these normal modes determine the pitch of the musical tones that these instruments produce. We'll discuss these instruments and many other aspects of sound in Chapter 16.

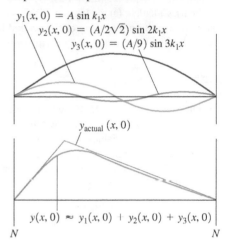

15.28 When a guitar string is plucked (pulled into a triangular shape) and released, a standing wave results. The standing wave is well represented (except at the sharp maximum point) by the sum of just three sinusoidal functions. Including additional sinusoidal functions further improves the representation.

$y_1(x, 0) = A \sin k_1 x$

$y_2(x, 0) = (A/2\sqrt{2}) \sin 2k_1 x$

$y_3(x, 0) = (A/9) \sin 3k_1 x$

$y_{\text{actual}}(x, 0)$

$y(x, 0) \approx y_1(x, 0) + y_2(x, 0) + y_3(x, 0)$

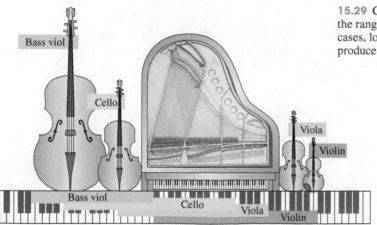

15.29 Comparing the range of a concert grand piano to the ranges of a bass viol, a cello, a viola, and a violin. In all cases, longer strings produce bass notes and shorter strings produce treble notes.

Bass viol

Cello

Viola

Violin

Bass viol

Cello

Viola

Violin

EXAMPLE 15.7 A GIANT BASS VIOL

In an attempt to get your name in *Guinness World Records,* you build a bass viol with strings of length 5.00 m between fixed points. One string, with linear mass density 40.0 g/m, is tuned to a 20.0-Hz fundamental frequency (the lowest frequency that the human ear can hear). Calculate (a) the tension of this string, (b) the frequency and wavelength on the string of the second harmonic, and (c) the frequency and wavelength on the string of the second overtone.

SOLUTION

IDENTIFY and SET UP: In part (a) the target variable is the string tension F; we'll use Eq. (15.35), which relates F to the known values $f_1 = 20.0$ Hz, $L = 5.00$ m, and $\mu = 40.0$ g/m. In parts (b) and (c) the target variables are the frequency and wavelength of a given harmonic and a given overtone. We determine these from the given length of the string and the fundamental frequency, using Eqs. (15.31) and (15.33).

EXECUTE: (a) We solve Eq. (15.35) for F:

$$F = 4\mu L^2 f_1^2 = 4(40.0 \times 10^{-3} \text{ kg/m})(5.00 \text{ m})^2(20.0 \text{ s}^{-1})^2$$

$$= 1600 \text{ N} = 360 \text{ lb}$$

(b) From Eqs. (15.33) and (15.31), the frequency and wavelength of the second harmonic ($n = 2$) are

$$f_2 = 2f_1 = 2(20.0 \text{ Hz}) = 40.0 \text{ Hz}$$

$$\lambda_2 = \frac{2L}{2} = \frac{2(5.00 \text{ m})}{2} = 5.00 \text{ m}$$

(c) The second overtone is the "second tone over" (above) the fundamental—that is, $n = 3$. Its frequency and wavelength are

$$f_3 = 3f_1 = 3(20.0 \text{ Hz}) = 60.0 \text{ Hz}$$

$$\lambda_3 = \frac{2L}{3} = \frac{2(5.00 \text{ m})}{3} = 3.33 \text{ m}$$

EVALUATE: The string tension in a real bass viol is typically a few hundred newtons; the tension in part (a) is a bit higher than that. The wavelengths in parts (b) and (c) are equal to the length of the string and two-thirds the length of the string, respectively, which agrees with the drawings of standing waves in Fig. 15.26.

EXAMPLE 15.8 FROM WAVES ON A STRING TO SOUND WAVES IN AIR

What are the frequency and wavelength of the sound waves produced in the air when the string in Example 15.7 is vibrating at its fundamental frequency? The speed of sound in air at 20°C is 344 m/s.

SOLUTION

IDENTIFY and SET UP: Our target variables are the frequency and wavelength for the *sound wave* produced by the bass viol string. The frequency of the sound wave is the same as the fundamental frequency f_1 of the standing wave, because the string forces the surrounding air to vibrate at the same frequency. The wavelength of the sound wave is $\lambda_{1(\text{sound})} = v_{\text{sound}}/f_1$.

EXECUTE: We have $f = f_1 = 20.0$ Hz, so

$$\lambda_{1(\text{sound})} = \frac{v_{\text{sound}}}{f_1} = \frac{344 \text{ m/s}}{20.0 \text{ Hz}} = 17.2 \text{ m}$$

EVALUATE: In Example 15.7, the wavelength of the fundamental on the string was $\lambda_{1(\text{string})} = 2L = 2(5.00 \text{ m}) = 10.0$ m. Here $\lambda_{1(\text{sound})} = 17.2$ m is greater than that by the factor of $17.2/10.0 = 1.72$. This is as it should be: Because the frequencies of the sound wave and the standing wave are equal, $\lambda = v/f$ says that the wavelengths in air and on the string are in the same ratio as the corresponding wave speeds; here $v_{\text{sound}} = 344$ m/s is greater than $v_{\text{string}} = (10.0 \text{ m})(20.0 \text{ Hz}) = 200$ m/s by just the factor 1.72.

TEST YOUR UNDERSTANDING OF SECTION 15.8 While a guitar string is vibrating, you gently touch the midpoint of the string to ensure that the string does not vibrate at that point. Which normal modes *cannot* be present on the string while you are touching it in this way? ∎

Waves and their properties: A wave is any disturbance that propagates from one region to another. A mechanical wave travels within some material called the medium. The wave speed v depends on the type of wave and the properties of the medium.

In a periodic wave, the motion of each point of the medium is periodic with frequency f and period T. The wavelength λ is the distance over which the wave pattern repeats, and the amplitude A is the maximum displacement of a particle in the medium. The product of λ and f equals the wave speed. A sinusoidal wave is a special periodic wave in which each point moves in simple harmonic motion. (See Example 15.1.)

$$v = \lambda f \qquad (15.1)$$

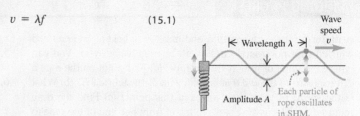

Wave functions and wave dynamics: The wave function $y(x, t)$ describes the displacements of individual particles in the medium. Equations (15.3), (15.4), and (15.7) give the wave equation for a sinusoidal wave traveling in the $+x$-direction. If the wave is moving in the $-x$-direction, the minus signs in the cosine functions are replaced by plus signs. (See Example 15.2.)

The wave function obeys a partial differential equation called the wave equation, Eq. (15.12).

The speed of transverse waves on a string depends on the tension F and mass per unit length μ. (See Example 15.3.)

$$y(x, t) = A \cos\left[\omega\left(\frac{x}{v} - t\right)\right] \qquad (15.3)$$

$$y(x, t) = A \cos 2\pi\left[\left(\frac{x}{\lambda} - \frac{t}{T}\right)\right] \qquad (15.4)$$

$$y(x, t) = A \cos(kx - \omega t) \qquad (15.7)$$

where $k = 2\pi/\lambda$ and $\omega = 2\pi f = vk$

$$\frac{\partial^2 y(x, t)}{\partial x^2} = \frac{1}{v^2}\frac{\partial^2 y(x, t)}{\partial t^2} \qquad (15.12)$$

$$v = \sqrt{\frac{F}{\mu}} \quad \text{(waves on a string)} \qquad (15.14)$$

Wavelength λ

Period T

Wave power: Wave motion conveys energy from one region to another. For a sinusoidal mechanical wave, the average power P_{av} is proportional to the square of the wave amplitude and the square of the frequency. For waves that spread out in three dimensions, the wave intensity I is inversely proportional to the square of the distance from the source. (See Examples 15.4 and 15.5.)

$$P_{av} = \frac{1}{2}\sqrt{\mu F}\,\omega^2 A^2 \qquad (15.25)$$
(average power, sinusoidal wave)

$$\frac{I_1}{I_2} = \frac{r_2^2}{r_1^2} \qquad (15.26)$$
(inverse-square law for intensity)

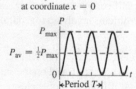

Wave power versus time t
at coordinate $x = 0$

$P_{av} = \frac{1}{2}P_{max}$

Period T

Wave superposition: A wave reflects when it reaches a boundary of its medium. At any point where two or more waves overlap, the total displacement is the sum of the displacements of the individual waves (principle of superposition).

$$y(x, t) = y_1(x, t) + y_2(x, t) \qquad (15.27)$$
(principle of superposition)

Standing waves on a string: When a sinusoidal wave is reflected from a fixed or free end of a stretched string, the incident and reflected waves combine to form a standing sinusoidal wave with nodes and antinodes. Adjacent nodes are spaced a distance $\lambda/2$ apart, as are adjacent antinodes. (See Example 15.6.)

When both ends of a string with length L are held fixed, standing waves can occur only when L is an integer multiple of $\lambda/2$. Each frequency with its associated vibration pattern is called a normal mode. (See Examples 15.7 and 15.8.)

$$y(x, t) = (A_{SW}\sin kx)\sin\omega t \qquad (15.28)$$
(standing wave on a string, fixed end at $x = 0$)

$$f_n = n\frac{v}{2L} = nf_1 \qquad (15.33)$$
$$(n = 1, 2, 3, \ldots)$$

$$f_1 = \frac{1}{2L}\sqrt{\frac{F}{\mu}} \qquad (15.35)$$
(string fixed at both ends)

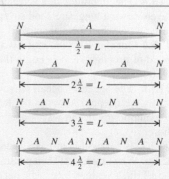

BRIDGING PROBLEM WAVES ON A ROTATING ROPE

A uniform rope with length L and mass m is held at one end and whirled in a horizontal circle with angular velocity ω. You can ignore the force of gravity on the rope. (a) At a point on the rope a distance r from the end that is held, what is the tension F? (b) What is the speed of transverse waves at this point? (c) Find the time required for a transverse wave to travel from one end of the rope to the other.

SOLUTION GUIDE

IDENTIFY and SET UP

1. Draw a sketch of the situation and label the distances r and L. The tension in the rope will be different at different values of r. Do you see why? Where on the rope do you expect the tension to be greatest? Where do you expect it will be least?

2. Where on the rope do you expect the wave speed to be greatest? Where do you expect it will be least?

3. Think about the portion of the rope that is farther out than r from the end that is held. What forces act on this portion? (Remember that you can ignore gravity.) What is the mass of this portion? How far is its center of mass from the rotation axis?

4. List the unknown quantities and decide which are your target variables.

EXECUTE

5. Draw a free-body diagram for the portion of the rope that is farther out than r from the end that is held.

6. Use your free-body diagram to help you determine the tension in the rope at distance r.

7. Use your result from step 6 to find the wave speed at distance r.

8. Use your result from step 7 to find the time for a wave to travel from one end to the other. (*Hint:* The wave speed is $v = dr/dt$, so the time for the wave to travel a distance dr along the rope is $dt = dr/v$. Integrate this to find the total time. See Appendix B.)

EVALUATE

9. Do your results for parts (a) and (b) agree with your expectations from steps 1 and 2? Are the units correct?

10. Check your result for part (a) by considering the net force on a small segment of the rope at distance r with length dr and mass $dm = (m/L)dr$. [*Hint:* The tension forces on this segment are $F(r)$ on one side and $F(r + dr)$ on the other side. You will get an equation for dF/dr that you can integrate to find F as a function of r.]

| **Problems** | For assigned homework and other learning materials, go to MasteringPhysics®. | |

•, ••, •••: Difficulty levels. **CP**: Cumulative problems incorporating material from earlier chapters. **CALC**: Problems requiring calculus. **DATA**: Problems involving real data, scientific evidence, experimental design, and/or statistical reasoning. **BIO**: Biosciences problems.

DISCUSSION QUESTIONS

Q15.1 Two waves travel on the same string. Is it possible for them to have (a) different frequencies; (b) different wavelengths; (c) different speeds; (d) different amplitudes; (e) the same frequency but different wavelengths? Explain your reasoning.

Q15.2 Under a tension F, it takes 2.00 s for a pulse to travel the length of a taut wire. What tension is required (in terms of F) for the pulse to take 6.00 s instead? Explain how you arrive at your answer.

Q15.3 What kinds of energy are associated with waves on a stretched string? How could you detect such energy experimentally?

Q15.4 The amplitude of a wave decreases gradually as the wave travels down a long, stretched string. What happens to the energy of the wave when this happens?

Q15.5 For the wave motions discussed in this chapter, does the speed of propagation depend on the amplitude? What makes you say this?

Q15.6 The speed of ocean waves depends on the depth of the water; the deeper the water, the faster the wave travels. Use this to explain why ocean waves crest and "break" as they near the shore.

Q15.7 Is it possible to have a longitudinal wave on a stretched string? Why or why not? Is it possible to have a transverse wave on a steel rod? Again, why or why not? If your answer is yes in either case, explain how you would create such a wave.

Q15.8 For transverse waves on a string, is the wave speed the same as the speed of any part of the string? Explain the difference between these two speeds. Which one is constant?

Q15.9 The four strings on a violin have different thicknesses, but are all under approximately the same tension. Do waves travel faster on the thick strings or the thin strings? Why? How does the fundamental vibration frequency compare for the thick versus the thin strings?

Q15.10 A sinusoidal wave can be described by a cosine function, which is negative just as often as positive. So why isn't the average power delivered by this wave zero?

Q15.11 Two strings of different mass per unit length μ_1 and μ_2 are tied together and stretched with a tension F. A wave travels along the string and passes the discontinuity in μ. Which of the following wave properties will be the same on both sides of the discontinuity, and which will change: speed of the wave; frequency; wavelength? Explain the physical reasoning behind each answer.

Q15.12 A long rope with mass m is suspended from the ceiling and hangs vertically. A wave pulse is produced at the lower end of the rope, and the pulse travels up the rope. Does the speed of the wave pulse change as it moves up the rope, and if so, does it increase or decrease? Explain.

Q15.13 In a transverse wave on a string, the motion of the string is perpendicular to the length of the string. How, then, is it possible for energy to move along the length of the string?

Q15.14 Energy can be transferred along a string by wave motion. However, in a standing wave on a string, no energy can ever be transferred past a node. Why not?

Q15.15 Can a standing wave be produced on a string by superposing two waves traveling in opposite directions with the same frequency but different amplitudes? Why or why not? Can a standing wave be produced by superposing two waves traveling in opposite directions with different frequencies but the same amplitude? Why or why not?

Q15.16 If you stretch a rubber band and pluck it, you hear a (somewhat) musical tone. How does the frequency of this tone change as you stretch the rubber band further? (Try it!) Does this agree with Eq. (15.35) for a string fixed at both ends? Explain.

Q15.17 A musical interval of an *octave* corresponds to a factor of 2 in frequency. By what factor must the tension in a guitar or violin string be increased to raise its pitch one octave? To raise it two octaves? Explain your reasoning. Is there any danger in attempting these changes in pitch?

Q15.18 By touching a string lightly at its center while bowing, a violinist can produce a note exactly one octave above the note to which the string is tuned—that is, a note with exactly twice the frequency. Why is this possible?

Q15.19 As we discussed in Section 15.1, water waves are a combination of longitudinal and transverse waves. Defend the following statement: "When water waves hit a vertical wall, the wall is a node of the longitudinal displacement but an antinode of the transverse displacement."

Q15.20 Violins are short instruments, while cellos and basses are long. In terms of the frequency of the waves they produce, explain why this is so.

Q15.21 What is the purpose of the frets on a guitar? In terms of the frequency of the vibration of the strings, explain their use.

EXERCISES

Section 15.2 Periodic Waves

15.1 • The speed of sound in air at $20°C$ is 344 m/s. (a) What is the wavelength of a sound wave with a frequency of 784 Hz, corresponding to the note G_5 on a piano, and how many milliseconds does each vibration take? (b) What is the wavelength of a sound wave one octave higher (twice the frequency) than the note in part (a)?

15.2 • BIO **Audible Sound.** Provided the amplitude is sufficiently great, the human ear can respond to longitudinal waves over a range of frequencies from about 20.0 Hz to about 20.0 kHz. (a) If you were to mark the beginning of each complete wave pattern with a red dot for the long-wavelength sound and a blue dot for the short-wavelength sound, how far apart would the red dots be, and how far apart would the blue dots be? (b) In reality would adjacent dots in each set be far enough apart for you to easily measure their separation with a meter stick? (c) Suppose you repeated part (a) in water, where sound travels at 1480 m/s. How far apart would the dots be in each set? Could you readily measure their separation with a meter stick?

15.3 • **Tsunami!** On December 26, 2004, a great earthquake occurred off the coast of Sumatra and triggered immense waves (tsunami) that killed some 200,000 people. Satellites observing these waves from space measured 800 km from one wave crest to the next and a period between waves of 1.0 hour. What was the speed of these waves in m/s and in km/h? Does your answer help you understand why the waves caused such devastation?

15.4 • BIO **Ultrasound Imaging.** Sound having frequencies above the range of human hearing (about 20,000 Hz) is called *ultrasound*. Waves above this frequency can be used to penetrate the body and to produce images by reflecting from surfaces. In a typical ultrasound scan, the waves travel through body tissue with a speed of 1500 m/s. For a good, detailed image, the wavelength should be no more than 1.0 mm. What frequency sound is required for a good scan?

15.5 • BIO (a) **Audible wavelengths.** The range of audible frequencies is from about 20 Hz to 20,000 Hz. What is the range of the wavelengths of audible sound in air? (b) **Visible light.** The range of visible light extends from 380 nm to 750 nm. What is the range of visible frequencies of light? (c) **Brain surgery.** Surgeons can remove brain tumors by using a cavitron ultrasonic surgical aspirator, which produces sound waves of frequency 23 kHz. What is the wavelength of these waves in air? (d) **Sound in the body.** What would be the wavelength of the sound in part (c) in bodily fluids in which the speed of sound is 1480 m/s but the frequency is unchanged?

15.6 •• A fisherman notices that his boat is moving up and down periodically, owing to waves on the surface of the water. It takes 2.5 s for the boat to travel from its highest point to its lowest, a total distance of 0.53 m. The fisherman sees that the wave crests are spaced 4.8 m apart. (a) How fast are the waves traveling? (b) What is the amplitude of each wave? (c) If the total vertical distance traveled by the boat were 0.30 m but the other data remained the same, how would the answers to parts (a) and (b) change?

Section 15.3 Mathematical Description of a Wave

15.7 • Transverse waves on a string have wave speed 8.00 m/s, amplitude 0.0700 m, and wavelength 0.320 m. The waves travel in the $-x$-direction, and at $t = 0$ the $x = 0$ end of the string has its maximum upward displacement. (a) Find the frequency, period, and wave number of these waves. (b) Write a wave function describing the wave. (c) Find the transverse displacement of a particle at $x = 0.360$ m at time $t = 0.150$ s. (d) How much time must elapse from the instant in part (c) until the particle at $x = 0.360$ m next has maximum upward displacement?

15.8 • A certain transverse wave is described by

$$y(x, t) = (6.50 \text{ mm}) \cos 2\pi \left(\frac{x}{28.0 \text{ cm}} - \frac{t}{0.0360 \text{ s}} \right)$$

Determine the wave's (a) amplitude; (b) wavelength; (c) frequency; (d) speed of propagation; (e) direction of propagation.

15.9 • CALC Which of the following wave functions satisfies the wave equation, Eq. (15.12)? (a) $y(x, t) = A \cos(kx + \omega t)$; (b) $y(x, t) = A \sin(kx + \omega t)$; (c) $y(x, t) = A(\cos kx + \cos \omega t)$. (d) For the wave of part (b), write the equations for the transverse velocity and transverse acceleration of a particle at point x.

15.10 • A water wave traveling in a straight line on a lake is described by the equation

$$y(x, t) = (2.75 \text{ cm}) \cos(0.410 \text{ rad/cm } x + 6.20 \text{ rad/s } t)$$

where y is the displacement perpendicular to the undisturbed surface of the lake. (a) How much time does it take for one complete wave pattern to go past a fisherman in a boat at anchor, and what horizontal distance does the wave crest travel in that time? (b) What are the wave number and the number of waves per second that pass the fisherman? (c) How fast does a wave crest travel past the fisherman, and what is the maximum speed of his cork floater as the wave causes it to bob up and down?

15.11 • A sinusoidal wave is propagating along a stretched string that lies along the x-axis. The displacement of the string as a function of time is graphed in **Fig. E15.11** for particles at $x = 0$ and at $x = 0.0900$ m.

Figure **E15.11**

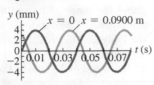

(a) What is the amplitude of the wave? (b) What is the period of the wave? (c) You are told that the two points $x = 0$ and $x = 0.0900$ m are within one wavelength of each other. If the wave is moving in the $+x$-direction, determine the wavelength and the wave speed. (d) If instead the wave is moving in the $-x$-direction, determine the wavelength and the wave speed. (e) Would it be possible to determine definitively the wavelengths in parts (c) and (d) if you were not told that the two points were within one wavelength of each other? Why or why not?

15.12 •• CALC **Speed of Propagation vs. Particle Speed.** (a) Show that Eq. (15.3) may be written as

$$y(x, t) = A \cos\left[\frac{2\pi}{\lambda}(x - vt)\right]$$

(b) Use $y(x, t)$ to find an expression for the transverse velocity v_y of a particle in the string on which the wave travels. (c) Find the maximum speed of a particle of the string. Under what circumstances is this equal to the propagation speed v? Less than v? Greater than v?

15.13 •• A transverse wave on a string has amplitude 0.300 cm, wavelength 12.0 cm, and speed 6.00 cm/s. It is represented by $y(x, t)$ as given in Exercise 15.12. (a) At time $t = 0$, compute y at 1.5-cm intervals of x (that is, at $x = 0, x = 1.5$ cm, $x = 3.0$ cm, and so on) from $x = 0$ to $x = 12.0$ cm. Graph the results. This is the shape of the string at time $t = 0$. (b) Repeat the calculations for the same values of x at times $t = 0.400$ s and $t = 0.800$ s. Graph the shape of the string at these instants. In what direction is the wave traveling?

15.14 • A wave on a string is described by $y(x, t) = A \cos(kx - \omega t)$. (a) Graph y, v_y, and a_y as functions of x for time $t = 0$. (b) Consider the following points on the string: (i) $x = 0$; (ii) $x = \pi/4k$; (iii) $x = \pi/2k$; (iv) $x = 3\pi/4k$; (v) $x = \pi/k$; (vi) $x = 5\pi/4k$; (vii) $x = 3\pi/2k$; (viii) $x = 7\pi/4k$. For a particle at each of these points at $t = 0$, describe in words whether the particle is moving and in what direction, and whether the particle is speeding up, slowing down, or instantaneously not accelerating.

Section 15.4 Speed of a Transverse Wave

15.15 • One end of a horizontal rope is attached to a prong of an electrically driven tuning fork that vibrates the rope transversely at 120 Hz. The other end passes over a pulley and supports a 1.50-kg mass. The linear mass density of the rope is 0.0480 kg/m. (a) What is the speed of a transverse wave on the rope? (b) What is the wavelength? (c) How would your answers to parts (a) and (b) change if the mass were increased to 3.00 kg?

15.16 • With what tension must a rope with length 2.50 m and mass 0.120 kg be stretched for transverse waves of frequency 40.0 Hz to have a wavelength of 0.750 m?

15.17 •• The upper end of a 3.80-m-long steel wire is fastened to the ceiling, and a 54.0-kg object is suspended from the lower end of the wire. You observe that it takes a transverse pulse 0.0492 s to travel from the bottom to the top of the wire. What is the mass of the wire?

15.18 •• A 1.50-m string of weight 0.0125 N is tied to the ceiling at its upper end, and the lower end supports a weight W. Ignore the very small variation in tension along the length of the string that is produced by the weight of the string. When you pluck the string slightly, the waves traveling up the string obey the equation

$$y(x, t) = (8.50 \text{ mm}) \cos(172 \text{ rad/m } x - 4830 \text{ rad/s } t)$$

Assume that the tension of the string is constant and equal to W. (a) How much time does it take a pulse to travel the full length of the string? (b) What is the weight W? (c) How many wavelengths are on the string at any instant of time? (d) What is the equation for waves traveling *down* the string?

15.19 • A thin, 75.0-cm wire has a mass of 16.5 g. One end is tied to a nail, and the other end is attached to a screw that can be adjusted to vary the tension in the wire. (a) To what tension (in newtons) must you adjust the screw so that a transverse wave of wavelength 3.33 cm makes 625 vibrations per second? (b) How fast would this wave travel?

15.20 •• A heavy rope 6.00 m long and weighing 29.4 N is attached at one end to a ceiling and hangs vertically. A 0.500-kg mass is suspended from the lower end of the rope. What is the speed of transverse waves on the rope at the (a) bottom of the rope, (b) middle of the rope, and (c) top of the rope? (d) Is the tension in the middle of the rope the average of the tensions at the top and bottom of the rope? Is the wave speed at the middle of the rope the average of the wave speeds at the top and bottom? Explain.

15.21 • A simple harmonic oscillator at the point $x = 0$ generates a wave on a rope. The oscillator operates at a frequency of 40.0 Hz and with an amplitude of 3.00 cm. The rope has a linear mass density of 50.0 g/m and is stretched with a tension of 5.00 N. (a) Determine the speed of the wave. (b) Find the wavelength. (c) Write the wave function $y(x, t)$ for the wave. Assume that the oscillator has its maximum upward displacement at time $t = 0$. (d) Find the maximum transverse acceleration of points on the rope. (e) In the discussion of transverse waves in this chapter, the force of gravity was ignored. Is that a reasonable approximation for this wave? Explain.

Section 15.5 Energy in Wave Motion

15.22 •• A piano wire with mass 3.00 g and length 80.0 cm is stretched with a tension of 25.0 N. A wave with frequency 120.0 Hz and amplitude 1.6 mm travels along the wire. (a) Calculate the average power carried by the wave. (b) What happens to the average power if the wave amplitude is halved?

15.23 • A horizontal wire is stretched with a tension of 94.0 N, and the speed of transverse waves for the wire is 406 m/s. What must the amplitude of a traveling wave of frequency 69.0 Hz be for the average power carried by the wave to be 0.365 W?

15.24 •• A light wire is tightly stretched with tension F. Transverse traveling waves of amplitude A and wavelength λ_1 carry average power $P_{av,1} = 0.400$ W. If the wavelength of the waves is doubled, so $\lambda_2 = 2\lambda_1$, while the tension F and amplitude A are not altered, what then is the average power $P_{av,2}$ carried by the waves?

15.25 •• A jet plane at takeoff can produce sound of intensity 10.0 W/m² at 30.0 m away. But you prefer the tranquil sound of normal conversation, which is 1.0 μW/m². Assume that the plane behaves like a point source of sound. (a) What is the closest distance you should live from the airport runway to preserve your peace of mind? (b) What intensity from the jet does your friend experience if she lives twice as far from the runway as you do? (c) What power of sound does the jet produce at takeoff?

15.26 •• **Threshold of Pain.** You are investigating the report of a UFO landing in an isolated portion of New Mexico, and you encounter a strange object that is radiating sound waves uniformly in all directions. Assume that the sound comes from a point source and that you can ignore reflections. You are slowly walking toward the source. When you are 7.5 m from it, you measure its intensity to be 0.11 W/m². An intensity of 1.0 W/m² is often used as the "threshold of pain." How much closer to the source can you move before the sound intensity reaches this threshold?

15.27 • **Energy Output.** By measurement you determine that sound waves are spreading out equally in all directions from a point source and that the intensity is 0.026 W/m² at a distance of 4.3 m from the source. (a) What is the intensity at a distance of 3.1 m from the source? (b) How much sound energy does the source emit in one hour if its power output remains constant?

15.28 • A fellow student with a mathematical bent tells you that the wave function of a traveling wave on a thin rope is $y(x, t) =$ 2.30 mm $\cos[(6.98 \text{ rad/m})x + (742 \text{ rad/s})t]$. Being more practical, you measure the rope to have a length of 1.35 m and a mass of 0.00338 kg. You are then asked to determine the following: (a) amplitude; (b) frequency; (c) wavelength; (d) wave speed; (e) direction the wave is traveling; (f) tension in the rope; (g) average power transmitted by the wave.

15.29 • At a distance of 7.00×10^{12} m from a star, the intensity of the radiation from the star is 15.4 W/m². Assuming that the star radiates uniformly in all directions, what is the total power output of the star?

Section 15.6 Wave Interference, Boundary Conditions, and Superposition

15.30 • **Reflection.** A wave pulse on a string has the dimensions shown in **Fig. E15.30** at $t = 0$. The wave speed is 40 cm/s. (a) If point O is a fixed end, draw the total wave on the string at $t = 15$ ms, 20 ms, 25 ms, 30 ms, 35 ms, 40 ms, and 45 ms. (b) Repeat part (a) for the case in which point O is a free end.

Figure **E15.30**

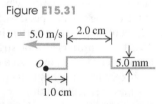
4.0 mm 4.0 mm
$v = 40$ cm/s
4.0 mm
O
8.0 mm

15.31 • **Reflection.** A wave pulse on a string has the dimensions shown in **Fig. E15.31** at $t = 0$. The wave speed is 5.0 m/s. (a) If point O is a fixed end, draw the total wave on the string at $t = 1.0$ ms, 2.0 ms, 3.0 ms, 4.0 ms, 5.0 ms, 6.0 ms, and 7.0 ms. (b) Repeat part (a) for the case in which point O is a free end.

Figure **E15.31**

$v = 5.0$ m/s
2.0 cm
O
5.0 mm
1.0 cm

15.32 • **Interference of Triangular Pulses.** Two triangular wave pulses are traveling toward each other on a stretched string as shown in **Fig. E15.32**. Each pulse is identical to the other and travels at 2.00 cm/s. The leading edges of the pulses are 1.00 cm apart at $t = 0$. Sketch the shape of the string at $t = 0.250$ s, $t = 0.500$ s, $t = 0.750$ s, $t = 1.000$ s, and $t = 1.250$ s.

Figure **E15.32**

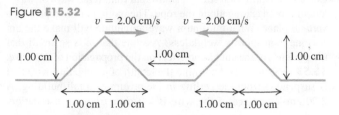
$v = 2.00$ cm/s $v = 2.00$ cm/s
1.00 cm   1.00 cm   1.00 cm
1.00 cm   1.00 cm   1.00 cm   1.00 cm

15.33 • Suppose that the left-traveling pulse in Exercise 15.32 is *below* the level of the unstretched string instead of above it. Make the same sketches that you did in that exercise.

15.34 •• Two pulses are moving in opposite directions at 1.0 cm/s on a taut string, as shown in **Fig. E15.34**. Each square is 1.0 cm. Sketch the shape of the string at the end of (a) 6.0 s; (b) 7.0 s; (c) 8.0 s.

Figure **E15.34**

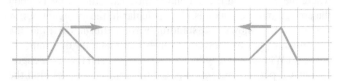

15.35 •• **Interference of Rectangular Pulses.** **Figure E15.35** shows two rectangular wave pulses on a stretched string traveling toward each other. Each pulse is traveling with a speed of 1.00 mm/s and has the height and width shown in the figure. If the leading edges of the pulses are 8.00 mm apart at $t = 0$, sketch the shape of the string at $t = 4.00$ s, $t = 6.00$ s, and $t = 10.0$ s.

Figure **E15.35**

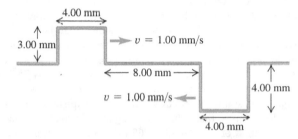
4.00 mm
3.00 mm
$v = 1.00$ mm/s
8.00 mm
$v = 1.00$ mm/s
4.00 mm
4.00 mm

Section 15.7 Standing Waves on a String
Section 15.8 Normal Modes of a String

15.36 •• CALC Adjacent antinodes of a standing wave on a string are 15.0 cm apart. A particle at an antinode oscillates in simple harmonic motion with amplitude 0.850 cm and period 0.0750 s. The string lies along the $+x$-axis and is fixed at $x = 0$. (a) How far apart are the adjacent nodes? (b) What are the wavelength, amplitude, and speed of the two traveling waves that form this pattern? (c) Find the maximum and minimum transverse speeds of a point at an antinode. (d) What is the shortest distance along the string between a node and an antinode?

15.37 • Standing waves on a wire are described by Eq. (15.28), with $A_{SW} = 2.50$ mm, $\omega = 942$ rad/s, and $k = 0.750\pi$ rad/m. The left end of the wire is at $x = 0$. At what distances from the left end are (a) the nodes of the standing wave and (b) the antinodes of the standing wave?

15.38 • A 1.50-m-long rope is stretched between two supports with a tension that makes the speed of transverse waves 62.0 m/s. What are the wavelength and frequency of (a) the fundamental; (b) the second overtone; (c) the fourth harmonic?

15.39 • A wire with mass 40.0 g is stretched so that its ends are tied down at points 80.0 cm apart. The wire vibrates in its fundamental mode with frequency 60.0 Hz and with an amplitude at the antinodes of 0.300 cm. (a) What is the speed of propagation of transverse waves in the wire? (b) Compute the tension in the wire. (c) Find the maximum transverse velocity and acceleration of particles in the wire.

15.40 • A piano tuner stretches a steel piano wire with a tension of 800 N. The steel wire is 0.400 m long and has a mass of 3.00 g. (a) What is the frequency of its fundamental mode of vibration? (b) What is the number of the highest harmonic that could be heard by a person who is capable of hearing frequencies up to 10,000 Hz?

15.41 • CALC A thin, taut string tied at both ends and oscillating in its third harmonic has its shape described by the equation $y(x, t) = (5.60 \text{ cm}) \sin[(0.0340 \text{ rad/cm})x] \sin[(50.0 \text{ rad/s})t]$, where the origin is at the left end of the string, the x-axis is along the string, and the y-axis is perpendicular to the string. (a) Draw a sketch that shows the standing-wave pattern. (b) Find the amplitude of the two traveling waves that make up this standing wave. (c) What is the length of the string? (d) Find the wavelength, frequency, period, and speed of the traveling waves. (e) Find the maximum transverse speed of a point on the string. (f) What would be the equation $y(x,t)$ for this string if it were vibrating in its eighth harmonic?

15.42 • The wave function of a standing wave is $y(x, t) = 4.44 \text{ mm} \sin[(32.5 \text{ rad/m})x] \sin[(754 \text{ rad/s})t]$. For the two traveling waves that make up this standing wave, find the (a) amplitude; (b) wavelength; (c) frequency; (d) wave speed; (e) wave functions. (f) From the information given, can you determine which harmonic this is? Explain.

15.43 • **Waves on a Stick.** A flexible stick 2.0 m long is not fixed in any way and is free to vibrate. Make clear drawings of this stick vibrating in its first three harmonics, and then use your drawings to find the wavelengths of each of these harmonics. (*Hint:* Should the ends be nodes or antinodes?)

15.44 •• One string of a certain musical instrument is 75.0 cm long and has a mass of 8.75 g. It is being played in a room where the speed of sound is 344 m/s. (a) To what tension must you adjust the string so that, when vibrating in its second overtone, it produces sound of wavelength 0.765 m? (Assume that the breaking stress of the wire is very large and isn't exceeded.) (b) What frequency sound does this string produce in its fundamental mode of vibration?

15.45 • The portion of the string of a certain musical instrument between the bridge and upper end of the finger board (that part of the string that is free to vibrate) is 60.0 cm long, and this length of the string has mass 2.00 g. The string sounds an A_4 note (440 Hz) when played. (a) Where must the player put a finger (what distance x from the bridge) to play a D_5 note (587 Hz)? (See **Fig. E15.45**.) For both the A_4 and D_5 notes, the string vibrates in its fundamental mode. (b) Without retuning, is it possible to play a G_4 note (392 Hz) on this string? Why or why not?

Figure **E15.45**

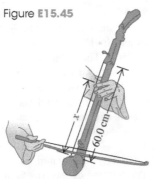

15.46 • (a) A horizontal string tied at both ends is vibrating in its fundamental mode. The traveling waves have speed v, frequency f, amplitude A, and wavelength λ. Calculate the maximum transverse velocity and maximum transverse acceleration of points located at (i) $x = \lambda/2$, (ii) $x = \lambda/4$, and (iii) $x = \lambda/8$, from the left-hand end of the string. (b) At each of the points in part (a), what is the amplitude of the motion? (c) At each of the points in part (a), how much time does it take the string to go from its largest upward displacement to its largest downward displacement?

15.47 • **Guitar String.** One of the 63.5-cm-long strings of an ordinary guitar is tuned to produce the note B_3 (frequency 245 Hz) when vibrating in its fundamental mode. (a) Find the speed of transverse waves on this string. (b) If the tension in this string is increased by 1.0%, what will be the new fundamental frequency of the string? (c) If the speed of sound in the surrounding air is 344 m/s, find the frequency and wavelength of the sound wave produced in the air by the vibration of the B_3 string. How do these compare to the frequency and wavelength of the standing wave on the string?

PROBLEMS

15.48 • A transverse wave on a rope is given by

$$y(x, t) = (0.750 \text{ cm}) \cos \pi[(0.400 \text{ cm}^{-1})x + (250 \text{ s}^{-1})t]$$

(a) Find the amplitude, period, frequency, wavelength, and speed of propagation. (b) Sketch the shape of the rope at these values of t: 0, 0.0005 s, 0.0010 s. (c) Is the wave traveling in the $+x$- or $-x$-direction? (d) The mass per unit length of the rope is 0.0500 kg/m. Find the tension. (e) Find the average power of this wave.

15.49 • CALC A transverse sine wave with an amplitude of 2.50 mm and a wavelength of 1.80 m travels from left to right along a long, horizontal, stretched string with a speed of 36.0 m/s. Take the origin at the left end of the undisturbed string. At time $t = 0$ the left end of the string has its maximum upward displacement. (a) What are the frequency, angular frequency, and wave number of the wave? (b) What is the function $y(x, t)$ that describes the wave? (c) What is $y(t)$ for a particle at the left end of the string? (d) What is $y(t)$ for a particle 1.35 m to the right of the origin? (e) What is the maximum magnitude of transverse velocity of any particle of the string? (f) Find the transverse displacement and the transverse velocity of a particle 1.35 m to the right of the origin at time $t = 0.0625$ s.

15.50 •• CP A 1750-N irregular beam is hanging horizontally by its ends from the ceiling by two vertical wires (A and B), each 1.25 m long and weighing 0.290 N. The center of gravity of this beam is one-third of the way along the beam from the end where wire A is attached. If you pluck both strings at the same time at the beam, what is the time delay between the arrival of the two pulses at the ceiling? Which pulse arrives first? (Ignore the effect of the weight of the wires on the tension in the wires.)

15.51 •• Three pieces of string, each of length L, are joined together end to end, to make a combined string of length $3L$. The first piece of string has mass per unit length μ_1, the second piece has mass per unit length $\mu_2 = 4\mu_1$, and the third piece has mass per unit length $\mu_3 = \mu_1/4$. (a) If the combined string is under tension F, how much time does it take a transverse wave to travel the entire length $3L$? Give your answer in terms of L, F, and μ_1. (b) Does your answer to part (a) depend on the order in which the three pieces are joined together? Explain.

15.52 •• **Weightless Ant.** An ant with mass m is standing peacefully on top of a horizontal, stretched rope. The rope has mass per unit length μ and is under tension F. Without warning, Cousin Throckmorton starts a sinusoidal transverse wave of wavelength λ propagating along the rope. The motion of the rope is in a vertical plane. What minimum wave amplitude will make the ant become momentarily weightless? Assume that m is so small that the presence of the ant has no effect on the propagation of the wave.

15.53 •• You must determine the length of a long, thin wire that is suspended from the ceiling in the atrium of a tall building. A 2.00-cm-long piece of the wire is left over from its installation.

Using an analytical balance, you determine that the mass of the spare piece is 14.5 μg. You then hang a 0.400-kg mass from the lower end of the long, suspended wire. When a small-amplitude transverse wave pulse is sent up that wire, sensors at both ends measure that it takes the wave pulse 26.7 ms to travel the length of the wire. (a) Use these measurements to calculate the length of the wire. Assume that the weight of the wire has a negligible effect on the speed of the transverse waves. (b) Discuss the accuracy of the approximation made in part (a).

15.54 •• **Music.** You are designing a two-string instrument with metal strings 35.0 cm long, as shown in **Fig. P15.54**. Both strings are under the *same tension*. String S_1 has a mass of 8.00 g and produces the note middle C (frequency 262 Hz) in its fundamental mode. (a) What should be the tension in the string? (b) What should be the mass of string S_2 so that it will produce A-sharp (frequency 466 Hz) as its fundamental? (c) To extend the range of your instrument, you include a fret located just under the strings but not normally touching them. How far from the upper end should you put this fret so that when you press S_1 tightly against it, this string will produce C-sharp (frequency 277 Hz) in its fundamental? That is, what is x in the figure? (d) If you press S_2 against the fret, what frequency of sound will it produce in its fundamental?

Figure **P15.54**

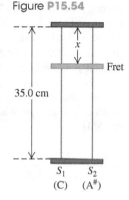

15.55 ••• **CP** A 5.00-m, 0.732-kg wire is used to support two uniform 235-N posts of equal length (**Fig. P15.55**). Assume that the wire is essentially horizontal and that the speed of sound is 344 m/s. A strong wind is blowing, causing the wire to vibrate in its 5th overtone. What are the frequency and wavelength of the sound this wire produces?

Figure **P15.55**

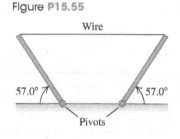

15.56 ••• **CP** You are exploring a newly discovered planet. The radius of the planet is 7.20×10^7 m. You suspend a lead weight from the lower end of a light string that is 4.00 m long and has mass 0.0280 kg. You measure that it takes 0.0685 s for a transverse pulse to travel from the lower end to the upper end of the string. On the earth, for the same string and lead weight, it takes 0.0390 s for a transverse pulse to travel the length of the string. The weight of the string is small enough that you ignore its effect on the tension in the string. Assuming that the mass of the planet is distributed with spherical symmetry, what is its mass?

15.57 •• For a string stretched between two supports, two successive standing-wave frequencies are 525 Hz and 630 Hz. There are other standing-wave frequencies lower than 525 Hz and higher than 630 Hz. If the speed of transverse waves on the string is 384 m/s, what is the length of the string? Assume that the mass of the wire is small enough for its effect on the tension in the wire to be ignored.

15.58 •• A 0.800-m-long string with linear mass density $\mu = 7.50$ g/m is stretched between two supports. The string has tension F and a standing-wave pattern (not the fundamental) of frequency 624 Hz. With the same tension, the next higher standing-wave frequency is 780 Hz. (a) What are the frequency

and wavelength of the fundamental standing wave for this string? (b) What is the value of F?

15.59 ••• **CP** A 1.80-m-long uniform bar that weighs 638 N is suspended in a horizontal position by two vertical wires that are attached to the ceiling. One wire is aluminum and the other is copper. The aluminum wire is attached to the left-hand end of the bar, and the copper wire is attached 0.40 m to the left of the right-hand end. Each wire has length 0.600 m and a circular cross section with radius 0.280 mm. What is the fundamental frequency of transverse standing waves for each wire?

15.60 ••• A continuous succession of sinusoidal wave pulses are produced at one end of a very long string and travel along the length of the string. The wave has frequency 70.0 Hz, amplitude 5.00 mm, and wavelength 0.600 m. (a) How long does it take the wave to travel a distance of 8.00 m along the length of the string? (b) How long does it take a point on the string to travel a distance of 8.00 m, once the wave train has reached the point and set it into motion? (c) In parts (a) and (b), how does the time change if the amplitude is doubled?

15.61 •• A horizontal wire is tied to supports at each end and vibrates in its second-overtone standing wave. The tension in the wire is 5.00 N, and the node-to-node distance in the standing wave is 6.28 cm. (a) What is the length of the wire? (b) A point at an antinode of the standing wave on the wire travels from its maximum upward displacement to its maximum downward displacement in 8.40 ms. What is the wire's mass?

15.62 ••• **CP** A vertical, 1.20-m length of 18-gauge (diameter of 1.024 mm) copper wire has a 100.0-N ball hanging from it. (a) What is the wavelength of the third harmonic for this wire? (b) A 500.0-N ball now *replaces* the original ball. What is the change in the wavelength of the third harmonic caused by replacing the light ball with the heavy one? (*Hint:* See Table 11.1 for Young's modulus.)

15.63 ••• A sinusoidal transverse wave travels on a string. The string has length 8.00 m and mass 6.00 g. The wave speed is 30.0 m/s, and the wavelength is 0.200 m. (a) If the wave is to have an average power of 50.0 W, what must be the amplitude of the wave? (b) For this same string, if the amplitude and wavelength are the same as in part (a), what is the average power for the wave if the tension is increased such that the wave speed is doubled?

15.64 •• A vibrating string 50.0 cm long is under a tension of 1.00 N. The results from five successive stroboscopic pictures are shown in **Fig. P15.64**. The strobe rate is set at 5000 flashes per minute, and observations reveal that the maximum displacement occurred at flashes 1 and 5 with no other maxima in between. (a) Find the period, frequency, and wavelength for the traveling waves on this string. (b) In what normal mode (harmonic) is the string vibrating? (c) What is the speed of the traveling waves on the string? (d) How fast is point P moving when the string is in (i) position 1 and (ii) position 3? (e) What is the mass of this string?

Figure **P15.64**

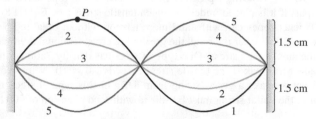

15.65 • **Clothesline Nodes.** Cousin Throckmorton is once again playing with the clothesline in Example 15.2 (Section 15.3). One end of the clothesline is attached to a vertical post. Throcky holds the other end loosely in his hand, so the speed of waves on the clothesline is a relatively slow 0.720 m/s. He finds several frequencies at which he can oscillate his end of the clothesline so that a light clothespin 45.0 cm from the post doesn't move. What are these frequencies?

15.66 •• A strong string of mass 3.00 g and length 2.20 m is tied to supports at each end and is vibrating in its fundamental mode. The maximum transverse speed of a point at the middle of the string is 9.00 m/s. The tension in the string is 330 N. (a) What is the amplitude of the standing wave at its antinode? (b) What is the magnitude of the maximum transverse acceleration of a point at the antinode?

15.67 •• A thin string 2.50 m in length is stretched with a tension of 90.0 N between two supports. When the string vibrates in its first overtone, a point at an antinode of the standing wave on the string has an amplitude of 3.50 cm and a maximum transverse speed of 28.0 m/s. (a) What is the string's mass? (b) What is the magnitude of the maximum transverse acceleration of this point on the string?

15.68 ••• CALC A guitar string is vibrating in its fundamental mode, with nodes at each end. The length of the segment of the string that is free to vibrate is 0.386 m. The maximum transverse acceleration of a point at the middle of the segment is 8.40×10^3 m/s^2 and the maximum transverse velocity is 3.80 m/s. (a) What is the amplitude of this standing wave? (b) What is the wave speed for the transverse traveling waves on this string?

15.69 ••• A uniform cylindrical steel wire, 55.0 cm long and 1.14 mm in diameter, is fixed at both ends. To what tension must it be adjusted so that, when vibrating in its first overtone, it produces the note D-sharp of frequency 311 Hz? Assume that it stretches an insignificant amount. (*Hint:* See Table 12.1.)

15.70 •• A string with both ends held fixed is vibrating in its third harmonic. The waves have a speed of 192 m/s and a frequency of 240 Hz. The amplitude of the standing wave at an antinode is 0.400 cm. (a) Calculate the amplitude at points on the string a distance of (i) 40.0 cm; (ii) 20.0 cm; and (iii) 10.0 cm from the left end of the string. (b) At each point in part (a), how much time does it take the string to go from its largest upward displacement to its largest downward displacement? (c) Calculate the maximum transverse velocity and the maximum transverse acceleration of the string at each of the points in part (a).

15.71 ••• CP A large rock that weighs 164.0 N is suspended from the lower end of a thin wire that is 3.00 m long. The density of the rock is 3200 kg/m^3. The mass of the wire is small enough that its effect on the tension in the wire can be ignored. The upper end of the wire is held fixed. When the rock is in air, the fundamental frequency for transverse standing waves on the wire is 42.0 Hz. When the rock is totally submerged in a liquid, with the top of the rock just below the surface, the fundamental frequency for the wire is 28.0 Hz. What is the density of the liquid?

15.72 • **Holding Up Under Stress.** A string or rope will break apart if it is placed under too much tensile stress [see Eq. (11.8)]. Thicker ropes can withstand more tension without breaking because the thicker the rope, the greater the cross-sectional area and the smaller the stress. One type of steel has density 7800 kg/m^3 and will break if the tensile stress exceeds 7.0×10^8 N/m^2. You want to make a guitar string from 4.0 g of this type of steel. In use, the guitar string must be able to withstand a tension of 900 N without breaking. Your job is to determine (a) the maximum length and minimum radius the string can have; (b) the highest possible fundamental frequency of standing waves on this string, if the entire length of the string is free to vibrate.

15.73 •• **Tuning an Instrument.** A musician tunes the C-string of her instrument to a fundamental frequency of 65.4 Hz. The vibrating portion of the string is 0.600 m long and has a mass of 14.4 g. (a) With what tension must the musician stretch it? (b) What percent increase in tension is needed to increase the frequency from 65.4 Hz to 73.4 Hz, corresponding to a rise in pitch from C to D?

15.74 •• **DATA** *Scale length* is the length of the part of a guitar string that is free to vibrate. A standard value of scale length for an acoustic guitar is 25.5 in. The frequency of the fundamental standing wave on a string is determined by the string's scale length, tension, and linear mass density. The standard frequencies f to which the strings of a six-string guitar are tuned are given in the table:

String	E2	A2	D3	G3	B3	E4
f (Hz)	82.4	110.0	146.8	196.0	246.9	329.6

Assume that a typical value of the tension of a guitar string is 78.0 N (although tension varies somewhat for different strings). (a) Calculate the linear mass density μ (in g/cm) for the E2, G3, and E4 strings. (b) Just before your band is going to perform, your G3 string breaks. The only replacement string you have is an E2. If your strings have the linear mass densities calculated in part (a), what must be the tension in the replacement string to bring its fundamental frequency to the G3 value of 196.0 Hz?

15.75 •• **DATA** In your physics lab, an oscillator is attached to one end of a horizontal string. The other end of the string passes over a frictionless pulley. You suspend a mass M from the free end of the string, producing tension Mg in the string. The oscillator produces transverse waves of frequency f on the string. You don't vary this frequency during the experiment, but you try strings with three different linear mass densities μ. You also keep a fixed distance between the end of the string where the oscillator is attached and the point where the string is in contact with the pulley's rim. To produce standing waves on the string, you vary M; then you measure the node-to-node distance d for each standing-wave pattern and obtain the following data:

String	A	A	B	B	C
μ (g/cm)	0.0260	0.0260	0.0374	0.0374	0.0482
M (g)	559	249	365	207	262
d (cm)	48.1	31.9	32.0	24.2	23.8

(a) Explain why you obtain only certain values of d. (b) Graph μd^2 (in kg · m) versus M (in kg). Explain why the data plotted this way should fall close to a straight line. (c) Use the slope of the best straight-line fit to the data to determine the frequency f of the waves produced on the string by the oscillator. Take $g = 9.80$ m/s^2. (d) For string A ($\mu = 0.0260$ g/cm), what value of M (in grams) would be required to produce a standing wave with a node-to-node distance of 24.0 cm? Use the value of f that you calculated in part (c).

15.76 •• **DATA** You are measuring the frequency dependence of the average power P_{av} transmitted by traveling waves on a wire. In your experiment you use a wire with linear mass density 3.5 g/m. For a transverse wave on the wire with amplitude 4.0 mm, you measure P_{av} (in watts) as a function of the frequency f of the wave (in Hz). You have chosen to plot P_{av} as a function of f^2 (**Fig. P15.76**). (a) Explain why values of P_{av} plotted versus f^2 should be well fit by a straight line. (b) Use the slope of the straight-line fit to the data shown in Fig P15.76 to calculate the speed of the waves. (c) What angular frequency ω would result in $P_{av} = 10.0$ W?

Figure **P15.76**

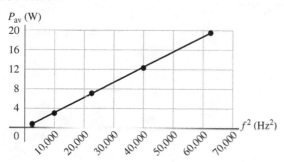

CHALLENGE PROBLEM

15.77 ••• **CP CALC** A deep-sea diver is suspended beneath the surface of Loch Ness by a 100-m-long cable that is attached to a boat on the surface (**Fig. P15.77**). The diver and his suit have a total mass of 120 kg and a volume of 0.0800 m³. The cable has a diameter of 2.00 cm and a linear mass density of $\mu = 1.10$ kg/m. The diver thinks he sees something moving in the murky depths and jerks the end of the cable back and forth to send transverse waves up the cable as a signal to his companions in the boat. (a) What is the tension in the cable at its lower end, where it is attached to the diver? Do not forget to include the buoyant force that the water (density 1000 kg/m³) exerts on him. (b) Calculate the tension in the cable a distance x above the diver. In your calculation, include the buoyant force on the cable. (c) The speed of transverse waves on the cable is given by $v = \sqrt{F/\mu}$ (Eq. 15.14). The speed therefore varies along the cable, since the tension is not constant. (This expression ignores the damping force that the water exerts on the moving cable.) Integrate to find the time required for the first signal to reach the surface.

Figure **P15.77**

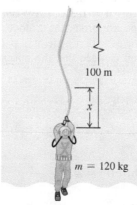

100 m

x

$m = 120$ kg

BIO **WAVES ON VOCAL FOLDS.** In the larynx, sound is produced by the vibration of the *vocal folds* (also called "vocal cords"). The accompanying figure is a cross section of the vocal tract at one instant in time. Air flows upward (in the +z-direction) through the vocal tract, causing a transverse wave to propagate vertically upward along the surface of the vocal folds. In a typical adult male, the thickness of

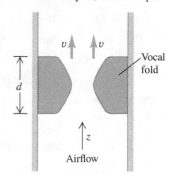

Vocal fold

Airflow

the vocal folds in the direction of airflow is $d = 2.0$ mm. High-speed photography shows that for a frequency of vibration of $f = 125$ Hz, the wave along the surface of the vocal folds travels upward at a speed of $v = 375$ cm/s. Use t for time, z for displacement in the +z-direction, and λ for wavelength.

15.78 What is the wavelength of the wave that travels on the surface of the vocal folds when they are vibrating at frequency f? (a) 2.0 mm; (b) 3.3 mm; (c) 0.50 cm; (d) 3.0 cm.

15.79 Which of these is a possible mathematical description of the wave in Problem 15.78? (a) $A\sin[2\pi f(t + z/v)]$; (b) $A\sin[2\pi f(t - z/v)]$; (c) $A\sin(2\pi ft)\cos(2\pi z/\lambda)$; (d) $A\sin(2\pi ft)\sin(2\pi z/\lambda)$.

15.80 The wave speed is measured for different vibration frequencies. A graph of the wave speed as a function of frequency (**Fig. P15.80**) indicates that as the frequency increases, the wavelength (a) increases; (b) decreases; (c) doesn't change; (d) becomes undefined.

Figure **P15.80**

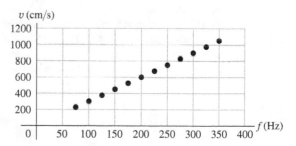

Answers

Chapter Opening Question ?

(iii) The power of a mechanical wave depends on both its amplitude and its frequency [see Eq. (15.25)].

Test Your Understanding Questions

15.1 (i) The "wave" travels horizontally from one spectator to the next along each row of the stadium, but the displacement of each spectator is vertically upward. Since the displacement is perpendicular to the direction in which the wave travels, the wave is transverse.

15.2 (iv) The speed of waves on a string, v, does not depend on the wavelength. We can rewrite the relationship $v = \lambda f$ as $f = v/\lambda$, which tells us that if the wavelength λ doubles, the frequency f becomes one-half as great.

15.3 (a) $\frac{2}{8}T$, **(b)** $\frac{4}{8}T$, **(c)** $\frac{5}{8}T$ Since the wave is sinusoidal, each point on the string oscillates in simple harmonic motion (SHM). Hence we can apply all of the ideas from Chapter 14 about SHM to the wave depicted in Fig. 15.8. (a) A particle in SHM has its maximum speed when it is passing through the equilibrium position ($y = 0$ in Fig. 15.8). The particle at point A is moving upward through this position at $t = \frac{2}{8}T$. (b) In vertical SHM the greatest *upward* acceleration occurs when a particle is at its maximum *downward* displacement. This occurs for the particle at point B at $t = \frac{4}{8}T$. (c) A particle in vertical SHM has a *downward* acceleration when its displacement is *upward*. The particle at C has an upward displacement and is moving downward at $t = \frac{5}{8}T$.

15.4 (ii) The relationship $v = \sqrt{F/\mu}$ [Eq. (15.14)] says that the wave speed is greatest on the string with the smallest linear mass density. This is the thinnest string, which has the smallest amount of mass m and hence the smallest linear mass density $\mu = m/L$ (all strings are the same length).

15.5 (iii), (iv), (ii), (i) Equation (15.25) says that the average power in a sinusoidal wave on a string is $P_{av} = \frac{1}{2}\sqrt{\mu F}\omega^2 A^2$. All four strings are identical, so all have the same mass, length, and linear mass density μ. The frequency f is the same for each wave, as is the angular frequency $\omega = 2\pi f$. Hence the average wave power for each string is proportional to the square root of the string tension F and the square of the amplitude A. Compared to string (i), the average power in each string is (ii) $\sqrt{4} = 2$ times greater; (iii) $4^2 = 16$ times greater; and (iv) $\sqrt{2}(2)^2 = 4\sqrt{2}$ times greater.

15.6

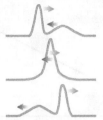

15.7 Yes, yes Doubling the frequency makes the wavelength half as large. Hence the spacing between nodes (equal to $\lambda/2$) is also half as large. There are nodes at all of the previous positions, but there is also a new node between every pair of old nodes.

15.8 $n = 1, 3, 5, \ldots$ When you touch the string at its center, you are producing a node at the center. Hence only standing waves with a node at $x = L/2$ are allowed. From Figure 15.26 you can see that the normal modes $n = 1, 3, 5, \ldots$ cannot be present.

Bridging Problem

(a) $F(r) = \dfrac{m\omega^2}{2L}(L^2 - r^2)$

(b) $v(r) = \omega\sqrt{\dfrac{L^2 - r^2}{2}}$

(c) $\dfrac{\pi}{\omega\sqrt{2}}$

? The sound from a horn travels more slowly on a cold winter day high in the mountains than on a warm summer day at sea level. This is because at high elevations in winter, the air has lower (i) pressure; (ii) density; (iii) humidity; (iv) temperature; (v) mass per mole.

16 SOUND AND HEARING

Of all the mechanical waves that occur in nature, the most important in our everyday lives are longitudinal waves in a medium—usually air—called *sound* waves. The reason is that the human ear is tremendously sensitive and can detect sound waves even of very low intensity. The ability to hear an unseen nocturnal predator was essential to the survival of our ancestors, so it is no exaggeration to say that we humans owe our existence to our highly evolved sense of hearing.

In Chapter 15 we described mechanical waves primarily in terms of displacement; however, because the ear is primarily sensitive to changes in pressure, it's often more appropriate to describe sound waves in terms of *pressure* fluctuations. We'll study the relationships among displacement, pressure fluctuation, and intensity and the connections between these quantities and human sound perception.

When a source of sound or a listener moves through the air, the listener may hear a frequency different from the one emitted by the source. This is the Doppler effect, which has important applications in medicine and technology.

16.1 SOUND WAVES

The most general definition of **sound** is a longitudinal wave in a medium. Our main concern is with sound waves in air, but sound can travel through any gas, liquid, or solid. You may be all too familiar with the propagation of sound through a solid if your neighbor's stereo speakers are right next to your wall.

The simplest sound waves are sinusoidal waves, which have definite frequency, amplitude, and wavelength. The human ear is sensitive to waves in the frequency range from about 20 to 20,000 Hz, called the **audible range,** but we also use the term "sound" for similar waves with frequencies above (**ultrasonic**) and below (**infrasonic**) the range of human hearing.

16.1 A sinusoidal longitudinal wave traveling to the right in a fluid. (Compare to Fig. 15.7.)

Longitudinal waves are shown at intervals of $\frac{1}{8}T$ for one period T.

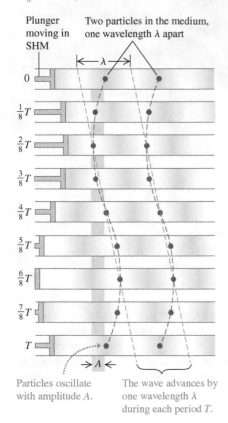

Plunger moving in SHM

Two particles in the medium, one wavelength λ apart

Particles oscillate with amplitude A.

The wave advances by one wavelength λ during each period T.

Sound waves usually travel outward in all directions from the source of sound, with an amplitude that depends on the direction and distance from the source. We'll return to this point in the next section. For now, we concentrate on the idealized case of a sound wave that propagates in the positive x-direction only. As we discussed in Section 15.3, for such a wave, the wave function $y(x, t)$ gives the instantaneous displacement y of a particle in the medium at position x at time t. If the wave is sinusoidal, we can express it by using Eq. (15.7):

$$y(x, t) = A\cos(kx - \omega t) \qquad \begin{array}{l}\text{(sound wave propagating} \\ \text{in the } +x\text{-direction)}\end{array} \qquad (16.1)$$

In a longitudinal wave the displacements are *parallel* to the direction of travel of the wave, so distances x and y are measured parallel to each other, not perpendicular as in a transverse wave. The amplitude A is the maximum displacement of a particle in the medium from its equilibrium position (**Fig. 16.1**). Hence A is also called the **displacement amplitude.**

Sound Waves As Pressure Fluctuations

We can also describe sound waves in terms of variations of *pressure* at various points. In a sinusoidal sound wave in air, the pressure fluctuates sinusoidally above and below atmospheric pressure p_a with the same frequency as the motions of the air particles. The human ear operates by sensing such pressure variations. A sound wave entering the ear canal exerts a fluctuating pressure on one side of the eardrum; the air on the other side of the eardrum, vented to the outside by the Eustachian tube, is at atmospheric pressure. The pressure difference on the two sides of the eardrum sets it into motion. Microphones and similar devices also usually sense pressure differences, not displacements.

Let $p(x, t)$ be the instantaneous pressure fluctuation in a sound wave at any point x at time t. That is, $p(x, t)$ is the amount by which the pressure *differs* from normal atmospheric pressure p_a. Think of $p(x, t)$ as the *gauge pressure* defined in Section 12.2; it can be either positive or negative. The *absolute* pressure at a point is then $p_a + p(x, t)$.

To see the connection between the pressure fluctuation $p(x, t)$ and the displacement $y(x, t)$ in a sound wave propagating in the $+x$-direction, consider an imaginary cylinder of a wave medium (gas, liquid, or solid) with cross-sectional area S and its axis along the direction of propagation (**Fig. 16.2**). When no sound wave is present, the cylinder has length Δx and volume $V = S\,\Delta x$, as shown by the shaded volume in Fig. 16.2. When a wave is present, at time t the end of the cylinder that is initially at x is displaced by $y_1 = y(x, t)$, and the end that is initially at $x + \Delta x$ is displaced by $y_2 = y(x + \Delta x, t)$; this is shown by the red lines. If $y_2 > y_1$, as shown in Fig. 16.2, the cylinder's volume has increased, which causes a decrease in pressure. If $y_2 < y_1$, the cylinder's volume has decreased and the pressure has increased. If $y_2 = y_1$, the cylinder is simply shifted to the left or right; there is no volume change and no pressure fluctuation. The pressure fluctuation depends on the *difference* between the displacements at neighboring points in the medium.

Quantitatively, the change in volume ΔV of the cylinder is

$$\Delta V = S(y_2 - y_1) = S[y(x + \Delta x, t) - y(x, t)]$$

In the limit as $\Delta x \to 0$, the fractional change in volume dV/V (volume change divided by original volume) is

16.2 As a sound wave propagates along the x-axis, the left and right ends undergo different displacements y_1 and y_2.

Undisturbed cylinder of fluid has cross-sectional area S, length Δx, and volume $S\,\Delta x$.

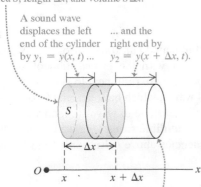

A sound wave displaces the left end of the cylinder by $y_1 = y(x, t)$ ...

... and the right end by $y_2 = y(x + \Delta x, t)$.

The change in volume of the disturbed cylinder of fluid is $S(y_2 - y_1)$.

$$\frac{dV}{V} = \lim_{\Delta x \to 0} \frac{S[y(x + \Delta x, t) - y(x, t)]}{S\,\Delta x} = \frac{\partial y(x, t)}{\partial x} \qquad (16.2)$$

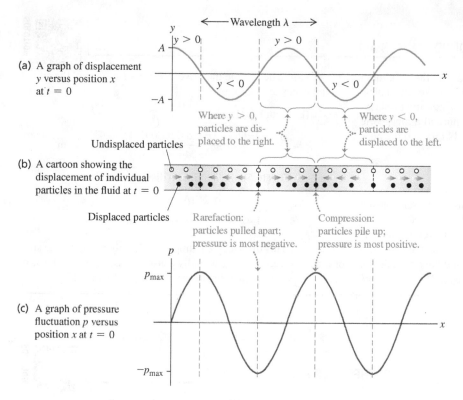

(a) A graph of displacement y versus position x at $t = 0$

(b) A cartoon showing the displacement of individual particles in the fluid at $t = 0$

(c) A graph of pressure fluctuation p versus position x at $t = 0$

The fractional volume change is related to the pressure fluctuation by the bulk modulus B, which by definition [Eq. (11.13)] is $B = -p(x, t)/(dV/V)$ (see Section 11.4). Solving for $p(x, t)$, we have

$$p(x, t) = -B\frac{\partial y(x, t)}{\partial x} \tag{16.3}$$

The negative sign arises because when $\partial y(x, t)/\partial x$ is positive, the displacement is greater at $x + \Delta x$ than at x, corresponding to an increase in volume, a decrease in pressure, and a negative pressure fluctuation.

When we evaluate $\partial y(x, t)/\partial x$ for the sinusoidal wave of Eq. (16.1), we find

$$p(x, t) = BkA\sin(kx - \omega t) \tag{16.4}$$

Figure 16.3 shows $y(x, t)$ and $p(x, t)$ for a sinusoidal sound wave at $t = 0$. It also shows how individual particles of the wave are displaced at this time. While $y(x, t)$ and $p(x, t)$ describe the same wave, these two functions are one-quarter cycle out of phase: At any time, the displacement is greatest where the pressure fluctuation is zero, and vice versa. In particular, note that the compressions (points of greatest pressure and density) and rarefactions (points of lowest pressure and density) are points of *zero* displacement.

Equation (16.4) shows that the quantity BkA represents the maximum pressure fluctuation. We call this the **pressure amplitude,** denoted by p_{max}:

Bulk modulus of medium

Pressure amplitude, sinusoidal sound wave $p_{max} = BkA$ Displacement amplitude   (16.5)

Wave number $= 2\pi/\lambda$

Waves of shorter wavelength λ (larger wave number $k = 2\pi/\lambda$) have greater pressure variations for a given displacement amplitude because the maxima and minima are squeezed closer together. A medium with a large value of bulk modulus B is less compressible and so requires a greater pressure amplitude for a given volume change (that is, a given displacement amplitude).

CAUTION **Graphs of a sound wave** The graphs in Fig. 16.3 show the wave at only *one* instant of time. Because the wave is propagating in the $+x$-direction, as time goes by the wave patterns described by the functions $y(x, t)$ and $p(x, t)$ move to the right at the wave speed $v = \omega/k$. The particles, by contrast, simply oscillate back and forth in simple harmonic motion as shown in Fig. 16.1. ∎

EXAMPLE 16.1 AMPLITUDE OF A SOUND WAVE IN AIR

In a sinusoidal sound wave of moderate loudness, the maximum pressure variations are about 3.0×10^{-2} Pa above and below atmospheric pressure. Find the corresponding maximum displacement if the frequency is 1000 Hz. In air at normal atmospheric pressure and density, the speed of sound is 344 m/s and the bulk modulus is 1.42×10^5 Pa.

SOLUTION

IDENTIFY and SET UP: This problem involves the relationship between two ways of describing a sound wave: in terms of displacement and in terms of pressure. The target variable is the displacement amplitude A. We are given the pressure amplitude p_{max}, wave speed v, frequency f, and bulk modulus B. Equation (16.5) relates the target variable A to p_{max}. We use $\omega = vk$

[Eq. (15.6)] to determine the wave number k from v and the angular frequency $\omega = 2\pi f$.

EXECUTE: From Eq. (15.6),

$$k = \frac{\omega}{v} = \frac{2\pi f}{v} = \frac{(2\pi \text{ rad})(1000 \text{ Hz})}{344 \text{ m/s}} = 18.3 \text{ rad/m}$$

Then from Eq. (16.5), the maximum displacement is

$$A = \frac{p_{max}}{Bk} = \frac{3.0 \times 10^{-2} \text{ Pa}}{(1.42 \times 10^5 \text{ Pa})(18.3 \text{ rad/m})} = 1.2 \times 10^{-8} \text{ m}$$

EVALUATE: This displacement amplitude is only about $\frac{1}{100}$ the size of a human cell. The ear actually senses pressure fluctuations; it detects these minuscule displacements only indirectly.

EXAMPLE 16.2 AMPLITUDE OF A SOUND WAVE IN THE INNER EAR

A sound wave that enters the human ear sets the eardrum into oscillation, which in turn causes oscillation of the *ossicles,* a chain of three tiny bones in the middle ear (**Fig. 16.4**). The ossicles transmit this oscillation to the fluid (mostly water) in the inner ear; there the fluid motion disturbs hair cells that send nerve impulses to the brain with information about the sound. The area of the moving part of the eardrum is about 43 mm^2, and that of the stapes (the smallest of the ossicles) where it connects to the inner ear is about 3.2 mm^2. For the sound in Example 16.1, determine (a) the pressure amplitude and (b) the displacement amplitude of the wave in the fluid of the inner ear, in which the speed of sound is 1500 m/s.

SOLUTION

IDENTIFY and SET UP: Although the sound wave here travels in liquid rather than air, the same principles and relationships among the properties of the wave apply. We can ignore the mass of the tiny ossicles (about 58 mg $= 5.8 \times 10^{-5}$ kg), so the force they exert on the inner-ear fluid is the same as that exerted on the eardrum and ossicles by the incident sound wave. (In Chapters 4 and 5 we used the same idea to say that the tension is the same at either end of a massless rope.) Hence the pressure amplitude in the inner ear, $p_{max(inner\,ear)}$, is greater than in the outside air, $p_{max(air)}$, because the same force is exerted on a smaller area (the area of the stapes versus the area of the eardrum). Given $p_{max(inner\,ear)}$, we find the displacement amplitude $A_{inner\,ear}$ from Eq. (16.5).

EXECUTE: (a) From the area of the eardrum and the pressure amplitude in air found in Example 16.1, the maximum force exerted by the sound wave in air on the eardrum is $F_{max} = p_{max(air)}S_{eardrum}$. Then

$$p_{max(inner\,ear)} = \frac{F_{max}}{S_{stapes}} = p_{max(air)} \frac{S_{eardrum}}{S_{stapes}}$$

$$= (3.0 \times 10^{-2} \text{ Pa}) \frac{43 \text{ mm}^2}{3.2 \text{ mm}^2} = 0.40 \text{ Pa}$$

16.4 The anatomy of the human ear. The middle ear is the size of a small marble; the ossicles (incus, malleus, and stapes) are the smallest bones in the human body.

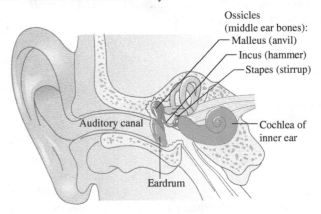

(b) To find the maximum displacement $A_{inner\,ear}$, we use $A = p_{max}/Bk$ as in Example 16.1. The inner-ear fluid is mostly water, which has a much greater bulk modulus B than air. From Table 11.2 the compressibility of water (unfortunately also called k) is 45.8×10^{-11} Pa^{-1}, so $B_{fluid} = 1/(45.8 \times 10^{-11}$ Pa$^{-1}) = 2.18 \times 10^9$ Pa.

The wave in the inner ear has the same angular frequency ω as the wave in the air because the air, eardrum, ossicles, and inner-ear fluid all oscillate together (see Example 15.8 in Section 15.8). But because the wave speed v is greater in the inner ear than in the air (1500 m/s versus 344 m/s), the wave number $k = \omega/v$ is smaller. Using the value of ω from Example 16.1,

$$k_{inner\,ear} = \frac{\omega}{v_{inner\,ear}} = \frac{(2\pi \text{ rad})(1000 \text{ Hz})}{1500 \text{ m/s}} = 4.2 \text{ rad/m}$$

Putting everything together, we have

$$A_{\text{inner ear}} = \frac{p_{\text{max (inner ear)}}}{B_{\text{fluid}} k_{\text{inner ear}}} = \frac{0.40 \text{ Pa}}{(2.18 \times 10^9 \text{ Pa})(4.2 \text{ rad/m})}$$

$$= \frac{0.40 \text{ Pa}}{(2.18 \times 10^9 \text{ Pa})(4.2 \text{ rad/m})}$$

$$= 4.4 \times 10^{-11} \text{ m}$$

EVALUATE: In part (a) we see that the ossicles increase the pressure amplitude by a factor of $(43 \text{ mm}^2)/(3.2 \text{ mm}^2) = 13$. This amplification helps give the human ear its great sensitivity.

The displacement amplitude in the inner ear is even smaller than in the air. But *pressure* variations within the inner-ear fluid are what set the hair cells into motion, so what matters is that the pressure amplitude is larger in the inner ear than in the air.

Perception of Sound Waves

The physical characteristics of a sound wave are directly related to the perception of that sound by a listener. For a given frequency, the greater the pressure amplitude of a sinusoidal sound wave, the greater the perceived **loudness.** The relationship between pressure amplitude and loudness is not a simple one, and it varies from one person to another. One important factor is that the ear is not equally sensitive to all frequencies in the audible range. A sound at one frequency may seem louder than one of equal pressure amplitude at a different frequency. At 1000 Hz the minimum pressure amplitude that can be perceived with normal hearing is about 3×10^{-5} Pa; to produce the same loudness at 200 Hz or 15,000 Hz requires about 3×10^{-4} Pa. Perceived loudness also depends on the health of the ear. Age usually brings a loss of sensitivity at high frequencies.

The frequency of a sound wave is the primary factor in determining the **pitch** of a sound, the quality that lets us classify the sound as "high" or "low." The higher the frequency of a sound (within the audible range), the higher the pitch that a listener will perceive. Pressure amplitude also plays a role in determining pitch. When a listener compares two sinusoidal sound waves with the same frequency but different pressure amplitudes, the one with the greater pressure amplitude is usually perceived as louder but also as slightly lower in pitch.

Musical sounds have wave functions that are more complicated than a simple sine function. **Figure 16.5a** shows the pressure fluctuation in the sound wave produced by a clarinet. The pattern is so complex because the column of air in a wind instrument like a clarinet vibrates at a fundamental frequency and at many harmonics at the same time. (In Section 15.8, we described this same behavior for a string that has been plucked, bowed, or struck. We'll examine the physics of wind instruments in Section 16.4.) The sound wave produced in the surrounding air has a similar amount of each harmonic—that is, a similar *harmonic content.* Figure 16.5b shows the harmonic content of the sound of a clarinet. The mathematical process of translating a pressure–time graph like Fig. 16.5a into a graph of harmonic content like Fig. 16.5b is called *Fourier analysis.*

Two tones produced by different instruments might have the same fundamental frequency (and thus the same pitch) but sound different because of different harmonic content. The difference in sound is called **timbre** and is often described in subjective terms such as reedy, mellow, and tinny. A tone that is rich in harmonics, like the clarinet tone in Figs. 16.5a and 16.5b, usually sounds thin and "reedy," while a tone containing mostly a fundamental, like the alto recorder tone in Figs. 16.5c and 16.5d, is more mellow and flutelike. The same principle applies to the human voice, which is another wind instrument; the vowels "a" and "e" sound different because of differences in harmonic content.

Another factor in determining tone quality is the behavior at the beginning (*attack*) and end (*decay*) of a tone. A piano tone begins with a thump and then dies away gradually. A harpsichord tone, in addition to having different harmonic content, begins much more quickly with a click, and the higher harmonics begin before the lower ones. When the key is released, the sound also dies away much more rapidly with a harpsichord than with a piano. Similar effects are present in other musical instruments.

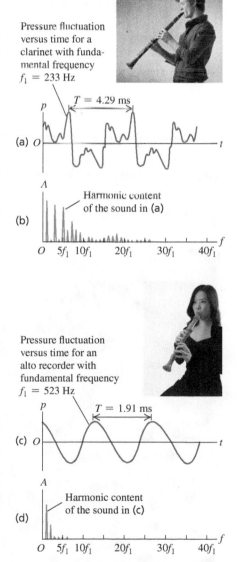

16.5 Different representations of the sound of (a), (b) a clarinet and (c), (d) an alto recorder. (Graphs adapted from R.E. Berg and D.G. Stork, *The Physics of Sound,* Prentice-Hall, 1982.)

Pressure fluctuation versus time for a clarinet with fundamental frequency $f_1 = 233$ Hz

(a) $T = 4.29$ ms

(b) Harmonic content of the sound in (a)

Pressure fluctuation versus time for an alto recorder with fundamental frequency $f_1 = 523$ Hz

(c) $T = 1.91$ ms

(d) Harmonic content of the sound in (c)

Unlike the tones made by musical instruments, **noise** is a combination of *all* frequencies, not just frequencies that are integer multiples of a fundamental frequency. (An extreme case is "white noise," which contains equal amounts of all frequencies across the audible range.) Examples include the sound of the wind and the hissing sound you make in saying the consonant "s."

TEST YOUR UNDERSTANDING OF SECTION 16.1 You use an electronic signal generator to produce a sinusoidal sound wave in air. You then increase the frequency of the wave from 100 Hz to 400 Hz while keeping the pressure amplitude constant. What effect does this have on the displacement amplitude of the sound wave? (i) It becomes four times greater; (ii) it becomes twice as great; (iii) it is unchanged; (iv) it becomes $\frac{1}{2}$ as great; (v) it becomes $\frac{1}{4}$ as great. ∎

16.2 SPEED OF SOUND WAVES

We found in Section 15.4 that the speed v of a transverse wave on a string depends on the string tension F and the linear mass density μ: $v = \sqrt{F/\mu}$. What, we may ask, is the corresponding expression for the speed of sound waves in a gas or liquid? On what properties of the medium does the speed depend?

We can make an educated guess about these questions by remembering a claim that we made in Section 15.4: For mechanical waves in general, the expression for the wave speed is of the form

$$v = \sqrt{\frac{\text{Restoring force returning the system to equilibrium}}{\text{Inertia resisting the return to equilibrium}}}$$

A sound wave in a bulk fluid causes compressions and rarefactions of the fluid, so the restoring-force term in the above expression must be related to how difficult it is to compress the fluid. This is precisely what the bulk modulus B of the medium tells us. According to Newton's second law, inertia is related to mass. The "massiveness" of a bulk fluid is described by its density, or mass per unit volume, ρ. Hence we expect that the speed of sound waves should be of the form $v = \sqrt{B/\rho}$.

To check our guess, we'll derive the speed of sound waves in a fluid in a pipe. This is a situation of some importance, since all musical wind instruments are pipes in which a longitudinal wave (sound) propagates in a fluid (air) (**Fig. 16.6**). Human speech works on the same principle; sound waves propagate in your vocal tract, which is an air-filled pipe connected to the lungs at one end (your larynx) and to the outside air at the other end (your mouth). The steps in our derivation are completely parallel to those we used in Section 15.4 to find the speed of transverse waves.

16.6 When a wind instrument like this French horn is played, sound waves propagate through the air within the instrument's pipes. The properties of the sound that emerges from the large bell depend on the speed of these waves.

Speed of Sound in a Fluid

Figure 16.7 shows a fluid with density ρ in a pipe with cross-sectional area A. In equilibrium (Fig. 16.7a), the fluid is at rest and under a uniform pressure p. We take the x-axis along the length of the pipe. This is also the direction in which we make a longitudinal wave propagate, so the displacement y is also measured along the pipe, just as in Section 16.1 (see Fig. 16.2).

At time $t = 0$ we start the piston at the left end moving toward the right with constant speed v_y. This initiates a wave motion that travels to the right along the length of the pipe, in which successive sections of fluid begin to move and become compressed at successively later times.

Figure 16.7b shows the fluid at time t. All portions of fluid to the left of point P are moving to the right with speed v_y, and all portions to the right of P are still at rest. The boundary between the moving and stationary portions travels to the right with a speed equal to the speed of propagation or wave speed v. At time t the piston has moved a distance $v_y t$, and the boundary has advanced a distance vt. As with a transverse disturbance in a string, we can compute the speed of propagation from the impulse–momentum theorem.

The quantity of fluid set in motion in time t originally occupied a section of the cylinder with length vt, cross-sectional area A, volume vtA, and mass ρvtA. Its longitudinal momentum (that is, momentum along the length of the pipe) is

$$\text{Longitudinal momentum} = (\rho vtA)v_y$$

Next we compute the increase of pressure, Δp, in the moving fluid. The original volume of the moving fluid, Avt, has decreased by an amount Av_yt. From the definition of the bulk modulus B, Eq. (11.13) in Section 11.5,

$$B = \frac{-\text{Pressure change}}{\text{Fractional volume change}} = \frac{-\Delta p}{-Av_yt/Avt} \quad \text{and} \quad \Delta p = B\frac{v_y}{v}$$

The pressure in the moving fluid is $p + \Delta p$, and the force exerted on it by the piston is $(p + \Delta p)A$. The net force on the moving fluid (see Fig. 16.7b) is ΔpA, and the longitudinal impulse is

$$\text{Longitudinal impulse} = \Delta pAt = B\frac{v_y}{v}At$$

Because the fluid was at rest at time $t = 0$, the change in momentum up to time t is equal to the momentum at that time. Applying the impulse–momentum theorem (see Section 8.1), we find

$$B\frac{v_y}{v}At = \rho vtAv_y \tag{16.6}$$

When we solve this expression for v, we get

Speed of a longitudinal wave in a fluid $\cdots\cdots\blacktriangleright v = \sqrt{\dfrac{B}{\rho}}$ $\quad\cdots$ Bulk modulus of fluid $\quad\cdots$ Density of fluid $\tag{16.7}$

which agrees with our educated guess.

While we derived Eq. (16.7) for waves in a pipe, it also applies to longitudinal waves in a bulk fluid, including sound waves traveling in air or water.

Speed of Sound in a Solid

When a longitudinal wave propagates in a *solid* rod or bar, the situation is somewhat different. The rod expands sideways slightly when it is compressed longitudinally, while a fluid in a pipe with constant cross section cannot move sideways. Using the same kind of reasoning that led us to Eq. (16.7), we can show that the speed of a longitudinal pulse in the rod is given by

Speed of a longitudinal wave in a solid rod $\cdots\cdots\blacktriangleright v = \sqrt{\dfrac{Y}{\rho}}$ $\quad\cdots$ Young's modulus of rod material $\quad\cdots$ Density of rod material $\tag{16.8}$

We defined Young's modulus in Section 11.4.

CAUTION **Solid rods vs. bulk solids** Equation (16.8) applies to only rods whose sides are free to bulge and shrink a little as the wave travels. It does not apply to longitudinal waves in a *bulk* solid because sideways motion in any element of material is prevented by the surrounding material. The speed of longitudinal waves in a bulk solid depends on the density, the bulk modulus, and the *shear* modulus. ▮

Note that Eqs. (16.7) and (16.8) are valid for sinusoidal and other periodic waves, not just for the special case discussed here.

Table 16.1 lists the speed of sound in several bulk materials. Sound waves travel more slowly in lead than in aluminum or steel because lead has a lower bulk modulus and shear modulus and a higher density.

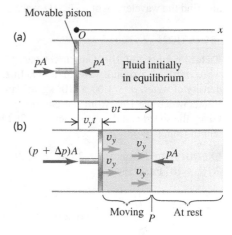

16.7 A sound wave propagating in a fluid confined to a tube. (a) Fluid in equilibrium. (b) A time t after the piston begins moving to the right at speed v_y, the fluid between the piston and point P is in motion. The speed of sound waves is v.

Speed of Sound in Various Bulk Materials

TABLE 16.1	
Material	**Speed of Sound (m/s)**
Gases	
Air (20°C)	344
Helium (20°C)	999
Hydrogen (20°C)	1330
Liquids	
Liquid helium (4 K)	211
Mercury (20°C)	1451
Water (0°C)	1402
Water (20°C)	1482
Water (100°C)	1543
Solids	
Aluminum	6420
Lead	1960
Steel	5941

EXAMPLE 16.3 WAVELENGTH OF SONAR WAVES

A ship uses a sonar system (**Fig. 16.8**) to locate underwater objects. Find the speed of sound waves in water using Eq. (16.7), and find the wavelength of a 262-Hz wave.

SOLUTION

IDENTIFY and SET UP: Our target variables are the speed and wavelength of a sound wave in water. In Eq. (16.7), we use the density of water, $\rho = 1.00 \times 10^3 \text{ kg/m}^3$, and the bulk modulus of water, which we find from the compressibility (see Table 11.2). Given the speed and the frequency $f = 262$ Hz, we find the wavelength from $v = f\lambda$.

EXECUTE: In Example 16.2, we used Table 11.2 to find $B = 2.18 \times 10^9$ Pa. Then

$$v = \sqrt{\frac{B}{\rho}} = \sqrt{\frac{2.18 \times 10^9 \text{ Pa}}{1.00 \times 10^3 \text{ kg/m}^3}} = 1480 \text{ m/s}$$

and

$$\lambda = \frac{v}{f} = \frac{1480 \text{ m/s}}{262 \text{ s}^{-1}} = 5.65 \text{ m}$$

EVALUATE: The calculated value of v agrees well with the value in Table 16.1. Water is denser than air (ρ is larger) but is also

16.8 A sonar system uses underwater sound waves to detect and locate submerged objects.

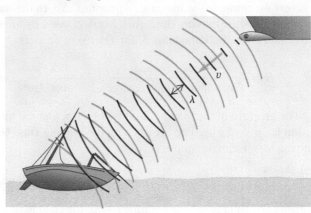

much more incompressible (B is much larger), and so the speed $v = \sqrt{B/\rho}$ is greater than the 344-m/s speed of sound in air at ordinary temperatures. The relationship $\lambda = v/f$ then says that a sound wave in water must have a longer wavelength than a wave of the same frequency in air. Indeed, we found in Example 15.1 (Section 15.2) that a 262-Hz sound wave in air has a wavelength of only 1.31 m.

16.9 This three-dimensional image of a fetus in the womb was made using a sequence of ultrasound scans. Each individual scan reveals a two-dimensional "slice" through the fetus; many such slices were then combined digitally. Ultrasound imaging is also used to study heart valve action and to detect tumors.

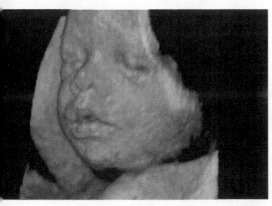

Dolphins emit high-frequency sound waves (typically 100,000 Hz) and use the echoes for guidance and for hunting. The corresponding wavelength in water is 1.48 cm. With this high-frequency "sonar" system they can sense objects that are roughly as small as the wavelength (but not much smaller). *Ultrasonic imaging* in medicine uses the same principle; sound waves of very high frequency and very short wavelength, called *ultrasound,* are scanned over the human body, and the "echoes" from interior organs are used to create an image. With ultrasound of frequency 5 MHz = 5×10^6 Hz, the wavelength in water (the primary constituent of the body) is 0.3 mm, and features as small as this can be discerned in the image (**Fig. 16.9**). Ultrasound is more sensitive than x rays in distinguishing various kinds of tissues and does not have the radiation hazards associated with x rays.

Speed of Sound in a Gas

Most of the sound waves that we encounter propagate in air. To use Eq. (16.7) to find the speed of sound waves in air, we note that the bulk modulus of a gas depends on pressure: The greater the pressure applied to compress a gas, the more it resists further compression and hence the greater the bulk modulus. (That's why specific values of the bulk modulus for gases are not given in Table 11.1.) The expression for the bulk modulus of a gas for use in Eq. (16.7) is

$$B = \gamma p_0 \tag{16.9}$$

where p_0 is the equilibrium pressure of the gas. The quantity γ (the Greek letter gamma) is called the *ratio of heat capacities.* It is a dimensionless number that characterizes the thermal properties of the gas. (We'll learn more about this quantity in Chapter 19.) As an example, the ratio of heat capacities for air is $\gamma = 1.40$. At normal atmospheric pressure $p_0 = 1.013 \times 10^5$ Pa, so $B = (1.40)(1.013 \times 10^5 \text{ Pa}) = 1.42 \times 10^5$ Pa. This value is minuscule compared to the bulk modulus of a typical solid (see Table 11.1), which is approximately 10^{10} to 10^{11} Pa. This shouldn't be surprising: It's simply a statement that air is far easier to compress than steel.

The density ρ of a gas also depends on the pressure, which in turn depends on the temperature. It turns out that the ratio B/ρ for a given type of ideal gas does *not* depend on the pressure at all, only the temperature. From Eq. (16.7), this means that the speed of sound in a gas is fundamentally a function of temperature T:

Ratio of heat capacities ⸱⸱⸱ ⸱⸱⸱ Gas constant

Speed of sound ⸱⸱⸱⸱⸱⸱⸱⸱ in an ideal gas
$$v = \sqrt{\frac{\gamma R T}{M}}$$
Absolute temperature

Molar mass

(16.10)

This expression incorporates several quantities that we will study in Chapters 17, 18, and 19. The temperature T is the *absolute* temperature in kelvins (K), equal to the Celsius temperature plus 273.15; thus 20.00°C corresponds to $T = 293.15$ K. The quantity M is the *molar mass,* or mass per mole of the substance of which the gas is composed. The *gas constant R* has the same value for all gases. The current best numerical value of R is

$$R = 8.3144621(75) \text{ J/mol} \cdot \text{K}$$

which for practical calculations we can write as $8.314 \text{ J/mol} \cdot \text{K}$.

For any particular gas, γ, R, and M are constants, and the wave speed is proportional to the square root of the absolute temperature. We will see in Chapter 18 that Eq. (16.10) is almost identical to the expression for the average speed of molecules in an ideal gas. This shows that sound speeds and molecular speeds are closely related.

EXAMPLE 16.4 **SPEED OF SOUND IN AIR**

Find the speed of sound in air at $T = 20$°C, and find the range of wavelengths in air to which the human ear (which can hear frequencies in the range of 20–20,000 Hz) is sensitive. The mean molar mass for air (a mixture of mostly nitrogen and oxygen) is $M = 28.8 \times 10^{-3}$ kg/mol and the ratio of heat capacities is $\gamma = 1.40$.

SOLUTION

IDENTIFY and SET UP: We use Eq. (16.10) to find the sound speed from γ, T, and M, and we use $v = f\lambda$ to find the wavelengths corresponding to the frequency limits. Note that in Eq. (16.10) temperature T *must* be expressed in kelvins, not Celsius degrees.

EXECUTE: At $T = 20$°C = 293 K, we find

$$v = \sqrt{\frac{\gamma R T}{M}} = \sqrt{\frac{(1.40)(8.314 \text{ J/mol} \cdot \text{K})(293 \text{ K})}{28.8 \times 10^{-3} \text{ kg/mol}}} = 344 \text{ m/s}$$

Using this value of v in $\lambda = v/f$, we find that at 20°C the frequency $f = 20$ Hz corresponds to $\lambda = 17$ m and $f = 20{,}000$ Hz to $\lambda = 1.7$ cm.

EVALUATE: Our calculated value of v agrees with the measured sound speed at $T = 20$°C.

A gas is actually composed of molecules in random motion, separated by distances that are large in comparison with their diameters. The vibrations that constitute a wave in a gas are superposed on the random thermal motion. At atmospheric pressure, a molecule travels an average distance of about 10^{-7} m between collisions, while the displacement amplitude of a faint sound may be only 10^{-9} m. We can think of a gas with a sound wave passing through as being comparable to a swarm of bees; the swarm as a whole oscillates slightly while individual insects move about within the swarm, apparently at random.

TEST YOUR UNDERSTANDING OF SECTION 16.2 Mercury is 13.6 times denser than water. Based on Table 16.1, at 20°C which of these liquids has the greater bulk modulus? (i) Mercury; (ii) water; (iii) both are about the same; (iv) not enough information is given to decide. ∎

16.3 SOUND INTENSITY

Traveling sound waves, like all other traveling waves, transfer energy from one region of space to another. In Section 15.5 we introduced the *wave intensity I*, equal to the time average rate at which wave energy is transported per unit area across a surface perpendicular to the direction of propagation. Let's see how to express the intensity of a sound wave in a fluid in terms of the displacement amplitude A or pressure amplitude p_{max}.

Let's consider a sound wave propagating in the $+x$-direction so that we can use our expressions from Section 16.1 for the displacement $y(x, t)$ [Eq. (16.1)] and pressure fluctuation $p(x, t)$ [Eq. (16.4)]. In Section 6.4 we saw that power equals the product of force and velocity [see Eq. (6.18)]. So the power per unit area in this sound wave equals the product of $p(x, t)$ (force per unit area) and the *particle* velocity $v_y(x, t)$, which is the velocity at time t of that portion of the wave medium at coordinate x. Using Eqs. (16.1) and (16.4), we find

$$v_y(x, t) = \frac{\partial y(x, t)}{\partial t} = \omega A \sin(kx - \omega t)$$

$$p(x, t)v_y(x, t) = \left[BkA \sin(kx - \omega t) \right]\left[\omega A \sin(kx - \omega t) \right]$$

$$= B\omega kA^2 \sin^2(kx - \omega t)$$

CAUTION **Wave velocity vs. particle velocity** Remember that the velocity of the wave as a whole is *not* the same as the particle velocity. While the wave continues to move in the direction of propagation, individual particles in the wave medium merely slosh back and forth, as shown in Fig. 16.1. Furthermore, the maximum speed of a particle of the medium can be very different from the wave speed.

The intensity is the time average value of the power per unit area $p(x, t)v_y(x, t)$. For any value of x the average value of the function $\sin^2(kx - \omega t)$ over one period $T = 2\pi/\omega$ is $\frac{1}{2}$, so

$$I = \tfrac{1}{2} B\omega kA^2 \tag{16.11}$$

Using the relationships $\omega = vk$ and $v = \sqrt{B/\rho}$, we can rewrite Eq. (16.11) as

Intensity of a sinusoidal sound wave in a fluid $\cdots\cdots I = \frac{1}{2}\sqrt{\rho B}\,\omega^2 A^2$ Angular frequency $= 2\pi f$ / Displacement amplitude / Density of fluid / Bulk modulus of fluid $\tag{16.12}$

It is usually more useful to express I in terms of the pressure amplitude p_{max}. Using Eqs. (16.5) and (16.12) and the relationship $\omega = vk$, we find

$$I = \frac{\omega p_{max}^2}{2Bk} = \frac{v p_{max}^2}{2B} \tag{16.13}$$

By using the wave speed relationship $v = \sqrt{B/\rho}$, we can also write Eq. (16.13) in the alternative forms

Intensity of a sinusoidal sound wave in a fluid $\cdots\cdots I = \frac{p_{max}^2}{2\rho v} = \frac{p_{max}^2}{2\sqrt{\rho B}}$ Pressure amplitude / Wave speed / Density of fluid / Bulk modulus of fluid $\tag{16.14}$

You should verify these expressions. Comparison of Eqs. (16.12) and (16.14) shows that sinusoidal sound waves of the same intensity but different frequency have different displacement amplitudes A but the *same* pressure amplitude p_{max}.

This is another reason it is usually more convenient to describe a sound wave in terms of pressure fluctuations, not displacement.

The *total* average power carried across a surface by a sound wave equals the product of the intensity at the surface and the surface area, if the intensity over the surface is uniform. The total average sound power emitted by a person speaking in an ordinary conversational tone is about 10^{-5} W, while a loud shout corresponds to about 3×10^{-2} W. If all the residents of New York City were to talk at the same time, the total sound power would be about 100 W, equivalent to the electric power requirement of a medium-sized light bulb. On the other hand, the power required to fill a large auditorium or stadium with loud sound is considerable (see Example 16.7.)

If the sound source emits waves in all directions equally, the intensity decreases with increasing distance r from the source according to the inverse-square law (Section 15.5): The intensity is proportional to $1/r^2$. The intensity can be increased by confining the sound waves to travel in the desired direction only (**Fig. 16.10**), although the $1/r^2$ law still applies.

The inverse-square relationship also does not apply indoors because sound energy can reach a listener by reflection from the walls and ceiling. Indeed, part of the architect's job in designing an auditorium is to tailor these reflections so that the intensity is as nearly uniform as possible over the entire auditorium.

16.10 By cupping your hands like this, you direct the sound waves emerging from your mouth so that they don't propagate to the sides. Hence you can be heard at greater distances.

PROBLEM-SOLVING STRATEGY 16.1) **SOUND INTENSITY**

IDENTIFY *the relevant concepts:* The relationships between the intensity and amplitude of a sound wave are straightforward. Other quantities are involved in these relationships, however, so it's particularly important to decide which is your target variable.

SET UP *the problem* using the following steps:
1. Sort the physical quantities into categories. Wave properties include the displacement and pressure amplitudes A and p_{max}. The frequency f can be determined from the angular frequency ω, the wave number k, or the wavelength λ. These quantities are related through the wave speed v, which is determined by properties of the medium (B and ρ for a liquid, and γ, T, and M for a gas).

2. List the given quantities and identify the target variables. Find relationships that take you where you want to go.

EXECUTE *the solution:* Use your selected equations to solve for the target variables. Express the temperature in kelvins (Celsius temperature plus 273.15) to calculate the speed of sound in a gas.

EVALUATE *your answer:* If possible, use an alternative relationship to check your results.

EXAMPLE 16.5 **INTENSITY OF A SOUND WAVE IN AIR**

Find the intensity of the sound wave in Example 16.1, with $p_{max} = 3.0 \times 10^{-2}$ Pa. Assume the temperature is 20°C so that the density of air is $\rho = 1.20$ kg/m^3 and the speed of sound is $v = 344$ m/s.

SOLUTION

IDENTIFY and SET UP: Our target variable is the intensity I of the sound wave. We are given the pressure amplitude p_{max} of the wave as well as the density ρ and wave speed v for the medium. We can determine I from p_{max}, ρ, and v from Eq. (16.14).

EXECUTE: From Eq. (16.14),

$$I = \frac{p_{max}^2}{2\rho v} = \frac{(3.0 \times 10^{-2} \text{ Pa})^2}{2(1.20 \text{ kg/m}^3)(344 \text{ m/s})}$$

$$= 1.1 \times 10^{-6} \text{ J/(s} \cdot \text{m}^2) = 1.1 \times 10^{-6} \text{ W/m}^2$$

EVALUATE: This seems like a very low intensity, but it is well within the range of sound intensities encountered on a daily basis. A very loud sound wave at the threshold of pain has a pressure amplitude of about 30 Pa and an intensity of about 1 W/m^2. The pressure amplitude of the faintest sound wave that can be heard is about 3×10^{-5} Pa, and the corresponding intensity is about 10^{-12} W/m^2. (Try these values of p_{max} in Eq. (16.14) to check that the corresponding intensities are as we have stated.)

SOLUTION

EXAMPLE 16.6   SAME INTENSITY, DIFFERENT FREQUENCIES

What are the pressure and displacement amplitudes of a 20-Hz sound wave with the same intensity as the 1000-Hz sound wave of Examples 16.1 and 16.5?

SOLUTION

IDENTIFY and SET UP: In Examples 16.1 and 16.5 we found that for a 1000-Hz sound wave with $p_{max} = 3.0 \times 10^{-2}$ Pa, $A = 1.2 \times 10^{-8}$ m and $I = 1.1 \times 10^{-6}$ W/m^2. Our target variables are p_{max} and A for a 20-Hz sound wave of the same intensity I. We can find these using Eqs. (16.14) and (16.12), respectively.

EXECUTE: We can rearrange Eqs. (16.14) and (16.12) as $p_{max}^2 = 2I\sqrt{\rho B}$ and $\omega^2 A^2 = 2I/\sqrt{\rho B}$, respectively. These tell us that for a given sound intensity I in a given medium (constant ρ and B), the

quantities p_{max} and ωA (or, equivalently, fA) are *constants* that don't depend on frequency. From the first result we immediately have $p_{max} = 3.0 \times 10^{-2}$ Pa for $f = 20$ Hz, the same as for $f = 1000$ Hz. If we write the second result as $f_{20}A_{20} = f_{1000}A_{1000}$, we have

$$A_{20} = \left(\frac{f_{1000}}{f_{20}}\right)A_{1000}$$

$$= \left(\frac{1000 \text{ Hz}}{20 \text{ Hz}}\right)(1.2 \times 10^{-8} \text{ m}) = 6.0 \times 10^{-7} \text{ m} = 0.60 \ \mu\text{m}$$

EVALUATE: Our result reinforces the idea that pressure amplitude is a more convenient description of a sound wave and its intensity than displacement amplitude.

EXAMPLE 16.7   "PLAY IT LOUD!"

For an outdoor concert we want the sound intensity to be 1 W/m^2 at a distance of 20 m from the speaker array. If the sound intensity is uniform in all directions, what is the required average acoustic power output of the array?

SOLUTION

IDENTIFY, SET UP, and EXECUTE: This example uses the definition of sound intensity as power per unit area. The total power is the target variable; the area in question is a hemisphere centered on the speaker array. We assume that the speakers are on the ground

and that none of the acoustic power is directed into the ground, so the acoustic power is uniform over a hemisphere 20 m in radius. The surface area of this hemisphere is $\left(\frac{1}{2}\right)(4\pi)(20 \text{ m})^2$, or about 2500 m^2. The required power is the product of this area and the intensity: $(1 \text{ W/m}^2)(2500 \text{ m}^2) = 2500 \text{ W} = 2.5 \text{ kW}$.

EVALUATE: The electrical power input to the speaker would need to be considerably greater than 2.5 kW, because speaker efficiency is not very high (typically a few percent for ordinary speakers, and up to 25% for horn-type speakers).

The Decibel Scale

Because the ear is sensitive over a broad range of intensities, a *logarithmic* measure of intensity called **sound intensity level** is often used:

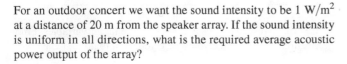

$$\text{Sound intensity level} \cdots \beta = (10 \text{ dB}) \log \frac{I}{I_0} \begin{array}{l} \text{Intensity of sound wave} \\ \text{Reference intensity} \\ = 10^{-12} \text{ W/m}^2 \end{array} \qquad (16.15)$$

Logarithm to base 10

The chosen reference intensity I_0 in Eq. (16.15) is approximately the threshold of human hearing at 1000 Hz. Sound intensity levels are expressed in **decibels,** abbreviated dB. A decibel is $\frac{1}{10}$ of a *bel*, a unit named for Alexander Graham Bell (the inventor of the telephone). The bel is inconveniently large for most purposes, and the decibel is the usual unit of sound intensity level.

If the intensity of a sound wave equals I_0 or 10^{-12} W/m^2, its sound intensity level is $\beta = 0$ dB. An intensity of 1 W/m^2 corresponds to 120 dB. **Table 16.2** gives the sound intensity levels of some familiar sounds. You can use Eq. (16.15) to check the value of β given for each intensity in the table.

Because the ear is not equally sensitive to all frequencies in the audible range, some sound-level meters weight the various frequencies unequally. One such scheme leads to the so-called dBA scale; this scale deemphasizes the low and very high frequencies, where the ear is less sensitive.

TABLE 16.2 | Sound Intensity Levels from Various Sources (Representative Values)

Source or Description of Sound	Sound Intensity Level, β (dB)	Intensity, I (W/m²)
Military jet aircraft 30 m away	140	10^2
Threshold of pain	120	1
Riveter	95	3.2×10^{-3}
Elevated train	90	10^{-3}
Busy street traffic	70	10^{-5}
Ordinary conversation	65	3.2×10^{-6}
Quiet automobile	50	10^{-7}
Quiet radio in home	40	10^{-8}
Average whisper	20	10^{-10}
Rustle of leaves	10	10^{-11}
Threshold of hearing at 1000 Hz	0	10^{-12}

EXAMPLE 16.8 TEMPORARY—OR PERMANENT—HEARING LOSS

A 10-min exposure to 120-dB sound will temporarily shift your threshold of hearing at 1000 Hz from 0 dB up to 28 dB. Ten years of exposure to 92-dB sound will cause a *permanent* shift to 28 dB. What sound intensities correspond to 28 dB and 92 dB?

SOLUTION

IDENTIFY and SET UP: We are given two sound intensity levels β; our target variables are the corresponding intensities. We can solve Eq. (16.15) to find the intensity I that corresponds to each value of β.

EXECUTE: We solve Eq. (16.15) for I by dividing both sides by 10 dB and using the relationship $10^{\log x} = x$:

$$I = I_0 10^{\beta/(10\ \text{dB})}$$

For $\beta = 28$ dB and $\beta = 92$ dB, the exponents are $\beta/(10\ \text{dB}) = 2.8$ and 9.2, respectively, so that

$$I_{28\ \text{dB}} = (10^{-12}\ \text{W/m}^2)10^{2.8} = 6.3 \times 10^{-10}\ \text{W/m}^2$$
$$I_{92\ \text{dB}} = (10^{-12}\ \text{W/m}^2)10^{9.2} = 1.6 \times 10^{-3}\ \text{W/m}^2$$

EVALUATE: If your answers are a factor of 10 too large, you may have entered 10×10^{-12} in your calculator instead of 1×10^{-12}. Be careful!

EXAMPLE 16.9 A BIRD SINGS IN A MEADOW

Consider an idealized bird (treated as a point source) that emits constant sound power, with intensity obeying the inverse-square law (**Fig. 16.11**). If you move twice the distance from the bird, by how many decibels does the sound intensity level drop?

SOLUTION

IDENTIFY and SET UP: The decibel scale is logarithmic, so the *difference* between two sound intensity levels (the target variable) corresponds to the *ratio* of the corresponding intensities, which is determined by the inverse-square law. We label the two points P_1 and P_2 (Fig. 16.11). We use Eq. (16.15), the definition of sound intensity level, at each point. We use Eq. (15.26), the inverse-square law, to relate the intensities at the two points.

EXECUTE: The difference $\beta_2 - \beta_1$ between any two sound intensity levels is related to the corresponding intensities by

$$\beta_2 - \beta_1 = (10\ \text{dB})\left(\log\frac{I_2}{I_0} - \log\frac{I_1}{I_0}\right)$$
$$= (10\ \text{dB})[(\log I_2 - \log I_0) - (\log I_1 - \log I_0)]$$
$$= (10\ \text{dB})\log\frac{I_2}{I_1}$$

16.11 When you double your distance from a point source of sound, by how much does the sound intensity level decrease?

For this inverse-square-law source, Eq. (15.26) yields $I_2/I_1 = r_1^2/r_2^2 = \frac{1}{4}$, so

$$\beta_2 - \beta_1 = (10\ \text{dB})\log\frac{I_2}{I_1} = (10\ \text{dB})\log\frac{1}{4} = -6.0\ \text{dB}$$

Continued

EVALUATE: Our result is negative, which tells us (correctly) that the sound intensity level is less at P_2 than at P_1. The 6-dB difference doesn't depend on the sound intensity level at P_1; *any* doubling of the distance from an inverse-square-law source reduces the sound intensity level by 6 dB.

Note that the perceived *loudness* of a sound is not directly proportional to its intensity. For example, most people interpret an increase of 8 dB to 10 dB in sound intensity level (corresponding to increasing intensity by a factor of 6 to 10) as a doubling of loudness.

TEST YOUR UNDERSTANDING OF SECTION 16.3   You double the intensity of a sound wave in air while leaving the frequency unchanged. (The pressure, density, and temperature of the air remain unchanged as well.) What effect does this have on the displacement amplitude, pressure amplitude, bulk modulus, sound speed, and sound intensity level? ▮

16.4 STANDING SOUND WAVES AND NORMAL MODES

When longitudinal (sound) waves propagate in a fluid in a pipe, the waves are reflected from the ends in the same way that transverse waves on a string are reflected at its ends. The superposition of the waves traveling in opposite directions again forms a standing wave. Just as for transverse standing waves on a string (see Section 15.7), standing sound waves in a pipe can be used to create sound waves in the surrounding air. This is the principle of the human voice as well as many musical instruments, including woodwinds, brasses, and pipe organs.

Transverse waves on a string, including standing waves, are usually described only in terms of the displacement of the string. But, as we have seen, sound waves in a fluid may be described either in terms of the displacement of the fluid or in terms of the pressure variation in the fluid. To avoid confusion, we'll use the terms **displacement node** and **displacement antinode** to refer to points where particles of the fluid have zero displacement and maximum displacement, respectively.

We can demonstrate standing sound waves in a column of gas using an apparatus called a Kundt's tube (**Fig. 16.12**). A horizontal glass tube a meter or so long is closed at one end and has a flexible diaphragm at the other end that can transmit vibrations. A nearby loudspeaker is driven by an audio oscillator and amplifier; this produces sound waves that force the diaphragm to vibrate sinusoidally with a frequency that we can vary. The sound waves within the tube are reflected at the other, closed end of the tube. We spread a small amount of light powder uniformly along the bottom of the tube. As we vary the frequency of the sound, we pass through frequencies at which the amplitude of the standing waves becomes large enough for the powder to be swept along the tube at those points where the gas is in motion. The powder therefore collects at the displacement nodes (where the gas is not moving). Adjacent nodes are separated by a distance equal to $\lambda/2$.

16.12 Demonstrating standing sound waves using a Kundt's tube. The blue shading represents the density of the gas at an instant when the gas pressure at the displacement nodes is a maximum or a minimum.

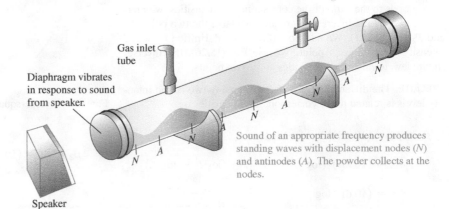

Gas inlet tube

Diaphragm vibrates in response to sound from speaker.

Sound of an appropriate frequency produces standing waves with displacement nodes (N) and antinodes (A). The powder collects at the nodes.

Speaker

Figure 16.13 shows the motions of nine different particles within a gas-filled tube in which there is a standing sound wave. A particle at a displacement node (N) does not move, while a particle at a displacement antinode (A) oscillates with maximum amplitude. Note that particles on opposite sides of a displacement node vibrate in opposite phase. When these particles approach each other, the gas between them is compressed and the pressure rises; when they recede from each other, there is an expansion and the pressure drops. Hence at a displacement *node* the gas undergoes the maximum amount of compression and expansion, and the variations in pressure and density above and below the average have their maximum value. By contrast, particles on opposite sides of a displacement *antinode* vibrate *in phase;* the distance between the particles is nearly constant, and there is *no* variation in pressure or density at a displacement antinode.

We use the term **pressure node** to describe a point in a standing sound wave at which the pressure and density do not vary and the term **pressure antinode** to describe a point at which the variations in pressure and density are greatest. Using these terms, we can summarize our observations as follows:

> **A pressure node is always a displacement antinode, and a pressure antinode is always a displacement node.**

Figure 16.12 depicts a standing sound wave at an instant at which the pressure variations are greatest; the blue shading shows that the density and pressure of the gas have their maximum and minimum values at the displacement nodes.

When reflection takes place at a *closed* end of a pipe (an end with a rigid barrier or plug), the displacement of the particles at this end must always be zero, analogous to a fixed end of a string. Thus a closed end of a pipe is a displacement node and a pressure antinode; the particles do not move, but the pressure variations are maximum. An *open* end of a pipe is a pressure node because it is open to the atmosphere, where the pressure is constant. Because of this, an open end is always a displacement *antinode,* in analogy to a free end of a string; the particles oscillate with maximum amplitude, but the pressure does not vary. (The pressure node actually occurs somewhat beyond an open end of a pipe. But if the diameter of the pipe is small in comparison to the wavelength, which is true for most musical instruments, this effect can safely be ignored.) Thus longitudinal sound waves are reflected at the closed and open ends of a pipe in the same way that transverse waves in a string are reflected at fixed and free ends, respectively.

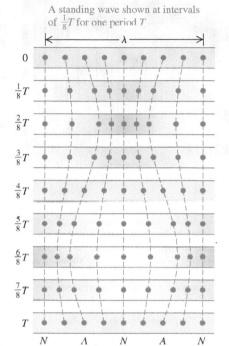

16.13 In a standing sound wave, a displacement node N is a pressure antinode (a point where the pressure fluctuates the most) and a displacement antinode A is a pressure node (a point where the pressure does not fluctuate at all).

A standing wave shown at intervals of $\frac{1}{8}T$ for one period T

N — a displacement node = a pressure antinode
A = a displacement antinode = a pressure node

CONCEPTUAL EXAMPLE 16.10   **THE SOUND OF SILENCE**

A directional loudspeaker directs a sound wave of wavelength λ at a wall (**Fig. 16.14**). At what distances from the wall could you stand and hear no sound at all?

SOLUTION

Your ear detects pressure variations in the air; you will therefore hear no sound if your ear is at a *pressure node,* which is a displacement antinode. The wall is at a displacement node; the distance from any node to an adjacent antinode is $\lambda/4$, and the distance from one antinode to the next is $\lambda/2$ (Fig. 16.14). Hence the displacement antinodes (pressure nodes), at which no sound will be heard, are at distances $d = \lambda/4$, $d = \lambda/4 + \lambda/2 = 3\lambda/4$, $d = 3\lambda/4 + \lambda/2 = 5\lambda/4, \ldots$ from the wall. If the loudspeaker is not highly directional, this effect is hard to notice because of reflections of sound waves from the floor, ceiling, and other walls.

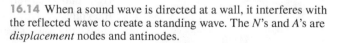

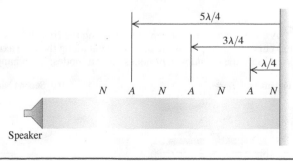

16.14 When a sound wave is directed at a wall, it interferes with the reflected wave to create a standing wave. The N's and A's are *displacement* nodes and antinodes.

Speaker

16.15 Organ pipes of different sizes produce tones with different frequencies.

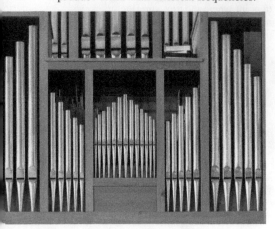

Organ Pipes and Wind Instruments

The most important application of standing sound waves is the production of musical tones. Organ pipes are one of the simplest examples (**Fig. 16.15**). Air is supplied by a blower to the bottom end of the pipe (**Fig. 16.16**). A stream of air emerges from the narrow opening at the edge of the horizontal surface and is directed against the top edge of the opening, which is called the *mouth* of the pipe. The column of air in the pipe is set into vibration, and there is a series of possible normal modes, just as with the stretched string. The mouth acts as an open end; it is a pressure node and a displacement antinode. The other end of the pipe (at the top in Fig. 16.16) may be either open or closed.

In **Fig. 16.17**, both ends of the pipe are open, so both ends are pressure nodes and displacement antinodes. An organ pipe that is open at both ends is called an *open pipe*. The fundamental frequency f_1 corresponds to a standing-wave pattern with a displacement antinode at each end and a displacement node in the middle (Fig. 16.17a). The distance between adjacent antinodes is always equal to one half-wavelength, and in this case that is equal to the length L of the pipe; $\lambda/2 = L$. The corresponding frequency, obtained from the relationship $f = v/\lambda$, is

$$f_1 = \frac{v}{2L} \quad \text{(open pipe)} \quad (16.16)$$

Figures 16.17b and 16.17c show the second and third harmonics; their vibration patterns have two and three displacement nodes, respectively. For these, a half-wavelength is equal to $L/2$ and $L/3$, respectively, and the frequencies are twice and three times the fundamental, respectively: $f_2 = 2f_1$ and $f_3 = 3f_1$. For *every* normal mode of an open pipe the length L must be an integer number of half-wavelengths, and the possible wavelengths λ_n are given by

$$L = n\frac{\lambda_n}{2} \quad \text{or} \quad \lambda_n = \frac{2L}{n} \quad (n = 1, 2, 3, \ldots) \quad \text{(open pipe)} \quad (16.17)$$

The corresponding frequencies f_n are given by $f_n = v/\lambda_n$, so all the normal-mode frequencies for a pipe that is open at both ends are given by

Standing waves, open pipe:
$$f_n = \frac{nv}{2L} \quad (16.18)$$
Frequency of nth harmonic ($n = 1, 2, 3, \ldots$)
Speed of sound in pipe
Length of pipe

The value $n = 1$ corresponds to the fundamental frequency, $n = 2$ to the second harmonic (or first overtone), and so on. Alternatively, we can say

$$f_n = nf_1 \quad (n = 1, 2, 3, \ldots) \quad \text{(open pipe)} \quad (16.19)$$

with f_1 given by Eq. (16.16).

Figure 16.18 shows a *stopped pipe*: It is open at the left end but closed at the right end. The left (open) end is a displacement antinode (pressure node), but the right (closed) end is a displacement node (pressure antinode). Figure 16.18a shows the lowest-frequency mode; the length of the pipe is the distance between

16.16 Cross sections of an organ pipe at two instants one half-period apart. The N's and A's are *displacement* nodes and antinodes; as the blue shading shows, these are points of maximum pressure variation and zero pressure variation, respectively.

Vibrations from turbulent airflow set up standing waves in the pipe.

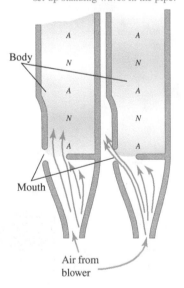

16.17 A cross section of an open pipe showing the first three normal modes. The shading indicates the pressure variations. The red curves are graphs of the displacement along the pipe axis at two instants separated in time by one half-period. The N's and A's are the *displacement* nodes and antinodes; interchange these to show the *pressure* nodes and antinodes.

(a) Fundamental: $f_1 = \frac{v}{2L}$

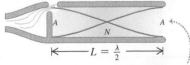

Open end is always a displacement antinode.

(b) Second harmonic: $f_2 = 2\frac{v}{2L} = 2f_1$

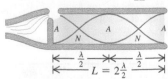

(c) Third harmonic: $f_3 = 3\frac{v}{2L} = 3f_1$

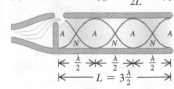

16.18 A cross section of a stopped pipe showing the first three normal modes as well as the *displacement* nodes and antinodes. Only odd harmonics are possible.

(a) Fundamental: $f_1 = \dfrac{v}{4L}$

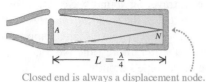

$L = \frac{\lambda}{4}$

Closed end is always a displacement node.

(b) Third harmonic: $f_3 = 3\dfrac{v}{4L} = 3f_1$

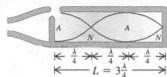

$\frac{\lambda}{4} \quad \frac{\lambda}{4} \quad \frac{\lambda}{4}$

$L = 3\frac{\lambda}{4}$

(c) Fifth harmonic: $f_5 = 5\dfrac{v}{4L} = 5f_1$

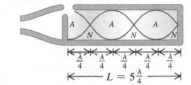

$\frac{\lambda}{4} \quad \frac{\lambda}{4} \quad \frac{\lambda}{4} \quad \frac{\lambda}{4} \quad \frac{\lambda}{4}$

$L = 5\frac{\lambda}{4}$

a node and the adjacent antinode, or a quarter-wavelength ($L = \lambda_1/4$). The fundamental frequency is $f_1 = v/\lambda_1$, or

$$f_1 = \frac{v}{4L} \qquad \text{(stopped pipe)} \qquad (16.20)$$

This is one-half the fundamental frequency for an *open* pipe of the same length. In musical language, the *pitch* of a closed pipe is one octave lower (a factor of 2 in frequency) than that of an open pipe of the same length. Figure 16.18b shows the next mode, for which the length of the pipe is *three-quarters* of a wavelength, corresponding to a frequency $3f_1$. For Fig. 16.18c, $L = 5\lambda/4$ and the frequency is $5f_1$. The possible wavelengths are given by

$$L = n\frac{\lambda_n}{4} \quad \text{or} \quad \lambda_n = \frac{4L}{n} \quad (n = 1, 3, 5, \ldots) \quad \text{(stopped pipe)} \quad (16.21)$$

The normal-mode frequencies are given by $f_n = v/\lambda_n$, or

Standing waves, stopped pipe:

Frequency of *n*th harmonic ($n = 1, 3, 5, \ldots$)

$$f_n = \frac{nv}{4L} \qquad (16.22)$$

Speed of sound in pipe

Length of pipe

or

$$f_n = nf_1 \quad (n = 1, 3, 5, \ldots) \quad \text{(stopped pipe)} \quad (16.23)$$

with f_1 given by Eq. (16.20). We see that the second, fourth, and all *even* harmonics are missing. In a stopped pipe, the fundamental frequency is $f_1 = v/4L$, and only the odd harmonics in the series ($3f_1, 5f_1, \ldots$) are possible.

A final possibility is a pipe that is closed at *both* ends, with displacement nodes and pressure antinodes at both ends. This wouldn't be of much use as a musical instrument because the vibrations couldn't get out of the pipe.

EXAMPLE 16.11 **A TALE OF TWO PIPES**

On a day when the speed of sound is 345 m/s, the fundamental frequency of a particular stopped organ pipe is 220 Hz. (a) How long is this pipe? (b) The second *overtone* of this pipe has the same wavelength as the third *harmonic* of an *open* pipe. How long is the open pipe?

SOLUTION

IDENTIFY and SET UP: This problem uses the relationship between the length and normal-mode frequencies of open pipes (Fig. 16.17) and stopped pipes (Fig. 16.18). In part (a), we determine the length of the stopped pipe from Eq. (16.22). In part (b), we must determine the length of an open pipe, for which Eq. (16.18) gives the frequencies.

EXECUTE: (a) For a stopped pipe $f_1 = v/4L$, so

$$L_{\text{stopped}} = \frac{v}{4f_1} = \frac{345 \text{ m/s}}{4(220 \text{ s}^{-1})} = 0.392 \text{ m}$$

(b) The frequency of the second overtone of a stopped pipe (the *third* possible frequency) is $f_5 = 5f_1 = 5(220 \text{ Hz}) = 1100 \text{ Hz}$. If the wavelengths for the two pipes are the same, the frequencies are also the same. Hence the frequency of the third harmonic of the open pipe, which is at $3f_1 = 3(v/2L)$, equals 1100 Hz. Then

$$1100 \text{ Hz} = 3\left(\frac{345 \text{ m/s}}{2L_{\text{open}}}\right) \quad \text{and} \quad L_{\text{open}} = 0.470 \text{ m}$$

EVALUATE: The 0.392-m stopped pipe has a fundamental frequency of 220 Hz; the *longer* (0.470-m) open pipe has a *higher* fundamental frequency, $(1100 \text{ Hz})/3 = 367 \text{ Hz}$. This is not a contradiction, as you can see if you compare Figs. 16.17a and 16.18a.

In an organ pipe in actual use, several modes are always present at once; the motion of the air is a superposition of these modes. This situation is analogous to a string that is struck or plucked, as in Fig. 15.28. Just as for a vibrating string, a complex standing wave in the pipe produces a traveling sound wave in the surrounding air with a harmonic content similar to that of the standing wave. A very narrow pipe produces a sound wave rich in higher harmonics; a fatter pipe produces mostly the fundamental mode, heard as a softer, more flutelike tone. The harmonic content also depends on the shape of the pipe's mouth.

We have talked about organ pipes, but this discussion is also applicable to other wind instruments. The flute and the recorder are directly analogous. The most significant difference is that those instruments have holes along the pipe. Opening and closing the holes with the fingers changes the effective length L of the air column and thus changes the pitch. Any individual organ pipe, by comparison, can play only a single note. The flute and recorder behave as *open* pipes, while the clarinet acts as a *stopped* pipe (closed at the reed end, open at the bell).

Equations (16.18) and (16.22) show that the frequencies of any wind instrument are proportional to the speed of sound v in the air column inside the instrument. As Eq. (16.10) shows, v depends on temperature; it increases when temperature increases. Thus the pitch of all wind instruments rises with increasing temperature. An organ that has some of its pipes at one temperature and others at a different temperature is bound to sound out of tune.

TEST YOUR UNDERSTANDING OF SECTION 16.4 If you connect a hose to one end of a metal pipe and blow compressed air into it, the pipe produces a musical tone. If instead you blow compressed helium into the pipe at the same pressure and temperature, will the pipe produce (i) the same tone, (ii) a higher-pitch tone, or (iii) a lower-pitch tone? ❚

16.5 RESONANCE AND SOUND

Many mechanical systems have normal modes of oscillation. As we have seen, these include columns of air (as in an organ pipe) and stretched strings (as in a guitar; see Section 15.8). In each mode, every particle of the system oscillates with simple harmonic motion at the same frequency as the mode. Air columns and stretched strings have an infinite series of normal modes, but the basic concept is closely related to the simple harmonic oscillator, discussed in Chapter 14, which has only a single normal mode (that is, only one frequency at which it oscillates after being disturbed).

Suppose we apply a periodically varying force to a system that can oscillate. The system is then forced to oscillate with a frequency equal to the frequency of the applied force (called the *driving frequency*). This motion is called a *forced oscillation*. We talked about forced oscillations of the harmonic oscillator in Section 14.8, including the phenomenon of mechanical **resonance.** A simple example of resonance is pushing Cousin Throckmorton on a swing. The swing is a pendulum; it has only a single normal mode, with a frequency determined by its length. If we push the swing periodically with this frequency, we can build up the amplitude of the motion. But if we push with a very different frequency, the swing hardly moves at all.

Resonance also occurs when a periodically varying force is applied to a system with many normal modes. In **Fig. 16.19a** an open organ pipe is placed next to a loudspeaker that emits pure sinusoidal sound waves of frequency f, which can be varied by adjusting the amplifier. The air in the pipe is forced to vibrate with the same frequency f as the *driving force* provided by the loudspeaker. In general the amplitude of this motion is relatively small, and the air inside the pipe will not move in any of the normal-mode patterns shown in Fig. 16.17. But if the frequency f of the force is close to one of the normal-mode frequencies, the air in the pipe moves in the normal-mode pattern for that frequency, and

16.19 (a) The air in an open pipe is forced to oscillate at the same frequency as the sinusoidal sound waves coming from the loudspeaker. (b) The resonance curve of the open pipe graphs the amplitude of the standing sound wave in the pipe as a function of the driving frequency.

(a)

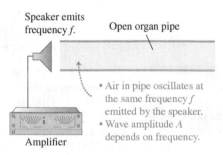

Speaker emits frequency f.   Open organ pipe

• Air in pipe oscillates at the same frequency f emitted by the speaker.
• Wave amplitude A depends on frequency.

Amplifier

(b) Resonance curve: graph of amplitude A versus driving frequency f. Peaks occur at normal-mode frequencies of the pipe: f_1, $f_2 = 2f_1$, $f_3 = 3f_1$, ...

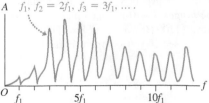

the amplitude can become quite large. Figure 16.19b shows the amplitude of oscillation of the air in the pipe as a function of the driving frequency f. This **resonance curve** of the pipe has peaks where f equals the normal-mode frequencies of the pipe. The detailed shape of the resonance curve depends on the geometry of the pipe.

If the frequency of the force is precisely *equal* to a normal-mode frequency, the system is in resonance, and the amplitude of the forced oscillation is maximum. If there were no friction or other energy-dissipating mechanism, a driving force at a normal-mode frequency would continue to add energy to the system, the amplitude would increase indefinitely, and the peaks in the resonance curve of Fig. 16.19b would be infinitely high. But in any real system there is always some dissipation of energy, or damping, as we discussed in Section 14.8; the amplitude of oscillation in resonance may be large, but it cannot be infinite.

The "sound of the ocean" you hear when you put your ear next to a large seashell is due to resonance. The noise of the outside air moving past the seashell is a mixture of sound waves of almost all audible frequencies, which forces the air inside the seashell to oscillate. The seashell behaves like an organ pipe, with a set of normal-mode frequencies; hence the inside air oscillates most strongly at those frequencies, producing the seashell's characteristic sound. To hear a similar phenomenon, uncap a full bottle of your favorite beverage and blow across the open top. The noise is provided by your breath blowing across the top, and the "organ pipe" is the column of air inside the bottle above the surface of the liquid. If you take a drink and repeat the experiment, you will hear a lower tone because the "pipe" is longer and the normal-mode frequencies are lower.

Resonance also occurs when a stretched string is forced to oscillate (see Section 15.8). Suppose that one end of a stretched string is held fixed while the other is given a transverse sinusoidal motion with small amplitude, setting up standing waves. If the frequency of the driving mechanism is *not* equal to one of the normal-mode frequencies of the string, the amplitude at the antinodes is fairly small. However, if the frequency is equal to any one of the normal-mode frequencies, the string is in resonance, and the amplitude at the antinodes is very much larger than that at the driven end. The driven end is not precisely a node, but it lies much closer to a node than to an antinode when the string is in resonance. The photographs of standing waves in Fig. 15.23 were made this way, with the left end of the string fixed and the right end oscillating vertically with small amplitude.

It is easy to demonstrate resonance with a piano. Push down the damper pedal (the right-hand pedal) so that the dampers are lifted and the strings are free to vibrate, and then sing a steady tone into the piano. When you stop singing, the piano seems to continue to sing the same note. The sound waves from your voice excite vibrations in the strings that have natural frequencies close to the frequencies (fundamental and harmonics) present in the note you sang.

A more spectacular example is a singer breaking a wine glass with her amplified voice. A good-quality wine glass has normal-mode frequencies that you can hear by tapping it. If the singer emits a loud note with a frequency corresponding exactly to one of these normal-mode frequencies, large-amplitude oscillations can build up and break the glass (**Fig. 16.20**).

BIO Application Resonance and the Sensitivity of the Ear The auditory canal of the human ear (see Fig. 16.4) is an air-filled pipe open at one end and closed at the other (eardrum) end. The canal is about 2.5 cm $=$ 0.025 m long, so it has a resonance at its fundamental frequency $f_1 = v/4L =$ (344 m/s)/[4(0.025 m)] $=$ 3440 Hz. The resonance means that a sound at this frequency produces a strong oscillation of the eardrum. That's why your ear is most sensitive to sounds near 3440 Hz.

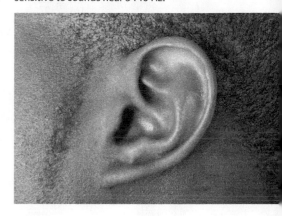

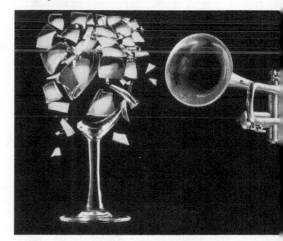

16.20 The frequency of the sound from this trumpet exactly matches one of the normal-mode frequencies of the goblet. The resonant vibrations of the goblet have such large amplitude that the goblet tears itself apart.

EXAMPLE 16.12 AN ORGAN–GUITAR DUET

A stopped organ pipe is sounded near a guitar, causing one of the strings to vibrate with large amplitude. We vary the string tension until we find the maximum amplitude. The string is 80% as long as the pipe. If both pipe and string vibrate at their fundamental frequency, calculate the ratio of the wave speed on the string to the speed of sound in air.

SOLUTION

IDENTIFY and SET UP: The large response of the string is an example of resonance. It occurs because the organ pipe and the guitar string have the same fundamental frequency. Letting the subscripts

Continued

a and s stand for the air in the pipe and the string, respectively, the condition for resonance is $f_{1a} = f_{1s}$. Equation (16.20) gives the fundamental frequency for a stopped pipe, and Eq. (15.32) gives the fundamental frequency for a guitar string held at both ends. These expressions involve the wave speed in air (v_a) and on the string (v_s) and the lengths of the pipe and string. We are given that $L_s = 0.80L_a$; our target variable is the ratio v_s/v_a.

EXECUTE: From Eqs. (16.20) and (15.32), $f_{1a} = v_a/4L_a$ and $f_{1s} = v_s/2L_s$. These frequencies are equal, so

$$\frac{v_a}{4L_a} = \frac{v_s}{2L_s}$$

Substituting $L_s = 0.80L_a$ and rearranging, we get $v_s/v_a = 0.40$.

EVALUATE: As an example, if the speed of sound in air is 345 m/s, the wave speed on the string is $(0.40)(345 \text{ m/s}) = 138 \text{ m/s}$. Note that while the standing waves in the pipe and on the string have the same frequency, they have different *wavelengths* $\lambda = v/f$ because the two media have different wave speeds v. Which standing wave has the greater wavelength?

TEST YOUR UNDERSTANDING OF SECTION 16.5 A stopped organ pipe of length L has a fundamental frequency of 220 Hz. For which of the following organ pipes will there be a resonance if a tuning fork of frequency 660 Hz is sounded next to the pipe? (There may be more than one correct answer.) (i) A stopped organ pipe of length L; (ii) a stopped organ pipe of length $2L$; (iii) an open organ pipe of length L; (iii) an open organ pipe of length $2L$. ▮

16.21 Two speakers driven by the same amplifier. Constructive interference occurs at point P, and destructive interference occurs at point Q.

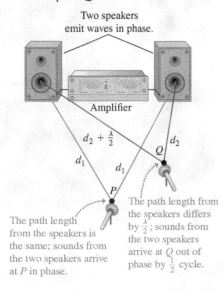

Two speakers emit waves in phase.

Amplifier

$d_2 + \frac{\lambda}{2}$

d_2

d_1

d_1

Q

P

The path length from the speakers is the same; sounds from the two speakers arrive at P in phase.

The path length from the speakers differs by $\frac{\lambda}{2}$; sounds from the two speakers arrive at Q out of phase by $\frac{1}{2}$ cycle.

16.6 INTERFERENCE OF WAVES

Wave phenomena that occur when two or more waves overlap in the same region of space are grouped under the heading *interference*. As we have seen, standing waves are a simple example of an interference effect: Two waves traveling in opposite directions in a medium can combine to produce a standing-wave pattern with nodes and antinodes that do not move.

Figure 16.21 shows an example of another type of interference that involves waves that spread out in space. Two speakers, driven in phase by the same amplifier, emit identical sinusoidal sound waves with the same constant frequency. We place a microphone at point P in the figure, equidistant from the speakers. Wave crests emitted from the two speakers at the same time travel equal distances and arrive at point P at the same time; hence the waves arrive in phase, and there is constructive interference. The total wave amplitude that we measure at P is twice the amplitude from each individual wave.

Now let's move the microphone to point Q, where the distances from the two speakers to the microphone differ by a half-wavelength. Then the two waves arrive a half-cycle out of step, or *out of phase;* a positive crest from one speaker arrives at the same time as a negative crest from the other. Destructive interference takes place, and the amplitude measured by the microphone is much *smaller* than when only one speaker is present. If the amplitudes from the two speakers are equal, the two waves cancel each other out completely at point Q, and the total amplitude there is zero.

CAUTION **Interference and traveling waves** The total wave in Fig. 16.21 is a *traveling* wave, not a standing wave. In a standing wave there is no net flow of energy in any direction; by contrast, in Fig. 16.21 there *is* an overall flow of energy from the speakers into the surrounding air, characteristic of a traveling wave. The interference between the waves from the two speakers simply causes the energy flow to be *channeled* into certain directions (for example, toward P) and away from other directions (for example, away from Q). You can see another difference between Fig. 16.21 and a standing wave by considering a point, such as Q, where destructive interference occurs. Such a point is *both* a displacement node *and* a pressure node because there is no wave at all at this point. In a standing wave, a pressure node is a displacement antinode, and vice versa. ▮

Page 163 of 456.

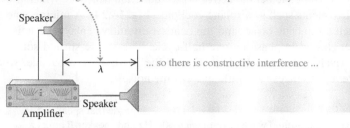

(a) The path lengths from the speakers to the microphone differ by λ ...

Speaker

λ

... so there is constructive interference ...

Speaker

Amplifier

... and the microphone detects a loud sound.

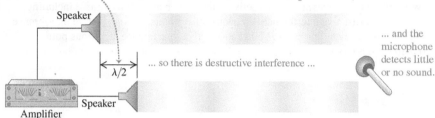

(b) The path lengths from the speakers to the microphone differ by $\frac{\lambda}{2}$ ...

Speaker

$\lambda/2$

... so there is destructive interference ...

Speaker

Amplifier

... and the microphone detects little or no sound.

16.22 Two speakers driven by the same amplifier, emitting waves in phase. Only the waves directed toward the microphone are shown, and they are separated for clarity. (a) Constructive interference occurs when the path difference is 0, λ, 2λ, 3λ, ... (b) Destructive interference occurs when the path difference is $\lambda/2$, $3\lambda/2$, $5\lambda/2$, ...

Constructive interference occurs wherever the distances traveled by the two waves differ by a whole number of wavelengths, 0, λ, 2λ, 3λ, ... ; then the waves arrive at the microphone in phase (**Fig. 16.22a**). If the distances from the two speakers to the microphone differ by any half-integer number of wavelengths, $\lambda/2$, $3\lambda/2$, $5\lambda/2$, ..., the waves arrive at the microphone out of phase and there will be destructive interference (Fig. 16.22b). In this case, little or no sound energy flows toward the microphone. The energy instead flows in other directions, to where constructive interference occurs.

SOLUTION

EXAMPLE 16.13 LOUDSPEAKER INTERFERENCE

Two small loudspeakers, A and B (**Fig. 16.23**), are driven by the same amplifier and emit pure sinusoidal waves in phase. (a) For what frequencies does constructive interference occur at point P? (b) For what frequencies does destructive interference occur? The speed of sound is 350 m/s.

SOLUTION

IDENTIFY and SET UP: The nature of the interference at P depends on the difference d in path lengths from point A to P and from point B to P. We calculate the path lengths using the Pythagorean theorem. Constructive interference occurs when d equals a whole number of wavelengths, while destructive interference occurs

16.23 What sort of interference occurs at P?

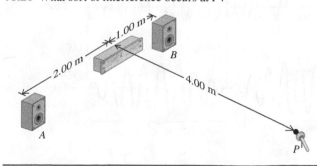

when d is a half-integer number of wavelengths. To find the corresponding frequencies, we use $v = f\lambda$.

EXECUTE: The A-to-P distance is $[(2.00\ \text{m})^2 + (4.00\ \text{m})^2]^{1/2} = 4.47\ \text{m}$, and the B-to-P distance is $[(1.00\ \text{m})^2 + (4.00\ \text{m})^2]^{1/2} = 4.12\ \text{m}$. The path difference is $d = 4.47\ \text{m} - 4.12\ \text{m} = 0.35\ \text{m}$.

(a) Constructive interference occurs when $d = 0$, λ, 2λ, ... or $d = 0$, v/f, $2v/f$, ... $= nv/f$. So the possible frequencies are

$$f_n = \frac{nv}{d} = n\frac{350\ \text{m/s}}{0.35\ \text{m}} \qquad (n = 1, 2, 3, \ldots)$$

$$= 1000\ \text{Hz}, 2000\ \text{Hz}, 3000\ \text{Hz}, \ldots$$

(b) Destructive interference occurs when $d = \lambda/2$, $3\lambda/2$, $5\lambda/2$, ... or $d = v/2f$, $3v/2f$, $5v/2f$, ... The possible frequencies are

$$f_n = \frac{nv}{2d} = n\frac{350\ \text{m/s}}{2(0.35\ \text{m})} \qquad (n = 1, 3, 5, \ldots)$$

$$= 500\ \text{Hz}, 1500\ \text{Hz}, 2500\ \text{Hz}, \ldots$$

EVALUATE: As we increase the frequency, the sound at point P alternates between large and small (near zero) amplitudes, with maxima and minima at the frequencies given above. This effect may not be strong in an ordinary room because of reflections from the walls, floor, and ceiling.

16.24 This aviation headset uses destructive interference to minimize the amount of noise from wind and propellers that reaches the wearer's ears.

Interference is the principle behind active noise-reduction headsets, which are used in loud environments such as airplane cockpits (**Fig. 16.24**). A microphone on the headset detects outside noise, and the headset circuitry replays the noise inside the headset shifted in phase by one half-cycle. This phase-shifted sound interferes destructively with the sounds that enter the headset from outside, so the headset wearer experiences very little unwelcome noise.

TEST YOUR UNDERSTANDING OF SECTION 16.6 Suppose that speaker A in Fig. 16.23 emits a sinusoidal sound wave of frequency 500 Hz and speaker B emits a sinusoidal sound wave of frequency 1000 Hz. What sort of interference will there be between these two waves? (i) Constructive interference at various points, including point P, and destructive interference at various other points; (ii) destructive interference at various points, including point P, and constructive interference at various points; (iii) neither (i) nor (ii). ▌

16.7 BEATS

In Section 16.6 we talked about *interference* effects that occur when two different waves with the same frequency overlap in the same region of space. Now let's look at what happens when we have two waves with equal amplitude but slightly different frequencies. This occurs, for example, when two tuning forks with slightly different frequencies are sounded together, or when two organ pipes that are supposed to have exactly the same frequency are slightly "out of tune."

Consider a particular point in space where the two waves overlap. In **Fig. 16.25a** we plot the displacements of the individual waves at this point as functions of time. The total length of the time axis represents 1 second, and the frequencies are 16 Hz (blue graph) and 18 Hz (red graph). Applying the principle of superposition, we add the two displacement functions to find the total displacement function. The result is the graph of Fig. 16.25b. At certain times the two waves are in phase; their maxima coincide and their amplitudes add. But at certain times (like $t = 0.50$ s in Fig. 16.25) the two waves are exactly *out* of phase. The two waves then cancel each other, and the total amplitude is zero.

The resultant wave in Fig. 16.25b looks like a single sinusoidal wave with an amplitude that varies from a maximum to zero and back. In this example the amplitude goes through two maxima and two minima in 1 second, so the frequency of this amplitude variation is 2 Hz. The amplitude variation causes variations of loudness called **beats,** and the frequency with which the loudness varies is called the **beat frequency.** In this example the beat frequency is the *difference* of the two frequencies. If the beat frequency is a few hertz, we hear it as a waver or pulsation in the tone.

16.25 Beats are fluctuations in amplitude produced by two sound waves of slightly different frequency, here 16 Hz and 18 Hz. (a) Individual waves. (b) Resultant wave formed by superposition of the two waves. The beat frequency is 18 Hz − 16 Hz = 2 Hz.

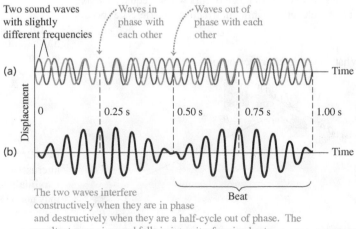

We can prove that the beat frequency is *always* the difference of the two frequencies f_a and f_b. Suppose f_a is larger than f_b; the corresponding periods are T_a and T_b, with $T_a < T_b$. If the two waves start out in phase at time $t = 0$, they are again in phase when the first wave has gone through exactly one more cycle than the second. This happens at a value of t equal to T_{beat}, the *period* of the beat. Let n be the number of cycles of the first wave in time T_{beat}; then the number of cycles of the second wave in the same time is $(n - 1)$, and we have the relationships

$$T_{\text{beat}} = nT_a \quad \text{and} \quad T_{\text{beat}} = (n - 1)T_b$$

Eliminating n between these two equations, we find

$$T_{\text{beat}} = \frac{T_a T_b}{T_b - T_a}$$

The reciprocal of the beat period is the beat *frequency*, $f_{\text{beat}} = 1/T_{\text{beat}}$, so

$$f_{\text{beat}} = \frac{T_b - T_a}{T_a T_b} = \frac{1}{T_a} - \frac{1}{T_b}$$

and finally

Beat frequency for ·········⟶ $f_{\text{beat}} = f_a - f_b$ ·······Frequency of wave a
waves a and b ⟵·······Frequency of wave b (16.24)
                                                 (lower than f_a)

As claimed, the beat frequency is the difference of the two frequencies.

An alternative way to derive Eq. (16.24) is to write functions to describe the curves in Fig. 16.25a and then add them. Suppose that at a certain position the two waves are given by $y_a(t) = A \sin 2\pi f_a t$ and $y_b(t) = -A \sin 2\pi f_b t$. We use the trigonometric identity

$$\sin a - \sin b = 2 \sin \tfrac{1}{2}(a - b) \cos \tfrac{1}{2}(a + b)$$

We can then express the total wave $y(t) = y_a(t) + y_b(t)$ as

$$y_a(t) + y_b(t) = \left[2A \sin \tfrac{1}{2}(2\pi)(f_a - f_b)t \right] \cos \tfrac{1}{2}(2\pi)(f_a + f_b)t$$

The amplitude factor (the quantity in brackets) varies slowly with frequency $\tfrac{1}{2}(f_a - f_b)$. The cosine factor varies with a frequency equal to the *average* frequency $\tfrac{1}{2}(f_a + f_b)$. The *square* of the amplitude factor, which is proportional to the intensity that the ear hears, goes through two maxima and two minima per cycle. So the beat frequency f_{beat} that is heard is twice the quantity $\tfrac{1}{2}(f_a - f_b)$, or just $f_a - f_b$, in agreement with Eq. (16.24).

Beats between two tones can be heard up to a beat frequency of about 6 or 7 Hz. Two piano strings or two organ pipes differing in frequency by 2 or 3 Hz sound wavery and "out of tune," although some organ stops contain two sets of pipes deliberately tuned to beat frequencies of about 1 to 2 Hz for a gently undulating effect. Listening for beats is an important technique in tuning all musical instruments. *Avoiding* beats is part of the task of flying a multiengine propeller airplane (**Fig. 16.26**).

At frequency differences greater than about 6 or 7 Hz, we no longer hear individual beats, and the sensation merges into one of *consonance* or *dissonance*, depending on the frequency ratio of the two tones. In some cases the ear perceives a tone called a *difference tone*, with a pitch equal to the beat frequency of the two tones. For example, if you listen to a whistle that produces sounds at 1800 Hz and 1900 Hz when blown, you will hear not only these tones but also a much lower 100-Hz tone.

16.26 If the two propellers on this airplane are not precisely synchronized, the pilots, passengers, and listeners on the ground will hear beats as loud, annoying, throbbing sounds. On some airplanes the propellers are synched electronically; on others the pilot does it by ear, like tuning a piano.

16.8 THE DOPPLER EFFECT

When a car approaches you with its horn sounding, the pitch seems to drop as the
car passes. This phenomenon, first described by the 19th-century Austrian scientist
Christian Doppler, is called the **Doppler effect.** When a source of sound and a
listener are in motion relative to each other, the frequency of the sound heard by
the listener is not the same as the source frequency. A similar effect occurs for
light and radio waves; we'll return to this later in this section.

To analyze the Doppler effect for sound, we'll work out a relationship between
the frequency shift and the velocities of source and listener relative to the medium
(usually air) through which the sound waves propagate. To keep things simple,
we consider only the special case in which the velocities of both source and listener lie along the line joining them. Let v_S and v_L be the velocity components
along this line for the source and the listener, respectively, relative to the medium.
We choose the positive direction for both v_S and v_L to be the direction from the
listener L to the source S. The speed of sound relative to the medium, v, is always
considered positive.

Moving Listener and Stationary Source

Let's think first about a listener L moving with velocity v_L toward a stationary
source S (**Fig. 16.27**). The source emits a sound wave with frequency f_S and
wavelength $\lambda = v/f_S$. The figure shows four wave crests, separated by equal distances λ. The wave crests approaching the moving listener have a speed of propagation *relative to the listener* of $(v + v_L)$. So the frequency f_L with which the
crests arrive at the listener's position (that is, the frequency the listener hears) is

$$f_L = \frac{v + v_L}{\lambda} = \frac{v + v_L}{v/f_S} \tag{16.25}$$

or

$$f_L = \left(\frac{v + v_L}{v}\right)f_S = \left(1 + \frac{v_L}{v}\right)f_S \qquad \begin{array}{l}\text{(moving listener,}\\ \text{stationary source)}\end{array} \tag{16.26}$$

16.27 A listener moving toward a stationary source hears a frequency that is higher
than the source frequency. This is because
the relative speed of listener and wave is
greater than the wave speed v.

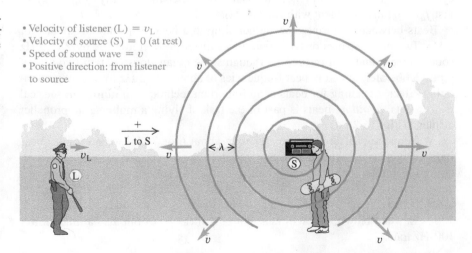

• Velocity of listener (L) = v_L
• Velocity of source (S) = 0 (at rest)
• Speed of sound wave = v
• Positive direction: from listener
  to source

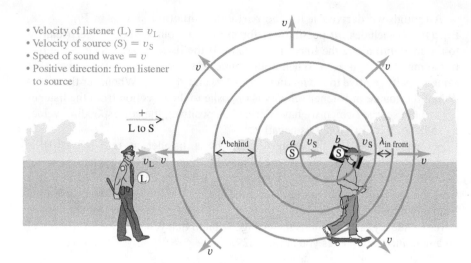

- Velocity of listener (L) = v_L
- Velocity of source (S) = v_S
- Speed of sound wave = v
- Positive direction: from listener to source

$\dfrac{+}{\text{L to S}}$

16.28 Wave crests emitted by a source moving from *a* to *b* are crowded together in front of the source (to the right of this source) and stretched out behind it (to the left of this source).

So a listener moving toward a source ($v_L > 0$), as in Fig. 16.27, hears a higher frequency (higher pitch) than does a stationary listener. A listener moving away from the source ($v_L < 0$) hears a lower frequency (lower pitch).

Moving Source and Moving Listener

Now suppose the source is also moving, with velocity v_S (**Fig. 16.28**). The wave speed relative to the wave medium (air) is still v; it is determined by the properties of the medium and is not changed by the motion of the source. But the wavelength is no longer equal to v/f_S. Here's why. The time for emission of one cycle of the wave is the period $T = 1/f_S$. During this time, the wave travels a distance $vT = v/f_S$ and the source moves a distance $v_S T = v_S/f_S$. The wavelength is the distance between successive wave crests, and this is determined by the *relative* displacement of source and wave. As Fig. 16.28 shows, this is different in front of and behind the source. In the region to the right of the source in Fig. 16.28 (that is, in front of the source), the wavelength is

$$\lambda_{\text{in front}} = \frac{v}{f_S} - \frac{v_S}{f_S} = \frac{v - v_S}{f_S} \qquad \text{(wavelength in front of a moving source)} \qquad (16.27)$$

In the region to the left of the source (that is, behind the source), it is

$$\lambda_{\text{behind}} = \frac{v + v_S}{f_S} \qquad \text{(wavelength behind a moving source)} \qquad (16.28)$$

The waves in front of and behind the source are compressed and stretched out, respectively, by the motion of the source.

To find the frequency heard by the listener behind the source, we substitute Eq. (16.28) into the first form of Eq. (16.25):

$$f_L = \frac{v + v_L}{\lambda_{\text{behind}}} = \frac{v + v_L}{(v + v_S)/f_S}$$

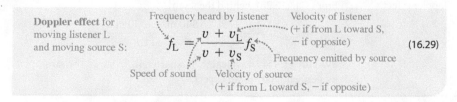

Doppler effect for moving listener L and moving source S:

Frequency heard by listener

Velocity of listener (+ if from L toward S, − if opposite)

$$f_L = \frac{v + v_L}{v + v_S} f_S \qquad (16.29)$$

Speed of sound

Velocity of source (+ if from L toward S, − if opposite)

Frequency emitted by source

16.29 The Doppler effect explains why the siren on a fire engine or ambulance has a high pitch ($f_L > f_S$) when it is approaching you ($v_S < 0$) and a low pitch ($f_L < f_S$) when it is moving away ($v_S > 0$).

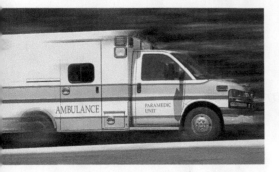

Although we derived it for the particular situation shown in Fig. 16.28, Eq. (16.29) includes *all* possibilities for motion of source and listener (relative to the medium) along the line joining them. If the listener happens to be at rest in the medium, v_L is zero. When both source and listener are at rest or have the same velocity relative to the medium, $v_L = v_S$ and $f_L = f_S$. Whenever the direction of the source or listener velocity is opposite to the direction from the listener toward the source (which we have defined as positive), the corresponding velocity to be used in Eq. (16.29) is negative.

As an example, the frequency heard by a listener at rest ($v_L = 0$) is $f_L = [v/(v + v_S)]f_S$. If the source is moving toward the listener (in the negative direction), then $v_S < 0, f_L > f_S$, and the listener hears a higher frequency than that emitted by the source. If instead the source is moving away from the listener (in the positive direction), then $v_S > 0$, $f_L < f_S$, and the listener hears a lower frequency. This explains the change in pitch that you hear from the siren of an ambulance as it passes you (**Fig. 16.29**).

PROBLEM-SOLVING STRATEGY 16.2 | DOPPLER EFFECT

IDENTIFY *the relevant concepts:* The Doppler effect occurs whenever the source of waves, the wave detector (listener), or both are in motion.

SET UP *the problem* using the following steps:

1. Establish a coordinate system, with the positive direction from the listener toward the source. Carefully determine the signs of all relevant velocities. A velocity in the direction from the listener toward the source is positive; a velocity in the opposite direction is negative. All velocities must be measured relative to the air in which the sound travels.
2. Use consistent subscripts to identify the various quantities: S for source and L for listener.
3. Identify which unknown quantities are the target variables.

EXECUTE *the solution* as follows:

1. Use Eq. (16.29) to relate the frequencies at the source and the listener, the sound speed, and the velocities of the source and

the listener according to the sign convention of step 1. If the source is moving, you can find the wavelength measured by the listener using Eq. (16.27) or (16.28).

2. When a wave is reflected from a stationary or moving surface, solve the problem in two steps. In the first, the surface is the "listener"; the frequency with which the wave crests arrive at the surface is f_L. In the second, the surface is the "source," emitting waves with this same frequency f_L. Finally, determine the frequency heard by a listener detecting this new wave.

EVALUATE *your answer:* Is the *direction* of the frequency shift reasonable? If the source and the listener are moving toward each other, $f_L > f_S$; if they are moving apart, $f_L < f_S$. If the source and the listener have no relative motion; $f_L = f_S$.

EXAMPLE 16.14 DOPPLER EFFECT I: WAVELENGTHS

A police car's siren emits a sinusoidal wave with frequency $f_S = 300$ Hz. The speed of sound is 340 m/s and the air is still. (a) Find the wavelength of the waves if the siren is at rest. (b) Find the wavelengths of the waves in front of and behind the siren if it is moving at 30 m/s.

SOLUTION

IDENTIFY and SET UP: In part (a) there is no Doppler effect because neither source nor listener is moving with respect to the air; $v = \lambda f$ gives the wavelength. **Figure 16.30** shows the situation in part (b): The source is in motion, so we find the wavelengths using Eqs. (16.27) and (16.28) for the Doppler effect.

EXECUTE: (a) When the source is at rest,

$$\lambda = \frac{v}{f_S} = \frac{340 \text{ m/s}}{300 \text{ Hz}} = 1.13 \text{ m}$$

16.30 Our sketch for this problem.

(b) From Eq. (16.27), in front of the siren

$$\lambda_{\text{in front}} = \frac{v - v_S}{f_S} = \frac{340 \text{ m/s} - 30 \text{ m/s}}{300 \text{ Hz}} = 1.03 \text{ m}$$

From Eq. (16.28), behind the siren

$$\lambda_{\text{behind}} = \frac{v + v_S}{f_S} = \frac{340 \text{ m/s} + 30 \text{ m/s}}{300 \text{ Hz}} = 1.23 \text{ m}$$

EVALUATE: The wavelength is shorter in front of the siren and longer behind it, as we expect.

EXAMPLE 16.15 DOPPLER EFFECT II: FREQUENCIES

If a listener L is at rest and the siren in Example 16.14 is moving away from L at 30 m/s, what frequency does the listener hear?

SOLUTION

IDENTIFY and SET UP: Our target variable is the frequency f_L heard by a listener behind the moving source. **Figure 16.31** shows the situation. We have $v_L = 0$ and $v_S = +30$ m/s (positive, since the velocity of the source is in the direction from listener to source).

EXECUTE: From Eq. (16.29),

$$f_L = \frac{v}{v + v_S}f_S = \frac{340 \text{ m/s}}{340 \text{ m/s} + 30 \text{ m/s}}(300 \text{ Hz}) = 276 \text{ Hz}$$

EVALUATE: The source and listener are moving apart, so $f_L < f_S$. Here's a check on our numerical result. From Example 16.14, the

16.31 Our sketch for this problem.

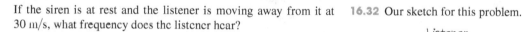
Listener at rest   Police car
$v_L = 0$ $v_S = 30$ m/s
$f_L = ?$ $\xrightarrow{+}$ L to S
Ⓛ   Ⓢ

wavelength behind the source (where the listener in Fig. 16.31 is located) is 1.23 m. The wave speed relative to the stationary listener is $v = 340$ m/s even though the source is moving, so

$$f_L = \frac{v}{\lambda} = \frac{340 \text{ m/s}}{1.23 \text{ m}} = 276 \text{ Hz}$$

EXAMPLE 16.16 DOPPLER EFFECT III: A MOVING LISTENER

If the siren is at rest and the listener is moving away from it at 30 m/s, what frequency does the listener hear?

SOLUTION

IDENTIFY and SET UP: Again our target variable is f_L, but now L is in motion and S is at rest. **Figure 16.32** shows the situation. The velocity of the listener is $v_L = -30$ m/s (negative, since the motion is in the direction from source to listener).

EXECUTE: From Eq. (16.29),

$$f_L = \frac{v + v_L}{v}f_S = \frac{340 \text{ m/s} + (-30 \text{ m/s})}{340 \text{ m/s}}(300 \text{ Hz}) = 274 \text{ Hz}$$

16.32 Our sketch for this problem.

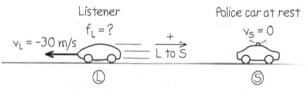
Listener   Police car at rest
$f_L = ?$ $v_S = 0$
$v_L = -30$ m/s $\xrightarrow{+}$ L to S
Ⓛ   Ⓢ

EVALUATE: Again the source and listener are moving apart, so $f_L < f_S$. Note that the *relative velocity* of source and listener is the same as in Example 16.15, but the Doppler shift is different because v_S and v_L are different.

EXAMPLE 16.17 DOPPLER EFFECT IV: MOVING SOURCE, MOVING LISTENER

The siren is moving away from the listener with a speed of 45 m/s relative to the air, and the listener is moving toward the siren with a speed of 15 m/s relative to the air. What frequency does the listener hear?

SOLUTION

IDENTIFY and SET UP: Now *both* L and S are in motion (**Fig. 16.33**). Again our target variable is f_L. Both the source velocity $v_S = +45$ m/s and the listener's velocity $v_L = +15$ m/s are positive because both velocities are in the direction from listener to source.

EXECUTE: From Eq. (16.29),

$$f_L = \frac{v + v_L}{v + v_S}f_S = \frac{340 \text{ m/s} + 15 \text{ m/s}}{340 \text{ m/s} + 45 \text{ m/s}}(300 \text{ Hz}) = 277 \text{ Hz}$$

16.33 Our sketch for this problem.

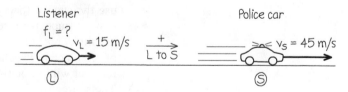
Listener   Police car
$f_L = ?$ $v_L = 15$ m/s $\xrightarrow{+}$ L to S $v_S = 45$ m/s
Ⓛ   Ⓢ

EVALUATE: As in Examples 16.15 and 16.16, the source and listener again move away from each other at 30 m/s, so again $f_L < f_S$. But f_L is different in all three cases because the Doppler effect for sound depends on how the source and listener are moving relative to the *air*, not simply on how they move relative to each other.

EXAMPLE 16.18   DOPPLER EFFECT V: A DOUBLE DOPPLER SHIFT

The police car is moving toward a warehouse at 30 m/s. What frequency does the driver hear reflected from the warehouse?

SOLUTION

IDENTIFY: This situation has *two* Doppler shifts (**Fig. 16.34**). In the first shift, the warehouse is the stationary "listener." The frequency of sound reaching the warehouse, which we call f_W, is greater than 300 Hz because the source is approaching. In the second shift, the warehouse acts as a source of sound with frequency f_W, and the listener is the driver of the police car; she hears a frequency greater than f_W because she is approaching the source.

SET UP: To determine f_W, we use Eq. (16.29) with f_L replaced by f_W. For this part of the problem, $v_L = v_W = 0$ (the warehouse is at rest) and $v_S = -30$ m/s (the siren is moving in the negative direction from source to listener).

  To determine the frequency heard by the driver (our target variable), we again use Eq. (16.29) but now with f_S replaced by f_W. For this second part of the problem, $v_S = 0$ because the stationary warehouse is the source and the velocity of the listener (the driver) is $v_L = +30$ m/s. (The listener's velocity is positive because it is in the direction from listener to source.)

EXECUTE: The frequency reaching the warehouse is

$$f_W = \frac{v}{v + v_S}f_S = \frac{340 \text{ m/s}}{340 \text{ m/s} + (-30 \text{ m/s})}(300 \text{ Hz}) = 329 \text{ Hz}$$

16.34 Two stages of the sound wave's motion from the police car to the warehouse and back to the police car.

(a) Sound travels from police car's siren (source S) to warehouse ("listener" L).

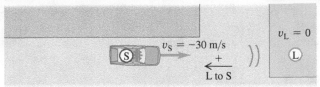

(b) Reflected sound travels from warehouse (source S) to police car (listener L).

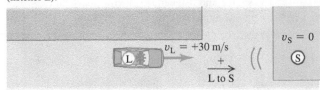

Then the frequency heard by the driver is

$$f_L = \frac{v + v_L}{v}f_W = \frac{340 \text{ m/s} + 30 \text{ m/s}}{340 \text{ m/s}}(329 \text{ Hz}) = 358 \text{ Hz}$$

EVALUATE: Because there are two Doppler shifts, the reflected sound heard by the driver has an even higher frequency than the sound heard by a stationary listener in the warehouse.

Doppler Effect for Electromagnetic Waves

In the Doppler effect for sound, the velocities v_L and v_S are always measured relative to the *air* or whatever medium we are considering. There is also a Doppler effect for *electromagnetic* waves in empty space, such as light waves or radio waves. In this case there is no medium that we can use as a reference to measure velocities, and all that matters is the *relative* velocity of source and receiver. (By contrast, the Doppler effect for sound does not depend simply on this relative velocity, as discussed in Example 16.17.)

  To derive the expression for the Doppler frequency shift for light, we have to use the special theory of relativity. We will discuss this in Chapter 37, but for now we quote the result without derivation. The wave speed is the speed of light, usually denoted by c, and it is the same for both source and receiver. In the frame of reference in which the receiver is at rest, the source is moving away from the receiver with velocity v. (If the source is *approaching* the receiver, v is negative.) The source frequency is again f_S. The frequency f_R measured by the receiver R (the frequency of arrival of the waves at the receiver) is then

$$f_R = \sqrt{\frac{c - v}{c + v}}f_S \qquad \text{(Doppler effect for light)} \qquad (16.30)$$

When v is positive, the source is moving directly *away* from the receiver and f_R is always *less* than f_S; when v is negative, the source is moving directly *toward* the receiver and f_R is *greater* than f_S. The qualitative effect is the same as for sound, but the quantitative relationship is different.

A familiar application of the Doppler effect for radio waves is the radar device mounted on the side window of a police car to check other cars' speeds. The electromagnetic wave emitted by the device is reflected from a moving car, which acts as a moving source, and the wave reflected back to the device is Doppler-shifted in frequency. The transmitted and reflected signals are combined to produce beats, and the speed can be computed from the frequency of the beats. Similar techniques ("Doppler radar") are used to measure wind velocities in the atmosphere.

The Doppler effect is also used to track satellites and other space vehicles. In **Fig. 16.35** a satellite emits a radio signal with constant frequency f_S. As the satellite orbits past, it first approaches and then moves away from the receiver; the frequency f_R of the signal received on earth changes from a value greater than f_S to a value less than f_S as the satellite passes overhead.

16.35 Change of velocity component along the line of sight of a satellite passing a tracking station. The frequency received at the tracking station changes from high to low as the satellite passes overhead.

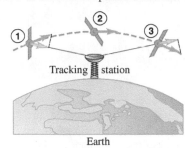

TEST YOUR UNDERSTANDING OF SECTION 16.8 You are at an outdoor concert with a wind blowing at 10 m/s from the performers toward you. Is the sound you hear Doppler-shifted? If so, is it shifted to lower or higher frequencies? ❚

16.9 SHOCK WAVES

You may have experienced "sonic booms" caused by an airplane flying overhead faster than the speed of sound. We can see qualitatively why this happens from **Fig. 16.36**. Let v_S denote the *speed* of the airplane relative to the air, so that it is always positive. The motion of the airplane through the air produces sound; if v_S is less than the speed of sound v, the waves in front of the airplane are crowded together with a wavelength given by Eq. (16.27):

$$\lambda_{\text{in front}} = \frac{v - v_S}{f_S}$$

As the speed v_S of the airplane approaches the speed of sound v, the wavelength approaches zero and the wave crests pile up on each other (Fig. 16.36a). The airplane must exert a large force to compress the air in front of it; by Newton's third law, the air exerts an equally large force back on the airplane. Hence there is a large increase in aerodynamic drag (air resistance) as the airplane approaches the speed of sound, a phenomenon known as the "sound barrier."

16.36 Wave crests around a sound source S moving (a) slightly slower than the speed of sound v and (b) faster than the sound speed v. (c) This photograph shows a T-38 jet airplane moving at 1.1 times the speed of sound. Separate shock waves are produced by the nose, wings, and tail. The angles of these waves vary because the air speeds up and slows down as it moves around the airplane, so the relative speed v_S of the airplane and air is different for shock waves produced at different points.

(a) Sound source S (airplane) moving at nearly the speed of sound

(b) Sound source moving faster than the speed of sound

(c) Shock waves around a supersonic airplane

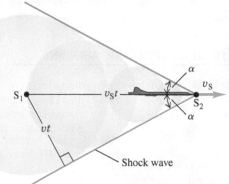

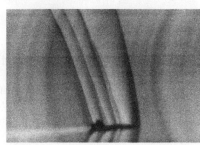

When v_S is greater in magnitude than v, the source of sound is **supersonic,** and Eqs. (16.27) and (16.29) for the Doppler effect no longer describe the sound wave in front of the source. Figure 16.36b shows a cross section of what happens. As the airplane moves, it displaces the surrounding air and produces sound. A series of wave crests is emitted from the nose of the airplane; each spreads out in a circle centered at the position of the airplane when it emitted the crest. After a time t the crest emitted from point S_1 has spread to a circle with radius vt, and the airplane has moved a greater distance v_St to position S_2. You can see that the circular crests interfere constructively at points along the blue line that makes an angle α with the direction of the airplane velocity, leading to a very-large-amplitude wave crest along this line. This large-amplitude crest is called a **shock wave** (Fig. 16.36c).

From the right triangle in Fig. 16.36b we can see that $\sin \alpha = vt/v_St$, or

16.37 The first supersonic airplane, the Bell X-1, was shaped much like a 50-caliber bullet—which was known to be able to travel faster than sound.

Shock wave produced by sound source moving faster than sound:

Angle of shock wave

$$\sin \alpha = \frac{v \cdots\text{Speed of sound}}{v_S \cdots\text{Speed of source}}$$ (16.31)

The ratio v_S/v is called the **Mach number.** It is greater than unity for all supersonic speeds, and $\sin \alpha$ in Eq. (16.31) is the reciprocal of the Mach number. The first person to break the sound barrier was Capt. Chuck Yeager of the U.S. Air Force, flying the Bell X-1 at Mach 1.06 on October 14, 1947 (**Fig. 16.37**).

Shock waves are actually three-dimensional; a shock wave forms a *cone* around the direction of motion of the source. If the source (possibly a supersonic jet airplane or a rifle bullet) moves with constant velocity, the angle α is constant, and the shock-wave cone moves along with the source. It's the arrival of this shock wave that causes the sonic boom you hear after a supersonic airplane has passed by. In front of the shock-wave cone, there is no sound. Inside the cone a stationary listener hears the Doppler-shifted sound of the airplane moving away.

CAUTION **Shock waves** A shock wave is produced *continuously* by any object that moves through the air at supersonic speed, not only at the instant that it "breaks the sound barrier." The sound waves that combine to form the shock wave, as in Fig. 16.36b, are created by the motion of the object itself, not by any sound source that the object may carry. The cracking noises of a bullet and of the tip of a circus whip are due to their supersonic motion. A supersonic jet airplane may have very loud engines, but these do not cause the shock wave. If the pilot were to shut the engines off, the airplane would continue to produce a shock wave as long as its speed remained supersonic. ∎

Shock waves have applications outside of aviation. They are used to break up kidney stones and gallstones without invasive surgery, using a technique with the impressive name *extracorporeal shock-wave lithotripsy.* A shock wave produced outside the body is focused by a reflector or acoustic lens so that as much of it as possible converges on the stone. When the resulting stresses in the stone exceed its tensile strength, it breaks into small pieces and can be eliminated. This technique requires accurate determination of the location of the stone, which may be done using ultrasonic imaging techniques (see Fig. 16.9).

EXAMPLE 16.19 | **SONIC BOOM FROM A SUPERSONIC AIRPLANE**

An airplane is flying at Mach 1.75 at an altitude of 8000 m, where the speed of sound is 320 m/s. How long after the plane passes directly overhead will you hear the sonic boom?

SOLUTION

IDENTIFY and SET UP: The shock wave forms a cone trailing backward from the airplane, so the problem is really asking for how much time elapses from when the airplane flies overhead to when

the shock wave reaches you at point L (**Fig. 16.38**). During the time t (our target variable) since the airplane traveling at speed v_S passed overhead, it has traveled a distance v_St. Equation (16.31) gives the shock cone angle α; we use trigonometry to solve for t.

EXECUTE: From Eq. (16.31) the angle α of the shock cone is

$$\alpha = \arcsin \frac{1}{1.75} = 34.8°$$

16.38 You hear a sonic boom when the shock wave reaches you at L (*not* just when the plane breaks the sound barrier). A listener to the right of L has not yet heard the sonic boom but will shortly; a listener to the left of L has already heard the sonic boom.

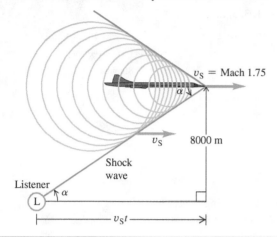

The speed of the plane is the speed of sound multiplied by the Mach number:

$$v_S = (1.75)(320 \text{ m/s}) = 560 \text{ m/s}$$

From Fig. 16.38 we have

$$\tan \alpha = \frac{8000 \text{ m}}{v_S t}$$

$$t = \frac{8000 \text{ m}}{(560 \text{ m/s})(\tan 34.8°)} = 20.5 \text{ s}$$

EVALUATE: You hear the boom 20.5 s after the airplane passes overhead, at which time it has traveled $(560 \text{ m/s})(20.5 \text{ s}) = 11.5$ km since it passed overhead. We have assumed that the speed of sound is the same at all altitudes, so that $\alpha = \arcsin v/v_S$ is constant and the shock wave forms a perfect cone. In fact, the speed of sound decreases with increasing altitude. How would this affect the value of t?

TEST YOUR UNDERSTANDING OF SECTION 16.9 What would you hear if you were directly behind (to the left of) the supersonic airplane in Fig. 16.38? (i) A sonic boom; (ii) the sound of the airplane, Doppler-shifted to higher frequencies; (iii) the sound of the airplane, Doppler-shifted to lower frequencies; (iv) nothing. ❙

CHAPTER 16 SUMMARY

SOLUTIONS TO ALL EXAMPLES

Sound waves: Sound consists of longitudinal waves in a medium. A sinusoidal sound wave is characterized by its frequency f and wavelength λ (or angular frequency ω and wave number k) and by its displacement amplitude A. The pressure amplitude p_{max} is directly proportional to the displacement amplitude, the wave number, and the bulk modulus B of the wave medium. (See Examples 16.1 and 16.2.)

The speed of a sound wave in a fluid depends on the bulk modulus B and density ρ. If the fluid is an ideal gas, the speed can be expressed in terms of the temperature T, molar mass M, and ratio of heat capacities γ of the gas. The speed of longitudinal waves in a solid rod depends on the density and Young's modulus Y. (See Examples 16.3 and 16.4.)

$$p_{max} = BkA \qquad (16.5)$$
(sinusoidal sound wave)

$$v = \sqrt{\frac{B}{\rho}} \qquad (16.7)$$
(longitudinal wave in a fluid)

$$v = \sqrt{\frac{\gamma RT}{M}} \qquad (16.10)$$
(sound wave in an ideal gas)

$$v = \sqrt{\frac{Y}{\rho}} \qquad (16.8)$$
(longitudinal wave in a solid rod)

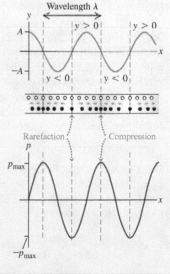

Intensity and sound intensity level: The intensity I of a sound wave is the time average rate at which energy is transported by the wave, per unit area. For a sinusoidal wave, the intensity can be expressed in terms of the displacement amplitude A or the pressure amplitude p_{max}. (See Examples 16.5–16.7.)

The sound intensity level β of a sound wave is a logarithmic measure of its intensity. It is measured relative to I_0, an arbitrary intensity defined to be 10^{-12} W/m². Sound intensity levels are expressed in decibels (dB). (See Examples 16.8 and 16.9.)

$$I = \tfrac{1}{2}\sqrt{\rho B}\,\omega^2 A^2 = \frac{p_{max}^2}{2\rho v}$$

$$= \frac{p_{max}^2}{2\sqrt{\rho B}} \qquad (16.12), (16.14)$$
(intensity of a sinusoidal sound wave in a fluid)

$$\beta = (10 \text{ dB}) \log \frac{I}{I_0} \qquad (16.15)$$
(definition of sound intensity level)

Standing sound waves: Standing sound waves can be set up in a pipe or tube. A closed end is a displacement node and a pressure antinode; an open end is a displacement antinode and a pressure node. For a pipe of length L open at both ends, the normal-mode frequencies are integer multiples of the sound speed divided by $2L$. For a stopped pipe (one that is open at only one end), the normal-mode frequencies are the odd multiples of the sound speed divided by $4L$. (See Examples 16.10 and 16.11.)

A pipe or other system with normal-mode frequencies can be driven to oscillate at any frequency. A maximum response, or resonance, occurs if the driving frequency is close to one of the normal-mode frequencies of the system. (See Example 16.12.)

$$f_n = \frac{nv}{2L} \quad (n = 1, 2, 3, \ldots) \quad (16.18)$$
(open pipe)

$$f_n = \frac{nv}{4L} \quad (n = 1, 3, 5, \ldots) \quad (16.22)$$
(stopped pipe)

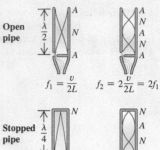

Interference: When two or more waves overlap in the same region of space, the resulting effects are called interference. The resulting amplitude can be either larger or smaller than the amplitude of each individual wave, depending on whether the waves are in phase (constructive interference) or out of phase (destructive interference). (See Example 16.13.)

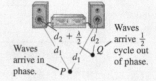

Beats: Beats are heard when two tones with slightly different frequencies f_a and f_b are sounded together. The beat frequency f_{beat} is the difference between f_a and f_b.

$$f_{\text{beat}} = f_a - f_b \quad (16.24)$$
(beat frequency)

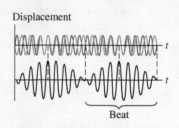

Doppler effect: The Doppler effect for sound is the frequency shift that occurs when there is motion of a source of sound, a listener, or both, relative to the medium. The source and listener frequencies f_S and f_L are related by the source and listener velocities v_S and v_L relative to the medium and to the speed of sound v. (See Examples 16.14–16.18.)

$$f_L = \frac{v + v_L}{v + v_S} f_S \quad (16.29)$$
(Doppler effect, moving source and moving listener)

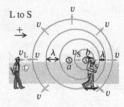

Shock waves: A sound source moving with a speed v_S greater than the speed of sound v creates a shock wave. The wave front is a cone with angle α. (See Example 16.19.)

$$\sin \alpha = \frac{v}{v_S} \quad \text{(shock wave)} \quad (16.31)$$

BRIDGING PROBLEM | **LOUDSPEAKER INTERFERENCE**

Loudspeakers A and B are 7.00 m apart and vibrate in phase at 172 Hz. They radiate sound uniformly in all directions. Their acoustic power outputs are 8.00×10^{-4} W and 6.00×10^{-5} W, respectively. The air temperature is 20°C. (a) Determine the difference in phase of the two signals at a point C along the line joining A and B, 3.00 m from B and 4.00 m from A (**Fig. 16.39**). (b) Determine the intensity and sound intensity level at C from speaker A alone (with B turned off) and from speaker B alone (with A turned off). (c) Determine the intensity and sound intensity level at C from both speakers together.

SOLUTION GUIDE

IDENTIFY and SET UP

1. Choose the equations that relate power, distance from the source, intensity, pressure amplitude, and sound intensity level.

16.39 The situation for this problem.

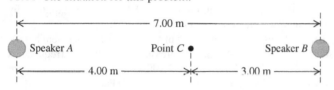

2. Decide how you will determine the phase difference in part (a). Once you have found the phase difference, how can you use it to find the amplitude of the combined wave at C due to both sources?
3. List the unknown quantities for each part of the problem and identify your target variables.

EXECUTE

4. Determine the phase difference at point C.
5. Find the intensity, sound intensity level, and pressure amplitude at C due to each speaker alone.
6. Use your results from steps 4 and 5 to find the pressure amplitude at C due to both loudspeakers together.
7. Use your result from step 6 to find the intensity and sound intensity level at C due to both loudspeakers together.

EVALUATE

8. How do your results from part (c) for intensity and sound intensity level at C compare to those from part (b)? Does this make sense?
9. What result would you have gotten in part (c) if you had (incorrectly) combined the *intensities* from A and B directly, rather than (correctly) combining the *pressure amplitudes* as you did in step 6?

Problems

 For assigned homework and other learning materials, go to MasteringPhysics®. **MP**

•, ••, •••: Difficulty levels. **CP**: Cumulative problems incorporating material from earlier chapters. **CALC**: Problems requiring calculus. **DATA**: Problems involving real data, scientific evidence, experimental design, and/or statistical reasoning. **BIO**: Biosciences problems.

DISCUSSION QUESTIONS

Q16.1 When sound travels from air into water, does the frequency of the wave change? The speed? The wavelength? Explain your reasoning.

Q16.2 The hero of a western movie listens for an oncoming train by putting his ear to the track. Why does this method give an earlier warning of the approach of a train than just listening in the usual way?

Q16.3 Would you expect the pitch (or frequency) of an organ pipe to increase or decrease with increasing temperature? Explain.

Q16.4 In most modern wind instruments the pitch is changed by using keys or valves to change the length of the vibrating air column. The bugle, however, has no valves or keys, yet it can play many notes. How might this be possible? Are there restrictions on what notes a bugle can play?

Q16.5 Symphonic musicians always "warm up" their wind instruments by blowing into them before a performance. What purpose does this serve?

Q16.6 In a popular and amusing science demonstration, a person inhales helium and then his voice becomes high and squeaky. Why does this happen? (*Warning:* Inhaling too much helium can cause unconsciousness or death.)

Q16.7 Lane dividers on highways sometimes have regularly spaced ridges or ripples. When the tires of a moving car roll along such a divider, a musical note is produced. Why? Explain how this phenomenon could be used to measure the car's speed.

Q16.8 (a) Does a sound level of 0 dB mean that there is no sound? (b) Is there any physical meaning to a sound having a negative intensity level? If so, what is it? (c) Does a sound intensity of zero mean that there is no sound? (d) Is there any physical meaning to a sound having a negative intensity? Why?

Q16.9 Which has a more direct influence on the loudness of a sound wave: the *displacement* amplitude or the *pressure* amplitude? Explain.

Q16.10 If the pressure amplitude of a sound wave is halved, by what factor does the intensity of the wave decrease? By what factor must the pressure amplitude of a sound wave be increased in order to increase the intensity by a factor of 16? Explain.

Q16.11 Does the sound intensity level β obey the inverse-square law? Why?

Q16.12 A small fraction of the energy in a sound wave is absorbed by the air through which the sound passes. How does this modify the inverse-square relationship between intensity and distance from the source? Explain.

Q16.13 A small metal band is slipped onto one of the tines of a tuning fork. As this band is moved closer and closer to the end of the tine, what effect does this have on the wavelength and frequency of the sound the tine produces? Why?

Q16.14 An organist in a cathedral plays a loud chord and then releases the keys. The sound persists for a few seconds and gradually dies away. Why does it persist? What happens to the sound energy when the sound dies away?

Q16.15 Two loudspeakers, *A* and *B*, are driven by the same amplifier and emit sinusoidal waves in phase. The frequency of the waves emitted by each speaker is 860 Hz. Point *P* is 12.0 m from *A* and 13.4 m from *B*. Is the interference at *P* constructive or destructive? Give the reasoning behind your answer.

Q16.16 Two vibrating tuning forks have identical frequencies, but one is stationary and the other is mounted at the rim of a rotating platform. What does a listener hear? Explain.

Q16.17 A large church has part of the organ in the front of the church and part in the back. A person walking rapidly down the aisle while both segments are playing at once reports that the two segments sound out of tune. Why?

Q16.18 A sound source and a listener are both at rest on the earth, but a strong wind is blowing from the source toward the listener. Is there a Doppler effect? Why or why not?

Q16.19 Can you think of circumstances in which a Doppler effect would be observed for surface waves in water? For elastic waves propagating in a body of water deep below the surface? If so, describe the circumstances and explain your reasoning. If not, explain why not.

Q16.20 Stars other than our sun normally appear featureless when viewed through telescopes. Yet astronomers can readily use the light from these stars to determine that they are rotating and even measure the speed of their surface. How do you think they can do this?

Q16.21 If you wait at a railroad crossing as a train approaches and passes, you hear a Doppler shift in its sound. But if you listen closely, you hear that the change in frequency is continuous; it does not suddenly go from one high frequency to another low frequency. Instead the frequency *smoothly* (but rather quickly) changes from high to low as the train passes. Why does this smooth change occur?

Q16.22 In case 1, a source of sound approaches a stationary observer at speed *u*. In case 2, the observer moves toward the stationary source at the same speed *u*. If the source is always producing the same frequency sound, will the observer hear the same frequency in both cases, since the relative speed is the same each time? Why or why not?

Q16.23 Does an aircraft make a sonic boom only at the instant its speed exceeds Mach 1? Explain.

Q16.24 If you are riding in a supersonic aircraft, what do you hear? Explain. In particular, do you hear a continuous sonic boom? Why or why not?

Q16.25 A jet airplane is flying at a constant altitude at a steady speed v_S greater than the speed of sound. Describe what observers at points *A*, *B*, and *C* hear at the instant shown in **Fig. Q16.25**, when the shock wave has just reached point *B*. Explain.

Figure **Q16.25**

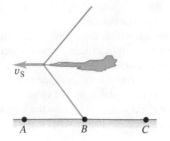

EXERCISES

Unless indicated otherwise, assume the speed of sound in air to be $v = 344$ m/s.

Section 16.1 Sound Waves

16.1 • Example 16.1 (Section 16.1) showed that for sound waves in air with frequency 1000 Hz, a displacement amplitude of 1.2×10^{-8} m produces a pressure amplitude of 3.0×10^{-2} Pa. (a) What is the wavelength of these waves? (b) For 1000-Hz waves in air, what displacement amplitude would be needed for the pressure amplitude to be at the pain threshold, which is 30 Pa? (c) For what wavelength and frequency will waves with a displacement amplitude of 1.2×10^{-8} m produce a pressure amplitude of 1.5×10^{-3} Pa?

16.2 • Example 16.1 (Section 16.1) showed that for sound waves in air with frequency 1000 Hz, a displacement amplitude of 1.2×10^{-8} m produces a pressure amplitude of 3.0×10^{-2} Pa. Water at 20°C has a bulk modulus of 2.2×10^9 Pa, and the speed of sound in water at this temperature is 1480 m/s. For 1000-Hz sound waves in 20°C water, what displacement amplitude is produced if the pressure amplitude is 3.0×10^{-2} Pa? Explain why your answer is much less than 1.2×10^{-8} m.

16.3 • Consider a sound wave in air that has displacement amplitude 0.0200 mm. Calculate the pressure amplitude for frequencies of (a) 150 Hz; (b) 1500 Hz; (c) 15,000 Hz. In each case compare the result to the pain threshold, which is 30 Pa.

16.4 • A loud factory machine produces sound having a displacement amplitude of 1.00 μm, but the frequency of this sound can be adjusted. In order to prevent ear damage to the workers, the maximum pressure amplitude of the sound waves is limited to 10.0 Pa. Under the conditions of this factory, the bulk modulus of air is 1.42×10^5 Pa. What is the highest-frequency sound to which this machine can be adjusted without exceeding the prescribed limit? Is this frequency audible to the workers?

16.5 • **BIO Ultrasound and Infrasound.** (a) **Whale communication.** Blue whales apparently communicate with each other using sound of frequency 17 Hz, which can be heard nearly 1000 km away in the ocean. What is the wavelength of such a sound in seawater, where the speed of sound is 1531 m/s? (b) **Dolphin clicks.** One type of sound that dolphins emit is a sharp click of wavelength 1.5 cm in the ocean. What is the frequency of such clicks? (c) **Dog whistles.** One brand of dog whistles claims a frequency of 25 kHz for its product. What is the wavelength of this sound? (d) **Bats.** While bats emit a wide variety of sounds, one type emits pulses of sound having a frequency between 39 kHz and 78 kHz. What is the range of wavelengths of this sound? (e) **Sonograms.** Ultrasound is used to view the interior of the body, much as x rays are utilized. For sharp imagery, the wavelength of the sound should be around one-fourth (or less) the size of the objects to be viewed. Approximately what frequency of sound is needed to produce a clear image of a tumor that is 1.0 mm across if the speed of sound in the tissue is 1550 m/s?

Section 16.2 Speed of Sound Waves

16.6 • (a) In a liquid with density 1300 kg/m³, longitudinal waves with frequency 400 Hz are found to have wavelength 8.00 m. Calculate the bulk modulus of the liquid. (b) A metal bar with a length of 1.50 m has density 6400 kg/m³. Longitudinal sound waves take 3.90×10^{-4} s to travel from one end of the bar to the other. What is Young's modulus for this metal?

16.7 • A submerged scuba diver hears the sound of a boat horn directly above her on the surface of the lake. At the same time, a friend on dry land 22.0 m from the boat also hears the horn (**Fig. E16.7**). The horn is 1.2 m above the surface of the water. What is the distance (labeled "?") from the horn to the diver? Both air and water are at 20°C.

Figure **E16.7**

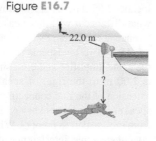

16.8 • At a temperature of 27.0°C, what is the speed of longitudinal waves in (a) hydrogen (molar mass 2.02 g/mol); (b) helium (molar mass 4.00 g/mol); (c) argon (molar mass 39.9 g/mol)? See Table 19.1 for values of γ. (d) Compare your answers for parts (a), (b), and (c) with the speed in air at the same temperature.

16.9 • An oscillator vibrating at 1250 Hz produces a sound wave that travels through an ideal gas at 325 m/s when the gas temperature is 22.0°C. For a certain experiment, you need to have the same oscillator produce sound of wavelength 28.5 cm in this gas. What should the gas temperature be to achieve this wavelength?

16.10 •• CALC (a) Show that the fractional change in the speed of sound (dv/v) due to a very small temperature change dT is given by $dv/v = \frac{1}{2}dT/T$. (*Hint:* Start with Eq. 16.10.) (b) The speed of sound in air at 20°C is found to be 344 m/s. Use the result in part (a) to find the change in the speed of sound for a 1.0°C change in air temperature.

16.11 •• A 60.0-m-long brass rod is struck at one end. A person at the other end hears two sounds as a result of two longitudinal waves, one traveling in the metal rod and the other traveling in air. What is the time interval between the two sounds? (The speed of sound in air is 344 m/s; see Tables 11.1 and 12.1 for relevant information about brass.)

16.12 •• What must be the stress (F/A) in a stretched wire of a material whose Young's modulus is Y for the speed of longitudinal waves to equal 30 times the speed of transverse waves?

Section 16.3 Sound Intensity

16.13 •• BIO **Energy Delivered to the Ear.** Sound is detected when a sound wave causes the tympanic membrane (the eardrum) to vibrate. Typically, the diameter of this membrane is about 8.4 mm in humans. (a) How much energy is delivered to the eardrum each second when someone whispers (20 dB) a secret in your ear? (b) To comprehend how sensitive the ear is to very small amounts of energy, calculate how fast a typical 2.0-mg mosquito would have to fly (in mm/s) to have this amount of kinetic energy.

16.14 • (a) By what factor must the sound intensity be increased to raise the sound intensity level by 13.0 dB? (b) Explain why you don't need to know the original sound intensity.

16.15 •• **Eavesdropping!** You are trying to overhear a juicy conversation, but from your distance of 15.0 m, it sounds like only an average whisper of 20.0 dB. How close should you move to the chatterboxes for the sound level to be 60.0 dB?

16.16 •• BIO **Human Hearing.** A fan at a rock concert is 30 m from the stage, and at this point the sound intensity level is 110 dB. (a) How much energy is transferred to her eardrums each second? (b) How fast would a 2.0-mg mosquito have to fly (in mm/s) to have this much kinetic energy? Compare the mosquito's speed with that found for the whisper in part (a) of Exercise 16.13.

16.17 • A sound wave in air at 20°C has a frequency of 320 Hz and a displacement amplitude of 5.00×10^{-3} mm. For this sound wave calculate the (a) pressure amplitude (in Pa); (b) intensity (in W/m²); (c) sound intensity level (in decibels).

16.18 •• You live on a busy street, but as a music lover, you want to reduce the traffic noise. (a) If you install special sound-reflecting windows that reduce the sound intensity level (in dB) by 30 dB, by what fraction have you lowered the sound intensity (in W/m²)? (b) If, instead, you reduce the intensity by half, what change (in dB) do you make in the sound intensity level?

16.19 • BIO For a person with normal hearing, the faintest sound that can be heard at a frequency of 400 Hz has a pressure amplitude of about 6.0×10^{-5} Pa. Calculate the (a) intensity; (b) sound intensity level; (c) displacement amplitude of this sound wave at 20°C.

16.20 •• The intensity due to a number of independent sound sources is the sum of the individual intensities. (a) When four quadruplets cry simultaneously, how many decibels greater is the sound intensity level than when a single one cries? (b) To increase the sound intensity level again by the same number of decibels as in part (a), how many more crying babies are required?

16.21 • CP A baby's mouth is 30 cm from her father's ear and 1.50 m from her mother's ear. What is the difference between the sound intensity levels heard by the father and by the mother?

16.22 •• The Sacramento City Council adopted a law to reduce the allowed sound intensity level of the much-despised leaf blowers from their current level of about 95 dB to 70 dB. With the new law, what is the ratio of the new allowed intensity to the previously allowed intensity?

16.23 •• CP At point A, 3.0 m from a small source of sound that is emitting uniformly in all directions, the sound intensity level is 53 dB. (a) What is the intensity of the sound at A? (b) How far from the source must you go so that the intensity is one-fourth of what it was at A? (c) How far must you go so that the sound intensity level is one-fourth of what it was at A? (d) Does intensity obey the inverse-square law? What about sound intensity level?

16.24 •• (a) If two sounds differ by 5.00 dB, find the ratio of the intensity of the louder sound to that of the softer one. (b) If one sound is 100 times as intense as another, by how much do they differ in sound intensity level (in decibels)? (c) If you increase the volume of your stereo so that the intensity doubles, by how much does the sound intensity level increase?

Section 16.4 Standing Sound Waves and Normal Modes

16.25 • Standing sound waves are produced in a pipe that is 1.20 m long. For the fundamental and first two overtones, determine the locations along the pipe (measured from the left end) of the displacement nodes and the pressure nodes if (a) the pipe is open at both ends and (b) the pipe is closed at the left end and open at the right end.

16.26 • The fundamental frequency of a pipe that is open at both ends is 524 Hz. (a) How long is this pipe? If one end is now closed, find (b) the wavelength and (c) the frequency of the new fundamental.

16.27 • BIO **The Human Voice.** The human vocal tract is a pipe that extends about 17 cm from the lips to the vocal folds (also called "vocal cords") near the middle of your throat. The vocal folds behave rather like the reed of a clarinet, and the vocal tract acts like a stopped pipe. Estimate the first three standing-wave frequencies of the vocal tract. Use $v = 344$ m/s. (The answers are only an estimate, since the position of lips and tongue affects the motion of air in the vocal tract.)

16.28 •• BIO **The Vocal Tract.** Many opera singers (and some pop singers) have a range of about $2\frac{1}{2}$ octaves or even greater. Suppose a soprano's range extends from A below middle C (frequency 220 Hz) up to E-flat above high C (frequency 1244 Hz). Although the vocal tract is quite complicated, we can model it as a resonating air column, like an organ pipe, that is open at the top and closed at the bottom. The column extends from the mouth down to the diaphragm in the chest cavity, and we can also assume that the lowest note is the fundamental. How long is this column of air if $v = 354$ m/s? Does your result seem reasonable, on the basis of observations of your own body?

16.29 • The longest pipe found in most medium-size pipe organs is 4.88 m (16 ft) long. What is the frequency of the note corresponding to the fundamental mode if the pipe is (a) open at both ends, (b) open at one end and closed at the other?

16.30 • **Singing in the Shower.** A pipe closed at both ends can have standing waves inside of it, but you normally don't hear them because little of the sound can get out. But you *can* hear them if you are *inside* the pipe, such as someone singing in the shower. (a) Show that the wavelengths of standing waves in a pipe of length L that is closed at both ends are $\lambda_n = 2L/n$ and the frequencies are given by $f_n = nv/2L = nf_1$, where $n = 1, 2, 3, \ldots$. (b) Modeling it as a pipe, find the frequency of the fundamental and the first two overtones for a shower 2.50 m tall. Are these frequencies audible?

Section 16.5 Resonance and Sound

16.31 • You blow across the open mouth of an empty test tube and produce the fundamental standing wave of the air column inside the test tube. The speed of sound in air is 344 m/s and the test tube acts as a stopped pipe. (a) If the length of the air column in the test tube is 14.0 cm, what is the frequency of this standing wave? (b) What is the frequency of the fundamental standing wave in the air column if the test tube is half filled with water?

16.32 •• CP You have a stopped pipe of adjustable length close to a taut 62.0-cm, 7.25-g wire under a tension of 4110 N. You want to adjust the length of the pipe so that, when it produces sound at its fundamental frequency, this sound causes the wire to vibrate in its second *overtone* with very large amplitude. How long should the pipe be?

16.33 •• A 75.0-cm-long wire of mass 5.625 g is tied at both ends and adjusted to a tension of 35.0 N. When it is vibrating in its second overtone, find (a) the frequency and wavelength at which it is vibrating and (b) the frequency and wavelength of the sound waves it is producing.

Section 16.6 Interference of Waves

16.34 • Small speakers A and B are driven in phase at 725 Hz by the same audio oscillator. Both speakers start out 4.50 m from the listener, but speaker A is slowly moved away (**Fig. E16.34**). (a) At what distance d will the sound from the speakers first produce destructive interference at the listener's location? (b) If A is moved even farther away than in part (a), at what distance d will the speakers next produce destructive interference at the listener's

Figure **E16.34**

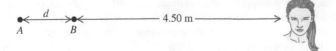

location? (c) After A starts moving away from its original spot, at what distance d will the speakers first produce constructive interference at the listener's location?

16.35 • Two loudspeakers, A and B (**Fig. E16.35**), are driven by the same amplifier and emit sinusoidal waves in phase. Speaker B is 2.00 m to the right of speaker A. Consider point Q along the extension of the line connecting the speakers, 1.00 m to the right of speaker B. Both speakers emit sound waves that travel directly from the speaker to point Q. What is the lowest frequency for which (a) *constructive* interference occurs at point Q; (b) *destructive* interference occurs at point Q?

Figure **E16.35**

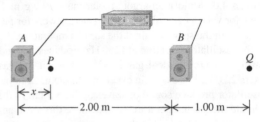

16.36 •• Two loudspeakers, A and B (see Fig. E16.35), are driven by the same amplifier and emit sinusoidal waves in phase. Speaker B is 2.00 m to the right of speaker A. The frequency of the sound waves produced by the loudspeakers is 206 Hz. Consider a point P between the speakers and along the line connecting them, a distance x to the right of A. Both speakers emit sound waves that travel directly from the speaker to point P. For what values of x will (a) *destructive* interference occur at P; (b) *constructive* interference occur at P? (c) Interference effects like those in parts (a) and (b) are almost never a factor in listening to home stereo equipment. Why not?

16.37 •• Two loudspeakers, A and B, are driven by the same amplifier and emit sinusoidal waves in phase. Speaker B is 12.0 m to the right of speaker A. The frequency of the waves emitted by each speaker is 688 Hz. You are standing between the speakers, along the line connecting them, and are at a point of constructive interference. How far must you walk toward speaker B to move to a point of destructive interference?

16.38 • Two loudspeakers, A and B, are driven by the same amplifier and emit sinusoidal waves in phase. The frequency of the waves emitted by each speaker is 172 Hz. You are 8.00 m from A. What is the closest you can be to B and be at a point of destructive interference?

16.39 •• Two small stereo speakers are driven in step by the same variable-frequency oscillator. Their sound is picked up by a microphone arranged as shown in **Fig. E16.39**. For what frequencies does their sound at the speakers produce (a) constructive interference and (b) destructive interference?

Figure **E16.39**

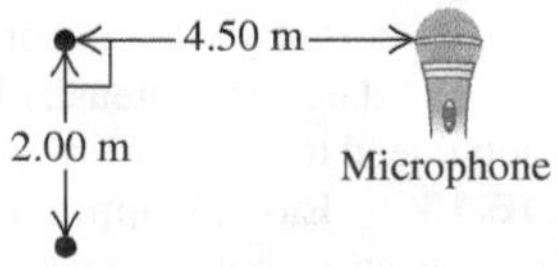

Section 16.7 Beats

16.40 •• Two guitarists attempt to play the same note of wavelength 64.8 cm at the same time, but one of the instruments is slightly out of tune and plays a note of wavelength 65.2 cm instead. What is the frequency of the beats these musicians hear when they play together?

16.41 •• **Tuning a Violin.** A violinist is tuning her instrument to concert A (440 Hz). She plays the note while listening to an electronically generated tone of exactly that frequency and hears a beat frequency of 3 Hz, which increases to 4 Hz when she tightens her violin string slightly. (a) What was the frequency of the note played by her violin when she heard the 3-Hz beats? (b) To get her violin perfectly tuned to concert A, should she tighten or loosen her string from what it was when she heard the 3-Hz beats?

16.42 •• **Adjusting Airplane Motors.** The motors that drive airplane propellers are, in some cases, tuned by using beats. The whirring motor produces a sound wave having the same frequency as the propeller. (a) If one single-bladed propeller is turning at 575 rpm and you hear 2.0-Hz beats when you run the second propeller, what are the two possible frequencies (in rpm) of the second propeller? (b) Suppose you increase the speed of the second propeller slightly and find that the beat frequency changes to 2.1 Hz. In part (a), which of the two answers was the correct one for the frequency of the second single-bladed propeller? How do you know?

16.43 •• Two organ pipes, open at one end but closed at the other, are each 1.14 m long. One is now lengthened by 2.00 cm. Find the beat frequency that they produce when playing together in their fundamentals.

Section 16.8 The Doppler Effect

16.44 •• In Example 16.18 (Section 16.8), suppose the police car is moving away from the warehouse at 20 m/s. What frequency does the driver of the police car hear reflected from the warehouse?

16.45 •• On the planet Arrakis a male ornithoid is flying toward his mate at 25.0 m/s while singing at a frequency of 1200 Hz. If the stationary female hears a tone of 1240 Hz, what is the speed of sound in the atmosphere of Arrakis?

16.46 • A railroad train is traveling at 25.0 m/s in still air. The frequency of the note emitted by the locomotive whistle is 400 Hz. What is the wavelength of the sound waves (a) in front of the locomotive and (b) behind the locomotive? What is the frequency of the sound heard by a stationary listener (c) in front of the locomotive and (d) behind the locomotive?

16.47 • Two train whistles, A and B, each have a frequency of 392 Hz. A is stationary and B is moving toward the right (away from A) at a speed of 35.0 m/s. A listener is between the two whistles and is moving toward the right with a speed of 15.0 m/s (**Fig. E16.47**). No wind is blowing. (a) What is the frequency from A as heard by the listener? (b) What is the frequency from B as heard by the listener? (c) What is the beat frequency detected by the listener?

Figure **E16.47**

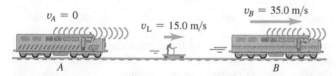

$v_A = 0$ $v_L = 15.0$ m/s $v_B = 35.0$ m/s

A   B

16.48 • **Moving Source vs. Moving Listener.** (a) A sound source producing 1.00-kHz waves moves toward a stationary listener at one-half the speed of sound. What frequency will the listener hear? (b) Suppose instead that the source is stationary and the listener moves toward the source at one-half the speed of sound. What frequency does the listener hear? How does your

answer compare to that in part (a)? Explain on physical grounds why the two answers differ.

16.49 • A swimming duck paddles the water with its feet once every 1.6 s, producing surface waves with this period. The duck is moving at constant speed in a pond where the speed of surface waves is 0.32 m/s, and the crests of the waves ahead of the duck are spaced 0.12 m apart. (a) What is the duck's speed? (b) How far apart are the crests behind the duck?

16.50 • A railroad train is traveling at 30.0 m/s in still air. The frequency of the note emitted by the train whistle is 352 Hz. What frequency is heard by a passenger on a train moving in the opposite direction to the first at 18.0 m/s and (a) approaching the first and (b) receding from the first?

16.51 • A car alarm is emitting sound waves of frequency 520 Hz. You are on a motorcycle, traveling directly away from the parked car. How fast must you be traveling if you detect a frequency of 490 Hz?

16.52 •• While sitting in your car by the side of a country road, you are approached by your friend, who happens to be in an identical car. You blow your car's horn, which has a frequency of 260 Hz. Your friend blows his car's horn, which is identical to yours, and you hear a beat frequency of 6.0 Hz. How fast is your friend approaching you?

16.53 • Two swift canaries fly toward each other, each moving at 15.0 m/s relative to the ground, each warbling a note of frequency 1750 Hz. (a) What frequency note does each bird hear from the other one? (b) What wavelength will each canary measure for the note from the other one?

16.54 •• The siren of a fire engine that is driving northward at 30.0 m/s emits a sound of frequency 2000 Hz. A truck in front of this fire engine is moving northward at 20.0 m/s. (a) What is the frequency of the siren's sound that the fire engine's driver hears reflected from the back of the truck? (b) What wavelength would this driver measure for these reflected sound waves?

16.55 •• A stationary police car emits a sound of frequency 1200 Hz that bounces off a car on the highway and returns with a frequency of 1250 Hz. The police car is right next to the highway, so the moving car is traveling directly toward or away from it. (a) How fast was the moving car going? Was it moving toward or away from the police car? (b) What frequency would the police car have received if it had been traveling toward the other car at 20.0 m/s?

16.56 •• How fast (as a percentage of light speed) would a star have to be moving so that the frequency of the light we receive from it is 10.0% higher than the frequency of the light it is emitting? Would it be moving away from us or toward us? (Assume it is moving either directly away from us or directly toward us.)

Section 16.9 Shock Waves

16.57 •• A jet plane flies overhead at Mach 1.70 and at a constant altitude of 1250 m. (a) What is the angle α of the shock-wave cone? (b) How much time after the plane passes directly overhead do you hear the sonic boom? Neglect the variation of the speed of sound with altitude.

16.58 • The shock-wave cone created by a space shuttle at one instant during its reentry into the atmosphere makes an angle of 58.0° with its direction of motion. The speed of sound at this altitude is 331 m/s. (a) What is the Mach number of the shuttle at this instant, and (b) how fast (in m/s and in mi/h) is it traveling relative to the atmosphere? (c) What would be its Mach number and the angle of its shock-wave cone if it flew at the same speed but at low altitude where the speed of sound is 344 m/s?

PROBLEMS

16.59 •• A soprano and a bass are singing a duet. While the soprano sings an A-sharp at 932 Hz, the bass sings an A-sharp but three octaves lower. In this concert hall, the density of air is 1.20 kg/m^3 and its bulk modulus is 1.42×10^5 Pa. In order for their notes to have the same sound intensity level, what must be (a) the ratio of the pressure amplitude of the bass to that of the soprano and (b) the ratio of the displacement amplitude of the bass to that of the soprano? (c) What displacement amplitude (in m and in nm) does the soprano produce to sing her A-sharp at 72.0 dB?

16.60 •• CP The sound from a trumpet radiates uniformly in all directions in 20°C air. At a distance of 5.00 m from the trumpet the sound intensity level is 52.0 dB. The frequency is 587 Hz. (a) What is the pressure amplitude at this distance? (b) What is the displacement amplitude? (c) At what distance is the sound intensity level 30.0 dB?

16.61 • CP A person is playing a small flute 10.75 cm long, open at one end and closed at the other, near a taut string having a fundamental frequency of 600.0 Hz. If the speed of sound is 344.0 m/s, for which harmonics of the flute will the string resonate? In each case, which harmonic of the string is in resonance?

16.62 •• CP A uniform 165-N bar is supported horizontally by two identical wires A and B (**Fig. P16.62**). A small 185-N cube of lead is placed three-fourths of the way from A to B. The wires are each 75.0 cm

Figure **P16.62**

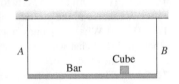

long and have a mass of 5.50 g. If both of them are simultaneously plucked at the center, what is the frequency of the beats that they will produce when vibrating in their fundamental?

16.63 • An organ pipe has two successive harmonics with frequencies 1372 and 1764 Hz. (a) Is this an open or a stopped pipe? Explain. (b) What two harmonics are these? (c) What is the length of the pipe?

16.64 ••• The frequency of the note F_4 is 349 Hz. (a) If an organ pipe is open at one end and closed at the other, what length must it have for its fundamental mode to produce this note at 20.0°C? (b) At what air temperature will the frequency be 370 Hz, corresponding to a rise in pitch from F to F-sharp? (Ignore the change in length of the pipe due to the temperature change.)

16.65 •• Two identical loudspeakers are located at points A and B, 2.00 m apart. The loudspeakers are driven by the same amplifier and produce sound waves with a frequency of 784 Hz. Take the speed of sound in air to be 344 m/s. A small microphone is moved out from point B along a line perpendicular to the line connecting A and B (line BC in **Fig. P16.65**). (a) At what distances from B will there be *destructive* interference? (b) At what distances from B will there be *constructive* interference? (c) If the frequency is made low enough, there will be no positions along the line BC at which destructive interference occurs. How low must the frequency be for this to be the case?

Figure **P16.65**

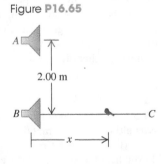

2.00 m

16.66 •• A bat flies toward a wall, emitting a steady sound of frequency 1.70 kHz. This bat hears its own sound plus the sound reflected by the wall. How fast should the bat fly in order to hear a beat frequency of 8.00 Hz?

16.67 •• The sound source of a ship's sonar system operates at a frequency of 18.0 kHz. The speed of sound in water (assumed to be at a uniform 20°C) is 1482 m/s. (a) What is the wavelength of the waves emitted by the source? (b) What is the difference in frequency between the directly radiated waves and the waves reflected from a whale traveling directly toward the ship at 4.95 m/s? The ship is at rest in the water.

16.68 ••• BIO **Ultrasound in Medicine.** A 2.00-MHz sound wave travels through a pregnant woman's abdomen and is reflected from the fetal heart wall of her unborn baby. The heart wall is moving toward the sound receiver as the heart beats. The reflected sound is then mixed with the transmitted sound, and 72 beats per second are detected. The speed of sound in body tissue is 1500 m/s. Calculate the speed of the fetal heart wall at the instant this measurement is made.

16.69 ••• BIO Horseshoe bats (genus *Rhinolophus*) emit sounds from their nostrils and then listen to the frequency of the sound reflected from their prey to determine the prey's speed. (The "horseshoe" that gives the bat its name is a depression around the nostrils that acts like a focusing mirror, so that the bat emits sound in a narrow beam like a flashlight.) A *Rhinolophus* flying at speed v_{bat} emits sound of frequency f_{bat}; the sound it hears reflected from an insect flying toward it has a higher frequency f_{refl}. (a) Show that the speed of the insect is

$$v_{insect} = v \left[\frac{f_{refl}(v - v_{bat}) - f_{bat}(v + v_{bat})}{f_{refl}(v - v_{bat}) + f_{bat}(v + v_{bat})} \right]$$

where v is the speed of sound. (b) If $f_{bat} = 80.7$ kHz, $f_{refl} = 83.5$ kHz, and $v_{bat} = 3.9$ m/s, calculate the speed of the insect.

16.70 • CP A police siren of frequency f_{siren} is attached to a vibrating platform. The platform and siren oscillate up and down in simple harmonic motion with amplitude A_p and frequency f_p. (a) Find the maximum and minimum sound frequencies that you would hear at a position directly above the siren. (b) At what point in the motion of the platform is the maximum frequency heard? The minimum frequency? Explain.

16.71 •• CP A turntable 1.50 m in diameter rotates at 75 rpm. Two speakers, each giving off sound of wavelength 31.3 cm, are attached to the rim of the table at opposite ends of a diameter. A listener stands in front of the turntable. (a) What is the greatest beat frequency the listener will receive from this system? (b) Will the listener be able to distinguish individual beats?

16.72 •• DATA A long, closed cylindrical tank contains a diatomic gas that is maintained at a uniform temperature that can be varied. When you measure the speed of sound v in the gas as a function of the temperature T of the gas, you obtain these results:

T (°C)	−20.0	0.0	20.0	40.0	60.0	80.0
v (m/s)	324	337	349	361	372	383

(a) Explain how you can plot these results so that the graph will be well fit by a straight line. Construct this graph and verify that the plotted points do lie close to a straight line. (b) Because the gas is diatomic, $\gamma = 1.40$. Use the slope of the line in part (a) to calculate M, the molar mass of the gas. Express M in grams/mole. What type of gas is in the tank?

16.73 •• DATA A long tube contains air at a pressure of 1.00 atm and a temperature of 77.0°C. The tube is open at one end and closed at the other by a movable piston. A tuning fork that vibrates with a frequency of 500 Hz is placed near the open end. Resonance is produced when the piston is at distances 18.0 cm, 55.5 cm, and 93.0 cm from the open end. (a) From these values, what is the speed of sound in air at 77.0°C? (b) From the result of part (a), what is the value of γ? (c) These results show that a displacement antinode is slightly outside the open end of the tube. How far outside is it?

16.74 ••• **DATA Supernova!** (a) Equation (16.30) can be written as

$$f_R = f_S\left(1 - \frac{v}{c}\right)^{1/2}\left(1 + \frac{v}{c}\right)^{-1/2}$$

where c is the speed of light in vacuum, 3.00×10^8 m/s. Most objects move much slower than this (v/c is very small), so calculations made with Eq. (16.30) must be done carefully to avoid rounding errors. Use the binomial theorem to show that if $v \ll c$, Eq. (16.30) approximately reduces to $f_R = f_S[1 - (v/c)]$. (b) The gas cloud known as the Crab Nebula can be seen with even a small telescope. It is the remnant of a *supernova*, a cataclysmic explosion of a star. (The explosion was seen on the earth on July 4, 1054 C.E.) Its streamers glow with the characteristic red color of heated hydrogen gas. In a laboratory on the earth, heated hydrogen produces red light with frequency 4.568×10^{14} Hz; the red light received from streamers in the Crab Nebula that are pointed toward the earth has frequency 4.586×10^{14} Hz. Estimate the speed with which the outer edges of the Crab Nebula are expanding. Assume that the speed of the center of the nebula relative to the earth is negligible. (c) Assuming that the expansion speed of the Crab Nebula has been constant since the supernova that produced it, estimate the diameter of the Crab Nebula. Give your answer in meters and in light-years. (d) The angular diameter of the Crab Nebula as seen from the earth is about 5 arc-minutes $\left(1 \text{ arc-minute} = \frac{1}{60} \text{ degree}\right)$. Estimate the distance (in light-years) to the Crab Nebula, and estimate the year in which the supernova actually took place.

CHALLENGE PROBLEMS

16.75 ••• **CALC Figure P16.75** shows the pressure fluctuation p of a nonsinusoidal sound wave as a function of x for $t = 0$. The wave is traveling in the $+x$-direction. (a) Graph the pressure fluctuation p as a function of t for $x = 0$. Show at least two cycles of oscillation. (b) Graph the displacement y in this sound wave as a function of x at $t = 0$. At $x = 0$, the displacement at $t = 0$ is zero. Show at least two wavelengths of the wave. (c) Graph the displacement y as a function of t for $x = 0$. Show at least two cycles of oscillation. (d) Calculate the maximum velocity and the maximum acceleration of an element of the air through which this sound wave is traveling. (e) Describe how the cone of a loudspeaker must move as a function of time to produce the sound wave in this problem.

Figure **P16.75**

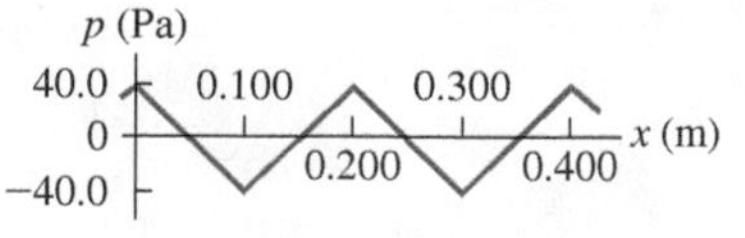

16.76 ••• **CP Longitudinal Waves on a Spring.** A long spring such as a Slinky™ is often used to demonstrate longitudinal waves. (a) Show that if a spring that obeys Hooke's law has mass m, length L, and force constant k', the speed of longitudinal waves on the spring is $v = L\sqrt{k'/m}$ (see Section 16.2). (b) Evaluate v for a spring with $m = 0.250$ kg, $L = 2.00$ m, and $k' = 1.50$ N/m.

PASSAGE PROBLEMS

BIO ULTRASOUND IMAGING. A typical ultrasound transducer used for medical diagnosis produces a beam of ultrasound with a frequency of 1.0 MHz. The beam travels from the transducer through tissue and partially reflects when it encounters different structures in the tissue. The same transducer that produces the ultrasound also detects the reflections. The transducer emits a short pulse of ultrasound and waits to receive the reflected echoes before emitting the next pulse. By measuring the time between the initial pulse and the arrival of the reflected signal, we can use the speed of ultrasound in tissue, 1540 m/s, to determine the distance from the transducer to the structure that produced the reflection.

As the ultrasound beam passes through tissue, the beam is attenuated through absorption. Thus deeper structures return weaker echoes. A typical attenuation in tissue is -100 dB/m · MHz; in bone it is -500 dB/m · MHz. In determining attenuation, we take the reference intensity to be the intensity produced by the transducer.

16.77 If the deepest structure you wish to image is 10.0 cm from the transducer, what is the maximum number of pulses per second that can be emitted? (a) 3850; (b) 7700; (c) 15,400; (d) 1,000,000.

16.78 After a beam passes through 10 cm of tissue, what is the beam's intensity as a fraction of its initial intensity from the transducer? (a) 1×10^{-11}; (b) 0.001; (c) 0.01; (d) 0.1.

16.79 Because the speed of ultrasound in bone is about twice the speed in soft tissue, the distance to a structure that lies beyond a bone can be measured incorrectly. If a beam passes through 4 cm of tissue, then 2 cm of bone, and then another 1 cm of tissue before echoing off a cyst and returning to the transducer, what is the difference between the true distance to the cyst and the distance that is measured by assuming the speed is always 1540 m/s? Compared with the measured distance, the structure is actually (a) 1 cm farther; (b) 2 cm farther; (c) 1 cm closer; (d) 2 cm closer.

16.80 In some applications of ultrasound, such as its use on cranial tissues, large reflections from the surrounding bones can produce standing waves. This is of concern because the large pressure amplitude in an antinode can damage tissues. For a frequency of 1.0 MHz, what is the distance between antinodes in tissue? (a) 0.38 mm; (b) 0.75 mm; (c) 1.5 mm; (d) 3.0 mm.

16.81 For cranial ultrasound, why is it advantageous to use frequencies in the kHZ range rather than the MHz range? (a) The antinodes of the standing waves will be closer together at the lower frequencies than at the higher frequencies; (b) there will be no standing waves at the lower frequencies; (c) cranial bones will attenuate the ultrasound more at the lower frequencies than at the higher frequencies; (d) cranial bones will attenuate the ultrasound less at the lower frequencies than at the higher frequencies.

Answers

Chapter Opening Question ?

(iv) Equation (16.10) in Section 16.2 says that the speed of sound in a gas depends on the temperature and on the kind of gas (through the ratio of heat capacities and the molar mass). Winter air in the mountains has a lower temperature than summer air at sea level, but they have essentially the same composition. Hence the lower temperature alone explains the slower speed of sound in winter in the mountains.

Test Your Understanding Questions

16.1 (v) From Eq. (16.5), the displacement amplitude is $A = p_{max}/Bk$. The pressure amplitude p_{max} and bulk modulus B remain the same, but the frequency f increases by a factor of 4. Hence the wave number $k = \omega/v = 2\pi f/v$ also increases by a factor of 4. Since A is inversely proportional to k, the displacement amplitude becomes $\frac{1}{4}$ as great. In other words, at higher frequency a smaller maximum displacement is required to produce the same maximum pressure fluctuation.

16.2 (i) From Eq. (16.7), the speed of longitudinal waves (sound) in a fluid is $v = \sqrt{B/\rho}$. We can rewrite this to give an expression for the bulk modulus B in terms of the fluid density ρ and the sound speed v: $B = \rho v^2$. At 20°C the speed of sound in mercury is slightly less than in water (1451 m/s versus 1482 m/s), but the density of mercury is greater than that of water by a large factor (13.6). Hence the bulk modulus of mercury is greater than that of water by a factor of $(13.6)(1451/1482)^2 = 13.0$.

16.3 A and p_{max} **increase by a factor of $\sqrt{2}$, B and v are unchanged, β increases by 3.0 dB** Equations (16.9) and (16.10) show that the bulk modulus B and sound speed v remain the same because the physical properties of the air are unchanged. From Eqs. (16.12) and (16.14), the intensity is proportional to the square of the displacement amplitude or the square of the pressure amplitude. Hence doubling the intensity means that A and p_{max} both increase by a factor of $\sqrt{2}$. Example 16.9 shows that *multiplying* the intensity by a factor of 2 $(I_2/I_1 = 2)$ corresponds to *adding* to the sound intensity level by $(10\text{ dB})\log(I_2/I_1) = (10\text{ dB})\log 2 = 3.0$ dB.

16.4 (ii) Helium is less dense and has a lower molar mass than air, so sound travels faster in helium than in air. The normal-mode frequencies for a pipe are proportional to the sound speed v, so the frequency and hence the pitch increase when the air in the pipe is replaced with helium.

16.5 (i) and (iv) There will be a resonance if 660 Hz is one of the pipe's normal-mode frequencies. A stopped organ pipe has normal-mode frequencies that are odd multiples of its fundamental frequency [see Eq. (16.22) and Fig. 16.18]. Hence pipe (i), which has fundamental frequency 220 Hz, also has a normal-mode frequency of $3(220\text{ Hz}) = 660$ Hz. Pipe (ii) has twice the length of pipe (i); from Eq. (16.20), the fundamental frequency of a stopped pipe is inversely proportional to the length, so pipe (ii) has a fundamental frequency of $\left(\frac{1}{2}\right)(220\text{ Hz}) = 110$ Hz. Its other normal-mode frequencies are 330 Hz, 550 Hz, 770 Hz, . . . , so a 660-Hz tuning fork will not cause resonance. Pipe (iii) is an open pipe of the same length as pipe (i), so its fundamental frequency is twice as great as for pipe (i) [compare Eqs. (16.16) and (16.20)], or $2(220\text{ Hz}) = 440$ Hz. Its other normal-mode frequencies are integer multiples of the fundamental frequency [see Eq. (16.19)], or 880 Hz, 1320 Hz, . . . , none of which match the 660-Hz frequency of the tuning fork. Pipe (iv) is also an open pipe but with twice the length of pipe (iii) [see Eq. (16.18)], so its normal-mode frequencies are one-half those of pipe (iii): 220 Hz, 440 Hz, 660 Hz, . . . , so the third harmonic will resonate with the tuning fork.

16.6 (iii) Constructive and destructive interference between two waves can occur only if the two waves have the same frequency. In this case the frequencies are different, so there are no points where the two waves always reinforce each other (constructive interference) or always cancel each other (destructive interference).

16.7 (vi) The beat frequency is 3 Hz, so the difference between the two tuning fork frequencies is also 3 Hz. Hence the second tuning fork vibrates at a frequency of either 443 Hz or 437 Hz. You can distinguish between the two possibilities by comparing the pitches of the two tuning forks sounded one at a time: The frequency is 437 Hz if the second tuning fork has a lower pitch and 443 Hz if it has a higher pitch.

16.8 no The air (the medium for sound waves) is moving from the source toward the listener. Hence, relative to the air, both the source and the listener are moving in the direction from listener to source. So both velocities are positive and $v_S = v_L = +10$ m/s. The equality of these two velocities means that the numerator and the denominator in Eq. (16.29) are the same, so $f_L = f_S$ and there is *no* Doppler shift.

16.9 (iii) Figure 16.38 shows that there are sound waves inside the cone of the shock wave. Behind the airplane the wave crests are spread apart, just as they are behind the moving source in Fig. 16.28. Hence the waves that reach you have an increased wavelength and a lower frequency.

Bridging Problem

(a) $180° = \pi$ rad
(b) A alone: $I = 3.98 \times 10^{-6}$ W/m^2, $\beta = 66.0$ dB;
   B alone: $I = 5.31 \times 10^{-7}$ W/m^2, $\beta = 57.2$ dB
(c) $I = 1.60 \times 10^{-6}$ W/m^2, $\beta = 62.1$ dB

At a steelworks, molten iron is heated to 1500° Celsius to remove impurities. It is most accurate to say that the molten iron contains a large amount of (i) temperature; (ii) heat; (iii) energy; (iv) two of these; (v) all three of these.

17

TEMPERATURE AND HEAT

Whether it's a sweltering summer day or a frozen midwinter night, your body needs to be kept at a nearly constant temperature. It has effective temperature-control mechanisms, but sometimes it needs help. On a hot day you wear less clothing to improve heat transfer from your body to the air and for better cooling by evaporation of perspiration. On a cold day you may sit by a roaring fire to absorb the energy that it radiates. The concepts in this chapter will help you understand the basic physics of keeping warm or cool.

The terms "temperature" and "heat" are often used interchangeably in everyday language. In physics, however, these two terms have very different meanings. In this chapter we'll define temperature in terms of how it's measured and see how temperature changes affect the dimensions of objects. We'll see that heat refers to energy transfer caused by temperature differences only and learn how to calculate and control such energy transfers.

Our emphasis in this chapter is on the concepts of temperature and heat as they relate to *macroscopic* objects such as cylinders of gas, ice cubes, and the human body. In Chapter 18 we'll look at these same concepts from a *microscopic* viewpoint in terms of the behavior of individual atoms and molecules. These two chapters lay the groundwork for the subject of **thermodynamics,** the study of energy transformations involving heat, mechanical work, and other aspects of energy and how these transformations relate to the properties of matter. Thermodynamics forms an indispensable part of the foundation of physics, chemistry, and the life sciences, and its applications turn up in such places as car engines, refrigerators, biochemical processes, and the structure of stars. We'll explore the key ideas of thermodynamics in Chapters 19 and 20.

17.1 TEMPERATURE AND THERMAL EQUILIBRIUM

The concept of **temperature** is rooted in qualitative ideas based on our sense of touch. A body that feels "hot" usually has a higher temperature than a similar body that feels "cold." That's pretty vague, and the senses can be deceived. But many properties of matter that we can *measure*—including the length of a metal

17.1 Two devices for measuring temperature.

(a) Changes in temperature cause the liquid's volume to change.

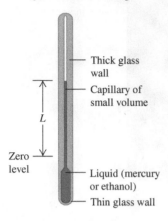
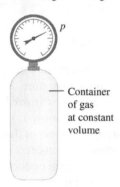

- Thick glass wall
- Capillary of small volume
- *L*
- Zero level
- Liquid (mercury or ethanol)
- Thin glass wall

(b) Changes in temperature cause the pressure of the gas to change.

- *p*
- Container of gas at constant volume

rod, steam pressure in a boiler, the ability of a wire to conduct an electric current, and the color of a very hot glowing object—depend on temperature.

Temperature is also related to the kinetic energies of the molecules of a material. In general this relationship is fairly complex, so it's not a good place to start in *defining* temperature. In Chapter 18 we will look at the relationship between temperature and the energy of molecular motion for an ideal gas. However, we can define temperature and heat independently of any detailed molecular picture. In this section we'll develop a *macroscopic* definition of temperature.

To use temperature as a measure of hotness or coldness, we need to construct a temperature scale. To do this, we can use any measurable property of a system that varies with its "hotness" or "coldness." **Figure 17.1a** shows a familiar system that is used to measure temperature. When the system becomes hotter, the colored liquid (usually mercury or ethanol) expands and rises in the tube, and the value of *L* increases. Another simple system is a quantity of gas in a constant-volume container (Fig. 17.1b). The pressure *p*, measured by the gauge, increases or decreases as the gas becomes hotter or colder. A third example is the electrical resistance *R* of a conducting wire, which also varies when the wire becomes hotter or colder. Each of these properties gives us a number (*L*, *p*, or *R*) that varies with hotness and coldness, so each property can be used to make a **thermometer.**

To measure the temperature of a body, you place the thermometer in contact with the body. If you want to know the temperature of a cup of hot coffee, you stick the thermometer in the coffee; as the two interact, the thermometer becomes hotter and the coffee cools off a little. After the thermometer settles down to a steady value, you read the temperature. The system has reached an *equilibrium* condition, in which the interaction between the thermometer and the coffee causes no further change in the system. We call this a state of **thermal equilibrium.**

If two systems are separated by an insulating material or **insulator** such as wood, plastic foam, or fiberglass, they influence each other more slowly. Camping coolers are made with insulating materials to delay the cold food inside from warming up and attaining thermal equilibrium with the hot summer air outside. An *ideal insulator* is an idealized material that permits no interaction at all between the two systems. It prevents the systems from attaining thermal equilibrium if they aren't in thermal equilibrium at the start. Real insulators, like those in camping coolers, aren't ideal, so the contents of the cooler will warm up eventually. But an ideal insulator is nonetheless a useful idealization, like a massless rope or a frictionless incline.

The Zeroth Law of Thermodynamics

We can discover an important property of thermal equilibrium by considering three systems, *A*, *B*, and *C*, that initially are not in thermal equilibrium (**Fig. 17.2**). We surround them with an ideal insulating box so that they cannot interact with anything except each other. We separate systems *A* and *B* with an ideal insulating wall (the green slab in Fig. 17.2a), but we let system *C* interact with both systems

17.2 The zeroth law of thermodynamics.

(a) If systems *A* and *B* are each in thermal equilibrium with system *C* ...

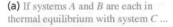
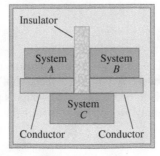

- Insulator
- System *A*
- System *B*
- System *C*
- Conductor
- Conductor

(b) ... then systems *A* and *B* are in thermal equilibrium with each other.

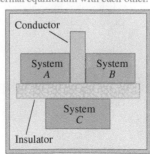

- Conductor
- System *A*
- System *B*
- System *C*
- Insulator

A and *B*. We show this interaction in the figure by a yellow slab representing a thermal **conductor,** a material that *permits* thermal interactions through it. We wait until thermal equilibrium is attained; then *A* and *B* are each in thermal equilibrium with *C*. But are they in thermal equilibrium *with each other?*

To find out, we separate system *C* from systems *A* and *B* with an ideal insulating wall (Fig. 17.2b), then replace the insulating wall between *A* and *B* with a *conducting* wall that lets *A* and *B* interact. What happens? Experiment shows that *nothing* happens; there are no additional changes to *A* or *B*. This result is called the **zeroth law of thermodynamics:**

> **If *C* is initially in thermal equilibrium with both *A* and *B*, then *A* and *B* are also in thermal equilibrium with each other.**

(The importance of this law was recognized only after the first, second, and third laws of thermodynamics had been named. Since it is fundamental to all of them, the name "zeroth" seemed appropriate.)

Now suppose system *C* is a thermometer, such as the liquid-in-tube system of Fig. 17.1a. In Fig. 17.2a the thermometer *C* is in contact with both *A* and *B*. In thermal equilibrium, when the thermometer reading reaches a stable value, the thermometer measures the temperature of both *A* and *B*; hence both *A* and *B* have the *same* temperature. Experiment shows that thermal equilibrium isn't affected by adding or removing insulators, so the reading of thermometer *C* wouldn't change if it were in contact only with *A* or only with *B*. We conclude:

> **Two systems are in thermal equilibrium if and only if they have the same temperature.**

This is what makes a thermometer useful; a thermometer actually measures *its own* temperature, but when a thermometer is in thermal equilibrium with another body, the temperatures must be equal. When the temperatures of two systems are different, they *cannot* be in thermal equilibrium.

TEST YOUR UNDERSTANDING OF SECTION 17.1 You put a thermometer in a pot of hot water and record the reading. What temperature have you recorded? (i) The temperature of the water; (ii) the temperature of the thermometer; (iii) an equal average of the temperatures of the water and thermometer; (iv) a weighted average of the temperatures of the water and thermometer, with more emphasis on the temperature of the water; (v) a weighted average of the water and thermometer, with more emphasis on the temperature of the thermometer. ∎

17.2 THERMOMETERS AND TEMPERATURE SCALES

To make the liquid-in-tube device shown in Fig. 17.1a into a useful thermometer, we need to mark a scale on the tube wall with numbers on it. Suppose we label the thermometer's liquid level at the freezing temperature of pure water "zero" and the level at the boiling temperature "100," and divide the distance between these two points into 100 equal intervals called *degrees.* The result is the **Celsius temperature scale** (formerly called the *centigrade* scale in English-speaking countries). The Celsius temperature for a state colder than freezing water is a negative number. The Celsius scale is used, both in everyday life and in science and industry, almost everywhere in the world.

Another common type of thermometer uses a *bimetallic strip,* made by bonding strips of two different metals together (**Fig. 17.3a**). When the temperature of the composite strip increases, one metal expands more than the other and the strip bends (Fig. 17.3b). This strip is usually formed into a spiral, with the outer end anchored to the thermometer case and the inner end attached to a pointer (Fig. 17.3c). The pointer rotates in response to temperature changes.

17.3 Use of a bimetallic strip as a thermometer.

(a) A bimetallic strip

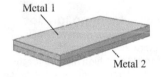

Metal 1

Metal 2

(b) The strip bends when its temperature is raised.

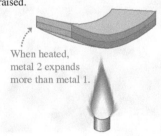

When heated, metal 2 expands more than metal 1.

(c) A bimetallic strip used in a thermometer

17.4 A temporal artery thermometer measures infrared radiation from the skin that overlies one of the important arteries in the head. Although the thermometer cover touches the skin, the infrared detector inside the cover does not.

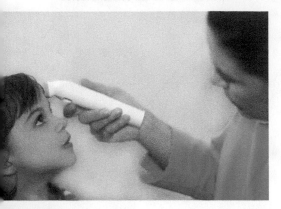

In a *resistance thermometer* the changing electrical resistance of a coil of fine wire, a carbon cylinder, or a germanium crystal is measured. Resistance thermometers are usually more precise than most other types.

Some thermometers detect the amount of infrared radiation emitted by an object. (We'll see in Section 17.7 that *all* objects emit electromagnetic radiation, including infrared, as a consequence of their temperature.) One example is a *temporal artery thermometer* (**Fig. 17.4**). A nurse runs this over a patient's forehead in the vicinity of the temporal artery, and an infrared sensor in the thermometer measures the radiation from the skin. This device gives more accurate values of body temperature than do oral or ear thermometers.

In the **Fahrenheit temperature scale,** still used in the United States, the freezing temperature of water is 32°F and the boiling temperature is 212°F, both at standard atmospheric pressure. There are 180 degrees between freezing and boiling, compared to 100 on the Celsius scale, so one Fahrenheit degree represents only $\frac{100}{180}$, or $\frac{5}{9}$, as great a temperature change as one Celsius degree.

To convert temperatures from Celsius to Fahrenheit, note that a Celsius temperature T_C is the number of Celsius degrees above freezing; the number of Fahrenheit degrees above freezing is $\frac{9}{5}$ of this. But freezing on the Fahrenheit scale is at 32°F, so to obtain the actual Fahrenheit temperature T_F, multiply the Celsius value by $\frac{9}{5}$ and then add 32°. Symbolically,

$$\underset{\text{temperature}}{\text{Fahrenheit}} \cdots\!\!\rightarrow T_\mathrm{F} = \tfrac{9}{5}T_\mathrm{C} \overset{\longleftarrow\cdots}{} + 32° \overset{\cdots}{\underset{\text{temperature}}{\text{Celsius}}} \tag{17.1}$$

To convert Fahrenheit to Celsius, solve this equation for T_C:

$$\underset{\text{temperature}}{\text{Celsius}} \cdots\!\!\rightarrow T_\mathrm{C} = \tfrac{5}{9}\big(T_\mathrm{F} \overset{\longleftarrow\cdots}{} - 32°\big) \overset{\cdots}{\underset{\text{temperature}}{\text{Fahrenheit}}} \tag{17.2}$$

In words, subtract 32° to get the number of Fahrenheit degrees above freezing, and then multiply by $\frac{5}{9}$ to obtain the number of Celsius degrees above freezing—that is, the Celsius temperature.

We don't recommend memorizing Eqs. (17.1) and (17.2). Instead, understand the reasoning that led to them so that you can derive them on the spot when you need them, checking your reasoning with the relationship 100°C = 212°F.

It is useful to distinguish between an actual temperature and a temperature *interval* (a difference or change in temperature). An actual temperature of 20° is stated as 20°C (twenty degrees Celsius), and a temperature *interval* of 10° is 10 C° (ten Celsius degrees). A beaker of water heated from 20°C to 30°C undergoes a temperature change of 10 C°.

BIO Application Mammalian Body Temperatures Most mammals maintain body temperatures in the range from 36°C to 40°C (309 K to 313 K). A high metabolic rate warms the animal from within, and insulation (such as fur and body fat) slows heat loss.

TEST YOUR UNDERSTANDING OF SECTION 17.2 Which of the following types of thermometers have to be in thermal equilibrium with the object being measured in order to give accurate readings? (i) A bimetallic strip; (ii) a resistance thermometer; (iii) a temporal artery thermometer; (iv) both (i) and (ii); (v) all of (i), (ii), and (iii). ∎

17.3 GAS THERMOMETERS AND THE KELVIN SCALE

When we calibrate two thermometers, such as a liquid-in-tube system and a resistance thermometer, so that they agree at 0°C and 100°C, they may not agree exactly at intermediate temperatures. Any temperature scale defined in this way always depends somewhat on the specific properties of the material used. Ideally, we would like to define a temperature scale that *doesn't* depend on the properties

17.5 (a) Using a constant-volume gas thermometer to measure temperature. (b) The greater the amount of gas in the thermometer, the higher the graph of pressure p versus temperature T.

(a) A constant-volume gas thermometer

(b) Graphs of pressure versus temperature at constant volume for three different types and quantities of gas

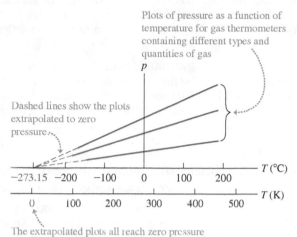

Plots of pressure as a function of temperature for gas thermometers containing different types and quantities of gas

Dashed lines show the plots extrapolated to zero pressure.

The extrapolated plots all reach zero pressure at the same temperature: −273.15°C.

of a particular material. To establish a truly material-independent scale, we first need to develop some principles of thermodynamics. We'll return to this fundamental problem in Chapter 20. Here we'll discuss a thermometer that comes close to the ideal, the *constant-volume gas thermometer.*

The principle of a constant-volume gas thermometer is that the pressure of a gas at constant volume increases with temperature. We place a quantity of gas in a constant-volume container (**Fig. 17.5a**) and measure its pressure by one of the devices described in Section 12.2. To calibrate this thermometer, we measure the pressure at two temperatures, say 0°C and 100°C, plot these points on a graph, and draw a straight line between them. Then we can read from the graph the temperature corresponding to any other pressure. Figure 17.5b shows the results of three such experiments, each using a different type and quantity of gas.

By extrapolating this graph, we see that there is a hypothetical temperature, −273.15°C, at which the absolute pressure of the gas would become zero. This temperature turns out to be the *same* for many different gases (at least in the limit of very low gas density). We can't actually observe this zero-pressure condition. Gases liquefy and solidify at very low temperatures, and the proportionality of pressure to temperature no longer holds.

We use this extrapolated zero-pressure temperature as the basis for a temperature scale with its zero at this temperature. This is the **Kelvin temperature scale,** named for the British physicist Lord Kelvin (1824–1907). The units are the same size as those on the Celsius scale, but the zero is shifted so that 0 K = −273.15°C and 273.15 K = 0°C (Fig. 17.5b); that is,

$$\underset{\text{temperature}}{\text{Kelvin}} \cdots\!\rightarrow T_K = T_C + 273.15 \overset{\text{Celsius}}{\underset{\text{temperature}}{\cdots}} \tag{17.3}$$

A common room temperature, 20°C (= 68°F), is 20 + 273.15, or about 293 K.

CAUTION **Never say "degrees kelvin"** In SI nomenclature, the temperature mentioned above is read "293 kelvins," not "degrees kelvin" (**Fig. 17.6**). We capitalize Kelvin when it refers to the temperature scale; however, the *unit* of temperature is the *kelvin,* which is not capitalized (but is nonetheless abbreviated as a capital K). ▮

DATA *SPEAKS*

Temperature Scales

When students were given a problem about converting among the Celsius, Fahrenheit, and Kelvin temperature scales, more than 46% gave an incorrect response. Common errors:

- Forgetting that Eqs. (17.1) and (17.2) apply to *temperatures,* not *temperature differences.* To convert a temperature difference in F° to one in C°, multiply by $\frac{5}{9}$; to convert a temperature difference in C° to one in F°, multiply by $\frac{9}{5}$.

- Forgetting that temperature differences are the same on the Celsius and Kelvin scales. Increasing the temperature by 5 C° is the same as increasing it by 5 K.

17.6 Correct and incorrect uses of the Kelvin scale.

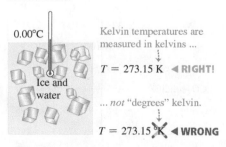

0.00°C

Ice and water

Kelvin temperatures are measured in kelvins ...

$T = 273.15\ \text{K}$ ◀ **RIGHT!**

... *not* "degrees" kelvin.

$T = 273.15\ °\text{K}$ ◀ **WRONG**

EXAMPLE 17.1   BODY TEMPERATURE

You place a small piece of ice in your mouth. Eventually, the water all converts from ice at $T_1 = 32.00°F$ to body temperature, $T_2 = 98.60°F$. Express these temperatures in both Celsius degrees and kelvins, and find $\Delta T = T_2 - T_1$ in both cases.

SOLUTION

IDENTIFY and SET UP: Our target variables are stated above. We convert Fahrenheit temperatures to Celsius by using Eq. (17.2), and Celsius temperatures to Kelvin by using Eq. (17.3).

EXECUTE: From Eq. (17.2), $T_1 = 0.00°C$ and $T_2 = 37.00°C$; then $\Delta T = T_2 - T_1 = 37.00$ C°. To get the Kelvin temperatures, just add 273.15 to each Celsius temperature: $T_1 = 273.15$ K and $T_2 = 310.15$ K. The temperature difference is $\Delta T = T_2 - T_1 = 37.00$ K.

EVALUATE: The Celsius and Kelvin scales have different zero points but the same size degrees. Therefore *any* temperature difference ΔT is the *same* on the Celsius and Kelvin scales. However, ΔT is *not* the same on the Fahrenheit scale; here, for example, $\Delta T = 66.60$ F°.

The Kelvin Scale and Absolute Temperature

The Celsius scale has two fixed points: the normal freezing and boiling temperatures of water. But we can define the Kelvin scale by using a gas thermometer with only a single reference temperature. Figure 17.5b shows that the pressure p in a gas thermometer is directly proportional to the Kelvin temperature. So we can define the ratio of any two Kelvin temperatures T_1 and T_2 as the ratio of the corresponding gas-thermometer pressures p_1 and p_2:

$$\text{Definition of Kelvin scale:} \quad \frac{T_2}{T_1} = \frac{p_2}{p_1} \quad \begin{array}{l}\text{... equals ratio of}\\\text{corresponding \textbf{pressures}}\\\text{in \textbf{constant-volume}}\\\text{\textbf{gas thermometer.}}\end{array} \quad (17.4)$$

Ratio of two **temperatures** in kelvins ...

To complete the definition of T, we need only specify the Kelvin temperature of a single state. For reasons of precision and reproducibility, the state chosen is the *triple point* of water, the unique combination of temperature and pressure at which solid water (ice), liquid water, and water vapor can all coexist. It occurs at a temperature of 0.01°C and a water-vapor pressure of 610 Pa (about 0.006 atm). (This is the pressure of the *water*, not the gas pressure in the *thermometer*.) The triple-point temperature of water is *defined* to have the value $T_{\text{triple}} = 273.16$ K, corresponding to 0.01°C. From Eq. (17.4), if p_{triple} is the pressure in a gas thermometer at temperature T_{triple} and p is the pressure at some other temperature T, then T is given on the Kelvin scale by

$$T = T_{\text{triple}} \frac{p}{p_{\text{triple}}} = (273.16 \text{ K}) \frac{p}{p_{\text{triple}}} \qquad (17.5)$$

Gas thermometers are impractical for everyday use. They are bulky and very slow to come to thermal equilibrium. They are used principally to establish high-precision standards and to calibrate other thermometers.

Figure 17.7 shows the relationships among the three temperature scales we have discussed. The Kelvin scale is called an **absolute temperature scale,** and its zero point ($T = 0$ K $= -273.15°C$, the temperature at which $p = 0$ in Eq. [17.5]) is called **absolute zero.** At absolute zero a system of molecules (such as a quantity of a gas, a liquid, or a solid) has its *minimum* possible total energy (kinetic plus potential); because of quantum effects, it is *not* correct to say that all molecular motion ceases at absolute zero. In Chapter 20 we'll define more completely what we mean by absolute zero through thermodynamic principles that we'll develop in the next several chapters.

17.7 Relationships among Kelvin (K), Celsius (C), and Fahrenheit (F) temperature scales. Temperatures have been rounded off to the nearest degree.

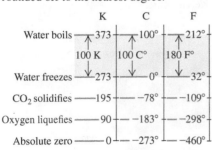

TEST YOUR UNDERSTANDING OF SECTION 17.3 Rank the following temperatures from highest to lowest: (i) 0.00°C; (ii) 0.00°F; (iii) 260.00 K; (iv) 77.00 K; (v) −180.00°C. ∎

17.4 THERMAL EXPANSION

Most materials expand when their temperatures increase. Rising temperatures make the liquid expand in a liquid-in-tube thermometer (Fig. 17.1a) and bend bimetallic strips (Fig. 17.3b). A completely filled and tightly capped bottle of water cracks when it is heated, but you can loosen a metal jar lid by running hot water over it. These are all examples of *thermal expansion.*

Linear Expansion

Suppose a solid rod has a length L_0 at some initial temperature T_0. When the temperature changes by ΔT, the length changes by ΔL. Experiments show that if ΔT is not too large (say, less than 100 C° or so), ΔL is *directly proportional* to ΔT (**Fig. 17.8a**). If two rods made of the same material have the same temperature change, but one is twice as long as the other, then the *change* in its length is also twice as great. Therefore ΔL must also be proportional to L_0 (Fig. 17.8b). We may express these relationships in an equation:

$$\underset{\text{Change in length}}{\underset{\text{Linear thermal expansion:}}{\quad}} \quad \Delta L = \alpha L_0 \Delta T \quad \underset{\text{Temperature change}}{\overset{\text{Original length}}{\quad}} \tag{17.6}$$

Coefficient of linear expansion

The constant α, which has different values for different materials, is called the **coefficient of linear expansion.** The units of α are K^{-1} or $(C°)^{-1}$. (Remember that a temperature interval is the same on the Kelvin and Celsius scales.) If a body has length L_0 at temperature T_0, then its length L at a temperature $T = T_0 + \Delta T$ is

$$L = L_0 + \Delta L = L_0 + \alpha L_0 \Delta T = L_0(1 + \alpha \Delta T) \tag{17.7}$$

For many materials, every linear dimension changes according to Eq. (17.6) or (17.7). Thus L could be the thickness of a rod, the side length of a square sheet, or the diameter of a hole. Some materials, such as wood or single crystals, expand differently in different directions. We won't consider this complication.

We can understand thermal expansion qualitatively on a molecular basis. Picture the interatomic forces in a solid as springs, as in **Fig. 17.9a**. (We explored the analogy between spring forces and interatomic forces in Section 14.4.) Each atom vibrates about its equilibrium position. When the temperature increases, the energy and amplitude of the vibration also increase. The interatomic spring forces are not symmetrical about the equilibrium position; they usually behave like a spring that is easier to stretch than to compress. As a result, when the amplitude of vibration increases, the *average* distance between atoms also increases (Fig. 17.9b). As the atoms get farther apart, every dimension increases.

17.8 How the length of a rod changes with a change in temperature. (Length changes are exaggerated for clarity.)

(a) For moderate temperature changes, ΔL is directly proportional to ΔT.

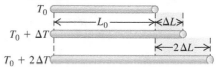

(b) ΔL is also directly proportional to L_0.

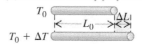

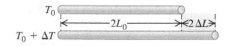

(a) A model of the forces between neighboring atoms in a solid

Average distance between atoms

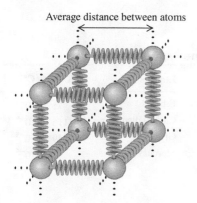

(b) A graph of the "spring" potential energy $U(x)$

x = distance between atoms
● = average distance between atoms

For each energy E, distance between atoms varies between the two values where $E = U$ (see Fig. 14.15a).

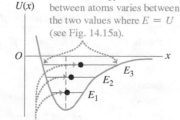

Average distance between atoms is midway between two limits. As energy increases from E_1 to E_2 to E_3, average distance increases.

17.9 (a) We can model atoms in a solid as being held together by "springs" that are easier to stretch than to compress. (b) A graph of the "spring" potential energy $U(x)$ versus distance x between neighboring atoms is *not* symmetrical (compare Fig. 14.20b). As the energy increases and the atoms oscillate with greater amplitude, the average distance increases.

17.10 When an object undergoes thermal expansion, any holes in the object expand as well. (The expansion is exaggerated.)

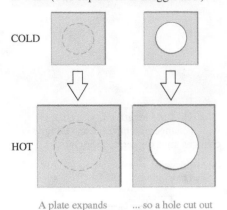

COLD

HOT

A plate expands when heated ...

... so a hole cut out of the plate must expand, too.

CAUTION **Heating an object with a hole** If a solid object has a hole in it, what happens to the size of the hole when the temperature of the object increases? A common misconception is that if the object expands, the hole will shrink because material expands into the hole. But, in fact, if the object expands, the hole will expand too (**Fig. 17.10**); *every* linear dimension of an object changes in the same way when the temperature changes. Think of the atoms in Fig. 17.9a as outlining a cubical hole. When the object expands, the atoms move apart and the hole increases in size. The only situation in which a "hole" will fill in due to thermal expansion is when two separate objects expand and close the gap between them (**Fig. 17.11**).

The direct proportionality in Eq. (17.6) is not exact; it is *approximately* correct only for sufficiently small temperature changes. For a given material, α varies somewhat with the initial temperature T_0 and the size of the temperature interval. We'll ignore this complication here, however. **Table 17.1** lists values of α for several materials. Within the precision of these values we don't need to worry whether T_0 is 0°C or 20°C or some other temperature. Typical values of α are very small; even for a temperature change of 100 C°, the fractional length change $\Delta L/L_0$ is only of the order of $\frac{1}{1000}$ for the metals in the table.

Volume Expansion

Increasing temperature usually causes increases in *volume* for both solids and liquids. Just as with linear expansion, experiments show that if the temperature change ΔT is less than 100 C° or so, the increase in volume ΔV is approximately proportional to both the temperature change ΔT and the initial volume V_0:

Volume thermal expansion:
Change in volume

$$\Delta V = \beta V_0 \, \Delta T$$

Original volume
Temperature change
Coefficient of volume expansion

(17.8)

The constant β characterizes the volume expansion properties of a particular material; it is called the **coefficient of volume expansion**. The units of β are K^{-1} or $(C°)^{-1}$. As with linear expansion, β varies somewhat with temperature, and Eq. (17.8) is an approximate relationship that is valid only for small temperature changes. For many substances, β decreases at low temperatures. **Table 17.2** lists values of β for several materials near room temperature. Note that the values for liquids are generally much larger than those for solids.

For solid materials we can find a simple relationship between the volume expansion coefficient β and the linear expansion coefficient α. Consider a cube of material with side length L and volume $V = L^3$. At the initial temperature the values are L_0 and V_0. When the temperature increases by dT, the side length increases by dL and the volume increases by an amount dV:

$$dV = \frac{dV}{dL} dL = 3L^2 \, dL$$

17.11 This railroad track has a gap between segments to allow for thermal expansion. (The "clickety-clack" sound familiar to railroad passengers comes from the wheels passing over such gaps.) On hot days, the segments expand and fill in the gap. If there were no gaps, the track could buckle under very hot conditions.

Gap

Coefficients of
TABLE 17.1	Linear Expansion
Material	α $[K^{-1}$ or $(C°)^{-1}]$
Aluminum	2.4×10^{-5}
Brass	2.0×10^{-5}
Copper	1.7×10^{-5}
Glass	$0.4–0.9 \times 10^{-5}$
Invar (nickel–iron alloy)	0.09×10^{-5}
Quartz (fused)	0.04×10^{-5}
Steel	1.2×10^{-5}

TABLE 17.2	Coefficients of Volume Expansion		
Solids	β $[K^{-1}$ or $(C°)^{-1}]$	**Liquids**	β $[K^{-1}$ or $(C°)^{-1}]$
Aluminum	7.2×10^{-5}	Ethanol	75×10^{-5}
Brass	6.0×10^{-5}	Carbon disulfide	115×10^{-5}
Copper	5.1×10^{-5}	Glycerin	49×10^{-5}
Glass	$1.2–2.7 \times 10^{-5}$	Mercury	18×10^{-5}
Invar	0.27×10^{-5}		
Quartz (fused)	0.12×10^{-5}		
Steel	3.6×10^{-5}		

Now we replace L and V by the initial values L_0 and V_0. From Eq. (17.6), dL is

$$dL = \alpha L_0 \, dT$$

Since $V_0 = L_0^3$, this means that dV can also be expressed as

$$dV = 3L_0^2 \alpha L_0 \, dT = 3\alpha V_0 \, dT$$

This is consistent with the infinitesimal form of Eq. (17.8), $dV = \beta V_0 \, dT$, only if

$$\beta = 3\alpha \qquad (17.9)$$

(Check this relationship for some of the materials listed in Tables 17.1 and 17.2.)

PROBLEM-SOLVING STRATEGY 17.1 | **THERMAL EXPANSION**

IDENTIFY *the relevant concepts:* Decide whether the problem involves changes in length (linear thermal expansion) or in volume (volume thermal expansion).

SET UP *the problem* using the following steps:
1. List the known and unknown quantities and identify the target variables.
2. Choose Eq. (17.6) for linear expansion and Eq. (17.8) for volume expansion.

EXECUTE *the solution* as follows:
1. Solve for the target variables. If you are given an initial temperature T_0 and must find a final temperature T corresponding to a given length or volume change, find ΔT and calculate $T = T_0 + \Delta T$. Remember that the size of a hole in a material varies with temperature just as any other linear dimension, and that the volume of a hole (such as the interior of a container) varies just as that of the corresponding solid shape.
2. Maintain unit consistency. Both L_0 and ΔL (or V_0 and ΔV) must have the same units. If you use a value of α or β in K^{-1} or $(C°)^{-1}$, then ΔT must be in either kelvins or Celsius degrees; from Example 17.1, the two scales are equivalent *for temperature differences.*

EVALUATE *your answer:* Check whether your results make sense.

EXAMPLE 17.2 **LENGTH CHANGE DUE TO TEMPERATURE CHANGE**

A surveyor uses a steel measuring tape that is exactly 50.000 m long at a temperature of 20°C. The markings on the tape are calibrated for this temperature. (a) What is the length of the tape when the temperature is 35°C? (b) When it is 35°C, the surveyor uses the tape to measure a distance. The value that she reads off the tape is 35.794 m. What is the actual distance?

SOLUTION

IDENTIFY and SET UP: This problem concerns the linear expansion of a measuring tape. We are given the tape's initial length $L_0 = 50.000$ m at $T_0 = 20$°C. In part (a) we use Eq. (17.6) to find the change ΔL in the tape's length at $T = 35$°C, and use Eq. (17.7) to find L. (Table 17.1 gives the value of α for steel.) Since the tape expands, at 35°C the distance between two successive meter marks is greater than 1 m. Hence the actual distance in part (b) is *larger* than the distance read off the tape by a factor equal to the ratio of the tape's length L at 35°C to its length L_0 at 20°C.

EXECUTE: (a) The temperature change is $\Delta T = T - T_0 = 15\ C°$; from Eqs. (17.6) and (17.7),

$$\Delta L = \alpha L_0 \, \Delta T = (1.2 \times 10^{-5}\ K^{-1})(50\ \text{m})(15\ \text{K})$$

$$= 9.0 \times 10^{-3}\ \text{m} = 9.0\ \text{mm}$$

$$L = L_0 + \Delta L = 50.000\ \text{m} + 0.009\ \text{m} = 50.009\ \text{m}$$

(b) Our result from part (a) shows that at 35°C, the slightly expanded tape reads a distance of 50.000 m when the true distance is 50.009 m. We can rewrite the algebra of part (a) as $L = L_0(1 + \alpha \, \Delta T)$; at 35°C, *any* true distance will be greater than the reading by the factor $50.009/50.000 = 1 + \alpha \, \Delta T = 1 + 1.8 \times 10^{-4}$. The true distance is therefore

$$(1 + 1.8 \times 10^{-4})(35.794\ \text{m}) = 35.800\ \text{m}$$

EVALUATE: In part (a) we needed only two of the five significant figures of L_0 to compute ΔL to the same number of decimal places as L_0. Our result shows that metals expand very little under moderate temperature changes. However, even the small difference 0.009 m = 9 mm found in part (b) between the scale reading and the true distance can be important in precision work.

EXAMPLE 17.3 VOLUME CHANGE DUE TO TEMPERATURE CHANGE

A 200-cm³ glass flask is filled to the brim with mercury at 20°C. How much mercury overflows when the temperature of the system is raised to 100°C? The coefficient of *linear* expansion of the glass is 0.40×10^{-5} K⁻¹.

SOLUTION

IDENTIFY and SET UP: This problem involves the volume expansion of the glass and of the mercury. The amount of overflow depends on the *difference* between the volume changes ΔV for these two materials, both given by Eq. (17.8). The mercury will overflow if its coefficient of volume expansion β (see Table 17.2) is greater than that of glass, which we find from Eq. (17.9) using the given value of α.

EXECUTE: From Table 17.2, $\beta_{Hg} = 18 \times 10^{-5}$ K⁻¹. That is indeed greater than $\beta_{glass} = 3\alpha_{glass} = 3(0.40 \times 10^{-5}$ K⁻¹$) = 1.2 \times 10^{-5}$ K⁻¹, from Eq. (17.9). The volume overflow is then

$$\Delta V_{Hg} - \Delta V_{glass} = \beta_{Hg}V_0\Delta T - \beta_{glass}V_0\Delta T$$
$$= V_0\Delta T(\beta_{Hg} - \beta_{glass})$$
$$= (200 \text{ cm}^3)(80 \text{ C}°)(18 \times 10^{-5} - 1.2 \times 10^{-5})$$
$$= 2.7 \text{ cm}^3$$

EVALUATE: This is basically how a mercury-in-glass thermometer works; the column of mercury inside a sealed tube rises as T increases because mercury expands faster than glass.

As Tables 17.1 and 17.2 show, glass has smaller coefficients of expansion α and β than do most metals. This is why you can use hot water to loosen a metal lid on a glass jar; the metal expands more than the glass does.

17.12 The volume of 1 gram of water in the temperature range from 0°C to 100°C. By 100°C the volume has increased to 1.043 cm³. If the coefficient of volume expansion were constant, the curve would be a straight line.

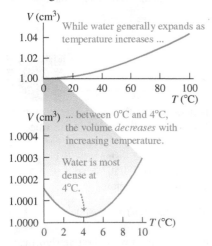

Thermal Expansion of Water

Water, in the temperature range from 0°C to 4°C, *decreases* in volume with increasing temperature. In this range its coefficient of volume expansion is *negative*. Above 4°C, water expands when heated (**Fig. 17.12**). Hence water has its greatest density at 4°C. Water also expands when it freezes, which is why ice humps up in the middle of the compartments in an ice cube tray. By contrast, most materials contract when they freeze.

This anomalous behavior of water has an important effect on plant and animal life in lakes. A lake cools from the surface down; above 4°C, the cooled water at the surface flows to the bottom because of its greater density. But when the surface temperature drops below 4°C, the water near the surface is less dense than the warmer water below. Hence the downward flow ceases, and the water near the surface remains colder than that at the bottom. As the surface freezes, the ice floats because it is less dense than water. The water at the bottom remains at 4°C until nearly the entire lake is frozen. If water behaved like most substances, contracting continuously on cooling and freezing, lakes would freeze from the bottom up. Circulation due to density differences would continuously carry warmer water to the surface for efficient cooling, and lakes would freeze solid much more easily. This would destroy all plant and animal life that cannot withstand freezing. If water did not have its special properties, the evolution of life would have taken a very different course.

17.13 Expansion joints on bridges are needed to accommodate changes in length that result from thermal expansion.

Thermal Stress

If we clamp the ends of a rod rigidly to prevent expansion or contraction and then change the temperature, **thermal stresses** develop. The rod would like to expand or contract, but the clamps won't let it. The resulting stresses may become large enough to strain the rod irreversibly or even break it. (You may want to review the discussion of stress and strain in Section 11.4).

Engineers must account for thermal stress when designing structures (see Fig. 17.11). Concrete highways and bridge decks usually have gaps between sections, filled with a flexible material or bridged by interlocking teeth (**Fig. 17.13**), to permit expansion and contraction of the concrete. Long steam pipes have expansion joints or U-shaped sections to prevent buckling or stretching with temperature changes. If one end of a steel bridge is rigidly fastened to its abutment, the other end usually rests on rollers.

To calculate the thermal stress in a clamped rod, we compute the amount the rod *would* expand (or contract) if not held and then find the stress needed to compress (or stretch) it back to its original length. Suppose that a rod with length L_0 and cross-sectional area A is held at constant length while the temperature is reduced (negative ΔT), causing a tensile stress. From Eq. (17.6), the fractional change in length if the rod were free to contract would be

$$\left(\frac{\Delta L}{L_0}\right)_{\text{thermal}} = \alpha \, \Delta T \qquad (17.10)$$

Both ΔL and ΔT are negative. The tension must increase by an amount F that is just enough to produce an equal and opposite fractional change in length $(\Delta L/L_0)_{\text{tension}}$. From the definition of Young's modulus, Eq. (11.10),

$$Y = \frac{F/A}{\Delta L/L_0} \qquad \text{so} \qquad \left(\frac{\Delta L}{L_0}\right)_{\text{tension}} = \frac{F}{AY} \qquad (17.11)$$

If the length is to be constant, the *total* fractional change in length must be zero. From Eqs. (17.10) and (17.11), this means that

$$\left(\frac{\Delta L}{L_0}\right)_{\text{thermal}} + \left(\frac{\Delta L}{L_0}\right)_{\text{tension}} = \alpha \, \Delta T + \frac{F}{AY} = 0$$

Solve for the tensile stress F/A required to keep the rod's length constant:

Thermal stress:
Force needed to keep length of rod constant $\longrightarrow \dfrac{F}{A} = -Y\alpha \, \Delta T$ $\qquad$ Young's modulus · Temperature change · Coefficient of linear expansion · Cross-sectional area of rod $\qquad (17.12)$

For a decrease in temperature, ΔT is negative, so F and F/A are positive; this means that a *tensile* force and stress are needed to maintain the length. If ΔT is positive, F and F/A are negative, and the required force and stress are *compressive*.

If there are temperature differences within a body, nonuniform expansion or contraction will result and thermal stresses can be induced. You can break a glass bowl by pouring very hot water into it; the thermal stress between the hot and cold parts of the bowl exceeds the breaking stress of the glass, causing cracks. The same phenomenon makes ice cubes crack when dropped into warm water.

EXAMPLE 17.4 THERMAL STRESS

An aluminum cylinder 10 cm long, with a cross-sectional area of 20 cm², is used as a spacer between two steel walls. At 17.2°C it just slips between the walls. Calculate the stress in the cylinder and the total force it exerts on each wall when it warms to 22.3°C, assuming that the walls are perfectly rigid and a constant distance apart.

SOLUTION

IDENTIFY and SET UP: See **Fig. 17.14**. Our target variables are the thermal stress F/A in the cylinder, whose cross-sectional area A is given, and the associated force F it exerts on the walls. We use Eq. (17.12) to relate F/A to the temperature change ΔT, and from

that calculate F. (The length of the cylinder is irrelevant.) We find Young's modulus Y_{Al} and the coefficient of linear expansion α_{Al} from Tables 11.1 and 17.1, respectively.

17.14 Our sketch for this problem.

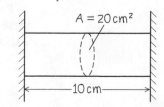

$A = 20\,\text{cm}^2$

$\longleftarrow$ 10 cm $\longrightarrow$

Continued

EXECUTE: We have $Y_{Al} = 7.0 \times 10^{10}\,\text{Pa}$ and $\alpha_{Al} = 2.4 \times 10^{-5}\,\text{K}^{-1}$, and $\Delta T = 22.3°\text{C} - 17.2°\text{C} = 5.1\,\text{C}° = 5.1\,\text{K}$. From Eq. (17.12), the stress is

$$\frac{F}{A} = -Y_{Al}\alpha_{Al}\Delta T$$

$$= -(7.0 \times 10^{10}\,\text{Pa})(2.4 \times 10^{-5}\,\text{K}^{-1})(5.1\,\text{K})$$

$$= -8.6 \times 10^6\,\text{Pa} = -1200\,\text{lb/in.}^2$$

The total force is the cross-sectional area times the stress:

$$F = A\left(\frac{F}{A}\right) = (20 \times 10^{-4}\,\text{m}^2)(-8.6 \times 10^6\,\text{Pa})$$

$$= -1.7 \times 10^4\,\text{N} = -1.9\,\text{tons}$$

EVALUATE: The stress on the cylinder and the force it exerts on each wall are immense. Such thermal stresses must be accounted for in engineering.

TEST YOUR UNDERSTANDING OF SECTION 17.4   In the bimetallic strip shown in Fig. 17.3a, metal 1 is copper. Which of the following materials could be used for metal 2? (There may be more than one correct answer). (i) Steel; (ii) brass; (iii) aluminum. ∎

17.5 QUANTITY OF HEAT

When you put a cold spoon into a cup of hot coffee, the spoon warms up and the coffee cools down as they approach thermal equilibrium. What causes these temperature changes is a transfer of *energy* from one substance to another. Energy transfer that takes place solely because of a temperature difference is called *heat flow* or *heat transfer,* and energy transferred in this way is called **heat.**

An understanding of the relationship between heat and other forms of energy emerged during the 18th and 19th centuries. Sir James Joule (1818–1889) studied how water can be warmed by vigorous stirring with a paddle wheel (**Fig. 17.15a**). The paddle wheel adds energy to the water by doing *work* on it, and Joule found that *the temperature rise is directly proportional to the amount of work done.* The same temperature change can also be caused by putting the water in contact with some hotter body (Fig. 17.15b); hence this interaction must also involve an energy exchange. We'll explore the relationship between heat and mechanical energy in Chapters 19 and 20.

17.15 The same temperature change of the same system may be accomplished by (a) doing work on it or (b) adding heat to it.

(a) Raising the temperature of water by doing work on it

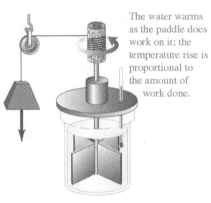

The water warms as the paddle does work on it; the temperature rise is proportional to the amount of work done.

(b) Raising the temperature of water by direct heating

Direct heating can produce the same temperature change as doing work on the water.

CAUTION **Temperature vs. heat** It is absolutely essential for you to distinguish between *temperature* and *heat.* Temperature depends on the physical state of a material and is a quantitative description of its hotness or coldness. In physics the term "heat" always refers to energy in transit from one body or system to another because of a temperature difference, never to the amount of energy contained within a particular system. We can change the temperature of a body by adding heat to it or taking heat away, or by adding or subtracting energy in other ways, such as mechanical work (Fig. 17.15a). If we cut a body in half, each half has the same temperature as the whole; but to raise the temperature of each half by a given interval, we add *half* as much heat as for the whole. ∎

We can define a *unit* of quantity of heat based on temperature changes of some specific material. The **calorie** (abbreviated cal) is *the amount of heat required to raise the temperature of 1 gram of water from 14.5°C to 15.5°C.* A food-value calorie is actually a kilocalorie (kcal), equal to 1000 cal. A corresponding unit of heat that uses Fahrenheit degrees and British units is the **British thermal unit,** or Btu. One Btu is the quantity of heat required to raise the temperature of 1 pound (weight) of water 1 F° from 63°F to 64°F.

Because heat is energy in transit, there must be a definite relationship between these units and the familiar mechanical energy units such as the joule (**Fig. 17.16**). Experiments similar in concept to Joule's have shown that

$$1\,\text{cal} = 4.186\,\text{J}$$

$$1\,\text{kcal} = 1000\,\text{cal} = 4186\,\text{J}$$

$$1\,\text{Btu} = 778\,\text{ft}\cdot\text{lb} = 252\,\text{cal} = 1055\,\text{J}$$

The calorie is not a fundamental SI unit. The International Committee on Weights and Measures recommends using the joule as the basic unit of energy in all forms, including heat. We will follow that recommendation in this book.

Specific Heat

We use the symbol Q for quantity of heat. When it is associated with an infinitesimal temperature change dT, we call it dQ. The quantity of heat Q required to increase the temperature of a mass m of a certain material from T_1 to T_2 is found to be approximately proportional to the temperature change $\Delta T = T_2 - T_1$. It is also proportional to the mass m of material. When you're heating water to make tea, you need twice as much heat for two cups as for one if the temperature change is the same. The quantity of heat needed also depends on the nature of the material; raising the temperature of 1 kilogram of water by 1 C° requires 4190 J of heat, but only 910 J is needed to raise the temperature of 1 kilogram of aluminum by 1 C°.

Putting all these relationships together, we have

Heat required to change temperature of a certain mass ⟶ $Q = mc\,\Delta T$ ⟵ Mass of material, Temperature change, Specific heat of material (17.13)

The **specific heat** c has different values for different materials. For an infinitesimal temperature change dT and corresponding quantity of heat dQ,

$$dQ = mc\,dT \qquad (17.14)$$

$$c = \frac{1}{m}\frac{dQ}{dT} \qquad \text{(specific heat)} \qquad (17.15)$$

In Eqs. (17.13), (17.14), and (17.15), when Q (or dQ) and ΔT (or dT) are positive, heat enters the body and its temperature increases. When they are negative, heat leaves the body and its temperature decreases.

CAUTION **The definition of heat** Remember that dQ does not represent a change in the amount of heat *contained* in a body. Heat is always energy *in transit* as a result of a temperature difference. There is no such thing as "the amount of heat in a body." ▮

The specific heat of water is approximately

$$4190 \text{ J/kg} \cdot \text{K} \qquad 1 \text{ cal/g} \cdot \text{C}° \qquad \text{or} \qquad 1 \text{ Btu/lb} \cdot \text{F}°$$

The specific heat of a material always depends somewhat on the initial temperature and the temperature interval. **Figure 17.17** shows this dependence for water. In this chapter we will usually ignore this small variation.

17.16 The word "energy" is of Greek origin. This label on a can of Greek coffee shows that 100 milliliters of prepared coffee have an energy content ($\varepsilon\nu\acute{\varepsilon}\rho\gamma\varepsilon\iota\alpha$) of 9.6 kilojoules or 2.3 kilocalories.

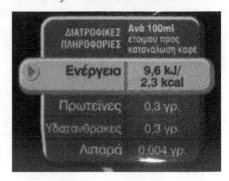

17.17 Specific heat of water as a function of temperature. The value of c varies by less than 1% between 0°C and 100°C.

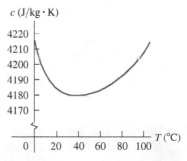

EXAMPLE 17.5 FEED A COLD, STARVE A FEVER

During a bout with the flu an 80-kg man ran a fever of 39.0°C (102.2°F) instead of the normal body temperature of 37.0°C (98.6°F). Assuming that the human body is mostly water, how much heat is required to raise his temperature by that amount?

SOLUTION

IDENTIFY and SET UP: This problem uses the relationship among heat (the target variable), mass, specific heat, and temperature change. We use Eq. (17.13) to determine the required heat Q, with $m = 80$ kg, $c = 4190$ J/kg·K (for water), and $\Delta T = 39.0°C - 37.0°C = 2.0$ C° = 2.0 K.

EXECUTE: From Eq. (17.13),

$$Q = mc\,\Delta T = (80 \text{ kg})(4190 \text{ J/kg}\cdot\text{K})(2.0 \text{ K}) = 6.7 \times 10^5 \text{ J}$$

EVALUATE: This corresponds to 160 kcal. In fact, the specific heat of the human body is about 3480 J/kg·K, 83% that of water, because protein, fat, and minerals have lower specific heats. Hence a more accurate answer is $Q = 5.6 \times 10^5$ J = 133 kcal. Either result shows us that were it not for the body's temperature-regulating systems, taking in energy in the form of food would produce measurable changes in body temperature. (The elevated temperature of a person with the flu results from the body's extra activity in response to infection.)

EXAMPLE 17.6   OVERHEATING ELECTRONICS

You are designing an electronic circuit element made of 23 mg of silicon. The electric current through it adds energy at the rate of 7.4 mW = 7.4×10^{-3} J/s. If your design doesn't allow any heat transfer out of the element, at what rate does its temperature increase? The specific heat of silicon is 705 J/kg·K.

SOLUTION

IDENTIFY and SET UP: The energy added to the circuit element gives rise to a temperature increase, just as if heat were flowing into the element at the rate $dQ/dt = 7.4 \times 10^{-3}$ J/s. Our target variable is the rate of temperature change dT/dt. We can use Eq. (17.14),

which relates infinitesimal temperature changes dT to the corresponding heat dQ, to obtain an expression for dQ/dt in terms of dT/dt.

EXECUTE: We divide both sides of Eq. (17.14) by dt and rearrange:

$$\frac{dT}{dt} = \frac{dQ/dt}{mc} = \frac{7.4 \times 10^{-3} \text{ J/s}}{(23 \times 10^{-6} \text{ kg})(705 \text{ J/kg·K})} = 0.46 \text{ K/s}$$

EVALUATE: At this rate of temperature rise (27 K/min), the circuit element would soon self-destruct. Heat transfer is an important design consideration in electronic circuit elements.

Molar Heat Capacity

Sometimes it's more convenient to describe a quantity of substance in terms of the number of *moles n* rather than the *mass m* of material. Recall from your study of chemistry that a mole of any pure substance always contains the same number of molecules. (We will discuss this point in more detail in Chapter 18.) The *molar mass* of any substance, denoted by M, is the mass per mole. (The quantity M is sometimes called *molecular weight*, but *molar mass* is preferable; the quantity depends on the mass of a molecule, not its weight.) For example, the molar mass of water is 18.0 g/mol = 18.0×10^{-3} kg/mol; 1 mole of water has a mass of 18.0 g = 0.0180 kg. The total mass m of material is equal to the mass per mole M times the number of moles n:

$$m = nM \tag{17.16}$$

Replacing the mass m in Eq. (17.13) by the product nM, we find

$$Q = nMc \, \Delta T \tag{17.17}$$

17.18 Water has a much higher specific heat than the glass or metals used to make cookware. This helps explain why it takes several minutes to boil water on a stove, even though the pot or kettle reaches a high temperature very quickly.

The product Mc is called the **molar heat capacity** (or *molar specific heat*) and is denoted by C (capitalized). With this notation we rewrite Eq. (17.17) as

Heat required to change temperature of a certain number of moles ⟶ $Q = nC \, \Delta T$ ⟵ Number of moles of material, Temperature change, Molar heat capacity of material $\tag{17.18}$

Comparing to Eq. (17.15), we can express the molar heat capacity C (heat per mole per temperature change) in terms of the specific heat c (heat per mass per temperature change) and the molar mass M (mass per mole):

$$C = \frac{1}{n}\frac{dQ}{dT} = Mc \qquad \text{(molar heat capacity)} \tag{17.19}$$

For example, the molar heat capacity of water is

$$C = Mc = (0.0180 \text{ kg/mol})(4190 \text{ J/kg·K}) = 75.4 \text{ J/mol·K}$$

Table 17.3 gives values of specific heat and molar heat capacity for several substances. Note the remarkably large specific heat for water (**Fig. 17.18**).

CAUTION **The meaning of "heat capacity"** The term "heat capacity" is unfortunate because it gives the erroneous impression that a body *contains* a certain amount of heat. Remember, heat is energy in transit to or from a body, not the energy residing in the body. ▌

DEMO

DEMO

TABLE 17.3 Approximate Specific Heats and Molar Heat Capacities (Constant Pressure)

Substance	Specific Heat, c $(J/kg \cdot K)$	Molar Mass, M (kg/mol)	Molar Heat Capacity, C $(J/mol \cdot K)$
Aluminum	910	0.0270	24.6
Beryllium	1970	0.00901	17.7
Copper	390	0.0635	24.8
Ethanol	2428	0.0461	111.9
Ethylene glycol	2386	0.0620	148.0
Ice (near 0°C)	2100	0.0180	37.8
Iron	470	0.0559	26.3
Lead	130	0.207	26.9
Marble ($CaCO_3$)	879	0.100	87.9
Mercury	138	0.201	27.7
Salt (NaCl)	879	0.0585	51.4
Silver	234	0.108	25.3
Water (liquid)	4190	0.0180	75.4

Measurements of specific heats and molar heat capacities for solid materials are usually made at constant atmospheric pressure; the corresponding values are called the *specific heat* and *molar heat capacity at constant pressure,* denoted by c_p and C_p. For a gas it is usually easier to keep the substance in a container with constant *volume;* the corresponding values are called the *specific heat* and *molar heat capacity at constant volume,* denoted by c_V and C_V. For a given substance, C_V and C_p are different. If the system can expand while heat is added, there is additional energy exchange through the performance of *work* by the system on its surroundings. If the volume is constant, the system does no work. For gases the difference between C_p and C_V is substantial. We will study heat capacities of gases in detail in Section 19.7.

The last column of Table 17.3 shows something interesting. The molar heat capacities for most elemental solids are about the same: about $25\ J/mol \cdot K$. This correlation, named the *rule of Dulong and Petit* (for its discoverers), forms the basis for a very important idea. The number of atoms in 1 mole is the same for all elemental substances. This means that on a *per atom* basis, about the same amount of heat is required to raise the temperature of each of these elements by a given amount, even though the *masses* of the atoms are very different. The heat required for a given temperature increase depends only on *how many* atoms the sample contains, not on the mass of an individual atom. We will see the reason the rule of Dulong and Petit works so well when we study the molecular basis of heat capacities in greater detail in Chapter 18.

TEST YOUR UNDERSTANDING OF SECTION 17.5 You wish to raise the temperature of each of the following samples from 20°C to 21°C. Rank these in order of the amount of heat needed to do this, from highest to lowest. (i) 1 kilogram of mercury; (ii) 1 kilogram of ethanol; (iii) 1 mole of mercury; (iv) 1 mole of ethanol. ∎

17.6 CALORIMETRY AND PHASE CHANGES

Calorimetry means "measuring heat." We have discussed the energy transfer (heat) involved in temperature changes. Heat is also involved in *phase changes,* such as the melting of ice or boiling of water. Once we understand these additional heat relationships, we can analyze a variety of problems involving quantity of heat.

17.19 The surrounding air is at room temperature, but this ice–water mixture remains at 0°C until all of the ice has melted and the phase change is complete.

PhET: States of Matter

Phase Changes

We use the term **phase** to describe a specific state of matter, such as a solid, liquid, or gas. The compound H_2O exists in the *solid phase* as ice, in the *liquid phase* as water, and in the *gaseous phase* as steam. (These are also referred to as **states of matter:** the solid state, the liquid state, and the gaseous state.) A transition from one phase to another is called a **phase change** or *phase transition*. For any given pressure a phase change takes place at a definite temperature, usually accompanied by heat flowing in or out and a change of volume and density.

A familiar phase change is the melting of ice. When we add heat to ice at 0°C and normal atmospheric pressure, the temperature of the ice *does not* increase. Instead, some of it melts to form liquid water. If we add the heat slowly, to maintain the system very close to thermal equilibrium, the temperature remains at 0°C until all the ice is melted (**Fig. 17.19**). The effect of adding heat to this system is not to raise its temperature but to change its *phase* from solid to liquid.

To change 1 kg of ice at 0°C to 1 kg of liquid water at 0°C and normal atmospheric pressure requires 3.34×10^5 J of heat. The heat required per unit mass is called the **heat of fusion** (or sometimes *latent heat of fusion*), denoted by L_f. For water at normal atmospheric pressure the heat of fusion is

$$L_f = 3.34 \times 10^5 \text{ J/kg} = 79.6 \text{ cal/g} = 143 \text{ Btu/lb}$$

More generally, to melt a mass m of material that has a heat of fusion L_f requires a quantity of heat Q given by

$$Q = mL_f$$

This process is *reversible*. To freeze liquid water to ice at 0°C, we have to *remove* heat; the magnitude is the same, but in this case, Q is negative because heat is removed rather than added. To cover both possibilities and to include other kinds of phase changes, we write

Heat transfer in ⋯⋯→ $Q = \pm mL$ ←⋯ Latent heat for this phase change (17.20)
a phase change ↗ Mass of material that changes phase
  ↖ + if heat enters material, − if heat leaves

The plus sign (heat entering) is used when the material melts; the minus sign (heat leaving) is used when it freezes. The heat of fusion is different for different materials, and it also varies somewhat with pressure.

For any given material at any given pressure, the freezing temperature is the same as the melting temperature. At this unique temperature the liquid and solid phases can coexist in a condition called **phase equilibrium.**

We can go through this whole story again for *boiling* or *evaporation,* a phase transition between liquid and gaseous phases. The corresponding heat (per unit mass) is called the **heat of vaporization** L_v. At normal atmospheric pressure the heat of vaporization L_v for water is

$$L_v = 2.256 \times 10^6 \text{ J/kg} = 539 \text{ cal/g} = 970 \text{ Btu/lb}$$

That is, it takes 2.256×10^6 J to change 1 kg of liquid water at 100°C to 1 kg of water vapor at 100°C. By comparison, to raise the temperature of 1 kg of water from 0°C to 100°C requires $Q = mc\,\Delta T = (1.00 \text{ kg})(4190 \text{ J/kg} \cdot \text{C°}) \times (100 \text{ C°}) = 4.19 \times 10^5$ J, less than one-fifth as much heat as is required for vaporization at 100°C. This agrees with everyday kitchen experience; a pot of water may reach boiling temperature in a few minutes, but it takes a much longer time to completely evaporate all the water away.

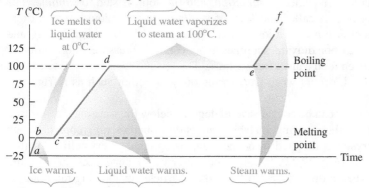

Phase **of water changes.** During these periods, temperature stays constant and the phase change proceeds as heat is added: $Q = +mL$.

Ice melts to liquid water at 0°C.

Liquid water vaporizes to steam at 100°C.

Boiling point

Melting point

Ice warms.

Liquid water warms.

Steam warms.

Temperature **of water changes.** During these periods, temperature rises as heat is added: $Q = mc\,\Delta T$.

17.20 Graph of temperature versus time for a specimen of water initially in the solid phase (ice). Heat is added to the specimen at a constant rate. The temperature remains constant during each change of phase, provided that the pressure remains constant.

$a \rightarrow b$: Ice initially at −25°C is warmed to 0°C.

$b \rightarrow c$: Temperature remains at 0°C until all ice melts.

$c \rightarrow d$: Water is warmed from 0°C to 100°C.

$d \rightarrow e$: Temperature remains at 100°C until all water vaporizes.

$e \rightarrow f$: Steam is warmed to temperatures above 100°C.

Like melting, boiling is a reversible transition. When heat is removed from a gas at the boiling temperature, the gas returns to the liquid phase, or *condenses*, giving up to its surroundings the same quantity of heat (heat of vaporization) that was needed to vaporize it. At a given pressure the boiling and condensation temperatures are always the same; at this temperature the liquid and gaseous phases can coexist in phase equilibrium.

Both L_v and the boiling temperature of a material depend on pressure. Water boils at a lower temperature (about 95°C) in Denver than in Pittsburgh because Denver is at higher elevation and the average atmospheric pressure is lower. The heat of vaporization is somewhat greater at this lower pressure, about 2.27×10^6 J/kg.

Figure 17.20 summarizes these ideas about phase changes. **Table 17.4** lists heats of fusion and vaporization for some materials and their melting and boiling temperatures at normal atmospheric pressure. Very few *elements* have melting temperatures in the vicinity of ordinary room temperatures; one of the few is the metal gallium, shown in **Fig. 17.21**.

17.21 The metal gallium, shown here melting in a person's hand, is one of the few elements that melt in the vicinity of room temperature. Its melting temperature is 29.8°C, and its heat of fusion is 8.04×10^4 J/kg.

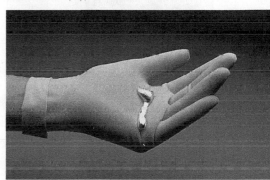

| TABLE 17.4 | **Heats of Fusion and Vaporization** | | | | | |

Substance	Normal Melting Point		Heat of Fusion, I_f (J/kg)	Normal Boiling Point		Heat of Vaporization, L_v (J/kg)
	K	**°C**		**K**	**°C**	
Helium	*	*	*	4.216	−268.93	20.9×10^3
Hydrogen	13.84	−259.31	58.6×10^3	20.26	−252.89	452×10^3
Nitrogen	63.18	−209.97	25.5×10^3	77.34	−195.8	201×10^3
Oxygen	54.36	−218.79	13.8×10^3	90.18	−183.0	213×10^3
Ethanol	159	−114	104.2×10^3	351	78	854×10^3
Mercury	234	−39	11.8×10^3	630	357	272×10^3
Water	273.15	0.00	334×10^3	373.15	100.00	2256×10^3
Sulfur	392	119	38.1×10^3	717.75	444.60	326×10^3
Lead	600.5	327.3	24.5×10^3	2023	1750	871×10^3
Antimony	903.65	630.50	165×10^3	1713	1440	561×10^3
Silver	1233.95	960.80	88.3×10^3	2466	2193	2336×10^3
Gold	1336.15	1063.00	64.5×10^3	2933	2660	1578×10^3
Copper	1356	1083	134×10^3	1460	1187	5069×10^3

*A pressure in excess of 25 atmospheres is required to make helium solidify. At 1 atmosphere pressure, helium remains a liquid down to absolute zero.

17.22 When this airplane flew into a cloud at a temperature just below freezing, the plane struck supercooled water droplets in the cloud that rapidly crystallized and formed ice on the plane's nose (shown here) and wings. Such inflight icing can be extremely hazardous, which is why commercial airliners are equipped with devices to remove ice.

A substance can sometimes change directly from the solid to the gaseous phase. This process is called *sublimation,* and the solid is said to *sublime.* The corresponding heat is called the *heat of sublimation, L_s.* Liquid carbon dioxide cannot exist at a pressure lower than about 5×10^5 Pa (about 5 atm), and "dry ice" (solid carbon dioxide) sublimes at atmospheric pressure. Sublimation of water from frozen food causes freezer burn. The reverse process, a phase change from gas to solid, occurs when frost forms on cold bodies such as refrigerator cooling coils.

Very pure water can be cooled several degrees below the freezing temperature without freezing; the resulting unstable state is described as *supercooled.* When a small ice crystal is dropped in or the water is agitated, it crystallizes within a second or less (**Fig. 17.22**). Supercooled water *vapor* condenses quickly into fog droplets when a disturbance, such as dust particles or ionizing radiation, is introduced. This principle is used in "seeding" clouds, which often contain supercooled water vapor, to cause condensation and rain.

A liquid can sometimes be *superheated* above its normal boiling temperature. Any small disturbance such as agitation causes local boiling with bubble formation.

Steam heating systems for buildings use a boiling–condensing process to transfer heat from the furnace to the radiators. Each kilogram of water that is turned to steam in the boiler absorbs over 2×10^6 J (the heat of vaporization L_v of water) from the boiler and gives it up when it condenses in the radiators. Boiling–condensing processes are also used in refrigerators, air conditioners, and heat pumps. We'll discuss these systems in Chapter 20.

The temperature-control mechanisms of many warm-blooded animals make use of heat of vaporization, removing heat from the body by using it to evaporate water from the tongue (panting) or from the skin (sweating). Such *evaporative cooling* enables humans to maintain normal body temperature in hot, dry desert climates where the air temperature may reach 55°C (about 130°F). The skin temperature may be as much as 30°C cooler than the surrounding air. Under these conditions a normal person may perspire several liters per day, and this lost water must be replaced. Evaporative cooling also explains why you feel cold when you first step out of a swimming pool (**Fig. 17.23**).

17.23 The water may be warm and it may be a hot day, but these children will feel cold when they first step out of the swimming pool. That's because as water evaporates from their skin, it removes the heat of vaporization from their bodies. To stay warm, they will need to dry off immediately.

Evaporative cooling is also used to condense and recirculate "used" steam in coal-fired or nuclear-powered electric-generating plants. That's what goes on in the large, tapered concrete towers that you see at such plants.

Chemical reactions such as combustion are analogous to phase changes in that they involve definite quantities of heat. Complete combustion of 1 gram of gasoline produces about 46,000 J or about 11,000 cal, so the **heat of combustion L_c** of gasoline is

$$L_c = 46,000 \text{ J/g} = 4.6 \times 10^7 \text{ J/kg}$$

Energy values of foods are defined similarly. When we say that a gram of peanut butter "contains 6 calories," we mean that 6 kcal of heat (6000 cal or 25,000 J) is released when the carbon and hydrogen atoms in the peanut butter react with oxygen (with the help of enzymes) and are completely converted to CO_2 and H_2O. Not all of this energy is directly useful for mechanical work. We'll study the *efficiency* of energy utilization in Chapter 20.

Heat Calculations

Let's look at some examples of calorimetry calculations (calculations with heat). The basic principle is very simple: When heat flow occurs between two bodies that are isolated from their surroundings, the amount of heat lost by one body must equal the amount gained by the other. Heat is energy in transit, so this principle is really just conservation of energy. Calorimetry, dealing entirely with one conserved quantity, is in many ways the simplest of all physical theories!

PROBLEM-SOLVING STRATEGY 17.2 | CALORIMETRY PROBLEMS

IDENTIFY *the relevant concepts:* When heat flow occurs between two or more bodies that are isolated from their surroundings, the *algebraic sum* of the quantities of heat transferred to all the bodies is zero. We take a quantity of heat *added* to a body as *positive* and a quantity *leaving* a body as *negative*.

SET UP *the problem* using the following steps:
1. Identify the objects that exchange heat.
2. Each object may undergo a temperature change only, a phase change at constant temperature, or both. Use Eq. (17.13) for the heat transferred in a temperature change and Eq. (17.20) for the heat transferred in a phase change.
3. Consult Table 17.3 for values of specific heat or molar heat capacity and Table 17.4 for heats of fusion or vaporization.
4. List the known and unknown quantities and identify the target variables.

EXECUTE *the solution* as follows:
1. Use Eq. (17.13) and/or Eq. (17.20) and the energy-conservation relation $\Sigma Q = 0$ to solve for the target variables. Ensure that you use the correct algebraic signs for Q and ΔT terms, and that you correctly write $\Delta T = T_{final} - T_{initial}$ and not the reverse.
2. If a phase change occurs, you may not know in advance whether all, or only part, of the material undergoes a phase change. Make a reasonable guess; if that leads to an unreasonable result (such as a final temperature higher or lower than any initial temperature), the guess was wrong. Try again!

EVALUATE *your answer:* Double-check your calculations, and ensure that the results are physically sensible.

EXAMPLE 17.7   A TEMPERATURE CHANGE WITH NO PHASE CHANGE

A camper pours 0.300 kg of coffee, initially in a pot at 70.0°C, into a 0.120-kg aluminum cup initially at 20.0°C. What is the equilibrium temperature? Assume that coffee has the same specific heat as water and that no heat is exchanged with the surroundings.

SOLUTION

IDENTIFY and SET UP: The target variable is the common final temperature T of the cup and coffee. No phase changes occur, so we need only Eq. (17.13). With subscripts C for coffee, W for water, and Al for aluminum, we have $T_{0C} = 70.0°$ and $T_{0Al} = 20.0°$; Table 17.3 gives $c_W = 4190$ J/kg·K and $c_{Al} = 910$ J/kg·K.

EXECUTE: The (negative) heat gained by the coffee is $Q_C = m_C c_W \Delta T_C$. The (positive) heat gained by the cup is $Q_{Al} = m_{Al} c_{Al} \Delta T_{Al}$. We set $Q_C + Q_{Al} = 0$ (see Problem-Solving Strategy 17.2) and substitute $\Delta T_C = T - T_{0C}$ and $\Delta T_{Al} = T - T_{0Al}$:

$$Q_C + Q_{Al} = m_C c_W \Delta T_C + m_{Al} c_{Al} \Delta T_{Al} = 0$$

$$m_C c_W (T - T_{0C}) + m_{Al} c_{Al} (T - T_{0Al}) = 0$$

Then we solve this expression for the final temperature T. A little algebra gives

$$T = \frac{m_C c_W T_{0C} + m_{Al} c_{Al} T_{0Al}}{m_C c_W + m_{Al} c_{Al}} = 66.0°C$$

EVALUATE: The final temperature is much closer to the initial temperature of the coffee than to that of the cup; water has a much higher specific heat than aluminum, and we have more than twice as much mass of water. We can also find the quantities of heat by substituting the value $T = 66.0°C$ back into the original equations. We find $Q_C = -5.0 \times 10^3$ J and $Q_{Al} = +5.0 \times 10^3$ J. As expected, Q_C is negative: The coffee loses heat to the cup.

EXAMPLE 17.8   CHANGES IN BOTH TEMPERATURE AND PHASE

A glass contains 0.25 kg of Omni-Cola (mostly water) initially at 25°C. How much ice, initially at −20°C, must you add to obtain a final temperature of 0°C with all the ice melted? Ignore the heat capacity of the glass.

SOLUTION

IDENTIFY and SET UP: The Omni-Cola and ice exchange heat. The cola undergoes a temperature change; the ice undergoes both a temperature change and a phase change from solid to liquid. We use subscripts C for cola, I for ice, and W for water. The target variable is the mass of ice, m_I. We use Eq. (17.13) to obtain an expression for the amount of heat involved in cooling the drink to $T = 0°C$ and warming the ice to $T = 0°C$, and Eq. (17.20) to obtain an expression for the heat required to melt the ice at 0°C. We have $T_{0C} = 25°C$ and $T_{0I} = −20°C$, Table 17.3 gives $c_W = 4190$ J/kg·K and $c_I = 2100$ J/kg·K, and Table 17.4 gives $L_f = 3.34 \times 10^5$ J/kg.

EXECUTE: From Eq. (17.13), the (negative) heat gained by the Omni-Cola is $Q_C = m_C c_W \Delta T_C$. The (positive) heat gained by the ice in warming is $Q_I = m_I c_I \Delta T_I$. The (positive) heat required to melt the ice is $Q_2 = m_I L_f$. We set $Q_C + Q_I + Q_2 = 0$, insert $\Delta T_C = T - T_{0C}$ and $\Delta T_I = T - T_{0I}$, and solve for m_I:

$$m_C c_W \Delta T_C + m_I c_I \Delta T_I + m_I L_f = 0$$

$$m_C c_W (T - T_{0C}) + m_I c_I (T - T_{0I}) + m_I L_f = 0$$

$$m_I [c_I (T - T_{0I}) + L_f] = -m_C c_W (T - T_{0C})$$

$$m_I = m_C \frac{c_W (T_{0C} - T)}{c_I (T - T_{0I}) + L_f}$$

Substituting numerical values, we find that $m_I = 0.070$ kg = 70 g.

EVALUATE: Three or four medium-size ice cubes would make about 70 g, which seems reasonable given the 250 g of Omni-Cola to be cooled.

EXAMPLE 17.9 WHAT'S COOKING?

A hot copper pot of mass 2.0 kg (including its copper lid) is at a temperature of 150°C. You pour 0.10 kg of cool water at 25°C into the pot, then quickly replace the lid so no steam can escape. Find the final temperature of the pot and its contents, and determine the phase of the water (liquid, gas, or a mixture). Assume that no heat is lost to the surroundings.

SOLUTION

IDENTIFY and SET UP: The water and the pot exchange heat. Three outcomes are possible: (1) No water boils, and the final temperature T is less than 100°C; (2) some water boils, giving a mixture of water and steam at 100°C; or (3) all the water boils, giving 0.10 kg of steam at 100°C or greater. We use Eq. (17.13) for the heat transferred in a temperature change and Eq. (17.20) for the heat transferred in a phase change.

EXECUTE: First consider case (1), which parallels Example 17.8 exactly. The equation that states that the heat flow into the water equals the heat flow out of the pot is

$$Q_W + Q_{Cu} = m_W c_W (T - T_{0W}) + m_{Cu} c_{Cu} (T - T_{0Cu}) = 0$$

Here we use subscripts W for water and Cu for copper, with $m_W = 0.10$ kg, $m_{Cu} = 2.0$ kg, $T_{0W} = 25°C$, and $T_{0Cu} = 150°C$. From Table 17.3, $c_W = 4190$ J/kg·K and $c_{Cu} = 390$ J/kg·K. Solving for the final temperature T and substituting these values, we get

$$T = \frac{m_W c_W T_{0W} + m_{Cu} c_{Cu} T_{0Cu}}{m_W c_W + m_{Cu} c_{Cu}} = 106°C$$

But this is above the boiling point of water, which contradicts our assumption that no water boils! So at least some of the water boils.

So consider case (2), in which the final temperature is $T = 100°C$ and some unknown fraction x of the water boils, where (if this case is correct) x is greater than zero and less than or equal to 1. The (positive) amount of heat needed to vaporize this water is $x m_W L_v$. The energy-conservation condition $Q_W + Q_{Cu} = 0$ is then

$$m_W c_W (100°C - T_{0W}) + x m_W L_v + m_{Cu} c_{Cu} (100°C - T_{0Cu}) = 0$$

We solve for the target variable x:

$$x = \frac{-m_{Cu} c_{Cu} (100°C - T_{0Cu}) - m_W c_W (100°C - T_{0W})}{m_W L_v}$$

With $L_v = 2.256 \times 10^6$ J from Table 17.4, this yields $x = 0.034$. We conclude that the final temperature of the water and copper is 100°C and that $0.034(0.10 \text{ kg}) = 0.0034 \text{ kg} = 3.4$ g of the water is converted to steam at 100°C.

EVALUATE: Had x turned out to be greater than 1, case (3) would have held; all the water would have vaporized, and the final temperature would have been greater than 100°C. Can you show that this would have been the case if we had originally poured less than 15 g of 25°C water into the pot?

EXAMPLE 17.10 COMBUSTION, TEMPERATURE CHANGE, AND PHASE CHANGE

In a particular camp stove, only 30% of the energy released in burning gasoline goes to heating the water in a pot on the stove. How much gasoline must we burn to heat 1.00 L (1.00 kg) of water from 20°C to 100°C and boil away 0.25 kg of it?

SOLUTION

IDENTIFY and SET UP: All of the water undergoes a temperature change and part of it undergoes a phase change, from liquid to gas. We determine the heat required to cause both of these changes, and then use the 30% combustion efficiency to determine the amount of gasoline that must be burned (the target variable). We use Eqs. (17.13) and (17.20) and the idea of heat of combustion.

EXECUTE: To raise the temperature of the water from 20°C to 100°C requires

$$Q_1 = mc \Delta T = (1.00 \text{ kg})(4190 \text{ J/kg·K})(80 \text{ K})$$
$$= 3.35 \times 10^5 \text{ J}$$

To boil 0.25 kg of water at 100°C requires

$$Q_2 = mL_v = (0.25 \text{ kg})(2.256 \times 10^6 \text{ J/kg}) = 5.64 \times 10^5 \text{ J}$$

The total energy needed is $Q_1 + Q_2 = 8.99 \times 10^5$ J. This is 30% = 0.30 of the total heat of combustion, which is therefore $(8.99 \times 10^5 \text{ J})/0.30 = 3.00 \times 10^6$ J. As we mentioned earlier, the combustion of 1 g of gasoline releases 46,000 J, so the mass of gasoline required is $(3.00 \times 10^6 \text{ J})/(46,000 \text{ J/g}) = 65$ g, or a volume of about 0.09 L of gasoline.

EVALUATE: This result suggests the tremendous amount of energy released in burning even a small quantity of gasoline. Another 123 g of gasoline would be required to boil away the remaining water; can you prove this?

TEST YOUR UNDERSTANDING OF SECTION 17.6 You take a block of ice at 0°C and add heat to it at a steady rate. It takes a time t to completely convert the block of ice to steam at 100°C. What do you have at time $t/2$? (i) All ice at 0°C; (ii) a mixture of ice and water at 0°C; (iii) water at a temperature between 0°C and 100°C; (iv) a mixture of water and steam at 100°C. ∎

17.7 MECHANISMS OF HEAT TRANSFER

We have talked about *conductors* and *insulators,* materials that permit or prevent heat transfer between bodies. Now let's look in more detail at *rates* of energy transfer. In the kitchen you use a metal or glass pot for good heat transfer from the stove to whatever you're cooking, but your refrigerator is insulated with a material that *prevents* heat from flowing into the food inside the refrigerator. How do we describe the difference between these two materials?

The three mechanisms of heat transfer are conduction, convection, and radiation. *Conduction* occurs within a body or between two bodies in contact. *Convection* depends on motion of mass from one region of space to another. *Radiation* is heat transfer by electromagnetic radiation, such as sunshine, with no need for matter to be present in the space between bodies.

Conduction

If you hold one end of a copper rod and place the other end in a flame, the end you are holding gets hotter and hotter, even though it is not in direct contact with the flame. Heat reaches the cooler end by **conduction** through the material. The atoms in the hotter regions have more kinetic energy, on the average, than their cooler neighbors. They jostle their neighbors, giving them some of their energy. The neighbors jostle *their* neighbors, and so on through the material. The atoms don't move from one region of material to another, but their energy does.

Most metals also conduct heat by another, more effective mechanism. Within the metal, some electrons can leave their parent atoms and wander through the metal. These "free" electrons can rapidly carry energy from hotter to cooler regions of the metal, so metals are generally good conductors of heat. A metal rod at 20°C feels colder than a piece of wood at 20°C because heat can flow more easily from your hand into the metal. The presence of "free" electrons also causes most metals to be good electrical conductors.

In conduction, the direction of heat flow is always from higher to lower temperature. **Figure 17.24a** shows a rod of conducting material with cross-sectional area A and length L. The left end of the rod is kept at a temperature T_H and the right end at a lower temperature T_C, so heat flows from left to right. The sides of the rod are covered by an ideal insulator, so no heat transfer occurs at the sides.

When a quantity of heat dQ is transferred through the rod in a time dt, the rate of heat flow is dQ/dt. We call this rate the **heat current,** denoted by H. That is, $H = dQ/dt$. Experiments show that the heat current is proportional to the cross-sectional area A of the rod (Fig. 17.24b) and to the temperature difference $(T_H - T_C)$ and is inversely proportional to the rod length L (Fig. 17.24c):

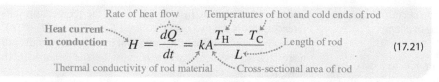

$$\text{Heat current in conduction} \quad H = \frac{dQ}{dt} = kA\frac{T_H - T_C}{L} \quad (17.21)$$

The quantity $(T_H - T_C)/L$ is the temperature difference *per unit length;* it is called the magnitude of the **temperature gradient.** The numerical value of the **thermal conductivity** k depends on the material of the rod. Materials with large k are good conductors of heat; materials with small k are poor conductors, or insulators. Equation (17.21) also gives the heat current through a slab or through *any* homogeneous body with uniform cross section A perpendicular to the direction of flow; L is the length of the heat-flow path.

The units of heat current H are units of energy per time, or power; the SI unit of heat current is the watt (1 W = 1 J/s). We can find the units of k by solving Eq. (17.21) for k; you can show that the SI units are W/m·K. **Table 17.5** gives some numerical values of k.

17.24 Steady-state heat flow due to conduction in a uniform rod.

(a) Heat current H

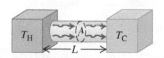

(b) Doubling the cross-sectional area of the conductor doubles the heat current (H is proportional to A).

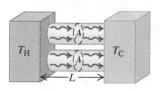

(c) Doubling the length of the conductor halves the heat current (H is inversely proportional to L).

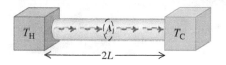

TABLE 17.5	Thermal Conductivities
Substance	**k (W/m · K)**
Metals	
Aluminum	205.0
Brass	109.0
Copper	385.0
Lead	34.7
Mercury	8.3
Silver	406.0
Steel	50.2
Solids (representative values)	
Brick, insulating	0.15
Brick, red	0.6
Concrete	0.8
Cork	0.04
Felt	0.04
Fiberglass	0.04
Glass	0.8
Ice	1.6
Rock wool	0.04
Styrofoam	0.027
Wood	0.12–0.04
Gases	
Air	0.024
Argon	0.016
Helium	0.14
Hydrogen	0.14
Oxygen	0.023

BIO **Application Fur Versus Blubber**
The fur of an arctic fox is a good thermal insulator because it traps air, which has a low thermal conductivity k. (The value $k = 0.04$ W/m · K for fur is higher than for air, $k = 0.024$ W/m · K, because fur also includes solid hairs.) The layer of fat beneath a bowhead whale's skin, called blubber, has six times the thermal conductivity of fur ($k = 0.24$ W/m · K). So a 6-cm thickness of blubber ($L = 6$ cm) is required to give the same insulation as 1 cm of fur.

The thermal conductivity of "dead" (nonmoving) air is very small. A wool sweater keeps you warm because it traps air between the fibers. Many insulating materials such as Styrofoam and fiberglass are mostly dead air.

If the temperature varies in a nonuniform way along the length of the conducting rod, we introduce a coordinate x along the length and generalize the temperature gradient to be dT/dx. The corresponding generalization of Eq. (17.21) is

$$H = \frac{dQ}{dt} = -kA\frac{dT}{dx} \qquad (17.22)$$

The negative sign indicates that heat flows in the direction of *decreasing* temperature. If temperature increases with increasing x, then $dT/dx > 0$ and $H < 0$; the negative value of H in this case means that heat flows in the negative x-direction, from high to low temperature.

For thermal insulation in buildings, engineers use the concept of **thermal resistance,** denoted by R. The thermal resistance R of a slab of material with area A is defined so that the heat current H through the slab is

$$H = \frac{A(T_H - T_C)}{R} \qquad (17.23)$$

where T_H and T_C are the temperatures on the two sides of the slab. Comparing this with Eq. (17.21), we see that R is given by

$$R = \frac{L}{k} \qquad (17.24)$$

where L is the thickness of the slab. The SI unit of R is 1 m^2 · K/W. In the units used for commercial insulating materials in the United States, H is expressed in Btu/h, A is in ft^2, and $T_H - T_C$ in F°. (1 Btu/h = 0.293 W.) The units of R are then ft^2 · F° · h/Btu, though values of R are usually quoted without units; a 6-inch-thick layer of fiberglass has an R value of 19 (that is, $R = 19$ ft^2 · F° · h/Btu), a 2-inch-thick slab of polyurethane foam has an R value of 12, and so on. Doubling the thickness doubles the R value. Common practice in new construction in severe northern climates is to specify R values of around 30 for exterior walls and ceilings. When the insulating material is in layers, such as a plastered wall, fiberglass insulation, and wood exterior siding, the R values are additive. Do you see why?

PROBLEM-SOLVING STRATEGY 17.3 HEAT CONDUCTION

IDENTIFY *the relevant concepts:* Heat conduction occurs whenever two objects at different temperatures are placed in contact.

SET UP *the problem* using the following steps:
1. Identify the direction of heat flow (from hot to cold). In Eq. (17.21), L is measured along this direction, and A is an area perpendicular to this direction. You can often approximate an irregular-shaped container with uniform wall thickness as a flat slab with the same thickness and total wall area.
2. List the known and unknown quantities and identify the target variable.

EXECUTE *the solution* as follows:
1. If heat flows through a single object, use Eq. (17.21) to solve for the target variable.
2. If the heat flows through two different materials in succession (in *series*), the temperature T at the interface between them is intermediate between T_H and T_C, so that the temperature differences across the two materials are $(T_H - T)$ and $(T - T_C)$. In steady-state heat flow, the same heat must pass through both materials, so the heat current H must be the *same* in both materials.
3. If heat flows through two or more *parallel* paths, then the total heat current H is the sum of the currents $H_1, H_2, \ldots$ for the separate paths. An example is heat flow from inside a room to outside, both through the glass in a window and through the surrounding wall. In parallel heat flow the temperature difference is the same for each path, but L, A, and k may be different for each path.
4. Be consistent with units. If k is expressed in W/m · K, for example, use distances in meters, heat in joules, and T in kelvins.

EVALUATE *your answer:* Are the results physically reasonable?

EXAMPLE 17.11   CONDUCTION INTO A PICNIC COOLER

A Styrofoam cooler (**Fig. 17.25a**) has total wall area (including the lid) of 0.80 m² and wall thickness 2.0 cm. It is filled with ice, water, and cans of Omni-Cola, all at 0°C. What is the rate of heat flow into the cooler if the temperature of the outside wall is 30°C? How much ice melts in 3 hours?

SOLUTION

IDENTIFY and SET UP: The target variables are the heat current H and the mass m of ice melted. We use Eq. (17.21) to determine H and Eq. (17.20) to determine m.

17.25 Conduction of heat across the walls of a Styrofoam cooler.

(a) A cooler at the beach   **(b)** Our sketch for this problem

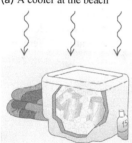

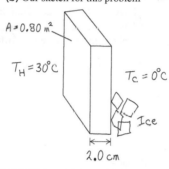

EXECUTE: We assume that the total heat flow is the same as it would be through a flat Styrofoam slab of area 0.80 m² and thickness 2.0 cm = 0.020 m (Fig. 17.25b). We find k from Table 17.5. From Eq. (17.21),

$$H = kA\frac{T_H - T_C}{L} = (0.027 \text{ W/m} \cdot \text{K})(0.80 \text{ m}^2)\frac{30°C - 0°C}{0.020 \text{ m}}$$

$$= 32.4 \text{ W} = 32.4 \text{ J/s}$$

The total heat flow is $Q = Ht$, with $t = 3 \text{ h} = 10,800$ s. From Table 17.4, the heat of fusion of ice is $L_f = 3.34 \times 10^5$ J/kg, so from Eq. (17.20) the mass of ice that melts is

$$m = \frac{Q}{L_f} = \frac{(32.4 \text{ J/s})(10,800 \text{ s})}{3.34 \times 10^5 \text{ J/kg}} = 1.0 \text{ kg}$$

EVALUATE: The low heat current is a result of the low thermal conductivity of Styrofoam.

EXAMPLE 17.12   CONDUCTION THROUGH TWO BARS I

A steel bar 10.0 cm long is welded end to end to a copper bar 20.0 cm long. Each bar has a square cross section, 2.00 cm on a side. The free end of the steel bar is kept at 100°C by placing it in contact with steam, and the free end of the copper bar is kept at 0°C by placing it in contact with ice. Both bars are perfectly insulated on their sides. Find the steady-state temperature at the junction of the two bars and the total rate of heat flow through the bars.

SOLUTION

IDENTIFY and SET UP: Figure 17.26 shows the situation. The heat currents in these end-to-end bars must be the same (see Problem-Solving Strategy 17.3). We are given "hot" and "cold" temperatures $T_H = 100°C$ and $T_C = 0°C$. With subscripts S for steel and Cu for copper, we write Eq. (17.21) separately for the heat currents H_S and H_{Cu} and set the resulting expressions equal to each other.

17.26 Our sketch for this problem.

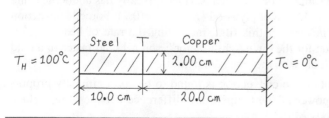

EXECUTE: Setting $H_S = H_{Cu}$, we have from Eq. (17.21)

$$H_S = k_S A\frac{T_H - T}{L_S} = H_{Cu} = k_{Cu}A\frac{T - T_C}{L_{Cu}}$$

We divide out the equal cross-sectional areas A and solve for T:

$$T = \frac{\dfrac{k_S}{L_S}T_H + \dfrac{k_{Cu}}{L_{Cu}}T_C}{\left(\dfrac{k_S}{L_S} + \dfrac{k_{Cu}}{L_{Cu}}\right)}$$

Substituting $L_S = 10.0$ cm and $L_{Cu} = 20.0$ cm, the given values of T_H and T_C, and the values of k_S and k_{Cu} from Table 17.5, we find $T = 20.7°C$.

We can find the total heat current by substituting this value of T into either the expression for H_S or the one for H_{Cu}:

$$H_S = (50.2 \text{ W/m} \cdot \text{K})(0.0200 \text{ m})^2\frac{100°C - 20.7°C}{0.100 \text{ m}}$$

$$= 15.9 \text{ W}$$

$$H_{Cu} = (385 \text{ W/m} \cdot \text{K})(0.0200 \text{ m})^2\frac{20.7°C}{0.200 \text{ m}} = 15.9 \text{ W}$$

EVALUATE: Even though the steel bar is shorter, the temperature drop across it is much greater (from 100°C to 20.7°C) than across the copper bar (from 20.7°C to 0°C). That's because steel is a much poorer conductor than copper.

EXAMPLE 17.13   CONDUCTION THROUGH TWO BARS II

Suppose the two bars of Example 17.12 are separated. One end of each bar is kept at 100°C and the other end of each bar is kept at 0°C. What is the *total* heat current in the two bars?

SOLUTION

IDENTIFY and SET UP: Figure 17.27 shows the situation. For each bar, $T_H - T_C = 100°C - 0°C = 100$ K. The total heat current is the sum of the currents in the two bars, $H_S + H_{Cu}$.

17.27 Our sketch for this problem.

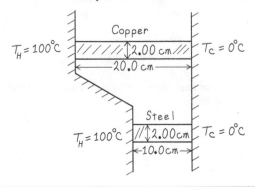

EXECUTE: We write the heat currents for the two rods individually, and then add them to get the total heat current:

$$H = H_S + H_{Cu} = k_S A \frac{T_H - T_C}{L_S} + k_{Cu} A \frac{T_H - T_C}{L_{Cu}}$$

$$= (50.2 \text{ W/m} \cdot \text{K})(0.0200 \text{ m})^2 \frac{100 \text{ K}}{0.100 \text{ m}}$$

$$+ (385 \text{ W/m} \cdot \text{K})(0.0200 \text{ m})^2 \frac{100 \text{ K}}{0.200 \text{ m}}$$

$$= 20.1 \text{ W} + 77.0 \text{ W} = 97.1 \text{ W}$$

EVALUATE: The heat flow in the copper bar is much greater than that in the steel bar, even though it is longer, because the thermal conductivity of copper is much larger. The total heat flow is greater than in Example 17.12 because the total cross section for heat flow is greater and because the full 100-K temperature difference appears across each bar.

Convection

DEMO

Convection is the transfer of heat by mass motion of a fluid from one region of space to another. Familiar examples include hot-air and hot-water home heating systems, the cooling system of an automobile engine, and the flow of blood in the body. If the fluid is circulated by a blower or pump, the process is called *forced convection;* if the flow is caused by differences in density due to thermal expansion, such as hot air rising, the process is called *free convection* (**Fig. 17.28**).

Free convection in the atmosphere plays a dominant role in determining the daily weather, and convection in the oceans is an important global heat-transfer mechanism. On a smaller scale, soaring hawks and glider pilots make use of thermal updrafts from the warm earth. The most important mechanism for heat transfer within the human body (needed to maintain nearly constant temperature in various environments) is *forced* convection of blood, with the heart as the pump.

Convective heat transfer is a very complex process, and there is no simple equation to describe it. Here are a few experimental facts:

1. The heat current due to convection is directly proportional to the surface area. That's why radiators and cooling fins, which use convection to transfer heat, have large surface areas.

2. The viscosity of fluids slows natural convection near a stationary surface, giving a surface film that on a vertical surface typically has about the same insulating value as 1.3 cm of plywood (R value = 0.7). Forced convection decreases the thickness of this film, increasing the rate of heat transfer. This is the reason for the "wind-chill factor"; you get cold faster in a cold wind than in still air with the same temperature.

3. The heat current due to convection is found to be approximately proportional to the $\frac{5}{4}$ power of the temperature difference between the surface and the main body of fluid.

17.28 A heating element in the tip of this submerged tube warms the surrounding water, producing a complex pattern of free convection.

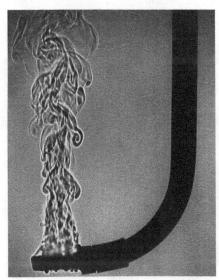

Radiation

Radiation is the transfer of heat by electromagnetic waves such as visible light, infrared, and ultraviolet radiation. Everyone has felt the warmth of the sun's radiation and the intense heat from a charcoal grill or the glowing coals in a fireplace. Most of the heat from these very hot bodies reaches you not by conduction or convection in the intervening air but by *radiation*. This heat transfer would occur even if there were nothing but vacuum between you and the source of heat.

Every body, even at ordinary temperatures, emits energy in the form of electromagnetic radiation. Around 20°C, nearly all the energy is carried by infrared waves with wavelengths much longer than those of visible light (see Fig. 17.4 and **Fig. 17.29**). As the temperature rises, the wavelengths shift to shorter values. At 800°C, a body emits enough visible radiation to appear "red-hot," although even at this temperature most of the energy is carried by infrared waves. At 3000°C, the temperature of an incandescent lamp filament, the radiation contains enough visible light that the body appears "white-hot."

The rate of energy radiation from a surface is proportional to the surface area A and to the fourth power of the absolute (Kelvin) temperature T. The rate also depends on the nature of the surface; we describe this dependence by a quantity e called **emissivity.** A dimensionless number between 0 and 1, e is the ratio of the rate of radiation from a particular surface to the rate of radiation from an equal area of an ideal radiating surface at the same temperature. Emissivity also depends somewhat on temperature. Thus we can express the heat current $H = dQ/dt$ due to radiation from a surface as

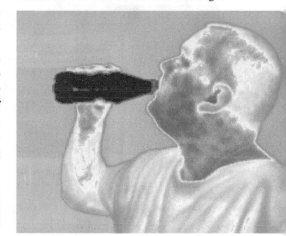

17.29 This false-color infrared photograph reveals radiation emitted by various parts of the man's body. The strongest emission (colored red) comes from the warmest areas, while there is very little emission from the bottle of cold beverage.

$$\underset{\substack{\text{Heat current}\\ \text{in radiation}}}{} \quad \overset{\substack{\text{Area of emitting surface}}}{} \quad H = Ae\sigma T^4 \quad \overset{\substack{\text{Emissivity of surface}}}{} \quad \underset{\substack{\text{of surface}}}{\overset{\substack{\text{Absolute temperature}}}{}} \qquad (17.25)$$

Stefan–Boltzmann constant

This relationship is called the **Stefan–Boltzmann law** in honor of its late-19th-century discoverers. The **Stefan–Boltzmann constant** σ (Greek sigma) is a fundamental constant; its current best numerical value is

$$\sigma = 5.670373(21) \times 10^{-8} \text{ W/m}^2 \cdot \text{K}^4$$

You should check unit consistency in Eq. (17.25). Emissivity (e) is often larger for dark surfaces than for light ones. The emissivity of a smooth copper surface is about 0.3, but e for a dull black surface can be close to unity.

EXAMPLE 17.14   HEAT TRANSFER BY RADIATION

A thin, square steel plate, 10 cm on a side, is heated in a blacksmith's forge to 800°C. If the emissivity is 0.60, what is the total rate of radiation of energy from the plate?

SOLUTION

IDENTIFY and SET UP: The target variable is H, the rate of emission of energy from the plate's two surfaces. We use Eq. (17.25) to calculate H.

EXECUTE: The total surface area is $2(0.10 \text{ m})^2 = 0.020 \text{ m}^2$, and $T = 800°C = 1073$ K. Then Eq. (17.25) gives

$$H = Ae\sigma T^4$$
$$= (0.020 \text{ m}^2)(0.60)(5.67 \times 10^{-8} \text{ W/m}^2 \cdot \text{K}^4)(1073 \text{ K})^4$$
$$= 900 \text{ W}$$

EVALUATE: The nearby blacksmith will easily feel the heat radiated from this plate.

Radiation and Absorption

While a body at absolute temperature T is radiating, its surroundings at temperature T_s are also radiating, and the body *absorbs* some of this radiation. If it is in thermal equilibrium with its surroundings, $T = T_s$ and the rates of radiation and absorption must be equal. For this to be true, the rate of absorption must be given in general by $H = Ae\sigma T_s^4$. Then the *net* rate of radiation from a body at temperature T with surroundings at temperature T_s is $Ae\sigma T^4 - Ae\sigma T_s^4$, or

Net heat current in radiation
Area of emitting surface ⋯⋯⋯ Emissivity of surface
$$H_{net} = Ae\sigma(T^4 - T_s^4)$$ (17.26)
Stefan–Boltzmann constant
Absolute temperatures of surface (T) and surroundings (T_s)

In Eq. (17.26) a positive value of H means a net heat flow *out of* the body. This will be the case if $T > T_s$.

EXAMPLE 17.15 RADIATION FROM THE HUMAN BODY

What is the total rate of radiation of energy from a human body with surface area 1.20 m^2 and surface temperature $30°C = 303 \text{ K}$? If the surroundings are at a temperature of $20°C$, what is the *net* rate of radiative heat loss from the body? The emissivity of the human body is very close to unity, irrespective of skin pigmentation.

SOLUTION

IDENTIFY and SET UP: We must consider both the radiation that the body emits and the radiation that it absorbs from its surroundings. Equation (17.25) gives the rate of radiation of energy from the body, and Eq. (17.26) gives the net rate of heat loss.

EXECUTE: Taking $e = 1$ in Eq. (17.25), we find that the body radiates at a rate

$$H = Ae\sigma T^4$$
$$= (1.20 \text{ m}^2)(1)(5.67 \times 10^{-8} \text{ W/m}^2 \cdot \text{K}^4)(303 \text{ K})^4 = 574 \text{ W}$$

This loss is partly offset by absorption of radiation, which depends on the temperature of the surroundings. From Eq. (17.26), the *net* rate of radiative energy transfer is

$$H_{net} = Ae\sigma(T^4 - T_s^4)$$
$$= (1.20 \text{ m}^2)(1)(5.67 \times 10^{-8} \text{ W/m}^2 \cdot \text{K}^4)$$
$$\times [(303 \text{ K}) - (293 \text{ K})^4]$$
$$= 72 \text{ W}$$

EVALUATE: The value of H_{net} is positive because the body is losing heat to its colder surroundings.

Applications of Radiation

Heat transfer by radiation is important in some surprising places. A premature baby in an incubator can be cooled dangerously by radiation if the walls of the incubator happen to be cold, even when the *air* in the incubator is warm. Some incubators regulate the air temperature by measuring the baby's skin temperature.

A body that is a good absorber must also be a good emitter. An ideal radiator, with emissivity $e = 1$, is also an ideal absorber, absorbing *all* of the radiation that strikes it. Such an ideal surface is called an ideal black body or simply a **blackbody.** Conversely, an ideal *reflector*, which absorbs *no* radiation at all, is also a very ineffective radiator.

This is the reason for the silver coatings on vacuum ("Thermos") bottles, invented by Sir James Dewar (1842–1923). A vacuum bottle has double glass walls. The air is pumped out of the spaces between the walls; this eliminates nearly all heat transfer by conduction and convection. The silver coating on the walls reflects most of the radiation from the contents back into the container, and the wall itself is a very poor emitter. Thus a vacuum bottle can keep coffee or soup hot for several hours. The Dewar flask, used to store very cold liquefied gases, is exactly the same in principle.

Radiation, Climate, and Climate Change

Our planet constantly absorbs radiation coming from the sun. In thermal equilibrium, the rate at which our planet absorbs solar radiation must equal the rate at which it emits radiation into space. The presence of an atmosphere on our planet has a significant effect on this equilibrium.

Most of the radiation emitted by the sun (which has a surface temperature of 5800 K) is in the visible part of the spectrum, to which our atmosphere is transparent. But the average surface temperature of the earth is only 287 K (14°C). Hence most of the radiation that our planet emits into space is infrared radiation, just like the radiation from the person shown in Fig. 17.29. However, our atmosphere is *not* completely transparent to infrared radiation. This is because our atmosphere contains carbon dioxide (CO_2), which is its fourth most abundant constituent (after nitrogen, oxygen, and argon). Molecules of CO_2 in the atmosphere *absorb* some of the infrared radiation coming upward from the surface. They then re-radiate the absorbed energy, but some of the re-radiated energy is directed back down toward the surface instead of escaping into space. In order to maintain thermal equilibrium, the earth's surface must compensate for this by increasing its temperature T and hence its total rate of radiating energy (which is proportional to T^4). This phenomenon, called the **greenhouse effect,** makes our planet's surface temperature about 33°C higher than it would be if there were no atmospheric CO_2. If CO_2 were absent, the earth's average surface temperature would be below the freezing point of water, and life as we know it would be impossible.

While atmospheric CO_2 has benefits, too much of it can have extremely negative consequences. Measurements of air trapped in ancient Antarctic ice show that over the past 650,000 years CO_2 has constituted less than 300 parts per million of our atmosphere. Since the beginning of the industrial age, however, the burning of fossil fuels such as coal and petroleum has elevated the atmospheric CO_2 concentration to unprecedented levels (**Fig. 17.30a**). As a consequence, since the 1950s the global average surface temperature has increased by 0.6°C and the earth has experienced the hottest years ever recorded (Fig. 17.30b). If we continue to consume fossil fuels at the same rate, by 2050 the atmospheric CO_2 concentration will reach 600 parts per million, well off the scale of Fig. 17.30a. The resulting temperature increase will have dramatic effects on global climate. In polar regions massive quantities of ice will melt and run from solid land to the sea, thus raising ocean levels worldwide and threatening the homes and lives of hundreds of millions of people who live near the coast. Coping with these threats is one of the greatest challenges facing 21st-century civilization.

PhET: The Greenhouse Effect

TEST YOUR UNDERSTANDING OF SECTION 17.7 A room has one wall made of concrete, one wall made of copper, and one wall made of steel. All of the walls are the same size and at the same temperature of 20°C. Which wall feels coldest to the touch? (i) The concrete wall; (ii) the copper wall; (iii) the steel wall; (iv) all three walls feel equally cold. ∎

17.30 (a) Due to humans burning fossil fuels, the concentration of carbon dioxide in the atmosphere is now more than 33% greater than in the pre-industrial era. (b) Due to the increased CO_2 concentration, during the past 50 years the global average temperature has increased at an average rate of approximately 0.13 C° per decade.

(a)

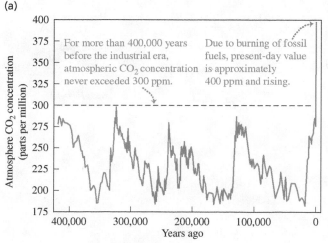

(b)

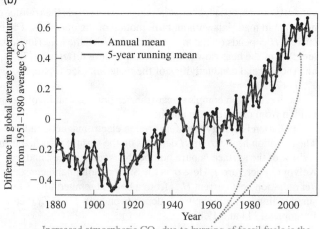

Increased atmospheric CO_2 due to burning of fossil fuels is the cause of this continuing increase in global average temperatures.

Temperature and temperature scales: Two bodies in thermal equilibrium must have the same temperature. A conducting material between two bodies permits them to interact and come to thermal equilibrium; an insulating material impedes this interaction.

The Celsius and Fahrenheit temperature scales are based on the freezing ($0°C = 32°F$) and boiling ($100°C = 212°F$) temperatures of water. One Celsius degree equals $\frac{9}{5}$ Fahrenheit degrees. (See Example 17.1.)

The Kelvin scale has its zero at the extrapolated zero-pressure temperature for a gas thermometer, $-273.15°C = 0$ K. In the gas-thermometer scale, the ratio of two temperatures T_1 and T_2 is defined to be equal to the ratio of the two corresponding gas-thermometer pressures p_1 and p_2.

$$T_F = \frac{9}{5}T_C + 32° \quad (17.1)$$

$$T_C = \frac{5}{9}(T_F - 32°) \quad (17.2)$$

$$T_K = T_C + 273.15 \quad (17.3)$$

$$\frac{T_2}{T_1} = \frac{p_2}{p_1} \quad (17.4)$$

If systems A and B are each in thermal equilibrium with system C ...

... then systems A and B are in thermal equilibrium with each other.

Thermal expansion and thermal stress: A temperature change ΔT causes a change in any linear dimension L_0 of a solid body. The change ΔL is approximately proportional to L_0 and ΔT. Similarly, a temperature change causes a change ΔV in the volume V_0 of any solid or liquid; ΔV is approximately proportional to V_0 and ΔT. The quantities α and β are the coefficients of linear expansion and volume expansion, respectively. For solids, $\beta = 3\alpha$. (See Examples 17.2 and 17.3.)

When a material is cooled or heated and held so it cannot contract or expand, it is under a tensile stress F/A. (See Example 17.4.)

$$\Delta L = \alpha L_0 \Delta T \quad (17.6)$$

$$\Delta V = \beta V_0 \Delta T \quad (17.8)$$

$$\frac{F}{A} = -Y\alpha \Delta T \quad (17.12)$$

$$L = L_0 + \Delta L$$
$$= L_0(1 + \alpha \Delta T)$$

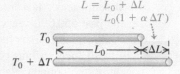

Heat, phase changes, and calorimetry: Heat is energy in transit from one body to another as a result of a temperature difference. Equations (17.13) and (17.18) give the quantity of heat Q required to cause a temperature change ΔT in a quantity of material with mass m and specific heat c (alternatively, with number of moles n and molar heat capacity $C = Mc$, where M is the molar mass and $m = nM$). When heat is added to a body, Q is positive; when it is removed, Q is negative. (See Examples 17.5 and 17.6.)

To change a mass m of a material to a different phase at the same temperature (such as liquid to vapor), a quantity of heat given by Eq. (17.20) must be added or subtracted. Here L is the heat of fusion, vaporization, or sublimation.

In an isolated system whose parts interact by heat exchange, the algebraic sum of the Q's for all parts of the system must be zero. (See Examples 17.7–17.10.)

$$Q = mc \Delta T \quad (17.13)$$

$$Q = nC \Delta T \quad (17.18)$$

$$Q = \pm mL \quad (17.20)$$

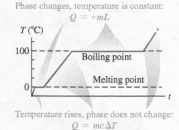

Phase changes, temperature is constant:
$Q = +mL$

Temperature rises, phase does not change:
$Q = mc \Delta T$

Conduction, convection, and radiation: Conduction is the transfer of heat within materials without bulk motion of the materials. The heat current H depends on the area A through which the heat flows, the length L of the heat-flow path, the temperature difference $(T_H - T_C)$, and the thermal conductivity k of the material. (See Examples 17.11–17.13.)

Convection is a complex heat-transfer process that involves mass motion from one region to another.

Radiation is energy transfer through electromagnetic radiation. The radiation heat current H depends on the surface area A, the emissivity e of the surface (a pure number between 0 and 1), and the Kelvin temperature T. Here σ is the Stefan–Boltzmann constant. The *net* radiation heat current H_{net} from a body at temperature T to its surroundings at temperature T_s depends on both T and T_s. (See Examples 17.14 and 17.15.)

$$H = \frac{dQ}{dt} = kA\frac{T_H - T_C}{L} \quad (17.21)$$

$$H = Ae\sigma T^4 \quad (17.25)$$

$$H_{net} = Ae\sigma(T^4 - T_s^4) \quad (17.26)$$

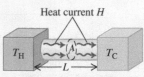

Heat current H

Heat current $H = kA\dfrac{T_H - T_C}{L}$

BRIDGING PROBLEM STEADY-STATE HEAT FLOW: RADIATION AND CONDUCTION

One end of a solid cylindrical copper rod 0.200 m long and 0.0250 m in radius is inserted into a large block of solid hydrogen at its melting temperature, 13.84 K. The other end is blackened and exposed to thermal radiation from surrounding walls at 500.0 K. (Some telescopes in space employ a similar setup. A solid refrigerant keeps the telescope very cold—required for proper operation—even though it is exposed to direct sunlight.) The sides of the rod are insulated, so no energy is lost or gained except at the ends of the rod. (a) When equilibrium is reached, what is the temperature of the blackened end? The thermal conductivity of copper at temperatures near 20 K is 1670 $W/m \cdot K$. b) At what rate (in kg/h) does the solid hydrogen melt?

SOLUTION GUIDE

IDENTIFY and SET UP

1. Draw a sketch of the situation, showing all relevant dimensions.
2. List the known and unknown quantities, and identify the target variables.
3. In order for the rod to be in equilibrium, how must the radiation heat current from the walls into the blackened end of the rod compare to the conduction heat current from this end to the other end and into the solid hydrogen? Use your answers to select the appropriate equations for part (a).
4. How does the heat current from the rod into the hydrogen determine the rate at which the hydrogen melts? (*Hint:* See Table 17.4.) Use your answer to select the appropriate equations for part (b).

EXECUTE

5. Solve for the temperature of the blackened end of the rod. (*Hint:* Since copper is an excellent conductor of heat at low temperature, you can assume that the temperature of the blackened end is only slightly higher than 13.84 K.)
6. Use your result from step 5 to find the rate at which the hydrogen melts.

EVALUATE

7. Is your result from step 5 consistent with the hint in that step?
8. How would your results from steps 5 and 6 be affected if the rod had twice the radius?

Problems For assigned homework and other learning materials, go to MasteringPhysics®. **MP**

•, ••, •••: Difficulty levels. **CP**: Cumulative problems incorporating material from earlier chapters. **CALC**: Problems requiring calculus. **DATA**: Problems involving real data, scientific evidence, experimental design, and/or statistical reasoning. **BIO**: Biosciences problems.

DISCUSSION QUESTIONS

Q17.1 Explain why it would not make sense to use a full-size glass thermometer to measure the temperature of a thimbleful of hot water.

Q17.2 If you heat the air inside a rigid, sealed container until its Kelvin temperature doubles, the air pressure in the container will also double. Is the same thing true if you double the Celsius temperature of the air in the container? Explain.

Q17.3 Many automobile engines have cast-iron cylinders and aluminum pistons. What kinds of problems could occur if the engine gets too hot? (The coefficient of volume expansion of cast iron is approximately the same as that of steel.)

Q17.4 Why do frozen water pipes burst? Would a mercury thermometer break if the temperature went below the freezing temperature of mercury? Why or why not?

Q17.5 Two bodies made of the same material have the same external dimensions and appearance, but one is solid and the other is hollow. When their temperature is increased, is the overall volume expansion the same or different? Why?

Q17.6 Why is it sometimes possible to loosen caps on screw-top bottles by dipping the capped bottle briefly into hot water?

Q17.7 The inside of an oven is at a temperature of 200°C (392°F). You can put your hand in the oven without injury as long as you don't touch anything. But since the air inside the oven is also at 200°C, why isn't your hand burned just the same?

Q17.8 A newspaper article about the weather states that "the temperature of a body measures how much heat the body contains." Is this description correct? Why or why not?

Q17.9 A student asserts that a suitable unit for specific heat is 1 $m^2/s^2 \cdot C°$. Is she correct? Why or why not?

Q17.10 In some household air conditioners used in dry climates, air is cooled by blowing it through a water-soaked filter, evaporating some of the water. How does this cool the air? Would such a system work well in a high-humidity climate? Why or why not?

Q17.11 The units of specific heat c are $J/kg \cdot K$, but the units of heat of fusion L_f or heat of vaporization L_v are simply J/kg. Why do the units of L_f and L_v not include a factor of $(K)^{-1}$ to account for a temperature change?

Q17.12 Why is a hot, humid day in the tropics generally more uncomfortable for human beings than a hot, dry day in the desert?

Q17.13 A piece of aluminum foil used to wrap a potato for baking in a hot oven can usually be handled safely within a few seconds after the potato is removed from the oven. The same is not true of the potato, however! Give two reasons for this difference.

Q17.14 Desert travelers sometimes keep water in a canvas bag. Some water seeps through the bag and evaporates. How does this cool the water inside the bag?

Q17.15 When you first step out of the shower, you feel cold. But as soon as you are dry you feel warmer, even though the room temperature does not change. Why?

Q17.16 The climate of regions adjacent to large bodies of water (like the Pacific and Atlantic coasts) usually features a narrower range of temperature than the climate of regions far from large bodies of water (like the prairies). Why?

Q17.17 When water is placed in ice-cube trays in a freezer, why doesn't the water freeze all at once when the temperature has reached 0°C? In fact, the water freezes first in a layer adjacent to the sides of the tray. Why?

Q17.18 Before giving you an injection, a physician swabs your arm with isopropyl alcohol at room temperature. Why does this make your arm feel cold? (*Hint:* The reason is *not* the fear of the injection! The boiling point of isopropyl alcohol is 82.4°C.)

Q17.19 A cold block of metal feels colder than a block of wood at the same temperature. Why? A *hot* block of metal feels hotter than a block of wood at the same temperature. Again, why? Is there any temperature at which the two blocks feel equally hot or cold? What temperature is this?

Q17.20 A person pours a cup of hot coffee, intending to drink it five minutes later. To keep the coffee as hot as possible, should she put cream in it now or wait until just before she drinks it? Explain.

Q17.21 When a freshly baked apple pie has just been removed from the oven, the crust and filling are both at the same temperature. Yet if you sample the pie, the filling will burn your tongue but the crust will not. Why is there a difference? (*Hint:* The filling is moist while the crust is dry.)

Q17.22 Old-time kitchen lore suggests that things cook better (evenly and without burning) in heavy cast-iron pots. What desirable characteristics do such pots have?

Q17.23 In coastal regions in the winter, the temperature over the land is generally colder than the temperature over the nearby ocean; in the summer, the reverse is usually true. Explain. (*Hint:* The specific heat of soil is only 0.2–0.8 times as great as that of water.)

Q17.24 It is well known that a potato bakes faster if a large nail is stuck through it. Why? Does an aluminum nail work better than a steel one? Why or why not? (*Note:* Don't try this in a microwave oven!) There is also a gadget on the market to hasten the roasting of meat; it consists of a hollow metal tube containing a wick and some water. This is claimed to work much better than a solid metal rod. How does it work?

Q17.25 Glider pilots in the Midwest know that thermal updrafts are likely to occur in the vicinity of freshly plowed fields. Why?

Q17.26 Some folks claim that ice cubes freeze faster if the trays are filled with hot water, because hot water cools off faster than cold water. What do you think?

Q17.27 We're lucky that the earth isn't in thermal equilibrium with the sun (which has a surface temperature of 5800 K). But why aren't the two bodies in thermal equilibrium?

Q17.28 When energy shortages occur, magazine articles sometimes urge us to keep our homes at a constant temperature day and night to conserve fuel. They argue that when we turn down the heat at night, the walls, ceilings, and other areas cool off and must be reheated in the morning. So if we keep the temperature constant, these parts of the house will not cool off and will not have to be reheated. Does this argument make sense? Would we really save energy by following this advice?

EXERCISES

Section 17.2 Thermometers and Temperature Scales

17.1 • Convert the following Celsius temperatures to Fahrenheit: (a) −62.8°C, the lowest temperature ever recorded in North America (February 3, 1947, Snag, Yukon); (b) 56.7°C, the highest temperature

ever recorded in the United States (July 10, 1913, Death Valley, California); (c) 31.1°C, the world's highest average annual temperature (Lugh Ferrandi, Somalia).

17.2 • BIO **Temperatures in Biomedicine.** (a) **Normal body temperature.** The average normal body temperature measured in the mouth is 310 K. What would Celsius and Fahrenheit thermometers read for this temperature? (b) **Elevated body temperature.** During very vigorous exercise, the body's temperature can go as high as 40°C. What would Kelvin and Fahrenheit thermometers read for this temperature? (c) **Temperature difference in the body.** The surface temperature of the body is normally about 7 C° lower than the internal temperature. Express this temperature difference in kelvins and in Fahrenheit degrees. (d) **Blood storage.** Blood stored at 4.0°C lasts safely for about 3 weeks, whereas blood stored at −160°C lasts for 5 years. Express both temperatures on the Fahrenheit and Kelvin scales. (e) **Heat stroke.** If the body's temperature is above 105°F for a prolonged period, heat stroke can result. Express this temperature on the Celsius and Kelvin scales.

17.3 • (a) On January 22, 1943, the temperature in Spearfish, South Dakota, rose from −4.0°F to 45.0°F in just 2 minutes. What was the temperature change in Celsius degrees? (b) The temperature in Browning, Montana, was 44.0°F on January 23, 1916. The next day the temperature plummeted to −56°F. What was the temperature change in Celsius degrees?

Section 17.3 Gas Thermometers and the Kelvin Scale

17.4 • (a) Calculate the one temperature at which Fahrenheit and Celsius thermometers agree with each other. (b) Calculate the one temperature at which Fahrenheit and Kelvin thermometers agree with each other.

17.5 •• You put a bottle of soft drink in a refrigerator and leave it until its temperature has dropped 10.0 K. What is its temperature change in (a) F° and (b) C°?

17.6 • Convert the following Kelvin temperatures to the Celsius and Fahrenheit scales: (a) the midday temperature at the surface of the moon (400 K); (b) the temperature at the tops of the clouds in the atmosphere of Saturn (95 K); (c) the temperature at the center of the sun (1.55×10^7 K).

17.7 • The pressure of a gas at the triple point of water is 1.35 atm. If its volume remains unchanged, what will its pressure be at the temperature at which CO_2 solidifies?

17.8 •• A constant-volume gas thermometer registers an absolute pressure corresponding to 325 mm of mercury when in contact with water at the triple point. What pressure does it read when in contact with water at the normal boiling point?

17.9 •• **A Constant-Volume Gas Thermometer.** An experimenter using a gas thermometer found the pressure at the triple point of water (0.01°C) to be 4.80×10^4 Pa and the pressure at the normal boiling point (100°C) to be 6.50×10^4 Pa. (a) Assuming that the pressure varies linearly with temperature, use these two data points to find the Celsius temperature at which the gas pressure would be zero (that is, find the Celsius temperature of absolute zero). (b) Does the gas in this thermometer obey Eq. (17.4) precisely? If that equation were precisely obeyed and the pressure at 100°C were 6.50×10^4 Pa, what pressure would the experimenter have measured at 0.01°C? (As we will learn in Section 18.1, Eq. (17.4) is accurate only for gases at very low density.)

17.10 • Like the Kelvin scale, the *Rankine scale* is an absolute temperature scale: Absolute zero is zero degrees Rankine (0°R). However, the units of this scale are the same size as those of the Fahrenheit scale rather than the Celsius scale. What is the numerical value of the triple-point temperature of water on the Rankine scale?

Section 17.4 Thermal Expansion

17.11 • The Humber Bridge in England has the world's longest single span, 1410 m. Calculate the change in length of the steel deck of the span when the temperature increases from $-5.0°C$ to $18.0°C$.

17.12 • One of the tallest buildings in the world is the Taipei 101 in Taiwan, at a height of 1671 feet. Assume that this height was measured on a cool spring day when the temperature was $15.5°C$. You could use the building as a sort of giant thermometer on a hot summer day by carefully measuring its height. Suppose you do this and discover that the Taipei 101 is 0.471 foot taller than its official height. What is the temperature, assuming that the building is in thermal equilibrium with the air and that its entire frame is made of steel?

17.13 • A U.S. penny has a diameter of 1.9000 cm at $20.0°C$. The coin is made of a metal alloy (mostly zinc) for which the coefficient of linear expansion is 2.6×10^{-5} K^{-1}. What would its diameter be on a hot day in Death Valley ($48.0°C$)? On a cold night in the mountains of Greenland ($-53°C$)?

17.14 • **Ensuring a Tight Fit.** Aluminum rivets used in airplane construction are made slightly larger than the rivet holes and cooled by "dry ice" (solid CO_2) before being driven. If the diameter of a hole is 4.500 mm, what should be the diameter of a rivet at $23.0°C$ if its diameter is to equal that of the hole when the rivet is cooled to $-78.0°C$, the temperature of dry ice? Assume that the expansion coefficient remains constant at the value given in Table 17.1.

17.15 •• A copper cylinder is initially at $20.0°C$. At what temperature will its volume be 0.150% larger than it is at $20.0°C$?

17.16 •• A geodesic dome constructed with an aluminum framework is a nearly perfect hemisphere; its diameter measures 55.0 m on a winter day at a temperature of $-15°C$. How much more interior space does the dome have in the summer, when the temperature is $35°C$?

17.17 •• A glass flask whose volume is 1000.00 cm^3 at $0.0°C$ is completely filled with mercury at this temperature. When flask and mercury are warmed to $55.0°C$, 8.95 cm^3 of mercury overflow. If the coefficient of volume expansion of mercury is 18.0×10^{-5} K^{-1}, compute the coefficient of volume expansion of the glass.

17.18 •• A steel tank is completely filled with 1.90 m^3 of ethanol when both the tank and the ethanol are at $32.0°C$. When the tank and its contents have cooled to $18.0°C$, what additional volume of ethanol can be put into the tank?

17.19 •• A machinist bores a hole of diameter 1.35 cm in a steel plate that is at $25.0°C$. What is the cross-sectional area of the hole (a) at $25.0°C$ and (b) when the temperature of the plate is increased to $175°C$? Assume that the coefficient of linear expansion remains constant over this temperature range.

17.20 •• As a new mechanical engineer for Engines Inc., you have been assigned to design brass pistons to slide inside steel cylinders. The engines in which these pistons will be used will operate between $20.0°C$ and $150.0°C$. Assume that the coefficients of expansion are constant over this temperature range. (a) If the piston just fits inside the chamber at $20.0°C$, will the engines be able to run at higher temperatures? Explain. (b) If the cylindrical pistons are 25.000 cm in diameter at $20.0°C$, what should be the minimum diameter of the cylinders at that temperature so the pistons will operate at $150.0°C$?

17.21 •• Steel train rails are laid in 12.0-m-long segments placed end to end. The rails are laid on a winter day when their temperature is $-9.0°C$. (a) How much space must be left between adjacent rails if they are just to touch on a summer day when their temperature is $33.0°C$? (b) If the rails are originally laid in contact, what is the stress in them on a summer day when their temperature is $33.0°C$?

17.22 •• A brass rod is 185 cm long and 1.60 cm in diameter. What force must be applied to each end of the rod to prevent it from contracting when it is cooled from $120.0°C$ to $10.0°C$?

Section 17.5 Quantity of Heat

17.23 •• An aluminum tea kettle with mass 1.10 kg and containing 1.80 kg of water is placed on a stove. If no heat is lost to the surroundings, how much heat must be added to raise the temperature from $20.0°C$ to $85.0°C$?

17.24 • In an effort to stay awake for an all-night study session, a student makes a cup of coffee by first placing a 200-W electric immersion heater in 0.320 kg of water. (a) How much heat must be added to the water to raise its temperature from $20.0°C$ to $80.0°C$? (b) How much time is required? Assume that all of the heater's power goes into heating the water.

17.25 • BIO While running, a 70-kg student generates thermal energy at a rate of 1200 W. For the runner to maintain a constant body temperature of $37°C$, this energy must be removed by perspiration or other mechanisms. If these mechanisms failed and the energy could not flow out of the student's body, for what amount of time could a student run before irreversible body damage occurred? (*Note:* Protein structures in the body are irreversibly damaged if body temperature rises to $44°C$ or higher. The specific heat of a typical human body is 3480 J/kg·K, slightly less than that of water. The difference is due to the presence of protein, fat, and minerals, which have lower specific heats.)

17.26 • BIO **Heat Loss During Breathing.** In very cold weather a significant mechanism for heat loss by the human body is energy expended in warming the air taken into the lungs with each breath. (a) On a cold winter day when the temperature is $-20°C$, what amount of heat is needed to warm to body temperature ($37°C$) the 0.50 L of air exchanged with each breath? Assume that the specific heat of air is 1020 J/kg·K and that 1.0 L of air has mass 1.3×10^{-3} kg. (b) How much heat is lost per hour if the respiration rate is 20 breaths per minute?

17.27 • You are given a sample of metal and asked to determine its specific heat. You weigh the sample and find that its weight is 28.4 N. You carefully add 1.25×10^4 J of heat energy to the sample and find that its temperature rises 18.0 C°. What is the sample's specific heat?

17.28 •• **On-Demand Water Heaters.** Conventional hot-water heaters consist of a tank of water maintained at a fixed temperature. The hot water is to be used when needed. The drawbacks are that energy is wasted because the tank loses heat when it is not in use and that you can run out of hot water if you use too much. Some utility companies are encouraging the use of *on-demand* water heaters (also known as *flash heaters*), which consist of heating units to heat the water as you use it. No water tank is involved, so no heat is wasted. A typical household shower flow rate is 2.5 gal/min (9.46 L/min) with the tap water being heated from $50°F$ ($10°C$) to $120°F$ ($49°C$) by the on-demand heater. What rate of heat input (either electrical or from gas) is required to operate such a unit, assuming that all the heat goes into the water?

17.29 • CP While painting the top of an antenna 225 m in height, a worker accidentally lets a 1.00-L water bottle fall from his lunchbox. The bottle lands in some bushes at ground level and does not break. If a quantity of heat equal to the magnitude of the change in mechanical energy of the water goes into the water, what is its increase in temperature?

17.30 • CP A 25,000-kg subway train initially traveling at 15.5 m/s slows to a stop in a station and then stays there long enough for its brakes to cool. The station's dimensions are 65.0 m long by 20.0 m wide by 12.0 m high. Assuming all the work done by the brakes in stopping the train is transferred as heat uniformly to all the air in the station, by how much does the air temperature in the station rise? Take the density of the air to be 1.20 kg/m^3 and its specific heat to be $1020 \text{ J/kg} \cdot \text{K}$.

17.31 • CP A nail driven into a board increases in temperature. If we assume that 60% of the kinetic energy delivered by a 1.80-kg hammer with a speed of 7.80 m/s is transformed into heat that flows into the nail and does not flow out, what is the temperature increase of an 8.00-g aluminum nail after it is struck ten times?

17.32 • A technician measures the specific heat of an unidentified liquid by immersing an electrical resistor in it. Electrical energy is converted to heat transferred to the liquid for 120 s at a constant rate of 65.0 W. The mass of the liquid is 0.780 kg, and its temperature increases from 18.55°C to 22.54°C. (a) Find the average specific heat of the liquid in this temperature range. Assume that negligible heat is transferred to the container that holds the liquid and that no heat is lost to the surroundings. (b) Suppose that in this experiment heat transfer from the liquid to the container or surroundings cannot be ignored. Is the result calculated in part (a) an *overestimate* or an *underestimate* of the average specific heat? Explain.

17.33 •• CP A 15.0-g bullet traveling horizontally at 865 m/s passes through a tank containing 13.5 kg of water and emerges with a speed of 534 m/s. What is the maximum temperature increase that the water could have as a result of this event?

Section 17.6 Calorimetry and Phase Changes

17.34 • You have 750 g of water at 10.0°C in a large insulated beaker. How much boiling water at 100.0°C must you add to this beaker so that the final temperature of the mixture will be 75°C?

17.35 •• A 500.0-g chunk of an unknown metal, which has been in boiling water for several minutes, is quickly dropped into an insulating Styrofoam beaker containing 1.00 kg of water at room temperature (20.0°C). After waiting and gently stirring for 5.00 minutes, you observe that the water's temperature has reached a constant value of 22.0°C. (a) Assuming that the Styrofoam absorbs a negligibly small amount of heat and that no heat was lost to the surroundings, what is the specific heat of the metal? (b) Which is more useful for storing thermal energy: this metal or an equal weight of water? Explain. (c) If the heat absorbed by the Styrofoam actually is not negligible, how would the specific heat you calculated in part (a) be in error? Would it be too large, too small, or still correct? Explain.

17.36 • BIO **Treatment for a Stroke.** One suggested treatment for a person who has suffered a stroke is immersion in an ice-water bath at 0°C to lower the body temperature, which prevents damage to the brain. In one set of tests, patients were cooled until their internal temperature reached 32.0°C. To treat a 70.0-kg patient, what is the minimum amount of ice (at 0°C) you need in the bath so that its temperature remains at 0°C? The specific heat of the human body is $3480 \text{ J/kg} \cdot \text{C°}$, and recall that normal body temperature is 37.0°C.

17.37 •• A blacksmith cools a 1.20-kg chunk of iron, initially at 650.0°C, by trickling 15.0°C water over it. All of the water boils away, and the iron ends up at 120.0°C. How much water did the blacksmith trickle over the iron?

17.38 •• A copper calorimeter can with mass 0.100 kg contains 0.160 kg of water and 0.0180 kg of ice in thermal equilibrium at atmospheric pressure. If 0.750 kg of lead at 255°C is dropped into the calorimeter can, what is the final temperature? Assume that no heat is lost to the surroundings.

17.39 •• A copper pot with a mass of 0.500 kg contains 0.170 kg of water, and both are at 20.0°C. A 0.250-kg block of iron at 85.0°C is dropped into the pot. Find the final temperature of the system, assuming no heat loss to the surroundings.

17.40 • In a container of negligible mass, 0.200 kg of ice at an initial temperature of −40.0°C is mixed with a mass m of water that has an initial temperature of 80.0°C. No heat is lost to the surroundings. If the final temperature of the system is 28.0°C, what is the mass m of the water that was initially at 80.0°C?

17.41 • A 6.00-kg piece of solid copper metal at an initial temperature T is placed with 2.00 kg of ice that is initially at −20.0°C. The ice is in an insulated container of negligible mass and no heat is exchanged with the surroundings. After thermal equilibrium is reached, there is 1.20 kg of ice and 0.80 kg of liquid water. What was the initial temperature of the piece of copper?

17.42 • BIO Before going in for his annual physical, a 70.0-kg man whose body temperature is 37.0°C consumes an entire 0.355-L can of a soft drink (mostly water) at 12.0°C. (a) What will his body temperature be after equilibrium is attained? Ignore any heating by the man's metabolism. The specific heat of the man's body is $3480 \text{ J/kg} \cdot \text{K}$. (b) Is the change in his body temperature great enough to be measured by a medical thermometer?

17.43 •• BIO **Basal Metabolic Rate.** In the situation described in Exercise 17.42, the man's metabolism will eventually return the temperature of his body (and of the soft drink that he consumed) to 37.0°C. If his body releases energy at a rate of $7.00 \times 10^3 \text{ kJ/day}$ (the *basal metabolic rate*, or BMR), how long does this take? Assume that all of the released energy goes into raising the temperature.

17.44 •• An ice-cube tray of negligible mass contains 0.290 kg of water at 18.0°C. How much heat must be removed to cool the water to 0.00°C and freeze it? Express your answer in joules, calories, and Btu.

17.45 • How much heat is required to convert 18.0 g of ice at −10.0°C to steam at 100.0°C? Express your answer in joules, calories, and Btu.

17.46 •• An open container holds 0.550 kg of ice at −15.0°C. The mass of the container can be ignored. Heat is supplied to the container at the constant rate of 800.0 J/min for 500.0 min. (a) After how many minutes does the ice *start* to melt? (b) After how many minutes, from the time when the heating is first started, does the temperature begin to rise above 0.0°C? (c) Plot a curve showing the temperature as a function of the elapsed time.

17.47 • CP What must the initial speed of a lead bullet be at 25.0°C so that the heat developed when it is brought to rest will be just sufficient to melt it? Assume that all the initial mechanical energy of the bullet is converted to heat and that no heat flows from the bullet to its surroundings. (Typical rifles have muzzle speeds that exceed the speed of sound in air, which is 347 m/s at 25.0°C.)

17.48 •• BIO **Steam Burns Versus Water Burns.** What is the amount of heat input to your skin when it receives the heat released (a) by 25.0 g of steam initially at 100.0°C, when it is cooled to skin temperature (34.0°C)? (b) By 25.0 g of water initially at 100.0°C, when it is cooled to 34.0°C? (c) What does this tell you about the relative severity of burns from steam versus burns from hot water?

17.49 • BIO **"The Ship of the Desert."** Camels require very little water because they are able to tolerate relatively large changes in their body temperature. While humans keep their body temperatures constant to within one or two Celsius degrees, a dehydrated camel permits its body temperature to drop to 34.0°C overnight and rise to 40.0°C during the day. To see how effective this mechanism is for saving water, calculate how many liters of water a 400-kg camel would have to drink if it attempted to keep its body temperature at a constant 34.0°C by evaporation of sweat during the day (12 hours) instead of letting it rise to 40.0°C. (*Note:* The specific heat of a camel or other mammal is about the same as that of a typical human, 3480 J/kg · K. The heat of vaporization of water at 34°C is 2.42×10^6 J/kg.)

17.50 • BIO Evaporation of sweat is an important mechanism for temperature control in some warm-blooded animals. (a) What mass of water must evaporate from the skin of a 70.0-kg man to cool his body 1.00 C°? The heat of vaporization of water at body temperature (37°C) is 2.42×10^6 J/kg. The specific heat of a typical human body is 3480 J/kg · K (see Exercise 17.25). (b) What volume of water must the man drink to replenish the evaporated water? Compare to the volume of a soft-drink can (355 cm^3).

17.51 •• CP An asteroid with a diameter of 10 km and a mass of 2.60×10^{15} kg impacts the earth at a speed of 32.0 km/s, landing in the Pacific Ocean. If 1.00% of the asteroid's kinetic energy goes to boiling the ocean water (assume an initial water temperature of 10.0°C), what mass of water will be boiled away by the collision? (For comparison, the mass of water contained in Lake Superior is about 2×10^{15} kg.)

17.52 • A laboratory technician drops a 0.0850-kg sample of unknown solid material, at 100.0°C, into a calorimeter. The calorimeter can, initially at 19.0°C, is made of 0.150 kg of copper and contains 0.200 kg of water. The final temperature of the calorimeter can and contents is 26.1°C. Compute the specific heat of the sample.

17.53 •• An insulated beaker with negligible mass contains 0.250 kg of water at 75.0°C. How many kilograms of ice at −20.0°C must be dropped into the water to make the final temperature of the system 40.0°C?

17.54 • A 4.00-kg silver ingot is taken from a furnace, where its temperature is 750.0°C, and placed on a large block of ice at 0.0°C. Assuming that all the heat given up by the silver is used to melt the ice, how much ice is melted?

17.55 •• A vessel whose walls are thermally insulated contains 2.40 kg of water and 0.450 kg of ice, all at 0.0°C. The outlet of a tube leading from a boiler in which water is boiling at atmospheric pressure is inserted into the water. How many grams of steam must condense inside the vessel (also at atmospheric pressure) to raise the temperature of the system to 28.0°C? You can ignore the heat transferred to the container.

Section 17.7 Mechanisms of Heat Transfer

17.56 •• Two rods, one made of brass and the other made of copper, are joined end to end. The length of the brass section is 0.300 m and the length of the copper section is 0.800 m. Each segment has cross-sectional area 0.00500 m^2. The free end of the brass segment is in boiling water and the free end of the copper segment is in an ice–water mixture, in both cases under normal atmospheric pressure. The sides of the rods are insulated so there is no heat loss to the surroundings. (a) What is the temperature of the point where the brass and copper segments are joined? (b) What mass of ice is melted in 5.00 min by the heat conducted by the composite rod?

17.57 • Suppose that the rod in Fig. 17.24a is made of copper, is 45.0 cm long, and has a cross-sectional area of 1.25 cm^2. Let $T_H = 100.0°C$ and $T_C = 0.0°C$. (a) What is the final steady-state temperature gradient along the rod? (b) What is the heat current in the rod in the final steady state? (c) What is the final steady-state temperature at a point in the rod 12.0 cm from its left end?

17.58 •• One end of an insulated metal rod is maintained at 100.0°C, and the other end is maintained at 0.00°C by an ice–water mixture. The rod is 60.0 cm long and has a cross-sectional area of 1.25 cm^2. The heat conducted by the rod melts 8.50 g of ice in 10.0 min. Find the thermal conductivity k of the metal.

17.59 •• A carpenter builds an exterior house wall with a layer of wood 3.0 cm thick on the outside and a layer of Styrofoam insulation 2.2 cm thick on the inside wall surface. The wood has $k = 0.080$ W/m · K, and the Styrofoam has $k = 0.027$ W/m · K. The interior surface temperature is 19.0°C, and the exterior surface temperature is −10.0°C. (a) What is the temperature at the plane where the wood meets the Styrofoam? (b) What is the rate of heat flow per square meter through this wall?

17.60 • An electric kitchen range has a total wall area of 1.40 m^2 and is insulated with a layer of fiberglass 4.00 cm thick. The inside surface of the fiberglass has a temperature of 175°C, and its outside surface is at 35.0°C. The fiberglass has a thermal conductivity of 0.040 W/m · K. (a) What is the heat current through the insulation, assuming it may be treated as a flat slab with an area of 1.40 m^2? (b) What electric-power input to the heating element is required to maintain this temperature?

17.61 • BIO **Conduction Through the Skin.** The blood plays an important role in removing heat from the body by bringing this energy directly to the surface where it can radiate away. Nevertheless, this heat must still travel through the skin before it can radiate away. Assume that the blood is brought to the bottom layer of skin at 37.0°C and that the outer surface of the skin is at 30.0°C. Skin varies in thickness from 0.50 mm to a few millimeters on the palms and soles, so assume an average thickness of 0.75 mm. A 165-lb, 6-ft-tall person has a surface area of about 2.0 m^2 and loses heat at a net rate of 75 W while resting. On the basis of our assumptions, what is the thermal conductivity of this person's skin?

17.62 • A long rod, insulated to prevent heat loss along its sides, is in perfect thermal contact with boiling water (at atmospheric pressure) at one end and with an ice–water mixture at the other (**Fig. E17.62**). The rod consists of a 1.00-m section of copper (one end in boiling water) joined end to end to a length L_2 of steel (one end in the ice–water mixture). Both sections of the rod have cross-sectional areas of 4.00 cm^2. The temperature of the copper–steel junction is 65.0°C after a steady state has been set up. (a) How much heat per second flows from the boiling water to the ice–water mixture? (b) What is the length L_2 of the steel section?

Figure **E17.62**

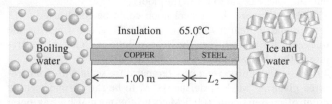

17.63 • A pot with a steel bottom 8.50 mm thick rests on a hot stove. The area of the bottom of the pot is 0.150 m^2. The water inside the pot is at 100.0°C, and 0.390 kg are evaporated every 3.00 min. Find the temperature of the lower surface of the pot, which is in contact with the stove.

17.64 •• You are asked to design a cylindrical steel rod 50.0 cm long, with a circular cross section, that will conduct 190.0 J/s from a furnace at 400.0°C to a container of boiling water under 1 atmosphere. What must the rod's diameter be?

17.65 •• A picture window has dimensions of 1.40 m × 2.50 m and is made of glass 5.20 mm thick. On a winter day, the temperature of the outside surface of the glass is −20.0°C, while the temperature of the inside surface is a comfortable 19.5°C. (a) At what rate is heat being lost through the window by conduction? (b) At what rate would heat be lost through the window if you covered it with a 0.750-mm-thick layer of paper (thermal conductivity 0.0500 W/m · K)?

17.66 • What is the rate of energy radiation per unit area of a blackbody at (a) 273 K and (b) 2730 K?

17.67 •• A spherical pot contains 0.75 L of hot coffee (essentially water) at an initial temperature of 95°C. The pot has an emissivity of 0.60, and the surroundings are at 20.0°C. Calculate the coffee's rate of heat loss by radiation.

17.68 •• The emissivity of tungsten is 0.350. A tungsten sphere with radius 1.50 cm is suspended within a large evacuated enclosure whose walls are at 290.0 K. What power input is required to maintain the sphere at 3000.0 K if heat conduction along the supports is ignored?

17.69 • **Size of a Light-Bulb Filament.** The operating temperature of a tungsten filament in an incandescent light bulb is 2450 K, and its emissivity is 0.350. Find the surface area of the filament of a 150-W bulb if all the electrical energy consumed by the bulb is radiated by the filament as electromagnetic waves. (Only a fraction of the radiation appears as visible light.)

17.70 • **The Sizes of Stars.** The hot glowing surfaces of stars emit energy in the form of electromagnetic radiation. It is a good approximation to assume $e = 1$ for these surfaces. Find the radii of the following stars (assumed to be spherical): (a) Rigel, the bright blue star in the constellation Orion, which radiates energy at a rate of 2.7×10^{32} W and has surface temperature 11,000 K; (b) Procyon B (visible only using a telescope), which radiates energy at a rate of 2.1×10^{23} W and has surface temperature 10,000 K. (c) Compare your answers to the radius of the earth, the radius of the sun, and the distance between the earth and the sun. (Rigel is an example of a *supergiant* star, and Procyon B is an example of a *white dwarf* star.)

PROBLEMS

17.71 •• CP A Foucault pendulum consists of a brass sphere with a diameter of 35.0 cm suspended from a steel cable 10.5 m long (both measurements made at 20.0°C). Due to a design oversight, the swinging sphere clears the floor by a distance of only 2.00 mm when the temperature is 20.0°C. At what temperature will the sphere begin to brush the floor?

17.72 •• Suppose that a steel hoop could be constructed to fit just around the earth's equator at 20.0°C. What would be the thickness of space between the hoop and the earth if the temperature of the hoop were increased by 0.500 C°?

17.73 ••• You propose a new temperature scale with temperatures given in °M. You define 0.0°M to be the normal melting point of mercury and 100.0°M to be the normal boiling point of mercury. (a) What is the normal boiling point of water in °M? (b) A temperature change of 10.0 M° corresponds to how many C°?

17.74 • CP CALC A 250-kg weight is hanging from the ceiling by a thin copper wire. In its fundamental mode, this wire vibrates at the frequency of concert A (440 Hz). You then increase the temperature of the wire by 40 C°. (a) By how much will the fundamental frequency change? Will it increase or decrease? (b) By what percentage will the speed of a wave on the wire change? (c) By what percentage will the wavelength of the fundamental standing wave change? Will it increase or decrease?

17.75 ••• You are making pesto for your pasta and have a cylindrical measuring cup 10.0 cm high made of ordinary glass $[\beta = 2.7 \times 10^{-5}(\text{C}°)^{-1}]$ that is filled with olive oil $[\beta = 6.8 \times 10^{-4}(\text{C}°)^{-1}]$ to a height of 3.00 mm below the top of the cup. Initially, the cup and oil are at room temperature (22.0°C). You get a phone call and forget about the olive oil, which you inadvertently leave on the hot stove. The cup and oil heat up slowly and have a common temperature. At what temperature will the olive oil start to spill out of the cup?

17.76 •• A surveyor's 30.0-m steel tape is correct at 20.0°C. The distance between two points, as measured by this tape on a day when its temperature is 5.00°C, is 25.970 m. What is the true distance between the points?

17.77 •• A metal rod that is 30.0 cm long expands by 0.0650 cm when its temperature is raised from 0.0°C to 100.0°C. A rod of a different metal and of the same length expands by 0.0350 cm for the same rise in temperature. A third rod, also 30.0 cm long, is made up of pieces of each of the above metals placed end to end and expands 0.0580 cm between 0.0°C and 100.0°C. Find the length of each portion of the composite rod.

17.78 •• On a cool (4.0°C) Saturday morning, a pilot fills the fuel tanks of her Pitts S-2C (a two-seat aerobatic airplane) to their full capacity of 106.0 L. Before flying on Sunday morning, when the temperature is again 4.0°C, she checks the fuel level and finds only 103.4 L of gasoline in the aluminum tanks. She realizes that it was hot on Saturday afternoon and that thermal expansion of the gasoline caused the missing fuel to empty out of the tank's vent. (a) What was the maximum temperature (in °C) of the fuel and the tank on Saturday afternoon? The coefficient of volume expansion of gasoline is 9.5×10^{-4} K^{-1}. (b) To have the maximum amount of fuel available for flight, when should the pilot have filled the fuel tanks?

17.79 ••• (a) Equation (17.12) gives the stress required to keep the length of a rod constant as its temperature changes. Show that if the length is permitted to change by an amount ΔL when its temperature changes by ΔT, the stress is equal to

$$\frac{F}{A} = Y\left(\frac{\Delta L}{L_0} - \alpha \Delta T\right)$$

where F is the tension on the rod, L_0 is the original length of the rod, A its cross-sectional area, α its coefficient of linear expansion, and Y its Young's modulus. (b) A heavy brass bar has projections at its ends (**Fig. P17.79**). Two fine steel wires, fastened between the projections, are just taut (zero tension) when the whole system is at 20°C. What is the tensile stress in the steel wires when the temperature of the system is raised to 140°C? Make any simplifying assumptions you think are justified, but state them.

Figure **P17.79**

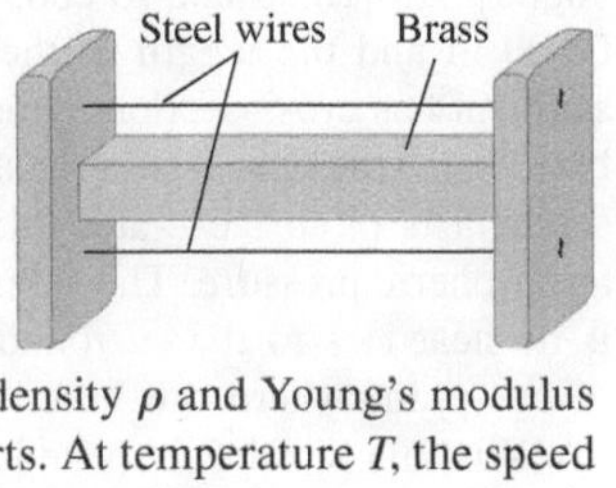

17.80 •• CP A metal wire, with density ρ and Young's modulus Y, is stretched between rigid supports. At temperature T, the speed of a transverse wave is found to be v_1. When the temperature is increased to $T + \Delta T$, the speed decreases to $v_2 < v_1$. Determine the coefficient of linear expansion of the wire.

17.81 •• A steel ring with a 2.5000-in. inside diameter at 20.0°C is to be warmed and slipped over a brass shaft with a 2.5020-in. outside diameter at 20.0°C. (a) To what temperature should the ring be warmed? (b) If the ring and the shaft together are cooled by some means such as liquid air, at what temperature will the ring just slip off the shaft?

17.82 • BIO **Doughnuts: Breakfast of Champions!** A typical doughnut contains 2.0 g of protein, 17.0 g of carbohydrates, and 7.0 g of fat. Average food energy values are 4.0 kcal/g for protein and carbohydrates and 9.0 kcal/g for fat. (a) During heavy exercise, an average person uses energy at a rate of 510 kcal/h. How long would you have to exercise to "work off" one doughnut? (b) If the energy in the doughnut could somehow be converted into the kinetic energy of your body as a whole, how fast could you move after eating the doughnut? Take your mass to be 60 kg, and express your answer in m/s and in km/h.

17.83 •• BIO **Shivering.** Shivering is your body's way of generating heat to restore its internal temperature to the normal 37°C, and it produces approximately 290 W of heat power per square meter of body area. A 68-kg, 1.78-m-tall woman has approximately 1.8 m² of surface area. How long would this woman have to shiver to raise her body temperature by 1.0 C°, assuming that the body loses none of this heat? The body's specific heat capacity is about 3500 J/kg·K.

17.84 •• You cool a 100.0-g slug of red-hot iron (temperature 745°C) by dropping it into an insulated cup of negligible mass containing 85.0 g of water at 20.0°C. Assuming no heat exchange with the surroundings, (a) what is the final temperature of the water and (b) what is the final mass of the iron and the remaining water?

17.85 •• CALC **Debye's T^3 Law.** At very low temperatures the molar heat capacity of rock salt varies with temperature according to Debye's T^3 law:

$$C = k\frac{T^3}{\theta^3}$$

where $k = 1940$ J/mol·K and $\theta = 281$ K. (a) How much heat is required to raise the temperature of 1.50 mol of rock salt from 10.0 K to 40.0 K? (*Hint:* Use Eq. (17.18) in the form $dQ = nC\,dT$ and integrate.) (b) What is the average molar heat capacity in this range? (c) What is the true molar heat capacity at 40.0 K?

17.86 •• CP A person of mass 70.0 kg is sitting in the bathtub. The bathtub is 190.0 cm by 80.0 cm; before the person got in, the water was 24.0 cm deep. The water is at 37.0°C. Suppose that the water were to cool down spontaneously to form ice at 0.0°C, and that all the energy released was used to launch the hapless bather vertically into the air. How high would the bather go? (As you will see in Chapter 20, this event is allowed by energy conservation but is prohibited by the second law of thermodynamics.)

17.87 • **Hot Air in a Physics Lecture.** (a) A typical student listening attentively to a physics lecture has a heat output of 100 W. How much heat energy does a class of 140 physics students release into a lecture hall over the course of a 50-min lecture? (b) Assume that all the heat energy in part (a) is transferred to the 3200 m³ of air in the room. The air has specific heat 1020 J/kg·K and density 1.20 kg/m³. If none of the heat escapes and the air conditioning system is off, how much will the temperature of the air in the room rise during the 50-min lecture? (c) If the class is taking an exam, the heat output per student rises to 280 W. What is the temperature rise during 50 min in this case?

17.88 ••• CALC The molar heat capacity of a certain substance varies with temperature according to the empirical equation

$$C = 29.5 \text{ J/mol·K} + (8.20 \times 10^{-3} \text{ J/mol·K}^2)T$$

How much heat is necessary to change the temperature of 3.00 mol of this substance from 27°C to 227°C? (*Hint:* Use Eq. (17.18) in the form $dQ = nC\,dT$ and integrate.)

17.89 •• BIO **Bicycling on a Warm Day.** If the air temperature is the same as the temperature of your skin (about 30°C), your body cannot get rid of heat by transferring it to the air. In that case, it gets rid of the heat by evaporating water (sweat). During bicycling, a typical 70-kg person's body produces energy at a rate of about 500 W due to metabolism, 80% of which is converted to heat. (a) How many kilograms of water must the person's body evaporate in an hour to get rid of this heat? The heat of vaporization of water at body temperature is 2.42×10^6 J/kg. (b) The evaporated water must, of course, be replenished, or the person will dehydrate. How many 750-mL bottles of water must the bicyclist drink per hour to replenish the lost water? (Recall that the mass of a liter of water is 1.0 kg.)

17.90 •• BIO **Overheating.** (a) By how much would the body temperature of the bicyclist in Problem 17.89 increase in an hour if he were unable to get rid of the excess heat? (b) Is this temperature increase large enough to be serious? To find out, how high a fever would it be equivalent to, in °F? (Recall that the normal internal body temperature is 98.6°F and the specific heat of the body is 3480 J/kg·C°.)

17.91 • BIO **A Thermodynamic Process in an Insect.** The African bombardier beetle (*Stenaptinus insignis*) can emit a jet of defensive spray from the movable tip of its abdomen (**Fig. P17.91**). The beetle's body has reservoirs containing two chemicals; when the beetle is disturbed, these chemicals combine in a reaction chamber, producing a compound that is warmed from 20°C to 100°C by the heat of reaction. The high pressure produced allows the compound to be sprayed out at speeds up to 19 m/s (68 km/h), soaring away from predators of all kinds. (The beetle shown in Fig. P17.91 is 2 cm long.) Calculate the heat of reaction of the two chemicals (in J/kg). Assume that the specific heat of the chemicals and of the spray is the same as that of water, 4.19×10^3 J/kg·K, and that the initial temperature of the chemicals is 20°C.

Figure **P17.91**

17.92 •• **Hot Water Versus Steam Heating.** In a household hot-water heating system, water is delivered to the radiators at 70.0°C (158.0°F) and leaves at 28.0°C (82.4°F). The system is to be replaced by a steam system in which steam at atmospheric pressure condenses in the radiators and the condensed steam leaves the radiators at 35.0°C (95.0°F). How many kilograms of steam will supply the same heat as was supplied by 1.00 kg of hot water in the first system?

17.93 •• You have 1.50 kg of water at 28.0°C in an insulated container of negligible mass. You add 0.600 kg of ice that is initially at −22.0°C. Assume that no heat exchanges with the surroundings. (a) After thermal equilibrium has been reached, has all of the ice melted? (b) If all of the ice has melted, what is the final temperature of the water in the container? If some ice remains, what is the final temperature of the water in the container, and how much ice remains?

17.94 •• A thirsty nurse cools a 2.00-L bottle of a soft drink (mostly water) by pouring it into a large aluminum mug of mass 0.257 kg and adding 0.120 kg of ice initially at −15.0°C. If the soft drink and mug are initially at 20.0°C, what is the final temperature of the system, assuming that no heat is lost?

17.95 ••• A copper calorimeter can with mass 0.446 kg contains 0.0950 kg of ice. The system is initially at 0.0°C. (a) If 0.0350 kg of steam at 100.0°C and 1.00 atm pressure is added to the can, what is the final temperature of the calorimeter can and its contents? (b) At the final temperature, how many kilograms are there of ice, how many of liquid water, and how many of steam?

17.96 • A Styrofoam bucket of negligible mass contains 1.75 kg of water and 0.450 kg of ice. More ice, from a refrigerator at −15.0°C, is added to the mixture in the bucket, and when thermal equilibrium has been reached, the total mass of ice in the bucket is 0.884 kg. Assuming no heat exchange with the surroundings, what mass of ice was added?

17.97 ••• In a container of negligible mass, 0.0400 kg of steam at 100°C and atmospheric pressure is added to 0.200 kg of water at 50.0°C. (a) If no heat is lost to the surroundings, what is the final temperature of the system? (b) At the final temperature, how many kilograms are there of steam and how many of liquid water?

17.98 •• BIO **Mammal Insulation.** Animals in cold climates often depend on *two* layers of insulation: a layer of body fat (of thermal conductivity 0.20 W/m · K) surrounded by a layer of air trapped inside fur or down. We can model a black bear (*Ursus americanus*) as a sphere 1.5 m in diameter having a layer of fat 4.0 cm thick. (Actually, the thickness varies with the season, but we are interested in hibernation, when the fat layer is thickest.) In studies of bear hibernation, it was found that the outer surface layer of the fur is at 2.7°C during hibernation, while the inner surface of the fat layer is at 31.0°C. (a) What is the temperature at the fat–inner fur boundary so that the bear loses heat at a rate of 50.0 W? (b) How thick should the air layer (contained within the fur) be?

17.99 •• **Effect of a Window in a Door.** A carpenter builds a solid wood door with dimensions 2.00 m × 0.95 m × 5.0 cm. Its thermal conductivity is $k = 0.120$ W/m · K. The air films on the inner and outer surfaces of the door have the same combined thermal resistance as an additional 1.8-cm thickness of solid wood. The inside air temperature is 20.0°C, and the outside air temperature is −8.0°C. (a) What is the rate of heat flow through the door? (b) By what factor is the heat flow increased if a window 0.500 m on a side is inserted in the door? The glass is 0.450 cm thick, and the glass has a thermal conductivity of 0.80 W/m · K. The air films on the two sides of the glass have a total thermal resistance that is the same as an additional 12.0 cm of glass.

17.100 •• One experimental method of measuring an insulating material's thermal conductivity is to construct a box of the material and measure the power input to an electric heater inside the box that maintains the interior at a measured temperature above the outside surface. Suppose that in such an apparatus a power input of 180 W is required to keep the interior surface of the box 65.0 C° (about 120 F°) above the temperature of the outer surface. The total area of the box is 2.18 m², and the wall thickness is 3.90 cm. Find the thermal conductivity of the material in SI units.

17.101 •• Compute the ratio of the rate of heat loss through a single-pane window with area 0.15 m² to that for a double-pane window with the same area. The glass of a single pane is 4.2 mm thick, and the air space between the two panes of the double-pane window is 7.0 mm thick. The glass has thermal conductivity 0.80 W/m · K. The air films on the room and outdoor surfaces of either window have a combined thermal resistance of 0.15 m² · K/W.

17.102 • Rods of copper, brass, and steel—each with cross-sectional area of 2.00 cm²—are welded together to form a Y-shaped figure. The free end of the copper rod is maintained at 100.0°C, and the free ends of the brass and steel rods at 0.0°C. Assume that there is no heat loss from the surfaces of the rods. The lengths of the rods are: copper, 13.0 cm; brass, 18.0 cm; steel, 24.0 cm. What is (a) the temperature of the junction point; (b) the heat current in each of the three rods?

17.103 ••• A brass rod 12.0 cm long, a copper rod 18.0 cm long, and an aluminum rod 24.0 cm long—each with cross-sectional area 2.30 cm³—are welded together end to end to form a rod 54.0 cm long, with copper as the middle section. The free end of the brass section is maintained at 100.0°C, and the free end of the aluminum section is maintained at 0.0°C. Assume that there is no heat loss from the curved surfaces and that the steady-state heat current has been established. What is (a) the temperature T_1 at the junction of the brass and copper sections; (b) the temperature T_2 at the junction of the copper and aluminum sections; (c) the heat current in the aluminum section?

17.104 •• BIO **Basal Metabolic Rate.** The *basal metabolic rate* is the rate at which energy is produced in the body when a person is at rest. A 75-kg (165-lb) person of height 1.83 m (6 ft) has a body surface area of approximately 2.0 m². (a) What is the net amount of heat this person could radiate per second into a room at 18°C (about 65°F) if his skin's surface temperature is 30°C? (At such temperatures, nearly all the heat is infrared radiation, for which the body's emissivity is 1.0, regardless of the amount of pigment.) (b) Normally, 80% of the energy produced by metabolism goes into heat, while the rest goes into things like pumping blood and repairing cells. Also normally, a person at rest can get rid of this excess heat just through radiation. Use your answer to part (a) to find this person's basal metabolic rate.

17.105 ••• CALC **Time Needed for a Lake to Freeze Over.** (a) When the air temperature is below 0°C, the water at the surface of a lake freezes to form an ice sheet. Why doesn't freezing occur throughout the entire volume of the lake? (b) Show that the thickness of the ice sheet formed on the surface of a lake is proportional to the square root of the time if the heat of fusion of the water freezing on the underside of the ice sheet is conducted through the sheet. (c) Assuming that the upper surface of the ice sheet is at −10°C and the bottom surface is at 0°C, calculate the time it will take to form an ice sheet 25 cm thick. (d) If the lake in part (c) is uniformly 40 m deep, how long would it take to freeze all the water in the lake? Is this likely to occur?

17.106 • The rate at which radiant energy from the sun reaches the earth's upper atmosphere is about 1.50 kW/m². The distance from the earth to the sun is 1.50×10^{11} m, and the radius of the sun is 6.96×10^8 m. (a) What is the rate of radiation of energy per unit area from the sun's surface? (b) If the sun radiates as an ideal blackbody, what is the temperature of its surface?

17.107 ••• **A Thermos for Liquid Helium.** A physicist uses a cylindrical metal can 0.250 m high and 0.090 m in diameter to store liquid helium at 4.22 K; at that temperature the heat of vaporization of helium is 2.09×10^4 J/kg. Completely surrounding the metal can are walls maintained at the temperature of liquid nitrogen, 77.3 K, with vacuum between the can and the surrounding walls. How much helium is lost per hour? The emissivity of the metal can is 0.200. The only heat transfer between the metal can and the surrounding walls is by radiation.

17.108 •• A metal sphere with radius 3.20 cm is suspended in a large metal box with interior walls that are maintained at 30.0°C. A small electric heater is embedded in the sphere. Heat energy must be supplied to the sphere at the rate of 0.660 J/s to maintain the sphere at a constant temperature of 41.0°C. (a) What is the emissivity of the metal sphere? (b) What power input to the sphere is required to maintain it at 82.0°C? What is the ratio of the power required for 82.0°C to the power required for 41.0°C? How does this ratio compare with 2^4? Explain.

17.109 •• BIO **Jogging in the Heat of the Day.** You have probably seen people jogging in extremely hot weather. There are good reasons not to do this! When jogging strenuously, an average runner of mass 68 kg and surface area 1.85 m² produces energy at a rate of up to 1300 W, 80% of which is converted to heat. The jogger radiates heat but actually absorbs more from the hot air than he radiates away. At such high levels of activity, the skin's temperature can be elevated to around 33°C instead of the usual 30°C. (Ignore conduction, which would bring even more heat into his body.) The only way for the body to get rid of this extra heat is by evaporating water (sweating). (a) How much heat per second is produced just by the act of jogging? (b) How much *net* heat per second does the runner gain just from radiation if the air temperature is 40.0°C (104°F)? (Remember: He radiates out, but the environment radiates back in.) (c) What is the *total* amount of excess heat this runner's body must get rid of per second? (d) How much water must his body evaporate every minute due to his activity? The heat of vaporization of water at body temperature is 2.42×10^6 J/kg. (e) How many 750-mL bottles of water must he drink after (or preferably before!) jogging for a half hour? Recall that a liter of water has a mass of 1.0 kg.

17.110 •• The icecaps of Greenland and Antarctica contain about 1.75% of the total water (by mass) on the earth's surface; the oceans contain about 97.5%, and the other 0.75% is mainly groundwater. Suppose the icecaps, currently at an average temperature of about −30°C, somehow slid into the ocean and melted. What would be the resulting temperature decrease of the ocean? Assume that the average temperature of ocean water is currently 5.00°C.

17.111 •• DATA As a physicist, you put heat into a 500.0-g solid sample at the rate of 10.0 kJ/min while recording its temperature as a function of time. You plot your data as shown in **Fig. P17.111**. (a) What is the latent heat of fusion for this solid? (b) What are the specific heats of the liquid and solid states of this material?

Figure **P17.111**

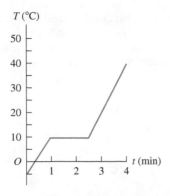

17.112 ••• DATA At a chemical plant where you are an engineer, a tank contains an unknown liquid. You must determine the liquid's specific heat capacity. You put 0.500 kg of the liquid into an insulated metal cup of mass 0.200 kg. Initially the liquid and cup are at 20.0°C. You add 0.500 kg of water that has a temperature of 80.0°C. After thermal equilibrium has been reached, the final temperature of the two liquids and the cup is 58.1°C. You then empty the cup and repeat the experiment with the same initial temperatures, but this time with 1.00 kg of the unknown liquid. The final temperature is 49.3°C. Assume that the specific heat capacities are constant over the temperature range of the experiment and that no heat is lost to the surroundings. Calculate the specific heat capacity of the liquid and of the metal from which the cup is made.

17.113 •• DATA During your mechanical engineering internship, you are given two uniform metal bars A and B, which are made from different metals, to determine their thermal conductivities. Measuring the bars, you determine that both have length 40.0 cm and uniform cross-sectional area 2.50 cm². You place one end of bar A in thermal contact with a very large vat of boiling water at 100.0°C and the other end in thermal contact with an ice–water mixture at 0.0°C. To prevent heat loss along the bar's sides, you wrap insulation around the bar. You weigh the amount of ice initially and find it to be 300 g. After 45.0 min has elapsed, you weigh the ice again and find that 191 g of ice remains. The ice–water mixture is in an insulated container, so the only heat entering or leaving it is the heat conducted by the metal bar.

You are confident that your data will allow you to calculate the thermal conductivity k_A of bar A. But this measurement was tedious—you don't want to repeat it for bar B. Instead, you glue the bars together end to end, with adhesive that has very large thermal conductivity, to make a composite bar 80.0 m long. You place the free end of A in thermal contact with the boiling water and the free end of B in thermal contact with the ice–water mixture. As in the first measurement, the composite bar is thermally insulated. You go to lunch; when you return, you notice that ice remains in the ice–water mixture. Measuring the temperature at the junction of the two bars, you find that it is 62.4°C. After 10 minutes you repeat that measurement and get the same temperature, with ice remaining in the ice–water mixture. From your data, calculate the thermal conductivities of bar A and of bar B.

CHALLENGE PROBLEMS

17.114 ••• BIO **A Walk in the Sun.** Consider a poor lost soul walking at 5 km/h on a hot day in the desert, wearing only a bathing suit. This person's skin temperature tends to rise due to four mechanisms: (i) energy is generated by metabolic reactions in the body at a rate of 280 W, and almost all of this energy is converted to heat that flows to the skin; (ii) heat is delivered to the skin by convection from the outside air at a rate equal to $k'A_{skin}(T_{air} - T_{skin})$, where k' is 54 J/h·C°·m², the exposed skin area A_{skin} is 1.5 m², the air temperature T_{air} is 47°C, and the skin temperature T_{skin} is 36°C; (iii) the skin absorbs radiant energy from the sun at a rate of 1400 W/m²; (iv) the skin absorbs radiant energy from the environment, which has temperature 47°C. (a) Calculate the net rate (in watts) at which the person's skin is heated by all four of these mechanisms. Assume that the emissivity of the skin is $e = 1$ and that the skin temperature is initially 36°C. Which mechanism is the most important? (b) At what rate (in L/h) must perspiration evaporate from this person's skin to maintain a constant skin temperature? (The heat of vaporization of water at 36°C is 2.42×10^6 J/kg.) (c) Suppose instead the person is protected by light-colored clothing ($e \approx 0$) so that the exposed skin area is only 0.45 m². What rate of perspiration is required now? Discuss the usefulness of the traditional clothing worn by desert peoples.

17.115 ••• A hollow cylinder has length L, inner radius a, and outer radius b, and the temperatures at the inner and outer surfaces are T_2 and T_1. (The cylinder could represent an insulated hot-water pipe.) The thermal conductivity of the material of which the cylinder is made is k. Derive an equation for (a) the total heat current through the walls of the cylinder; (b) the temperature variation inside the cylinder walls. (c) Show that the equation for the total heat current reduces to Eq. (17.21) for linear heat flow when the cylinder wall is very thin. (d) A steam pipe with a radius of 2.00 cm, carrying steam at 140°C, is surrounded by a cylindrical jacket with inner and outer radii 2.00 cm and 4.00 cm and made of a type of cork with thermal conductivity 4.00×10^{-2} W/m·K. This in turn is surrounded by a cylindrical jacket made of a brand of Styrofoam with thermal conductivity 2.70×10^{-2} W/m·K and having inner and outer radii 4.00 cm and 6.00 cm (**Fig. P17.115**). The outer surface of the Styrofoam has a temperature of 15°C. What is the temperature at a radius of 4.00 cm, where the two insulating layers meet? (e) What is the total rate of transfer of heat out of a 2.00-m length of pipe?

Figure **P17.115**

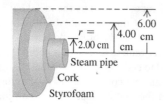

PASSAGE PROBLEMS

BIO **PRESERVING CELLS AT COLD TEMPERATURES.** In cryopreservation, biological materials are cooled to a very low temperature to slow down chemical reactions that might damage the cells or tissues. It is important to prevent the materials from forming ice crystals during freezing. One method for preventing ice formation is to place the material in a protective solution called a *cryoprotectant*. Stated values of the thermal properties of one cryoprotectant are listed here:

Melting point	−20°C
Latent heat of fusion	2.80×10^5 J/kg
Specific heat (liquid)	4.5×10^3 J/kg·K
Specific heat (solid)	2.0×10^3 J/kg·K
Thermal conductivity (liquid)	1.2 W/m·K
Thermal conductivity (solid)	2.5 W/m·K

17.116 You place 35 g of this cryoprotectant at 22°C in contact with a cold plate that is maintained at the boiling temperature of liquid nitrogen (77 K). The cryoprotectant is thermally insulated from everything but the cold plate. Use the values in the table to determine how much heat will be transferred from the cryoprotectant as it reaches thermal equilibrium with the cold plate. (a) 1.5×10^4 J; (b) 2.9×10^4 J; (c) 3.4×10^4 J; (d) 4.4×10^4 J.

17.117 Careful measurements show that the specific heat of the solid phase depends on temperature (**Fig. P17.117**). How will the actual time needed for this cryoprotectant to come to equilibrium with the cold plate compare with the time predicted by using the values in the table? Assume that all values other than the specific heat (solid) are correct. The actual time (a) will be shorter; (b) will be longer; (c) will be the same; (d) depends on the density of the cryoprotectant.

Figure **P17.117**

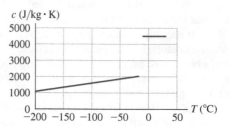

17.118 In another experiment, you place a layer of this cryoprotectant between one 10 cm × 10 cm cold plate maintained at −40°C and a second cold plate of the same size maintained at liquid nitrogen's boiling temperature (77 K). Then you measure the rate of heat transfer. Another lab wants to repeat the experiment but uses cold plates that are 20 cm × 20 cm, with one at −40°C and the other at 77 K. How thick does the layer of cryoprotectant have to be so that the rate of heat transfer by conduction is the same as that when you use the smaller plates? (a) One-quarter the thickness; (b) half the thickness; (c) twice the thickness; (d) four times the thickness.

17.119 To measure the specific heat in the liquid phase of a newly developed cryoprotectant, you place a sample of the new cryoprotectant in contact with a cold plate until the solution's temperature drops from room temperature to its freezing point. Then you measure the heat transferred to the cold plate. If the system isn't sufficiently isolated from its room-temperature surroundings, what will be the effect on the measurement of the specific heat? (a) The measured specific heat will be greater than the actual specific heat; (b) the measured specific heat will be less than the actual specific heat; (c) there will be no effect because the thermal conductivity of the cryoprotectant is so low; (d) there will be no effect on the specific heat, but the temperature of the freezing point will change.

Answers

Chapter Opening Question ?

(iii) The molten iron contains a large amount of energy. A body *has* a temperature but does not *contain* temperature. By "heat" we mean energy that is in transit from one body to another as a result of temperature difference between the bodies. Bodies do not *contain* heat.

Test Your Understanding Questions

17.1 (ii) A liquid-in-tube thermometer actually measures its own temperature. If the thermometer stays in the hot water long enough, it will come to thermal equilibrium with the water and its temperature will be the same as that of the water.

17.2 (iv) Both a bimetallic strip and a resistance thermometer measure their own temperature. For this to be equal to the temperature of the object being measured, the thermometer and object must be in thermal equilibrium. A temporal artery thermometer detects the infrared radiation from a person's skin; the detector and skin need not be at the same temperature.

17.3 (i), (iii), (ii), (v), (iv) To compare these temperatures, convert them all to the Kelvin scale. For (i), the Kelvin temperature is $T_K = T_C + 273.15 = 0.00 + 273.15 = 273.15$ K; for (ii), $T_C = \frac{5}{9}(T_F - 32°) = \frac{5}{9}(0.00° - 32°) = -17.78°C$ and $T_K = T_C + 273.15 = -17.78 + 273.15 = 255.37$ K; for (iii), $T_K = 260.00$ K; for (iv), $T_K = 77.00$ K; and for (v), $T_K = T_C + 273.15 = -180.00 + 273.15 = 93.15$ K.

17.4 (ii) and (iii) Metal 2 must expand more than metal 1 when heated and so must have a larger coefficient of linear expansion α. From Table 17.1, brass and aluminum have larger values of α than copper, but steel does not.

17.5 (ii), (i), (iv), (iii) For (i) and (ii), the relevant quantity is the specific heat c of the substance, which is the amount of heat required to raise the temperature of 1 *kilogram* of that substance by 1 K (1 C°). From Table 17.3, these values are (i) 138 J for mercury and (ii) 2428 J for ethanol. For (iii) and (iv) we need the molar heat capacity C, which is the amount of heat required to raise the temperature of 1 *mole* of that substance by 1 C°. Again from Table 17.3, these values are (iii) 27.7 J for mercury and (iv) 111.9 J for ethanol. (The ratio of molar heat capacities is different from the ratio of the specific heats because a mole of mercury and a mole of ethanol have different masses.)

17.6 (iv) In time t the system goes from point b to point e in Fig. 17.20. According to this figure, at time $t/2$ (halfway along the horizontal axis from b to e), the system is at 100°C and is still boiling; that is, it is a mixture of liquid and gas. This says that most of the heat added goes into boiling the water.

17.7 (ii) When you touch one of the walls, heat flows from your hand to the lower-temperature wall. The more rapidly heat flows from your hand, the colder you will feel. Equation (17.21) shows that the rate of heat flow is proportional to the thermal conductivity k. From Table 17.5, copper has a much higher thermal conductivity (385.0 W/m·K) than steel (50.2 W/m·K) or concrete (0.8 W/m·K), and so the copper wall feels the coldest.

Bridging Problem

(a) 14.26 K   **(b)** 0.427 kg/h

? The higher the temperature of a gas, the greater the average kinetic energy of its molecules. How much faster are molecules moving in the air above a frying pan (100°C) than in the surrounding kitchen air (25°C)? (i) 4 times faster; (ii) twice as fast; (iii) 1.25 times as fast; (iv) 1.12 times as fast; (v) 1.06 times as fast.

18 THERMAL PROPERTIES OF MATTER

The kitchen is a great place to learn about how the properties of matter depend on temperature. When you boil water in a tea kettle, the increase in temperature produces steam that whistles out of the spout at high pressure. If you forget to poke holes in a potato before baking it, the high-pressure steam produced inside the potato can cause it to explode messily. Water vapor in the air can condense into liquid on the sides of a glass of ice water; if the glass is just out of the freezer, water vapor will solidify and form frost on its sides.

These examples show the relationships among the large-scale or *macroscopic* properties of a substance, such as pressure, volume, temperature, and mass. But we can also describe a substance by using a *microscopic* perspective. This means investigating small-scale quantities such as the masses, speeds, kinetic energies, and momenta of the individual molecules that make up a substance.

The macroscopic and microscopic descriptions are intimately related. For example, the (microscopic) forces that occur when air molecules strike a solid surface (such as your skin) cause (macroscopic) atmospheric pressure. To produce standard atmospheric pressure of 1.01×10^5 Pa, 10^{32} molecules strike your skin every day with an average speed of over 1700 km/h (1000 mi/h)!

In this chapter we'll begin by looking at some macroscopic aspects of matter in general. We'll pay special attention to the *ideal gas*, one of the simplest types of matter to understand. We'll relate the macroscopic properties of an ideal gas to the microscopic behavior of its molecules. We'll also use microscopic ideas to understand the heat capacities of gases and solids. Finally, we'll look at the various phases of matter—gas, liquid, and solid—and the conditions under which each occurs.

18.1 EQUATIONS OF STATE

Quantities such as pressure, volume, temperature, and amount of substance describe the conditions, or *state,* in which a particular material exists. (For example, a tank of medical oxygen has a pressure gauge and a label stating the volume within the tank. We can add a thermometer and put the tank on a scale to measure the mass of oxygen.) These quantities are called **state variables**.

The volume V of a substance is usually determined by its pressure p, temperature T, and amount of substance, described by the mass m_{total} or number of moles n. (We are calling the total mass of a substance m_{total} because later in the chapter we will use m for the mass of one molecule.) Ordinarily, we can't change one of these variables without causing a change in another. When the tank of oxygen gets hotter, the pressure increases. If the tank gets too hot, it explodes.

In a few cases the relationship among p, V, T, and m_{total} (or n) is simple enough that we can express it as an equation called the **equation of state.** When it's too complicated for that, we can use graphs or numerical tables. Even then, the relationship among the variables still exists; we call it an equation of state even when we don't know the actual equation.

Here's a simple (though approximate) equation of state for a solid material. The temperature coefficient of volume expansion β (see Section 17.4) is the fractional volume change $\Delta V/V_0$ per unit temperature change, and the compressibility k (see Section 11.4) is the negative of the fractional volume change $\Delta V/V_0$ per unit pressure change. If a certain amount of material has volume V_0 when the pressure is p_0 and the temperature is T_0, the volume V at slightly differing pressure p and temperature T is approximately

$$V = V_0[1 + \beta(T - T_0) - k(p - p_0)] \qquad (18.1)$$

(There is a negative sign in front of the term $k(p - p_0)$ because an *increase* in pressure causes a *decrease* in volume.)

The Ideal-Gas Equation

Another simple equation of state is the one for an *ideal gas.* **Figure 18.1** shows an experimental setup to study the behavior of a gas. The cylinder has a movable piston to vary the volume, the temperature can be varied by heating, and we can pump in any desired amount of gas. We then measure the pressure, volume, temperature, and amount of gas. Note that *pressure* refers both to the force per unit area exerted by the cylinder on the gas and to that exerted by the gas on the cylinder; by Newton's third law, these must be equal.

It is usually easiest to describe the amount of gas in terms of the number of moles n, rather than the mass. (We did this when we defined molar heat capacity in Section 17.5.) The **molar mass** M of a compound (sometimes confusingly called *molecular weight*) is the mass per mole:

Total mass of substance $\longrightarrow m_{\text{total}} = nM \longleftarrow$ Number of moles of substance
$\qquad\qquad\qquad\qquad\qquad\qquad\longleftarrow$ Molar mass of substance $\qquad (18.2)$

Hence if we know the number of moles of gas in the cylinder, we can determine the mass of gas from Eq. (18.2).

18.1 A hypothetical setup for studying the behavior of gases. By heating the gas, varying the volume with a movable piston, and adding more gas, we can control the gas pressure p, volume V, temperature T, and number of moles n.

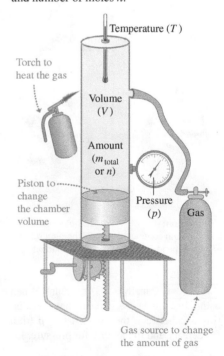

Gas source to change the amount of gas

18.2 The ideal-gas equation $pV = nRT$ gives a good description of the air inside an inflated vehicle tire, where the pressure is about 3 atmospheres and the temperature is much too high for nitrogen or oxygen to liquefy. As the tire warms (T increases), the volume V changes only slightly but the pressure p increases.

BIO Application Respiration and the Ideal-Gas Equation To breathe, you rely on the ideal-gas equation $pV = nRT$. Contraction of the dome-shaped diaphragm muscle increases the volume V of the thoracic cavity (which encloses the lungs), decreasing its pressure p. The lowered pressure causes the lungs to expand and fill with air. (The temperature T is kept constant.) When you exhale, the diaphragm relaxes, allowing the lungs to contract and expel the air.

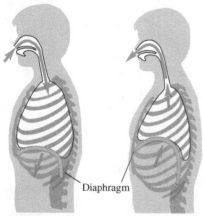

Diaphragm

Inhalation:
Diaphragm contracts;
lungs expand.

Exhalation:
Diaphragm relaxes;
lungs contract.

CAUTION **Density vs. pressure** When using Eq. (18.5), be certain that you distinguish between the Greek letter ρ (rho) for density and the letter p for pressure. ▮

Measurements of the behavior of various gases lead to three conclusions:

1. The volume V is proportional to the number of moles n. If we double n, keeping pressure and temperature constant, the volume doubles.

2. The volume varies *inversely* with the absolute pressure p. If we double p while holding the temperature T and number of moles n constant, the gas compresses to one-half of its initial volume. In other words, $pV = $ constant when n and T are constant.

3. The pressure is proportional to the *absolute* temperature T. If we double T, keeping the volume and number of moles constant, the pressure doubles. In other words, $p = $ (constant) $\times T$ when n and V are constant.

We can combine these three relationships into a single **ideal-gas equation:**

$$\text{Ideal-gas equation:} \quad \underset{\text{Gas volume}}{\underset{\text{Gas pressure}}{pV}} = \underset{\underset{\text{Gas constant}}{\text{Absolute temperature of gas}}}{\overset{\text{Number of moles of gas}}{nRT}} \qquad (18.3)$$

An **ideal gas** is one for which Eq. (18.3) holds precisely for *all* pressures and temperatures. This is an idealized model; it works best at very low pressures and high temperatures, when the gas molecules are far apart and in rapid motion. It is valid within a few percent at moderate pressures (such as a few atmospheres) and at temperatures well above those at which the gas liquefies (**Fig. 18.2**).

We might expect that the proportionality constant R in the ideal-gas equation would have different values for different gases, but it turns out to have the same value for *all* gases, at least at sufficiently high temperature and low pressure. It is called the **gas constant** (or *ideal-gas constant*). In SI units, in which the unit of p is Pa ($1\text{ Pa} = 1\text{ N/m}^2$) and the unit of V is m^3, the current best numerical value of R is

$$R = 8.3144621(75) \text{ J/mol} \cdot \text{K}$$

or $R = 8.314 \text{ J/mol} \cdot \text{K}$ to four significant figures. Note that the units of pressure times volume are the same as the units of work or energy (for example, N/m^2 times m^3); that's why R has units of energy per mole per unit of absolute temperature. In chemical calculations, volumes are often expressed in liters (L) and pressures in atmospheres (atm). In this system, to four significant figures,

$$R = 0.08206 \frac{\text{L} \cdot \text{atm}}{\text{mol} \cdot \text{K}}$$

We can express the ideal-gas equation, Eq. (18.3), in terms of the mass m_{total} of gas, using $m_{\text{total}} = nM$ from Eq. (18.2):

$$pV = \frac{m_{\text{total}}}{M} RT \qquad (18.4)$$

From this we can get an expression for the density $\rho = m_{\text{total}}/V$ of the gas:

$$\rho = \frac{pM}{RT} \qquad (18.5)$$

For a *constant mass* (or constant number of moles) of an ideal gas the product nR is constant, so the quantity pV/T is also constant. If the subscripts 1 and 2 refer to any two states of the same mass of a gas, then

$$\frac{p_1 V_1}{T_1} = \frac{p_2 V_2}{T_2} = \text{constant} \qquad \text{(ideal gas, constant mass)} \qquad (18.6)$$

Notice that you don't need the value of R to use this equation.

We used the proportionality of pressure to absolute temperature in Chapter 17 to define a temperature scale in terms of pressure in a constant-volume gas thermometer. That may make it seem that the pressure–temperature relationship in the ideal-gas equation, Eq. (18.3), is just a result of the way we define temperature. But the ideal-gas equation also tells us what happens when we change the volume or the amount of substance. Also, we'll see in Chapter 20 that the gas-thermometer scale corresponds closely to a temperature scale that does *not* depend on the properties of any particular material. For now, consider Eq. (18.6) as being based on this genuinely material-independent temperature scale.

DATA *SPEAKS*

The Ideal-Gas Equation

When students were given a problem using Eq. (18.3), more than 47% gave an incorrect response. Common errors:

- Forgetting that in Eq. (18.3) pressure p is *absolute*, not gauge, pressure (Section 12.2), and temperature T is *absolute* (Kelvin), not Celsius, temperature.
- Not correctly interpreting Eq. (18.3) to graph p versus V for constant T, p versus T for constant V, or V versus T for constant p.

PROBLEM-SOLVING STRATEGY 18.1 | IDEAL GASES

IDENTIFY *the relevant concepts:* Unless the problem states otherwise, you can use the ideal-gas equation to find quantities related to the state of a gas, such as pressure p, volume V, temperature T, and/or number of moles n.

SET UP *the problem* using the following steps:
1. List the known and unknown quantities. Identify the target variables.
2. If the problem concerns only one state of the system, use Eq. (18.3), $pV = nRT$ (or Eq. (18.5), $\rho = pM/RT$ if the problem involves the density ρ rather than n and V).
3. In problems that concern two states (call them 1 and 2) of the same amount of gas, if all but one of the six quantities p_1, p_2, V_1, V_2, T_1, and T_2 are known, use Eq. (18.6), $p_1V_1/T_1 = p_2V_2/T_2 = $ constant. Otherwise, use Eq. (18.3) or Eq. (18.5).

EXECUTE *the solution* as follows:
1. Use consistent units. (SI units are entirely consistent.) The problem statement may make one system of units more convenient than others. Make appropriate unit conversions, such as from atmospheres to pascals or from liters to cubic meters.
2. You may have to convert between mass m_{total} and number of moles n, using $m_{total} = Mn$, where M is the molar mass. If you

use Eq. (18.4), you *must* use the same mass units for m_{total} and M. So if M is in grams per mole (the usual units for molar mass), then m_{total} must also be in grams. To use m_{total} in kilograms, you must convert M to kg/mol. For example, the molar mass of oxygen is 32 g/mol or 32×10^{-3} kg/mol.
3. Remember that in the ideal-gas equations, T is always an *absolute* (Kelvin) temperature and p is always an absolute (not gauge) pressure.
4. Solve for the target variables.

EVALUATE *your answer:* Do your results make physical sense? Use benchmarks, such as the result of Example 18.1 below that a mole of an ideal gas at 1 atmosphere pressure occupies a volume of 22.4 liters.

EXAMPLE 18.1   VOLUME OF AN IDEAL GAS AT STP

What is the volume of a container that holds exactly 1 mole of an ideal gas at *standard temperature and pressure* (STP), defined as $T = 0°C = 273.15$ K and $p = 1$ atm $= 1.013 \times 10^5$ Pa?

SOLUTION

IDENTIFY and SET UP: This problem involves the properties of a single state of an ideal gas, so we use Eq. (18.3). We are given the pressure p, temperature T, and number of moles n; our target variable is the corresponding volume V.

EXECUTE: From Eq. (18.3), using R in J/mol·K, we get

$$V = \frac{nRT}{p} = \frac{(1 \text{ mol})(8.314 \text{ J/mol·K})(273.15 \text{ K})}{1.013 \times 10^5 \text{ Pa}}$$

$$= 0.0224 \text{ m}^3 = 22.4 \text{ L}$$

EVALUATE: At STP, 1 mole of an ideal gas occupies 22.4 L. This is the volume of a cube 0.282 m (11.1 in.) on a side, or of a sphere 0.350 m (13.8 in.) in diameter.

EXAMPLE 18.2 COMPRESSING GAS IN AN AUTOMOBILE ENGINE

In an automobile engine, a mixture of air and vaporized gasoline is compressed in the cylinders before being ignited. A typical engine has a compression ratio of 9.00 to 1; that is, the gas in the cylinders is compressed to $\frac{1}{9.00}$ of its original volume (**Fig. 18.3**). The intake and exhaust valves are closed during the compression, so the quantity of gas is constant. What is the final temperature of the compressed gas if its initial temperature is 27°C and the initial and final pressures are 1.00 atm and 21.7 atm, respectively?

SOLUTION

IDENTIFY and SET UP: We must compare two states of the same quantity of ideal gas, so we use Eq. (18.6). In the uncompressed state 1, $p_1 = 1.00$ atm and $T_1 = 27°C = 300$ K. In the compressed state 2, $p_2 = 21.7$ atm. The cylinder volumes are not given, but we have $V_1 = 9.00V_2$. The temperature T_2 of the compressed gas is the target variable.

EXECUTE: We solve Eq. (18.6) for T_2:

$$T_2 = T_1 \frac{p_2 V_2}{p_1 V_1} = (300 \text{ K}) \frac{(21.7 \text{ atm})V_2}{(1.00 \text{ atm})(9.00V_2)} = 723 \text{ K} = 450°C$$

18.3 Cutaway of an automobile engine. While the air–gasoline mixture is being compressed prior to ignition, both the intake and exhaust valves are in the closed (up) position.

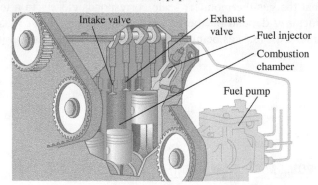

Intake valve

Exhaust valve

Fuel injector

Combustion chamber

Fuel pump

EVALUATE: This is the temperature of the air–gasoline mixture *before* the mixture is ignited; when burning starts, the temperature becomes higher still.

EXAMPLE 18.3 MASS OF AIR IN A SCUBA TANK

An "empty" aluminum scuba tank contains 11.0 L of air at 21°C and 1 atm. When the tank is filled rapidly from a compressor, the air temperature is 42°C and the gauge pressure is 2.10×10^7 Pa. What mass of air was added? (Air is about 78% nitrogen, 21% oxygen, and 1% miscellaneous; its average molar mass is 28.8 g/mol = 28.8×10^{-3} kg/mol.)

SOLUTION

IDENTIFY and SET UP: Our target variable is the difference $m_2 - m_1$ between the masses present at the end (state 2) and at the beginning (state 1). We are given the molar mass M of air, so we can use Eq. (18.2) to find the target variable if we know the number of moles present in states 1 and 2. We determine n_1 and n_2 by applying Eq. (18.3) to each state individually.

EXECUTE: We convert temperatures to the Kelvin scale by adding 273 and convert the pressure to absolute by adding 1.013×10^5 Pa.

The tank's volume is hardly affected by the increased temperature and pressure, so $V_2 = V_1$. From Eq. (18.3), the numbers of moles in the empty tank (n_1) and the full tank (n_2) are

$$n_1 = \frac{p_1 V_1}{RT_1} = \frac{(1.013 \times 10^5 \text{ Pa})(11.0 \times 10^{-3} \text{ m}^3)}{(8.314 \text{ J/mol} \cdot \text{K})(294 \text{ K})} = 0.46 \text{ mol}$$

$$n_2 = \frac{p_2 V_2}{RT_2} = \frac{(2.11 \times 10^7 \text{ Pa})(11.0 \times 10^{-3} \text{ m}^3)}{(8.314 \text{ J/mol} \cdot \text{K})(315 \text{ K})} = 88.6 \text{ mol}$$

We added $n_2 - n_1 = 88.6$ mol $- 0.46$ mol $= 88.1$ mol to the tank. From Eq. (18.2), the added mass is $M(n_2 - n_1) = (28.8 \times 10^{-3}$ kg/mol$)(88.1$ mol$) = 2.54$ kg.

EVALUATE: The added mass is not insubstantial: You could certainly use a scale to determine whether the tank was empty or full.

EXAMPLE 18.4 VARIATION OF ATMOSPHERIC PRESSURE WITH ELEVATION

Find the variation of atmospheric pressure with elevation in the earth's atmosphere. Assume that at all elevations, $T = 0°C$ and $g = 9.80$ m/s².

SOLUTION

IDENTIFY and SET UP: As the elevation y increases, both the atmospheric pressure p and the density ρ decrease. Hence we have *two* unknown functions of y; to solve for them, we need two independent equations. One is the ideal-gas equation, Eq. (18.5), which is expressed in terms of p and ρ. The other is Eq. (12.4), the rela-

tionship that we found in Section 12.2 among p, ρ, and y in a fluid in equilibrium: $dp/dy = -\rho g$. We are told to assume that g and T are the same at all elevations; we also assume that the atmosphere has the same chemical composition, and hence the same molar mass M, at all heights. We combine the two equations and solve for $p(y)$.

EXECUTE: We substitute $\rho = pM/RT$ into $dp/dy = -\rho g$, separate variables, and integrate, letting p_1 be the pressure at elevation y_1 and p_2 be the pressure at y_2:

$$\frac{dp}{dy} = -\frac{pM}{RT}g$$

$$\int_{p_1}^{p_2}\frac{dp}{p} = -\frac{Mg}{RT}\int_{y_1}^{y_2}dy$$

$$\ln\frac{p_2}{p_1} = -\frac{Mg}{RT}(y_2 - y_1)$$

$$\frac{p_2}{p_1} = e^{-Mg(y_2-y_1)/RT}$$

Now let $y_1 = 0$ be at sea level and let the pressure at that point be $p_0 = 1.013 \times 10^5$ Pa. Then the pressure p at any height y is

$$p = p_0e^{-Mgy/RT}$$

18.4 The variation of atmospheric pressure p with elevation y, assuming a constant temperature T.

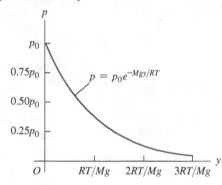

EVALUATE: According to our calculation, the pressure decreases exponentially with elevation. The graph in **Fig. 18.4** shows that the slope dp/dy becomes less negative with greater elevation. That result makes sense, since $dp/dy = -\rho g$ and the density also decreases with elevation. At the summit of Mount Everest, where $y = 8848$ m,

$$\frac{Mgy}{RT} = \frac{(28.8 \times 10^{-3}\text{ kg/mol})(9.80\text{ m/s}^2)(8848\text{ m})}{(8.314\text{ J/mol}\cdot\text{K})(273\text{ K})} = 1.10$$

$$p = (1.013 \times 10^5\text{ Pa})e^{-1.10} = 0.337 \times 10^5\text{ Pa} = 0.33\text{ atm}$$

The assumption of constant temperature isn't realistic, and g decreases a little with increasing elevation (see Challenge Problem 18.84). Even so, this example shows why most mountaineers carry oxygen on Mount Everest. It also shows why jet airliners, which typically fly at altitudes of 8000 to 12,000 m, *must* have pressurized cabins for passenger comfort and health.

The van der Waals Equation

In Section 18.3 we'll obtain the ideal-gas equation, Eq. (18.3), from a simple molecular model that ignores the volumes of the molecules themselves and the attractive forces between them (**Fig. 18.5a**). Another equation of state, the **van der Waals equation,** makes approximate corrections for these two omissions (Fig. 18.5b). This equation was developed by the 19th-century Dutch physicistJ. D. van der Waals; the interaction between atoms that we discussed in Section 14.4 is named the *van der Waals interaction*. The van der Waals equation is

$$\left(p + \frac{an^2}{V^2}\right)(V - nb) = nRT \tag{18.7}$$

The constants a and b are different for different gases. Roughly speaking, b represents the volume of a mole of molecules; the total volume of the molecules is nb, and the volume remaining in which the molecules can move is $V - nb$. The constant a depends on the attractive intermolecular forces, which reduce the pressure of the gas by *pulling* the molecules together as they *push* on the walls of the container. The decrease in pressure is proportional to the number of molecules per unit volume in a layer near the wall (which are exerting the pressure on the wall) and is also proportional to the number per unit volume in the next layer beyond the wall (which are doing the attracting). Hence the decrease in pressure due to intermolecular forces is proportional to n^2/V^2.

When n/V is small (that is, when the gas is *dilute*), the average distance between molecules is large, the corrections in the van der Waals equation become insignificant, and Eq. (18.7) reduces to the ideal-gas equation. As an example, for carbon dioxide gas (CO_2) the constants in the van der Waals equation are $a = 0.364$ J$\cdot$m^3/mol^2 and $b = 4.27 \times 10^{-5}$ m^3/mol. We saw in Example 18.1

18.5 A gas as modeled by (a) the ideal-gas equation and (b) the van der Waals equation.

(a) An idealized model of a gas

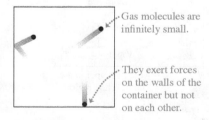

Gas molecules are infinitely small.

They exert forces on the walls of the container but not on each other.

(b) A more realistic model of a gas

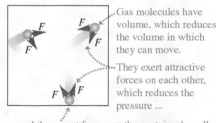

Gas molecules have volume, which reduces the volume in which they can move.

They exert attractive forces on each other, which reduces the pressure ...

... and they exert forces on the container's walls.

that 1 mole of an ideal gas at $T = 0°C = 273.15$ K and $p = 1$ atm $= 1.013 \times 10^5$ Pa occupies a volume $V = 0.0224$ m^3; according to Eq. (18.7), 1 mole of CO_2 occupying this volume at this temperature would be at a pressure 532 Pa less than 1 atm, a difference of only 0.5% from the ideal-gas value.

pV-Diagrams

We could in principle represent the p-V-T relationship graphically as a *surface* in a three-dimensional space with coordinates p, V, and T. This representation is useful (see Section 18.6), but ordinary two-dimensional graphs are usually more convenient. One of the most useful of these is a set of graphs of pressure as a function of volume, each for a particular constant temperature. Such a diagram is called a ***pV*-diagram.** Each curve, representing behavior at a specific temperature, is called an **isotherm,** or a *pV-isotherm*.

Figure 18.6 shows pV-isotherms for a constant amount of an ideal gas. Since $p = nRT/V$ from Eq. (18.3), along an isotherm (constant T) the pressure p is inversely proportional to the volume V and the isotherms are hyperbolic curves.

Figure 18.7 shows a pV-diagram for a material that *does not* obey the ideal-gas equation. At temperatures below T_c the isotherms develop flat regions in which we can compress the material (that is, reduce the volume V) without increasing the pressure p. Observation shows that the gas is *condensing* from the vapor (gas) to the liquid phase. The flat parts of the isotherms in the shaded area of Fig. 18.7 represent conditions of liquid-vapor *phase equilibrium*. As the volume decreases, more and more material goes from vapor to liquid, but the pressure does not change. (To keep the temperature constant during condensation, we have to remove the heat of vaporization, discussed in Section 17.6.)

When we compress such a gas at a constant temperature T_2 in Fig. 18.7, it is vapor until point a is reached. Then it begins to liquefy; as the volume decreases further, more material liquefies, and *both* the pressure and the temperature remain constant. At point b, all the material is in the liquid state. After this, any further compression requires a very rapid rise of pressure, because liquids are in general much less compressible than gases. At a lower constant temperature T_1, similar behavior occurs, but the condensation begins at lower pressure and greater volume than at the constant temperature T_2. At temperatures greater than T_c, *no phase transition occurs as the material is compressed*; at the highest temperatures, such as T_4, the curves resemble the ideal-gas curves of Fig. 18.6. We call T_c the *critical temperature* for this material. In Section 18.6 we'll discuss what happens to the phase of the gas above the critical temperature.

We will use pV-diagrams often in the next two chapters. We will show that the *area* under a pV-curve (whether or not it is an isotherm) represents the *work* done by the system during a volume change. This work, in turn, is directly related to heat transfer and changes in the *internal energy* of the system.

TEST YOUR UNDERSTANDING OF SECTION 18.1   Rank the following ideal gases in order from highest to lowest number of moles: (i) Pressure 1 atm, volume 1 L, and temperature 300 K; (ii) pressure 2 atm, volume 1 L, and temperature 300 K; (iii) pressure 1 atm, volume 2 L, and temperature 300 K; (iv) pressure 1 atm, volume 1 L, and temperature 600 K; (v) pressure 2 atm, volume 1 L, and temperature 600 K. ▌

18.2 MOLECULAR PROPERTIES OF MATTER

We have studied several properties of matter in bulk, including elasticity, density, surface tension, heat capacities, and equations of state. Now we want to look in more detail at the relationship of bulk behavior to *molecular* structure. We begin with a general discussion of the molecular structure of matter. Then in the next two sections we develop the kinetic-molecular model of an ideal gas, obtaining from this molecular model the equation of state and an expression for heat capacity.

18.6 Isotherms, or constant-temperature curves, for a constant amount of an ideal gas. The highest temperature is T_4; the lowest is T_1. This is a graphical representation of the ideal-gas equation of state.

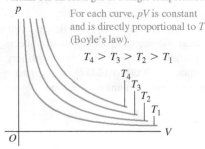

Each curve represents pressure as a function of volume for an ideal gas at a single temperature.

For each curve, pV is constant and is directly proportional to T (Boyle's law).

$$T_4 > T_3 > T_2 > T_1$$

18.7 A pV-diagram for a nonideal gas, showing isotherms for temperatures above and below the critical temperature T_c. The liquid–vapor equilibrium region is shown as a green shaded area. At still lower temperatures the material might undergo phase transitions from liquid to solid or from gas to solid; these are not shown here.

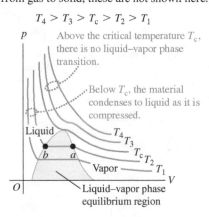

$$T_4 > T_3 > T_c > T_2 > T_1$$

Above the critical temperature T_c, there is no liquid–vapor phase transition.

Below T_c, the material condenses to liquid as it is compressed.

Liquid

Vapor

Liquid–vapor phase equilibrium region

Molecules and Intermolecular Forces

Any specific chemical compound is made up of identical **molecules.** The smallest molecules contain one atom each and are of the order of 10^{-10} m in size; the largest contain many atoms and are at least 10,000 times larger. In gases the molecules move nearly independently; in liquids and solids they are held together by intermolecular forces. These forces arise from interactions among the electrically charged particles that make up the molecules. Gravitational forces between molecules are negligible in comparison with electric forces.

The interaction of two *point* electric charges is described by a force (repulsive for like charges, attractive for unlike charges) with a magnitude proportional to $1/r^2$, where r is the distance between the points. We will study this relationship, called *Coulomb's law,* in Chapter 21. Molecules are *not* point charges but complex structures containing both positive and negative charge, and their interactions are more complex. The force between molecules in a gas varies with the distance r between molecules somewhat as shown in **Fig. 18.8**, where a positive F_r corresponds to a repulsive force and a negative F_r to an attractive force. When molecules are far apart, the intermolecular forces are very small and usually attractive. As a gas is compressed and its molecules are brought closer together, the attractive forces increase. The intermolecular force becomes zero at an equilibrium spacing r_0, corresponding roughly to the spacing between molecules in the liquid and solid states. In liquids and solids, relatively large pressures are needed to compress the substance appreciably. This shows that at molecular distances slightly *less* than r_0, the forces become *repulsive* and relatively large.

Figure 18.8 also shows the potential energy as a function of r. This function has a *minimum* at r_0, where the force is zero. The two curves are related by $F_r(r) = -dU/dr$, as we showed in Section 7.4. Such a potential-energy function is often called a **potential well.** A molecule at rest at a distance r_0 from a second molecule would need an additional energy $|U_0|$, the "depth" of the potential well, to "escape" to an indefinitely large value of r.

Molecules are always in motion; their kinetic energies usually increase with temperature. At very low temperatures the average kinetic energy of a molecule may be much *less* than the depth of the potential well. The molecules then condense into the liquid or solid phase with average intermolecular spacings of about r_0. But at higher temperatures the average kinetic energy becomes larger than the depth $|U_0|$ of the potential well. Molecules can then escape the intermolecular force and become free to move independently, as in the gaseous phase of matter.

In *solids,* molecules vibrate about more or less fixed points. (See Section 17.4.) In a crystalline solid these points are arranged in a *crystal lattice.* **Figure 18.9** shows the cubic crystal structure of sodium chloride, and **Fig. 18.10** shows a scanning tunneling microscope image of individual silicon atoms on the surface of a crystal.

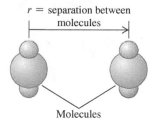

18.8 How the force between molecules and their potential energy of interaction depend on their separation r.

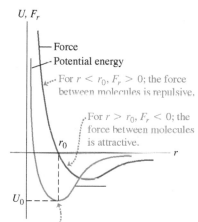

r = separation between molecules

Molecules

U, F_r

Force

Potential energy

For $r < r_0$, $F_r > 0$; the force between molecules is repulsive.

For $r > r_0$, $F_r < 0$; the force between molecules is attractive.

r_0

r

U_0

At a separation $r = r_0$, the potential energy of the two molecules is minimum and the force between the molecules is zero.

18.9 Schematic representation of the cubic crystal structure of sodium chloride (ordinary salt).

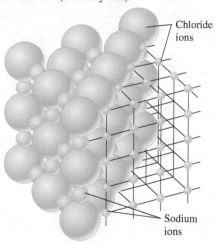

Chloride ions

Sodium ions

18.10 A scanning tunneling microscope image of the surface of a silicon crystal. The area shown is only 9.0 nm (9.0×10^{-9} m) across. Each blue "bead" is one silicon atom; these atoms are arranged in a (nearly) perfect array of hexagons.

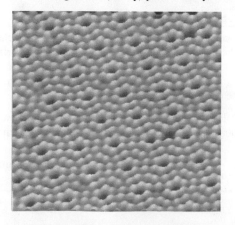

In a *liquid,* the intermolecular distances are usually only slightly greater than in the solid phase of the same substance, but the molecules have much greater freedom of movement. Liquids show regularity of structure only in the immediate neighborhood of a few molecules.

The molecules of a *gas* are usually widely separated and so have only very small attractive forces. A gas molecule moves in a straight line until it collides with another molecule or with a wall of the container. In molecular terms, an *ideal gas* is a gas whose molecules exert *no* attractive forces on each other (see Fig. 18.5a) and therefore have no *potential* energy.

At low temperatures, most common substances are in the solid phase. As the temperature rises, a substance melts and then vaporizes. From a molecular point of view, these transitions are in the direction of increasing molecular kinetic energy. Thus temperature and molecular kinetic energy are closely related.

Moles and Avogadro's Number

We have used the mole as a measure of quantity of substance. One **mole** of any pure chemical element or compound contains a definite number of molecules, the same number for all elements and compounds. The official SI definition is:

> **One mole is the amount of substance that contains as many elementary entities as there are atoms in 0.012 kilogram of carbon-12.**

In our discussion, the "elementary entities" are molecules. (In a monatomic substance such as carbon or helium, each molecule is a single atom.) Atoms of a given element may occur in any of several isotopes, which are chemically identical but have different atomic masses; "carbon-12" is a specific isotope of carbon.

The number of molecules in a mole is called **Avogadro's number,** denoted by N_A. The current best numerical value of N_A is

$$N_A = 6.02214129(27) \times 10^{23} \text{ molecules/mol (Avogadro's number)}$$

The *molar mass M* of a compound is the mass of 1 mole. It is equal to the mass m of a single molecule multiplied by Avogadro's number:

$$\underset{\text{of a substance}}{\overset{\text{Molar mass}}{\cdots\cdots}} M = N_A m \overset{\text{Avogadro's number}}{\underset{\text{Mass of a molecule of substance}}{\cdots\cdots}} \tag{18.8}$$

When the molecule consists of a single atom, the term *atomic mass* is often used instead of molar mass.

EXAMPLE 18.5 ATOMIC AND MOLECULAR MASS

Find the mass of a single hydrogen atom and of a single oxygen molecule.

SOLUTION

IDENTIFY and SET UP: This problem involves the relationship between the mass of a molecule or atom (our target variable) and the corresponding molar mass M. We use Eq. (18.8) in the form $m = M/N_A$ and the values of the atomic masses from the periodic table of the elements (see Appendix D).

EXECUTE: For atomic hydrogen the atomic mass (molar mass) is $M_H = 1.008$ g/mol, so the mass m_H of a single hydrogen atom is

$$m_H = \frac{1.008 \text{ g/mol}}{6.022 \times 10^{23} \text{ atoms/mol}} = 1.674 \times 10^{-24} \text{ g/atom}$$

For oxygen the atomic mass is 16.0 g/mol, so for the diatomic (two-atom) oxygen molecule the molar mass is 32.0 g/mol. Then the mass of a single oxygen molecule is

$$m_{O_2} = \frac{32.0 \text{ g/mol}}{6.022 \times 10^{23} \text{ molecules/mol}} = 53.1 \times 10^{-24} \text{ g/molecule}$$

EVALUATE: We note that the values in Appendix D are for the *average* atomic masses of a natural sample of each element. Such a sample may contain several *isotopes* of the element, each with a different atomic mass. Natural samples of hydrogen and oxygen are almost entirely made up of just one isotope.

TEST YOUR UNDERSTANDING OF SECTION 18.2   Suppose you could adjust the value of r_0 for the molecules of a certain chemical compound (Fig. 18.8) by turning a dial. If you doubled the value of r_0, the density of the solid form of this compound would become (i) twice as great; (ii) four times as great; (iii) eight times as great; (iv) $\frac{1}{2}$ as great; (v) $\frac{1}{4}$ as great; (vi) $\frac{1}{8}$ as great. ▮

18.3 KINETIC-MOLECULAR MODEL OF AN IDEAL GAS

PhET: Balloons & Buoyancy
PhET: Friction
PhET: Gas Properties

The goal of any molecular theory of matter is to understand the *macroscopic* properties of matter in terms of its atomic or molecular structure and behavior. Once we have this understanding, we can design materials to have specific desired properties. Theories have led to the development of high-strength steels, semiconductor materials for electronic devices, and countless other materials essential to contemporary technology.

Let's consider a simple molecular model of an ideal gas. This *kinetic-molecular model* represents the gas as a large number of particles bouncing around in a closed container. In this section we use the kinetic-molecular model to understand how the ideal-gas equation of state, Eq. (18.3), is related to Newton's laws. In the following section we use the kinetic-molecular model to predict the molar heat capacity of an ideal gas. We'll go on to elaborate the model to include "particles" that are not points but have a finite size.

Our discussion of the kinetic-molecular model has several steps, and you may need to go over them several times. Don't get discouraged!

Here are the assumptions of our model:

1. A container with volume V contains a very large number N of identical molecules, each with mass m.

2. The molecules behave as point particles that are small compared to the size of the container and to the average distance between molecules.

3. The molecules are in constant motion. Each molecule collides occasionally with a wall of the container. These collisions are perfectly elastic.

4. The container walls are rigid and infinitely massive and do not move.

CAUTION Molecules vs. moles Don't confuse N, the number of *molecules* in the gas, with n, the number of *moles*. The number of molecules is equal to the number of moles multiplied by Avogadro's number: $N = nN_A$. ▮

Collisions and Gas Pressure

During collisions the molecules exert *forces* on the walls of the container; this is the origin of the *pressure* that the gas exerts. In a typical collision (**Fig. 18.11**) the velocity component parallel to the wall is unchanged, and the component perpendicular to the wall reverses direction but does not change in magnitude.

We'll first determine the *number* of collisions that occur per unit time for a certain area A of wall. Then we find the total momentum change associated with these collisions and the force needed to cause this momentum change. From this we can determine the pressure (force per unit area) and compare to the ideal-gas equation. We'll find a direct connection between the temperature of the gas and the kinetic energy of its molecules.

To begin, we will assume that all molecules in the gas have the same *magnitude* of x-velocity, $|v_x|$. Later we'll see that our results don't depend on making this overly simplistic assumption.

As Fig. 18.11 shows, for each collision the x-component of velocity changes from $-|v_x|$ to $+|v_x|$. So the x-component of momentum p_x changes from $-m|v_x|$ to $+m|v_x|$, and the *change* in p_x is $m|v_x| - (-m|v_x|) = 2m|v_x|$.

18.11 Elastic collision of a molecule with an idealized container wall.

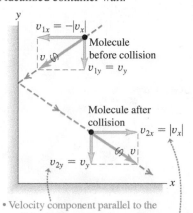

- Velocity component parallel to the wall (y-component) does not change.
- Velocity component perpendicular to the wall (x-component) reverses direction.
- Speed v does not change.

18.12 For a molecule to strike the wall in area A during a time interval dt, the molecule must be headed for the wall and be within the shaded cylinder of length $|v_x|\,dt$ at the beginning of the interval.

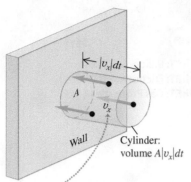

All molecules are assumed to have the same magnitude $|v_x|$ of x-velocity.

If a molecule is going to collide with a given wall area A during a small time interval dt, then at the beginning of dt it must be within a distance $|v_x|\,dt$ from the wall (**Fig. 18.12**) and it must be headed toward the wall. So the number of molecules that collide with A during dt is equal to the number of molecules within a cylinder with base area A and length $|v_x|\,dt$ that have their x-velocity aimed toward the wall. The volume of such a cylinder is $A|v_x|\,dt$. Assuming that the number of molecules per unit volume (N/V) is uniform, the *number* of molecules in this cylinder is $(N/V)(A|v_x|\,dt)$. On the average, half of these molecules are moving toward the wall and half are moving away from it. So the number of collisions with A during dt is

$$\tfrac{1}{2}\left(\frac{N}{V}\right)(A|v_x|\,dt)$$

For the system of all molecules in the gas, the total momentum change dP_x during dt is the *number* of collisions multiplied by $2m|v_x|$:

$$dP_x = \tfrac{1}{2}\left(\frac{N}{V}\right)(A|v_x|\,dt)(2m|v_x|) = \frac{NAmv_x^2\,dt}{V} \tag{18.9}$$

(We are using capital P for total momentum and lowercase p for pressure. Be careful!) We wrote v_x^2 rather than $|v_x|^2$ in the final expression because the square of the absolute value of a number is equal to the square of that number. The *rate* of change of momentum component P_x is

$$\frac{dP_x}{dt} = \frac{NAmv_x^2}{V} \tag{18.10}$$

According to Newton's second law, this rate of change of momentum equals the force exerted by the wall area A on the gas molecules. From Newton's *third* law this is equal and opposite to the force exerted *on* the wall *by* the molecules. Pressure p is the magnitude of the force exerted on the wall per unit area:

$$p = \frac{F}{A} = \frac{Nmv_x^2}{V} \tag{18.11}$$

The pressure exerted by the gas depends on the number of molecules per volume (N/V), the mass m per molecule, and the speed of the molecules.

Pressure and Molecular Kinetic Energies

We mentioned that $|v_x|$ is really *not* the same for all the molecules. But we could have sorted the molecules into groups having the same $|v_x|$ within each group, then added up the resulting contributions to the pressure. The net effect of all this is just to replace v_x^2 in Eq. (18.11) by the *average* value of v_x^2, which we denote by $(v_x^2)_{\text{av}}$. We can relate $(v_x^2)_{\text{av}}$ to the *speeds* of the molecules. The speed v of a molecule is related to the velocity components v_x, v_y, and v_z by

$$v^2 = v_x^2 + v_y^2 + v_z^2$$

We can average this relation over all molecules:

$$(v^2)_{\text{av}} = (v_x^2)_{\text{av}} + (v_y^2)_{\text{av}} + (v_z^2)_{\text{av}}$$

But there is no real difference in our model between the x-, y-, and z-directions. (Molecular speeds are very fast in a typical gas, so the effects of gravity are negligibly small.) It follows that $(v_x^2)_{\text{av}}$, $(v_y^2)_{\text{av}}$, and $(v_z^2)_{\text{av}}$ must all be *equal*. Hence $(v^2)_{\text{av}}$ is equal to $3(v_x^2)_{\text{av}}$ and

$$(v_x^2)_{\text{av}} = \tfrac{1}{3}(v^2)_{\text{av}}$$

so Eq. (18.11) becomes

$$pV = \tfrac{1}{3}Nm(v^2)_{\text{av}} = \tfrac{2}{3}N\left[\tfrac{1}{2}m(v^2)_{\text{av}}\right] \tag{18.12}$$

We notice that $\frac{1}{2}m(v^2)_{av}$ is the average translational kinetic energy of a single molecule. The product of this and the total number of molecules N equals the total random kinetic energy K_{tr} of translational motion of all the molecules. (The notation K_{tr} reminds us that this is the energy of *translational* motion. There may also be energies associated with molecular rotation and vibration.) The product pV equals two-thirds of the total translational kinetic energy:

$$pV = \tfrac{2}{3}K_{tr} \tag{18.13}$$

Now compare Eq. (18.13) to the ideal-gas equation $pV = nRT$, Eq. (18.3), which is based on experimental studies of gas behavior. For the two equations to agree, we must have

18.13 Summer air (top) is warmer than winter air (bottom); that is, the average translational kinetic energy of air molecules is greater in summer.

Average translational ⋯⋯ $K_{tr} = \frac{3}{2}nRT$ ⋯⋯ Number of moles of gas
kinetic energy of an ⋯⋯ Absolute temperature of gas   (18.14)
ideal gas ⋯⋯ Gas constant

So K_{tr} is *directly proportional* to the absolute temperature T (**Fig. 18.13**).

The average translational kinetic energy of a single molecule is the total translational kinetic energy K_{tr} of all molecules divided by the number of molecules, N:

$$\frac{K_{tr}}{N} = \tfrac{1}{2}m(v^2)_{av} = \frac{3nRT}{2N}$$

Also, the total number of molecules N is the number of moles n multiplied by Avogadro's number N_A, so $N = nN_A$ and $n/N = 1/N_A$. Thus the above equation becomes

$$\frac{K_{tr}}{N} = \tfrac{1}{2}m(v^2)_{av} = \frac{3}{2}\left(\frac{R}{N_A}\right)T \tag{18.15}$$

The ratio R/N_A is called the **Boltzmann constant,** k:

$$k = \frac{R}{N_A} = \frac{8.314 \text{ J/mol} \cdot \text{K}}{6.022 \times 10^{23} \text{ molecules/mol}} = 1.381 \times 10^{-23} \text{ J/molecule} \cdot \text{K}$$

(The current best numerical value of k is $1.3806488(13) \times 10^{-23}$ J/molecule · K). In terms of k we can rewrite Eq. (18.15) as

Average translational ⋯⋯ Mass of a molecule
kinetic energy of a $\frac{1}{2}m(v^2)_{av} = \frac{3}{2}kT$ ⋯⋯ Absolute temperature   (18.16)
gas molecule   of gas
                        Average value of the ⋯⋯ Boltzmann constant
                        square of molecular speeds

This shows that the average translational kinetic energy *per molecule* depends only on the temperature, not on the pressure, volume, or kind of molecule. We can obtain the average translational kinetic energy *per mole* by multiplying Eq. (18.16) by Avogadro's number and using the relation $M = N_A m$:

$$N_A \tfrac{1}{2}m(v^2)_{av} = \tfrac{1}{2}M(v^2)_{av} = \tfrac{3}{2}RT \qquad \begin{matrix}\text{(average translational kinetic}\\ \text{energy per mole of gas)}\end{matrix} \tag{18.17}$$

The translational kinetic energy of a mole of an ideal gas depends only on T.

Finally, it can be helpful to rewrite the ideal-gas equation on a "per-molecule" basis. We use $N = N_A n$ and $R = N_A k$ to obtain this alternative form:

$$pV = NkT \tag{18.18}$$

This shows that we can think of the Boltzmann constant k as a gas constant on a "per-molecule" basis instead of the usual "per-mole" basis for R.

Molecular Speeds

From Eqs. (18.16) and (18.17) we can obtain expressions for the square root of $(v^2)_{\text{av}}$, called the **root-mean-square speed** (or **rms speed**) v_{rms}:

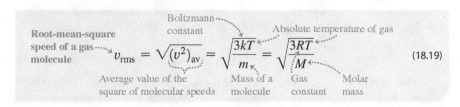

$$v_{\text{rms}} = \sqrt{(v^2)_{\text{av}}} = \sqrt{\frac{3kT}{m}} = \sqrt{\frac{3RT}{M}} \qquad (18.19)$$

Root-mean-square speed of a gas molecule; Boltzmann constant; Absolute temperature of gas; Average value of the square of molecular speeds; Mass of a molecule; Gas constant; Molar mass

It might seem more natural to give the *average* speed rather than v_{rms}, but v_{rms} follows more directly from Eqs. (18.16) and (18.17). To compute the rms speed, we square each molecular speed, add, divide by the number of molecules, and take the square root; v_{rms} is the *root* of the *mean* of the *squares*.

Equations (18.16) and (18.19) show that at a given temperature T, gas molecules of different mass m have the same average kinetic energy but different root-mean-square speeds. On average, the nitrogen molecules ($M = 28$ g/mol) in the air around you are moving faster than are the oxygen molecules ($M = 32$ g/mol). Hydrogen molecules ($M = 2$ g/mol) are fastest of all; this is why there is hardly any hydrogen in the earth's atmosphere, despite its being the most common element in the universe (**Fig. 18.14**). A sizable fraction of any H_2 molecules in the atmosphere would have speeds greater than the earth's escape speed of 1.12×10^4 m/s (calculated in Example 13.5 in Section 13.3) and would escape into space. The heavier, slower-moving gases cannot escape so easily, which is why they predominate in our atmosphere.

The assumption that individual molecules undergo perfectly elastic collisions with the container wall is a little too simple. In most cases, molecules actually adhere to the wall for a short time and then leave again with speeds that are characteristic of the temperature *of the wall*. However, the gas and the wall are ordinarily in thermal equilibrium and have the same temperature. So there is no net energy transfer between gas and wall, and our conclusions remain valid.

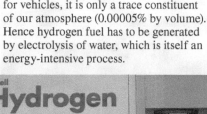

18.14 While hydrogen is a desirable fuel for vehicles, it is only a trace constituent of our atmosphere (0.00005% by volume). Hence hydrogen fuel has to be generated by electrolysis of water, which is itself an energy-intensive process.

PROBLEM-SOLVING STRATEGY 18.2 | KINETIC-MOLECULAR THEORY

IDENTIFY *the relevant concepts:* Use the results of the kinetic-molecular model to relate the macroscopic properties of a gas, such as temperature and pressure, to microscopic properties, such as molecular speeds.

SET UP *the problem* using the following steps:
1. List knowns and unknowns; identify the target variables.
2. Choose appropriate equation(s) from among Eqs. (18.14), (18.16), and (18.19).

EXECUTE *the solution* as follows: Maintain consistency in units.
1. The usual units for molar mass M are grams per mole; these units are often omitted in tables. In equations such as Eq. (18.19), when you use SI units you must express M in kilograms per mole. For example, for oxygen $M_{O_2} = 32$ g/mol $= 32 \times 10^{-3}$ kg/mol.

2. Are you working on a "per-molecule" basis (with m, N, and k) or a "per-mole" basis (with M, n, and R)? To check units, think of N as having units of "molecules"; then m has units of mass per molecule, and k has units of joules per molecule per kelvin. Similarly, n has units of moles; then M has units of mass per mole and R has units of joules per mole per kelvin.
3. Remember that T is always *absolute* (Kelvin) temperature.

EVALUATE *your answer:* Are your answers reasonable? Here's a benchmark: Typical molecular speeds at room temperature are several hundred meters per second.

EXAMPLE 18.6 MOLECULAR KINETIC ENERGY AND v_{rms}

(a) What is the average translational kinetic energy of an ideal-gas molecule at 27°C? (b) What is the total random translational kinetic energy of the molecules in 1 mole of this gas? (c) What is the rms speed of oxygen molecules at this temperature?

SOLUTION

IDENTIFY and SET UP: This problem involves the translational kinetic energy of an ideal gas on a per-molecule and per-mole basis, as well as the root-mean-square molecular speed v_{rms}. We are given $T = 27°C = 300$ K and $n = 1$ mol; we use the molecular mass m for oxygen. We use Eq. (18.16) to determine the average kinetic energy of a molecule, Eq. (18.14) to find the total molecular kinetic energy K_{tr} of 1 mole, and Eq. (18.19) to find v_{rms}.

EXECUTE: (a) From Eq. (18.16),

$$\tfrac{1}{2}m(v^2)_{av} = \tfrac{3}{2}kT = \tfrac{3}{2}(1.38 \times 10^{-23} \text{ J/K})(300 \text{ K})$$
$$= 6.21 \times 10^{-21} \text{ J}$$

(b) From Eq. (18.14), the kinetic energy of one mole is

$$K_{tr} = \tfrac{3}{2}nRT = \tfrac{3}{2}(1 \text{ mol})(8.314 \text{ J/mol} \cdot \text{K})(300 \text{ K}) = 3740 \text{ J}$$

(c) We found the mass per molecule m and molar mass M of molecular oxygen in Example 18.5. Using Eq. (18.19), we can calculate v_{rms} in two ways:

$$v_{rms} = \sqrt{\frac{3kT}{m}} = \sqrt{\frac{3(1.38 \times 10^{-23} \text{ J/K})(300 \text{ K})}{5.31 \times 10^{-26} \text{ kg}}}$$
$$= 484 \text{ m/s} = 1740 \text{ km/h} = 1080 \text{ mi/h}$$

$$v_{rms} = \sqrt{\frac{3RT}{M}} = \sqrt{\frac{3(8.314 \text{ J/mol} \cdot \text{K})(300 \text{ K})}{32.0 \times 10^{-3} \text{ kg/mol}}} = 484 \text{ m/s}$$

EVALUATE: The answer in part (a) does not depend on the mass of the molecule. We can check our result in part (b) by noting that the translational kinetic energy per mole must be equal to the product of the average translational kinetic energy per molecule from part (a) and Avogadro's number N_A: $K_{tr} = (6.21 \times 10^{-21} \text{ J/molecule}) \times (6.022 \times 10^{23} \text{ molecules}) = 3740 \text{ J}$.

EXAMPLE 18.7 CALCULATING RMS AND AVERAGE SPEEDS

Five gas molecules have speeds of 500, 600, 700, 800, and 900 m/s. What is the rms speed? What is the *average* speed?

SOLUTION

IDENTIFY and SET UP: We use the definitions of the root mean square and the average of a collection of numbers. To find v_{rms}, we square each speed, find the average (mean) of the squares, and take the square root of the result. We find v_{av} as usual.

EXECUTE: The average value of v^2 and the resulting v_{rms} for the five molecules are

$$(v^2)_{av} = \frac{500^2 + 600^2 + 700^2 + 800^2 + 900^2}{5} \text{ m}^2/\text{s}^2$$
$$= 5.10 \times 10^5 \text{ m}^2/\text{s}^2$$
$$v_{rms} = \sqrt{(v^2)_{av}} = 714 \text{ m/s}$$

The average speed v_{av} is

$$v_{av} = \frac{500 + 600 + 700 + 800 + 900}{5} \text{ m/s} = 700 \text{ m/s}$$

EVALUATE: In general v_{rms} and v_{av} are *not* the same. Roughly speaking, v_{rms} gives greater weight to the higher speeds than does v_{av}.

Collisions Between Molecules

We have ignored the possibility that two gas molecules might collide. If they are really points, they *never* collide. But consider a more realistic model in which the molecules are rigid spheres with radius r. How often do they collide with other molecules? How far do they travel, on average, between collisions? We can get approximate answers from the following rather primitive model.

Consider N spherical molecules with radius r in a volume V. Suppose only one molecule is moving. When it collides with another molecule, the distance between centers is $2r$. Suppose we draw a cylinder with radius $2r$, with its axis

18.15 In a time dt a molecule with radius r will collide with any other molecule within a cylindrical volume of radius $2r$ and length $v\,dt$.

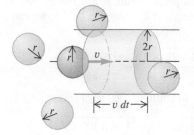

parallel to the velocity of the molecule (**Fig. 18.15**). The moving molecule collides with any other molecule whose center is inside this cylinder. In a short time dt a molecule with speed v travels a distance $v\,dt$; during this time it collides with any molecule that is in the cylindrical volume of radius $2r$ and length $v\,dt$. The volume of the cylinder is $4\pi r^2 v\,dt$. There are N/V molecules per unit volume, so the number dN with centers in this cylinder is

$$dN = 4\pi r^2 v\,dt\,N/V$$

Thus the number of collisions *per unit time* is

$$\frac{dN}{dt} = \frac{4\pi r^2 vN}{V}$$

This result assumes that only one molecule is moving. It turns out that collisions are more frequent when all the molecules move at once, and the above equation has to be multiplied by a factor of $\sqrt{2}$:

$$\frac{dN}{dt} = \frac{4\pi \sqrt{2}\,r^2 vN}{V}$$

The average time t_{mean} between collisions, called the *mean free time,* is the reciprocal of this expression:

$$t_{\text{mean}} = \frac{V}{4\pi \sqrt{2}\,r^2 vN} \tag{18.20}$$

The average distance traveled between collisions is called the **mean free path.** In our model, this is just the molecule's speed v multiplied by t_{mean}:

18.16 If you try to walk through a crowd, your mean free path—the distance you can travel on average without running into another person—depends on how large the people are and how closely they are spaced.

Speed of molecule   Volume of gas

$$\text{Mean free path of a gas molecule} \quad \lambda = vt_{\text{mean}} = \frac{V}{4\pi\sqrt{2}r^2 N} \tag{18.21}$$

Mean free time between collisions   Radius of a molecule   Number of molecules in gas

The mean free path λ (the Greek letter lambda) is inversely proportional to the number of molecules per unit volume (N/V) and inversely proportional to the cross-sectional area πr^2 of a molecule; the more molecules there are and the larger the molecule, the shorter the mean distance between collisions (**Fig. 18.16**). Note that the mean free path *does not* depend on the speed of the molecule.

We can express Eq. (18.21) in terms of macroscopic properties of the gas, using the ideal-gas equation in the form of Eq. (18.18), $pV = NkT$. We find

$$\lambda = \frac{kT}{4\pi \sqrt{2}\,r^2 p} \tag{18.22}$$

If the temperature is increased at constant pressure, the gas expands, the average distance between molecules increases, and λ increases. If the pressure is increased at constant temperature, the gas compresses and λ decreases.

EXAMPLE 18.8   **CALCULATING MEAN FREE PATH**

(a) Estimate the mean free path of a molecule of air at 27°C and 1 atm. Model the molecules as spheres with radius $r = 2.0 \times 10^{-10}$ m. (b) Estimate the mean free time of an oxygen molecule with $v = v_{\text{rms}}$ at 27°C and 1 atm.

SOLUTION

IDENTIFY and SET UP: This problem uses the concepts of mean free path and mean free time (our target variables). We use Eq. (18.22)

to determine the mean free path λ. We then use $\lambda = vt_{\text{mean}}$ in Eq. (18.21), with $v = v_{\text{rms}}$, to find the mean free time t_{mean}.

EXECUTE: (a) From Eq. (18.22),

$$\lambda = \frac{kT}{4\pi\sqrt{2}r^2 p} = \frac{(1.38 \times 10^{-23}\ \text{J/K})(300\ \text{K})}{4\pi\sqrt{2}(2.0 \times 10^{-10}\ \text{m})^2(1.01 \times 10^5\ \text{Pa})}$$

$$= 5.8 \times 10^{-8}\ \text{m}$$

(b) From Example 18.6, for oxygen at 27°C the root-mean-square speed is $v_{rms} = 484$ m/s, so the mean free time for a molecule with this speed is

$$t_{mean} = \frac{\lambda}{v} = \frac{5.8 \times 10^{-8} \text{ m}}{484 \text{ m/s}} = 1.2 \times 10^{-10} \text{ s}$$

This molecule undergoes about 10^{10} collisions per second!

EVALUATE: Note that from Eqs. (18.21) and (18.22) the mean free *path* doesn't depend on the molecule's speed, but the mean free *time* does. Slower molecules have a longer average time interval t_{mean} between collisions than do fast ones, but the average *distance* λ between collisions is the same no matter what the molecule's speed. Our answer to part (a) says that the molecule doesn't go far between collisions, but the mean free path is still several hundred times the molecular radius r.

TEST YOUR UNDERSTANDING OF SECTION 18.3 Rank the following gases in order from (a) highest to lowest rms speed of molecules and (b) highest to lowest average translational kinetic energy of a molecule: (i) oxygen ($M = 32.0$ g/mol) at 300 K; (ii) nitrogen ($M = 28.0$ g/mol) at 300 K; (iii) oxygen at 330 K; (iv) nitrogen at 330 K. ❙

18.4 HEAT CAPACITIES

When we introduced the concept of heat capacity in Section 17.5, we talked about ways to *measure* the specific heat or molar heat capacity of a particular material. Now we'll see how to *predict* these on theoretical grounds.

Heat Capacities of Gases

The basis of our analysis is that heat is *energy* in transit. When we add heat to a substance, we are increasing its molecular energy. We'll assume that the volume of the gas remains constant; if we were to let the gas expand, it would do work by pushing on the moving walls of its container, and this additional energy transfer would have to be included in our calculations. We'll return to this more general case in Chapter 19. For now we are concerned with C_V, the molar heat capacity *at constant volume*.

In the simple kinetic-molecular model of Section 18.3 the molecular energy consists of only the translational kinetic energy K_{tr} of the pointlike molecules. This energy is directly proportional to the absolute temperature T, as shown by Eq. (18.14), $K_{tr} = \frac{3}{2}nRT$. When the temperature changes by a small amount dT, the corresponding change in kinetic energy is

$$dK_{tr} = \tfrac{3}{2}nR\,dT \tag{18.23}$$

From the definition of molar heat capacity at constant volume, C_V (see Section 17.5), we also have

$$dQ = nC_V\,dT \tag{18.24}$$

where dQ is the heat input needed for a temperature change dT. Now if K_{tr} represents the total molecular energy, as we have assumed, then dQ and dK_{tr} must be equal (**Fig. 18.17**). From Eqs. (18.23) and (18.24), this says

$$nC_V\,dT = \tfrac{3}{2}nR\,dT$$

> Molar heat capacity
> at constant volume, $\quad C_V = \tfrac{3}{2}R \longleftarrow$ Gas constant $\qquad$ (18.25)
> ideal gas of point particles

This surprisingly simple result says that the molar heat capacity at constant volume is $3R/2$ for *any* gas whose molecules can be represented as points.

Does Eq. (18.25) agree with experiment? In SI units, Eq. (18.25) gives

$$C_V = \tfrac{3}{2}(8.314 \text{ J/mol}\cdot\text{K}) = 12.47 \text{ J/mol}\cdot\text{K}$$

18.17 (a) A fixed volume V of a monatomic ideal gas. (b) When an amount of heat dQ is added to the gas, the total translational kinetic energy increases by $dK_{tr} = dQ$ and the temperature increases by $dT = dQ/nC_V$.

(a)

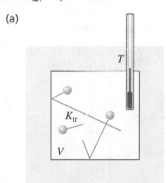

(b)

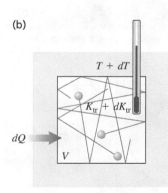

Type of Gas	Gas	C_V (J/mol · K)
Monatomic	He	12.47
	Ar	12.47
Diatomic	H_2	20.42
	N_2	20.76
	O_2	20.85
	CO	20.85
Polyatomic	CO_2	28.46
	SO_2	31.39
	H_2S	25.95

18.18 Motions of a diatomic molecule.

(a) Translational motion. The molecule moves as a whole; its velocity may be described as the x-, y-, and z-velocity components of its center of mass.

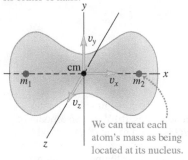

We can treat each atom's mass as being located at its nucleus.

(b) Rotational motion. The molecule rotates about its center of mass. This molecule has two independent axes of rotation.

Independent axes of rotation

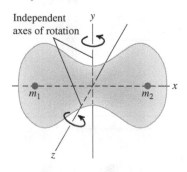

(c) Vibrational motion. The molecule oscillates as though the nuclei were connected by a spring.

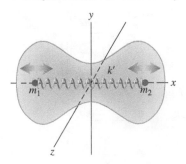

For comparison, **Table 18.1** gives measured values of C_V for several gases. We see that for *monatomic* gases our prediction is right on the money, but that it is way off for diatomic and polyatomic gases.

This comparison tells us that our point-molecule model is good enough for monatomic gases but that for diatomic and polyatomic molecules we need something more sophisticated. For example, we can picture a diatomic molecule as *two* point masses, like a little elastic dumbbell (see **Fig. 18.18**), with an interaction force between the atoms of the kind shown in Fig. 18.8. Such a molecule can have additional kinetic energy associated with *rotation* about axes through its center of mass. The atoms may also *vibrate* along the line joining them, with additional kinetic and potential energies.

When heat flows into a *monatomic* gas at constant volume, *all* of the added energy goes into an increase in random *translational* molecular kinetic energy. Equation (18.23) shows that this gives rise to an increase in temperature. But when the temperature is increased by the same amount in a *diatomic* or *polyatomic* gas, additional heat is needed to supply the increased rotational and vibrational energies. Thus polyatomic gases have *larger* molar heat capacities than monatomic gases, as Table 18.1 shows.

But how do we know how much energy is associated with each additional kind of motion of a complex molecule, compared to the translational kinetic energy? The new principle that we need is called the principle of **equipartition of energy.** It can be derived from sophisticated statistical-mechanics considerations; that derivation is beyond our scope, and we will treat the principle as an axiom.

The principle of equipartition of energy states that each velocity component (either linear or angular) has, on average, an associated kinetic energy per molecule of $\frac{1}{2}kT$, or one-half the product of the Boltzmann constant and the absolute temperature. The number of velocity components needed to describe the motion of a molecule completely is called the number of **degrees of freedom.** For a monatomic gas, there are three degrees of freedom (for the velocity components v_x, v_y, and v_z); this gives a total average kinetic energy per molecule of $3\left(\frac{1}{2}kT\right)$, consistent with Eq. (18.16).

For a *diatomic* molecule there are two possible axes of rotation, perpendicular to each other and to the molecule's axis. (We don't include rotation about the molecule's own axis because in ordinary collisions there is no way for this rotational motion to change.) If we add two rotational degrees of freedom for a diatomic molecule, the average total kinetic energy per molecule is $\frac{5}{2}kT$ instead of $\frac{3}{2}kT$. The total kinetic energy of n moles is $K_{\text{total}} = nN_A\left(\frac{5}{2}kT\right) = \frac{5}{2}n(kN_A)T = \frac{5}{2}nRT$, and the molar heat capacity (at constant volume) is

> Molar heat capacity at constant volume, ideal diatomic gas $\quad C_V = \frac{5}{2}R \quad$ Gas constant $\qquad$ (18.26)

In SI units,

$$C_V = \frac{5}{2}(8.314 \text{ J/mol} \cdot \text{K}) = 20.79 \text{ J/mol} \cdot \text{K}$$

This value is close to the measured values for diatomic gases in Table 18.1.

Vibrational motion can also contribute to the heat capacities of gases. Molecular bonds can stretch and bend, and the resulting vibrations lead to additional degrees of freedom and additional energies. For most diatomic gases, however, vibration does *not* contribute appreciably to heat capacity. The reason for this involves some concepts of quantum mechanics. Briefly, vibrational energy can change only in finite steps. If the energy change of the first step is much larger than the energy possessed by most molecules, then nearly all the molecules remain in the minimum-energy state of motion. Changing the temperature does not change their average vibrational energy appreciably, and the vibrational degrees of freedom are said to be "frozen out." In more complex molecules the

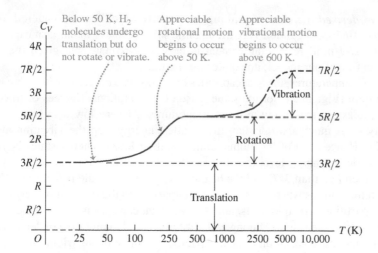

18.19 Experimental values of C_V, the molar heat capacity at constant volume, for hydrogen gas (H_2). The temperature is plotted on a logarithmic scale.

gaps between permitted energy levels can be much smaller, and then vibration *does* contribute to heat capacity. The rotational energy of a molecule also changes by finite steps, but they are usually much smaller; the "freezing out" of rotational degrees of freedom occurs only in rare instances.

In Table 18.1 the large values of C_V for polyatomic molecules show the effects of vibrational energy. In addition, a molecule with three or more atoms that are not in a straight line has *three* rotational degrees of freedom.

From this discussion we expect heat capacities to be temperature-dependent, generally increasing with increasing temperature. **Figure 18.19** is a graph of the temperature dependence of C_V for hydrogen gas (H_2), showing the temperatures at which the rotational and vibrational energies begin to contribute.

Heat Capacities of Solids

We can carry out a similar heat-capacity analysis for a crystalline solid. Consider a crystal consisting of N identical atoms (a *monatomic solid*). Each atom is bound to an equilibrium position by interatomic forces. Solid materials are elastic, so forces must permit stretching and bending of the bonds. We can think of a crystal as an array of atoms connected by little springs (**Fig. 18.20**).

Each atom can *vibrate* around its equilibrium position and has three degrees of freedom, corresponding to its three components of velocity. According to the equipartition principle, each atom has an average kinetic energy of $\frac{1}{2}kT$ for each degree of freedom. In addition, there is *potential* energy associated with the elastic deformation. For a simple harmonic oscillator (discussed in Chapter 14) it is not hard to show that the average kinetic energy is *equal* to the average potential energy. In our model of a crystal, each atom is a three-dimensional harmonic oscillator; it can be shown that the equality of average kinetic and potential energies also holds here, provided that the "spring" forces obey Hooke's law.

Thus we expect each atom to have an average kinetic energy $\frac{3}{2}kT$ and an average potential energy $\frac{3}{2}kT$, or an average total energy $3kT$ per atom. If the crystal contains N atoms or n moles, its total energy is

$$E_{\text{total}} = 3NkT = 3nRT \tag{18.27}$$

From this we conclude that the molar heat capacity of a crystal should be

Molar heat capacity of an ideal monatomic solid (rule of Dulong and Petit) $\quad C_V = 3R \quad$ Gas constant $\tag{18.28}$

In SI units,

$$C_V = (3)(8.314 \text{ J/mol} \cdot \text{K}) = 24.9 \text{ J/mol} \cdot \text{K}$$

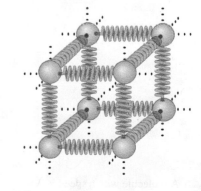

18.20 To visualize the forces between neighboring atoms in a crystal, envision every atom as being attached to its neighbors by springs.

We have *derived* the **rule of Dulong and Petit,** which we encountered as an *empirical* finding in Section 17.5: Monatomic solids all have molar heat capacities of about 25 J/mol·K. The agreement is only approximate, but given the very simple nature of our model, it is quite significant.

At low temperatures, the heat capacities of most solids *decrease* with decreasing temperature (**Fig. 18.21**) for the same reason that vibrational degrees of freedom of molecules are frozen out at low temperatures. At very low temperatures the quantity kT is much *smaller* than the smallest energy step the vibrating atoms can take. Hence most of the atoms remain in their lowest energy states because the next higher energy level is out of reach. The average vibrational energy per atom is then *less* than $3kT$, and the heat capacity per molecule is *less* than $3k$. At higher temperatures when kT is *large* in comparison to the minimum energy step, the equipartition principle holds, and the total heat capacity is $3k$ per molecule or $3R$ per mole as the rule of Dulong and Petit predicts. Quantitative understanding of the temperature variation of heat capacities was one of the triumphs of quantum mechanics during its initial development in the 1920s.

TEST YOUR UNDERSTANDING OF SECTION 18.4 A cylinder with a fixed volume contains hydrogen gas (H_2) at 25 K. You then add heat to the gas at a constant rate until its temperature reaches 500 K. Does the temperature of the gas increase at a constant rate? Why or why not? If not, does the temperature increase most rapidly near the beginning or near the end of this process? ▌

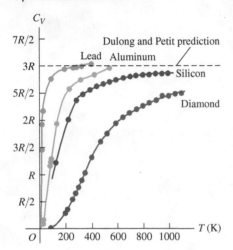

18.21 Experimental values of C_V for lead, aluminum, silicon, and diamond. At high temperatures, C_V for each solid approaches about $3R$, in agreement with the rule of Dulong and Petit. At low temperatures, C_V is much less than $3R$.

18.5 MOLECULAR SPEEDS

As we mentioned in Section 18.3, the molecules in a gas don't all have the same speed. **Figure 18.22** shows one experimental scheme for measuring the distribution of molecular speeds. A substance is vaporized in a hot oven; molecules of the vapor escape through an aperture in the oven wall and into a vacuum chamber. A series of slits blocks all molecules except those in a narrow beam, which is aimed at a pair of rotating disks. A molecule passing through the slit in the first disk is blocked by the second disk unless it arrives just as the slit in the second disk is lined up with the beam. The disks function as a speed selector that passes only molecules within a certain narrow speed range. This range can be varied by changing the disk rotation speed, and we can measure how many molecules lie within each of various speed ranges.

To describe the results of such measurements, we define a function $f(v)$ called a *distribution function*. If we observe a total of N molecules, the number dN having speeds in the range between v and $v + dv$ is given by

$$dN = Nf(v)\,dv \tag{18.29}$$

18.22 A molecule with a speed v passes through the slit in the first rotating disk. When the molecule reaches the second rotating disk, the disks have rotated through the offset angle θ. If $v = \omega x/\theta$, the molecule passes through the slit in the second rotating disk and reaches the detector.

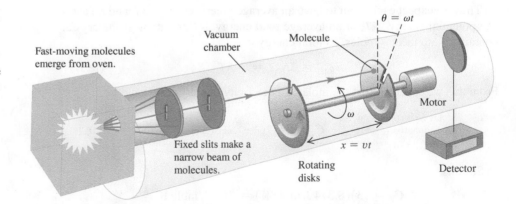

The *probability* that a randomly chosen molecule will have a speed in the interval v to $v + dv$ is $f(v)dv$. Hence $f(v)$ is the probability per unit speed *interval*; it is *not* the probability that a molecule has speed exactly equal to v. Since a probability is a pure number, $f(v)$ has units of reciprocal speed (s/m).

Figure 18.23a shows distribution functions for three different temperatures. At each temperature the height of the curve for any value of v is proportional to the number of molecules with speeds near v. The peak of the curve represents the *most probable speed* v_{mp} for the corresponding temperature. As the temperature increases, the average molecular kinetic energy increases, and so the peak of $f(v)$ shifts to higher and higher speeds.

Figure 18.23b shows that the area under a curve between any two values of v represents the fraction of all the molecules having speeds in that range. Every molecule must have *some* value of v, so the integral of $f(v)$ over all v must be unity for any T.

If we know $f(v)$, we can calculate the most probable speed v_{mp}, the average speed v_{av}, and the rms speed v_{rms}. To find v_{mp}, we simply find the point where $df/dv = 0$; this gives the value of the speed where the curve has its peak. To find v_{av}, we take the number $Nf(v)dv$ having speeds in each interval dv, multiply each number by the corresponding speed v, add all these products (by integrating over all v from zero to infinity), and finally divide by N. That is,

$$v_{av} = \int_0^\infty v f(v)\, dv \qquad (18.30)$$

We can find the rms speed in a similar way; the average of v^2 is

$$(v^2)_{av} = \int_0^\infty v^2 f(v)\, dv \qquad (18.31)$$

and v_{rms} is the square root of this.

The Maxwell–Boltzmann Distribution

The function $f(v)$ describing the actual distribution of molecular speeds is called the **Maxwell–Boltzmann distribution.** It can be derived from statistical mechanics considerations, but that derivation is beyond our scope. Here is the result:

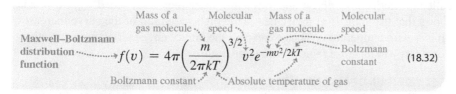

Maxwell–Boltzmann distribution function

Mass of a gas molecule ... Molecular speed ... Mass of a gas molecule ... Molecular speed

$$f(v) = 4\pi \left(\frac{m}{2\pi kT}\right)^{3/2} v^2 e^{-mv^2/2kT} \qquad (18.32)$$

Boltzmann constant ... Absolute temperature of gas ... Boltzmann constant

We can also express this function in terms of the translational kinetic energy of a molecule, which we denote by ϵ; that is, $\epsilon = \frac{1}{2}mv^2$. We invite you to verify that when this is substituted into Eq. (18.32), the result is

$$f(\epsilon) = \frac{8\pi}{m} \left(\frac{m}{2\pi kT}\right)^{3/2} \epsilon e^{-\epsilon/kT} \qquad (18.33)$$

This form shows that the exponent in the Maxwell–Boltzmann distribution function is $-\epsilon/kT$; the shape of the curve is determined by the relative magnitude of ϵ and kT at any point. You can prove that the *peak* of each curve occurs where $\epsilon = kT$, corresponding to a most probable speed v_{mp}:

$$v_{mp} = \sqrt{\frac{2kT}{m}} \qquad (18.34)$$

18.23 (a) Curves of the Maxwell–Boltzmann distribution function $f(v)$ for three temperatures. (b) The shaded areas under the curve represent the fractions of molecules within certain speed ranges. The most probable speed v_{mp} for a given temperature is at the peak of the curve.

(a)

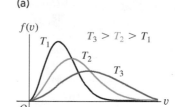

As temperature increases:
- the curve flattens.
- the maximum shifts to higher speeds.

(b)

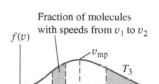

Fraction of molecules with speeds from v_1 to v_2

Fraction of molecules with speeds greater than v_A

TABLE 18.2	Fractions of Molecules in an Ideal Gas with Speeds Less Than Various Multiples of v_{rms}	
v/v_{rms}	Fraction	
0.20	0.011	
0.40	0.077	
0.60	0.218	
0.80	0.411	
1.00	0.608	
1.20	0.771	
1.40	0.882	
1.60	0.947	
1.80	0.979	
2.00	0.993	

To find the average speed, we substitute Eq. (18.32) into Eq. (18.30), make a change of variable $v^2 = x$, and integrate by parts. The result is

$$v_{av} = \sqrt{\frac{8kT}{\pi m}} \qquad (18.35)$$

Finally, to find the rms speed, we substitute Eq. (18.32) into Eq. (18.31). Evaluating the resulting integral takes some mathematical acrobatics, but we can find it in a table of integrals. The result is

$$v_{rms} = \sqrt{\frac{3kT}{m}} \qquad (18.36)$$

This result agrees with Eq. (18.19); it *must* agree if the Maxwell–Boltzmann distribution is to be consistent with our kinetic-theory calculations.

Table 18.2 shows the fraction of all the molecules in an ideal gas that have speeds *less than* various multiples of v_{rms}. These numbers were obtained by numerical integration; they are the same for all ideal gases.

The distribution of molecular speeds in liquids is similar, although not identical, to that for gases. We can understand evaporation and the vapor pressure of a liquid on this basis. Suppose a molecule must have a speed at least as great as v_A in Fig. 18.23b to escape from the surface of a liquid into the adjacent vapor. The number of such molecules, represented by the area under the "tail" of each curve (to the right of v_A), increases rapidly with temperature. Thus the rate at which molecules can escape is strongly temperature-dependent. This process is balanced by one in which molecules in the vapor phase collide inelastically with the surface and are trapped into the liquid phase. The number of molecules suffering this fate per unit time is proportional to the pressure in the vapor phase. Phase equilibrium between liquid and vapor occurs when these two competing processes proceed at the same rate. So if the molecular speed distributions are known for various temperatures, we can make a theoretical prediction of vapor pressure as a function of temperature. When liquid evaporates, it's the high-speed molecules that escape from the surface. The ones that are left have less energy on average; this gives us a molecular view of evaporative cooling.

Rates of chemical reactions are often strongly temperature-dependent, and the reason is contained in the Maxwell–Boltzmann distribution. When two reacting molecules collide, the reaction can occur only when the molecules are close enough for their electrons to interact strongly. This requires a minimum energy, called the *activation energy,* and thus a minimum molecular speed. Figure 18.23a shows that the number of molecules in the high-speed tail of the curve increases rapidly with temperature. Thus we expect the rate of any reaction with an activation energy to increase rapidly with temperature.

BIO Application Activation Energy and Moth Activity This hawkmoth of genus *Manduca* cannot fly if the temperature of its muscles is below 29°C. The reason is that the enzyme-catalyzed reactions that power aerobic metabolism and enable muscle action require a minimum molecular energy (activation energy). Just like the molecules in an ideal gas, at low temperatures very few of the molecules involved in these reactions have high energy. As the temperature increases, more molecules have the required minimum energy and the reactions take place at a greater rate. Above 29°C, enough power is generated to allow the hawkmoth to fly.

TEST YOUR UNDERSTANDING OF SECTION 18.5 A quantity of gas containing N molecules has a speed distribution function $f(v)$. How many molecules have speeds between v_1 and $v_2 > v_1$? (i) $\int_0^{v_2} f(v)\,dv - \int_0^{v_1} f(v)\,dv$; (ii) $N[\int_0^{v_2} f(v)\,dv - \int_0^{v_1} f(v)\,dv]$; (iii) $\int_0^{v_1} f(v)\,dv - \int_0^{v_2} f(v)\,dv$; (iv) $N[\int_0^{v_1} f(v)\,dv - \int_0^{v_2} f(v)\,dv]$; (v) none of these. ∎

18.6 PHASES OF MATTER

An ideal gas is the simplest system to analyze from a molecular viewpoint because we ignore the interactions between molecules. But those interactions are the very thing that makes matter condense into the liquid and solid phases under some conditions. So it's not surprising that theoretical analysis of liquid and solid structure and behavior is a lot more complicated than that for gases. We won't try to go far here with a microscopic picture, but we can talk in general about phases of matter, phase equilibrium, and phase transitions.

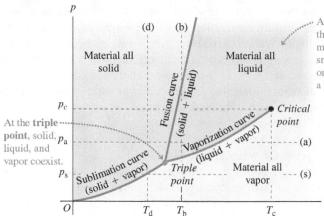

18.24 A typical pT phase diagram, showing regions of temperature and pressure at which the various phases exist and where phase changes occur.

In Section 17.6 we learned that each phase is stable in only certain ranges of temperature and pressure. A transition from one phase to another ordinarily requires **phase equilibrium** between the two phases, and for a given pressure this occurs at only one specific temperature. We can represent these conditions on a graph with axes p and T, called a **phase diagram; Fig. 18.24** shows an example. Each point on the diagram represents a pair of values of p and T.

Only a single phase can exist at each point in Fig. 18.24, except for points on the solid lines, where two phases can coexist in phase equilibrium. The fusion curve separates the solid and liquid areas and represents possible conditions of solid-liquid phase equilibrium. The vaporization curve separates the liquid and vapor areas, and the sublimation curve separates the solid and vapor areas. All three curves meet at the **triple point,** the only condition under which all three phases can coexist (**Fig. 18.25**). In Section 17.3 we used the triple-point temperature of water to define the Kelvin temperature scale. **Table 18.3** gives triple-point data for several substances.

If we heat a substance at a constant pressure p_a, it goes through a series of states represented by the horizontal line (a) in Fig. 18.24. The melting and boiling temperatures at this pressure are the temperatures at which the line intersects the fusion and vaporization curves, respectively. When the pressure is p_s, constant-pressure heating transforms a substance from solid directly to vapor. This process is called *sublimation;* the intersection of line (s) with the sublimation curve gives the temperature T_s at which it occurs for a pressure p_s. At any pressure less than the triple-point pressure, no liquid phase is possible. The triple-point pressure for carbon dioxide (CO_2) is 5.1 atm. At normal atmospheric pressure, solid CO_2 ("dry ice") undergoes sublimation; there is no liquid phase.

Line (b) in Fig. 18.24 represents compression at a constant temperature T_b. The material passes from vapor to liquid and then to solid at the points where line (b) crosses the vaporization curve and fusion curve, respectively. Line (d) shows constant-temperature compression at a lower temperature T_d; the material passes from vapor to solid at the point where line (d) crosses the sublimation curve.

We saw in the pV-diagram of Fig. 18.7 that a liquid-vapor phase transition occurs only when the temperature and pressure are less than those at the point at the top of the green shaded area labeled "Liquid-vapor phase equilibrium region." This point corresponds to the endpoint at the top of the vaporization curve in Fig. 18.24. It is called the **critical point,** and the corresponding values of p and T are called the critical pressure and temperature, p_c and T_c. A gas at a pressure *above* the critical pressure does not separate into two phases when it is cooled at constant pressure (along a horizontal line above the critical point in Fig. 18.24). Instead, its properties change gradually and continuously from those we ordinarily associate with a gas (low density, large compressibility) to those of a liquid (high density, small compressibility) *without a phase transition*.

18.25 Atmospheric pressure on earth is higher than the triple-point pressure of water (see line (a) in Fig. 18.24). Depending on the temperature, water can exist as a vapor (in the atmosphere), as a liquid (in the ocean), or as a solid (like the iceberg shown here).

TABLE 18.3	Triple-Point Data	
Substance	**Temperature (K)**	**Pressure (Pa)**
Hydrogen	13.80	0.0704×10^5
Deuterium	18.63	0.171×10^5
Neon	24.56	0.432×10^5
Nitrogen	63.18	0.125×10^5
Oxygen	54.36	0.00152×10^5
Ammonia	195.40	0.0607×10^5
Carbon dioxide	216.55	5.17×10^5
Sulfur dioxide	197.68	0.00167×10^5
Water	273.16	0.00610×10^5

You can understand this by thinking about liquid-phase transitions at successively higher points on the vaporization curve. As we approach the critical point, the *differences* in physical properties (such as density and compressibility) between the liquid and vapor phases become smaller. Exactly *at* the critical point they all become zero, and at this point the distinction between liquid and vapor disappears. The heat of vaporization also grows smaller as we approach the critical point, and it too becomes zero at the critical point.

For nearly all familiar materials the critical pressures are much greater than atmospheric pressure, so we don't observe this behavior in everyday life. For example, the critical point for water is at 647.4 K and 221.2×10^5 Pa (about 218 atm or 3210 psi). But high-pressure steam boilers in electric generating plants regularly run at pressures and temperatures well above the critical point.

Many substances can exist in more than one solid phase. A familiar example is carbon, which exists as noncrystalline soot and crystalline graphite and diamond. Water is another example; more than a dozen types of ice, differing in crystal structure and physical properties, have been observed at very high pressures.

pVT-Surfaces

We remarked in Section 18.1 that for any material, it can be useful to represent the equation of state as a surface in a three-dimensional space with coordinates *p*, *V*, and *T*. **Figure 18.26** shows a typical *pVT*-surface. The light lines represent *pV*-isotherms; projecting them onto the *pV*-plane gives a diagram similar to Fig. 18.7. The *pV*-isotherms represent contour lines on the *pVT*-surface, just as contour lines on a topographic map represent the elevation (the third dimension) at each point. The projections of the edges of the surface onto the *pT*-plane give the *pT* phase diagram of Fig. 18.24.

Line *abcdef* in Fig. 18.26 represents constant-pressure heating, with melting along *bc* and vaporization along *de*. Note the volume changes that occur as *T* increases along this line. Line *ghjklm* corresponds to an isothermal (constant temperature) compression, with liquefaction along *hj* and solidification along *kl*. Between these, segments *gh* and *jk* represent isothermal compression with increase in pressure; the pressure increases are much greater in the liquid region *jk* and the solid region *lm* than in the vapor region *gh*. Finally, line *nopq* represents isothermal solidification directly from vapor, as in the formation of snowflakes or frost.

18.26 A *pVT*-surface for a substance that expands on melting. Projections of the boundaries on the surface onto the *pT*- and *pV*-planes are also shown.

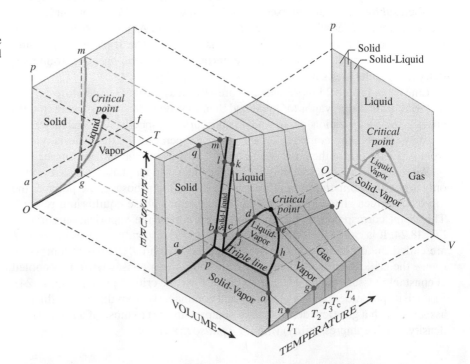

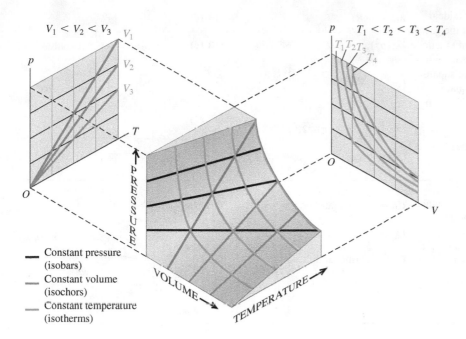

18.27 A pVT-surface for an ideal gas. At the left, each orange line corresponds to a certain constant volume; at the right, each green line corresponds to a certain constant temperature.

Figure 18.27 shows the much simpler pVT-surface for a substance that obeys the ideal-gas equation of state under all conditions. The projections of the constant-temperature curves onto the pV-plane correspond to the curves of Fig. 18.6, and the projections of the constant-volume curves onto the pT-plane show that pressure is directly proportional to absolute temperature. Figure 18.27 also shows the *isobars* (curves of constant pressure) and *isochors* (curves of constant volume) for an ideal gas.

TEST YOUR UNDERSTANDING OF SECTION 18.6 The average atmospheric pressure on Mars is 6.0×10^2 Pa. Could there be lakes or rivers of liquid water on Mars today? What about in the past, when the atmospheric pressure is thought to have been substantially greater than today? ▮

CHAPTER 18 SUMMARY

SOLUTIONS TO ALL EXAMPLES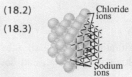

Equations of state: The pressure p, volume V, and absolute temperature T of a given quantity of a substance are related by an equation of state. This relationship applies only for equilibrium states, in which p and T are uniform throughout the system. The ideal-gas equation of state, Eq. (18.3), involves the number of moles n and a constant R that is the same for all gases. (See Examples 18.1–18.4.)

$$pV = nRT \qquad (18.3)$$

Molecular properties of matter: The molar mass M of a pure substance is the mass per mole. The mass m_{total} of a quantity of substance equals M multiplied by the number of moles n. Avogadro's number N_A is the number of molecules in a mole. The mass m of an individual molecule is M divided by N_A. (See Example 18.5.)

$$m_{total} = nM \qquad (18.2)$$
$$M = N_A m \qquad (18.3)$$

Kinetic-molecular model of an ideal gas: In an ideal gas, the total translational kinetic energy of the gas as a whole (K_{tr}) and the average translational kinetic energy per molecule $[\frac{1}{2}m(v^2)_{av}]$ are proportional to the absolute temperature T, and the root-mean-square speed of molecules is proportional to the square root of T. These expressions involve the Boltzmann constant $k = R/N_A$. (See Examples 18.6 and 18.7.) The mean free path λ of molecules in an ideal gas depends on the number of molecules per volume (N/V) and the molecular radius r. (See Example 18.8.)

$$K_{tr} = \tfrac{3}{2}nRT \tag{18.14}$$

$$\tfrac{1}{2}m(v^2)_{av} = \tfrac{3}{2}kT \tag{18.16}$$

$$v_{rms} = \sqrt{(v^2)_{av}} = \sqrt{\frac{3kT}{m}} \tag{18.19}$$

$$\lambda = vt_{mean} = \frac{V}{4\pi\sqrt{2}\,r^2 N} \tag{18.21}$$

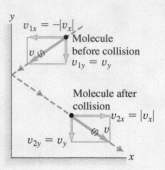

Heat capacities: The molar heat capacity at constant volume C_V is a simple multiple of the gas constant R for certain idealized cases: an ideal monatomic gas [Eq. (18.25)]; an ideal diatomic gas including rotational energy [Eq. (18.26)]; and an ideal monatomic solid [Eq. (18.28)]. Many real systems are approximated well by these idealizations.

$$C_V = \tfrac{3}{2}R \text{ (monatomic gas)} \tag{18.25}$$

$$C_V = \tfrac{5}{2}R \text{ (diatomic gas)} \tag{18.26}$$

$$C_V = 3R \text{ (monatomic solid)} \tag{18.28}$$

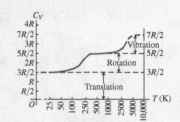

Molecular speeds: The speeds of molecules in an ideal gas are distributed according to the Maxwell–Boltzmann distribution $f(v)$. The quantity $f(v)\,dv$ describes what fraction of the molecules have speeds between v and $v + dv$.

$$f(v) = 4\pi\left(\frac{m}{2\pi kT}\right)^{3/2}v^2 e^{-mv^2/2kT} \tag{18.32}$$

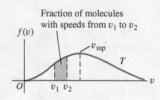

Phases of matter: Ordinary matter exists in the solid, liquid, and gas phases. A phase diagram shows conditions under which two phases can coexist in phase equilibrium. All three phases can coexist at the triple point. The vaporization curve ends at the critical point, above which the distinction between the liquid and gas phases disappears.

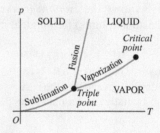

BRIDGING PROBLEM GAS ON JUPITER'S MOON EUROPA

An astronaut visiting Jupiter's satellite Europa leaves a canister of 1.20 mol of nitrogen gas (28.0 g/mol) at 25.0°C on the satellite's surface. Europa has no significant atmosphere, and the acceleration due to gravity at its surface is 1.30 m/s². The canister springs a leak, allowing molecules to escape from a small hole. (a) What is the maximum height (in km) above Europa's surface that is reached by a nitrogen molecule whose speed equals the rms speed? Assume that the molecule is shot straight up out of the hole in the canister, and ignore the variation in g with altitude. (b) The escape speed from Europa is 2025 m/s. Can any of the nitrogen molecules escape from Europa and into space?

SOLUTION GUIDE

IDENTIFY AND SET UP

1. Sketch the situation, showing all relevant dimensions.
2. List the unknown quantities, and decide which are the target variables.

3. How will you find the rms speed of the nitrogen molecules? What principle will you use to find the maximum height that a molecule with this speed can reach?
4. Does the rms molecular speed in the gas represent the maximum molecular speed? If not, what is the maximum speed?

EXECUTE

5. Solve for the rms speed. Use this to calculate the maximum height that a molecule with this speed can reach.
6. Use your result from step 5 to answer the question in part (b).

EVALUATE

7. Do your results depend on the amount of gas in the container? Why or why not?
8. How would your results from steps 5 and 6 be affected if the gas cylinder were instead left on Jupiter's satellite Ganymede, which has higher surface gravity than Europa and a higher escape speed? Like Europa, Ganymede has no significant atmosphere.

Problems

For assigned homework and other learning materials, go to MasteringPhysics®.

•, ••, •••: Difficulty levels. **CP**: Cumulative problems incorporating material from earlier chapters. **CALC**: Problems requiring calculus. **DATA**: Problems involving real data, scientific evidence, experimental design, and/or statistical reasoning. **BIO**: Biosciences problems.

DISCUSSION QUESTIONS

Q18.1 Section 18.1 states that ordinarily, pressure, volume, and temperature cannot change individually without one affecting the others. Yet when a liquid evaporates, its volume changes, even though its pressure and temperature are constant. Is this inconsistent? Why or why not?

Q18.2 In the ideal-gas equation, could an equivalent Celsius temperature be used instead of the Kelvin one if an appropriate numerical value of the constant R is used? Why or why not?

Q18.3 When a car is driven some distance, the air pressure in the tires increases. Why? Should you let out some air to reduce the pressure? Why or why not?

Q18.4 The coolant in an automobile radiator is kept at a pressure higher than atmospheric pressure. Why is this desirable? The radiator cap will release coolant when the gauge pressure of the coolant reaches a certain value, typically 15 lb/in.^{2} or so. Why not just seal the system completely?

Q18.5 Unwrapped food placed in a freezer experiences dehydration, known as "freezer burn." Why?

Q18.6 A group of students drove from their university (near sea level) up into the mountains for a skiing weekend. Upon arriving at the slopes, they discovered that the bags of potato chips they had brought for snacks had all burst open. What caused this to happen?

Q18.7 The derivation of the ideal-gas equation included the assumption that the number of molecules is very large, so that we could compute the average force due to many collisions. However, the ideal-gas equation holds accurately only at low pressures, where the molecules are few and far between. Is this inconsistent? Why or why not?

Q18.8 A rigid, perfectly insulated container has a membrane dividing its volume in half. One side contains a gas at an absolute temperature T_0 and pressure p_0, while the other half is completely empty. Suddenly a small hole develops in the membrane, allowing the gas to leak out into the other half until it eventually occupies twice its original volume. In terms of T_0 and p_0, what will be the new temperature and pressure of the gas when it is distributed equally in both halves of the container? Explain your reasoning.

Q18.9 (a) Which has more atoms: a kilogram of hydrogen or a kilogram of lead? Which has more mass? (b) Which has more atoms: a mole of hydrogen or a mole of lead? Which has more mass? Explain your reasoning.

Q18.10 Use the concepts of the kinetic-molecular model to explain: (a) why the pressure of a gas in a rigid container increases as heat is added to the gas and (b) why the pressure of a gas increases as we compress it, even if we do not change its temperature.

Q18.11 The proportions of various gases in the earth's atmosphere change somewhat with altitude. Would you expect the proportion of oxygen at high altitude to be greater or less than at sea level compared to the proportion of nitrogen? Why?

Q18.12 Comment on the following statement: *When two gases are mixed, if they are to be in thermal equilibrium, they must have the same average molecular speed.* Is the statement correct? Why or why not?

Q18.13 The kinetic-molecular model contains a hidden assumption about the temperature of the container walls. What is this assumption? What would happen if this assumption were not valid?

Q18.14 The temperature of an ideal gas is directly proportional to the average kinetic energy of its molecules. If a container of ideal gas is moving past you at 2000 m/s, is the temperature of the gas higher than if the container was at rest? Explain your reasoning.

Q18.15 If the pressure of an ideal monatomic gas is increased while the number of moles is kept constant, what happens to the average translational kinetic energy of one atom of the gas? Is it possible to change *both* the volume and the pressure of an ideal gas and keep the average translational kinetic energy of the atoms constant? Explain.

Q18.16 In deriving the ideal-gas equation from the kinetic-molecular model, we ignored potential energy due to the earth's gravity. Is this omission justified? Why or why not?

Q18.17 Imagine a special air filter placed in a window of a house. The tiny holes in the filter allow only air molecules moving faster than a certain speed to exit the house, and allow only air molecules moving slower than that speed to enter the house from outside. What effect would this filter have on the temperature inside the house? (It turns out that the second law of thermodynamics—which we will discuss in Chapter 20—tells us that such a wonderful air filter would be impossible to make.)

Q18.18 A gas storage tank has a small leak. The pressure in the tank drops more quickly if the gas is hydrogen or helium than if it is oxygen. Why?

Q18.19 Consider two specimens of ideal gas at the same temperature. Specimen A has the same total mass as specimen B, but the molecules in specimen A have greater molar mass than they do in specimen B. In which specimen is the total kinetic energy of the gas greater? Does your answer depend on the molecular structure of the gases? Why or why not?

Q18.20 The temperature of an ideal monatomic gas is increased from 25°C to 50°C. Does the average translational kinetic energy of each gas atom double? Explain. If your answer is no, what would the final temperature be if the average translational kinetic energy was doubled?

Q18.21 If the root-mean-square speed of the atoms of an ideal gas is to be doubled, by what factor must the Kelvin temperature of the gas be increased? Explain.

Q18.22 (a) If you apply the same amount of heat to 1.00 mol of an ideal monatomic gas and 1.00 mol of an ideal diatomic gas, which one (if any) will increase more in temperature? (b) Physically, *why* do diatomic gases have a greater molar heat capacity than monatomic gases?

Q18.23 The discussion in Section 18.4 concluded that all ideal monatomic gases have the same heat capacity C_V. Does this mean that it takes the same amount of heat to raise the temperature of 1.0 g of each one by 1.0 K? Explain your reasoning.

Q18.24 In a gas that contains N molecules, is it accurate to say that the number of molecules with speed v is equal to $f(v)$? Is it accurate to say that this number is given by $Nf(v)$? Explain your answers.

Q18.25 The atmosphere of the planet Mars is 95.3% carbon dioxide (CO_2) and about 0.03% water vapor. The atmospheric pressure is only about 600 Pa, and the surface temperature varies from −30°C to −100°C. The polar ice caps contain both CO_2 ice and water ice. Could there be *liquid* CO_2 on the surface of Mars? Could there be liquid water? Why or why not?

Q18.26 A beaker of water at room temperature is placed in an enclosure, and the air pressure in the enclosure is slowly reduced. When the air pressure is reduced sufficiently, the water begins to boil. The temperature of the water does not rise when it boils; in fact, the temperature *drops* slightly. Explain these phenomena.

Q18.27 Ice is slippery to walk on, and especially slippery if you wear ice skates. What does this tell you about how the melting temperature of ice depends on pressure? Explain.

Q18.28 Hydrothermal vents are openings in the ocean floor that discharge very hot water. The water emerging from one such vent off the Oregon coast, 2400 m below the surface, is at 279°C. Despite its high temperature, the water doesn't boil. Why not?

Q18.29 The dark areas on the moon's surface are called *maria*, Latin for "seas," and were once thought to be bodies of water. In fact, the maria are not "seas" at all, but plains of solidified lava. Given that there is no atmosphere on the moon, how can you explain the absence of liquid water on the moon's surface?

Q18.30 In addition to the normal cooking directions printed on the back of a box of rice, there are also "high-altitude directions." The only difference is that the "high-altitude directions" suggest increasing the cooking time and using a greater volume of boiling water in which to cook the rice. Why should the directions depend on the altitude in this way?

EXERCISES

Section 18.1 Equations of State

18.1 • A 20.0-L tank contains 4.86×10^{-4} kg of helium at 18.0°C. The molar mass of helium is 4.00 g/mol. (a) How many moles of helium are in the tank? (b) What is the pressure in the tank, in pascals and in atmospheres?

18.2 ••• Helium gas with a volume of 3.20 L, under a pressure of 0.180 atm and at 41.0°C, is warmed until both pressure and volume are doubled. (a) What is the final temperature? (b) How many grams of helium are there? The molar mass of helium is 4.00 g/mol.

18.3 • A cylindrical tank has a tight-fitting piston that allows the volume of the tank to be changed. The tank originally contains 0.110 m³ of air at a pressure of 0.355 atm. The piston is slowly pulled out until the volume of the gas is increased to 0.390 m³. If the temperature remains constant, what is the final value of the pressure?

18.4 • A 3.00-L tank contains air at 3.00 atm and 20.0°C. The tank is sealed and cooled until the pressure is 1.00 atm. (a) What is the temperature then in degrees Celsius? Assume that the volume of the tank is constant. (b) If the temperature is kept at the value found in part (a) and the gas is compressed, what is the volume when the pressure again becomes 3.00 atm?

18.5 • **Planetary Atmospheres.** (a) Calculate the density of the atmosphere at the surface of Mars (where the pressure is 650 Pa and the temperature is typically 253 K, with a CO_2 atmosphere), Venus (with an average temperature of 730 K and pressure of 92 atm, with a CO_2 atmosphere), and Saturn's moon Titan (where the pressure is 1.5 atm and the temperature is −178°C, with a N_2 atmosphere). (b) Compare each of these densities with that of the earth's atmosphere, which is 1.20 kg/m³. Consult Appendix D to determine molar masses.

18.6 •• You have several identical balloons. You experimentally determine that a balloon will break if its volume exceeds 0.900 L. The pressure of the gas inside the balloon equals air pressure (1.00 atm). (a) If the air inside the balloon is at a constant 22.0°C and behaves as an ideal gas, what mass of air can you blow into one of the balloons before it bursts? (b) Repeat part (a) if the gas is helium rather than air.

18.7 •• A Jaguar XK8 convertible has an eight-cylinder engine. At the beginning of its compression stroke, one of the cylinders contains 499 cm³ of air at atmospheric pressure (1.01×10^5 Pa) and a temperature of 27.0°C. At the end of the stroke, the air has been compressed to a volume of 46.2 cm³ and the gauge pressure has increased to 2.72×10^6 Pa. Compute the final temperature.

18.8 •• A welder using a tank of volume 0.0750 m³ fills it with oxygen (molar mass 32.0 g/mol) at a gauge pressure of 3.00×10^5 Pa and temperature of 37.0°C. The tank has a small leak, and in time some of the oxygen leaks out. On a day when the temperature is 22.0°C, the gauge pressure of the oxygen in the tank is 1.80×10^5 Pa. Find (a) the initial mass of oxygen and (b) the mass of oxygen that has leaked out.

18.9 •• A large cylindrical tank contains 0.750 m³ of nitrogen gas at 27°C and 7.50×10^3 Pa (absolute pressure). The tank has a tight-fitting piston that allows the volume to be changed. What will be the pressure if the volume is decreased to 0.410 m³ and the temperature is increased to 157°C?

18.10 • An empty cylindrical canister 1.50 m long and 90.0 cm in diameter is to be filled with pure oxygen at 22.0°C to store in a space station. To hold as much gas as possible, the absolute pressure of the oxygen will be 21.0 atm. The molar mass of oxygen is 32.0 g/mol. (a) How many moles of oxygen does this canister hold? (b) For someone lifting this canister, by how many kilograms does this gas increase the mass to be lifted?

18.11 • The gas inside a balloon will always have a pressure nearly equal to atmospheric pressure, since that is the pressure applied to the outside of the balloon. You fill a balloon with helium (a nearly ideal gas) to a volume of 0.600 L at 19.0°C. What is the volume of the balloon if you cool it to the boiling point of liquid nitrogen (77.3 K)?

18.12 • An ideal gas has a density of 1.33×10^{-6} g/cm³ at 1.00×10^{-3} atm and 20.0°C. Identify the gas.

18.13 •• If a certain amount of ideal gas occupies a volume V at STP on earth, what would be its volume (in terms of V) on Venus, where the temperature is 1003°C and the pressure is 92 atm?

18.14 • A diver observes a bubble of air rising from the bottom of a lake (where the absolute pressure is 3.50 atm) to the surface (where the pressure is 1.00 atm). The temperature at the bottom is 4.0°C, and the temperature at the surface is 23.0°C. (a) What is the ratio of the volume of the bubble as it reaches the surface to its volume at the bottom? (b) Would it be safe for the diver to hold his breath while ascending from the bottom of the lake to the surface? Why or why not?

18.15 • A metal tank with volume 3.10 L will burst if the absolute pressure of the gas it contains exceeds 100 atm. (a) If 11.0 mol of an ideal gas is put into the tank at 23.0°C, to what temperature can the gas be warmed before the tank ruptures? Ignore the thermal expansion of the tank. (b) Based on your answer to part (a), is it reasonable to ignore the thermal expansion of the tank? Explain.

18.16 • Three moles of an ideal gas are in a rigid cubical box with sides of length 0.300 m. (a) What is the force that the gas exerts on each of the six sides of the box when the gas temperature is 20.0°C? (b) What is the force when the temperature of the gas is increased to 100.0°C?

18.17 • With the assumptions of Example 18.4 (Section 18.1), at what elevation above sea level is air pressure 90% of the pressure at sea level?

18.18 •• With the assumption that the air temperature is a uniform 0.0°C, what is the density of the air at an altitude of 1.00 km as a percentage of the density at the surface?

18.19 •• (a) Calculate the mass of nitrogen present in a volume of 3000 cm³ if the gas is at 22.0°C and the absolute pressure of 2.00×10^{-13} atm is a partial vacuum easily obtained in laboratories. (b) What is the density (in kg/m³) of the N_2?

18.20 • At an altitude of 11,000 m (a typical cruising altitude for a jet airliner), the air temperature is −56.5°C and the air density is 0.364 kg/m³. What is the pressure of the atmosphere at that altitude? (*Note:* The temperature at this altitude is not the same as at the surface of the earth, so the calculation of Example 18.4 in Section 18.1 doesn't apply.)

Section 18.2 Molecular Properties of Matter

18.21 • How many moles are in a 1.00-kg bottle of water? How many molecules? The molar mass of water is 18.0 g/mol.

18.22 • A large organic molecule has a mass of 1.41×10^{-21} kg. What is the molar mass of this compound?

18.23 •• Modern vacuum pumps make it easy to attain pressures of the order of 10^{-13} atm in the laboratory. Consider a volume of air and treat the air as an ideal gas. (a) At a pressure of 9.00×10^{-14} atm and an ordinary temperature of 300.0 K, how many molecules are present in a volume of 1.00 cm³? (b) How many molecules would be present at the same temperature but at 1.00 atm instead?

18.24 •• The Lagoon Nebula (**Fig. E18.24**) is a cloud of hydrogen gas located 3900 light-years from the earth. The cloud is about 45 light-years in diameter and glows because of its high temperature of 7500 K. (The gas is raised to this temperature by the stars that lie within the nebula.) The cloud is also very thin; there are only 80 molecules per cubic centimeter. (a) Find the gas pressure (in atmospheres) in the Lagoon Nebula. Compare it to the laboratory pressure referred to in Exercise 18.23. (b) Science-fiction films sometimes show starships being buffeted by turbulence as they fly through gas clouds such as the Lagoon Nebula. Does this seem realistic? Why or why not?

Figure **E18.24**

18.25 •• In a gas at standard conditions, what is the length of the side of a cube that contains a number of molecules equal to the population of the earth (about 7×10^9 people)?

18.26 •• **How Close Together Are Gas Molecules?** Consider an ideal gas at 27°C and 1.00 atm. To get some idea how close these molecules are to each other, on the average, imagine them to be uniformly spaced, with each molecule at the center of a small cube. (a) What is the length of an edge of each cube if adjacent cubes touch but do not overlap? (b) How does this distance compare with the diameter of a typical molecule? (c) How does their separation compare with the spacing of atoms in solids, which typically are about 0.3 nm apart?

Section 18.3 Kinetic-Molecular Model of an Ideal Gas

18.27 • (a) What is the total translational kinetic energy of the air in an empty room that has dimensions 8.00 m × 12.00 m × 4.00 m if the air is treated as an ideal gas at 1.00 atm? (b) What is the speed of a 2000-kg automobile if its kinetic energy equals the translational kinetic energy calculated in part (a)?

18.28 • A flask contains a mixture of neon (Ne), krypton (Kr), and radon (Rn) gases. Compare (a) the average kinetic energies of the three types of atoms and (b) the root-mean-square speeds. (*Hint:* Appendix D shows the molar mass (in g/mol) of each element under the chemical symbol for that element.)

18.29 • We have two equal-size boxes, A and B. Each box contains gas that behaves as an ideal gas. We insert a thermometer into each box and find that the gas in box A is at 50°C while the gas in box B is at 10°C. This is all we know about the gas in the boxes. Which of the following statements *must* be true? Which *could* be true? Explain your reasoning. (a) The pressure in A is higher than in B. (b) There are more molecules in A than in B. (c) A and B do not contain the same type of gas. (d) The molecules in A have more average kinetic energy per molecule than those in B. (e) The molecules in A are moving faster than those in B.

18.30 • A container with volume 1.64 L is initially evacuated. Then it is filled with 0.226 g of N_2. Assume that the pressure of the gas is low enough for the gas to obey the ideal-gas law to a high degree of accuracy. If the root-mean-square speed of the gas molecules is 182 m/s, what is the pressure of the gas?

18.31 •• (a) A deuteron, ^2_1H, is the nucleus of a hydrogen isotope and consists of one proton and one neutron. The plasma of deuterons in a nuclear fusion reactor must be heated to about 300 million K. What is the rms speed of the deuterons? Is this a significant fraction of the speed of light in vacuum ($c = 3.0 \times 10^8$ m/s)? (b) What would the temperature of the plasma be if the deuterons had an rms speed equal to $0.10c$?

18.32 • **Martian Climate.** The atmosphere of Mars is mostly CO_2 (molar mass 44.0 g/mol) under a pressure of 650 Pa, which we shall assume remains constant. In many places the temperature varies from 0.0°C in summer to −100°C in winter. Over the course of a Martian year, what are the ranges of (a) the rms speeds of the CO_2 molecules and (b) the density (in mol/m³) of the atmosphere?

18.33 •• Oxygen (O_2) has a molar mass of 32.0 g/mol. What is (a) the average translational kinetic energy of an oxygen molecule at a temperature of 300 K; (b) the average value of the square of its speed; (c) the root-mean-square speed; (d) the momentum of an oxygen molecule traveling at this speed? (e) Suppose an oxygen molecule traveling at this speed bounces back and forth between opposite sides of a cubical vessel 0.10 m on a side. What is the average force the molecule exerts on one of the walls of the container? (Assume that the molecule's velocity is perpendicular to the two sides that it strikes.) (f) What is the average force per unit area? (g) How many oxygen molecules traveling at this speed are necessary to produce an average pressure of 1 atm? (h) Compute the number of oxygen molecules that are contained in a vessel of this size at 300 K and atmospheric pressure. (i) Your answer for part (h) should be three times as large as the answer for part (g). Where does this discrepancy arise?

18.34 •• Calculate the mean free path of air molecules at 3.50×10^{-13} atm and 300 K. (This pressure is readily attainable in the laboratory; see Exercise 18.23.) As in Example 18.8, model the air molecules as spheres of radius 2.0×10^{-10} m.

18.35 •• At what temperature is the root-mean-square speed of nitrogen molecules equal to the root-mean-square speed of hydrogen molecules at 20.0°C? (*Hint:* Appendix D shows the molar mass (in g/mol) of each element under the chemical symbol for that element. The molar mass of H_2 is twice the molar mass of hydrogen atoms, and similarly for N_2.)

18.36 • Smoke particles in the air typically have masses of the order of 10^{-16} kg. The Brownian motion (rapid, irregular movement) of these particles, resulting from collisions with air molecules, can be observed with a microscope. (a) Find the root-mean-square speed of Brownian motion for a particle with a mass of 3.00×10^{-16} kg in air at 300 K. (b) Would the root-mean-square speed be different if the particle were in hydrogen gas at the same temperature? Explain.

Section 18.4 Heat Capacities

18.37 • How much heat does it take to increase the temperature of 1.80 mol of an ideal gas by 50.0 K near room temperature if the gas is held at constant volume and is (a) diatomic; (b) monatomic?

18.38 •• Perfectly rigid containers each hold n moles of ideal gas, one being hydrogen (H_2) and the other being neon (Ne). If it takes 300 J of heat to increase the temperature of the hydrogen by 2.50°C, by how many degrees will the same amount of heat raise the temperature of the neon?

18.39 •• (a) Compute the specific heat at constant volume of nitrogen (N_2) gas, and compare it with the specific heat of liquid water. The molar mass of N_2 is 28.0 g/mol. (b) You warm 1.00 kg of water at a constant volume of 1.00 L from 20.0°C to 30.0°C in a kettle. For the same amount of heat, how many kilograms of 20.0°C air would you be able to warm to 30.0°C? What volume (in liters) would this air occupy at 20.0°C and a pressure of 1.00 atm? Make the simplifying assumption that air is 100% N_2.

18.40 •• (a) Calculate the specific heat at constant volume of water vapor, assuming the nonlinear triatomic molecule has three translational and three rotational degrees of freedom and that vibrational motion does not contribute. The molar mass of water is 18.0 g/mol. (b) The actual specific heat of water vapor at low pressures is about 2000 J/kg · K. Compare this with your calculation and comment on the actual role of vibrational motion.

Section 18.5 Molecular Speeds

18.41 • For diatomic carbon dioxide gas (CO_2, molar mass 44.0 g/mol) at $T = 300$ K, calculate (a) the most probable speed v_{mp}; (b) the average speed v_{av}; (c) the root-mean-square speed v_{rms}.

18.42 • For a gas of nitrogen molecules (N_2), what must the temperature be if 94.7% of all the molecules have speeds less than (a) 1500 m/s; (b) 1000 m/s; (c) 500 m/s? Use Table 18.2. The molar mass of N_2 is 28.0 g/mol.

Section 18.6 Phases of Matter

18.43 • Solid water (ice) is slowly warmed from a very low temperature. (a) What minimum external pressure p_1 must be applied to the solid if a melting phase transition is to be observed? Describe the sequence of phase transitions that occur if the applied pressure p is such that $p < p_1$. (b) Above a certain maximum pressure p_2, no boiling transition is observed. What is this pressure? Describe the sequence of phase transitions that occur if $p_1 < p < p_2$.

18.44 • **Meteorology.** The *vapor pressure* is the pressure of the vapor phase of a substance when it is in equilibrium with the solid or liquid phase of the substance. The *relative humidity* is the partial pressure of water vapor in the air divided by the vapor pressure of water at that same temperature, expressed as a percentage. The air is saturated when the humidity is 100%. (a) The vapor pressure of water at 20.0°C is 2.34×10^3 Pa. If the air temperature is 20.0°C and the relative humidity is 60%, what is the partial pressure of water vapor in the atmosphere (that is, the pressure due to water vapor alone)? (b) Under the conditions of part (a), what is the mass of water in 1.00 m³ of air? (The molar mass of water is 18.0 g/mol. Assume that water vapor can be treated as an ideal gas.)

18.45 • Calculate the volume of 1.00 mol of liquid water at 20°C (at which its density is 998 kg/m³), and compare that with the volume occupied by 1.00 mol of water at the critical point, which is 56×10^{-6} m³. Water has a molar mass of 18.0 g/mol.

PROBLEMS

18.46 • A physics lecture room at 1.00 atm and 27.0°C has a volume of 216 m³. (a) Use the ideal-gas law to estimate the number of air molecules in the room. Assume that all of the air is N_2. Calculate (b) the particle density—that is, the number of N_2 molecules per cubic centimeter—and (c) the mass of the air in the room.

18.47 •• CP BIO **The Effect of Altitude on the Lungs.** (a) Calculate the *change* in air pressure you will experience if you climb a 1000-m mountain, assuming that the temperature and air density do not change over this distance and that they were 22°C and 1.2 kg/m³, respectively, at the bottom of the mountain. (*Note:* The result of Example 18.4 doesn't apply, since the expression derived in that example accounts for the variation of air density with altitude and we are told to ignore that here.) (b) If you took a 0.50-L breath at the foot of the mountain and managed to hold it until you reached the top, what would be the volume of this breath when you exhaled it there?

18.48 •• CP BIO **The Bends.** If deep-sea divers rise to the surface too quickly, nitrogen bubbles in their blood can expand and prove fatal. This phenomenon is known as the *bends*. If a scuba diver rises quickly from a depth of 25 m in Lake Michigan (which is fresh water), what will be the volume at the surface of an N_2 bubble that occupied 1.0 mm³ in his blood at the lower depth? Does it seem that this difference is large enough to be a problem? (Assume that the pressure difference is due to only the changing water pressure, not to any temperature difference. This assumption is reasonable, since we are warm-blooded creatures.)

18.49 ••• CP A hot-air balloon stays aloft because hot air at atmospheric pressure is less dense than cooler air at the same pressure. If the volume of the balloon is 500.0 m³ and the surrounding air is at 15.0°C, what must the temperature of the air in the balloon be for it to lift a total load of 290 kg (in addition to the mass of the hot air)? The density of air at 15.0°C and atmospheric pressure is 1.23 kg/m³.

18.50 ·· In an evacuated enclosure, a vertical cylindrical tank of diameter D is sealed by a 3.00-kg circular disk that can move up and down without friction. Beneath the disk is a quantity of ideal gas at temperature T in the cylinder (**Fig. P18.50**). Initially the disk is at rest at a distance of $h = 4.00$ m above the bottom of the tank. When a lead brick of mass 9.00 kg is gently placed on the disk, the disk moves downward. If the temperature of the gas is kept constant and no gas escapes from the tank, what distance above the bottom of the tank is the disk when it again comes to rest?

Figure **P18.50**

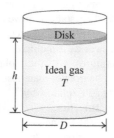

Disk

Ideal gas
T

h

D

18.51 ··· A cylinder 1.00 m tall with inside diameter 0.120 m is used to hold propane gas (molar mass 44.1 g/mol) for use in a barbecue. It is initially filled with gas until the gauge pressure is 1.30×10^6 Pa at 22.0°C. The temperature of the gas remains constant as it is partially emptied out of the tank, until the gauge pressure is 3.40×10^5 Pa. Calculate the mass of propane that has been used.

18.52 · CP During a test dive in 1939, prior to being accepted by the U.S. Navy, the submarine *Squalus* sank at a point where the depth of water was 73.0 m. The temperature was 27.0°C at the surface and 7.0°C at the bottom. The density of seawater is 1030 kg/m³. (a) A diving bell was used to rescue 33 trapped crewmen from the *Squalus*. The diving bell was in the form of a circular cylinder 2.30 m high, open at the bottom and closed at the top. When the diving bell was lowered to the bottom of the sea, to what height did water rise within the diving bell? (*Hint:* Ignore the relatively small variation in water pressure between the bottom of the bell and the surface of the water within the bell.) (b) At what gauge pressure must compressed air have been supplied to the bell while on the bottom to expel all the water from it?

18.53 · **Atmosphere of Titan.** Titan, the largest satellite of Saturn, has a thick nitrogen atmosphere. At its surface, the pressure is 1.5 earth-atmospheres and the temperature is 94 K. (a) What is the surface temperature in °C? (b) Calculate the surface density in Titan's atmosphere in molecules per cubic meter. (c) Compare the density of Titan's surface atmosphere to the density of earth's atmosphere at 22°C. Which body has denser atmosphere?

18.54 · **Pressure on Venus.** At the surface of Venus the average temperature is a balmy 460°C due to the greenhouse effect (global warming!), the pressure is 92 earth-atmospheres, and the acceleration due to gravity is 0.894g_{earth}. The atmosphere is nearly all CO_2 (molar mass 44.0 g/mol), and the temperature remains remarkably constant. Assume that the temperature does not change with altitude. (a) What is the atmospheric pressure 1.00 km above the surface of Venus? Express your answer in Venus-atmospheres and earth-atmospheres. (b) What is the root-mean-square speed of the CO_2 molecules at the surface of Venus and at an altitude of 1.00 km?

18.55 ·· An automobile tire has a volume of 0.0150 m³ on a cold day when the temperature of the air in the tire is 5.0°C and atmospheric pressure is 1.02 atm. Under these conditions the gauge pressure is measured to be 1.70 atm (about 25 lb/in.²).

After the car is driven on the highway for 30 min, the temperature of the air in the tires has risen to 45.0°C and the volume has risen to 0.0159 m³. What then is the gauge pressure?

18.56 ·· A flask with a volume of 1.50 L, provided with a stopcock, contains ethane gas (C_2H_6) at 300 K and atmospheric pressure (1.013×10^5 Pa). The molar mass of ethane is 30.1 g/mol. The system is warmed to a temperature of 550 K, with the stopcock open to the atmosphere. The stopcock is then closed, and the flask is cooled to its original temperature. (a) What is the final pressure of the ethane in the flask? (b) How many grams of ethane remain in the flask?

18.57 ·· CP A balloon of volume 750 m³ is to be filled with hydrogen at atmospheric pressure (1.01×10^5 Pa). (a) If the hydrogen is stored in cylinders with volumes of 1.90 m³ at a gauge pressure of 1.20×10^6 Pa, how many cylinders are required? Assume that the temperature of the hydrogen remains constant. (b) What is the total weight (in addition to the weight of the gas) that can be supported by the balloon if both the gas in the balloon and the surrounding air are at 15.0°C? The molar mass of hydrogen (H_2) is 2.02 g/mol. The density of air at 15.0°C and atmospheric pressure is 1.23 kg/m³. See Chapter 12 for a discussion of buoyancy. (c) What weight could be supported if the balloon were filled with helium (molar mass 4.00 g/mol) instead of hydrogen, again at 15.0°C?

18.58 ·· A vertical cylindrical tank contains 1.80 mol of an ideal gas under a pressure of 0.300 atm at 20.0°C. The round part of the tank has a radius of 10.0 cm, and the gas is supporting a piston that can move up and down in the cylinder without friction. There is a vacuum above the piston. (a) What is the mass of this piston? (b) How tall is the column of gas that is supporting the piston?

18.59 ·· CP A large tank of water has a hose connected to it (**Fig. P18.59**). The tank is sealed at the top and has compressed air between the water surface and the top. When the water height h has the value 3.50 m, the absolute pressure p of the compressed air is 4.20×10^5 Pa. Assume that the air above the water expands at constant temperature, and take the atmospheric pressure to be 1.00×10^5 Pa. (a) What is the speed with which water flows out of the hose when $h = 3.50$ m? (b) As water flows out of the tank, h decreases. Calculate the speed of flow for $h = 3.00$ m and for $h = 2.00$ m. (c) At what value of h does the flow stop?

Figure **P18.59**

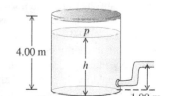

4.00 m

p

h

1.00 m

18.60 ·· CP A light, plastic sphere with mass $m = 9.00$ g and density $\rho = 4.00$ kg/m³ is suspended in air by thread of negligible mass. (a) What is the tension T in the thread if the air is at 5.00°C and $p = 1.00$ atm? The molar mass of air is 28.8 g/mol. (b) How much does the tension in the thread change if the temperature of the gas is increased to 35.0°C? Ignore the change in volume of the plastic sphere when the temperature is changed.

18.61 ·· BIO **How Many Atoms Are You?** Estimate the number of atoms in the body of a 50-kg physics student. Note that the human body is mostly water, which has molar mass 18.0 g/mol, and that each water molecule contains three atoms.

18.62 ·· BIO A person at rest inhales 0.50 L of air with each breath at a pressure of 1.00 atm and a temperature of 20.0°C. The inhaled air is 21.0% oxygen. (a) How many oxygen molecules does this person inhale with each breath? (b) Suppose this person is now resting at an elevation of 2000 m but the temperature is still 20.0°C. Assuming that the oxygen percentage and volume per inhalation are the same as stated above, how many oxygen molecules does this person now inhale with each breath? (c) Given that the body still requires the same number of oxygen molecules per second as at sea level to maintain its functions, explain why some people report "shortness of breath" at high elevations.

18.63 •• You have two identical containers, one containing gas A and the other gas B. The masses of these molecules are $m_A = 3.34 \times 10^{-27}$ kg and $m_B = 5.34 \times 10^{-26}$ kg. Both gases are under the same pressure and are at 10.0°C. (a) Which molecules (A or B) have greater translational kinetic energy per molecule and rms speeds? (b) Now you want to raise the temperature of only one of these containers so that both gases will have the same rms speed. For which gas should you raise the temperature? (c) At what temperature will you accomplish your goal? (d) Once you have accomplished your goal, which molecules (A or B) now have greater average translational kinetic energy per molecule?

18.64 • The size of an oxygen molecule is about 2.0×10^{-10} m. Make a rough estimate of the pressure at which the finite volume of the molecules should cause noticeable deviations from ideal-gas behavior at ordinary temperatures ($T = 300$ K).

18.65 •• A sealed box contains a monatomic ideal gas. The number of gas atoms per unit volume is 5.00×10^{20} atoms/cm³, and the average translational kinetic energy of each atom is 1.80×10^{-23} J. (a) What is the gas pressure? (b) If the gas is neon (molar mass 20.18 g/mol), what is v_{rms} for the gas atoms?

18.66 •• Helium gas is in a cylinder that has rigid walls. If the pressure of the gas is 2.00 atm, then the root-mean-square speed of the helium atoms is $v_{rms} = 176$ m/s. By how much (in atmospheres) must the pressure be increased to increase the v_{rms} of the He atoms by 100 m/s? Ignore any change in the volume of the cylinder.

18.67 •• You blow up a spherical balloon to a diameter of 50.0 cm until the absolute pressure inside is 1.25 atm and the temperature is 22.0°C. Assume that all the gas is N_2, of molar mass 28.0 g/mol. (a) Find the mass of a single N_2 molecule. (b) How much translational kinetic energy does an average N_2 molecule have? (c) How many N_2 molecules are in this balloon? (d) What is the *total* translational kinetic energy of all the molecules in the balloon?

18.68 • CP (a) Compute the increase in gravitational potential energy for a nitrogen molecule (molar mass 28.0 g/mol) for an increase in elevation of 400 m near the earth's surface. (b) At what temperature is this equal to the average kinetic energy of a nitrogen molecule? (c) Is it possible that a nitrogen molecule near sea level where $T = 15.0°C$ could rise to an altitude of 400 m? Is it likely that it could do so without hitting any other molecules along the way? Explain.

18.69 •• CP CALC **The Lennard-Jones Potential.** A commonly used potential-energy function for the interaction of two molecules (see Fig. 18.8) is the Lennard-Jones 6-12 potential:

$$U(r) = U_0\left[\left(\frac{R_0}{r}\right)^{12} - 2\left(\frac{R_0}{r}\right)^6\right]$$

where r is the distance between the centers of the molecules and U_0 and R_0 are positive constants. The corresponding force $F(r)$ is given in Eq. (14.26). (a) Graph $U(r)$ and $F(r)$ versus r. (b) Let r_1 be the value of r at which $U(r) = 0$, and let r_2 be the value of r at which $F(r) = 0$. Show the locations of r_1 and r_2 on your graphs of $U(r)$ and $F(r)$. Which of these values represents the equilibrium separation between the molecules? (c) Find the values of r_1 and r_2 in terms of R_0, and find the ratio r_1/r_2. (d) If the molecules are located a distance r_2 apart [as calculated in part (c)], how much work must be done to pull them apart so that $r \rightarrow \infty$?

18.70 • (a) What is the total random translational kinetic energy of 5.00 L of hydrogen gas (molar mass 2.016 g/mol) with pressure 1.01×10^5 Pa and temperature 300 K? (*Hint:* Use the procedure of Problem 18.67 as a guide.) (b) If the tank containing the gas is placed on a swift jet moving at 300.0 m/s, by what percentage is the *total* kinetic energy of the gas increased? (c) Since the kinetic energy of the gas molecules is greater when it is on the jet, does this mean that its temperature has gone up? Explain.

18.71 •• It is possible to make crystalline solids that are only one layer of atoms thick. Such "two-dimensional" crystals can be created by depositing atoms on a very flat surface. (a) If the atoms in such a two-dimensional crystal can move only within the plane of the crystal, what will be its molar heat capacity near room temperature? Give your answer as a multiple of R and in J/mol·K. (b) At very low temperatures, will the molar heat capacity of a two-dimensional crystal be greater than, less than, or equal to the result you found in part (a)? Explain why.

18.72 • **Hydrogen on the Sun.** The surface of the sun has a temperature of about 5800 K and consists largely of hydrogen atoms. (a) Find the rms speed of a hydrogen atom at this temperature. (The mass of a single hydrogen atom is 1.67×10^{-27} kg.) (b) The escape speed for a particle to leave the gravitational influence of the sun is given by $(2GM/R)^{1/2}$, where M is the sun's mass, R its radius, and G the gravitational constant (see Example 13.5 of Section 13.3). Use Appendix F to calculate this escape speed. (c) Can appreciable quantities of hydrogen escape from the sun? Can *any* hydrogen escape? Explain.

18.73 •• CP (a) Show that a projectile with mass m can "escape" from the surface of a planet if it is launched vertically upward with a kinetic energy greater than mgR_p, where g is the acceleration due to gravity at the planet's surface and R_p is the planet's radius. Ignore air resistance. (See Problem 18.72.) (b) If the planet in question is the earth, at what temperature does the average translational kinetic energy of a nitrogen molecule (molar mass 28.0 g/mol) equal that required to escape? What about a hydrogen molecule (molar mass 2.02 g/mol?) (c) Repeat part (b) for the moon, for which $g = 1.63$ m/s² and $R_p = 1740$ km. (d) While the earth and the moon have similar average surface temperatures, the moon has essentially no atmosphere. Use your results from parts (b) and (c) to explain why.

18.74 • **Planetary Atmospheres.** (a) The temperature near the top of Jupiter's multicolored cloud layer is about 140 K. The temperature at the top of the earth's troposphere, at an altitude of about 20 km, is about 220 K. Calculate the rms speed of hydrogen molecules in both these environments. Give your answers in m/s and as a fraction of the escape speed from the respective planet (see Problem 18.72). (b) Hydrogen gas (H_2) is a rare element in the earth's atmosphere. In the atmosphere of Jupiter, by contrast, 89% of all molecules are H_2. Explain why, using your results from part (a). (c) Suppose an astronomer claims to have discovered an oxygen (O_2) atmosphere on the asteroid Ceres. How likely is this? Ceres has a mass equal to 0.014 times the mass of the moon, a density of 2400 kg/m³, and a surface temperature of about 200 K.

18.75 •• CALC Calculate the integral in Eq. (18.31), $\int_0^\infty v^2 f(v) \, dv$, and compare this result to $(v^2)_{av}$ as given by Eq. (18.16). (*Hint:* You may use the tabulated integral

$$\int_0^\infty x^{2n}e^{-\alpha x^2}dx = \frac{1 \cdot 3 \cdot 5 \cdots (2n-1)}{2^{n+1}\alpha^n}\sqrt{\frac{\pi}{\alpha}}$$

where n is a positive integer and α is a positive constant.)

18.76 •• (a) Calculate the total *rotational* kinetic energy of the molecules in 1.00 mol of a diatomic gas at 300 K. (b) Calculate the moment of inertia of an oxygen molecule (O_2) for rotation about either the y- or z-axis shown in Fig. 18.18b. Treat the molecule as two massive points (representing the oxygen atoms) separated by a distance of 1.21×10^{-10} m. The molar mass of oxygen *atoms* is 16.0 g/mol. (c) Find the rms angular velocity of rotation of an oxygen molecule about either the y- or z-axis shown in Fig. 18.18b. How does your answer compare to the angular velocity of a typical piece of rapidly rotating machinery (10,000 rev/min)?

18.77 •• **CALC** (a) Explain why in a gas of N molecules, the number of molecules having speeds in the *finite* interval v to $v + \Delta v$ is $\Delta N = N \int_v^{v+\Delta v} f(v)\, dv$. (b) If Δv is small, then $f(v)$ is approximately constant over the interval and $\Delta N \approx Nf(v)\Delta v$. For oxygen gas ($O_2$, molar mass 32.0 g/mol) at $T = 300$ K, use this approximation to calculate the number of molecules with speeds within $\Delta v = 20$ m/s of v_{mp}. Express your answer as a multiple of N. (c) Repeat part (b) for speeds within $\Delta v = 20$ m/s of $7v_{mp}$. (d) Repeat parts (b) and (c) for a temperature of 600 K. (e) Repeat parts (b) and (c) for a temperature of 150 K. (f) What do your results tell you about the shape of the distribution as a function of temperature? Do your conclusions agree with what is shown in Fig. 18.23?

18.78 •• **CALC** Calculate the integral in Eq. (18.30), $\int_0^\infty vf(v)\, dv$, and compare this result to v_{av} as given by Eq. (18.35). (*Hint:* Make the change of variable $v^2 = x$ and use the tabulated integral

$$\int_0^\infty x^n e^{-\alpha x} dx = \frac{n!}{\alpha^{n+1}}$$

where n is a positive integer and α is a positive constant.)

18.79 ••• **CP Oscillations of a Piston.** A vertical cylinder of radius r contains an ideal gas and is fitted with a piston of mass m that is free to move (**Fig. P18.79**). The piston and the walls of the cylinder are frictionless, and the entire cylinder is placed in a constant-temperature bath. The outside air pressure is p_0. In equilibrium, the piston sits at a height h above the bottom of the cylinder. (a) Find the absolute pressure of the gas trapped below the piston when in equilibrium.
(b) The piston is pulled up by a small distance and released. Find the net force acting on the piston when its base is a distance $h + y$ above the bottom of the cylinder, where $y \ll h$. (c) After the piston is displaced from equilibrium and released, it oscillates up and down. Find the frequency of these small oscillations. If the displacement is not small, are the oscillations simple harmonic? How can you tell?

Figure **P18.79**

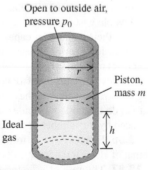
Open to outside air, pressure p_0

r

Piston, mass m

Ideal gas

h

18.80 •• **DATA** A steel cylinder with rigid walls is evacuated to a high degree of vacuum; you then put a small amount of helium into the cylinder. The cylinder has a pressure gauge that measures the pressure of the gas inside the cylinder. You place the cylinder in various temperature environments, wait for thermal equilibrium to be established, and then measure the pressure of the gas. You obtain these results:

	T (°C)	p (Pa)
Normal boiling point of nitrogen	−195.8	254
Ice–water mixture	0.0	890
Outdoors on a warm day	33.3	999
Normal boiling point of water	100.0	1214
Hot oven	232	1635

(a) Recall (Chapter 17) that absolute zero is the temperature at which the pressure of an ideal gas becomes zero. Use the data in the table to calculate the value of absolute zero in °C. Assume that the pressure of the gas is low enough for it to be treated as an ideal gas, and ignore the change in volume of the cylinder as its temperature is changed. (b) Use the coefficient of volume expansion for steel in Table 17.2 to calculate the percentage change in the volume of the cylinder between the lowest and highest temperatures in the table. Is it accurate to ignore the volume change of the cylinder as the temperature changes? Justify your answer.

18.81 ••• **DATA The Dew Point and Clouds.** The vapor pressure of water (see Exercise 18.44) decreases as the temperature decreases. The table lists the vapor pressure of water at various temperatures:

Temperature (°C)	Vapor Pressure (Pa)
10.0	1.23×10^3
12.0	1.40×10^3
14.0	1.60×10^3
16.0	1.81×10^3
18.0	2.06×10^3
20.0	2.34×10^3
22.0	2.65×10^3
24.0	2.99×10^3
26.0	3.36×10^3
28.0	3.78×10^3
30.0	4.25×10^3

If the amount of water vapor in the air is kept constant as the air is cooled, the *dew point* temperature is reached, at which the partial pressure and vapor pressure coincide and the vapor is saturated. If the air is cooled further, the vapor condenses to liquid until the partial pressure again equals the vapor pressure at that temperature. The temperature in a room is 30.0°C. (a) A meteorologist cools a metal can by gradually adding cold water. When the can's temperature reaches 16.0°C, water droplets form on its outside surface. What is the relative humidity of the 30.0°C air in the room? On a spring day in the midwestern United States, the air temperature at the surface is 28.0°C. Puffy cumulus clouds form at an altitude where the air temperature equals the dew point. If the air temperature decreases with altitude at a rate of 0.6 C°/100 m, at approximately what height above the ground will clouds form if the relative humidity at the surface is (b) 35%; (c) 80%?

18.82 •• **DATA** The statistical quantities "average value" and "root-mean-square value" can be applied to any distribution. **Figure P18.82** shows the scores of a class of 150 students on a 100-point quiz. (a) Find the average score for the class. (b) Find the rms score for the class. (c) Which is higher: the average score or the rms score? Why?

Figure **P18.82**

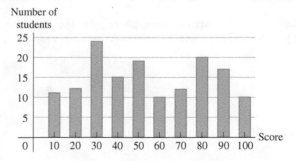

Number of students

CHALLENGE PROBLEMS

18.83 ••• CP **Dark Nebulae and the Interstellar Medium.**
The dark area in **Fig. P18.83** that appears devoid of stars is a *dark nebula*, a cold gas cloud in interstellar space that contains enough material to block out light from the stars behind it. A typical dark nebula is about 20 light-years in diameter and contains about 50 hydrogen atoms per cubic centimeter (monatomic hydrogen, *not* H_2) at about 20 K. (A light-year is the distance light travels in vacuum in one year and is equal to 9.46×10^{15} m.) (a) Estimate the mean free path for a hydrogen atom in a dark nebula. The radius of a hydrogen atom is 5.0×10^{-11} m. (b) Estimate the rms speed of a hydrogen atom and the mean free time (the average time between collisions for a given atom). Based on this result, do you think that atomic collisions, such as those leading to H_2 molecule formation, are very important in determining the composition of the nebula? (c) Estimate the pressure inside a dark nebula. (d) Compare the rms speed of a hydrogen atom to the escape speed at the surface of the nebula (assumed spherical). If the space around the nebula were a vacuum, would such a cloud be stable or would it tend to evaporate? (e) The stability of dark nebulae is explained by the presence of the *interstellar medium* (ISM), an even thinner gas that permeates space and in which the dark nebulae are embedded. Show that for dark nebulae to be in equilibrium with the ISM, the numbers of atoms per volume (N/V) and the temperatures (T) of dark nebulae and the ISM must be related by

$$\frac{(N/V)_{\text{nebula}}}{(N/V)_{\text{ISM}}} = \frac{T_{\text{ISM}}}{T_{\text{nebula}}}$$

(f) In the vicinity of the sun, the ISM contains about 1 hydrogen atom per 200 cm³. Estimate the temperature of the ISM in the vicinity of the sun. Compare to the temperature of the sun's surface, about 5800 K. Would a spacecraft coasting through interstellar space burn up? Why or why not?

Figure **P18.83**

18.84 ••• CALC **Earth's Atmosphere.** In the *troposphere*, the part of the atmosphere that extends from earth's surface to an altitude of about 11 km, the temperature is not uniform but decreases with increasing elevation. (a) Show that if the temperature variation is approximated by the linear relationship

$$T = T_0 - \alpha y$$

where T_0 is the temperature at the earth's surface and T is the temperature at height y, the pressure p at height y is

$$\ln\left(\frac{p}{p_0}\right) = \frac{Mg}{R\alpha} \ln\left(\frac{T_0 - \alpha y}{T_0}\right)$$

where p_0 is the pressure at the earth's surface and M is the molar mass for air. The coefficient α is called the lapse rate of temperature. It varies with atmospheric conditions, but an average value is about 0.6 C°/100 m. (b) Show that the above result reduces to the result of Example 18.4 (Section 18.1) in the limit that $\alpha \to 0$. (c) With $\alpha = 0.6$ C°/100 m, calculate p for $y = 8863$ m and compare your answer to the result of Example 18.4. Take $T_0 = 288$ K and $p_0 = 1.00$ atm.

PASSAGE PROBLEMS

INSULATING WINDOWS. One way to improve insulation in windows is to fill a sealed space between two glass panes with a gas that has a lower thermal conductivity than that of air. The thermal conductivity k of a gas depends on its molar heat capacity C_V, molar mass M, and molecular radius r. The dependence on those quantities at a given temperature is approximated by $k \propto C_V/r^2\sqrt{M}$. The noble gases have properties that make them particularly good choices as insulating gases. Noble gases range from helium (molar mass 4.0 g/mol, molecular radius 0.13 nm) to xenon (molar mass 131 g/mol, molecular radius 0.22 nm). (The noble gas radon is heavier than xenon, but radon is radioactive and so is not suitable for this purpose.)

18.85 What is one reason the noble gases are *preferable* to air (which is mostly nitrogen and oxygen) as an insulating material? (a) Noble gases are monatomic, so no rotational modes contribute to their molar heat capacity; (b) noble gases are monatomic, so they have lower molecular masses than do nitrogen and oxygen; (c) molecular radii in noble gases are much larger than those of gases that consist of diatomic molecules; (d) because noble gases are monatomic, they have many more degrees of freedom than do diatomic molecules, and their molar heat capacity is reduced by the number of degrees of freedom.

18.86 Estimate the ratio of the thermal conductivity of Xe to that of He. (a) 0.015; (b) 0.061; (c) 0.10; (d) 0.17.

18.87 The rate of *effusion*—that is, leakage of a gas through tiny cracks—is proportional to v_{rms}. If tiny cracks exist in the material that's used to seal the space between two glass panes, how many times greater is the rate of He leakage out of the space between the panes than the rate of Xe leakage at the same temperature? (a) 370 times; (b) 19 times; (c) 6 times; (d) no greater—the He leakage rate is the same as for Xe.

Answers

Chapter Opening Question ?

(iv) From Eq. (18.19), the root-mean-square speed of a gas molecule is proportional to the square root of the absolute temperature T. The temperature range we're considering is $(25 + 273.15)$ K = 298 K to $(100 + 273.15)$ K = 373 K. Hence the speeds increase by a factor of $\sqrt{(373\ \text{K})/(298\ \text{K})} = 1.12$; that is, there is a 12% increase. While 100°C feels far warmer than 25°C, the difference in molecular speeds is relatively small.

Test Your Understanding Questions

18.1 (ii) and (iii) (tie), (i) and (v) (tie), (iv) We can rewrite the ideal-gas equation, Eq. (18.3), as $n = pV/RT$. This tells us that the number of moles n is proportional to the pressure and volume and inversely proportional to the absolute temperature. Hence, compared to (i), the number of moles in each case is (ii) $(2)(1)/(1) = 2$ times as much, (iii) $(1)(2)/(1) = 2$ times as much, (iv) $(1)(1)/(2) = \frac{1}{2}$ as much, and (v) $(2)(1)/(2) = 1$ time as much (that is, equal).

18.2 (vi) The value of r_0 determines the equilibrium separation of the molecules in the solid phase, so doubling r_0 means that the separation doubles as well. Hence a solid cube of this compound might grow from 1 cm on a side to 2 cm on a side. The volume would then be $2^3 = 8$ times larger, and the density (mass divided by volume) would be $\frac{1}{8}$ as great.

18.3 (a) (iv), (ii), (iii), (i); (b) (iii) and (iv) (tie), (i) and (ii) (tie) (a) Equation (18.19) tells us that $v_{\text{rms}} = \sqrt{3RT/M}$, so the rms speed is proportional to the square root of the ratio of absolute temperature T to molar mass M. Compared to (i) oxygen at 300 K, v_{rms} in the other cases is (ii) $\sqrt{(32.0\ \text{g/mol})/(28.0\ \text{g/mol})} = 1.07$ times faster, (iii) $\sqrt{(330\ \text{K})/(300\ \text{K})} = 1.05$ times faster, and (iv) $\sqrt{(330\ \text{K})(32.0\ \text{g/mol})/(300\ \text{K})(28.0\ \text{g/mol})} = 1.12$ times faster. (b) From Eq. (18.16), the average translational kinetic energy per molecule is $\frac{1}{2}m(v^2)_{\text{av}} = \frac{3}{2}kT$, which is directly proportional to T and independent of M. We have $T = 300$ K for cases (i) and (ii) and $T = 330$ K for cases (iii) and (iv), so $\frac{1}{2}m(v^2)_{\text{av}}$ has equal values for cases (iii) and (iv) and equal (but smaller) values for cases (i) and (ii).

18.4 no, near the beginning Adding a small amount of heat dQ to the gas changes the temperature by dT, where $dQ = nC_V dT$ from Eq. (18.24). Figure 18.19 shows that C_V for H_2 varies with temperature between 25 K and 500 K, so a given amount of heat gives rise to different amounts of temperature change during the process. Hence the temperature will *not* increase at a constant rate. The temperature change $dT = dQ/nC_V$ is inversely proportional to C_V, so the temperature increases most rapidly at the beginning of the process when the temperature is lowest and C_V is smallest (see Fig. 18.19).

18.5 (ii) Figure 18.23b shows that the *fraction* of molecules with speeds between v_1 and v_2 equals the area under the curve of $f(v)$ versus v from $v = v_1$ to $v = v_2$. This is equal to the integral $\int_{v_1}^{v_2} f(v)\,dv$, which in turn is equal to the difference between the integrals $\int_0^{v_2} f(v)\,dv$ (the fraction of molecules with speeds from 0 to v_2) and $\int_0^{v_1} f(v)\,dv$ (the fraction of molecules with speeds from 0 to the slower speed v_1). The *number* of molecules with speeds from v_1 to v_2 equals the fraction of molecules in this speed range multiplied by N, the total number of molecules.

18.6 no, yes The triple-point pressure of water from Table 18.3 is 6.10×10^2 Pa. The present-day pressure on Mars is just less than this value, corresponding to the line labeled p_s in Fig. 18.24. Hence liquid water cannot exist on the present-day Martian surface, and there are no rivers or lakes. Planetary scientists conclude that liquid water could have existed and almost certainly did exist on Mars in the past, when the atmosphere was thicker.

Bridging Problem

(a) 102 km   **(b)** yes

? A steam locomotive uses the first law of thermodynamics: Water is heated and boils, and the expanding steam does work to propel the locomotive. Would it be possible for the steam to propel the locomotive by doing work as it *condenses?* (i) Yes; (ii) no; (iii) answer depends on the details of how the steam condenses.

19 THE FIRST LAW OF THERMODYNAMICS

E very time you drive a gasoline-powered car, turn on an air conditioner, or cook a meal, you reap the benefits of *thermodynamics,* the study of relationships involving heat, mechanical work, and other aspects of energy and energy transfer. For example, in a car engine heat is generated by the chemical reaction of oxygen and vaporized gasoline in the engine's cylinders. The heated gas pushes on the pistons within the cylinders, doing mechanical work that is used to propel the car. This is an example of a *thermodynamic process.*

The first law of thermodynamics, central to the understanding of such processes, is an extension of the principle of conservation of energy. It broadens this principle to include energy exchange by both heat transfer and mechanical work and introduces the concept of the *internal energy* of a system. Conservation of energy plays a vital role in every area of physical science, and the first law has extremely broad usefulness. To state energy relationships precisely, we need the concept of a *thermodynamic system.* We'll discuss *heat* and *work* as two means of transferring energy into or out of such a system.

19.1 THERMODYNAMIC SYSTEMS

We have studied energy transfer through mechanical work (Chapter 6) and through heat transfer (Chapters 17 and 18). Now we are ready to combine and generalize these principles.

We always talk about energy transfer to or from some specific *system.* The system might be a mechanical device, a biological organism, or a specified quantity of material, such as the refrigerant in an air conditioner or steam expanding in a turbine. In general, a **thermodynamic system** is any collection of objects that is convenient to regard as a unit, and that may have the potential to exchange energy with its surroundings. A familiar example is a quantity of popcorn kernels in a pot with a lid. When the pot is placed on a stove, energy is added to the popcorn by conduction of heat. As the popcorn pops and expands, it does work as it exerts an upward force on the lid and moves it through a displacement (**Fig. 19.1**). The *state* of the popcorn—its volume, temperature, and pressure—changes as it pops. A process such as this one, in which there are changes in the state of a thermodynamic system, is called a **thermodynamic process.**

In mechanics we used the concept of *system* with free-body diagrams and with conservation of energy and momentum. For *thermodynamic* systems, as for all others, it is essential to define clearly at the start exactly what is and is not included in the system. Only then can we describe unambiguously the energy transfers into and out of that system. For instance, in our popcorn example we defined the system to include the popcorn but not the pot, lid, or stove.

Thermodynamics has its roots in many practical problems other than popping popcorn (**Fig. 19.2**). The gasoline engine in an automobile, the jet engines in an airplane, and the rocket engines in a launch vehicle use the heat of combustion of their fuel to perform mechanical work in propelling the vehicle. Muscle tissue in living organisms metabolizes chemical energy in food and performs mechanical work on the organism's surroundings. A steam engine or steam turbine uses the heat of combustion of coal or other fuel to perform mechanical work such as driving an electric generator or pulling a train.

19.1 The popcorn in the pot is a thermodynamic system. In the thermodynamic process shown here, heat is added to the system, and the system does work on its surroundings to lift the lid of the pot.

Signs for Heat and Work in Thermodynamics

We describe the energy relationships in any thermodynamic process in terms of the quantity of heat Q added *to* the system and the work W done *by* the system. Both Q and W may be positive, negative, or zero (**Fig. 19.3**). A positive value of Q represents heat flow *into* the system, with a corresponding input of energy to it; negative Q represents heat flow *out of* the system. A positive value of W represents work done *by* the system against its surroundings, such as work done by an expanding gas, and hence corresponds to energy *leaving* the system. Negative W, such as work done during compression of a gas in which work is done *on the gas* by its surroundings, represents energy *entering* the system. We will use these conventions consistently in the examples in this chapter and the next.

CAUTION **Be careful with the sign of work** W Note that our sign rule for work is *opposite* to the one we used in mechanics, in which we always spoke of the work done by the forces acting *on* a body. In thermodynamics it is usually more convenient to call W the work done *by* the system so that when a system expands, the pressure, volume change, and work are all positive. Use the sign rules for work and heat consistently! ▮

TEST YOUR UNDERSTANDING OF SECTION 19.1 In Example 17.7 (Section 17.6), what is the sign of Q for the coffee? For the aluminum cup? If a block slides along a horizontal surface with friction, what is the sign of W for the block? ▮

19.2 (a) A rocket engine uses the heat of combustion of its fuel to do work propelling the launch vehicle. (b) Humans and other biological organisms are more complicated systems than we can analyze fully in this book, but the same basic principles of thermodynamics apply to them.

(a)   (b)

19.3 A thermodynamic system may exchange energy with its surroundings (environment) by means of heat, work, or both. Note the sign conventions for Q and W.

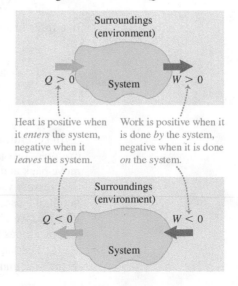

19.4 A molecule striking a piston (a) does positive work if the piston is moving away from the molecule and (b) does negative work if the piston is moving toward the molecule. Hence a gas does positive work when it expands as in (a) but does negative work when it compresses as in (b).

(a)

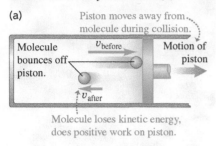

Molecule loses kinetic energy, does positive work on piston.

(b)

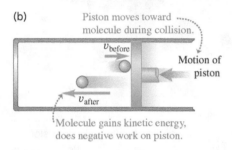

Molecule gains kinetic energy, does negative work on piston.

19.5 The infinitesimal work done by the system during the small expansion dx is $dW = pA\ dx$.

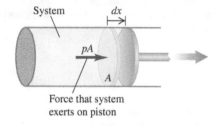

Force that system exerts on piston

19.2 WORK DONE DURING VOLUME CHANGES

A simple example of a thermodynamic system is a quantity of gas enclosed in a cylinder with a movable piston. Internal-combustion engines, steam engines, and compressors in refrigerators and air conditioners all use some version of such a system. In the next several sections we will use the gas-in-cylinder system to explore several kinds of thermodynamic processes.

We'll use a microscopic viewpoint, based on the kinetic and potential energies of individual molecules in a material, to develop intuition about thermodynamic quantities. But it is important to understand that the central principles of thermodynamics can be treated in a completely *macroscopic* way, without reference to microscopic models. Indeed, part of the great power and generality of thermodynamics is that it does *not* depend on details of the structure of matter.

First we consider the *work* done by the system during a volume change. When a gas expands, it pushes outward on its boundary surfaces as they move outward. Hence an expanding gas always does positive work. The same thing is true of any material that expands under pressure, such as the popcorn in Fig. 19.1.

We can understand the work done by a gas in a volume change by considering the molecules that make up the gas. When one such molecule **?** collides with a stationary surface, it exerts a momentary force on the wall but does no work because the wall does not move. But if the surface is moving, like a piston in a gasoline engine, the molecule *does* do work on the surface during the collision. If the piston in **Fig. 19.4a** moves to the right, so the volume of the gas increases, the molecules that strike the piston exert a force through a distance and do *positive* work on the piston. If the piston moves toward the left as in Fig. 19.4b, so the volume of the gas decreases, positive work is done *on* the molecule during the collision. Hence the gas molecules do *negative* work on the piston.

Figure 19.5 shows a system whose volume can change (a gas, liquid, or solid) in a cylinder with a movable piston. Suppose that the cylinder has cross-sectional area A and that the pressure exerted by the system at the piston face is p. The total force F exerted by the system on the piston is $F = pA$. When the piston moves out an infinitesimal distance dx, the work dW done by this force is

$$dW = F\ dx = pA\ dx$$

But

$$A\ dx = dV$$

where dV is the infinitesimal change of volume of the system. Thus we can express the work done by the system in this infinitesimal volume change as

$$dW = p\ dV \tag{19.1}$$

In a finite change of volume from V_1 to V_2,

Work done in a volume change $\longrightarrow W = \int_{V_1}^{V_2} p\ dV$ · · · Upper limit = final volume
Integral of the pressure with respect to volume
· · · Lower limit = initial volume $\qquad$ (19.2)

In general, the pressure of the system may vary during the volume change. For example, this is the case in the cylinders of an automobile engine as the pistons move back and forth. To evaluate the integral in Eq. (19.2), we have to know how the pressure varies as a function of volume. We can represent this relationship as a graph of p as a function of V (a pV-diagram, described at the end of Section 18.1). **Figure 19.6** shows a simple example. In this figure, Eq. (19.2) is represented graphically as the *area* under the curve of p versus V between the limits V_1 and V_2. (In Section 6.3 we used a similar interpretation of the work done by a force F as the area under the curve of F versus x between the limits x_1 and x_2.)

19.6 The work done equals the area under the curve on a *pV*-diagram.

(a) *pV*-diagram for a system undergoing an expansion with varying pressure

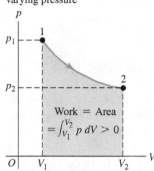

(b) *pV*-diagram for a system undergoing a compression with varying pressure

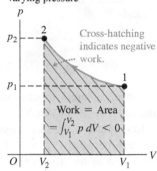

Cross-hatching indicates negative work.

(c) *pV*-diagram for a system undergoing an expansion with constant pressure

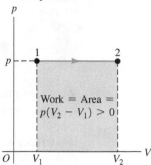

According to the rule we stated in Section 19.1, work is *positive* when a system *expands*. In an expansion from state 1 to state 2 in Fig. 19.6a, the area under the curve and the work are positive. A *compression* from 1 to 2 in Fig. 19.6b gives a *negative* area; when a system is compressed, its volume decreases and it does *negative* work on its surroundings (see also Fig. 19.4b).

If the pressure *p* remains constant while the volume changes from V_1 to V_2 (Fig. 19.6c), the work done by the system is

Work done in a volume change at constant pressure

$$W = p(V_2 - V_1) \qquad (19.3)$$

Pressure · · · Final volume · Initial volume

CAUTION Be careful with subscripts 1 and 2 In Eq. (19.2), V_1 is the *initial* volume and V_2 is the *final* volume. That's why labels 1 and 2 are reversed in Fig. 19.6b compared to Fig. 19.6a, even though both processes move between the same two thermodynamic states. ∎

If the volume is *constant*, there is no displacement and the system does no work.

EXAMPLE 19.1 **ISOTHERMAL EXPANSION OF AN IDEAL GAS**

As an ideal gas undergoes an *isothermal* (constant-temperature) expansion at temperature *T*, its volume changes from V_1 to V_2. How much work does the gas do?

SOLUTION

IDENTIFY and SET UP: The ideal-gas equation, Eq. (18.3), tells us that if the temperature *T* of *n* moles of an ideal gas is constant, the quantity $pV = nRT$ is also constant. If *V* changes, *p* changes as well, so we *cannot* use Eq. (19.3) to calculate the work done. Instead we must evaluate the integral in Eq. (19.2), so we must know *p* as a function of *V*; for this we use Eq. (18.3).

EXECUTE: From Eq. (18.3),

$$p = \frac{nRT}{V}$$

We substitute this into the integral of Eq. (19.2), take the constant factor *nRT* outside, and evaluate the integral:

$$W = \int_{V_1}^{V_2} p \, dV = nRT \int_{V_1}^{V_2} \frac{dV}{V}$$

$$= nRT \ln\frac{V_2}{V_1} \quad \text{(ideal gas, isothermal process)}$$

We can rewrite this expression for *W* in terms of p_1 and p_2. Because $pV = nRT$ is constant,

$$p_1V_1 = p_2V_2 \qquad \text{or} \qquad \frac{V_2}{V_1} = \frac{p_1}{p_2}$$

so

$$W = nRT \ln\frac{p_1}{p_2} \quad \text{(ideal gas, isothermal process)}$$

EVALUATE: We check our result by noting that in an expansion $V_2 > V_1$ and the ratio V_2/V_1 is greater than 1. The logarithm of a number greater than 1 is positive, so $W > 0$, as it should be. As an additional check, look at our second expression for *W*: In an isothermal expansion the volume increases and the pressure drops, so $p_2 < p_1$, the ratio $p_1/p_2 > 1$, and $W = nRT \ln(p_1/p_2)$ is again positive.

Our result for *W* also applies to an isothermal *compression* of a gas, for which $V_2 < V_1$ and $p_2 > p_1$.

19.3 PATHS BETWEEN THERMODYNAMIC STATES

We've seen that if a thermodynamic process involves a change in volume, the system undergoing the process does work (either positive or negative) on its surroundings. Heat also flows into or out of the system during the process if there is a temperature difference between the system and its surroundings. Let's now examine how the work done by and the heat added to the system during a thermodynamic process depend on the details of how the process takes place.

Work Done in a Thermodynamic Process

When a thermodynamic system changes from an initial state to a final state, it passes through a series of intermediate states. We call this series of states a **path.** There are always infinitely many possibilities for these intermediate states. When all are equilibrium states, the path can be plotted on a *pV*-diagram (**Fig. 19.7a**). Point 1 represents an initial state with pressure p_1 and volume V_1, and point 2 represents a final state with pressure p_2 and volume V_2. To pass from state 1 to state 2, we could keep the pressure constant at p_1 while the system expands to volume V_2 (point 3 in Fig. 19.7b), then reduce the pressure to p_2 (probably by decreasing the temperature) while keeping the volume constant at V_2 (to point 2). The work done by the system during this process is the area under the line $1 \rightarrow 3$; no work is done during the constant-volume process $3 \rightarrow 2$. Or the system might traverse the path $1 \rightarrow 4 \rightarrow 2$ (Fig. 19.7c); then the work is the area under the line $4 \rightarrow 2$, since no work is done during the constant-volume process $1 \rightarrow 4$. The smooth curve from 1 to 2 is another possibility (Fig. 19.7d), and the work for this path is different from that for either of the other paths.

We conclude that *the work done by the system depends not only on the initial and final states, but also on the intermediate states—that is, on the path.* Furthermore, we can take the system through a series of states forming a closed loop, such as $1 \rightarrow 3 \rightarrow 2 \rightarrow 4 \rightarrow 1$. In this case the final state is the same as the initial state, but the total work done by the system is *not* zero. (In fact, it is represented on the graph by the area enclosed by the loop; see Exercise 19.7.) So we can't talk about the amount of work *contained in* a system. In a particular state, a system may have definite values of the state coordinates *p*, *V*, and *T*, but it wouldn't make sense to say that it has a definite value of *W*.

Heat Added in a Thermodynamic Process

Like work, the *heat* added to a thermodynamic system when it undergoes a change of state depends on the path from the initial state to the final state. Here's an example. Suppose we want to change the volume of a certain quantity of an ideal gas from 2.0 L to 5.0 L while keeping the temperature constant at $T = 300$ K. **Figure 19.8** shows two different ways to do this. In Fig. 19.8a the gas is contained in a cylinder with a piston, with an initial volume of 2.0 L. We let the gas expand slowly, supplying heat from the electric heater to keep the temperature at 300 K until the gas reaches its final volume of 5.0 L. The gas absorbs a definite amount of heat in this isothermal process.

Figure 19.8b shows a different process leading to the same final state. The container is surrounded by insulating walls and is divided by a thin, breakable partition into two compartments. The lower part has volume 2.0 L and the upper part has volume 3.0 L. In the lower compartment we place the same amount of

19.7 The work done by a system during a transition between two states depends on the path chosen.

(a)

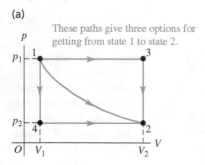

These paths give three options for getting from state 1 to state 2.

(b)

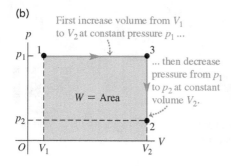

First increase volume from V_1 to V_2 at constant pressure p_1 ...

... then decrease pressure from p_1 to p_2 at constant volume V_2.

$W = $ Area

(c)

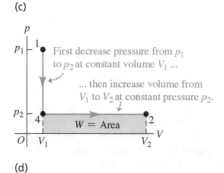

First decrease pressure from p_1 to p_2 at constant volume V_1 ...

... then increase volume from V_1 to V_2 at constant pressure p_2.

$W = $ Area

(d)

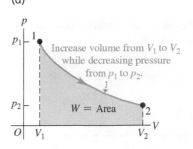

Increase volume from V_1 to V_2 while decreasing pressure from p_1 to p_2.

$W = $ Area

the same gas as in Fig. 19.8a, again at $T = 300$ K. The initial state is the same as before. Now we break the partition; the gas expands rapidly, with no heat passing through the insulating walls. The final volume is 5.0 L, the same as in Fig. 19.8a. The expanding gas does no work because it doesn't push against anything that moves. This uncontrolled expansion of a gas into vacuum is called a **free expansion;** we'll discuss it further in Section 19.6.

Experiments show that when an ideal gas undergoes a free expansion, there is no temperature change. So the final state of the gas is the same as in Fig. 19.8a. The intermediate pressures and volumes during the transition from state 1 to state 2 are entirely different in the two cases; Figs. 19.8a and 19.8b represent *two different paths* connecting the *same states* 1 and 2. For the path in Fig. 19.8b, *no* heat is transferred into the system, and the system does no work. Like work, *heat depends not only on the initial and final states but also on the path.*

Because of this path dependence, it would not make sense to say that a system "contains" a certain quantity of heat. To see this, suppose we assign an arbitrary value to the "heat in a body" in some reference state. Then presumably the "heat in the body" in some other state would equal the heat in the reference state plus the heat added when the body goes to the second state. But that's ambiguous, as we have just seen; the heat added depends on the *path* we take from the reference state to the second state. We are forced to conclude that there is *no* consistent way to define "heat in a body"; it is not a useful concept.

While it doesn't make sense to talk about "work in a body" or "heat in a body," it *does* make sense to speak of the amount of *internal energy* in a body. This important concept is our next topic.

TEST YOUR UNDERSTANDING OF SECTION 19.3 The system described in Fig. 19.7a undergoes four different thermodynamic processes. Each process is represented in a pV-diagram as a straight line from the initial state to the final state. (These processes are different from those shown in the pV-diagrams of Fig. 19.7.) Rank the processes in order of the amount of work done by the system, from the most positive to the most negative. (i) $1 \rightarrow 2$; (ii) $2 \rightarrow 1$; (iii) $3 \rightarrow 4$; (iv) $4 \rightarrow 3$. ❚

19.4 INTERNAL ENERGY AND THE FIRST LAW OF THERMODYNAMICS

Internal energy is one of the most important concepts in thermodynamics. In Section 7.3, when we discussed energy changes for a body sliding with friction, we stated that warming a body increased its internal energy and that cooling the body decreased its internal energy. But what *is* internal energy? We can look at it in various ways; let's start with one based on the ideas of mechanics. Matter consists of atoms and molecules, and these are made up of particles having kinetic and potential energies. We *tentatively* define the **internal energy** of a system as the sum of the kinetic energies of all of its constituent particles, plus the sum of all the potential energies of interaction among these particles.

CAUTION **Is it internal?** Internal energy does *not* include potential energy arising from the interaction between the system and its surroundings. If the system is a glass of water, placing it on a high shelf increases the gravitational potential energy arising from the interaction between the glass and the earth. But this has no effect on the interactions among the water molecules, and so the internal energy of the water does not change. ❚

We use the symbol U for internal energy. (We used this symbol in our study of mechanics to represent potential energy. However, U has a different meaning in thermodynamics.) During a change of state of the system, the internal energy may change from an initial value U_1 to a final value U_2. We denote the change in internal energy as $\Delta U = U_2 - U_1$.

19.8 (a) Slow, controlled isothermal expansion of a gas from an initial state 1 to a final state 2 with the same temperature but lower pressure. (b) Rapid, uncontrolled expansion of the same gas starting at the same state 1 and ending at the same state 2.

(a) System does work on piston; hot plate adds heat to system ($W > 0$ and $Q > 0$).

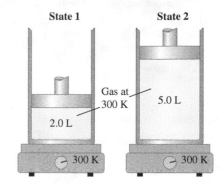

(b) System does no work; no heat enters or leaves system ($W = 0$ and $Q = 0$).

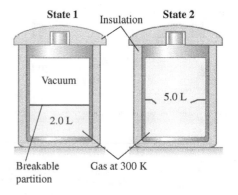

19.9 In a thermodynamic process, the internal energy U of a system may (a) increase ($\Delta U > 0$), (b) decrease ($\Delta U < 0$), or (c) remain the same ($\Delta U = 0$).

(a) More heat is added to system than system does work: Internal energy of system increases.

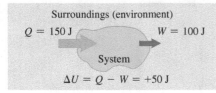

$$\Delta U = Q - W = +50 \text{ J}$$

(b) More heat flows out of system than work is done: Internal energy of system decreases.

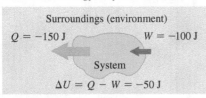

$$\Delta U = Q - W = -50 \text{ J}$$

(c) Heat added to system equals work done by system: Internal energy of system unchanged.

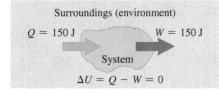

$$\Delta U = Q - W = 0$$

BIO Application The First Law of Exercise Thermodynamics Your body is a thermodynamic system. When you exercise, your body does work (such as the work done to lift your body as a whole in a push-up). Hence $W > 0$. Your body also warms up during exercise; by perspiration and other means the body rids itself of this heat, so $Q < 0$. Since Q is negative and W is positive, $\Delta U = Q - W < 0$ and the body's internal energy decreases. That's why exercise helps you lose weight: It uses up some of the internal energy stored in your body in the form of fat.

When we add a quantity of heat Q to a system and the system does no work during the process (so $W = 0$), the internal energy increases by an amount equal to Q; that is, $\Delta U = Q$. When a system does work W by expanding against its surroundings and no heat is added during the process, energy leaves the system and the internal energy decreases: W is positive, Q is zero, and $\Delta U = -W$. When *both* heat transfer and work occur, the *total* change in internal energy is

First law of thermodynamics:

Internal energy change of thermodynamic system

$$\Delta U = Q - W \tag{19.4}$$

Heat added to system ····⟶ ⟵···· Work done by system

We can rearrange this to the form

$$Q = \Delta U + W \tag{19.5}$$

The message of Eq. (19.5) is that when heat Q is added to a system, some of this added energy remains within the system, changing its internal energy by ΔU; the remainder leaves the system as the system does work W on its surroundings. Because W and Q may be positive, negative, or zero, ΔU can be positive, negative, or zero for different processes (**Fig. 19.9**).

Equation (19.4) or (19.5) is the **first law of thermodynamics.** It is a generalization of the principle of conservation of energy to include energy transfer through heat as well as mechanical work. As you will see in later chapters, this principle can be extended to ever-broader classes of phenomena by identifying additional forms of energy and energy transfer. In every situation in which it seems that the total energy in all known forms is not conserved, it has been possible to identify a new form of energy such that the total energy, including the new form, *is* conserved.

Understanding the First Law of Thermodynamics

At the beginning of this discussion we tentatively defined internal energy in terms of microscopic kinetic and potential energies. But actually *calculating* internal energy in this way for any real system would be hopelessly complicated. Furthermore, this definition isn't an *operational* one: It doesn't describe how to determine internal energy from physical quantities that we can measure.

So let's look at internal energy in another way. Starting over, we define the *change* in internal energy ΔU during any change of a system as the quantity given by Eq. (19.4), $\Delta U = Q - W$. This *is* an operational definition because we can measure Q and W. It does not define U itself, only ΔU. This is not a shortcoming because we can *define* the internal energy of a system to have a specified value in some reference state, and then use Eq. (19.4) to define the internal energy in any other state. This is analogous to our treatment of potential energy in Chapter 7, in which we arbitrarily defined the potential energy of a mechanical system to be zero at a certain position.

This new definition trades one difficulty for another. If we define ΔU by Eq. (19.4), then when the system goes from state 1 to state 2 by two different paths, how do we know that ΔU is the same for the two paths? We have already seen that Q and W are, in general, *not* the same for different paths. If ΔU, which equals $Q - W$, is also path dependent, then ΔU is ambiguous. If so, the concept of internal energy of a system is subject to the same criticism as the erroneous concept of quantity of heat in a system, as we discussed at the end of Section 19.3.

The only way to answer this question is through *experiment*. For various materials we measure Q and W for various changes of state and various paths to learn whether ΔU is or is not path dependent. The results of many such investigations are clear and unambiguous: While Q and W depend on the path, $\Delta U = Q - W$ is independent of path. *The change in internal energy of a system during any thermodynamic process depends only on the initial and final states, not on the path leading from one to the other.*

Experiment, then, is the ultimate justification for believing that a thermodynamic system in a specific state has a unique internal energy that depends only on that state. An equivalent statement is that the internal energy U of a system is a function of the state coordinates p, V, and T (actually, any two of these, since the three variables are related by the equation of state).

To say that the first law of thermodynamics, given by Eq. (19.4) or (19.5), represents conservation of energy for thermodynamic processes is correct, as far as it goes. But an important *additional* aspect of the first law is the fact that internal energy depends only on the state of a system (**Fig. 19.10**). In changes of state, the change in internal energy is independent of the path.

All this may seem a little abstract if you are satisfied to think of internal energy as microscopic mechanical energy. There's nothing wrong with that view, and we will make use of it at various times during our discussion. But as for heat, a precise *operational* definition of internal energy must be independent of the detailed microscopic structure of the material.

19.10 The internal energy of a cup of coffee depends on just its thermodynamic state—how much water and ground coffee it contains, and what its temperature is. It does not depend on the history of how the coffee was prepared—that is, the thermodynamic path that led to its current state.

Cyclic Processes and Isolated Systems

Two special cases of the first law of thermodynamics are worth mentioning. A process that eventually returns a system to its initial state is called a *cyclic process*. For such a process, the final state is the same as the initial state, and so the *total* internal energy change must be zero. Then

$$U_2 = U_1 \quad \text{and} \quad Q = W$$

If a net quantity of work W is done by the system during this process, an equal amount of energy must have flowed into the system as heat Q. But there is no reason either Q or W individually has to be zero (**Fig. 19.11**).

Another special case occurs in an *isolated system,* one that does no work on its surroundings and has no heat flow to or from its surroundings. For any process taking place in an isolated system,

$$W = Q = 0$$

and therefore

$$U_2 = U_1 = \Delta U = 0$$

In other words, *the internal energy of an isolated system is constant.*

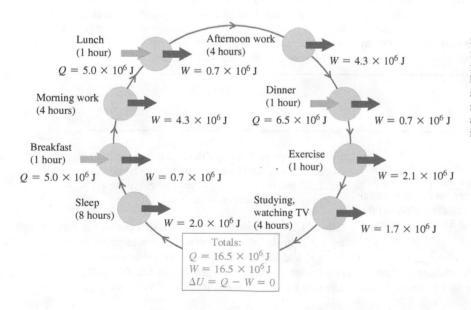

Lunch
(1 hour)

Afternoon work
(4 hours)

$Q = 5.0 \times 10^6$ J

$W = 0.7 \times 10^6$ J

$W = 4.3 \times 10^6$ J

Morning work
(4 hours)

Dinner
(1 hour)

$W = 4.3 \times 10^6$ J

$Q = 6.5 \times 10^6$ J

$W = 0.7 \times 10^6$ J

Breakfast
(1 hour)

Exercise
(1 hour)

$Q = 5.0 \times 10^6$ J

$W = 0.7 \times 10^6$ J

$W = 2.1 \times 10^6$ J

Sleep
(8 hours)

Studying,
watching TV
(4 hours)

$W = 2.0 \times 10^6$ J

$W = 1.7 \times 10^6$ J

Totals:
$Q = 16.5 \times 10^6$ J
$W = 16.5 \times 10^6$ J
$\Delta U = Q - W = 0$

19.11 Every day, your body (a thermodynamic system) goes through a cyclic thermodynamic process like this one. Heat Q is added by metabolizing food, and your body does work W in breathing, walking, and other activities. If you return to the same state at the end of the day, $Q = W$ and the net change in your internal energy is zero.

PROBLEM-SOLVING STRATEGY 19.1 **THE FIRST LAW OF THERMODYNAMICS**

IDENTIFY *the relevant concepts:* The first law of thermodynamics is the statement of the law of conservation of energy in its most general form. You can apply it to *any* thermodynamic process in which the internal energy of a system changes, heat flows into or out of the system, and/or work is done by or on the system.

SET UP *the problem* using the following steps:
1. Define the thermodynamic system to be considered.
2. If the thermodynamic process has more than one step, identify the initial and final states for each step.
3. List the known and unknown quantities and identify the target variables.
4. Confirm that you have enough equations. You can apply the first law, $\Delta U = Q - W$, just once to each step in a thermodynamic process, so you will often need additional equations. These may include Eq. (19.2), $W = \int_{V_1}^{V_2} p\,dV$, which gives the work W done in a volume change, and the equation of state of the material that makes up the thermodynamic system (for an ideal gas, $pV = nRT$).

EXECUTE *the solution* as follows:
1. Be sure to use consistent units. If p is in Pa and V in m^3, then W is in joules. If a heat capacity is given in terms of calories,

convert it to joules. When you use $n = m_{total}/M$ to relate total mass m_{total} to number of moles n, remember that if m_{total} is in kilograms, M must be in *kilograms* per mole; M is usually tabulated in *grams* per mole.
2. The internal energy change ΔU in any thermodynamic process or series of processes is independent of the path, whether the substance is an ideal gas or not. If you can calculate ΔU for *any* path between given initial and final states, you know ΔU for *every possible path* between those states; you can then relate the various energy quantities for any of those other paths.
3. In a process comprising several steps, tabulate Q, W, and ΔU for each step, with one line per step and with the Q's, W's, and ΔU's forming columns (see Example 19.4). You can apply the first law to each line, and you can add each column and apply the first law to the sums. Do you see why?
4. Using steps 1–3, solve for the target variables.

EVALUATE *your answer:* Check your results for reasonableness. Ensure that each of your answers has the correct algebraic sign. A positive Q means that heat flows *into* the system; a negative Q means that heat flows *out of* the system. A positive W means that work is done *by* the system on its environment; a negative W means that work is done *on* the system by its environment.

EXAMPLE 19.2 **WORKING OFF YOUR DESSERT**

You propose to climb several flights of stairs to work off the energy you took in by eating a 900-calorie hot fudge sundae. How high must you climb? Assume that your mass is 60.0 kg.

SOLUTION

IDENTIFY and SET UP: The thermodynamic system is your body. You climb the stairs to make the final state of the system the same as the initial state (no fatter, no leaner). There is therefore no net change in internal energy: $\Delta U = 0$. Eating the hot fudge sundae corresponds to a heat flow into your body, and you do work climbing the stairs. We can relate these quantities by using the first law of thermodynamics. We are given that $Q = 900$ food calories (900 kcal) of heat flow into your body. The work you must do to raise your mass m a height h is $W = mgh$; our target variable is h.

EXECUTE: From the first law of thermodynamics, $\Delta U = 0 = Q - W$, so $W = mgh = Q$. Hence you must climb to height $h = Q/mg$. First convert units: $Q = (900 \text{ kcal})(4186 \text{ J}/1 \text{ kcal}) = 3.77 \times 10^6$ J. Then

$$h = \frac{Q}{mg} = \frac{3.77 \times 10^6 \text{ J}}{(60.0 \text{ kg})(9.80 \text{ m/s}^2)} = 6410 \text{ m}$$

EVALUATE: We have unrealistically assumed 100% efficiency in the conversion of food energy into mechanical work. The actual efficiency is roughly 25%, so the work W you do as you "burn off" the sundae is only about $(0.25)(900 \text{ kcal}) = 225$ kcal. (The remaining 75%, or 675 kcal, is transferred to your surroundings as heat.) Hence you actually must climb about $(0.25)(6410 \text{ m}) = 1600$ m, or one *mile*! Do you really want that sundae?

EXAMPLE 19.3 **A CYCLIC PROCESS**

Figure 19.12 shows a *pV*-diagram for a *cyclic* process in which the initial and final states of some thermodynamic system are the same. The state of the system starts at point a and proceeds counterclockwise in the *pV*-diagram to point b, then back to a; the total work is $W = -500$ J. (a) Why is the work negative? (b) Find the change in internal energy and the heat added during this process.

SOLUTION

IDENTIFY and SET UP: We must relate the change in internal energy, the heat added, and the work done in a thermodynamic

process. Hence we can apply the first law of thermodynamics. The process is cyclic, and it has two steps: $a \rightarrow b$ via the lower curve in Fig. 19.12 and $b \rightarrow a$ via the upper curve. We are asked only about the *entire* cyclic process $a \rightarrow b \rightarrow a$.

EXECUTE: (a) The work done in any step equals the area under the curve in the *pV*-diagram, with the area taken as positive if $V_2 > V_1$ and negative if $V_2 < V_1$; this rule yields the signs that result from the actual integrations in Eq. (19.2), $W = \int_{V_1}^{V_2} p\,dV$. The area under the lower curve $a \rightarrow b$ is therefore positive, but it

19.12 The net work done by the system in process $a \to b \to a$ is -500 J. What would it have been if the process had proceeded clockwise in this pV-diagram?

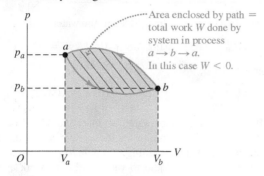

Area enclosed by path = total work W done by system in process $a \to b \to a$. In this case $W < 0$.

is smaller than the absolute value of the (negative) area under the upper curve $b \to a$. Therefore the net area (the area enclosed by the path, shown with red stripes) and the net work W are negative. In other words, 500 J more work is done *on* the system than *by* the system in the complete process.

(b) In any cyclic process, $\Delta U = 0$, so $Q = W$. Here, that means $Q = -500$ J; that is, 500 J of heat flows *out of* the system.

EVALUATE: In cyclic processes, the total work is positive if the process goes clockwise around the pV-diagram representing the cycle, and negative if the process goes counterclockwise (as here).

EXAMPLE 19.4 COMPARING THERMODYNAMIC PROCESSES

The pV-diagram of **Fig. 19.13** shows a series of thermodynamic processes. In process ab, 150 J of heat is added to the system; in process bd, 600 J of heat is added. Find (a) the internal energy change in process ab; (b) the internal energy change in process abd (shown in light blue); and (c) the total heat added in process acd (shown in dark blue).

SOLUTION

IDENTIFY and SET UP: In each process we use $\Delta U = Q - W$ to determine the desired quantity. We are given $Q_{ab} = +150$ J and $Q_{bd} = +600$ J (both values are positive because heat is *added* to the system). Our target variables are (a) ΔU_{ab}, (b) ΔU_{abd}, and (c) Q_{acd}.

EXECUTE: (a) No volume change occurs during process ab, so the system does no work: $W_{ab} = 0$ and so $\Delta U_{ab} = Q_{ab} = 150$ J.

(b) Process bd is an expansion at constant pressure, so from Eq. (19.3),

$$W_{bd} = p(V_2 - V_1)$$
$$= (8.0 \times 10^4 \text{ Pa})(5.0 \times 10^{-3} \text{ m}^3 - 2.0 \times 10^{-3} \text{ m}^3)$$
$$= 240 \text{ J}$$

The total work for the two-step process abd is then

$$W_{abd} = W_{ab} + W_{bd} = 0 + 240 \text{ J} = 240 \text{ J}$$

and the total heat is

$$Q_{abd} = Q_{ab} + Q_{bd} = 150 \text{ J} + 600 \text{ J} = 750 \text{ J}$$

Applying Eq. (19.4) to abd, we then have

$$\Delta U_{abd} = Q_{abd} - W_{abd} = 750 \text{ J} - 240 \text{ J} = 510 \text{ J}$$

(c) Because ΔU is *independent of the path* from a to d, the internal energy change is the same for path acd as for path abd:

$$\Delta U_{acd} = \Delta U_{abd} = 510 \text{ J}$$

The total work for path acd is

$$W_{acd} = W_{ac} + W_{cd} = p(V_2 - V_1) + 0$$
$$= (3.0 \times 10^4 \text{ Pa})(5.0 \times 10^{-3} \text{ m}^3 - 2.0 \times 10^{-3} \text{ m}^3)$$
$$= 90 \text{ J}$$

Now we apply Eq. (19.5) to process acd:

$$Q_{acd} = \Delta U_{acd} + W_{acd} = 510 \text{ J} + 90 \text{ J} = 600 \text{ J}$$

We tabulate the quantities above:

19.13 A pV-diagram showing the various thermodynamic processes.

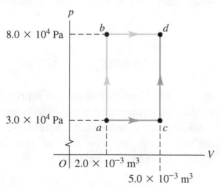

Step	Q	W	$\Delta U = Q - W$	Step	Q	W	$\Delta U = Q - W$
ab	150 J	0 J	150 J	ac	?	90 J	?
bd	600 J	240 J	360 J	cd	?	0 J	?
abd	750 J	240 J	510 J	acd	600 J	90 J	510 J

EVALUATE: Be sure that you understand how each entry in the table above was determined. Although ΔU is the same (510 J) for abd and acd, W (240 J versus 90 J) and Q (750 J versus 600 J) are quite different. Although we couldn't find Q or ΔU for processes ac and cd, we could analyze the composite process acd by comparing it with process abd, which has the same initial and final states and for which we have more information.

EXAMPLE 19.5   **THERMODYNAMICS OF BOILING WATER**

One gram of water (1 cm³) becomes 1671 cm³ of steam when boiled at a constant pressure of 1 atm (1.013×10^5 Pa). The heat of vaporization at this pressure is $L_v = 2.256 \times 10^6$ J/kg. Compute (a) the work done by the water when it vaporizes and (b) its increase in internal energy.

SOLUTION

IDENTIFY and SET UP: The heat added causes the system (water) to change phase from liquid to vapor. We can analyze this process by using the first law of thermodynamics. The water is boiled at constant pressure, so we can use Eq. (19.3) to calculate the work W done by the vaporizing water as it expands. We are given the mass of water and the heat of vaporization, so we can use Eq. (17.20), $Q = mL_v$, to calculate the heat Q added to the water. We can then find the internal energy change from Eq. (19.4), $\Delta U = Q - W$.

EXECUTE: (a) From Eq. (19.3), the water does work

$$W = p(V_2 - V_1)$$
$$= (1.013 \times 10^5 \text{ Pa})(1671 \times 10^{-6} \text{ m}^3 - 1 \times 10^{-6} \text{ m}^3)$$
$$= 169 \text{ J}$$

(b) From Eq. (17.20), the heat added to the water is

$$Q = mL_v = (10^{-3} \text{ kg})(2.256 \times 10^6 \text{ J/kg}) = 2256 \text{ J}$$

Then from Eq. (19.4),

$$\Delta U = Q - W = 2256 \text{ J} - 169 \text{ J} = 2087 \text{ J}$$

EVALUATE: To vaporize 1 g of water, we must add 2256 J of heat, most of which (2087 J) remains in the system as an increase in internal energy. The remaining 169 J leaves the system as the system expands from liquid to vapor and does work against the surroundings. (The increase in internal energy is associated mostly with the attractive intermolecular forces. The associated potential energies are greater after work has been done to pull apart the molecules in the liquid, forming the vapor state. It's like increasing gravitational potential energy by pulling an elevator farther from the center of the earth.)

Infinitesimal Changes of State

In the preceding examples the initial and final states differ by a finite amount. Later we will consider *infinitesimal* changes of state in which a small amount of heat dQ is added to the system, the system does a small amount of work dW, and its internal energy changes by an amount dU. For such a process,

First law of thermodynamics, infinitesimal process:

Infinitesimal internal energy change

$$dU = dQ - dW \qquad (19.6)$$

Infinitesimal heat added   Infinitesimal work done

For the systems we will discuss, the work dW is given by $dW = p\,dV$, so we can also state the first law as

$$dU = dQ - p\,dV \qquad (19.7)$$

TEST YOUR UNDERSTANDING OF SECTION 19.4   Rank the following thermodynamic processes according to the change in internal energy in each process, from most positive to most negative. (i) As you do 250 J of work on a system, it transfers 250 J of heat to its surroundings; (ii) as you do 250 J of work on a system, it absorbs 250 J of heat from its surroundings; (iii) as a system does 250 J of work on you, it transfers 250 J of heat to its surroundings; (iv) as a system does 250 J of work on you, it absorbs 250 J of heat from its surroundings. ▮

19.5 KINDS OF THERMODYNAMIC PROCESSES

In this section we describe four specific kinds of thermodynamic processes that occur often in practical situations. We can summarize these briefly as "no heat transfer" or *adiabatic*, "constant volume" or *isochoric*, "constant pressure" or *isobaric,* and "constant temperature" or *isothermal*. For some of these processes we can use a simplified form of the first law of thermodynamics.

Adiabatic Process

An **adiabatic process** (pronounced "ay-dee-ah-*bat*-ic") is defined as one with no heat transfer into or out of a system; $Q = 0$. We can prevent heat flow either by surrounding the system with thermally insulating material or by carrying out the process so quickly that there is not enough time for appreciable heat flow. From the first law we find that for every adiabatic process,

$$U_2 - U_1 = \Delta U = -W \qquad \text{(adiabatic process)} \qquad (19.8)$$

When a system expands adiabatically, W is positive (the system does work on its surroundings), so ΔU is negative and the internal energy decreases. When a system is *compressed* adiabatically, W is negative (work is done on the system by its surroundings) and U increases. In many (but not all) systems an increase of internal energy is accompanied by a rise in temperature, and a decrease in internal energy by a drop in temperature (**Fig. 19.14**).

The compression stroke in an internal-combustion engine is an approximately adiabatic process. The temperature rises as the air–fuel mixture in the cylinder is compressed. The expansion of the burned fuel during the power stroke is also an approximately adiabatic expansion with a drop in temperature. In Section 19.8 we'll consider adiabatic processes in an ideal gas.

19.14 When the cork is popped on a bottle of champagne, the pressurized gases inside the bottle expand rapidly and do work on the outside air ($W > 0$). There is little time for the gases to exchange heat with their surroundings, so the expansion is nearly adiabatic ($Q = 0$). Hence the internal energy of the expanding gases decreases ($\Delta U = -W < 0$) and their temperature drops. This makes water vapor condense and form a miniature cloud.

Isochoric Process

An **isochoric process** (pronounced "eye-so-*kor*-ic") is a *constant-volume* process. When the volume of a thermodynamic system is constant, it does no work on its surroundings. Then $W = 0$ and

$$U_2 - U_1 = \Delta U = Q \qquad \text{(isochoric process)} \qquad (19.9)$$

In an isochoric process, all the energy added as heat remains in the system as an increase in internal energy. Heating a gas in a closed constant-volume container is an example of an isochoric process. The processes ab and cd in Example 19.4 are also examples of isochoric processes. (Note that there are types of work that do not involve a volume change. For example, we can do work on a fluid by stirring it. In some literature, "isochoric" is used to mean that no work of any kind is done.)

Isobaric Process

An **isobaric process** (pronounced "cyc-so-*bear*-ic") is a *constant-pressure* process. In general, none of the three quantities ΔU, Q, and W is zero in an isobaric process, but calculating W is easy nonetheless. From Eq. (19.3),

$$W = p(V_2 - V_1) \qquad \text{(isobaric process)} \qquad (19.10)$$

Boiling water at constant pressure is an isobaric process (**Fig. 19.15**).

19.15 Most cooking involves isobaric processes. That's because the air pressure above a saucepan or frying pan, or inside a microwave oven, remains essentially constant while the food is being heated.

Isothermal Process

An **isothermal process** is a *constant-temperature* process. For a process to be isothermal, any heat flow into or out of the system must occur slowly enough that thermal equilibrium is maintained. In general, none of the quantities ΔU, Q, or W is zero in an isothermal process.

In some special cases the internal energy of a system depends *only* on its temperature, not on its pressure or volume. The most familiar system having this special property is an ideal gas, as we'll discuss in the next section. For such systems, if the temperature is constant, the internal energy is also constant;

19.16 Four different processes for a constant amount of an ideal gas, all starting at state a. For the adiabatic process, $Q = 0$; for the isochoric process, $W = 0$; and for the isothermal process, $\Delta U = 0$. The temperature increases only during the isobaric expansion.

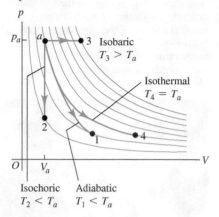

Isochoric   Adiabatic
$T_2 < T_a$ $T_1 < T_a$

19.17 The partition is broken (or removed) to start the free expansion of gas into the vacuum region.

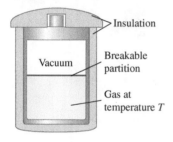

$\Delta U = 0$ and $Q = W$. That is, any energy entering the system as heat Q must leave it again as work W done by the system. Example 19.1, involving an ideal gas, is an example of an isothermal process in which U is also constant. For most systems other than ideal gases, the internal energy depends on pressure as well as temperature, so U may vary even when T is constant.

Figure 19.16 shows a pV-diagram for these four processes for a constant amount of an ideal gas. The path followed in an adiabatic process (a to 1) is called an **adiabat.** A vertical line (constant volume) is an **isochor,** a horizontal line (constant pressure) is an **isobar,** and a curve of constant temperature (shown as light blue lines in Fig. 19.16) is an **isotherm.**

TEST YOUR UNDERSTANDING OF SECTION 19.5 Which of the processes in Fig. 19.7 are isochoric? Which are isobaric? Is it possible to tell if any of the processes are isothermal or adiabatic? ❚

19.6 INTERNAL ENERGY OF AN IDEAL GAS

We now show that for an ideal gas, the internal energy U depends only on temperature, not on pressure or volume. Let's think again about the free-expansion experiment described in Section 19.3. A thermally insulated container with rigid walls is divided into two compartments by a partition (**Fig. 19.17**). One compartment has a quantity of an ideal gas and the other is evacuated.

When the partition is removed or broken, the gas expands to fill both parts of the container. There is no heat flow through the insulation, and the gas does no work on its surroundings because the walls of the container don't move. So both Q and W are zero and the internal energy U is constant.

Does the *temperature T* change during a free expansion? Suppose it *does* change, while the internal energy stays the same. In that case we have to conclude that the internal energy depends on both T and the volume V or on both T and the pressure p, but certainly not on T alone. But if T is constant during a free expansion, for which we know that U is constant even though both p and V change, then we have to conclude that U depends only on T, not on p or V.

Many experiments have shown that when a low-density gas (essentially an ideal gas) undergoes a free expansion, its temperature *does not* change. The conclusion is:

> The internal energy U of an ideal gas depends only on its temperature T, not on its pressure or volume.

This property, in addition to the ideal-gas equation of state, is part of the ideal-gas model. We'll make frequent use of this property.

For nonideal gases, some temperature change occurs during free expansions, even though the internal energy is constant. This shows that the internal energy cannot depend *only* on temperature; it must depend on pressure as well. From the microscopic viewpoint, in which internal energy U is the sum of the kinetic and potential energies for all the particles that make up the system, this is not surprising. Nonideal gases usually have attractive intermolecular forces, and when molecules move farther apart, the associated potential energies increase. If the total internal energy is constant, the kinetic energies must decrease. Temperature is directly related to molecular *kinetic* energy, and for such a gas a free expansion is usually accompanied by a *drop* in temperature.

TEST YOUR UNDERSTANDING OF SECTION 19.6 Is the internal energy of a solid likely to be independent of its volume, as is the case for an ideal gas? Explain your reasoning. (*Hint:* See Fig. 18.20.) ❚

19.7 HEAT CAPACITIES OF AN IDEAL GAS

We defined specific heat and molar heat capacity in Section 17.5. We also remarked at the end of that section that the specific heat or molar heat capacity of a substance depends on the conditions under which the heat is added. The heat capacity of a gas is usually measured in a closed container under constant-volume conditions. The corresponding heat capacity is the **molar heat capacity at constant volume,** denoted by C_V. Heat capacity measurements for solids and liquids are usually carried out under constant atmospheric pressure, and we call the corresponding heat capacity the **molar heat capacity at constant pressure,** C_p.

Let's consider C_V and C_p for an ideal gas. To measure C_V, we raise the temperature of an ideal gas in a rigid container with constant volume, ignoring its thermal expansion (**Fig. 19.18a**). To measure C_p, we let the gas expand just enough to keep the pressure constant as the temperature rises (Fig. 19.18b).

Why should these two molar heat capacities be different? The answer lies in the first law of thermodynamics. In a constant-volume temperature increase, the system does no work, and the change in internal energy ΔU equals the heat added Q. In a constant-pressure temperature increase, on the other hand, the volume *must* increase; otherwise, the pressure (given by the ideal-gas equation of state, $p = nRT/V$) could not remain constant. As the material expands, it does an amount of work W. According to the first law,

$$Q = \Delta U + W \qquad (19.11)$$

For a given temperature increase, the internal energy change ΔU of an ideal gas has the same value no matter what the process (remember that the internal energy of an ideal gas depends only on temperature, not on pressure or volume). Equation (19.11) then shows that the heat input for a constant-pressure process must be *greater* than that for a constant-volume process because additional energy must be supplied to account for the work W done during the expansion. So C_p is greater than C_V for an ideal gas. The pV-diagram in **Fig. 19.19** shows this relationship. For air, C_p is 40% greater than C_V.

For a very few substances (one of which is water between 0°C and 4°C) the volume *decreases* during heating. In this case, W is negative and the internal energy change ΔU is greater than the heat input Q.

Relating C_p and C_V for an Ideal Gas

We can derive a simple relationship between C_p and C_V for an ideal gas. First consider the constant-*volume* process. We place n moles of an ideal gas at temperature T in a constant-volume container. We place it in thermal contact with a hotter body; an infinitesimal quantity of heat dQ flows into the gas, and its temperature increases by an infinitesimal amount dT. By the definition of C_V, the molar heat capacity at constant volume,

$$dQ = nC_V \, dT \qquad (19.12)$$

The pressure increases during this process, but the gas does no work ($dW = 0$) because the volume is constant. The first law in differential form, Eq. (19.6), is $dQ = dU + dW$. Since $dW = 0$, $dQ = dU$ and Eq. (19.12) can also be written as

$$dU = nC_V \, dT \qquad (19.13)$$

Now consider a constant-*pressure* process with the same temperature change dT. We place the same gas in a cylinder with a piston that we allow to move just enough to maintain constant pressure (Fig. 19.18b). Again we bring the system into contact with a hotter body. As heat flows into the gas, it expands at constant pressure and does work. By the definition of C_p, the molar heat capacity at

19.18 Measuring the molar heat capacity of an ideal gas (a) at constant volume and (b) at constant pressure.

(a) Constant volume: $dQ = nC_V \, dT$

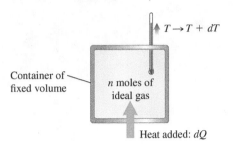

(b) Constant pressure: $dQ = nC_p \, dT$

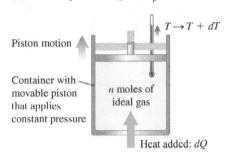

19.19 Raising the temperature of an ideal gas from T_1 to T_2 by a constant-volume or a constant-pressure process. For an ideal gas, U depends only on T, so ΔU is the same for both processes. But for the constant-pressure process, more heat Q must be added to both increase U and do work W. Hence $C_p > C_V$.

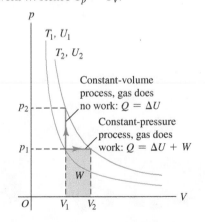

constant pressure, the amount of heat entering the gas is

$$dQ = nC_p \, dT \tag{19.14}$$

The work dW done by the gas in this constant-pressure process is

$$dW = p \, dV$$

We can also express dW in terms of the temperature change dT by using the ideal-gas equation of state, $pV = nRT$. Because p is constant, the change in V is proportional to the change in T:

$$dW = p \, dV = nR \, dT \tag{19.15}$$

Now substitute Eqs. (19.14) and (19.15) into the first law, $dQ = dU + dW$:

$$nC_p \, dT = dU + nR \, dT \tag{19.16}$$

Here comes the crux of the calculation. The internal energy change dU for the constant-pressure process is again given by Eq. (19.13), $dU = nC_V \, dT$, *even though now the volume is not constant.* Why is this so? From Section 19.6, one of the special properties of an ideal gas is that its internal energy depends *only* on temperature. Thus the *change* in internal energy during any process must be determined only by the temperature change. If Eq. (19.13) is valid for an ideal gas for one particular kind of process, it must be valid for an ideal gas for *every* kind of process with the same dT. So we may replace dU in Eq. (19.16) by $nC_V \, dT$:

$$nC_p \, dT = nC_V \, dT + nR \, dT$$

When we divide each term by the common factor $n \, dT$, we get

Molar heat capacity at constant *pressure*

For an ideal gas: $$C_p = C_V + R \quad \leftarrow \text{Gas constant} \tag{19.17}$$

Molar heat capacity at constant *volume*

As we predicted, the molar heat capacity of an ideal gas at constant pressure is *greater* than the molar heat capacity at constant volume; the difference is the gas constant R.

We have used the ideal-gas model to derive Eq. (19.17), but it turns out to be obeyed to within a few percent by many real gases at moderate pressures. **Table 19.1** gives measured values of C_p and C_V for several real gases at low pressures; the difference in most cases is approximately $R = 8.314 \text{ J/mol} \cdot \text{K}$.

The table also shows that the molar heat capacity of a gas is related to its molecular structure, as we discussed in Section 18.4. In fact, the first two columns of Table 19.1 are the same as Table 18.1.

TABLE 19.1 **Molar Heat Capacities of Gases at Low Pressure**

Type of Gas	Gas	C_V (J/mol $\cdot$ K)	C_p (J/mol $\cdot$ K)	$C_p - C_V$ (J/mol $\cdot$ K)	$\gamma = C_p/C_V$
Monatomic	He	12.47	20.78	8.31	1.67
	Ar	12.47	20.78	8.31	1.67
Diatomic	H_2	20.42	28.74	8.32	1.41
	N_2	20.76	29.07	8.31	1.40
	O_2	20.85	29.17	8.32	1.40
	CO	20.85	29.16	8.31	1.40
Polyatomic	CO_2	28.46	36.94	8.48	1.30
	SO_2	31.39	40.37	8.98	1.29
	H_2S	25.95	34.60	8.65	1.33

The Ratio of Heat Capacities

The last column of Table 19.1 lists the values of the dimensionless **ratio of heat capacities,** C_p/C_V, denoted by γ (the Greek letter gamma):

$$\text{Ratio of heat capacities} \cdots\!\rightarrow \gamma = \frac{C_p}{C_V} \begin{array}{l} \cdots\text{Molar heat capacity at} \\ \quad\text{constant } pressure \\ \cdots\text{Molar heat capacity at} \\ \quad\text{constant } volume \end{array} \qquad (19.18)$$

(This is sometimes called the "ratio of specific heats.") For gases, C_p is always greater than C_V and γ is always greater than unity. We'll see in the next section that γ plays an important role in adiabatic processes for an ideal gas.

We can use our kinetic-theory discussion of the molar heat capacity of an ideal gas (see Section 18.4) to predict values of γ. As an example, an ideal monatomic gas has $C_V = \frac{3}{2}R$. From Eq. (19.17),

$$C_p = C_V + R = \tfrac{3}{2}R + R = \tfrac{5}{2}R$$

so

$$\gamma = \frac{C_p}{C_V} = \frac{\frac{5}{2}R}{\frac{3}{2}R} = \tfrac{5}{3} = 1.67$$

As Table 19.1 shows, this agrees well with values of γ computed from measured heat capacities. For most diatomic gases near room temperature, $C_V = \frac{5}{2}R$, $C_p = C_V + R = \frac{7}{2}R$, and

$$\gamma = \frac{C_p}{C_V} = \frac{\frac{7}{2}R}{\frac{5}{2}R} = \tfrac{7}{5} = 1.40$$

also in good agreement with measured values.

Here's a final reminder: For an ideal gas, the internal energy change in *any* process is given by $\Delta U = nC_V \Delta T$, *whether the volume is constant or not.* This relationship holds for other substances *only* when the volume is constant.

EXAMPLE 19.6   **COOLING YOUR ROOM**

A typical dorm room or bedroom contains about 2500 moles of air. Find the change in the internal energy of this much air when it is cooled from 35.0°C to 26.0°C at a constant pressure of 1.00 atm. Treat the air as an ideal gas with $\gamma = 1.400$.

SOLUTION

IDENTIFY and SET UP: Our target variable is the change in the internal energy ΔU of an ideal gas in a constant-pressure process. We are given the number of moles, the temperature change, and the value of γ for air. We use Eq. (19.13), $\Delta U = nC_V \Delta T$, which gives the internal energy change for an ideal gas in *any* process, *whether the volume is constant or not.* [See the discussion following Eq. (19.16).] We use Eqs. (19.17) and (19.18) to find C_V.

EXECUTE: From Eqs. (19.17) and (19.18),

$$\gamma = \frac{C_p}{C_V} = \frac{C_V + R}{C_V} = 1 + \frac{R}{C_V}$$

$$C_V = \frac{R}{\gamma - 1} = \frac{8.314 \text{ J/mol} \cdot \text{K}}{1.400 - 1} = 20.79 \text{ J/mol} \cdot \text{K}$$

Then from Eq. (19.13),

$$\Delta U = nC_V \Delta T$$
$$= (2500 \text{ mol})(20.79 \text{ J/mol} \cdot \text{K})(26.0°\text{C} - 35.0°\text{C})$$
$$= -4.68 \times 10^5 \text{ J}$$

EVALUATE: To cool 2500 moles of air from 35.0°C to 26.0°C, a room air conditioner must extract this much internal energy from the air and transfer it to the air outside. In Chapter 20 we'll discuss how this is done.

TEST YOUR UNDERSTANDING OF SECTION 19.7   You want to cool a storage cylinder containing 10 moles of compressed gas from 30°C to 20°C. For which kind of gas would this be easiest? (i) A monatomic gas; (ii) a diatomic gas; (iii) a polyatomic gas; (iv) it would be equally easy for all of these. ∎

19.8 ADIABATIC PROCESSES FOR AN IDEAL GAS

An adiabatic process, defined in Section 19.5, is a process in which no heat transfer takes place between a system and its surroundings. Zero heat transfer is an idealization, but a process is approximately adiabatic if the system is well insulated or if the process takes place so quickly that there is not enough time for appreciable heat flow to occur.

In an adiabatic process, $Q = 0$, so from the first law, $\Delta U = -W$. An adiabatic process for an ideal gas is shown in the pV-diagram of **Fig. 19.20**. As the gas expands from volume V_a to V_b, it does positive work, so its internal energy decreases and its temperature drops. If point a, representing the initial state, lies on an isotherm at temperature $T + dT$, then point b for the final state is on a different isotherm at a lower temperature T. For an adiabatic *compression* from V_b to V_a the situation is reversed and the temperature rises.

The air in the output hoses of air compressors used to inflate tires and to fill scuba tanks is always warmer than the air entering the compressor; this is because the compression is rapid and hence approximately adiabatic. Adiabatic *cooling* occurs when you open a bottle of your favorite carbonated beverage. The gas just above the beverage surface expands rapidly in a nearly adiabatic process; the gas temperature drops so much that water vapor in the gas condenses, forming a miniature cloud (see Fig. 19.14).

CAUTION "Heating" and "cooling" without heat When we talk about "adiabatic heating" and "adiabatic cooling," we really mean "raising the temperature" and "lowering the temperature," respectively. In an adiabatic process, the temperature change is due to work done by or on the system; there is *no* heat flow at all. ∎

19.20 A pV-diagram of an adiabatic $(Q = 0)$ process for an ideal gas. As the gas expands from V_a to V_b, it does positive work W on its environment, its internal energy decreases $(\Delta U = -W < 0)$, and its temperature drops from $T + dT$ to T. (An adiabatic process is also shown in Fig. 19.16.)

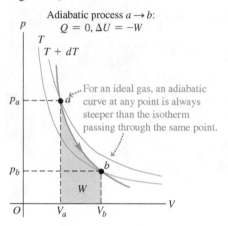

Adiabatic process $a \rightarrow b$:
$$Q = 0, \Delta U = -W$$

For an ideal gas, an adiabatic curve at any point is always steeper than the isotherm passing through the same point.

Adiabatic Ideal Gas: Relating V, T, and p

We can derive a relationship between volume and temperature changes for an infinitesimal adiabatic process in an ideal gas. Equation (19.13) gives the internal energy change dU for *any* process for an ideal gas, adiabatic or not, so we have $dU = nC_V\,dT$. Also, the work done by the gas during the process is given by $dW = p\,dV$. Then, since $dU = -dW$ for an adiabatic process, we have

$$nC_V\,dT = -p\,dV \qquad (19.19)$$

To obtain a relationship containing only the volume V and temperature T, we eliminate p by using the ideal-gas equation in the form $p = nRT/V$. Substituting this into Eq. (19.19) and rearranging, we get

$$nC_V\,dT = -\frac{nRT}{V}dV$$

$$\frac{dT}{T} + \frac{R}{C_V}\frac{dV}{V} = 0$$

The coefficient R/C_V can be expressed in terms of $\gamma = C_p/C_V$. We have

$$\frac{R}{C_V} = \frac{C_p - C_V}{C_V} = \frac{C_p}{C_V} - 1 = \gamma - 1$$

$$\frac{dT}{T} + (\gamma - 1)\frac{dV}{V} = 0 \qquad (19.20)$$

Because γ is always greater than unity for a gas, $(\gamma - 1)$ is always positive. This means that in Eq. (19.20), dV and dT always have opposite signs. An adiabatic *expansion* of an ideal gas $(dV > 0)$ always occurs with a *drop* in temperature $(dT < 0)$, and an adiabatic *compression* $(dV < 0)$ always occurs with a *rise* in temperature $(dT > 0)$; this confirms our earlier prediction.

For finite changes in temperature and volume we integrate Eq. (19.20), obtaining

$$\ln T + (\gamma - 1) \ln V = \text{constant}$$

$$\ln T + \ln V^{\gamma-1} = \text{constant}$$

$$\ln (TV^{\gamma-1}) = \text{constant}$$

and finally,

$$TV^{\gamma-1} = \text{constant} \tag{19.21}$$

Thus for an initial state (T_1, V_1) and a final state (T_2, V_2),

$$T_1 V_1^{\gamma-1} = T_2 V_2^{\gamma-1} \qquad \text{(adiabatic process, ideal gas)} \tag{19.22}$$

Because we have used the ideal-gas equation in our derivation of Eqs. (19.21) and (19.22), the T's must always be *absolute* (Kelvin) temperatures.

We can also convert Eq. (19.21) into a relationship between pressure and volume by eliminating T, using the ideal-gas equation in the form $T = pV/nR$. Substituting this into Eq. (19.21), we find

$$\frac{pV}{nR} V^{\gamma-1} = \text{constant}$$

or, because n and R are constant,

$$pV^{\gamma} = \text{constant} \tag{19.23}$$

For an initial state (p_1, V_1) and a final state (p_2, V_2), Eq. (19.23) becomes

$$p_1 V_1^{\gamma} = p_2 V_2^{\gamma} \qquad \text{(adiabatic process, ideal gas)} \tag{19.24}$$

We can also calculate the *work* done by an ideal gas during an adiabatic process. We know that $Q = 0$ and $W = -\Delta U$ for *any* adiabatic process. For an ideal gas, $\Delta U = nC_V(T_2 - T_1)$. If the number of moles n and the initial and final temperatures T_1 and T_2 are known, we have simply

> Work done by an ideal gas, adiabatic process
>
> Number of moles ····→
> Initial temperature ·····
> Final temperature ·····
>
> $$W = nC_V(T_1 - T_2) \tag{19.25}$$
>
> Molar heat capacity at constant volume

We may also use $pV = nRT$ in this equation to obtain

> Work done by an ideal gas, adiabatic process
>
> Molar heat capacity at constant volume ····
> Initial pressure, volume ·····
>
> $$W = \frac{C_V}{R}(p_1V_1 - p_2V_2) = \frac{1}{\gamma - 1}(p_1V_1 - p_2V_2) \tag{19.26}$$
>
> Gas constant
> Ratio of heat capacities
> Final pressure, volume

(We used the result $C_V = R/(\gamma - 1)$ from Example 19.6.) If the process is an expansion, the temperature drops, T_1 is greater than T_2, p_1V_1 is greater than p_2V_2, and the work is *positive*. If the process is a compression, the work is negative.

Throughout this analysis of adiabatic processes we have used the ideal-gas equation of state, which is valid only for *equilibrium* states. Strictly speaking, our results are valid only for a process that is fast enough to prevent appreciable heat exchange with the surroundings (so that $Q = 0$ and the process is adiabatic), yet slow enough that the system does not depart very much from thermal and mechanical equilibrium. Even when these conditions are not strictly satisfied, though, Eqs. (19.22), (19.24), and (19.26) give useful approximate results.

BIO **Application Exhaling Adiabatically** Put your hand a few centimeters in front of your mouth, open your mouth wide, and exhale. Your breath will feel warm on your hand, because the exhaled gases emerge at roughly the temperature of your body's interior. Now purse your lips as though you were going to whistle, and again blow on your hand. The exhaled gases will feel much cooler. In this case the gases undergo a rapid, essentially adiabatic expansion as they emerge from between your lips, so the temperature of the exhaled gases decreases.

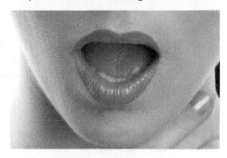

EXAMPLE 19.7 ADIABATIC COMPRESSION IN A DIESEL ENGINE

The compression ratio of a diesel engine is 15.0 to 1; that is, air in a cylinder is compressed to $\frac{1}{(15.0)}$ of its initial volume (**Fig. 19.21**). (a) If the initial pressure is 1.01×10^5 Pa and the initial temperature is 27°C (300 K), find the final pressure and the temperature after adiabatic compression. (b) How much work does the gas do during the compression if the initial volume of the cylinder is $1.00\,\text{L} = 1.00 \times 10^{-3}\,\text{m}^3$? Use the values $C_V = 20.8\,\text{J/mol}\cdot\text{K}$ and $\gamma = 1.400$ for air.

SOLUTION

IDENTIFY and SET UP: This problem involves the adiabatic compression of an ideal gas, so we can use the ideas of this section. In part (a) we are given the initial pressure and temperature $p_1 = 1.01 \times 10^5$ Pa and $T_1 = 300$ K; the ratio of initial and final volumes is $V_1/V_2 = 15.0$. We use Eq. (19.22) to find the final temperature T_2 and Eq. (19.24) to find the final pressure p_2. In part (b) our target variable is W, the work done *by* the gas during the adiabatic compression. We use Eq. (19.26) to calculate W.

EXECUTE: (a) From Eqs. (19.22) and (19.24),

$$T_2 = T_1\left(\frac{V_1}{V_2}\right)^{\gamma-1} = (300\,\text{K})(15.0)^{0.40} = 886\,\text{K} = 613°\text{C}$$

$$p_2 = p_1\left(\frac{V_1}{V_2}\right)^{\gamma} = (1.01 \times 10^5\,\text{Pa})(15.0)^{1.40}$$

$$= 44.8 \times 10^5\,\text{Pa} = 44\,\text{atm}$$

(b) From Eq. (19.26), the work done is

$$W = \frac{1}{\gamma-1}(p_1V_1 - p_2V_2)$$

Using $V_1/V_2 = 15.0$, we have

$$W = \frac{1}{1.400-1}\left[\begin{array}{l}(1.01 \times 10^5\,\text{Pa})(1.00 \times 10^{-3}\,\text{m}^3) \\ -\,(44.8 \times 10^5\,\text{Pa})\left(\dfrac{1.00 \times 10^{-3}\,\text{m}^3}{15.0}\right)\end{array}\right]$$

$$= -494\,\text{J}$$

19.21 Adiabatic compression of air in a cylinder of a diesel engine.

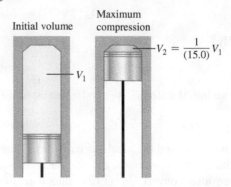

$$V_2 = \frac{1}{(15.0)}V_1$$

EVALUATE: If the compression had been isothermal, the final pressure would have been 15.0 atm. Because the temperature also increases during an adiabatic compression, the final pressure is much greater. When fuel is injected into the cylinders near the end of the compression stroke, the high temperature of the air attained during compression causes the fuel to ignite spontaneously without the need for spark plugs.

We can check our result in part (b) by using Eq. (19.25). The number of moles of gas in the cylinder is

$$n = \frac{p_1V_1}{RT_1} = \frac{(1.01 \times 10^5\,\text{Pa})(1.00 \times 10^{-3}\,\text{m}^3)}{(8.314\,\text{J/mol}\cdot\text{K})(300\,\text{K})} = 0.0405\,\text{mol}$$

Then Eq. (19.25) gives

$$W = nC_V(T_1 - T_2)$$

$$= (0.0405\,\text{mol})(20.8\,\text{J/mol}\cdot\text{K})(300\,\text{K} - 886\,\text{K})$$

$$= -494\,\text{J}$$

The work is negative because the gas is compressed.

TEST YOUR UNDERSTANDING OF SECTION 19.8 You have four samples of ideal gas, each of which contains the same number of moles of gas and has the same initial temperature, volume, and pressure. You compress each sample to one-half of its initial volume. Rank the four samples in order from highest to lowest value of the final pressure. (i) A monatomic gas compressed isothermally; (ii) a monatomic gas compressed adiabatically; (iii) a diatomic gas compressed isothermally; (iv) a diatomic gas compressed adiabatically. ∎

Heat and work in thermodynamic processes: A thermodynamic system has the potential to exchange energy with its surroundings by heat transfer or by mechanical work. When a system at pressure p changes volume from V_1 to V_2, it does an amount of work W given by the integral of p with respect to volume. If the pressure is constant, the work done is equal to p times the change in volume. A negative value of W means that work is done on the system. (See Example 19.1.)

In any thermodynamic process, the heat added to the system and the work done by the system depend not only on the initial and final states, but also on the path (the series of intermediate states through which the system passes).

$$W = \int_{V_1}^{V_2} p \, dV \qquad (19.2)$$

$$W = p(V_2 - V_1) \qquad (19.3)$$
(constant pressure only)

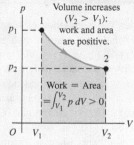

The first law of thermodynamics: The first law of thermodynamics states that when heat Q is added to a system while the system does work W, the internal energy U changes by an amount equal to $Q - W$. This law can also be expressed for an infinitesimal process. (See Examples 19.2, 19.3, and 19.5.)

The internal energy of any thermodynamic system depends only on its state. The change in internal energy in any process depends only on the initial and final states, not on the path. The internal energy of an isolated system is constant. (See Example 19.4.)

$$\Delta U = Q - W \qquad (19.4)$$

$$dU = dQ - dW \qquad (19.6)$$
(infinitesimal process)

Surroundings (environment)
$Q = 150 \text{ J}$　　$W = 100 \text{ J}$

System

$\Delta U = Q - W = +50 \text{ J}$

Important kinds of thermodynamic processes:

- Adiabatic process: No heat transfer into or out of a system; $Q = 0$.
- Isochoric process: Constant volume; $W = 0$.
- Isobaric process: Constant pressure; $W = p(V_2 - V_1)$.
- Isothermal process: Constant temperature.

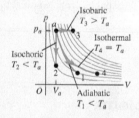

Thermodynamics of ideal gases: The internal energy of an ideal gas depends only on its temperature, not on its pressure or volume. For other substances the internal energy generally depends on both pressure and temperature.

The molar heat capacities C_V and C_p of an ideal gas differ by R, the ideal-gas constant. The dimensionless ratio of heat capacities, C_p/C_V, is denoted by γ. (See Example 19.6.)

$$C_p = C_V + R \qquad (19.17)$$

$$\gamma = \frac{C_p}{C_V} \qquad (19.18)$$

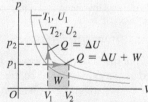

Adiabatic processes in ideal gases: For an adiabatic process for an ideal gas, the quantities $TV^{\gamma-1}$ and pV^γ are constant. The work done by an ideal gas during an adiabatic expansion can be expressed in terms of the initial and final values of temperature, or in terms of the initial and final values of pressure and volume. (See Example 19.7.)

$$W = nC_V(T_1 - T_2) \qquad (19.25)$$

$$= \frac{C_V}{R}(p_1V_1 - p_2V_2)$$

$$= \frac{1}{\gamma - 1}(p_1V_1 - p_2V_2) \qquad (19.26)$$

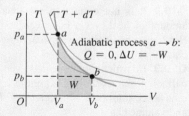

BRIDGING PROBLEM WORK DONE BY A VAN DER WAALS GAS

The van der Waals equation of state, an approximate representation of the behavior of gases at high pressure, is given by Eq. (18.7): $[p + (an^2/V^2)](V - nb) = nRT$, where a and b are constants having different values for different gases. (In the special case of $a = b = 0$, this is the ideal-gas equation.) (a) Calculate the work done by a gas with this equation of state in an isothermal expansion from V_1 to V_2. (b) For ethane gas (C_2H_6), $a = 0.554 \, J \cdot m^3/mol^2$ and $b = 6.38 \times 10^{-5} \, m^3/mol$. Calculate the work W done by 1.80 mol of ethane when it expands from $2.00 \times 10^{-3} \, m^3$ to $4.00 \times 10^{-3} \, m^3$ at a constant temperature of 300 K. Do the calculation by using (i) the van der Waals equation of state and (ii) the ideal-gas equation of state. (c) For which equation of state is W larger? Why should this be so?

SOLUTION GUIDE

IDENTIFY and SET UP

1. Review the discussion of the van der Waals equation of state in Section 18.1. What is the significance of the quantities a and b?
2. Decide how to find the work done by an expanding gas whose pressure p does not depend on V in the same way as for an ideal gas. (*Hint:* See Section 19.2.)
3. How will you find the work done by an expanding ideal gas?

EXECUTE

4. Find the general expression for the work done by a van der Waals gas as it expands from volume V_1 to volume V_2 (**Fig. 19.22**).

(*Hint:* If you set $a = b = 0$ in your result, it should reduce to the expression for the work done by an expanding ideal gas.)
5. Use your result from step 4 to solve part (b) for ethane treated as a van der Waals gas.
6. Use the formula you chose in step 3 to solve part (b) for ethane treated as an ideal gas.

EVALUATE

7. Is the difference between W for the two equations of state large enough to be significant?
8. Does the term with a in the van der Waals equation of state increase or decrease the amount of work done? What about the term with b? Which one is more important for the ethane in this problem?

19.22 A gas undergoes an isothermal expansion.

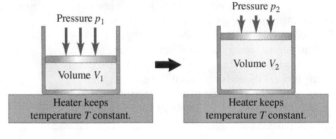

Problems   For assigned homework and other learning materials, go to MasteringPhysics®.   (MP)

•, ••, •••: Difficulty levels. **CP**: Cumulative problems incorporating material from earlier chapters. **CALC**: Problems requiring calculus. **DATA**: Problems involving real data, scientific evidence, experimental design, and/or statistical reasoning. **BIO**: Biosciences problems.

DISCUSSION QUESTIONS

Q19.1 For the following processes, is the work done by the system (defined as the expanding or contracting gas) on the environment positive or negative? (a) expansion of the burned gasoline–air mixture in the cylinder of an automobile engine; (b) opening a bottle of champagne; (c) filling a scuba tank with compressed air; (d) partial crumpling of a sealed, empty water bottle as you drive from the mountains down to sea level.

Q19.2 It is not correct to say that a body contains a certain amount of heat, yet a body can transfer heat to another body. How can a body give away something it does not have in the first place?

Q19.3 In which situation must you do more work: inflating a balloon at sea level or inflating the same balloon to the same volume at the summit of Mt. McKinley? Explain in terms of pressure and volume change.

Q19.4 If you are told the initial and final states of a system and the associated change in internal energy, can you determine whether the internal energy change was due to work or to heat transfer? Explain.

Q19.5 Discuss the application of the first law of thermodynamics to a mountaineer who eats food, gets warm and perspires a lot during a climb, and does a lot of mechanical work in raising herself to the summit. The mountaineer also gets warm during the descent. Is the source of this energy the same as the source during the ascent?

Q19.6 When ice melts at 0°C, its volume decreases. Is the internal energy change greater than, less than, or equal to the heat added? How can you tell?

Q19.7 You hold an inflated balloon over a hot-air vent in your house and watch it slowly expand. You then remove it and let it cool back to room temperature. During the expansion, which was larger: the heat added to the balloon or the work done by the air inside it? Explain. (Assume that air is an ideal gas.) Once the balloon has returned to room temperature, how does the net heat gained or lost by the air inside it compare to the net work done on or by the surrounding air?

Q19.8 You bake chocolate chip cookies and put them, still warm, in a container with a loose (not airtight) lid. What kind of process does the air inside the container undergo as the cookies gradually cool to room temperature (isothermal, isochoric, adiabatic, isobaric, or some combination)? Explain.

Q19.9 Imagine a gas made up entirely of negatively charged electrons. Like charges repel, so the electrons exert repulsive forces on each other. Would you expect that the temperature of such a gas would rise, fall, or stay the same in a free expansion? Why?

Q19.10 In an adiabatic process for an ideal gas, the pressure decreases. In this process does the internal energy of the gas increase or decrease? Explain.

Q19.11 When you blow on the back of your hand with your mouth wide open, your breath feels warm. But if you partially close your mouth to form an "o" and then blow on your hand, your breath feels cool. Why?

Q19.12 An ideal gas expands while the pressure is kept constant. During this process, does heat flow into the gas or out of the gas? Justify your answer.

Q19.13 A liquid is irregularly stirred in a well-insulated container and thereby undergoes a rise in temperature. Regard the liquid as the system. Has heat been transferred? How can you tell? Has work been done? How can you tell? Why is it important that the stirring is irregular? What is the sign of ΔU? How can you tell?

Q19.14 When you use a hand pump to inflate the tires of your bicycle, the pump gets warm after a while. Why? What happens to the temperature of the air in the pump as you compress it? Why does this happen? When you raise the pump handle to draw outside air into the pump, what happens to the temperature of the air taken in? Again, why does this happen?

Q19.15 In the carburetor of an aircraft or automobile engine, air flows through a relatively small aperture and then expands. In cool, foggy weather, ice sometimes forms in this aperture even though the outside air temperature is above freezing. Why?

Q19.16 On a sunny day, large "bubbles" of air form on the sun-warmed earth, gradually expand, and finally break free to rise through the atmosphere. Soaring birds and glider pilots are fond of using these "thermals" to gain altitude easily. This expansion is essentially an adiabatic process. Why?

Q19.17 The prevailing winds on the Hawaiian island of Kauai blow from the northeast. The winds cool as they go up the slope of Mt. Waialeale (elevation 1523 m), causing water vapor to condense and rain to fall. There is much more precipitation at the summit than at the base of the mountain. In fact, Mt. Waialeale is the rainiest spot on earth, averaging 11.7 m of rainfall a year. But what makes the winds cool?

Q19.18 Applying the same considerations as in Question Q19.17, explain why the island of Niihau, a few kilometers to the southwest of Kauai, is almost a desert and farms there need to be irrigated.

Q19.19 In a constant-volume process, $dU = nC_V \, dT$. But in a constant-pressure process, it is *not* true that $dU = nC_p \, dT$. Why not?

Q19.20 When a gas surrounded by air is compressed adiabatically, its temperature rises even though there is no heat input to the gas. Where does the energy come from to raise the temperature?

Q19.21 When a gas expands adiabatically, it does work on its surroundings. But if there is no heat input to the gas, where does the energy come from to do the work?

Q19.22 The gas used in separating the two uranium isotopes ^{235}U and ^{238}U has the formula UF_6. If you added heat at equal rates to a mole of UF_6 gas and a mole of H_2 gas, which one's temperature would you expect to rise faster? Explain.

Q19.23 A system is taken from state a to state b along the three paths shown in **Fig. Q19.23**. (a) Along which path is the work done by the system the greatest? The least? (b) If $U_b > U_a$, along which path is the absolute value of the heat transfer, $|Q|$, the greatest? For this path, is heat absorbed or liberated by the system? Explain.

Figure **Q19.23**

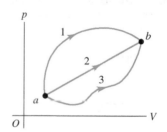

Q19.24 A thermodynamic system undergoes a cyclic process as shown in **Fig. Q19.24**. The cycle consists of two closed loops: I and II. (a) Over one complete cycle, does the system do positive or negative work? (b) In each loop, is the net work done by the system positive or negative? (c) Over one complete cycle, does heat flow into or out of the system? (d) In each loop, does heat flow into or out of the system? Explain.

Figure **Q19.24**

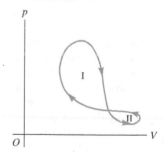

EXERCISES

Section 19.2 Work Done During Volume Changes and Section 19.3 Paths Between Thermodynamic States

19.1 •• Two moles of an ideal gas are heated at constant pressure from $T = 27°C$ to $T = 107°C$. (a) Draw a pV-diagram for this process. (b) Calculate the work done by the gas.

19.2 • Six moles of an ideal gas are in a cylinder fitted at one end with a movable piston. The initial temperature of the gas is $27.0°C$ and the pressure is constant. As part of a machine design project, calculate the final temperature of the gas after it has done 2.40×10^3 J of work.

19.3 •• **CALC** Two moles of an ideal gas are compressed in a cylinder at a constant temperature of $65.0°C$ until the original pressure has tripled. (a) Sketch a pV-diagram for this process. (b) Calculate the amount of work done.

19.4 •• BIO **Work Done by the Lungs.** The graph in **Fig. E19.4** shows a pV-diagram of the air in a human lung when a person is inhaling and then exhaling a deep breath. Such graphs, obtained in clinical practice, are normally somewhat curved, but we have modeled one as a set of straight lines of the same general shape. (*Important:* The pressure shown is the *gauge* pressure, *not* the absolute pressure.) (a) How many joules of *net* work does this person's lung do during one complete breath? (b) The process illustrated here is somewhat different from those we have been studying, because the pressure change is due to changes in the amount of gas in the lung, not to temperature changes. (Think of your own breathing. Your lungs do not expand because they've gotten hot.) If the temperature of the air in the lung remains a reasonable 20°C, what is the maximum number of moles in this person's lung during a breath?

Figure **E19.4**

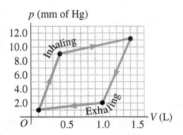

19.5 •• CALC During the time 0.305 mol of an ideal gas undergoes an isothermal compression at 22.0°C, 392 J of work is done on it by the surroundings. (a) If the final pressure is 1.76 atm, what was the initial pressure? (b) Sketch a pV-diagram for the process.

19.6 •• A gas undergoes two processes. In the first, the volume remains constant at 0.200 m³ and the pressure increases from 2.00×10^5 Pa to 5.00×10^5 Pa. The second process is a compression to a volume of 0.120 m³ at a constant pressure of 5.00×10^5 Pa. (a) In a pV-diagram, show both processes. (b) Find the total work done by the gas during both processes.

19.7 • **Work Done in a Cyclic Process.** (a) In Fig. 19.7a, consider the closed loop $1 \rightarrow 3 \rightarrow 2 \rightarrow 4 \rightarrow 1$. This is a *cyclic* process in which the initial and final states are the same. Find the total work done by the system in this cyclic process, and show that it is equal to the area enclosed by the loop. (b) How is the work done for the process in part (a) related to the work done if the loop is traversed in the opposite direction, $1 \rightarrow 4 \rightarrow 2 \rightarrow 3 \rightarrow 1$? Explain.

Section 19.4 Internal Energy and the First Law of Thermodynamics

19.8 •• **Figure E19.8** shows a pV-diagram for an ideal gas in which its absolute temperature at b is one-fourth of its absolute temperature at a. (a) What volume does this gas occupy at point b? (b) How many joules of work was done by or on the gas in this process? Was it done by or on the gas? (c) Did the internal energy of the gas increase or decrease from a to b? How do you know? (d) Did heat enter or leave the gas from a to b? How do you know?

Figure **E19.8**

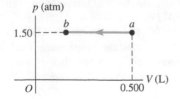

19.9 • A gas in a cylinder expands from a volume of 0.110 m³ to 0.320 m³. Heat flows into the gas just rapidly enough to keep the pressure constant at 1.65×10^5 Pa during the expansion. The total heat added is 1.15×10^5 J. (a) Find the work done by the gas. (b) Find the change in internal energy of the gas. (c) Does it matter whether the gas is ideal? Why or why not?

19.10 •• Five moles of an ideal monatomic gas with an initial temperature of 127°C expand and, in the process, absorb 1500 J of heat and do 2100 J of work. What is the final temperature of the gas?

19.11 •• The process abc shown in the pV-diagram in **Fig. E19.11** involves 0.0175 mol of an ideal gas. (a) What was the lowest temperature the gas reached in this process? Where did it occur? (b) How much work was done by or on the gas from a to b? From b to c? (c) If 215 J of heat was put into the gas during abc, how many of those joules went into internal energy?

Figure **E19.11**

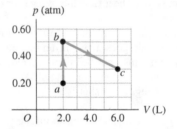

19.12 • A gas in a cylinder is held at a constant pressure of 1.80×10^5 Pa and is cooled and compressed from 1.70 m³ to 1.20 m³. The internal energy of the gas decreases by 1.40×10^5 J. (a) Find the work done by the gas. (b) Find the absolute value of the heat flow, $|Q|$, into or out of the gas, and state the direction of the heat flow. (c) Does it matter whether the gas is ideal? Why or why not?

19.13 •• The pV-diagram in **Fig. E19.13** shows a process abc involving 0.450 mol of an ideal gas. (a) What was the temperature of this gas at points a, b, and c? (b) How much work was done by or on the gas in this process? (c) How much heat had to be added during the process to increase the internal energy of the gas by 15,000 J?

Figure **E19.13**

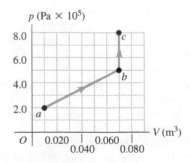

19.14 • **Boiling Water at High Pressure.** When water is boiled at a pressure of 2.00 atm, the heat of vaporization is 2.20×10^6 J/kg and the boiling point is 120°C. At this pressure, 1.00 kg of water has a volume of 1.00×10^{-3} m³, and 1.00 kg of steam has a volume of 0.824 m³. (a) Compute the work done when 1.00 kg of steam is formed at this temperature. (b) Compute the increase in internal energy of the water.

19.15 • An ideal gas is taken from a to b on the pV-diagram shown in **Fig. E19.15**. During this process, 700 J of heat is added and the pressure doubles. (a) How much work is done by or on the gas? Explain. (b) How does the temperature of the gas at a compare to its temperature at b? Be specific. (c) How does the internal energy of the gas at a compare to the internal energy at b? Be specific and explain.

Figure **E19.15**

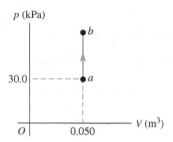

Section 19.5 Kinds of Thermodynamic Processes, Section 19.6 Internal Energy of an Ideal Gas, and Section 19.7 Heat Capacities of an Ideal Gas

19.16 • During an isothermal compression of an ideal gas, 410 J of heat must be removed from the gas to maintain constant temperature. How much work is done by the gas during the process?

19.17 • A cylinder contains 0.250 mol of carbon dioxide (CO_2) gas at a temperature of 27.0°C. The cylinder is provided with a frictionless piston, which maintains a constant pressure of 1.00 atm on the gas. The gas is heated until its temperature increases to 127.0°C. Assume that the CO_2 may be treated as an ideal gas. (a) Draw a pV diagram for this process. (b) How much work is done by the gas in this process? (c) On what is this work done? (d) What is the change in internal energy of the gas? (e) How much heat was supplied to the gas? (f) How much work would have been done if the pressure had been 0.50 atm?

19.18 • A cylinder contains 0.0100 mol of helium at $T = 27.0$°C. (a) How much heat is needed to raise the temperature to 67.0°C while keeping the volume constant? Draw a pV-diagram for this process. (b) If instead the pressure of the helium is kept constant, how much heat is needed to raise the temperature from 27.0°C to 67.0°C? Draw a pV-diagram for this process. (c) What accounts for the difference between your answers to parts (a) and (b)? In which case is more heat required? What becomes of the additional heat? (d) If the gas is ideal, what is the change in its internal energy in part (a)? In part (b)? How do the two answers compare? Why?

19.19 • In an experiment to simulate conditions inside an automobile engine, 0.185 mol of air at 780 K and 3.00×10^6 Pa is contained in a cylinder of volume 40.0 cm³. Then 645 J of heat is transferred to the cylinder. (a) If the volume of the cylinder is constant while the heat is added, what is the final temperature of the air? Assume that the air is essentially nitrogen gas, and use the data in Table 19.1 even though the pressure is not low. Draw a pV-diagram for this process. (b) If instead the volume of the cylinder is allowed to increase while the pressure remains constant, repeat part (a).

19.20 •• When a quantity of monatomic ideal gas expands at a constant pressure of 4.00×10^4 Pa, the volume of the gas increases from 2.00×10^{-3} m³ to 8.00×10^{-3} m³. What is the change in the internal energy of the gas?

19.21 • Heat Q flows into a monatomic ideal gas, and the volume increases while the pressure is kept constant. What fraction of the heat energy is used to do the expansion work of the gas?

19.22 • Three moles of an ideal monatomic gas expands at a constant pressure of 2.50 atm; the volume of the gas changes from 3.20×10^{-2} m³ to 4.50×10^{-2} m³. Calculate (a) the initial and final temperatures of the gas; (b) the amount of work the gas does in expanding; (c) the amount of heat added to the gas; (d) the change in internal energy of the gas.

19.23 • An experimenter adds 970 J of heat to 1.75 mol of an ideal gas to heat it from 10.0°C to 25.0°C at constant pressure. The gas does +223 J of work during the expansion. (a) Calculate the change in internal energy of the gas. (b) Calculate γ for the gas.

19.24 • Propane gas (C_3H_8) behaves like an ideal gas with $\gamma = 1.127$. Determine the molar heat capacity at constant volume and the molar heat capacity at constant pressure.

19.25 • CALC The temperature of 0.150 mol of an ideal gas is held constant at 77.0°C while its volume is reduced to 25.0% of its initial volume. The initial pressure of the gas is 1.25 atm. (a) Determine the work done by the gas. (b) What is the change in its internal energy? (c) Does the gas exchange heat with its surroundings? If so, how much? Does the gas absorb or liberate heat?

Section 19.8 Adiabatic Processes for an Ideal Gas

19.26 •• Five moles of monatomic ideal gas have initial pressure 2.50×10^3 Pa and initial volume 2.10 m³. While undergoing an adiabatic expansion, the gas does 1480 J of work. What is the final pressure of the gas after the expansion?

19.27 • A monatomic ideal gas that is initially at 1.50×10^5 Pa and has a volume of 0.0800 m³ is compressed adiabatically to a volume of 0.0400 m³. (a) What is the final pressure? (b) How much work is done by the gas? (c) What is the ratio of the final temperature of the gas to its initial temperature? Is the gas heated or cooled by this compression?

19.28 • The engine of a Ferrari F355 F1 sports car takes in air at 20.0°C and 1.00 atm and compresses it adiabatically to 0.0900 times the original volume. The air may be treated as an ideal gas with $\gamma = 1.40$. (a) Draw a pV-diagram for this process. (b) Find the final temperature and pressure.

19.29 • During an adiabatic expansion the temperature of 0.450 mol of argon (Ar) drops from 66.0°C to 10.0°C. The argon may be treated as an ideal gas. (a) Draw a pV-diagram for this process. (b) How much work does the gas do? (c) What is the change in internal energy of the gas?

19.30 •• A player bounces a basketball on the floor, compressing it to 80.0% of its original volume. The air (assume it is essentially N_2 gas) inside the ball is originally at 20.0°C and 2.00 atm. The ball's inside diameter is 23.9 cm. (a) What temperature does the air in the ball reach at its maximum compression? Assume the compression is adiabatic and treat the gas as ideal. (b) By how much does the internal energy of the air change between the ball's original state and its maximum compression?

19.31 •• On a warm summer day, a large mass of air (atmospheric pressure 1.01×10^5 Pa) is heated by the ground to 26.0°C and then begins to rise through the cooler surrounding air. (This can be treated approximately as an adiabatic process; why?) Calculate the temperature of the air mass when it has risen to a level at which atmospheric pressure is only 0.850×10^5 Pa. Assume that air is an ideal gas, with $\gamma = 1.40$. (This rate of cooling for dry, rising air, corresponding to roughly 1 C° per 100 m of altitude, is called the *dry adiabatic lapse rate*.)

19.32 • A cylinder contains 0.100 mol of an ideal monatomic gas. Initially the gas is at 1.00×10^5 Pa and occupies a volume of 2.50×10^{-3} m^3. (a) Find the initial temperature of the gas in kelvins. (b) If the gas is allowed to expand to twice the initial volume, find the final temperature (in kelvins) and pressure of the gas if the expansion is (i) isothermal; (ii) isobaric; (iii) adiabatic.

PROBLEMS

19.33 •• A quantity of air is taken from state a to state b along a path that is a straight line in the pV-diagram (**Fig. P19.33**). (a) In this process, does the temperature of the gas increase, decrease, or stay the same? Explain. (b) If $V_a = 0.0700$ m^3, $V_b = 0.1100$ m^3, $p_a = 1.00 \times 10^5$ Pa, and $p_b = 1.40 \times 10^5$ Pa, what is the work W done by the gas in this process? Assume that the gas may be treated as ideal.

Figure **P19.33**

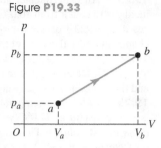

19.34 • One-half mole of an ideal gas is taken from state a to state c as shown in **Fig. P19.34**. (a) Calculate the final temperature of the gas. (b) Calculate the work done on (or by) the gas as it moves from state a to state c. (c) Does heat leave the system or enter the system during this process? How much heat? Explain.

Figure **P19.34**

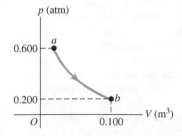

19.35 •• **Figure P19.35** shows the pV-diagram for a process in which the temperature of the ideal gas remains constant at 85°C. (a) How many moles of gas are involved? (b) What volume does this gas occupy at a? (c) How much work was done by or on the gas from a to b? (d) By how much did the internal energy of the gas change during this process?

Figure **P19.35**

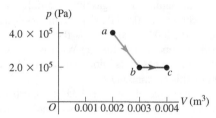

19.36 •• The graph in **Fig. P19.36** shows a pV-diagram for 3.25 mol of *ideal* helium (He) gas. Part ca of this process is isothermal. (a) Find the pressure of the He at point a. (b) Find the temperature

Figure **P19.36**

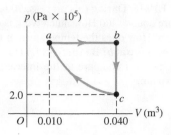

of the He at points a, b, and c. (c) How much heat entered or left the He during segments ab, bc, and ca? In each segment, did the heat enter or leave? (d) By how much did the internal energy of the He change from a to b, from b to c, and from c to a? Indicate whether this energy increased or decreased.

19.37 •• When a system is taken from state a to state b in **Fig. P19.37** along path acb, 90.0 J of heat flows into the system and 60.0 J of work is done by the system. (a) How much heat flows into the system along path adb if the work done by the system is 15.0 J? (b) When the system is returned from b to a along the curved path, the absolute value of the work done by the system is 35.0 J. Does the system absorb or liberate heat? How much heat? (c) If $U_a = 0$ and $U_d = 8.0$ J, find the heat absorbed in the processes ad and db.

Figure **P19.37**

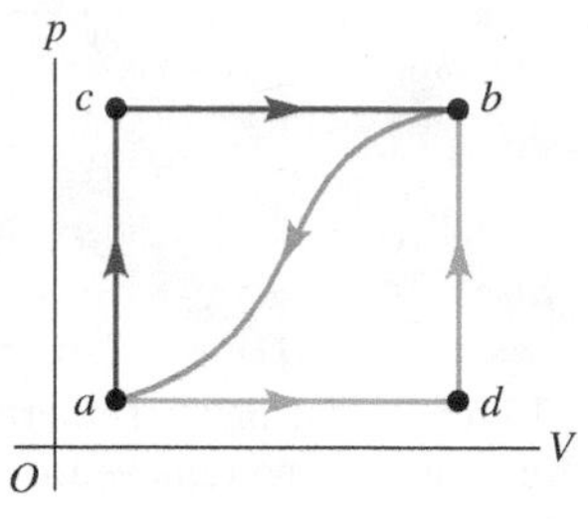

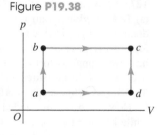

19.38 • A thermodynamic system is taken from state a to state c in **Fig. P19.38** along either path abc or path adc. Along path abc, the work W done by the system is 450 J. Along path adc, W is 120 J. The internal energies of each of the four states shown in the figure are $U_a = 150$ J, $U_b = 240$ J, $U_c = 680$ J, and $U_d = 330$ J. Calculate the heat flow Q for each of the four processes ab, bc, ad, and dc. In each process, does the system absorb or liberate heat?

Figure **P19.38**

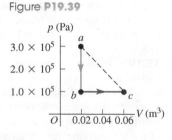

19.39 • A volume of air (assumed to be an ideal gas) is first cooled without changing its volume and then expanded without changing its pressure, as shown by path abc in **Fig. P19.39**. (a) How does the final temperature of the gas compare with its initial temperature? (b) How much heat does the air exchange with its surroundings during process abc? Does the air absorb heat or release heat during this process? Explain. (c) If the air instead expands from state a to state c by the straight-line path shown, how much heat does it exchange with its surroundings?

Figure **P19.39**

19.40 • Three moles of argon gas (assumed to be an ideal gas) originally at 1.50×10^4 Pa and a volume of 0.0280 m^3 are first heated and expanded at constant pressure to a volume of 0.0435 m³, then heated at constant volume until the pressure reaches 3.50×10^4 Pa, then cooled and compressed at constant pressure until the volume is again 0.0280 m³, and finally cooled at constant volume until the pressure drops to its original value of 1.50×10^4 Pa. (a) Draw the pV-diagram for this cycle. (b) Calculate the total work done by (or on) the gas during the cycle. (c) Calculate the net heat exchanged with the surroundings. Does the gas gain or lose heat overall?

19.41 •• Two moles of an ideal monatomic gas go through the cycle abc. For the complete cycle, 800 J of heat flows out of the gas. Process ab is at constant pressure, and process bc is at constant volume. States a and b have temperatures $T_a = 200$ K and $T_b = 300$ K. (a) Sketch the pV-diagram for the cycle. (b) What is the work W for the process ca?

19.42 •• Three moles of an ideal gas are taken around cycle acb shown in **Fig. P19.42**. For this gas, $C_p = 29.1$ J/mol·K. Process ac is at constant pressure, process ba is at constant volume, and process cb is adiabatic. The temperatures of the gas in states a, c, and b are $T_a = 300$ K, $T_c = 492$ K, and $T_b = 600$ K. Calculate the total work W for the cycle.

Figure **P19.42**

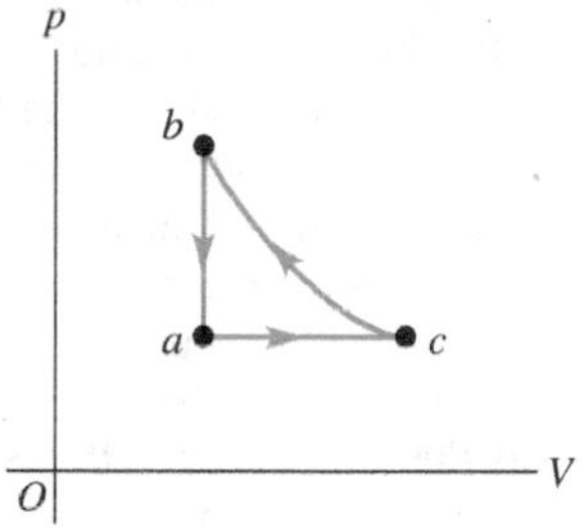

19.43 •• **Figure P19.43** shows a pV-diagram for 0.0040 mol of ideal H_2 gas. The temperature of the gas does not change during segment bc. (a) What volume does this gas occupy at point c? (b) Find the temperature of the gas at points a, b, and c. (c) How much heat went into or out of the gas during segments ab, ca, and bc? Indicate whether the heat has gone into or out of the gas. (d) Find the change in the internal energy of this hydrogen during segments ab, bc, and ca. Indicate whether the internal energy increased or decreased during each segment.

Figure **P19.43**

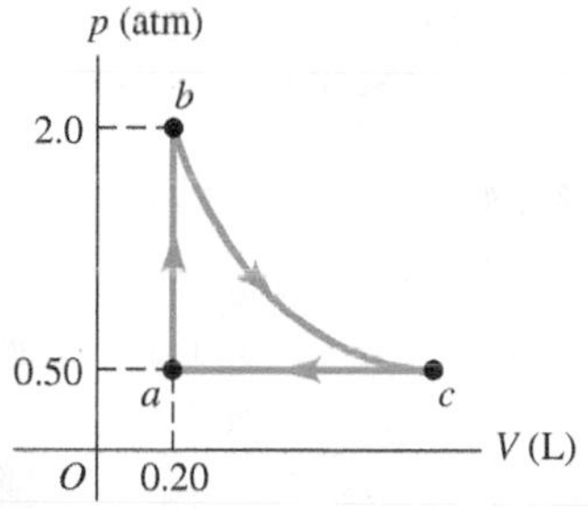

19.44 •• (a) One-third of a mole of He gas is taken along the path abc shown in **Fig. P19.44**. Assume that the gas may be treated as ideal. How much heat is transferred into or out of the gas? (b) If the gas instead went directly from state a to state c

Figure **P19.44**

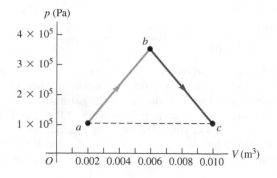

along the horizontal dashed line in Fig. P19.44, how much heat would be transferred into or out of the gas? (c) How does Q in part (b) compare with Q in part (a)? Explain.

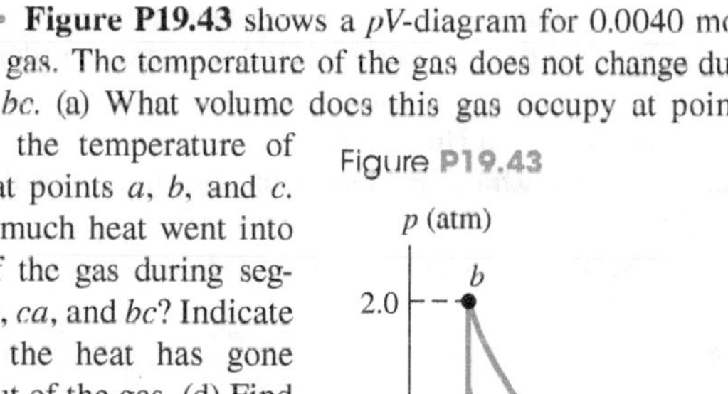

19.45 ••• Starting with 2.50 mol of N_2 gas (assumed to be ideal) in a cylinder at 1.00 atm and 20.0°C, a chemist first heats the gas at constant volume, adding 1.36×10^4 J of heat, then continues heating and allows the gas to expand at constant pressure to twice its original volume. Calculate (a) the final temperature of the gas; (b) the amount of work done by the gas; (c) the amount of heat added to the gas while it was expanding; (d) the change in internal energy of the gas for the whole process.

19.46 •• Nitrogen gas in an expandable container is cooled from 50.0°C to 10.0°C with the pressure held constant at 3.00×10^5 Pa. The total heat liberated by the gas is 2.50×10^4 J. Assume that the gas may be treated as ideal. Find (a) the number of moles of gas; (b) the change in internal energy of the gas; (c) the work done by the gas. (d) How much heat would be liberated by the gas for the same temperature change if the volume were constant?

19.47 • CALC A cylinder with a frictionless, movable piston like that shown in Fig. 19.5 contains a quantity of helium gas. Initially the gas is at 1.00×10^5 Pa and 300 K and occupies a volume of 1.50 L. The gas then undergoes two processes. In the first, the gas is heated and the piston is allowed to move to keep the temperature at 300 K. This continues until the pressure reaches 2.50×10^4 Pa. In the second process, the gas is compressed at constant pressure until it returns to its original volume of 1.50 L. Assume that the gas may be treated as ideal. (a) In a pV-diagram, show both processes. (b) Find the volume of the gas at the end of the first process, and the pressure and temperature at the end of the second process. (c) Find the total work done by the gas during both processes. (d) What would you have to do to the gas to return it to its original pressure and temperature?

19.48 • CP A Thermodynamic Process in a Solid. A cube of copper 2.00 cm on a side is suspended by a string. (The physical properties of copper are given in Tables 14.1, 17.2, and 17.3.) The cube is heated with a burner from 20.0°C to 90.0°C. The air surrounding the cube is at atmospheric pressure (1.01×10^5 Pa). Find (a) the increase in volume of the cube; (b) the mechanical work done by the cube to expand against the pressure of the surrounding air; (c) the amount of heat added to the cube; (d) the change in internal energy of the cube. (e) Based on your results, explain whether there is any substantial difference between the specific heats c_p (at constant pressure) and c_V (at constant volume) for copper under these conditions.

19.49 ••• Chinook. During certain seasons strong winds called chinooks blow from the west across the eastern slopes of the Rockies and downhill into Denver and nearby areas. Although the mountains are cool, the wind in Denver is very hot; within a few minutes after the chinook wind arrives, the temperature can climb 20 C° ("chinook" refers to a Native American people of the Pacific Northwest). Similar winds occur in the Alps (called foehns) and in southern California (called Santa Anas). (a) Explain why the temperature of the chinook wind rises as it descends the slopes. Why is it important that the wind be fast moving? (b) Suppose a strong wind is blowing toward Denver (elevation 1630 m) from Grays Peak (80 km west of Denver, at an elevation of 4350 m), where the air pressure is 5.60×10^4 Pa and the air temperature is -15.0°C. The temperature and pressure in Denver before the wind arrives are 2.0°C and 8.12×10^4 Pa. By how many Celsius degrees will the temperature in Denver rise when the chinook arrives?

19.50 ••• **High-Altitude Research.** A large research balloon containing 2.00×10^3 m^3 of helium gas at 1.00 atm and a temperature of 15.0°C rises rapidly from ground level to an altitude at which the atmospheric pressure is only 0.900 atm (**Fig. P19.50**). Assume the helium behaves like an ideal gas and the balloon's ascent is too rapid to permit much heat exchange with the surrounding air. (a) Calculate the volume of the gas at the higher altitude. (b) Calculate the temperature of the gas at the higher altitude. (c) What is the change in internal energy of the helium as the balloon rises to the higher altitude?

Figure **P19.50**

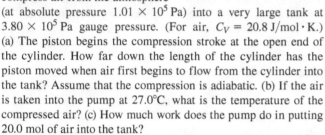

19.51 ••• An air pump has a cylinder 0.250 m long with a movable piston. The pump is used to compress air from the atmosphere (at absolute pressure 1.01×10^5 Pa) into a very large tank at 3.80×10^5 Pa gauge pressure. (For air, $C_V = 20.8$ J/mol·K.) (a) The piston begins the compression stroke at the open end of the cylinder. How far down the length of the cylinder has the piston moved when air first begins to flow from the cylinder into the tank? Assume that the compression is adiabatic. (b) If the air is taken into the pump at 27.0°C, what is the temperature of the compressed air? (c) How much work does the pump do in putting 20.0 mol of air into the tank?

19.52 •• A certain ideal gas has molar heat capacity at constant volume C_V. A sample of this gas initially occupies a volume V_0 at pressure p_0 and absolute temperature T_0. The gas expands isobarically to a volume $2V_0$ and then expands further adiabatically to a final volume $4V_0$. (a) Draw a pV-diagram for this sequence of processes. (b) Compute the total work done by the gas for this sequence of processes. (c) Find the final temperature of the gas. (d) Find the absolute value of the total heat flow $|Q|$ into or out of the gas for this sequence of processes, and state the direction of heat flow.

19.53 • A monatomic ideal gas expands slowly to twice its original volume, doing 450 J of work in the process. Find the heat added to the gas and the change in internal energy of the gas if the process is (a) isothermal; (b) adiabatic; (c) isobaric.

19.54 •• **CALC** A cylinder with a piston contains 0.250 mol of oxygen at 2.40×10^5 Pa and 355 K. The oxygen may be treated as an ideal gas. The gas first expands isobarically to twice its original volume. It is then compressed isothermally back to its original volume, and finally it is cooled isochorically to its original pressure. (a) Show the series of processes on a pV-diagram. Compute (b) the temperature during the isothermal compression; (c) the maximum pressure; (d) the total work done by the piston on the gas during the series of processes.

19.55 • Use the conditions and processes of Problem 19.54 to compute (a) the work done by the gas, the heat added to it, and its internal energy change during the initial expansion; (b) the work done, the heat added, and the internal energy change during the final cooling; (c) the internal energy change during the isothermal compression.

19.56 •• **CALC** A cylinder with a piston contains 0.150 mol of nitrogen at 1.80×10^5 Pa and 300 K. The nitrogen may be treated as an ideal gas. The gas is first compressed isobarically to half its original volume. It then expands adiabatically back to its original volume, and finally it is heated isochorically to its original pressure. (a) Show the series of processes in a pV-diagram. (b) Compute the temperatures at the beginning and end of the adiabatic expansion. (c) Compute the minimum pressure.

19.57 • Use the conditions and processes of Problem 19.56 to compute (a) the work done by the gas, the heat added to it, and its internal energy change during the initial compression; (b) the work done by the gas, the heat added to it, and its internal energy change during the adiabatic expansion; (c) the work done, the heat added, and the internal energy change during the final heating.

19.58 • **Comparing Thermodynamic Processes.** In a cylinder, 1.20 mol of an ideal monatomic gas, initially at 3.60×10^5 Pa and 300 K, expands until its volume triples. Compute the work done by the gas if the expansion is (a) isothermal; (b) adiabatic; (c) isobaric. (d) Show each process in a pV-diagram. In which case is the absolute value of the work done by the gas greatest? Least? (e) In which case is the absolute value of the heat transfer greatest? Least? (f) In which case is the absolute value of the change in internal energy of the gas greatest? Least?

19.59 •• **DATA** You have recorded measurements of the heat flow Q into 0.300 mol of a gas that starts at $T_1 = 20.0$°C and ends at a temperature T_2. You measured Q for three processes: one isobaric, one isochoric, and one adiabatic. In each case, T_2 was the same. **Figure P19.59** summarizes your results. But you lost a page from your lab notebook and don't have a record of the value of T_2; you also don't know which process was isobaric, isochoric, or adiabatic. Each process was done at a sufficiently low pressure for the gas to be treated as ideal. (a) Identify each process a, b, or c as isobaric, isochoric, or adiabatic. (b) What is the value of T_2? (c) How much work is done by the gas in each process? (d) For which process is the magnitude of the volume change the greatest? (e) For each process, does the volume of the gas increase, decrease, or stay the same?

Figure **P19.59**

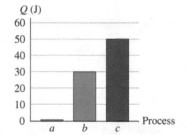

19.60 •• **DATA** You compress a gas in an insulated cylinder—no heat flows into or out of the gas. The gas pressure is fairly low, so treating the gas as ideal is a good approximation. When you measure the pressure as a function of the volume of the gas, you obtain these results:

V (L)	2.50	2.02	1.48	1.01	0.50
p (atm)	0.101	0.139	0.202	0.361	0.952

(a) Graph $\log{(p)}$ versus $\log{(V)}$, with p in Pa and V in m^3. Explain why the data points fall close to a straight line. (b) Use your graph to calculate γ for the gas. Is the gas monatomic, diatomic, or polyatomic? (c) When $p = 0.101$ atm and $V = 2.50$ L, the temperature is 22.0°C. Apply the ideal-gas equation and calculate the temperature for each of the other pairs of p and V values. In this compression, does the temperature of the gas increase, decrease, or stay constant?

19.61 ·· **DATA** You place a quantity of gas into a metal cylinder that has a movable piston at one end. No gas leaks out of the cylinder as the piston moves. The external force applied to the piston can be varied to change the gas pressure as you move the piston to change the volume of the gas. A pressure gauge attached to the interior wall of the cylinder measures the gas pressure, and you can calculate the volume of the gas from a measurement of the piston's position in the cylinder.

You start with a pressure of 1.0 atm and a gas volume of 3.0 L. Holding the pressure constant, you increase the volume to 5.0 L. Then, keeping the volume constant at 5.0 L, you increase the pressure to 3.0 atm. Next you decrease the pressure linearly as a function of volume until the volume is 3.0 L and the pressure is 2.0 atm. Finally, you keep the volume constant at 3.0 L and decrease the pressure to 1.0 atm, returning the gas to its initial pressure and volume. The walls of the cylinder are good conductors of heat, and you provide the required heat sources and heat sinks so that the necessary heat flows can occur. At these relatively high pressures, you suspect that the ideal-gas equation will not apply with much accuracy. You don't know what gas is in the cylinder or whether it is monatomic, diatomic, or polyatomic. (a) Plot the cycle in the pV-plane. (b) What is the net heat flow for the gas during this cycle? Is there net heat flow into or out of the gas?

CHALLENGE PROBLEM

19.62 ·· **Engine Turbochargers and Intercoolers.** The power output of an automobile engine is directly proportional to the mass of air that can be forced into the volume of the engine's cylinders to react chemically with gasoline. Many cars have a *turbocharger*, which compresses the air before it enters the engine, giving a greater mass of air per volume. This rapid, essentially adiabatic compression also heats the air. To compress it further, the air then passes through an *intercooler* in which the air exchanges heat with its surroundings at essentially constant pressure. The air is then drawn into the cylinders. In a typical installation, air is taken into the turbocharger at atmospheric pressure (1.01×10^5 Pa), density $\rho = 1.23$ kg/m^3, and temperature 15.0°C. It is compressed adiabatically to 1.45×10^5 Pa. In the intercooler, the air is cooled to the original temperature of 15.0°C at a constant pressure of 1.45×10^5 Pa. (a) Draw a pV-diagram for this sequence of processes. (b) If the volume of one of the engine's cylinders is 575 cm^3, what mass of air exiting from the intercooler will fill the cylinder at 1.45×10^5 Pa? Compared to the power output of an engine that takes in air at 1.01×10^5 Pa at 15.0°C, what percentage increase in power is obtained by using the turbocharger and intercooler? (c) If the intercooler is not used, what

mass of air exiting from the turbocharger will fill the cylinder at 1.45×10^5 Pa? Compared to the power output of an engine that takes in air at 1.01×10^5 Pa at 15.0°C, what percentage increase in power is obtained by using the turbocharger alone?

PASSAGE PROBLEMS

BIO **ANESTHETIC GASES.** One type of gas mixture used in anesthesiology is a 50%/50% mixture (by volume) of nitrous oxide (N_2O) and oxygen (O_2), which can be premixed and kept in a cylinder for later use. Because these two gases don't react chemically at or below 2000 psi, at typical room temperatures they form a homogeneous single gas phase, which can be considered an ideal gas. If the temperature drops below −6°C, however, N_2O may begin to condense out of the gas phase. Then any gas removed from the cylinder will initially be nearly pure O_2; as the cylinder empties, the proportion of O_2 will decrease until the gas coming from the cylinder is nearly pure N_2O.

19.63 In a test of the effects of low temperatures on the gas mixture, a cylinder filled at 20.0°C to 2000 psi (gauge pressure) is cooled slowly and the pressure is monitored. What is the expected pressure at −5.00°C if the gas remains a homogeneous mixture? (a) 500 psi; (b) 1500 psi; (c) 1830 psi; (d) 1920 psi.

19.64 In another test, the valve of a 500-L cylinder full of the gas mixture at 2000 psi (gauge pressure) is opened wide so that the gas rushes out of the cylinder very rapidly. Why might some N_2O condense during this process? (a) This is an isochoric process in which the pressure decreases, so the temperature also decreases. (b) Because of the rapid expansion, heat is removed from the system, so the internal energy and temperature of the gas decrease. (c) This is an isobaric process, so as the volume increases, the temperature decreases proportionally. (d) With the rapid expansion, the expanding gas does work with no heat input, so the internal energy and temperature of the gas decrease.

19.65 You have a cylinder that contains 500 L of the gas mixture pressurized to 2000 psi (gauge pressure). A regulator sets the gas flow to deliver 8.2 L/min at atmospheric pressure. Assume that this flow is slow enough that the expansion is isothermal and the gases remain mixed. How much time will it take to empty the cylinder? (a) 1 h; (b) 33 h; (c) 57 h; (d) 140 h.

19.66 In a hospital, pure oxygen may be delivered at 50 psi (gauge pressure) and then mixed with N_2O. What volume of oxygen at 20°C and 50 psi (gauge pressure) should be mixed with 1.7 kg of N_2O to get a 50%/50% mixture by volume at 20°C? (a) 0.21 m^3; (b) 0.27 m^3; (c) 1.9 m^3; (d) 100 m^3.

Answers

Chapter Opening Question **?**

(ii) The work done by a gas as its volume changes from V_1 to V_2 is equal to the integral $\int p \, dV$ between those two volume limits. If the volume of the gas contracts, the final volume V_2 is less than the initial volume V_1 and the gas does negative work. Propelling the locomotive requires that the gas do positive work, so the gas doesn't contribute to propulsion while contracting.

Test Your Understanding Questions

19.1 negative, positive, positive Heat flows out of the coffee, so $Q_{\text{coffee}} < 0$; heat flows into the aluminum cup, so $Q_{\text{aluminum}} > 0$. In mechanics, we would say that negative work is done *on* the block, since the surface exerts a force on the block that opposes the block's motion. But in thermodynamics we use the opposite convention and say that $W > 0$, which means that positive work is done *by* the block on the surface.

19.2 (ii) The work done in an expansion is represented by the area under the curve of pressure p versus volume V. In an isothermal expansion the pressure decreases as the volume increases, so the pV-diagram looks like Fig. 19.6a and the work done equals the shaded area under the blue curve from point 1 to point 2. If, however, the expansion is at constant pressure, the curve of p versus V would be the same as the dashed horizontal line at pressure p_2 in Fig. 19.6a. The area under this dashed line is smaller than the area under the blue curve for an isothermal expansion, so less work is done in the constant-pressure expansion than in the isothermal expansion.

19.3 (i) and (iv) (tie), (ii) and (iii) (tie) The accompanying figure shows the pV-diagrams for each of the four processes. The trapezoidal area under the curve, and hence the absolute value of the work, is the same in all four cases. In cases (i) and (iv) the volume increases, so the system does positive work as it expands against its surroundings. In cases (ii) and (iii) the volume decreases, so the system does negative work (shown by cross-hatching) as the surroundings push inward on it.

19.4 (ii), (i) and (iv) (tie), (iii) In the expression $\Delta U = Q - W$, Q is the heat *added* to the system and W is the work done *by* the system. If heat is transferred from the system to its surroundings, Q is negative; if work is done on the system, W is negative. Hence we have (i) $Q = -250 \, \text{J}$, $W = -250 \, \text{J}$, $\Delta U = -250 \, \text{J} - (-250 \, \text{J}) = 0$; (ii) $Q = 250 \, \text{J}$, $W = -250 \, \text{J}$, $\Delta U = 250 \, \text{J} - (-250 \, \text{J}) = 500 \, \text{J}$; (iii) $Q = -250 \, \text{J}$, $W = 250 \, \text{J}$, $\Delta U = -250 \, \text{J} - 250 \, \text{J} = -500 \, \text{J}$; and (iv) $Q = 250 \, \text{J}$, $W = 250 \, \text{J}$, $\Delta U = 250 \, \text{J} - 250 \, \text{J} = 0$.

19.5 $1 \rightarrow 4$ and $3 \rightarrow 2$ are isochoric; $1 \rightarrow 3$ and $4 \rightarrow 2$ are isobaric; no In a pV-diagram like those shown in Fig. 19.7, isochoric processes are represented by vertical lines (lines of constant volume) and isobaric processes are represented by horizontal lines (lines of constant pressure). The process $1 \rightarrow 2$ in Fig. 19.7 is shown as a curved line, which superficially resembles the adiabatic and isothermal processes for an ideal gas in Fig. 19.16. Without more information we can't tell whether process $1 \rightarrow 2$ is isothermal, adiabatic, or neither.

19.6 no Using the model of a solid in Fig. 18.20, we can see that the internal energy of a solid *does* depend on its volume. Compressing the solid means compressing the "springs" between the atoms, thereby increasing their stored potential energy and hence the internal energy of the solid.

19.7 (i) For a given number of moles n and a given temperature change ΔT, the amount of heat that must be transferred out of a fixed volume of air is $Q = nC_V \Delta T$. Hence the amount of heat transfer required is least for the gas with the smallest value of C_V. From Table 19.1, C_V is smallest for monatomic gases.

19.8 (ii), (iv), (i) and (iii) (tie) Samples (i) and (iii) are compressed isothermally, so $pV = $ constant. The volume of each sample decreases to one-half of its initial value, so the final pressure is twice the initial pressure. Samples (ii) and (iv) are compressed adiabatically, so $pV^\gamma = $ constant and the pressure increases by a factor of 2^γ. Sample (ii) is a monatomic gas for which $\gamma = \frac{5}{3}$, so its final pressure is $2^{5/3} = 3.17$ times greater than the initial pressure. Sample (iv) is a diatomic gas for which $\gamma = \frac{7}{5}$, so its final pressure is greater than the initial pressure by a factor of $2^{7/5} = 2.64$.

Bridging Problem

(a) $W = nRT \ln \left[\dfrac{V_2 - nb}{V_1 - nb} \right] + an^2 \left[\dfrac{1}{V_2} - \dfrac{1}{V_1} \right]$

(b) (i) $W = 2.80 \times 10^3 \, \text{J}$, (ii) $W = 3.11 \times 10^3 \, \text{J}$

(c) Ideal gas, for which there is no attraction between molecules

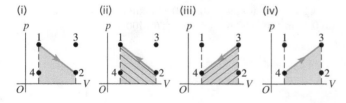

(i)   (ii)   (iii)   (iv)

? The second law of thermodynamics tells us that heat
naturally flows from a hot body
(such as molten lava, shown
here flowing into the ocean in
Hawaii) to a cold one (such as
ocean water, which is heated to
make steam). Is it *ever* possible
for heat to flow from a cold
body to a hot one? (i) Yes, no
matter what the temperature
difference; (ii) yes, but for only
certain temperature differences;
(iii) no; (iv) answer depends on
the compositions of the two
bodies.

20 THE SECOND LAW OF THERMODYNAMICS

Many thermodynamic processes proceed naturally in one direction but not the opposite. For example, heat by itself always flows from a hot body to a cooler body, never the reverse. Heat flow from a cool body to a hot body would not violate the first law of thermodynamics; energy would be conserved. But it doesn't happen in nature. Why not? As another example, note that it is easy to convert mechanical energy completely into heat; this happens every time we use a car's brakes to stop it. In the reverse direction, there are plenty of devices that convert heat *partially* into mechanical energy. (An automobile engine is an example.) But no one has ever managed to build a machine that converts heat *completely* into mechanical energy. Again, why not?

The answer to both of these questions has to do with the *directions* of thermodynamic processes and is called the *second law of thermodynamics*. This law places fundamental limitations on the efficiency of an engine or a power plant. It also places limitations on the minimum energy input needed to operate a refrigerator. So the second law is directly relevant for many important practical problems.

We can also state the second law in terms of the concept of *entropy*, a quantitative measure of the degree of randomness of a system. The idea of entropy helps explain why ink mixed with water never spontaneously unmixes and why we never observe a host of other seemingly possible processes.

20.1 DIRECTIONS OF THERMODYNAMIC PROCESSES

Thermodynamic processes that occur in nature are all **irreversible processes.** These are processes that proceed spontaneously in one direction but not the other (**Fig. 20.1a**, next page). The flow of heat from a hot body to a cooler body is irreversible, as is the free expansion of a gas discussed in Sections 19.3 and 19.6. Sliding a book across a table converts mechanical energy into heat by friction; this process is

20.1 Reversible and irreversible processes.

(a) A block of ice melts *irreversibly* when we place it in a hot (70°C) metal box.

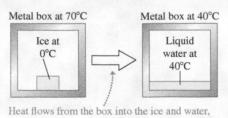

Heat flows from the box into the ice and water, never the reverse.

(b) A block of ice at 0°C can be melted *reversibly* if we put it in a 0°C metal box.

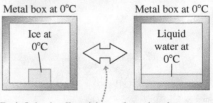

By infinitesimally raising or lowering the temperature of the box, we can make heat flow into the ice to melt it or make heat flow out of the water to refreeze it.

irreversible, for no one has ever observed the reverse process (in which a book initially at rest on the table would spontaneously start moving and the table and book would cool down). Our main topic for this chapter is the *second law of thermodynamics,* which determines the preferred direction for such processes.

Despite this preferred direction for every natural process, we can think of a class of idealized processes that *would* be reversible. A system that undergoes such an idealized **reversible process** is always very close to being in thermodynamic equilibrium within itself and with its surroundings. Any change of state that takes place can then be reversed by making only an infinitesimal change in the conditions of the system. For example, we can reverse heat flow between two bodies whose temperatures differ only infinitesimally by making only a very small change in one temperature or the other (Fig. 20.1b).

Reversible processes are thus **equilibrium processes,** with the system always in thermodynamic equilibrium. Of course, if a system were *truly* in thermodynamic equilibrium, no change of state would take place. Heat would not flow into or out of a system with truly uniform temperature throughout, and a system that is truly in mechanical equilibrium would not expand and do work against its surroundings. A reversible process is an idealization that can never be precisely attained in the real world. But by making the temperature gradients and the pressure differences in the substance very small, we can keep the system very close to equilibrium states and make the process nearly reversible.

By contrast, heat flow with finite temperature difference, free expansion of a gas, and conversion of work to heat by friction are all *irreversible* processes; no small change in conditions could make any of them go the other way. They are also all *nonequilibrium* processes, in that the system is not in thermodynamic equilibrium at any point until the end of the process.

Disorder and Thermodynamic Processes

There is a relationship between the direction of a process and the *disorder* or *randomness* of the resulting state. For example, imagine a thousand names written on file cards and arranged in alphabetical order. Throw the alphabetized stack of cards into the air, and they will likely come down in a random, disordered state. In the free expansion of a gas discussed in Sections 19.3 and 19.6, the air is more disordered after it has expanded into the entire box than when it was confined in one side, just as your clothes are more disordered when scattered all over your floor than when confined to your closet.

Similarly, macroscopic kinetic energy is energy associated with organized, coordinated motions of many molecules, but heat transfer involves changes in energy of random, disordered molecular motion. Therefore conversion of mechanical energy into heat involves an increase of randomness or disorder.

In the following sections we will introduce the second law of thermodynamics by considering two broad classes of devices: *heat engines,* which are partly successful in converting heat into work, and *refrigerators,* which are partly successful in transporting heat from cooler to hotter bodies.

TEST YOUR UNDERSTANDING OF SECTION 20.1   Your left and right hands are normally at the same temperature, just like the metal box and ice in Fig. 20.1b. Is rubbing your hands together to warm them (i) a reversible process or (ii) an irreversible process? ∎

20.2 HEAT ENGINES

The essence of our technological society is the ability to use sources of energy other than muscle power. Sometimes, mechanical energy is directly available; water power and wind power are examples. But most of our energy comes from the burning of fossil fuels (coal, oil, and gas) and from nuclear reactions. They supply energy that is transferred as *heat*. This is directly useful for heating buildings, for cooking, and for chemical processing, but to operate a machine or propel a vehicle, we need *mechanical* energy.

Thus it's important to know how to take heat from a source and convert as much of it as possible into mechanical energy or work. This is what happens in gasoline engines in automobiles, jet engines in airplanes, steam turbines in electric power plants, and many other systems. Closely related processes occur in the animal kingdom; food energy is "burned" (that is, carbohydrates combine with oxygen to yield water, carbon dioxide, and energy) and partly converted to mechanical energy as an animal's muscles do work on its surroundings.

Any device that transforms heat partly into work or mechanical energy is called a **heat engine** (**Fig. 20.2**). Usually, a quantity of matter inside the engine undergoes inflow and outflow of heat, expansion and compression, and sometimes change of phase. We call this matter the **working substance** of the engine. In internal-combustion engines, such as those used in automobiles, the working substance is a mixture of air and fuel; in a steam turbine it is water.

The simplest kind of engine to analyze is one in which the working substance undergoes a **cyclic process,** a sequence of processes that eventually leaves the substance in the same state in which it started. In a steam turbine the water is recycled and used over and over. Internal-combustion engines do not use the same air over and over, but we can still analyze them in terms of cyclic processes that approximate their actual operation.

20.2 All motorized vehicles other than purely electric vehicles use heat engines for propulsion. (Hybrid vehicles use their internal-combustion engine to help charge the batteries for the electric motor.)

Hot and Cold Reservoirs

All heat engines *absorb* heat from a source at a relatively high temperature, perform some mechanical work, and *discard* or *reject* some heat at a lower temperature. As far as the engine is concerned, the discarded heat is wasted. In internal-combustion engines the waste heat is that discarded in the hot exhaust gases and the cooling system; in a steam turbine it is the heat that must flow out of the used steam to condense and recycle the water.

When a system is carried through a cyclic process, its initial and final internal energies are equal, so the first law of thermodynamics requires that

$$U_2 - U_1 = 0 = Q - W \qquad \text{so} \qquad Q = W$$

That is, the net heat flowing into the engine in a cyclic process equals the net work done by the engine.

When we analyze heat engines, it helps to think of two bodies with which the working substance of the engine can interact. One of these, called the *hot reservoir,* represents the heat source; it can give the working substance large amounts of heat at a constant temperature T_H without appreciably changing its own temperature. The other body, called the *cold reservoir,* can absorb large amounts of discarded heat from the engine at a constant lower temperature T_C.

In a steam-turbine system the flames and hot gases in the boiler are the hot reservoir, and the cold water and air used to condense and cool the used steam are the cold reservoir.

We denote the quantities of heat transferred from the hot and cold reservoirs as Q_H and Q_C, respectively. A quantity of heat Q is positive when heat is transferred *into* the working substance and is negative when heat leaves the working substance. Thus in a heat engine, Q_H is positive but Q_C is negative, representing heat *leaving* the working substance. This sign convention is consistent with the rules we stated in Section 19.1; we will continue to use those rules here. For clarity, we'll often state the relationships in terms of the absolute values of the Q's and W's because absolute values are always positive.

20.3 Schematic energy-flow diagram for a heat engine.

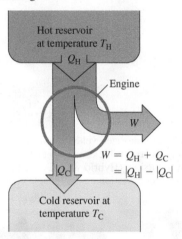

Energy-Flow Diagrams and Efficiency

We can represent the energy transformations in a heat engine by the *energy-flow diagram* of **Fig. 20.3**. The engine itself is represented by the circle. The amount of heat Q_H supplied to the engine by the hot reservoir is proportional to the width of the incoming "pipeline" at the top of the diagram. The width of the outgoing pipeline at the bottom is proportional to the magnitude $|Q_C|$ of the heat rejected in the exhaust. The branch line to the right represents the portion of the heat supplied that the engine converts to mechanical work, W.

When an engine repeats the same cycle over and over, Q_H and Q_C represent the quantities of heat absorbed and rejected by the engine *during one cycle*; Q_H is positive, and Q_C is negative. The *net* heat Q absorbed per cycle is

$$Q = Q_H + Q_C = |Q_H| - |Q_C| \tag{20.1}$$

The useful output of the engine is the net work W done by the working substance. From the first law,

$$W = Q = Q_H + Q_C = |Q_H| - |Q_C| \tag{20.2}$$

Ideally, we would like to convert *all* the heat Q_H into work; in that case we would have $Q_H = W$ and $Q_C = 0$. Experience shows that this is impossible; there is always some heat wasted, and Q_C *is never zero*. We define the **thermal efficiency** of an engine, denoted by e, as the quotient

$$e = \frac{W}{Q_H} \tag{20.3}$$

The thermal efficiency e represents the fraction of Q_H that *is* converted to work. To put it another way, e is what you get divided by what you pay for. This is always less than unity, an all-too-familiar experience! In terms of the flow diagram of Fig. 20.3, the most efficient engine is one for which the branch pipeline representing the work output is as wide as possible and the exhaust pipeline representing the heat thrown away is as narrow as possible.

When we substitute the two expressions for W given by Eq. (20.2) into Eq. (20.3), we get the following equivalent expressions for e:

BIO **Application Biological Efficiency** Although a biological organism is not a heat engine, the concept of efficiency still applies: Here e is the ratio of the work done to the energy that was used to do that work. To exercise on a stationary bike, your body must first convert the chemical-bond energy in glucose to chemical-bond energy in ATP (adenosine triphosphate), then convert energy from ATP into motion of your leg muscles, and finally convert muscular motion into motion of the pedals. The overall efficiency of this entire process is only about 25%. The remaining 75% of the energy liberated from glucose goes into heating your body.

Work done by engine ⟶ Heat rejected by engine ⟶

Thermal efficiency of an engine
$$e = \frac{W}{Q_H} = 1 + \frac{Q_C}{Q_H} = 1 - \left|\frac{Q_C}{Q_H}\right| \tag{20.4}$$

Heat absorbed by engine ⟶

Note that e is a quotient of two energy quantities and thus is a pure number, without units. Of course, we must always express W, Q_H, and Q_C in the same units.

PROBLEM-SOLVING STRATEGY 20.1 HEAT ENGINES

Problems involving heat engines are, fundamentally, problems in the first law of thermodynamics. You should review Problem-Solving Strategy 19.1 (Section 19.4).

IDENTIFY *the relevant concepts:* A heat engine is any device that converts heat partially to work, as shown schematically in Fig. 20.3. We will see in Section 20.4 that a refrigerator is essentially a heat engine running in reverse, so many of the same concepts apply.

SET UP *the problem* as suggested in Problem-Solving Strategy 19.1. Use Eq. (20.4) if the thermal efficiency of the engine is relevant. Sketch an energy-flow diagram like Fig. 20.3.

EXECUTE *the solution* as follows:
1. Be careful with the sign conventions for W and the various Q's. W is positive when the system expands and does work; W is

negative when the system is compressed and work is done on it. Each Q is positive if it represents heat entering the system and is negative if it represents heat leaving the system. When you know that a quantity is negative, such as Q_C in the above discussion, it sometimes helps to write it as $Q_C = -|Q_C|$.
2. Power is work per unit time ($P = W/t$), and rate of heat transfer (heat current) H is heat transfer per unit time ($H = Q/t$). In problems involving these concepts it helps to ask, "What is W or Q in one second (or one hour)?"
3. Keeping steps 1 and 2 in mind, solve for the target variables.

EVALUATE *your answer:* Use the first law of thermodynamics to check your results. Pay particular attention to algebraic signs.

EXAMPLE 20.1 ANALYZING A HEAT ENGINE

A gasoline truck engine takes in 10,000 J of heat and delivers 2000 J of mechanical work per cycle. The heat is obtained by burning gasoline with heat of combustion $L_c = 5.0 \times 10^4$ J/g. (a) What is the thermal efficiency of this engine? (b) How much heat is discarded in each cycle? (c) If the engine goes through 25 cycles per second, what is its power output in watts? In horsepower? (d) How much gasoline is burned in each cycle? (e) How much gasoline is burned per second? Per hour?

SOLUTION

IDENTIFY and SET UP: This problem concerns a heat engine, so we can use the ideas of this section. **Figure 20.4** is our energy flow diagram for one cycle. In each cycle the engine does $W = 2000$ J of work and takes in heat $Q_H = 10,000$ J. We use Eq. (20.4), in the form $e = W/Q_H$, to find the thermal efficiency. We use Eq. (20.2) to find the amount of heat Q_C rejected per cycle. The heat of combustion tells us how much gasoline must be burned per cycle and hence per unit time. The power output is the time rate at which the work W is done.

20.4 Our sketch for this problem.

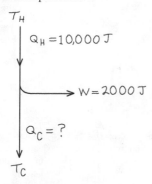

EXECUTE: (a) From Eq. (20.4), the thermal efficiency is

$$e = \frac{W}{Q_H} = \frac{2000 \text{ J}}{10,000 \text{ J}} = 0.20 = 20\%$$

(b) From Eq. (20.2), $W = Q_H + Q_C$, so

$$Q_C = W - Q_H = 2000 \text{ J} - 10,000 \text{ J} = -8000 \text{ J}$$

That is, 8000 J of heat leaves the engine during each cycle.

(c) The power P equals the work per cycle multiplied by the number of cycles per second:

$$P = (2000 \text{ J/cycle})(25 \text{ cycles/s}) = 50,000 \text{ W} = 50 \text{ kW}$$

$$= (50,000 \text{ W})\frac{1 \text{ hp}}{746 \text{ W}} = 67 \text{ hp}$$

(d) Let m be the mass of gasoline burned during each cycle. Then $Q_H = mL_c$ and

$$m = \frac{Q_H}{L_c} = \frac{10,000 \text{ J}}{5.0 \times 10^4 \text{ J/g}} = 0.20 \text{ g}$$

(e) The mass of gasoline burned per second equals the mass per cycle multiplied by the number of cycles per second:

$$(0.20 \text{ g/cycle})(25 \text{ cycles/s}) = 5.0 \text{ g/s}$$

The mass burned per hour is

$$(5.0 \text{ g/s})\frac{3600 \text{ s}}{1 \text{ h}} = 18,000 \text{ g/h} = 18 \text{ kg/h}$$

EVALUATE: An efficiency of 20% is fairly typical for cars and trucks if W includes only the work delivered to the wheels. We can check the mass burned per hour by expressing it in miles per gallon ("mileage"). The density of gasoline is about 0.70 g/cm³, so this is about 25,700 cm³, 25.7 L, or 6.8 gallons of gasoline per hour. If the truck is traveling at 55 mi/h (88 km/h), this represents fuel consumption of 8.1 miles/gallon (3.4 km/L). This is a fairly typical mileage for large trucks.

20.3 INTERNAL-COMBUSTION ENGINES

The gasoline engine, used in automobiles and many other types of machinery, is a familiar example of a heat engine. Let's look at its thermal efficiency. **Figure 20.5** shows the operation of one type of gasoline engine. First a mixture of air and gasoline vapor flows into a cylinder through an open intake valve while the piston descends, increasing the volume of the cylinder from a minimum of V (when the piston is all the way up) to a maximum of rV (when it is all the way down). The quantity r is called the **compression ratio;** for present-day automobile engines its value is typically 8 to 10. At the end of this *intake stroke,* the intake valve closes and the mixture is compressed, approximately adiabatically, to volume V during the *compression stroke.* The mixture is then ignited by the spark plug, and the heated gas expands, approximately adiabatically, back to volume rV, pushing on the piston and doing work; this is the *power stroke.* Finally, the exhaust valve opens, and the combustion products are pushed out (during the *exhaust stroke*), leaving the cylinder ready for the next intake stroke.

The Otto Cycle

Figure 20.6 is a pV-diagram for an idealized model of the thermodynamic processes in a gasoline engine. This model is called the **Otto cycle.** At point a the gasoline–air mixture has entered the cylinder. The mixture is compressed adiabatically to point b and is then ignited. Heat Q_H is added to the system by the burning gasoline along line bc, and the power stroke is the adiabatic expansion to d. The gas is cooled to the temperature of the outside air along line da; during this process, heat $|Q_C|$ is rejected. This gas leaves the engine as exhaust and does not enter the engine again. But since an equivalent amount of gasoline and air enters, we may consider the process to be cyclic.

20.5 Cycle of a four-stroke internal-combustion engine.

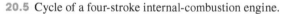

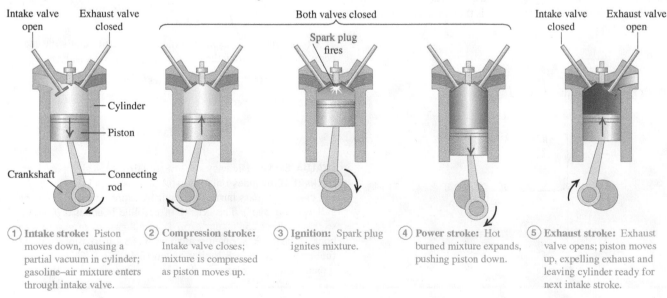

(1) **Intake stroke:** Piston moves down, causing a partial vacuum in cylinder; gasoline–air mixture enters through intake valve.

(2) **Compression stroke:** Intake valve closes; mixture is compressed as piston moves up.

(3) **Ignition:** Spark plug ignites mixture.

(4) **Power stroke:** Hot burned mixture expands, pushing piston down.

(5) **Exhaust stroke:** Exhaust valve opens; piston moves up, expelling exhaust and leaving cylinder ready for next intake stroke.

We can calculate the efficiency of this idealized cycle. Processes bc and da are constant-volume, so the heats Q_H and Q_C are related simply to the temperatures at points a, b, c, and d:

$$Q_H = nC_V(T_c - T_b) > 0$$

$$Q_C = nC_V(T_a - T_d) < 0$$

The thermal efficiency is given by Eq. (20.4). Inserting the above expressions and cancelling out the common factor nC_V, we find

$$e = \frac{Q_H + Q_C}{Q_H} = \frac{T_c - T_b + T_a - T_d}{T_c - T_b} \tag{20.5}$$

To simplify this further, we use the temperature–volume relationship for adiabatic processes for an ideal gas, Eq. (19.22). For the two adiabatic processes ab and cd,

$$T_a(rV)^{\gamma-1} = T_bV^{\gamma-1} \quad \text{and} \quad T_d(rV)^{\gamma-1} = T_cV^{\gamma-1}$$

where γ is the ratio of heat capacities for the gas in the engine (see Section 19.7). We divide each of these equations by the common factor $V^{\gamma-1}$ and substitute the resulting expressions for T_b and T_c back into Eq. (20.5). The result is

$$e = \frac{T_dr^{\gamma-1} - T_ar^{\gamma-1} + T_a - T_d}{T_dr^{\gamma-1} - T_ar^{\gamma-1}} = \frac{(T_d - T_a)(r^{\gamma-1} - 1)}{(T_d - T_a)r^{\gamma-1}}$$

Dividing out the common factor $(T_d - T_a)$, we get

Thermal efficiency ⋯ in Otto cycle
$$e = 1 - \frac{1}{r^{\gamma-1}} \tag{20.6}$$
Compression ratio ⋯ Ratio of heat capacities

The thermal efficiency given by Eq. (20.6) is always less than unity, even for this idealized model. With $r = 8$ and $\gamma = 1.4$ (the value for air) the theoretical efficiency is $e = 0.56$, or 56%. The efficiency can be increased by increasing r. However, this also increases the temperature at the end of the adiabatic compression of the air–fuel mixture. If the temperature is too high, the mixture explodes spontaneously during compression instead of burning evenly after the spark plug ignites it. This is called *pre-ignition* or *detonation;* it causes a knocking sound and can damage the engine. The octane rating of a gasoline is a measure of its antiknock qualities. The maximum practical compression ratio for high-octane, or "premium," gasoline is about 10 to 13.

The Otto cycle is a highly idealized model. It assumes that the mixture behaves as an ideal gas; it ignores friction, turbulence, loss of heat to cylinder walls, and many other effects that reduce the efficiency of an engine. Efficiencies of real gasoline engines are typically around 35%.

The Diesel Cycle

The Diesel engine is similar in operation to the gasoline engine. The most important difference is that there is no fuel in the cylinder at the beginning of the compression stroke. A little before the beginning of the power stroke, the injectors start to inject fuel directly into the cylinder, just fast enough to keep the pressure approximately constant during the first part of the power stroke. Because of the high temperature developed during the adiabatic compression, the fuel ignites spontaneously as it is injected; no spark plugs are needed.

Figure 20.7 shows the idealized **Diesel cycle.** Starting at point a, air is compressed adiabatically to point b, heated at constant pressure to point c, expanded adiabatically to point d, and cooled at constant volume to point a. Because there is no fuel in the cylinder during most of the compression stroke,

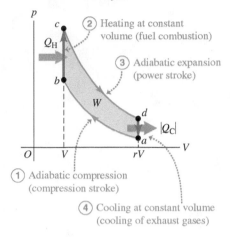

20.6 The pV-diagram for the Otto cycle, an idealized model of the thermodynamic processes in a gasoline engine.

Otto cycle

② Heating at constant volume (fuel combustion)
③ Adiabatic expansion (power stroke)
① Adiabatic compression (compression stroke)
④ Cooling at constant volume (cooling of exhaust gases)

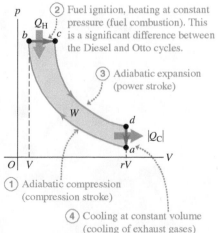

20.7 The pV-diagram for the idealized Diesel cycle.

Diesel cycle

② Fuel ignition, heating at constant pressure (fuel combustion). This is a significant difference between the Diesel and Otto cycles.
③ Adiabatic expansion (power stroke)
① Adiabatic compression (compression stroke)
④ Cooling at constant volume (cooling of exhaust gases)

pre-ignition cannot occur, and the compression ratio r can be much higher than for a gasoline engine. This improves efficiency and ensures reliable ignition when the fuel is injected (because of the high temperature reached during the adiabatic compression). Values of r of 15 to 20 are typical; with these values and $\gamma = 1.4$, the theoretical efficiency of the idealized Diesel cycle is about 0.65 to 0.70. As with the Otto cycle, the efficiency of any actual engine is substantially less than this. While Diesel engines are very efficient, they must be built to much tighter tolerances than gasoline engines and the fuel-injection system requires careful maintenance.

TEST YOUR UNDERSTANDING OF SECTION 20.3   For an Otto-cycle engine with cylinders of a fixed size and a fixed compression ratio, which of the following aspects of the pV-diagram in Fig. 20.6 would change if you doubled the amount of fuel burned per cycle? (There may be more than one correct answer.) (i) The vertical distance between points b and c; (ii) the vertical distance between points a and d; (iii) the horizontal distance between points b and a. ▮

20.4 REFRIGERATORS

We can think of a **refrigerator** as a heat engine operating in reverse. A heat engine takes heat from a hot place and gives off heat to a colder place. A refrigerator does the opposite; it takes heat from a cold place (the inside of the refrigerator) and gives it off to a warmer place (usually the air in the room where the refrigerator is located). A heat engine has a net *output* of mechanical work; the refrigerator requires a net *input* of mechanical work. With the sign conventions from Section 20.2, for a refrigerator Q_C is positive but both W and Q_H are negative; hence $|W| = -W$ and $|Q_H| = -Q_H$.

Figure 20.8 shows an energy-flow diagram for a refrigerator. From the first law for a cyclic process,

$$Q_H + Q_C - W = 0 \quad \text{or} \quad -Q_H = Q_C - W$$

or, because both Q_H and W are negative,

$$|Q_H| = Q_C + |W| \tag{20.7}$$

Thus, as the diagram shows, the heat $|Q_H|$ leaving the working substance and given to the hot reservoir is always *greater* than the heat Q_C taken from the cold reservoir. Note that the absolute-value relationship

$$|Q_H| = |Q_C| + |W| \tag{20.8}$$

is valid for both heat engines and refrigerators.

From an economic point of view, the best refrigeration cycle is one that removes the greatest amount of heat $|Q_C|$ from the inside of the refrigerator for the least expenditure of mechanical work, $|W|$. The relevant ratio is therefore $|Q_C|/|W|$; the larger this ratio, the better the refrigerator. We call this ratio the **coefficient of performance**, K. From Eq. (20.8), $|W| = |Q_H| - |Q_C|$, so

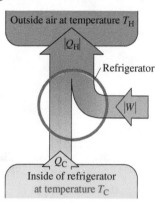

20.8 Schematic energy-flow diagram of a refrigerator.

Outside air at temperature T_H

$|Q_H|$

Refrigerator

$|W|$

Q_C

Inside of refrigerator at temperature T_C

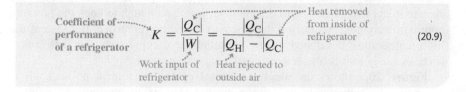

$$\begin{array}{c} \text{Coefficient of} \\ \text{performance} \\ \text{of a refrigerator} \end{array} \quad K = \frac{|Q_C|}{|W|} = \frac{|Q_C|}{|Q_H| - |Q_C|} \tag{20.9}$$

Heat removed from inside of refrigerator

Work input of refrigerator

Heat rejected to outside air

As always, we measure Q_H, Q_C, and W all in the same energy units; K is then a dimensionless number.

20.9 (a) Principle of the mechanical refrigeration cycle. (b) How the key elements are arranged in a practical refrigerator.

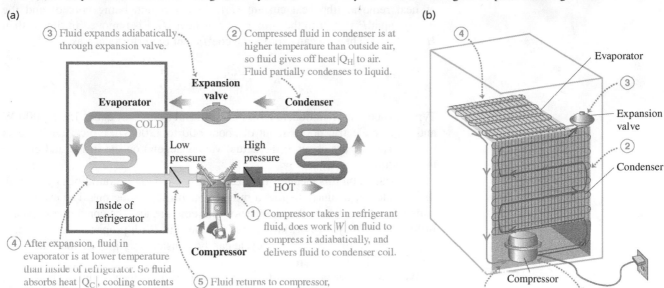

(a)

③ Fluid expands adiabatically through expansion valve.

② Compressed fluid in condenser is at higher temperature than outside air, so fluid gives off heat $|Q_H|$ to air. Fluid partially condenses to liquid.

Expansion valve

Evaporator

COLD

Condenser

Low pressure

High pressure

HOT

Inside of refrigerator

Compressor

① Compressor takes in refrigerant fluid, does work $|W|$ on fluid to compress it adiabatically, and delivers fluid to condenser coil.

④ After expansion, fluid in evaporator is at lower temperature than inside of refrigerator. So fluid absorbs heat $|Q_C|$, cooling contents of refrigerator. Fluid partially evaporates to vapor.

⑤ Fluid returns to compressor, and another cycle begins.

(b)

④ Evaporator ③ Expansion valve ② Condenser

Compressor ⑤ ①

Practical Refrigerators

Figure 20.9a shows the principles of the cycle used in home refrigerators. The fluid "circuit" contains a refrigerant fluid (the working substance). The left side of the circuit (including the cooling coils inside the refrigerator) is at low temperature and low pressure; the right side (including the condenser coils outside the refrigerator) is at high temperature and high pressure. Ordinarily, both sides contain liquid and vapor in phase equilibrium. In each cycle the fluid absorbs heat $|Q_C|$ from the inside of the refrigerator on the left side and gives off heat $|Q_H|$ to the surrounding air on the right side. The compressor, usually driven by an electric motor (Fig. 20.9b), does work $|W|$ *on* the fluid during each cycle. So the compressor requires energy input, which is why refrigerators have to be plugged in.

An air conditioner operates on exactly the same principle. In this case the refrigerator box becomes a room or an entire building. The evaporator coils are inside, the condenser is outside, and fans circulate air through these (**Fig. 20.10**). In large installations the condenser coils are often cooled by water.

20.10 An air conditioner works on the same principle as a refrigerator.

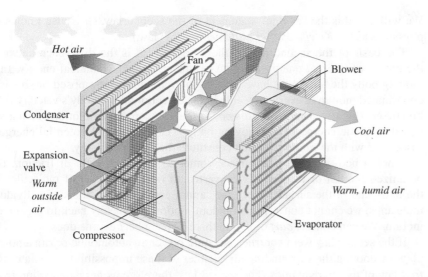

Hot air

Fan

Blower

Condenser

Cool air

Expansion valve

Warm outside air

Warm, humid air

Compressor

Evaporator

For air conditioners the quantities of greatest practical importance are the *rate of heat removal* (the heat current H from the region being cooled) and the *power* input $P = W/t$ to the compressor. If heat $|Q_C|$ is removed in time t, then $H = |Q_C|/t$. Then we can express the coefficient of performance as

$$K = \frac{|Q_C|}{|W|} = \frac{Ht}{Pt} = \frac{H}{P}$$

Typical room air conditioners have heat removal rates H of about 1500–3000 W and require electric power input of about 600 to 1200 W. Typical coefficients of performance are about 3; the actual values depend on the inside and outside temperatures.

A variation on this theme is the **heat pump,** used to heat buildings by cooling the outside air. It functions like a refrigerator turned inside out. The evaporator coils are outside, where they take heat from cold air, and the condenser coils are inside, where they give off heat to the warmer air. With proper design, the heat $|Q_H|$ delivered to the inside per cycle can be considerably greater than the work $|W|$ required to get it there.

Work is *always* needed to transfer heat from a colder to a hotter body. Heat flows spontaneously from hotter to colder, and to reverse this flow requires the addition of work from the outside. Experience shows that it is impossible to make a refrigerator that transports heat from a colder body to a hotter body without the addition of work. If no work were needed, the coefficient of performance would be infinite. We call such a device a *workless refrigerator;* it is a mythical beast, like the unicorn and the free lunch.

TEST YOUR UNDERSTANDING OF SECTION 20.4 Can you cool your house by leaving the refrigerator door open? ∎

20.5 THE SECOND LAW OF THERMODYNAMICS

Experimental evidence suggests strongly that it is *impossible* to build a heat engine that converts heat completely to work—that is, an engine with 100% thermal efficiency. This impossibility is the basis of one statement of the **second law of thermodynamics,** as follows:

> It is impossible for any system to undergo a process in which it absorbs heat from a reservoir at a single temperature and converts the heat completely into mechanical work, with the system ending in the same state in which it began.

We will call this the "engine" statement of the second law. (It is also known to physicists as the *Kelvin–Planck statement* of this law.)

The basis of the second law of thermodynamics is the difference between the nature of internal energy and that of macroscopic mechanical energy. In a moving body the molecules have random motion, but superimposed on this is a coordinated motion of every molecule in the direction of the body's velocity. The kinetic energy associated with this *coordinated* macroscopic motion is what we call the kinetic energy of the moving body. The kinetic and potential energies associated with the *random* motion constitute the internal energy.

When a body sliding on a surface comes to rest as a result of friction, the organized motion of the body is converted to random motion of molecules in the body and in the surface. Since we cannot control the motions of individual molecules, we cannot convert this random motion completely back to organized motion. We can convert *part* of it, and this is what a heat engine does.

If the second law were *not* true, we could power an automobile or run a power plant by cooling the surrounding air. Neither of these impossibilities violates the *first* law of thermodynamics. The second law, therefore, is not a deduction from the first but stands by itself as a separate law of nature. The first law denies the possibility of creating or destroying energy; the second law limits the *availability* of energy and the ways in which it can be used and converted.

Restating the Second Law

Our analysis of refrigerators in Section 20.4 forms the basis for an alternative statement of the second law of thermodynamics. Heat flows spontaneously from hotter to colder bodies, never the reverse. A refrigerator does take heat from a colder to a hotter body, but its operation requires an input of mechanical energy or work. We can generalize this observation:

> **It is impossible for any process to have as its sole result the transfer of heat from a cooler to a hotter body.**

We'll call this the "refrigerator" statement of the second law. (It is also known as the *Clausius statement*.) It may not seem to be very closely related to the "engine" statement. In fact, though, the two statements are completely equivalent. For example, if we could build a workless refrigerator, violating the second or "refrigerator" statement of the second law, we could use it in conjunction with a heat engine, pumping the heat rejected by the engine back to the hot reservoir to be reused. This composite machine (**Fig. 20.11a**) would violate the "engine" statement of the second law because its net effect would be to take a net quantity of heat $Q_H - |Q_C|$ from the hot reservoir and convert it completely to work W.

20.11 Energy-flow diagrams showing that the two forms of the second law are equivalent.

(a) The "engine" statement of the second law of thermodynamics

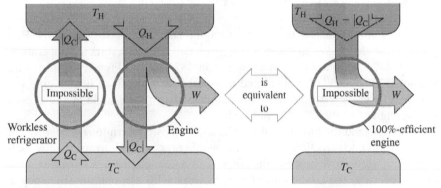

If a workless refrigerator were possible, it could be used in conjunction with an ordinary heat engine to form a 100%-efficient engine, converting heat $Q_H - |Q_C|$ completely to work.

(b) The "refrigerator" statement of the second law of thermodynamics

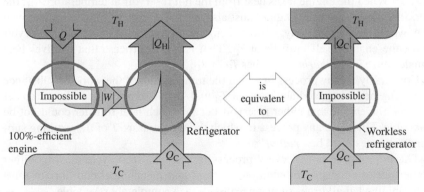

If a 100%-efficient engine were possible, it could be used in conjunction with an ordinary refrigerator to form a workless refrigerator, transferring heat Q_C from the cold to the hot reservoir with no input of work.

Alternatively, if we could make an engine with 100% thermal efficiency, in violation of the first statement, we could run it using heat from the hot reservoir and use the work output to drive a refrigerator that pumps heat from the cold reservoir to the hot (Fig. 20.11b). This composite device would violate the "refrigerator" statement because its net effect would be to take heat Q_C from the cold reservoir and deliver it to the hot reservoir without requiring any input of work. Thus any device that violates one form of the second law can be used to make a device that violates the other form. If violations of the first form are impossible, so are violations of the second!

The conversion of work to heat and the heat flow from hot to cold across a finite temperature gradient are *irreversible* processes. The "engine" and "refrigerator" statements of the second law state that these processes can be only partially reversed. We could cite other examples. Gases naturally flow from a region of high pressure to a region of low pressure; gases and miscible liquids left by themselves always tend to mix, not to unmix. The second law of thermodynamics is an expression of the inherent one-way aspect of these and many other irreversible processes. Energy conversion is an essential aspect of all plant and animal life and of human technology, so the second law of thermodynamics is of fundamental importance.

TEST YOUR UNDERSTANDING OF SECTION 20.5 Would a 100%-efficient engine (Fig. 20.11a) violate the *first* law of thermodynamics? What about a workless refrigerator (Fig. 20.11b)? ∎

20.6 THE CARNOT CYCLE

According to the second law, no heat engine can have 100% efficiency. How great an efficiency *can* an engine have, given two heat reservoirs at temperatures T_H and T_C? This question was answered in 1824 by the French engineer Sadi Carnot (1796–1832), who developed a hypothetical, idealized heat engine that has the maximum possible efficiency consistent with the second law. The cycle of this engine is called the **Carnot cycle.**

To understand the rationale of the Carnot cycle, we return to *reversibility* and its relationship to directions of thermodynamic processes. Conversion of work to heat is an irreversible process; the purpose of a heat engine is a *partial* reversal of this process, the conversion of heat to work with as great an efficiency as possible. For maximum heat-engine efficiency, therefore, *we must avoid all irreversible processes* (**Fig. 20.12**).

Heat flow through a finite temperature drop is an irreversible process. Therefore, during heat transfer in the Carnot cycle there must be *no* finite temperature difference. When the engine takes heat from the hot reservoir at temperature T_H, the working substance of the engine must also be at T_H; otherwise, irreversible heat flow would occur. Similarly, when the engine discards heat to the cold reservoir at T_C, the engine itself must be at T_C. That is, every process that involves heat transfer must be *isothermal* at either T_H or T_C.

Conversely, in any process in which the temperature of the working substance of the engine is intermediate between T_H and T_C, there must be *no* heat transfer between the engine and either reservoir because such heat transfer could not be reversible. Therefore any process in which the temperature T of the working substance changes must be *adiabatic*.

The bottom line is that every process in our idealized cycle must be either isothermal or adiabatic. In addition, thermal and mechanical equilibrium must be maintained at all times so that each process is completely reversible.

20.12 The temperature of the firebox of a steam engine is much higher than the temperature of water in the boiler, so heat flows irreversibly from firebox to water. Carnot's quest to understand the efficiency of steam engines led him to the idea that an ideal engine would involve only *reversible* processes.

20.13 The Carnot cycle for an ideal gas. The light blue lines in the pV-diagram are isotherms (curves of constant temperature) and the dark blue lines are adiabats (curves of zero heat flow).

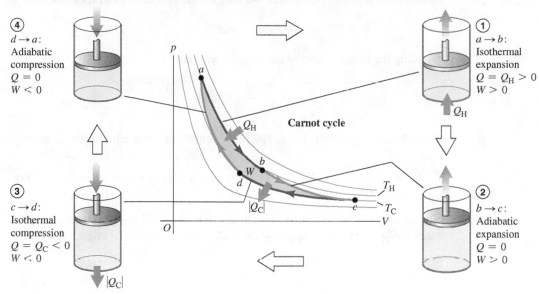

④

$d \rightarrow a$:
Adiabatic
compression
$Q = 0$
$W < 0$

①

$a \rightarrow b$:
Isothermal
expansion
$Q = Q_H > 0$
$W > 0$

③

$c \rightarrow d$:
Isothermal
compression
$Q = Q_C < 0$
$W < 0$

②

$b \rightarrow c$:
Adiabatic
expansion
$Q = 0$
$W > 0$

Steps of the Carnot Cycle

The Carnot cycle consists of two reversible isothermal and two reversible adiabatic processes. **Figure 20.13** shows a Carnot cycle using as its working substance an ideal gas in a cylinder with a piston. It consists of the following steps:

1. The gas expands isothermally at temperature T_H, absorbing heat Q_H (ab).
2. It expands adiabatically until its temperature drops to T_C (bc).
3. It is compressed isothermally at T_C, rejecting heat $|Q_C|$ (cd).
4. It is compressed adiabatically back to its initial state at temperature T_H (da).

We can calculate the thermal efficiency e of a Carnot engine in the special case shown in Fig. 20.13 in which the working substance is an *ideal gas*. To do this, we'll first find the ratio Q_C/Q_H of the quantities of heat transferred in the two isothermal processes and then use Eq. (20.4) to find e.

For an ideal gas the internal energy U depends only on temperature and is thus constant in any isothermal process. For the isothermal expansion ab, $\Delta U_{ab} = 0$ and Q_H is equal to the work W_{ab} done by the gas during its isothermal expansion at temperature T_H. We calculated this work in Example 19.1 (Section 19.2); using that result, we have

$$Q_H = W_{ab} = nRT_H \ln \frac{V_b}{V_a} \qquad (20.10)$$

Similarly,

$$Q_C = W_{cd} = nRT_C \ln \frac{V_d}{V_c} = -nRT_C \ln \frac{V_c}{V_d} \qquad (20.11)$$

Because V_d is less than V_c, Q_C is negative ($Q_C = -|Q_C|$); heat flows out of the gas during the isothermal compression at temperature T_C.

The ratio of the two quantities of heat is thus

$$\frac{Q_C}{Q_H} = -\left(\frac{T_C}{T_H}\right) \frac{\ln (V_c/V_d)}{\ln (V_b/V_a)} \qquad (20.12)$$

This can be simplified further by use of the temperature–volume relationship for an adiabatic process, Eq. (19.22). We find for the two adiabatic processes:

$$T_H V_b^{\gamma-1} = T_C V_c^{\gamma-1} \quad \text{and} \quad T_H V_a^{\gamma-1} = T_C V_d^{\gamma-1}$$

Dividing the first of these by the second, we find

$$\frac{V_b^{\gamma-1}}{V_a^{\gamma-1}} = \frac{V_c^{\gamma-1}}{V_d^{\gamma-1}} \quad \text{and} \quad \frac{V_b}{V_a} = \frac{V_c}{V_d}$$

Thus the two logarithms in Eq. (20.12) are equal, and that equation reduces to

$$\frac{Q_C}{Q_H} = -\frac{T_C}{T_H} \quad \text{or} \quad \frac{|Q_C|}{|Q_H|} = \frac{T_C}{T_H} \quad \text{(heat transfer in a Carnot engine)} \quad (20.13)$$

The ratio of the heat rejected at T_C to the heat absorbed at T_H is just equal to the ratio T_C/T_H. Then from Eq. (20.4) the efficiency of the Carnot engine is

Efficiency of a Carnot engine
$$e_{\text{Carnot}} = 1 - \frac{T_C}{T_H} = \frac{T_H - T_C}{T_H} \quad (20.14)$$
Temperature of cold reservoir
Temperature of hot reservoir

CAUTION **Use Kelvin temperature in all Carnot calculations** In Carnot-cycle calculations, you must use *absolute* (Kelvin) temperatures only. That's because Eqs. (20.10) through (20.14) come from the ideal-gas equation $pV = nRT$, in which T is absolute temperature. ∎

This simple result says that the efficiency of a Carnot engine depends only on the temperatures of the two heat reservoirs. The efficiency is large when the temperature *difference* is large, and it is very small when the temperatures are nearly equal. The efficiency can never be exactly unity unless $T_C = 0$; we'll see later that this, too, is impossible.

EXAMPLE 20.2 **ANALYZING A CARNOT ENGINE I**

A Carnot engine takes 2000 J of heat from a reservoir at 500 K, does some work, and discards some heat to a reservoir at 350 K. How much work does it do, how much heat is discarded, and what is its efficiency?

SOLUTION

IDENTIFY and SET UP: This problem involves a Carnot engine, so we can use the ideas of this section and those of Section 20.2 (which apply to heat engines of all kinds). **Figure 20.14** shows the energy-flow diagram. We have $Q_H = 2000$ J, $T_H = 500$ K, and $T_C = 350$ K. We use Eq. (20.13) to find Q_C, and then use the first law of thermodynamics as given by Eq. (20.2) to find W. We find the efficiency e from T_C and T_H from Eq. (20.14).

EXECUTE: From Eq. (20.13),

$$Q_C = -Q_H \frac{T_C}{T_H} = -(2000 \text{ J}) \frac{350 \text{ K}}{500 \text{ K}} = -1400 \text{ J}$$

Then from Eq. (20.2), the work done is

$$W = Q_H + Q_C = 2000 \text{ J} + (-1400 \text{ J}) = 600 \text{ J}$$

From Eq. (20.14), the thermal efficiency is

$$e = 1 - \frac{T_C}{T_H} = 1 - \frac{350 \text{ K}}{500 \text{ K}} = 0.30 = 30\%$$

EVALUATE: The negative sign of Q_C is correct: It shows that 1400 J of heat flows *out* of the engine and into the cold reservoir. We can check our result for e by using the basic definition of thermal efficiency, Eq. (20.3):

$$e = \frac{W}{Q_H} = \frac{600 \text{ J}}{2000 \text{ J}} = 0.30 = 30\%$$

20.14 Our sketch for this problem.

$T_H = 500$ K
$Q_H = 2000$ J
$W = ?$
$e = ?$
$Q_C = ?$
$T_C = 350$ K

SOLUTION

EXAMPLE 20.3 ANALYZING A CARNOT ENGINE II

Suppose 0.200 mol of an ideal diatomic gas ($\gamma = 1.40$) undergoes a Carnot cycle between 227°C and 27°C, starting at $p_a = 10.0 \times 10^5$ Pa at point a in the pV-diagram of Fig. 20.13. The volume doubles during the isothermal expansion step $a \rightarrow b$. (a) Find the pressure and volume at points a, b, c, and d. (b) Find Q, W, and ΔU for each step and for the entire cycle. (c) Find the efficiency directly from the results of part (b), and compare with the value calculated from Eq. (20.14).

SOLUTION

IDENTIFY and SET UP: This problem involves the properties of the Carnot cycle and those of an ideal gas. We are given the number of moles n and the pressure and temperature at point a (which is at the higher of the two reservoir temperatures); we can find the volume at a from the ideal-gas equation $pV = nRT$. We then find the pressure and volume at points b, c, and d from the known doubling of volume in step $a \rightarrow b$, from equations given in this section, and from $pV = nRT$. In each step we use Eqs. (20.10) and (20.11) to find the heat flow and work done and Eq. (19.13) to find the internal energy change.

EXECUTE: (a) With $T_H = (227 + 273.15)$ K $= 500$ K and $T_C = (27 + 273.15)$ K $= 300$ K, $pV = nRT$ yields

$$V_a = \frac{nRT_H}{p_a} = \frac{(0.200 \text{ mol})(8.314 \text{ J/mol} \cdot \text{K})(500 \text{ K})}{10.0 \times 10^5 \text{ Pa}}$$

$$= 8.31 \times 10^{-4} \text{ m}^3$$

The volume doubles during the isothermal expansion $a \rightarrow b$:

$$V_b = 2V_a = 2(8.31 \times 10^{-4} \text{ m}^3) = 16.6 \times 10^{-4} \text{ m}^3$$

Because the expansion $a \rightarrow b$ is isothermal, $p_a V_a = p_b V_b$, so

$$p_b = \frac{p_a V_a}{V_b} = 5.00 \times 10^5 \text{ Pa}$$

For the adiabatic expansion $b \rightarrow c$, we use the equation $T_H V_b^{\gamma-1} = T_C V_c^{\gamma-1}$ that follows Eq. (20.12) as well as the ideal-gas equation:

$$V_c = V_b \left(\frac{T_H}{T_C}\right)^{1/(\gamma-1)} = (16.6 \times 10^{-4} \text{ m}^3)\left(\frac{500 \text{ K}}{300 \text{ K}}\right)^{2.5}$$

$$= 59.6 \times 10^{-4} \text{ m}^3$$

$$p_c = \frac{nRT_C}{V_c} = \frac{(0.200 \text{ mol})(8.314 \text{ J/mol} \cdot \text{K})(300 \text{ K})}{59.6 \times 10^{-4} \text{ m}^3}$$

$$= 0.837 \times 10^5 \text{ Pa}$$

For the adiabatic compression $d \rightarrow a$, we have $T_C V_d^{\gamma-1} = T_H V_a^{\gamma-1}$ and so

$$V_d = V_a \left(\frac{T_H}{T_C}\right)^{1/(\gamma-1)} = (8.31 \times 10^{-4} \text{ m}^3)\left(\frac{500 \text{ K}}{300 \text{ K}}\right)^{2.5}$$

$$= 29.8 \times 10^{-4} \text{ m}^3$$

$$p_d = \frac{nRT_C}{V_d} = \frac{(0.200 \text{ mol})(8.314 \text{ J/mol} \cdot \text{K})(300 \text{ K})}{29.8 \times 10^{-4} \text{ m}^3}$$

$$= 1.67 \times 10^5 \text{ Pa}$$

(b) For the isothermal expansion $a \rightarrow b$, $\Delta U_{ab} = 0$. From Eq. (20.10),

$$W_{ab} = Q_H = nRT_H \ln \frac{V_b}{V_a}$$

$$= (0.200 \text{ mol})(8.314 \text{ J/mol} \cdot \text{K})(500 \text{ K})(\ln 2) = 576 \text{ J}$$

For the adiabatic expansion $b \rightarrow c$, $Q_{bc} = 0$. From the first law of thermodynamics, $\Delta U_{bc} = Q_{bc} - W_{bc} = -W_{bc}$; the work W_{bc} done by the gas in this adiabatic expansion equals the negative of the change in internal energy of the gas. From Eq. (19.13) we have $\Delta U = nC_V\Delta T$, where $\Delta T = T_C - T_H$. Using $C_V = 20.8$ J/mol $\cdot$ K for an ideal diatomic gas, we find

$$W_{bc} = -\Delta U_{bc} = -nC_V(T_C - T_H) = nC_V(T_H - T_C)$$

$$= (0.200 \text{ mol})(20.8 \text{ J/mol} \cdot \text{K})(500 \text{ K} - 300 \text{ K}) = 832 \text{ J}$$

For the isothermal compression $c \rightarrow d$, $\Delta U_{cd} = 0$; Eq. (20.11) gives

$$W_{cd} = Q_C = nRT_C \ln \frac{V_d}{V_c}$$

$$= (0.200 \text{ mol})(8.314 \text{ J/mol} \cdot \text{K})(300 \text{ K})\left(\ln \frac{29.8 \times 10^{-4} \text{ m}^3}{59.6 \times 10^{-4} \text{ m}^3}\right)$$

$$= -346 \text{ J}$$

For the adiabatic compression $d \rightarrow a$, $Q_{da} = 0$ and

$$W_{da} = -\Delta U_{da} = -nC_V(T_H - T_C) = nC_V(T_C - T_H)$$

$$= (0.200 \text{ mol})(20.8 \text{ J/mol} \cdot \text{K})(300 \text{ K} - 500 \text{ K}) = -832 \text{ J}$$

We can tabulate these results as follows:

Process	Q	W	ΔU
$a \rightarrow b$	576 J	576 J	0
$b \rightarrow c$	0	832 J	−832 J
$c \rightarrow d$	−346 J	−346 J	0
$d \rightarrow a$	0	−832 J	832 J
Total	230 J	230 J	0

(c) From the above table, $Q_H = 576$ J and the total work is 230 J. Thus

$$e = \frac{W}{Q_H} = \frac{230 \text{ J}}{576 \text{ J}} = 0.40 = 40\%$$

We can compare this to the result from Eq. (20.14),

$$e = \frac{T_H - T_C}{T_H} = \frac{500 \text{ K} - 300 \text{ K}}{500 \text{ K}} = 0.40 = 40\%$$

EVALUATE: The table in part (b) shows that for the entire cycle $Q = W$ and $\Delta U = 0$, just as we would expect: In a complete cycle, the *net* heat input is used to do work, and there is zero net change in the internal energy of the system. Note also that the quantities of work in the two adiabatic processes are negatives of each other. Can you show from the analysis leading to Eq. (20.13) that this must *always* be the case in a Carnot cycle?

The Carnot Refrigerator

Because each step in the Carnot cycle is reversible, the *entire cycle* may be reversed, converting the engine into a refrigerator. The coefficient of performance of the Carnot refrigerator is obtained by combining the general definition of K, Eq. (20.9), with Eq. (20.13) for the Carnot cycle. We first rewrite Eq. (20.9) as

$$K = \frac{|Q_C|}{|Q_H| - |Q_C|} = \frac{|Q_C|/|Q_H|}{1 - |Q_C|/|Q_H|}$$

Then we substitute Eq. (20.13), $|Q_C|/|Q_H| = T_C/T_H$, into this expression:

Coefficient of performance of a Carnot refrigerator .... $K_{\text{Carnot}} = \dfrac{T_C}{T_H - T_C}$ .... Temperature of cold reservoir (20.15)

Temperature of hot reservoir

When the temperature difference $T_H - T_C$ is small, K is much larger than unity; in this case a lot of heat can be "pumped" from the lower to the higher temperature with only a little expenditure of work. But the greater the temperature difference, the smaller the value of K and the more work is required to transfer a given quantity of heat.

EXAMPLE 20.4   ANALYZING A CARNOT REFRIGERATOR

If the cycle described in Example 20.3 is run backward as a refrigerator, what is its coefficient of performance?

SOLUTION

IDENTIFY and SET UP: This problem uses the ideas of Section 20.3 (for refrigerators in general) and the above discussion of Carnot refrigerators. Equation (20.9) gives the coefficient of performance K of *any* refrigerator in terms of the heat Q_C extracted from the cold reservoir per cycle and the work W that must be done per cycle.

EXECUTE: In Example 20.3 we found that in one cycle the Carnot engine rejects heat $Q_C = -346$ J to the cold reservoir and does work $W = 230$ J. When run in reverse as a refrigerator, the system

extracts heat $Q_C = +346$ J from the cold reservoir while requiring a work input of $W = -230$ J. From Eq. (20.9),

$$K = \frac{|Q_C|}{|W|} = \frac{346 \text{ J}}{230 \text{ J}} = 1.50$$

Because this is a Carnot cycle, we can also use Eq. (20.15):

$$K = \frac{T_C}{T_H - T_C} = \frac{300 \text{ K}}{500 \text{ K} - 300 \text{ K}} = 1.50$$

EVALUATE: Equations (20.14) and (20.15) show that e and K for a Carnot cycle depend only on T_H and T_C, and we don't need to calculate Q and W. For cycles containing irreversible processes, however, these two equations are not valid, and more detailed calculations are necessary.

The Carnot Cycle and the Second Law

We can prove that **no engine can be more efficient than a Carnot engine operating between the same two temperatures.** The key to the proof is the above observation that since each step in the Carnot cycle is reversible, the *entire cycle* may be reversed. Run backward, the engine becomes a refrigerator. Suppose we have an engine that is more efficient than a Carnot engine (**Fig. 20.15**). Let the Carnot engine, run backward as a refrigerator by negative work $-|W|$, take in heat Q_C from the cold reservoir and expel heat $|Q_H|$ to the hot reservoir. The superefficient engine expels heat $|Q_C|$, but to do this, it takes in a greater amount of heat $Q_H + \Delta$. Its work output is then $W + \Delta$, and the net effect of the two machines together is to take a quantity of heat Δ and convert it completely into work. This violates the "engine" statement of the second law. We could construct a similar argument that a superefficient engine could be used to violate the "refrigerator" statement of the second law. Note that we don't have to assume that the superefficient engine is reversible. In a similar way we can

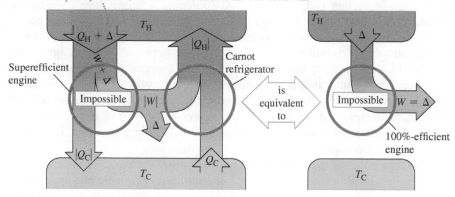

If a superefficient engine were possible, it could be used in conjunction with a Carnot refrigerator to convert the heat Δ completely to work, with no net transfer to the cold reservoir.

20.15 Proving that the Carnot engine has the highest possible efficiency. A "superefficient" engine (more efficient than a Carnot engine) combined with a Carnot refrigerator could convert heat completely into work with no net heat transfer to the cold reservoir. This would violate the second law of thermodynamics.

show that *no refrigerator can have a greater coefficient of performance than a Carnot refrigerator operating between the same two temperatures.*

Thus the statement that no engine can be more efficient than a Carnot engine is yet another equivalent statement of the second law of thermodynamics. It also follows directly that **all Carnot engines operating between the same two temperatures have the same efficiency, irrespective of the nature of the working substance.** Although we derived Eq. (20.14) for a Carnot engine by using an ideal gas as its working substance, it is in fact valid for *any* Carnot engine, no matter what its working substance.

Equation (20.14), the expression for the efficiency of a Carnot engine, sets an upper limit to the efficiency of a real engine such as a steam turbine. To maximize this upper limit and the actual efficiency of the real engine, the designer must make the intake temperature T_H as high as possible and the exhaust temperature T_C as low as possible (**Fig. 20.16**).

The exhaust temperature cannot be lower than the lowest temperature available for cooling the exhaust. For a steam turbine at an electric power plant, T_C may be the temperature of river or lake water; then we want the boiler temperature T_H to be as high as possible. The vapor pressures of all liquids increase rapidly with temperature, so we are limited by the mechanical strength of the boiler. At 500°C the vapor pressure of water is about 240×10^5 Pa (235 atm); this is about the maximum practical pressure in large present-day steam boilers.

20.16 To maximize efficiency, the temperatures inside a jet engine are made as high as possible. Exotic ceramic materials are used that can withstand temperatures in excess of 1000°C without melting or becoming soft.

The Kelvin Temperature Scale

In Chapter 17 we expressed the need for a temperature scale that doesn't depend on the properties of any particular material. We can now use the Carnot cycle to define such a scale. The thermal efficiency of a Carnot engine operating between two heat reservoirs at temperatures T_H and T_C is independent of the nature of the working substance and depends only on the temperatures. From Eq. (20.4), this thermal efficiency is

$$e = \frac{Q_H + Q_C}{Q_H} = 1 + \frac{Q_C}{Q_H}$$

Therefore the ratio Q_C/Q_H is the same for *all* Carnot engines operating between two given temperatures T_H and T_C.

Kelvin proposed that we *define* the ratio of the temperatures, T_C/T_H, to be equal to the magnitude of the ratio Q_C/Q_H of the quantities of heat absorbed and rejected:

$$\frac{T_C}{T_H} = \frac{|Q_C|}{|Q_H|} = -\frac{Q_C}{Q_H} \qquad \text{(definition of Kelvin temperature)} \qquad (20.16)$$

Equation (20.16) looks identical to Eq. (20.13), but there is a subtle and crucial difference. The temperatures in Eq. (20.13) are based on an ideal-gas thermometer, as defined in Section 17.3, while Eq. (20.16) *defines* a temperature scale based on the Carnot cycle and the second law of thermodynamics and is independent of the behavior of any particular substance. Thus the **Kelvin temperature scale** is truly *absolute*. To complete the definition of the Kelvin scale, we assign, as in Section 17.3, the arbitrary value of 273.16 K to the temperature of the triple point of water. When a substance is taken around a Carnot cycle, the ratio of the heats absorbed and rejected, $|Q_H|/|Q_C|$, is equal to the ratio of the temperatures of the reservoirs *as expressed on the gas-thermometer scale* defined in Section 17.3. Since the triple point of water is chosen to be 273.16 K in both scales, it follows that *the Kelvin and ideal-gas scales are identical.*

The zero point on the Kelvin scale is called **absolute zero.** At absolute zero a system has its *minimum* possible total internal energy (kinetic plus potential). Because of quantum effects, however, it is *not* true that at $T = 0$, all molecular motion ceases. There are theoretical reasons for believing that absolute zero cannot be attained experimentally, although temperatures below 10^{-7} K have been achieved. The more closely we approach absolute zero, the more difficult it is to get closer. One statement of the *third law of thermodynamics* is that it is impossible to reach absolute zero in a finite number of thermodynamic steps.

TEST YOUR UNDERSTANDING OF SECTION 20.6 An inventor looking for financial support comes to you with an idea for a gasoline engine that runs on a novel type of thermodynamic cycle. His design is made entirely of copper and is air-cooled. He claims that the engine will be 85% efficient. Should you invest in this marvelous new engine? (*Hint:* See Table 17.4.) ▮

20.7 ENTROPY

The second law of thermodynamics, as we have stated it, is not an equation or a quantitative relationship but rather a statement of *impossibility*. However, the second law *can* be stated as a quantitative relationship with the concept of *entropy,* the subject of this section.

We have talked about several processes that proceed naturally in the direction of increasing randomness. Irreversible heat flow increases randomness: The molecules are initially sorted into hotter and cooler regions, but this sorting is lost when the system comes to thermal equilibrium. Adding heat to a body also increases average molecular speeds; therefore, molecular motion becomes more random. In the free expansion of a gas, the molecules have greater randomness of position after the expansion than before. **Figure 20.17** shows another process in which randomness increases.

20.17 When firecrackers explode, randomness increases: The neatly packaged chemicals within each firecracker are dispersed in all directions, and the stored chemical energy is converted to random kinetic energy of the fragments.

Entropy and Randomness

Entropy provides a *quantitative* measure of randomness. To introduce this concept, let's consider an infinitesimal isothermal expansion of an ideal gas. We add heat dQ and let the gas expand just enough to keep the temperature constant. Because the internal energy of an ideal gas depends on only its temperature, the internal energy is also constant; thus from the first law, the work dW done by the gas is equal to the heat dQ added. That is,

$$dQ = dW = p\,dV = \frac{nRT}{V}dV \quad \text{so} \quad \frac{dV}{V} = \frac{dQ}{nRT}$$

The gas is more disordered after the expansion than before: The molecules are moving in a larger volume and have more randomness of position. Thus the fractional volume change dV/V is a measure of the increase in randomness, and the above equation shows that it is proportional to the quantity dQ/T. We introduce the symbol S for the entropy of the system, and we define the infinitesimal entropy change dS during an infinitesimal reversible process at absolute temperature T as

$$dS = \frac{dQ}{T} \quad \text{(infinitesimal reversible process)} \qquad (20.17)$$

If a total amount of heat Q is added during a reversible isothermal process at absolute temperature T, the total entropy change $\Delta S = S_2 - S_1$ is given by

$$\Delta S = S_2 - S_1 = \frac{Q}{T} \quad \text{(reversible isothermal process)} \qquad (20.18)$$

Entropy has units of energy divided by temperature; the SI unit of entropy is 1 J/K.

We can see how the quotient Q/T is related to the increase in randomness. Higher temperature means greater randomness of motion. If the substance is initially cold, with little molecular motion, adding heat Q causes a substantial fractional increase in molecular motion and randomness. But if the substance is already hot, the same quantity of heat adds relatively little to the greater molecular motion already present. So Q/T is an appropriate characterization of the increase in randomness when heat flows into a system.

EXAMPLE 20.5   ENTROPY CHANGE IN MELTING

What is the change of entropy of 1 kg of ice that is melted reversibly at 0°C and converted to water at 0°C? The heat of fusion of water is $L_f = 3.34 \times 10^5$ J/kg.

SOLUTION

IDENTIFY and SET UP: The melting occurs at a constant temperature $T = 0°C = 273$ K, so this is an *isothermal* reversible process. We can calculate the added heat Q required to melt the ice, then calculate the entropy change ΔS from Eq. (20.18).

EXECUTE: The heat needed to melt the ice is $Q = mL_f = 3.34 \times 10^5$ J. Then from Eq. (20.18),

$$\Delta S = S_2 - S_1 = \frac{Q}{T} = \frac{3.34 \times 10^5 \text{ J}}{273 \text{ K}} = 1.22 \times 10^3 \text{ J/K}$$

EVALUATE: This entropy increase corresponds to the increase in disorder when the water molecules go from the state of a crystalline solid to the much more randomly arranged state of a liquid. In *any* isothermal reversible process, the entropy change equals the heat transferred divided by the absolute temperature. When we refreeze the water, Q has the opposite sign, and the entropy change is $\Delta S = -1.22 \times 10^3$ J/K. The water molecules rearrange themselves into a crystal to form ice, so both randomness and entropy decrease.

Entropy in Reversible Processes

We can generalize the definition of entropy change to include *any* reversible process leading from one state to another, whether it is isothermal or not. We represent the process as a series of infinitesimal reversible steps. During a typical step, an infinitesimal quantity of heat dQ is added to the system at absolute temperature T. Then we sum (integrate) the quotients dQ/T for the entire process; that is,

Entropy change in a reversible process $\cdots\!\!\rightarrow \Delta S = \int_1^2 \dfrac{dQ}{T}$

Upper limit = final state
Infinitesimal heat flow into system
Lower limit = initial state   Absolute temperature

(20.19)

Because entropy is a measure of the randomness of a system in any specific state, it must depend only on the current state of the system, not on its past history. (We will verify this later.) When a system proceeds from an initial state with entropy S_1 to a final state with entropy S_2, the change in entropy $\Delta S = S_2 - S_1$ defined by Eq. (20.19) does not depend on the path leading from the initial to the final state but is the same for *all possible* processes leading from state 1 to state 2. Thus the entropy of a system must also have a definite value for any given state of the system. *Internal energy,* introduced in Chapter 19, also has this property, although entropy and internal energy are very different quantities.

Since entropy is a function only of the state of a system, we can also compute entropy changes in *irreversible* (nonequilibrium) processes for which Eqs. (20.17) and (20.19) are not applicable. We simply invent a path connecting the given initial and final states that *does* consist entirely of reversible equilibrium processes and compute the total entropy change for that path. It is not the actual path, but the entropy change must be the same as for the actual path.

As with internal energy, the above discussion does not tell us how to calculate entropy itself, but only the change in entropy in any given process. Just as with internal energy, we may arbitrarily assign a value to the entropy of a system in a specified reference state and then calculate the entropy of any other state with reference to this.

EXAMPLE 20.6   ENTROPY CHANGE IN A TEMPERATURE CHANGE

One kilogram of water at 0°C is heated to 100°C. Compute its change in entropy. Assume that the specific heat of water is constant at 4190 J/kg·K over this temperature range.

SOLUTION

IDENTIFY and SET UP: The entropy change of the water depends only on the initial and final states of the system, no matter whether the process is reversible or irreversible. We can imagine a reversible process in which the water temperature is increased in a sequence of infinitesimal steps dT. We can use Eq. (20.19) to integrate over all these steps and calculate the entropy change for such a reversible process. (Heating the water on a stove whose cooking surface is maintained at 100°C would be an irreversible process. The entropy change would be the same, however.)

EXECUTE: From Eq. (17.14) the heat required to carry out each infinitesimal step is $dQ = mc\,dT$. Substituting this into Eq. (20.19) and integrating, we find

$$\Delta S = S_2 - S_1 = \int_1^2 \frac{dQ}{T} = \int_{T_1}^{T_2} mc\frac{dT}{T} = mc\ln\frac{T_2}{T_1}$$

$$= (1.00\text{ kg})(4190\text{ J/kg·K})\left(\ln\frac{373\text{ K}}{273\text{ K}}\right) = 1.31 \times 10^3\text{ J/K}$$

EVALUATE: The entropy change is positive, as it must be for a process in which the system absorbs heat. Our assumption about the specific heat is a pretty good one, since c for water varies by less than 1% between 0°C and 100°C (see Fig. 17.17).

CAUTION **When $\Delta S = Q/T$ can (and cannot) be used** In solving this problem you might be tempted to avoid doing an integral by using the simpler expression in Eq. (20.18), $\Delta S = Q/T$. This would be incorrect, however, because Eq. (20.18) is applicable only to *isothermal* processes, and the initial and final temperatures in our example are *not* the same. The *only* correct way to find the entropy change in a process with different initial and final temperatures is to use Eq. (20.19). ∎

CONCEPTUAL EXAMPLE 20.7 | ENTROPY CHANGE IN A REVERSIBLE ADIABATIC PROCESS

A gas expands adiabatically and reversibly. What is its change in entropy?

SOLUTION

In an adiabatic process, no heat enters or leaves the system. Hence $dQ = 0$ and there is *no* change in entropy in this reversible process:

$\Delta S = 0$. Every *reversible* adiabatic process is a constant-entropy process. (That's why such processes are also called *isentropic* processes.) The increase in randomness resulting from the gas occupying a greater volume is exactly balanced by the decrease in randomness associated with the lowered temperature and reduced molecular speeds.

EXAMPLE 20.8 | ENTROPY CHANGE IN A FREE EXPANSION

A partition divides a thermally insulated box into two compartments, each of volume V (**Fig. 20.18**). Initially, one compartment contains n moles of an ideal gas at temperature T, and the other compartment is evacuated. We break the partition and the gas expands, filling both compartments. What is the entropy change in this free-expansion process?

SOLUTION

IDENTIFY and SET UP: For this process, $Q = 0$, $W = 0$, $\Delta U = 0$, and therefore (because the system is an ideal gas) $\Delta T = 0$. We might think that the entropy change is zero because there is no heat exchange. But Eq. (20.19) can be used to calculate entropy changes for *reversible* processes only; this free expansion is *not*

reversible, and there *is* an entropy change. As we mentioned at the beginning of this section, entropy increases in a free expansion because the positions of the molecules are more random than before the expansion. To calculate ΔS, we recall that the entropy change depends only on the initial and final states. We can devise a *reversible* process having the same endpoints as this free expansion, and in general we can then use Eq. (20.19) to calculate its entropy change, which will be the same as for the free expansion. An appropriate reversible process is an *isothermal* expansion from V to $2V$ at temperature T, which allows us to use the simpler Eq. (20.18) to calculate ΔS. The gas does work W during this expansion, so an equal amount of heat Q must be supplied to keep the internal energy constant.

EXECUTE: We saw in Example 19.1 that the work done by n moles of ideal gas in an isothermal expansion from V_1 to V_2 is $W = nRT \ln(V_2/V_1)$. With $V_1 = V$ and $V_2 = 2V$, we have

$$Q = W = nRT \ln\frac{2V}{V} = nRT \ln 2$$

From Eq. (20.18), the entropy change is

$$\Delta S = \frac{Q}{T} = nR \ln 2$$

20.18 (a, b) Free expansion of an insulated ideal gas. (c) The free-expansion process doesn't pass through equilibrium states from a to b. However, the entropy change $S_b - S_a$ can be calculated by using the isothermal path shown or *any* reversible path from a to b.

(a)   (b)   (c)

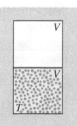 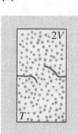 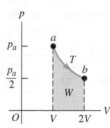

EVALUATE: For 1 mole, $\Delta S = (1 \text{ mol})(8.314 \text{ J/mol·K})(\ln 2) = 5.76 \text{ J/K}$. The entropy change is positive, as we predicted. The factor $(\ln 2)$ in our answer is a result of the volume having increased by a factor of 2, from V to $2V$. Can you show that if the volume increases in a free expansion from V to xV, where x is an arbitrary number, the entropy change is $\Delta S = nR \ln x$?

EXAMPLE 20.9 | ENTROPY AND THE CARNOT CYCLE

For the Carnot engine in Example 20.2 (Section 20.6), what is the total entropy change during one cycle?

SOLUTION

IDENTIFY and SET UP: All four steps in the Carnot cycle (see Fig. 20.13) are reversible, so we can use our expressions for the entropy change ΔS in a reversible process. We find ΔS for each step and add them to get ΔS for the complete cycle.

EXECUTE: There is no entropy change during the adiabatic expansion $b \to c$ or the adiabatic compression $d \to a$. During the isothermal expansion $a \to b$ at $T_H = 500$ K, the engine takes in 2000 J of heat, and from Eq. (20.18),

$$\Delta S_H = \frac{Q_H}{T_H} = \frac{2000 \text{ J}}{500 \text{ K}} = 4.0 \text{ J/K}$$

Continued

During the isothermal compression $c \rightarrow d$ at $T_C = 350$ K, the engine gives off 1400 J of heat, and

$$\Delta S_C = \frac{Q_C}{T_C} = \frac{-1400 \text{ J}}{350 \text{ K}} = -4.0 \text{ J/K}$$

The total entropy change in the engine during one cycle is $\Delta S_{tot} = \Delta S_H + \Delta S_C = 4.0 \text{ J/K} + (-4.0 \text{ J/K}) = 0$.

EVALUATE: The result $\Delta S_{total} = 0$ tells us that when the Carnot engine completes a cycle, it has the same entropy as it did at the beginning of the cycle. We'll explore this result in the next subsection.

What is the total entropy change of the engine's *environment* during this cycle? During the reversible isothermal expansion $a \rightarrow b$, the hot (500 K) reservoir gives off 2000 J of heat, so its entropy change is $(-2000 \text{ J})/(500 \text{ K}) = -4.0 \text{ J/K}$. During the reversible isothermal compression $c \rightarrow d$, the cold (350 K) reservoir absorbs 1400 J of heat, so its entropy change is $(+1400 \text{ J})/(350 \text{ K}) = +4.0 \text{ J/K}$. Thus the hot and cold reservoirs each have an entropy change, but the sum of these changes—that is, the total entropy change of the system's environment—is zero.

These results apply to the special case of the Carnot cycle, for which *all* of the processes are reversible. In this case the total entropy change of the system and the environment together is zero. We will see that if the cycle includes irreversible processes (as is the case for the Otto and Diesel cycles of Section 20.3), the total entropy change of the system and the environment *cannot* be zero, but rather must be positive.

Entropy in Cyclic Processes

Example 20.9 showed that the total entropy change for a cycle of a particular Carnot engine, which uses an ideal gas as its working substance, is zero. This result follows directly from Eq. (20.13), which we can rewrite as

$$\frac{Q_H}{T_H} + \frac{Q_C}{T_C} = 0 \qquad (20.20)$$

The quotient Q_H/T_H equals ΔS_H, the entropy change of the engine that occurs at $T = T_H$. Likewise, Q_C/T_C equals ΔS_C, the (negative) entropy change of the engine that occurs at $T = T_C$. Hence Eq. (20.20) says that $\Delta S_H + \Delta S_C = 0$; that is, there is zero net entropy change in one cycle.

What about Carnot engines that use a different working substance? According to the second law, *any* Carnot engine operating between given temperatures T_H and T_C has the same efficiency $e = 1 - T_C/T_H$ [Eq. (20.14)]. Combining this expression for e with Eq. (20.4), $e = 1 + Q_C/Q_H$, just reproduces Eq. (20.20). So Eq. (20.20) is valid for any Carnot engine working between these temperatures, whether its working substance is an ideal gas or not. We conclude that *the total entropy change in one cycle of any Carnot engine is zero.*

This result can be generalized to show that the total entropy change during *any* reversible cyclic process is zero. A reversible cyclic process appears on a pV-diagram as a closed path (**Fig. 20.19a**). We can approximate such a path as closely as we like by a sequence of isothermal and adiabatic processes forming parts of many long, thin Carnot cycles (Fig. 20.19b). The total entropy change

20.19 (a) A reversible cyclic process for an ideal gas is shown as a red closed path on a pV-diagram. Several ideal-gas isotherms are shown in blue. (b) We can approximate the path in (a) by a series of long, thin Carnot cycles; one of these is highlighted in gold. The total entropy change is zero for each Carnot cycle and for the actual cyclic process. (c) The entropy change between points a and b is independent of the path.

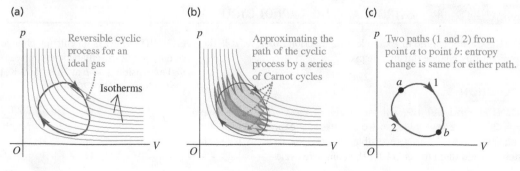

(a) Reversible cyclic process for an ideal gas

Isotherms

(b) Approximating the path of the cyclic process by a series of Carnot cycles

(c) Two paths (1 and 2) from point a to point b: entropy change is same for either path.

for the full cycle is the sum of the entropy changes for each small Carnot cycle, each of which is zero. So **the total entropy change during** *any* **reversible cycle is zero:**

$$\int \frac{dQ}{T} = 0 \qquad \text{(reversible cyclic process)} \qquad (20.21)$$

It follows that when a system undergoes a reversible process leading from any state *a* to any other state *b*, *the entropy change of the system is independent of the path* (Fig. 20.19c). If the entropy change for path 1 were different from the change for path 2, the system could be taken along path 1 and then backward along path 2 to the starting point, with a nonzero net change in entropy. This would violate the conclusion that the total entropy change in such a cyclic process must be zero. Because the entropy change in such processes is independent of path, we conclude that in any given state, the system has a definite value of entropy that depends only on the state, not on the processes that led to that state.

Entropy in Irreversible Processes

In an idealized, reversible process involving only equilibrium states, the total entropy change of the system and its surroundings is zero. But all *irreversible* processes involve an increase in entropy. Unlike energy, *entropy is not a conserved quantity*. The entropy of an isolated system *can* change, but as we shall see, it can never decrease. The free expansion of a gas (Example 20.8) is an irreversible process in an isolated system in which there is an entropy increase.

BIO **Application Entropy Changes in a Living Organism** When a puppy or other growing animal eats, it takes organized chemical energy from the food and uses it to make new cells that are even more highly organized. This process alone lowers entropy. But most of the energy in the food is either excreted in the animal's feces or used to generate heat, processes that lead to a large increase in entropy. So while the entropy of the animal alone decreases, the *total* entropy of animal plus food *increases*.

EXAMPLE 20.10   **ENTROPY CHANGE IN AN IRREVERSIBLE PROCESS**

Suppose 1.00 kg of water at 100°C is placed in thermal contact with 1.00 kg of water at 0°C. What is the total change in entropy? Assume that the specific heat of water is constant at 4190 J/kg · K over this temperature range.

SOLUTION

IDENTIFY and SET UP: This process involves irreversible heat flow because of the temperature differences. There are equal masses of 0°C water and 100°C water, so the final temperature is the average of these two temperatures: 50°C = 323 K. Although the processes are irreversible, we can calculate the entropy changes for the (initially) hot water and the (initially) cold water by assuming that the process occurs reversibly. As in Example 20.6, we must use Eq. (20.19) to calculate ΔS for each substance because the temperatures are not constant.

EXECUTE: The entropy changes of the hot water (subscript H) and the cold water (subscript C) are

$$\Delta S_{\text{H}} = mc \int_{T_1}^{T_2} \frac{dT}{T} = (1.00 \text{ kg})(4190 \text{ J/kg} \cdot \text{K}) \int_{373 \text{ K}}^{323 \text{ K}} \frac{dT}{T}$$

$$= (4190 \text{ J/K})\left(\ln \frac{323 \text{ K}}{373 \text{ K}} \right) = -603 \text{ J/K}$$

$$\Delta S_{\text{C}} = (4190 \text{ J/K})\left(\ln \frac{323 \text{ K}}{273 \text{ K}} \right) = +705 \text{ J/K}$$

The *total* entropy change of the system is

$$\Delta S_{\text{tot}} = \Delta S_{\text{H}} + \Delta S_{\text{C}} = (-603 \text{ J/K}) + 705 \text{ J/K} = +102 \text{ J/K}$$

EVALUATE: An irreversible heat flow in an isolated system is accompanied by an increase in entropy. We could reach the same end state by mixing the hot and cold water, which is also an irreversible process; the total entropy change, which depends only on the initial and final states of the system, would again be 102 J/K.

Note that the entropy of the system increases *continuously* as the two quantities of water come to equilibrium. For example, the first 4190 J of heat transferred cools the hot water to 99°C and warms the cold water to 1°C. The net change in entropy for this step is approximately

$$\Delta S = \frac{-4190 \text{ J}}{373 \text{ K}} + \frac{4190 \text{ J}}{273 \text{ K}} = +4.1 \text{ J/K}$$

Can you show in a similar way that the net entropy change is positive for *any* one-degree temperature change leading to the equilibrium condition?

SOLUTION

20.20 The mixing of colored ink and water starts from a state of low entropy in which each fluid is separate and distinct from the other. In the final state, both the ink and water molecules are spread randomly throughout the volume of liquid, so the entropy is greater. Spontaneous unmixing of the ink and water, a process in which there would be a net decrease in entropy, is never observed.

DATA *SPEAKS*

Entropy and the Second Law

The results of Example 20.10 about the flow of heat from a higher to a lower temperature are characteristic of *all* natural (that is, irreversible) processes. When we include the entropy changes of all the systems taking part in the process, the increases in entropy are always greater than the decreases. In the special case of a *reversible* process, the increases and decreases are equal. Hence we can state the general principle: **When all systems taking part in a process are included, the entropy either remains constant or increases.** In other words: **No process is possible in which the total entropy decreases, when all systems taking part in the process are included.** This is an alternative statement of the second law of thermodynamics in terms of entropy. Thus it is equivalent to the "engine" and "refrigerator" statements discussed earlier. **Figure 20.20** shows a specific example of this general principle.

The increase of entropy in every natural, irreversible process measures the increase of randomness in the universe associated with that process. Consider again the example of mixing hot and cold water (Example 20.10). We *might* have used the hot and cold water as the high- and low-temperature reservoirs of a heat engine. While removing heat from the hot water and giving heat to the cold water, we could have obtained some mechanical work. But once the hot and cold water have been mixed and have come to a uniform temperature, this opportunity to convert heat to mechanical work is lost irretrievably. The lukewarm water will never *unmix* itself and separate into hotter and colder portions. No decrease in *energy* occurs when the hot and cold water are mixed. What has been lost is the *opportunity* to convert part of the heat from the hot water into mechanical work. Hence when entropy increases, energy becomes less *available*, and the universe becomes more random or "run down."

TEST YOUR UNDERSTANDING OF SECTION 20.7 Suppose 2.00 kg of water at 50°C spontaneously changes temperature, so that half of the water cools to 0°C while the other half spontaneously warms to 100°C. (All of the water remains liquid, so it doesn't freeze or boil.) What would be the entropy change of the water? Is this process possible? (*Hint:* See Example 20.10.) ∎

20.8 MICROSCOPIC INTERPRETATION OF ENTROPY

We described in Section 19.4 how the internal energy of a system could be calculated, at least in principle, by adding up all the kinetic energies of its constituent particles and all the potential energies of interaction among the particles. This is called a *microscopic* calculation of the internal energy. We can also make a microscopic calculation of the entropy S of a system. Unlike energy, however, entropy is not something that belongs to each individual particle or pair of particles in the system. Rather, entropy is a measure of the randomness of the system as a whole. To see how to calculate entropy microscopically, we first have to introduce the idea of *macroscopic* and *microscopic states*.

Suppose you toss N identical coins on the floor, and half of them show heads and half show tails. This is a description of the large-scale or **macroscopic state** of the system of N coins. A description of the **microscopic state** of the system includes information about each individual coin: Coin 1 was heads, coin 2 was tails, coin 3 was tails, and so on. There can be many microscopic states that correspond to the same macroscopic description. For instance, with $N = 4$ coins there are six possible states in which half are heads and half are tails (**Fig. 20.21**). The number of microscopic states grows rapidly with increasing N; for $N = 100$ there are $2^{100} = 1.27 \times 10^{30}$ microscopic states, of which 1.01×10^{29} are half heads and half tails.

The least probable outcomes of the coin toss are the states that are either all heads or all tails. It is certainly possible that you could throw 100 heads in a row, but don't bet on it; the probability of doing this is only 1 in 1.27×10^{30}. The most probable outcome of tossing N coins is that half are heads and half are tails. The reason is that this *macroscopic* state has the greatest number of corresponding *microscopic* states, as Fig. 20.21 shows.

To make the connection to the concept of entropy, note that the macroscopic description "all heads" completely specifies the state of each one of the N coins. The same is true if the coins are all tails. But the macroscopic description "half heads, half tails" by itself tells you very little about the state (heads or tails) of each individual coin. Compared to the state "all heads" or "all tails," the state "half heads, half tails" has much greater *randomness* because the system could be in any of a much greater number of possible microscopic states. Hence the "half heads, half tails" state has much greater entropy (which is a quantitative measure of randomness).

Now instead of N coins, consider a mole of an ideal gas containing Avogadro's number of molecules. The macroscopic state of this gas is given by its pressure p, volume V, and temperature T; a description of the microscopic state involves stating the position and velocity for each molecule in the gas. At a given pressure, volume, and temperature, the gas may be in any one of an astronomically large number of microscopic states, depending on the positions and velocities of its 6.02×10^{23} molecules. If the gas undergoes a free expansion into a greater volume, the range of possible positions increases, as does the number of possible microscopic states. The system becomes more random, and the entropy increases as calculated in Example 20.8 (Section 20.7).

We can draw the following general conclusion: **For any thermodynamic system, the most probable macroscopic state is the one with the greatest number of corresponding microscopic states, which is also the macroscopic state with the greatest randomness and the greatest entropy.**

Calculating Entropy: Microscopic States

Let w represent the number of possible microscopic states for a given macroscopic state. (For the four coins shown in Fig. 20.21 the state of four heads has $w = 1$, the state of three heads and one tails has $w = 4$, and so on.) Then the entropy S of a macroscopic state can be shown to be given by

Expression for entropy in microscopic terms
$$S = k \ln w$$
Boltzmann constant (gas constant per molecule) — Number of microscopic states for the given macroscopic state (20.22)

(We introduced the Boltzmann constant in Section 18.3.) As Eq. (20.22) shows, increasing the number of possible microscopic states w increases the entropy S.

20.21 All possible microscopic states of four coins. There can be several possible microscopic states for each macroscopic state.

Macroscopic state	Corresponding microscopic states
Four heads	
Three heads, one tails	
Two heads, two tails	
One heads, three tails	
Four tails	

What matters in a thermodynamic process is not the absolute entropy S but the *difference* in entropy between the initial and final states. Hence an equally valid and useful definition would be $S = k \ln w + C$, where C is a constant, since C cancels in any calculation of an entropy difference between two states. But it's convenient to set this constant equal to zero and use Eq. (20.22). With this choice, since the smallest possible value of w is unity, the smallest possible value of S for any system is $k \ln 1 = 0$. Entropy can *never* be negative.

In practice, calculating w is a difficult task, so Eq. (20.22) is typically used only to calculate the absolute entropy S of certain special systems. But we can use this relationship to calculate *differences* in entropy between one state and another. Consider a system that undergoes a thermodynamic process that takes it from macroscopic state 1, for which there are w_1 possible microscopic states, to macroscopic state 2, with w_2 associated microscopic states. The change in entropy in this process is

$$\Delta S = S_2 - S_1 = k \ln w_2 - k \ln w_1 = k \ln \frac{w_2}{w_1} \qquad (20.23)$$

The *difference* in entropy between the two macroscopic states depends on the *ratio* of the numbers of possible microscopic states.

As the following example shows, using Eq. (20.23) to calculate a change in entropy from one macroscopic state to another gives the same results as considering a reversible process connecting those two states and using Eq. (20.19).

EXAMPLE 20.11   A MICROSCOPIC CALCULATION OF ENTROPY CHANGE

Use Eq. (20.23) to calculate the entropy change in the free expansion of n moles of gas at temperature T described in Example 20.8 (**Fig. 20.22**).

SOLUTION

IDENTIFY and SET UP: We are asked to calculate the entropy change by using the number of microscopic states in the initial and final macroscopic states (Figs. 20.22a and b). When the partition is broken, no work is done, so the velocities of the molecules are unaffected. But each molecule now has twice as much volume in which it can move and hence has twice the number of possible positions. This is all we need to calculate the entropy change using Eq. (20.23).

EXECUTE: Let w_1 be the number of microscopic states of the system as a whole when the gas occupies volume V (Fig. 20.22a). The number of molecules is $N = nN_A$, and each of these N molecules has twice as many possible states after the partition is broken. Hence the number w_2 of microscopic states when the gas occupies volume $2V$ (Fig. 20.22b) is greater by a factor of 2^N; that is, $w_2 = 2^N w_1$. The change in entropy in this process is

$$\Delta S = k \ln \frac{w_2}{w_1} = k \ln \frac{2^N w_1}{w_1}$$
$$= k \ln 2^N = Nk \ln 2$$

Since $N = nN_A$ and $k = R/N_A$, this becomes

$$\Delta S = (nN_A)(R/N_A) \ln 2$$
$$= nR \ln 2$$

EVALUATE: We found the same result as in Example 20.8, but without any reference to the thermodynamic path taken.

20.22 In a free expansion of N molecules in which the volume doubles, the number of possible microscopic states increases by a factor of 2^N.

(a) Gas occupies volume V; number of microscopic states $= w_1$.

(b) Gas occupies volume $2V$; number of microscopic states $= w_2 = 2^N w_1$.

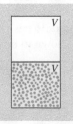
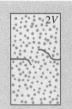

Microscopic States and the Second Law

The relationship between entropy and the number of microscopic states gives us new insight into the entropy statement of the second law of thermodynamics: that the entropy of a closed system can never decrease. From Eq. (20.22) this means that a closed system can never spontaneously undergo a process that decreases the number of possible microscopic states.

An example of such a forbidden process would be if all of the air in your room spontaneously moved to one half of the room, leaving a vacuum in the other half. Such a "free compression" would be the reverse of the free expansion of Examples 20.8 and 20.11. This would decrease the number of possible microscopic states by a factor of 2^N. Strictly speaking, this process is not impossible! The probability of finding a given molecule in one half of the room is $\frac{1}{2}$, so the probability of finding all of the molecules in one half of the room at once is $\left(\frac{1}{2}\right)^N$. (This is exactly the same as the probability of having a tossed coin come up heads N times in a row.) This probability is *not* zero. But lest you worry about suddenly finding yourself gasping for breath in the evacuated half of your room, consider that a typical room might hold 1000 moles of air, and so $N = 1000N_A = 6.02 \times 10^{26}$ molecules. The probability of all the molecules being in the same half of the room is therefore $\left(\frac{1}{2}\right)^{6.02\times10^{26}}$. Expressed as a decimal, this number has more than 10^{26} zeros to the right of the decimal point!

Because the probability of such a "free compression" taking place is so vanishingly small, it has almost certainly never occurred anywhere in the universe since the beginning of time. We conclude that for all practical purposes the second law of thermodynamics is never violated.

TEST YOUR UNDERSTANDING OF SECTION 20.8 A quantity of N molecules of an ideal gas initially occupies volume V. The gas then expands to volume $2V$. The number of microscopic states of the gas increases in this expansion. Under which of the following circumstances will this number increase the most? (i) If the expansion is reversible and isothermal; (ii) if the expansion is reversible and adiabatic; (iii) the number will change by the same amount for both circumstances. ∎

A polyethylene molecule ... ... is a chain of C_2H_4 monomers. Hydrogen atom. Carbon atom.

Straight polymer chains

Coiled polymer chains

Reversible and irreversible processes: A reversible process is one whose direction can be reversed by an infinitesimal change in the conditions of the process, and in which the system is always in or very close to thermal equilibrium. All other thermodynamic processes are irreversible.

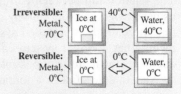
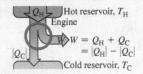

Heat engines: A heat engine takes heat Q_H from a source, converts part of it to work W, and discards the remainder $|Q_C|$ at a lower temperature. The thermal efficiency e of a heat engine measures how much of the absorbed heat is converted to work. (See Example 20.1.)

$$e = \frac{W}{Q_H} = 1 + \frac{Q_C}{Q_H} = 1 - \left| \frac{Q_C}{Q_H} \right| \quad (20.4)$$

The Otto cycle: A gasoline engine operating on the Otto cycle has a theoretical maximum thermal efficiency e that depends on the compression ratio r and the ratio of heat capacities γ of the working substance.

$$e = 1 - \frac{1}{r^{\gamma-1}} \quad (20.6)$$

Refrigerators: A refrigerator takes heat Q_C from a colder place, has a work input $|W|$, and discards heat $|Q_H|$ at a warmer place. The effectiveness of the refrigerator is given by its coefficient of performance K.

$$K = \frac{|Q_C|}{|W|} = \frac{|Q_C|}{|Q_H| - |Q_C|} \quad (20.9)$$

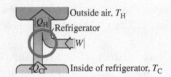

The second law of thermodynamics: The second law of thermodynamics describes the directionality of natural thermodynamic processes. It can be stated in several equivalent forms. The *engine* statement is that no cyclic process can convert heat completely into work. The *refrigerator* statement is that no cyclic process can transfer heat from a colder place to a hotter place with no input of mechanical work.

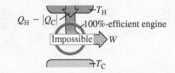

The Carnot cycle: The Carnot cycle operates between two heat reservoirs at temperatures T_H and T_C and uses only reversible processes. Its thermal efficiency depends only on T_H and T_C. An additional equivalent statement of the second law is that no engine operating between the same two temperatures can be more efficient than a Carnot engine. (See Examples 20.2 and 20.3.)

A Carnot engine run backward is a Carnot refrigerator. Its coefficient of performance depends on only T_H and T_C. Another form of the second law states that no refrigerator operating between the same two temperatures can have a larger coefficient of performance than a Carnot refrigerator. (See Example 20.4.)

$$e_{Carnot} = 1 - \frac{T_C}{T_H} = \frac{T_H - T_C}{T_H} \quad (20.14)$$

$$K_{Carnot} = \frac{T_C}{T_H - T_C} \quad (20.15)$$

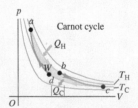

Entropy: Entropy is a quantitative measure of the randomness of a system. The entropy change in any reversible process depends on the amount of heat flow and the absolute temperature T. Entropy depends only on the state of the system, and the change in entropy between given initial and final states is the same for all processes leading from one state to the other. This fact can be used to find the entropy change in an irreversible process. (See Examples 20.5–20.10.)

$$\Delta S = \int_1^2 \frac{dQ}{T}$$
(reversible process)

$$(20.19)$$

An important statement of the second law of thermodynamics is that the entropy of an isolated system may increase but can never decrease. When a system interacts with its surroundings, the total entropy change of system and surroundings can never decrease. When the interaction involves only reversible processes, the total entropy is constant and $\Delta S = 0$; when there is any irreversible process, the total entropy increases and $\Delta S > 0$.

Entropy and microscopic states: When a system is in a particular macroscopic state, the particles that make up the system may be in any of w possible microscopic states. The greater the number w, the greater the entropy. (See Example 20.11.)

$$S = k \ln w$$

$$(20.22)$$

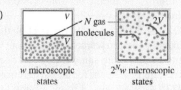

w microscopic states

$2^N w$ microscopic states

BRIDGING PROBLEM ENTROPY CHANGES: COLD ICE IN HOT WATER

An insulated container of negligible mass holds 0.600 kg of water at 45.0°C. You put a 0.0500-kg ice cube at −15.0°C in the water (**Fig. 20.23**). (a) Calculate the final temperature of the water once the ice has melted. (b) Calculate the change in entropy of the system.

SOLUTION GUIDE

IDENTIFY and SET UP

1. Make a list of the known and unknown quantities, and identify the target variables.
2. How will you find the final temperature of the ice–water mixture? How will you decide whether or not all the ice melts?
3. Once you find the final temperature of the mixture, how will you determine the changes in entropy of (i) the ice initially at −15.0°C and (ii) the water initially at 45.0°C?

EXECUTE

4. Use the methods of Chapter 17 to calculate the final temperature T. (*Hint:* First assume that all of the ice melts, then write an equation which says that the heat that flows into the ice equals the heat that flows out of the water. If your assumption is correct, the final temperature that you calculate will be greater than 0°C. If your assumption is incorrect, the final temperature will be 0°C or less, which means that some ice remains. You'll then need to redo the calculation to account for this.)

5. Use your result from step 4 to calculate the entropy changes of the ice and the water. (*Hint:* You must include the heat flow associated with temperature changes, as in Example 20.6, as well as the heat flow associated with the change of phase.)
6. Find the total change in entropy of the system.

EVALUATE

7. Do the signs of the entropy changes make sense? Why or why not?

20.23 What becomes of this ice–water mixture?

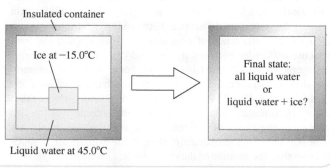

Insulated container

Ice at −15.0°C

Final state: all liquid water or liquid water + ice?

Liquid water at 45.0°C

Problems

•, ••, •••: Difficulty levels. **CP:** Cumulative problems incorporating material from earlier chapters. **CALC:** Problems requiring calculus. **DATA:** Problems involving real data, scientific evidence, experimental design, and/or statistical reasoning. **BIO:** Biosciences problems.

DISCUSSION QUESTIONS

Q20.1 A pot is half-filled with water, and a lid is placed on it, forming a tight seal so that no water vapor can escape. The pot is heated on a stove, forming water vapor inside the pot. The heat is then turned off and the water vapor condenses back to liquid. Is this cycle reversible or irreversible? Why?

Q20.2 Give two examples of reversible processes and two examples of irreversible processes in purely mechanical systems, such as blocks sliding on planes, springs, pulleys, and strings. Explain what makes each process reversible or irreversible.

Q20.3 Household refrigerators have arrays or coils of tubing on the outside, usually at the back or bottom. When the refrigerator is running, the tubing becomes quite hot. Where does the heat come from?

Q20.4 Suppose you try to cool the kitchen of your house by leaving the refrigerator door open. What happens? Why? Would the result be the same if you left open a picnic cooler full of ice? Explain the reason for any differences.

Q20.5 Why must a room air conditioner be placed in a window rather than just set on the floor and plugged in? Why can a refrigerator be set on the floor and plugged in?

Q20.6 Is it a violation of the second law of thermodynamics to convert mechanical energy completely into heat? To convert heat completely into work? Explain your answers.

Q20.7 Imagine a special air filter placed in a window of a house. The tiny holes in the filter allow only air molecules moving faster than a certain speed to exit the house, and allow only air molecules moving slower than that speed to enter the house from outside. Explain why such an air filter would cool the house, and why the second law of thermodynamics makes building such a filter an impossible task.

Q20.8 An electric motor has its shaft coupled to that of an electric generator. The motor drives the generator, and some current from the generator is used to run the motor. The excess current is used to light a home. What is wrong with this scheme?

Q20.9 When a wet cloth is hung up in a hot wind in the desert, it is cooled by evaporation to a temperature that may be 20 C° or so below that of the air. Discuss this process in light of the second law of thermodynamics.

Q20.10 Compare the pV-diagram for the Otto cycle in Fig. 20.6 with the diagram for the Carnot heat engine in Fig. 20.13. Explain some of the important differences between the two cycles.

Q20.11 The efficiency of heat engines is high when the temperature difference between the hot and cold reservoirs is large. Refrigerators, on the other hand, work better when the temperature difference is small. Thinking of the mechanical refrigeration cycle shown in Fig. 20.9, explain in physical terms why it takes less work to remove heat from the working substance if the two reservoirs (the inside of the refrigerator and the outside air) are at nearly the same temperature, than if the outside air is much warmer than the interior of the refrigerator.

Q20.12 What would be the efficiency of a Carnot engine operating with $T_H = T_C$? What would be the efficiency if $T_C = 0$ K and T_H were any temperature above 0 K? Interpret your answers.

Q20.13 Real heat engines, like the gasoline engine in a car, always have some friction between their moving parts, although

lubricants keep the friction to a minimum. Would a heat engine with completely frictionless parts be 100% efficient? Why or why not? Does the answer depend on whether or not the engine runs on the Carnot cycle? Again, why or why not?

Q20.14 Does a refrigerator full of food consume more power if the room temperature is 20°C than if it is 15°C? Or is the power consumption the same? Explain your reasoning.

Q20.15 In Example 20.4, a Carnot refrigerator requires a work input of only 230 J to extract 346 J of heat from the cold reservoir. Doesn't this discrepancy imply a violation of the law of conservation of energy? Explain why or why not.

Q20.16 How can the thermal conduction of heat from a hot object to a cold object increase entropy when the same amount of heat that flows out of the hot object flows into the cold one?

Q20.17 Explain why each of the following processes is an example of increasing randomness: mixing hot and cold water; free expansion of a gas; irreversible heat flow; developing heat by mechanical friction. Are entropy increases involved in all of these? Why or why not?

Q20.18 The free expansion of an ideal gas is an adiabatic process and so no heat is transferred. No work is done, so the internal energy does not change. Thus, $Q/T = 0$, yet the randomness of the system and thus its entropy have increased after the expansion. Why does Eq. (20.19) not apply to this situation?

Q20.19 Are the earth and sun in thermal equilibrium? Are there entropy changes associated with the transmission of energy from the sun to the earth? Does radiation differ from other modes of heat transfer with respect to entropy changes? Explain your reasoning.

Q20.20 Suppose that you put a hot object in thermal contact with a cold object and observe (much to your surprise) that heat flows from the cold object to the hot object, making the cold one colder and the hot one hotter. Does this process necessarily violate the first law of thermodynamics? The second law of thermodynamics? Explain.

Q20.21 If you run a movie film backward, it is as if the direction of time were reversed. In the time-reversed movie, would you see processes that violate conservation of energy? Conservation of linear momentum? Would you see processes that violate the second law of thermodynamics? In each case, if law-breaking processes could occur, give some examples.

Q20.22 BIO Some critics of biological evolution claim that it violates the second law of thermodynamics, since evolution involves simple life forms developing into more complex and more highly ordered organisms. Explain why this is not a valid argument against evolution.

Q20.23 BIO A growing plant creates a highly complex and organized structure out of simple materials such as air, water, and trace minerals. Does this violate the second law of thermodynamics? Why or why not? What is the plant's ultimate source of energy? Explain.

EXERCISES

Section 20.2 Heat Engines

20.1 • A diesel engine performs 2200 J of mechanical work and discards 4300 J of heat each cycle. (a) How much heat must be supplied to the engine in each cycle? (b) What is the thermal efficiency of the engine?

20.2 • An aircraft engine takes in 9000 J of heat and discards 6400 J each cycle. (a) What is the mechanical work output of the engine during one cycle? (b) What is the thermal efficiency of the engine?

20.3 • **A Gasoline Engine.** A gasoline engine takes in 1.61 × 10⁴ J of heat and delivers 3700 J of work per cycle. The heat is obtained by burning gasoline with a heat of combustion of 4.60 × 10⁴ J/g. (a) What is the thermal efficiency? (b) How much heat is discarded in each cycle? (c) What mass of fuel is burned in each cycle? (d) If the engine goes through 60.0 cycles per second, what is its power output in kilowatts? In horsepower?

20.4 • A gasoline engine has a power output of 180 kW (about 241 hp). Its thermal efficiency is 28.0%. (a) How much heat must be supplied to the engine per second? (b) How much heat is discarded by the engine per second?

20.5 •• The pV-diagram in **Fig. E20.5** shows a cycle of a heat engine that uses 0.250 mol of an ideal gas with $\gamma = 1.40$. Process ab is adiabatic. (a) Find the pressure of the gas at point a. (b) How much heat enters this gas per cycle, and where does it happen? (c) How much heat leaves this gas in a cycle, and where does it occur? (d) How much work does this engine do in a cycle? (e) What is the thermal efficiency of the engine?

Figure **E20.5**

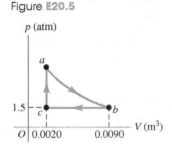

Section 20.3 Internal-Combustion Engines

20.6 • (a) Calculate the theoretical efficiency for an Otto-cycle engine with $\gamma = 1.40$ and $r = 9.50$. (b) If this engine takes in 10,000 J of heat from burning its fuel, how much heat does it discard to the outside air?

20.7 •• The Otto-cycle engine in a Mercedes-Benz SLK230 has a compression ratio of 8.8. (a) What is the ideal efficiency of the engine? Use $\gamma = 1.40$. (b) The engine in a Dodge Viper GT2 has a slightly higher compression ratio of 9.6. How much increase in the ideal efficiency results from this increase in the compression ratio?

Section 20.4 Refrigerators

20.8 • The coefficient of performance $K = H/P$ is a dimensionless quantity. Its value is independent of the units used for H and P, as long as the same units, such as watts, are used for both quantities. However, it is common practice to express H in Btu/h and P in watts. When these mixed units are used, the ratio H/P is called the *energy efficiency ratio* (*EER*). If a room air conditioner has $K = 3.0$, what is its EER?

20.9 • A refrigerator has a coefficient of performance of 2.10. In each cycle it absorbs 3.10 × 10⁴ J of heat from the cold reservoir. (a) How much mechanical energy is required each cycle to operate the refrigerator? (b) During each cycle, how much heat is discarded to the high-temperature reservoir?

20.10 •• A freezer has a coefficient of performance of 2.40. The freezer is to convert 1.80 kg of water at 25.0°C to 1.80 kg of ice at −5.0°C in one hour. (a) What amount of heat must be removed from the water at 25.0°C to convert it to ice at −5.0°C? (b) How much electrical energy is consumed by the freezer during this hour? (c) How much wasted heat is delivered to the room in which the freezer sits?

20.11 •• A refrigerator has a coefficient of performance of 2.25, runs on an input of 135 W of electrical power, and keeps its inside compartment at 5°C. If you put a dozen 1.0-L plastic bottles of water at 31°C into this refrigerator, how long will it take for them to be cooled down to 5°C? (Ignore any heat that leaves the plastic.)

Section 20.6 The Carnot Cycle

20.12 • A Carnot engine is operated between two heat reservoirs at temperatures of 520 K and 300 K. (a) If the engine receives 6.45 kJ of heat energy from the reservoir at 520 K in each cycle, how many joules per cycle does it discard to the reservoir at 300 K? (b) How much mechanical work is performed by the engine during each cycle? (c) What is the thermal efficiency of the engine?

20.13 • A Carnot engine whose high-temperature reservoir is at 620 K takes in 550 J of heat at this temperature in each cycle and gives up 335 J to the low-temperature reservoir. (a) How much mechanical work does the engine perform during each cycle? What is (b) the temperature of the low-temperature reservoir; (c) the thermal efficiency of the cycle?

20.14 •• An ice-making machine operates in a Carnot cycle. It takes heat from water at 0.0°C and rejects heat to a room at 24.0°C. Suppose that 85.0 kg of water at 0.0°C are converted to ice at 0.0°C. (a) How much heat is discharged into the room? (b) How much energy must be supplied to the device?

20.15 • A Carnot engine has an efficiency of 66% and performs 2.5 × 10⁴ J of work in each cycle. (a) How much heat does the engine extract from its heat source in each cycle? (b) Suppose the engine exhausts heat at room temperature (20.0°C). What is the temperature of its heat source?

20.16 •• A certain brand of freezer is advertised to use 730 kW · h of energy per year. (a) Assuming the freezer operates for 5 hours each day, how much power does it require while operating? (b) If the freezer keeps its interior at −5.0°C in a 20.0°C room, what is its theoretical maximum performance coefficient? (c) What is the theoretical maximum amount of ice this freezer could make in an hour, starting with water at 20.0°C?

20.17 • A Carnot refrigerator is operated between two heat reservoirs at temperatures of 320 K and 270 K. (a) If in each cycle the refrigerator receives 415 J of heat energy from the reservoir at 270 K, how many joules of heat energy does it deliver to the reservoir at 320 K? (b) If the refrigerator completes 165 cycles each minute, what power input is required to operate it? (c) What is the coefficient of performance of the refrigerator?

20.18 •• A Carnot heat engine uses a hot reservoir consisting of a large amount of boiling water and a cold reservoir consisting of a large tub of ice and water. In 5 minutes of operation, the heat rejected by the engine melts 0.0400 kg of ice. During this time, how much work W is performed by the engine?

20.19 •• You design an engine that takes in 1.50 × 10⁴ J of heat at 650 K in each cycle and rejects heat at a temperature of 290 K. The engine completes 240 cycles in 1 minute. What is the theoretical maximum power output of your engine, in horsepower?

Section 20.7 Entropy

20.20 • A 4.50-kg block of ice at 0.00°C falls into the ocean and melts. The average temperature of the ocean is 3.50°C, including all the deep water. By how much does the change of this ice to water at 3.50°C alter the entropy of the world? Does the entropy increase or decrease? (*Hint:* Do you think that the ocean temperature will change appreciably as the ice melts?)

20.21 • A sophomore with nothing better to do adds heat to 0.350 kg of ice at 0.0°C until it is all melted. (a) What is the change in entropy of the water? (b) The source of heat is a very massive body at 25.0°C. What is the change in entropy of this body? (c) What is the total change in entropy of the water and the heat source?

20.22 • CALC You decide to take a nice hot bath but discover that your thoughtless roommate has used up most of the hot water. You fill the tub with 195 kg of 30.0°C water and attempt to warm it further by pouring in 5.00 kg of boiling water from the stove. (a) Is this a reversible or an irreversible process? Use physical reasoning to explain. (b) Calculate the final temperature of the bath water. (c) Calculate the net change in entropy of the system (bath water + boiling water), assuming no heat exchange with the air or the tub itself.

20.23 •• A 15.0-kg block of ice at 0.0°C melts to liquid water at 0.0°C inside a large room at 20.0°C. Treat the ice and the room as an isolated system, and assume that the room is large enough for its temperature change to be ignored. (a) Is the melting of the ice reversible or irreversible? Explain, using simple physical reasoning without resorting to any equations. (b) Calculate the net entropy change of the system during this process. Explain whether or not this result is consistent with your answer to part (a).

20.24 •• CALC You make tea with 0.250 kg of 85.0°C water and let it cool to room temperature (20.0°C). (a) Calculate the entropy change of the water while it cools. (b) The cooling process is essentially isothermal for the air in your kitchen. Calculate the change in entropy of the air while the tea cools, assuming that all of the heat lost by the water goes into the air. What is the total entropy change of the system tea + air?

20.25 • Three moles of an ideal gas undergo a reversible isothermal compression at 20.0°C. During this compression, 1850 J of work is done on the gas. What is the change of entropy of the gas?

20.26 •• What is the change in entropy of 0.130 kg of helium gas at the normal boiling point of helium when it all condenses isothermally to 1.00 L of liquid helium? (*Hint:* See Table 17.4 in Section 17.6.)

20.27 • (a) Calculate the change in entropy when 1.00 kg of water at 100°C is vaporized and converted to steam at 100°C (see Table 17.4). (b) Compare your answer to the change in entropy when 1.00 kg of ice is melted at 0°C, calculated in Example 20.5 (Section 20.7). Is the change in entropy greater for melting or for vaporization? Interpret your answer using the idea that entropy is a measure of the randomness of a system.

20.28 •• **Entropy Change Due to Driving.** Premium gasoline produces 1.23×10^8 J of heat per gallon when it is burned at approximately 400°C (although the amount can vary with the fuel mixture). If a car's engine is 25% efficient, three-fourths of that heat is expelled into the air, typically at 20°C. If your car gets 35 miles per gallon of gas, by how much does the car's engine change the entropy of the world when you drive 1.0 mi? Does it decrease or increase it?

Section 20.8 Microscopic Interpretation of Entropy

20.29 • CALC Two moles of an ideal gas occupy a volume V. The gas expands isothermally and reversibly to a volume $3V$. (a) Is the velocity distribution changed by the isothermal expansion? Explain. (b) Use Eq. (20.23) to calculate the change in entropy of the gas. (c) Use Eq. (20.18) to calculate the change in entropy of the gas. Compare this result to that obtained in part (b).

20.30 • A box is separated by a partition into two parts of equal volume. The left side of the box contains 500 molecules of nitrogen gas; the right side contains 100 molecules of oxygen gas. The two gases are at the same temperature. The partition is punctured, and equilibrium is eventually attained. Assume that the volume of the box is large enough for each gas to undergo a free expansion and not change temperature. (a) On average, how many molecules of each type will there be in either half of the box? (b) What is the change in entropy of the system when the partition is punctured? (c) What is the probability that the molecules will be found in the same distribution as they were before the partition was punctured— that is, 500 nitrogen molecules in the left half and 100 oxygen molecules in the right half?

20.31 • CALC A lonely party balloon with a volume of 2.40 L and containing 0.100 mol of air is left behind to drift in the temporarily uninhabited and depressurized International Space Station. Sunlight coming through a porthole heats and explodes the balloon, causing the air in it to undergo a free expansion into the empty station, whose total volume is 425 m³. Calculate the entropy change of the air during the expansion.

PROBLEMS

20.32 • You are designing a Carnot engine that has 2 mol of CO_2 as its working substance; the gas may be treated as ideal. The gas is to have a maximum temperature of 527°C and a maximum pressure of 5.00 atm. With a heat input of 400 J per cycle, you want 300 J of useful work. (a) Find the temperature of the cold reservoir. (b) For how many cycles must this engine run to melt completely a 10.0-kg block of ice originally at 0.0°C, using only the heat rejected by the engine?

20.33 •• CP An ideal Carnot engine operates between 500°C and 100°C with a heat input of 250 J per cycle. (a) How much heat is delivered to the cold reservoir in each cycle? (b) What minimum number of cycles is necessary for the engine to lift a 500-kg rock through a height of 100 m?

20.34 •• BIO **Entropy of Metabolism.** An average sleeping person metabolizes at a rate of about 80 W by digesting food or burning fat. Typically, 20% of this energy goes into bodily functions, such as cell repair, pumping blood, and other uses of mechanical energy, while the rest goes to heat. Most people get rid of all this excess heat by transferring it (by conduction and the flow of blood) to the surface of the body, where it is radiated away. The normal internal temperature of the body (where the metabolism takes place) is 37°C, and the skin is typically 7 C° cooler. By how much does the person's entropy change per second due to this heat transfer?

20.35 •• CP A certain heat engine operating on a Carnot cycle absorbs 410 J of heat per cycle at its hot reservoir at 135°C and has a thermal efficiency of 22.0%. (a) How much work does this engine do per cycle? (b) How much heat does the engine waste each cycle? (c) What is the temperature of the cold reservoir? (d) By how much does the engine change the entropy of the world each cycle? (e) What mass of water could this engine pump per cycle from a well 35.0 m deep?

20.36 • A heat engine takes 0.350 mol of a diatomic ideal gas around the cycle shown in the pV-diagram of **Fig. P20.36**. Process $1 \to 2$ is at constant volume, process $2 \to 3$ is

Figure **P20.36**

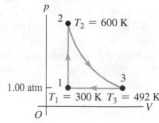

adiabatic, and process $3 \rightarrow 1$ is at a constant pressure of 1.00 atm. The value of γ for this gas is 1.40. (a) Find the pressure and volume at points 1, 2, and 3. (b) Calculate Q, W, and ΔU for each of the three processes. (c) Find the net work done by the gas in the cycle. (d) Find the net heat flow into the engine in one cycle. (e) What is the thermal efficiency of the engine? How does this compare to the efficiency of a Carnot-cycle engine operating between the same minimum and maximum temperatures T_1 and T_2?

20.37 •• BIO **Entropy Change from Digesting Fat.** Digesting fat produces 9.3 food calories per gram of fat, and typically 80% of this energy goes to heat when metabolized. (One food calorie is 1000 calories and therefore equals 4186 J.) The body then moves all this heat to the surface by a combination of thermal conductivity and motion of the blood. The internal temperature of the body (where digestion occurs) is normally 37°C, and the surface is usually about 30°C. By how much do the digestion and metabolism of a 2.50-g pat of butter change your body's entropy? Does it increase or decrease?

Figure **P20.38**

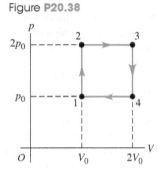

20.38 •• What is the thermal efficiency of an engine that operates by taking n moles of diatomic ideal gas through the cycle $1 \rightarrow 2 \rightarrow 3 \rightarrow 4 \rightarrow 1$ shown in **Fig. P20.38**?

20.39 •• CALC You build a heat engine that takes 1.00 mol of an ideal diatomic gas through the cycle shown in **Fig. P20.39**. (a) Show that process ab is an isothermal compression. (b) During which process(es) of the cycle is heat absorbed by the gas? During which process(es) is heat rejected? How do you know? Calculate (c) the temperature at points a, b, and c; (d) the net heat exchanged with the surroundings and net work done by the engine in one cycle; (e) the thermal efficiency of the engine.

Figure **P20.39**

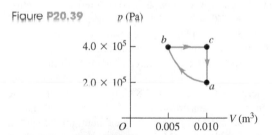

20.40 • CP As a budding mechanical engineer, you are called upon to design a Carnot engine that has 2.00 mol of a monatomic ideal gas as its working substance and operates from a high-temperature reservoir at 500°C. The engine is to lift a 15.0-kg weight 2.00 m per cycle, using 500 J of heat input. The gas in the engine chamber can have a minimum volume of 5.00 L during the cycle. (a) Draw a pV-diagram for this cycle. Show in your diagram where heat enters and leaves the gas. (b) What must be the temperature of the cold reservoir? (c) What is the thermal efficiency of the engine? (d) How much heat energy does this engine waste per cycle? (e) What is the maximum pressure that the gas chamber will have to withstand?

20.41 • CALC A heat engine operates using the cycle shown in **Fig. P20.41**. The working substance is 2.00 mol of helium gas, which reaches a maximum temperature of 327°C. Assume the helium can be treated as an ideal gas. Process bc is isothermal.

The pressure in states a and c is 1.00×10^5 Pa, and the pressure in state b is 3.00×10^5 Pa. (a) How much heat enters the gas and how much leaves the gas each cycle? (b) How much work does the engine do each cycle, and what is its efficiency? (c) Compare this engine's efficiency with the maximum possible efficiency attainable with the hot and cold reservoirs used by this cycle.

Figure **P20.41**

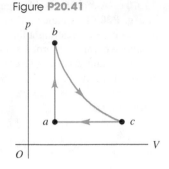

20.42 •• CP BIO **Human Entropy.** A person who has skin of surface area 1.85 m² and temperature 30.0°C is resting in an insulated room where the ambient air temperature is 20.0°C. In this state, a person gets rid of excess heat by radiation. By how much does the person change the entropy of the air in this room each second? (Recall that the room radiates back into the person and that the emissivity of the skin is 1.00.)

20.43 ••• An experimental power plant at the Natural Energy Laboratory of Hawaii generates electricity from the temperature gradient of the ocean. The surface and deep-water temperatures are 27°C and 6°C, respectively. (a) What is the maximum theoretical efficiency of this power plant? (b) If the power plant is to produce 210 kW of power, at what rate must heat be extracted from the warm water? At what rate must heat be absorbed by the cold water? Assume the maximum theoretical efficiency. (c) The cold water that enters the plant leaves it at a temperature of 10°C. What must be the flow rate of cold water through the system? Give your answer in kg/h and in L/h.

20.44 •• CP BIO **A Human Engine.** You decide to use your body as a Carnot heat engine. The operating gas is in a tube with one end in your mouth (where the temperature is 37.0°C) and the other end at the surface of your skin, at 30.0°C. (a) What is the maximum efficiency of such a heat engine? Would it be a very useful engine? (b) Suppose you want to use this human engine to lift a 2.50-kg box from the floor to a tabletop 1.20 m above the floor. How much must you increase the gravitational potential energy, and how much heat input is needed to accomplish this? (c) If your favorite candy bar has 350 food calories (1 food calorie = 4186 J) and 80% of the food energy goes into heat, how many of these candy bars must you eat to lift the box in this way?

20.45 • CALC A cylinder contains oxygen at a pressure of 2.00 atm. The volume is 4.00 L, and the temperature is 300 K. Assume that the oxygen may be treated as an ideal gas. The oxygen is carried through the following processes:

(i) Heated at constant pressure from the initial state (state 1) to state 2, which has $T = 450$ K.

(ii) Cooled at constant volume to 250 K (state 3).

(iii) Compressed at constant temperature to a volume of 4.00 L (state 4).

(iv) Heated at constant volume to 300 K, which takes the system back to state 1.

(a) Show these four processes in a pV-diagram, giving the numerical values of p and V in each of the four states. (b) Calculate Q and W for each of the four processes. (c) Calculate the net work done by the oxygen in the complete cycle. (d) What is the efficiency of this device as a heat engine? How does this compare to the efficiency of a Carnot-cycle engine operating between the same minimum and maximum temperatures of 250 K and 450 K?

20.46 • A monatomic ideal gas is taken around the cycle shown in **Fig. P20.46** in the direction shown in the figure. The path for process $c \to a$ is a straight line in the pV-diagram. (a) Calculate Q, W, and ΔU for each process $a \to b$, $b \to c$, and $c \to a$. (b) What are Q, W, and ΔU for one complete cycle? (c) What is the efficiency of the cycle?

Figure **P20.46**

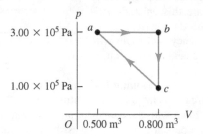

20.47 •• A Carnot engine operates between two heat reservoirs at temperatures T_H and T_C. An inventor proposes to increase the efficiency by running one engine between T_H and an intermediate temperature T' and a second engine between T' and T_C, using as input the heat expelled by the first engine. Compute the efficiency of this composite system, and compare it to that of the original engine.

20.48 ••• A typical coal-fired power plant generates 1000 MW of usable power at an overall thermal efficiency of 40%. (a) What is the rate of heat input to the plant? (b) The plant burns anthracite coal, which has a heat of combustion of 2.65×10^7 J/kg. How much coal does the plant use per day, if it operates continuously? (c) At what rate is heat ejected into the cool reservoir, which is the nearby river? (d) The river is at 18.0°C before it reaches the power plant and 18.5°C after it has received the plant's waste heat. Calculate the river's flow rate, in cubic meters per second. (e) By how much does the river's entropy increase each second?

20.49 • **Automotive Thermodynamics.** A Volkswagen Passat has a six-cylinder Otto-cycle engine with compression ratio $r = 10.6$. The diameter of each cylinder, called the *bore* of the engine, is 82.5 mm. The distance that the piston moves during the compression in Fig. 20.5, called the *stroke* of the engine, is 86.4 mm. The initial pressure of the air–fuel mixture (at point a in Fig. 20.6) is 8.50×10^4 Pa, and the initial temperature is 300 K (the same as the outside air). Assume that 200 J of heat is added to each cylinder in each cycle by the burning gasoline, and that the gas has $C_V = 20.5$ J/mol·K and $\gamma = 1.40$. (a) Calculate the total work done in one cycle in each cylinder of the engine, and the heat released when the gas is cooled to the temperature of the outside air. (b) Calculate the volume of the air–fuel mixture at point a in the cycle. (c) Calculate the pressure, volume, and temperature of the gas at points b, c, and d in the cycle. In a pV-diagram, show the numerical values of p, V, and T for each of the four states. (d) Compare the efficiency of this engine with the efficiency of a Carnot-cycle engine operating between the same maximum and minimum temperatures.

20.50 • An air conditioner operates on 800 W of power and has a performance coefficient of 2.80 with a room temperature of 21.0°C and an outside temperature of 35.0°C. (a) Calculate the rate of heat removal for this unit. (b) Calculate the rate at which heat is discharged to the outside air. (c) Calculate the total entropy change in the room if the air conditioner runs for 1 hour. Calculate the total entropy change in the outside air for the same time period. (d) What is the net change in entropy for the system (room + outside air)?

20.51 •• The pV-diagram in **Fig. P20.51** shows the cycle for a refrigerator operating on 0.850 mol of H_2. Assume that the gas can be treated as ideal. Process ab is isothermal. Find the coefficient of performance of this refrigerator.

Figure **P20.51**

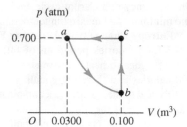

20.52 •• **BIO Human Entropy.** A person with skin of surface area 1.85 m² and temperature 30.0°C is resting in an insulated room where the ambient air temperature is 20.0°C. In this state, a person gets rid of excess heat by radiation. By how much does the person change the entropy of the air in this room each second? (Recall that the room radiates back into the person and that the emissivity of the skin is 1.00.)

20.53 •• **CALC** An object of mass m_1, specific heat c_1, and temperature T_1 is placed in contact with a second object of mass m_2, specific heat c_2, and temperature $T_2 > T_1$. As a result, the temperature of the first object increases to T and the temperature of the second object decreases to T'. (a) Show that the entropy increase of the system is

$$\Delta S = m_1 c_1 \ln\frac{T}{T_1} + m_2 c_2 \ln\frac{T'}{T_2}$$

and show that energy conservation requires that

$$m_1 c_1 (T - T_1) = m_2 c_2 (T_2 - T')$$

(b) Show that the entropy change ΔS, considered as a function of T, is a *maximum* if $T = T'$, which is just the condition of thermodynamic equilibrium. (c) Discuss the result of part (b) in terms of the idea of entropy as a measure of randomness.

20.54 •• **CALC** To heat 1 cup of water (250 cm³) to make coffee, you place an electric heating element in the cup. As the water temperature increases from 20°C to 78°C, the temperature of the heating element remains at a constant 120°C. Calculate the change in entropy of (a) the water; (b) the heating element; (c) the system of water and heating element. (Make the same assumption about the specific heat of water as in Example 20.10 in Section 20.7, and ignore the heat that flows into the ceramic coffee cup itself.) (d) Is this process reversible or irreversible? Explain.

20.55 •• **DATA** In your summer job with a venture capital firm, you are given funding requests from four inventors of heat engines. The inventors claim the following data for their operating prototypes:

	Prototype			
	A	**B**	**C**	**D**
T_C (°C), low-temperature reservoir	47	17	−33	37
T_H (°C), high-temperature reservoir	177	197	247	137
Claimed efficiency e (%)	21	35	56	20

(a) Based on the T_C and T_H values for each prototype, find the maximum possible efficiency for each. (b) Are any of the claimed efficiencies impossible? Explain. (c) For all prototypes with an efficiency that is possible, rank the prototypes in decreasing order of the ratio of claimed efficiency to maximum possible efficiency.

20.56 •• **DATA** For a refrigerator or air conditioner, the coefficient of performance K (often denoted as COP) is, as in Eq. (20.9), the ratio of cooling output $|Q_C|$ to the required electrical energy input $|W|$, both in joules. The coefficient of performance is also expressed as a ratio of powers,

$$K = \frac{|Q_C|/t}{|W|/t}$$

where $|Q_C|/t$ is the cooling power and $|W|/t$ is the electrical power input to the device, both in watts. The energy efficiency ratio (EER) is the same quantity expressed in units of Btu for $|Q_C|$ and W·h for $|W|$. (a) Derive a general relationship that expresses EER in terms of K. (b) For a home air conditioner, EER is generally determined for a 95°F outside temperature and an 80°F return air temperature. Calculate EER for a Carnot device that operates between 95°F and 80°F. (c) You have an air conditioner with an EER of 10.9. Your home on average requires a total cooling output of $|Q_C| = 1.9 \times 10^{10}$ J per year. If electricity costs you 15.3 cents per kW·h, how much do you spend per year, on average, to operate your air conditioner? (Assume that the unit's EER accurately represents the operation of your air conditioner. A *seasonal energy efficiency ratio* (SEER) is often used. The SEER is calculated over a range of outside temperatures to get a more accurate seasonal average.) (d) You are considering replacing your air conditioner with a more efficient one with an EER of 14.6. Based on the EER, how much would that save you on electricity costs in an average year?

20.57 ••• **DATA** You are conducting experiments to study prototype heat engines. In one test, 4.00 mol of argon gas are taken around the cycle shown in **Fig. P20.57**. The pressure is low enough for the gas to be treated as ideal. You measure the gas temperature in states a, b, c, and d and find $T_a = 250.0$ K, $T_b = 300.0$ K, $T_c = 380.0$ K, and $T_d = 316.7$ K. (a) Calculate the efficiency e of the cycle. (b) Disappointed by the cycle's low efficiency, you consider doubling the number of moles of gas while keeping the pressure and volume the same. What would e be then? (c) You remember that the efficiency of a Carnot cycle increases if the temperature of the hot reservoir is increased. So, you return to using 4.00 mol of gas but double the volume in states c and d while keeping the pressures the same. The resulting temperatures in these states are $T_c = 760.0$ K and $T_d = 633.4$ K. T_a and T_b remain the same as in part (a). Calculate e for this cycle with the new T_c and T_d values. (d) Encouraged by the increase in efficiency, you raise T_c and T_d still further. But e doesn't increase very much; it seems to be approaching a limiting value. If $T_a = 250.0$ K and $T_b = 300.0$ K and you keep volumes V_a and V_b the same as in part (a), then $T_c/T_d = T_b/T_a$ and $T_c = 1.20T_d$. Derive an expression for e as a function of T_d for this cycle. What value does e approach as T_d becomes very large?

Figure **P20.57**

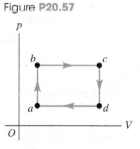

20.58 ••• Consider a Diesel cycle that starts (at point a in Fig. 20.7) with air at temperature T_a. The air may be treated as an ideal gas. (a) If the temperature at point c is T_c, derive an expression for the efficiency of the cycle in terms of the compression ratio r. (b) What is the efficiency if $T_a = 300$ K, $T_c = 950$ K, $\gamma = 1.40$, and $r = 21.0$?

| PASSAGE PROBLEMS |

POWER FROM THE SEA. *Ocean thermal energy conversion* is a process that uses the temperature difference between the warm surface water of tropical oceans and the cold deep-ocean water to run a heat engine. The graph shows a typical decrease of temperature with depth below the surface in tropical oceans. In the heat engine, the warmer surface water vaporizes a low-boiling-point fluid, such as ammonia. The heat of vaporization of ammonia is 260 cal/g at 27°C, the surface-water temperature. The vapor is used to turn a turbine and is then condensed back into a liquid by means of cold water brought from deep below the surface through a large intake pipe. A power plant producing 10 MW of useful power would require a cold seawater flow rate of about 30,000 kg/s.

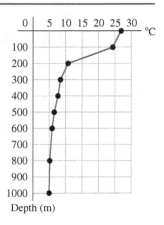

20.59 If the power plant uses a Carnot cycle and the desired theoretical efficiency is 6.5%, from what depth must cold water be brought? (a) 100 m; (b) 400 m; (c) 800 m; (d) deeper than 1000 m.

20.60 What is the change in entropy of the ammonia vaporized per second in the 10-MW power plant, assuming an ideal Carnot efficiency of 6.5%? (a) $+6 \times 10^6$ J/K per second; (b) $+5 \times 10^5$ J/K per second; (c) $+1 \times 10^5$ J/K per second; (d) 0.

20.61 Compare the entropy change of the warmer water to that of the colder water during one cycle of the heat engine, assuming an ideal Carnot cycle. (a) The entropy does not change during one cycle in either case. (b) The entropy of both increases, but the entropy of the colder water increases by more because its initial temperature is lower. (c) The entropy of the warmer water decreases by more than the entropy of the colder water increases, because some of the heat removed from the warmer water goes to the work done by the engine. (d) The entropy of the warmer water decreases by the same amount that the entropy of the colder water increases.

20.62 If the proposed plant is built and produces 10 MW but the rate at which waste heat is exhausted to the cold water is 165 MW, what is the plant's actual efficiency? (a) 5.7%; (b) 6.1%; (c) 6.5%; (d) 16.5%.

Answers

Chapter Opening Question ?

(i) This is what a refrigerator does: It makes heat flow from the cold interior of the refrigerator to the warm outside. The second law of thermodynamics says that heat cannot *spontaneously* flow from a cold body to a hot one. A refrigerator has a motor that does work on the system to *force* the heat to flow in that way.

Test Your Understanding Questions

20.1 (ii) Like sliding a book across a table, rubbing your hands together uses friction to convert mechanical energy into heat. The (impossible) reverse process would involve your hands spontaneously getting colder, with the released energy forcing your hands to move rhythmically back and forth!

20.2 (iii), (i), (ii) From Eq. (20.4) the efficiency is $e = W/Q_H$, and from Eq. (20.2) $W = Q_H + Q_C = |Q_H| - |Q_C|$. For engine (i) $Q_H = 5000$ J and $Q_C = -4500$ J, so $W = 5000$ J $+ (-4500$ J$) = 500$ J and $e = (500$ J$)/(5000$ J$) = 0.100$. For engine (ii) $Q_H = 25{,}000$ J and $W = 2000$ J, so $e = (2000$ J$)/(25{,}000$ J$) = 0.080$. For engine (iii) $W = 400$ J and $Q_C = -2800$ J, so $Q_H = W - Q_C = 400$ J $- (-2800$ J$) = 3200$ J and $e = (400$ J$)/(3200$ J$) = 0.125$.

20.3 (i), (ii) Doubling the amount of fuel burned per cycle means that Q_H is doubled, so the resulting pressure increase from b to c in Fig. 20.6 is greater. The compression ratio and hence the efficiency remain the same, so $|Q_C|$ (the amount of heat rejected to the environment) must increase by the same factor as Q_H. Hence the pressure drop from d to a in Fig. 20.6 is also greater. The volume V and the compression ratio r don't change, so the horizontal dimensions of the pV-diagram don't change.

20.4 no A refrigerator uses an input of work to transfer heat from one system (the refrigerator's interior) to another system (its exterior, which includes the house in which the refrigerator is installed). If the door is open, these two systems are really the *same* system and will eventually come to the same temperature. By the first law of thermodynamics, all of the work input to the refrigerator motor will be converted into heat and the temperature in your house will actually *increase*. To cool the house you need a system that will transfer heat from it to the outside world, such as an air conditioner or heat pump.

20.5 no, no Both the 100%-efficient engine of Fig. 20.11a and the workless refrigerator of Fig. 20.11b return to the same state at the end of a cycle as at the beginning, so the net change in internal energy of each system is zero ($\Delta U = 0$). For the 100%-efficient engine, the net heat flow into the engine equals the net work done, so $Q = W$, $Q - W = 0$, and the first law ($\Delta U = Q - W$) is obeyed. For the workless refrigerator, no net work is done (so $W = 0$) and as much heat flows into it as out (so $Q = 0$), so again $Q - W = 0$ and $\Delta U = Q - W$ in accordance with the first law. It is the *second* law of thermodynamics that tells us that both the 100%-efficient engine and the workless refrigerator are impossible.

20.6 no The efficiency can be no better than that of a Carnot engine running between the same two temperature limits, $e_{Carnot} = 1 - (T_C/T_H)$ [Eq. (20.14)]. The temperature T_C of the cold reservoir for this air-cooled engine is about 300 K (ambient temperature), and the temperature T_H of the hot reservoir cannot exceed the melting point of copper, 1356 K (see Table 17.4). Hence the maximum possible Carnot efficiency is $e = 1 - (300$ K$)/(1356$ K$) = 0.78$, or 78%. The temperature of any real engine would be less than this, so it would be impossible for the inventor's engine to attain 85% efficiency. You should invest your money elsewhere.

20.7 -102 J/K, no The process described is exactly the opposite of the process used in Example 20.10. The result violates the second law of thermodynamics, which states that the entropy of an isolated system cannot decrease.

20.8 (i) For case (i), we saw in Example 20.8 (Section 20.7) that for an ideal gas, the entropy change in a free expansion is the same as in an isothermal expansion. From Eq. (20.23), this implies that the ratio of the number of microscopic states after and before the expansion, w_2/w_1, is also the same for these two cases. From Example 20.11, $w_2/w_1 = 2^N$, so the number of microscopic states increases by a factor 2^N. For case (ii), in a reversible expansion the entropy change is $\Delta S = \int dQ/T = 0$; if the expansion is adiabatic there is no heat flow, so $\Delta S = 0$. From Eq. (20.23), $w_2/w_1 = 1$ and there is *no* change in the number of microscopic states. The difference is that in an adiabatic expansion the temperature drops and the molecules move more slowly, so they have fewer microscopic states available to them than in an isothermal expansion.

Bridging Problem

(a) 34.8°C **(b)** +10 J/K

CHAPTER 23

Entropy

23.1
REVERSIBLE PART OF THE SECOND LAW

Work diagrams in which a generalized force such as P, $\mathcal{F}$, γ, $\mathcal{E}$, or $\mu_0 \mathcal{H}$ is plotted against the corresponding generalized displacement V, L, A, Z, or $\mathcal{M}$ have been used to indicate processes of various systems. An isothermal process or an adiabatic process is represented by a different curve on each diagram. In this chapter, it is desired to formulate general principles that apply to all systems. If we let the symbol Y denote any generalized force and the symbol X its corresponding generalized displacement, a generalized work diagram in which Y is plotted against X may be used to depict processes common to all systems and will thus be suitable for general discussions.

Consider a reversible process represented by the smooth curve $i \rightarrow f$ on the generalized work diagram shown in Fig. 23-1. The nature of the system is not essential. The dashed curves through i and f, respectively, represent portions of adiabatic processes. Let us draw a curve $a \rightarrow b$, representing an isothermal process, in such a way that the area under the smooth curve if is equal to the area under the zigzag sequence of processes, path $iabf$. Then, the work done in traversing both paths is the same, or

$$W_{if} = W_{iabf}.$$

From the first law,

$$Q_{if} = U_f - U_i - W_{if},$$

and

$$Q_{iabf} = U_f - U_i - W_{iabf}.$$

Therefore,

$$Q_{if} = Q_{iabf}.$$

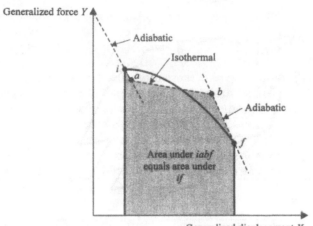

FIGURE 23-1
Generalized work diagram, where $i \rightarrow f$ is any reversible process; $i \rightarrow a$ is a reversible adiabatic process; $a \rightarrow b$ is a reversible isothermal process; and $b \rightarrow f$ is a reversible adiabatic process.

But, since no heat is transferred in the two adiabatic processes ia and bf, we have

$$Q_{if} = Q_{ab}. \tag{23.1}$$

If we are given, therefore, a reversible process in which the temperature may change in any manner, it is always possible to find a reversible zigzag path between the same two states, consisting of an adiabatic process followed by an isothermal process followed by an adiabatic process, such that the heat transferred during the isothermal segment is the same as that transferred during the original process.

Now, consider the smooth closed curve on the generalized work diagram shown in Fig. 23-2. Since no two adiabatic lines can intersect, a number of adiabatic lines may be drawn, dividing the cycle into a number of adjacent strips. A zigzag closed path may now be drawn, consisting of alternate adia-batic and isothermal portions, such that the heat transferred during all the isothermal portions is equal to the heat transferred in the original cycle. Consider the two isothermal processes ab at the temperature T_1, during which heat Q_1 is absorbed, and cd at the temperature T_2, during which heat Q_2 is rejected. Since ab and cd are bounded by the same adiabatic curves, $abcd$ is a Carnot cycle.

$$\frac{|Q_1|}{T_1} = \frac{|Q_2|}{T_2}.$$

For the sake of clearness and simplicity, we have been considering only the absolute values of heat entering or leaving a system, thus ignoring the sign

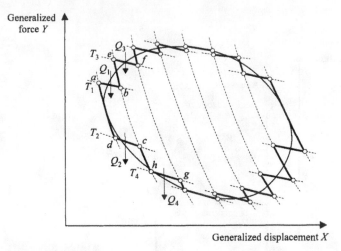

FIGURE 23-2
Generalized work diagram, where the smooth closed curve is a reversible cycle and the zigzag closed path is made up of alternating reversible isothermal and reversible adiabatic processes.

Let us now return to the sign convention and regard any Q as an algebraic symbol, positive for heat absorbed by a system and negative for heat rejected from a system. We may then write the equation cited above as

$$\frac{Q_1}{T_1} + \frac{Q_2}{T_2} = 0,$$

where Q_1 is a positive number and Q_2 is a negative number. Since the isothermal curves ef and gh are bounded by the same two adiabatic curves, $efgh$ is also a Carnot cycle, and

$$\frac{Q_3}{T_3} + \frac{Q_4}{T_4} = 0.$$

If a similar equation is written for each pair of isothermal curves bounded by the same two adiabatic curves and if all the equations are added, then the result obtained is that

$$\frac{Q_1}{T_1} + \frac{Q_2}{T_2} + \frac{Q_3}{T_3} + \frac{Q_4}{T_4} + \cdots = 0.$$

Since no heat is transferred during the adiabatic portions of the zigzag cycle, we may write

$$\sum_j \frac{Q_j}{T_j} = 0, \tag{23.2}$$

where the summation is taken over the entire zigzag cycle consisting of Carnot cycles, j in number.

Now, imagine the cycle divided into a very large number of strips by drawing a large number of adiabatic curves close together. If we connect these adiabatic curves with small isothermal curves, in the manner already described, then a zigzag path may be traced that can be made to approximate the original cycle as closely as we please. When these isothermal processes become infinitesimal, the ratio dQ/T for an infinitesimal isothermal between two adjacent adiabatic curves is equal to the ratio dQ/T for the infinitesimal piece of the original cycle bounded by the same two adiabatic curves. In the limit, therefore, we may write for Eq. (23.2) any reversible cycle,

$$\oint_R \frac{dQ}{T} = 0. \tag{23.3}$$

The circle through the integral sign signifies that the integration takes place over the complete cycle, and the letter R emphasizes the fact that the equation is true only for a reversible cycle. This result, known as *Clausius' theorem*, is one part of Clausius' mathematical statement of the second law. The other part applicable to irreversible cycles will be presented in Sec. 23.8.

23.2
ENTROPY

Let an initial equilibrium state of any thermodynamic system be represented by the point i on any convenient diagram, such as the generalized work diagram of Fig. 23-3. Denote a final equilibrium state by the point f. It is possible to take the system from i to f along any number of different reversible paths, since i and f are equilibrium states. Suppose the system is taken from i to f along the reversible path R_1 and then back to i again along another reversible path R_2. The two paths form a reversible cycle, and from Clausius' theorem we may write

$$\oint_{R_1 R_2} \frac{dQ}{T} = 0.$$

The above integral may be expressed as the sum of two integrals, one for the path R_1 and the other for the path R_2. Then, we have

$$\int_{R_1}{}_i^f \frac{dQ}{T} + \int_{R_2}{}_f^i \frac{dQ}{T} = 0,$$

or

$$\int_{R_1}{}_i^f \frac{dQ}{T} = - \int_{R_2}{}_f^i \frac{dQ}{T}.$$

Since R_2 is a reversible path,

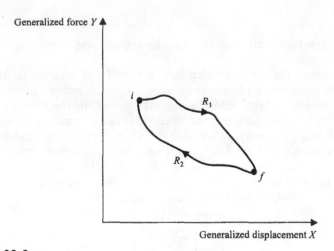

FIGURE 23-3
Two reversible paths joining two equilibrium states of a system.

$$-{}_{R_2}\int_f^i \frac{dQ}{T} = {}_{R_2}\int_i^f \frac{dQ}{T},$$

and, finally,

$$_{R_1}\int_i^f \frac{dQ}{T} = {}_{R_2}\int_i^f \frac{dQ}{T}. \tag{23.4}$$

Since R_1 and R_2 were chosen at random and represent *any* two reversible paths, the above equation expresses the important fact that $_R\int_i^f dQ/T$ *is independent of the reversible path connecting i and f*. Therefore, it follows from Eq. (23.4) that *there exists a function of the thermodynamic coordinates of a system whose value at the final state minus its value at the initial state equals the integral* $_R\int_i^f dQ/T$. This state function was named the *entropy* by Rudolf Clausius in 1865 and is denoted by S. If S_i is the entropy at the initial state and S_f the entropy at the final state, then we have a finite *change of entropy $S_f - S_i$* from state i to state f, given by

$$S_f - S_i = {}_R\int_i^f \frac{dQ}{T}, \tag{23.5}$$

where the path from state i to state f is *any* reversible path R. Thus, the entropy change of the system between states i and f is independent of the path. This is a very remarkable result. Although the heat entering the system depends on the path between the states i and f, the entropy change does *not* depend on the path.

The existence of an entropy function S is deduced in the same way as that of the internal-energy function U, that is, by showing that a certain quantity is independent of choice of reversible processes connecting the initial equilibrium state with the final equilibrium state. Both U and S are state functions, which means that the difference of either function evaluated at the final and initial equilibrium states is independent of the path connecting the two states. In neither function, however, does the defining equation enable us to calculate a single value of the function, only the difference of two values.

If the two equilibrium states i and f are infinitesimally near, then the integral sign may be eliminated and $S_f - S_i$ becomes dS, an *infinitesimal* change of entropy of the system. Equation (23.5) then becomes

$$dS = \frac{đQ_R}{T},$$

(23.6)

where dS is an exact differential, since it is the differential of an actual function and not a small inexact quantity, such as $đQ$ or $đW$. The subscript R to $đQ$ indicates that the preceding equation is true *only* if a small amount of heat $đQ$ is transferred reversibly.

When Eq. (23.6) is written in the form $đQ_R = T\,dS$, it is seen that the difficulty of dealing with the inexact differential of heat is eliminated by substituting the product of the temperature and exact differential of the entropy. This is a major advancement in the formalism of thermodynamics, comparable to replacing $đW$ with $-P\,dV$ in a hydrostatic system. Entropy S joins P, V, and T as a thermodynamic variable to be used in the development of the formalism and mathematical methods of thermodynamics.

It is instructive to calculate a unit of entropy, a joule per kelvin, in order to gain a feeling for this new variable. Consider the Joule paddle wheel apparatus shown in Fig. 23-4. The system is a kilogram of water at room temperature T. The surroundings are the adiabatic cylindrical wall and top, the

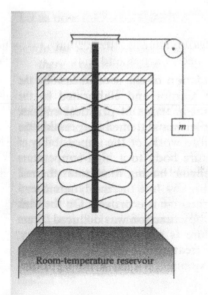

FIGURE 23-4
Joule paddle wheel apparatus, an "entropy generator."

diathermic bottom in contact with a heat reservoir, also at temperature T, and the paddle wheels. A slowly falling mass m causes the paddle wheels to turn, so the portion of the boundary formed by the paddle wheels moves. The falling mass does work on the system, which tends to experience an increase in the temperature of the water. However, the diathermic bottom prevents the temperature from rising by removing energy from the system in the form of heat.

The change of entropy of the reservoir ΔS is given by

$$\Delta S = \int \frac{dQ_R}{T} = \frac{Q}{T},$$

which is also the total change of entropy for the composite system of liquid plus reservoir, since the state of the water in the apparatus is unchanged at the end of the process. Furthermore, since the temperature of the water and the volume of the water are both unchanged, the internal energy is unchanged. Thus, the work done by the falling mass equals the heat that enters the reservoir. If the paddle wheel is driven by a mass of 29.9 kg (approximately 66 lb) that falls 1 m, then the change of entropy is given by

$$\Delta S = \frac{W}{T} = \frac{(29.9\,\text{kg})(9.8\,\text{N/kg})(1\,\text{m})}{293\,\text{K}}$$
$$= 1.00\,\text{J/K}.$$

The entropy of the mass turning the paddle wheels is not changed during the process, because no heat enters or leaves the mass. Rather, the entropy is generated by the conversion of work (done by the mass) into heat (entering the reservoir). Thus, the paddle wheel apparatus serves as an entropy generator.

23.3
PRINCIPLE OF CARATHÉODORY

We have arrived at the mathematical formulation of the second law by the historical method initiated by the engineer Carnot and elaborated by the physicists Kelvin and Clausius. They thought in terms of practical engines, ideal engines, and physical models. Starting with a statement expressing the impossibility of converting heat completely into work, or the impossibility of spontaneous heat flow from a low-temperature body to a high-temperature body, they conceived of the ideal Carnot engine having maximum thermal efficiency. With the aid of this ideal engine, an absolute thermodynamic temperature scale was defined, and the Clausius theorem was proved. On the basis of Clausius' theorem, the existence of an entropy function was deduced. From a mathematical point of view, this procedure is somewhat unsatisfactory. Mathematicians often prefer an "axiomatic treatment," that is, a statement of the minimum number of fundamental axioms and then a purely formal mathematical deduction from these axioms.

In 1909, the mathematician Carathéodory sought to find a statement of the second law which, without the aid of Carnot engines and refrigerators but only by mathematical deduction, would lead to the existence of an entropy function satisfying the equation $dQ_R = T\,dS$. He was led to his formulation of the second law by a mathematical theorem that he proved and which may be stated in simple form[†] as follows.

Imagine a space of three dimensions with rectangular coordinates x, y, z. Carathéodory's theorem states that, *in the neighborhood of any arbitrary point P_0, there are points that are not accessible from P_0 along solution curves of the equation*

$$A(x, y, z)\,dx + B(x, y, z)\,dy + C(x, y, z)\,dz = 0,$$

if, and only if, the equation is integrable. The equation is said to be integrable if there exist functions $\lambda(x, y, z)$ and $F(x, y, z)$ such that

$$A\,dx + B\,dy + C\,dz = \lambda\,dF.$$

The proof of this purely mathematical theorem is somewhat involved and it will not be given here. It holds for any number of variables.

Let us now consider how this theorem has a bearing on thermodynamics. Consider a system whose states are determined, for the sake of argument, by three thermodynamic coordinates $x, y,$ and z. Then, the first law in differential form may be written

$$dQ = A\,dx + B\,dy + C\,dz,$$

where $A, B,$ and C are functions of $x, y,$ and z. The adiabatic, reversible transitions of this system are subject to the condition

$$dQ = A\,dx + B\,dy + C\,dz = 0.$$

Let us now take as Carathéodory's statement of the second law the following:

In the neighborhood of any arbitrary initial state P_0 of a physical system, there exist neighboring states that are not accessible from P_0 along quasistatic adiabatic paths.

It follows from Carathéodory's theorem that his statement of the second law is possible if, and only if, there exist functions T and S such that

$$dQ = A\,dx + B\,dy + C\,dz = T\,dS.$$

Thus, by stating the second law in terms of the inaccessibility of certain states by adiabatic paths, and by using a mathematical theorem, Carathéodory deduced the existence of an entropy function and an integrating factor connected with Kelvin temperature, which reassures us of the validity of Clausius'

---

† For a complete discussion, see H. A. Buchdahl: *Twenty Lectures on Thermodynamics*, Pergamon, Elmsford, NY, 1975.

theorem. The difficulty with Carathéodory's statement of the second law is that no physical intuition is developed, as is in the study of the characteristics of heat engines.

23.4
ENTROPY OF THE IDEAL GAS

If a system absorbs an infinitesimal amount of heat $đQ_R$ during a reversible process, the entropy change of the system is given by Eq. (23.6),

$$dS = \frac{đQ_R}{T}.$$

It is interesting to notice that, although $đQ_R$ is an inexact differential, the ratio $đQ_R/T$ is exact. The reciprocal of the absolute thermodynamic temperature is, therefore, the integrating factor of $đQ_R$. If $đQ_R$ is expressed as a sum of differentials involving thermodynamic coordinates, then, upon dividing by T, the expression may be integrated and the entropy of the system obtained. As an example of this procedure, consider one of the expressions for $đQ_R$ of the ideal gas, namely, Eq. (5.10),

$$đQ_R = C_P \, dT - V \, dP.$$

Dividing by T, we get

$$\frac{đQ_R}{T} = C_P \frac{dT}{T} - \frac{V}{T} \, dP,$$

or

$$dS = C_P \frac{dT}{T} - nR \frac{dP}{P}. \tag{23.7}$$

Let us now calculate the entropy change ΔS of the ideal gas between an arbitrarily chosen *reference state r* with coordinates T_r, P_r, and any other state with coordinates T, P. Integrating between these two states, we get

$$\Delta S = \int_{T_r}^{T} C_P \frac{dT}{T} - nR \ln \frac{P}{P_r}.$$

Suppose we assign to the reference state an entropy S_r and choose *any arbitrary numerical value* for this quantity. Then, an entropy S may be associated with the other state where $S - S_r = \Delta S$. To make the discussion simpler, let C_P be constant. Then,

$$S - S_r = C_P \ln \frac{T}{T_r} - nR \ln \frac{P}{P_r},$$

and this may be rewritten

$$S = C_P \ln T - nR \ln P + (S_r - C_P \ln T_r + nR \ln P_r).$$

Denoting the quantity in parentheses by the *constant* S_0, we get, finally,

$$S = C_P \ln T - nR \ln P + S_0. \tag{23.8}$$

Substituting for T and P thousands of different values, we may calculate thousands of corresponding values of S, which form an *entropy table*. Any one value from this table, taken alone, will have no meaning. The difference between two values, however, will be an actual change of entropy.

Let us investigate the meaning of the standard state entropy S_0 by returning to Eq. (23.7),

$$dS = C_P \frac{dT}{T} - nR \frac{dP}{P}.$$

Again, for simplicity, assuming C_P to be constant, we may take the indefinite integral and obtain

$$S = C_P \ln T - nR \ln P + S_0,$$

where S_0 is the constant of integration. This result is precisely Eq.(23.8) obtained previously by taking into account the reference state. We see that, in taking the indefinite integral of dS, we do not obtain an "absolute entropy," but merely an entropy referred to an unspecified reference state whose coordinates are contained within the constant of integration. The reference state is arbitrarily chosen, usually for convenience and practicality. Thus, chemists use $0.1\,\text{MPa}$ and $25°\text{C}$ ($298\,\text{K}$) as the reference state for chemical reactions; engineers use the triple point of water for steam processes; and physicists use $0.1\,\text{MPa}$ and absolute zero for low-temperature calculations. Once the reference state is chosen, the constant of integration S_0 can be evaluated and entropy tables constructed.

Let us calculate the *change of* entropy of the ideal gas as a function of T and V by using the expression for $đQ_R$ of the ideal gas. Thus,

$$\frac{đQ_R}{T} = C_V \frac{dT}{T} + \frac{P}{T}\, dV,$$

and

$$dS = C_V \frac{dT}{T} + nR \frac{dV}{V},$$

where C_V is the heat capacity at constant volume. Integrating dS, we obtain

$$S = \int C_V \frac{dT}{T} + nR \ln V + S_0. \tag{23.9}$$

In terms of the molar specific heat at constant volume c_V, the change of entropy of the ideal gas between an initial state and final state is given by

$$\boxed{\Delta S = n \int_i^f c_V \frac{dT}{T} + nR \ln \frac{V_f}{V_i}.} \tag{23.10}$$

Similarly, for the change of entropy of an ideal gas as a function of T and P, we use Eq. (23.7) to obtain

$$\Delta S = n \int_i^f c_P \frac{dT}{T} + nR \ln \frac{P_f}{P_i}, \qquad (23.11)$$

where c_P is the molar specific heat at constant pressure.

23.5
TS DIAGRAM

For every infinitesimal amount of heat that enters a system during an infinitesimal portion of a reversible process, there is an equation

$$đQ_R = T\, dS.$$

It follows, therefore, that the total amount of heat transferred in a reversible process is given by

$$Q_R = \int_i^f T\, dS.$$

This integral can be interpreted graphically as the area under a curve on a diagram in which T is plotted along the y-axis and S along the x-axis, a so-called "TS diagram." The shape of the curve on the TS diagram is determined by the kind of reversible process that the system undergoes. Obviously, an isothermal process is a horizontal line, but in the case of a reversible adiabatic process, we have

$$dS = \frac{đQ_R}{T}.$$

Also, for an adiabatic process,

$$đQ = 0.$$

So, if T is not zero, then

$$dS = 0,$$

and S is constant. Therefore, during a reversible adiabatic process, the entropy of a system remains constant, or, in other words, the system undergoes an *isentropic process*. An isentropic process on a TS diagram is obviously a vertical line, called an "isentrope." Also obvious is that an isothermal process on a TS diagram is a horizontal line, called an "isotherm."

It is clear that the two isothermal and the two adiabatic process that make up any Carnot cycle form a rectangle on a TS diagram, regardless of the nature of the working substance, unlike the many shapes found in work diagrams for the heat engines. It was with this knowledge that we represented a Carnot engine. Only reversible processes may be plotted on a TS diagram, because of the definition of entropy in Eq. (23.6). The TS diagram is particularly convenient for representing all the idealized reversible cycles for various heat engines. The closed curve shown in Fig. 23-5 consisting of an upper portion R_1 and a lower portion R_2 represents any reversible engine cycle that is not a Carnot cycle. The area under R_1 (positive area) is equal to the positive heat Q_1 absorbed by the system, and the area under R_2 (negative area) is equal to the negative heat Q_2 rejected by the system. The area inside the closed curve is, therefore, $Q_1 - Q_2$, or W. The thermal efficiency of the engine is W/Q_1, which may be measured directly from the diagram.

Other processes are also plotted on a TS diagram. For a reversible *isobaric* process, the curve has a slope that follows from Eq.(23.7) by imposing constant pressure; thus,

$$\left(\frac{\partial T}{\partial S}\right)_P = \frac{T}{C_P}. \tag{23.12}$$

Similarly, by imposing the condition of constant volume on the equation preceding Eq. (23.9), the slope of a reversible *isochoric* process is given by

$$\left(\frac{\partial T}{\partial S}\right)_V = \frac{T}{C_V}. \tag{23.13}$$

The slopes given by Eqs. (23.12) and (23.13) are independent of the nature of the hydrostatic system, because the requirement of constant pressure and constant volume eliminated the equation of state of the ideal gas used in Eqs. (23.7) and

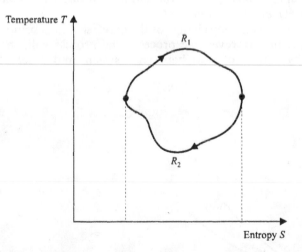

FIGURE 23-5
An arbitrary reversible cycle on a TS diagram. The area under upper portion R_1 equals the positive heat Q_1 absorbed by the system; the area under lower portion R_2 equals the negative heat Q_2 rejected by the system. The Carnot cycle for the same system would be represented by a rectangle enclosing the closed curve.

(23.10). Curves representing various types of processes of a hydrostatic system are shown on a *TS* diagram in Fig. 23-6.

23.6
ENTROPY AND REVERSIBILITY

In order to understand the physical meaning of entropy and its significance, it is necessary to study *all* the entropy changes that take place when a system undergoes a reversible process. If we calculate the entropy change of the system and add the calculated entropy change of the surroundings, then we obtain the sum of the entropy changes brought about by this particular process. We may call this sum the *entropy change of the universe* due to the process in question.

When a finite amount of heat is absorbed or rejected by a reservoir, extremely small changes in the coordinates occur in every unit of mass of the reservoir. The entropy change of a unit of mass is, therefore, very small. However, since the total mass of a reservoir is large, the total entropy change of the reservoir is finite. Suppose that a reservoir is in contact with a system and that heat Q is absorbed irreversibly by the reservoir at the temperature T. The reservoir undergoes nondissipative changes determined entirely by the quantity of heat absorbed. Exactly the same changes *in the reservoir* would occur if the same amount of heat Q were transferred reversibly. Hence, the entropy change of the reservoir is Q/T. Therefore, *whenever a reservoir absorbs heat Q at the temperature T from any system during any kind of process, the entropy change of the* **reservoir** *is Q/T*.

Consider now the entropy change of the universe that is brought about by the performance of any reversible process. The process will, in general, be accompanied by a flow of heat between a system and a set of reservoirs

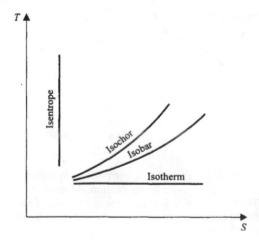

FIGURE 23-6
Curves representing reversible processes of a hydrostatic system on a *TS* diagram.

ranging in temperature from T_i to T_f. During *any* infinitesimal portion of the process, an amount of heat dQ_R is transferred between the system and one of the reservoirs at the temperature T. If dQ_R is absorbed by the system, then

$$dS \text{ of the system } = +\frac{dQ_R}{T},$$

$$dS \text{ of the reservoir } = -\frac{dQ_R}{T},$$

and the entropy change of the universe, which is the sum of these two changes, is zero. If dQ_R is rejected by the system, then, obviously,

$$dS \text{ of the system } = -\frac{dQ_R}{T},$$

$$dS \text{ of the reservoir } = +\frac{dQ_R}{T},$$

and the entropy change of the universe is again zero. If no heat is transferred, then dQ_R is zero. Neither the system nor the reservoir will have an entropy change, and the entropy change of the universe is still zero. Since there is no infinitesimal entropy change of the universe for any infinitesimal portion of the reversible process, then there is no entropy change for all such portions. In general, *the change of entropy of the universe is zero for a reversible process.* In other words, when a reversible process is performed, the entropy of the universe remains unchanged. However, all natural processes are irreversible and only ideal processes are reversible.

23.7
ENTROPY AND IRREVERSIBILITY

During an *irreversible* process, there is a different situation for the entropy change of the universe. When a system undergoes an irreversible process between an initial equilibrium state and a final equilibrium state, the irreversible process is replaced by a reversible one. This replacement is permitted when the initial and the final state of the system are equilibrium states. No integration is performed over the original irreversible path, because the path is not known. The entropy change of the system is equal to

$$S_f - S_i = _R\!\!\int_i^f \frac{dQ}{T},$$

where R indicates *any arbitrarily chosen* reversible process by which the system is brought from the given initial state to the given final state of the irreversible process. When either the initial or the final state is a nonequilibrium state, special methods must be used, which will discussed in Sec. 23.10. For the present, we shall limit ourselves to irreversible processes, all of which involve initial and final states of equilibrium.

Processes exhibiting external mechanical irreversibility

(*a*) Examples are those processes involving the isothermal dissipation of work through a system (which remains unchanged) into internal energy of a reservoir, such as:

1. Friction from two solids in contact with a reservoir.
2. Irregular stirring of a viscous liquid in contact with a reservoir (e.g., Joule paddle wheel apparatus).
3. Inelastic deformation of a solid in contact with a reservoir.
4. Transfer of charge through a resistor in contact with a reservoir.
5. Magnetic hysteresis of a material in contact with a reservoir.

In the case of any process involving the *isothermal* transformation of work W done by a system into internal energy of a reservoir, there is no entropy change of the system because the thermodynamic coordinates of the system do not change. Heat Q is absorbed by the reservoir, where $Q = W$ from the work done on the reservoir. Since the reservoir absorbs $+Q$ units of heat at the temperature T, the entropy change of the reservoir is $+Q/T$ or $+W/T$. The entropy change of the universe is, therefore, also $+W/T$, which is a positive quantity.

(*b*) Further examples are those processes involving the adiabatic dissipation of work into internal energy of a system open to the atmosphere, such as:

1. Friction from rubbing thermally insulated liquids.
2. Irregular stirring of a viscous thermally insulated liquid.
3. Inelastic deformation of a thermally insulated solid.
4. Transfer of charge through a thermally insulated resistor.
5. Magnetic hysteresis of a thermally insulated material.

In the case of any process involving the *adiabatic* transformation of work W into internal energy of a system whose temperature *rises* from T_i to T_f at constant atmospheric pressure, there is no flow of heat to or from the surroundings, and, therefore, the entropy change of the local surroundings is zero. To calculate the entropy change of the system, the original irreversible process must be replaced by a reversible one that will take the system from the given initial state (temperature T_i, pressure P) to the final state (temperature T_f, pressure P). Let us replace the irreversible performance of work by a reversible isobaric flow of heat from a series of reservoirs ranging in temperature from T_i to T_f. The entropy change of the system will then be

$$S_f - S_i \,(\text{system}) = {}_R\!\!\int_{T_i}^{T_f} \frac{dQ}{T}.$$

For an isobaric process,

$$ đQ = C_P\, dT, $$

and, so,

$$ S_f - S_i\ (\text{system}) = \int_{T_i}^{T_f} C_P\, \frac{dT}{T}. $$

Finally, if C_P is assumed not to be a function of temperature, then the entropy change of the system is

$$ S_f - S_i\ (\text{system}) = C_P \ln \frac{T_f}{T_i}. \qquad (23.14) $$

Thus, the entropy change of the universe is also $C_P \ln (T_f/T_i)$, which is a positive quantity.

Processes exhibiting internal mechanical irreversibility. Examples are those processes involving the transformation of internal energy of a system enclosed by adiabatic walls into mechanical energy and then back into internal energy again, such as:

1. Ideal gas rushing into a vacuum (free expansion, i.e., Joule expansion).
2. Gas flowing through a porous plug (throttling process, i.e., Joule-Thomson expansion).
3. Snapping of a stretched wire after it is cut.
4. Collapse of a soap film after it is punctured.

In the case of a free expansion of the ideal gas, the entropy change of the local surroundings is zero, because there is no heat transfer through the adiabatic walls. In order to calculate the entropy change of the system, the free expansion must be replaced by a reversible process that will take the gas from its original state (volume V_i, temperature T) to the final state (volume V_f, temperature T), where temperature does not change for the ideal gas during expansion. Evidently, the most convenient reversible process to replace the irreversible process, for the purpose of calculation, is a reversible isothermal expansion at the temperature T from a volume V_i to the volume V_f. The entropy change of the system is then

$$ S_f - S_i\ (\text{system}) = {}_R\!\int_{V_i}^{V_f} \frac{đQ}{T}. $$

For an isothermal process of the ideal gas,

$$ đQ_R = P\, dV, $$

and

$$ \frac{đQ_R}{T} = nR\, \frac{dV}{V}, $$

which yields, for the entropy change of the system,

$$S_f - S_i \text{ (system)} = nR \ln \frac{V_f}{V_i}. \tag{23.15}$$

The entropy change of the universe is, therefore, $nR \ln (V_f/V_i)$, which is a positive number.

Once again, we see that the entropy of the universe, which is the system, has increased, even though no heat entered or left the system. This result may seem puzzling, because entropy is defined in terms of the heat entering or leaving a system. The puzzle is resolved by recognizing that the free expansion of the ideal gas within an adiabatic container is not a *reversible* process. During an irreversible process, the entropy change of the universe, even if the process is adiabatic, is always positive.

Processes exhibiting external thermal irreversibility. Examples are those processes involving a transfer of heat by virtue of a *finite* temperature difference, such as:

1. Conduction or radiation of heat from a system to its cooler surroundings.
2. Conduction or radiation of heat through a system (which remains unchanged) from a hot reservoir to a cooler one.

In the case of the conduction of Q units of heat from one end to the other end of a system (which remains unchanged) from a hotter reservoir at T_1 to a cooler reservoir at T_2, the following steps are obvious:

$$S_f - S_i \text{ (system)} = 0.$$

$$S_f - S_i \text{ (hotter reservoir)} = -\frac{Q}{T_1}.$$

$$S_f - S_i \text{ (cooler reservoir)} = +\frac{Q}{T_2}.$$

$$S_f - S_i \text{ (universe)} = \frac{Q}{T_2} - \frac{Q}{T_1}. \tag{23.16}$$

The entropy change of the universe is positive, because T_2 is less than T_1.

Processes exhibiting chemical irreversibility. Examples are those processes involving a spontaneous change of internal structure, density, chemical composition, etc., such as:

1. Diffusion of two dissimilar inert ideal gases.
2. Mixing of alcohol and water.
3. Osmosis.
4. Freezing of supercooled liquid.
5. Condensation of a supersaturated vapor.
6. Dissolution of a solid in water.
7. A chemical reaction.

Assume that the diffusion of two dissimilar inert ideal gases is equivalent to two separate free expansions in an adiabatic enclosure with chambers of equal volume. For one of the gases, the change of entropy is given by Eq. (23.15),

$$S_f - S_i \text{ (system)} = nR \ln \frac{V_f}{V_i},$$

namely,

$$S_f - S_i \text{ (one gas)} = nR \ln \frac{V_f}{V_i},$$

which is a positive number, because $V_f/V_i > 1$. The other half of the system experiences the same entropy change. Since there is no entropy change of the reservoir, the entropy change of the universe is

$$S_f - S_i \text{ (universe)} = 2nR \ln \frac{V_f}{V_i}, \qquad (23.17)$$

which is a positive number. In general, *the change of entropy is positive for any irreversible process*. All the results of this section are summarized in Table (23.1.)

TABLE 23.1
Entropy change of the universe due to natural processes

Type of irreversibility	Irreversible process	Entropy change of the system	Entropy change of the local surroundings	Entropy change of the universe
External mechanical irreversibility	Isothermal dissipation of work through a system into internal energy of a reservoir	0	$\dfrac{W}{T}$	$\dfrac{W}{T}$
	Adiabatic dissipation of work into internal energy of a system	$C_P \ln \dfrac{T_f}{T_i}$	0	$C_P \ln \dfrac{T_f}{T_i}$
Internal mechanical irreversibility	Free expansion of an ideal gas	$nR \ln \dfrac{V_f}{V_i}$	0	$nR \ln \dfrac{V_f}{V_i}$
External thermal irreversibility	Transfer of heat through a medium from a hotter to a cooler reservoir	0	$\dfrac{Q}{T_2} - \dfrac{Q}{T_1}$	$\dfrac{Q}{T_2} - \dfrac{Q}{T_1}$
Chemical irreversibility	Diffusion of two dissimilar inert ideal gases	$2nR \ln \dfrac{V_f}{V_i}$	0	$2nR \ln \dfrac{V_f}{V_i}$

23.8
IRREVERSIBLE PART OF THE SECOND LAW

The first part of the second law considered only reversible processes. The second part deals with irreversible processes. Recall that for a reversible cycle, Eq. (23.3) states that

$$\oint_R \frac{đQ}{T} = 0 \qquad \text{(reversible)}. \tag{23.3}$$

Let us consider an *irreversible* cycle and calculate its closed integral. Figure 23-7 shows a high-temperature reservoir at T_1 supplying a small quantity of heat $đQ_1$ to an auxiliary reversible engine R. The purpose of R is to provide reversible heat for the irreversible engine I. Engine R rejects a small amount of heat $đQ$ at temperature T that is supplied to the irreversible engine I. Engine I does a small amount of work $đW$ during an irreversible cycle, so the combined system of engine R and engine I also performs an irreversible cycle. The net work of the combined system, according to the first law, equals $\oint đQ_1$. But the net work cannot be positive, according to the Kelvin-Planck statement of the second law, since the combined system exchanges heat with a single reservoir. So, $\oint đQ_1$ cannot be positive. Moreover, if $\oint đQ_1$ equals zero, then, at the end of the cycle, engine I and its surroundings have returned to their original state. This result, however, is contrary to the irreversibility of engine I. So, we conclude,

$$\oint_R đQ_1 < 0; \tag{23.18}$$

that is, engine I generates heat that flows out of the system. From the definition of the thermodynamic temperature scale. We have, in differential form for reversible engine R,

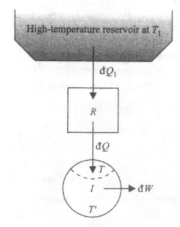

FIGURE 23-7
A high-temperature reservoir at temperature T_1 supplies heat $đQ_1$ to an auxiliary reversible engine R. Irreversible engine I receives heat $đQ$ at temperature T, even though the system was initially at temperature T'.

$$\frac{dQ_1}{T_1} = -\frac{dQ}{T}.$$

Integrating around a cycle,

$$\oint_R \frac{-dQ}{T} = \oint_R \frac{dQ_1}{T_1}.$$

However, T_1 is the constant temperature of the reservoir, so

$$-\oint_R \frac{dQ}{T} = \frac{1}{T_1} \oint_R dQ_1. \qquad (23.19)$$

The heat dQ rejected from R is absorbed by I, so, $-dQ_R = dQ_I$. Substituting this expression in Eq. (23.19) and recognizing that the closed integral on the left now applies to the irreversible system, we obtain

$$\oint_I \frac{dQ}{T} = \frac{1}{T_1} \oint_R dQ_1,$$

or

$$T_1 \oint_I \frac{dQ}{T} = \oint_R dQ_1 < 0$$

from Eq. (23.18). Since $T_1 > 0$, the result is

$$\boxed{\oint_I \frac{dQ}{T} < 0} \qquad \text{(irreversible)}. \qquad (23.20)$$

Equation (23.20) provides the second part of the second law and is known as the *Inequality of Clausius*. It states that *for an internally irreversible cycle, the closed integral* $_I \oint dQ/T$ *of the ratio of the heat absorbed by a system to the temperature* **at which the heat is received** *is always less than zero.* Compare Eq. (23.20) with Eq. (23.3) and notice that the closed integral is less than zero for an irreversible cycle and equal to zero for a reversible cycle. Combining the two equations yields Clausius' mathematical statement of the second law:

$$\boxed{\oint \frac{dQ}{T} \leq 0.} \qquad (23.21)$$

In order to avoid misunderstandings as to the meaning of Eq. (23.3), the equality for reversible cycles, and Eq. (23.20), the inequality for irreversible cycles, we must point out that T represents the temperature of the reservoir or auxiliary reversible engine that provides the small quantity of heat dQ, and is *not* necessarily equal to the temperature T' of the system (or part of the system) that receives the heat dQ. Indeed, if the cycle is irreversible, then $T' \leq T$ when dQ is positive, because heat cannot flow spontaneously from a cooler to a hotter body. Similarly, $T' \geq T$ when dQ is negative. On the other hand, if the cycle is reversible, then we must always have $T' = T$, because an exchange of heat between two bodies at different temperatures is not reversible. In Eq. (23.3), we may take T to be the temperature of the reservoir or auxiliary surroundings and also the temperature of the part of the system that absorbs the heat $đQ$. In Eq.(23.3), all quantities refer to the system itself, and the integral is evaluated for a closed path taken by the reversible system. In Eq. (23.20), everything refers to the auxiliary reservoirs, and the integral is evaluated for a closed range of reservoir temperatures through which, incidentally, the irreversible system is brought back to its initial state.

23.9
HEAT AND ENTROPY IN IRREVERSIBLE PROCESSES

In order to relate change of entropy to heat in irreversible processes, consider a cycle in which a system begins in an initial equilibrium state i, passes during an irreversible process I to a final equilibrium state f, and then returns by a reversible process R to the initial state i, as shown in Fig. 23-8. Since entropy is a state function, its closed integral is always zero:

$$\oint dS = {}_I\!\int_i^f dS + {}_R\!\int_f^i dS = 0. \tag{23.22}$$

From Eq. (23.20) we obtain

$$_I\!\oint \frac{đQ}{T} = {}_I\!\int_i^f \frac{đQ}{T} + {}_R\!\int_f^i \frac{đQ}{T} < 0. \tag{23.23}$$

From Eq. (23.6), the definition of entropy, we can write

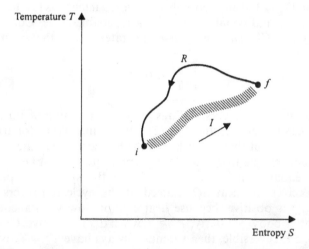

FIGURE 23-8
An irreversible process followed by a reversible process to complete an irreversible cycle.

$$\int_R \int_i^f \frac{\text{d}Q}{T} = \int_R \int_i^f dS.$$

Subtract Eq. (23.23) from Eq. (23.22) and substitute the equation cited above; then,

$$\int_I \int_i^f dS - \int_I \int_i^f \frac{\text{d}Q}{T} > 0,$$

or

$$\int_I \int_i^f dS > \int_I \int_i^f \frac{\text{d}Q}{T}, \tag{23.24}$$

which means that the change of entropy during an irreversible process is greater than the integral of the heat divided by the temperature of the auxiliary reservoirs.

For small changes in state, Eq. (23.24) can be written

$$dS_I > \left(\frac{\text{d}Q}{T}\right)_I. \tag{23.25}$$

In general, we have

$$dS \geq \frac{\text{d}Q}{T}, \tag{23.26}$$

where the equality applies to reversible processes and the inequality applies to irreversible processes.

Various expressions for conditions involving entropy require careful consideration. According to the definition of entropy in Eq. (23.6),

$$dS - \frac{\text{d}Q_R}{T},$$

the change in entropy in a reversible and adiabatic process ($\text{d}Q_R = 0$) is zero. Thus, the term *reversible adiabatic* implies the term *isentropic*. *Isentropic*, however, does not necessarily imply *reversible adiabatic*. For an isentropic process, in general, we have

$$dS = 0.$$

Substituting Eq. (23.26) into this expression, we have

$$\frac{\text{d}Q}{T} \leq 0.$$

It follows that for an isentropic process, *either*

$$\text{d}Q = 0 \qquad \text{(reversible)},$$

or

$$\text{d}Q < 0 \qquad \text{(irreversible)}.$$

Thus, *reversible isentropic* implies *adiabatic*, and *isentropic adiabatic* implies *reversible*. But, *irreversible isentropic* is *not* adiabatic ($\text{d}Q < 0$) and implies that heat flows out of the system. Of course, if the process is *irreversible adiabatic*, then it is *not* isentropic (T not constant) and implies that the temperature increases. Finally, if the process is *isentropic adiabatic*, then it is *not* irreversible ($dQ_R = 0$) and implies that the process is reversible.

23.10
ENTROPY AND NONEQUILIBRIUM STATES

The calculation of the entropy changes associated with the irreversible processes discussed in Sec. 23.7 presented no special difficulties because, in all cases, the system either did not change at all (in which case, only the entropy changes of reservoirs had to be calculated) or *both* the initial and final states of a system were equilibrium states that could be connected by a suitable reversible process. Consider, however, the following process involving internal thermal irreversibility with equilibrium only in the final state. A thermally conducting bar has a nonuniform temperature distribution by connecting one end to a high-temperature reservoir and the other end to a low-temperature reservoir. The bar is removed from the reservoirs and is then thermally insulated with adiabatic walls at constant pressure. An internal flow of heat will finally bring the bar to a uniform temperature, so the irreversible process will be from an initial nonequilibrium state to a final equilibrium state. It is obviously impossible to replace the irreversible process with a reversible process, because the initial state is a nonequilibrium state. What meaning, therefore, may be attached to the entropy change associated with this irreversible process?

Let us consider a bar to be composed of an infinite number of infinitesimally thin slices (volume elements), each of which has a different initial temperature but all of which have the same final temperature. Suppose we imagine that all the slices are insulated from one another and all are kept at the same pressure, and then each slice is put in contact successively with a series of reservoirs ranging in temperature from the initial temperature of the particular section to the common final temperature. This model defines an infinite number of reversible isobaric processes for each slice, which may be used to take each slice of the system from its initial nonequilibrium state to its final equilibrium state. We shall now define the entropy change as the result of integrating dQ/T over all of these reversible processes. In other words, in the absence of one reversible process to take the system from i to f, we conceive of an infinite number of reversible processes for each volume element.

Consider a uniform bar of length L as depicted in Fig. 23-9. A typical volume element at x has a mass

$$dm = \rho A \, dx,$$

where ρ is the density and A is the cross-sectional area of the bar. The heat capacity of the *volume element* is

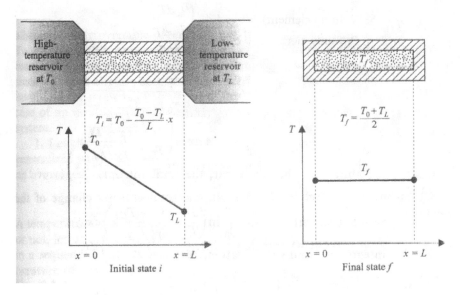

FIGURE 23.9
Process exhibiting internal thermal irreversibility.

$$c_P \, dm = c_P \rho A \, dx.$$

Let us suppose that the initial temperature distribution is linear along the length of the bar, so that the volume element at x has an initial temperature

$$T_i = T_0 - \frac{T_0 - T_L}{L} x,$$

where the temperature is T_0 at $x = 0$, and T_L at $x = L$. If no heat is lost and if we assume for the sake of simplicity that the thermal conductivity, density, and heat capacity of all volume elements remain constant, then the final temperature of the entire length of the bar will be

$$T_f = \frac{T_0 + T_L}{2}.$$

Integrating dQ/T over a reversible isobaric transfer of heat between a particular volume element and a series of reservoirs ranging in temperature from T_i to T_f, we get, for the entropy change of *this one volume element*,

$$S_f - S_i \text{ (volume element)} = c_P \rho A \, dx \int_{T_i}^{T_f} \frac{dT}{T}$$

$$= c_P \rho A \, dx \ln \frac{T_f}{T_i}$$

$$= c_P \rho A \, dx \ln \frac{T_f}{T_0 - \dfrac{T_0 - T_L}{L} x}$$

$$= -c_P \dot{\rho} A \, dx \ln \left(\frac{T_0}{T_f} - \frac{T_0 - T_L}{L T_f} x \right).$$

Upon integrating over the whole bar, the total entropy change of the system is

$$S_f - S_i \text{ (system)} = -c_P \rho A \int_0^L \ln \left(\frac{T_0}{T_f} - \frac{T_0 - T_L}{L T_f} x \right) dx,$$

which, after integration[†] and simplification, becomes

$$S_f - S_i \text{ (system)} = C_P \left[1 - \ln \left(\frac{T_L}{T_f} \right) + \frac{T_0}{T_0 - T_L} \ln \left(\frac{T_L}{T_0} \right) \right]. \qquad (23.27)$$

Since the bar is enclosed by an adiabatic enclosure, there is no entropy change of the surroundings. Hence, the entropy change of the universe is also given by Eq. (23.27). In order to show that the entropy change is positive, let us take a convenient numerical case, such as $T_0 = 400 \, \text{K}$, $T_L = 200 \, \text{K}$; hence, $T_f = 300 \, \text{K}$. Then,

$$S_f - S_i \text{ (universe)} = C_P (1 - \ln \tfrac{2}{3} + 2 \ln \tfrac{1}{2}) = C_P (1 + \ln 3 - 3 \ln 2)$$
$$= 0.018 \, C_P,$$

where it is seen that entropy and heat capacity have the same units: joule per kelvin.

The same method may be used to compute the entropy change of a system during a process from an initial nonequilibrium state, characterized by a nonuniform pressure distribution, to a final equilibrium state where the pressure is uniform. Examples of such processes are given in the problems at the end of the chapter.

23.11
PRINCIPLE OF INCREASE OF ENTROPY

The entropy change of the universe was found to be positive for each of the irreversible processes treated so far. We are led to believe, therefore, that

---

[†] $\int \ln (a + bx) \, dx = \frac{1}{b} (a + bx)[\ln (a + bx) - 1]$.

whenever an irreversible process occurs, the entropy of the universe increases. To establish this proposition, known as the *entropy principle*, in a general manner, it is sufficient to confine our attention to adiabatic processes only, since we have already seen that the entropy principle is true for all processes involving the irreversible transfer of heat. We start by considering the special case of an adiabatic irreversible process between two equilibrium states of a system.

1. Let the initial state of the system be represented by the point i on the generalized work diagram of Fig. 23-10, and suppose that the system undergoes an *irreversible adiabatic process* to the state f. Then the entropy change is

$$\Delta S = S_f - S_i. \tag{23.28}$$

A temperature change may or may not have occurred in the system. Whether or not, let us cause the system to undergo a *reversible adiabatic process* $f \rightarrow k$ in a sequence of steps that brings the temperature of the system to the temperature of any arbitrarily chosen reservoir, say, at T'. Then, since $S_f = S_k$, Eq. (23.28) becomes

$$\Delta S = S_k - S_i. \tag{23.29}$$

Now, suppose that the system is brought into contact with the reservoir at T' and the system undergoes a *reversible isothermal process* $k \rightarrow j$ until its entropy is the same in state j as in the initial state i. A final *reversible adiabatic process* $j \rightarrow i$ will now bring the system back to its initial state with no change of entropy; and, since $S_j = S_i$, Eq. (23.29) becomes

$$\Delta S = S_k - S_j. \tag{23.30}$$

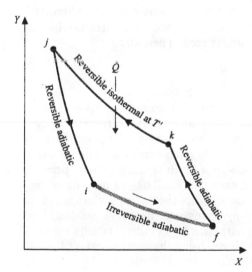

FIGURE 23-10
A cycle that contradicts the second law unless $S_f > S_i$.

The only heat transfer Q_R occurred in the cycle during the reversible isothermal process $k \rightarrow j$, where

$$Q_R = T'(S_j - S_k).$$

A net amount of work W has been done in the cycle, where

$$W = Q_R.$$

It is clear from the second law of thermodynamics that the heat Q_R cannot have entered the system, that is, Q_R cannot be positive, for then we would have a cyclic process where the only effect would be the absorption of heat from a single reservoir and the performance of an equivalent amount of work. Therefore, $Q_R \leq 0$, and

$$T'(S_j - S_k) \leq 0,$$

and, finally, since the process went from state k to state j,

$$T'(S_k - S_j) \geq 0.$$

However, $T' \geq 0$, so

$$S_k - S_j = \Delta S \geq 0. \tag{23.31}$$

2. If we assume that the original irreversible adiabatic process occurred without any change in entropy, then it would be possible to bring the system back to i by means of one reversible adiabatic process. Moreover, since the net heat transferred in this cycle is zero, the net work would also be zero. Therefore, under these circumstances, the system and its surroundings would have been restored to their initial states without producing changes elsewhere, which implies that the original process was reversible. Since this is contrary to our original assertion that the process was irreversible, the entropy of the system cannot remain unchanged. Therefore,

$$\Delta S > 0, \tag{23.32}$$

because the entropy change could not have decreased.

3. Let us now suppose that the system is not homogeneous and not at uniform temperature and pressure and that it undergoes an irreversible adiabatic process in which mixing and chemical reaction may take place. First, we assume that the system may be subdivided into parts (each one infinitesimal, if necessary) and that it is possible to assign a definite temperature, pressure, composition, etc., to each part, so that each part shall have a definite entropy depending on its coordinates, so we may define the entropy changes of the whole system as the sum of the entropy changes of its parts. Second, if we assume that it is possible to take *each part* back to its initial state by means of the reversible processes described in 1 above, using the same reservoir for each part, then it follows that ΔS of the whole system is positive.

It should be emphasized that we have had to make two assumptions, namely: (1) that the entropy change of a system may be defined by subdividing the system into parts and summing the entropy changes of these parts; and (2) that reversible processes may be found or imagined by which mixtures may be unmixed and reactions may be caused to proceed in the opposite direction. The justification for these assumptions rests, to a small extent, on experimental grounds. Thus, in a later chapter, there will be described a device involving semipermeable membranes whereby a mixture of two different inert ideal gases may be separated reversibly. A similar device through which a chemical reaction may be caused to proceed reversibly through any set of equilibrium states may also be conceived. Nevertheless, the main justification for these assumptions is that experiment completely agrees with the *entropy principle*, which states that the change of entropy of the universe increases in an irreversible process.

The behavior of the entropy of the universe as a result of *any* kind of process may now be represented simply.

$$\boxed{\Delta S \text{ (universe)} \geq 0,}$$

(23.33)

where the equality sign refers to reversible processes and the inequality sign to irreversible processes. Equation (23.33) is a succinct statement of the second law of thermodynamics.

23.12
APPLICATION OF THE ENTROPY PRINCIPLE

We have seen that whenever irreversible processes occur, the entropy of the universe increases. In the actual operation of a machine, such as an engine or a refrigerator, it is often possible to calculate the sum of all the entropy changes. The fact that this sum is positive enables us to draw useful conclusions concerning the behavior of the machine. An important example from the field of low-temperature physics will illustrate the power and simplicity of the entropy principle. Suppose one wants to cool an object with a refrigerator to a desired low temperature, that is, to lower the temperature of a body of finite mass from the temperature T_1 of its surroundings to any desired low temperature T_2. A refrigerator operating in a cycle between a reservoir at T_1 and the body itself is utilized, and, after several complete cycles have been completed, a quantity of heat Q has been removed from the body, a quantity of work W has been supplied to the refrigerator, and a quantity of heat $Q + W$ has been rejected to the reservoir, as shown in Fig. 23-11. Listing the entropy changes, we have

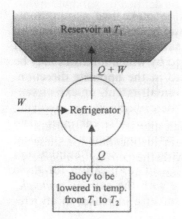

FIGURE 23-11
Operation of a refrigerator in lowering the temperature of a body from that of its surroundings T_1 to any desired temperature T_2.

$$\Delta S \text{ of the body} = S_2 - S_1,$$

$$\Delta S \text{ of the refrigerant} = 0,$$

and
$$\Delta S \text{ of the reservoir} = \frac{Q + W}{T_1}.$$

Applying the entropy principle, we obtain

$$S_2 - S_1 + \frac{Q + W}{T_1} \geq 0.$$

Multiplying by T_1 and transposing, we get

$$W \geq T_1(S_1 - S_2) - Q.$$

It follows that the smallest possible value for W is

$$W(\text{min}) = T_1(S_1 - S_2) - Q.$$

If tables of the thermodynamic properties of the material are available, then a knowledge of the initial and final states is all that is needed to read from the tables the values of $S_1 - S_2$ and, if the body undergoes an isobaric process, the values of Q. The calculated value of W (min) is used to provide an estimate of the minimum cost of operation of the refrigerator.

23.13
ENTROPY AND DISORDER

When applied to an irreversible process, Eq. (23.33) is very unusual in being an inequality. Unlike most quantities in physics and chemistry, the change of entropy of the system and its surroundings is not conserved, rather, it increases. In order to appreciate the concept of entropy, let us consider various natural processes and look for insights that are consistent with calculations.

First-order phase changes are irreversible,[†] isothermal processes that lend themselves to a descriptive discussion of entropy. For example, consider the phase change of sublimation, the transition of a solid to a vapor that occurs in dry ice. The change of entropy, which is the amount of heat absorbed during the sublimation divided by the sublimation temperature, increases as expected. But what can be said about the microscopic changes that occur when carbon dioxide molecules of dry ice escape from the solid into the vapor?

A solid is capable of supporting itself, whether in a crystalline state or amorphous state. Moreover, the material in the solid phase retains its size and shape, which means that the microscopic components (particles) of the system form a rigid structure. Simply stated, each particle retains its location in an organized strucure; that is, the solid is in a state of *order*.

As latent heat is supplied to a solid, the process of sublimation changes the solid into a vapor with no change of temperature. A vapor has no fixed size and shape; in fact, a vapor must be placed in a closed container or it is lost. The particles in the vapor are not individually restrained into any organized structure; rather, the vapor particles are free to move independently throughout the volume of the container. In other words, the vapor is in a state of *disorder*, relative to its solid phase. *An increase in entropy of a system can be described as an increase in the disorder of the system.* Notice that the concept of disorder is relative to a reference state, just as entropy is.

The use of disorder as a synonym for entropy can be extended beyond phase transitions as the following examples show.

1. The temperature of an ideal gas does not change and heat is not added to the system during a free expansion, yet the entropy increases, as seen in Eq. (23.15). The only difference between the initial state and the final state of the ideal gas is an increase of volume, which provides the gas particles with more space for their motion. Disorder, in this case, is not linked to a structural change that provides freedom of movement, as in the case of sublimation, but, rather, *more* freedom of movement is provided in a larger volume.

2. When the temperature of a ferromagnetic material is raised above its Curie point, the material suddenly loses its ferromagnetism and becomes paramagnetic. In the microscopic picture, the magnetic moments of the ferromagnetic material are mostly aligned in one direction (ordered). At temperatures above the Curie point, the magnetic moments are randomly

---

† Ordinarily, there is a finite difference in temperature between the reservoir and a system experiencing a phase transition; hence, Eq. (23.16) applies and the process is irreversible. If the difference in temperature is made increasingly smaller, then the process becomes more nearly reversible, but at the expense of slowing the rate of heat-flow between the reservoir and the system, which slows the rate of the transition from one phase to the other phase.

oriented (disordered) to produce paramagnetic behavior. From a thermodynamic point of view, the entropy increases in the transition from ferromagnetism to paramagnetism.

3. In the case of conduction of heat through a metal bar from a high-temperature reservoir to a low-temperature reservoir, there is no change of phase, volume, or temperature of the conductor, but the entropy of the universe increases, as seen in Eq. (23.16). The internal energy becomes disordered in its passage between reservoirs, because the internal energy has been dissipated in the low-temperature reservoir and cannot be used to run a heat engine.

4. The entropy increases in an isothermal conversion of work into internal energy, which then flows into a heat reservoir, such as occurs with the Joule paddle wheel shown in Fig. 23.4. It has been emphasized that work is a macroscopic concept. Changes must be describable by macroscopic coordinates external to the system, although the internal situation may be discussed, at least in the equilibrium state. Haphazard motions of individual particles do not constitute work. Thus, during the isothermal dissipation of work into heat, the disorderly motion of the particles in the reservoir is increased. The process increases the entropy of the reservoir, since the system is unchanged.

All these examples, involving irreversible processes, show that the entropy of the universe increases. It is possible to regard all natural processes from the point of view of orderliness, and, in all cases, the result obtained is that *isolated systems or systems plus surroundings experiencing irreversible processes proceed toward a state of greater disorder.* The increase of entropy of the universe during natural processes is an expression of this tendency. Living processes, such as growth or decay, are natural processes that increase disorder, when both the system and surroundings are considered, but the calculation of the increase of entropy is not simple, even in idealized cases.

The concept of entropy has importance in the discussion of time, a topic usually avoided in thermodynamics. The increase of entropy (disorder) of a system and its surroundings occurs in all aging processes, whether in a living organism or in an inanimate system. There is no doubt which condition is prior in time: youth or maturity, green apple or overripe apple, structure or erosion. One condition always precedes the other; order precedes disorder. Entropy always increases during an aging process. So, in a metaphorical sense, *entropy is the arrow of time.* Furthermore, the arrow has only one direction: it points forward into the future. True, special relativity provides that the forward progress of time slows down when masses approach the speed of light. But, so far, there is no consensus that time can be reversed to move backward into the past.

23.14
EXACT DIFFERENTIALS

Experiment shows that internal energy is related to heat and work in the following equation,

$$dU = đW + đQ,$$

which is, of course, the first law of thermodynamics. Apart from the obvious observation that energy is conserved in all its forms, there are two other insights important for thermodynamics. First, the small quantities of heat and work are *not* differentials of a mathematical function; that is, they are inexact differentials. But, more importantly, the sum of two inexact differentials yields an exact differential! The mathematical problem is to convert the inexact differentials into exact differentials.

The situation for dW is solved in mechanics, where the generalized work is the product of the generalized force and the generalized displacement. The The situation for dQ is more complicated.

In order to clarify the notion of heat, the concept of temperature had first to be refined. That required a detailed discussion of thermometers, experimental temperature, and the second law of thermodynamics applied to the Carnot cycle. As a result, the concept of temperature was detached from experiment to become the theoretical absolute thermodynamic temperature. Furthermore, Clausius introduced a totally new concept based on his analysis of a reversible cycle composed of many infinitesimal Carnot cycles, namely, the concept of entropy. The union of the concepts of temperature and entropy produced a way to express the inexact differential of heat in terms of exact differentials,

$$đQ = T \, dS.$$

Now, the first law can be rewritten in usable mathematical form, as, for example, in a hydrostatic system,

$$dU = -P \, dV + T \, dS.$$

In some ways, the thermodynamics is complete now that the inexact differentials for work and heat have been replaced with exact differentials. The only other fundamental law in thermodynamics is the third law, which sets entropy to zero at absolute zero, rather than setting it to zero at an arbitrary state. The remainder of this book is devoted to developing more mathematical functions and methods to aid in the calculation of the thermodynamic quantities, and bringing in quantum mechanics in the calculation of statistical mechanical quantities.

PROBLEMS

23.1. (*a*) Derive the expression for the efficiency of a Carnot engine directly from a *TS* diagram.
  (*b*) Compare the efficiencies of cycles *A* and *B* of Fig. P23-1

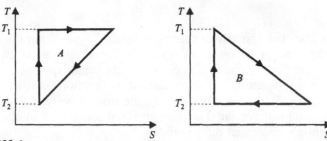

FIGURE P23-1

23.2. Prove that the slope on a *TS* diagram of:
  (*a*) An isochoric curve is T/C_V.
  (*b*) An isobaric curve is T/C_P.

23.3. Show that the partial derivatives given in Eqs. (23.12) and (23.13) are independent of the equation of state for the hydrostatic system.

23.4. Why does an isochoric curve plotted on a *TS* diagram have a greater slope than an isobaric curve at the same temperature?

23.5. Sketch *TS* diagrams for the following four ideal gas cycles: Otto; Diesel; a rectangle on a *PV* diagram; and a "right triangle" on a *PV* diagram in which the base is an isobaric, the altitude is an isochoric, and the "hypotenuse" is an adiabatic.

23.6. A current of 10 A is maintained for 1 s in a resistor of 25 Ω while the temperature of the resistor is kept constant at 27°C.
  (*a*) What is the entropy change of the resistor?
  (*b*) What is the entropy change of the universe?
  The same current is maintained for the same time in the same resistor, but now thermally insulated, with the same initial temperature. If the resistor has a mass of 10 g and a specific heat of 836 J/kg · K:
  (*c*) What is the entropy change of the resistor?
  (*d*) What is the entropy change of the universe?

23.7. (*a*) One kilogram of water at 273 K is brought into contact with a heat reservoir at 373 K. When the water has reached 373 K, what is the entropy change of the water, of the heat reservoir, and of the universe?
  (*b*) If the water had been heated from 273 to 373 K by first bringing it into contact with a reservoir at 323 K and then with a reservoir at 373 K, what would have been the entropy change of the universe?

(c) Explain how the water might be heated from 273 to 373 K with almost no change of entropy of the universe.

23.8. A body of constant heat capacity C_P and at a temperature T_i is put in contact with a reservoir at a higher temperature T_f. The pressure remains constant while the body comes to equilibrium with the reservoir. Show that the entropy change of the universe is equal to

$$\Delta S = C_P[x - \ln(1 + x)],$$

where $x = -(T_f - T_i)/T_f$. Prove that the entropy change is positive.

23.9. The molar heat capacity at constant magnetic field of a paramagnetic solid at low temperatures varies with the temperature and field according to the relation

$$c_{\mathscr{H}} = \frac{B + C\mathscr{H}^2}{T^2} + DT^2,$$

where B, C, and D are constants. What is the entropy change of n moles of material when the temperature changes from T_i to T_f while $\mathscr{H}$ remains constant at the value $\mathscr{H}_0$?

23.10. According to Debye's law, the molar heat capacity at constant volume of a diamond varies with the temperature as follows:

$$c_V = 3R \frac{4\pi^4}{5} \left(\frac{T}{\Theta}\right)^3.$$

What is the entropy change in units of R of a diamond of 1.2 g mass when it is heated at constant volume from 10 to 350 K? The molar mass of diamond is 12 g, and Θ is 2230 K.

23.11. A thermally insulated cylinder, closed at both ends, is fitted with a frictionless heat-conducting piston that divides the cylinder into two parts. Initially, the piston is clamped in the center with 1 liter of air at 300 K and 2 atm pressure on one side and 1 liter of air at 300 K at 1 atm pressure on the other side. The piston is released and reaches equilibrium in pressure and temperature at a new position. Compute the final pressure and temperature and increase of entropy if air is assumed to be the ideal gas. What irreversible process has taken place?

23.12. An adiabatic cylinder, closed at both ends, is fitted with a frictionless *adiabatic* piston that divides the cylinder into two parts. Initially the pressure, volume, and temperature are the same on both sides of the piston (P_0, V_0, and T_0). The gas is ideal with C_V independent of temperature and $\gamma = 1.5$. By means of a heating coil in the gas on the left side, heat is slowly supplied to the gas on the left until the pressure reaches $27P_0/8$. In terms of nR, V_0, and T_0:
(a) What is the final volume on the right side?
(b) What is the final temperature on the right side?
(c) What is the final temperature on the left side?
(d) How much heat must be supplied to the *gas* on the left side? (*Note*: Ignore the coil!)
(e) How much work is done on the gas on the right side?

(f) What is the entropy change of the gas on the right side?

(g) What is the entropy change of the gas on the left side?

(h) What is the entropy change of the universe?

23.13. Solve the problem of the uniform bar shown in Fig. 23-9 if only the hot reservoir is removed by showing that the entropy change of the universe is

$$\Delta S = C_P \left(1 + \frac{T_0 - T_L}{2T_L} - \frac{T_0}{T_0 - T_L} \ln \frac{T_o}{T_L} \right).$$

23.14. Calculate the entropy change of the universe as a result of the following processes:

(a) A copper block of 0.4 kg mass and with heat capacity at constant pressure of 150 J/K at 100°C is placed in a lake at 10°C.

(b) The same block at 10°C is dropped from a height of 100 m into the lake.

(c) Two such blocks at 100°C and 0°C are joined together.

23.15. What is the entropy change of the universe as a result of each of the following processes?

(a) A 1-μF capacitor is connected to a 100-V electrochemical cell at 0°C?

(b) The same capacitor, after being charged to 100 V, is discharged through a resistor kept at 0°C.

23.16. An ideal-gas cycle suggested by A. S. Arrott of British Columbia, Canada, is shown in Fig. P23-2, where there are shown on a PV two isothermal curves intersected by an adiabatic curve, referring to 1 mol of an ideal monatomic gas. A process takes the gas from the upper intersection point A and expands it isothermally at 600 K to a very special state B. The gas is then put in contact with a low-temperature reservoir at

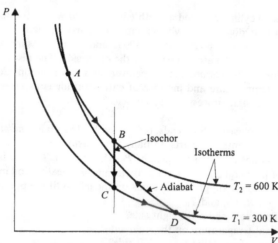

FIGURE P23-2

The zilch cycle for 1 mol of an ideal monatomic gas. (A. S. Arrott: *American Journal of Physics*, vol. 45, pp. 672–673, 1977. See also R. H. Dickerson and J. Mottmann: *American Journal of Physics*, vol. 62, pp. 558–562, 1994.)

300 K so that it cools isochorically to state C. Then, there is a further isothermal expansion from C to the lower intersection point D. The remainder of the zilch cycle is accomplished by an adiabatic compression from D back to A. The isochoric process BC is chosen to satisfy the condition that the net work in the cycle is zero.

(a) Calculate the work W_{DA}.

(b) Calculate the heat Q_{BC}.

(c) Calculate the net entropy change of the gas (*not the reservoirs*) and obtain the relationship

$$\frac{Q_{AB}}{600\,\text{K}} + \frac{Q_{CD}}{300\,\text{K}} = 8.64\,\frac{\text{J}}{\text{K}}.$$

(d) Calculate the work W_{AB}.

(e) Calculate the work W_{CD}.

(f) Calculate the net entropy change of the reservoirs.

(g) Draw the TS diagram.

23.17. (a) Prove that two isentropic curves do not intersect for systems of two independent variables.

(b) Show that isentropic curves *do* generally intersect for systems with more than two independent variables.

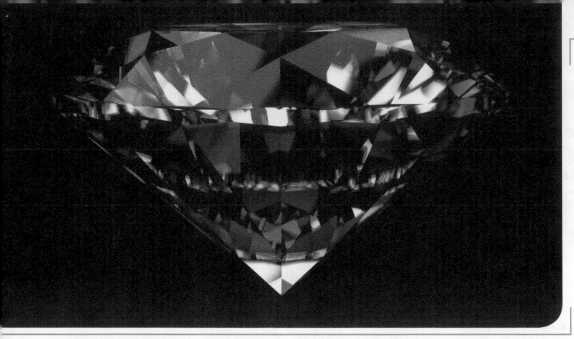

? When a cut diamond is illuminated with white light, it sparkles brilliantly with a spectrum of vivid colors. These distinctive visual features are a result of (i) light traveling much slower in diamond than in air; (ii) light of different colors traveling at different speeds in diamond; (iii) diamond absorbing light of certain colors; (iv) both (i) and (ii); (v) all of (i), (ii), and (iii).

33 THE NATURE AND PROPAGATION OF LIGHT

Blue lakes, ochre deserts, green forests, and multicolored rainbows can be enjoyed by anyone who has eyes with which to see them. But by studying the branch of physics called **optics,** which deals with the behavior of light and other electromagnetic waves, we can reach a deeper appreciation of the visible world. A knowledge of the properties of light allows us to understand the blue color of the sky and the design of optical devices such as telescopes, microscopes, cameras, eyeglasses, and the human eye. The same basic principles of optics also lie at the heart of modern developments such as the laser, optical fibers, holograms, and new techniques in medical imaging.

The importance of optics to physics, and to science and engineering in general, is so great that we will devote the next four chapters to its study. In this chapter we begin with a study of the laws of reflection and refraction and the concepts of dispersion, polarization, and scattering of light. Along the way we compare the various possible descriptions of light in terms of particles, rays, or waves, and we introduce Huygens's principle, an important link that connects the ray and wave viewpoints. In Chapter 34 we'll use the ray description of light to understand how mirrors and lenses work, and we'll see how mirrors and lenses are used in optical instruments such as cameras, microscopes, and telescopes. We'll explore the wave characteristics of light further in Chapters 35 and 36.

33.1 THE NATURE OF LIGHT

Until the time of Isaac Newton (1642–1727), most scientists thought that light consisted of streams of particles (called *corpuscles*) emitted by light sources. Galileo and others tried (unsuccessfully) to measure the speed of light. Around 1665, evidence of *wave* properties of light began to be discovered. By the early 19th century, evidence that light is a wave had grown very persuasive.

In 1873, James Clerk Maxwell predicted the existence of electromagnetic waves and calculated their speed of propagation, as we learned in Section 32.2. This development, along with the experimental work of Heinrich Hertz starting in 1887, showed conclusively that light is indeed an electromagnetic wave.

The Two Personalities of Light

The wave picture of light is not the whole story, however. Several effects associated with emission and absorption of light reveal a particle aspect, in that the energy carried by light waves is packaged in discrete bundles called *photons* or *quanta*. These apparently contradictory wave and particle properties have been reconciled since 1930 with the development of quantum electrodynamics, a comprehensive theory that includes *both* wave and particle properties. The *propagation* of light is best described by a wave model, but understanding emission and absorption requires a particle approach.

The fundamental sources of all electromagnetic radiation are electric charges in accelerated motion. All bodies emit electromagnetic radiation as a result of thermal motion of their molecules; this radiation, called *thermal radiation*, is a mixture of different wavelengths. At sufficiently high temperatures, all matter emits enough visible light to be self-luminous; a very hot body appears "red-hot" (**Fig. 33.1**) or "white-hot." Thus hot matter in any form is a light source. Familiar examples are a candle flame, hot coals in a campfire, and the coils in an electric toaster oven or room heater.

Light is also produced during electrical discharges through ionized gases. The bluish light of mercury-arc lamps, the orange-yellow of sodium-vapor lamps, and the various colors of "neon" signs are familiar. A variation of the mercury-arc lamp is the *fluorescent* lamp (see Fig. 30.7). This light source uses a material called a *phosphor* to convert the ultraviolet radiation from a mercury arc into visible light. This conversion makes fluorescent lamps more efficient than incandescent lamps in transforming electrical energy into light.

In most light sources, light is emitted independently by different atoms within the source; in a *laser,* by contrast, atoms are induced to emit light in a cooperative, coherent fashion. The result is a very narrow beam of radiation that can be enormously intense and that is much more nearly *monochromatic*, or single-frequency, than light from any other source. Lasers are used by physicians for microsurgery, in a DVD or Blu-ray player to scan the information recorded on a video disc, in industry to cut through steel and to fuse high-melting-point materials, and in many other applications (**Fig. 33.2**).

No matter what its source, electromagnetic radiation travels in vacuum at the same speed c. As we saw in Sections 1.3 and 32.1, this speed is defined to be

$$c = 2.99792458 \times 10^8 \text{ m/s}$$

or 3.00×10^8 m/s to three significant figures. The duration of one second is defined by the cesium clock (see Section 1.3), so one meter is defined to be the distance that light travels in 1/299,792,458 s.

Waves, Wave Fronts, and Rays

We often use the concept of a **wave front** to describe wave propagation. We introduced this concept in Section 32.2 to describe the leading edge of a wave. More generally, we define a wave front as *the locus of all adjacent points at which the phase of vibration of a physical quantity associated with the wave is the same.* That is, at any instant, all points on a wave front are at the same part of the cycle of their variation.

When we drop a pebble into a calm pool, the expanding circles formed by the wave crests, as well as the circles formed by the wave troughs between them, are wave fronts. Similarly, when sound waves spread out in still air from a

33.1 An electric heating element emits primarily infrared radiation. But if its temperature is high enough, it also emits a discernible amount of visible light.

33.2 Ophthalmic surgeons use lasers for repairing detached retinas and for cauterizing blood vessels in retinopathy. Pulses of blue-green light from an argon laser are ideal for this purpose, since they pass harmlessly through the transparent part of the eye but are absorbed by red pigments in the retina.

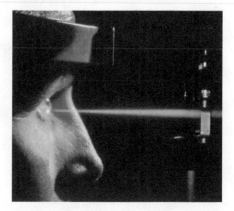

33.3 Spherical wave fronts of sound spread out uniformly in all directions from a point source in a motionless medium, such as still air, that has the same properties in all regions and in all directions. Electromagnetic waves in vacuum also spread out as shown here.

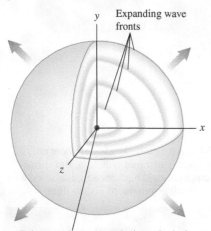

Point sound source producing spherical sound waves (alternating compressions and rarefactions of air)

33.4 Wave fronts (blue) and rays (purple).

(a)

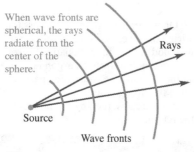

When wave fronts are spherical, the rays radiate from the center of the sphere.

Rays

Source

Wave fronts

(b)

When wave fronts are planar, the rays are perpendicular to the wave fronts and parallel to each other.

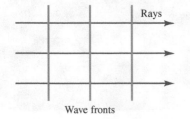

Rays

Wave fronts

pointlike source, or when electromagnetic radiation spreads out from a pointlike emitter, any spherical surface that is concentric with the source is a wave front, as shown in **Fig. 33.3**. In diagrams of wave motion we usually draw only parts of a few wave fronts, often choosing consecutive wave fronts that have the same phase and thus are one wavelength apart, such as crests of water waves. Similarly, a diagram for sound waves might show only the "pressure crests," the surfaces over which the pressure is maximum, and a diagram for electromagnetic waves might show only the "crests" on which the electric or magnetic field is maximum.

We will often use diagrams that show the shapes of the wave fronts or their cross sections in some reference plane. For example, when electromagnetic waves are radiated by a small light source, we can represent the wave fronts as spherical surfaces concentric with the source or, as in **Fig. 33.4a**, by the circular intersections of these surfaces with the plane of the diagram. Far away from the source, where the radii of the spheres have become very large, a section of a spherical surface can be considered as a plane, and we have a *plane* wave like those discussed in Sections 32.2 and 32.3 (Fig. 33.4b).

To describe the directions in which light propagates, it's often convenient to represent a light wave by **rays** rather than by wave fronts. In a particle theory of light, rays are the paths of the particles. From the wave viewpoint *a ray is an imaginary line along the direction of travel of the wave*. In Fig. 33.4a the rays are the radii of the spherical wave fronts, and in Fig. 33.4b they are straight lines perpendicular to the wave fronts. When waves travel in a homogeneous isotropic material (a material with the same properties in all regions and in all directions), the rays are always straight lines normal to the wave fronts. At a boundary surface between two materials, such as the surface of a glass plate in air, the wave speed and the direction of a ray may change, but the ray segments in the air and in the glass are straight lines.

The next several chapters will give you many opportunities to see the interplay of the ray, wave, and particle descriptions of light. The branch of optics for which the ray description is adequate is called **geometric optics;** the branch dealing specifically with wave behavior is called **physical optics.** This chapter and the following one are concerned mostly with geometric optics. In Chapters 35 and 36 we will study wave phenomena and physical optics.

TEST YOUR UNDERSTANDING OF SECTION 33.1   Some crystals are *not* isotropic: Light travels through the crystal at a higher speed in some directions than in others. In a crystal in which light travels at the same speed in the *x*- and *z*-directions but faster in the *y*-direction, what would be the shape of the wave fronts produced by a light source at the origin? (i) Spherical, like those shown in Fig. 33.3; (ii) ellipsoidal, flattened along the *y*-axis; (iii) ellipsoidal, stretched out along the *y*-axis. ∥

33.2 REFLECTION AND REFRACTION

In this section we'll use the *ray* model of light to explore two of the most important aspects of light propagation: **reflection** and **refraction.** When a light wave strikes a smooth interface separating two transparent materials (such as air and glass or water and glass), the wave is in general partly *reflected* and partly *refracted* (transmitted) into the second material, as shown in **Fig. 33.5a**. For example, when you look into a restaurant window from the street, you see a reflection of the street scene, but a person inside the restaurant can look out through the window at the same scene as light reaches him by refraction.

The segments of plane waves shown in Fig. 33.5a can be represented by bundles of rays forming *beams* of light (Fig. 33.5b). For simplicity we often draw only one ray in each beam (Fig. 33.5c). Representing these waves in terms of rays is the basis of geometric optics. We begin our study with the behavior of an individual ray.

33.5 (a) A plane wave is in part reflected and in part refracted at the boundary between two media (in this case, air and glass). The light that reaches the inside of the coffee shop is refracted twice, once entering the glass and once exiting the glass. (b), (c) How light behaves at the interface between the air outside the coffee shop (material a) and the glass (material b). For the case shown here, material b has a larger index of refraction than material a ($n_b > n_a$) and the angle θ_b is smaller than θ_a.

(a) Plane waves reflected and refracted from a window

(b) The waves in the outside air and glass represented by rays

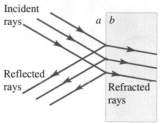

(c) The representation simplified to show just one set of rays

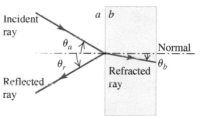

We describe the directions of the incident, reflected, and refracted (transmitted) rays at a smooth interface between two optical materials in terms of the angles they make with the *normal* (perpendicular) to the surface at the point of incidence, as shown in Fig. 33.5c. If the interface is rough, both the transmitted light and the reflected light are scattered in various directions, and there is no single angle of transmission or reflection. Reflection at a definite angle from a very smooth surface is called **specular reflection** (from the Latin word for "mirror"); scattered reflection from a rough surface is called **diffuse reflection** (**Fig. 33.6**). Both kinds of reflection can occur with either transparent materials or *opaque* materials that do not transmit light. The vast majority of objects in your environment (including plants, other people, and this book) are visible to you because they reflect light in a diffuse manner from their surfaces. Our primary concern, however, will be with specular reflection from a very smooth surface such as highly polished glass or metal. Unless stated otherwise, when referring to "reflection" we will always mean *specular* reflection.

The **index of refraction** of an optical material (also called the **refractive index**), denoted by n, plays a central role in geometric optics:

$$\underset{\substack{\text{Index of refraction} \\ \text{of an optical material}}}{} n = \frac{c}{v} \quad \substack{\text{Speed of light in vacuum} \\ \text{Speed of light in the material}} \tag{33.1}$$

Light always travels *more slowly* in a material than in vacuum, so the value of n in anything other than vacuum is always greater than unity. For vacuum, $n = 1$. Since n is a ratio of two speeds, it is a pure number without units. (In Section 32.3 we described the relationship of the value of n to the electric and magnetic properties of a material.)

CAUTION **Wave speed and index of refraction** Keep in mind that the wave speed v is *inversely* proportional to the index of refraction n. The greater the index of refraction in a material, the *slower* the wave speed in that material. ▌

33.6 Two types of reflection.

(a) Specular reflection

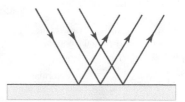

(b) Diffuse reflection

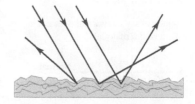

33.7 The laws of reflection and refraction.

1. The incident, reflected, and refracted rays and the normal to the surface all lie in the same plane.

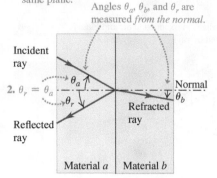

Angles θ_a, θ_b, and θ_r are measured *from the normal.*

Incident ray

2. $\theta_r = \theta_a$

Reflected ray

Normal

Refracted ray

Material *a* | Material *b*

3. When a monochromatic light ray crosses the interface between two given materials *a* and *b*, the angles θ_a and θ_b are related to the indexes of refraction of *a* and *b* by

$$\frac{\sin \theta_a}{\sin \theta_b} = \frac{n_b}{n_a}$$

33.8 Refraction and reflection in three cases. **(a)** Material *b* has a larger index of refraction than material *a*. **(b)** Material *b* has a smaller index of refraction than material *a*. **(c)** The incident light ray is normal to the interface between the materials.

(a) A ray entering a material of *larger* index of refraction bends *toward* the normal.

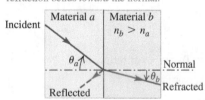

Material *a* | Material *b* $n_b > n_a$

Incident

θ_a

Normal

θ_b

Reflected | Refracted

(b) A ray entering a material of *smaller* index of refraction bends *away from* the normal.

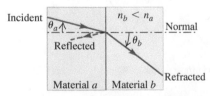

Incident

θ_a | $n_b < n_a$ | Normal

Reflected

θ_b

Material *a* | Material *b* | Refracted

(c) A ray oriented along the normal does not bend, regardless of the materials.

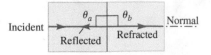

Incident | θ_a | θ_b | Normal

Reflected | Refracted

The Laws of Reflection and Refraction

Experimental studies of reflection and refraction at a smooth interface between two optical materials lead to the following conclusions (**Fig. 33.7**):

1. **The incident, reflected, and refracted rays and the normal to the surface all lie in the same plane.** This plane, called the **plane of incidence,** is perpendicular to the plane of the boundary surface between the two materials. We always draw ray diagrams so that the incident, reflected, and refracted rays are in the plane of the diagram.

2. **The angle of reflection θ_r is equal to the angle of incidence θ_a for all wavelengths and for any pair of materials.** That is, in Fig. 33.5c,

Angle of reflection (measured from normal)

Law of reflection: $\theta_r = \theta_a$ Angle of incidence (measured from normal)   (33.2)

This relationship, together with the observation that the incident and reflected rays and the normal all lie in the same plane, is called the **law of reflection.**

3. For monochromatic light and for a given pair of materials, *a* and *b*, on opposite sides of the interface, **the ratio of the sines of the angles θ_a and θ_b, where both angles are measured from the normal to the surface, is equal to the inverse ratio of the two indexes of refraction:**

$$\frac{\sin \theta_a}{\sin \theta_b} = \frac{n_b}{n_a} \qquad (33.3)$$

or

Angle of incidence (measured from normal)

Law of refraction: $n_a \sin \theta_a = n_b \sin \theta_b$ Angle of refraction (measured from normal)   (33.4)

Index of refraction for material with incident light   Index of refraction for material with refracted light

This result, together with the observation that the incident and refracted rays and the normal all lie in the same plane, is called the **law of refraction** or **Snell's law,** after the Dutch scientist Willebrord Snell (1591–1626). This law was actually first discovered in the 10th century by the Persian scientist Ibn Sahl. The discovery that $n = c/v$ came much later.

While these results were first observed experimentally, they can be derived theoretically from a wave description of light. We do this in Section 33.7.

Equations (33.3) and (33.4) show that when a ray passes from one material (a) into another material (b) having a larger index of refraction ($n_b > n_a$) and hence a slower wave speed, the angle θ_b with the normal is *smaller* in the second material than the angle θ_a in the first; hence the ray is bent *toward* the normal (**Fig. 33.8a**). When the second material has a *smaller* index of refraction than the first material ($n_b < n_a$) and hence a faster wave speed, the ray is bent *away from* the normal (Fig. 33.8b).

No matter what the materials on either side of the interface, in the case of *normal* incidence the transmitted ray is not bent at all (Fig. 33.8c). In this case $\theta_a = 0$ and $\sin \theta_a = 0$, so from Eq. (33.4) θ_b is also equal to zero; the transmitted ray is also normal to the interface. From Eq. (33.2), θ_r is also equal to zero, so the reflected ray travels back along the same path as the incident ray.

The law of refraction explains why a partially submerged ruler or drinking straw appears bent; light rays coming from below the surface change in direction at the air–water interface, so the rays appear to be coming from a position above

33.9 (a) This ruler is actually straight, but it appears to bend at the surface of the water. (b) Light rays from any submerged object bend away from the normal when they emerge into the air. As seen by an observer above the surface of the water, the object appears to be much closer to the surface than it actually is.

(a) A straight ruler half-immersed in water

(b) Why the ruler appears bent

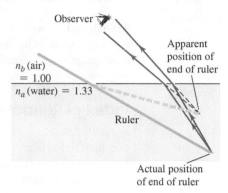

their actual point of origin (**Fig. 33.9**). A similar effect explains the appearance of the setting sun (**Fig. 33.10**).

An important special case is refraction that occurs at an interface between vacuum, for which the index of refraction is unity by definition, and a material. When a ray passes from vacuum into a material (b), so that $n_a = 1$ and $n_b > 1$, the ray is always bent *toward* the normal. When a ray passes from a material into vacuum, so that $n_a > 1$ and $n_b = 1$, the ray is always bent *away from* the normal.

The laws of reflection and refraction apply regardless of which side of the interface the incident ray comes from. If a ray of light approaches the interface in Fig. 33.8a or 33.8b from the right rather than from the left, there are again reflected and refracted rays, and they lie in the same plane as the incident ray and the normal to the surface. Furthermore, the path of a refracted ray is *reversible;* it follows the same path when going from b to a as when going from a to b. [You can verify this by using Eq. (33.4).] Since the reflected and incident angles are the same, the path of a reflected ray is also reversible. That's why when you see someone's eyes in a mirror, they can also see you.

The *intensities* of the reflected and refracted rays depend on the angle of incidence, the two indexes of refraction, and the polarization (that is, the direction of the electric-field vector) of the incident ray. The fraction reflected is smallest at normal incidence $(\theta_a = 0°)$, where it is about 4% for an air–glass interface. This fraction increases with increasing angle of incidence to 100% at grazing incidence, when $\theta_a = 90°$. (It's possible to use Maxwell's equations to predict the amplitude, intensity, phase, and polarization states of the reflected and refracted waves. Such an analysis is beyond our scope, however.)

BIO **Application Transparency and Index of Refraction** An eel in its larval stage is nearly as transparent as the seawater in which it swims. The larva in this photo is nonetheless easy to see because its index of refraction is higher than that of seawater, so that some of the light striking it is reflected instead of transmitted. The larva appears particularly shiny around its edges because the light reaching the camera from those points struck the larva at near-grazing incidence $(\theta_a = 90°)$, resulting in almost 100% reflection.

(a)

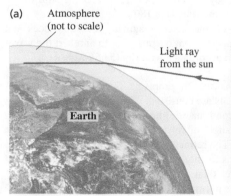

(b)

33.10 (a) The index of refraction of air is slightly greater than 1, so light rays from the setting sun bend downward when they enter our atmosphere. (The effect is exaggerated in this figure.) (b) Stronger refraction occurs for light coming from the lower limb of the sun (the part that appears closest to the horizon), which passes through denser air in the lower atmosphere. As a result, the setting sun appears flattened vertically. (See Problem 33.51.)

Index of Refraction for Yellow Sodium Light,

| TABLE 33.1 | $\lambda_0 = 589$ nm |

Substance	Index of Refraction, n
Solids	
Ice (H_2O)	1.309
Fluorite (CaF_2)	1.434
Polystyrene	1.49
Rock salt (NaCl)	1.544
Quartz (SiO_2)	1.544
Zircon ($ZrO_2 \cdot SiO_2$)	1.923
Diamond (C)	2.417
Fabulite ($SrTiO_3$)	2.409
Rutile (TiO_2)	2.62
Glasses (typical values)	
Crown	1.52
Light flint	1.58
Medium flint	1.62
Dense flint	1.66
Lanthanum flint	1.80
Liquids at 20°C	
Methanol (CH_3OH)	1.329
Water (H_2O)	1.333
Ethanol (C_2H_5OH)	1.36
Carbon tetrachloride (CCl_4)	1.460
Turpentine	1.472
Glycerine	1.473
Benzene	1.501
Carbon disulfide (CS_2)	1.628

The index of refraction depends not only on the substance but also on the wavelength of the light. The dependence on wavelength is called *dispersion;* we will consider it in Section 33.4. Indexes of refraction for several solids and liquids are given in **Table 33.1** for a particular wavelength of yellow light.

The index of refraction of air at standard temperature and pressure is about 1.0003, and we will usually take it to be exactly unity. The index of refraction of a gas increases as its density increases. Most glasses used in optical instruments have indexes of refraction between about 1.5 and 2.0. A few substances have larger indexes; one example is diamond, with 2.417 (see Table 33.1).

Index of Refraction and the Wave Aspects of Light

We have discussed how the direction of a light ray changes when it passes from one material to another material with a different index of refraction. What aspects of the *wave* characteristics of the light change when this happens?

First, the frequency f of the wave does *not* change when passing from one material to another. That is, the number of wave cycles arriving per unit time must equal the number leaving per unit time; this is a statement that the boundary surface cannot create or destroy waves.

Second, the wavelength λ of the wave *is* different in general in different materials. This is because in any material, $v = \lambda f$; since f is the same in any material as in vacuum and v is always less than the wave speed c in vacuum, λ is also correspondingly reduced. Thus the wavelength λ of light in a material is *less than* the wavelength λ_0 of the same light in vacuum. From the above discussion, $f = c/\lambda_0 = v/\lambda$. Combining this with Eq. (33.1), $n = c/v$, we find

$$\text{Wavelength of light in a material} \quad \lambda = \frac{\lambda_0 \;\cdots\; \text{Wavelength of light in vacuum}}{n \;\cdots\; \text{Index of refraction of the material}} \tag{33.5}$$

When a wave passes from one material into a second material with larger index of refraction, so $n_b > n_a$, the wave speed decreases. The wavelength $\lambda_b = \lambda_0/n_b$ in the second material is then shorter than the wavelength $\lambda_a = \lambda_0/n_a$ in the first material. If instead the second material has a smaller index of refraction than the first material, so $n_b < n_a$, then the wave speed increases. Then the wavelength λ_b in the second material is longer than the wavelength λ_a in the first material. This makes intuitive sense; the waves get "squeezed" (the wavelength gets shorter) if the wave speed decreases and get "stretched" (the wavelength gets longer) if the wave speed increases.

| PROBLEM-SOLVING STRATEGY 33.1 | **REFLECTION AND REFRACTION** |

IDENTIFY *the relevant concepts:* Use geometric optics, discussed in this section, whenever light (or electromagnetic radiation of *any* frequency and wavelength) encounters a boundary between materials. In general, part of the light is reflected back into the first material and part is refracted into the second material.

SET UP *the problem* using the following steps:
1. In problems involving rays and angles, start by drawing a large, neat diagram. Label all known angles and indexes of refraction.
2. Identify the target variables.

EXECUTE *the solution* as follows:
1. Apply the laws of reflection, Eq. (33.2), and refraction, Eq. (33.4). Measure angles of incidence, reflection, and refraction with respect to the *normal* to the surface, *never* from the surface itself.

2. Apply geometry or trigonometry in working out angular relationships. Remember that the sum of the acute angles of a right triangle is 90° (they are *complementary*) and the sum of the interior angles in any triangle is 180°.
3. The frequency of the electromagnetic radiation does not change when it moves from one material to another; the wavelength changes in accordance with Eq. (33.5), $\lambda = \lambda_0/n$.

EVALUATE *your answer:* In problems that involve refraction, check that your results are consistent with Snell's law ($n_a \sin \theta_a = n_b \sin \theta_b$). If the second material has a higher index of refraction than the first, the angle of refraction must be *smaller* than the angle of incidence: The refracted ray bends toward the normal. If the first material has the higher index of refraction, the refracted angle must be larger than the incident angle: The refracted ray bends away from the normal.

EXAMPLE 33.1 REFLECTION AND REFRACTION

In **Fig. 33.11**, material a is water and material b is glass with index of refraction 1.52. The incident ray makes an angle of 60.0° with the normal; find the directions of the reflected and refracted rays.

SOLUTION

IDENTIFY and SET UP: This is a problem in geometric optics. We are given the angle of incidence $\theta_a = 60.0°$ and the indexes of

33.11 Reflection and refraction of light passing from water to glass.

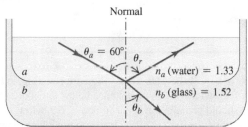

refraction $n_a = 1.33$ and $n_b = 1.52$. We must find the angles of reflection and refraction θ_r and θ_b; to do this we use Eqs. (33.2) and (33.4), respectively. Figure 33.11 shows the rays and angles; n_b is slightly greater than n_a, so by Snell's law [Eq. (33.4)] θ_b is slightly smaller than θ_a.

EXECUTE: According to Eq. (33.2), the angle the reflected ray makes with the normal is the same as that of the incident ray, so $\theta_r = \theta_a = 60.0°$.

To find the direction of the refracted ray we use Snell's law, Eq. (33.4):

$$n_a \sin\theta_a = n_b \sin\theta_b$$

$$\sin\theta_b = \frac{n_a}{n_b}\sin\theta_a = \frac{1.33}{1.52}\sin 60.0° = 0.758$$

$$\theta_b = \arcsin(0.758) = 49.3°$$

EVALUATE: The second material has a larger refractive index than the first, as in Fig. 33.8a. Hence the refracted ray is bent toward the normal and $\theta_b < \theta_a$.

EXAMPLE 33.2 INDEX OF REFRACTION IN THE EYE

The wavelength of the red light from a helium-neon laser is 633 nm in air but 474 nm in the aqueous humor inside your eyeball. Calculate the index of refraction of the aqueous humor and the speed and frequency of the light in it.

SOLUTION

IDENTIFY and SET UP: The key ideas here are (i) the definition of index of refraction n in terms of the wave speed v in a medium and the speed c in vacuum, and (ii) the relationship between wavelength λ_0 in vacuum and wavelength λ in a medium of index n. We use Eq. (33.1), $n = c/v$; Eq. (33.5), $\lambda = \lambda_0/n$; and $v = \lambda f$.

EXECUTE: The index of refraction of air is very close to unity, so we assume that the wavelength λ_0 in vacuum is the same as that in air, 633 nm. Then from Eq. (33.5),

$$\lambda = \frac{\lambda_0}{n} \qquad n = \frac{\lambda_0}{\lambda} = \frac{633 \text{ nm}}{474 \text{ nm}} = 1.34$$

This is about the same index of refraction as for water. Then, using $n = c/v$ and $v = \lambda f$, we find

$$v = \frac{c}{n} = \frac{3.00 \times 10^8 \text{ m/s}}{1.34} = 2.25 \times 10^8 \text{ m/s}$$

$$f = \frac{v}{\lambda} = \frac{2.25 \times 10^8 \text{ m/s}}{474 \times 10^{-9} \text{ m}} = 4.74 \times 10^{14} \text{ Hz}$$

EVALUATE: Although the speed and wavelength have different values in air and in the aqueous humor, the *frequency* in air, f_0, is the same as the frequency f in the aqueous humor:

$$f_0 = \frac{c}{\lambda_0} = \frac{3.00 \times 10^8 \text{ m/s}}{633 \times 10^{-9} \text{ m}} = 4.74 \times 10^{14} \text{ Hz}$$

When a light wave passes from one material into another, both the wave speed and wavelength change but the wave frequency is unchanged.

EXAMPLE 33.3 A TWICE-REFLECTED RAY

Two mirrors are perpendicular to each other. A ray traveling in a plane perpendicular to both mirrors is reflected from one mirror at P, then the other at Q, as shown in **Fig. 33.12** (next page). What is the ray's final direction relative to its original direction?

SOLUTION

IDENTIFY and SET UP: This problem involves the law of reflection, which we must apply twice (once for each mirror).

EXECUTE: For mirror 1 the angle of incidence is θ_1, and this equals the angle of reflection. The sum of interior angles in the triangle PQR is 180°, so we see that the angles of both incidence and reflection for mirror 2 are $90° - \theta_1$. The total change in direction of the ray after both reflections is therefore $2(90° - \theta_1) + 2\theta_1 = 180°$. That is, the ray's final direction is opposite to its original direction.

Continued

33.12 A ray moving in the xy-plane. The first reflection changes the sign of the y-component of its velocity, and the second reflection changes the sign of the x-component.

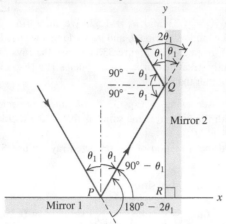

EVALUATE: An alternative viewpoint is that reflection reverses the sign of the component of light velocity perpendicular to the surface but leaves the other components unchanged. We invite you to verify this in detail. You should also be able to use this result to show that when a ray of light is successively reflected by three mirrors forming a corner of a cube (a "corner reflector"), its final direction is again opposite to its original direction. This principle is widely used in tail-light lenses and bicycle reflectors to improve their night-time visibility. *Apollo* astronauts placed arrays of corner reflectors on the moon. By use of laser beams reflected from these arrays, the earth–moon distance has been measured to within 0.15 m.

TEST YOUR UNDERSTANDING OF SECTION 33.2 You are standing on the shore of a lake. You spot a tasty fish swimming some distance below the lake surface. (a) If you want to spear the fish, should you aim the spear (i) above, (ii) below, or (iii) directly at the apparent position of the fish? (b) If instead you use a high-power laser to simultaneously kill and cook the fish, should you aim the laser (i) above, (ii) below, or (iii) directly at the apparent position of the fish? ∎

33.3 TOTAL INTERNAL REFLECTION

We have described how light is partially reflected and partially transmitted at an interface between two materials with different indexes of refraction. Under certain circumstances, however, *all* of the light can be reflected back from the interface, with none of it being transmitted, even though the second material is transparent. **Figure 33.13a** shows how this can occur. Several rays are shown radiating from a point source in material a with index of refraction n_a. The rays strike the surface of a second material b with index n_b, where $n_a > n_b$. (Materials a and b could be water and air, respectively.) From Snell's law of refraction,

$$\sin\theta_b = \frac{n_a}{n_b}\sin\theta_a$$

Because n_a/n_b is greater than unity, $\sin\theta_b$ is larger than $\sin\theta_a$; the ray is bent *away from* the normal. Thus there must be some value of θ_a *less than* 90° for which $\sin\theta_b = 1$ and $\theta_b = 90°$. This is shown by ray 3 in the diagram, which emerges just grazing the surface at an angle of refraction of 90°. Compare Fig. 33.13a to the photograph of light rays in Fig. 33.13b.

33.13 (a) Total internal reflection. The angle of incidence for which the angle of refraction is 90° is called the critical angle: This is the case for ray 3. The reflected portions of rays 1, 2, and 3 are omitted for clarity. (b) Rays of laser light enter the water in the fishbowl from above; they are reflected at the bottom by mirrors tilted at slightly different angles. One ray undergoes total internal reflection at the air–water interface.

(a) Total internal reflection

Total internal reflection occurs only if $n_b < n_a$.

At the critical angle of incidence, θ_{crit}, the angle of refraction $\theta_b = 90°$.

Any ray with $\theta_a > \theta_{crit}$ shows total internal reflection.

(b) A light beam enters the top left of the tank, then reflects at the bottom from mirrors tilted at different angles. One beam undergoes total internal reflection at the air–water interface.

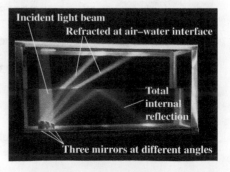

Incident light beam
Refracted at air–water interface
Total internal reflection
Three mirrors at different angles

The angle of incidence for which the refracted ray emerges tangent to the surface is called the **critical angle,** denoted by θ_{crit}. (A more detailed analysis using Maxwell's equations shows that as the incident angle approaches the critical angle, the transmitted intensity approaches zero.) If the angle of incidence is *larger* than the critical angle, $\sin \theta_b$ would have to be greater than unity, which is impossible. Beyond the critical angle, the ray *cannot* pass into the upper material; it is trapped in the lower material and is completely reflected at the boundary surface. This situation, called **total internal reflection,** occurs only when a ray in material a is incident on a second material b whose index of refraction is *smaller* than that of material a (that is, $n_b < n_a$).

We can find the critical angle for two given materials a and b by setting $\theta_b = 90°$ ($\sin \theta_b = 1$) in Snell's law. We then have

$$\underset{\substack{\text{Critical angle for} \\ \text{total internal reflection}}}{} \quad \sin \theta_{crit} = \frac{n_b}{n_a} \quad \begin{array}{l}\text{Index of refraction} \\ \text{of second material} \\ \text{Index of refraction} \\ \text{of first material}\end{array} \qquad (33.6)$$

Total internal reflection will occur if the angle of incidence θ_a is larger than or equal to θ_{crit}.

Applications of Total Internal Reflection

Total internal reflection finds numerous uses in optical technology. As an example, consider glass with index of refraction $n = 1.52$. If light propagating within this glass encounters a glass–air interface, the critical angle is

$$\sin \theta_{crit} = \frac{1}{1.52} = 0.658 \qquad \theta_{crit} = 41.1°$$

The light will be *totally reflected* if it strikes the glass–air surface at an angle of 41.1° or larger. Because the critical angle is slightly smaller than 45°, it is possible to use a prism with angles of 45°–45°–90° as a totally reflecting surface. As reflectors, totally reflecting prisms have some advantages over metallic surfaces such as ordinary coated-glass mirrors. While no metallic surface reflects 100% of the light incident on it, light can be *totally* reflected by a prism. These reflecting properties of a prism are unaffected by tarnishing.

A 45°–45°–90° prism, used as in **Fig. 33.14a**, is called a *Porro* prism. Light enters and leaves at right angles to the hypotenuse and is totally reflected at each of the shorter faces. The total change of direction of the rays is 180°. Binoculars often use combinations of two Porro prisms, as in Fig. 33.14b.

(a) Total internal reflection in a Porro prism

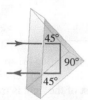

45°
90°
45°

If the incident beam is oriented as shown, total internal reflection occurs on the 45° faces (because, for a glass–air interface, $\theta_{crit} = 41.1$).

(b) Binoculars use Porro prisms to reflect the light to each eyepiece.

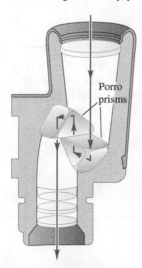

Porro prisms

33.14 (a) Total internal reflection in a Porro prism. **(b)** A combination of two Porro prisms in binoculars.

33.15 A transparent rod with refractive index greater than that of the surrounding material.

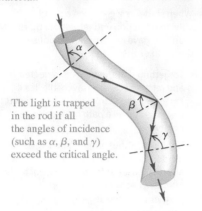

The light is trapped in the rod if all the angles of incidence (such as α, β, and γ) exceed the critical angle.

33.16 This colored x-ray image of a patient's abdomen shows an endoscope winding through the colon.

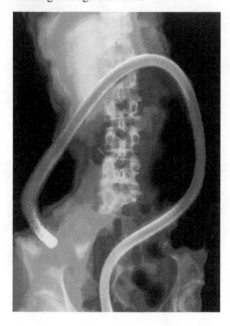

When a beam of light enters at one end of a transparent rod (**Fig. 33.15**), the light can be totally reflected internally if the index of refraction of the rod is greater than that of the surrounding material. The light is "trapped" within even a curved rod, provided that the curvature is not too great. A bundle of fine glass or plastic fibers behaves in the same way and has the advantage of being flexible. A bundle may consist of thousands of individual fibers, each of the order of 0.002 to 0.01 mm in diameter. If the fibers are assembled in the bundle so that the relative positions of the ends are the same (or mirror images) at both ends, the bundle can transmit an image.

Fiber-optic devices have found a wide range of medical applications in instruments called *endoscopes,* which can be inserted directly into the bronchial tubes, the bladder, the colon, and other organs for direct visual examination (**Fig. 33.16**). A bundle of fibers can even be enclosed in a hypodermic needle for studying tissues and blood vessels far beneath the skin.

Fiber optics also have applications in communication systems. The rate at which information can be transmitted by a wave (light, radio, or whatever) is proportional to the frequency. To see qualitatively why this is so, consider modulating (modifying) the wave by chopping off some of the wave crests. Suppose each crest represents a binary digit, with a chopped-off crest representing a zero and an unmodified crest representing a one. The number of binary digits we can transmit per unit time is thus proportional to the frequency of the wave. Infrared and visible-light waves have much higher frequency than do radio waves, so a modulated laser beam can transmit an enormous amount of information through a single fiber-optic cable.

Another advantage of optical fibers is that they can be made thinner than conventional copper wire, so more fibers can be bundled together in a cable of a given diameter. Hence more distinct signals (for instance, different phone lines) can be sent over the same cable. Because fiber-optic cables are electrical insulators, they are immune to electrical interference from lightning and other sources, and they don't allow unwanted currents between source and receiver. For these and other reasons, fiber-optic cables play an important role in long-distance telephone, television, and Internet communication.

Total internal reflection also plays an important role in the design of jewelry. The brilliance of diamond is due in large measure to its very high index of refraction ($n = 2.417$) and correspondingly small critical angle. Light entering a cut diamond is totally internally reflected from facets on its back surface and then emerges from its front surface (see the photograph that opens this chapter). "Imitation diamond" gems, such as cubic zirconia, are made from less expensive crystalline materials with comparable indexes of refraction.

CONCEPTUAL EXAMPLE 33.4 A LEAKY PERISCOPE

A submarine periscope uses two totally reflecting 45°–45°–90° prisms with total internal reflection on the sides adjacent to the 45° angles. Explain why the periscope will no longer work if it springs a leak and the bottom prism is covered with water.

SOLUTION

The critical angle for water ($n_b = 1.33$) on glass ($n_a = 1.52$) is

$$\theta_{\text{crit}} = \arcsin\frac{1.33}{1.52} = 61.0°$$

The 45° angle of incidence for a totally reflecting prism is *smaller* than this new 61° critical angle, so total internal reflection does not occur at the glass–water interface. Most of the light is transmitted into the water, and very little is reflected back into the prism.

In which of the following situations is there total internal reflection? (i) Light propagating in water ($n = 1.33$) strikes a water–air interface at an incident angle of 70°; (ii) light propagating in glass ($n = 1.52$) strikes a glass–water interface at an incident angle of 70°; (iii) light propagating in water strikes a water–glass interface at an incident angle of 70°. ∎

33.4 DISPERSION

Ordinary white light is a superposition of waves with all visible wavelengths. The speed of light *in vacuum* is the same for all wavelengths, but the speed in a material substance is different for different wavelengths. Therefore the index of refraction of a material depends on wavelength. The dependence of wave speed and index of refraction on wavelength is called **dispersion.**

Figure 33.17 shows the variation of index of refraction n with wavelength for some common optical materials. Note that the horizontal axis of this figure is the wavelength of the light *in vacuum*, λ_0; the wavelength in the material is given by Eq. (33.5), $\lambda = \lambda_0/n$. In most materials the value of n *decreases* with increasing wavelength and decreasing frequency, and thus n *increases* with decreasing wavelength and increasing frequency. In such a material, light of longer wavelength has greater speed than light of shorter wavelength.

Figure 33.18 shows a ray of white light incident on a prism. The deviation (change of direction) produced by the prism increases with increasing index of refraction and frequency and decreasing wavelength. So violet light is deviated most, and red is deviated least. When it comes out of the prism, the light is spread out into a fan-shaped beam, as shown. The light is said to be *dispersed* into a spectrum. The amount of dispersion depends on the *difference* between the refractive indexes for violet light and for red light. From Fig. 33.17 we can see that for fluorite, the difference between the indexes for red and violet is small, and the dispersion will also be small. A better choice of material for a prism whose purpose is to produce a spectrum would be silicate flint glass, for which there is a larger difference in the value of n between red and violet.

As we mentioned in Section 33.3, the brilliance of diamond is due in part to its unusually large refractive index; another important factor is its large dispersion, which causes white light entering a diamond to emerge as a multicolored spectrum. Crystals of rutile and of strontium titanate, which can be produced synthetically, have about eight times the dispersion of diamond.

33.17 Variation of index of refraction n with wavelength for different transparent materials. The horizontal axis shows the wavelength λ_0 of the light *in vacuum;* the wavelength in the material is equal to $\lambda = \lambda_0/n$.

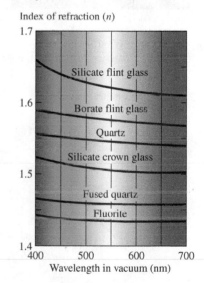

Index of refraction (n)

33.18 Dispersion of light by a prism. The band of colors is called a spectrum.

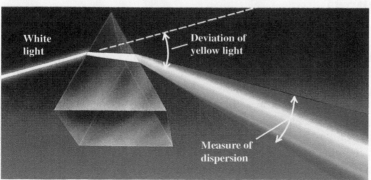

33.19 How rainbows form.

(a) A double rainbow

Secondary rainbow
(note reversed colors)

Primary rainbow

(b) The paths of light rays entering the upper half of a raindrop

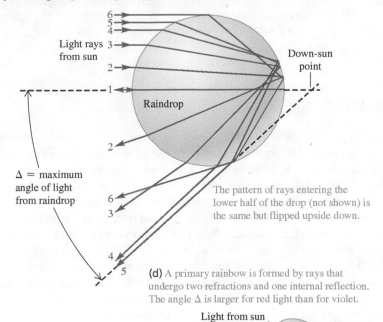

Light rays from sun

Raindrop

Down-sun point

Δ = maximum angle of light from raindrop

The pattern of rays entering the lower half of the drop (not shown) is the same but flipped upside down.

(d) A primary rainbow is formed by rays that undergo two refractions and one internal reflection. The angle Δ is larger for red light than for violet.

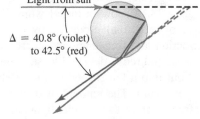

Light from sun

$\Delta = 40.8°$ (violet) to $42.5°$ (red)

(c) Forming a rainbow. The sun in this illustration is directly behind the observer at P.

The rays of sunlight that form the primary rainbow refract into the droplets, undergo internal reflection, and refract out.

The two refractions disperse the colors.

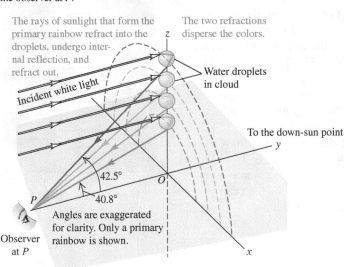

Incident white light

Water droplets in cloud

To the down-sun point

$42.5°$

$40.8°$

P

Angles are exaggerated for clarity. Only a primary rainbow is shown.

Observer at P

(e) A secondary rainbow is formed by rays that undergo two refractions and *two* internal reflections. The angle Δ is larger for violet light than for red.

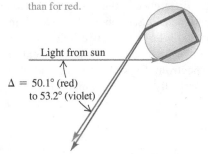

Light from sun

$\Delta = 50.1°$ (red) to $53.2°$ (violet)

Rainbows

When you experience the beauty of a rainbow, as in **Fig. 33.19a**, you are seeing the combined effects of dispersion, refraction, and reflection. Sunlight comes from behind you, enters a water droplet, is (partially) reflected from the back surface of the droplet, and is refracted again upon exiting the droplet (Fig. 33.19b). A light ray that enters the middle of the raindrop is reflected straight back. All other rays exit the raindrop within an angle Δ of that middle ray, with many rays "piling up" at the angle Δ. What you see is a disk of light of angular radius Δ centered on the down-sun point (the point in the sky opposite the sun); due to the "piling up" of light rays, the disk is brightest around its rim, which we see as a rainbow (Fig. 33.19c). Because no light reaches your eye from angles larger than Δ, the sky looks dark outside the rainbow (see Fig. 33.19a). The value of the angle Δ depends on the index of refraction of the water that makes up the raindrops, which in turn depends on the wavelength (Fig. 33.19d). The bright disk of red light is slightly larger than that for orange light, which in turn is slightly larger than that for yellow light, and so on. As a result, you see the rainbow as a band of colors.

In many cases you can see a second, larger rainbow. It is the result of dispersion, refraction, and *two* reflections from the back surface of the droplet (Fig. 33.19e). Each time a light ray hits the back surface, part of the light is refracted out of the drop (not shown in Fig. 33.19); after two such hits, relatively little light is left inside the drop, which is why the secondary rainbow is noticeably fainter than the primary rainbow. Just as a mirror held up to a book reverses the printed letters, so the second reflection reverses the sequence of colors in the secondary rainbow. You can see this effect in Fig. 33.19a.

33.5 POLARIZATION

Polarization is a characteristic of all transverse waves. This chapter is about light, but to introduce some basic polarization concepts, let's go back to the transverse waves on a string that we studied in Chapter 15. For a string that in equilibrium lies along the *x*-axis, the displacements may be along the *y*-direction, as in **Fig. 33.20a**. In this case the string always lies in the *xy*-plane. But the displacements might instead be along the *z*-axis, as in Fig. 33.20b; then the string always lies in the *xz*-plane.

When a wave has only *y*-displacements, we say that it is **linearly polarized** in the *y*-direction; a wave with only *z*-displacements is linearly polarized in the *z*-direction. For mechanical waves we can build a **polarizing filter,** or **polarizer,** that permits only waves with a certain polarization direction to pass. In Fig. 33.20c the string can slide vertically in the slot without friction, but no horizontal motion is possible. This filter passes waves that are polarized in the *y*-direction but blocks those that are polarized in the *z*-direction.

This same language can be applied to electromagnetic waves, which also have polarization. As we learned in Chapter 32, an electromagnetic wave is a transverse wave; the fluctuating electric and magnetic fields are perpendicular to each other and to the direction of propagation. We always define the direction of polarization of an electromagnetic wave to be the direction of the *electric*-field vector $\vec{E}$, not the magnetic field, because many common electromagnetic-wave detectors respond to the electric forces on electrons in materials, not the magnetic forces. Thus the electromagnetic wave described by Eq. (32.17),

$$\vec{E}(x, t) = \hat{\jmath} E_{max} \cos(kx - \omega t)$$

$$\vec{B}(x, t) = \hat{k} B_{max} \cos(kx - \omega t)$$

is said to be polarized in the *y*-direction because the electric field has only a *y*-component.

CAUTION The meaning of "polarization" It's unfortunate that the same word "polarization" that is used to describe the direction of $\vec{E}$ in an electromagnetic wave is also used to describe the shifting of electric charge within a body, such as in response to a nearby charged body; we described this latter kind of polarization in Section 21.2 (see Fig. 21.7). Don't confuse these two concepts! ▌

33.20 (a), (b) Polarized waves on a string. (c) Making a polarized wave on a string from an unpolarized one using a polarizing filter.

(a) Transverse wave linearly polarized in the *y*-direction

(b) Transverse wave linearly polarized in the *z*-direction

(c) The slot functions as a polarizing filter, passing only components polarized in the *y*-direction.

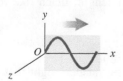
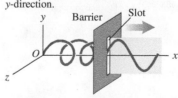

33.21 (a) Electrons in the red and white broadcast antenna oscillate vertically, producing vertically polarized electromagnetic waves that propagate away from the antenna in the horizontal direction. (The small gray antennas are for relaying cellular phone signals.) (b) No matter how this light bulb is oriented, the random motion of electrons in the filament produces unpolarized light waves.

(a)

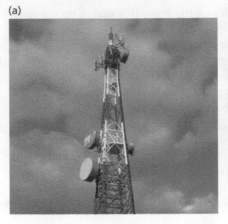

(b)

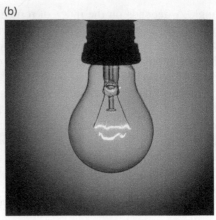

Polarizing Filters

Waves emitted by a radio transmitter are usually linearly polarized. The vertical antennas that are used for radio broadcasting emit waves that, in a horizontal plane around the antenna, are polarized in the vertical direction (parallel to the antenna) (**Fig. 33.21a**).

The situation is different for visible light. Light from incandescent light bulbs and fluorescent light fixtures is *not* polarized (Fig. 33.21b). The "antennas" that radiate light waves are the molecules that make up the sources. The waves emitted by any one molecule may be linearly polarized, like those from a radio antenna. But any actual light source contains a tremendous number of molecules with random orientations, so the emitted light is a random mixture of waves linearly polarized in all possible transverse directions. Such light is called **unpolarized light** or **natural light.** To create polarized light from unpolarized natural light requires a filter that is analogous to the slot for mechanical waves in Fig. 33.20c.

Polarizing filters for electromagnetic waves have different details of construction, depending on the wavelength. For microwaves with a wavelength of a few centimeters, a good polarizer is an array of closely spaced, parallel conducting wires that are insulated from each other. (Think of a barbecue grill with the outer metal ring replaced by an insulating one.) Electrons are free to move along the length of the conducting wires and will do so in response to a wave whose $\vec{E}$ field is parallel to the wires. The resulting currents in the wires dissipate energy by I^2R heating; the dissipated energy comes from the wave, so whatever wave passes through the grid is greatly reduced in amplitude. Waves with $\vec{E}$ oriented perpendicular to the wires pass through almost unaffected, since electrons cannot move through the air between the wires. Hence a wave that passes through such a filter will be predominantly polarized in the direction perpendicular to the wires.

The most common polarizing filter for visible light is a material known by the trade name Polaroid, widely used for sunglasses and polarizing filters for camera lenses. This material incorporates substances that have **dichroism,** a selective absorption in which one of the polarized components is absorbed much more strongly than the other (**Fig. 33.22**). A Polaroid filter transmits 80% or more of the intensity of a wave that is polarized parallel to the **polarizing axis** of the material, but only 1% or less for waves that are polarized perpendicular to this axis. In one type of Polaroid filter, long-chain molecules within the filter are oriented with their axis perpendicular to the polarizing axis; these molecules preferentially absorb light that is polarized along their length, much like the conducting wires in a polarizing filter for microwaves.

33.22 A Polaroid filter is illuminated by unpolarized natural light (shown by $\vec{E}$ vectors that point in all directions perpendicular to the direction of propagation). The transmitted light is linearly polarized along the polarizing axis (shown by $\vec{E}$ vectors along the polarization direction only).

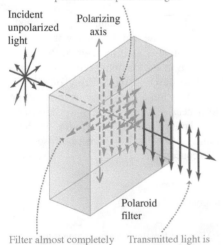

Filter only partially absorbs vertically polarized component of light.

Incident unpolarized light

Polarizing axis

Polaroid filter

Filter almost completely absorbs horizontally polarized component of light.

Transmitted light is linearly polarized in the vertical direction.

Using Polarizing Filters

An *ideal* polarizing filter (polarizer) passes 100% of the incident light that is polarized parallel to the filter's polarizing axis but completely blocks all light

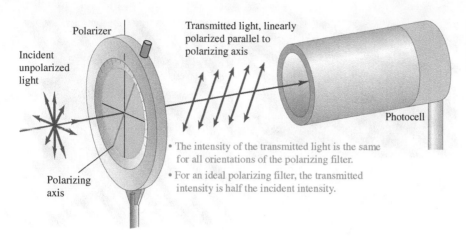

33.23 Unpolarized natural light is incident on the polarizing filter. The photocell measures the intensity of the transmitted linearly polarized light.

that is polarized perpendicular to this axis. Such a device is an unattainable idealization, but the concept is useful in clarifying the basic ideas. In the following discussion we will assume that all polarizing filters are ideal. In **Fig. 33.23** unpolarized light is incident on a flat polarizing filter. The $\vec{E}$ vector of the incident wave can be represented in terms of components parallel and perpendicular to the polarizer axis (shown in blue); only the component of $\vec{E}$ parallel to the polarizing axis is transmitted. Hence the light emerging from the polarizer is linearly polarized parallel to the polarizing axis.

When unpolarized light is incident on an ideal polarizer as in Fig. 33.23, the intensity of the transmitted light is *exactly half* that of the incident unpolarized light, no matter how the polarizing axis is oriented. Here's why: We can resolve the $\vec{E}$ field of the incident wave into a component parallel to the polarizing axis and a component perpendicular to it. Because the incident light is a random mixture of all states of polarization, these two components are, on average, equal. The ideal polarizer transmits only the component that is parallel to the polarizing axis, so half the incident intensity is transmitted.

What happens when the linearly polarized light emerging from a polarizer passes through a second polarizer, or *analyzer,* as in **Fig. 33.24**? Suppose the polarizing axis of the analyzer makes an angle ϕ with the polarizing axis of the first polarizer. We can resolve the linearly polarized light that is transmitted by the first polarizer into two components, as shown in Fig. 33.24, one parallel and the other perpendicular to the axis of the analyzer. Only the parallel component, with amplitude $E\cos\phi$, is transmitted by the analyzer. The transmitted intensity is greatest when $\phi = 0$, and it is zero when the polarizer and analyzer are *crossed*

DEMO

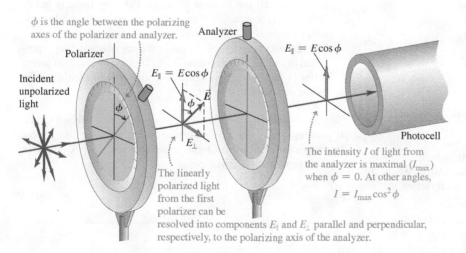

ϕ is the angle between the polarizing axes of the polarizer and analyzer.

The linearly polarized light from the first polarizer can be resolved into components $E_{\parallel}$ and $E_{\perp}$ parallel and perpendicular, respectively, to the polarizing axis of the analyzer.

The intensity I of light from the analyzer is maximal (I_{max}) when $\phi = 0$. At other angles,

$$I = I_{max}\cos^2\phi$$

33.24 An ideal analyzer transmits only the electric field component parallel to its transmission direction (that is, its polarizing axis).

33.25 These photos show the view through Polaroid sunglasses whose polarizing axes are (left) aligned ($\phi = 0$) and (right) perpendicular ($\phi = 90°$). The transmitted intensity is greatest when the axes are aligned; it is zero when the axes are perpendicular.

so that $\phi = 90°$ (**Fig. 33.25**). To determine the direction of polarization of the light transmitted by the first polarizer, rotate the analyzer until the photocell in Fig. 33.24 measures zero intensity; the polarization axis of the first polarizer is then perpendicular to that of the analyzer.

To find the transmitted intensity at intermediate values of the angle ϕ, we recall from Section 32.4 that the intensity of an electromagnetic wave is proportional to the *square* of the amplitude of the wave [see Eq. (32.29)]. The ratio of transmitted to incident *amplitude* is $\cos\phi$, so the ratio of transmitted to incident *intensity* is $\cos^2\phi$. Thus the intensity transmitted is

Intensity of polarized light passed through an analyzer

Malus's law:
$$I = I_{max}\cos^2\phi \quad \text{Angle between polarization axis of light and polarizing axis of analyzer}$$ (33.7)

Maximum transmitted intensity

This relationship, discovered experimentally by Étienne-Louis Malus in 1809, is called **Malus's law.** Malus's law applies *only* if the incident light passing through the analyzer is already linearly polarized.

PROBLEM-SOLVING STRATEGY 33.2 | **LINEAR POLARIZATION**

IDENTIFY *the relevant concepts:* In all electromagnetic waves, including light waves, the direction of polarization is the direction of the $\vec{E}$ field and is perpendicular to the propagation direction. Problems about polarizers are therefore about the components of $\vec{E}$ parallel and perpendicular to the polarizing axis.

SET UP *the problem* using the following steps:
1. Start by drawing a large, neat diagram. Label all known angles, including the angles of all polarizing axes.
2. Identify the target variables.

EXECUTE *the solution* as follows:
1. Remember that a polarizer lets pass only electric-field components parallel to its polarizing axis.
2. If the incident light is linearly polarized and has amplitude E and intensity I_{max}, the light that passes through an ideal polarizer has amplitude $E\cos\phi$ and intensity $I_{max}\cos^2\phi$, where ϕ is the angle between the incident polarization direction and the filter's polarizing axis.

3. Unpolarized light is a random mixture of all possible polarization states, so on the average it has equal components in any two perpendicular directions. When passed through an ideal polarizer, unpolarized light becomes linearly polarized light with half the incident intensity. Partially linearly polarized light is a superposition of linearly polarized and unpolarized light.
4. The intensity (average power per unit area) of a wave is proportional to the *square* of its amplitude. If you find that two waves differ in amplitude by a certain factor, their intensities differ by the square of that factor.

EVALUATE *your answer:* Check your answer for any obvious errors. If your results say that light emerging from a polarizer has greater intensity than the incident light, something's wrong: A polarizer can't add energy to a light wave.

EXAMPLE 33.5   TWO POLARIZERS IN COMBINATION

In Fig. 33.24 the incident unpolarized light has intensity I_0. Find the intensities transmitted by the first and second polarizers if the angle between the axes of the two filters is 30°.

SOLUTION

IDENTIFY and SET UP: This problem involves a polarizer (a polarizing filter on which unpolarized light shines, producing polarized light) and an analyzer (a second polarizing filter on which the polarized light shines). We are given the intensity I_0 of the incident light and the angle $\phi = 30°$ between the axes of the polarizers. We use Malus's law, Eq. (33.7), to solve for the intensities of the light emerging from each polarizer.

EXECUTE: The incident light is unpolarized, so the intensity of the linearly polarized light transmitted by the first polarizer is $I_0/2$. From Eq. (33.7) with $\phi = 30°$, the second polarizer reduces the intensity by a further factor of $\cos^2 30° = \frac{3}{4}$. Thus the intensity transmitted by the second polarizer is

$$\left(\frac{I_0}{2}\right)\left(\frac{3}{4}\right) = \frac{3}{8}I_0$$

EVALUATE: Note that the intensity decreases after each passage through a polarizer. The only situation in which the transmitted intensity does *not* decrease is if the polarizer is ideal (so it absorbs none of the light that passes through it) and if the incident light is linearly polarized along the polarizing axis, so $\phi = 0$.

Polarization by Reflection

Unpolarized light can be polarized, either partially or totally, by *reflection*. In **Fig. 33.26**, unpolarized natural light is incident on a reflecting surface between two transparent optical materials. For most angles of incidence, waves for which the electric-field vector $\vec{E}$ is perpendicular to the plane of incidence (that is, parallel to the reflecting surface) are reflected more strongly than those for which $\vec{E}$ lies in this plane. In this case the reflected light is *partially polarized* in the direction perpendicular to the plane of incidence.

But at one particular angle of incidence, called the **polarizing angle** θ_p, the light for which $\vec{E}$ lies in the plane of incidence is *not reflected at all* but is completely refracted. At this same angle of incidence the light for which $\vec{E}$ is perpendicular to the plane of incidence is partially reflected and partially refracted. The *reflected* light is therefore *completely* polarized perpendicular to the plane of incidence, as shown in Fig. 33.26. The *refracted* (transmitted) light is *partially* polarized parallel to this plane; the refracted light is a mixture of the component parallel to the plane of incidence, all of which is refracted, and the remainder of the perpendicular component.

In 1812 the British scientist Sir David Brewster discovered that when the angle of incidence is equal to the polarizing angle θ_p, the reflected ray and the refracted

33.26 When light is incident on a reflecting surface at the polarizing angle, the reflected light is linearly polarized.

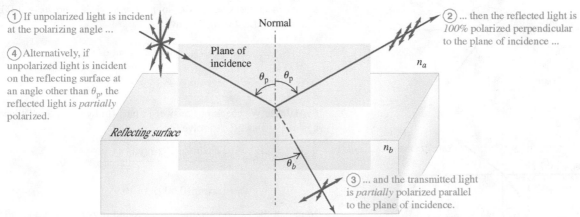

33.27 The significance of the polarizing angle. The open circles represent a component of $\vec{E}$ that is perpendicular to the plane of the figure (the plane of incidence) and parallel to the surface between the two materials.

Note: This is a side view of the situation shown in Fig. 33.26.

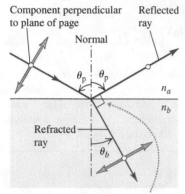

When light strikes a surface at the polarizing angle, the reflected and refracted rays are perpendicular to each other and

$$\tan\theta_p = \frac{n_b}{n_a}$$

ray are perpendicular to each other (**Fig. 33.27**). In this case the angle of refraction θ_b equals $90° - \theta_p$. From the law of refraction,

$$n_a\sin\theta_p = n_b\sin\theta_b = n_b\sin(90° - \theta_p) = n_b\cos\theta_p$$

Since $(\sin\theta_p)/(\cos\theta_p) = \tan\theta_p$, we can rewrite this equation as

Polarizing angle (angle of incidence for which reflected light is 100% polarized)

Brewster's law for the polarizing angle: $\tan\theta_p = \dfrac{n_b}{n_a}$ Index of refraction of second material   Index of refraction of first material   (33.8)

This relationship is known as **Brewster's law.** Although discovered experimentally, it can also be *derived* from a wave model by using Maxwell's equations.

Polarization by reflection is the reason polarizing filters are widely used in sunglasses (Fig. 33.25). When sunlight is reflected from a horizontal surface, the plane of incidence is vertical, and the reflected light contains a preponderance of light that is polarized in the horizontal direction. When the reflection occurs at a smooth asphalt road surface, it causes unwanted glare. To eliminate this glare, the polarizing axis of the lens material is made vertical, so very little of the horizontally polarized light reflected from the road is transmitted to the eyes. The glasses also reduce the overall intensity of the transmitted light to somewhat less than 50% of the intensity of the unpolarized incident light.

EXAMPLE 33.6   **REFLECTION FROM A SWIMMING POOL'S SURFACE**

Sunlight reflects off the smooth surface of a swimming pool. (a) For what angle of reflection is the reflected light completely polarized? (b) What is the corresponding angle of refraction? (c) At night, an underwater floodlight is turned on in the pool. Repeat parts (a) and (b) for rays from the floodlight that strike the surface from below.

SOLUTION

IDENTIFY and SET UP: This problem involves polarization by reflection at an air–water interface in parts (a) and (b) and at a water–air interface in part (c). **Figure 33.28** shows our sketches.

33.28 Our sketches for this problem.

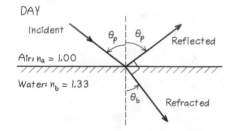

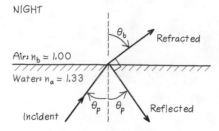

For both cases our first target variable is the polarizing angle θ_p, which we find from Brewster's law, Eq. (33.8). For this angle of reflection, the angle of refraction θ_b is the complement of θ_p (that is, $\theta_b = 90° - \theta_p$).

EXECUTE: (a) During the day (shown in the upper part of Fig. 33.28) the light moves in air toward water, so $n_a = 1.00$ (air) and $n_b = 1.33$ (water). From Eq. (33.8),

$$\theta_p = \arctan\frac{n_b}{n_a} = \arctan\frac{1.33}{1.00} = 53.1°$$

(b) The incident light is at the polarizing angle, so the reflected and refracted rays are perpendicular; hence

$$\theta_b = 90° - \theta_p = 90° - 53.1° = 36.9°$$

(c) At night (shown in the lower part of Fig. 33.28) the light moves in water toward air, so now $n_a = 1.33$ and $n_b = 1.00$. Again using Eq. (33.8), we have

$$\theta_p = \arctan\frac{1.00}{1.33} = 36.9°$$

$$\theta_b = 90° - 36.9° = 53.1°$$

EVALUATE: We check our answer in part (b) by using Snell's law, $n_a\sin\theta_a = n_b\sin\theta_b$, to solve for θ_b:

$$\sin\theta_b = \frac{n_a\sin\theta_p}{n_b} = \frac{1.00\sin 53.1°}{1.33} = 0.600$$

$$\theta_b = \arcsin(0.600) = 36.9°$$

Note that the two polarizing angles found in parts (b) and (c) add to 90°. This is *not* an accident; can you see why?

Circular and Elliptical Polarization

Light and other electromagnetic radiation can also have *circular* or *elliptical* polarization. To introduce these concepts, let's return once more to mechanical waves on a stretched string. In Fig. 33.20, suppose the two linearly polarized waves in parts (a) and (b) are in phase and have equal amplitude. When they are superposed, each point in the string has simultaneous y- and z-displacements of equal magnitude. A little thought shows that the resultant wave lies in a plane oriented at 45° to the y- and z-axes (i.e., in a plane making a 45° angle with the xy- and xz-planes). The amplitude of the resultant wave is larger by a factor of $\sqrt{2}$ than that of either component wave, and the resultant wave is linearly polarized.

But now suppose the two equal-amplitude waves differ in phase by a quarter-cycle. Then the resultant motion of each point corresponds to a superposition of two simple harmonic motions at right angles, with a quarter-cycle phase difference. The y-displacement at a point is greatest at times when the z-displacement is zero, and vice versa. The string as a whole then no longer moves in a single plane. It can be shown that each point on the rope moves in a *circle* in a plane parallel to the yz-plane. Successive points on the rope have successive phase differences, and the overall motion of the string has the appearance of a rotating helix, as shown to the left of the polarizing filter in Fig. 33.20c. Such a superposition of two linearly polarized waves is called **circular polarization.**

Figure 33.29 shows the analogous situation for an electromagnetic wave. Two sinusoidal waves of equal amplitude, polarized in the y- and z-directions and with a quarter-cycle phase difference, are superposed. The result is a wave in which the $\vec{E}$ vector at each point has a constant magnitude but *rotates* around the direction of propagation. The wave in Fig. 33.29 is propagating toward you and the $\vec{E}$ vector appears to be rotating clockwise, so it is called a *right circularly polarized* electromagnetic wave. If instead the $\vec{E}$ vector of a wave coming toward you appears to be rotating counterclockwise, it is called a *left circularly polarized* electromagnetic wave.

If the phase difference between the two component waves is something other than a quarter-cycle, or if the two component waves have different amplitudes, then each point on the string traces out not a circle but an *ellipse*. The resulting wave is said to be **elliptically polarized.**

For electromagnetic waves with radio frequencies, circular or elliptical polarization can be produced by using two antennas at right angles, fed from the same transmitter but with a phase-shifting network that introduces the appropriate phase difference. For light, the phase shift can be introduced by use of a material

Application Circular Polarization and 3-D Movies The lenses of the special glasses you wear to see a 3-D movie are circular polarizing filters. The lens over one eye allows only right circularly polarized light to pass; the other lens allows only left circularly polarized light to pass. The projector alternately projects the images intended for the left eye and those intended for the right eye. A special filter synchronized with the projector and in front of its lens circularly polarizes the projected light, with alternate polarization for each frame. Hence alternate images go to your left and right eyes, with such a short time interval between them that they produce the illusion of viewing with both eyes simultaneously.

33.29 Circular polarization of an electromagnetic wave moving toward you parallel to the x-axis. The y-component of $\vec{E}$ lags the z-component by a quarter-cycle. This phase difference results in right circular polarization.

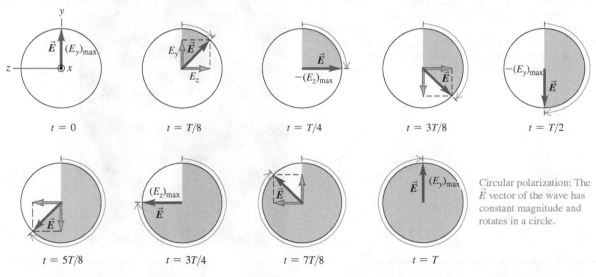

$t = 0 \qquad t = T/8 \qquad t = T/4 \qquad t = 3T/8 \qquad t = T/2$

$t = 5T/8 \qquad t = 3T/4 \qquad t = 7T/8 \qquad t = T$

Circular polarization: The $\vec{E}$ vector of the wave has constant magnitude and rotates in a circle.

Application **Birefringence and Liquid Crystal Displays** In each pixel of an LCD computer screen is a birefringent material called a liquid crystal. This material is composed of rod-shaped molecules that align to produce a fluid with two different indexes of refraction. The liquid crystal is placed between linear polarizing filters with perpendicular polarizing axes, and the sandwich of filters and liquid crystal is backlighted. The two polarizers by themselves would not transmit light, but like the birefringent object in Fig. 33.30, the liquid crystal allows light to pass through. Varying the voltage across a pixel turns the birefringence effect on and off, changing the pixel from bright to dark and back again.

Microscope image of a liquid crystal

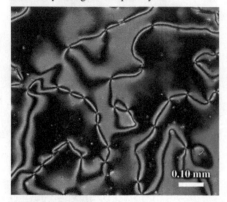

0.10 mm

Liquid crystal display

that exhibits *birefringence*—that is, has different indexes of refraction for different directions of polarization. A common example is calcite ($CaCO_3$). When a calcite crystal is oriented appropriately in a beam of unpolarized light, its refractive index (for a wavelength in vacuum of 589 nm) is 1.658 for one direction of polarization and 1.486 for the perpendicular direction. When two waves with equal amplitude and with perpendicular directions of polarization enter such a material, they travel with different speeds. If they are in phase when they enter the material, then in general they are no longer in phase when they emerge. If the crystal is just thick enough to introduce a quarter-cycle phase difference, then the crystal converts linearly polarized light to circularly polarized light. Such a crystal is called a *quarter-wave plate*. Such a plate also converts circularly polarized light to linearly polarized light. Can you prove this?

Photoelasticity

Some optical materials that are not normally birefringent become so when they are subjected to mechanical stress. This is the basis of the science of *photoelasticity*. Stresses in girders, boiler plates, gear teeth, and cathedral pillars can be analyzed by constructing a transparent model of the object, usually of a plastic material, subjecting it to stress, and examining it between a polarizer and an analyzer in the crossed position. Very complicated stress distributions can be studied by these optical methods.

Figure 33.30 is a photograph of a photoelastic model under stress. The polarized light that enters the model can be thought of as having a component along each of the two directions of the birefringent plastic. Since these two components travel through the plastic at different speeds, the light that emerges from the other side of the model can have a different overall direction of polarization. Hence some of this transmitted light will be able to pass through the analyzer even though its polarization axis is at a 90° angle to the polarizer's axis, and the stressed areas in the plastic will appear as bright spots. The amount of birefringence is different for different wavelengths and hence different colors of light; the color that appears at each location in Fig. 33.30 is that for which the transmitted light is most nearly polarized along the analyzer's polarization axis.

TEST YOUR UNDERSTANDING OF SECTION 33.5 You are taking a photograph of a sunlit office building at sunrise, so the plane of incidence is nearly horizontal. In order to minimize the reflections from the building's windows, you place a polarizing filter on the camera lens. How should you orient the filter? (i) With the polarizing axis vertical; (ii) with the polarizing axis horizontal; (iii) either orientation will minimize the reflections just as well; (iv) neither orientation will have any effect. |

33.30 This plastic model of an artificial hip joint was photographed between two polarizing filters (a polarizer and an analyzer) with perpendicular polarizing axes. The colored interference pattern reveals the direction and magnitude of stresses in the model. Engineers use these results to help design the actual hip joint (used in hip replacement surgery), which is made of metal.

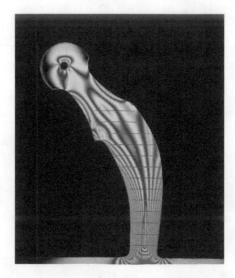

33.6 SCATTERING OF LIGHT

The sky is blue. Sunsets are red. Skylight is partially polarized; that's why the sky looks darker from some angles than from others when it is viewed through Polaroid sunglasses. As we will see, a single phenomenon is responsible for all of these effects.

When you look at the daytime sky, the light that you see is sunlight that has been absorbed and then re-radiated in a variety of directions. This process is called **scattering.** (If the earth had no atmosphere, the sky would appear as black in the daytime as it does at night, just as it does to an astronaut in space or on the moon.) **Figure 33.31** shows some of the details of the scattering process. Sunlight, which is unpolarized, comes from the left along the x-axis and passes over an observer looking vertically upward along the y-axis. (We are viewing the situation from the side.) Consider the molecules of the earth's atmosphere located at point O. The electric field in the beam of sunlight sets the electric charges in these molecules into vibration. Since light is a transverse wave, the direction of the electric field in any component of the sunlight lies in the yz-plane, and the motion of the charges takes place in this plane. There is no field, and hence no motion of charges, in the direction of the x-axis.

An incident light wave sets the electric charges in the molecules at point O vibrating along the line of $\vec{E}$. We can resolve this vibration into two components, one along the y-axis and the other along the z-axis. Each component in the incident light produces the equivalent of two molecular "antennas," oscillating with the same frequency as the incident light and lying along the y- and z-axes.

We mentioned in Chapter 32 that an oscillating charge, like those in an antenna, does not radiate in the direction of its oscillation. (See Fig. 32.3 in Section 32.1.) Thus the "antenna" along the y-axis does not send any light to the observer directly below it, although it does emit light in other directions. Therefore the only light reaching this observer comes from the other molecular "antenna," corresponding to the oscillation of charge along the z-axis. This light is linearly polarized, with its electric field along the z-axis (parallel to the "antenna"). The red vectors on the y-axis below point O in Fig. 33.31 show the direction of polarization of the light reaching the observer.

As the original beam of sunlight passes though the atmosphere, its intensity decreases as its energy goes into the scattered light. Detailed analysis of the scattering process shows that the intensity of the light scattered from air molecules increases in proportion to the fourth power of the frequency (inversely to the fourth power of the wavelength). Thus the intensity ratio for the two ends of the visible spectrum is $(750\ \text{nm}/380\ \text{nm})^4 = 15$. Roughly speaking, scattered light contains 15 times as much blue light as red, and that's why the sky is blue.

BIO Application Bee Vision and Polarized Light from the Sky The eyes of a bee can detect the polarization of light. Bees use this ability when they navigate between the hive and food sources. As Fig. 33.31 would suggest, a bee sees unpolarized light if it looks directly toward the sun and sees completely polarized light if it looks 90° away from the sun. These polarizations are unaffected by the presence of clouds, so a bee can navigate relative to the sun even on an overcast day.

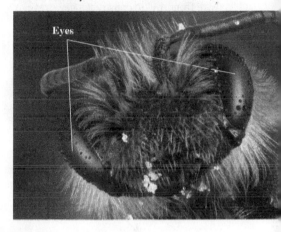

33.31 When the sunbathing observer on the left looks up, he sees blue, polarized sunlight that has been scattered by air molecules. The observer on the right sees reddened, unpolarized light when he looks at the sun.

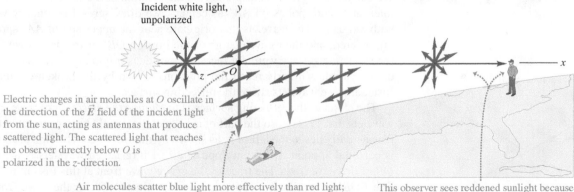

Incident white light, y unpolarized

Electric charges in air molecules at O oscillate in the direction of the $\vec{E}$ field of the incident light from the sun, acting as antennas that produce scattered light. The scattered light that reaches the observer directly below O is polarized in the z-direction.

Air molecules scatter blue light more effectively than red light; we see the sky overhead by scattered light, so it looks blue.

This observer sees reddened sunlight because most of the blue light has been scattered out.

33.32 Clouds are white because they efficiently scatter sunlight of all wavelengths.

Clouds contain a high concentration of suspended water droplets or ice crystals, which also scatter light. Because of this high concentration, light passing through the cloud has many more opportunities for scattering than does light passing through a clear sky. Thus light of *all* wavelengths is eventually scattered out of the cloud, so the cloud looks white (**Fig. 33.32**). Milk looks white for the same reason; the scattering is due to fat globules suspended in the milk.

Near sunset, when sunlight has to travel a long distance through the earth's atmosphere, a substantial fraction of the blue light is removed by scattering. White light minus blue light looks yellow or red. This explains the yellow or red hue that we so often see from the setting sun (and that is seen by the observer at the far right of Fig. 33.31).

33.7 HUYGENS'S PRINCIPLE

The laws of reflection and refraction of light rays, as introduced in Section 33.2, were discovered experimentally long before the wave nature of light was firmly established. However, we can *derive* these laws from wave considerations and show that they are consistent with the wave nature of light.

We begin with a principle called **Huygens's principle.** This principle, stated originally by the Dutch scientist Christiaan Huygens in 1678, is a geometrical method for finding, from the known shape of a wave front at some instant, the shape of the wave front at some later time. Huygens assumed that **every point of a wave front may be considered the source of secondary wavelets that spread out in all directions with a speed equal to the speed of propagation of the wave.** The new wave front at a later time is then found by constructing a surface *tangent* to the secondary wavelets or, as it is called, the *envelope* of the wavelets. All the results that we obtain from Huygens's principle can also be obtained from Maxwell's equations, but Huygens's simple model is easier to use.

Figure 33.33 illustrates Huygens's principle. The original wave front AA' is traveling outward from a source, as indicated by the arrows. We want to find the shape of the wave front after a time interval t. We assume that v, the speed of propagation of the wave, is the same at all points. Then in time t the wave front travels a distance vt. We construct several circles (traces of spherical wavelets) with radius $r = vt$, centered at points along AA'. The trace of the envelope of these wavelets, which is the new wave front, is the curve BB'.

33.33 Applying Huygens's principle to wave front AA' to construct a new wave front BB'.

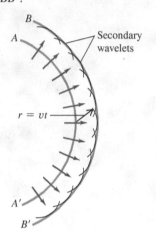

Reflection and Huygens's Principle

To derive the law of reflection from Huygens's principle, we consider a plane wave approaching a plane reflecting surface. In **Fig. 33.34a** the lines AA', OB', and NC' represent successive positions of a wave front approaching the surface MM'. Point A on the wave front AA' has just arrived at the reflecting surface. We can use Huygens's principle to find the position of the wave front after a time interval t. With points on AA' as centers, we draw several secondary wavelets with radius vt. The wavelets that originate near the upper end of AA' spread out unhindered, and their envelope gives the portion OB' of the new wave front. If the reflecting surface were not there, the wavelets originating near the lower end of AA' would similarly reach the positions shown by the broken circular arcs. Instead, these wavelets strike the reflecting surface.

The effect of the reflecting surface is to *change the direction* of travel of those wavelets that strike it, so the part of a wavelet that would have penetrated the surface actually lies to the left of it, as shown by the full lines. The first such wavelet is centered at point A; the envelope of all such reflected wavelets is the portion OB of the wave front. The trace of the entire wave front at this instant is the bent line BOB'. A similar construction gives the line CNC' for the wave front after another interval t.

33.34 Using Huygens's principle to derive the law of reflection.

(a) Successive positions of a plane wave AA' as it is reflected from a plane surface

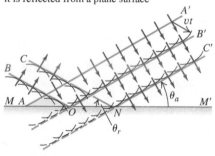

(b) Magnified portion of (a)

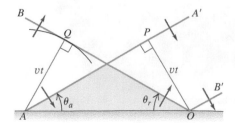

From plane geometry the angle θ_a between the incident *wave front* and the *surface* is the same as that between the incident *ray* and the *normal* to the surface and is therefore the angle of incidence. Similarly, θ_r is the angle of reflection. To find the relationship between these angles, we consider Fig. 33.34b. From O we draw $OP = vt$, perpendicular to AA'. Now OB, by construction, is tangent to a circle of radius vt with center at A. If we draw AQ from A to the point of tangency, the triangles APO and OQA are congruent because they are right triangles with the side AO in common and with $AQ = OP = vt$. The angle θ_a therefore equals the angle θ_r, and we have the law of reflection.

Refraction and Huygens's Principle

We can derive the law of *refraction* by a similar procedure. In **Fig. 33.35a** we consider a wave front, represented by line AA', for which point A has just arrived at the boundary surface SS' between two transparent materials a and b, with indexes of refraction n_a and n_b and wave speeds v_a and v_b. (The *reflected* waves are not shown; they proceed as in Fig. 33.34.) We can apply Huygens's principle to find the position of the refracted wave fronts after a time t.

With points on AA' as centers, we draw several secondary wavelets. Those originating near the upper end of AA' travel with speed v_a and, after a time interval t, are spherical surfaces of radius $v_a t$. The wavelet originating at point A, however, is traveling in the second material b with speed v_b and at time t is a spherical surface of radius $v_b t$. The envelope of the wavelets from the original wave front is the plane whose trace is the bent line BOB'. A similar construction leads to the trace CPC' after a second interval t.

The angles θ_a and θ_b between the surface and the incident and refracted wave fronts are the angle of incidence and the angle of refraction, respectively. To find the relationship between these angles, refer to Fig. 33.35b. We draw $OQ = v_a t$, perpendicular to AQ, and we draw $AB = v_b t$, perpendicular to BO. From the right triangle AOQ,

$$\sin\theta_a = \frac{v_a t}{AO}$$

and from the right triangle AOB,

$$\sin\theta_b = \frac{v_b t}{AO}$$

Combining these, we find

$$\frac{\sin\theta_a}{\sin\theta_b} = \frac{v_a}{v_b} \tag{33.9}$$

We have defined the index of refraction n of a material as the ratio of the speed of light c in vacuum to its speed v in the material: $n_a = c/v_a$ and $n_b = c/v_b$. Thus

$$\frac{n_b}{n_a} = \frac{c/v_b}{c/v_a} = \frac{v_a}{v_b}$$

and we can rewrite Eq. (33.9) as

$$\frac{\sin\theta_a}{\sin\theta_b} = \frac{n_b}{n_a} \quad \text{or}$$

$$n_a \sin\theta_a = n_b \sin\theta_b$$

which we recognize as Snell's law, Eq. (33.4). So we have derived Snell's law from a wave theory. Alternatively, we can regard Snell's law as an experimental result that defines the index of refraction of a material; in that case this analysis helps confirm the relationship $v = c/n$ for the speed of light in a material.

33.35 Using Huygens's principle to derive the law of refraction. The case $v_b < v_a$ ($n_b > n_a$) is shown.

(a) Successive positions of a plane wave AA' as it is refracted by a plane surface

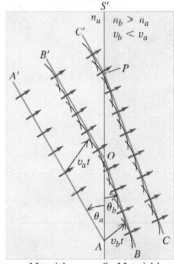

(b) Magnified portion of (a)

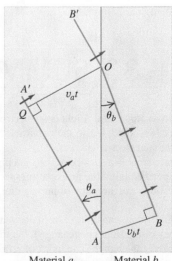

33.36 How mirages are formed.

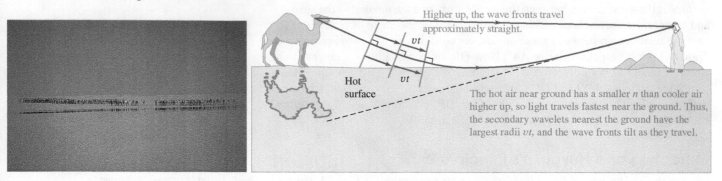

Mirages are an example of Huygens's principle in action. When the surface of pavement or desert sand is heated intensely by the sun, a hot, less dense, smaller-n layer of air forms near the surface. The speed of light is slightly greater in the hotter air near the ground, the Huygens wavelets have slightly larger radii, the wave fronts tilt slightly, and rays that were headed toward the surface with a large angle of incidence (near 90°) can be bent up as shown in **Fig. 33.36**. Light farther from the ground is bent less and travels nearly in a straight line. The observer sees the object in its natural position, with an inverted image below it, as though seen in a horizontal reflecting surface. A thirsty traveler can interpret the apparent reflecting surface as a sheet of water.

It is important to keep in mind that Maxwell's equations are the fundamental relationships for electromagnetic wave propagation. But Huygens's principle provides a convenient way to visualize this propagation.

TEST YOUR UNDERSTANDING OF SECTION 33.7   Sound travels faster in warm air than in cold air. Imagine a weather front that runs north-south, with warm air to the west of the front and cold air to the east. A sound wave traveling in a northeast direction in the warm air encounters this front. How will the direction of this sound wave change when it passes into the cold air? (i) The wave direction will deflect toward the north; (ii) the wave direction will deflect toward the east; (iii) the wave direction will be unchanged. ▌

| CHAPTER 33 SUMMARY

SOLUTIONS TO ALL EXAMPLES

Light and its properties: Light is an electromagnetic wave. When emitted or absorbed, it also shows particle properties. It is emitted by accelerated electric charges.

A wave front is a surface of constant phase; wave fronts move with a speed equal to the propagation speed of the wave. A ray is a line along the direction of propagation, perpendicular to the wave fronts.

When light is transmitted from one material to another, the frequency of the light is unchanged, but the wavelength and wave speed can change. The index of refraction n of a material is the ratio of the speed of light in vacuum c to the speed v in the material. If λ_0 is the wavelength in vacuum, the same wave has a shorter wavelength λ in a medium with index of refraction n. (See Example 33.2.)

$$n = \frac{c}{v} \tag{33.1}$$

$$\lambda = \frac{\lambda_0}{n} \tag{33.5}$$

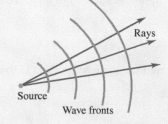

Reflection and refraction: At a smooth interface between two optical materials, the incident, reflected, and refracted rays and the normal to the interface all lie in a single plane called the plane of incidence. The law of reflection states that the angles of incidence and reflection are equal. The law of refraction relates the angles of incidence and refraction to the indexes of refraction of the materials. (See Examples 33.1 and 33.3.)

$$\theta_r = \theta_a \quad (33.2)$$
(law of reflection)

$$n_a \sin\theta_a = n_b \sin\theta_b \quad (33.4)$$
(law of refraction)

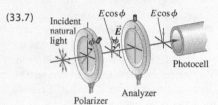

Total internal reflection: When a ray travels in a material of index of refraction n_a toward a material of index $n_b < n_a$, total internal reflection occurs at the interface when the angle of incidence equals or exceeds a critical angle θ_{crit}. (See Example 33.4.)

$$\sin\theta_{crit} = \frac{n_b}{n_a} \quad (33.6)$$

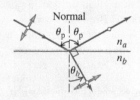

Polarization of light: The direction of polarization of a linearly polarized electromagnetic wave is the direction of the $\vec{E}$ field. A polarizing filter passes waves that are linearly polarized along its polarizing axis and blocks waves polarized perpendicularly to that axis. When polarized light of intensity I_{max} is incident on a polarizing filter used as an analyzer, the intensity I of the light transmitted through the analyzer depends on the angle ϕ between the polarization direction of the incident light and the polarizing axis of the analyzer. (See Example 33.5.)

$$I = I_{max} \cos^2\phi \quad (33.7)$$
(Malus's law)

Polarization by reflection: When unpolarized light strikes an interface between two materials, Brewster's law states that the reflected light is completely polarized perpendicular to the plane of incidence (parallel to the interface) if the angle of incidence equals the polarizing angle θ_p. (See Example 33.6.)

$$\tan\theta_p = \frac{n_b}{n_a} \quad (33.8)$$
(Brewster's law)

Huygens's principle: Huygens's principle states that if the position of a wave front at one instant is known, then the position of the front at a later time can be constructed by imagining the front as a source of secondary wavelets. Huygens's principle can be used to derive the laws of reflection and refraction.

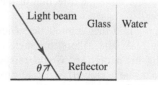

SOLUTION

BRIDGING PROBLEM | REFLECTION AND REFRACTION

Figure 33.37 shows a rectangular glass block that has a metal reflector on one face and water on an adjoining face. A light beam strikes the reflector as shown. You gradually increase the angle θ of the light beam. If $\theta \geq 59.2°$, no light enters the water. What is the speed of light in this glass?

33.37 Glass bounded by water and a metal reflector.

SOLUTION GUIDE

IDENTIFY and SET UP

1. Specular reflection occurs where the light ray in the glass strikes the reflector. If no light is to enter the water, we require that there be reflection only and no refraction where this ray strikes the glass–water interface—that is, there must be total internal reflection.
2. The target variable is the speed of light v in the glass, which you can determine from the index of refraction n of the glass. (Table 33.1 gives the index of refraction of water.) Write down the equations you will use to find n and v.

EXECUTE

3. Use the figure to find the angle of incidence of the ray at the glass–water interface.
4. Use the result of step 3 to find n.
5. Use the result of step 4 to find v.

EVALUATE

6. How does the speed of light in the glass compare to the speed in water? Does this make sense?

Problems

For assigned homework and other learning materials, go to MasteringPhysics®. MP°

•, ••, •••: Difficulty levels. CP: Cumulative problems incorporating material from earlier chapters. CALC: Problems requiring calculus. DATA: Problems involving real data, scientific evidence, experimental design, and/or statistical reasoning. BIO: Biosciences problems.

DISCUSSION QUESTIONS

Q33.1 Light requires about 8 minutes to travel from the sun to the earth. Is it delayed appreciably by the earth's atmosphere? Explain.

Q33.2 Sunlight or starlight passing through the earth's atmosphere is always bent toward the vertical. Why? Does this mean that a star is not really where it appears to be? Explain.

Q33.3 A beam of light goes from one material into another. On *physical* grounds, explain *why* the wavelength changes but the frequency and period do not.

Q33.4 A student claimed that, because of atmospheric refraction (see Discussion Question Q33.2), the sun can be seen after it has set and that the day is therefore longer than it would be if the earth had no atmosphere. First, what does she mean by saying that the sun can be seen after it has set? Second, comment on the validity of her conclusion.

Q33.5 When hot air rises from a radiator or heating duct, objects behind it appear to shimmer or waver. What causes this?

Q33.6 Devise straightforward experiments to measure the speed of light in a given glass using (a) Snell's law; (b) total internal reflection; (c) Brewster's law.

Q33.7 Sometimes when looking at a window, you see two reflected images slightly displaced from each other. What causes this?

Q33.8 If you look up from underneath toward the surface of the water in your aquarium, you may see an upside-down reflection of your pet fish in the surface of the water. Explain how this can happen.

Q33.9 A ray of light in air strikes a glass surface. Is there a range of angles for which total internal reflection occurs? Explain.

Q33.10 When light is incident on an interface between two materials, the angle of the refracted ray depends on the wavelength, but the angle of the reflected ray does not. Why should this be?

Q33.11 A salesperson at a bargain counter claims that a certain pair of sunglasses has Polaroid filters; you suspect that the glasses are just tinted plastic. How could you find out for sure?

Q33.12 Does it make sense to talk about the polarization of a *longitudinal* wave, such as a sound wave? Why or why not?

Q33.13 How can you determine the direction of the polarizing axis of a single polarizer?

Q33.14 It has been proposed that automobile windshields and headlights should have polarizing filters to reduce the glare of oncoming lights during night driving. Would this work? How should the polarizing axes be arranged? What advantages would this scheme have? What disadvantages?

Q33.15 When a sheet of plastic food wrap is placed between two crossed polarizers, no light is transmitted. When the sheet is stretched in one direction, some light passes through the crossed polarizers. What is happening?

Q33.16 If you sit on the beach and look at the ocean through Polaroid sunglasses, the glasses help to reduce the glare from sunlight reflecting off the water. But if you lie on your side on the beach, there is little reduction in the glare. Explain why there is a difference.

Q33.17 When unpolarized light is incident on two crossed polarizers, no light is transmitted. A student asserted that if a third polarizer is inserted between the other two, some transmission will occur. Does this make sense? How can adding a third filter *increase* transmission?

Q33.18 For the old "rabbit-ear" style TV antennas, it's possible to alter the quality of reception considerably simply by changing the orientation of the antenna. Why?

Q33.19 In Fig. 33.31, since the light that is scattered out of the incident beam is polarized, why is the transmitted beam not also partially polarized?

Q33.20 You are sunbathing in the late afternoon when the sun is relatively low in the western sky. You are lying flat on your back, looking straight up through Polaroid sunglasses. To minimize the amount of sky light reaching your eyes, how should you lie: with your feet pointing north, east, south, west, or in some other direction? Explain your reasoning.

Q33.21 Light scattered from blue sky is strongly polarized because of the nature of the scattering process described in Section 33.6. But light scattered from white clouds is usually *not* polarized. Why not?

Q33.22 Atmospheric haze is due to water droplets or smoke particles ("smog"). Such haze reduces visibility by scattering light, so that the light from distant objects becomes randomized and images become indistinct. Explain why visibility through haze can be improved by wearing red-tinted sunglasses, which filter out blue light.

Q33.23 The explanation given in Section 33.6 for the color of the setting sun should apply equally well to the *rising* sun, since sunlight travels the same distance through the atmosphere to reach your eyes at either sunrise or sunset. Typically, however, sunsets are redder than sunrises. Why? (*Hint:* Particles of all kinds in the atmosphere contribute to scattering.)

Q33.24 Huygens's principle also applies to sound waves. During the day, the temperature of the atmosphere decreases with increasing altitude above the ground. But at night, when the ground cools, there is a layer of air just above the surface in which the temperature *increases* with altitude. Use this to explain why sound waves from distant sources can be heard more clearly at night than in the daytime. (*Hint:* The speed of sound increases with increasing temperature. Use the ideas displayed in Fig. 33.36 for light.)

Q33.25 Can water waves be reflected and refracted? Give examples. Does Huygens's principle apply to water waves? Explain.

EXERCISES

Section 33.2 Reflection and Refraction

33.1 • Two plane mirrors intersect at right angles. A laser beam strikes the first of them at a point 11.5 cm from their point of intersection, as shown in **Fig. E33.1**. For what angle of incidence at the first mirror will this ray strike the midpoint of the second mirror (which is 28.0 cm long) after reflecting from the first mirror?

Figure **E33.1**

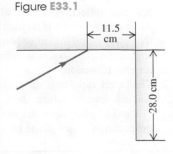

33.2 • BIO **Light Inside the Eye.** The vitreous humor, a transparent, gelatinous fluid that fills most of the eyeball, has an index of refraction of 1.34. Visible light ranges in wavelength from 380 nm (violet) to 750 nm (red), as measured in air. This light travels through the vitreous humor and strikes the rods and cones at the surface of the retina. What are the ranges of (a) the wavelength, (b) the frequency, and (c) the speed of the light just as it approaches the retina within the vitreous humor?

33.3 • A beam of light has a wavelength of 650 nm in vacuum. (a) What is the speed of this light in a liquid whose index of refraction at this wavelength is 1.47? (b) What is the wavelength of these waves in the liquid?

33.4 • Light with a frequency of 5.80×10^{14} Hz travels in a block of glass that has an index of refraction of 1.52. What is the wavelength of the light (a) in vacuum and (b) in the glass?

33.5 • A light beam travels at 1.94×10^8 m/s in quartz. The wavelength of the light in quartz is 355 nm. (a) What is the index of refraction of quartz at this wavelength? (b) If this same light travels through air, what is its wavelength there?

33.6 •• Light of a certain frequency has a wavelength of 526 nm in water. What is the wavelength of this light in benzene?

33.7 •• A parallel beam of light in air makes an angle of 47.5° with the surface of a glass plate having a refractive index of 1.66. (a) What is the angle between the reflected part of the beam and the surface of the glass? (b) What is the angle between the refracted beam and the surface of the glass?

33.8 •• A laser beam shines along the surface of a block of transparent material (see **Fig. E33.8**). Half of the beam goes straight to a detector, while the other half travels through the block and then hits the detector. The time delay between the arrival of the two light beams at the detector is 6.25 ns. What is the index of refraction of this material?

Figure E33.8

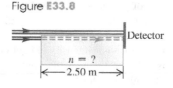

Detector

$n = ?$

←——2.50 m——→

33.9 • Light traveling in air is incident on the surface of a block of plastic at an angle of 62.7° to the normal and is bent so that it makes a 48.1° angle with the normal in the plastic. Find the speed of light in the plastic.

33.10 • (a) A tank containing methanol has walls 2.50 cm thick made of glass of refractive index 1.550. Light from the outside air strikes the glass at a 41.3° angle with the normal to the glass. Find the angle the light makes with the normal in the methanol. (b) The tank is emptied and refilled with an unknown liquid. If light incident at the same angle as in part (a) enters the liquid in the tank at an angle of 20.2° from the normal, what is the refractive index of the unknown liquid?

33.11 •• As shown in **Fig. E33.11**, a layer of water covers a slab of material X in a beaker. A ray of light traveling upward follows the path indicated. Using the information on the figure, find (a) the index of refraction of material X and (b) the angle the light makes with the normal in the *air.*

Figure E33.11

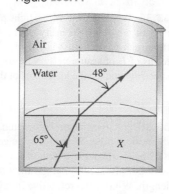

Air

Water   48°

65°   X

33.12 •• A horizontal, parallel-sided plate of glass having a refractive index of 1.52 is in contact with the surface of water in a tank. A ray coming from above in air makes an angle of incidence of 35.0° with the normal to the top surface of the glass. (a) What angle does the ray refracted into the water make with the normal to the surface? (b) What is the dependence of this angle on the refractive index of the glass?

33.13 • A ray of light is incident on a plane surface separating two sheets of glass with refractive indexes 1.70 and 1.58. The angle of incidence is 62.0°, and the ray originates in the glass with $n = 1.70$. Compute the angle of refraction.

33.14 • A ray of light traveling in water is incident on an interface with a flat piece of glass. The wavelength of the light in the water is 726 nm, and its wavelength in the glass is 544 nm. If the ray in water makes an angle of 56.0° with respect to the normal to the interface, what angle does the refracted ray in the glass make with respect to the normal?

Section 33.3 Total Internal Reflection

33.15 • **Light Pipe.** Light enters a solid pipe made of plastic having an index of refraction of 1.60. The light travels parallel to the upper part of the pipe (**Fig. E33.15**). You want to cut the face *AB* so that all the light will reflect back into the pipe after it first strikes that face. (a) What is the largest that θ can be if the pipe is in air? (b) If the pipe is immersed in water of refractive index 1.33, what is the largest that θ can be?

Figure E33.15

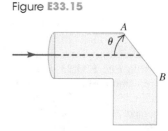

33.16 • A flat piece of glass covers the top of a vertical cylinder that is completely filled with water. If a ray of light traveling in the glass is incident on the interface with the water at an angle of $\theta_a = 36.2°$, the ray refracted into the water makes an angle of 49.8° with the normal to the interface. What is the smallest value of the incident angle θ_a for which none of the ray refracts into the water?

33.17 •• The critical angle for total internal reflection at a liquid–air interface is 42.5°. (a) If a ray of light traveling in the liquid has an angle of incidence at the interface of 35.0°, what angle does the refracted ray in the air make with the normal? (b) If a ray of light traveling in air has an angle of incidence at the interface of 35.0°, what angle does the refracted ray in the liquid make with the normal?

33.18 • A beam of light is traveling inside a solid glass cube that has index of refraction 1.62. It strikes the surface of the cube from the inside. (a) If the cube is in air, at what minimum angle with the normal inside the glass will this light *not* enter the air at this surface? (b) What would be the minimum angle in part (a) if the cube were immersed in water?

33.19 • A ray of light is traveling in a glass cube that is totally immersed in water. You find that if the ray is incident on the glass–water interface at an angle to the normal larger than 48.7°, no light is refracted into the water. What is the refractive index of the glass?

33.20 • At the very end of Wagner's series of operas *Ring of the Nibelung*, Brünnhilde takes the golden ring from the finger of the dead Siegfried and throws it into the Rhine, where it sinks to the bottom of the river. Assuming that the ring is small enough compared to the depth of the river to be treated as a point and that the Rhine is 10.0 m deep where the ring goes in, what is the area of the largest circle at the surface of the water over which light from the ring could escape from the water?

33.21 • Light is incident along the normal on face AB of a glass prism of refractive index 1.52, as shown in **Fig. E33.21**. Find the largest value the angle α can have without any light refracted out of the prism at face AC if (a) the prism is immersed in air and (b) the prism is immersed in water.

Figure **E33.21**

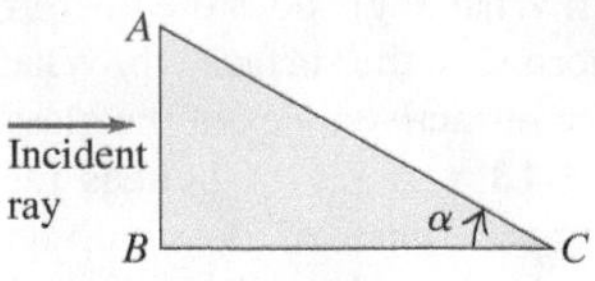

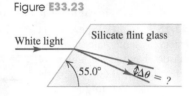

Section 33.4 Dispersion

33.22 • The indexes of refraction for violet light ($\lambda = 400$ nm) and red light ($\lambda = 700$ nm) in diamond are 2.46 and 2.41, respectively. A ray of light traveling through air strikes the diamond surface at an angle of 53.5° to the normal. Calculate the angular separation between these two colors of light in the refracted ray.

33.23 •• A narrow beam of white light strikes one face of a slab of silicate flint glass. The light is traveling parallel to the two adjoining faces, as shown in **Fig. E33.23**. For the transmitted light inside the glass, through what angle $\Delta\theta$ is the portion of the visible spectrum between 400 nm and 700 nm dispersed? (Consult the graph in Fig. 33.17.)

Figure **E33.23**

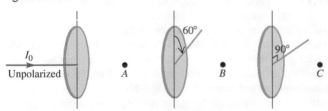

33.24 • A beam of light strikes a sheet of glass at an angle of 57.0° with the normal in air. You observe that red light makes an angle of 38.1° with the normal in the glass, while violet light makes a 36.7° angle. (a) What are the indexes of refraction of this glass for these colors of light? (b) What are the speeds of red and violet light in the glass?

Section 33.5 Polarization

33.25 • Unpolarized light with intensity I_0 is incident on two polarizing filters. The axis of the first filter makes an angle of 60.0° with the vertical, and the axis of the second filter is horizontal. What is the intensity of the light after it has passed through the second filter?

33.26 •• (a) At what angle above the horizontal is the sun if sunlight reflected from the surface of a calm lake is completely polarized? (b) What is the plane of the electric-field vector in the reflected light?

33.27 •• A beam of unpolarized light of intensity I_0 passes through a series of ideal polarizing filters with their polarizing axes turned to various angles as shown in **Fig. E33.27**. (a) What is the light intensity (in terms of I_0) at points A, B, and C? (b) If we remove the middle filter, what will be the light intensity at point C?

Figure **E33.27**

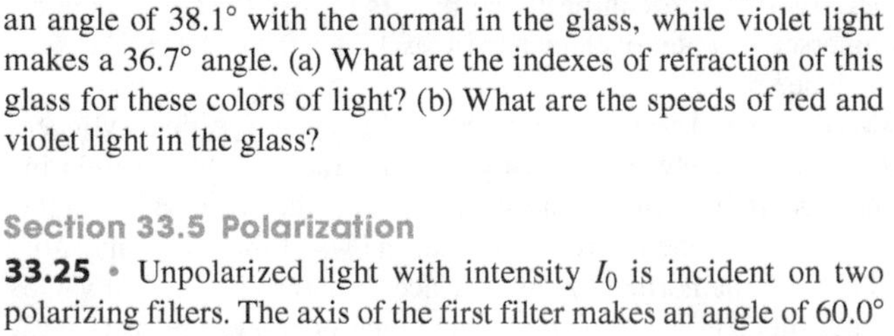

33.28 •• Light of original intensity I_0 passes through two ideal polarizing filters having their polarizing axes oriented as shown in **Fig. E33.28**. You want to adjust the angle ϕ so that the intensity at point P is equal to $I_0/10$. (a) If the original light is unpolarized, what should ϕ be? (b) If the original light is linearly polarized in the same direction as the polarizing axis of the first polarizer the light reaches, what should ϕ be?

Figure **E33.28**

33.29 • A parallel beam of unpolarized light in air is incident at an angle of 54.5° (with respect to the normal) on a plane glass surface. The reflected beam is completely linearly polarized. (a) What is the refractive index of the glass? (b) What is the angle of refraction of the transmitted beam?

33.30 • The refractive index of a certain glass is 1.66. For what incident angle is light reflected from the surface of this glass completely polarized if the glass is immersed in (a) air and (b) water?

33.31 •• A beam of polarized light passes through a polarizing filter. When the angle between the polarizing axis of the filter and the direction of polarization of the light is θ, the intensity of the emerging beam is I. If you now want the intensity to be $I/2$, what should be the angle (in terms of θ) between the polarizing angle of the filter and the original direction of polarization of the light?

33.32 ••• Three polarizing filters are stacked, with the polarizing axis of the second and third filters at 23.0° and 62.0°, respectively, to that of the first. If unpolarized light is incident on the stack, the light has intensity 55.0 W/cm² after it passes through the stack. If the incident intensity is kept constant but the second polarizer is removed, what is the intensity of the light after it has passed through the stack?

33.33 •• Unpolarized light of intensity 20.0 W/cm² is incident on two polarizing filters. The axis of the first filter is at an angle of 25.0° counterclockwise from the vertical (viewed in the direction the light is traveling), and the axis of the second filter is at 62.0° counterclockwise from the vertical. What is the intensity of the light after it has passed through the second polarizer?

33.34 • **Three Polarizing Filters.** Three polarizing filters are stacked with the polarizing axes of the second and third at 45.0° and 90.0°, respectively, with that of the first. (a) If unpolarized light of intensity I_0 is incident on the stack, find the intensity and state of polarization of light emerging from each filter. (b) If the second filter is removed, what is the intensity of the light emerging from each remaining filter?

Section 33.6 Scattering of Light

33.35 • A beam of white light passes through a uniform thickness of air. If the intensity of the scattered light in the middle of the green part of the visible spectrum is I, find the intensity (in terms of I) of scattered light in the middle of (a) the red part of the spectrum and (b) the violet part of the spectrum. Consult Table 32.1.

PROBLEMS

33.36 • A light beam is directed parallel to the axis of a hollow cylindrical tube. When the tube contains only air, the light takes 8.72 ns to travel the length of the tube, but when the tube is filled with a transparent jelly, the light takes 1.82 ns longer to travel its length. What is the refractive index of this jelly?

33.37 •• BIO **Heart Sonogram.** Physicians use high-frequency (f = 1–5 MHz) sound waves, called ultrasound, to image internal organs. The speed of these ultrasound waves is 1480 m/s in muscle and 344 m/s in air. We define the index of refraction of a material for sound waves to be the ratio of the speed of sound in air to the speed of sound in the material. Snell's law then applies to the refraction of sound waves. (a) At what angle from the normal does an ultrasound beam enter the heart if it leaves the lungs at an angle of 9.73° from the normal to the heart wall? (Assume that the speed of sound in the lungs is 344 m/s.) (b) What is the critical angle for sound waves in air incident on muscle?

33.38 ••• In a physics lab, light with wavelength 490 nm travels in air from a laser to a photocell in 17.0 ns. When a slab of glass 0.840 m thick is placed in the light beam, with the beam incident along the normal to the parallel faces of the slab, it takes the light 21.2 ns to travel from the laser to the photocell. What is the wavelength of the light in the glass?

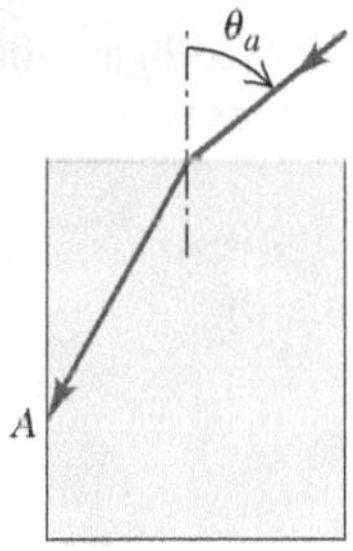

33.39 •• A ray of light is incident in air on a block of a transparent solid whose index of refraction is n. If n = 1.38, what is the *largest* angle of incidence θ_a for which total internal reflection will occur at the vertical face (point A shown in **Fig. P33.39**)?

Figure **P33.39**

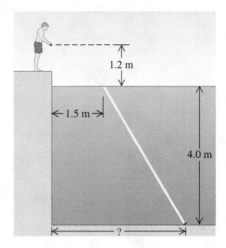

33.40 • A light ray in air strikes the right-angle prism shown in **Fig. P33.40**. The prism angle at B is 30.0°. This ray consists of two different wavelengths. When it emerges at face AB, it has been split into two different rays that diverge from each other by 8.50°. Find the index of refraction of the prism for each of the two wavelengths.

Figure **P33.40**

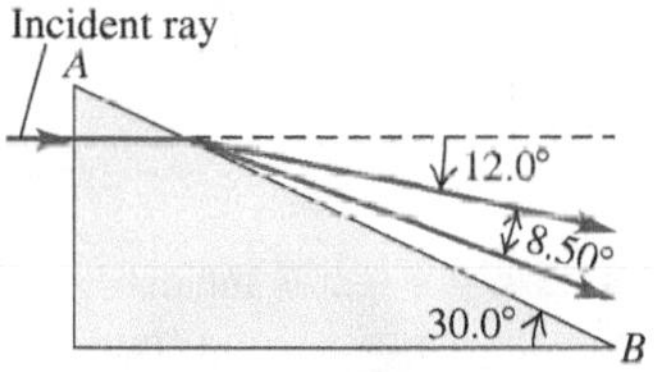

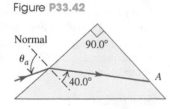

33.41 •• A ray of light traveling *in* a block of glass (n = 1.52) is incident on the top surface at an angle of 57.2° with respect to the normal in the glass. If a layer of oil is placed on the top surface of the glass, the ray is totally reflected. What is the maximum possible index of refraction of the oil?

33.42 •• A ray of light traveling in air is incident at angle θ_a on one face of a 90.0° prism made of glass. Part of the light refracts into the prism and strikes the opposite face at point A (**Fig. P33.42**). If the ray at A is at the critical angle, what is the value of θ_a?

Figure **P33.42**

33.43 ••• A glass plate 2.50 mm thick, with an index of refraction of 1.40, is placed between a point source of light with wavelength 540 nm (in vacuum) and a screen. The distance from source to screen is 1.80 cm. How many wavelengths are there between the source and the screen?

33.44 • After a long day of driving you take a late-night swim in a motel swimming pool. When you go to your room, you realize that you have lost your room key in the pool. You borrow a powerful flashlight and walk around the pool, shining the light into it. The light shines on the key, which is lying on the bottom of the pool, when the flashlight is held 1.2 m above the water surface and is directed at the surface a horizontal distance of 1.5 m from the

edge (**Fig. P33.44**). If the water here is 4.0 m deep, how far is the key from the edge of the pool?

Figure **P33.44**

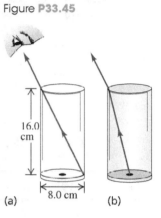

33.45 • You sight along the rim of a glass with vertical sides so that the top rim is lined up with the opposite edge of the bottom (**Fig. P33.45a**). The glass is a thin-walled, hollow cylinder 16.0 cm high. The diameter of the top and bottom of the glass is 8.0 cm. While you keep your eye in the same position, a friend fills the glass with a transparent liquid, and you then see a dime that is lying at the center of the bottom of the glass (Fig. P33.45b). What is the index of refraction of the liquid?

Figure **P33.45**

33.46 •• Optical fibers are constructed with a cylindrical core surrounded by a sheath of cladding material. Common materials used are pure silica (n_2 = 1.450) for the cladding and silica doped with germanium (n_1 = 1.465) for the core. (a) What is the critical angle θ_{crit} for light traveling in the core and reflecting at the interface with the cladding material? (b) The numerical aperture (NA) is defined as the angle of incidence θ_i at the flat end of the cable for which light is incident on the core–cladding interface at angle θ_{crit} (**Fig. P33.46**). Show that $\sin\theta_i = \sqrt{n_1^2 - n_2^2}$. (c) What is the value of θ_i for n_1 = 1.465 and n_2 = 1.450?

Figure **P33.46**

33.47 • A thin layer of ice (n = 1.309) floats on the surface of water (n = 1.333) in a bucket. A ray of light from the bottom of the bucket travels upward through the water. (a) What is the largest angle with respect to the normal that the ray can make at the ice–water interface and still pass out into the air above the ice? (b) What is this angle after the ice melts?

33.48 •• A 45°–45°–90° prism is immersed in water. A ray of light is incident normally on one of its shorter faces. What is the minimum index of refraction that the prism must have if this ray is to be totally reflected within the glass at the long face of the prism?

33.49 •• The prism shown in **Fig. P33.49** has a refractive index of 1.66, and the angles A are 25.0°. Two light rays m and n are parallel as they enter the prism. What is the angle between them after they emerge?

Figure **P33.49**

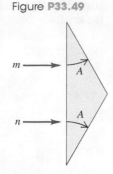

33.50 •• Light is incident normally on the short face of a 30°–60°–90° prism (**Fig. P33.50**). A drop of liquid is placed on the hypotenuse of the prism. If the index of refraction of the prism is 1.56, find the maximum index that the liquid may have for the light to be totally reflected.

Figure **P33.50**

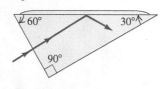

33.51 •• When the sun is either rising or setting and appears to be just on the horizon, it is in fact *below* the horizon. The explanation for this seeming paradox is that light from the sun bends slightly when entering the earth's atmosphere, as shown in **Fig. P33.51**. Since our perception is based on the idea that light travels in straight lines, we perceive the light to be coming from an apparent position that is an angle δ above the sun's true position. (a) Make the simplifying assumptions that the atmosphere has uniform density, and hence uniform index of refraction n, and extends to a height h above the earth's surface, at which point it abruptly stops. Show that the angle δ is given by

$$\delta = \arcsin\left(\frac{nR}{R+h}\right) - \arcsin\left(\frac{R}{R+h}\right)$$

where $R = 6378$ km is the radius of the earth. (b) Calculate δ using $n = 1.0003$ and $h = 20$ km. How does this compare to the angular radius of the sun, which is about one quarter of a degree? (In actuality a light ray from the sun bends gradually, not abruptly, since the density and refractive index of the atmosphere change gradually with altitude.)

Figure **P33.51**

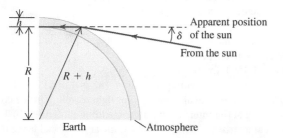

33.52 •• A horizontal cylindrical tank 2.20 m in diameter is half full of water. The space above the water is filled with a pressurized gas of unknown refractive index. A small laser can move along the curved bottom of the water and aims a light beam toward the center of the water surface (**Fig. P33.52**). You observe that when the laser has moved a distance $S = 1.09$ m or more (measured along the

Figure **P33.52**

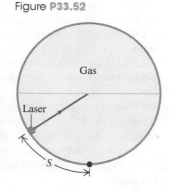

curved surface) from the lowest point in the water, no light enters the gas. (a) What is the index of refraction of the gas? (b) What minimum time does it take the light beam to travel from the laser to the rim of the tank when (i) $S > 1.09$ m and (ii) $S < 1.09$ m?

33.53 •• **Angle of Deviation.** The incident angle θ_a shown in **Fig. P33.53** is chosen so that the light passes symmetrically through the prism, which has refractive index n and apex angle A. (a) Show that the angle of deviation δ (the angle between the initial and final directions of the ray) is given by

$$\sin\frac{A+\delta}{2} = n\sin\frac{A}{2}$$

(When the light passes through symmetrically, as shown, the angle of deviation is a minimum.) (b) Use the result of part (a) to find the angle of deviation for a ray of light passing symmetrically through a prism having three equal angles ($A = 60.0°$) and $n = 1.52$. (c) A certain glass has a refractive index of 1.61 for red light (700 nm) and 1.66 for violet light (400 nm). If both colors pass through symmetrically, as described in part (a), and if $A = 60.0°$, find the difference between the angles of deviation for the two colors.

Figure **P33.53**

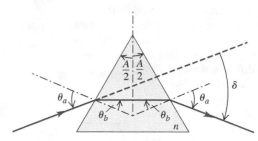

33.54 •• Light is incident in air at an angle θ_a (**Fig. P33.54**) on the upper surface of a transparent plate, the surfaces of the plate being plane and parallel to each other. (a) Prove that $\theta_a = \theta'_a$. (b) Show that this is true for any number of different parallel plates. (c) Prove that the lateral displacement d of the emergent beam is given by the relationship

$$d = t\frac{\sin(\theta_a - \theta'_b)}{\cos\theta'}$$

where t is the thickness of the plate. (d) A ray of light is incident at an angle of 66.0° on one surface of a glass plate 2.40 cm thick with an index of refraction of 1.80. The medium on either side of the plate is air. Find the lateral displacement between the incident and emergent rays.

Figure **P33.54**

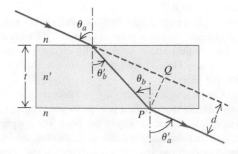

33.55 •• A beam of unpolarized sunlight strikes the vertical plastic wall of a water tank at an unknown angle. Some of the light reflects from the wall and enters the water (**Fig. P33.55**). The refractive index of the plastic wall is 1.61. If the light that has been reflected from the wall into the water is observed to be completely polarized, what angle does this beam make with the normal inside the water?

33.56 • A thin beam of white light is directed at a flat sheet of silicate flint glass at an angle of 20.0° to the surface of the sheet. Due to dispersion in the glass, the beam is spread out in a spectrum as shown in **Fig. P33.56**. The refractive index of silicate flint glass versus wavelength is graphed in Fig. 33.17. (a) The rays a and b shown in Fig. P33.56 correspond to the extreme wavelengths shown in Fig. 33.17. Which corresponds to red and which to violet? Explain your reasoning. (b) For what thickness d of the glass sheet will the spectrum be 1.0 mm wide, as shown (see Problem 33.54)?

33.57 •• DATA In physics lab, you are studying the properties of four transparent liquids. You shine a ray of light (in air) onto the surface of each liquid—A, B, C, and D—one at a time, at a 60.0° angle of incidence; you then measure the angle of refraction. The table gives your data:

Liquid	A	B	C	D
θ_a (°)	36.4	40.5	32.1	35.2

The wavelength of the light when it is traveling in air is 589 nm. (a) Find the refractive index of each liquid at this wavelength. Use Table 33.1 to identify each liquid, assuming that all four are listed in the table. (b) For each liquid, what is the dielectric constant K at the frequency of the 589-nm light? For each liquid, the relative permeability (K_m) is very close to unity. (c) What is the frequency of the light in air and in each liquid?

33.58 •• DATA Given small samples of three liquids, you are asked to determine their refractive indexes. However, you do not have enough of each liquid to measure the angle of refraction for light refracting from air into the liquid. Instead, for each liquid, you take a rectangular block of glass ($n = 1.52$) and place a drop of the liquid on the top surface of the block. You shine a laser beam with wavelength 638 nm in vacuum at one side of the block and measure the largest angle of incidence θ_a for which there is total internal reflection at the interface between the glass and the liquid (**Fig. P33.58**). Your results are given in the table:

Liquid	A	B	C
θ_a (°)	52.0	44.3	36.3

What is the refractive index of each liquid at this wavelength?

Figure **P33.55**

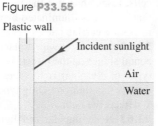

Plastic wall
Incident sunlight
Air
Water

Figure **P33.56**

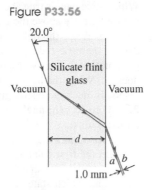

20.0°
Silicate flint glass
Vacuum
Vacuum
d
a b
1.0 mm

Figure **P33.58**

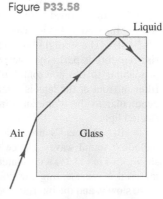

Liquid
Air
Glass

33.59 •• DATA A beam of light traveling horizontally is made of an unpolarized component with intensity I_0 and a polarized component with intensity I_p. The plane of polarization of the polarized component is oriented at an angle θ with respect to the vertical. **Figure P33.59** is a graph of the total intensity I_{total} after the light passes through a polarizer versus the angle α that the polarizer's axis makes with respect to the vertical. (a) What is the orientation of the polarized component? (That is, what is θ?) (b) What are the values of I_0 and I_p?

Figure **P33.59**

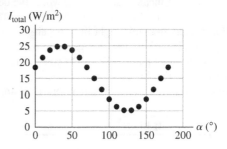

I_{total} (W/m²)

CHALLENGE PROBLEMS

33.60 ••• CALC A rainbow is produced by the reflection of sunlight by spherical drops of water in the air. **Figure P33.60** shows a ray that refracts into a drop at point A, is reflected from the back surface of the drop at point B, and refracts back into the air at point C. The angles of incidence and refraction, θ_a and θ_b, are shown at points A and C, and the angles of incidence and reflection, θ_a and θ_r, are shown at point B. (a) Show that $\theta_a^B = \theta_b^A$, $\theta_a^C = \theta_b^A$, and $\theta_b^C = \theta_a^A$. (b) Show that the angle in radians between the ray before it enters the drop at A and after it exits at C (the total angular deflection of the ray) is $\Delta = 2\theta_a^A - 4\theta_b^A + \pi$. (*Hint:* Find the angular deflections that occur at A, B, and C, and add them to get Δ.) (c) Use Snell's law to write Δ in terms of θ_a^A and n, the refractive index of the water in the drop. (d) A rainbow will form when the angular deflection Δ is *stationary* in the incident angle θ_a^A—that is, when $d\Delta/d\theta_a^A = 0$. If this condition is satisfied, all the rays with incident angles close to θ_a^A will be sent back in the same direction, producing a bright zone in the sky. Let θ_1 be the value of θ_a^A for which this occurs. Show that $\cos^2\theta_1 = \frac{1}{3}(n^2 - 1)$. (*Hint:* You may find the derivative formula $d(\arcsin u(x))/dx = (1 - u^2)^{-1/2}(du/dx)$ helpful.) (e) The index

Figure **P33.60**

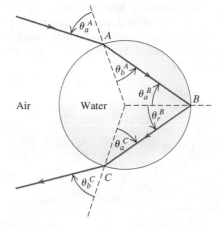

θ_a^A
A
θ_b^A
θ_a^B
B
θ_r^B
θ_a^C
Air
Water
θ_b^C
C

of refraction in water is 1.342 for violet light and 1.330 for red light. Use the results of parts (c) and (d) to find θ_1 and Δ for violet and red light. Do your results agree with the angles shown in Fig. 33.19d? When you view the rainbow, which color, red or violet, is higher above the horizon?

33.61 ••• **CALC** A *secondary rainbow* is formed when the incident light undergoes two internal reflections in a spherical drop of water as shown in Fig. 33.19e. (See Challenge Problem 33.60.) (a) In terms of the incident angle θ_a^A and the refractive index n of the drop, what is the angular deflection Δ of the ray? That is, what is the angle between the ray before it enters the drop and after it exits? (b) What is the incident angle θ_2 for which the derivative of Δ with respect to the incident angle θ_a^A is zero? (c) The indexes of refraction for red and violet light in water are given in part (e) of Challenge Problem 33.60. Use the results of parts (a) and (b) to find θ_2 and Δ for violet and red light. Do your results agree with the angles shown in Fig. 33.19e? When you view a secondary rainbow, is red or violet higher above the horizon? Explain.

PASSAGE PROBLEMS

BIO SEEING POLARIZED LIGHT. Some insect eyes have two types of cells that are sensitive to the plane of polarization of light. In a simple model, one cell type (type H) is sensitive to horizontally polarized light only, and the other cell type (type V) is sensitive to vertically polarized light only. To study the responses of these cells, researchers fix the insect in a normal, upright position so that one eye is illuminated by a light source. Then several experiments are carried out.

33.62 First, light with a plane of polarization at 45° to the horizontal shines on the insect. Which statement is true about the two types of cells? (a) Both types detect this light. (b) Neither type detects this light. (c) Only type H detects the light. (d) Only type V detects the light.

33.63 Next, unpolarized light is reflected off a smooth horizontal piece of glass, and the reflected light shines on the insect. Which statement is true about the two types of cells? (a) When the light is directly above the glass, only type V detects the reflected light. (b) When the light is directly above the glass, only type H detects the reflected light. (c) When the light is about 35° above the horizontal, type V responds much more strongly than type H does. (d) When the light is about 35° above the horizontal, type H responds much more strongly than type V does.

33.64 To vary the angle as well as the intensity of polarized light, ordinary unpolarized light is passed through one polarizer with its transmission axis vertical, and then a second polarizer is placed between the first polarizer and the insect. When the light leaving the second polarizer has half the intensity of the original unpolarized light, which statement is true about the two types of cells? (a) Only type H detects this light. (b) Only type V detects this light. (c) Both types detect this light, but type H detects more light. (d) Both types detect this light, but type V detects more light.

Answers

Chapter Opening Question ?

(iv) The brilliance and color of a diamond are due to total internal reflection from its surfaces (Section 33.3) and to dispersion, which spreads this light into a spectrum (Section 33.4).

Test Your Understanding Questions

33.1 (iii) The waves go farther in the y-direction in a given amount of time than in the other directions, so the wave fronts are elongated in the y-direction.

33.2 (a) (ii), (b) (iii) As shown in the figure, light rays coming from the fish bend away from the normal when they pass from the water ($n = 1.33$) into the air ($n = 1.00$). As a result, the fish appears to be higher in the water than it actually is. Hence you should aim a spear *below* the apparent position of the fish. If you use a laser beam, you should aim *at* the apparent position of the fish: The beam of laser light takes the same path from you to the fish as ordinary light takes from the fish to you (though in the opposite direction).

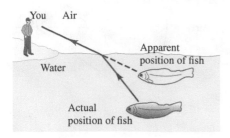

33.3 (i), (ii) Total internal reflection can occur only if two conditions are met: n_b must be less than n_a, and the critical angle θ_{crit} (where $\sin\theta_{\text{crit}} = n_b/n_a$) must be smaller than the angle of incidence θ_a. In the first two cases both conditions are met: The critical angles are (i) $\theta_{\text{crit}} = \sin^{-1}(1/1.33) = 48.8°$ and (ii) $\theta_{\text{crit}} = \sin^{-1}(1.33/1.52) = 61.0°$, both of which are smaller than $\theta_a = 70°$. In the third case $n_b = 1.52$ is greater than $n_a = 1.33$, so total internal reflection cannot occur for any incident angle.

33.5 (ii) The sunlight reflected from the windows of the high-rise building is partially polarized in the vertical direction, perpendicular to the horizontal plane of incidence. The Polaroid filter in front of the lens is oriented with its polarizing axis perpendicular to the dominant direction of polarization of the reflected light.

33.7 (ii) Huygens's principle applies to waves of all kinds, including sound waves. Hence this situation is exactly like that shown in Fig. 33.35, with material a representing the warm air, material b representing the cold air in which the waves travel more slowly, and the interface between the materials representing the weather front. North is toward the top of the figure and east is toward the right, so Fig. 33.35 shows that the rays (which indicate the direction of propagation) deflect toward the east.

Bridging Problem

1.93×10^8 m/s

? When white light shines downward on a thin, horizontal layer of oil, light waves reflected from the upper and lower surfaces of the film of oil interfere, producing vibrant colors. The color that you see reflected from a certain spot on the film depends on (i) the film thickness at that spot; (ii) the index of refraction of the oil; (iii) the index of refraction of the material below the oil; (iv) both (i) and (ii); (v) all of (i), (ii), and (iii).

35 INTERFERENCE

LEARNING GOALS

Looking forward at ...

35.1 What happens when two waves combine, or interfere, in space.

35.2 How to understand the interference pattern formed by the interference of two coherent light waves.

35.3 How to calculate the intensity at various points in an interference pattern.

35.4 How interference occurs when light reflects from the two surfaces of a thin film.

35.5 How interference makes it possible to measure extremely small distances.

Looking back at ...

14.2, 31.1 Phasors.

15.3, 15.6, 15.7 Wave number, wave superposition, standing waves on a string.

16.4 Standing sound waves.

An ugly black oil spot on the pavement can become a thing of beauty after a rain, when the oil reflects a rainbow of colors. Multicolored reflections can also be seen from the surfaces of soap bubbles and DVDs. How is it possible for colorless objects to produce these remarkable colors?

In our discussion of lenses, mirrors, and optical instruments we used the model of *geometric optics,* in which we represent light as *rays,* straight lines that are bent at a reflecting or refracting surface. But light is fundamentally a *wave,* and in some situations we have to consider its wave properties explicitly. If two or more light waves of the same frequency overlap at a point, the total effect depends on the *phases* of the waves as well as their amplitudes. The resulting patterns of light are a result of the *wave* nature of light and cannot be understood on the basis of rays. Optical effects that depend on the wave nature of light are grouped under the heading **physical optics.**

In this chapter we'll look at *interference* phenomena that occur when two waves combine. Effects that occur when *many* sources of waves are present are called *diffraction* phenomena; we'll study these in Chapter 36. In that chapter we'll see that diffraction effects occur whenever a wave passes through an aperture or around an obstacle. They are important in practical applications of physical optics such as diffraction gratings, x-ray diffraction, and holography.

While our primary concern is with light, interference and diffraction can occur with waves of *any* kind. As we go along, we'll point out applications to other types of waves such as sound and water waves.

35.1 INTERFERENCE AND COHERENT SOURCES

As we discussed in Chapter 15, the term **interference** refers to any situation in which two or more waves overlap in space. When this occurs, the total wave at any point at any instant of time is governed by the **principle of superposition,** which we introduced in Section 15.6 in the context of waves on a string. This principle also applies to electromagnetic waves and is the most important principle in all of physical optics. The principle of superposition states:

> **When two or more waves overlap, the resultant displacement at any point and at any instant is found by adding the instantaneous displacements that would be produced at the point by the individual waves if each were present alone.**

(In some special situations, such as electromagnetic waves propagating in a crystal, this principle may not apply. A discussion of these is beyond our scope.)

We use the term "displacement" in a general sense. With waves on the surface of a liquid, we mean the actual displacement of the surface above or below its normal level. With sound waves, the term refers to the excess or deficiency of pressure. For electromagnetic waves, we usually mean a specific component of electric or magnetic field.

Interference in Two or Three Dimensions

We have already discussed one important case of interference, in which two identical waves propagating in opposite directions combine to produce a *standing wave*. We saw this in Section 15.7 for transverse waves on a string and in Section 16.4 for longitudinal waves in a fluid filling a pipe; we described the same phenomenon for electromagnetic waves in Section 32.5. In all of these cases the waves propagated along only a single axis: along a string, along the length of a fluid-filled pipe, or along the propagation direction of an electromagnetic plane wave. But light waves can (and do) travel in *two* or *three* dimensions, as can any kind of wave that propagates in a two- or three-dimensional medium. In this section we'll see what happens when we combine waves that spread out in two or three dimensions from a pair of identical wave sources.

Interference effects are most easily seen when we combine *sinusoidal* waves with a single frequency f and wavelength λ. **Figure 35.1** shows a "snapshot" of a *single* source S_1 of sinusoidal waves and some of the wave fronts produced by this source. The figure shows only the wave fronts corresponding to wave *crests*, so the spacing between successive wave fronts is one wavelength. The material surrounding S_1 is uniform, so the wave speed is the same in all directions, and there is no refraction (and hence no bending of the wave fronts). If the waves are two-dimensional, like waves on the surface of a liquid, the circles in Fig. 35.1 represent circular wave fronts; if the waves propagate in three dimensions, the circles represent spherical wave fronts spreading away from S_1.

In optics, sinusoidal waves are characteristic of **monochromatic light** (light of a single color). While it's fairly easy to make water waves or sound waves of a single frequency, common sources of light *do not* emit monochromatic (single-frequency) light. For example, incandescent light bulbs and flames emit a continuous distribution of wavelengths. By far the most nearly monochromatic light source is the *laser*. An example is the helium–neon laser, which emits red light at 632.8 nm with a wavelength range of the order of ± 0.000001 nm, or about one part in 10^9. In this chapter and the next, we will assume that we are working with monochromatic waves (unless we explicitly state otherwise).

Constructive and Destructive Interference

Figure 35.2a (next page) shows two identical sources of monochromatic waves, S_1 and S_2. The two sources produce waves of the same amplitude and the same wavelength λ. In addition, the two sources are permanently *in phase;* they vibrate in unison. They might be two loudspeakers driven by the same amplifier, two radio antennas powered by the same transmitter, or two small slits in an opaque screen, illuminated by the same monochromatic light source. We will see that if

35.1 A "snapshot" of sinusoidal waves of frequency f and wavelength λ spreading out from source S_1 in all directions.

Wave fronts: crests of the wave (frequency f) separated by one wavelength λ

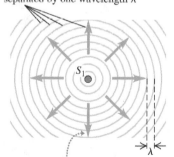

The wave fronts move outward from source S_1 at the wave speed $v = f\lambda$.

35.2 (a) A "snapshot" of sinusoidal waves spreading out from two coherent sources S_1 and S_2. Constructive interference occurs at point a (equidistant from the two sources) and (b) at point b. (c) Destructive interference occurs at point c.

(a) Two coherent wave sources separated by a distance 4λ

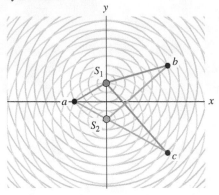

(b) Conditions for constructive interference: Waves interfere constructively if their path lengths differ by an integral number of wavelengths: $r_2 - r_1 = m\lambda$.

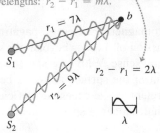

(c) Conditions for destructive interference: Waves interfere destructively if their path lengths differ by a half-integral number of wavelengths: $r_2 - r_1 = (m + \frac{1}{2})\lambda$.

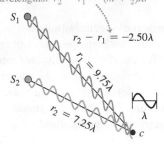

there were not a constant phase relationship between the two sources, the phenomena we are about to discuss would not occur. Two monochromatic sources of the same frequency and with a constant phase relationship (not necessarily in phase) are said to be **coherent.** We also use the term *coherent waves* (or, for light waves, *coherent light*) to refer to the waves emitted by two such sources.

If the waves emitted by the two coherent sources are *transverse,* like electromagnetic waves, then we will also assume that the wave disturbances produced by both sources have the same *polarization* (that is, they lie along the same line). For example, the sources S_1 and S_2 in Fig. 35.2a could be two radio antennas in the form of long rods oriented parallel to the z-axis (perpendicular to the plane of the figure); at any point in the xy-plane the waves produced by both antennas have $\vec{E}$ fields with only a z-component. Then we need only a single scalar function to describe each wave; this makes the analysis much easier.

We position the two sources of equal amplitude, equal wavelength, and (if the waves are transverse) the same polarization along the y-axis in Fig. 35.2a, equidistant from the origin. Consider a point a on the x-axis. From symmetry the two distances from S_1 to a and from S_2 to a are *equal*; waves from the two sources thus require equal times to travel to a. Hence waves that leave S_1 and S_2 in phase arrive at a in phase, and the total amplitude at a is *twice* the amplitude of each individual wave. This is true for *any* point on the x-axis.

Similarly, the distance from S_2 to point b is exactly two wavelengths *greater* than the distance from S_1 to b. A wave crest from S_1 arrives at b exactly two cycles earlier than a crest emitted at the same time from S_2, and again the two waves arrive in phase. As at point a, the total amplitude is the sum of the amplitudes of the waves from S_1 and S_2.

In general, when waves from two or more sources arrive at a point *in phase,* they reinforce each other: The amplitude of the resultant wave is the *sum* of the amplitudes of the individual waves. This is called **constructive interference** (Fig. 35.2b). Let the distance from S_1 to any point P be r_1, and let the distance from S_2 to P be r_2. For constructive interference to occur at P, the path difference $r_2 - r_1$ for the two sources must be an integral multiple of the wavelength λ:

$$r_2 - r_1 = m\lambda \qquad (m = 0, \pm 1, \pm 2, \pm 3, \dots)$$

(constructive interference, sources in phase) (35.1)

In Fig. 35.2a, points a and b satisfy Eq. (35.1) with $m = 0$ and $m = +2$, respectively.

Something different occurs at point c in Fig. 35.2a. At this point, the path difference $r_2 - r_1 = -2.50\lambda$, which is a *half-integral* number of wavelengths. Waves from the two sources arrive at point c exactly a half-cycle out of phase. A crest of one wave arrives at the same time as a crest in the opposite direction (a "trough") of the other wave (Fig. 35.2c). The resultant amplitude is the *difference* between the two individual amplitudes. If the individual amplitudes are equal, then the total amplitude is *zero*! This cancellation or partial cancellation of the individual waves is called **destructive interference.** The condition for destructive interference in the situation shown in Fig. 35.2a is

$$r_2 - r_1 = \left(m + \tfrac{1}{2}\right)\lambda \quad (m = 0, \pm 1, \pm 2, \pm 3, \dots) \quad \text{(35.2)}$$

(destructive interference, sources in phase)

The path difference at point c in Fig. 35.2a satisfies Eq. (35.2) with $m = -3$.

Figure 35.3 shows the same situation as in Fig. 35.2a, but with red curves that show all positions where *constructive* interference occurs. On each curve, the path difference $r_2 - r_1$ is equal to an integer m times the wavelength, as in Eq. (35.1). These curves are called **antinodal curves.** They are directly analogous to *antinodes* in the standing-wave patterns described in Chapters 15 and 16 and Section 32.5. In a standing wave formed by interference between waves propagating in opposite directions, the antinodes are points at which the amplitude is maximum; likewise, the wave amplitude in the situation of Fig. 35.3 is maximum along the antinodal curves. Not shown in Fig. 35.3 are the **nodal curves,** which are the curves that show where *destructive* interference occurs in accordance with Eq. (35.2); these are analogous to the *nodes* in a standing-wave pattern. A nodal curve lies between each two adjacent antinodal curves in Fig. 35.3; one such curve, corresponding to $r_2 - r_1 = -2.50\lambda$, passes through point c.

In some cases, such as two loudspeakers or two radio-transmitter antennas, the interference pattern is three-dimensional. Think of rotating the color curves of Fig. 35.3 around the y-axis; then maximum constructive interference occurs at all points on the resulting surfaces of revolution.

CAUTION Interference patterns are not standing waves In the standing waves described in Sections 15.7, 16.4, and 32.5, the interference is between two waves propagating in opposite directions; there is *no* net energy flow in either direction (the energy in the wave is left "standing"). In the situations shown in Figs. 35.2a and 35.3, there is likewise a stationary pattern of antinodal and nodal curves, but there is a net flow of energy *outward* from the two sources. All that interference does is to "channel" the energy flow so that it is greatest along the antinodal curves and least along the nodal curves. ▮

For Eqs. (35.1) and (35.2) to hold, the two sources must have the same wavelength and must *always* be in phase. These conditions are rather easy to satisfy for sound waves. But with *light* waves there is no practical way to achieve a constant phase relationship (coherence) with two independent sources. This is because of the way light is emitted. In ordinary light sources, atoms gain excess energy by thermal agitation or by impact with accelerated electrons. Such an "excited" atom begins to radiate energy and continues until it has lost all the energy it can, typically in a time of the order of 10^{-8} s. The many atoms in a source ordinarily radiate in an unsynchronized and random phase relationship, and the light that is emitted from *two* such sources has no definite phase relationship.

However, the light from a single source can be split so that parts of it emerge from two or more regions of space, forming two or more *secondary sources*. Then any random phase change in the source affects these secondary sources equally and does not change their *relative* phase.

The distinguishing feature of light from a *laser* is that the emission of light from many atoms is synchronized in frequency and phase. As a result, the random phase changes mentioned above occur much less frequently. Definite phase relationships are preserved over correspondingly much greater lengths in the beam, and laser light is much more coherent than ordinary light.

TEST YOUR UNDERSTANDING OF SECTION 35.1 Consider a point in Fig. 35.3 on the positive y-axis above S_1. Does this point lie on (i) an antinodal curve; (ii) a nodal curve; or (iii) neither? (*Hint:* The distance between S_1 and S_2 is 4λ.) ▮

35.3 The same as Fig. 35.2a, but with red antinodal curves (curves of maximum amplitude) superimposed. All points on each curve satisfy Eq. (35.1) with the value of m shown. The nodal curves (not shown) lie between each adjacent pair of antinodal curves.

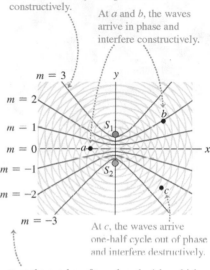

Antinodal curves (red) mark positions where the waves from S_1 and S_2 interfere constructively.

At a and b, the waves arrive in phase and interfere constructively.

At c, the waves arrive one-half cycle out of phase and interfere destructively.

$m =$ the number of wavelengths λ by which the path lengths from S_1 and S_2 differ.

BIO Application Phase Difference, Path Difference, and Localization in Human Hearing Your auditory system uses the phase differences between sounds received by your left and your right ears for *localization*—determining the direction from which the sounds are coming. For sound waves with frequencies lower than about 800 Hz (which are important in speech and music), the distance between your ears is less than a half-wavelength and the phase difference between the waves detected by each ear is less than a half cycle. Remarkably, your brain can detect this phase difference, determine the corresponding path difference, and use this information to localize the direction of the sound source.

35.4 The concepts of constructive interference and destructive interference apply to these water waves as well as to light waves and sound waves.

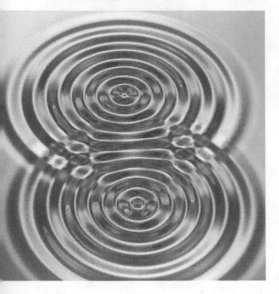

35.2 TWO-SOURCE INTERFERENCE OF LIGHT

The interference pattern produced by two coherent sources of *water* waves of the same wavelength can be readily seen in a ripple tank with a shallow layer of water (**Fig. 35.4**). This pattern is not directly visible when the interference is between *light* waves, since light traveling in a uniform medium cannot be seen. (Sunlight in a room is made visible by scattering from airborne dust.)

Figure 35.5a shows one of the earliest quantitative experiments to reveal the interference of light from two sources, first performed in 1800 by the English scientist Thomas Young. Let's examine this important experiment in detail. A light source (not shown) emits monochromatic light; however, this light is not suitable for use in an interference experiment because emissions from different parts of an ordinary source are not synchronized. To remedy this, the light is directed at a screen with a narrow slit S_0, 1 μm or so wide. The light emerging from the slit originated from only a small region of the light source; thus slit S_0 behaves more nearly like the idealized source shown in Fig. 35.1. (In modern versions of the experiment, a laser is used as a source of coherent light, and the slit S_0 isn't needed.) The light from slit S_0 falls on a screen with two other narrow slits S_1 and S_2, each 1 μm or so wide and a few tens or hundreds of micrometers apart. Cylindrical wave fronts spread out from slit S_0 and reach slits S_1 and S_2 *in phase* because they travel equal distances from S_0. The waves *emerging* from slits S_1 and S_2 are therefore also always in phase, so S_1 and S_2 are *coherent* sources. The interference of waves from S_1 and S_2 produces a pattern in space like that to the right of the sources in Figs. 35.2a and 35.3.

To visualize the interference pattern, a screen is placed so that the light from S_1 and S_2 falls on it (Fig. 35.5b). The screen will be most brightly illuminated at points P, where the light waves from the slits interfere constructively, and will be darkest at points where the interference is destructive.

To simplify the analysis of Young's experiment, we assume that the distance R from the slits to the screen is so large in comparison to the distance d between the slits that the lines from S_1 and S_2 to P are very nearly parallel, as in Fig. 35.5c.

35.5 (a) Young's experiment to show interference of light passing through two slits. A pattern of bright and dark areas appears on the screen (see Fig. 35.6). (b) Geometrical analysis of Young's experiment. For the case shown, $r_2 > r_1$ and both y and θ are positive. If point P is on the other side of the screen's center, $r_2 < r_1$ and both y and θ are negative. (c) Approximate geometry when the distance R to the screen is much greater than the distance d between the slits.

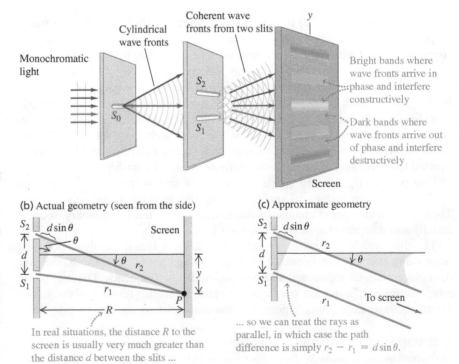

(a) Interference of light waves passing through two slits

(b) Actual geometry (seen from the side)

(c) Approximate geometry

This is usually the case for experiments with light; the slit separation is typically a few millimeters, while the screen may be a meter or more away. The difference in path length is then given by

$$r_2 - r_1 = d \sin \theta \qquad (35.3)$$

where θ is the angle between a line from slits to screen (shown in blue in Fig. 35.5c) and the normal to the plane of the slits (shown as a thin black line).

Constructive and Destructive Two-Slit Interference

We found in Section 35.1 that constructive interference (reinforcement) occurs at points where the path difference is an integral number of wavelengths, $m\lambda$, where $m = 0, \pm 1, \pm 2, \pm 3, \ldots$. So the bright regions on the screen in Fig. 35.5a occur at angles θ for which

Constructive interference, two slits:	Distance between slits Wavelength
	$d \sin \theta = m\lambda \quad (m = 0, \pm 1, \pm 2, \ldots)$ (35.4)
	Angle of line from slits to mth bright region on screen

Similarly, destructive interference (cancellation) occurs, forming dark regions on the screen, at points for which the path difference is a half-integral number of wavelengths, $\left(m + \frac{1}{2}\right)\lambda$;

Destructive interference, two slits:	Distance between slits Wavelength
	$d \sin \theta = \left(m + \frac{1}{2}\right)\lambda \quad (m = 0, \pm 1, \pm 2, \ldots)$ (35.5)
	Angle of line from slits to mth dark region on screen

Thus the pattern on the screen of Figs. 35.5a and 35.5b is a succession of bright and dark bands, or **interference fringes,** parallel to the slits S_1 and S_2. A photograph of such a pattern is shown in **Fig. 35.6**.

We can derive an expression for the positions of the centers of the bright bands on the screen. In Fig. 35.5b, y is measured from the center of the pattern, corresponding to the distance from the center of Fig. 35.6. Let y_m be the distance from the center of the pattern ($\theta = 0$) to the center of the mth bright band. Let θ_m be the corresponding value of θ; then

$$y_m = R \tan \theta_m$$

In such experiments, the distances y_m are often much smaller than the distance R from the slits to the screen. Hence θ_m is very small, $\tan \theta_m \approx \sin \theta_m$, and

$$y_m = R \sin \theta_m$$

Combining this with Eq. (35.4), we find that *for small angles only,*

Constructive interference, Young's experiment (small angles only):	Position of mth bright band Wavelength
	$y_m = R\dfrac{m\lambda}{d} \quad (m = 0, \pm 1, \pm 2, \ldots)$ (35.6)
	Distance from slits to screen Distance between slits

We can measure R and d, as well as the positions y_m of the bright fringes, so this experiment provides a direct measurement of the wavelength λ. Young's experiment was in fact the first direct measurement of wavelengths of light.

The distance between adjacent bright bands in the pattern is *inversely* proportional to the distance d between the slits. The closer together the slits are, the more the pattern spreads out. When the slits are far apart, the bands in the pattern are closer together.

PhET: Wave Interference

35.6 Photograph of interference fringes produced on a screen in Young's double-slit experiment. The center of the pattern is a bright band corresponding to $m = 0$ in Eq. (35.4); this point on the screen is equidistant from the two slits.

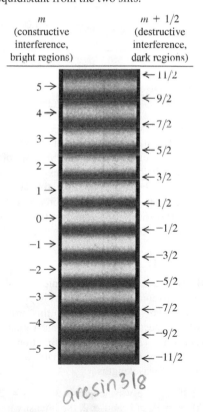

aresin3l8

CAUTION Equation (35.6) is for small angles only While Eqs. (35.4) and (35.5) are valid for any angle, Eq. (35.6) is valid for *small* angles only. It can be used *only* if the distance R from slits to screen is much greater than the slit separation d and if R is much greater than the distance y_m from the center of the interference pattern to the mth bright band. ▌

While we have described the experiment that Young performed with visible light, the results given in Eqs. (35.4) and (35.5) are valid for *any* type of wave, provided that the resultant wave from two coherent sources is detected at a point that is far away in comparison to the separation d.

EXAMPLE 35.1   TWO-SLIT INTERFERENCE

Figure 35.7 shows a two-slit interference experiment in which the slits are 0.200 mm apart and the screen is 1.00 m from the slits. The $m = 3$ bright fringe in the figure is 9.49 mm from the central fringe. Find the wavelength of the light.

35.7 Using a two-slit interference experiment to measure the wavelength of light.

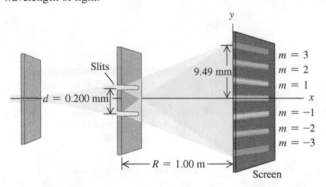

SOLUTION

IDENTIFY and SET UP: Our target variable in this two-slit interference problem is the wavelength λ. We are given the slit separation $d = 0.200$ mm, the distance from slits to screen $R = 1.00$ m, and the distance $y_3 = 9.49$ mm on the screen from the center of the interference pattern to the $m = 3$ bright fringe. We may use Eq. (35.6) to find λ, since the value of R is so much greater than the values of d or y_3.

EXECUTE: We solve Eq. (35.6) for λ for the case $m = 3$:

$$\lambda = \frac{y_m d}{mR} = \frac{(9.49 \times 10^{-3}\text{ m})(0.200 \times 10^{-3}\text{ m})}{(3)(1.00\text{ m})}$$

$$= 633 \times 10^{-9}\text{ m} = 633\text{ nm}$$

EVALUATE: This bright fringe could also correspond to $m = -3$. Can you show that this gives the same result for λ?

EXAMPLE 35.2   BROADCAST PATTERN OF A RADIO STATION

It is often desirable to radiate most of the energy from a radio transmitter in particular directions rather than uniformly in all directions. Pairs or rows of antennas are often used to produce the desired radiation pattern. As an example, consider two identical vertical antennas 400 m apart, operating at 1500 kHz = 1.5×10^6 Hz (near the top end of the AM broadcast band) and oscillating in phase. At distances much greater than 400 m, in what directions is the intensity from the two antennas greatest?

SOLUTION

IDENTIFY and SET UP: The antennas, shown in **Fig. 35.8**, correspond to sources S_1 and S_2 in Fig. 35.5. Hence we can apply the ideas of two-slit interference to this problem. Since the resultant wave is detected at distances much greater than $d = 400$ m, we may use Eq. (35.4) to give the directions of the intensity maxima, the values of θ for which the path difference is zero or a whole number of wavelengths.

EXECUTE: The wavelength is $\lambda = c/f = 200$ m. From Eq. (35.4) with $m = 0$, ± 1, and ± 2, the intensity maxima are given by

$$\sin \theta = \frac{m\lambda}{d} = \frac{m(200\text{ m})}{400\text{ m}} = \frac{m}{2} \qquad \theta = 0, \pm 30°, \pm 90°$$

In this example, values of m greater than 2 or less than -2 give values of $\sin\theta$ greater than 1 or less than -1, which is impossible. There is *no* direction for which the path difference is three or more wavelengths, so values of m of ± 3 or beyond have no meaning in this example.

35.8 Two radio antennas broadcasting in phase. The purple arrows indicate the directions of maximum intensity. The waves that are emitted toward the lower half of the figure are not shown.

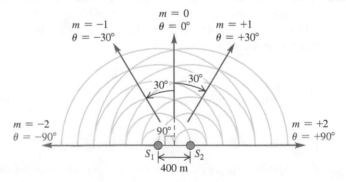

EVALUATE: We can check our result by calculating the angles for *minimum* intensity, using Eq. (35.5). There should be one intensity minimum between each pair of intensity maxima, just as in Fig. 35.6. From Eq. (35.5), with $m = -2, -1, 0$, and 1,

$$\sin \theta = \frac{\left(m + \frac{1}{2}\right)\lambda}{d} = \frac{m + \frac{1}{2}}{2} \qquad \theta = \pm 14.5°, \pm 48.6°$$

These angles fall between the angles for intensity maxima, as they should. The angles are not small, so the angles for the minima are *not* exactly halfway between the angles for the maxima.

TEST YOUR UNDERSTANDING OF SECTION 35.2   You shine a tunable laser (whose wavelength can be adjusted by turning a knob) on a pair of closely spaced slits. The light emerging from the two slits produces an interference pattern on a screen like that shown in Fig. 35.6. If you adjust the wavelength so that the laser light changes from red to blue, how will the spacing between bright fringes change? (i) The spacing increases; (ii) the spacing decreases; (iii) the spacing is unchanged; (iv) not enough information is given to decide. ∎

35.3 INTENSITY IN INTERFERENCE PATTERNS

In Section 35.2 we found the positions of maximum and minimum intensity in a two-source interference pattern. Let's now see how to find the intensity at *any* point in the pattern. To do this, we have to combine the two sinusoidally varying fields (from the two sources) at a point P in the radiation pattern, taking proper account of the phase difference of the two waves at point P, which results from the path difference. The intensity is then proportional to the square of the resultant electric-field amplitude, as we learned in Section 32.4.

To calculate the intensity, we will assume, as in Section 35.2, that the waves from the two sources have equal amplitude E and the same polarization. This assumes that the sources are identical and ignores the slight amplitude difference caused by the unequal path lengths (the amplitude decreases with increasing distance from the source). From Eq. (32.29), each source by itself would give an intensity $\frac{1}{2}\epsilon_0 cE^2$ at point P. If the two sources are in phase, then the waves that arrive at P differ in phase by an amount ϕ that is proportional to the difference in their path lengths, $(r_2 - r_1)$. Then we can use the following expressions for the two electric fields superposed at P:

$$E_1(t) = E\cos(\omega t + \phi)$$

$$E_2(t) = E\cos\omega t$$

The superposition of the two fields at P is a sinusoidal function with some amplitude E_P that depends on E and the phase difference ϕ. First we'll work on finding the amplitude E_P if E and ϕ are known. Then we'll find the intensity I of the resultant wave, which is proportional to E_P^2. Finally, we'll relate the phase difference ϕ to the path difference, which is determined by the geometry of the situation.

Amplitude in Two-Source Interference

To add the two sinusoidal functions with a phase difference, we use the same *phasor* representation that we used for simple harmonic motion (see Section 14.2) and for voltages and currents in ac circuits (see Section 31.1). We suggest that you review these sections now. Each sinusoidal function is represented by a rotating vector (phasor) whose projection on the horizontal axis at any instant represents the instantaneous value of the sinusoidal function.

In **Fig. 35.9**, E_1 is the horizontal component of the phasor representing the wave from source S_1, and E_2 is the horizontal component of the phasor for the wave from S_2. As shown in the diagram, both phasors have the same magnitude E, but E_1 is *ahead* of E_2 in phase by an angle ϕ. Both phasors rotate counterclockwise with constant angular speed ω, and the sum of the projections on the horizontal axis at any time gives the instantaneous value of the total E field at point P. Thus the amplitude E_P of the resultant sinusoidal wave at P is the magnitude of the dark red phasor in the diagram (labeled E_P); this is the *vector sum* of the other two phasors. To find E_P, we use the law of cosines and the trigonometric identity $\cos(\pi - \phi) = -\cos\phi$:

$$E_P^2 = E^2 + E^2 - 2E^2\cos(\pi - \phi)$$

$$= E^2 + E^2 + 2E^2\cos\phi$$

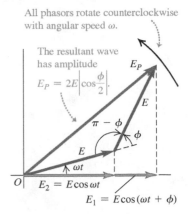

35.9 Phasor diagram for the superposition at a point P of two waves of equal amplitude E with a phase difference ϕ.

Then, using the identity $1 + \cos\phi = 2\cos^2(\phi/2)$, we obtain

$$E_P^2 = 2E^2(1 + \cos\phi) = 4E^2\cos^2\left(\frac{\phi}{2}\right)$$

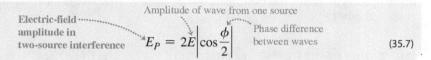

Electric-field amplitude in two-source interference $\cdots\rightarrow E_P = 2E\left|\cos\dfrac{\phi}{2}\right|$ — Amplitude of wave from one source; Phase difference between waves (35.7)

You can also obtain this result without using phasors.

When the two waves are in phase, $\phi = 0$ and $E_P = 2E$. When they are exactly a half-cycle out of phase, $\phi = \pi$ rad $= 180°$, $\cos(\phi/2) = \cos(\pi/2) = 0$, and $E_P = 0$. Thus the superposition of two sinusoidal waves with the same frequency and amplitude but with a phase difference yields a sinusoidal wave with the same frequency and an amplitude between zero and twice the individual amplitudes, depending on the phase difference.

Intensity in Two-Source Interference

To obtain the intensity I at point P, we recall from Section 32.4 that I is equal to the average magnitude of the Poynting vector, S_{av}. For a sinusoidal wave with electric-field amplitude E_P, this is given by Eq. (32.29) with E_{max} replaced by E_P. Thus we can express the intensity in several equivalent forms:

$$I = S_{av} = \frac{E_P^2}{2\mu_0 c} = \frac{1}{2}\sqrt{\frac{\epsilon_0}{\mu_0}}E_P^2 = \frac{1}{2}\epsilon_0 c E_P^2 \tag{35.8}$$

The essential content of these expressions is that I is proportional to E_P^2. When we substitute Eq. (35.7) into the last expression in Eq. (35.8), we get

$$I = \frac{1}{2}\epsilon_0 c E_P^2 = 2\epsilon_0 c E^2 \cos^2\frac{\phi}{2} \tag{35.9}$$

In particular, the *maximum* intensity I_0, which occurs at points where the phase difference is zero ($\phi = 0$), is

$$I_0 = 2\epsilon_0 c E^2$$

Note that the maximum intensity I_0 is *four times* (not twice) as great as the intensity $\frac{1}{2}\epsilon_0 c E^2$ from each individual source. Substituting the expression for I_0 into Eq. (35.9), we find

Intensity in two-source interference $\cdots\rightarrow I = I_0\cos^2\dfrac{\phi}{2}$ — Maximum intensity; Phase difference between waves (35.10)

The intensity depends on the phase difference ϕ and varies between I_0 and zero. If we average Eq. (35.10) over all possible phase differences, the result is $I_0/2 = \epsilon_0 c E^2$ [the average of $\cos^2(\phi/2)$ is $\frac{1}{2}$]. This is just twice the intensity from each individual source, as we should expect. The total energy output from the two sources isn't changed by the interference effects, but the energy is redistributed (see Section 35.1).

Phase Difference and Path Difference

Our next task is to find the phase difference ϕ between the two fields at any point P. We know that ϕ is proportional to the difference in path length from the two sources to point P. When the path difference is one wavelength, the phase difference is one cycle, and $\phi = 2\pi$ rad $= 360°$. When the path difference is $\lambda/2$, $\phi = \pi$ rad $= 180°$, and so on. That is, the ratio of the phase difference ϕ to 2π is equal to the ratio of the path difference $r_2 - r_1$ to λ:

$$\frac{\phi}{2\pi} = \frac{r_2 - r_1}{\lambda}$$

Phase difference in two-source interference $\cdots\cdots\cdots\blacktriangleright$ $\phi = \dfrac{2\pi}{\lambda}(r_2 - r_1) = k(r_2 - r_1)$ $\qquad$ (35.11)

Path difference $\qquad$ Wave number $= 2\pi/\lambda$
Wavelength $\qquad$ Distance from source 2 $\qquad$ Distance from source 1

We introduced the wave number $k = 2\pi/\lambda$ in Section 15.3.

If the material in the space between the sources and P is anything other than vacuum, we must use the wavelength *in the material* in Eq. (35.11). If λ_0 and k_0 are the wavelength and wave number, respectively, in vacuum and the material has index of refraction n, then

$$\lambda = \frac{\lambda_0}{n} \qquad \text{and} \qquad k = nk_0 \qquad (35.12)$$

Finally, if the point P is far away from the sources in comparison to their separation d, the path difference is given by Eq. (35.3):

$$r_2 - r_1 = d\sin\theta$$

Combining this with Eq. (35.11), we find

$$\phi = k(r_2 - r_1) = kd\sin\theta = \frac{2\pi d}{\lambda}\sin\theta \qquad (35.13)$$

When we substitute this into Eq. (35.10), we find

$$I = I_0\cos^2\left(\tfrac{1}{2}kd\sin\theta\right) = I_0\cos^2\left(\frac{\pi d}{\lambda}\sin\theta\right) \qquad \begin{array}{l}\text{(intensity far from}\\ \text{two sources)}\end{array} \qquad (35.14)$$

Maximum intensity occurs when the cosine has the values ± 1—that is, when

$$\frac{\pi d}{\lambda}\sin\theta = m\pi \qquad (m = 0, \pm 1, \pm 2, \ldots)$$

or

$$d\sin\theta = m\lambda$$

in agreement with Eq. (35.4). You can also derive Eq. (35.5) for the zero-intensity directions from Eq. (35.14).

As we noted in Section 35.2, in experiments with light we visualize the interference pattern due to two slits by using a screen placed at a distance R from the slits. We can describe positions on the screen with the coordinate y; the positions of the bright fringes are given by Eq. (35.6), where ordinarily $y \ll R$. In that case, $\sin\theta$ is approximately equal to y/R, and we obtain the following expressions for the intensity at *any* point on the screen as a function of y:

$$I = I_0\cos^2\left(\frac{kdy}{2R}\right) = I_0\cos^2\left(\frac{\pi dy}{\lambda R}\right) \qquad \begin{array}{l}\text{(intensity in two-slit}\\ \text{interference)}\end{array} \qquad (35.15)$$

35.10 Intensity distribution in the interference pattern from two identical slits.

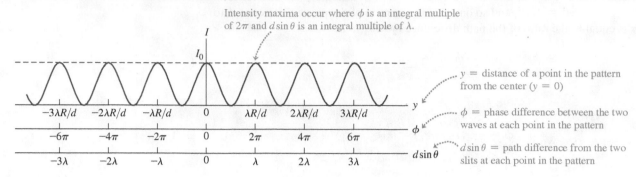

Intensity maxima occur where ϕ is an integral multiple of 2π and $d\sin\theta$ is an integral multiple of λ.

y = distance of a point in the pattern from the center ($y = 0$)

ϕ = phase difference between the two waves at each point in the pattern

$d\sin\theta$ = path difference from the two slits at each point in the pattern

Figure 35.10 shows a graph of Eq. (35.15); we can compare this with the photographically recorded pattern of Fig. 35.6. All peaks in Fig. 35.10 have the same intensity, while those in Fig. 35.6 fade off as we go away from the center. We'll explore the reasons for this variation in peak intensity in Chapter 36.

EXAMPLE 35.3 **A DIRECTIONAL TRANSMITTING ANTENNA ARRAY**

Suppose the two identical radio antennas of Fig. 35.8 are moved to be only 10.0 m apart and the broadcast frequency is increased to $f = 60.0$ MHz. At a distance of 700 m from the point midway between the antennas and in the direction $\theta = 0$ (see Fig. 35.8), the intensity is $I_0 = 0.020$ W/m^2. At this same distance, find (a) the intensity in the direction $\theta = 4.0°$; (b) the direction near $\theta = 0$ for which the intensity is $I_0/2$; and (c) the directions in which the intensity is zero.

SOLUTION

IDENTIFY and SET UP: This problem involves the intensity distribution as a function of angle. Because the 700-m distance from the antennas to the point at which the intensity is measured is much greater than the distance $d = 10.0$ m between the antennas, the amplitudes of the waves from the two antennas are very nearly equal. Hence we can use Eq. (35.14) to relate intensity I and angle θ.

EXECUTE: The wavelength is $\lambda = c/f = 5.00$ m. The spacing $d = 10.0$ m between the antennas is just twice the wavelength (as was the case in Example 35.2), so $d/\lambda = 2.00$ and Eq. (35.14) becomes

$$I = I_0\cos^2\left(\frac{\pi d}{\lambda}\sin\theta\right) = I_0\cos^2[(2.00\pi \text{ rad})\sin\theta]$$

(a) When $\theta = 4.0°$,

$$I = I_0\cos^2[(2.00\pi \text{ rad})\sin 4.0°] = 0.82I_0$$
$$= (0.82)(0.020 \text{ W/m}^2) = 0.016 \text{ W/m}^2$$

(b) The intensity I equals $I_0/2$ when the cosine in Eq. (35.14) has the value $\pm 1/\sqrt{2}$. The smallest angles at which this occurs correspond to $2.00\pi\sin\theta = \pm\pi/4$ rad, so $\sin\theta = \pm(1/8.00) = \pm 0.125$ and $\theta = \pm 7.2°$.

(c) The intensity is zero when $\cos[(2.00\pi \text{ rad})\sin\theta] = 0$. This occurs for $2.00\pi\sin\theta = \pm\pi/2, \pm 3\pi/2, \pm 5\pi/2, \ldots,$ or $\sin\theta = \pm 0.250, \pm 0.750, \pm 1.25, \ldots$. Values of $\sin\theta$ greater than 1 have no meaning, so the answers are

$$\theta = \pm 14.5°, \pm 48.6°$$

EVALUATE: The condition in part (b) that $I = I_0/2$, so that $(2.00\pi \text{ rad})\sin\theta = \pm\pi/4$ rad, is also satisfied when $\sin\theta = \pm 0.375, \pm 0.625,$ or ± 0.875 so that $\theta = \pm 22.0°, \pm 38.7°,$ or $\pm 61.0°$. (Can you verify this?) It would be incorrect to include these angles in the solution, however, because the problem asked for the angle *near* $\theta = 0$ at which $I = I_0/2$. These additional values of θ aren't the ones we're looking for.

TEST YOUR UNDERSTANDING OF SECTION 35.3 A two-slit interference experiment uses coherent light of wavelength 5.00×10^{-7} m. Rank the following points in the interference pattern according to the intensity at each point, from highest to lowest. (i) A point that is closer to one slit than the other by 4.00×10^{-7} m; (ii) a point where the light waves received from the two slits are out of phase by 4.00 rad; (iii) a point that is closer to one slit than the other by 7.50×10^{-7} m; (iv) a point where the light waves received by the two slits are out of phase by 2.00 rad. ∎

35.4 INTERFERENCE IN THIN FILMS

You often see bright bands of color when light reflects from a thin layer of oil floating on water or from a soap bubble (see the photograph that opens this chapter). These are the results of interference. Light waves are reflected from the front and back surfaces of such thin films, and constructive interference between the two reflected waves (with different path lengths) occurs in different places for different wavelengths. **Figure 35.11a** shows the situation. Light shining on the upper surface of a thin film with thickness t is partly reflected at the upper surface (path abc). Light *transmitted* through the upper surface is partly reflected at the lower surface (path $abdef$). The two reflected waves come together at point P on the retina of the eye. Depending on the phase relationship, they may interfere constructively or destructively. Different colors have different wavelengths, so the interference may be constructive for some colors and destructive for others. That's why we see colored patterns in the photograph that opens this chapter (which shows a thin film of oil floating on water) and in Fig. 35.11b (which shows thin films of soap solution that make up the bubble walls). The complex shapes of the colored patterns result from variations in the thickness of the film.

Thin-Film Interference and Phase Shifts During Reflection

Let's look at a simplified situation in which *monochromatic* light reflects from two nearly parallel surfaces at nearly normal incidence. **Figure 35.12** shows two plates of glass separated by a thin wedge, or film, of air. We want to consider interference between the two light waves reflected from the surfaces adjacent to the air wedge. (Reflections also occur at the top surface of the upper plate and the bottom surface of the lower plate; to keep our discussion simple, we won't include these.) The situation is the same as in Fig. 35.11a except that the film (wedge) thickness is not uniform. The path difference between the two waves is just twice the thickness t of the air wedge at each point. At points where $2t$ is an integer number of wavelengths, we expect to see constructive interference and a bright area; where it is a half-integer number of wavelengths, we expect to see destructive interference and a dark area. Where the plates are in contact, there is practically *no* path difference, and we expect a bright area.

When we carry out the experiment, the bright and dark fringes appear, but they are interchanged! Along the line where the plates are in contact, we find a *dark* fringe, not a bright one. This suggests that one or the other of the reflected waves has undergone a half-cycle phase shift during its reflection. In that case the two waves that are reflected at the line of contact are a half-cycle out of phase even though they have the same path length.

In fact, this phase shift can be predicted from Maxwell's equations and the electromagnetic nature of light. The details of the derivation are beyond our scope, but here is the result. Suppose a light wave with electric-field amplitude E_i is traveling in an optical material with index of refraction n_a. It strikes, at normal incidence, an interface with another optical material with index n_b. The amplitude E_r of the wave reflected from the interface is given by

$$E_r = \frac{n_a - n_b}{n_a + n_b} E_i \quad \text{(normal incidence)} \quad (35.16)$$

This result shows that the incident and reflected amplitudes have the same sign when n_a is larger than n_b and opposite signs when n_b is larger than n_a. Because amplitudes must always be positive or zero, a *negative* value means that the

35.11 (a) A diagram and (b) a photograph showing interference of light reflected from a thin film.

(a) Interference between rays reflected from the two surfaces of a thin film

Light reflected from the upper and lower surfaces of the film comes together in the eye at P and undergoes interference.

Some colors interfere constructively and others destructively, creating the color bands we see.

(b) Colorful reflections from a soap bubble

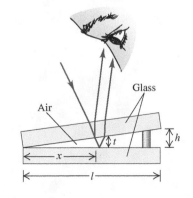

35.12 Interference between light waves reflected from the two sides of an air wedge separating two glass plates. The angles and the thickness of the air wedge have been exaggerated for clarity; in the text we assume that the light strikes the upper plate at normal incidence and that the distances h and t are much less than l.

35.13 Upper figures: electromagnetic waves striking an interface between optical materials at normal incidence (shown as a small angle for clarity). Lower figures: mechanical wave pulses on ropes.

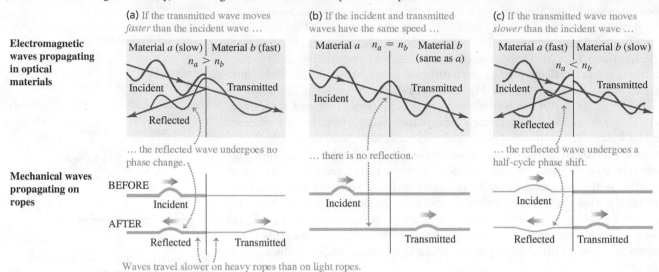

Electromagnetic waves propagating in optical materials

(a) If the transmitted wave moves *faster* than the incident wave ...

Material a (slow) | Material b (fast)
$n_a > n_b$
Incident | Transmitted
Reflected
... the reflected wave undergoes no phase change.

(b) If the incident and transmitted waves have the same speed ...

Material a $\quad n_a = n_b \quad$ Material b (same as a)
Transmitted
Incident
... there is no reflection.

(c) If the transmitted wave moves *slower* than the incident wave ...

Material a (fast) | Material b (slow)
$n_a < n_b$
Incident | Transmitted
Reflected
... the reflected wave undergoes a half-cycle phase shift.

Mechanical waves propagating on ropes

BEFORE
Incident
AFTER
Reflected | Transmitted

Incident
Transmitted

Incident
Reflected | Transmitted

Waves travel slower on heavy ropes than on light ropes.

wave actually undergoes a half-cycle (180°) phase shift. **Figure 35.13** shows three possibilities:

Figure 35.13a: When $n_a > n_b$, light travels more slowly in the first material than in the second. In this case, E_r and E_i have the same sign, and the phase shift of the reflected wave relative to the incident wave is zero. This is analogous to reflection of a transverse mechanical wave on a heavy rope at a point where it is tied to a lighter rope.

Figure 35.13b: When $n_a = n_b$, the amplitude E_r of the reflected wave is zero. In effect there is no interface, so there is *no* reflected wave.

Figure 35.13c: When $n_a < n_b$, light travels more slowly in the second material than in the first. In this case, E_r and E_i have opposite signs, and the phase shift of the reflected wave relative to the incident wave is π rad (a half-cycle). This is analogous to reflection (with inversion) of a transverse mechanical wave on a light rope at a point where it is tied to a heavier rope.

Let's compare with the situation of Fig. 35.12. For the wave reflected from the upper surface of the air wedge, n_a (glass) is greater than n_b, so this wave has zero phase shift. For the wave reflected from the lower surface, n_a (air) is less than n_b (glass), so this wave has a half-cycle phase shift. Waves that are reflected from the line of contact have no path difference to give additional phase shifts, and they interfere destructively; this is what we observe. You can use the above principle to show that for normal incidence, the wave reflected at point b in Fig. 35.11a is shifted by a half-cycle, while the wave reflected at d is not (if there is air below the film).

We can summarize this discussion mathematically. If the film has thickness t, the light is at normal incidence and has wavelength λ in the film; if neither or both of the reflected waves from the two surfaces have a half-cycle reflection phase shift, the conditions for constructive and destructive interference are

Constructive reflection	$2t = m\lambda \quad (m = 0, 1, 2, \dots)$	(35.17a)
(From thin film, no relative phase shift)	Thickness of film $\quad$ Wavelength	
Destructive reflection	$2t = \left(m + \tfrac{1}{2}\right)\lambda \quad (m = 0, 1, 2, \dots)$	(35.17b)

If *one* of the two waves has a half-cycle reflection phase shift, the conditions for constructive and destructive interference are reversed:

Constructive reflection	$2t = \left(m + \tfrac{1}{2}\right)\lambda \quad (m = 0, 1, 2, \dots)$	(35.18a)
(From thin film, half-cycle phase shift)	Thickness of film Wavelength	
Destructive reflection	$2t = m\lambda \quad (m = 0, 1, 2, \dots)$	(35.18b)

Thin and Thick Films

We have emphasized *thin* films in our discussion because of a principle we introduced in Section 35.1: In order for two waves to cause a steady interference pattern, the waves must be *coherent,* with a definite and constant phase relationship. The sun and light bulbs emit light in a stream of short bursts, each of which is only a few micrometers long (1 micrometer = $1\ \mu m = 10^{-6}$ m). If light reflects from the two surfaces of a thin film, the two reflected waves are part of the same burst (**Fig. 35.14a**). Hence these waves are coherent and interference occurs as we have described. If the film is too thick, however, the two reflected waves will belong to different bursts (Fig. 35.14b). There is no definite phase relationship between different light bursts, so the two waves are incoherent and there is no fixed interference pattern. That's why you see interference colors in light reflected from a soap bubble a few micrometers thick (see Fig. 35.11b), but you do *not* see such colors in the light reflected from a pane of window glass with a thickness of a few millimeters (a thousand times greater).

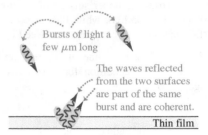

35.14 (a) Light reflecting from a thin film produces a steady interference pattern, but (b) light reflecting from a thick film does not.

(a) Light reflecting from a thin film

Bursts of light a few μm long

The waves reflected from the two surfaces are part of the same burst and are coherent.

Thin film

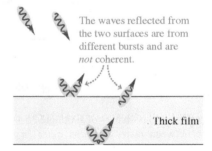

(b) Light reflecting from a thick film

The waves reflected from the two surfaces are from different bursts and are *not* coherent.

Thick film

| PROBLEM-SOLVING STRATEGY 35.1 | INTERFERENCE IN THIN FILMS |

IDENTIFY *the relevant concepts:* Problems with thin films involve interference of two waves, one reflected from the film's front surface and one reflected from the back surface. Typically you will be asked to relate the wavelength, the film thickness, and the index of refraction of the film.

SET UP *the problem* using the following steps:
1. Make a drawing showing the geometry of the film. Identify the materials that adjoin the film; their properties determine whether one or both of the reflected waves have a half-cycle phase shift.
2. Identify the target variable.

EXECUTE *the solution* as follows:
1. Apply the rule for phase changes to each reflected wave: There is a half-cycle phase shift when $n_b > n_a$ and none when $n_b < n_a$.

2. If *neither* reflected wave undergoes a phase shift, or if *both* do, use Eqs. (35.17). If only one reflected wave undergoes a phase shift, use Eqs. (35.18).
3. Solve the resulting equation for the target variable. Use the wavelength $\lambda = \lambda_0/n$ of light *in the film* in your calculations, where n is the index of refraction of the film. (For air, $n = 1.000$ to four-figure precision.)
4. If you are asked about the wave that is transmitted through the film, remember that minimum intensity in the reflected wave corresponds to maximum *transmitted* intensity, and vice versa.

EVALUATE *your answer:* Interpret your results by examining what would happen if the wavelength were changed or if the film had a different thickness.

| EXAMPLE 35.4 | THIN-FILM INTERFERENCE I |

Suppose the two glass plates in Fig. 35.12 are two microscope slides 10.0 cm long. At one end they are in contact; at the other end they are separated by a piece of paper 0.0200 mm thick. What is the spacing of the interference fringes seen by reflection? Is the fringe at the line of contact bright or dark? Assume monochromatic light with a wavelength in air of $\lambda = \lambda_0 = 500$ nm.

SOLUTION

IDENTIFY and SET UP: Figure 35.15 depicts the situation. We'll consider only interference between the light reflected from the

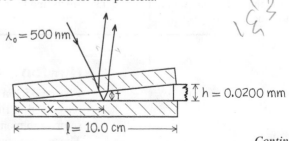

35.15 Our sketch for this problem.

$\lambda_0 = 500$ nm

$h = 0.0200$ mm

$l = 10.0$ cm

Continued

upper and lower surfaces of the air wedge between the microscope slides. [The top slide has a relatively great thickness, about 1 mm, so we can ignore interference between the light reflected from its upper and lower surfaces (see Fig. 35.14b).] Light travels more slowly in the glass of the slides than it does in air. Hence the wave reflected from the upper surface of the air wedge has no phase shift (see Fig. 35.13a), while the wave reflected from the lower surface has a half-cycle phase shift (see Fig. 35.13c).

EXECUTE: Since only one of the reflected waves undergoes a phase shift, the condition for *destructive* interference (a dark fringe) is Eq. (35.18b):

$$2t = m\lambda_0 \qquad (m = 0, 1, 2, \ldots)$$

From similar triangles in Fig. 35.15 the thickness t of the air wedge at each point is proportional to the distance x from the line of contact:

$$\frac{t}{x} = \frac{h}{l}$$

Combining this with Eq. (35.18b), we find

$$\frac{2xh}{l} = m\lambda_0$$

$$x = m\frac{l\lambda_0}{2h} = m\frac{(0.100 \text{ m})(500 \times 10^{-9} \text{ m})}{(2)(0.0200 \times 10^{-3} \text{ m})} = m(1.25 \text{ mm})$$

Successive dark fringes, corresponding to $m = 1, 2, 3, \ldots$, are spaced 1.25 mm apart. Substituting $m = 0$ into this equation gives $x = 0$, which is where the two slides touch (at the left-hand side of Fig. 35.15). Hence there is a dark fringe at the line of contact.

EVALUATE: Our result shows that the fringe spacing is proportional to the wavelength of the light used; the fringes would be farther apart with red light (larger λ_0) than with blue light (smaller λ_0). If we use white light, the reflected light at any point is a mixture of wavelengths for which constructive interference occurs; the wavelengths that interfere destructively are weak or absent in the reflected light. (This same effect explains the colors seen when a soap bubble is illuminated by white light, as in Fig. 35.11b.)

EXAMPLE 35.5   THIN-FILM INTERFERENCE II

Suppose the glass plates of Example 35.4 have $n = 1.52$ and the space between plates contains water ($n = 1.33$) instead of air. What happens now?

SOLUTION

IDENTIFY and SET UP: The index of refraction of the water wedge is still less than that of the glass on either side of it, so the phase shifts are the same as in Example 35.4. Once again we use Eq. (35.18b) to find the positions of the dark fringes; the only difference is that the wavelength λ in this equation is now the wavelength in water instead of in air.

EXECUTE: In the film of water ($n = 1.33$), the wavelength is $\lambda = \lambda_0/n = (500 \text{ nm})/(1.33) = 376 \text{ nm}$. When we replace λ_0 by λ in the expression from Example 35.4 for the position x of the mth dark fringe, we find that the fringe spacing is reduced by the same factor of 1.33 and is equal to 0.940 mm. There is still a dark fringe at the line of contact.

EVALUATE: Can you see that to obtain the same fringe spacing as in Example 35.4, the dimension h in Fig. 35.15 would have to be reduced to $(0.0200 \text{ mm})/1.33 = 0.0150 \text{ mm}$? This shows that what matters in thin-film interference is the *ratio* t/λ between film thickness and wavelength. [Consider Eqs. (35.17) and (35.18).]

EXAMPLE 35.6   THIN-FILM INTERFERENCE III

Suppose the upper of the two plates of Example 35.4 is a plastic with $n = 1.40$, the wedge is filled with a silicone grease with $n = 1.50$, and the bottom plate is a dense flint glass with $n = 1.60$. What happens now?

SOLUTION

IDENTIFY and SET UP: The geometry is again the same as shown in Fig. 35.15, but now half-cycle phase shifts occur at *both* surfaces of the grease wedge (see Fig. 35.13c). Hence there is no *relative* phase shift and we must use Eq. (35.17b) to find the positions of the dark fringes.

EXECUTE: The value of λ to use in Eq. (35.17b) is the wavelength in the silicone grease, $\lambda = \lambda_0/n = (500 \text{ nm})/1.50 = 333$ nm. You can readily show that the fringe spacing is 0.833 mm. Note that the two reflected waves from the line of contact are in phase (they both undergo the same phase shift), so the line of contact is at a *bright* fringe.

EVALUATE: What would happen if you carefully removed the upper microscope slide so that the grease wedge retained its shape? There would still be half-cycle phase changes at the upper and lower surfaces of the wedge, so the pattern of fringes would be the same as with the upper slide present.

Newton's Rings

Figure 35.16a shows the convex surface of a lens in contact with a plane glass plate. A thin film of air is formed between the two surfaces. When you view the setup with monochromatic light, you see circular interference fringes (Fig. 35.16b). These were studied by Newton and are called **Newton's rings.**

(a) A convex lens in contact with a glass plane

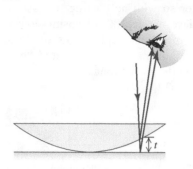

(b) Newton's rings: circular interference fringes

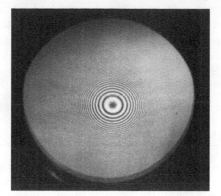

35.16 (a) Air film between a convex lens and a plane surface. The thickness of the film t increases from zero as we move out from the center, giving (b) a series of alternating dark and bright rings for monochromatic light.

We can use interference fringes to compare the surfaces of two optical parts by placing the two in contact and observing the interference fringes. **Figure 35.17** is a photograph made during the grinding of a telescope objective lens. The lower, larger-diameter, thicker disk is the correctly shaped master, and the smaller, upper disk is the lens under test. The "contour lines" are Newton's interference fringes; each one indicates an additional distance between the specimen and the master of one half-wavelength. At 10 lines from the center spot the distance between the two surfaces is five wavelengths, or about 0.003 mm. This isn't very good; high-quality lenses are routinely ground with a precision of less than one wavelength. The surface of the primary mirror of the Hubble Space Telescope was ground to a precision of better than $\frac{1}{50}$ wavelength. Unfortunately, it was ground to incorrect specifications, creating one of the most precise errors in the history of optical technology (see Section 34.2).

Nonreflective and Reflective Coatings

Nonreflective coatings for lens surfaces make use of thin-film interference. A thin layer or film of hard transparent material with an index of refraction smaller than that of the glass is deposited on the lens surface, as in **Fig. 35.18**. Light is reflected from both surfaces of the layer. In both reflections the light is reflected from a medium of greater index than that in which it is traveling, so the same phase change occurs in both reflections. If the film thickness is a quarter (one-fourth) of the wavelength *in the film* (assuming normal incidence), the total path difference is a half-wavelength. Light reflected from the first surface is then a half-cycle out of phase with light reflected from the second, and there is destructive interference.

The thickness of the nonreflective coating can be a quarter-wavelength for only one particular wavelength. This is usually chosen in the central yellow-green portion of the spectrum ($\lambda = 550$ nm), where the eye is most sensitive. Then there is somewhat more reflection at both longer (red) and shorter (blue) wavelengths, and the reflected light has a purple hue. The overall reflection from a lens or prism surface can be reduced in this way from 4–5% to less than 1%. This also increases the net amount of light that is *transmitted* through the lens, since light that is not reflected will be transmitted. The same principle is used to minimize reflection from silicon photovoltaic solar cells ($n = 3.5$) by use of a thin surface layer of silicon monoxide (SiO, $n = 1.45$); this helps to increase the amount of light that actually reaches the solar cells.

If a quarter-wavelength thickness of a material with an index of refraction *greater* than that of glass is deposited on glass, then the reflectivity is *increased*, and the deposited material is called a **reflective coating.** In this case there is a half-cycle phase shift at the air–film interface but none at the film–glass interface, and reflections from the two sides of the film interfere constructively.

35.17 The surface of a telescope objective lens under inspection during manufacture.

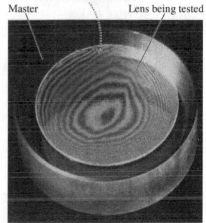

Fringes map lack of fit between lens and master.

Master   Lens being tested

35.18 A nonreflective coating has an index of refraction intermediate between those of glass and air.

Destructive interference occurs when
- the film is about $\frac{1}{4}\lambda$ thick and
- the light undergoes a phase change at both reflecting surfaces,

so that the two reflected waves emerge from the film about $\frac{1}{2}$ cycle out of phase.

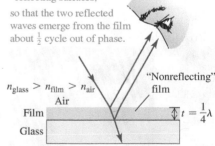

$n_{glass} > n_{film} > n_{air}$

"Nonreflecting" film

Air

Film

Glass

$t = \frac{1}{4}\lambda$

For example, a coating with refractive index 2.5 causes 38% of the incident energy to be reflected, compared with 4% or so with no coating. By use of multiple-layer coatings, it is possible to achieve nearly 100% transmission or reflection for particular wavelengths. Some practical applications of these coatings are for color separation in television cameras and for infrared "heat reflectors" in motion-picture projectors, solar cells, and astronauts' visors.

EXAMPLE 35.7   A NONREFLECTIVE COATING

A common lens coating material is magnesium fluoride (MgF_2), with $n = 1.38$. What thickness should a nonreflective coating have for 550-nm light if it is applied to glass with $n = 1.52$?

SOLUTION

IDENTIFY and SET UP: This coating is of the sort shown in Fig. 35.18. The thickness must be one-quarter of the wavelength of this light *in the coating*.

EXECUTE: The wavelength in air is $\lambda_0 = 550$ nm, so its wavelength in the MgF_2 coating is $\lambda = \lambda_0/n = (550 \text{ nm})/1.38 = 400$ nm. The coating thickness should be one-quarter of this, or $\lambda/4 = 100$ nm.

EVALUATE: This is a very thin film, no more than a few hundred molecules thick. Note that this coating is *reflective* for light whose wavelength is *twice* the coating thickness; light of that wavelength reflected from the coating's lower surface travels one wavelength farther than light reflected from the upper surface, so the two waves are in phase and interfere constructively. This occurs for light with a wavelength in MgF_2 of 200 nm and a wavelength in air of $(200 \text{ nm})(1.38) = 276$ nm. This is an ultraviolet wavelength (see Section 32.1), so designers of optical lenses with nonreflective coatings need not worry about such enhanced reflection.

TEST YOUR UNDERSTANDING OF SECTION 35.4 A thin layer of benzene ($n = 1.501$) lies on top of a sheet of fluorite ($n = 1.434$). It is illuminated from above with light whose wavelength in benzene is 400 nm. Which of the following possible thicknesses of the benzene layer will maximize the brightness of the reflected light? (i) 100 nm; (ii) 200 nm; (iii) 300 nm; (iv) 400 nm. ∎

BIO Application Interference and Butterfly Wings Many of the most brilliant colors in the animal world are created by *interference* rather than by pigments. These photos show the butterfly *Morpho rhetenor* and the microscopic scales that cover the upper surfaces of its wings. The scales have a profusion of tiny ridges (middle photo); these carry regularly spaced flanges (bottom photo) that function as reflectors. These are spaced so that the reflections interfere constructively for blue light. The multilayered structure reflects 70% of the blue light that strikes it, giving the wings a mirrorlike brilliance. (The undersides of the wings do not have these structures and are a dull brown.)

35.5 THE MICHELSON INTERFEROMETER

An important experimental device that uses interference is the **Michelson interferometer.** Michelson interferometers are used to make precise measurements of wavelengths and of very small distances, such as the minute changes in thickness of an axon when a nerve impulse propagates along its length. Like the Young two-slit experiment, a Michelson interferometer takes monochromatic light from a single source and divides it into two waves that follow different paths. In Young's experiment, this is done by sending part of the light through one slit and part through another; in a Michelson interferometer a device called a *beam splitter* is used. Interference occurs in both experiments when the two light waves are recombined.

How a Michelson Interferometer Works

Figure 35.19 shows the principal components of a Michelson interferometer. A ray of light from a monochromatic source A strikes the beam splitter C, which is a glass plate with a thin coating of silver on its right side. Part of the light (ray 1) passes through the silvered surface and the compensator plate D and is reflected from mirror M_1. It then returns through D and is reflected from the silvered surface of C to the observer. The remainder of the light (ray 2) is reflected from the silvered surface at point P to the mirror M_2 and back through C to the observer's eye. The purpose of the compensator plate D is to ensure that rays 1 and 2 pass through the same thickness of glass; plate D is cut from the same piece of glass as plate C, so their thicknesses are identical to within a fraction of a wavelength.

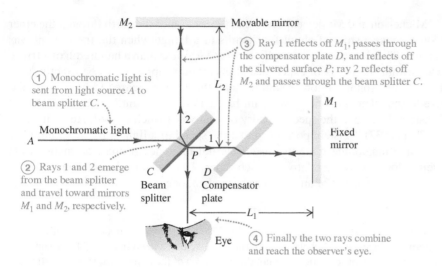

① Monochromatic light is sent from light source A to beam splitter C.

Monochromatic light

A

② Rays 1 and 2 emerge from the beam splitter and travel toward mirrors M_1 and M_2, respectively.

M_2 — Movable mirror

③ Ray 1 reflects off M_1, passes through the compensator plate D, and reflects off the silvered surface P; ray 2 reflects off M_2 and passes through the beam splitter C.

L_2

M_1

Fixed mirror

C
Beam splitter

D
Compensator plate

P

L_1

Eye ④ Finally the two rays combine and reach the observer's eye.

35.19 A schematic Michelson interferometer. The observer sees an interference pattern that results from the difference in path lengths for rays 1 and 2.

The whole apparatus in Fig. 35.19 is mounted on a very rigid frame, and the position of mirror M_2 can be adjusted with a fine, very accurate micrometer screw. If the distances L_1 and L_2 are exactly equal and the mirrors M_1 and M_2 are exactly at right angles, the virtual image of M_1 formed by reflection at the silvered surface of plate C coincides with mirror M_2. If L_1 and L_2 are *not* exactly equal, the image of M_1 is displaced slightly from M_2; and if the mirrors are not exactly perpendicular, the image of M_1 makes a slight angle with M_2. Then the mirror M_2 and the virtual image of M_1 play the same roles as the two surfaces of a wedge-shaped thin film (see Section 35.4), and light reflected from these surfaces forms the same sort of interference fringes.

Suppose the angle between mirror M_2 and the virtual image of M_1 is just large enough that five or six vertical fringes are present in the field of view. If we now move the mirror M_2 slowly either backward or forward a distance $\lambda/2$, the difference in path length between rays 1 and 2 changes by λ, and each fringe moves to the left or right a distance equal to the fringe spacing. If we observe the fringe positions through a telescope with a crosshair eyepiece and m fringes cross the crosshairs when we move the mirror a distance y, then

$$y = m\frac{\lambda}{2} \qquad \text{or} \qquad \lambda = \frac{2y}{m} \qquad (35.19)$$

If m is several thousand, the distance y is large enough that it can be measured with good accuracy, and we can obtain an accurate value for the wavelength λ. Alternatively, if the wavelength is known, a distance y can be measured by simply counting fringes when M_2 is moved by this distance. In this way, distances that are comparable to a wavelength of light can be measured with relative ease.

The Michelson-Morley Experiment

The original application of the Michelson interferometer was to the historic **Michelson-Morley experiment.** Before the electromagnetic theory of light became established, most physicists thought that the propagation of light waves occurred in a medium called the **ether,** which was believed to permeate all space. In 1887 the American scientists Albert Michelson and Edward Morley used the Michelson interferometer in an attempt to detect the motion of the earth through the ether. Suppose the interferometer in Fig. 35.19 is moving from left to right relative to the ether. According to the ether theory, this would lead to changes in the speed of light in the portions of the path shown as horizontal lines in the figure. There would be fringe shifts relative to the positions that the fringes would have if the instrument were at rest in the ether. Then when the entire instrument was rotated 90°, the other portions of the paths would be similarly affected, giving a fringe shift in the opposite direction.

BIO **Application Imaging Cells with a Michelson Interferometer** This false-color image of a human colon cancer cell was made by using a microscope that was mated to a Michelson interferometer. The cell is in one arm of the interferometer, and light passing through the cell undergoes a phase shift that depends on the cell thickness and the organelles within the cell. The fringe pattern can then be used to construct a three-dimensional view of the cell. Scientists have used this technique to observe how different types of cells behave when prodded by microscopic probes. Cancer cells turn out to be "softer" than normal cells, a distinction that may make cancer stem cells easier to identify.

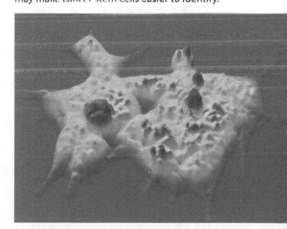

Michelson and Morley expected that the motion of the earth through the ether would cause a shift of about four-tenths of a fringe when the instrument was rotated. The shift that was actually observed was less than a hundredth of a fringe and, within the limits of experimental uncertainty, appeared to be exactly zero. Despite its orbital motion around the sun, the earth appeared to be *at rest* relative to the ether. This negative result baffled physicists until 1905, when Albert Einstein developed the special theory of relativity (which we will study in detail in Chapter 37). Einstein postulated that the speed of a light wave in vacuum has the same magnitude c relative to *all* inertial reference frames, no matter what their velocity may be relative to each other. The presumed ether then plays no role, and the concept of an ether has been abandoned.

TEST YOUR UNDERSTANDING OF SECTION 35.5 You are observing the pattern of fringes in a Michelson interferometer like that shown in Fig. 35.19. If you change the index of refraction (but not the thickness) of the compensator plate, will the pattern change? ▌

CHAPTER **35 SUMMARY**

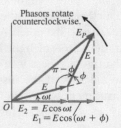

Interference and coherent sources: Monochromatic light is light with a single frequency. Coherence is a definite, unchanging phase relationship between two waves. The overlap of waves from two coherent sources of monochromatic light forms an interference pattern. The principle of superposition states that the total wave disturbance at any point is the sum of the disturbances from the separate waves.

Two-source interference of light: When two sources are in phase, constructive interference occurs where the difference in path length from the two sources is zero or an integer number of wavelengths; destructive interference occurs where the path difference is a half-integer number of wavelengths. If two sources separated by a distance d are both very far from a point P, and the line from the sources to P makes an angle θ with the line perpendicular to the line of the sources, then the condition for constructive interference at P is Eq. (35.4). The condition for destructive interference is Eq. (35.5). When θ is very small, the position y_m of the mth bright fringe on a screen located a distance R from the sources is given by Eq. (35.6). (See Examples 35.1 and 35.2.)

$$d\sin\theta = m\lambda \quad (m = 0, \pm 1, \pm 2, \ldots)$$
(constructive interference) $\quad$ (35.4)

$$d\sin\theta = \left(m + \tfrac{1}{2}\right)\lambda$$
$$(m = 0, \pm 1, \pm 2, \ldots)$$
(destructive interference) $\quad$ (35.5)

$$y_m = R\frac{m\lambda}{d} \quad (m = 0, \pm 1, \pm 2, \ldots)$$
(bright fringes) $\quad$ (35.6)

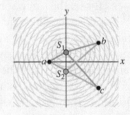

Intensity in interference patterns: When two sinusoidal waves with equal amplitude E and phase difference ϕ are superimposed, the resultant amplitude E_P and intensity I are given by Eqs. (35.7) and (35.10), respectively. If the two sources emit in phase, the phase difference ϕ at a point P (located a distance r_1 from source 1 and a distance r_2 from source 2) is directly proportional to the path difference $r_2 - r_1$. (See Example 35.3.)

$$E_P = 2E\left|\cos\frac{\phi}{2}\right| \quad (35.7)$$

$$I = I_0\cos^2\frac{\phi}{2} \quad (35.10)$$

$$\phi = \frac{2\pi}{\lambda}(r_2 - r_1) = k(r_2 - r_1) \quad (35.11)$$

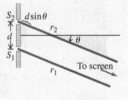

Interference in thin films: When light is reflected from both sides of a thin film of thickness t and no phase shift occurs at either surface, constructive interference between the reflected waves occurs when $2t$ is equal to an integral number of wavelengths. If a half-cycle phase shift occurs at one surface, this is the condition for destructive interference. A half-cycle phase shift occurs during reflection whenever the index of refraction in the second material is greater than that in the first. (See Examples 35.4–35.7.)

$2t = m\lambda \quad (m = 0, 1, 2, \ldots)$
(constructive reflection from   (35.17a)
thin film, no relative phase shift)

$2t = \left(m + \tfrac{1}{2}\right)\lambda \quad (m = 0, 1, 2, \ldots)$
(destructive reflection from   (35.17b)
thin film, no relative phase shift)

$2t = \left(m + \tfrac{1}{2}\right)\lambda \quad (m - 0, 1, 2, \ldots)$
(constructive reflection from   (35.18a)
thin film, half-cycle phase shift)

$2t = m\lambda \quad (m = 0, 1, 2, \ldots)$
(destructive reflection from   (35.18b)
thin film, half-cycle phase shift)

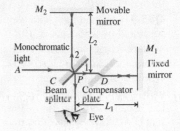

Michelson interferometer: The Michelson interferometer uses a monochromatic light source and can be used for high-precision measurements of wavelengths. Its original purpose was to detect motion of the earth relative to a hypothetical ether, the supposed medium for electromagnetic waves. The ether has never been detected, and the concept has been abandoned; the speed of light is the same relative to all observers. This is part of the foundation of the special theory of relativity.

BRIDGING PROBLEM   THIN-FILM INTERFERENCE IN AN OIL SLICK

An oil tanker spills a large amount of oil ($n = 1.45$) into the sea ($n = 1.33$). (a) If you look down onto the oil spill from overhead, what predominant wavelength of light do you see at a point where the oil is 380 nm thick? What color is the light? (*Hint:* See Table 32.1.) (b) In the water under the slick, what visible wavelength (as measured in air) is predominant in the transmitted light at the same place in the slick as in part (a)?

SOLUTION GUIDE

IDENTIFY and SET UP

1. The oil layer acts as a thin film, so we must consider interference between light that reflects from the top and bottom surfaces of the oil. If a wavelength is prominent in the *transmitted* light, there is destructive interference for that wavelength in the *reflected* light.

2. Choose the appropriate interference equations that relate the thickness of the oil film and the wavelength of light. Take account of the indexes of refraction of the air, oil, and water.

EXECUTE

3. For part (a), find the wavelengths for which there is constructive interference as seen from above the oil film. Which of these are in the visible spectrum?

4. For part (b), find the visible wavelength for which there is destructive interference as seen from above the film. (This will ensure that there is substantial transmitted light at the wavelength.)

EVALUATE

5. If a diver below the water's surface shines a light up at the bottom of the oil film, at what wavelengths would there be constructive interference in the light that reflects back downward?

Problems   For assigned homework and other learning materials, go to MasteringPhysics®.   **MP**

•, ••, •••: Difficulty levels. **CP**: Cumulative problems incorporating material from earlier chapters. **CALC**: Problems requiring calculus.
DATA: Problems involving real data, scientific evidence, experimental design, and/or statistical reasoning. **BIO**: Biosciences problems.

DISCUSSION QUESTIONS

Q35.1 A two-slit interference experiment is set up, and the fringes are displayed on a screen. Then the whole apparatus is immersed in the nearest swimming pool. How does the fringe pattern change?

Q35.2 Could an experiment similar to Young's two-slit experiment be performed with sound? How might this be carried out? Does it matter that sound waves are longitudinal and electromagnetic waves are transverse? Explain.

Q35.3 Monochromatic coherent light passing through two thin slits is viewed on a distant screen. Are the bright fringes equally spaced on the screen? If so, why? If not, which ones are closest to being equally spaced?

Q35.4 In a two-slit interference pattern on a distant screen, are the bright fringes midway between the dark fringes? Is this ever a good approximation?

Q35.5 Would the headlights of a distant car form a two-source interference pattern? If so, how might it be observed? If not, why not?

Q35.6 The two sources S_1 and S_2 shown in Fig. 35.3 emit waves of the same wavelength λ and are in phase with each other. Suppose S_1 is a weaker source, so that the waves emitted by S_1 have half the amplitude of the waves emitted by S_2. How would this affect the positions of the antinodal lines and nodal lines? Would there be total reinforcement at points on the antinodal curves? Would there be total cancellation at points on the nodal curves? Explain your answers.

Q35.7 Could the Young two-slit interference experiment be performed with gamma rays? If not, why not? If so, discuss differences in the experimental design compared to the experiment with visible light.

Q35.8 Coherent red light illuminates two narrow slits that are 25 cm apart. Will a two-slit interference pattern be observed when the light from the slits falls on a screen? Explain.

Q35.9 Coherent light with wavelength λ falls on two narrow slits separated by a distance d. If d is less than some minimum value, no dark fringes are observed. Explain. In terms of λ, what is this minimum value of d?

Q35.10 A fellow student, who values memorizing equations above understanding them, combines Eqs. (35.4) and (35.13) to "prove" that ϕ can *only* equal $2\pi m$. How would you explain to this student that ϕ can have values other than $2\pi m$?

Q35.11 If the monochromatic light shown in Fig. 35.5a were replaced by white light, would a two-slit interference pattern be seen on the screen? Explain.

Q35.12 In using the superposition principle to calculate intensities in interference patterns, could you add the intensities of the waves instead of their amplitudes? Explain.

Q35.13 A glass windowpane with a thin film of water on it reflects less than when it is perfectly dry. Why?

Q35.14 A *very* thin soap film ($n = 1.33$), whose thickness is much less than a wavelength of visible light, looks black; it appears to reflect no light at all. Why? By contrast, an equally thin layer of soapy water ($n = 1.33$) on glass ($n = 1.50$) appears quite shiny. Why is there a difference?

Q35.15 Interference can occur in thin films. Why is it important that the films be *thin*? Why don't you get these effects with a relatively *thick* film? Where should you put the dividing line between "thin" and "thick"? Explain your reasoning.

Q35.16 If we shine white light on an air wedge like that shown in Fig. 35.12, the colors that are weak in the light *reflected* from any point along the wedge are strong in the light *transmitted* through the wedge. Explain why this should be so.

Q35.17 Monochromatic light is directed at normal incidence on a thin film. There is destructive interference for the reflected light, so the intensity of the reflected light is very low. What happened to the energy of the incident light?

Q35.18 When a thin oil film spreads out on a puddle of water, the thinnest part of the film looks dark in the resulting interference pattern. What does this tell you about the relative magnitudes of the refractive indexes of oil and water?

EXERCISES

Section 35.1 Interference and Coherent Sources

35.1 • Two small stereo speakers A and B that are 1.40 m apart are sending out sound of wavelength 34 cm in all directions and all in phase. A person at point P starts out equidistant from both speakers and walks so that he is always 1.50 m from speaker B (**Fig. E35.1**). For what values of x will the sound this person hears

Figure **E35.1**

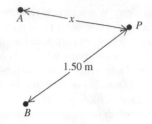

be (a) maximally reinforced, (b) cancelled? Limit your solution to the cases where $x \leq 1.50$ m.

35.2 •• Two speakers that are 15.0 m apart produce in-phase sound waves of frequency 250.0 Hz in a room where the speed of sound is 340.0 m/s. A woman starts out at the midpoint between the two speakers. The room's walls and ceiling are covered with absorbers to eliminate reflections, and she listens with only one ear for best precision. (a) What does she hear: constructive or destructive interference? Why? (b) She now walks slowly toward one of the speakers. How far from the center must she walk before she first hears the sound reach a minimum intensity? (c) How far from the center must she walk before she first hears the sound maximally enhanced?

35.3 •• A radio transmitting station operating at a frequency of 120 MHz has two identical antennas that radiate in phase. Antenna B is 9.00 m to the right of antenna A. Consider point P between the antennas and along the line connecting them, a horizontal distance x to the right of antenna A. For what values of x will constructive interference occur at point P?

35.4 • **Radio Interference.** Two radio antennas A and B radiate in phase. Antenna B is 120 m to the right of antenna A. Consider point Q along the extension of the line connecting the antennas, a horizontal distance of 40 m to the right of antenna B. The frequency, and hence the wavelength, of the emitted waves can be varied. (a) What is the longest wavelength for which there will be destructive interference at point Q? (b) What is the longest wavelength for which there will be constructive interference at point Q?

35.5 • Two speakers, emitting identical sound waves of wavelength 2.0 m in phase with each other, and an observer are located as shown in **Fig. E35.5**. (a) At the observer's location, what is the path difference for waves from the two speakers? (b) Will the sound waves interfere constructively or destructively at the observer's location—or something in between constructive and destructive? (c) Suppose the observer now increases her distance from the closest speaker to 17.0 m, staying directly in front of the same speaker as initially. Answer the questions of parts (a) and (b) for this new situation.

Figure **E35.5**

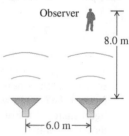

35.6 • Two light sources can be adjusted to emit monochromatic light of any visible wavelength. The two sources are coherent, 2.04 μm apart, and in line with an observer, so that one source is 2.04 μm farther from the observer than the other. (a) For what visible wavelengths (380 to 750 nm) will the observer see the brightest light, owing to constructive interference? (b) How would your answers to part (a) be affected if the two sources were not in line with the observer, but were still arranged so that one source is 2.04 μm farther away from the observer than the other? (c) For what visible wavelengths will there be *destructive* interference at the location of the observer?

Section 35.2 Two-Source Interference of Light

35.7 • Young's experiment is performed with light from excited helium atoms ($\lambda = 502$ nm). Fringes are measured carefully on a screen 1.20 m away from the double slit, and the center of the 20th fringe (not counting the central bright fringe) is found to be 10.6 mm from the center of the central bright fringe. What is the separation of the two slits?

35.8 •• Coherent light with wavelength 450 nm falls on a pair of slits. On a screen 1.80 m away, the distance between dark fringes is 3.90 mm. What is the slit separation?

35.9 •• Two slits spaced 0.450 mm apart are placed 75.0 cm from a screen. What is the distance between the second and third dark lines of the interference pattern on the screen when the slits are illuminated with coherent light with a wavelength of 500 nm?

35.10 •• If the entire apparatus of Exercise 35.9 (slits, screen, and space in between) is immersed in water, what then is the distance between the second and third dark lines?

35.11 •• Two thin parallel slits that are 0.0116 mm apart are illuminated by a laser beam of wavelength 585 nm. (a) On a very large distant screen, what is the *total* number of bright fringes (those indicating complete constructive interference), including the central fringe and those on both sides of it? Solve this problem without calculating all the angles! (*Hint:* What is the largest that $\sin\theta$ can be? What does this tell you is the largest value of m?) (b) At what angle, relative to the original direction of the beam, will the fringe that is most distant from the central bright fringe occur?

35.12 • Coherent light with wavelength 400 nm passes through two very narrow slits that are separated by 0.200 mm, and the interference pattern is observed on a screen 4.00 m from the slits. (a) What is the width (in mm) of the central interference maximum? (b) What is the width of the first-order bright fringe?

35.13 •• Two very narrow slits are spaced 1.80 μm apart and are placed 35.0 cm from a screen. What is the distance between the first and second dark lines of the interference pattern when the slits are illuminated with coherent light with $\lambda = 550$ nm? (*Hint:* The angle θ in Eq. (35.5) is *not* small.)

35.14 •• Coherent light that contains two wavelengths, 660 nm (red) and 470 nm (blue), passes through two narrow slits that are separated by 0.300 mm. Their interference pattern is observed on a screen 4.00 m from the slits. What is the distance on the screen between the first-order bright fringes for the two wavelengths?

35.15 •• Coherent light with wavelength 600 nm passes through two very narrow slits and the interference pattern is observed on a screen 3.00 m from the slits. The first-order bright fringe is at 4.84 mm from the center of the central bright fringe. For what wavelength of light will the first-order dark fringe be observed at this same point on the screen?

35.16 •• Coherent light of frequency 6.32×10^{14} Hz passes through two thin slits and falls on a screen 85.0 cm away. You observe that the third bright fringe occurs at ± 3.11 cm on either side of the central bright fringe. (a) How far apart are the two slits? (b) At what distance from the central bright fringe will the third dark fringe occur?

Section 35.3 Intensity in Interference Patterns

35.17 •• In a two-slit interference pattern, the intensity at the peak of the central maximum is I_0. (a) At a point in the pattern where the phase difference between the waves from the two slits is 60.0°, what is the intensity? (b) What is the path difference for 480-nm light from the two slits at a point where the phase difference is 60.0°?

35.18 • Coherent sources A and B emit electromagnetic waves with wavelength 2.00 cm. Point P is 4.86 m from A and 5.24 m from B. What is the phase difference at P between these two waves?

35.19 • Coherent light with wavelength 500 nm passes through narrow slits separated by 0.340 mm. At a distance from the slits large compared to their separation, what is the phase difference (in radians) in the light from the two slits at an angle of 23.0° from the centerline?

35.20 • Two slits spaced 0.260 mm apart are 0.900 m from a screen and illuminated by coherent light of wavelength 660 nm. The intensity at the center of the central maximum ($\theta = 0°$) is I_0. What is the distance on the screen from the center of the central maximum (a) to the first minimum; (b) to the point where the intensity has fallen to $I_0/2$?

35.21 • Consider two antennas separated by 9.00 m that radiate in phase at 120 MHz, as described in Exercise 35.3. A receiver placed 150 m from both antennas measures an intensity I_0. The receiver is moved so that it is 1.8 m closer to one antenna than to the other. (a) What is the phase difference ϕ between the two radio waves produced by this path difference? (b) In terms of I_0, what is the intensity measured by the receiver at its new position?

35.22 •• Two slits spaced 0.0720 mm apart are 0.800 m from a screen. Coherent light of wavelength λ passes through the two slits. In their interference pattern on the screen, the distance from the center of the central maximum to the first minimum is 3.00 mm. If the intensity at the peak of the central maximum is 0.0600 W/m², what is the intensity at points on the screen that are (a) 2.00 mm and (b) 1.50 mm from the center of the central maximum?

Section 35.4 Interference in Thin Films

35.23 • What is the thinnest film of a coating with $n = 1.42$ on glass ($n = 1.52$) for which destructive interference of the red component (650 nm) of an incident white light beam in air can take place by reflection?

35.24 •• **Nonglare Glass.** When viewing a piece of art that is behind glass, one often is affected by the light that is reflected off the front of the glass (called *glare*), which can make it difficult to see the art clearly. One solution is to coat the outer surface of the glass with a film to cancel part of the glare. (a) If the glass has a refractive index of 1.62 and you use TiO_2, which has an index of refraction of 2.62, as the coating, what is the minimum film thickness that will cancel light of wavelength 505 nm? (b) If this coating is too thin to stand up to wear, what other thickness would also work? Find only the three thinnest ones.

35.25 •• Two rectangular pieces of plane glass are laid one upon the other on a table. A thin strip of paper is placed between them at one edge so that a very thin wedge of air is formed. The plates are illuminated at normal incidence by 546-nm light from a mercury-vapor lamp. Interference fringes are formed, with 15.0 fringes per centimeter. Find the angle of the wedge.

35.26 •• A plate of glass 9.00 cm long is placed in contact with a second plate and is held at a small angle with it by a metal strip 0.0800 mm thick placed under one end. The space between the plates is filled with air. The glass is illuminated from above with light having a wavelength in air of 656 nm. How many interference fringes are observed per centimeter in the reflected light?

35.27 •• A uniform film of TiO_2, 1036 nm thick and having index of refraction 2.62, is spread uniformly over the surface of crown glass of refractive index 1.52. Light of wavelength 520.0 nm falls at normal incidence onto the film from air. You want to increase the thickness of this film so that the reflected light cancels. (a) What is the *minimum* thickness of TiO_2 that you must *add* so the reflected light cancels as desired? (b) After you make the adjustment in part (a), what is the path difference between the light reflected off the top of the film and the light that cancels it after traveling through the film? Express your answer in (i) nanometers and (ii) wavelengths of the light in the TiO_2 film.

35.28 • A plastic film with index of refraction 1.70 is applied to the surface of a car window to increase the reflectivity and thus to keep the car's interior cooler. The window glass has index of refraction 1.52. (a) What minimum thickness is required if light of wavelength 550 nm in air reflected from the two sides of the film is to interfere constructively? (b) Coatings as thin as that calculated in part (a) are difficult to manufacture and install. What is the next greater thickness for which constructive interference will also occur?

35.29 • The walls of a soap bubble have about the same index of refraction as that of plain water, $n = 1.33$. There is air both inside and outside the bubble. (a) What wavelength (in air) of visible light is most strongly reflected from a point on a soap bubble where its wall is 290 nm thick? To what color does this correspond (see Fig. 32.4 and Table 32.1)? (b) Repeat part (a) for a wall thickness of 340 nm.

35.30 •• A researcher measures the thickness of a layer of benzene ($n = 1.50$) floating on water by shining monochromatic light onto the film and varying the wavelength of the light. She finds that light of wavelength 575 nm is reflected most strongly from the film. What does she calculate for the minimum thickness of the film?

35.31 •• **Compact Disc Player.** A compact disc (CD) is read from the bottom by a semiconductor laser with wavelength 790 nm passing through a plastic substrate of refractive index 1.8. When the beam encounters a pit, part of the beam is reflected from the pit and part from the flat region between the pits, so these two beams interfere with each other (**Fig. E35.31**). What must the minimum pit depth be so that the part of the beam reflected from a pit cancels the part of the beam reflected from the flat region? (It is this cancellation that allows the player to recognize the beginning and end of a pit.)

Figure **E35.31**

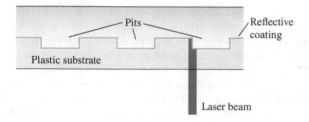

35.32 • What is the thinnest soap film (excluding the case of zero thickness) that appears black when illuminated with light with wavelength 480 nm? The index of refraction of the film is 1.33, and there is air on both sides of the film.

Section 35.5 The Michelson Interferometer

35.33 • How far must the mirror M_2 (see Fig. 35.19) of the Michelson interferometer be moved so that 1800 fringes of He-Ne laser light ($\lambda = 633$ nm) move across a line in the field of view?

35.34 • Jan first uses a Michelson interferometer with the 606-nm light from a krypton-86 lamp. He displaces the movable mirror away from him, counting 818 fringes moving across a line in his field of view. Then Linda replaces the krypton lamp with filtered 502-nm light from a helium lamp and displaces the movable mirror toward her. She also counts 818 fringes, but they move across the line in her field of view opposite to the direction they moved for Jan. Assume that both Jan and Linda counted to 818 correctly. (a) What distance did each person move the mirror? (b) What is the resultant displacement of the mirror?

PROBLEMS

35.35 •• One round face of a 3.25-m, solid, cylindrical plastic pipe is covered with a thin black coating that completely blocks light. The opposite face is covered with a fluorescent coating that glows when it is struck by light. Two straight, thin, parallel scratches, 0.225 mm apart, are made in the center of the black face. When laser light of wavelength 632.8 nm shines through the slits perpendicular to the black face, you find that the central bright fringe on the opposite face is 5.82 mm wide, measured between the dark fringes that border it on either side. What is the index of refraction of the plastic?

35.36 ••• Newton's rings are visible when a planoconvex lens is placed on a flat glass surface. For a particular lens with an index of refraction of $n = 1.50$ and a glass plate with an index of $n = 1.80$, the diameter of the third bright ring is 0.640 mm. If water ($n = 1.33$) now fills the space between the lens and the glass plate, what is the new diameter of this ring? Assume the radius of curvature of the lens is much greater than the wavelength of the light.

35.37 • BIO **Coating Eyeglass Lenses.** Eyeglass lenses can be coated on the *inner* surfaces to reduce the reflection of stray light to the eye. If the lenses are medium flint glass of refractive index 1.62 and the coating is fluorite of refractive index 1.432, (a) what minimum thickness of film is needed on the lenses to cancel light of wavelength 550 nm reflected toward the eye at normal incidence? (b) Will any other wavelengths of visible light be cancelled or enhanced in the reflected light?

35.38 •• BIO **Sensitive Eyes.** After an eye examination, you put some eyedrops on your sensitive eyes. The cornea (the front part of the eye) has an index of refraction of 1.38, while the eyedrops have a refractive index of 1.45. After you put in the drops, your friends notice that your eyes look red, because red light of wavelength 600 nm has been reinforced in the reflected light. (a) What is the minimum thickness of the film of eyedrops on your cornea? (b) Will any other wavelengths of visible light be reinforced in the reflected light? Will any be cancelled? (c) Suppose you had contact lenses, so that the eyedrops went on them instead of on your corneas. If the refractive index of the lens material is 1.50 and the layer of eyedrops has the same thickness as in part (a), what wavelengths of visible light will be reinforced? What wavelengths will be cancelled?

35.39 •• Two flat plates of glass with parallel faces are on a table, one plate on the other. Each plate is 11.0 cm long and has a refractive index of 1.55. A very thin sheet of metal foil is inserted under the end of the upper plate to raise it slightly at that end, in a manner similar to that discussed in Example 35.4. When you view the glass plates from above with reflected white light, you observe that, at 1.15 mm from the line where the sheets are in contact, the violet light of wavelength 400.0 nm is enhanced in this reflected light, but no visible light is enhanced closer to the line of contact. (a) How far from the line of contact will green light (of wavelength 550.0 nm) and orange light (of wavelength 600.0 nm) first be enhanced? (b) How far from the line of contact will the violet, green, and orange light again be enhanced in the reflected light? (c) How thick is the metal foil holding the ends of the plates apart?

35.40 •• In a setup similar to that of Problem 35.39, the glass has an index of refraction of 1.53, the plates are each 8.00 cm long, and the metal foil is 0.015 mm thick. The space between the plates is filled with a jelly whose refractive index is not known precisely, but is known to be greater than that of the glass. When you illuminate these plates from above with light of wavelength 525 nm, you observe a series of equally spaced dark fringes in the reflected light. You measure the spacing of these fringes and find that there are 10 of them every 6.33 mm. What is the index of refraction of the jelly?

35.41 ••• Suppose you illuminate two thin slits by monochromatic coherent light in air and find that they produce their first interference *minima* at ± 35.20° on either side of the central bright spot. You then immerse these slits in a transparent liquid and illuminate them with the same light. Now you find that the first minima occur at ± 19.46° instead. What is the index of refraction of this liquid?

35.42 •• **CP CALC** A very thin sheet of brass contains two thin parallel slits. When a laser beam shines on these slits at normal incidence and room temperature (20.0°C), the first interference dark fringes occur at ± 26.6° from the original direction of the laser beam when viewed from some distance. If this sheet is now slowly heated to 135°C, by how many degrees do these dark fringes change position? Do they move closer together or farther apart? See Table 17.1 for pertinent information, and ignore any effects that might occur due to a change in the thickness of the slits. (*Hint:* Thermal expansion normally produces very small changes in length, so you can use differentials to find the change in the angle.)

35.43 •• Two radio antennas radiating in phase are located at points *A* and *B*, 200 m apart (**Fig. P35.43**). The radio waves have a frequency of 5.80 MHz. A radio receiver is moved out from point *B* along a line perpendicular to the line connecting *A* and *B* (line *BC* shown in Fig. P35.43). At what distances from *B* will there be *destructive* interference? (*Note:* The distance of the receiver from the sources is not large in comparison to the separation of the sources, so Eq. (35.5) does not apply.)

Figure **P35.43**

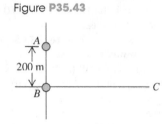

35.44 •• Two speakers *A* and *B* are 3.50 m apart, and each one is emitting a frequency of 444 Hz. However, because of signal delays in the cables, speaker *A* is one-fourth of a period *ahead* of speaker *B*. For points far from the speakers, find all the angles relative to the centerline (**Fig. P35.44**) at which the sound from these speakers cancels. Include angles on *both* sides of the centerline. The speed of sound is 340 m/s.

Figure **P35.44**

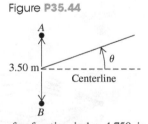

35.45 •• **CP** A thin uniform film of refractive index 1.750 is placed on a sheet of glass of refractive index 1.50. At room temperature (20.0°C), this film is just thick enough for light with wavelength 582.4 nm reflected off the top of the film to be cancelled by light reflected from the top of the glass. After the glass is placed in an oven and slowly heated to 170°C, you find that the film cancels reflected light with wavelength 588.5 nm. What is the coefficient of linear expansion of the film? (Ignore any changes in the refractive index of the film due to the temperature change.)

35.46 ••• **GPS Transmission.** The GPS (Global Positioning System) satellites are approximately 5.18 m across and transmit two low-power signals, one of which is at 1575.42 MHz (in the UHF band). In a series of laboratory tests on the satellite, you put two 1575.42-MHz UHF transmitters at opposite ends of the satellite. These broadcast in phase uniformly in all directions. You measure the intensity at points on a circle that is several hundred meters in radius and centered on the satellite. You measure angles on this circle relative to a point that lies along the centerline of the satellite (that is, the perpendicular bisector of a line that extends from one transmitter to the other). At this point on the circle, the measured intensity is 2.00 W/m². (a) At how many other angles in the range 0° < θ < 90° is the intensity also 2.00 W/m²? (b) Find the four smallest angles in the range 0° < θ < 90° for which the intensity is 2.00 W/m². (c) What is the intensity at a point on the circle at an angle of 4.65° from the centerline?

35.47 •• White light reflects at normal incidence from the top and bottom surfaces of a glass plate ($n = 1.52$). There is air above and below the plate. Constructive interference is observed for light whose wavelength in air is 477.0 nm. What is the thickness of the plate if the next longer wavelength for which there is constructive interference is 540.6 nm?

35.48 •• Laser light of wavelength 510 nm is traveling in air and shines at normal incidence onto the flat end of a transparent plastic rod that has $n = 1.30$. The end of the rod has a thin coating of a transparent material that has refractive index 1.65. What is the minimum (nonzero) thickness of the coating (a) for which there is maximum transmission of the light into the rod; (b) for which transmission into the rod is minimized?

35.49 •• Red light with wavelength 700 nm is passed through a two-slit apparatus. At the same time, monochromatic visible light with another wavelength passes through the same apparatus. As a result, most of the pattern that appears on the screen is a mixture of two colors; however, the center of the third bright fringe ($m = 3$) of the red light appears pure red, with none of the other color. What are the possible wavelengths of the second type of visible light? Do you need to know the slit spacing to answer this question? Why or why not?

35.50 •• **BIO** **Reflective Coatings and Herring.** Herring and related fish have a brilliant silvery appearance that camouflages them while they are swimming in a sunlit ocean. The silveriness is due to *platelets* attached to the surfaces of these fish. Each platelet is made up of several alternating layers of crystalline guanine ($n = 1.80$) and of cytoplasm ($n = 1.333$, the same as water), with a guanine layer on the outside in contact with the surrounding water (**Fig. P35.50**). In one typical platelet, the guanine

Figure **P35.50**

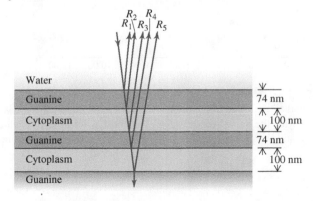

layers are 74 nm thick and the cytoplasm layers are 100 nm thick. (a) For light striking the platelet surface at normal incidence, for which vacuum wavelengths of visible light will all of the reflections R_1, R_2, R_3, R_4, and R_5, shown in Fig. P35.50, be approximately in phase? If white light is shone on this platelet, what color will be most strongly reflected (see Fig. 32.4)? The surface of a herring has very many platelets side by side with layers of different thickness, so that *all* visible wavelengths are reflected. (b) Explain why such a "stack" of layers is more reflective than a single layer of guanine with cytoplasm underneath. (A stack of five guanine layers separated by cytoplasm layers reflects more than 80% of incident light at the wavelength for which it is "tuned.") (c) The color that is most strongly reflected from a platelet depends on the angle at which it is viewed. Explain why this should be so. (You can see these changes in color by examining a herring from different angles. Most of the platelets on these fish are oriented in the same way, so that they are vertical when the fish is swimming.)

35.51 •• After a laser beam passes through two thin parallel slits, the first completely dark fringes occur at $\pm 19.0°$ with the original direction of the beam, as viewed on a screen far from the slits. (a) What is the ratio of the distance between the slits to the wavelength of the light illuminating the slits? (b) What is the smallest angle, relative to the original direction of the laser beam, at which the intensity of the light is $\frac{1}{10}$ the maximum intensity on the screen?

35.52 •• DATA In your summer job at an optics company, you are asked to measure the wavelength λ of the light that is produced by a laser. To do so, you pass the laser light through two narrow slits that are separated by a distance d. You observe the interference pattern on a screen that is 0.900 m from the slits and measure the separation Δy between adjacent bright fringes in the portion of the pattern that is near the center of the screen. Using a microscope, you measure d. But both Δy and d are small and difficult to measure accurately, so you repeat the measurements for several pairs of slits, each with a different value of d. Your results are shown in **Fig. P35.52**, where you have plotted Δy versus $1/d$. The line in the graph is the best-fit straight line for the data. (a) Explain why the data points plotted this way fall close to a straight line. (b) Use Fig. P35.52 to calculate λ.

Figure **P35.52**

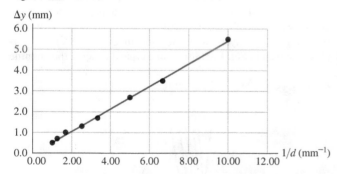

35.53 •• DATA Short-wave radio antennas A and B are connected to the same transmitter and emit coherent waves in phase and with the same frequency f. You must determine the value of f and the placement of the antennas that produce a maximum

intensity through constructive interference at a receiving antenna that is located at point P, which is at the corner of your garage. First you place antenna A at a point 240.0 m due east of P. Next you place antenna B on the line that connects A and P, a distance x due east of P, where $x < 240.0$ m. Then you measure that a maximum in the total intensity from the two antennas occurs when $x = 210.0$ m, 216.0 m, and 222.0 m. You don't investigate smaller or larger values of x. (Treat the antennas as point sources.) (a) What is the frequency f of the waves that are emitted by the antennas? (b) What is the greatest value of x, with $x < 240.0$ m, for which the interference at P is destructive?

35.54 •• DATA In your research lab, a very thin, flat piece of glass with refractive index 1.40 and uniform thickness covers the opening of a chamber that holds a gas sample. The refractive indexes of the gases on either side of the glass are very close to unity. To determine the thickness of the glass, you shine coherent light of wavelength λ_0 in vacuum at normal incidence onto the surface of the glass. When $\lambda_0 = 496$ nm, constructive interference occurs for light that is reflected at the two surfaces of the glass. You find that the next shorter wavelength in vacuum for which there is constructive interference is 386 nm. (a) Use these measurements to calculate the thickness of the glass. (b) What is the longest wavelength in vacuum for which there is constructive interference for the reflected light?

CHALLENGE PROBLEMS

35.55 ••• CP The index of refraction of a glass rod is 1.48 at $T = 20.0°C$ and varies linearly with temperature, with a coefficient of $2.50 \times 10^{-5}/C°$. The coefficient of linear expansion of the glass is $5.00 \times 10^{-6}/C°$. At 20.0°C the length of the rod is 3.00 cm. A Michelson interferometer has this glass rod in one arm, and the rod is being heated so that its temperature increases at a rate of 5.00 C°/min. The light source has wavelength $\lambda = 589$ nm, and the rod initially is at $T = 20.0°C$. How many fringes cross the field of view each minute?

35.56 ••• CP **Figure P35.56** shows an interferometer known as *Fresnel's biprism*. The magnitude of the prism angle A is extremely small. (a) If S_0 is a very narrow source slit, show that the separation of the two virtual coherent sources S_1 and S_2 is given by $d = 2aA(n - 1)$, where n is the index of refraction of the material of the prism. (b) Calculate the spacing of the fringes of green light with wavelength 500 nm on a screen 2.00 m from the biprism. Take $a = 0.200$ m, $A = 3.50$ mrad, and $n = 1.50$.

Figure **P35.56**

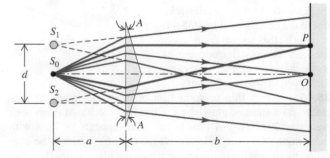

PASSAGE PROBLEMS

INTERFERENCE AND SOUND WAVES. Interference occurs with not only light waves but also all frequencies of electromagnetic waves and all other types of waves, such as sound and water waves. Suppose that your physics professor sets up two sound speakers in the front of your classroom and uses an electronic oscillator to produce sound waves of a single frequency. When she turns the oscillator on (take this to be its original setting), you and many students hear a loud tone while other students hear nothing. (The speed of sound in air is 340 m/s.)

35.57 The professor then adjusts the apparatus. The frequency that you hear does not change, but the loudness decreases. Now all of your fellow students can hear the tone. What did the professor do? (a) She turned off the oscillator. (b) She turned down the volume of the speakers. (c) She changed the phase relationship of the speakers. (d) She disconnected one speaker.

35.58 The professor returns the apparatus to the original setting. She then adjusts the speakers again. All of the students who had heard nothing originally now hear a loud tone, while you and the others who had originally heard the loud tone hear nothing.

What did the professor do? (a) She turned off the oscillator. (b) She turned down the volume of the speakers. (c) She changed the phase relationship of the speakers. (d) She disconnected one speaker.

35.59 The professor again returns the apparatus to its original setting, so you again hear the original loud tone. She then slowly moves one speaker away from you until it reaches a point at which you can no longer hear the tone. If she has moved the speaker by 0.34 m (farther from you), what is the frequency of the tone? (a) 1000 Hz; (b) 2000 Hz; (c) 500 Hz; (d) 250 Hz.

35.60 The professor once again returns the apparatus to its original setting, but now she adjusts the oscillator to produce sound waves of half the original frequency. What happens? (a) The students who originally heard a loud tone again hear a loud tone, and the students who originally heard nothing still hear nothing. (b) The students who originally heard a loud tone now hear nothing, and the students who originally heard nothing now hear a loud tone. (c) Some of the students who originally heard a loud tone again hear a loud tone, but others in that group now hear nothing. (d) Among the students who originally heard nothing, some still hear nothing but others now hear a loud tone.

Answers

Chapter Opening Question ?

(v) The colors appear as a result of constructive interference between light waves reflected from the upper and lower surfaces of the oil film. The wavelength of light for which the most constructive interference occurs at a point, and hence the color that appears the brightest at that point, depends on (1) the thickness of the film (which determines the path difference between light waves that reflect off the two surfaces), (2) the oil's index of refraction (which gives the wavelength of light in the oil a different value than in air), and (3) the index of refraction of the material below the oil (which determines whether the wave that reflects from the lower surface undergoes a half-cycle phase shift). (See Examples 35.4, 35.5, and 35.6 in Section 35.4.)

Test Your Understanding Questions

35.1 (i) At any point P on the positive y-axis above S_1, the distance r_2 from S_2 to P is greater than the distance r_1 from S_1 to P by 4λ. This corresponds to $m = 4$ in Eq. (35.1), the equation for constructive interference. Hence all such points make up an antinodal curve.

35.2 (ii) Blue light has a shorter wavelength than red light (see Section 32.1). Equation (35.6) tells us that the distance y_m from the center of the pattern to the mth bright fringe is proportional to the wavelength λ. Hence all of the fringes will move toward the center of the pattern as the wavelength decreases, and the spacing between fringes will decrease.

35.3 (i), (iv), (ii), (iii) In cases (i) and (iii) we are given the wavelength λ and path difference $d\sin\theta$. Hence we use Eq. (35.14),

$I = I_0\cos^2[(\pi d\sin\theta)/\lambda]$. In parts (ii) and (iii) we are given the phase difference ϕ and we use Eq. (35.10), $I = I_0\cos^2(\phi/2)$. We find:

(i) $I = I_0\cos^2[\pi(4.00 \times 10^{-7}\text{ m})/(5.00 \times 10^{-7}\text{ m})] = I_0\cos^2(0.800\pi\text{ rad}) = 0.655I_0$;

(ii) $I = I_0\cos^2[(4.00\text{ rad})/2] = I_0\cos^2(2.00\text{ rad}) = 0.173I_0$;

(iii) $I = I_0\cos^2[\pi(7.50 \times 10^{-7}\text{ m})/(5.00 \times 10^{-7}\text{ m})] = I_0\cos^2(1.50\pi\text{ rad}) = 0$;

(iv) $I = I_0\cos^2[(2.00\text{ rad})/2] = I_0\cos^2(1.00\text{ rad}) = 0.292I_0$.

35.4 (i) and (iii) Benzene has a larger index of refraction than air, so light that reflects off the upper surface of the benzene undergoes a half-cycle phase shift. Fluorite has a *smaller* index of refraction than benzene, so light that reflects off the benzene–fluorite interface does not undergo a phase shift. Hence the equation for constructive reflection is Eq. (35.18a), $2t = \left(m + \frac{1}{2}\right)\lambda$, which we can rewrite as $t = \left(m + \frac{1}{2}\right)\lambda/2 = \left(m + \frac{1}{2}\right)(400\text{ mm})/2 = 100\text{ nm}, 300\text{ nm}, 500\text{ nm},\dots$.

35.5 yes Changing the index of refraction changes the wavelength of the light inside the compensator plate, and so changes the number of wavelengths within the thickness of the plate. Hence this has the same effect as changing the distance L_1 from the beam splitter to mirror M_1, which would change the interference pattern.

Bridging Problem

(a) 441 nm

(b) 551 nm

APPENDIX A

THE INTERNATIONAL SYSTEM OF UNITS

The Système International d'Unités, abbreviated SI, is the system developed by the General Conference on Weights and Measures and adopted by nearly all the industrial nations of the world. The following material is adapted from the National Institute of Standards and Technology (**http://physics.nist.gov/cuu**).

Quantity	Name of unit	Symbol	
SI base units			
length	meter	m	
mass	kilogram	kg	
time	second	s	
electric current	ampere	A	
thermodynamic temperature	kelvin	K	
amount of substance	mole	mol	
luminous intensity	candela	cd	
SI derived units			**Equivalent units**
area	square meter	m^2	
volume	cubic meter	m^3	
frequency	hertz	Hz	s^{-1}
mass density (density)	kilogram per cubic meter	kg/m^3	
speed, velocity	meter per second	m/s	
angular velocity	radian per second	rad/s	
acceleration	meter per second squared	m/s^2	
angular acceleration	radian per second squared	rad/s^2	
force	newton	N	$kg \cdot m/s^2$
pressure (mechanical stress)	pascal	Pa	N/m^2
kinematic viscosity	square meter per second	m^2/s	
dynamic viscosity	newton-second per square meter	$N \cdot s/m^2$	
work, energy, quantity of heat	joule	J	$N \cdot m$
power	watt	W	J/s
quantity of electricity	coulomb	C	$A \cdot s$
potential difference, electromotive force	volt	V	J/C, W/A
electric field strength	volt per meter	V/m	N/C
electrical resistance	ohm	Ω	V/A
capacitance	farad	F	$A \cdot s/V$
magnetic flux	weber	Wb	$V \cdot s$
inductance	henry	H	$V \cdot s/A$
magnetic flux density	tesla	T	Wb/m^2
magnetic field strength	ampere per meter	A/m	
magnetomotive force	ampere	A	
luminous flux	lumen	lm	$cd \cdot sr$
luminance	candela per square meter	cd/m^2	
illuminance	lux	lx	lm/m^2
wave number	1 per meter	m^{-1}	
entropy	joule per kelvin	J/K	
specific heat capacity	joule per kilogram-kelvin	$J/kg \cdot K$	
thermal conductivity	watt per meter-kelvin	$W/m \cdot K$	

Quantity	Name of unit	Symbol	Equivalent units
radiant intensity	watt per steradian	W/sr	
activity (of a radioactive source)	becquerel	Bq	s^{-1}
radiation dose	gray	Gy	J/kg
radiation dose equivalent	sievert	Sv	J/kg
SI supplementary units			
plane angle	radian	rad	
solid angle	steradian	sr	

Definitions of SI Units

meter (m) The *meter* is the length equal to the distance traveled by light, in vacuum, in a time of 1/299,792,458 second.

kilogram (kg) The *kilogram* is the unit of mass; it is equal to the mass of the international prototype of the kilogram. (The international prototype of the kilogram is a particular cylinder of platinum-iridium alloy that is preserved in a vault at Sévres, France, by the International Bureau of Weights and Measures.)

second (s) The *second* is the duration of 9,192,631,770 periods of the radiation corresponding to the transition between the two hyperfine levels of the ground state of the cesium-133 atom.

ampere (A) The *ampere* is that constant current that, if maintained in two straight parallel conductors of infinite length, of negligible circular cross section, and placed 1 meter apart in vacuum, would produce between these conductors a force equal to 2×10^{-7} newton per meter of length.

kelvin (K) The *kelvin,* unit of thermodynamic temperature, is the fraction 1/273.16 of the thermodynamic temperature of the triple point of water.

ohm (Ω) The *ohm* is the electric resistance between two points of a conductor when a constant difference of potential of 1 volt, applied between these two points, produces in this conductor a current of 1 ampere, this conductor not being the source of any electromotive force.

coulomb (C) The *coulomb* is the quantity of electricity transported in 1 second by a current of 1 ampere.

candela (cd) The *candela* is the luminous intensity, in a given direction, of a source that emits monochromatic radiation of frequency 540×10^{12} hertz and that has a radiant intensity in that direction of 1/683 watt per steradian.

mole (mol) The *mole* is the amount of substance of a system that contains as many elementary entities as there are carbon atoms in 0.012 kg of carbon 12. The elementary entities must be specified and may be atoms, molecules, ions, electrons, other particles, or specified groups of such particles.

newton (N) The *newton* is that force that gives to a mass of 1 kilogram an acceleration of 1 meter per second per second.

joule (J) The *joule* is the work done when the point of application of a constant force of 1 newton is displaced a distance of 1 meter in the direction of the force.

watt (W) The *watt* is the power that gives rise to the production of energy at the rate of 1 joule per second.

volt (V) The *volt* is the difference of electric potential between two points of a conducting wire carrying a constant current of 1 ampere, when the power dissipated between these points is equal to 1 watt.

weber (Wb) The *weber* is the magnetic flux that, linking a circuit of one turn, produces in it an electromotive force of 1 volt as it is reduced to zero at a uniform rate in 1 second.

lumen (lm) The *lumen* is the luminous flux emitted in a solid angle of 1 steradian by a uniform point source having an intensity of 1 candela.

farad (F) The *farad* is the capacitance of a capacitor between the plates of which there appears a difference of potential of 1 volt when it is charged by a quantity of electricity equal to 1 coulomb.

henry (H) The *henry* is the inductance of a closed circuit in which an electromotive force of 1 volt is produced when the electric current in the circuit varies uniformly at a rate of 1 ampere per second.

radian (rad) The *radian* is the plane angle between two radii of a circle that cut off on the circumference an arc equal in length to the radius.

steradian (sr) The *steradian* is the solid angle that, having its vertex in the center of a sphere, cuts off an area of the surface of the sphere equal to that of a square with sides of length equal to the radius of the sphere.

SI Prefixes To form the names of multiples and submultiples of SI units, apply the prefixes listed in Appendix F.

APPENDIX B

USEFUL MATHEMATICAL RELATIONS

Algebra

$$a^{-x} = \frac{1}{a^x} \qquad a^{(x+y)} = a^x a^y \qquad a^{(x-y)} = \frac{a^x}{a^y}$$

Logarithms: If $\log a = x$, then $a = 10^x$. $\log a + \log b = \log(ab)$ $\log a - \log b = \log(a/b)$ $\log(a^n) = n\log a$

If $\ln a = x$, then $a = e^x$. $\ln a + \ln b = \ln(ab)$ $\ln a - \ln b = \ln(a/b)$ $\ln(a^n) = n\ln a$

Quadratic formula: If $ax^2 + bx + c = 0$, $x = \dfrac{-b \pm \sqrt{b^2 - 4ac}}{2a}$.

Binomial Theorem

$$(a + b)^n = a^n + na^{n-1}b + \frac{n(n-1)a^{n-2}b^2}{2!} + \frac{n(n-1)(n-2)a^{n-3}b^3}{3!} + \cdots$$

Trigonometry
In the right triangle ABC, $x^2 + y^2 = r^2$.

Definitions of the trigonometric functions:
$\sin\alpha = y/r \qquad \cos\alpha - x/r \qquad \tan\alpha = y/x$

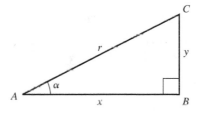

Identities:

$$\sin^2\alpha + \cos^2\alpha = 1 \qquad\qquad \tan\alpha = \frac{\sin\alpha}{\cos\alpha}$$

$$\sin 2\alpha = 2\sin\alpha\cos\alpha \qquad\qquad \cos 2\alpha = \cos^2\alpha - \sin^2\alpha = 2\cos^2\alpha - 1$$
$$= 1 - 2\sin^2\alpha$$

$$\sin\tfrac{1}{2}\alpha = \sqrt{\frac{1 - \cos\alpha}{2}} \qquad\qquad \cos\tfrac{1}{2}\alpha = \sqrt{\frac{1 + \cos\alpha}{2}}$$

$$\sin(-\alpha) = -\sin\alpha \qquad\qquad \sin(\alpha \pm \beta) = \sin\alpha\cos\beta \pm \cos\alpha\sin\beta$$

$$\cos(-\alpha) = \cos\alpha \qquad\qquad \cos(\alpha \pm \beta) = \cos\alpha\cos\beta \mp \sin\alpha\sin\beta$$

$$\sin(\alpha \pm \pi/2) = \pm\cos\alpha \qquad\qquad \sin\alpha + \sin\beta = 2\sin\tfrac{1}{2}(\alpha + \beta)\cos\tfrac{1}{2}(\alpha - \beta)$$

$$\cos(\alpha \pm \pi/2) = \mp\sin\alpha \qquad\qquad \cos\alpha + \cos\beta = 2\cos\tfrac{1}{2}(\alpha + \beta)\cos\tfrac{1}{2}(\alpha - \beta)$$

For *any* triangle $A'B'C'$ (not necessarily a right triangle) with sides a, b, and c and angles α, β, and γ:

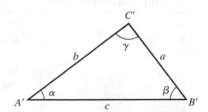

Law of sines: $\dfrac{\sin\alpha}{a} = \dfrac{\sin\beta}{b} = \dfrac{\sin\gamma}{c}$

Law of cosines: $c^2 = a^2 + b^2 - 2ab\cos\gamma$

Geometry

Circumference of circle of radius r:	$C = 2\pi r$	Surface area of sphere of radius r:	$A = 4\pi r^2$
Area of circle of radius r:	$A = \pi r^2$	Volume of cylinder of radius r and height h:	$V = \pi r^2 h$
Volume of sphere of radius r:	$V = 4\pi r^3/3$		

Calculus

Derivatives:

$$\frac{d}{dx}x^n = nx^{n-1}$$

$$\frac{d}{dx}\ln ax = \frac{1}{x}$$

$$\frac{d}{dx}e^{ax} = ae^{ax}$$

$$\frac{d}{dx}\sin ax = a\cos ax$$

$$\frac{d}{dx}\cos ax = -a\sin ax$$

Integrals:

$$\int x^n\,dx = \frac{x^{n+1}}{n+1} \quad (n \neq -1)$$

$$\int \frac{dx}{x} = \ln x$$

$$\int e^{ax}\,dx = \frac{1}{a}e^{ax}$$

$$\int \sin ax\,dx = -\frac{1}{a}\cos ax$$

$$\int \cos ax\,dx = \frac{1}{a}\sin ax$$

$$\int \frac{dx}{\sqrt{a^2 - x^2}} = \arcsin\frac{x}{a}$$

$$\int \frac{dx}{\sqrt{x^2 + a^2}} = \ln\left(x + \sqrt{x^2 + a^2}\right)$$

$$\int \frac{dx}{x^2 + a^2} = \frac{1}{a}\arctan\frac{x}{a}$$

$$\int \frac{dx}{(x^2 + a^2)^{3/2}} = \frac{1}{a^2}\frac{x}{\sqrt{x^2 + a^2}}$$

$$\int \frac{x\,dx}{(x^2 + a^2)^{3/2}} = -\frac{1}{\sqrt{x^2 + a^2}}$$

Power series (convergent for range of x shown):

$$(1 + x)^n = 1 + nx + \frac{n(n-1)x^2}{2!} + \frac{n(n-1)(n-2)}{3!}x^3 + \cdots (|x| < 1)$$

$$\tan x = x + \frac{x^3}{3} + \frac{2x^5}{15} + \frac{17x^7}{315} + \cdots (|x| < \pi/2)$$

$$e^x = 1 + x + \frac{x^2}{2!} + \frac{x^3}{3!} + \cdots (\text{all } x)$$

$$\sin x = x - \frac{x^3}{3!} + \frac{x^5}{5!} - \frac{x^7}{7!} + \cdots (\text{all } x)$$

$$\ln(1 + x) = x - \frac{x^2}{2} + \frac{x^3}{3} - \frac{x^4}{4} + \cdots (|x| < 1)$$

$$\cos x = 1 - \frac{x^2}{2!} + \frac{x^4}{4!} - \frac{x^6}{6!} + \cdots (\text{all } x)$$

APPENDIX C

THE GREEK ALPHABET

Name	Capital	Lowercase	Name	Capital	Lowercase	Name	Capital	Lowercase
Alpha	A	α	Iota	I	ι	Rho	P	ρ
Beta	B	β	Kappa	K	κ	Sigma	Σ	σ
Gamma	Γ	γ	Lambda	Λ	λ	Tau	T	τ
Delta	Δ	δ	Mu	M	μ	Upsilon	Υ	υ
Epsilon	E	ϵ	Nu	N	ν	Phi	Φ	ϕ
Zeta	Z	ζ	Xi	Ξ	ξ	Chi	X	χ
Eta	H	η	Omicron	O	o	Psi	Ψ	ψ
Theta	Θ	θ	Pi	Π	π	Omega	Ω	ω

PERIODIC TABLE OF THE ELEMENTS

Group	1	2	3	4	5	6	7	8	9	10	11	12	13	14	15	16	17	18
Period																		
1	1 **H** 1.008																	2 **He** 4.003
2	3 **Li** 6.941	4 **Be** 9.012											5 **B** 10.811	6 **C** 12.011	7 **N** 14.007	8 **O** 15.999	9 **F** 18.998	10 **Ne** 20.180
3	11 **Na** 22.990	12 **Mg** 24.305											13 **Al** 26.982	14 **Si** 28.086	15 **P** 30.974	16 **S** 32.065	17 **Cl** 35.453	18 **Ar** 39.948
4	19 **K** 39.098	20 **Ca** 40.078	21 **Sc** 44.956	22 **Ti** 47.867	23 **V** 50.942	24 **Cr** 51.996	25 **Mn** 54.938	26 **Fe** 55.845	27 **Co** 58.933	28 **Ni** 58.693	29 **Cu** 63.546	30 **Zn** 65.409	31 **Ga** 69.723	32 **Ge** 72.64	33 **As** 74.922	34 **Se** 78.96	35 **Br** 79.904	36 **Kr** 83.798
5	37 **Rb** 85.468	38 **Sr** 87.62	39 **Y** 88.906	40 **Zr** 91.224	41 **Nb** 92.906	42 **Mo** 95.94	43 **Tc** (98)	44 **Ru** 101.07	45 **Rh** 102.906	46 **Pd** 106.42	47 **Ag** 107.868	48 **Cd** 112.411	49 **In** 114.818	50 **Sn** 118.710	51 **Sb** 121.760	52 **Te** 127.60	53 **I** 126.904	54 **Xe** 131.293
6	55 **Cs** 132.905	56 **Ba** 137.327	71 **Lu** 174.967	72 **Hf** 178.49	73 **Ta** 180.948	74 **W** 183.84	75 **Re** 186.207	76 **Os** 190.23	77 **Ir** 192.217	78 **Pt** 195.078	79 **Au** 196.967	80 **Hg** 200.59	81 **Tl** 204.383	82 **Pb** 207.2	83 **Bi** 208.980	84 **Po** (209)	85 **At** (210)	86 **Rn** (222)
7	87 **Fr** (223)	88 **Ra** (226)	103 **Lr** (262)	104 **Rf** (261)	105 **Db** (262)	106 **Sg** (266)	107 **Bh** (270)	108 **Hs** (269)	109 **Mt** (278)	110 **Ds** (281)	111 **Rg** (281)	112 **Cn** (285)	113 **Uut** (284)	114 **Fl** (289)	115 **Uup** (288)	116 **Lv** (292)	117 **Uus** (294)	118 **Uuo** (294)

Lanthanoids

57 **La** 138.905	58 **Ce** 140.116	59 **Pr** 140.908	60 **Nd** 144.24	61 **Pm** (145)	62 **Sm** 150.36	63 **Eu** 151.964	64 **Gd** 157.25	65 **Tb** 158.925	66 **Dy** 162.500	67 **Ho** 164.930	68 **Er** 167.259	69 **Tm** 168.934	70 **Yb** 173.04

Actinoids

89 **Ac** (227)	90 **Th** (232)	91 **Pa** (231)	92 **U** (238)	93 **Np** (237)	94 **Pu** (244)	95 **Am** (243)	96 **Cm** (247)	97 **Bk** (247)	98 **Cf** (251)	99 **Es** (252)	100 **Fm** (257)	101 **Md** (258)	102 **No** (259)

For each element, the average atomic mass of the mixture of isotopes occurring in nature is shown. For elements having no stable isotope, the approximate atomic mass of the longest-lived isotope is shown in parentheses. All atomic masses are expressed in atomic mass units ($1 \text{ u} = 1.660538921(73) \times 10^{-27}$ kg), equivalent to grams per mole (g/mol).

APPENDIX E

UNIT CONVERSION FACTORS

Length
1 m = 100 cm = 1000 mm = $10^6 \mu$m = 10^9 nm
1 km = 1000 m = 0.6214 mi
1 m = 3.281 ft = 39.37 in.
1 cm = 0.3937 in.
1 in. = 2.540 cm
1 ft = 30.48 cm
1 yd = 91.44 cm
1 mi = 5280 ft = 1.609 km
1 Å = 10^{-10} m = 10^{-8} cm = 10^{-1} nm
1 nautical mile = 6080 ft
1 light-year = 9.461 × 10^{15} m

Area
1 cm^2 = 0.155 in.^{2}
1 m^2 = 10^4 cm^2 = 10.76 ft^2
1 in.^{2} = 6.452 cm^2
1 ft^2 = 144 in.^{2} = 0.0929 m^2

Volume
1 liter = 1000 cm^3 = 10^{-3} m^3 = 0.03531 ft^3 = 61.02 in.^{3}
1 ft^3 = 0.02832 m^3 = 28.32 liters = 7.477 gallons
1 gallon = 3.788 liters

Time
1 min = 60 s
1 h = 3600 s
1 d = 86,400 s
1 y = 365.24 d = 3.156 × 10^7 s

Angle
1 rad = 57.30° = 180°/π
1° = 0.01745 rad = π/180 rad
1 revolution = 360° = 2π rad
1 rev/min (rpm) = 0.1047 rad/s

Speed
1 m/s = 3.281 ft/s
1 ft/s = 0.3048 m/s
1 mi/min = 60 mi/h = 88 ft/s
1 km/h = 0.2778 m/s = 0.6214 mi/h
1 mi/h = 1.466 ft/s = 0.4470 m/s = 1.609 km/h
1 furlong/fortnight = 1.662 × 10^{-4} m/s

Acceleration
1 m/s^2 = 100 cm/s^2 = 3.281 ft/s^2
1 cm/s^2 = 0.01 m/s^2 = 0.03281 ft/s^2
1 ft/s^2 = 0.3048 m/s^2 = 30.48 cm/s^2
1 mi/h·s = 1.467 ft/s^2

Mass
1 kg = 10^3 g = 0.0685 slug
1 g = 6.85 × 10^{-5} slug
1 slug = 14.59 kg
1 u = 1.661 × 10^{-27} kg
1 kg has a weight of 2.205 lb when g = 9.80 m/s^2

Force
1 N = 10^5 dyn = 0.2248 lb
1 lb = 4.448 N = 4.448 × 10^5 dyn

Pressure
1 Pa = 1 N/m^2 = 1.450 × 10^{-4} lb/in.^{2} = 0.0209 lb/ft^2
1 bar = 10^5 Pa
1 lb/in.^{2} = 6895 Pa
1 lb/ft^2 = 47.88 Pa
1 atm = 1.013 × 10^5 Pa = 1.013 bar
    = 14.7 lb/in.^{2} = 2117 lb/ft^2
1 mm Hg = 1 torr = 133.3 Pa

Energy
1 J = 10^7 ergs = 0.239 cal
1 cal = 4.186 J (based on 15° calorie)
1 ft·lb = 1.356 J
1 Btu = 1055 J = 252 cal = 778 ft·lb
1 eV = 1.602 × 10^{-19} J
1 kWh = 3.600 × 10^6 J

Mass-Energy Equivalence
1 kg $\leftrightarrow$ 8.988 × 10^{16} J
1 u $\leftrightarrow$ 931.5 MeV
1 eV $\leftrightarrow$ 1.074 × 10^{-9} u

Power
1 W = 1 J/s
1 hp = 746 W = 550 ft·lb/s
1 Btu/h = 0.293 W

APPENDIX F

NUMERICAL CONSTANTS

Fundamental Physical Constants*

Name	Symbol	Value
Speed of light in vacuum	c	2.99792458×10^8 m/s
Magnitude of charge of electron	e	$1.602176565(35) \times 10^{-19}$ C
Gravitational constant	G	$6.67384(80) \times 10^{-11}$ N $\cdot$ m^2/kg^2
Planck's constant	h	$6.62606957(29) \times 10^{-34}$ J $\cdot$ s
Boltzmann constant	k	$1.3806488(13) \times 10^{-23}$ J/K
Avogadro's number	N_A	$6.02214129(27) \times 10^{23}$ molecules/mol
Gas constant	R	$8.3144621(75)$ J/mol $\cdot$ K
Mass of electron	m_e	$9.10938291(40) \times 10^{-31}$ kg
Mass of proton	m_p	$1.672621777(74) \times 10^{-27}$ kg
Mass of neutron	m_n	$1.674927351(74) \times 10^{-27}$ kg
Magnetic constant	μ_0	$4\pi \times 10^{-7}$ Wb/A $\cdot$ m
Electric constant	$\epsilon_0 = 1/\mu_0 c^2$	$8.854187817\ldots \times 10^{-12}$ C^2/N $\cdot$ m^2
	$1/4\pi\epsilon_0$	$8.987551787\ldots \times 10^9$ N $\cdot$ m^2/C^2

Other Useful Constants*

Name	Symbol	Value
Mechanical equivalent of heat		4.186 J/cal (15° calorie)
Standard atmospheric pressure	1 atm	1.01325×10^5 Pa
Absolute zero	0 K	-273.15°C
Electron volt	1 eV	$1.602176565(35) \times 10^{-19}$ J
Atomic mass unit	1 u	$1.660538921(73) \times 10^{-27}$ kg
Electron rest energy	$m_e c^2$	0.510998928(11) MeV
Volume of ideal gas (0°C and 1 atm)		22.413968(20) liter/mol
Acceleration due to gravity (standard)	g	9.80665 m/s^2

*Source: National Institute of Standards and Technology (**http://physics.nist.gov/cuu**). Numbers in parentheses show the uncertainty in the final digits of the main number; for example, the number 1.6454(21) means 1.6454 ± 0.0021. Values shown without uncertainties are exact.

Body	Mass (kg)	Radius (m)	Orbit radius (m)	Orbital period
Sun	1.99×10^{30}	6.96×10^{8}	—	—
Moon	7.35×10^{22}	1.74×10^{6}	3.84×10^{8}	27.3 d
Mercury	3.30×10^{23}	2.44×10^{6}	5.79×10^{10}	88.0 d
Venus	4.87×10^{24}	6.05×10^{6}	1.08×10^{11}	224.7 d
Earth	5.97×10^{24}	6.37×10^{6}	1.50×10^{11}	365.3 d
Mars	6.42×10^{23}	3.39×10^{6}	2.28×10^{11}	687.0 d
Jupiter	1.90×10^{27}	6.99×10^{7}	7.78×10^{11}	11.86 y
Saturn	5.68×10^{26}	5.82×10^{7}	1.43×10^{12}	29.45 y
Uranus	8.68×10^{25}	2.54×10^{7}	2.87×10^{12}	84.02 y
Neptune	1.02×10^{26}	2.46×10^{7}	4.50×10^{12}	164.8 y
Pluto‡	1.31×10^{22}	1.15×10^{6}	5.91×10^{12}	247.9 y

†Source: NASA (**http://solarsystem.nasa.gov/planets/**). For each body, "radius" is its average radius and "orbit radius" is its average distance from the sun or (for the moon) from the earth.

‡In August 2006, the International Astronomical Union reclassified Pluto and similar small objects that orbit the sun as "dwarf planets."

Prefixes for Powers of 10

Power of ten	Prefix	Abbreviation	Pronunciation
10^{-24}	yocto-	y	*yoc*-toe
10^{-21}	zepto-	z	*zep*-toe
10^{-18}	atto-	a	*at*-toe
10^{-15}	femto-	f	*fem*-toe
10^{-12}	pico-	p	*pee*-koe
10^{-9}	nano-	n	*nan*-oe
10^{-6}	micro-	μ	*my*-crow
10^{-3}	milli-	m	*mil*-i
10^{-2}	centi-	c	*cen*-ti
10^{3}	kilo-	k	*kil*-oe
10^{6}	mega-	M	*meg*-a
10^{9}	giga-	G	*jig*-a or *gig*-a
10^{12}	tera-	T	*ter*-a
10^{15}	peta-	P	*pet*-a
10^{18}	exa-	E	*ex*-a
10^{21}	zetta-	Z	*zet*-a
10^{24}	yotta-	Y	*yot*-a

Examples:

1 femtometer = 1 fm = 10^{-15} m   1 millivolt = 1 mV = 10^{-3} V

1 picosecond = 1 ps = 10^{-12} s   1 kilopascal = 1 kPa = 10^{3} Pa

1 nanocoulomb = 1 nC = 10^{-9} C   1 megawatt = 1 MW = 10^{6} W

1 microkelvin = 1 μK = 10^{-6} K   1 gigahertz = 1 GHz = 10^{9} Hz

ANSWERS TO ODD-NUMBERED PROBLEMS

Chapter 6

6.1 a) 3.60 J b) −0.900 J c) 0 d) 0 e) 2.70 J
6.3 a) 74 N b) 333 J c) −330 J d) 0,0 e) 0
6.5 a) −1750 J b) no
6.7 a) (i) 9.00 J (ii) −9.00 J
    b) (i) 0 (ii) 9.00 J (iii) −9.00 J (iv) 0
    c) zero for each block
6.9 a) (i) 0 (ii) 0 b) (i) 0 (ii) −25.1 J
6.11 a) 374 J b) −333 J c) 0 d) 41 J
    e) 352 J
6.13 −572 J
6.15 a) 120 J b) −108 J c) 24.3 J
6.17 a) 36,000 J b) 4
6.19 a) 1.0×10^{16} J b) 2.4 times
6.21 a) 43.2 m/s b) 101 m/s
6.23 $\sqrt{2gh(1 + \mu_k/\tan\alpha)}$
6.25 48.0 N
6.27 a) 4.48 m/s b) 3.61 m/s
6.29 a) 4.96 m/s b) 1.43 m/s²; 4.96 m/s, same
6.31 a) $v_0^2/2\mu_k g$ b) (i) $\frac{1}{2}$ (ii) 4 (iii) 2
6.33 a) 40.0 N/m b) 0.456 N
6.35 b) 13.1 cm (bottom), 14.1 cm (middle),
    15.2 cm (top)
6.37 a) 2.83 m/s b) 3.46 m/s
6.39 8.5 cm
6.41 a) 1.76 b) 0.666 m/s
6.43 a) 4.0 J b) 0 c) −1.0 J d) 3.0 J
    e) −1.0 J
6.45 a) 2.83 m/s b) 2.40 m/s
6.47 a) 0.0565 m b) no, 0.57 J
6.49 8.17 m/s
6.51 360,000 J; 100 m/s
6.53 $(3.9 \times 10^{13})P$
6.55 745 W ≈ 1 hp
6.57 a) 84.6/min b) 22.7/min
6.59 29.6 kW
6.61 0.20 W
6.63 a) 608 J b) −395 J c) 0 d) −189 J
    e) 24 J f) 1.5 m/s
6.65 a) 5.62 J (20.0-N block), 3.38 J (12.0-N
    block) b) 2.58 J (20.0-N block), 1.54 J
    (12.0-N block)
6.67 a) 1.8 m/s = 4.0 mi/h
    b) 180 m/s² ≈ 18g, 900 N
6.69 a) 5.11 m b) 0.304 c) 10.3 m
6.71 a) 0.074 N b) 4.7 N c) 0.22 J
6.73 6.3×10^4 N/m
6.75 1.1 m
6.77 a) 2.39 m/s b) 9.42 m/s, away from the wall
6.79 a) 0.600 m b) 1.50 m/s
6.81 0.786
6.83 1.3 m
6.85 a) 1.10×10^5 J b) 1.30×10^5 J
    c) 3.99 kW
6.87 3.6 h
6.89 a) 1.26×10^5 J b) 1.46 W
6.91 b) $v^2 = -\dfrac{k}{m}d^2 + 2d\left[\dfrac{k}{m}(0.400 \text{ m}) - \mu_k g\right]$
    c) 1.29 m/s, 0.204 m d) 12.0 N/m, 0.800
6.93 a) $Mv^2/6$ b) 6.1 m/s c) 3.9 m/s
    d) 0.40 J, 0.60 J
6.95 choice (a)
6.97 choice (d)

Chapter 11

11.1 29.8 cm
11.3 1.35 m
11.5 6.6 kN
11.7 a) 1000 N, 0.800 m from end where 600-N
    force is applied b) 800 N, 0.75 m from end
    where 600-N force is applied
11.9 a) 550 N b) 0.614 m from A
11.11 a) 1920 N b) 1140 N
11.13 a) T = 2.60w; 3.28w, 37.6°
    b) T = 4.10w; 5.39w, 48.8°
11.15 a) 3410 N b) 3410 N, 7600 N
11.17 b) 533 N c) 600 N, 267 N; downward
11.19 220 N (left), 255 N (right), 42°
11.21 a) 0.800 m b) clockwise
    c) 0.800 m, clockwise
11.23 b) 208 N
11.25 1.9 mm
11.27 2.0×10^{11} Pa
11.29 a) 3.1×10^{-3} (upper), 2.0×10^{-3} (lower)
    b) 1.6 mm (upper), 1.0 mm (lower)
11.31 a) 150 atm b) 1.5 km, no
11.33 4.8×10^9 Pa, 2.1×10^{-10} Pa^{-1}
11.35 b) 6.6×10^5 N c) 1.8 mm
11.37 7.36×10^6 Pa
11.39 3.41×10^7 Pa
11.41 10.2 m/s²
11.43 20.0 kg
11.45 a) 525 N b) 222 N, 328 N c) 1.48
11.47 a) 140 N b) 6 cm to the right
11.49 a) 409 N b) 161 N
11.51 49.9 cm
11.53 a) 370 N b) when he starts to raise his leg
    c) no
11.55 a) 3 cm b) lean backward
11.57 5500 N
11.59 b) 2000 N = 2.72mg c) 4.4 mm
11.61 a) 4.90 m b) 60 N
11.63 a) 175 N at each hand, 200 N at each foot
    b) 91 N at each hand and at each foot
11.65 a) 1150 N b) 1940 N c) 918 N d) 0.473
11.67 590 N (person above), 1370 N (person below);
    person above
11.69 a) $\dfrac{T_{max}hD}{L\sqrt{h^2 + D^2}}$
    b) $\dfrac{T_{max}h}{L\sqrt{h^2 + D^2}}\left(1 - \dfrac{D^2}{h^2 + D^2}\right)$, positive
11.71 a) 71.5 kg
    b) 380 N, 25.2° above the horizontal
11.73 a) 375 N b) 325 N c) 512 N
11.75 a) 0.424 N (A), 1.47 N (B), 0.424 N (C)
    b) 0.848 N
11.77 a) 27° to tip, 31° to slip, tips first
    b) 27° to tip, 22° to slip, slips first
11.79 a) 80 N (A), 870 N (B) b) 1.92 m
11.81 a) 1.0 cm b) 0.86 cm
11.83 a) 0.70 m from A b) 0.60 m from A
11.85 a) 4.2×10^4 N b) 65 m
11.87 b) $x = 1.50 \text{ m} + \dfrac{(1.30 \text{ m})m_1 - (0.38 \text{ m})M}{m_2}$
    c) 1.59 kg d) 1.50 m
11.89 a) 391 N (4.00-m ladder), 449 N (3.00-m ladder)
    b) 322 N c) 334 N d) 937 N

11.91 a) 0.66 mm b) 0.022 J c) 8.35×10^{-3} J
    d) -3.04×10^{-2} J e) 3.04×10^{-2} J
11.93 choice (a)
11.95 choice (d)

Chapter 14

14.1 a) 2.15 ms, 2930 rad/s
    b) 2.00×10^4 Hz, 1.26×10^5 rad/s
    c) 1.3×10^{-15} s ≤ T ≤ 2.3×10^{-15} s,
    4.3×10^{14} Hz ≤ f ≤ 7.5×10^{14} Hz
    d) 2.0×10^{-7} s, 3.1×10^7 rad/s
14.3 5530 rad/s, 1.14 ms
14.5 0.0625 s
14.7 a) 0.80 s b) 1.25 Hz c) 7.85 rad/s
    d) 3.0 cm e) 148 N/m
14.9 a) 0.167 s b) 37.7 rad/s c) 0.0844 kg
14.11 a) 0.150 s b) 0.0750 s
14.13 a) 0.98 m b) π/2 rad
    c) x = (−0.98 m) sin[(12.2 rad/s)t]
14.15 a) −2.71 m/s² b) x = (1.46 cm) ×
    cos[(15.7 rad/s)t + 0.715 rad],
    $v_x = (-22.9$ cm/s) ×
    sin[(15.7 rad/s)t + 0.715 rad],
    $a_x = (-359$ cm/s²) ×
    cos[(15.7 rad/s)t + 0.715 rad]
14.17 120 kg
14.19 a) 0.253 kg b) 1.21 cm c) 3.03 N
14.21 a) 1.51 s b) 26.0 N/m
    c) 30.8 cm/s d) 1.92 N
    e) −0.0125 m, 30.4 cm/s, 0.216 m/s²
    f) 0.324 N
14.23 a) x = (0.0030 m) cos[(2760 rad/s)t]
    b) 8.3 m/s, 2.3×10^4 m/s²
    c) $da_x/dt = (6.3 \times 10^7$ m/s³) ×
    sin[(2760 rad/s)t], 6.3×10^7 m/s³
14.25 92.2 m/s²
14.27 a) 0.0336 J b) 0.0150 m c) 0.669 m/s
14.29 a) 1.20 m/s b) 1.11 m/s c) 36 m/s²
    d) 13.5 m/s² e) 0.36 J
14.31 3M; $\frac{3}{4}$
14.33 0.240 m
14.35 a) 0.376 m b) 59.3 m/s² c) 119 N
14.37 a) 4.06 cm b) 1.21 m/s c) 29.8 rad/s
14.39 a) 0, 0, 3.92 J, 3.92 J b) 3.92 J, 0, 0, 3.92 J
    c) 0.98 J, 0.98 J, 1.96 J, 3.92 J
14.41 a) 2.7×10^{-8} kg·m²
    b) 4.3×10^{-6} N·m/rad
14.43 0.0294 kg·m²
14.45 a) 0.25 s b) 0.25 s
14.47 0.407 swing per second
14.49 10.7 m/s²
14.51 a) 2.84 s b) 2.89 s c) 2.89 s; −2%
14.53 A: $2\pi\sqrt{\dfrac{L}{g}}$, B: $\dfrac{2\sqrt{2}}{3}\left(2\pi\sqrt{\dfrac{L}{g}}\right)$; pendulum A
14.55 0.129 kg·m²
14.57 A: $2\pi\sqrt{\dfrac{L}{g}}$, B: $\sqrt{\dfrac{11}{10}}\left(2\pi\sqrt{\dfrac{L}{g}}\right)$, pendulum B
14.59 a) 0.30 J
14.61 a) 0.393 Hz b) 1.73 kg/s
14.63 a) $A_1/3$ b) $2A_1$
14.65 0.353 m
14.67 a) 1.34 m/s b) 1.90 m/s²
14.69 a) 24.4 cm b) 0.221 s c) 1.19 m/s

14.71 2.00 m

14.73 $0.921\left(\dfrac{1}{2\pi}\sqrt{\dfrac{g}{L}}\right)$

14.75 a) 0.784 s   b) -1.12×10^{-4} s per s; shorter
  c) 0.419 s

14.77 a) 0.150 m/s   b) 0.112 m/s^2 downward
  c) 0.700 s   d) 4.38 m

14.79 a) 2.6 m/s   b) 0.21 m   c) 0.49 s

14.81 1.17 s

14.83 0.421 s

14.85 0.705 Hz, 14.5°

14.87 $2\pi\sqrt{\dfrac{M}{3k}}$

14.89 a) 1.60 s   b) 0.625 Hz   c) 3.93 rad/s
  d) 5.1 cm; 0.4 s, 1.2 s, 1.8 s
  e) 79 cm/s^2; 0.4 s, 1.2 s, 1.8 s   f) 4.9 kg

14.91 b) The angular amplitude increases as L
  decreases.   c) about 53°

14.93 a) $Mv^2/6$ c) $\omega = \sqrt{3k/M}, M' = M/3$

14.95 choice (a)

Chapter 15

15.1 a) 0.439 m, 1.28 ms   b) 0.219 m

15.3 220 m/s = 800 km/h

15.5 a) 1.7 cm to 17 m
  b) 4.3×10^{14} Hz to 7.5×10^{14} Hz
  c) 1.5 cm   d) 6.4 cm

15.7 a) 25.0 Hz, 0.0400 s, 19.6 rad/m
  b) $y(x, t) = (0.0700 \text{ m}) \times$
  $\cos[(19.6 \text{ m}^{-1})x + (157 \text{ rad/s})t]$
  c) 4.95 cm   d) 0.0050 s

15.9 a) yes   b) yes   c) no
  d) $v_y = \omega A \cos(kx + \omega t)$,
  $a_y = -\omega^2 A \sin(kx + \omega t)$

15.11 a) 4 mm   b) 0.040 s   c) 0.14 m, 3.6 m/s
  d) 0.24 m, 6.0 m/s   e) no

15.13 b) $+x$-direction

15.15 a) 17.5 m/s   b) 0.146 m
  c) both would increase by a factor of $\sqrt{2}$

15.17 0.337 kg

15.19 a) 9.53 N   b) 20.8 m/s

15.21 a) 10.0 m/s   b) 0.250 m
  c) $y(x, t) = (3.00 \text{ cm}) \times$
  $\cos[(8.00\pi \text{ rad/m})x - (80.0\pi \text{ rad/s})t]$
  d) 1890 m/s^2 e) yes

15.23 4.10 mm

15.25 a) 95 km   b) 0.25 μW/m^2 c) 110 kW

15.27 a) 0.050 W/m^2 b) 22 kJ

15.29 9.48×10^{27} W

15.37 a) $(1.33 \text{ m})n, n = 0, 1, 2, \ldots$
  b) $(1.33 \text{ m})\left(n + \frac{1}{2}\right), n = 0, 1, 2, \ldots$

15.39 a) 96.0 m/s   b) 461 N
  c) 1.13 m/s, 4.26 m/s^2

15.41 b) 2.80 cm   c) 277 cm
  d) 185 cm, 7.96 Hz, 0.126 s, 1470 cm/s
  e) 280 cm/s
  f) $y(x, t) = (5.60 \text{ cm}) \times$
  $\sin[(0.0906 \text{ rad/cm})x] \sin[(133 \text{ rad/s})t]$

15.43 4.0 m, 2.0 m, 1.33 m

15.45 a) 45.0 cm   b) no

15.47 a) 311 m/s   b) 246 Hz   c) 245 Hz, 1.40 m

15.49 a) 20.0 Hz, 126 rad/s, 3.49 rad/m
  b) $y(x, t) = (2.50 \times 10^{-3} \text{ m}) \times$
  $\cos[(3.49 \text{ rad/m})x - (126 \text{ rad/s})t]$
  c) $y(0, t) = (2.50 \times 10^{-3} \text{ m}) \cos[(126 \text{ rad/s})t]$
  d) $y(1.35 \text{ m}, t) = (2.50 \times 10^{-3} \text{ m}) \times$
  $\cos[(126 \text{ rad/s})t - 3\pi/2 \text{ rad}]$
  e) 0.315 m/s   f) -2.50×10^{-3} m, 0

15.51 a) $\dfrac{7L}{2}\sqrt{\dfrac{\mu_1}{F}}$ b) no

15.53 a) 62.1 m

15.55 13.7 Hz, 25.0 m

15.57 1.83 m

15.59 361 Hz (copper), 488 Hz (aluminum)

15.61 a) 18.8 cm   b) 0.0169 kg

15.63 a) 7.07 cm   b) 0.400 kW

15.65 $(0.800 \text{ Hz})n, n = 1, 2, 3, \ldots$

15.67 a) 2.22 g   b) 2.24×10^4 m/s^2

15.69 233 N

15.71 1780 kg/m^3

15.73 a) 148 N   b) 26%

15.75 c) 47.5 Hz   d) 138 g

15.77 a) 392 N   b) 392 N + (7.70 N/m)x
  c) 3.89 s

15.79 choice (b)

Chapter 16

16.1 a) 0.344 m   b) 1.2×10^{-5} m
  c) 6.9 m, 50 Hz

16.3 a) 7.78 Pa   b) 77.8 Pa   c) 778 Pa

16.5 a) 90 m   b) 102 kHz   c) 1.4 cm
  d) 4.4 mm to 8.8 mm   e) 6.2 MHz

16.7 90.8 m

16.9 81.4°C

16.11 0.16 s

16.13 a) 5.5×10^{-15} J   b) 0.074 mm/s

16.15 15.0 cm

16.17 a) 4.14 Pa   b) 0.0208 W/m^2 c) 103 dB

16.19 a) 4.4×10^{-12} W/m^2 b) 6.4 dB
  c) 5.8×10^{-11} m

16.21 14.0 dB

16.23 a) 2.0×10^{-7} W/m^2 b) 6.0 m
  c) 290 m   d) yes, no

16.25 a) fundamental: 0.60 m; 0, 1.20 m; first overtone: 0.30 m, 0.90 m; 0, 0.60 m, 1.20 m;
  second overtone: 0.20 m, 0.60 m, 1.00 m;
  0, 0.40 m, 0.80 m, 1.20 m
  b) fundamental: 0; 1.20 m; first overtone:
  0, 0.80 m; 0.40 m, 1.20 m; second overtone:
  0, 0.48 m, 0.96 m; 0.24 m, 0.72 m, 1.20 m

16.27 506 Hz, 1517 Hz, 2529 Hz

16.29 a) 35.2 Hz   b) 17.6 Hz

16.31 a) 614 Hz   b) 1230 Hz

16.33 a) 137 Hz, 0.50 m   b) 137 Hz, 2.51 m

16.35 a) 172 Hz   b) 86 Hz

16.37 0.125 m

16.39 a) $(820 \text{ Hz})n, n = 1, 2, 3, \ldots$
  b) $(410 \text{ Hz})(2n + 1), n = 0, 1, 2, \ldots$

16.41 a) 433 Hz   b) loosen

16.43 1.3 Hz

16.45 780 m/s

16.47 a) 375 Hz   b) 371 Hz   c) 4 Hz

16.49 a) 0.25 m/s   b) 0.91 m

16.51 19.8 m/s

16.53 a) 1910 Hz   b) 0.188 m

16.55 a) 7.02 m/s, toward   b) 1404 Hz

16.57 a) 36.0°   b) 2.94 s

16.59 a) 1.00   b) 8.00
  c) 4.73×10^{-8} m = 47.3 nm

16.61 flute harmonic $3n$ resonates with string
  harmonic $4n, n = 1, 3, 5, \ldots$

16.63 a) stopped   b) 7th and 9th   c) 0.439 m

16.65 a) 0.026 m, 0.53 m, 1.27 m, 2.71 m, 9.01 m
  b) 0.26 m, 0.86 m, 1.84 m, 4.34 m   c) 86 Hz

16.67 a) 0.0823 m   b) 120 Hz

16.69 b) 2.0 m/s

16.71 a) 38 Hz   b) no

16.73 a) 375 m/s   b) 1.39   c) 0.8 cm

16.75 d) 9.69 cm/s, 667 m/s^2

16.77 choice (b)

16.79 choice (a)

16.81 choice (b)

Chapter 17

17.1 a) -81.0°F   b) 134.1°F   c) 88.0°F

17.3 a) 27.2 C°   b) -55.6 C°

17.5 a) -18.0 F°   b) -10.0 C°

17.7 0.964 atm

17.9 a) -282°C   b) no, 47,600 Pa

17.11 0.39 m

17.13 1.9014 cm; 1.8964 cm

17.15 49.4°C

17.17 1.7×10^{-5} (C°)$^{-1}$

17.19 a) 1.431 cm^2 b) 1.436 cm^2

17.21 a) 6.0 mm   b) -1.0×10^8 Pa

17.23 555 kJ

17.25 23 min

17.27 240 J/kg·K

17.29 0.526 C°

17.31 45.2 C°

17.33 0.0613 C°

17.35 a) 215 J/kg·K   b) water   c) too small

17.37 0.114 kg

17.39 27.5°C

17.41 150°C

17.43 7.6 min

17.45 54.5 kJ, 13.0 kcal, 51.7 Btu

17.47 357 m/s

17.49 3.45 L

17.51 5.05×10^{15} kg

17.53 0.0674 kg

17.55 190 g

17.57 a) 222 K/m   b) 10.7 W   c) 73.3°C

17.59 a) -0.86°C   b) 24 W/m^2

17.61 4.0×10^{-3} W/m·C°

17.63 105.5°C

17.65 a) 21 kW   b) 6.4 kW

17.67 15 W

17.69 2.1 cm^2

17.71 35.0°C

17.73 a) 35.1°M   b) 39.6 C°

17.75 69.4°C

17.77 23.0 cm (first rod), 7.0 cm (second rod)

17.79 1.9×10^8 Pa

17.81 a) 87°C   b) -80°C

17.83 460 s

17.85 a) 83.6 J   b) 1.86 J/mol·K
  c) 5.60 J/mol·K

17.87 a) 4.20×10^7 J   b) 10.7 C°   c) 30.0 C°

17.89 a) 0.60 kg   b) 0.80 bottle/h

17.91 3.4×10^5 J/kg

17.93 a) no   b) 0.0°C, 0.156 kg

17.95 a) 86.1°C
  b) no ice, 0.130 kg liquid water, no steam

17.97 a) 100°C
  b) 0.0214 kg steam, 0.219 kg liquid water

17.99 a) 93.9 W   b) 1.35

17.101 2.9

17.103 a) 59.8°C   b) 42.7°C   c) 8.40 W

17.105 c) 170 h   d) 1.5×10^{10} s $\approx$ 500 y, no

17.107 5.82 g

17.109 a) 1.04 kW   b) 87.1 W   c) 1.13 kW
  d) 28 g   e) 1.1 bottles

17.111 a) 3.00×10^4 J/kg   b) 1.00×10^3 J/kg·K
  (liquid), 1.33×10^3 J/kg·K (solid)

17.113 A: 216 W/m·K, B: 130 W/m·K

17.115 a) $H = \dfrac{(T_2 - T_1)2\pi kL}{\ln(b/a)}$

b) $T = T_2 - \dfrac{(T_2 - T_1)\ln(r/a)}{\ln(b/a)}$

d) 73°C e) 49 W

17.117 choice (a)

17.119 choice (a)

Chapter 18

18.1 a) 0.122 mol b) 14,700 Pa, 0.145 atm

18.3 0.100 atm

18.5 a) 0.0136 kg/m³, 67.6 kg/m³, 5.39 kg/m³

b) $0.011\rho_E$, $56\rho_E$, $4.5\rho_E$

18.7 503°C

18.9 19.7 kPa

18.11 0.159 L

18.13 0.0508V

18.15 a) 70.2°C b) yes

18.17 850 m

18.19 a) 6.95×10^{-16} kg b) 2.32×10^{-13} kg/m³

18.21 55.6 mol, 3.35×10^{25} molecules

18.23 a) 2.20×10^6 molecules

b) 2.44×10^{19} molecules

18.25 6.4×10^{-6} m

18.27 a) 5.83×10^7 J b) 242 m/s

18.29 (d) must be true; the others could be true.

18.31 a) 1.93×10^6 m/s, no b) 7.3×10^{10} K

18.33 a) 6.21×10^{-21} J b) 2.34×10^5 m²/s²

c) 484 m/s d) 2.57×10^{-23} kg·m/s

e) 1.24×10^{-19} N f) 1.24×10^{-17} Pa

g) 8.17×10^{21} molecules

h) 2.45×10^{22} molecules

18.35 3800°C

18.37 a) 1870 J b) 1120 J

18.39 a) 741 J/kg·K, $c_w = 5.65c_{N_2}$

b) 5.65 kg; 4850 L

18.41 a) 337 m/s b) 380 m/s c) 412 m/s

18.43 a) 610 Pa b) 22.12 MPa

18.45 18.0 cm³, $V_{20°C} = 0.32V_{cp}$

18.47 a) 11.8 kPa b) 0.566 L

18.49 272°C

18.51 0.195 kg

18.53 a) −179°C b) 1.2×10^{26} molecules/m³

c) $\rho_T = 4.0\rho_e$

18.55 1.92 atm

18.57 a) 30.7 cylinders b) 8420 N c) 7800 N

18.59 a) 26.2 m/s b) 16.1 m/s, 5.44 m/s c) 1.74 m

18.61 $\approx 5 \times 10^{27}$ atoms

18.63 a) A b) B c) 4250°C d) B

18.65 a) 6.00×10^3 Pa b) 32.8 m/s

18.67 a) 4.65×10^{-26} kg b) 6.11×10^{-21} J

c) 2.04×10^{24} molecules d) 12.5 kJ

18.69 b) r_2 c) $r_1 = \dfrac{R_0}{2^{1/6}}$, $r_2 = R_0$, $2^{-1/6}$ d) U_0

18.71 a) $2R = 16.6$ J/mol·K b) less than

18.73 b) 1.40×10^5 K (N₂), 1.01×10^4 K (H₂)

c) 6370 K (N₂), 459 K (H₂)

18.75 $3kT/m$, same

18.77 b) 0.0421N c) $(2.94 \times 10^{-21})N$

d) $0.0297N$, $(2.08 \times 10^{-21})N$

e) $0.0595N$, $(4.15 \times 10^{-21})N$

18.79 a) $p_0 + \dfrac{mg}{\pi r^2}$ b) $-\left(\dfrac{y}{h}\right)(p_0\pi r^2 + mg)$

c) $\dfrac{1}{2\pi}\sqrt{\dfrac{g}{h}\left(1 + \dfrac{p_0\pi r^2}{mg}\right)}$, no

18.81 a) 42.6% b) 3 km c) 1 km

18.83 a) 4.5×10^{11} m

b) 703 m/s, 6.4×10^8 s (≈ 20 y)

c) 1.4×10^{-14} Pa

d) 650 m/s, $v_H > v_{esc}$, evaporate

f) 2×10^5 K, $> 3T_{sun}$, no

18.85 choice (a)

18.87 choice (c)

Chapter 19

19.1 b) 1330 J

19.3 b) −6180 J

19.5 a) 1.04 atm

19.7 a) $(p_1 - p_2)(V_2 - V_1)$

b) negative of work done in reverse direction

19.9 a) 34.7 kJ b) 80.4 kJ c) no

19.11 a) 278 K, at a b) 0; 162 J c) 53 J

19.13 a) $T_a = 535$ K, $T_b = 9350$ K, $T_c = 15{,}000$ K

b) 21 kJ done by gas c) 36 kJ

19.15 a) 0 b) $T_b = 2T_a$ c) $U_b = U_a + 700$ J

19.17 b) 208 J c) on the piston d) 712 J

e) 920 J f) 208 J

19.19 a) 948 K b) 900 K

19.21 $\frac{2}{5}$

19.23 a) 747 J b) 1.30

19.25 a) −605 J b) 0 c) yes, 605 J, liberate

19.27 a) 476 kPa b) −10.6 kJ c) 1.59, heated

19.29 b) 314 J c) −314 J

19.31 11.6°C

19.33 a) increase b) 4.8 kJ

19.35 a) 0.681 mol b) 0.0333 m³

c) 2.23 kJ d) 0

19.37 a) 45.0 J b) liberate, 65.0 J c) 23.0 J, 22.0 J

19.39 a) the same b) 4.0 kJ, absorb c) 8.0 kJ

19.41 b) −2460 J

19.43 a) 0.80 L b) 305 K, 1220 K, 1220 K

c) ab: 76 J, into the gas

ca: −107 J, out of the gas

bc: 56 J, into the gas

d) ab: 76 J, increased

bc: 0, no change

ca: −76 J, decreased

19.45 a) 837°C b) 11.5 kJ c) 40.3 kJ d) 42.4 kJ

19.47 b) 6.00 L, 2.5×10^4 Pa, 75.0 K

c) 95 J d) heat it at constant volume

19.49 b) 11.9 C°

19.51 a) 0.168 m b) 196°C c) 70.1 kJ

19.53 a) $Q = 450$ J, $\Delta U = 0$

b) $Q = 0$, $\Delta U = -450$ J

c) $Q = 1125$ J, $\Delta U = 675$ J

19.55 a) $W = 738$ J, $Q = 2590$ J, $\Delta U = 1850$ J

b) $W = 0$, $Q = -1850$ J, $\Delta U = -1850$ J

c) $\Delta U = 0$

19.57 a) $W = -187$ J, $Q = -654$ J, $\Delta U = -467$ J

b) $W = 113$ J, $Q = 0$, $\Delta U = -113$ J

c) $W = 0$, $Q = 580$ J, $\Delta U = 580$ J

19.59 a) a: adiabatic, b: isochoric, c: isobaric

b) 28.0°C c) a: −30.0 J, b: 0, a: 20.0 J

d) a

e) a: decrease, b: stay the same, c: increase

19.61 b) −300 J, out of the gas

19.63 choice (c)

19.65 choice (d)

Chapter 20

20.1 a) 6500 J b) 34%

20.3 a) 23% b) 12,400 J c) 0.350 g

d) 222 kW = 298 hp

20.5 a) 12.3 atm b) 5470 J, ca c) 3723 J, bc

d) 1747 J e) 31.9%

20.7 a) 58% b) 1.4%

20.9 a) 14.8 kJ b) 45.8 kJ

20.11 1.2 h

20.13 a) 215 J b) 378 K c) 39.0%

20.15 a) 38 kJ b) 590°C

20.17 a) 492 J b) 212 W c) 5.4

20.19 44.5 hp

20.21 a) 429 J/K b) −393 J/K c) 36 J/K

20.23 a) irreversible b) 1250 J/K

20.25 −6.31 J/K

20.27 a) 6.05×10^3 J/K

b) about five times greater for vaporization

20.29 a) no b) 18.3 J/K c) 18.3 J/K

20.31 10.0 J/K

20.33 a) 121 J b) 3800 cycles

20.35 a) 90.2 J b) 320 J c) 45°C d) 0

e) 263 g

20.37 −5.8 J/K, decrease

20.39 b) absorbed: bc; rejected: ab and ca

c) $T_a = T_b = 241$ K, $T_c = 481$ K

d) 610 J, 610 J e) 8.7%

20.41 a) 21.0 kJ (enters), 16.6 kJ (leaves)

b) 4.4 kJ, 21% c) $e = 0.31e_{max}$

20.43 a) 7.0% b) 3.0 MW; 2.8 MW

c) 6×10^5 kg/h = 6×10^5 L/h

20.45 a) 1: 2.00 atm, 4.00 L; 2: 2.00 atm, 6.00 L;

3: 1.11 atm, 6.00 L; 4: 1.67 atm, 4.00 L

b) $1 \to 2$: 1422 J, 405 J; $2 \to 3$: −1355 J, 0;

$3 \to 4$: −274 J, −274 J; $4 \to 1$: 339 J, 0

c) 131 J d) 7.44%; $e = 0.168e_C$

20.47 $1 - T_c/T_h$, same

20.49 a) 122 J, −78 J b) 5.10×10^{-4} m³

c) b: 2.32 MPa, 4.81×10^{-5} m³, 771 K

c: 4.01 MPa, 4.81×10^{-5} m³, 1332 K

d: 0.147 MPa, 5.10×10^{-4} m³, 518 K

d) 61.1%, 77.5%

20.51 6.23

20.55 a) A: 28.9%, B: 38.3%, C: 53.8%, D: 24.4%

b) C c) $B > D > A$

20.57 a) 4.83% b) 4.83% c) 6.25%

d) $e = \dfrac{0.80T_d - 200}{12T_d - 2700}$, 6.67%

20.59 choice (b)

20.61 choice (d)

Chapter 23

23.6. (a) 0 (b) 8.33 J/K (c) 5.82 J/K (d) 5.82 J/K

23.7. (a) 1311 K, −1126 J/K, 185 J/K (b) 1310 K,
−1210 J/K, 98 J/K

23.10. 0.0301 R

23.11. 1.5 atm, 300 K, 0.0566 J/K

23.12. (a) $\dfrac{4}{9}V_0$ (b) $\dfrac{3}{2}T_0$ (c) $\dfrac{21}{4}T_0$ (d) $\dfrac{19}{4}nC_VT_0$,

(e) $\dfrac{1}{2}nC_VT_0$ (f) 0 (g) $nC_p\ln\dfrac{21}{4} - nR\ln\dfrac{27}{8}$,

(h) $nC_p\ln\dfrac{63}{84} - 2nR\ln\dfrac{27}{8}$

23.14. (a) 6.28 J/K (b) 1.385 J/K (c) 3.64 J/K

23.15. (a) 1.83×10^{-5} J/K (b) 1.83×10^{-5} J/K

23.16. (a) 3740 J/mol (b) 3740 J/mol (d) −2296 J/mol,

(e) −1444 J/mol (f) 3.82 J/mol·K

Chapter 33

33.1 39.4°

33.3 a) 2.04×10^8 m/s b) 442 nm

33.5 a) 1.55 b) 550 nm

33.7 a) 47.5° b) 66.0°

33.9 2.51×10^8 m/s

33.11 a) 2.34 b) 82°

33.13 71.8°

33.15 a) 51.3° b) 33.6°

33.17 a) 58.1° b) 22.8°

33.19 1.77

33.21 a) 48.9° b) 28.7°

33.23 $0.6°$

33.25 $0.375I_0$

33.27 a) A: $I_0/2$, B: $0.125I_0$, C: $0.0938I_0$ b) 0

33.29 a) 1.40   b) $35.5°$

33.31 $\arccos\left(\dfrac{\cos\theta}{\sqrt{2}}\right)$

33.33 6.38 W/cm^2

33.35 a) $0.364I$ b) $2.70I$

33.37 a) $46.7°$ b) $13.4°$

33.39 $72.1°$

33.41 1.28

33.43 3.52×10^4

33.45 1.84

33.47 a) $48.6°$ b) $48.6°$

33.49 $39.1°$

33.51 b) $0.23°$; about the same

33.53 b) $38.9°$ c) $5.0°$

33.55 $23.3°$

33.57 a) A: 1.46, carbon tetrachloride; B: 1.33, water;
       C: 1.63, carbon disulfide; D: 1.50, benzene
       b) A: 2.13, B: 1.77, C: 2.66, D: 2.25
       c) all: $5.09 \times 10^{14} \text{ Hz}$

33.59 a) $35°$ b) $I_0 = 10 \text{ W/m}^2$, $I_p = 20 \text{ W/m}^2$

33.61 a) $\Delta = 2\theta_a^A - 6 \arcsin\left(\dfrac{\sin\theta_a^A}{n}\right) + 2\pi$

       b) $\theta_2 = \arccos\sqrt{\dfrac{n^2 - 1}{8}}$

       c) violet: $\theta_2 = 71.55°$, $\Delta = 233.2°$
       red: $\theta_2 = 71.94°$, $\Delta = 230.1°$; violet

33.63 choice (d)

Chapter 35

35.1 a) 14 cm, 48 cm, 82 cm, 116 cm, 150 cm
      b) 31 cm, 65 cm, 99 cm, 133 cm

35.3 0.75 m, 2.00 m, 3.25 m, 4.50 m, 5.75 m,
      7.00 m, 8.25 m

35.5 a) 2.0 m   b) constructively
      c) 1.0 m, destructively

35.7 1.14 mm

35.9 0.83 mm

35.11 a) 39   b) $\pm 73.3°$

35.13 12.6 cm

35.15 1200 nm

35.17 a) $0.750I_0$ b) 80 nm

35.19 1670 rad

35.21 a) 4.52 rad   b) $0.404I_0$

35.23 114 nm

35.25 $0.0234°$

35.27 a) 55.6 nm
       b) (i) 2180 nm   (ii) 11.0 wavelengths

35.29 a) 514 nm; green   b) 603 nm; orange

35.31 $0.11 \ \mu m$

35.33 0.570 mm

35.35 1.57

35.37 a) 96.0 nm   b) no, no

35.39 a) 1.58 mm (green), 1.72 mm (orange)
       b) 3.45 mm (violet), 4.74 mm (green),
       5.16 mm (orange)   c) $9.57 \ \mu m$

35.41 1.730

35.43 761 m, 219 m, 90.1 m, 20.0 m

35.45 $6.8 \times 10^{-5} \ (\text{C}°)^{-1}$

35.47 $1.33 \ \mu m$

35.49 600 nm, 467 nm; no

35.51 a) 1.54   b) $\pm 15.0°$

35.53 a) 50 MHz   b) 237.0 m

35.55 14.0

35.57 choice (d)

35.59 choice (c)

CREDITS

Chapter 6 Opener: Brocreative/Shutterstock; 6.1: mariiya/Fotolia; Appl. p. 173: Steve Gschmeissner/Science Source; 6.13: Mikadun/Shutterstock; Appl. p. 186: Steve Gschmeissner/Science Source; 6.26: Fox Photos/Hulton Archive/Getty Images; Appl. p. 190: Gayvoronskaya_Yana/Shutterstock; 6.27a: Keystone/Hulton Archive/Getty Images; 6.27b: Anthony Hall/Fotolia; 6.28: Fandu/Fotolia; P6.90 (chart): Data from Science Buddies. www.sciencebuddies.org/science-fair-projects/project_ideas/Physics_Springs_Tutorial.shtml

Chapter 11 Opener: nito/Shutterstock; 11.3: Turleyt/Fotolia; 11.8a: Maridav/Shutterstock; 11.12a: Benjamin Marin Rubio/Shutterstock; 11.12b: Richard Carey/Fotolia; 11.12c: Andrew Bret Wallis/Photodisc/Getty Images; 11.13: Djomas/Shutterstock; Appl. p. 350: Dante Fenolio/Science Source

Chapter 14 Opener: blurAZ/Shutterstock; Appl. p. 434: Steve Byland/Shutterstock; 14.7: American Diagnostic Corporation; 14.21a: Zurijeta/Shutterstock; 14.25: Christopher Griffin/Alamy; Appl. p. 455: Symbiot/Shutterstock; Appl. p. 456: Sonya Etchison/Shutterstock

Chapter 15 Opener: Walter D. Mooney/U.S. Geological Survey; Appl. p. 469: Marco PoloCollection/Balan Madhavan/Alamy; 15.2: Charles Platiau/Reuters; 15.5: EpicStockMedia/Shutterstock; 15.12: Kodda/Shutterstock; Appl. p. 482: Christian Delbert/Shutterstock; 15.23a–d: Richard Megna/Fundamental Photographs; 15.25: Shmeliova Natalia/Shutterstock; 15.27: National Optical Astronomy Observatories

Chapter 16 Opener: Eduard Kyslynskyy/Shutterstock; 16.5 (line art): Berg, Richard E.; Stork, David G., *The Physics Of Sound*, 1st Ed., ©1982. Reprinted and electronically reproduced by permission of Pearson Education, Inc., Upper Saddle River, New Jersey; 16.5a: olly/Shutterstock; 16.5b: Lebrecht Music and Arts Photo Library/Alamy; Appl. p. 510: Steve Thorne/Getty Images; 16.6: Geoff Dann/DK Images; 16.9: Kretztechnik/Science Source; 16.10: auremar/Shutterstock; 16.15: Digoarpi/Shutterstock; Appl. p. 523: Piotr Marcinski/Shutterstock; 16.20: Martin Bough/Fundamental Photographs; 16.24: Roger A. Freedman; 16.26: R. Gino Santa Maria/Shutterstock; 16.29: Aaron Kohr/Shutterstock; 16.36c: NASA; 16.37: NASA

Chapter 17 Opener: huyangshu/Shutterstock; 17.4: PRNewsFoto/Exergen TemporalScanner/AP Images; Appl. p. 548 (top): David Thyberg/Shutterstock; Appl. p. 548 (bottom): Hofhauser/Shutterstock; 17.5a: Roger A. Freedman; 17.11: Eugene Sergeev/Shutterstock; 17.13: Eric Schrader/Pearson Education; 17.16: Hugh D. Young; 17.18: Roman Sigaev/Shutterstock; 17.19: Science Source; 17.21: Richard Megna/Fundamental Photographs; 17.22: NASA; 17.23: MaszaS/Shutterstock; Appl. p. 566 (top): Dmitry Deshevykh/Getty Images; Appl. p. 566 (bottom): Paul Nicklen/National Geographic/Getty Images; 17.28: Hugh D. Young; 17.29: Steve Gschmeissner/Science

Source; 17.30a: Source: *Trends: A Compendium of Data on Global Change*, U.S. Department of Energy's Carbon Dioxide Information Analysis Center, http://cdiac.esd.ornl.gov/trends/co2/contents.htm; 17.30b: Source: http://data.giss.nasa.gov/gistemp/graphs_v3/, first graph; P17.91: Satoshi Kuribayashi/Nature Production/Nature Picture Library

Chapter 18 Opener: stockyimages/Shutterstock; 18.2: Topham/The Image Works; 18.10: Courtesy of Bruker Corporation; 18.13: Rich Iwasaki/Stone/Getty Images; 18.14: Arctic Images/Alamy; 18.16: David Grossman/The Image Works; Appl. p. 604: Ray Coleman/Science Source; 18.25: PhotoDisc/Getty Images; E18.24: National Optical Astronomy Observatory; P18.83: National Optical Astronomy Observatory

Chapter 19 Opener: Ken Paul/All Canada Photos/Getty Images; 19.1: Roger A. Freedman via John P. Surey; 19.2a: Stocktrek/Photodisc/Getty Images; 19.2b: Alin Dragulin/Alamy; Appl. p. 624: Diego Cervo/Shutterstock; 19.10: Liv friis-larsen/Shutterstock; 19.14: Tom Branch/Science Source; 19.15: Rob Byron/Shutterstock; Appl. p. 635: Dean Bertoncelj/Shutterstock

Chapter 20 Opener: George Burba/Shutterstock; 20.2: James Morgan/Shutterstock; Appl. p. 650: Tyler Olson/Shutterstock; 20.12: Bill Bachman/Science Source; 20.16: U.S. Air Force photo by Staff Sgt. Robert Zoellner; 20.17: cowardlion/Shutterstock; Appl. p. 669: DenisNata/Shutterstock; 20.20 abc: Eric Schrader/Pearson Education; Summ. p. 675: Eric Schrader/Pearson Education; PP20.59–62 (chart): Source: Public domain from Wikimedia Commons: http://commons.wikimedia.org/wiki/File:Thermocline.jpg

Chapter 33 Opener: Rozaliya/Getty Images; 33.1: bradleym/E+/Getty Images; 33.2: National Institute of Health/Science Source; 33.9a: Roger A. Freedman; Appl. p. 1083: Image Quest Marine; 33.10a: NASA; 33.10b: Stephen Meese/Getty Images; 33.13b: Ken Kay/Fundamental Photographs; 33.16: VEM/Science Source; 33.19a: mtilghma/Fotolia; 33.21a: Dougal Waters/Photographer's Choice/Getty Images; 33.21b: Pixtal/AGE Fotostock; 33.25: Diane Hirsch/Fundamental Photographs; Appl. p. 1097: Kzenon/Shutterstock; Appl. p. 1098 (top): Linda Hirst; Appl. p. 1098 (bottom): Cefo design/Shutterstock; 33.30: Peter Aprahamian/Sharples Stress Engineers Ltd./Science Source; Appl. p. 1099: Laurie Knight/Getty Images; 33.32: Roger A. Freedman; 33.36 (left): K.Nomachi/Science Source

Chapter 35 Opener: Ilya Andriyanov/Shutterstock; Appl. p. 1163: Peter Dazeley/The Image Bank/Getty Images; 35.4: Roger A. Freedman; 35.6: Pearson; 35.11b: Rob Friedman/E+/Getty Images; 35.16b: Bausch & Lomb Incorporated; 35.17: Bausch & Lomb Incorporated; Appl. p. 1176 (top left): Laurie Knight/Getty Images; Appl. p. 1176 (top right, bottom): Peter Vukusic; Appl. p. 1177: Jason Reed

INDEX

For users of the three-volume edition: pages 1–682 are in Volume 1; pages 683–1253 are in Volume 2; pages 1218–1522 are in Volume 3. Pages 1254–1522 are not in the Standard Edition.

NOTE: Page numbers followed by f indicate figures; those followed by t indicate tables.

Astronomical Data[†]

Body	Mass (kg)	Radius (m)	Orbit radius (m)	Orbital period
Sun	1.99×10^{30}	6.96×10^8	—	—
Moon	7.35×10^{22}	1.74×10^6	3.84×10^8	27.3 d
Mercury	3.30×10^{23}	2.44×10^6	5.79×10^{10}	88.0 d
Venus	4.87×10^{24}	6.05×10^6	1.08×10^{11}	224.7 d
Earth	5.97×10^{24}	6.37×10^6	1.50×10^{11}	365.3 d
Mars	6.42×10^{23}	3.39×10^6	2.28×10^{11}	687.0 d
Jupiter	1.90×10^{27}	6.99×10^7	7.78×10^{11}	11.86 y
Saturn	5.68×10^{26}	5.82×10^7	1.43×10^{12}	29.45 y
Uranus	8.68×10^{25}	2.54×10^7	2.87×10^{12}	84.02 y
Neptune	1.02×10^{26}	2.46×10^7	4.50×10^{12}	164.8 y
Pluto[‡]	1.31×10^{22}	1.15×10^6	5.91×10^{12}	247.9 y

[†]Source: NASA (**http://solarsystem.nasa.gov/planets/**). For each body, "radius" is its average radius and "orbit radius" is its average distance from the sun or (for the moon) from the earth.

[‡]In August 2006, the International Astronomical Union reclassified Pluto and similar small objects that orbit the sun as "dwarf planets."

Prefixes for Powers of 10

Power of ten	Prefix	Abbreviation	Pronunciation
10^{-24}	yocto-	y	*yoc*-toe
10^{-21}	zepto-	z	*zep*-toe
10^{-18}	atto-	a	*at*-toe
10^{-15}	femto-	f	*fem*-toe
10^{-12}	pico-	p	*pee*-koe
10^{-9}	nano-	n	*nan*-oe
10^{-6}	micro-	μ	*my*-crow
10^{-3}	milli-	m	*mil*-i
10^{-2}	centi-	c	*cen*-ti
10^3	kilo-	k	*kil*-oe
10^6	mega-	M	*meg*-a
10^9	giga-	G	*jig*-a or *gig*-a
10^{12}	tera-	T	*ter*-a
10^{15}	peta-	P	*pet*-a
10^{18}	exa-	E	*ex*-a
10^{21}	zetta-	Z	*zet*-a
10^{24}	yotta-	Y	*yot*-a

Examples:

1 femtometer = 1 fm = 10^{-15} m

1 picosecond = 1 ps = 10^{-12} s

1 nanocoulomb = 1 nC = 10^{-9} C

1 microkelvin = 1 μK = 10^{-6} K

1 millivolt = 1 mV = 10^{-3} V

1 kilopascal = 1 kPa = 10^3 Pa

1 megawatt = 1 MW = 10^6 W

1 gigahertz = 1 GHz = 10^9 Hz